Psychology

ABOUT THE COVER . . .

The marble's play with light seemed a metaphor for the ways in which we process experience. Light enlivens the glass, and light is changed by the glass—focused, diffused, curved, given color. Experience, similarly, stirs us, and we modify experience within. The patterns according to which we perceive and act upon the world are very much the subject matter of psychology. Moreover, no two of us perceive the world and behave in quite the same way—just as no two marbles process light in just the same way. Psychology focuses upon the behavior—and the dignity—of the individual.

The Author

Holt, Rinehart and Winston
New York Chicago San Francisco Philadelphia
Montreal Toronto London Sydney
Tokyo Mexico City Rio de Janeiro Madrid

Psychology

Third Edition

Spencer A. Rathus
Marist College
Poughkeepsie, N.Y.

Editor-in-Chief: *Susan Katz*
Publisher: *Robert Woodbury*
Acquisitions Editor: *Susan Meyers*
Senior Project Editor: *Françoise Bartlett*
Production Manager: *Pat Sarcuni*
Art Director: *Louis Scardino*
Design Concept: *Harushi Matsui*
Text Design: *Caliber Design Planning, Inc.*
Cover Photograph: *Al Francekevich*
Line Art: *Caliber Design Planning, Inc.*
Anatomical Art: *D.L. Cramer*
Photo Research: *Cheryl Mannes*

Library of Congress Cataloging-in-Publication Data
Rathus, Spencer A.

   Psychology.

   Bibliography: p. R1
   Includes index.
   1. Psychology. I. Title.
BF121.R34 1987   150   86–11973

ISBN 0-03-001608-8

Printed in the United States of America
Published simultaneously in Canada
All rights reserved
7 8 9 0   039   9 8 7 6 5 4 3 2 1

Address correspondence to:
383 Madison Avenue
New York, NY 10017

CBS COLLEGE PUBLISHING
Holt, Rinehart and Winston
The Dryden Press
Saunders College Publishing

PHOTO CREDITS

CHAPTER 1: *page 4*, Art Resource Center; *page 8*, Michel
Heron/Woodfin Camp & Associates; *page 10*, The Museum
of Modern Art/Film Stills Archive; *page 11*, Sepp Seitz/
Woodfin Camp & Associates; *page 12*, Steve Dunwell/The
Image Bank; *page 14*, Peter Schaaf/Time Pix Syndication;
page 16, The Bettmann Archive; *page 18 (left)*, The
Bettmann Archive; *(right)*, Ken Heyman.
                    (Continued following References)

For my daughters
Jill, Allyn, Jordan

PREFACE

Writing a textbook can engulf you. Family and friends have a way of asking that you play the basic role of citizen by attending dinner, going to an occasional film, taking a turn at mowing the lawn, and remembering to close the refrigerator door. Under normal circumstances, requests like these are reasonable enough. But composing a book like *Psychology* demands that you lock yourself in your study, spend evenings at the library, and develop a hearing deficit that allows you to ignore most household events except for the occasional emergency. In my case, it also requires bumping into walls and wearing a perpetual distracted look.

Composing the third edition of *Psychology* turned out to be as demanding as writing the first and second editions. When I started this project, I had the misconception that revisions would come easy. Not so. For one thing, psychology is a dynamic, evolving field. Keeping up with the literature is a full-time job, as any instructor of introductory psychology will gladly testify. Because of the changes that have occurred in psychology, it was necessary for me to integrate the findings of hundreds of studies that have been carried out since the second edition was published. For another, I have now had the benefit of feedback from colleagues who have used the second edition. While they agreed that the second edition was superior to the first, they let me know of the many ways in which the second edition still fell short of perfection. In this edition, I have integrated the comments and suggestions of dozens of colleagues who used the second edition in the classroom and who reviewed early drafts of the third.

WHAT'S NEW IN THIS EDITION

1. A major innovation of the third edition will be made immediately apparent by leafing through the pages. The third edition uses full-color illustrations throughout. In some cases, the use of color serves mainly to

motivate students or to illustrate the topics being discussed in the text. But in many cases, such as throughout Chapters 2 and 3, the color also serves as a carefully planned teaching tool that clarifies anatomical and conceptual distinctions.

2. To show the relevance of contemporary psychological research in our lives, this new edition of *Psychology* includes thematic boxes devoted to applied research. For example, "Psychology and Health" boxes highlight research in health psychology and behavioral medicine. "Psychology in the Workplace" items feature discussions pertaining to industrial/organizational psychology and careers. There are also "60 Minutes" features that show how the contemporary media have communicated psychological issues to the public. Videotapes of the "60 Minutes" segments accompany the text.*

3. One of the most popular features in earlier editions of *Psychology* has been the "Truth or Fiction?" sections that open each chapter. In the third edition, we have retained this feature, but have modified the items so that each is now an application of a chapter Learning Objective. The Learning Objectives, with the "Truth or Fiction?" items, appear in the student *Study Guide, Test Bank,* and *Instructor's Manual.*

4. To highlight the distinctions between topics, chapter summaries are numbered in the present edition.

5. Each chapter has been revised to reflect changes in the discipline and reviewer/user suggestions. Specific chapter-by-chapter changes include:

Chapter 1 ("What Is Psychology?") now contains a separate section on the history of psychology, which traces the development of psychology from the writings of Aristotle and Socrates to the modern day. There is expanded coverage of ethical issues, including the treatment of animal subjects in research.

Chapter 2 ("Biology and Behavior") has greatly expanded coverage of neurotransmitters, in keeping with developments of recent years. There is now also coverage of mitosis and meiosis and expanded coverage of genetic abnormalities. The promises of genetic counseling and genetic engineering are now explored.

Chapter 3 ("Sensation and Perception") has greatly expanded coverage of color vision, including the psychological dimensions of color, analogous versus complementary colors, and ways in which artists use color to achieve various effects. Coverage of the skin senses is expanded, with special focus on the topic of pain — its transmission and control. There is now coverage of psychophysical methods in studying the sense of taste and of use of biofeedback to help patients with problems in kinesthesis.

Chapter 4 ("States of Consciousness") includes updated information on psychoactive drugs. There are also revised appraisals of meditation and hypnosis, including the latest research on the effects of meditation versus simply sitting or resting quietly.

Chapter 5 ("Learning and Memory") now better brings home the many applications of learning theory. There is now coverage, for example, of the use of the bell-and-pad method for controlling bedwetting, of programed

---

*Instructors may check with their local Holt, Rinehart and Winston representative to learn how to acquire these videotapes.

learning, of the use of behavior modification in management and in the classroom, and of computer-assisted learning.

Chapter 6 ("Language, Thought, and Intelligence") has more extended coverage of language development, including a report on what is communicated by an infant's crying. The discussion of problem solving now includes algorithms and heuristic devices. There is mention of sex differences in creativity. There is, finally, greatly expanded coverage of the types of research that provide psychologists with data concerning the genetic and environmental determinants of intelligence.

Chapter 7 ("Motivation and Emotion") begins with a new section called "Theoretical Perspectives on Motivation" and a comparative evaluation of instinct theory, drive-reduction theory, and humanistic theory. There is coverage of motives for working. The section on emotions now includes Plutchik's emotion wheel and the most recent thinking of Izard, Zajonc, and Ekman.

Chapter 8 ("Developmental Psychology") includes up-to-date findings on agents that can harm the fetus. There is expanded coverage of perceptual development, including discussion of newborn babies' preferences for their mothers' voices. There is practical advice on selecting a day-care center and a new section on child abuse. Material on middle age and late adulthood is expanded, including empirical research on reactions to impending death.

Chapter 9 ("Personality: Theory and Measurement") now includes a section on the psychoanalytic theory of Karen Horney. Coverage of the role of computers in psychological assessment and report writing is expanded. Now there is also solid coverage of the use of psychological tests in making occupational choices.

Chapter 10 is now called "Stress, Health, and Adjustment" rather than just "Stress and Adjustment," because of expanded coverage of the influence of stress on health. There is now a discussion of the effects of stress on cancer. Research on the Type A personality is updated. There is a discussion of stress in the workplace and what companies are doing to help workers cope with stress.

Chapter 11 ("Abnormal Behavior") now gives the cognitive model of abnormal behavior the prominence it deserves. There is a new section on panic disorder. There is now a discussion of workaholism. The sections on cognitive factors in depression and on the roles of neurotransmitters in affective disorders and schizophrenic disorders are expanded and updated.

Chapter 12 is now called "Methods of Therapy" rather than "Psychotherapy" in order to better encompass psychological and biological methods. There is a new section on modern psychoanalytic approaches, which now shows how contemporary followers of Freud tend to differ with Freud in their methods. There is superior evaluation of psychotherapies, with greater reliance on meta-analytic studies. The discussion of cognitive therapy was reworked to clearly describe the views and methods of Ellis, Beck, and others. The section on biological therapies was also reworked, with focus on the types of psychosurgery carried out today, rather than on the old prefrontal lobotomy.

Chapter 13, formerly called "Sexual Behavior," was reworked into a chapter on "Sex Roles and Sexual Behavior." There is major focus on the adjustment of working wives and their children. A new section called "On Becoming a Man or a Woman" reviews research on the biological and psychological determinants of sex differences in behavior. A new section on sexual motivation ties together a discussion of the maternal drive, pornography, homosexuality, and rape. There is exploration of the effects of AIDS on sexual behavior.

Chapter 14 ("Social Psychology") includes expanded coverage of approaches to advertising and ways in which advertisements persuade audiences. There is also expanded coverage of biases in the attribution process, factors that contribute to physical attractiveness, social facilitation and social loafing, group decision-making, altruism and helping behavior, and the effects of extremes of temperature.

WHAT'S MUCH THE SAME

Many features of *Psychology* helped to make earlier editions successful. My goal in this third edition, therefore, was to present the dynamic nature of psychological research while retaining the basic features that have been popular with instructors and students. To this end, you will find the following in *Psychology*, third edition:

COMPREHENSIVE AND BALANCED COVERAGE

As in earlier editions, the aim of this edition of *Psychology* is to communicate in content and form the excitement, relevance, and true scientific nature of psychology. The text provides students with a straightforward introduction to the basic research areas in psychology, such as biological psychology, sensation and perception, learning and memory, cognitive processes, motivation and emotion, and personality and social psychology. With that knowledge as a base, the text also makes explicit for students many of psychology's evolving applications in the areas of human growth and development, states of consciousness, stress and adjustment, abnormal behavior and psychotherapy, and sexual behavior.

Because no introductory psychology textbook can pursue every important area within the broad science of psychology in the depth these areas deserve, *Psychology* is succinct in presentation. A number of areas are combined to receive single-chapter coverage: "Sensation and Perception" (Chapter 3); "Learning and Memory" (Chapter 5); "Language, Thought, and Intelligence" (Chapter 6); "Motivation and Emotion" (Chapter 7); and "Personality: Theory and Measurement" (Chapter 9). Clear, concise, accurate coverage of these areas permits full chapter treatment of topics that immediately touch students' lives: "States of Consciousness" (Chapter 4), including sleep and dreams, drugs, meditation, biofeedback, and hypnosis; "Stress, Health, and Adjustment" (Chapter 10), including methods of coping with frustration, conflict, and the Type A behavior pattern; and "Sex Roles and Sexual Behavior" (Chapter 13), including sex roles and their acquisition, sex differences, the problems (and rewards!) of working wives, varieties of sexual experience, and sexual problems or dysfunctions. The applied areas of psychology, as all areas, are treated with academic rigor. Great emphasis is placed on research methodology and up-to-date research findings.

THE WRITING STYLE

The third edition of *Psychology* was deliberately written with the needs of students in mind. The third edition also had the advantage of feedback from dozens of instructors and hundreds of students who used the second edition. I believe that their input has enabled me to retain the engaging and motivating qualities of previous editions while avoiding frivolity and condescension. Colleagues and students have helped me in my continuing quest to craft the language and the vocabulary so that psychological concepts are made accessible to the student. It is my belief that even the most abstract concepts can be presented in energetic prose that is easy to retain when one writes and rewrites according to the suggestions of the readers.

Psychology was also explicitly written for the instructor—the instructor who wants to teach from a textbook that is:

comprehensive and balanced
accurate and up-to-date
applied as well as theoretical
clearly written
succinct in presentation
interest-arousing
easily understood
well-illustrated

LEARNING AIDS

The central task of a textbook is to provide students with clear information in a format that promotes learning. *Psychology* contains seven specific elements designed to meet this goal:

Chapter Outlines   Each chapter begins with an outline that helps organize the subject matter for the student. Care was taken to present the headings used in the chapter outlines in a succinct and clear manner.

"Truth-or-Fiction?" Sections   These sections follow the chapter outlines. "Truth-or-Fiction?" items are intimately related to Learning Objectives, which are listed in the student *Study Guide* and in the *Instructor's Manual*. But the "Truth-or-Fiction?" items go beyond a matter-of-fact list; they stimulate student interest by highlighting some of the fascinating research findings in psychology and by challenging common knowledge and folklore.

Many students consider themselves psychologists. After all, even by the age at which they first attend college, they have already observed human nature for many years. The "Truth-or-Fiction?" items prod them to reflect upon the accuracy of their observations and to reconsider the conclusions they may have drawn about human nature.

Glossary Items Defined in the Margins   Technical terms and, occasionally, other words are defined in the margins, at the point where they
occur in the text. Research indicates that many students do not make use
of a glossary at the back of a book. Moreover, ready access to glossary
items permits students to maintain concentration on the chapter; they need
not flip back and forth between different sections of the book in order to
understand the material.

When needed, technical terms are writen phonetically to help the
students pronounce them. Students will not have to ''unlearn'' mispro-
nunciations through embarrassing verbal errors made in the classroom. In
many cases, word origins are also provided. Word origins always helped
me to understand the meanings of technical terms, and I wanted to share
this information with students.

The definitions may be repeated in the margins of several chapters,
as they are brought up in the text. This repetition reinforces learning and
gives the instructor flexibility in the sequencing of reading assignments. All
technical terms are boldfaced on the pages on which they appear, so that
students will be made immediately aware as to whether definitions for them
are available.

Illustrations   A generous supply of full-color photographs, figures,
and drawings illustrates the themes and research findings of the text. All
figures and drawings have been redone for the third edition, so that their
pedagogical value will match the excellence of the text per se.

Figure captions are extensive, where needed, to reinforce the explanatory power of illustrations.

Chapter Summaries   Numbered chapter summaries review the material in a logical step-by-step manner. Care was taken to include as many
technical terms as possible in the summaries.

''Truth-or-Fiction Revisited'' Sections   ''Truth-or-Fiction Revisited''
sections complete each chapter. In this way, each chapter comes full circle:
a sense of psychological closure is provided by returning to the issues raised
in the chapter-opening ''Truth-or-Fiction?'' sections. By now the material
has been discussed in the chapter and reviewed in the chapter summary.
The ''Truth-or-Fiction Revisited'' sections provide students with feedback as
to whether the objectives of the chapter have been met and erroneous views
have been dispelled.

Applications   While *Psychology* avoids deceivingly simple answers
to complex human problems, it offers numerous examples of how psychological principles and research have been applied in such areas as:

control of pain
coping with insomnia
cutting down and quitting smoking
weight control
methods of meditation
biofeedback

methods of relaxation
reducing test anxiety
coping with Type A behavior
selecting a day-care center
decision-making
suicide prevention
rape prevention

THE ANCILLARIES

The needs of today's instructors and students demand a full and broad array of ancillary materials to make learning and teaching more effective. *Psychology* is accompanied by a complete, convenient, and carefully conceived package.

For the student, a *Study Guide*, written by the author, features an all-new format that is equally useful in traditional or individualized (PSI) instructional settings. The guide features an opening chapter on "How to Succeed in College." Each chapter includes Learning Objectives with "Truth-or-Fiction?" applications, key terms, exercises, pre- and post-tests, and a comprehensive programed learning section that is organized both by Learning Objectives and major text headings. The *Study Guide* also includes a complete end-of-text glossary to aid students in mastering the vocabulary of psychology.

For the instructor, *Psychology*, third edition, includes the most comprehensive teaching package available. Features include an *Instructor's Manual* that is designed to make even the newest instructor look like a veteran; a *Whole Psychology Catalog* that contains handouts, demonstrations, experiments, and transparency masters; a set of transparency acetates; a comprehensive *Test Bank* that includes 120 multiple-choice items per chapter, organized by Learning Objectives; a *Computerized Test Bank* available on Apple or IBM; videotapes; and a software package. For more information, please contact your local Holt, Rinehart and Winston representative or regional office.

ACKNOWLEDGMENTS

The discipline of psychology owes its progress and its scientific standing to experts who conduct research in many different areas. Similarly, the textbook *Psychology* and its ancillaries owe a great deal of their substance and form to my colleagues, who provided expert suggestions and insights at various stages in their development. My sincere thanks to the following: Mark H. Ashcraft, Cleveland State University; Gladys J. Baez-Dickreiter, St. Philip's College; Patricia Barker, Schenectady County Community College; Thomas L. Bennett, Colorado State University; Otto Berliner, SUNY–Alfred; Richard A. Block, Montana State University; C. Robert Borresen, Wichita State University; Theodore N. Bosack, Providence College; Betty Bowers, North Central Technical Institute; Peter J. Brady, Clark Technical College;

Richard Day, Manchester Community College; Donald L. Daoust, Southern Oregon State College; Carl L. Denti, Dutchess County Community College; Carol Doolin, Henderson County Jr. College; Wendy L. Dunn, Coe College; John Foust, Parkland College; Morton P. Friedman, University of California at Los Angeles; Marvin Goldstein, Rider College; Bernard Gorman, Nassau Community College; Sandra L. Groeltz, DeVry Institute of Technology at Chicago; Arthur Gutman, Florida Institute of Technology; Jim Hail, McLellan Community College; Robert W. Hayes, Boston University; George Herrick, SUNY–Alfred; Sidney Hochman, Nassau Community College; Morton Hoffman, Metropolitan State College; Betsy Howton, Western Kentucky University; John H. Hummel, University of Houston; Sam L. Hutchinson, Radford University; Jarvel Jackson, McLellan Community College; Robert L. Johnson, Umpqua Community College; Eve Jones, Los Angeles City College; Charles Karis, Northwestern University; Mary-Louise Kean, University of California–Irvine; Richard Kellogg, SUNY–Alfred; Richard A. King, University of North Carolina–Chapel Hill; Alan Lanning, College of DuPage; Patsy Lawson, Volunteer State Community College; John D. Lawry, Marymount College; Charles Levinthal, Hofstra University; Robert MacAleese, Spring Hill College; Daniel Madsen, University of Minnesota–Duluth; S. R. Mathews, Converse College; Juan Mercado, McLellan Community College; Richard McCarbery, Lorain College; Derrill McGuigan, Rider College; Leroy Metze, Western Kentucky University; Richard E. Miller, Navarro College; Thomas Minor, SUNY at Stony Brook; Thomas Moeschl, Broward Community College; Joel Morgovsky, Brookdale Community College; Walena C. Morse, West Chester University; Basil Najjar, College of DuPage; Jeffrey Nevid, St. John's University; John W. Nichols, Tulsa Junior College; Joseph Palladino, Indiana State University–Evansville; John Pennachio, Adirondack Community College; Terry Pettijohn, Ohio State University–Marion; Gregory Pezzeti, Santa Ana College; Walter Pieper, Georgia State University; Donis Price, Mesa Community College; Louis Primavera, St. John's University; Richard A. Rare, University of Maine; Valda Robinson, Hillsborough Community College; Rene A. Ruiz, New Mexico State University; Patrick J. Ryan, Tompkins-Cortland Community College; H. R. Schiffman, Rutgers University; Jacob Steinberg, Fairleigh Dickinson University; Ann Swint, North Harris County College; Robert S. Tacker, East Carolina University; Francis Terrell, North Texas State University; Harry A. Tiemann, Jr., Mesa College; Douglas Wallen, Mankato State University; Charles Weichert, San Antonio College; Paul Wellman, Texas A&M; Richard Whinery, Ohio University–Chillicothe; Robert Williams, William Jewel College; Keith A. Wollen, Washington State University; Walter Zimmerman, New Hampshire College.

The publishing professionals at Holt, Rinehart and Winston are a particularly able group of individuals, and it is a continuing privilege to work with them. Foremost among them is Susan Meyers, Psychology Editor, who brought a new vision and vitality to *Psychology*. Susan is that rare individual who has the courage to tamper with the successful, to attempt to improve upon that which is already well-received. In doing so, she literally and figuratively brought *Psychology* much of its color.

Lisa Bayard, President of CBS College Publishing, Susan Katz, Editor-in-Chief, and Bob Woodbury, Publisher of the Liberal Arts Group, also gambled; they poured the resources into the third edition that made the enhanced format possible. Steve Helba, Associate Psychology Editor, offered numerous valuable insights and suggestions. David DeCampo, assistant editor, handled so many day-to-day problems and chores that I cannot begin to recall them, much less list them here. My gratitude to John Yarley for marketing the third edition of this textbook. Fran Bartlett, Senior Project Editor, is to be credited for overseeing the editing and coordinating all the activities necessary to turning a manuscript into a bound book. Lou Scardino directed the art program for the book and is to be credited for giving the text much of its visual impact. Pat Sarcuni has once again ably managed the production of the book. Cheryl Mannes brought imagination to the task of photo research.

Many of the publishing professionals at Holt, Rinehart and Winston have become old friends. They have enriched the text as they have enriched my life.

Chappaqua, New York   S.A.R.
August 1986

CONTENTS
IN BRIEF

CONTENTS

FEATURES

A CLOSER LOOK

PSYCHOLOGY AND HEALTH

PSYCHOLOGY IN THE WORKPLACE

PSYCHOLOGY TODAY

60 MINUTES

QUESTIONNAIRES

Psychology

OUTLINE

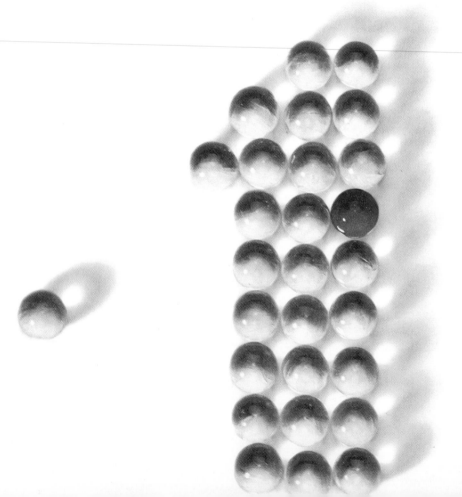

What Is Psychology?

TRUTH OR FICTION?

- Psychology is the study of the mind.
- Psychologists attempt to control behavior.
- A book on psychology, whose contents were similar to those of the book you are now holding in your hands, was written by Aristotle more than 2,000 years ago.
- Some psychologists measure the effectiveness of television commercials.
- Other psychologists serve as expert witnesses in court.
- Still other psychologists guide people into eating more healthful diets.
- Only people use tools.
- Alcohol causes aggression.
- You could survey 20 million Americans and still not predict accurately the outcome of a presidential election.

WHAT IS PSYCHOLOGY?

"What a piece of work is man!" wrote William Shakespeare. "How noble in reason! how infinite in faculty! in form, in moving, how express and admirable! in action how like an angel! in apprehension how like a god! the beauty of the world! the paragon of animals!"

You probably had no trouble recognizing yourself in Shakespeare's description—"noble in reason," "admirable," godlike in understanding, head and shoulders above all other animals. That's you to a "t," isn't it? But human behavior is greatly varied, and much of it is not so admirable. And a good deal of human behavior, even familiar behavior, is rather puzzling. Consider these examples:

> Most adults on crowded city streets will not stop to help a person lying on the sidewalk, or to help a lost child. Why?

> While most of us watch television, ride a bicycle, jog, or go for a swim, some people seek excitement by driving motorcycles at breakneck speed, skydiving, or taking "uppers." Why?

> Most adults who smoke cigarettes or overeat know that they are probably jeopardizing their health. Yet they continue their hazardous habits. Why?

> Some children seem capable of learning more in school than others. Their teachers scan their records and find that more capable children usually have higher scores on intelligence tests. But what is intelligence? How is intelligence measured? Why do some people have, or seem to have, more of "it" than others?

> A rapist or murderer claims to have committed his crime because another "personality" living in him took over, or because a dog prompted him with "mental messages." What is wrong with such people? What can be done about it?

Human behavior has always fascinated other human beings. Sometimes we are even "surprised at ourselves." Psychologists, like other people, are intrigued by the mysteries of behavior and make an effort to answer questions such as we have posed. But while most people try to satisfy their curiosity about behavior in their spare time, or through casual observations, psychologists make the study of behavior their lifework.

Psychology may be defined as a scientific approach to the study of behavior. As a science, it brings carefully controlled methods of observation, such as the survey and the experiment, to bear on its subject matter whenever possible. Most psychologists are interested primarily in human behavior, yet many of them focus much or all of their research on the behavior of animals ranging from rats and pigeons to flatworms and gorillas. Some psychologists believe that research findings about lower animals can be applied to humans. Others argue that people are so distinct from other animals that we can learn about people only by studying people. As with many such controversies, both views hold much truth. For instance, laboratory studies of the nerve cells of animals like the squid have given us much insight into the workings of the nerve cells of people. But only by studying people can we understand the purely human inventions of morality, values, and romantic love. Yet many psychologists study the behavior

"WHAT A PIECE OF WORK IS MAN!" "What a piece of work is man!" wrote William Shakespeare. Psychologists agree. Psychologists use the scientific method to study the observable behavior and mental processes of this most complex and subtle of creatures. Michelangelo's *David*, pictured here, captures the awesome beauty and power of human beings.

Behavior The observable actions and mental processes of people and lower animals.

Self-report (1) A subject's testimony about his or her own thoughts, feelings, or behaviors; (2) a method of investigation in which information is obtained through the report of the subject.

Theory A formulation of relationships underlying observed events. A theory involves assumptions and logically derived explanations and predictions. (From the Greek *theoria,* meaning "a looking at.")

of lower animals simply because they enjoy doing so. They are under no obligation to justify their interests on the basis of applicability to people.

Psychologists generally agree that psychology is the science of **behavior,** but they do not all agree on what behavior is. Some psychologists limit their definition to observable behavior—for example, to activities like pressing a lever, turning left or right, eating and mating, or even involuntary bodily functions like heart rate, dilation of the pupils of the eyes, blood pressure, or emission of a certain brain wave. All these behaviors can be measured by simple observation or by laboratory instruments. Other psychologists extend the definition of behavior to include mental processes like images, concepts, thoughts, dreams, and emotions. The difficulty in studying mental processes is that they are private events that cannot be fully verified through use of laboratory instruments. They are usually assumed to be present on the basis of the **self-report** of the person experiencing them. However, psychologists have found that mental processes often can be at least partially verified by laboratory instruments. Dreams, for instance, are most likely to occur when certain brain waves are being emitted (see Chapter 4). Strong emotions are usually accompanied by increases in heart rate and breathing (see Chapter 7). In this way psychologists who study mental processes can often tie them to a number of observable behaviors. This allows them to verify self-reports with some confidence.

THE GOALS OF PSYCHOLOGY

Psychology, like other sciences, seeks to describe, explain, predict, and control the events it studies. Thus, psychology seeks to describe, explain, predict, and control observable behavior and mental processes.

Psychologists attempt to describe and explain behavior in terms of psychological concepts like learning, motivation, emotion, intelligence, personality, and attitudes. For example, we may describe learning as a process in which behavior changes as a result of experience. We can be more specific and also describe instances of learning in which children memorize the alphabet through repetition or acquire gymnastic skills through practice in which their performance becomes gradually closer to desired behavior. We would explain learning in terms of rules or principles that govern learning. We might explain the trainer's use of words like "fine" and "good" as "reinforcers" that provide "feedback" to the gymnast, or "knowledge of results."

When possible, descriptive terms and concepts are interwoven into **theories.** Theories are related sets of statements about events. Theories are based on certain assumptions about behavior, and they allow us to derive explanations and predictions. Many psychological theories combine statements about psychological concepts (like learning and motivation), behavior (like eating or problem solving), and anatomical structures or biological processes. For instance, our responses to drugs like alcohol and marijuana reflect the biochemical actions of these drugs and our psychological expectations or beliefs about the drugs, as we shall see in Chapter 4.

A satisfactory psychological theory must allow us to predict behavior. For instance, a satisfactory theory of hunger will allow us to predict when people will eat and not eat. A broadly satisfying, comprehensive theory should have a wide range of applicability. A broad theory of hunger might apply to human beings and lower animals, to normal-weight and over-weight people, and to people who have been deprived of food for differing lengths of time. If our observations cannot be adequately explained by or predicted from a given theory, we should consider revising or replacing that theory.

In psychology many theories have been found to be incapable of explaining or predicting new observations. As a result they have been re-vised extensively. For example, the theory that hunger results from stomach contractions may be partially correct for normal-weight individuals, but it is inadequate as an explanation for feelings of hunger among the over-weight. In Chapter 7 we shall see that stomach contractions are only one of many factors, or **variables,** involved in hunger. Contemporary theories also focus on biological variables, such as fat cells and brain structures, and situational variables, such as the presence of other people who are eating and the time of day.

The notion of controlling behavior is highly controversial. Some peo-ple erroneously think that psychologists seek ways to make people do their bidding—like puppets dangling on strings. This could not be farther from the truth. Psychologists are generally committed to belief in the dignity of human beings, and human dignity demands that people be free to make their own decisions and choose their own behavior. Psychologists are learn-ing more all the time about the various influences on human behavior, but they apply this knowledge only upon request and in ways they believe will be helpful to an individual or an institution. Later in this chapter you will see that ethical standards prevent psychologists from using any method in research or practice that might harm or injure an individual.

The remainder of this chapter provides an overview of psychology and psychologists. You will see that psychologists have diverse interests and fields of specialization. We discuss the history of psychology and the major perspectives from which today's psychologists view behavior. Then we ex-plore methods psychologists use to test their theoretical assumptions and gather new information about behavior.

WHAT PSYCHOLOGISTS DO

Psychologists share a keen interest in behavior, but in other ways they may differ markedly. Some psychologists engage primarily in basic or **pure re-search.** Pure research has no immediate application to personal or social problems, and has thus been characterized as research for its own sake. Other psychologists engage in **applied research,** which is designed to find solutions to specific personal or social problems. Although pure research is spurred onward by curiosity and the desires to know and to understand, today's pure research frequently enhances tomorrow's way of life. For ex-ample, pure research in learning and motivation with lower animals early in the century has found widespread applications in today's school systems.

Variable A condition that is measured or controlled in a scientific study. A variable can vary in a measurable manner.

Pure research Research conducted without concern for immediate applications. Also called *basic research.*

Applied research Research conducted in an effort to find solutions to particular problems.

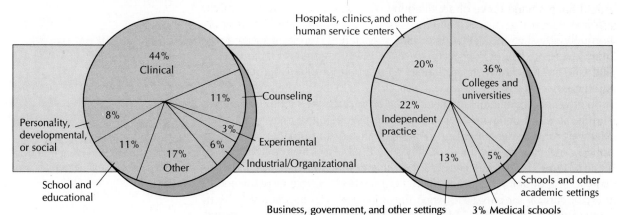

MAJOR SPECIALTIES OF PSYCHOLOGISTS

44% Clinical

11% Counseling

8%

3%

Personality, developmental, or social

11%

17% Other

6%

Experimental

Industrial/Organizational

School and educational

WHERE PSYCHOLOGISTS WORK

Hospitals, clinics, and other human service centers

20%

36% Colleges and universities

22% Independent practice

13%

5%

Schools and other academic settings

Business, government, and other settings

3% Medical schools

FIGURE 1.1 **SPECIALTIES AND WORK SETTINGS OF PSYCHOLOGISTS** A recent survey of doctoral-level psychologists by the American Psychological Association (Stapp, Tucker, & VandenBos, 1985) showed that 44 percent identified themselves as clinical psychologists (see chart at left). The single largest group of psychologists works in colleges and universities, while large numbers of psychologists also work in independent practice and in hospitals, clinics, and other human-service settings (see chart at right).

As we shall see in Chapter 6, pure research in teaching sign language to chimpanzees and gorillas has led to ways of improving the communications skills of severely retarded humans.

Many psychologists do not engage in research at all. They are concerned with applying psychological knowledge to help individuals change their behavior so that they can be more effective in meeting their goals. A number of psychologists are also engaged primarily in teaching. They disseminate psychological knowledge in classrooms, seminars, and workshops. Figure 1.1 shows that a large percentage of psychologists are employed by colleges and universities, but some of these psychologists counsel students rather than teach.

Many psychologists are involved in all the activities described above: research, **consultation,** and teaching. For example, professors of psychology usually conduct pure or applied research and consult with individuals or industrial clients as well as instruct in the classroom. Full-time researchers may be called upon to consult with industrial clients and to organize seminars or workshops in which they help others acquire some of their skills. Practitioners, like clinical and industrial psychologists, may also engage in research—which is usually applied—and teach in the classroom or workshop. Unfortunately for psychologists who teach, conduct research, and also carry on a practice, research into expanding the week to 250 hours does not look promising.

Let us now explore some of the specialties of psychologists. Although psychologists tend to wear more than one hat, most of them carry out their functions in the following fields.

Consultation The provision of professional advice or services.

CLINICAL, COMMUNITY, AND COUNSELING PSYCHOLOGISTS

Clinical psychologists specialize in helping people who are behaving abnormally adjust to the demands of life. Their clients' problems may range from severe anxiety or depression to sexual dysfunctions to loss of goals in life. Clinical psychologists are trained to evaluate problems through structured interviews and psychological tests. They help their clients resolve their problems and change maladaptive behavior through the techniques of **psychotherapy** and **behavior therapy**. Clinical psychologists may work in institutions for the mentally ill or mentally retarded, in outpatient clinics, in college and university clinics, or they may establish private practices.

As you can see in Figure 1.1, clinical psychologists comprise the largest subgroup of psychologists. So it is not surprising that most lay people think of clinical psychologists when they hear the term *psychologist*. Many clinical psychologists divide their time between clinical practice, teaching, and research.

Community psychologists are similar to clinical psychologists in their training and functions. However, they more often work in community agencies—such as community mental-health centers—and they tend to focus on the prevention as well as the treatment of abnormal behavior. They consult with community organizations to develop ways of educating the public about personal and social problems, such as drug abuse and child abuse.

Counseling psychologists, like clinical psychologists, use interviews and tests to define their clients' problems. Clients of counseling psychologists typically have adjustment problems but do not behave in seriously abnormal ways. These problems may include difficulty making academic or vocational decisions, difficulty making friends in college, marital or family conflict, physical handicaps, or the adjustment problems of an offender who is returning to the community from prison. Counseling psychologists use various counseling methods to help clients clarify their goals and find ways of surmounting obstacles so that they can meet their goals. Counseling psychologists are often employed in college and university counseling and testing centers. They are also found in rehabilitation agencies.

SCHOOL AND EDUCATIONAL PSYCHOLOGISTS

School psychologists are employed by school systems to help identify and assist students who encounter problems that interfere with learning. These problems range from social and family problems to emotional disturbances and learning disabilities such as **dyslexia**. School psychologists define students' problems through interviews with teachers, parents, and students themselves, through psychological tests such as intelligence and achievement tests, and through direct observation of student behavior in the classroom. They consult with teachers, school officials, parents, and other professionals in an effort to help students overcome obstacles to learning. They help make decisions about placement of students in special education and remediation programs.

Educational psychologists, like school psychologists, are concerned with optimizing classroom conditions to facilitate learning. But they usually

CLINICAL PSYCHOLOGY Clinical psychologists are trained to evaluate problems through structured interviews and psychological tests. They help their clients resolve problems through techniques such as psychotherapy and behavior therapy.

Psychotherapy The systematic application of psychological knowledge to the treatment of problem behavior. Psychotherapy frequently encourages clients to express feelings and develop insight into motives; see Chapter 12. (From the Greek *psyche*, meaning "soul" or "mind," and *therapeuein*, meaning "to treat.")

Behavior therapy Application of principles of learning (see Chapter 5) to the direct modification of problem behavior. In contrast to psychotherapy, behavior therapy may be conducted without the development of client self-insight; see Chapter 12.

Dyslexia (dis-LEGS-see-uh). Impaired reading ability. (From the Greek prefix *dys-*, meaning "bad," and *lexis*, meaning "speech.")

focus on improvement of course planning and instructional methods for a school system rather than on the identification and assistance of children with learning problems.

Educational psychologists are often more concerned than school psychologists about theoretical issues relating to learning and child development. They are more likely to engage in pure and applied research and to hold faculty posts in colleges and universities. Educational psychologists who hold academic posts are likely to engage in research as to how variables like motivation, personality, intelligence, rewards and punishments, and teacher expectations influence learning. Some educational psychologists specialize in preparing standardized tests, such as the Scholastic Aptitude Tests.

DEVELOPMENTAL PSYCHOLOGISTS

Developmental psychologists study the changes—physical, emotional, cognitive, and social—that occur in people throughout the life span. They attempt to sort out the relative influences of heredity and the environment on certain types of growth and to learn the causes of developmental abnormalities.

We find developmental psychologists conducting research on a wide variety of issues. These may include the effects of maternal use of aspirin or heroin on an unborn child, the value of breast-feeding as compared with bottle feeding, children's concepts of space and time, adolescent sexual behavior, and factors that may help the elderly adjust to forced retirement.

PERSONALITY, SOCIAL, AND ENVIRONMENTAL PSYCHOLOGISTS

Personality psychologists attempt to define human traits; to determine influences on human thought processes, feelings, and behavior; and to explain both normal and abnormal behaviors. They are particularly concerned with human issues such as **anxiety,** aggression, **sex-typing,** and learning by observing others. Other topics of interest to personality psychologists include **repression** as a way in which we defend ourselves from feelings of anxiety and guilt, and the effects of television violence.

Social psychologists are primarily concerned with ways in which individuals and groups of people influence the behavior of other people. Whereas personality psychologists tend to look within the person for explanations of behavior, social psychologists tend to focus on social or external influences.

Social psychologists have historically focused on topics including attitude formation and attitude change, interpersonal attraction and liking, sex roles and **stereotypes,** obedience to authority, conformity to group norms, and group decision-making processes. Social psychologists, like personality psychologists, study the problem of human aggression.

Environmental psychologists are closely related to social psychologists. However, instead of focusing on how people behave in social situations, environmental psychologists study the ways in which behavior influ-

Anxiety A psychological state characterized by tension and apprehension, foreboding and dread. The causes of anxiety are usually less specific than the causes of fear. (From the Latin *angere,* meaning "to choke" or "to give pain.")

Sex-typing The process through which people acquire a sense of being male or being female and the traits considered typical of males or females.

Repression In personality theory, an automatic tendency to force anxiety-provoking thoughts, images, or impulses out of awareness. A type of defense mechanism. See Chapters 9 and 10.

Stereotype A fixed, conventional idea about a group. (From the Greek *stereos,* meaning "hard" or "fixed.")

ON HURRICANES, HIM-ICANES, AND SEX ROLES

Today the World Meteorological Association assigns men's as well as women's names to hurricanes. Since 1953, when storms were first named, a number of "female" storms had done their damage. But beginning in 1979, storms named Frederick and David joined their impetuous "sisters" in devastating the islands of the Caribbean and the southern coastline of the United States.

The World Meteorological Association added men's names to this frightening roster in response to protests from women's groups. The women had been outraged by the exclusive use of women's names, because of the implication that storminess and unpredictability were feminine traits.

A sex role is a cluster of traits considered masculine or feminine in our culture. Personality and social psychologists are vitally concerned about sex roles. Later in this book you will see that they have found at least partial answers to a number of provocative questions:

What traits are considered masculine? What traits are considered feminine?
Are women more emotional and less logical than men?
Are women more talkative than men?
Are men more aggressive than women?
How do men and women compare in their verbal and math skills?
Do women make natural mothers?

Sex roles have been changing in the United States. It used to be that a woman's place was in the home. But the majority of women now work—including most mothers of even young children. Here and there a handful of men are becoming househusbands, while their wives trek to the office each morning. For those who believe that women must devote themselves to their families, these events hinge on blasphemy. For those who see it as the man's role to be aggressive, competitive, and achievement-oriented, they are puz-

SEX ROLES In recent years, men and women have felt more free to express traits considered part of the sex role of the opposite sex. In this scene from the film *Kramer vs. Kramer*, Dustin Hoffman learns that he can be warm and supportive of his son—that he can show traits that have been traditionally considered feminine—after his wife leaves them.

zling. Yet it would appear that an increasing number of people, men and women, are challenging traditional sex roles by showing psychological androgyny. That is, they feel free to express traditionally masculine traits and traditionally feminine traits. They are self-assertive yet supportive, logical yet warm. In Chapter 13 we shall see that research suggests that psychologically androgynous people may be better able to adjust to life's challenges, because they can bring a wider range of traits to bear on them.

ences and is influenced by the physical environment. Like social psychologists, environmental psychologists are concerned with the effects of crowding on the behavior of city dwellers. Environmental psychologists study ways in which buildings and cities can be designed to better serve human needs. They also investigate the effects of extremes of temperature, noise, and air pollution on people and lower animals.

TABLE 1.1   Divisions of the American Psychological Association

General Psychology	Theoretical and Philosophical Psychology
The Teaching of Psychology	Experimental Analysis of Behavior
Experimental Psychology	History of Psychology
Evaluation and Measurement	Community Psychology
Physiological and Comparative Psychology	Psychopharmacology
Developmental Psychology	Psychotherapy
Personality and Social Psychology	Psychological Hypnosis
The Society for the Psychological Study of Social Issues	State Psychological Association Affairs
Psychology and the Arts	Humanistic Psychology
Clinical Psychology	Mental Retardation
Consulting Psychology	Population and Environmental Psychology
Society for Industrial and Organizational Psychology	Psychology of Women
Educational Psychology	Psychologists Interested in Religious Issues
School Psychology	Child, Youth, and Family Services
Counseling Psychology	Health Psychology
Psychologists in Public Service	Psychoanalysis
Military Psychology	Clinical Neuropsychology
Adult Development and Aging	American Psychology-Law Society
Applied and Experimental Engineering Psychology	Psychologists in Independent Practice
Rehabilitation Psychology	Family Psychology
Consumer Psychology	Society for the Psychological Study of Lesbian and Gay Issues

This constantly evolving list reflects the diversity of interests found among psychologists, as well as areas of social concern and individual specialties. Many psychologists are active in several divisions.

EXPERIMENTAL PSYCHOLOGISTS

Psychologists in all specialties may conduct experimental research. However, those called experimental psychologists conduct research into fundamental processes relevant to all other specializations. These include the functions of the nervous system, sensation and perception, learning and memory, thinking, language, motivation, and emotion, to name but a few. Experimental psychologists who focus on the biological foundations of behavior and seek to understand the relationships between biological changes and psychological events are called biological psychologists.

Experimental psychologists are more likely than other psychologists to engage in basic or pure research. Still, their findings are often applied by other specialists in psychological practice. Pure research in motivation, for example, has helped clinical and counseling psychologists devise strategies for helping people with weight problems. As noted earlier, pure research in learning and memory has helped school and educational psychologists optimize learning conditions in the schools.

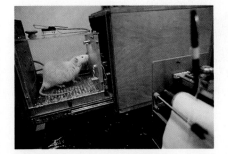

EXPERIMENTAL PSYCHOLOGY Experimental psychologists conduct research into fundamental psychological processes, such as the functions of the nervous system, sensation and perception, learning and memory, thinking, language, motivation, and emotion. Many experimental psychologists use rats as their subjects.

PSYCHOLOGISTS IN INDUSTRY

Industrial and organizational psychology are closely related fields. Industrial psychologists focus on the relationships between people and work, while organizational psychologists study the behavior of people in organizations (such as business organizations), and how organizations may function more efficiently. However, many psychologists are trained in both areas, and both industrial and organizational psychologists are employed by business firms to improve working conditions, enhance productivity, and—if they have counseling skills—to work with employees who encounter problems on the job. They assist in the processes of hiring, training, and promotion. They may use psychological tests and interviews to help determine whether job applicants have abilities, interests, and traits that predict successful performance of certain job responsibilities. They help with the innovation of concepts like **job sharing** and **flextime,** and their research skills equip them to evaluate the results.

Industrial psychology is a rapidly expanding specialization. As you can see in the nearby box on enhancing the quality of work life and productivity, businesses have been learning that psychological expertise can

Job sharing Dividing a full-time job into part-time work that is shared by two or more workers. Also called work sharing.

Flextime A flexible work schedule which attempts to meet worker as well as company needs.

PSYCHOLOGY IN THE WORKPLACE

HOW TO ENHANCE JOB SATISFACTION *AND PRODUCTIVITY:* IMPROVING THE QUALITY OF WORK LIFE IS ALSO GOOD BUSINESS

The history of the work place in the United States has too often pitted management against labor. Stories are rife about the long hours and back-breaking labor that antedated the union movement. Even today, companies fold because of demands for high wages that management is not able to meet.

Amidst this strife, industrial-organizational psychologists have applied their expertise in an effort to make the work place more satisfying to workers and also enhance productivity. Their research affords us more than just a glimmer of hope. Research suggests that management as well as labor has a vested interest in improving the quality of work life for at least two reasons. First, increased job satisfaction decreases employee turnover and absenteeism—two expensive measures of job *dis*satisfaction. Second, there is a positive relationship between productivity and the quality of work life. That is, many of the methods for increasing productivity also contribute to the satisfaction of the worker.

Industrial-organizational psychologists (Hunter & Schmidt, 1983; Katzell & Guzzo, 1983) have found that methods such as the following help make the difference:

Improved Recruitment and Placement. Part of the satisfaction/productivity issue is solved by using appropriate application forms, interviews, and tests to recruit the right person for the job (Hunter & Schmidt, 1983). Psychologists increase the adequacy of recruitment procedures by constructing tests and specifying the skills and personal attributes that are needed in a position.

Training and Instruction. Psychologists are well versed in principles of learning, and learning from training and instruction is the most commonly reported way of enhancing productivity (Katzell & Guzzo, 1983). Adequate training provides workers with appropriate skills and reduces the stresses impacting on them by equipping

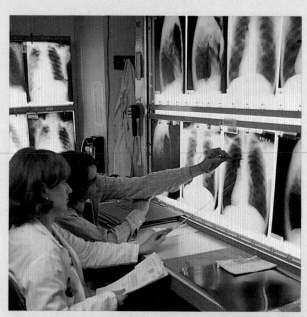

AN EXAMPLE OF PSYCHOLOGY IN THE WORKPLACE
Industrial-organizational psychologists are well versed in principles of learning and help fashion effective on-the-job training techniques. On-the-job training enhances workers' skills, reduces the stresses impacting upon them, and increases productivity.

them to solve the problems they will face. Capacity to solve challenging problems enhances workers' feelings of self-worth.

Appraisal and Feedback. Workers profit and productivity is enhanced when they receive individualized guidance, based on an accurate appraisal of their performance. Psychologists suggest that the focus should

help them increase productivity while at the same time decreasing employee turnover and absenteeism.

Consumer psychologists study the behavior of consumers in an effort to predict and influence their behavior. Their functions include advising store managers how to lay out the aisles of a supermarket to increase impulse buying and how to arrange window displays to draw customers in. They also devise strategies for making newspaper ads and television commercials more effective. Interestingly, they have found that while some ads may catch the eye, like the photo of Brooke Shields on p. 14, you may remember the photo but forget the product when the ad is too sexy (La-Chance et al., 1978; Schultz, 1978).

be on the positive reinforcement of skillful behavior, not the punishment of the inadequate.

Goal Setting. When goals are set at high but attainable levels, work is challenging but not excessively stressful. Psychologists know that, when workers are concretely aware of what is expected of them, they are better able to conform their behavior to expectation.

Financial Compensation. Psychologists are knowledgeable about the potentials and pitfalls of rewards. When possible, performance should be linked to financial reward. In many instances it is demoralizing when productive workers receive no more pay than nonproductive workers. If financial incentives for productivity are to be used, the assessment of productivity must be made in an absolutely fair, objective manner. If objective assessment is not possible, workers may become demoralized because of actual or suspected favoritism.

Work Redesign. Psychologists understand the importance of creating work settings in which workers can feel pride and a sense of closure. An assembly-line worker may repeat one task hundreds of times a day and never see the finished product. In order to make factory work more meaningful, workers at one Volvo assembly plant in Sweden have been organized into small groups that elect leaders and distribute tasks among themselves. In another work-redesign program, workers move along the assembly line with "their" truck chassis, providing them the satisfaction of seeing their product take shape (Blackler & Brown, 1978). In an experiment at Motorola, one worker builds an entire pocket radio pager and signs the product when finished. The janitorial staff at a Texas Instruments worksite meets in small groups to set goals and distribute cleaning tasks among themselves. Texas Instruments reports a cleaner plant, lowered costs, and decreased turnover (Dickson, 1975).

Supervisory Methods. Lombardo and McCall (1984) note that some intolerable bosses—little dictators, know-it-all's, incompetents and the like—aid the careers of supervisees. How? The supervisees learn what behavior to *avoid.* (But at an unforgivably high cost.) Democratic supervisors are usually liked better than authoritarian bosses, and democracy in the workplace usually pays off in enhanced productivity.

How can *you* cope with an intolerable boss? Lombardo and McCall (1984) suggest viewing your situation as a learning experience, not a disaster. Reinforce positive behavior from the boss and try to ignore (fail to reinforce) the negative. Search for common ground, common goals. But when all else fails, find a new job or bring the situation to a head with a (carefully detailed) interview with your boss's supervisor. When you become a boss, remember what you've learned. Try giving supervisees helpful criticism and recognizing their achievements. Give supervisees some responsibility, a chance to show what they can do.

Decision Making. Psychologists suggest that we are more motivated to carry out our jobs when we have had a role in deciding what to do. Management may have to carefully define the limits of jobs, but it is also wise for management to allow workers, and groups of workers, to make whatever decisions they can at their level. A worker who makes decisions not only increases the intrinsic rewards of the job; he or she also makes a commitment to behave in accord with them and enhance productivity.

Work Schedules. When there is no company reason for maintaining a rigid 9–5 schedule, workers frequently profit from flextime, being able to modify their own schedules to meet their personal needs. In one variation on flextime, workers put in four ten-hour workdays, rather than five eight-hour days (Ronen, 1981). At Honeywell, a "mothers' shift" allows women to coordinate their work schedules with their children's school hours. Mothers may also have college students fill in for them during their children's summer vacations. Are we ready for a "fathers' shift"?

Increasing the quality of work life turns out to be very good business for everyone.

CONSUMER PSYCHOLOGY Consumer psychologists study human behavior in an attempt to predict and influence our behavior as consumers. For example, consumer psychologists have found that if ads are too sexy, they may indeed catch the eye; however, the viewer may not be able to recall the name of the product. Does this photo of Brooke Shields in her Calvins help viewers recall the brand of jeans, or do they just remember Brooke Shields?

EMERGING FIELDS

There are many other fields and subfields in psychology today. The behavior problems that affect children can be very different from those encountered by adults; child clinical psychologists assess these problems and work with parents, teachers, and children themselves to overcome or adjust to them.

Health psychologists engage in research into the ways in which stress and other psychological factors can contribute to and influence the courses of diseases ranging from high blood pressure and heart problems to diabetes and cancer. Health psychologists also work with clients to help them discontinue harmful habits and engage in more healthful lifestyles; for example, they help clients to start exercising, to lose weight, and to stop or cut down smoking and alcohol intake.

Forensic psychologists apply psychological expertise within the criminal justice system. They may serve as expert witnesses in the courtroom, testifying as to the competence of defendants to stand trial, or describing mental disorders and how they may influence criminal behavior. Psychologists are employed by police departments to assist in the selection of stable applicants, to counsel officers as to how to cope with stress, and to train police in the handling of suicide threats, hostage crises, family disputes, and a host of other human problems.

Psychologists are continually finding new areas in which to apply their knowledge and skills.

WHERE PSYCHOLOGY COMES FROM: A BRIEF HISTORY

Psychology is as old as history and as modern as today. Although theoretical developments and research seem to dramatically change the face of contemporary psychology every few years, the outline for this textbook could have been written by the Greek philosopher Aristotle, who lived from 384 to 323 B.C. One of Aristotle's works was called *Peri Psyches*, which translates as "About the Psyche." *Peri Psyches* began with a history of psychological thought and historical perspectives on the nature of the mind and behavior! Given his scientific approach, Aristotle made the case that human behavior was subject to rules and laws, just as was the behavior of the stars and of the seas. Then Aristotle delved into his subject matter topic by topic: personality, sensation and perception, thought, intelligence, needs and motives, feelings and emotion, and memory. This book reorganizes these topics somewhat, but each is here.

There are many other contributors from ancient Greece. Democritus, for instance, suggested that we could think of behavior in terms of a body and a mind at about 400 B.C. (Contemporary psychologists prefer to talk about the interaction of physiological and cognitive processes.) Democritus also pointed out that our behavior was influenced by external stimulation, and he was one of the first to raise the issue of whether there is such a thing as free will or choice. After all, if we are influenced by external forces, can we be said to control our own behavior? This is a theme which will be repeatedly addressed in this book.

Plato (ca. 427–347 B.C.), the disciple of Socrates, recorded Socrates' advice, "Know thyself," which has remained a sort of motto of psychological thought ever since. Socrates claimed that we could not gain reliable self-knowledge through our senses, because the senses do not reflect reality with perfection; they even give rise to illusions. Since the senses provide imperfect knowledge, Socrates suggested that we should rely upon processes such as rational thought and **introspection** to gain self-knowledge. Today we are more willing to accept the accuracy of sensory information under most circumstances, but we still make the distinction between the stimuli that impact upon our sensory receptors—and presumably reflect the external world as it is—and our sometimes distorted perceptions of the world. Socrates can also be said to have stressed the importance of social psychology by pointing out how people are social creatures who are deeply influenced by one another.

If we had time, we could trace psychology's roots to more distant thinkers than the ancient Greeks, and we could trace its development through the great thinkers of the Renaissance. We could point to the influences of nineteenth-century developments such as the theory of evolution; atomic theory; theories as to how brain cells transmit messages to one another; theories as to how thoughts and memories are associated—even the development of statistics, which, as you will see in Appendix A, psychologists use to help determine the results of their research.

But as it is we must move to the development of psychology as a laboratory science during the second half of the nineteenth century.

Introspection A method of describing one's mental content as objectively as possible. (From the Latin *intro-*, meaning "inward," and *specere*, meaning "to look.")

STRUCTURALISM

There are so many controversies in psychology that it seems excessive to debate when modern psychology had its debut as an experimental science. But we should note that some historians set the marker date as 1860, when Gustav Theodor Fechner (1801–1887) published his *Elements of Psychophysics.* Fechner's book showed how physical events (such as lights and sounds) were related to psychological sensation and perception, and he showed how we could scientifically measure the impact of these events. However, most historians set the birth of psychology as a science in the year 1879, when Wilhelm Wundt (1832–1920) established the first psychological laboratory in Leipzig, Germany.

Wundt, as did Aristotle, claimed that the mind was a natural event and could be studied scientifically, just as light, heat, and the flow of blood. Wundt used the method of introspection, recommended by Socrates, to try to discover the basic elements of experience. When presented with various sights and sounds, he and his colleagues tried to look inward as objectively as possible to describe their sensations and feelings.

Wundt and his students—among them Edward Bradford Titchener, who brought Wundt's methodology to Cornell University in the United States—founded the school of psychology known as **structuralism.** Structuralism attempted to define the makeup of conscious experience, breaking it down into **objective** sensations, such as sight or taste, and **subjective** feelings, such as emotional responses, will, and mental images (for example, memories or dreams). Structuralists believed that the mind functioned by creatively combining the elements of experience.

Another of Wundt's American students was G. Stanley Hall (1844–1924), whose main interests included the psychological developments of childhood, adolescence, and old age. Hall founded the American Psychological Association.

Wilhelm Wundt.

FUNCTIONALISM

Toward the end of the nineteenth century, William James (1842–1910), brother of the novelist Henry James, adopted a broader view of psychology that focused on the relationships between conscious experience and behavior. James was a major figure in shifting the center of gravity of psychology from Germany to the United States. James received an MD from Harvard University, then spent his professional career teaching at Harvard—first in physiology, then in philosophy, and then in psychology. He described his views in the first modern psychology textbook, *The Principles of Psychology,* published in 1890 by the same publisher as the book you are now reading. Though it is almost a hundred years old, James's book is still considered by some to be the "single greatest work in American psychology" (Adelson, 1982, p. 52). In *Principles,* which became known to students as the "Jimmy," James argued that the stream of consciousness is fluid and continuous. James's experiences with introspection assured him that experience cannot be broken down into basic units as readily as the structuralists maintained.

Structuralism The school of psychology, founded by Wundt and his students, which argues that the mind consists of three basic elements—sensations, feelings, and images—that combine to form experience.

Objective Of known or perceived objects rather than existing only in the mind; real.

Subjective Of the mind; personal; determined by thoughts and feelings rather than by external objects.

William James.

James also founded the school of **functionalism,** which dealt with overt behavior as well as consciousness. Functionalism addressed the ways in which experience permits us to function more adaptively in our environments and used behavioral observation in the laboratory to supplement introspection. James was heavily influenced by Charles Darwin's theory of evolution. Darwin argued that organisms with adaptive features survive and reproduce, while those without them are doomed to extinction. James adapted Darwin's view to behavior and proposed that more adaptive actions are learned and maintained, while less adaptive behavior patterns are discontinued. Adaptive actions tend to be repeated and become **habits.** In his chapter on habit, James wrote that "habit is the enormous flywheel of society." Habit, in other words, largely supplies the power that keeps things going from day to day.

The formation of habits is seen in acts such as lifting forks to our mouths and turning doorknobs. These acts require our full attention at first. If you don't believe this, stand by with paper towels and watch a baby's first efforts at self-feeding. But through repetition, self-feeding responses become automatic, or habitual. The multiple acts involved in learning to drive a car also become habitual through repetition. We can then carry them out without much attention at all, freeing ourselves to focus on other matters, such as our witty conversation and the tasteful sounds emanating from the radio. The concept of learning by repetition is also basic to the behavioral tradition.

BEHAVIORISM

Think of placing a hungry rat in a maze. It meanders down a pathway that comes to an end, and it can then turn left or right. If you consistently reward the rat with food for turning right at this choice-point, it will learn to turn right when it arrives there, at least when it is hungry. But what does the rat *think* when it is learning to turn right? "Hmm, last time I was in this situation and turned to the right, I was given some food. Think I'll try that again"?

Does it seem ridiculous to try to place yourself in the "mind" of a rat? So it seemed to John Broadus Watson (1878–1958), the founder of American **behaviorism.** But Watson was asked to consider just such a question as one of the requirements for his doctoral degree, which he received from the University of Chicago in 1903. Functionalism was abroad in the land and dominant at the University of Chicago at the time, and functionalists were concerned with the stream of consciousness as well as overt behavior. Watson bridled at the introspective efforts of the functionalists to study consciousness—especially the consciousness of lower animals. He asserted that if psychology were to be a natural science, like physics or chemistry, it must limit itself to observable, measurable events or behavior. It must not concern itself with "elements of consciousness" that were accessible only to the organism experiencing them.

Watson agreed with the functionalist focus on the importance of learning, however, and suggested that psychology address the learning of measurable **responses** to environmental **stimuli.** He pointed to the laboratory

Functionalism The school of psychology, founded by William James, that emphasizes the uses or functions of the mind rather than the elements of experience.

Habit A response to a stimulus that becomes automatic with repetition.

Behaviorism The school of psychology that defines psychology as the study of observable behavior only, and investigates relationships between stimuli and responses.

Response In behavioral theory, a movement or other observable reaction to a stimulus.

Stimuli (STIM-you-lie, or STIM-you-lee). Plural of *stimulus.* (1) A change in the environment that leads to a change in behavior (a response). (2) Any form of physical energy, like light or sound, that impinges on the sensory receptors of an organism. (A Latin word meaning "goad," "pang," "spur," or "incentive.")

John B. Watson.

B. F. Skinner.

experiments being conducted by Ivan Pavlov in Russia as a model. Pavlov had found that dogs will learn to salivate when a bell is rung, if ringing the bell has been repeatedly associated with feeding. Pavlov explained the salivation in terms of the laboratory conditions, or **conditioning,** that led to it—not in terms of the imagined mental processes of the dogs. Moreover, the response that Pavlov chose to study, salivation, was a public event that could be measured by laboratory instruments. It was absurd to try to determine what a dog, or person, is thinking.

Watson went to Johns Hopkins University in 1908, where behaviorism took root and soon became firmly planted in American psychology. In 1920 Watson got a divorce so that he could marry a former student, and the scandal forced him to leave academic life. For a while Watson sold coffee and worked as a clerk in a department store. Then he undertook a second profitable career in advertising, and he eventually became a vice-president in a New York agency.

Harvard University psychologist B. F. Skinner took up the behaviorist call and introduced the concept of **reinforcement** to behaviorism. Organisms, Skinner maintained, learn to behave in certain ways because they have been reinforced for doing so. Skinner demonstrated that laboratory animals would carry out various simple and complex behaviors because of reinforcement. They will peck buttons (Figure 1.2) or turn in circles, then climb ladders and push toys across the floor (see Barnabus the Rat in Chapter 5). Many psychologists adopted the view that, in principle, one could explain complex human behavior as the summation of instances of learning through reinforcement. Nevertheless, as a practical matter, they recognized that trying to list even one person's complete history of reinforcement would be a hopeless task.

Conditioning In behavioral theory, a simple form of learning in which responses become associated with stimuli. See Chapter 5.

Reinforcement In behavioral theory, a stimulus that follows a response and increases the frequency of the response. See Chapter 5.

Gestalt psychology (gesh-TALT). The school of psychology that emphasizes the tendency to organize perceptions into wholes, to integrate separate stimuli into meaningful patterns. (*Gestalt* is a German word meaning "shape" or "form.")

FIGURE 1.2 A COUPLE OF EXAMPLES OF THE POWER OF REINFORCEMENT
In the photo on the left, we see how our feathered gift to city life has earned its keep in many behavioral experiments on the effects of reinforcement. Here the pigeon pecks the blue button because pecking this button has been followed (reinforced) by the dropping of a food pellet into the cage. In the photo on the right, Magic Raccoon shoots a basket. Behaviorists teach animals complex behaviors, like shooting baskets, by first reinforcing approximations to the goal (or target behavior). As time progresses, closer approximations are demanded before reinforcement is given.

GESTALT PSYCHOLOGY

In the 1920s, another school of psychology was quite active in Germany: **Gestalt psychology.** In the 1930s, the three founders of the school, Max Wertheimer (1880–1943), Kurt Koffka (1886–1941), and Wolfgang Köhler (1887–1967), left Europe to escape the Nazi threat. They carried on their work in the United States, giving further impetus to America's ascendance in psychology.

Wertheimer and his colleagues focused on perception, and on how perception influences thinking and problem solving. In contrast to the behaviorists, Gestalt psychologists argued that one cannot hope to understand human nature by focusing on overt behavior alone. In contrast to the structuralists, they claimed that one cannot explain human perceptions, emotions, or thought processes in terms of basic units. Perceptions were *more* than the sums of their parts; Gestalt psychologists saw our perceptions as wholes that give meanings to parts.

Gestalt psychologists illustrated how we tend to perceive separate pieces of information as integrated wholes, including the contexts in which they occur. As an example, note Figure 1.3. The dots in the centers of the configurations at the left are the same size, yet we may perceive them as being of different sizes because of the contexts in which they appear. The gray squares in the center figure are equally bright, but they may look different because of their differing backgrounds. The second symbol in each line at the right is identical. But in the top row we may perceive it as a B,

Max Wertheimer.

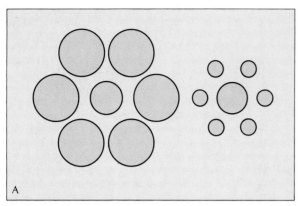
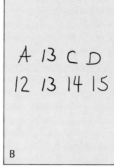
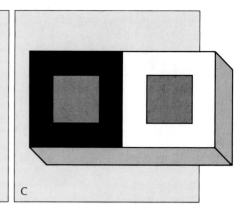

(A) Are the dots in the center of the configuration the same size? Why not take a ruler and measure their diameters?

(B) Is the second symbol in each line the letter B or the number 13?

(C) Which of the gray squares is brighter?

FIGURE 1.3 **THE IMPORTANCE OF CONTEXT** Gestalt psychologists have shown that our perceptions depend not only on our sensory impressions, but also on the context of our impressions. They argue that human perception cannot be explained in terms of basic units, because we tend to interpret our perceptions of things as wholes, in terms of the contexts in which they occur. You will interpret a man's running in your direction very differently depending on whether you are on a deserted street at night or at a track in the morning.

and in the bottom row as the number 13. The symbol has not changed, only the context in which it appears. In *The Prince and the Pauper*, Mark Twain dressed a peasant boy as a prince, and the kingdom bowed to him. Do clothes sometimes make the man, or woman?

Gestalt psychologists believed that learning could be active and purposeful, not merely responsive and mechanical, as in Pavlov's experiments. Wolfgang Köhler and the others demonstrated that much learning, especially in learning to solve problems, is accomplished by **insight,** not by mechanical repetition. Köhler was marooned by the First World War on one of the Canary Islands, where the Prussian Academy of Science kept a colony of apes, and his research on the island gave him, well, insight into the process of learning by insight.

Consider the chimpanzee in Figure 1.4. At first it is unsuccessful in reaching for bananas hanging from the ceiling. Then it suddenly piles the boxes atop one another and climbs them to reach the banana. It seems that the chimp has experienced a sudden reorganization of the mental elements that represent the problem—that is, has had a "flash of insight." Köhler's findings suggest that we often manipulate the mentally represented elements of problems until we group them in such a way that we believe that we shall be able to reach our goal. The manipulations may take quite some time in a sort of mental trial and error. But once the proper grouping has been found, we seem to perceive it all at once.

Insight In Gestalt psychology, the sudden reorganization of perceptions, allowing the sudden solution of a problem.

FIGURE 1.4 SOME INSIGHT INTO THE ROLE OF INSIGHT At first the chimpanzee cannot reach the bananas hanging from the ceiling. After some time has passed, it suddenly piles the boxes on top of one another to reach the fruit, behavior suggestive of a "flash of insight." Gestalt psychologists argue that behavior is often too complex to be explained in terms of learning mechanical responses to environmental stimulation.

Have you ever sat pondering a problem for quite a while, and then suddenly the solution has appeared? Did it seem to "come out of nowhere"? In a flash? Was it difficult at that point to understand how it could have taken so long?

Gestalt principles of perceptual organization will be discussed in Chapter 3, and learning by insight will be expanded in Chapter 5.

PSYCHOANALYSIS

Psychoanalysis, the school of psychology founded by Sigmund Freud, is very different from the other schools in its background and in its approach. Psychoanalytic theory, more than the others, has invaded the popular culture, and you may already be familiar with a number of its concepts.

Think of television crime shows for a moment. Every year on at least one show, a mentally unbalanced person goes on a killing spree. At the show's conclusion a **psychiatrist** explains that the killer was "unconsciously" doing away with his own mother or father. Or perhaps a friend has tried to "interpret" a slip of the tongue you made, or asked you what you thought might be the symbolic "meaning" of a dream.

The notions that people are driven by deeply hidden impulses, and that verbal slips and dreams represent unconscious wishes, reflect the influence of one man, Sigmund Freud (1856–1939), a Viennese physician

Psychoanalysis The school of psychology, founded by Sigmund Freud, that emphasizes the importance of unconscious motives and conflicts as determinants of human behavior. (Also the name of Freud's method of psychotherapy.)

Psychiatrist A physician who specializes in the application of medical treatments to abnormal behavior.

who fled to England in the 1930s to escape the Nazi tyranny. In contrast to the academic psychologists, who conducted research mainly in the laboratory, Freud gained his understanding of human thoughts, emotions, and behavior through clinical interviews with his patients. He was astounded at how little insight his patients seemed to have into their motives. Some patients justified the most abominable behavior with absurd explanations. Others, by contrast, seized the opportunity to blame themselves for nearly every misfortune that had befallen the human species.

Freud came to believe that hidden impulses, especially primitive sexual and aggressive impulses, were more influential than conscious thought in determining human behavior. As you will see in later chapters, Freud thought that most of the mind was unconscious, consisting of a seething cauldron of conflicting impulses, urges, and wishes. People were motivated to gratify these impulses, ugly as some of them were, but at the same time they were motivated to think positively of themselves. Thus, they would often delude themselves about their own motives.

Freud devised a method of psychotherapy called psychoanalysis. Psychoanalysis aims to help patients gain insight into many of their deep-seated conflicts and to find socially acceptable ways of expressing wishes and gratifying needs. Psychoanalytic therapy is a long-term process that can last several years, and we shall describe it at length in Chapter 12.

Today we no longer find psychologists who describe themselves as structuralists or functionalists. Although the school of Gestalt psychology gave birth to current research approaches in perception and problem solving, few would consider themselves Gestalt psychologists. So too are there relatively few "traditional" behaviorists or psychoanalysts. As we shall see in the following section, many contemporary psychologists in the behaviorist tradition look upon themselves as social-learning theorists, and most psychoanalysts consider themselves neoanalysts as opposed to traditional "Freudians." Still, the historical traditions of psychology find expression in many contemporary fields and schools of psychology, as we shall see throughout the book.

Sigmund Freud.

HOW TODAY'S PSYCHOLOGISTS VIEW BEHAVIOR

In order to understand the various perspectives from which today's psychologists view behavior, let us use the example of the continuing human problem of violence. It turns out that for violence, there's no place like home. Consider the following statistics:

Half of all American wives have been physically assaulted by their husbands at least once.

In a given year, 16 of every 100 couples have conflicts that involve biting, kicking, punching, or worse.

Each year more than a million American children are brought to the attention of authorities as victims of child abuse.

We know to avoid dark streets and alleyways and not to frequent unknown bars. We know that the world at large is a violent place, with open warfare and guerrilla conflict. But for many Americans, the most dangerous place is home. In *Behind Closed Doors: A Survey of Family Violence in America,* Murray Strauss and his colleagues (1979) estimate that as many as eight million Americans are assaulted by family members each year.

Psychologists tend to view problems like human violence and aggression from a variety of perspectives, or broad psychological theories. There are at least five major perspectives in contemporary psychology: the biological, the cognitive, the humanistic, the psychoanalytic, and learning-theory perspectives. Let us have a look at each of them to see what they have to say about human nature. We shall also note what each perspective suggests about the origins and control of human aggression. While it is simplistic to make broad generalizations about these perspectives, let us note that the first four tend to look within the person for explanations of behavior. The fifth—learning theory—tends to focus on the person's situation, or circumstances.

THE BIOLOGICAL PERSPECTIVE

Psychologists assume that every thought, fantasy, dream, and mental image is made possible by the nervous system, and especially by that central part of the nervous system we call the brain. Biologically oriented psychologists seek links between measurable events in the brain—such as the "firing" of brain cells—and mental processes. They have used techniques such as electrical stimulation of certain sites in the brain to show that these areas are involved in a wide range of emotional and behavioral responses—for example, mating behavior and aggression.

Psychologists who focus on biological **determinants** of behavior also study the influence of hormones and genes. For instance, the **hormone** prolactin stimulates not only production of milk in rats but also maternal behavior. In lower animals, sex hormones not only spur development of the sex organs, but also determine whether mating behavior will follow stereotypical male or female behavior patterns. **Genes** are the basic units of heredity. Psychologists are vitally interested in the extent of genetic influences on human traits and behaviors such as intelligence, abnormal behaviors, criminal behaviors, and even the tendency to become addicted to alcohol and **morphine.** Recent studies (see Chapter 2) have shown that identical twins (who share the same genetic endowment) are more likely than fraternal twins (who are no more closely related than other brothers and sisters) to share such broad personality traits as sociability, emotionality, and level of activity. In Chapter 6 we shall see that the degree to which intelligence reflects heredity (*"nature"*) or environmental influences (*"nurture"*) is a hotly debated issue, with major political implications.

The Biological Perspective and Aggression Electrical stimulation of the brain triggers aggressive behaviors and **rage responses** in a number of lower animals. Thus, some psychologists have suggested that human aggres-

Determinants Factors that set limits.

Hormone A chemical substance that promotes development of bodily structures and regulates various bodily functions. (From the Greek *horman,* meaning "to stimulate" or "to excite.")

Genes The basic building blocks of heredity.

Morphine (MORE-feen). A narcotic derived from opium that produces feelings of well-being. (From *Morpheus,* the Greek god of dreams.)

Rage response Stereotypical aggressive behavior that can be brought forth in lower animals by electrical stimulation of the brain.

ELICITING A RAGE RESPONSE BY ELECTRICAL STIMULATION OF THE BRAIN Biological psychologists use electrical stimulation of the brain (ESB) and other techniques to learn what parts of the brain are linked to such behaviors as mating and aggression. The monkey in this photo is exhibiting a rage response, not because the other monkey in the cage has provoked him, but because certain areas deep within his brain are receiving electrical stimulation.

sion may someday be controlled through ESB or other biological means of changing behavior. This concept conjures up the spectre of people being made into docile, compliant robots, then manipulated into doing the bidding of others. But this type of control apparently is not possible with humans; aggression seems less localized and mechanical in people than in lower animals.

Sociobiology   The offshoot of the biological perspective called **sociobiology** became popular in the 1970s. Sociobiology views the gene as the "ultimate unit of life," or the "hereditary units . . . which either fail or prosper as a result of (natural) selection" (Leak & Christopher, 1982, pp. 313–314). Sociobiology argues that the underlying purpose of animal behavior is to contribute as many genes as possible to the next generation. More aggressive individuals are usually more likely to survive to maturity and reproduce. Therefore, whatever genes are linked to aggressive behavior may be more likely to be transmitted to the following generation. This view is thought to apply to people as well as lower animals, although our intelligence—our capacity to outwit other species—may be a more central factor in our survival.

Sociobiological theory also attempts to explain **altruism** among animals and people—for example, why some animals (e.g., some monkeys and apes) will sacrifice themselves (say, by attacking a leopard that has broken into a colony of monkeys), so that the remainder of the colony has time to flee the predator. From the sociobiological perspective, altruistic behavior is basically selfish. Sociobiologists argue that the self-sacrificing animal shares a large gene pool with relatives in the colony, and so the act of self-sacrifice actually increases the chances that one's genes will survive.

Sociobiology A biological theory of social behavior which assumes that the primary purpose of behavior is to insure the transmission of an organism's genes from generation to generation.

Altruism Selflessness; unselfish concern for the welfare of others. (From the Latin *alter,* meaning "another.")

Sociobiology has been severely attacked on various grounds. Many scientists argue that it is absurd to suggest that genes can harbor anything akin to an "intent" to be transmitted. Sociobiology also seems to suggest that aggressiveness is natural and desirable. Thus, efforts to control aggression can be seen as doomed to failure and even morally questionable, because they interfere with with the natural order of things.

But do not confuse sociobiology with the biological perspective at large. While the role of sociobiology remains controversial, the biological perspective makes regular vital contributions to our understanding of behavior and to human welfare, as we shall see in later chapters.

THE COGNITIVE PERSPECTIVE

Psychologists with a **cognitive** perspective are interested in studying our mental processes. They investigate how we perceive and mentally represent the outside world, how we go about solving problems, how we dream and daydream. Cognitive psychologists, in short, attempt to study all those things we refer to as the *mind*.

The cognitive tradition has clear roots in Socrates' advice "Know thyself," and in Socrates' suggested method of looking inward to find truth. We also find cognitive psychology's roots in structuralism, functionalism, and Gestalt psychology, each of which, in its own way, addressed issues that are still of interest to cognitive psychologists.

Today the cognitive perspective has many faces. For instance, Swiss psychologist Jean Piaget's (1896–1980) innovative study of the intellectual or cognitive development of children has inspired thousands of research projects by developmental and educational psychologists. The focus of this research is to learn how children and adults mentally represent and reason about the world.

As we shall see in Chapter 8, Piaget has shown us that the child's conception of the world seems to develop through various stages of sophistication. Although the role of experience is essential to children, their cognitive understanding also seems to develop according to something akin to an inner clock.

Another area of interest to cognitive psychologists is **information processing**—the processes by which information is perceived, stored, and retrieved (recalled). Psychologists are given to thinking of human processes in terms of the status of the physical sciences of the day. So it is not surprising that a number of cognitive psychologists describe human information processing in computer science concepts such as input and output and bits of information.

The Cognitive Perspective and Aggression Cognitive psychologists assert that our behavior is influenced by our values, our perceptions of our situations, and by choice. For example, people who believe that aggression is necessary and justified, as in wartime, are likely to act aggressively in that situation. People who believe that a particular war or act of aggression is unjust, or who oppose aggression under all circumstances, are less likely to behave aggressively. Piaget noted that the bases of our moral judgments

Cognitive Having to do with mental processes. Cognitive psychologists are concerned with topics such as sensation and perception, memory, intelligence, language, thought, and problem solving. (From the Latin *cognito,* meaning "knowledge.")

Information processing The ways in which knowledge is perceived, stored, and retrieved.

change as we mature. For instance, five-year-old children might consider an act of aggression wrong, simply because they have been told that aggression is bad. However, an eight-year-old child would also be likely to consider the motives of the aggressor.

Cognitively oriented psychologists also focus on the ways in which our thoughts **mediate** behavior, or come between environmental events and our overt responses to them. Cognitively oriented psychotherapists, for example, note that we are more likely to respond aggressively to a provocation when our thoughts magnify the insult or otherwise stir feelings of anger. In Chapter 12 you will see how a number of explosive people gained control of aggressive impulses when they learned to perceive a provocation as a problem demanding a solution, rather than as an insult demanding retaliation.

Psychologists in the behaviorist tradition argue that cognitions are not directly observable, and that cognitive psychologists do not place adequate emphasis on the situational determinants of behavior. Cognitive psychologists counter that human behavior cannot be understood without reference to cognition. Below we shall see that social-learning theorists straddle the cognitive and behaviorist perspectives, and balance the roles of cognitive and situational influences on behavior.

THE HUMANISTIC PERSPECTIVE

Humanistic psychology is a recent school of psychology that is strongly related to Gestalt psychology and has a cognitive flavor. Humanism stresses the human capacity for self-fulfillment and the central roles of human consciousness, self-awareness, and the capacity to make choices. Consciousness is seen as the unifying force underlying our personalities.

Because of its focuses on consciousness and self-awareness, humanistic psychology is also labeled **phenomenological.** The word *phenomenon* is derived from the same Greek root as the word *fantasy*. However, fantasy implies that one's perceptions are inaccurate and unreal, while a phenomenon is an event as perceived by a person, and may be quite realistic. In any event, humanistic psychology considers the person's experience, as perceived by the person, to be the most important event in psychology. Humanists believe that self-awareness, experience, and choice permit us to a large extent to "invent ourselves"—to fashion our growth and our ways of responding to the world—as we go through life.

In the previous section it was mentioned that there is an ongoing debate in psychology as to whether we are free to choose or whether our behavior is determined by external factors. John Watson's behaviorism was a deterministic stance. The humanistic approach of American psychologists like Carl Rogers (born 1902), Rollo May (born 1909), and Abraham Maslow (1916–1972) asserts that we are basically free. To humanists, freedom is a source of both pride and great responsibility. Humanistic psychologists suggest that we are engaged in quests to discover our personal identities and the meanings of our lives.

The goals of humanistic psychology have been more applied than academic. Humanistic psychologists have been involved in devising ways to help people "get in touch" with their feelings and realize their potentials.

Mediate To go between.

Humanistic psychology The school of psychology that assumes the existence of the self and emphasizes the importance of consciousness and self-awareness.

Phenomenological (feh-NOM-men-no-LODGE-uh-cal). Having to do with the human experience of perceiving the world.

Humanistic psychology reached the peak of its popularity in the 1970s with encounter groups, gestalt therapy, meditation, and a number of other methods that have been referred to, collectively, as the Human Potential Movement. We shall discuss some of these techniques in Chapters 4 and 12.

The Humanistic Perspective and Aggression   Humanistic psychologists are generally optimistic about human nature. They do not see aggression as an inevitable state of affairs, but rather as a defensive reaction to frustrations imposed upon us by people who, for their own reasons, do not want us to develop into what we are capable of being. Humanistic psychotherapists have sought to help clients get in touch with their true motives and potentials, and have encouraged them to express their genuine feelings. The faith is that, when people are truly free to choose their own directions in life and express their own feelings, they do not choose violence.

Critics, including those in the behaviorist tradition, insist that psychology must be a natural science and address itself to observable events. They argue that our experiences are subjective events that are poorly suited to objective observation and measurement. Humanists like Carl Rogers (1985) may agree that the observation methods of humanists have sometimes been less than scientific, but they argue that subjective human experience remains vital to the understanding of human nature and that research methods can be improved.

THE PSYCHOANALYTIC PERSPECTIVE

Contemporary followers of Freud are likely to consider themselves neoanalysts. Neoanalysts like Karen Horney, Erich Fromm, and Erik Erikson tend to focus less on the roles of unconscious sexual and aggressive impulses in human behavior, and more on conscious choice and self-direction. In this sense they are more humanistic than Freud was, a point that will be elaborated in Chapter 9.

The Psychoanalytic Perspective and Aggression   While many neoanalysts may be humanistic in their approach, Sigmund Freud's view of aggression and human nature was quite different from that of the humanists. Freud believed that aggressive impulses were an inevitable result of the frustrations of daily life, even if others tried to give us the freedom to develop as we wished. Children (and adults) would normally desire to vent aggressive impulses on other people, including parents, because even the most attentive parents could not meet all their children's demands immediately. Yet children, also fearing their parents' retribution and loss of love, would come to repress most aggressive impulses. Still, aggressive impulses might be expressed toward the parents in other ways, or they might be expressed against strangers later in life.

In his later years Freud became so despondent about the mass slaughter of World War I and other human tragedies that he also proposed the existence of a death instinct, **thanatos.** Thanatos was the ultimate expression of what Freud saw as the unconscious human wish to return to the stress-free days prior to birth—not a very pretty picture of human nature.

Thanatos (THAN-uh-toes). In psychoanalytic theory, the death instinct. (A Greek word meaning "death.")

Research has been somewhat hard on the psychoanalytic perspective. Still, psychoanalysts claim, with some justification, that their views have not been tested adequately in the laboratory. We shall expand our discussion and evaluation of psychoanalysis in Chapter 9.

LEARNING-THEORY PERSPECTIVES

Many psychologists today focus on the effects of experience upon behavior. Learning, to them, is the essential factor in describing, explaining, predicting, and controlling behavior. However, there are different kinds of learning, and some of them have a role for consciousness and self-awareness, while others do not, as we see in the behavioral and the social-learning perspectives.

The Behavioral Perspective John B. Watson was a **radical behaviorist.** Behaviorism for him was a philosophy of life as well as a broad guideline for psychological research. Not only did Watson despair of measuring consciousness and mental processes in the laboratory; he also denied their influence on behavior in his private conversations.

Learning, for Watson and his followers, is exemplified by experiments in conditioning. The results of conditioning are explained in terms of external laboratory procedures and not what changes have occurred within the organism. Behaviorists do not attempt to find out what an organism has come to "know" through learning.

The Social-Learning Perspective **Social-learning theorists** may well comprise the largest group of learning theorists today. Albert Bandura of Stanford University and other social-learning theorists see themselves as within the behaviorist tradition because of their strong focus on the role of learning in human behavior. However, they also return to their functionalist roots in the sense that they perceive a major role for cognition. Whereas behaviorists emphasize the importance of learning habits through repetition and reinforcement, social-learning theorists emphasize the importance of learning by observing others. Observational learning, as we shall see in Chapters 5 and 9, is not mechanical; instead, we acquire a storehouse of possible responses through observation. Social-learning theorists are also humanistic in that they believe that our expectations and values play a role in determining whether we shall do the things we have learned how to do.

Albert Bandura.

Learning-Theory Perspectives and Aggression From the behavioral perspective, learning is acquired through principles of reinforcement. Organisms that are reinforced for aggressive behavior become more likely to behave aggressively in similar situations. From the social-learning perspective, as we shall see in Chapter 9, aggressive skills are acquired predominantly by observing others. However, social-learning theorists find roles for consciousness and choice. They believe that we are not likely to act aggressively, unless we also believe that aggression is appropriate for us under the circumstances.

The social-learning perspective in a sense integrates the behavioral, cognitive, and humanistic perspectives. Some psychologists believe that the future of psychology will see continued efforts to integrate these approaches. The behaviorist tradition, they assert, has served its historic purpose of highlighting some of the nonscientific excesses that have characterized cognitive and humanistic efforts to explore the "stream of consciousness." But no approach that diminishes the roles of human values and personal choice can be adequate to explain the complexity and richness of human behavior. Fully consistent with the history and traditions of psychology, other psychologists would disagree with this assessment of future directions.

Historic traditions and theoretical perspectives encourage psychologists to focus on various psychological questions and issues in their research. Their research findings are also made meaningful by integrating them with existing perspectives, or by creating new perspectives that will encompass them when current perspectives fail. In the next section, we survey the methods that today's psychologists use in their investigation of behavior. Just as there are many traditions in psychology, there are also many ways of conducting research.

HOW PSYCHOLOGISTS STUDY BEHAVIOR

Do only people use tools? Does alcohol cause aggression? Does pornography trigger crimes of violence?

Many of us have expressed opinions on questions like these at one time or another. But psychology is a science. Within a science, assumptions about the behavior of cosmic rays, chemical compounds, cells, or people must be supported by evidence. Strong arguments, reference to authority figures, even tightly knit theories are not considered evidence in psychology. While psychology is a theoretical science, it is also an **empirical** science. Evidence must thus be based upon carefully controlled observations in the laboratory and elsewhere.

Psychologists gather evidence for their assumptions about behavior in a number of ways. In this section we examine the naturalistic-observation method, the experimental method, the survey method, the testing method, the case-study method, and the correlational method.

THE NATURALISTIC-OBSERVATION METHOD

The next time you go to McDonald's or Burger King for lunch, have a look around. Pick out slender people and overweight people and observe whether they eat their burgers and fries differently. Do the overweight eat more rapidly? Chew less frequently? Leave less food on their plates? This is precisely the type of research psychologists have recently used to study the eating habits of normal- and overweight people. In fact, if you notice some mysterious-looking people at McDonald's watching others over sunglasses and occasionally tapping the head of a partly concealed microphone, per-

Empirical Emphasizing or based on observation and experiment, in contrast to theory. (From the Greek *empeiria,* meaning "experience.")

FIGURE 1.5 **THE NATURALISTIC-OBSERVATION METHOD** In the naturalistic-observation method, psychologists study behavior in the field, "where it happens." For example, psychologists have recorded patterns of eating at fast-food restaurants to learn whether obese people eat more rapidly, or take larger bites, than normal-weight people.

haps they are recording their observations of other people's eating habits—even as you watch.

This method of scientific investigation is called **naturalistic observation** (Figure 1.5). Psychologists and other scientists use it to observe behavior in the field, or "where it happens." They try to avoid interfering with the behaviors they are observing by using **unobtrusive** measures. Jane Goodall has observed the behavior of chimpanzees in their natural environment in order to learn about their social behavior, sexual behavior, use of tools, and other facts of chimp life. Her observations have shown us that (1) we were incorrect to think that only people use tools; and (2) kissing, as a greeting, is used by **primates** other than humans. But don't conclude that using tools or kissing are inborn or **instinctive** behaviors among primates. Chimps, like people, can learn from experience. It may be that they learned how to use tools and to kiss. The naturalistic-observation method may tell us what is happening as we watch, but it is not the best method for determining the causes of behavior.

Other scientists have observed the Tasaday, a recently discovered primitive tribe in the Philippine Islands. Aggressive behavior is unknown among the Tasaday. It may be somewhat romantic to conclude that aggressive behavior results from civilization, especially since many other primitive tribes have been known to be quite aggressive. Still, the findings on the Tasaday show that aggression is not universal among human beings. Thus, aggression may not be an unavoidable part of the human condition.

There are many problems with the naturalistic-observation method. For instance, sometimes we see what we want to see. Kissing behavior among chimps seems to serve a social function similar to human kissing, but "kissing" by the kissing gourami, a tropical fish, seems to be a test of strength. We must be cautious in our interpretations. In Chapter 6 we shall

Naturalistic observation A method of scientific investigation in which organisms are observed carefully in their natural environments.

Unobtrusive Avoiding interfering. (From the Latin *trudere*, meaning "to thrust.")

Primate (PRY-mate). A member of an order of mammals including people, apes, and monkeys.

Instinctive Inborn, natural, unlearned. (From the Latin *instinguere*, meaning "to impel" or "to instigate.")

see that there is also a controversy concerning observation of the use of sign language in chimps and gorillas.

We must also be certain that the animals or people we are observing represent the target **population,** such as citizens of the United States (rather than young business people in Southern California or white, middle-class Americans). Visitors from space who encountered only the Tasaday would gain an erroneous impression of the human potential for violence. Visitors who observed the Times Square area in New York might conclude that only men are sexually aroused by pornography, since very few women attend such films and are usually accompanied by men when they do. In Chapter 13 you will see that other types of observations lead to very different conclusions.

Finally, it is difficult to determine the causes of behavior through naturalistic observation. After visiting a few bars near the university where I teach, you might conclude that alcohol causes aggressive behavior as you duck to avoid the flying ashtrays and chairs. There is little doubt that aggression often accompanies drinking, but you will soon learn that alcohol may not cause aggression—at least among college males who are social drinkers.

THE EXPERIMENTAL METHOD

Most psychologists would agree that the preferred method for answering research questions, such as whether alcohol causes aggression, is the experimental method. In an **experiment** a group of participants receives a **treatment,** such as a dosage of alcohol. The participants, or **subjects,** are then observed carefully to determine whether the treatment makes a difference in their behavior. In another example, environmental psychologists have varied room temperatures and the background levels of noise to see whether these treatments have an effect on subjects' behavior.

Experiments are used whenever possible in contemporary psychological research because they allow psychologists to directly control the experiences of animals and people in their effort to determine the results of a treatment. Experiments are usually undertaken to test a **hypothesis,** an assumption or proposition about behavior. Hypotheses are often derived from theory. For example, a psychologist may theorize that alcohol leads to aggression by reducing fear of consequences or generally energizing the activity levels of drinkers. He or she may then hypothesize that the treatment of a specified dosage of alcohol will lead to increases in aggression.

Independent and Dependent Variables   In an experiment to determine whether alcohol causes aggression, experimental subjects would be given a quantity of alcohol and its effects would be measured. Alcohol would be considered an **independent variable.** The presence of an independent variable is manipulated by the experimenters so that its effects may be determined. The independent variable of alcohol may be administered at different levels, or doses, from none or very little to enough to cause **intoxication.**

The measured results or outcomes in an experiment are called **dependent variables.** The presence of dependent variables presumably de-

Population A complete group of organisms or events.

Experiment A method of scientific investigation that seeks to discover cause-and-effect relationships by introducing independent variables and observing their effects on dependent variables. (From a Latin word meaning "trial" or "test.")

Treatment In experiments, a condition received by participants so that its effects may be observed.

Subjects Participants in a scientific study. Many psychologists consider this term dehumanizing and no longer use it in reference to human participants.

Hypothesis (high-POTH-uh-sis). An assumption about behavior that is tested through research. (A Greek word meaning "groundwork" or "foundation.")

Independent variable A condition in a scientific study that is manipulated so that its effects may be observed.

Intoxication Drunkenness. (From the Latin *toxicare,* meaning "to smear with poison.")

Dependent variable A measure of an assumed effect of an independent variable.

pends on the independent variables. In an experiment to determine whether alcohol influences aggression, aggressive behavior would be a dependent variable. Other dependent variables of interest in an experiment on the effects of alcohol might include sexual arousal (see Chapter 4), visual-motor coordination, and performance on intellectual tasks such as defining words or numerical computations.

In an experiment on the relationships between temperature and aggression, temperature would be an independent variable and aggressive behavior would be a dependent variable. We might use various temperature settings, from below freezing to blistering hot, and study the effects of each. We might also use a second independent variable, such as social provocation, and insult certain subjects but not others. Then we could also study the interaction between temperature and social provocation as they influence aggression. The results of studies on the effects of temperature are reported in Chapter 14.

Experiments can be quite complex, with several independent and dependent variables. Psychologists often use complex experimental designs and sophisticated statistical techniques to determine the effect of each independent variable, acting alone and in combination with others, on each dependent variable.

Experimental and Control Groups   Ideal experiments use experimental and control subjects, or experimental and control groups. **Experimental subjects** receive the treatment while **control subjects** do not. Every effort is made to ensure that all other conditions are held constant both for experimental and control subjects, so that we can have confidence that the experimental outcomes reflect the treatments, and not chance factors or variation.

In an experiment concerning the effects of alcohol on aggression, experimental subjects would be given alcohol, and control subjects would not. In a complex experiment, different experimental groups might receive (1) different dosages of alcohol and (2) different types of provocations.

Blinds and Double Blinds   One experiment on the effects of alcohol on aggression (Boyatzis, 1974) reported that men at parties where beer and liquor were served acted more aggressively than control subjects at parties where only soft drinks were served. But we must be cautious in interpreting these findings, because the experimental subjects *knew* that they had drunk alcohol, and the control subjects *knew* that they had not. And so aggression that appeared to result from alcohol may not have reflected drinking itself, but subjects' expectations about the effects of alcohol instead. There is reason to be suspicious, because other experiments show that people "act in stereotyped ways" when they think they have been drinking alcohol (Marlatt & Rohsenow, 1981). For instance, men will become less anxious in social situations, more aggressive, and more sexually aroused—even though they have drunk only a **placebo** like tonic water.

A placebo, sometimes referred to as a "sugar pill," often results in the behavior that people expect. Physicians have been known to give sugar pills to demanding but healthy patients, and they claim that some patients receiving placebos report that they feel better. When subjects in psycho-

Experimental subjects (1) Subjects receiving a treatment in an experiment. (2) More generally, participants in an experiment.

Control subjects Experimental participants who do not receive the experimental treatment, but for whom all other conditions are comparable to those of experimental subjects.

Placebo (pluh-SEE-bow). A bogus treatment that has the appearance of being genuine. (The Latin phrase meaning "I shall please," reflecting the old medical practice of giving a *placebo*, also referred to as a "sugar pill," to a demanding patient.)

Blind In experimental terminology, unaware as to whether one has received a treatment.

Double-blind study A study in which neither the subjects nor the persons measuring results know who has received the treatment.

logical experiments are given placebos like tonic water, but they think that they have drunk alcohol, we can conclude that any behavioral changes stem from their beliefs and expectations about alcohol.

Well-designed experiments control for the possible effects of expectations by creating conditions under which the subjects are unaware of, or **blind** to, the treatment they have received. But researchers may also have expectations. They may, in effect, be ''rooting for'' a certain treatment. For instance, tobacco-company executives may wish to show that cigarette smoking is harmless. For this reason it is useful if the people measuring the experimental outcomes are also unaware of who has received the treatment. Studies in which both subjects and experimenters are unaware of who has received the treatment are called **double-blind studies.**

Double-blind studies are also used in medicine as the standard method of determining the usefulness of new drugs. The drug and the placebo are made up to look and taste the same. Subjects are assigned to the new drug or the placebo at random, and the key for determining who has taken what is ''locked away'' until the study is completed. Neither the subjects who take the drugs, the people who hand them out, nor the people who measure the subjects' progress know who has received the drug and who has received the placebo. Only after the final measurements of progress are made is the key unlocked. Then an impartial panel can determine whether the outcomes differed for people who took the drug and people who took the placebo.

In one well-designed study on the effects of alcohol, Alan Lang of the University of Wisconsin and his colleagues (1975) pretested a highball of vodka and tonic water to determine that it could not be discriminated by taste from tonic water alone. They recruited college men as subjects. Some subjects received vodka and tonic water while others received tonic water only. Of subjects who received vodka, half were misled into believing that they had drunk tonic water only (Figure 1.6). Of subjects receiving tonic

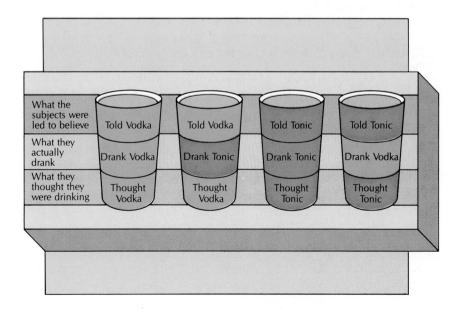

FIGURE 1.6 THE EXPERIMENTAL CONDITIONS IN THE LANG STUDY
The taste of vodka cannot be discerned when vodka is mixed with tonic water. For this reason, it was possible for subjects in the Lang study on the effects of alcohol to be kept ''blind'' as to whether or not they had actually drunk alcohol. Blind studies allow psychologists to control for the effects of subject expectations.

What the subjects were led to believe	Told Vodka	Told Vodka	Told Tonic	Told Tonic
What they actually drank	Drank Vodka	Drank Tonic	Drank Tonic	Drank Vodka
What they thought they were drinking	Thought Vodka	Thought Vodka	Thought Tonic	Thought Tonic

water only, half were misled into believing that their drink contained vodka. Thus half the subjects were blind to the treatment they received. Experimenters who measured aggressive responses were also blind as to which subjects had received vodka.

The research team found that men who believed that they had drunk vodka responded more aggressively to a provocation than men who believed that they had drunk tonic water only. The actual content of the drink was immaterial. That is, men who had actually drunk alcohol acted no more aggressively than men who had drunk tonic water only. The results of the Lang study differ dramatically from those reported by Boyatzis, perhaps because the Boyatzis study did not control for the effects of expectations or beliefs about alcohol.

Is it possible that alcohol does not cause aggression? That centuries of folklore have been in error? Quite possible. Other studies that control for the effects of expectations have shown that alcohol can even decrease aggressive behavior (Marlatt & Rohsenow, 1981). Actually, this finding should not be so surprising. We acknowledge that alcohol can lead to a stupor, even to passing out. Why should such a substance cause aggressive outbursts prior to its depressing effects on the nervous system? Psychology is an empirical science. Centuries of folklore may stimulate research into certain topics, but folklore is not acceptable evidence within science.

So what do we make of it? Why does belief that one has drunk alcohol increase aggression, while alcohol itself may not? Perhaps alcohol gives one a certain social role to play in our culture—the role of the uninhibited social mover. Perhaps alcohol also provides an excuse for aggressive or other antisocial behavior. After all, the drinker can always claim, "It wasn't me, it was the alcohol." How do you think you will respond the next time someone says "It was the alcohol" to you?

Generalizing from Experimental Results   Many factors must be considered in interpreting the results of experiments. In the Lang study the subjects represented a **sample** of male college students. In the discussion of the naturalistic-observation method, it was noted that we need to be certain that the sample under study represents the target population. Whom do male college students represent, other than themselves? To whom can we extend or **generalize** the results?

For one thing, the results may not extend to women, not even college women. Women, as we shall see in Chapter 13, tend to behave aggressively under circumstances that differ from those under which men act aggressively. College men also tend to fall within a certain age range (about 18 to 22) and are more intelligent than the general population. We cannot be certain that the findings extend to older men of average intelligence, although it seems reasonable to **infer** that they do. Subjects in the Lang study also reported themselves to be social drinkers. In Chapter 4 we shall see that alcoholics may differ biologically and psychologically from people who can control their drinking. Nor can we be certain that college social drinkers represent people who do not drink at all.

There is a quip in psychology that experiments tend to be run with "rats, sophomores, and soldiers." Why? Because these subjects are readily

Sample Part of a population.

Generalize To go from the particular to the general; to extend.

Infer (in-FUR). Draw a conclusion.

Operational definition. A definition of a variable in terms of the methods used to create or measure the variable. For example, an operational definition of intelligence is that which is measured by intelligence tests.

Replicate Repeat or duplicate. In science, research must be reported in sufficient detail to permit other investigators to replicate it.

available. Still, science is a conservative enterprise, and scientists are cautious about generalizing experimental results to populations other than those from which their samples were drawn.

Operational Definitions   Our ability to generalize experimental results also relates to the operational definitions of the independent and dependent variables. The **operational definition** of a variable is limited to the methods used to create or measure that variable. For example, sexual arousal may be operationally defined as subjects' self-reports (based on introspection) that they feel sexually aroused. This would also be considered a subjective definition of arousal, since it depends on subjects' private feelings. Unfortunately, self-reports can fall prey to accidental or purposeful inaccuracies, as we shall see in the next section. Thus, psychologists prefer to use objective measures whenever possible. For this reason, many recent studies define sexual arousal in the male as size of erection and in the female as vaginal blood pressure. Both can be measured directly by objective laboratory instruments.

In the Lang study on alcohol and aggression, alcohol was operationally defined as a certain dose of vodka. Other types of drinks and other dosages of vodka might have had different effects. Aggression was operationally defined as selecting a certain amount of electric shock and administering it to another student participating in a psychological experiment. College men might behave differently when they drink in other situations— for example, when they are insulted by a supporter of an opposing football team or are threatened outside a bar. Still, some psychologists argue that subjects in a laboratory may assign a meaning to the laboratory setting and their actions that makes them comparable to the real-life situation (e.g., Berkowitz & Donnerstein, 1982).

Does it sound as if we are speaking from both corners of our mouth? As if we're praising the Lang study, on the one hand, but telling you not to believe it, on the other? Not quite. The Lang study is worthy of praise for reasons discussed earlier. It has also been **replicated** to some degree with subjects other than college men and other dosages of alcohol. We can also say, with some justification, that only studies that control for the effects of expectations should receive our attention. Thus, the Lang study and studies showing similar results (see Chapter 4) are, in a sense, all we have on the behavioral effects of alcohol—despite centuries of folklore.

THE SURVEY METHOD

In the good old days, when being "sound as a dollar" was a sign of good health, one had to wait until the wee hours of the morning to learn the results of local and national elections. Throughout the evening and early morning hours, suspense would build as ballots from distant neighborhoods and states were tallied. Nowadays one is barely settled with an after-dinner cup of coffee on election night when the CBS News computer cheerfully announces (computers do not, of course, have emotions or make "cheerful" announcements, but they certainly seem rather smug at times) that it has examined the ballots of a "scientifically selected sample" and then predicts

PSYCHOLOGY TODAY

DOES PORNOGRAPHY ENCOURAGE VIOLENCE AGAINST WOMEN?

On what issue do radical feminists and right-wing fundamentalists agree? Certainly not on how to balance the budget or on how to conduct foreign policy. Instead, both groups tend to affirm the belief that pornography should be stamped out.

But their reasons differ. The fundamentalists usually assail pornography from a moral standpoint. Feminists, on the other hand, assert that pornography encourages violence against women and generally degrades women by portraying them as subservient to the wishes of men. Feminists and many other women particularly object to pornographic films and books that portray women being raped, tortured, and killed.

There is also concern about the widespread availability of pornography. Pornography today is found not only in New York's Times Square and San Francisco's North Beach after dark. "First-run" skin flicks are also advertised on theater marquees in heartland cities such as Peoria and Topeka. Cable TV and VCRs, moreover, have brought pornography right into average homes in living color.

According to a 1985 NEWSWEEK/Gallup survey of a nationally drawn sample of 1,020 adults, 7 percent of the public went to an X-rated film during the past year, and 9 percent bought or rented an X-rated movie or cassette. The sample was evenly divided as to whether community standards regarding the sale of pornographic materials should be tightened: 43 percent wanted stricter standards, but 48 percent wanted the

A DEMONSTRATION AGAINST PORNOGRAPHY Some opponents of pornography argue that pornography encourages violence against women and generally degrades women by portraying them as subservient to the wishes of men.

the next president of the United States. All this may occur with less than one percent of the vote tallied. Polls taken before elections also do their share of eroding wonderment and doubt—so much so that supporters of projected winners must sometimes be encouraged to actually vote on Election Day so that predictions will be borne out.

Just as computers and pollsters predict election results and report national opinion on the basis of scientifically selected samples, psychologists conduct **surveys** in order to learn about behavior that cannot be observed in the natural setting or studied experimentally. Psychologists making surveys may employ questionnaires and interviews or examine public records. By distributing questionnaires and analyzing answers with a computer, psychologists can survey many thousands of people at a time.

In the late 1940s and early 1950s Alfred Kinsey of Indiana University and his colleagues published two surveys of sexual behavior, based on interviews, that shocked the nation: *Sexual Behavior in the Human Male* (1948) and *Sexual Behavior in the Human Female* (1953). Kinsey reported that masturbation was practically universal in his sample of men at a time

Survey A method of scientific investigation in which large samples of people are questioned.

standards kept as they were. Table 1.2 shows how the sample answered the question, "Do you think laws should totally ban any of the following activities in your community, allow them as long as there is no public display—or impose no restrictions at all for adult audiences?" As you can see, the sample was consistently in favor of banning only those materials that depicted sexual violence.

Pornography is a highly charged issue, but psychologists are committed to the objective study of all aspects of human behavior, including responses to pornography. Recent psychological experiments have addressed questions such as:

Does violent pornography lead to crimes of violence?
Does repeated exposure to pornography transform the average male into an insatiable Casanova?
Is pornography for men only, or does it also sexually arouse women?

Some findings reported in Chapter 13 concerning the effects of pornography may surprise you. For instance, Julia Heiman (1975) found that pornography sexually arouses women as well as men. Howard and his colleagues (1973) found that continued exposure to pornography does not drive college men to sexual abandon. Instead, sexual arousal diminished with repeated exposure. But other findings reported in Chapter 13 suggest that the NEWSWEEK sample may be quite justified in its opposition to *violent* pornography.

Psychologists, like other people, may harbor strong moral opinions on controversial issues such as por-

TABLE 1.2 Responses of the NEWSWEEK/Gallup Survey Sample to the Question as to Whether Pornographic Materials Should be Banned Outright, Permitted for Private Adult Use Only, or Be Unrestricted, Percentages

	Ban	No Public Display	No Restriction
Magazines that show nudity	21	52	26
Magazines that show adults having sexual relations	47	40	12
Magazines that show sexual violence	73	20	6
Theaters showing X-rated movies	40	37	20
Theaters showing movies that depict sexual violence	68	21	9
Sale or rental of X-rated video cassettes for home viewing	32	39	27
Sale or rental of video cassettes featuring sexual violence	63	23	13

In the 1985 NEWSWEEK/Gallup Poll, a majority of those sampled agreed that pornographic materials depicting sexual violence should be banned. However, the sample was more lenient concerning nonviolent materials. Source: NEWSWEEK, March 18, 1985, p. 60.

nography. But, as scientists, it is their responsibility to run their experiments without bias and to report the results objectively.

when masturbation was still widely thought to impair physical or mental health. He also reported that about one woman in three still single at age 25 had engaged in premarital intercourse.

The survey was the appropriate method for attaining these data, since Kinsey wished to learn what was happening in the United States rather than study the causes of sexual behavior in depth. And if Kinsey had tried to use the naturalistic-observation method, he and his colleagues might have been tossed into jail as Peeping Toms.

In addition to compiling self-reports of behavior, surveys are also used to learn about people's opinions, attitudes, and values. For example, more recent surveys concerning sex have found that during the 1970s people were less likely to condemn masturbation and premarital intercourse than were people in Kinsey's era (Hunt, 1974).

Interviews and questionnaires are not foolproof, of course. People may inaccurately recall their behavior or purposefully misrepresent it. Some people try to ingratiate themselves with their interviewers by answering in what they perceive to be the socially desirable direction. The Kinsey studies all

"Would you say Attila is doing an excellent job, a good job, a fair job, or a poor job?"

relied on male interviewers, for example, and it has been speculated that women interviewees may have been more open and honest with women interviewers. Similar problems may occur when interviewers and those surveyed are from different racial or socioeconomic backgrounds. Other people may falsify attitudes and exaggerate problems to draw attention to themselves, or even purposefully to foul up the results.

The *Literary Digest* **Survey: A Case Study in the Importance of Random Sampling**   You recall President Landon, don't you? Elected in 1936, he defeated the incumbent president, Franklin D. Roosevelt? If this sounds wrong, it may be because it is wrong. Roosevelt defeated Landon in a landslide of about 11 million votes. Still, the *Literary Digest,* a popular magazine of the day, had predicted a Landon victory.

The *Digest,* you see, had phoned the voters it surveyed. Today telephone sampling is a widely practiced and reasonably legitimate technique. But the *Digest* poll was taken during the Great Depression, when Americans who had telephones were decidedly higher in socioeconomic status than Americans without phones. Americans at higher income levels are also more likely to vote Republican, and Alf Landon was heading the Republican ticket. No surprise, then, that the people sampled said they would vote overwhelmingly for Landon.

Survey samples must accurately represent the population they are meant to reflect. One way to accomplish this is through a **random sample.** In a

Random sample A sample drawn such that every member of a population has an equal chance of being selected.

random sample, each member of a population has an equal chance of being selected to participate. Researchers can also use a **stratified sample,** which is drawn so that known subgroups in the population are represented proportionately in the sample. For instance, 12 percent of the United States population is black. Thus, a racially stratified sample would be 12 percent black. As a practical matter, a large randomly selected sample will show reasonably accurate stratification. In any event an appropriately selected random sample of 1,500 Americans will represent the general United States population reasonably well. But a haphazardly drawn sample of 20 million may not.

The Kinsey studies on sexual behavior did not adequately represent blacks, poor Americans, the elderly, and other groups. Large-scale magazine surveys of sexual behavior run by *Redbook* (Tavris & Sadd, 1977) and *Cosmopolitan* (Wolfe, 1981) asked readers to fill out and return questionnaires. Although many thousands of readers responded, did they represent the general American population? Probably not. They may have represented only a subgroup of readers of these magazines who were willing to fill out candid questionnaires about their sexual behavior. Shere Hite (1976, 1981) distributed well over 100,000 questionnaires for each of her surveys of sexual behavior, but had returns of about 3,000 for the 1976 report, and about 7,000 for the 1981 report. Do the people who returned her questionnaires accurately represent those who received them? What do you think?

THE TESTING METHOD

Psychologists also use psychological tests, like intelligence, aptitude, and personality tests, to measure various traits and characteristics among a population. In Chapters 6 and 9 we shall see that there is a wide range of psychological tests, and that they measure traits ranging from verbal ability and achievement to anxiety, depression, the need for social dominance, musical aptitude, and vocational interests.

Psychological test results, like the results of surveys, can also be distorted by respondents who answer in a socially desirable direction or attempt to exaggerate problems. For these reasons some commonly used psychological tests have items built into them called **validity scales.** Validity scales are sensitive to misrepresentations and alert the psychologist when test results may be deceptive.

Because of validity problems, many psychologists prefer to observe behavior directly when possible.

THE CASE-STUDY METHOD

Sigmund Freud developed psychoanalytic theory largely on the basis of **case studies,** or carefully drawn biographies of the lives of individuals. In the case study, as opposed to most other research methods, the psychologist studies one or a handful of individuals in great depth, seeking out the factors that seem to contribute to notable patterns of behavior. Freud studied some patients over a period of several years, meeting with them several times a week.

Stratified sample A sample drawn such that known subgroups within a population are represented in proportion to their numbers in the population.

Validity scales Groups of test items that suggest whether or not the test results are valid, that is, whether they measure what they are supposed to measure.

Case study A carefully drawn biography that may be obtained through interviews, questionnaires, and psychological tests.

QUESTIONNAIRE

THE SOCIAL-DESIRABILITY SCALE

Do you say what you think, or do you tend to misrepresent your beliefs to earn the approval of others? Do you answer questions honestly, or do you say what you think other people want to hear?

Telling others what we think they want to hear is making the socially desirable response. Falling prey to social desirability may cause us to distort our beliefs and experiences in interviews or on psychological tests. You can complete the following test devised by Crowne and Marlowe (1960) to gain insight into whether you have a tendency to produce socially desirable responses. Read each item and decide whether it is true (T) or false (F) for you. Try to work rapidly and answer each question by circling the T or the F. Then turn to the scoring key in Appendix B to interpret your answers.

T   F

_____ 1. Before voting I thoroughly investigate the qualifications of all the candidates.

_____ 2. I never hesitate to go out of my way to help someone in trouble.

_____ 3. It is sometimes hard for me to go on with my work if I am not encouraged.

_____ 4. I have never intensely disliked anyone.

_____ 5. I have sometimes doubted my ability to succeed in life.

_____ 6. I sometimes feel resentful when I don't get my way.

_____ 7. I am always careful about my manner of dress.

_____ 8. My table manners at home are as good as when I eat out in a restaurant.

_____ 9. If I could get into a movie without paying and be sure I was not seen I would probably do it.

_____ 10. On a few occasions, I have given up something because I thought too little of my ability.

_____ 11. I like to gossip at times.

_____ 12. There have been times when I felt like rebelling against people in authority even though I knew they were right.

_____ 13. No matter who I'm talking to, I'm always a good listener.

_____ 14. I can remember "playing sick" to get out of something.

_____ 15. There have been occasions when I have taken advantage of someone.

_____ 16. I'm always willing to admit it when I make a mistake.

_____ 17. I always try to practice what I preach.

_____ 18. I don't find it particularly difficult to get along with loud-mouthed, obnoxious people.

_____ 19. I sometimes try to get even rather than forgive and forget.

_____ 20. When I don't know something I don't mind at all admitting it.

_____ 21. I am always courteous, even to people who are disagreeable.

_____ 22. At times I have really insisted on having things my own way.

_____ 23. There have been occasions when I felt like smashing things.

_____ 24. I would never think of letting someone else be punished for my wrong-doings.

_____ 25. I never resent being asked to return a favor.

_____ 26. I have never been irked when people expressed ideas very different from my own.

_____ 27. I never make a long trip without checking the safety of my car.

_____ 28. There have been times when I was quite jealous of the good fortune of others.

_____ 29. I have almost never felt the urge to tell someone off.

_____ 30. I am sometimes irritated by people who ask favors of me.

_____ 31. I have never felt that I was punished without cause.

_____ 32. I sometimes think when people have a misfortune they only got what they deserved.

_____ 33. I have never deliberately said something that hurt someone's feelings.

Source: Crowne, D. P., and Marlowe, D. A new scale of social desirability independent of pathology, *Journal of Consulting Psychology*, 1960, *24*, p. 351, Table 1. Copyright 1960 by the American Psychological Association. Reprinted by permission.

Of course, there are bound to be gaps in memory when people are interviewed, and people may distort their pasts because of social desirability or other factors. Interviewers may also have certain expectations and subtly encourage their subjects to fill in gaps in ways that are consistent with their theoretical perspectives. Psychoanalysts have been criticized, for example, for guiding their patients into viewing their own lives from the psychoanalytic perspective. No wonder, then, that many patients provide "evidence" that is consistent with psychoanalytic theory. However, interviewers who hold any theoretical viewpoint run the risk of indirectly prodding their subjects into producing what they want to hear.

When doing a case study, of course it is useful to have regular access to the person being studied, as Freud did with his patients. But case studies of prominent historical figures have also been carried out. These figures include powerful political leaders like Napoleon and Hitler, great artists like Michelangelo and Vincent van Gogh, and ingenious scientists like Leonardo da Vinci and Madame Curie. The goals are usually to discover the factors that led to the dominant traits of these figures. In these cases, the task is to reconstruct traits and motives on the basis of the figure's writings, public and private records, and, if possible, interviews with people who have known the figure.

Case studies are also used to investigate rare occurrences, as in the cases of "Eve" and "Genie." "Eve" (in real life, Chris Sizemore) was a multiple personality (discussed in Chapter 11). "Eve White," as we shall see, was a mousy, well-intentioned woman who had two other "personalities" living inside her, including "Eve Black," a promiscuous personality who now and then emerged and "took control" of her behavior.

"Genie's" father locked her in a small room at the age of 20 months and kept her there until she was discovered at the age of 13½ (Curtiss, 1977). Her social contacts were limited to her nearly blind mother, who entered the room only to feed her, and to beatings at the hands of her father. No one spoke to her throughout this period. After her rescue, Genie's language development followed the normal sequence, as outlined in Chapter 6, suggesting the universality of this sequence. However, Genie did not reach normal proficiency in her use of language, also suggesting that there may be a sensitive period for learning language in early childhood.

The case study is also used in psychological consultation. Psychologists learn whatever they can about individuals, agencies, and business firms so that they can suggest ways in which these clients can more effectively meet the challenges in their lives. Psychologists base their suggestions on laboratory research whenever possible, but psychological practice is also sometimes an art in which psychologist and client agree that a suggestion or a treatment has been helpful on the basis of the client's self-report.

The case study can be used quite scientifically in clinical practice if the psychologist repeatedly applies and removes a treatment, attempts to control for variables such as client expectations, or takes repeated measures through behavioral observations, psychological tests, or structured interviews (Hayes, 1981; Kazdin, 1981). If the treatment leads to consistent changes in the client, it may be concluded that these are not chance fluctuations in behavior. But this approach is unlikely to be used in clinical practice. Some "treatments," such as helping a client gain insight into the meaning of events that occurred prior to the age of five, cannot be repeatedly applied then removed. In other cases rather concrete treatments may be used to help clients quit smoking, lose weight, or resolve sexual problems. But it would be harmful to the client to reinstate these problems—even with the intention of resolving them a second time—to determine whether treatment has been effective. Even so, psychologists encourage laboratory experiments in these problem areas, so that they will know that their treatments are backed by research whenever possible.

The case study looks for relationships between variables within individuals or within small groups. The correlational method seeks out relationships between variables among larger groups.

THE CORRELATIONAL METHOD

Are people with higher intelligence more likely to do well in school? Are people with a stronger need for achievement likely to climb higher up the corporate ladder? Are we more or less likely to behave aggressively as the temperature soars through the 80s and 90s F?

In **correlational research,** psychologists investigate whether one kind of behavior or trait is related to, or correlated with, another. Consider the variables of intelligence and academic performance. Numerous studies report **positive correlations** between intelligence and achievement. This means that by and large the higher people score on intelligence tests, the better their academic performance is likely to be. In these studies, the variables of intelligence and academic performance are assigned numbers, such as intelligence test scores and academic averages. These numbers are mathematically related and expressed as a **correlation coefficient.*** In Chapter 6 you will see that there is a controversy as to exactly what intelligence tests measure. Still, the scores attained on these tests are positively correlated with overall academic achievement.

Correlational research A method of scientific investigation that studies the relationships between variables. Correlational research can imply but cannot show cause and effect, because no experimental treatment is introduced.

Positive correlation A relationship between variables in which one variable increases as the other variable also increases.

Correlation coefficient A number ranging from +1.00 to −1.00 that expresses the strength and direction (positive or negative) of the relationship between two variables.

*The mathematics of the correlation coefficient are discussed in Appendix A.

Negative correlation A relationship between two variables in which one variable
increases as the other variable decreases.

Ethical Moral; referring to one's system of
deriving standards for determining what is
moral.

What of the need for achievement and getting ahead? In Chapter 7 we shall see that the need for achievement can be assessed by rating stories told by subjects for the presence of the need. Getting ahead can be assessed in many ways—salary and the prestige of one's occupation or level within the corporation are just a few of them. It may come as no surprise that the need for achievement and success are also positively correlated; however, as we shall also see in Chapter 7, factors other than the need for achievement may be even stronger predictors of success in the business world.

The correlations between aggression and temperature are not so straightforward. In Chapter 14 we shall see that there is a positive correlation between temperature and aggression as the numbers rise through the 70s and the low 80s F. However, past this point, there is a **negative correlation** between temperature and aggression. That is, when the heat is really on—as in the 90s—we tend to "cool it." In the case of the negative correlation, as one variable (in this case, temperature) increases in value, the other variable (in this case, aggression) decreases in value.

Correlational research may suggest but does not show cause and effect. For instance, it may seem logical to assume that high intelligence makes it possible for children to profit from education. However, research has also shown that education contributes to higher scores on intelligence tests. Children placed in richly stimulating Head Start programs at an early age later do better on intelligence tests than agemates who do not have this experience! The relationship between intelligence and academic performance may not be so simple as you might have thought. In Chapter 6 we shall see that motivation and adjustment to the school also enter the picture, by contributing to both academic performance and scores on tests, such as intelligence tests.

Despite the inability of correlational research to place clear "cause" and "effect" labels on variables, correlational research does point the way toward profitable experimental research. That is, if there were no correlation between intelligence and achievement, there would be little purpose to running experiments to try to determine causal relationships. If there were no relationship between the need for achievement and success, it would be pointless to ask whether the need for achievement contributes to success.

In order to properly study behavior, psychologists must not only be skilled in the uses and limitations of various kinds of research methods. They must also adhere to a number of ethical guidelines that govern the treatment of human and animal participants in research, as we shall see in the following section.

ETHICS IN PSYCHOLOGICAL RESEARCH AND PRACTICE

Psychologists adhere to a number of **ethical** standards in research and practice. All of them are basically intended to assure that psychologists do not undertake research methods or treatments which they believe are harmful to subjects or clients (American Psychological Association, 1981). However, some exceptions may be necessary, as we shall see.

RESEARCH WITH HUMAN SUBJECTS

Human subjects must provide **informed consent** before they participate in research programs. Having a general overview of the research and the opportunity to choose not to participate apparently gives subjects a sense of control and decreases the stress of participating (Dill et al., 1982).

Psychologists treat the records of research subjects and clients as **confidential.** They do not divulge the names of participants in research and in therapy, unless participants specifically request that they do so.

Ethical standards tend to limit the types of research that psychologists may conduct. For example, how can we determine whether early separation from one's mother impairs social development? One research direction is to observe the development of children who have been separated from their mothers from an early age. But it is difficult to draw conclusions from such research because the same factors that led to the separation, such as family tragedy or irresponsible parents, rather than the separation itself, may have led to the observed outcomes.

Scientifically, it would be more sound to run experiments in which children are purposefully separated from their mothers at an early age and compared with children who are not. But psychologists would not seriously consider such research because of ethical standards. However, experiments in which infants are purposefully separated from mothers have been run with lower animals, as we shall see below.

THE USE OF DECEPTION

A number of psychological experiments could not be run without deceiving their human subjects. But the use of deception raises ethical issues. Before we explore these issues, let us first return briefly to the Lang (Lang et al., 1975) study on alcohol and aggression. In that study, the researchers had to (1) misinform half their subjects about the beverage they had drunk; and (2) mislead subjects to believe that they were giving other participants electric shock when they were actually only pressing switches on a dead control board. (Pressing these switches was the operational definition of aggression in the study.)

We saw that students in this study who believed they had drunk vodka were more aggressive than students who believed they had not. The actual content of the beverages was immaterial. But this study could not have been run without deceiving the subjects. Foiling their expectations or beliefs was at the heart of the experiment, and the potential benefits of the research may well outweigh the possible harmful effects of the deceptions. Certainly it seems preferable that subjects only thought they were shocking other people. After all, would we prefer them actually to deliver painful electric shock?

But it should be noted that some psychologists are opposed to the use of deception under any circumstances. Diane Baumrind (1985) argues, for example, that deception-based research is unacceptable because it can harm not only research subjects, but also the reputation of the profession of psychology and society at large. In a study that supports Baumrind's views, one group of students participated in experiments in which they were de-

Informed consent   The term used by psychologists to indicate that a person has agreed to participate in research after receiving information about the purposes of the study and the nature of the treatments.

Confidential   Secret, not to be disclosed.

Debrief To receive information about a just-completed procedure.

Breathalyzer A device that measures the quantity of alcohol in the body by analyzing the breath.

Lesion (LEE-shun). An injury that results in impaired behavior or loss of a function. (From the Latin *laedere,* meaning "to harm" or "to injure.")

ceived. Afterwards they regarded psychologists as less trustworthy than did students who were not deceived (Smith & Richardson, 1983). Baumrind argues that such deception might eventually cause the public to lose trust in expert authorities in general.

In any event, many research endeavors continue to rely upon the use of deception (Adair et al., 1985). The code of ethics of the American Psychological Association requires that research participants who are deceived be **debriefed** afterward to help eliminate any harmful effects, and the incidence of debriefing has increased in recent years (Adair et al., 1985). Sieber (1983) argues that debriefing must be carried out honestly, skillfully, and sympathetically. After the Lang study was carried out, the subjects were informed of the deceptions and of the rationale for them. Students who had actually drunk alcohol were given coffee and a **breathalyzer** test, so that the researchers could be sure that they were not leaving the laboratory in an intoxicated state.

Psychologists use deception in research only when the research could not be run without it. As with other ethical dilemmas, deception is used when the psychologist believes that its benefits will outweigh its potential harm.

RESEARCH WITH ANIMAL SUBJECTS

Psychologists and other scientists frequently turn to animal subjects to conduct research that cannot be carried out with humans. For example, as suggested above, experiments on the effects of early separation from the mother have been carried out with monkeys and other animals. As you will see in later chapters, this research has allowed psychologists to investigate the formation of parent-child bonds of attachment.

Experiments with infant monkeys highlight some of the dilemmas faced by psychologists and other scientists when they contemplate research with people or animals that has or may have harmful effects. Psychologists and biologists who study the workings of the brain have destroyed sections of the brains of laboratory animals to learn how these areas of the brain influence behavior. For instance, as you will see in Chapter 7, a **lesion** in one part of a brain structure will cause a rat to overeat. A lesion elsewhere will cause the rat to go on a crash diet. Psychologists generalize to people from experiments like these in the hope that we may find solutions to persistent human problems, such as obesity.

But, as noted in the nearby box, "King of the Jungle," psychologists must still face the ethical dilemma of subjecting animals to harm. By and large, psychologists follow the principle that they should do so only when they believe that the eventual benefits to people of their research justify the harm done to animals (Rollin, 1985). Still, tradition and law suggest that "there is a limit to the amount of pain an animal should endure in the name of science" (Larson, 1982).

Psychologists are human, of course, and capable of making errors. Occasionally human and animal research participants may be exposed to more harm than anticipated. But generally speaking, psychologists make every effort to minimize the possible harmful effects of their research.

KING OF THE JUNGLE

When you were a child, you may have been told that the lion was the king of the jungle. However, in the 60 Minutes segment "King of the Jungle," we and not lions are portrayed as the kings of the jungle because of our domination over lower animals. One aspect of our domination is expressed in our use of animal subjects in research. And, as noted by correspondent Ed Bradley,

In the name of science, animals have been drugged, shocked, radiated, castrated. Cats have had their eyelids sewn shut so scientists could study vision deprivation. Monkeys have had electrodes implanted in their brains. Rabbits have had chemicals and drugs put in their eyes to determine the damage caused. Primates have sustained head injuries so their behavioral changes could then be observed.

This 60 Minutes segment addresses questions such as, How ethical is it to harm animals for the sake of science and the well-being of people? To just how much pain can we expose animals to find the answers to such human problems as obesity and diabetes?

Supporters of the use of animals in research argue that many of the major advances in medicine and psychology over the past century could not have taken place without the use of animals in the laboratory (Gallup & Suarez, 1985).

Psychologist Neal E. Miller (1985) points out that behavioral research with animals has led to important advances in animal welfare as well as human welfare. For example, using animal subjects, effective scarecrows for owls (Conover, 1982) and cost-effective electrical fences for deer have been developed (Dowlin, 1981), so that farmers need no longer kill these animals to protect their crops. Research with animal subjects has benefited people in areas such as **behavioral medicine,** rehabilitation or neuromuscular disorders, development of drugs, coping with stress and pain, and the survival of premature infants.

Ed Bradley asked Donald Kennedy, the president of Stanford University, whether it was immoral to give a disease to a healthy animal in order to develop techniques of treating the illness in humans. Dr. Kennedy replied that giving the animal the disease was justified "if the experiment is a soundly planned one and care is used as much as possible to make it a humane experiment as far as the animals are concerned." Similarly, Dr. Frances Conley, the brain surgeon, claims that the "study of tumors going to the brain from another site in the body would be stopped" if animals could no longer be used in research.

"KING OF THE JUNGLE" Now and then psychologists and other scientists must do animals some harm if they are to answer research questions that may yield important benefits for people. Justifying such harm is a major ethical dilemma.

Actress Gretchen Wyler, head of the California chapter of the Fund for Animals, counters:

I believe some day this will be looked on as the "horse and buggy" days of medical research. We live in a computer age right now, computer models, mathematical models, cell culture, tissue culture—all sorts of alternatives that could be available. I think it's an insult to the intelligence of our species to say that we are still vivisecting animals to find cures for diseases.

Dr. Norman Shumway, the heart-transplant surgeon, responds to Wyler by noting that the "computer will only respond to the information that one gives it, and what we're looking for are the responses we can't anticipate, and those are the ones that will be derived from animal work." The debate over the subjecting of animals to harm in scientific research will go on.

Behavioral medicine An interdisciplinary field in which psychological principles are applied to the treatment of health problems.

SUMMARY

1. Psychology is a scientific approach to the study of behavior. Some psychologists limit their definition of behavior to observable behavior, while others include mental processes like images, concepts, thoughts, and dreams.

2. Psychology seeks to describe, explain, predict, and control behavior. But psychologists do not attempt to control the behavior of other people against their wills. Instead, they help clients modify their behavior for their own benefit.

3. Behavior is explained through psychological theories, which are sets of statements that involve assumptions about behavior. Explanations and predictions are derived from theories. Theories are revised, as needed, to accommodate new observations. If necessary, they are discarded.

4. Some psychologists engage in basic or pure research, which has no immediate applications. Others engage in applied research, which seeks solutions to specific problems. In addition to research, many psychologists are found in teaching and consultation.

5. Clinical psychologists help people who are behaving abnormally adjust to the demands of life. Community psychologists focus on the prevention as well as treatment of abnormal behavior. Counseling psychologists work with individuals who have adjustment problems but do not show abnormal behavior.

6. School psychologists assist students with problems that interfere with learning, while educational psychologists are more concerned with theoretical issues concerning human learning.

7. Developmental psychologists study the changes that occur throughout the life span. Personality psychologists study influences on our thought processes, feelings, and behaviors, while social psychologists focus on the ways in which people influence the behavior of other people. Experimental psychologists conduct research into basic psychological processes, such as sensation and perception, learning and memory, and motivation and emotion.

8. Industrial psychologists focus on the relationships between people and work, while organizational psychologists study the behavior of people in organizations.

9. The Greek philosopher Aristotle was among the first to argue that human behavior is subject to rules and laws. Socrates proclaimed "Know thyself" and suggested the use of introspection to gain self-knowledge.

10. Wilhelm Wundt established the first psychological laboratory in 1879. Wundt also founded the school of structuralism and used introspection to study the objective and subjective elements of experience.

11. William James founded the school of functionalism, which dealt with observable behavior as well as conscious experience, and focused on the importance of habit.

12. John B. Watson founded behaviorism, which argues that psychology must limit itself to observable behavior and forgo excursions into subjective consciousness. Behaviorism focused on learning by conditioning, and B. F. Skinner introduced the concept of reinforcement as an explanation of how learning occurs.

13. Gestalt psychology focused on perception and argued that psychologists must focus on the wholeness of human experience.

14. Sigmund Freud founded the school of psychoanalysis, which asserts that people are driven by hidden impulses and distort reality in order to protect themselves from anxiety.

15. The five major perspectives in contemporary psychology include the biological, cognitive, humanistic, psychoanalytic, and learning-theory perspectives. Biologically oriented psychologists study the links between behavior and biological events, such as brain activity and the release of hormones. Cognitive psychologists study the ways in which we perceive and mentally represent the world. Humanistic psychologists, like Gestalt psychologists, stress the importance of human experience; they also assert that people have the freedom to make choices. Contemporary psychoanalysts generally follow Freud's views, but tend to see people as less driven by hidden impulses and more capable of making conscious choices. Social-learning theorists are in the behaviorist tradition, but also find roles for observational learning, expectations, and values in explaining human behavior.

16. Theory may lead to predictions, or hypotheses, about behavior, but psychologists confirm or disconfirm hypotheses through empirical research. The naturalistic-observation method studies behavior where it happens—in the "field."

17. Experiments are used to seek cause and effect, or the effects of independent variables on dependent variables. Experimental subjects are given a treatment, while control subjects are not. Blinds and double blinds may be used to control for the effects of the expectations

of the subjects and the researchers themselves. Results can be generalized only to populations that have been adequately represented in research samples.

18. In the survey method, psychologists may use interviews or questionnaires or examine public records to learn about behavior that cannot be observed directly. It is important to use random or stratified samples to represent the population one is surveying.

19. Psychologists also use psychological tests, like intelligence, aptitude, and personality tests, to measure various traits and characteristics among a population.

20. Case studies are carefully drawn biographies of the lives of individuals. The case-study approach is also widely used in psychological consultation and clinical practice.

21. Correlational research shows relationships between variables, but does not determine cause and effect.

22. Ethical standards of psychologists prevent mistreatment of human and animal subjects. Limits are set on the discomfort that may be imposed on animals. Records of human behavior are kept confidential. Human subjects are required to give informed consent prior to participating in research.

23. Some psychological studies cannot be run unless participants are deceived about their purposes. In such cases, participants are debriefed after the research is completed.

TRUTH OR FICTION REVISITED

Psychology is the study of the mind.
False. While psychology may be translated from its Greek roots as the study of the soul or mind, scientific psychology is defined as the study of behavior. Some psychologists restrict their definition of behavior to observable behavior, but others include such mental processes as thoughts, images, and dreams.

Psychologists attempt to control behavior.
True. The goals of psychology include the description, explanation, prediction, and control of behavior. However, as explained, psychologists also believe in the dignity of other people, and do not attempt to foster behavior that is harmful or opposed to the desires of the individual.

A book on psychology, whose contents were similar to those of the one you are now holding in your hands, was written by Aristotle more than 2,000 years ago.
True. The name of the book was *About the Psyche,* and it was written in the fourth century B.C. It included topics such as sensation and perception, development, intelligence, thought, personality, and motivation and emotion.

Some psychologists measure the effectiveness of television commercials.
True. They are called consumer psychologists.

Other psychologists serve as expert witnesses in court.
True. Forensic psychologists may testify as to the competence of defendants to stand trial, and also about psychological factors that may influence criminal behavior.

Still other psychologists guide people into eating more healthful diets.
True. Psychology is found in the worlds of academia, business, law, and health. Health psychologists—along with clinical and counseling psychologists—may help clients with problems in weight control and smoking, and with stress-related problems that have an impact upon physical illness.

Only people use tools.

False. Naturalistic-observation methods have found that chimpanzees and other animals also use tools.

Alcohol causes aggression.

False. But people who drink may act aggressively because of their beliefs about the effects of alcohol.

You could survey 20 million Americans and still not predict accurately the outcome of a presidential election.

True. It is most important that a sample represent the population it is meant to represent. If the sample is not representative, sample size is immaterial.

OUTLINE

CHAPTER 2

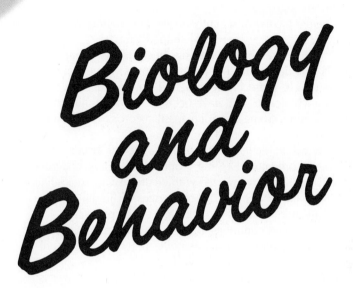

Biology and Behavior

TRUTH OR FICTION?

- Some cells in your body stretch all the way down your back to your big toe.
- We lose brain cells as we grow older.
- Messages travel in the brain by means of electricity.
- Our bodies produce natural pain killers that are more powerful than morphine.
- The human brain is larger than that of any other animal.
- Many men who are paralyzed below the waist can still achieve erection and ejaculate.
- Fear can give you indigestion.
- If a surgeon were to stimulate a certain part of your brain electrically, you might swear in court that someone had stroked your leg.
- If a certain area in your brain were damaged, your ability to speak would be impaired, but you could still understand the written or spoken language.
- Women body-builders can achieve as much muscle mass and definition as men can by working as hard at "pumping iron."
- Some people grow into "giants" because of "glands."
- With so many billions of people in the world, you are bound to have a "double" somewhere, even if you are not an identical twin.
- You can learn the sex of your child several months before it is born.
- Inventors are applying for patents on new life forms.

According to one theory, our universe began with a "big bang" that sent countless atoms and other particles hurtling at fantastic speeds into every corner of space. For 15 to 20 billion years, galaxies and solar systems have been condensing from immense gas clouds, sparkling for some eons, then winking out. Human beings have only recently evolved on an unremarkable rock circling an average star in a typical spiral-shaped galaxy.

Since the beginning of time, the universe has been in flux—changing. Change has brought life and death and countless challenges. Some creatures have adapted successfully to these challenges and continued to evolve. Others have not met the challenges and have become extinct, falling back into the distant mists of time. Some have left fossil records. Others have disappeared without a trace.

At first human survival on planet Earth required a greater struggle than it does today. We fought predators like the leopard. We foraged across parched lands for food. We may have warred with creatures very much like ourselves—creatures who failed to meet the challenges of life and whose bones are now being unearthed on digs in Africa. Yet we prevailed. The human species has survived and continues to pass on its unique characteristics from generation to generation through genetic material whose complex chemical codes are only now being cracked.

Yet what is passed on from generation to generation? The answer is: biological or **physiological** structures. There is no evidence that we can inherit thoughts or ideas or images or plans. But we inherit physiological structures that serve as the material base for our observable behaviors, our emotions, and our cognitions—our thoughts, images, and plans.

Just how our mental processes and observable behaviors are linked to physiological structures is the fascinating question being answered piece by piece by a group of psychologists referred to as either **biological psychologists** or **physiological psychologists.** Through systematic probing of the brain and other structures, biological psychologists in recent years have been seemingly on the threshold of exciting discoveries. Biological psychologists today are unlocking the mysteries of:

1. *Neurons*. Neurons are the building blocks of the nervous system. There are billions of neurons in the body, all transmitting messages of one kind or another.
2. *The nervous system*. Neurons join to form a nervous system with subdivisions that are responsible for muscle movement; perception; automatic functions such as breathing and the secretion of hormones; and psychological phenomena such as thoughts and feelings.
3. *The cerebral cortex*. The cerebral cortex is the large, wrinkled mass inside your head that you think of as your brain. Actually, it is only one part of the brain—the part that is the most characteristically human.
4. *The endocrine system*. Through secretion of hormones, the endocrine system controls functions ranging from growth in children to production of milk in nursing women.
5. *Heredity*. Within every cell of your body are hundreds of thousands of genes. These complex chemical substances determine just what type of creature you are, from the color of your hair to your body temperature and the fact that you have arms and legs rather than wings or fins.

Physiological Having to do with the biological functions and vital processes of living organisms.

Biological psychologists Psychologists who study the relationships between biological processes, on the one hand, and observable behaviors and mental processes, on the other.

Physiological psychologists Same as biological psychologists.

Neurotransmitters Chemical substances involved in the transmission of neural impulses from one neuron to another.

Neuron (NEW-ron). A single nerve cell. (A Greek word meaning "nerve.")

Glial cells (GLEE-al). Cells that produce myelin and engage in housekeeping chores for neurons.

NEURONS

Let us begin our journey in a fabulous forest of nerve cells that can be visualized as having branches, trunks, and roots very much like trees. As in other "forests," many of these nerve cells ("trees") are next to one another. But unlike other forests, these "trees" sometimes lie end to end; their "roots" are intertwined with the "branches" of many nerve cells, or other "trees" below. Messages can be transmitted from nerve cell to nerve cell, or "tree" to "tree." Nerve cells communicate through chemical substances, called **neurotransmitters,** that are released by the "branches" of one and taken up by the "roots" of the next. Neurotransmitters may lead to chemical changes in the receiving nerve cell that cause the message to travel along its "trunk," be translated back into neurotransmitters in its "branches," and then travel through the small spaces between nerve cells to be received by the "roots" of yet other nerve cells.

Each "tree" in this forest is a nerve cell, or **neuron,** that transmits and coordinates messages in the form of neural impulses (Figure 2.1). The nervous system also contains billions of **glial cells.** Glial cells outnumber neurons. Their functions appear to include nourishment and direction of the pattern of growth of neurons, and the removal of waste products from the nervous system. But neurons occupy center stage in the nervous system. The messages transmitted by neurons somehow account for phenomena ranging from perception of an itch from a mosquito bite and the coordination of a skier's vision and muscles to the composition of a concerto and the solution of an algebraic equation.

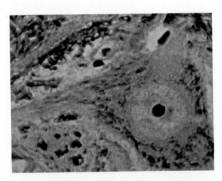

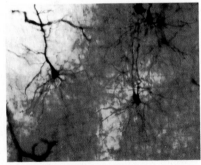

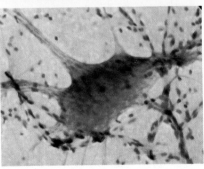

FIGURE 2.1 **NEURONS** Neurons take different forms in different parts of the nervous system. **Above left:** the large cell body belongs to a motor neuron (multipolar) from the gray matter in the spinal cord. **Above right:** pyramidal neurons in the cerebral cortex. **Left:** a large multipolar neuron from the myenteric (intestinal) plexus.

THE MAKEUP OF NEURONS

Neurons vary according to their functions and their location in the body. Some in the brain are only a fraction of an inch in length, while others in the legs are several feet long. But every neuron is a single nerve cell with a number of common features: a cell body, or **soma,** dendrites, and axon (Figure 2.2). The cell body is enclosed by the cell membrane and contains the nucleus of the cell. The cell body uses oxygen to create energy to carry out the work of the cell. Anywhere from a few to several hundred short fibers, or **dendrites,** extend from the cell body to receive incoming messages from up to 1,000 adjoining neurons. In the analogy of the neuron to a tree, dendrites serve as the roots. Each neuron has one **axon** that extends trunk-like from the cell body. Axons are very thin, but they may be quite short or extend for several feet if they are carrying messages from the toes to the spinal cord. Like tree trunks, axons too may branch and extend in different directions. Axons end in smaller branching structures that are aptly named **terminals.** At the tips of the axon terminals are swellings called **knobs** (Figure 2.3). Neurons carry messages in one direction only, from the dendrites or cell body through the axon to the axon terminals. The messages are then transmitted from the terminal knobs to other neurons, to muscles or to glands.

Myelin Many neurons are wrapped tightly with white, fatty **myelin sheaths.** Myelin is produced by glial cells. Myelin sheaths insulate the axon from electrically charged atoms, or ions, found in the bodily fluids that surround the nervous system, and facilitate the transmission of messages. Myelin does not uniformly coat the surface of an axon. It is missing at points called **nodes of Ranvier,** where the axon is exposed. Neural messages, or impulses, seem to skip rapidly from node to node rather than travel more slowly through the length of the axon.

The process of myelinization is not complete at birth. The growth of myelin is part of the maturation process that leads to the abilities to crawl and walk during the first year of life. It may be that babies are not physiologically "ready" to engage in visual-motor coordination and other types of learning until the coating process has been completed. In the disease multiple sclerosis, myelin is replaced with a hard fibrous tissue that throws off the timing of nerve impulses and interferes with muscular control. If neurons that control breathing are afflicted, the person can die from suffocation.

Opposite: FIGURE 2.2 **THE ANATOMY OF A NEURON** "Messages" enter neurons through dendrites, are transmitted along the trunklike axon, and then are sent through axon terminals to muscles, glands, and other neurons. A neuron relays its message to another neuron across a junction called a synapse, which consists of an axon terminal from the transmitting neuron, a dendrite of the receiving neuron, and a small gap between the neurons referred to as the synaptic cleft. Axon terminals contain sacs of chemicals called neurotransmitters. Neurotransmitters are released by the transmitting neuron into the synaptic cleft, and many of them are taken up by receptor sites on the dendrites of the receiving neuron. Some neurotransmitters (called "excitatory") influence receiving neurons in the direction of firing; others (called "inhibitory") influence them in the direction of *not* firing. To date, a few dozen possible neurotransmitters have been identified.

Soma A cell body. (A Greek word meaning "body.")

Dendrites Rootlike structures attached to the soma of a neuron. Dendrites receive impulses from other neurons. (From the Greek *dendron,* meaning "tree.")

Axon A long, thin part of a neuron that transmits impulses to other neurons from small branching structures called terminals.

Terminals Small, branching structures at the tips of axons.

Knobs Swellings at the ends of terminals. Also referred to as *bulbs* or *buttons*.

Myelin sheath (MY-uh-lin). A fatty substance that encases and insulates axons, permitting more rapid transmission of neural impulses. (From the Greek *myelos,* meaning "marrow.")

Node of Ranvier A noninsulated segment of a generally myelinated axon.

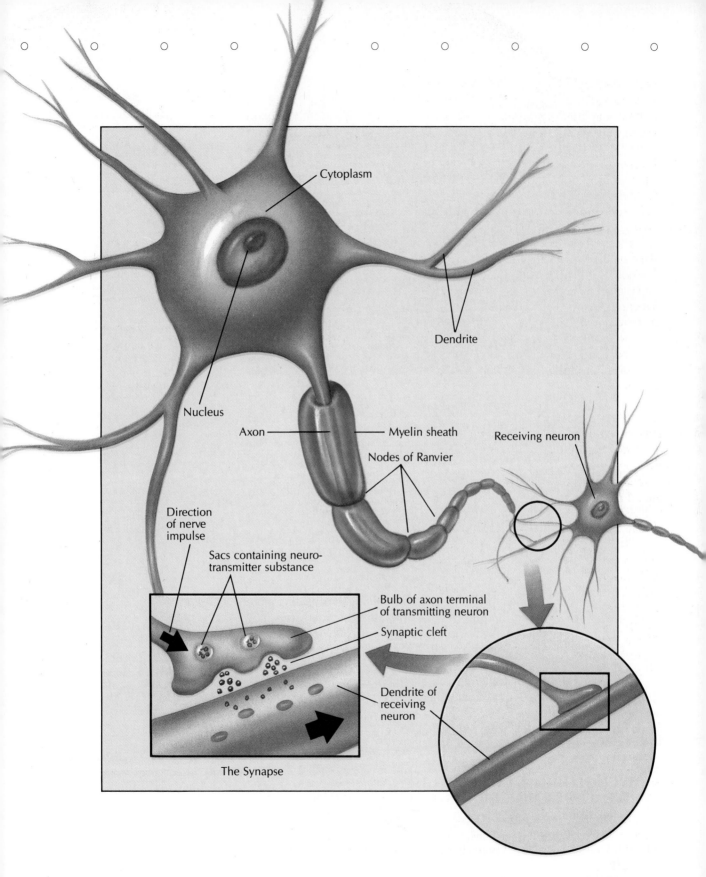

Cytoplasm

Dendrite

Nucleus

Axon

Myelin sheath

Nodes of Ranvier

Receiving neuron

Direction
of nerve
impulse

Sacs containing neuro-
transmitter substance

Bulb of axon terminal
of transmitting neuron

Synaptic cleft

Dendrite of
receiving
neuron

The Synapse

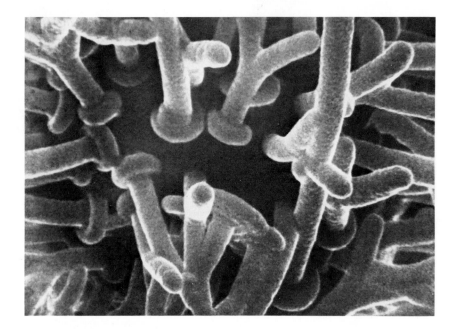

FIGURE 2.3 AXON TERMINALS A much-enlarged photograph of axon terminals, showing the terminal knobs or bulbs.

Afferent and Efferent Neurons If someone steps on your big toe, the sensation is registered by receptors or sensory neurons near the surface of your skin. Then it is transmitted to the spinal cord and brain through **afferent neurons** that are perhaps two to three feet long. In the brain, subsequent messages may be buffeted about by associative neurons that are only a few thousandths of an inch long. You experience the pain through this process and perhaps entertain some rather nasty thoughts about the perpetrator who is now apologizing and begging for understanding. Long before you arrive at any logical conclusions, however, motor neurons, or **efferent neurons,** will have sent messages back to your toe and foot so that you have withdrawn them and begun an impressive hopping routine. Other efferent neurons may have stimulated glands, so that by now your heart is beating more rapidly, you are sweating, and the hairs on the backs of your arms may have even become erect! Being a sport, you may say, "Oh, it's nothing." But considering all the neurons involved, it was really something, wasn't it?

In case you think that afferent and efferent neurons will be hard to distinguish because they sound pretty much the SAME to you, simply remember that they are the "SAME." That is, Sensory = Afferent, and Motor = Efferent. But don't tell your professor I let you in on this **mnemonic** device.

A PSYCHOLOGICAL CONTROVERSY: DO WE LOSE BRAIN CELLS AS WE GROW OLDER?

I've waited awhile, but now I'll come out with it. Although you have many billions of neurons, practically all of them were present at birth, and they have probably been dying off at the rate of several thousand a day. Yes,

Afferent neurons Neurons that transmit messages from sensory receptors to the spinal cord and brain. Also called sensory neurons. (From the Latin *afferre,* meaning "to carry.")

Efferent neurons Neurons that transmit messages from the brain or spinal cord to muscles and glands. Also called motor neurons. (From the Latin *efferre,* meaning "to carry outward.")

Mnemonic (neh-MON-ick). Aiding memory, usually by linking chunks of new information to well-known schemes. See Chapter 5. (From the Greek *mnemon,* meaning "mindful.")

the brain and other parts of the nervous system grew larger as you matured, but this growth has been largely due to the development of existing neurons through myelinization, the proliferation of dendrites and axon terminals, and an increase in the number of glial cells.

No doubt about it, you're losing some cells. But don't despair: We probably have more cells than we need. And many brain functions seem to be duplicated in different groups of cells. And if you started with, say, 12 billion neurons in the brain and were losing 10,000 a day, or three million a year, it would take a while to make a dent.

Yet Marian Diamond (1978) of the University of California maintains that we have no basis for affixing any number to the daily loss of brain cells. She claims that no reports of loss of brain cells have been supported by adequate research methodology. And she warns that one sinister effect of theorizing that we lose vast numbers of brain cells as we age is that it seems to justify the tossing of elderly workers onto the scrap heap of forced retirement.

Diamond and her colleagues decided that it was high time that a careful study on brain-cell counts was done. Rats journey through the life cycle more rapidly than we slowpoke humans, and so they compared the numbers of cells in rats' brains at the ages of 26 days (weaning), 41 days (onset of puberty), 108 days (young adulthood), and 650 days (old age).

The brains were cut into thin slices and stained so that neurons could be differentiated under the microscope from glial cells. The greatest decrease in neurons and glial cells occurred prior to 108 days, or young adulthood. Decreases at later ages were trivial by comparison. We must be cautious in generalizing from rats to people, but these findings suggest that intellectual deficits found in some elderly people may have little if anything to do with loss of brain cells.

Diamond also reports that rats raised in enriched environments—with ladders, mazes, tunnels, and many companions—developed thicker cerebral **cortices** with larger numbers of glial cells than rats raised in plain cages with fewer companions. The same thickening of the cerebral cortex occurred in rats who were first placed in enriched environments at the advanced age of 766 days! In other words, neurological development in response to experience can take place even in very old age—at least with rats and probably with humans (Diamond, 1984). Not only does the brain shape our experience. Experience to some degree can also shape the brain, apparently at any age.

THE NEURAL IMPULSE

In the late 1700s, Italian physiologist Luigi Galvani engaged in a shocking experiment in a rainstorm. While his neighbors had the sense to remain indoors, Galvani and his wife were out on the porch connecting lightning rods to the heads of dissected frogs whose legs were connected by wire to a well of water. When lightning blazed above, the frogs' muscles contracted repeatedly and violently. This is not a recommended way to prepare frogs' legs—Galvani was demonstrating that the messages (**neural impulses**) that travel along neurons are electrical in nature.

Cortices (CORE-tih-seas). Plural of cortex.

Neural impulse The electrochemical discharge of a nerve cell, or neuron.

Neural impulses travel somewhere between two (in nonmyelinated neurons) and 225 miles an hour (in myelinated neurons). This speed is not impressive when compared with that of an electric current in a toaster oven or a lamp, which can travel at the speed of light—over 186,000 miles per second. But distances in the body are short, and a message will travel from a toe to the brain in perhaps one-fiftieth of a second.

An Electrochemical Process The process by which neural impulses travel is electrochemical. Chemical changes take place within neurons that cause an electric charge to be transmitted along their lengths. In a resting state, when a neuron is not being stimulated by its neighbors, there are relatively greater numbers of positively charged sodium ions (Na+) and negatively charged chloride (Cl−) ions in the body fluid outside the neuron than in the fluid within the neuron. Positively charged potassium (K+) ions are more plentiful inside. This difference in electrical charge **polarizes** the neuron with a negative **resting potential** of about −70 millivolts in relation to the body fluid outside the cell membrane.

When an area on the surface of the resting neuron is adequately stimulated by other neurons, the cell membrane in the area changes its **permeability** to allow sodium ions to enter. As a consequence, the area of entry becomes positively charged or **depolarized** with respect to the outside (Figure 2.4). The permeability of the cell membrane changes again, allowing no more sodium ions to enter.

The inside of the cell at the disturbed area is now said to have an **action potential,** or positive charge, of about +40 millivolts. This inner change causes the next section of the cell to become permeable to sodium ions, while at the same time sodium ions are being pumped out of the area of the cell previously affected, which then returns to its resting potential. In this way the neural impulse is transmitted continuously along an axon that is not myelinated. Because the impulse is created anew as it progresses, its strength does not change. As noted earlier, neural impulses are conducted more rapidly along myelinated axons because they jump from node to node.

The conduction of the neural impulse along the length of a neuron is what is meant by "firing." A neuron "fires" in less than one thousandth of a second. In firing, it "attempts" to transmit the "message" to other neurons, muscles, or glands. However, other neurons will not fire unless the incoming messages combine to reach an adequate **threshold.** A weak message may cause a temporary shift in electrical charge at some point along the cell membrane of a neuron; but this charge will dissipate if the neuron is not stimulated to threshold.

A neuron may transmit several hundred such messages in a second. Yet, in accord with the **all-or-none principle,** each time a neuron fires it transmits an impulse of the same strength. Neurons fire more frequently when they have been stimulated by larger numbers of other neurons; stronger stimuli result in firing with greater frequency.

For a thousandth of a second or so after firing, a neuron enters an **absolute refractory period** during which it will not fire in response to stim-

Polarize To ready a neuron for firing by creating an internal negative charge in relation to the body fluid outside the cell membrane.

Resting potential The electrical potential across the neural membrane when it is not responding to other neurons.

Permeability The degree to which a membrane allows a substance to pass through it.

Depolarize To reduce the resting potential of a cell membrane from about −70 millivolts toward zero.

Action potential The electrical impulse that provides the basis for the conduction of a neural impulse along an axon of a neuron.

Threshold The point at which a stimulus is just strong enough to produce a response.

All-or-none principle The fact that a neuron fires an impulse of the same strength whenever its action potential has been triggered.

Absolute refractory period A phase following firing during which a neuron's action potential cannot be triggered.

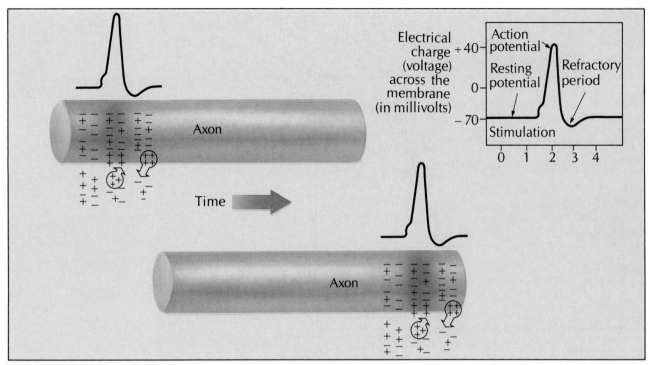

FIGURE 2.4 THE NEURAL IMPULSE In the resting state, a section of a neuron has a charge of about −70 millivolts. When it is stimulated by other neurons, the cell membrane becomes permeable to sodium ions so that an action potential of about +40 millivolts is induced. This action potential is transmitted along the axon. Eventually the neuron fires (or fails to fire) according to the all-or-none principle.

ulation from other neurons. Then, for another few thousandths of a second, the neuron is said to be in a **relative refractory period,** during which it will fire, but only in response to messages that are stronger than usual. The refractory period is a time of recovery, when the chemical balance is being restored to the resting potential. When we realize that such periods of recovery may take place hundreds of times per second, it seems a rapid recovery and a short rest indeed.

THE SYNAPSE

A neuron relays its message to another neuron across a junction called a **synapse.** A synapse consists of a "branch," or axon terminal from the transmitting neuron; a "root," or dendrite of a receiving neuron; and a small fluid-filled gap between the neurons that is called the synaptic cleft (Figure 2.5). Although the neural impulse is electrical, it does not just jump across the synaptic cleft like a spark. Instead, when a nerve impulse reaches them, axon terminals release chemicals into the synaptic cleft like a myriad of ships being cast off into the sea.

Relative refractory period A phase following the absolute refractory period during which a neuron will fire in response to stronger-than-usual messages.

Synapse (SIN-apps). A space or junction between the terminal knobs of an axon and the dendrites or soma of another neuron. (From the Greek *synapsis,* meaning "junction" or "connection.")

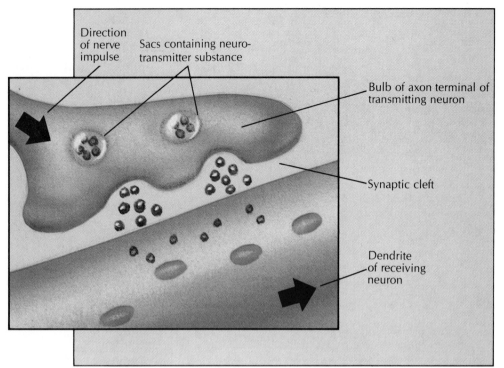

FIGURE 2.5 THE SYNAPSE Neurons relay their messages to other neurons across junctions called synapses. A synapse consists of an axon terminal from the transmitting neuron, a dendrite of the receiving neuron, and a fluid-filled gap between the two which is referred to as the synaptic cleft. Molecules of neurotransmitters are released into the synaptic cleft from vesicles within the axon terminal. Many molecules are taken up by receptor sites on the dendrite; others are broken down or "re-uptaked" by the transmitting neuron.

NEUROTRANSMITTERS

In the knobs at the tips of the axon terminals are sacs or synaptic vesicles that contain chemicals called neurotransmitters. When a neural impulse reaches the axon terminal, the vesicles release varying amounts of these neurotransmitters into the synaptic cleft. From there they influence the receiving neuron. If adequate quantities of neurotransmitters are released by transmitting cells, the receiving neuron will also fire.

As of today, some three dozen different possible neurotransmitters have been identified, and it has been estimated that there may be hundreds of them (Snyder, 1980). Each neurotransmitter has its own chemical structure, and each can fit into a specifically tailored harbor, or **receptor site,** on the dendrite of the receiving neuron. The analogy of a key fitting into a lock has also been used. Once released, not all molecules of a neurotransmitter find their ways into receptor sites of other neurons. "Loose" neurotransmitters are usually either broken down or reabsorbed by the axon terminal (a process called "re-uptake").

Some neurotransmitters act to excite other neurons; that is, to influence receiving neurons in the direction of firing. The synapses between

Receptor site A location on a dendrite of a receiving neuron tailored to receive a neurotransmitter.

Excitatory synapse A synapse that influences receiving neurons in the direction of firing by increasing depolarization of their cell membranes.

Inhibitory synapse A synapse that influences receiving neurons in the direction of not firing by encouraging changes in their membrane permeability in the direction of the resting potential.

Acetylcholine (uh-see-till-CO-lean). A neurotransmitter that controls muscle contractions. Abbreviated *ACh*.

Dopamine (DOPE-uh-mean). A neurotransmitter that is involved in Parkinson's disease and appears to play a major role in schizophrenia. See Chapter 11.

Norepinephrine (nor-ep-pee-NEFF-rin). A neurotransmitter whose action is similar to that of the hormone *epinephrine,* and which may play a role in depression. See Chapter 11.

axon terminals with excitatory neurotransmitters and receiving neurons are called **excitatory synapses.** Other neurotransmitters inhibit receiving neurons; that is, they influence them in the direction of not firing. The synapses between axon terminals with inhibitory neurotransmitters and receiving neurons are called **inhibitory synapses.** Neurons may be influenced by neurotransmitters that have been released by up to 1,000 other neurons. The additive stimulation received from all these cells determines whether a particular neuron will also fire and which neurotransmitters will be released in the process.

Neurotransmitters are involved in processes ranging from muscle contraction to emotional response. Excesses or deficiencies of neurotransmitters have been linked to diseases and abnormal behavior.

Acetylcholine   **Acetylcholine** (ACh) is a neurotransmitter that controls muscle contractions. ACh is excitatory at synapses between nerves and muscles that involve voluntary movement, but inhibitory at the heart and some other locations.

The functioning of ACh is highlighted by the effects of curare. Curare is a poison that was extracted from plants by South American Indians and used in hunting. If an arrow tipped with curare pierced the skin and the poison entered the body, it would prevent ACh from lodging within receptor sites in neurons, resulting in paralysis. The victim would be prevented from contracting the muscles used in breathing and would die from suffocation. Botulism, a disease that stems from food poisoning, prevents the release of ACh and has the same effect as curare.

Dopamine   **Dopamine** is primarily an inhibitory neurotransmitter. Dopamine is involved in voluntary movements, learning and memory, and emotional arousal. Deficiencies of dopamine are linked to Parkinson's disease, a disorder in which patients progressively lose control over their muscles. They come to show muscle tremors and jerky, uncoordinated movements. The drug L-Dopa, a substance that the brain converts to dopamine, helps slow the progress of Parkinson's disease.

The mental disorder schizophrenia (see Chapter 12) has also been linked to dopamine. Schizophrenic individuals may have more receptor sites for dopamine in an area of the brain that is involved in emotional responding. For this reason, they may *overutilize* the dopamine that is available in the brain, leading to hallucinations and disturbances of thought and emotion. The phenothiazines, a group of drugs used in the treatment of schizophrenia, are thought to work by blocking the action of dopamine—by locking some dopamine out of these receptor sites (Snyder, 1984). Not surprisingly, phenothiazines may have Parkinson-like side effects, which are usually then treated by additional drugs, adjustment of the dose of phenothiazine, or switching to another drug.

Norepinephrine   **Norepinephrine** is chemically similar to the hormone epinephrine, which we shall discuss later in the chapter. Norepinephrine is both a neurotransmitter and a hormone. Norepinephrine, like epinephrine, speeds up the heartbeat and other bodily processes. Norepinephrine is involved in general arousal, learning and memory, and eating. Deficiencies of norepinephrine have been linked to depression (Ellison, 1977).

Amphetamines ("speed") increase the release of dopamine and norepinephrine, and also impede their reabsorption by the releasing synaptic vesicles after neurons have fired. As a result, there are excesses of these neurotransmitters in the nervous system, vastly increasing the firing of neurons and leading to a persistent state of high arousal. The stimulant caffeine, found in coffee, is thought to prevent reabsorption of these neurotransmitters by blocking the action of the enzymes that break them down. Until the caffeine has been removed from the system, we may encounter "coffee nerves."

Serotonin   **Serotonin** is also primarily an inhibitory transmitter. Serotonin is involved in emotional arousal and sleep. Deficiencies of serotonin have been linked to anxiety, depression, and insomnia. The drug LSD (see Chapter 4) decreases the action of serotonin and may also influence the utilization of dopamine. With LSD, "two no's make a yes." By inhibiting an inhibitor, brain activity increases, in this case frequently leading to hallucinations.

NEUROPEPTIDES

Jogging and running have become something of a fad in the United States, and not only because running promotes cardiovascular conditioning, firms the muscles, and helps us to control weight. There are also at least two common psychological effects: (1) an increased sense of self-competence, and (2) the so-called "runner's high."

Endorphins   "Runner's high" may be caused by the release of chains of amino acids called **endorphins.** Endorphins are a member of a family of recently discovered chemicals known as **neuropeptides** (Krieger, 1983). The word *endorphin* is the contraction of *endogenous morphine. Endogenous* means "developing from within." Endorphins, then, are similar to the narcotic morphine in their functions and are produced by our own bodies. They occur naturally in the brain and in the bloodstream.

It turns out that endorphins have effects that are similar to those of morphine (Bolles & Faneslow, 1982). Endorphins act like inhibitory neurotransmitters. As we shall see in Chapter 3, endorphins act by locking into the receptor sites for chemicals that transmit pain messages to the brain. Once the endorphin "key" is in the "lock," pain-causing chemicals cannot transmit their (frequently unwelcome) messages. There are a number of endorphins. Beta-endorphin has been found to be many times more powerful than morphine, molecule for molecule, whether injected into the bloodstream or directly into the brain (Snyder, 1977).

In addition to relieving pain, endorphins play a role in regulating respiration, hunger, memory, sexual behavior, blood pressure, mood, and body temperature.

Serotonin A neurotransmitter, deficiencies of which have been linked to affective disorders, anxiety, and insomnia.

Endorphins (en-DOOR-fins). Mostly inhibitory neurotranmitters that are composed of chains of amino acids and are functionally similar to morphine.

Neuropeptides A group of compounds formed from amino acids (peptides) that function as neurotransmitters.

A VIEW OF THE NEW YORK CITY MARATHON Why have thousands of people taken up long-distance running? Running, of course, promotes cardiovascular conditioning, firms the muscles, and helps us to control weight. But long-distance running may also induce the so-called "runner's high" by stimulating the release of endorphins—naturally occurring substances that are similar in function to the narcotic morphine.

Enkephalins (en-KEFF-uh-lins). Types of endorphins that are weaker and shorter-acting than beta-endorphin.

Dynorphin (die-NOR-fin). A neuropeptide that is more powerful than beta-endorphin in its pain-relieving effects.

Nerve A bundle of axons from many neurons.

Nuclei (NEW-klee-eye). Plural of *nucleus*. A group of neural cell bodies found in the brain or spinal cord.

Ganglia Plural of *ganglion*. A group of neural cell bodies found elsewhere in the body other than the brain or spinal cord.

Enkephalins   **Enkephalins** are one specific type of endorphins and, as such, also occur naturally in the brain. The word *enkephalin* derives from roots meaning "in" and the Greek *kephale,* meaning "head." Enkephalins share the pain-relieving effects of endorphins, but may be somewhat weaker and shorter-acting.

Dynorphin   Yet another recently discovered neuropeptide, **dynorphin,** turns out to be many times more powerful than beta-endorphin (Whitehall et al., 1983). Dynorphin, like the word dynamic, derives from the Greek *dynamis,* meaning "power" or "strength." It is possible that a new generation of powerful pain-killing drugs may be synthetic neuropeptides.

There you have it—a fabulous "forest" of neurons in which billions upon billions of vesicles are pouring neurotransmitters into synaptic clefts at any given time, when you are involved in strenuous activity, now as you are reading this page, even as you are passively watching television. This microscopic picture is repeated several hundred times every second. The combined activity of all these neurotransmitters determines which messages will be transmitted and which will not. Your experience of sensations, your thoughts, and your psychological sense of control over your body are very different from the electrochemical processes we have described. Yet somehow these many electrochemical events are responsible for your psychological sense of yourself and of the world.

THE NERVOUS SYSTEM

There was a time during my childhood when it seemed to me that it was not a very good thing to have a "nervous" system. For instance, if your system were not so nervous, you might be less likely to jump at strange noises.

At some point I learned that a nervous system was not a system that was nervous, but a system of nerves that were involved in thought processes, heart beat, visual-motor coordination, and so on. I also learned that the human nervous system was more complex than that of any other animal, and that our brains were larger than those of any other animal. Now this last piece of business is not exactly true. A human brain weighs about three pounds, but elephant and whale brains may be four times as heavy. Still, our brains comprise a greater part of our body weight than do those of elephants or whales. Our brains weigh about one-sixtieth of our body weight. Elephant brains weigh about one-thousandth of their total weight, and whale brains a paltry $1/10,000$th of their weight. So if we wish, we can still find figures to make us proud.

The brain is but one part of the nervous system. A **nerve** is a bundle of axons. The cell bodies of these neurons are not considered part of the nerve. The cell bodies are gathered into clumps called **nuclei** in the brain and spinal cord, and **ganglia** elsewhere.

The nervous system consists of the brain, the spinal cord, and nerves linking them to receptors in the sensory organs and effectors in the muscles and glands. As shown in Figure 2.6, the brain and spinal cord compose

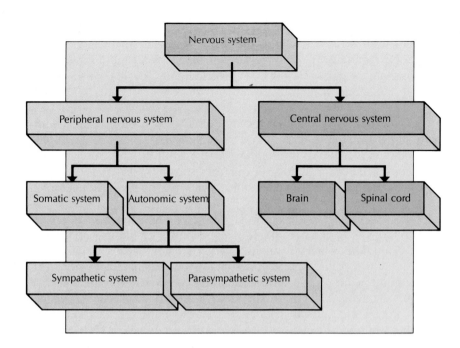

FIGURE 2.6 **DIVISIONS OF THE NERVOUS SYSTEM**

what we refer to as the **central nervous system.** The sensory (afferent) neurons, which receive and transmit messages to the brain and spinal cord, and the motor (efferent) neurons, which transmit messages from the brain or spinal cord to the muscles and glands, compose the **peripheral nervous system.** There is no deep, complex reason for labeling the two major divisions of the nervous system in this way. It is just geography. The peripheral nervous system extends more into the edges or periphery of the body.

Let us now examine the nature and functions of the central and peripheral nervous systems.

THE CENTRAL NERVOUS SYSTEM

The central nervous system consists of the spinal cord and the brain.

The Spinal Cord The **spinal cord** is a column of nerves about as thick as a thumb. It transmits messages from receptors to the brain, and from the brain to muscles and glands throughout the body (Figure 2.7). The spinal cord is also capable of some "local government" of responses to external stimulation through **spinal reflexes.** A spinal reflex is an unlearned response to a stimulus that may involve only two neurons—a sensory (afferent) neuron and a motor (efferent) neuron. In some reflexes a third neuron, called an **interneuron,** transmits the neural impulse from the sensory neuron through the spinal cord to the motor neuron (Figure 2.8).

The spinal cord includes both gray matter and white matter. The **gray matter** consists of nonmyelinated neurons. Some of these nonmyelinated neurons are involved in spinal reflexes, while others send axons to the brain. The **white matter** is composed of bundles of longer, myelinated (and thus whitish) axons that carry messages back and forth to and from the brain.

Central nervous system The brain and spinal cord.

Peripheral nervous system (pair-IF-fur-al). The part of the nervous system consisting of the somatic nervous system and the autonomic nervous system.

Spinal cord A column of nerves within the spine that transmits messages from sensory receptors to the brain, and from the brain to muscles and glands throughout the body.

Spinal reflex A simple unlearned response to a stimulus that may involve as few as two neurons. (From the Latin *reflectere,* meaning "to bend back" or "to reflect.")

Interneuron A neuron that transmits a neural impulse from a sensory neuron to a motor neuron.

Gray matter In the spinal cord, the neurons and neural segments that are involved in spinal reflexes. They are gray in appearance.

White matter In the spinal cord, axon bundles that carry messages back and forth from and to the brain.

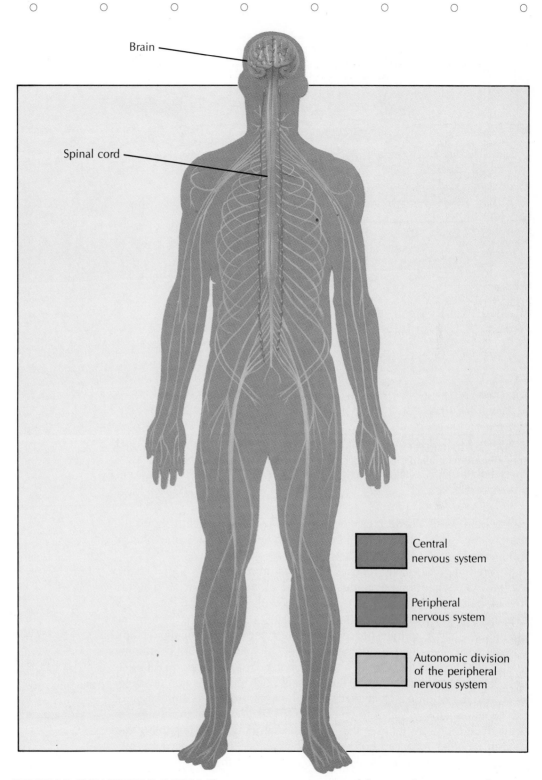

Brain

Spinal cord

Central
nervous system

Peripheral
nervous system

Autonomic division
of the peripheral
nervous system

FIGURE 2.7 THE NERVOUS SYSTEM The nervous system consists of the central
nervous system (brain and spinal cord) and the peripheral nervous system. The
autonomic nervous system is a division of the peripheral nervous system.

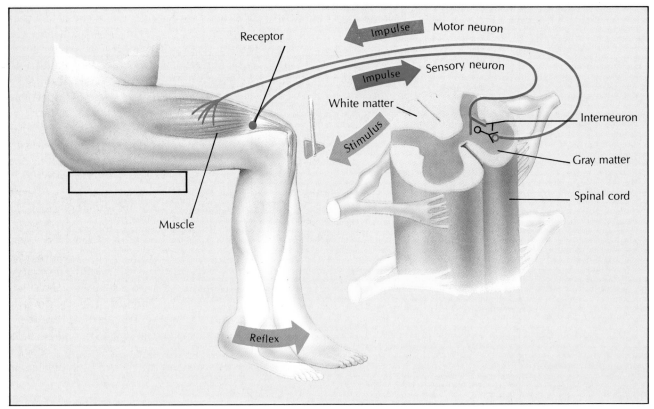

FIGURE 2.8 **THE REFLEX ARC** A cross-section of the spinal cord, showing a sensory neuron, interneuron, and motor neuron—a combination involved in many spinal reflexes, such as the knee-jerk reflex.

As you can see in Figure 2.8, a cross section of the spinal cord shows the gray matter, which includes cell bodies, to be distributed in something of a butterfly-shaped pattern.*

We engage in many reflexes. We blink in response to a puff of air. We swallow when food accumulates in the mouth. A physician may tap the leg below the knee to see if we will show the knee-jerk reflex, a sign that the nervous system is operating adequately. Urinating and defecating are reflexes that occur in response to pressure in the bladder and the rectum. Parents typically spend a number of weeks or months in toilet training infants, or teaching them to involve their brains in the process of elimination. Learning to inhibit these reflexes makes civilized interaction possible.

Sexual response also involves many reflexes. Adequate stimulation of the genital organs will lead to erection in the male, vaginal lubrication in the female (both are reflexes that make sexual intercourse possible), and orgasm (another reflex) in both sexes. These processes *can* be quite mechanical, not involving the brain at all, but most often they are not. Feelings

*If you turn to the Rorschach inkblot shown on p. 451, you can see why many biology and nursing students report that it reminds them of the spinal cord.

of passion, memories of an enjoyable sexual encounter, and sexual fantasies usually contribute to sexual response by transmitting messages from the brain to the genitals through the spinal cord (Rathus, 1983). Awareness of pleasurable sexual sensations in the genitals also works to heighten sexual response, but is not biologically required. (In fact, some people can reach orgasm without touching the genitals—through fantasy alone—usually by imagining sexual stimulation of the genitals by an exciting sex partner.)

Although sexual response in humans is rarely fully mechanical, we can, as noted, respond purely on a reflexive level. Some men and women have spinal-cord injuries that prevent genital sensations from reaching the brain. But genital stimulation in many instances can still lead to the reflexes of sexual arousal and orgasm (Money, 1960; Comarr, 1970). In experiments with dogs in which messages were prevented from reaching the brain by way of the spinal cord, the animals have achieved erection, shown pelvic thrusting, and ejaculated (Hart, 1967). After ejaculation, in fact, they were usually responsive to additional sexual stimulation *earlier* than dogs whose spinal columns were intact. It seems that the brain can inhibit sexual response as well as promote it. Many men paralyzed below the waist have similarly achieved erection and ejaculated in response to genital stimulation, although they have not experienced sexual sensations. In this way, even paralyzed people often have sexually active relationships and become parents. Do they "enjoy" their sexual activity? Why not? They achieve common sexual goals with their partners and observe the pleasure their partners experience.

The Brain   Every show has a star, and the brain is the undisputed star of the human nervous system. The size and shape of your brain are responsible for your large, delightfully rounded head. In all the animal kingdom, you (and about five billion other human beings) are unique because of the capacities for learning and thought made possible by the human brain.

Let us have a look at the brain, as shown in Figure 2.9. We shall begin with the back of the head, where the spinal cord rises to meet the brain, and work our way forward. The lower part of the brain, referred to as the or hindbrain, consists of three major structures: the medulla, the pons, and the cerebellum.

Many nerves that connect the spinal cord to higher levels of the brain pass through the **medulla.** The medulla regulates vital functions such as heart rate, blood pressure, and respiration. The medulla also plays a role in sleep, sneezing, and coughing. The **pons** is a bulge in the hindbrain that lies forward of the medulla. Pons is the Latin word for "bridge," and the pons is so named because of the bundles of nerves that pass through it. The pons transmits information concerning bodily movement, and is also involved in functions related to attention, sleep and alertness, and respiration.

Behind the pons lies the **cerebellum,** which means "little brain" in Latin. The two hemispheres of the cerebellum are involved in maintaining balance and in controlling motor (muscle) behavior. Injury to the cerebellum may lead to lack of motor coordination, stumbling, and loss of muscle tone.

Medulla (meh-DULL-ah). An oblong-shaped area of the hindbrain involved in heartbeat and respiration.

Pons A structure of the hindbrain that is involved in respiration.

Cerebellum A part of the hindbrain involved in muscle coordination and balance.

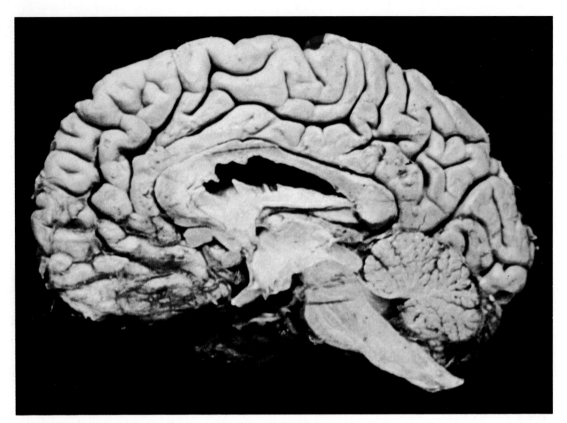

A PHOTO OF THE HUMAN BRAIN, SPLIT TOP TO BOTTOM

The **reticular activating system** (RAS) begins in the hindbrain and ascends through the region of the midbrain into the lower part of the forebrain. The RAS is vital in the functions of attention, sleep, and arousal. Injury to the RAS may leave an animal **comatose.** Stimulation of the RAS causes it to send messages to the cortex, making us more alert to sensory information. Electrical stimulation of the RAS awakens sleeping animals, and certain drugs called central-nervous-system depressants, like alcohol, are thought to work in part by lowering RAS activity.

Sudden loud noises will stimulate the RAS and awaken a sleeping animal or person. But the RAS may become selective, or acquire the capacity to play a filtering role through learning. It may allow some messages to filter through to higher brain levels and awareness, while screening out others. For example, the parent who has primary responsibility for child care may be awakened by the stirring sounds of an infant, while louder sounds of traffic or street noise are filtered out. The other parent, by contrast, may usually sleep through even loud cries. But if the first parent must be away for several days, the second parent's RAS may quickly acquire sensitivity to noises produced by the child. This sensitivity may rapidly fade again when the first parent returns.

Reticular-activating system A part of the brain involved in attention, sleep, and arousal. (From the Latin *rete*, meaning "net.")

Comatose In a coma, a state resembling sleep from which it is difficult to be aroused.

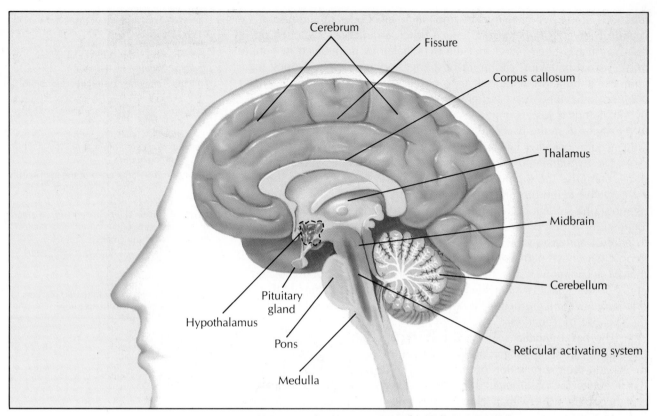

FIGURE 2.9 **A CUTAWAY VIEW OF THE HUMAN BRAIN** This view of the brain, also split top to bottom, labels some of the most important structures.

Also located in the midbrain are areas involved in vision and hearing. These include the area that controls eye reflexes such as dilation of the pupils and eye movements.

Five major areas of the frontmost part of the brain, or forebrain, are the thalamus, the hypothalamus, the limbic system, the basal ganglia, and the cerebrum.

The **thalamus** is located near the center of the brain. It consists of two joined lobes that have egg or football shapes. The thalamus serves as a relay station for sensory stimulation. Nerve fibers from our sensory systems enter from below; the information carried by them is then transmitted to the cerebral cortex by way of fibers that exit from above. For instance, the thalamus relays sensory input from the eyes to the visual areas of the cerebral cortex. The thalamus is also involved in controlling sleep and attention, in coordination with other brain structures, including the RAS.

The **hypothalamus** is a tiny collection of nuclei located beneath the thalamus and above the pituitary gland. The hypothalamus is about the size of a pea and weighs only four grams, yet it is vital in the control of body temperature, the concentration of fluids, the storage of nutrients, and various aspects of motivation and emotion. Experimenters learn many of the

Thalamus An area near the center of the brain that is involved in the relay of sensory information to the cortex, and in the functions of sleep and attention. (From the Latin *thalamos,* meaning "inner chamber.")

Hypothalamus A bundle of nuclei below the thalamus involved in body temperature, motivation, and emotion. See Chapter 7. (From the Greek *hypo-,* meaning "under," and *thalamos.)*

functions of the hypothalamus by implanting electrodes in various parts of it and observing the behavioral effects when a current is switched on. In this way it has been found that the hypothalamus is involved in hunger, thirst, sexual behavior, caring for offspring, and aggression. Among lower animals, stimulation of various areas of the hypothalamus can trigger stereotyped behaviors, such as fighting, mating, or even nest building. The hypothalamus is just as important to people, but our behavior in response to messages from the hypothalamus is less stereotyped and relatively more influenced by cognitive functions such as thought, choice, and value systems.

The hypothalamus, along with parts of the thalamus and other structures, comprise the **limbic system.** The limbic system lies along the inner edge of the cerebrum and is found in mammals only. It is involved in memory (the storage of information), and in the drives of hunger, sex, and aggression. A part of the limbic system is sometimes removed in an effort to control **epilepsy,** or seizures that stem from sudden neural discharges. People who have had such operations can recall material learned prior to them, but cannot permanently store new information. Destruction of certain areas of the limbic system leads monkeys and other mammals to show docile behavior. Destruction of other areas will lead to a rage reaction at the slightest provocation.

The **basal ganglia** are buried beneath the cortex to the front of the thalamus. The basal ganglia are involved in the control of postural movements and the coordination of the limbs. The death of a group of neurons that regulate the basal ganglia has been linked to Parkinson's disease, in which people walk with a clumsy, shuffling gait and find it difficult to initiate movement.

The **cerebrum** is the crowning glory of the brain. Only in human beings does the cerebrum comprise such a large proportion of the brain (Figure 2.9).

The surface of the cerebrum is wrinkled, or convoluted, with ridges and valleys. This surface is the **cerebral cortex.** The convolutions allow a great deal of surface area to be packed into the brain. We shall explore the cerebral cortex in depth in a later section of this chapter.

Valleys in the cortex are called **fissures.** A most significant fissure practically divides the cerebrum in half.* The hemispheres of the cerebral cortex are connected by the **corpus callosum** (Latin for "thick body" or "hard body"), a thick fiber bundle. Later we shall see that severing the corpus callosum is not life-threatening and leads to some interesting behavior.

THE PERIPHERAL NERVOUS SYSTEM

The peripheral nervous system consists of sensory and motor neurons that transmit messages to and from the central nervous system. Without the peripheral nervous system, our brains would be isolated from the world: they would not be able to perceive it, and they would not be able to act upon it. The two main divisions of the peripheral nervous system are the somatic nervous system and the autonomic nervous system.

*I was going to note that this fissure ran from front to back, under the line covered by Mr. T's Mohawk-style hair, but my editor convinced me to omit this descriptive information.

Limbic system A group of structures that form a fringe along the inner edge of the cerebrum. They are involved in memory and motivation. (From the Latin *limbus,* meaning "border" or "fringe.")

Epilepsy Temporary disturbances of brain functions that involve sudden neural discharges. (From the Greek *epilepsia,* meaning "seizure.")

Basal ganglia Ganglia located between the thalamus and cerebrum that are involved in motor coordination.

Cerebrum The large mass of the forebrain, which consists of two hemispheres. (Latin word meaning "brain.")

Cerebral cortex The wrinkled surface area of the cerebrum, often called "gray matter" because of the appearance afforded by the many cell bodies. (*Cortex* is a Latin word meaning "bark.")

Fissures. Valleys.

Corpus callosum A thick bundle of fibers that connects the two hemispheres.

Somatic nervous system The divison of the peripheral nervous system that connects the central nervous system with sensory receptors, muscles, and the surface of the body.

Autonomic nervous system The division of the peripheral nervous system that regulates glands and involuntary activities like heartbeat, respiration, digestion, and dilation of the pupils. Abbreviated *ANS.* (From the Greek *autonomos,* meaning "independent.")

Involuntary Automatic, not consciously controlled.

Sympathetic The branch of the ANS that is most active during emotional responses that spend the body's reserves of energy, such as fear and anxiety. (From the Greek *syn-,* meaning "together," and *pathos,* meaning "feeling.")

Parasympathetic The branch of the ANS that is most active during processes that restore the body's reserves of energy, like digestion. Parasympathetic activities are frequently, but not always, antagonistic to sympathetic activities. (From the Greek *para-,* meaning "alongside," and *sympathetic.)*

The Somatic Nervous System The **somatic nervous system** consists of our sensory (afferent) and motor (efferent) neurons. It transmits messages about sights, sounds, smells, temperature, our bodily positions, and so on to the central nervous system. As a result we can experience the beauties and the horrors of the world, its physical ecstasies and agonies. Messages from the brain and spinal cord to the somatic nervous system control purposeful body movements, like raising a hand, winking, or running; breathing; and movements which we hardly attend to—movements that maintain our posture and balance.

The Autonomic Nervous System *Autonomic* means "automatic." The **autonomic nervous system** (ANS) regulates the glands and **involuntary** activities like heartbeat, digestion, and dilation of the pupils of the eyes— even while we are asleep. In Chapter 4 we shall see that people have also learned to gain conscious control over a number of autonomic functions, such as the rate of the heartbeat, through biofeedback training.

The ANS has two branches or divisions, the **sympathetic** and the **parasympathetic.** These branches have largely opposing effects; when they work at the same time, their effects can be something of an averaging out of their influences. Many organs and glands are stimulated by both branches of the ANS (Figure 2.10). In general, the sympathetic division is most active during processes that involve the spending of bodily energy from stored reserves, such as in a fight-or-flight response to a predator or when you find out that your mortgage payment is going to be increased. The parasympathetic division is most active during processes that replenish reserves of energy, as during eating (Levitt, 1981). For instance, when we are afraid, the sympathetic division of the ANS accelerates the heart rate. But when we relax, it is the parasympathetic division that decelerates the heart rate. The parasympathetic division stimulates digestive processes, but the sympathetic branch inhibits digestive activity. Since the sympathetic division predominates when we feel fear or anxiety, fear or anxiety can lead to indigestion.

The autonomic nervous system is of particular interest to psychologists, because its activities are linked to the experiencing of various emotions, such as anxiety and love. Some of us appear to have overactive sympathetic nervous systems; our bodies respond as though we were faced with great danger in the absence of outside threats. In Chapter 10 we shall see that prolonged activity of the sympathetic nervous system has been linked to various kinds of illnesses, and that there are many things that we can do directly or indirectly to reduce sympathetic activity.

In the area of sexual behavior, we see how sympathetic and parasympathetic activities can interact to facilitate pleasurable performance or to lead to frustration. To begin with, a small amount of anxiety (characterized by sympathetic activity), as is normal when a couple first engage in sexual activity, can enhance sexual response by generally activating the body. However, the reflexes of erection and vaginal lubrication are largely under parasympathetic control. For that reason, too much anxiety (sympathetic activity) can inhibit erection or lubrication from occurring. Ejaculation is largely under sympathetic control. Even though a great deal of

AUTONOMIC NERVOUS SYSTEM

Parasympathetic Branch

Sympathetic Branch

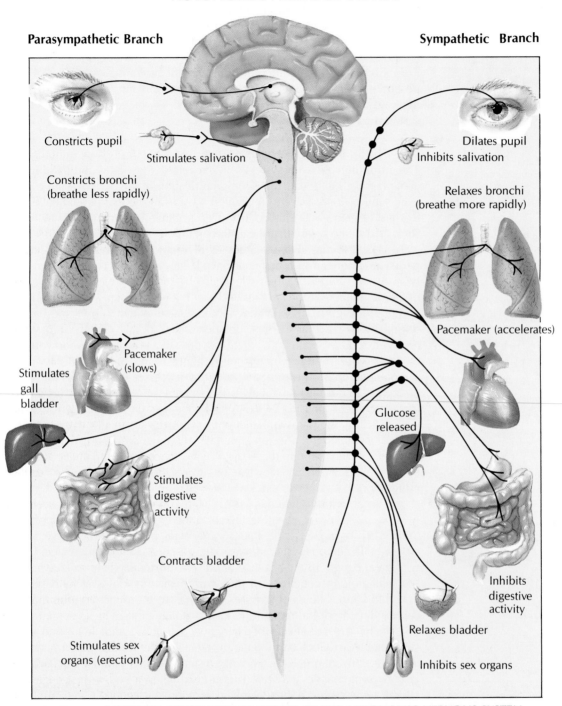

Constricts pupil

Stimulates salivation

Constricts bronchi
(breathe less rapidly)

Pacemaker
(slows)

Stimulates
gall
bladder

Stimulates
digestive
activity

Contracts bladder

Stimulates sex
organs (erection)

Dilates pupil

Inhibits salivation

Relaxes bronchi
(breathe more rapidly)

Pacemaker (accelerates)

Glucose
released

Inhibits
digestive
activity

Relaxes bladder

Inhibits sex organs

FIGURE 2.10 ACTIVITIES OF THE TWO BRANCHES OF THE AUTONOMIC NERVOUS SYSTEM
The parasympathetic branch of the ANS is generally dominant during activities that replenish the
body's stores of energy, such as eating and relaxing. The sympathetic branch is most active during
activities that spend energy, such as fighting or fleeing from an enemy, and when we experience
emotions such as fear and anxiety. For this reason, most of the organs shown are stimulated to
heightened activity by the sympathetic branch of the ANS. Digestive processes are an exception;
they are inhibited by sympathetic activity.

anxiety can inhibit erection, it can produce early or premature ejaculation. In Chapter 13 we shall see that sex-therapy techniques for treating sexual problems rely, in part, on helping people reduce sympathetic nervous system activity—that is, their sexual anxieties.

THE CEREBRAL CORTEX

Just where is that elusive piece of business you think of as your "mind"? Thousands of years ago it was not generally thought that the mind had a place to hang its hat within the body. It was common to assume that the body was inhabited by demons or souls that could not be explained in terms of substance at all. After all, if you look inside a human being, the biological structures you find do not look all that different in quality from those of many lower animals. So it seemed to make sense that those qualities that made us distinctly human—thinking, planning, talking, dreaming, composing—were unrelated to substances that you could actually see, feel, and weigh on a scale.

Some ancient Egyptians attributed control of the human being to a little person, or **homunculus,** who dwelled within the skull and regulated our behavior. The Greek philosopher Aristotle thought that the soul had set up living quarters in the heart. After all, serious injury to the heart could be said to cause the soul to take flight from the body.

Through a variety of accidents and research projects, we have come to recognize that "mind," or consciousness, dwells essentially within the brain. Within the brain, it is located largely in the cerebral cortex. Different sorts of bodily injuries have distinct effects. It became increasingly apparent that injuries to the head can lead to impairments of consciousness and awareness, such as loss of vision and hearing, general confusion, or loss of memory. Experiments in stimulating or destroying specific areas in animal brains and human brains* have also shown that certain areas of the brain are associated with specific types of sensations or activities.

From the perspective of biological psychologists today, the mind is a manifestation of the brain. Without the brain, in other words, there is no mind. Within the brain lies the potential for self-awareness and purposeful activity. Somehow the brain gives rise to mind. Whether thought is then self-initiated, merely responsive to external stimulation, or reflects an ongoing interaction between people and the environment is a hotly debated issue in psychology. But it is generally agreed that for every **phenomenological** event, like a "thought" or a "feeling," there are accompanying, underlying neurological events.

When you realize that a neuron may fire hundreds of times a second, and that thoughts may involve the firing of millions or billions of neurons, you can understand that it will never become practical to try to explain a thought in terms of the firing of a particular combination of neurons. And so, we shall never be able to outline all the biological events that are involved in the functions of the "mind." Still, it is assumed that the mind

---

Homunculus (ho-MUN-cue-luss). Latin for "little man." A homunculus within the brain was once thought to govern human behavior.

Phenomenological Having to do with subjective, conscious experience.

---

*Experiments are not intended to harm people, but local injuries are sometimes unavoidable in operations that are intended to save life or cure certain disorders.

is generally based on the substance of the brain. All this adds to the fascination of the work of biological psychologists.

We have seen that sensation and muscle activity involve many parts of the nervous system. But the essential human activities of thought and language involve the hemispheres of the cerebrum.

THE GEOGRAPHY OF THE CEREBRAL CORTEX

Each of the two hemispheres of the cerebral cortex is divided into four parts or lobes, as shown in Figure 2.11. The **frontal lobe** lies in front of the central fissure, and the **parietal lobe** lies behind it. The **temporal lobe** lies below the side, or lateral, fissure, across from the frontal and parietal lobes. The **occipital lobe** lies behind the temporal lobe and behind and below the parietal lobe.

When light strikes the retinas of the eyes, neurons in the occipital lobe fire and we ''see.'' Direct artificial stimulation of the occipital lobe also produces visual sensations. You would ''see'' flashes of light if neurons in the occipital region of the cortex were stimulated with electricity, even if it were pitch black out or your eyes were covered. The hearing or auditory area of the cortex lies in the temporal lobe along the lateral fissure. As we shall see in Chapter 3, sounds cause structures in the ear to vibrate. Messages are relayed to the auditory area of the cortex, and when you hear a noise, neurons in this area are firing.

Just behind the central fissure in the parietal lobe lies an area of **sensory cortex** in which the messages received from skin senses all over the body are projected. These sensations include heat and cold, touch, pain, and movement. Neurons in different parts of this sensory cortex fire, depending on whether you wiggle your finger or raise your leg. And if a brain surgeon were to stimulate the proper area of your sensory cortex with a small probe known as a ''pencil electrode,'' you might testify in court that someone had touched your arm or leg. Figure 2.11 suggests how our faces and heads are overrepresented on this cortex as compared with, say, our trunks and legs. For this reason, our faces and heads are relatively more sensitive to touch.

Many years ago it was discovered that patients with injuries to one hemisphere of the brain would show sensory or motor deficits on the opposite side of the body below the head. Experimentation since that time has made it clear that sensory and motor nerves cross in the brain and elsewhere. The left hemisphere controls functions on, and receives inputs from, the right side of the body. The right hemisphere controls functions on, and receives inputs from, the left side of the body.

The **motor cortex** lies in the frontal lobe, just across the valley of the central fissure from the sensory cortex. Neurons in the motor cortex fire when we move certain parts of our body. If a surgeon were to stimulate a certain area of the right hemisphere of the motor cortex with a pencil electrode, you would raise your left leg. Raising the leg would be sensed in the sensory cortex, and you might have a devil of a time trying to figure out whether you had ''intended'' to raise that leg! How do you like this as an example of brain control?

Frontal lobe The lobe of the cerebral cortex that lies to the front of the central fissure.

Parietal lobe (par-RYE-uh-tal). The lobe that lies just behind the central fissure. (From the Latin *paries,* meaning ''wall.'')

Temporal lobe The lobe that lies below the lateral fissure, near the temples of the head.

Occipital lobe (ox-SIP-it-tal). The lobe that lies behind and below the parietal lobe, and behind the temporal lobe. (From the Latin *ob-,* meaning ''in the way'' or ''against,'' and *caput,* meaning ''head.'')

Sensory cortex The section of cortex that lies just behind the central fissure in the parietal lobe. Sensory stimulation is projected in this section of cortex.

Motor cortex The section of cortex that lies in the frontal lobe, just across the central fissure from the sensory cortex. Neural impulses in the motor cortex are linked to muscular responses throughout the body.

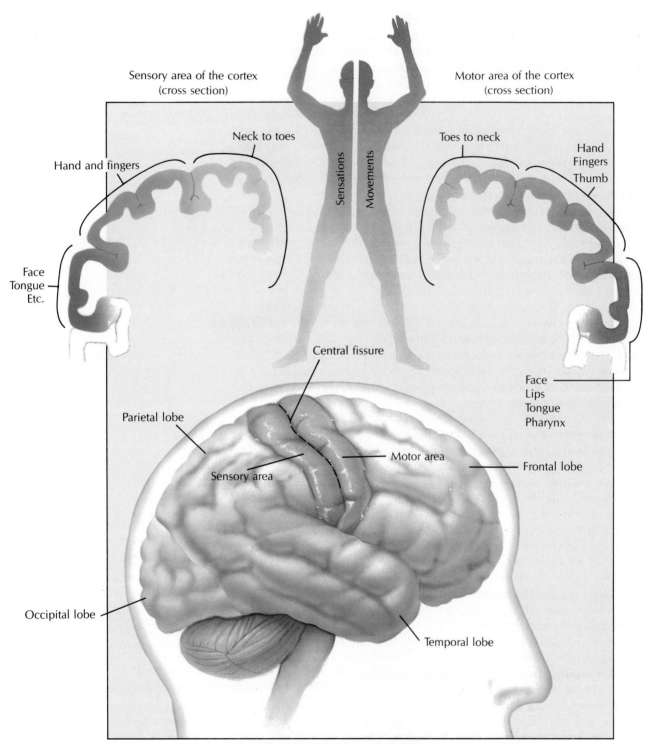

FIGURE 2.11 THE GEOGRAPHY OF THE CEREBRAL CORTEX The cortex is divided into four lobes: frontal, parietal, temporal, and occipital. The visual area of the cortex is located in the occipital lobe. The hearing or auditory cortex lies in the temporal lobe. The sensory and motor areas face each other across the central fissure. What happens when surgeons stimulate areas of the sensory or motor cortex during operations?

THOUGHT, LANGUAGE, AND THE CORTEX

Areas of the cerebral cortex that are not primarily involved in sensation or motor activity are called **association areas.** Their functions appear largely to involve learning, thought, memory, and language.

Association areas, for example, involve memory functions required for simple problem solving. Monkeys with **lesions** in certain association areas have difficulty remembering which of a pair of cups holds food when the cups have been screened off from them for a few seconds (Bauer & Fuster, 1976; French & Harlow, 1962). Stimulation of many association areas with pencil electrodes during surgery leads people to recall memories vividly, along with the emotions linked to them (Penfield, 1969).

Some association areas seem involved in integrating sensory information. Certain neurons in the visual area of the occipital lobe fire in response to visual presentation of vertical lines. Others fire in response to horizontal lines. Although single cells may respond only to part of the visual field, association areas "put it all together" so that you see a box, or an automobile, or a road map, and not a confusing array of verticals and horizontals.

Language Functions   The left and right hemispheres of the brain tend to duplicate each other's functions to some degree, but they are not entirely equal. For the nine of ten people who are right-handed, the left hemisphere contains language functions and dominates. For about half the people who are left-handed, the right hemisphere is dominant. The left hemisphere thus contains language functions for about 95 percent of us.

Dennis and Victoria Molfese (1979) have found that even at birth the sounds of speech elicit greater electrical activity in the left hemisphere than the right, as indicated by the activity of brain waves. Children are more likely to report hearing the sounds of speech with the right ear at the age of three, and the right ear becomes progressively more dominant through age seven (Geffen, 1976). This pattern does not hold for nonspeech-related sounds. Music tends to elicit greater electrical activity in the right hemispheres of the brains of infants (Molfese et al., 1975)—a finding that has contributed to some fascinating notions about the functioning of the hemispheres of the brain, as we shall see below.

Within the dominant (usually left) hemisphere of the cortex, the two areas most involved in speech are Broca's area and Wernicke's area (see Figure 2.12). Damage to either area is likely to cause an **aphasia,** that is, a disruption of the ability to understand or produce language.

Broca's area is located in the frontal lobe, near the section of the motor cortex that controls the muscles of the tongue and throat, and of other areas of the face that are used when speaking. When Broca's area is damaged, people speak slowly and laboriously, with simple sentences—a pattern termed **Broca's aphasia.** In more severe cases, their comprehension and use of proper syntax may be seriously impaired (Schwartz et al., 1980).

Wernicke's area lies in the temporal lobe near the auditory cortex. This area appears to be involved in the integration of auditory and visual information. Broca's area and Wernicke's area are connected by nerve fibers. People with damage to Wernicke's area may show **Wernicke's aphasia,**

Association areas Areas of the cortex involved in learning, thought, memory, and language.

Lesion An injury that results in impaired behavior or loss of a function.

Aphasia Impaired ability to comprehend or express oneself through speech. (From the Greek a-, meaning "not," and *phasis,* meaning "utterance.")

Broca's aphasia Slow, laborious speech; difficulty in articulating words and forming grammatical sentences.

Wernicke's aphasia Difficulty comprehending the meaning of the spoken language; the production of language that is grammatically correct but confused or meaningless in content.

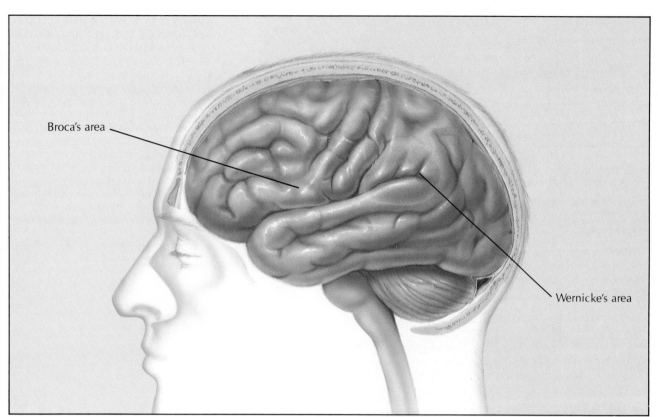

FIGURE 2.12 BROCA'S AND WERNICKE'S AREAS OF THE CEREBRAL CORTEX
The two areas of the dominant cortex most involved in speech are Broca's area and Wernicke's area. Damage to either area can produce a characteristic aphasia—that is, a predictable disruption of the ability to understand or produce language.

in which they usually speak freely and with proper syntax; however, their abilities to comprehend other people's speech and to think of the proper words to express their own thoughts are impaired (Gardner, 1978). And so Wernicke's area seems essential to understanding the relationships between words and their meanings.

Are Some People "Left-Brained" or "Right-Brained"? In recent years it has become popular to speak of people as being either "left-brained" or "right-brained." The notion is that the hemispheres of the brain are involved in very different kinds of intellectual and emotional functions and responses, along the lines suggested in Figure 2.13. According to this view, people whose "left brains" are dominant would be basically logical and intellectual, while people whose "right brains" are dominant would be intuitive, creative, and emotional. Those of us fortunate enough to have our "brains" in balance would presumably have the best of it—the capacity for logic combined with emotional richness.

Like so many other popular ideas, the "left-brain–right-brain" notion is at best exaggerated. Research does suggest that the dominant (usually the

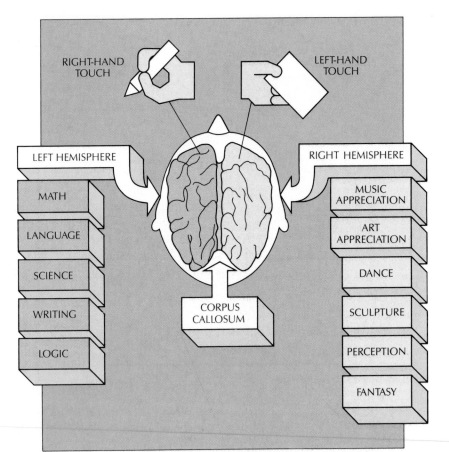

FIGURE 2.13 SOME OF THE SPECIALIZATIONS OF THE LEFT AND RIGHT HEMISPHERES OF THE CEREBRAL CORTEX This diagram exaggerates the "left-brain–right-brain" notion. It seems to be true that the dominant (usually left) hemisphere is somewhat more involved in intellectual undertakings that require logic and problem solving, while the nondominant (usually right) hemisphere is relatively more concerned with decoding visual information, esthetic and emotional responses, and imagination. However, each hemisphere has some involvement with logic and with creativity and intuition.

left) hemisphere is somewhat more involved in intellectual undertakings that require logic and problem solving, understanding syntax, associating written words with their sounds, and the general comprehension and production of speech (Levy, 1985). The nondominant (usually right) hemisphere is relatively more concerned with decoding visual information, esthetic and emotional responses, imagination, and understanding metaphors. However, it would be erroneous to think that the hemispheres of the brain act independently, or that some people are "left-brained" while others are "right-brained."

Biological psychologist Jerre Levy (1985) summarizes left-brain and right-brain similarities and differences as follows:

1. The hemispheres are similar enough so that each can function quite well independently, but not as well as they function in normal combined usage.
2. The left hemisphere does seem to play a special role in understanding and producing language, while the right hemisphere does seem to play a special role in emotional response.
3. Both hemispheres are involved in logic.

Split-brain operation An operation in which the corpus callosum is severed, usually in an effort to control epileptic seizures.

Tactile Of the sense of touch. (From the Latin *tangere,* meaning "to touch.")

4. Creativity and intuition are not confined to the right hemisphere.
5. Both hemispheres are educated at the same time, even when instruction is intended to "appeal" to the right hemisphere (as in music) or the left (in a logic class).

DIVIDED-BRAIN EXPERIMENTS: WHEN TWO HEMISPHERES STOP TALKING TO EACH OTHER

A number of patients suffering from severe cases of epilepsy have undergone **split-brain operations** to try to confine the disorder to one hemisphere of the cerebral cortex, rather than allow one hemisphere to agitate the other through transmitting a "violent storm of neural impulses" (Carlson, 1980). The surgeon severs the corpus callosum, the thick band of nervous fibers that, in the main, connect the hemispheres. These operations do seem to help epilepsy patients. People who have undergone them wind up with two brains that function somewhat independently, yet under most circumstances their behavior remains perfectly normal. But some of the effects of two hemispheres that have stopped talking to one another can be rather intriguing.

Gazzaniga (1972, 1983, 1985) has shown that split-brain patients whose eyes are closed may be able to verbally describe an object like a key that is held in one hand, but cannot do so when the object is held in the other. As shown in Figure 2.14, if a split-brain patient handles a key with his left hand behind a screen, **tactile** impressions of the key are projected into the right hemisphere, which has little or no language ability. Thus he will not be able to describe the key. If it were held in his right hand, he would have no trouble describing it, because sensory impressions would be projected into the left hemisphere of the cortex, which contains language functions. To further confound matters, if the word *ring* is projected into the dominant (left) hemisphere while the patient is asked what he is handling, he will say "ring," not "key."

However, this discrepancy between what is felt and what is said occurs only in split-brain patients. As noted earlier, most of the time the hemispheres work together, even when we are playing the piano or are involved in scientific thought.

In case you have ever wondered whether other people could make us play the piano or engage in scientific thinking by "pressing the right buttons" in us, let us consider some of the effects of electrical stimulation of the brain.

A PSYCHOLOGICAL CONTROVERSY: CAN BEHAVIOR BE CONTROLLED BY ELECTRICAL STIMULATION OF THE BRAIN?

Some years ago, José Delgado astounded the scientific world by stepping into a bullring armed only with a radio transmitter, a cape, and, perhaps, crossed fingers (Figure 2.15). As he described his experiment in *Physical Control of the Mind* (1969), Delgado implanted a radio-controlled electrode in the limbic system of a "brave bull"—a variety bred to respond with a raging charge when it sees any human being. But when Delgado pressed

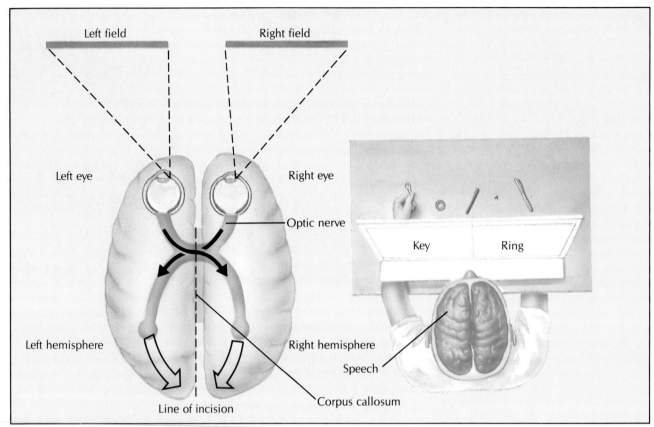

FIGURE 2.14 A DIVIDED-BRAIN EXPERIMENT The drawing on the left shows how visual sensations in the left visual field cross over and are projected in the occipital cortex of the right hemisphere. Visual sensations from the right visual field are projected in the occipital cortex in the left hemisphere. In the divided-brain experiment diagrammed on the right, a subject with a severed corpus callosum handles a key with his left hand and perceives the written word *key* with his left eye. The word "key" is projected in the right hemisphere. But speech is usually a function of the left (dominant) hemisphere. The written word "ring," perceived by the right eye, is projected in the left hemisphere. So, when asked what he is handling, the divided-brain subject reports "ring," not "key."

a button on the transmitter, sending a signal to a battery-powered receiver attached to the bull's horns, an electrical impulse went into the bull's brain and the animal ceased his charge. After several repetitions, the bull no longer attempted to charge Delgado.

During the 1950s, James Olds and Peter Milner (Olds, 1969) accidentally discovered (how many important discoveries are made by accident!) that electrical stimulation of an area of the hypothalamus of a rat would increase the frequency of whatever the rat was doing at the time (Figure 2.16). Rats would also rapidly learn to do things, such as pressing a lever (Figure 2.16), that would result in more stimulation. Rats, in fact, will stimulate themselves in this area repeatedly, up to 100 times a minute and over 1,900 times an hour. For this reason, Olds and Milner labeled this area of the hypothalamus the rat's "pleasure center."

FIGURE 2.15 AN EXPERIMENT IN ELECTRICAL STIMULATION OF THE BRAIN
Brave bulls are dangerous animals that will attack an intruder in the arena. Even in full charge, however, a bull can be stopped abruptly by radio-triggered electrical stimulation of the brain. After several stimulations, there is a lasting inhibition of aggressive behavior.

An experiment with a monkey produced even more astonishing results. Electrical stimulation (ESB) of one part of her brain caused her to (1) stop whatever she was doing; (2) alter expression; (3) turn her head; (4) stand on two feet and circle; (5) climb up and down a pole; (6) growl; and then (7) attack another monkey (Delgado, 1969).

Since these early days, ESB has been used with people to address a number of problems. For example, Robert Heath of Tulane University claims that ESB has helped some severely disturbed schizophrenia patients (Valenstein, 1978). Cancer or trauma patients suffering unrelenting pain have used ESB to block pain messages in the spinal cord before they reach the brain (Restak, 1975). It has even been suggested that ESB be used to block criminal behavior. Electrodes implanted in habitual criminals would be

FIGURE 2.16 THE "PLEASURE CENTER" OF THE BRAIN A rat with an electrode implanted in a section of the hyothalamus that has been termed the "pleasure center" of the brain learns to press a lever in order to receive electrical stimulation.

monitored by a distant computer. When the computer interpreted data like muscle tension and heavy breathing to mean that a crime was being considered, it could use ESB to cause the criminals to forget what they were about to do!

But psychologist Elliot Valenstein (1978) is not quite so impressed by the potential of ESB. He notes, for example, that the bull in the Delgado demonstration did not actually have its aggressive tendencies eliminated by ESB. Instead, the electrical impulses caused the bull to circle to the right. The bull might have become confused, not pacified.

Also, ESB-provoked behavior does not perfectly mimic natural behavior. Behavior brought about by ESB is stereotyped and compulsive. For example, an animal whose "hunger" has been prodded by ESB may eat one type of food only. And ESB in the same site may produce different effects on different occasions. On one occasion a rat may eat when receiving ESB. On another, it may drink. ESB may not be as predictable as had been thought.

The sites for producing pleasant or unpleasant sensations in people may vary from person to person and from day to day. As Valenstein notes, "The impression that brain stimulation in humans can repeatedly evoke the same emotional state, the same memory, or the same behavior is simply a myth. The brain is not organized into neat compartments that correspond to the . . . labels we assign to behavior" (1978, p. 31). I find that thought more than a little comforting.

In our discussion of the nervous system, we have described naturally occurring chemical substances that facilitate or inhibit the transmission of neural messages—neurotransmitters. Let us now turn our attention to other naturally occurring chemical substances that influence behavior—hormones. We shall see that some hormones actually function as neurotransmitters.

THE ENDOCRINE SYSTEM

Here are some things you may have heard about hormones and behavior. Are they truth or fiction?

Some obese people actually eat very little, and their excess weight is caused by "glands."

A boy whose growth was "stunted" began to catch up with his agemates after receiving injections of "growth hormone."

A woman who becomes anxious and depressed just before menstruating is suffering from "raging hormones."

Women who "pump iron" frequently use hormones to achieve the muscle definition that is needed to win body-building contests.

People who receive injections of adrenalin often report that they feel "as if" they are about to experience some emotion, but they're not sure which one.

Let us consider each of these items. The obese may often attribute their weight problems to glands, but most of the time they simply eat too

Pituitary gland The body's "master gland," which secretes growth hormone, prolactin, antidiuretic hormone, and others.

Adrenal cortex One of the two adrenal glands located above the kidneys. The adrenal cortex produces steroids. (From the Latin *ad-*, meaning "at" or "near," and *renes*, meaning "kidneys.")

Adrenal medulla One of the adrenal glands. The adrenal medulla produces adrenalin.

Duct A passageway or channel. (From the Latin *ducere*, meaning "to lead.")

Endocrine system Ductless glands that secrete hormones and release them directly into the bloodstream.

Hormone A chemical substance secreted by an endocrine gland. Hormones promote development of bodily structures and regulate a variety of bodily functions.

Growth hormone A pituitary hormone that regulates growth.

Prolactin (pro-LACK-tin). A pituitary hormone that regulates production of milk and, in lower animals, maternal behavior.

much. Growth hormone, a secretion of the **pituitary gland,** can promote growth. Women may become somewhat more anxious or depressed at the time of menstruation, but the effects of hormones have been exaggerated. Later in this section we shall see that women's response to menstruation reflects their attitudes as well as biological changes. It is an "open secret" that many top women body-builders use steroids, hormones that are produced by the **adrenal cortex,** and human growth hormone, in order to achieve the muscle mass and definition sought by judges in competition (Leerhsen & Abramson, 1985). Steroids and growth hormone promote resistance to stress and muscle growth in both men and women. Finally, adrenalin, a hormone produced by the **adrenal medulla,** does generally arouse people and thereby heighten general emotional responsiveness. In Chapter 7 you will see that the specific emotion to which this arousal is attributed may depend on the person's situation.

DUCTLESS GLANDS

The body contains two types of glands: glands with **ducts** and glands without ducts. A duct is a passageway that carries substances to specific locations. Saliva, sweat, and tears (the name of a new singing group?) all reach their destinations by ducts. Psychologists are more likely to show interest in the substances secreted by ductless glands because of their behavioral effects (see the summary in Table 2.1). The ductless glands constitute the **endocrine system** of the body, and they secrete substances called **hormones** (from the Greek *horman*, meaning "to stimulate" or "to excite") (see Figure 2.17).

Let us now examine the functions of several glands of the endocrine system.

THE PITUITARY GLAND

The pituitary gland is located just below the hypothalamus. It is so central to the body's functioning that it is referred to as the "master gland." But today we know that the hypothalamus controls much of the activity of the pituitary gland. Even the master gland serves a master. The anterior (front) and posterior (back) lobes of the pituitary gland produce or secrete many hormones, some of which are listed in Table 2.1.

Growth hormone regulates the growth of muscles, bones, and glands. As noted in the nearby box, "André the Giant," an excess of growth hormone can lead to *acromegaly,* a condition in which people may grow two to three feet taller than they would normally. Children whose growth patterns seem abnormally slow often catch up to their agemates when growth hormone is administered by a physician. A recently discovered substance, growth-hormone releasing factor (or hGRF), is produced by the hypothalamus and causes the pituitary to produce growth hormone (Taylor, 1985).

Prolactin largely regulates maternal behavior in lower mammals, such as rats, and stimulates production of milk in women. As you will see in Chapter 7, transfusion of blood from a new mother rat to another female rat will cause the recipient to display typical mothering behaviors.

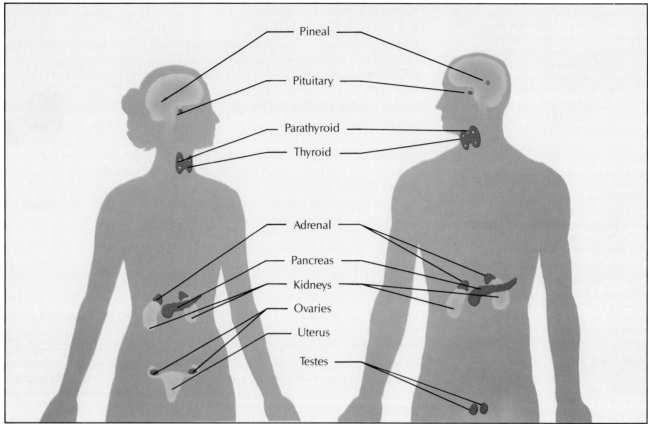

FIGURE 2.17 LOCATION OF MAJOR GLANDS OF THE ENDOCRINE SYSTEM

When the fluid level of the body is low, the hypothalamus stimulates the pituitary gland to secrete **antidiuretic hormone,** which is abbreviated *ADH* and also referred to as *vasopressin.* ADH increases the reabsorption of urine in order to conserve fluid. ADH also has effects on memory, as we shall see in Chapter 5.

Oxytocin stimulates labor in pregnant women. Obstetricians may induce labor or increase the strength of uterine contractions during labor by injecting pregnant women with oxytocin.

THE PANCREAS

The **pancreas** is influential in controlling the level of sugar in the blood and the urine through the hormones **insulin** and **glucagon.** One form of diabetes (diabetes mellitus) is characterized by excess sugar in the blood (**hyperglycemia**) and in the urine, a condition that can lead to coma and death. Diabetes stems from inadequate secretion or utilization of insulin. People who do not secrete enough insulin of their own may need to inject this hormone daily in order to control diabetes.

Antidiuretic hormone (ant-eye-dye-you-RET-ick). A pituitary hormone that inhibits the production of urine. Abbreviated *ADH.*

Oxytocin (ox-see-TOE-sin). A pituitary hormone that stimulates labor. (From the Greek *oxys,* meaning "quick," and *tokos,* meaning "birth.")

Pancreas (PAN-kree-us). A gland behind the stomach whose secretions influence the level of sugar in the blood.

Insulin A pancreatic hormone that stimulates the metabolism of sugar.

Glucagon A pancreatic hormone that increases the levels of sugar and fat in the blood.

Hyperglycemia (high-purr-gly-SEEM-me-uh). A disorder caused by excess sugar in the blood. (From the Greek *hyper-,* meaning "above," and *glykys,* meaning "sweet.")

TABLE 2.1   An Overview of Some Major Glands of the Endocrine System

Gland	Hormone	Major Effects
Pituitary		
ANTERIOR LOBE	Growth hormone	Causes growth of muscles, bones, and glands
	Adrenocorticotrophic hormone (ACTH)	Regulates adrenal cortex
	Thyrotrophin	Causes thyroid gland to secrete thyroxin
	Follicle-stimulating hormone	Causes formation of sperm and egg cells
	Luteinizing hormone	Causes ovulation, maturation of sperm and egg cells
	Prolactin	Stimulates production of milk
POSTERIOR LOBE	Antidiuretic hormone (ADH)	Inhibits production of urine
	Oxytocin	Stimulates uterine contractions during delivery and release of milk during nursing
Pancreas	Insulin	Enables body to metabolize sugar, regulates storage of fats
	Glucagon	Increases levels of sugar and fats in blood
	Somatostatin	Regulates secretion of insulin and glucagon
Thyroid	Thyroxin	Increases metabolic rate
Parathyroid	Parathormone	Increases blood calcium level
Pineal	Melatonin	Regulates reproductive behavior and growth of secondary sex characteristics
Adrenal		
CORTEX	Steroids	Increase resistance to stress, regulate carbohydrate metabolism
MEDULLA	Adrenalin (Epinephrine)	Increases metabolic activity (heart and respiration rates, blood sugar level, etc.)
	Noradrenalin (Norepinephrine)	Raises blood pressure, acts as neurotransmitter
Testes	Testosterone	Promotes growth of male sex characteristics
Ovaries	Estrogen	Regulates menstrual cycle
	Progesterone	Promotes growth of female reproductive tissues, maintains pregnancy
Uterus	(Several)	Maintain pregnancy

The condition **hypoglycemia** is characterized by too little sugar in the blood. Symptoms of hypoglycemia include shakiness, dizziness, and lack of energy, a **syndrome** that is easily confused with anxiety. Many people have sought help for anxiety and learned through a series of blood tests that they are actually suffering from hypoglycemia. This disorder is generally controlled through dietary restrictions.

Hypoglycemia A disorder caused by too little sugar in the blood. (From the Greek *hypo-*, meaning "under.")

Syndrome (SIN-drome). A cluster of symptoms characteristic of a disorder.

PSYCHOLOGY AND HEALTH

ANDRÉ THE GIANT

André Rousimoff, known to wrestling fans as "André the Giant," is one living example of the effects of an excess of growth hormone. Over seven feet tall, and weighing in at nearly 500 pounds, André has made a fortune on the pro wrestling circuit.

André's condition is called Acromegaly, and it is known by symptoms such as a protruding forehead, lantern jaw, and broad nose. "Giants" like André also have enlarged internal organs and higher-than-normal blood sugar levels, which frequently lead to death before the victim's 45th birthday.

As a child, André naturally produced too much growth hormone. But today, as pointed out by CBS News correspondent Morley Safer in 1985, many professional athletes are injecting growth hormone as adults. The payoff? As reported by a former pro football player who also competed as a weightlifter:

> I trained for six or seven months [doing] heavy lifting, really peaked out in my training, [took a] heavy dose of steroids, peaked my dose of steroids out, and I got on growth hormones two weeks before the contest. My lifts went up a hundred pounds in two weeks. . . . You don't just get gains like that. You train for months just to get five or ten pounds increase when you're at the high level. Yet, in two weeks, my lifts went up a hundred pounds. (CBS News, 1985)

Although adults who use human growth hormone may not show the symptoms of acromegaly, as André the Giant does, there are other side effects. Two of

André the Giant meets his fans.

them were apparently encountered by nine-time world-champion power lifter Larry Pacifico, who admits that several of his titles followed the use of steroids and human growth hormone. Pacifico suffers from blocked arteries and has had two heart attacks.

With the possibility of such an outcome, why do athletes resort to growth hormone? According to Dr. Robert Kerr of San Gabriel, California, who openly prescribes steroids and human growth hormone for athletes, "When you consider that in some sports practically everyone is taking these products, then you're at a distinct disadvantage if you do not." As pointed out by Safer, however, Kerr is also being sued for malpractice by three athletes who claim that they have suffered irreversible damage from growth hormone.

THE THYROID GLAND

Thyroxin is produced by the thyroid gland. Thyroxin affects the body's **metabolism,** or rate of using oxygen and producing energy. Some people who are overweight are suffering from a condition known as **hypothyroidism,** which results from abnormally low secretions of thyroxin. Deficiency of thyroxin can lead to **cretinism** in children, a disorder characterized by stunted growth and mental retardation. Adults who secrete too little thyroxin may feel tired and sluggish, and may put on weight. People who produce excesses of thyroxin may develop **hyperthyroidism,** a disorder characterized by excitability, insomnia, and weight loss.

THE ADRENAL GLANDS

The adrenal glands, located above the kidneys, have an outer layer, or cortex, and an inner core, or medulla. The adrenal cortex is regulated by the pituitary hormone ACTH. The cortex secretes as many as 20 different

Thyroxin (thigh-ROCKS-sin). The thyroid hormone that increases metabolic rate. (From the Latin *thyroides,* meaning "shield-shaped.")

Metabolism (met-TAB-bowl-ism). In organisms, a continuous process that converts food into energy. (From the Greek *metabole,* meaning "change.")

Hypothyroidism A condition caused by a deficiency of thyroxin and characterized by sluggish behavior and a low metabolic rate.

Cretinism A condition caused by thyroid deficiency in childhood and characterized by mental retardation and stunted growth.

Hyperthyroidism A condition caused by excess thyroxin and characterized by excitability, weight loss, and insomnia.

PSYCHOLOGY TODAY

IN SPORTS, "LIONS VS. TIGERS"

When Don Schollander swam the 400-meter freestyle in 4 minutes, 12.2 seconds at the 1964 Olympics, he set a world record and took home a gold medal. Had he clocked the same time against the women racing at the 1984 Los Angeles Games, he would have finished way back in the pack. In the pool and on the track, women have closed to within 10 percent or less of the best male times, [but] physiologists, coaches, and trainers generally agree that while women will continue to improve their performances, they will never fully overcome inherent differences in size and strength. In sports where power is a key ingredient of success, the best women will remain a stroke behind or a stride slower than the best man.

Muscle vs. Fat A man's biggest advantage is his muscle mass. Puberty stokes male bodies with the hormone testosterone, which adds bulk to muscles. A girl's puberty brings her an increase in fat. When growth ends, an average man is 40 percent muscle and 15 percent fat; a woman 23 percent muscle, 25 percent fat. Training reduces fat, but no amount of working out will give a woman the physique of a man. Male and female athletes sometimes try to build bigger muscles by use of anabolic steroids—artificial male hormones that stimulate muscle growth—even though they may be dangerous and all major sports have outlawed them.

Bulging muscles alone can't make a woman as strong as a man. Men have larger hearts and lungs and more hemoglobin in their blood, which enables them to pump oxygen to their muscles more efficiently than women can. A man's wider shoulders and longer arms also increase leverage, and his longer legs move him farther with each step. Although highly conditioned women can achieve pound-for-pound parity with men in leg strength, their upper-body power is usually only one-half to two-thirds that of an equally well-conditioned male athlete.

A few sports make a virtue of anatomy for women. Extra body fat gives a woman English Channel swimmer better buoyancy and more insulation from the cold, and narrow shoulders reduce her resistance in the water. As a result, women have beaten the fastest male's round

BODYBUILDERS Many women in recent years have taken to bodybuilding, a sport previously reserved for men. Although highly conditioned women can achieve pound-for-pound parity with men in leg strength, their upper-body power is usually only one-half to two-thirds that of an equally well-conditioned male athlete.

trip by a full three hours. In long-distance running contests, women may also be on an equal footing with men. Under the body-draining demands of extended exertion, a woman's fat may provide her with deeper energy reserves.

Tough Women athletes have dispelled the myths about their susceptibility to injury. The uterus and ovaries are surrounded by shock-absorbing fluids—far better protected than a man's exposed reproductive equipment. And the bouncing of the breasts doesn't make them more prone to cancer, or even to sagging. As for psychological toughness, Penn State sports psychologist Dorothy Harris says that "if you give a woman a shot at a $100,000 prize, you discover that she can be every bit as aggressive as a man."

Going one-on-one with a man is not the goal of most women in sports. "It's like pitting lions against tigers," declares Joan Ullyot. "Women's achievements should not be downgraded by comparing them to men's."

hormones known as **steroids.** Steroids increase resistance to stress; promote muscle development; and cause the liver to release stored sugar, making energy available for emergencies. As noted in the nearby box "In Sports, 'Lions vs. Tigers,'" anabolic steroids (synthetic versions of the male sex hormone testosterone) have been used to enhance athletic prowess. Anabolic steroids also have psychological effects. They increase self-esteem,

---

Steroids Hormones produced by the adrenal cortex that increase resistance to stress and regulate carbohydrate metabolism.

the sex drive, and one's energy level (Taylor, 1985). However, they may also cause sleep disturbances and be linked with depression and apathy when usage is discontinued.

Adrenalin, also known as epinephrine, is secreted by the adrenal medulla. It acts on the sympathetic branch of the ANS and on the RAS to arouse the body in preparation for threats and stress. As noted earlier and in Chapter 7, adrenalin is also implicated in general emotional arousal.

Adrenalin A hormone produced by the adrenal medulla that stimulates sympathetic ANS activity. Also called *epinephrine.*

PSYCHOLOGY AND HEALTH

WOMEN AND PMS: DOES PREMENSTRUAL SYNDROME DOOM WOMEN TO MISERY?

For several days prior to and during menstruation, the stereotype has been that "raging hormones" doom women to irritability and poor judgment—two facets of premenstrual syndrome (PMS). This view, as noted by Karen Paige (1973) has cost women many opportunities to assume responsible positions in society:

> Women, the old argument goes, are eternally subject to the whims and wherefores of their biological clocks. Their raging hormonal cycles make them emotionally unstable and intellectually unreliable. If women have second-class status, we are told, it is because they cannot control the implacable demands of that bouncing estrogen (p. 41).

Do women show behavioral and emotional deficits prior to and during menstruation? The evidence is mixed.

Psychologist Judith Bardwick (Bardwick, 1971; Ivey & Bardwick, 1968) found women's moods to be most positive halfway through their menstrual cycles (during release of an ovum). But a number of women show significant levels of anxiety, depression, and fatigue for two to three days before menstruating (Money, 1980). British investigator Katharina Dalton (1972, 1980) reported that women are more likely to commit suicide or crimes, call in sick at work, and develop physical and emotional problems before or during menstruation.

Dalton (1968) also reported that the grades of English schoolgirls decline during the eight-day period prior to and including menstruation. However, investigators in the United States have found no reliable decline in academic performance at this time (Walsh et al., 1981).

There is evidence showing a link between hormone levels and mood in women. Paige (1971) studied women whose hormone levels were kept rather even by birth-control pills and whose hormone levels varied naturally throughout the cycle. She found that women whose hormone levels fluctuated appeared to show somewhat greater anxiety and hostility prior to and during menstruation. However, they did not commit crimes or wind up on mental wards. Other studies suggest that even among women who report premenstrual syndrome, the symptoms are most often mild, although a small percentage of women may have symptoms that are strong enough to interfere with their functioning (Keye, 1983).

We must note also that women may be responding to negative cultural attitudes toward menstruation as well as to menstrual symptoms themselves (Brooks-Gunn & Ruble, 1980; Sherif, 1980). In some societies, menstruating women have been consigned to special living quarters because of expectations of foul temper (Paige, 1977). The historical view of menstruation as a time of pollution (Fisher, 1980; Paige, 1978) may make women highly sensitive to internal sensations at certain times of the month, as well as concerned about discreet disposal of the menstrual flow. Other research (Paige, 1973) shows that women who do not share highly traditional cultural attitudes—including attitudes about the debilitating nature of menstruation—are less likely to show mood changes throughout the different phases of the menstrual cycle.

However, some hormonal changes at time of menstruation can cause some very real and painful problems. For instance, prostaglandins, which cause uterine contractions, may in some women cause painful cramping. In such cases prostaglandin-inhibiting drugs, like Motrin and Indocin, are showing promise in helping women (Rathus, 1983). Unfortunately, the medical establishment has often treated women's menstrual complaints as hysterical. And so many women have not received what medical help is available (Toufexis, 1981).

In summary, (1) hormone levels seem to exert some influence over mood shifts in women, but most often these shifts are minor; (2) much of the evidence that women show performance deficits prior to and during menstruation is unreliable; (3) traditional views of (perfectly harmless) menstrual flow as polluting may contribute to any problems women may encounter; but (4) some women experience very real menstrual discomfort, like menstrual cramping, and such problems need to be treated medically.

Testosterone A male sex hormone produced by the testes that promotes growth of male sexual characteristics and sperm.

Primary sex characteristics Physical traits that distinguish the sexes and are directly involved in reproduction.

Secondary sex characteristics Physical traits that differentiate the sexes but are not directly involved in reproduction.

Estrogen A generic term for several female sex hormones that promote growth of female sexual characteristics and regulate the menstrual cycle.

Progesterone (pro-JESS-ter-own). A female sex hormone that promotes growth of the sexual organs and helps maintain pregnancy.

Menstruation The monthly shedding of the lining of the uterus by women who are not pregnant. (From the Latin *menstruus,* meaning "monthly.")

THE TESTES AND THE OVARIES

Did you know that if it were not for the secretion of the male sex hormone **testosterone** about six weeks after conception, we would all develop into females? Testosterone is produced by the testes and, a few weeks following fertilization of an ovum, it stimulates prenatal differentiation of male sex organs. During puberty it promotes the growth of muscle and bone, and the development of **primary** and **secondary sex characteristics.** Primary sex characteristics are directly involved in reproduction, such as the growth of the penis and of the sperm-producing ability of the testes. Secondary sex characteristics, such as the growth of the beard and the deepening of the voice, differentiate the sexes but are not directly involved in reproduction.

Testosterone levels vary slightly with stress, time of the day or month, and other factors, but are maintained at fairly even levels by the hypothalamus, pituitary gland, and testes. Low blood levels of testosterone signal the hypothalamus to produce releasing hormones. Releasing hormones, in turn, signals the pituitary to secrete luteinizing hormone, which then stimulates the testes to secrete testosterone. Conversely, high blood levels of testosterone signal the hypothalamus not to secrete releasing hormones, so that further testosterone is not produced.

The ovaries produce **estrogen** and **progesterone.** Estrogen is a generic name for several female sex hormones that lead to development of reproductive capacity and development of female secondary sexual characteristics at puberty. Progesterone also has multiple functions. It stimulates growth of the female reproductive organs and maintains pregnancy. As is the case with testosterone, estrogen and progesterone levels influence and are also influenced by hormones of the hypothalamus and pituitary gland.

Hormonal Regulation of the Menstrual Cycle   While testosterone levels remain fairly stable, estrogen and progesterone levels vary markedly and regulate the menstrual cycle. Following **menstruation**—the monthly sloughing off of the inner lining of the uterus—estrogen levels increase, leading to the development of an ovum (egg cell) and growth of the inner lining of the uterus. The ovum is released by the ovary when estrogens reach peak blood levels. Then the inner lining of the uterus thickens in response to secretion of progesterone, gaining the capacity to support an embryo if fertilization should occur. If the ovum is not fertilized, estrogen and progesterone levels drop suddenly, triggering menstruation once more.

HEREDITY

Spend a moment or two reflecting on some facts of life:

People cannot breathe underwater (without special equipment).
People cannot fly (again, without some rather special equipment).
Fish cannot learn to speak French or do an Irish jig even if you raise them in enriched environments and send them to finishing school (which is why we look for tuna that tastes good, not for tuna with good taste).
Chimpanzees and gorillas can learn to use sign language.

People cannot breathe underwater or fly (without oxygen tanks, airplanes, or other devices) because of the structures they have inherited. Fish are similarly limited by their **heredity**, or the biological transmission of traits and characteristics from one generation to another. Because of their heredity, fish cannot speak French or do a jig. Although the language ability of apes is a controversial topic (as we shall see in Chapter 6), some psychologists believe that chimpanzees and gorillas are capable of understanding and expressing some verbal concepts through American sign language (Bazar, 1980). But chimps and gorillas have shown no ability to speak, even though they can make sounds and have voice boxes somewhat similar to ours in their throats. They have probably failed to inherit humanlike speech areas of the cerebral cortex.

GENES AND CHROMOSOMES

Genes are the basic building blocks of heredity. Genes are the biochemical materials that regulate the development of traits. Some traits, such as blood type, are transmitted by a single pair of genes. Other traits, referred to as **polygenic,** are determined by combinations of genes.

Chromosomes, the rod-shaped genetic structures found in the nuclei of the body's cells, each consist of a large number of genes. A normal human cell contains forty-six chromosomes, which are organized into twenty-three pairs.

We have thousands upon thousands of genes in every cell in our bodies. Chromosomes consist of large, complex molecules of deoxyribonucleic acid, which has several chemical components. (You can breathe a sigh of relief: behavior geneticists refer to this acid simply as DNA.) Genes occupy various segments along the length of chromosomes. As you can see in Figure 2.18, DNA takes the form of a double spiral, or helix, that is similar in appearance to a twisting ladder. In all living things, from one-celled animals to fish to people, the sides of the "ladder" consist of alternating segments of phosphate (P) and a simple sugar (S). The "rungs" of the ladder are always attached to the sugars and consist of one of two pairs of bases, either *adenine* with *thymine* (A with T), or *cytosine* with *guanine* (C with G). The sequence of the rungs is the genetic code that will cause the unfolding organism to grow arms or wings, skin or scales.

GENETICS AND BEHAVIOR GENETICS

Heredity, or the biological transmission of traits from one generation to another, plays a significant role in the determination of traits we consider human, and nonhuman. The biological structures we inherit at once make our behaviors possible and place limits on them. The field within the science of biology that studies heredity is called **genetics. Behavior genetics** is a specialty that bridges the sciences of psychology and biology. It is concerned with the transmission of structures and traits that give rise to behavior.

Research suggests that heredity is a major factor in the origin of per-

Heredity The tranmission of characteristics from one generation to another through genes. (From the Latin *heres*, meaning "heir.")

Genes The basic building blocks of heredity, which consist of deoxyribonucleic acid.

Polygenic Determined by several genes.

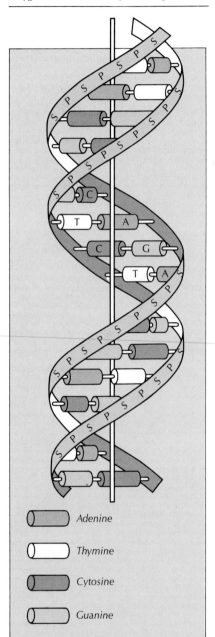

Adenine

Thymine

Cytosine

Guanine

FIGURE 2.18 THE DOUBLE HELIX OF DNA

Chromosomes Rodlike structures consisting of genes which are found in the nuclei of the body's cells.

Genetics The branch of biology that studies heredity. (From the Latin *genesis,* meaning "birth.")

Behavior genetics The study of the genetic transmission of structures and traits that give rise to behavior.

Extraversion A trait in which a person directs his or her interest to persons and things outside the self. See Chapter 9.

Neuroticism A trait in which a person is given to anxiety, foreboding, and avoidance reactions. See Chapters 9 and 11.

Genotype (JEAN-oh-type). The sum total of our traits as inherited from our parents.

Phenotype (FEEN-oh-type). The sum total of our traits at a given point in time, as inherited from our parents and influenced by environmental factors.

Nature In behavior genetics, heredity.

Nurture In behavior genetics, environmental influences on behavior, such as nutrition, culture, socioeconomic status, and learning.

Mitosis (my-TOE-sis). The process of cell division by which the identical genetic code is carried into new cells in the body.

sonality traits such as **extraversion** (Loehlin et al., 1982); **neuroticism** (Scarr et al., 1981); shyness (Kagan, 1984; Plomin, 1982); dominance and aggressiveness (Goldsmith, 1983); and criminal behavior (Mednick, 1985). Personality traits, as we shall see in Chapter 9, are believed to give rise to relatively enduring patterns of behavior. Consider the example of neuroticism. Neuroticism may in part stem from the genetic transmission of a highly active autonomic nervous system, and neuroticism is associated with high levels of emotional responsiveness and anxiety. On the other hand, in Chapter 11 we shall see that antisocial behavior patterns may well reflect the genetic transmission of relatively *unresponsive* autonomic nervous systems. There even appears to be a genetic influence on infants' communicative development, as measured by their production of words, use of gesturing, and vocal imitation within a week of their first birthdays (Hardy-Brown & Plomin, 1985). The development of verbal behavior seems to be influenced by the rate of maturation of certain areas of the brain, including the speech areas. The rate of maturation of these areas of the brain, in turn, appears to be at least in part determined by genes.

The sets of traits that we inherit from our parents are referred to as our **genotypes.** But none of us, as we appear, is the result of heredity, or genotype, alone. We are also influenced by environmental factors such as nutrition, learning, exercise, and, unfortunately, accident and illness, so that our actual characteristics at any point in time are our **phenotypes.** That is, our traits as they are expressed are the product of genetic and environmental influences.

Behavior geneticists are attempting to sort out the relative importance of **nature** (heredity) and **nurture** (environmental influences) in the development of various behavior patterns. Psychologists are especially interested in the roles of nature and nurture in intelligence (Plomin & DeFries, 1980), abnormal behavior patterns like schizophrenia, and social problems like sociopathy and aggression. We shall be pursuing these particular themes throughout this book.

In a general sense it can be argued that all behavior reflects the influences of both nature and nurture. All organisms inherit a range of structures that set the stage for certain behaviors. Yet environmental influences such as nutrition and learning also figure in to whether genetically possible behaviors will be displayed. A potential Shakespeare who is raised in an impoverished neighborhood and never taught to read or write is unlikely to create a *Hamlet.* For this reason it may be most accurate to state that behavior represents an interaction between nature and nurture.

MITOSIS AND MEIOSIS

We all begin life as a single cell that divides again and again. There are two types of cell division: *mitosis* and *meiosis.* **Mitosis** is the cell-division process by which growth occurs and tissues are replaced. Through mitosis, the identical genetic code is carried into each new cell in the body. In order to accomplish this, the chromosomal strands of DNA "unzip" (see Figure 2.19). One side of the "ladder" and one of the two elements of each "rung"

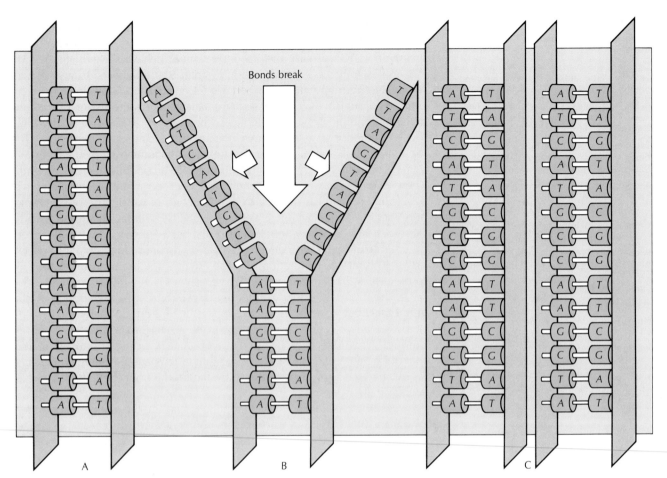

FIGURE 2.19 THE "UNZIPPING" OF DNA Part A shows a segment of a strand of DNA prior to mitosis. During the cell-division process of mitosis, chromosomal strands of DNA "unzip" (Part B). One side of the "ladder" and one element of each "rung" remain in each new cell following division. The double helix is then rebuilt in each new cell (Part C), as each incomplete rung combines with the appropriate base from the chemicals within the cell.

remain in the nucleus of each new cell after division takes place. The double helix is then rebuilt in each cell: each incomplete rung combines with the appropriate base from the chemicals within the cell (that is, G with C, A with T, C with G, and T with A) to form a complete ladder. As a consequence the genetic code is identical in every cell unless **mutations** occur through radiation or other environmental influences.

Sperm and ova are produced through **meiosis,** or reduction division. In meiosis, the forty-six chromosomes within the nucleus first divide into twenty-three pairs. When the cell divides, one member of each pair goes to each newly formed cell. As a consequence, each new cell contains only twenty-three chromosomes, not forty-six. And so, a cell that results from meiosis has half the genetic material of one that results from mitosis.

Through reduction division, or meiosis, we receive twenty-three chromosomes from our fathers and twenty-three chromosomes from our moth-

Mutation Sudden variations in the genetic code that usually occur as a result of environmental influences.

Meiosis (my-OH-sis). A process of reduction division in which sperm and ova are formed that each contain 23 chromosomes instead of 46.

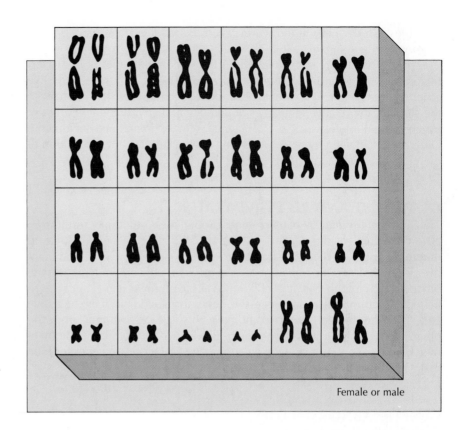

Female or male

FIGURE 2.20 **THE 23 PAIRS OF HU-MAN CHROMOSOMES** Sex is determined by the twenty-third pair of chromosomes. Females have two X sex chromosomes, while males have an X and a Y sex chromosome.

Autosomes Chromosomes that look alike and possess information concerning the same sets of traits. One autosome is received from the father and the corresponding autosome is received from the mother.

Sex chromosomes The twenty-third pair of chromosomes which determine sex and, in the case of males, do not look alike.

Zygote (ZY-goat). A fertilized egg cell. (From the Greek *zygon,* meaning "yoke"— two things harnessed together.)

Monozygotic twins Identical twins. Twins who develop from a single zygote, thus carrying the same genetic instructions. (From the Greek *monos,* meaning "single.")

ers. When a sperm cell fertilizes an ovum, they join into twenty-three pairs of chromosomes (Figure 2.20). Twenty-two of the pairs contain **autosomes,** which are chromosomes that look alike and possess information concerning the same set of traits. The twenty-third pair consists of **sex chromosomes** which determine our sex and, in the case of males, look different. We all receive an X sex chromosome (so called because of the "X" shape) from our mothers. If we also receive an X sex chromosome from our fathers, we develop into females. If we receive a Y sex chromosome (named after the "Y" shape) from our fathers, we develop into males.

MONOZYGOTIC AND DIZYGOTIC TWINS
The fertilized ovum that carries genetic messages from both parents is called a **zygote.** Now and then a zygote divides into two cells that separate, so that each develops into an individual with the same genetic makeup. These persons are known as identical or **monozygotic twins.** The possible combinations of traits that can result from the coming together of so many thousands of genes is, for all practical purposes, unlimited. The chances that any two people will show completely identical traits, with the exception of monozygotic twins (or triplets, etc.), are essentially nil. With the exception of identical twins or triplets, the odds are clearly against our having

"doubles" somewhere in the world, even though there are many billions of people.

If the woman releases two ova in the same month and both are fertilized, they develop into fraternal or **dizygotic twins,** and are related like other brothers and sisters. Identical or monozygotic twins are important in the study of the relative influences of heredity and environment in areas of psychological interest such as intelligence, schizophrenia, and sociopathy. Differences between monozygotic twins are the result of the interaction of the genotype and the environment.

DOMINANT AND RECESSIVE TRAITS

Traits are determined by pairs of genes. Sometimes a trait may result from an "averaging" of the genetic instructions. But many genes give rise to **dominant traits** or **recessive traits.** Brown hair, for instance, is dominant over blond hair. So if one parent carries genes for only brown hair, and the other for only blond hair, the children will have brown hair.* But brown-haired parents may also carry recessive genes for blond hair. If the recessive gene from one parent should combine with the recessive gene from the other, the recessive trait will be shown. Brown eyes are similarly dominant over blue eyes, and brown-eyed persons may carry recessive genes for blue eyes, as shown in Figure 2.21.

GENETIC ABNORMALITIES

Occasionally children do not have the normal complement of 46 chromosomes, and behavioral as well as physical abnormalities result.

In **Down syndrome** (formerly referred to as Down's syndrome), the twenty-first pair of chromosomes has an extra, or third, chromosome. Down syndrome is thought to be caused by faulty division of the twenty-first pair of chromosomes during meiosis, an abnormality that becomes increasingly likely among older parents. While this abnormality is usually attributed to the mother, it should be noted that fathers can also be responsible for Down syndrome. Persons with Down syndrome have eyes with an upward slant and thickened eyelids—hence the unfortunate term *mongolism*—a protruding tongue, and a broad nose. Such individuals are frequently mentally retarded, and they may suffer from respiratory problems and malformations of the heart.

An extra Y sex chromosome is associated with heightening of male secondary sexual characteristics in men labeled "supermales." XYY males are somewhat taller than average and develop heavier beards. At one point it was speculated that XYY syndrome was linked to aggressive criminal behavior, but in Chapter 11 you will see that evidence for this assertion is sketchy at best.

Other sex chromosomal abnormalities include Klinefelter's syndrome, Turner's syndrome, and the XXX "superfemale" syndrome. About one male in 500 has **Klinefelter's syndrome,** which is caused by an extra X sex chro-

*An exception would occur if the children also inherit a gene for albinism, in which case their hair and eyes would be colorless.

Dizygotic twins Fraternal twins. Twins who develop from separate zygotes. (From the Greek *di-*, meaning "two.")

Dominant trait In genetics, a trait that is expressed.

Recessive trait In genetics, a trait that is not expressed when the gene or genes involved have been paired with dominant genes. But recessive traits are transmitted to future generations and expressed if paired with other recessive genes.

Down syndrome A chromosomal abnormality characterized by slanted eyelids and mental retardation, and caused by an extra chromosome in the twenty-first pair.

Klinefelter's syndrome A chromosomal disorder found among males that is caused by an extra X sex chromosome and characterized by infertility and mild mental retardation.

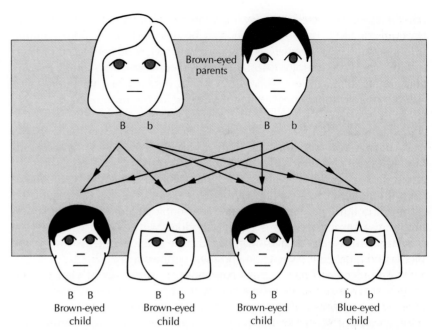

FIGURE 2.21 Two brown-eyed parents each carry a recessive gene for blue eyes. Their children have an equal opportunity of receiving genes for brown eyes and blue eyes. In such cases, 25 percent of the children show the recessive trait—blue eyes. The other 75 percent show the dominant trait, or brown eyes. But two of three who show brown eyes carry the recessive trait for transmittal to future generations. If a blue-eyed person has a child with someone who has brown eyes but carries a recessive gene for blue eyes, what is the probability that the child will have blue eyes?

mosome (XXY). XXY males produce less testosterone than normal males and are infertile. XXY males usually have enlarged breasts and poor muscular development. In terms of cognitive functioning and personality, they are frequently mildly mentally retarded, more passive, and less ambitious than most males.

Girls with a single X sex chromosome are said to have **Turner's syndrome.** Their external genitals are normal, because we all develop as females in the absence of a Y sex chromosome. However, their ovaries are poorly developed, and they produce reduced amounts of estrogen. Females with Turner's syndrome are shorter than average and infertile.

XXX "superfemales" reach normal height and look like XX women. However, they may be mildly mentally retarded and show particularly poor verbal ability (Rovet & Netley, 1983).

Other disorders have been attributed to genes. One of them, **phenylketonuria** (PKU), is transmitted by a recessive gene. Therefore, if both parents are carriers, PKU will be transmitted to about one child in four (as in Figure 2.21). One child in four will not carry the recessive gene, and the other two, as their parents, will be carriers.

Children with PKU cannot metabolize the amino acid *phenylalanine*, which builds up in their bodies as phenylpyruvic acid and leads to mental retardation. Amino acids are the structural units that compose proteins, and

Turner's syndrome A chromosomal disorder found among females that is caused by having a single X sex chromosome and characterized by infertility.

Phenylketonuria (fee-nill-key-tone-NEW-ree-uh). A genetic abnormality in which phenylpyruvic acid builds up and leads to mental retardation.

phenylalanine is present in many important foods, including milk. We have no cure for PKU, but the disorder can be detected in newborn children through blood or urine analysis. Children with PKU who are placed on diets low in phenylalanine, the substance that is converted into phenylpyruvic acid, right after birth show little or no mental deficiency. The children also receive protein supplements that compensate for the nutritional loss.

Amniocentesis and CVS   Today pregnant women who have reason to suspect genetic abnormalities in their children are likely to have an **amniocentesis** or **chorionic villus sampling** (CVS). Amniocentesis is performed about fifteen weeks following conception (Figure 2.22). Fluid is withdrawn from the amniotic sac containing the fetus. Fetal cells that have sloughed off into the fluid are then examined microscopically for chromosomal abnormalities. Amniocentesis is commonly done with women who become pregnant past the age of thirty-five, because the chances of Down syndrome increase dramatically as women and their partners age.

Amniocentesis also permits parents to learn the sex of their unborn child through examination of the twenty-third pair of chromosomes. However, amniocentesis carries some risks, and it would be unwise to have the procedure done solely for this purpose. If you were having an amniocentesis, would you want to know the sex of your unborn child, or would you prefer to wait?

CVS is carried out during the seventh or eighth week of pregnancy by inserting a small tube through the vagina and into the uterus, and snipping off pieces of material from the outer membrane that contains the amniotic sac (with the fetus inside). CVS is carried out in only a small number of medical centers today, and it is somewhat more risky to the fetus than amniocentesis (Waldholz, 1985). Still, it allows detection of some disorders, including Tay-Sachs disease, in half the time.

In the future it may be that we shall be able to modify problem genes while babies are still developing within the uterus. For the time being, however, families whose unborn children face serious genetic disorders can only choose whether or not to have an abortion, which often raises painful moral and personal dilemmas. Families who do choose abortion usually find it relatively less painful to do so earlier in their pregnancies.

Amniocentesis (am-knee-oh-cent-TEE-sis). A method for detecting the presence of genetic abnormalities in an unborn child by examining fluid drawn from the amniotic sac. (From the Greek *amnion,* meaning "lamb," and *kentesis,* meaning "tapping," as by a needle.)

Chorionic villus sampling Another method for detecting genetic abnormalities. CVS samples the membrane that envelops the amniotic sac and the fetus within.

EXPERIMENTS IN SELECTIVE BREEDING

You need not be a psychologist to know that animals can be selectively bred to enhance desired traits over the generations. Simply compare wild African dogs with their descendants—varieties as diverse as the Great Dane, the tiny, nervous Chihuahua, and the pug-nosed, white-trimmed Boston terrier. We breed our cattle and chickens bigger and fatter, so that they provide the most food calories for the minimum amount of feed. It also seems that we can selectively breed animals to enhance the presence of traits that are of more interest to psychologists, such as intelligence (although "intelligence" in lower animals does not correspond directly to human intelligence), aggressiveness, and even preference for alcohol over water (Eriksson, 1972).

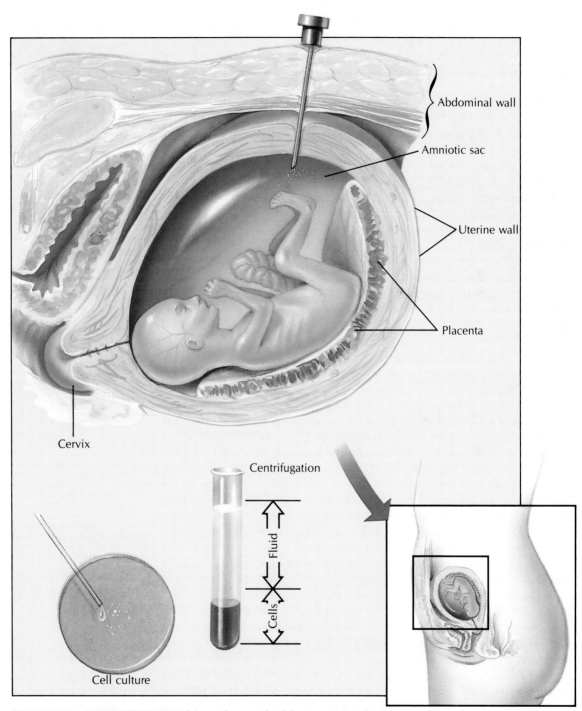

Abdominal wall

Amniotic sac

Uterine wall

Placenta

Cervix

Centrifugation

Fluid

Cells

Cell culture

FIGURE 2.22 AMNIOCENTESIS This modern method for examining the chromosomes sloughed off by a fetus into amniotic fluid permits the prenatal identification of certain hereditary diseases. Amniocentesis also allows parents to learn the sex of their unborn child. Would you want to know?

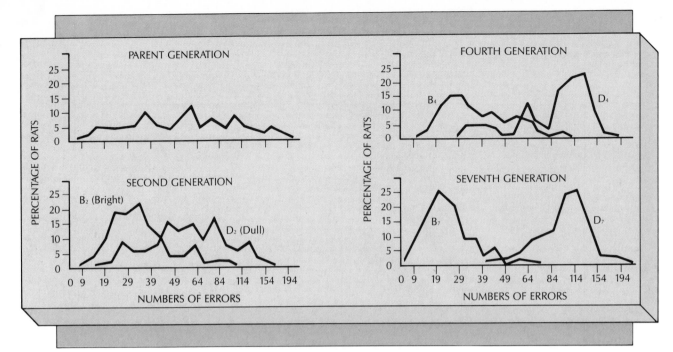

FIGURE 2.23 SELECTIVE BREEDING FOR MAZE-LEARNING ABILITY IN RATS
In the Tryon study, the offspring of maze-bright rats were inbred for six generations. So were the offspring of maze-dull rats. As the generations became further
removed, there was progressively less overlap in the maze-learning ability of the
offspring of the two groups, even though environmental influences were held as
constant as possible for all offspring. Is maze-learning ability in rats similar to intelligence in human beings?

There is an extensive discussion of the roles of heredity (nature) and
the environment (nurture) in human intelligence in Chapter 6. Here let us
illustrate the concept of selective breeding with rats, which have been bred
selectively for maze-learning ability (Rosenzweig, 1969; Tryon, 1940) and
many other traits.

In such studies, an initial group of rats is tested for maze-learning
ability by measuring the number of mistakes they make in repeated trials
as they learn to find a food goal. Rats making the fewest mistakes are labeled
B_1, signifying the first generation of "maze-bright" rats. "Maze-dull" rats
are labeled D_1. The total distribution of errors, or blind-alley entrances,
made by the first (parent) generation is shown in Figure 2.23. These errors
were made over a series of nineteen runs in the Tryon study.

Maze-bright rats from the first generation were then bred with other
maze-bright rats, while maze-dull rats were similarly interbred. The second
graph in Figure 2.23 shows how the offspring (B_2) of the maze-bright parents
compared with the offspring (D_2) of the maze-dull parents in numbers of
errors (blind-alley entrances). The offspring of the maze-bright rats, as a
group, clearly made fewer errors than the offspring of the maze-dull, although there was considerable overlap between groups. The brightest offspring of the maze-bright were then interbred as were the dullest of the
maze-dull for six consecutive generations. Fortunately for experimental psychologists, rat generations are measured in months, not decades. Through-

PSYCHOLOGY TODAY

GENETIC ENGINEERING

In the recently developed technology of genetic engineering, the genetic structures of organisms are changed by direct manipulation of their reproductive cells. Even as you read these words, patents are pending on new life forms—mostly microscopic—that biologists and corporations hope will be marketable.

Current research suggests that genetic engineering may lead to some exciting discoveries (McAuliffe & McAuliffe, 1983) in the not-too-distant future. These include:

New vaccines for diseases like hepatitis and herpes
Ways of detecting predispositions for disorders such as cancer, heart disease, and emphysema by studying a newborn's (or fetus's) genetic code

Prenatal screening for fatal hereditary diseases such as Huntington's chorea, cystic fibrosis, and muscular dystrophy*
Learning how "spelling errors" in the genetic code (for example, ATTC rather than ATGC in a given segment of DNA) may cause inherited diseases such as sickle-cell anemia
Modifying the genetic codes of unborn children to prevent disease
Creating new wonder drugs from the materials that compose DNA

*In amniocentesis the general chromosomal structure, rather than the intricate and elusive genetic code, is examined.

out these generations, the environments of the rats were kept as constant as possible. Dull rats were often raised by bright mothers, and vice versa, so that a critic could not argue that the maze-learning ability of bright offspring could be attributed to an enriched environment provided by a bright mother.

After six generations there was little overlap in maze-learning performance between maze-bright and maze-dull rats. The (spatial relations) superiority of the maze-bright rats did not generalize to all types of learning tasks. We also cannot emphasize too strongly that maze-learning ability in rats is not comparable to the complex groupings of behavior that define human intelligence. Still, experiments such as these suggest that it would be foolhardy to completely overlook possible genetic influences on human intelligence.

Some breeds of dogs, like Doberman pinschers and German shepherds, have been bred to be more aggressive than other varieties. Within breeds, however, dogs have been selectively bred to show high or low activity levels. Chickens have also been selectively bred for aggressiveness (consider the "sport" of cockfighting) and for level of sexual activity (McClearn & DeFries, 1973; Scott & Fuller, 1965).

GENETICS AND THE FUTURE

The future of selective breeding and other methods for modifying living organisms seems at once promising and frightening. On the positive side, selective breeding practices have given birth (literally) to superchickens, superwheat, and super fir trees. These are oversized organisms that mature early, reproduce early, and are more disease resistant than their ancestors. There may be yet more promise in genetic engineering, in which the genetic structures of organisms are changed by direct manipulation of their reproductive cells.

On another level, **genetic counseling** has become more common. In this procedure, information about a couple's genetic backgrounds is compiled to determine the possibility that their union may result in genetically defective children. Some couples whose natural children would be at high risk for genetic diseases elect to adopt. Among the disorders that genetic counseling can prevent are sickle-cell anemia, which mainly afflicts blacks; Tay-Sachs disease, which afflicts Jews of European origin; cystic fibrosis; and Huntington's chorea.

Some fear that increasing control of genetics will make possible future scenarios like that portrayed by Aldous Huxley in his still powerful 1932 novel *Brave New World*. Through a fictitious method called "Bokanovsky's Process," egg cells from parents who are identically suited for certain types of labor are made to "bud." From these buds up to 96 people with identical genetic makeups can be developed—filling whatever labor niches are required by society.

In the novel the director of a "hatchery" is leading a group of students on a tour. One student is foolish enough to question the advantage of Bokanovsky's Process:

> "My good boy!" The Director wheeled sharply round on him. "Can't you see? Can't you see?" He raised a hand; his expression was solemn. "Bokanovsky's Process is one of the major instruments of social stability!"
>
> Major instruments of social stability (wrote the student).
>
> Standard men and women; in uniform batches. The whole of a small factory staffed with the products of a single Bokanovskied egg.
>
> "Ninety-six identical twins working 96 identical machines!" The voice was almost tremulous with enthusiasm. "You really know where you are. For the first time in history." He quoted the planetary motto. "Community, Identity, Stability." Grand words. "If we could Bokanovskify indefinitely the whole problem would be solved."

Through Bokanovsky's Process we might be able to eliminate certain genetic disorders. We might even be able to lower the incidence of crime, aggression, and abnormal behaviors. But I ask those of you who think that all this might be a good idea to consider that from none of these "Bokanovskied" eggs would there emerge a Shakespeare, a Beethoven, or an Einstein. Perhaps we would avoid tyrants, but we would also be bereft of geniuses and individuals who might shape the world in ways we cannot foresee.

And those of you who think that genetic research ought to be stopped might consider that there is no such thing as bad knowledge—only bad use of knowledge.

GENETIC COUNSELING In genetic counseling, information about a couple's genetic backgrounds is examined to determine the possibility that their children may be genetically defective. Genetic counseling can prevent disorders such as sickle-cell anemia, which afflicts mainly blacks; Tay-Sachs disease; cystic fibrosis; and Huntington's chorea.

Genetic counseling Counseling concerning the probability that a couple's children will have genetic abnormalities and what to do about it.

SUMMARY

1. The nervous system consists of neurons, which transmit information through neural impulses, and glial cells, which serve support functions. Neurons have a cell body (soma), dendrites, which receive transmissions, and axons. Chemicals called neurotransmitters travel across synapses to transmit messages to other neurons.

2. Many neurons have fatty myelin sheaths, which

are missing at the nodes of Ranvier. Neural impulses can jump from node to node.

3. Afferent neurons transmit sensory messages to the central nervous system, and efferent neurons conduct messages from the central nervous system that stimulate glands or cause muscles to contract.

4. Although it has been estimated that we lose several thousand neurons daily through the aging process, there is little reliable evidence for this view. Moreover, the nervous system can apparently continue to develop, even in old age.

5. Neural transmission is electrochemical. An electric charge is conducted along an axon through a process that allows sodium ions into the cell and then pumps them out. The neuron has a resting potential of -70 millivolts, and an action potential of $+30$ to $+40$ millivolts.

6. Excitatory synapses stimulate neurons to fire; inhibitory neurons influence them not to. Neurons fire on an all-or-none principle. Neurons may fire hundreds of times per second, and absolute and relative refractory (insensitive) periods follow each firing.

7. Important neurotransmitters include acetylcholine, which is involved in muscle contractions; dopamine, imbalances of which have been linked to Parkinson's disease and schizophrenia; and norepinephrine, which accelerates the heartbeat and other bodily processes. A number of neuropeptides, such as beta-endorphin, serve as naturally occurring pain-killers.

8. The brain and spinal cord compose the central nervous system. Reflexes involve the spinal cord, but not the brain. The somatic and autonomic systems compose the peripheral nervous system.

9. The hindbrain includes the medulla, pons, and cerebellum. The reticular-activating system begins in the hindbrain and continues through the midbrain into the forebrain. Important structures of the forebrain include the thalamus, hypothalamus, limbic system, basal ganglia, and cerebrum. The hypothalamus is involved in controlling body temperature and regulating motivation and emotion.

10. The somatic nervous system transmits sensory information about muscles, skin, and joints to the central nervous system; it also controls muscular activity from the central nervous system. The autonomic nervous system (ANS) regulates the glands and involuntary activities like heartbeat, digestion, and dilation of the pupils. The sympathetic division of the ANS dominates in activities that expend the body's resources, such as fleeing from a predator, and the parasympathetic division dominates during processes that build the body's reserves, like eating.

11. The cerebral cortex is divided into the frontal, parietal, temporal, and occipital lobes. The visual cortex is in the occipital lobe, and the auditory cortex is in the temporal lobe. The sensory cortex lies behind the central fissure in the parietal lobe, and the motor cortex lies in the frontal lobe, across the central fissure from the sensory cortex.

12. Association areas of the cortex are involved in thought and language. The language areas of the cortex lie near the intersection of the frontal, temporal, and parietal lobes in the dominant hemisphere. For right-handed people the left hemisphere of the cortex is dominant; for half the left-handed people the right hemisphere is dominant. The notion that some people are "left-brained" while others are "right-brained" is exaggerated and largely inaccurate.

13. Split-brain patients may be able to verbally describe a screened-off object like a pencil that is held in the hand connected to the dominant hemisphere, but cannot do so when the object is held in the other hand.

14. The endocrine system consists of ductless glands that secrete hormones. The pituitary gland secretes growth hormone; prolactin, which regulates maternal behavior in lower animals and stimulates production of milk in women; ADH, which inhibits the production of urine; and oxytocin, which stimulates labor in pregnant women.

15. The pancreas secretes insulin, which enables the body to metabolize sugar. Diabetes, hyperglycemia, and hypoglycemia are all linked to imbalances in insulin.

16. The adrenal cortex produces steroids, which promote development of muscle mass and increase activity level. The adrenal medulla secretes adrenalin (epinephrine), which increases the metabolic rate and is involved in general emotional arousal.

17. Sex hormones secreted by the testes and ovaries are responsible for prenatal sexual differentiation, and female sex hormones regulate the menstrual cycle. Premenstrual syndrome (PMS) is usually mild, but prostaglandins can cause painful cramping. PMS is often complicated by negative cultural attitudes toward menstruation.

18. Genes are the basic building blocks of heredity and consist of DNA. A large number of genes make up each chromosome. People normally have forty-six

chromosomes. They receive twenty-three from the father and twenty-three from the mother.

19. Genetics is concerned with transmission of traits from generation to generation.

20. Our genotypes are the sets of traits we inherit from our parents, while our phenotypes—the characteristics that we show at any point in time—are also influenced by environmental factors.

21. Through the cell-division process of mitosis, the identical genetic code is carried to each new cell in the body. Chromosomal strands of DNA "unzip" and are rebuilt in each new cell. Sperm and ova are produced through reduction division, or meiosis, in which each new cell contains only twenty-three chromosomes.

22. A fertilized egg cell is a zygote. Identical twins are monozygotic, while fraternal twins are dizygotic. Monozygotic twins are important in the study of the relative influences of nature and nurture.

23. Dominant traits are shown, while recessive traits are shown only if a recessive gene from one parent combines with a recessive gene from the other. People with recessive genes for illnesses are said to be carriers of those illnesses.

24. Down syndrome is caused by an extra chromosome on the twenty-first pair and is more common among children of older parents. "Supermale" syndrome, Klinefelter's syndrome, and Turner's syndrome are all caused by abnormal numbers of sex chromosomes. Phenylketonuria, which leads to mental retardation, is transmitted by a recessive gene and controlled by diet. New methods, including amniocentesis and CVS, permit parents to learn whether their children will have certain inherited disorders before they are born.

25. Experiments show that animals can be selectively bred to heighten the influence of many traits. Rats, for example, can be selectively bred for maze-learning ability, but we cannot assume that maze-learning ability in rats corresponds directly to human intelligence.

26. In the future, genetic engineering may lead to new prenatal screening methods for disease, new wonder drugs, and manipulation of the genetic codes of unborn children to prevent disease.

TRUTH OR FICTION REVISITED

Some cells in your body stretch all the way down your back to your big toe.

True. Some neurons span the length from your brain stem to your toes, while other neurons are only a few thousandths of an inch long.

We lose brain cells as we grow older.

True. However, we have so many brain cells (neurons) that this loss probably has little or no influence on our abilities to learn, think, or remember.

Messages travel in the brain by means of electricity.

True—up to a point. Messages (neural impulses) travel along the length of a neuron by means of an electrochemical process. However, messages are transmitted to other neurons by means of chemicals called neurotransmitters.

Our bodies produce natural pain killers that are more powerful than the narcotic morphine.

True. They are called endorphins.

The human brain is larger than that of any other animal.

False. Elephant and whale brains are larger, but our brains have a higher brain-to-body-weight ratio.

Many men who are paralyzed below the waist can still achieve erection and ejaculate.

True. These sexual responses are reflexes that do not require input from the brain. But it is necessary that the appropriate section of the spine be intact.

Fear can give you indigestion.

True. Fear stimulates (and is stimulated by) the sympathetic branch of the ANS, but digestion involves parasympathetic activity. These two branches of the ANS service many of the same organs and have largely opposing effects.

If a surgeon were to stimulate a certain part of your brain electrically, you might swear in court that someone had stroked your leg.

True. Stimulation of areas of the sensory cortex leads to the perception of sensation in corresponding parts of the body.

If a certain area in your brain were damaged, your ability to speak would be impaired, but you could still understand the written or spoken language.

True. This is one form of aphasia.

Women body-builders can achieve as much muscle mass and definition as men do by working as hard at "pumping iron."

False. Because of their different genetic makeup, women must also take anabolic steroids and other dangerous substances to achieve similar effects.

Some people grow into "giants" because of "glands."

True. The condition known as acromegaly is produced by an excess of growth hormone, which is secreted by the pituitary gland.

With so many billions of people in the world, you are bound to have a "double" somewhere, even if you are not an identical twin.

False. The number of possible combinations of genetic material is so vast that only identical twins can be "doubles," although some people, especially close relatives, may bear a resemblance to you.

You can learn the sex of your child several months before it is born.

True. One method for doing so is amniocentesis.

Inventors are applying for patents on new life forms.

True. These life forms, mostly microscopic, are being created through genetic engineering.

OUTLINE

CHAPTER 3

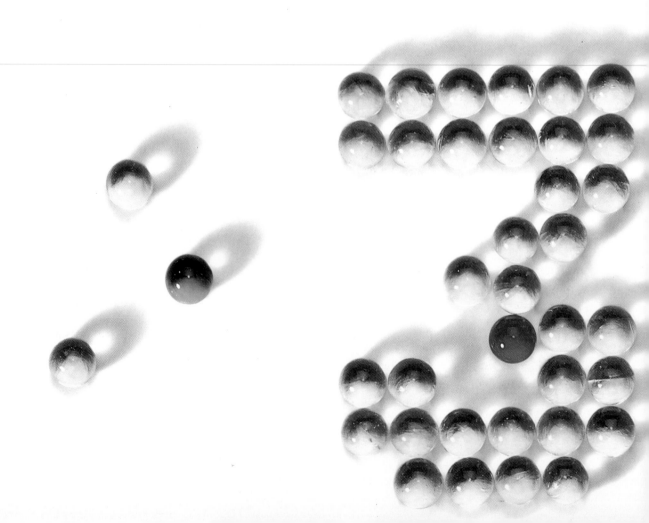

Sensation and Perception

TRUTH OR FICTION?

- White sunlight is actually composed of all the colors of the rainbow.
- On a clear, dark night you could probably see the light from a single candle burning thirty miles away.
- We all have blind spots in our eyes.
- At first we may not be able to see other viewers when we enter a dark movie theater, but after several minutes we can discriminate other people and the features of the theater interior much more clearly.
- As we approach late adulthood, we become likely to need reading glasses, even if our visual acuity has been perfect at younger ages.
- When we mix blue light and yellow light, we attain green light.
- "Motion pictures" do not move at all.
- We need two eyes in order to perceive depth.
- The advertising slogan for the film *Alien* was accurate: "In space, no one can hear you scream."
- The menstrual cycles of women who live together tend to become synchronized.
- Perfume and cologne manufacturers have placed chemical substances in their products that sexually arouse us.
- Onions and apples have the same taste.
- We have no sensory receptors for perceiving hotness.
- Some people have the ability to read other people's minds.

Five thousand years ago in China, give or take a day or two, an arrow was shot into the air. Where did it land? Ancient records tell us precisely where: in the hand of a fierce warrior and master of the martial arts.

As the story was told to me, the warrior had grown so fierce because of a chronic toothache. The unrelenting pain had simply ruined his disposition.

On one fateful day our hero watched as invading hordes assembled on surrounding hills. His troops were trembling, and he raised his arms in wild gestures in an effort to boost their morale in the face of the invaders' superior numbers. A slender wooden shaft lifted into the air from a nearby rise, arced, and then descended—right into the warrior's palm. His troops cringed and muttered among themselves, but our hero said nothing. Although he saw the arrow through his palm, he did not scream. He did not run. He did not even complain.

He was astounded. His toothache had vanished. His entire jaw was numb.

Meanwhile the invaders looked on—horrified. They, too, muttered among themselves. What sort of warrior could look upon an arrow through his hand with such indifference? Even with a growing smile? If this was the caliber of warrior in this village, they'd be better off traveling west and looking for a brawl in ancient Sumer, or in Egypt. They sounded the retreat and withdrew.

Our warrior received a hero's welcome back in town. A physician offered to remove the arrow without a fee—a tribute to bravery. But our warrior would have none of it. The arrow had done wonders for his toothache, and he would permit no meddling. He had discovered already that if the pain threatened to return, he need only twirl the arrow and it would recede once more.

But things were not so rosy on the home front. His wife was thrilled to find him jovial once more, but the arrow put a crimp in romance. When he put his arm around her, she was in dire danger of being stabbed. Finally she gave him an ultimatum: It was she or the arrow.

Placed in deep conflict, our warrior consulted a psychologist, who then huddled with the physician and the village elders. After much todo, they asked the warrior to participate in an experiment. They would remove the arrow and replace it with a pin that the warrior could twirl as needed. If the pin didn't do the trick, they could always fall back on the arrow, so to speak.

To his wife's relief, the pin worked. And here, in ancient China, lay the origins of the art of **acupuncture**—the use of needles to relieve pain and treat a variety of ills ranging from **hypertension** to some forms of blindness.

I confess that this tale is not entirely accurate. To my knowledge, there were no psychologists in ancient China. (Their loss.) Moreover, the part about the warrior's wife is fictitious. But it is claimed that acupuncture, as a means for dealing with pain, originated in ancient China when a soldier was, in fact, wounded in a hand by an arrow and discovered that a chronic toothache had disappeared. The Chinese, historians claim, then set out to "map" the body by sticking pins here and there to learn how they influenced the perception of pain.

Acupuncture (ACK-you-PUNK-tyour). The ancient Chinese practice of piercing parts of the body with needles in order to deaden pain and treat illness. (From the Latin *acus,* meaning "needle.")

Hypertension High blood pressure.

Sensation The stimulation of sensory receptors and the transmission of sensory information to the central nervous system. (From the Latin *sensus,* meaning "sense.")

Perception The process by which sensations are organized into an inner representation of the world—a psychological process through which we interpret sensory information. (From the Latin *percipere,* meaning "to take hold of," or "to comprehend.")

Visual capture The tendency of vision to dominate the other senses.

Light Electromagnetic energy of various wavelengths. The part of this spectrum of energy that stimulates the eye and produces visual sensations. (From the Latin *lux,* meaning "light.")

Control of pain is just one of the many issues that interest psychologists who study the closely related concepts of sensation and perception. **Sensation** is the stimulation of sensory receptors and the transmission of sensory information to the central nervous system (the spinal cord or brain). Sensory receptors are located in sensory organs like the eyes and ears, and, as we shall see, in the skin and elsewhere in the body. The stimulation of the senses is mechanical; it results from sources of energy like light and sound, or from the presence of chemicals, as in smell and taste.

Perception is not mechanical at all. Perception is the process by which sensations are organized and interpreted, forming an inner representation of the world. Perception involves much more than sensation. Perception involves learning and expectations and the ways in which we organize incoming information about the world. Perception is an active process through which we make sense of sensory stimulation. A human shape and a twelve-inch ruler may stimulate paths of equal length among the sensory receptors in our eyes. But whether we interpret the human shape to be a foot-long doll or a full-grown person fifteen to twenty feet away is a matter of perception.

In this chapter we shall see that your personal map of reality—your ticket of admission to a world of changing sights, sounds, and other sources of sensory input—depends largely on the "five senses" of vision, hearing, smell, taste, and touch. We shall see, however, that touch is just one of several "skin senses," which also include pressure, warmth, cold, and pain. There are also other senses that alert you to your own body position without your having literally to watch every step you take. We shall explore the nature of each of these senses, and we shall find that highly similar sensations may lead to quite different perceptions in different people—or among the same people in different situations.

VISION

Our eyes are said to be our "windows on the world." We consider information from vision more essential than that from hearing, smell, taste, and touch. Studies in **visual capture** have shown, for example, that when we perceive a square object through lenses that distort it into a rectangle, we report the object to be a rectangle even when we can feel it with our hands (Rock & Victor, 1964). Because vision is our dominant sense, we consider blindness our most debilitating sensory loss. An understanding of vision requires discussion of the nature of light and of the master of the sensory organs, the eye.

LIGHT

According to the Bible, in the beginning the **light** was set apart from the dark. The light was good and the potential for evil lay in darkness. In almost all cultures light is a symbol of goodness and knowledge. We describe capable people as being "bright" or "brilliant." If we are not being complimentary, we label them as "dull." People who aren't "in the know" are said to be "in the dark." Just what is this stuff called light?

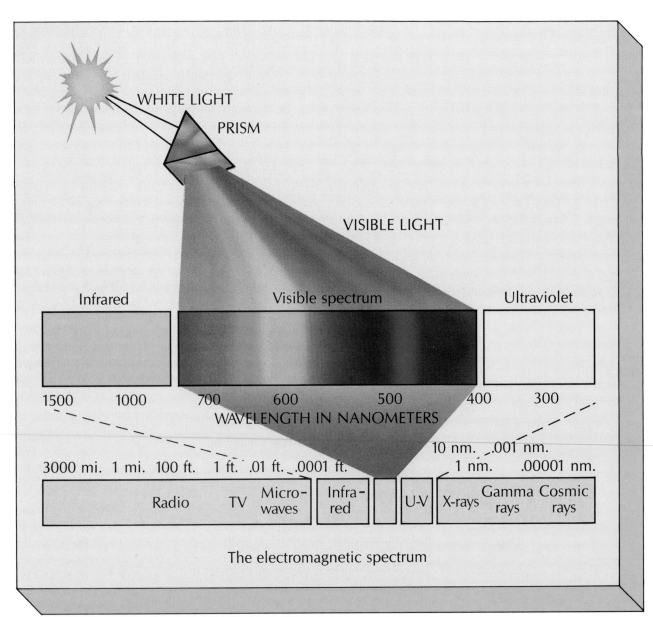

FIGURE 3.1 **THE VISIBLE SPECTRUM** By passing a source of white light, such as sunlight, through a prism, we break it down into the colors of the visible spectrum. The visible spectrum is just one part—and a narrow part indeed—of the electromagnetic spectrum. The electromagnetic spectrum also includes radio waves, microwaves, X-rays, cosmic rays, and many others. Different forms of electromagnetic energy have different wavelengths, which vary from a few trillionths of a meter to thousands of miles. Visible light varies in wavelength from about 400 to 700 nanometers. What is a nanometer? One *billionth* of a meter. (A meter = 39.37 inches.)

Visible light The band of electromagnetic energy that produces visual sensations. (Usually simply referred to as *light*.)

Prism A transparent triangular solid that breaks down visible light into the colors of the spectrum. (From the Greek *prisma,* meaning "something sawed," referring to the construction of a prism.)

Hue The color of light, as determined by its wavelength. (From the Old English *hiw,* meaning "appearance.")

Amplitude Height. The extreme range of a variable quantity.

Absolute threshold The minimal amount of energy that can produce a sensation.

Psychophysicist A person who studies the relationships between physical stimuli, like light or sound, and their perception.

Difference threshold The minimal difference in intensity required between two sources of energy so that they will be perceived as different.

Weber's constant The fraction of the intensity by which a source of physical energy must be increased or decreased so that a difference in intensity will be perceived.

Just noticeable difference The minimal amount by which a source of energy must be increased or decreased so that a difference in intensity will be perceived.

Visible light is the stuff that triggers visual sensations. Visible light is just one small part of a spectrum of electromagnetic energy (see Figure 3.1) that is described in terms of wavelengths. These wavelengths vary from those of cosmic rays, which are only a few trillionths of an inch long, to some radio waves that extend for many miles. Radar, microwaves, and X-rays are also forms of electromagnetic energy.

You have probably seen rainbows or seen light broken down into several colors as it filtered through your windows. Sir Isaac Newton, the British scientist, discovered that sunlight could be broken down into different colors by means of a triangular solid of glass called a **prism** (Figure 3.1). When I took introductory psychology, I was taught that I could remember the colors of the spectrum, from longest to shortest wavelengths, by using the mnemonic device *Mr. Roy G. Biv* (red, orange, yellow, green, blue, indigo, violet). I must have been a backward student because I found it easier to recall them in reverse order, using the meaningless acronym *vibgyor.*

The wavelength of visible light determines its color, or **hue.** The wavelength for red is longer than that for orange, and so on through the spectrum.

To gain a clearer idea of the meaning of waves of light, think for a moment of waves crashing on a shore. The wavelength—or length of waves—corresponds to the frequency with which a wave hits the shore—or *how often* a new wave comes. But waves also have height, or **amplitude.** Light waves of greater "height" or amplitude are seen as brighter, or more intense.

ABSOLUTE AND DIFFERENCE THRESHOLDS: TWO PSYCHOPHYSICAL CONCEPTS

The weakest amount of light that a person can see is called the **absolute threshold** for light. It may also be defined as the amount of physical energy required to activate the visual sensory system. Beneath this threshold, detection of light is impossible (Haber & Hershenson, 1980).

Psychophysicists experiment to determine the absolute threshold for vision by presenting visual stimuli of progressively greater intensity. They begin with an intensity of light that is not detectable, increase it step by step, and ask subjects to report when they can detect a visual stimulus. A person's absolute threshold is the lowest intensity of light that he or she can see 50 percent of the time. The relationship between the intensity of the light (a physical stimulus) and its perception (a psychological event) is considered *psychophysical*—it bridges psychological and physical events.

As you can see in Table 3.1, absolute thresholds have been determined for the senses of vision, hearing, taste, smell, and touch.

How much of a difference in intensity between two lights is required before you will perceive one as brighter than the other? The minimum required difference in intensity is defined as the **difference threshold** for light. Psychophysicist Ernst Weber discovered through laboratory research that the difference threshold for perceiving differences in the intensity of light is about 2 percent (actually closer to 1/60th) of their intensity. This fraction, 1/60th, is known as **Weber's constant** for light. It has also been called the **just noticeable difference,** or *jnd,* for light, indicating that people can perceive a difference in intensity when the brightness of a light is in-

TABLE 3.1 Absolute Thresholds and Other Characteristics of Our Sensory Systems

Sense	Stimulus	Receptors	Threshold
Vision	Electromagnetic energy	Rods and cones in the retina	A candle flame viewed from a distance of about 30 miles (48 km) on a clear, dark night
Hearing	Sound pressure waves	Hair cells on the basilar membrane of the inner ear	The ticking of a watch from about 20 feet (6 m) away in a quiet room
Taste	Chemical substances dissolved in saliva	Taste buds on the tongue in the mouth	About one teaspoon of sugar dissolved in 2 gallons of water
Smell	Chemical substances in the air	Receptor cells in the upper nasal cavity (the nose)	About one drop of perfume diffused throughout a small house (1 part in 500 million)
Touch	Mechanical displacement or pressure on the skin	Nerve endings located in the skin	The wing of a fly falling on a cheek from a distance of about 0.4 inch (1 cm)

SOURCE: Adapted from Galanter (1962).

creased or decreased by 1/60th. Remarkably, Weber's constant (1/60) for light holds whether we are comparing two quite bright or rather dull lights. However, it becomes inaccurate when we compare extremely bright or extremely dull lights.

As you can see in Table 3.2, Weber's research in psychophysics touched on many senses. He derived difference thresholds for different types of sensory stimulation.

TABLE 3.2 Weber's Constant for Various Sensory Discriminations

Sense	Type of Discrimination	Weber's Constant
Vision	Brightness of a light	1/60
Hearing	Pitch (frequency) of a tone	1/333
	Loudness of a tone	1/10
Taste	Difference in saltiness	1/5
Smell	Amount of rubber smell	1/10
Touch	Pressure on the skin surface	1/7
	Deep pressure	1/77
	Difference in lifted weights	1/53

Signal detection theory The view that the perception of sensory stimuli involves the interaction of physical, biological, and psychological factors.

Cornea (CORE-knee-uh). Transparent tissue forming the outer surface of the eyeball. (From the Latin *cornu,* meaning "horn" and referring to the appearance of the cornea.)

Iris A muscular membrane whose dilation regulates the amount of light that enters the eye.

Pupil The apparently black opening in the center of the iris, through which light enters the eye. (From the Latin *pupilla,* meaning one's figure as reflected in the eye of another.)

Lens A transparent body that focuses an image on the retina. (From the Latin *lentil,* referring to the shape of a lens.)

Retina The area of the inner surface of the eye that contains rods and cones. (Probably from the Latin *rete,* meaning "net.")

Photoreceptors Cells that respond to light.

Bipolar cells Neurons that conduct neural impulses from rods and cones to ganglion cells.

Ganglion cells Neurons whose axons form the optic nerve.

According to **signal detection theory,** several factors determine whether people will be able to perceive sensory stimuli or a difference between two sensory stimuli. These factors concern the sensory stimuli themselves, the biological sensory system of the person, and psychological factors. For example, how intense are the sensory stimuli? Can they be distinguished from background stimuli? How sharp or acute is the individual's sensory system? Is sensory capacity diminished because of illness or advanced years? Psychological factors include motivation, expectations, and learning. For example, is the individual motivated to try to perceive the stimulus? Does the person know what to expect? People who are experienced in psychophysical procedures may be more alert or sensitive to stimuli of low intensities.

And so, a combination of physical, biological, and psychological factors determine whether sensory stimuli will be perceived. Let us now turn our attention to the biological system that is involved in the sense of vision, beginning with the eye.

THE EYE: OUR LIVING CAMERA

Consider for a moment that magnificent invention called the camera, which records visual experiences. In the camera, light enters an opening and is focused onto a sensitive surface, or film. Chemical reactions then take place on this surface which create a lasting impression of the image that entered the camera.

The eye—our living camera—is no less remarkable. Consider the major parts of the eye (Figure 3.2). As with a film or television camera, light enters through a narrow opening and is projected onto a sensitive surface. Light first passes through the transparent **cornea.** The amount of light that passes is determined by the size of the opening of the muscle called the **iris.** The opening in the iris is called the **pupil.** Pupil size adjusts automatically to the amount of light; you do not have to try to purposefully open the eye farther to see better under conditions of low lighting. The more intense the light, the smaller the opening. We similarly adjust the amount of light allowed into a camera according to its brightness.

Once light passes through the iris, it encounters the **lens.** The lens adjusts or accommodates to the image by changing its thickness. Changes in thickness permit projection of a clear image of the object onto the retina—that is, they focus the light according to the distance of the object. If you hold a finger at arm's length, then slowly bring it toward your nose, you will feel tension in the eye as the thickness of the lens accommodates to keep the retinal image in focus (Haber & Hershenson, 1980). When people "squint" to bring an object into focus, they are adjusting the thickness of the lens. The lens in a camera does not accommodate to the distance of objects. Instead, in order to focus the light that is projected onto the film, the camera lens is moved farther away from or closer to the film.

The **retina** is like the film or image surface of the camera. But instead of being composed of film that is sensitive to light (photosensitive), the retina consists of photosensitive cells, or **photoreceptors,** called *rods* and *cones.* The retina (Figure 3.3) contains several layers of cells: the rods and cones, **bipolar cells,** and **ganglion cells.** Light travels past the ganglion cells and

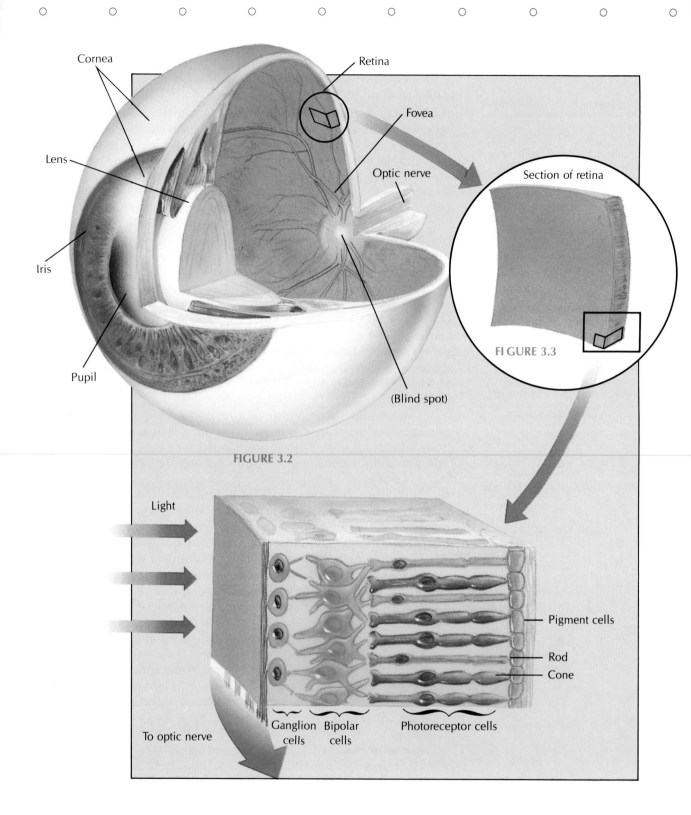

Cornea

Retina

Fovea

Lens

Optic nerve

Iris

Section of retina

Pupil

FIGURE 3.3

(Blind spot)

FIGURE 3.2

Light

Pigment cells

Rod

Cone

To optic nerve

Ganglion cells

Bipolar cells

Photoreceptor cells

Opposite: FIGURES 3.2 AND 3.3 THE HUMAN EYE Figure 3.2 shows the entire human eye. In both the eye and a camera, light enters through a narrow opening and is projected onto a sensitive surface. In the eye, the photosensitive surface is called the retina, and information concerning the changing images on the retina is transmitted to the brain. In a camera, the photosensitive surface is usually film, which captures a single image. Figure 3.3 shows the retina of the human eye. Light finds its way through ganglion neurons and bipolar neurons to the photosensitive rods and cones. These photoreceptors then transmit sensory input back through the bipolar neurons to the ganglion neurons. The axons of the ganglion neurons form the optic nerve, which transmits sensory stimulation through the brain to the visual cortex of the occipital lobe.

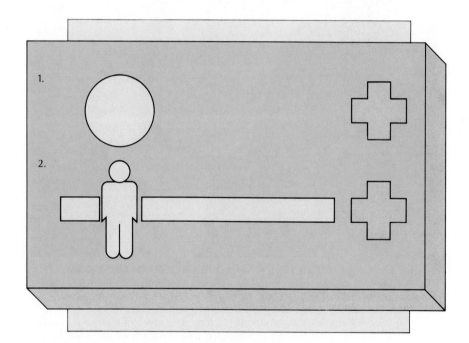

FIGURE 3.4 LOCATING THE BLIND SPOT In order to try a "disappearing act," first look at Drawing 1. Close your right eye. Then move the book back and forth about one foot from your left eye while you stare at the plus sign. You will notice the circle disappear. When the circle disappears it is being projected onto the blind spot of your retina, the point at which the axons of ganglion neurons collect to form the optic nerve. Then close your left eye. Stare at the circle with your right eye, and move the book back and forth. When the plus sign disappears, it is being projected onto the blind spot of your right eye. Now look at Drawing 2. You can make this figure disappear and "see" the black line continue through the spot where it was by closing your right eye and staring at the plus sign with your left. When this figure is projected onto your blind spot, your brain "fills in" the line, which is one reason that we're not usually aware that we have blind spots.

bipolar cells and stimulates the rods and cones. The rods and cones then send neural messages through the bipolar cells to the ganglion cells. The axons of the ganglion cells constitute the **optic nerve.** The optic nerve conducts the sensory input to the brain and, eventually, the visual area of the occipital lobe.

The **fovea** is the most sensitive area of the retina (see Figure 3.2). The **blind spot,** by contrast, is insensitive to visual stimulation. The blind spot is the part of the retina where the axons of the ganglion cells congregate to form the optic nerve (Figure 3.3).

Optic nerve The nerve that transmits sensory information from the eye to the brain. (From the Greek *optikos,* meaning "seeing.")

Fovea (FOE-vee-uh). A rodless area near the center of the retina where vision is most acute. (A Latin word meaning "pit.")

Blind spot The area of the retina where axons from ganglion cells meet to form the optic nerve. It is insensitive to light.

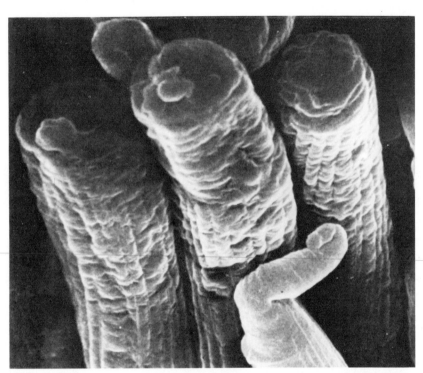

FIGURE 3.5 A MUCH (MUCH!) ENLARGED PHOTOGRAPH OF SEVERAL RODS AND A CONE Cones are usually upright fellows. However, the cone at the bottom right of this photo has been bent by the photographic process. You have more than 100 million rods and six million cones distributed across the retina of each eye. Only cones provide sensations of color. The fovea of the eye is populated by cones only, which are then distributed more sparsely as you work forward toward the lens. Rods, by contrast, are absent at the fovea and become more densely packed as you work forward.

Rods and Cones **Rods** and **cones** are the photoreceptors in the retina (Figure 3.5). Over 100 million rods and six million cones are distributed across the retina. The fovea contains cones only. Cones then become more sparsely distributed as you work forward from the fovea toward the lens. Rods, by contrast, are absent at the fovea but distributed more densely as you approach the lens.

Rods are sensitive to the intensity of light only. They allow us to see in "black and white." Cones provide color vision. If you are a camera buff,

Rods Rod-shaped photoreceptors that are sensitive only to the intensity of light. Rods permit black-and-white vision.

Cones Cone-shaped photoreceptors that transmit sensations of color.

Dark adaptation The process of adjusting to conditions of lower lighting through increasing the sensitivity of rods and cones.

Visual acuity Keenness or sharpness of vision. (From the Latin *acus,* meaning "needle." What other term in this chapter shares this derivation?)

you know that black-and-white films are generally "faster," or more responsive to light, than color film. In the same way, rods are more sensitive than cones to light. Therefore, under dim illumination, as during nighttime, objects appear to lose their color.

Dark Adaptation   Have you ever entered a movie theater on a bright afternoon and had to feel your way to a seat by holding onto the backs of the chairs near the aisle? You may have thought at first that the theater was too dark. But after several minutes you were able to see other people clearly, even in the darkest recesses of the theater. Adjusting to lower lighting is called **dark adaptation.**

Figure 3.6 shows the amount of light needed for detection as a function of the amount of time spent in the dark. The cones and rods adapt at different rates. The cones, which permit perception of color, reach their maximum adaptation to darkness in about ten minutes. The rods, which allow perception of light and dark only, are more sensitive and continue to adapt to darkness for up to about forty-five minutes.

Visual Acuity   You may recall from geometry that an acute angle is a sharp angle. Your **visual acuity** is the sharpness of your vision—your ability to discriminate visual details.

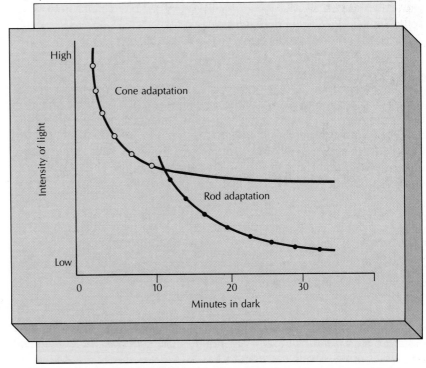

FIGURE 3.6 DARK ADAPTATION This illustration shows the amount of light necessary for detection as a function of the amount of time spent in the dark. Cones and rods adapt at different rates. Cones, which permit perception of color, reach maximum dark adaptation in about ten minutes. Rods, which permit perception of dark and light only, are more sensitive than cones. Rods continue to adapt for up to about forty-five minutes.

A familiar means of measuring visual acuity is the Snellen Chart (Figure 3.7). If you were to stand 20 feet from the Snellen Chart and could only discriminate the E, we would say that your vision is "20/200." This would mean that you can see from a distance of 20 feet what a person with normal vision can discriminate from a distance of 200 feet. In such a case you would be quite **nearsighted.** You would have to be unusually close to an object to discriminate its details. A person who could read the smallest line on the chart from 20 feet would have 20/15 vision and be somewhat **farsighted.** It is not unusual for eyes to differ somewhat in their visual acuity, although people tend to be generally nearsighted or farsighted when their vision is not normal.

You may have noticed that elderly people often hold newspapers or books at a distance. As you grow older, the lenses of the eyes become relatively brittle, making it more difficult to accommodate to, or focus on, objects. This condition is called **presbyopia,** from the Greek for "old man." The lens structure of elderly people with presbyopia differs from that of farsighted young people. Still, the effect of presbyopia in the elderly is to make it difficult to perceive nearby visual stimuli.

If you are nearsighted in youth, you may welcome presbyopia, since your vision will tend to normalize. But people who had normal visual acuity in their youth typically find that they must use corrective lenses to read in old age. And people who were initially farsighted often suffer from headaches linked to eyestrain during the later years.

COLOR VISION

For most of us, the world is a place of brilliant colors. The blue-greens of the ocean, the red-oranges of the setting sun, the deepened greens of June, the glories of rhododendron and hibiscus—color is an emotional and aesthetic part of our everyday lives. In this section we explore psychological dimensions of color and then examine theories as to how we manage to convert different wavelengths of light into perceptions of color.

PSYCHOLOGICAL DIMENSIONS OF COLOR: HUE, BRIGHTNESS, AND SATURATION

As noted earlier, the wavelength of light determines its color, or hue. The brightness of a color, like the brightness of any light, is its degree of lightness or darkness. The brighter the color, the lighter it is.

If we bend the colors of the spectrum around into a circle, we create a color wheel as in Figure 3.8. Yellow is the lightest of the colors on the color wheel. As we work our way around from yellow to violet-blue, we encounter progressively darker colors.

Warm and Cool Colors   Psychologically, the colors on the green-blue side of the color wheel are considered cool in temperature, while the colors on the yellow-orange-red side are considered warm. Perhaps greens and blues suggest the coolness of the ocean and the sky, while things tend

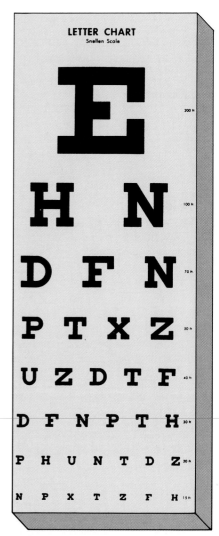

FIGURE 3.7 THE SNELLEN CHART
The Snellen Chart and others like it are used to assess visual acuity.

Nearsighted Capable of seeing nearby objects with greater acuity than distant objects.

Farsighted Capable of seeing distant objects with greater acuity than nearby objects.

Presbyopia Brittleness of the lens, a condition that permits greater visual acuity with distant objects.

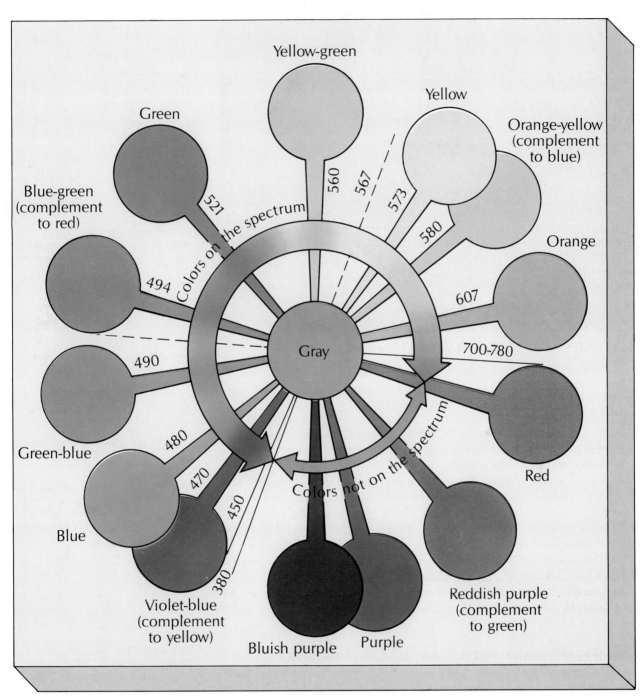

FIGURE 3.8 THE COLOR WHEEL A color wheel can be formed by bending the colors of the spectrum into a circle and placing complementary colors across from one another. (A few colors between violet and red that are not found on the spectrum must be added to complete the circle.) When lights of complementary colors, such as yellow and violet-blue, are mixed, they dissolve into neutral gray. The afterimage of a color is also the color's complement.

THE CHILD'S WORLD OF COLOR Children can discriminate the colors of the spectrum early in infancy. Toy manufacturers usually make infants' toys in bright colors that catch the eye and are easy for parents to label.

to burn red or orange. A room decorated in green or blue may seem more appealing on a hot day in July than a room decorated in red or orange.

When we look at a painting, warm colors seem to advance toward the viewer, which explains, in part, why the oranges and yellows of Mark Rothko's "Orange and Yellow" (Figure 3.9) seem to pulsate toward the observer. Cool colors seem to recede. Similarly the warm Sunoco sign in Allan d'Arcangelo's "Highway No. 2" (Figure 3.10) leaps out toward the viewer; however, the cool blue sky seems to recede into the distance.

The **saturation** of a color is its pureness. Pure hues have the greatest intensity, or brightness. The saturation, and thus the brightness, decreases when another hue or black, gray, or white is added. Artists produce shades of a given hue by adding black, and tints by adding white.

COMPLEMENTARY VERSUS ANALOGOUS COLORS

Complementary Colors   The colors across from one another on the color wheel are labeled **complementary.** Red-green and blue-yellow are the major complementary pairs. If we mix complementary colors together, they dissolve into gray.

But wait! you say: Blue and yellow cannot be complementary because by mixing *pigments* of blue and yellow we create green, not gray. True enough, but we have been talking about mixing *light,* not pigment. Light is

Saturation The degree of purity of a color, as measured by its freedom from mixture with white or black.

Complementary Descriptive of colors of the spectrum which, when combined, produce neutral gray.

Primary colors Colors that we cannot produce from mixing other hues; colors from which other colors are derived.

Secondary colors Colors derived from mixing primary colors.

FIGURE 3.9 **"ORANGE AND YELLOW"** Warm colors such as orange and yellow seem to advance toward the viewer, while cool colors such as blue and green seem to recede. The oranges and yellows of Rothko's painting seem to pulsate toward the observer.

FIGURE 3.10 **"HIGHWAY NO. 2"** The "warm" Sunoco sign in d'Arcangelo's painting leaps out toward the viewer, while the "cool" blue sky recedes into the distance.

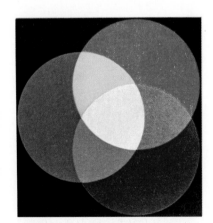

FIGURE 3.11 **ADDITIVE COLOR MIXTURES PRODUCED BY LIGHTS OF THREE COLORS: RED, GREEN, AND VIOLET-BLUE** In the early 1800s, British scientist Thomas Young discovered that white light and all the colors of the spectrum could be produced by adding various combinations of lights of three colors and varying their intensities.

the source of all color. Pigments reflect and absorb different wavelengths of light selectively. The mixture of lights is an *additive* process, while the mixture of pigments is *subtractive* (see Figure 3.11).

Pigments attain their colors by absorbing light from certain segments of the spectrum and reflecting the rest. For example, we see most plant life as green because the pigment in chlorophyll absorbs most of the red, blue, and violet wavelengths of light. The remaining green is reflected. A red pigment absorbs most of the spectrum but reflects red. White pigments reflect all colors equally. Black pigments reflect very little light; they absorb all colors without prejudice.

In works of art, complementary colors placed next to one another clash, and there seems to be a pulsating where they meet. Note Richard Anuszkiewicz's painting, "Entrance to Green" (Figure 3.12). If you look at the picture from a foot or so away and allow your eyes to relax, you are likely to perceive vibrations in the areas of the lines separating the reddish and greenish colors.

Primary, Secondary, and Tertiary Colors   The pigments of red, blue, and yellow are the **primary colors**—those that we cannot produce by mixing pigments of other hues. **Secondary colors** are created by mixing pigments of primary colors. The three secondary colors are orange (derived from

FIGURE 3.12 **"ENTRANCE TO GREEN"** In works of art, there seems to be a pulsating where complementary colors come together. If you look at Anuszkiewicz's painting for a while from a foot or so away, you are likely to perceive vibrations where the red and green meet. So-called Op Art works rely on vibrations and other visual responses for their effect.

mixing red and yellow), green (blue and yellow), and purple (red and blue). **Tertiary colors** are created by mixing pigments of primary and adjoining secondary colors, as in the cases of yellow-green and bluish-purple.

In his "Sunday Afternoon on the Island of La Grande Jatte" (Figure 3.13), French painter Georges Seurat molded his figures and forms from dabs of pure and complementary colors. Instead of mixing his pigments, he placed points of pure color next to one another. The sensations are of pure color when the painting is viewed from very close (see detail, Figure 3.13); however, from a distance, the juxtaposition of pure colors creates the impression of mixtures of color.

Tertiary colors Colors derived from mixing primary and adjoining secondary colors.

FIGURE 3.13 **"SUNDAY AFTERNOON ON THE ISLAND OF LA GRANDE JATTE"** The French painter Seurat molded his figures and forms from dabs of pure and complementary colors. Up close, the dabs of pure color are visible. From afar, they create the impression of color mixtures. (The Art Institute of Chicago. Helen Birch Bartlett Memorial Collection)

Afterimages Before reading on, why don't you try a brief experiment? Look at the strangely colored American flag in Figure 3.14 for at least half a minute. Then look at a sheet of white or gray paper. What has happened to the flag? If your color vision is working properly, and if you looked at the miscolored flag long enough, you should see a flag composed of the familiar red, white, and blue. The flag you perceive on the white sheet of paper is an **afterimage** of the first. (If you didn't look at the green, black, and yellow flag long enough the first time, you may wish to try it again. It will work any number of times.)

In afterimages, persistent sensations of color are followed by perception of the complementary color when the first color is removed. (The same holds true for black and white; staring at one will create an afterimage of the others. Stare at d'Arcangelo's "Highway No. 2" [Figure 3.10] for thirty seconds, then look at a sheet of white paper, and you are likely to perceive

Afterimage The lingering impression made by a stimulus that has been removed. The afterimage of red is green, and vice versa.

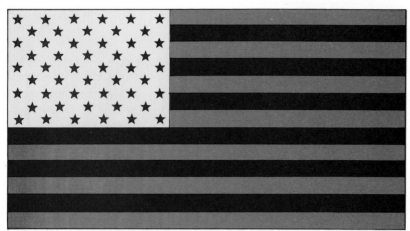

FIGURE 3.14 THREE CHEERS FOR THE GREEN, BLACK, AND YELLOW? Don't be concerned. We can readily restore Old Glory to its familiar hues. Place a sheet of white paper beneath the book, and then stare at the center of the flag for thirty seconds. Then remove the book. You will see a more familiar image on the paper beneath. This is an afterimage. Afterimages such as this led Ewald Hering to doubt the trichromatic theory of color vision and to propose the opponent-process theory in its place. The text points out that both theories have received some empirical support.

a black stripe down a white highway—along with a blue Sunoco sign and a yellow sky.) The phenomenon of afterimages has contributed to one of the theories of color vision, as we shall see later in the section.

Analogous Colors   **Analogous** hues lie next to one another on the color wheel, forming families of colors like yellow and orange, orange and red, and green and blue. As we work our way around the wheel, the families intermarry, as blue with violet and violet with red. Works of art that use closely related families of color seem harmonious, e.g., Rothko's "Orange and Yellow," which draws on the color family containing analogous oranges and yellows. The title of a Barnett Newman painting, "Who's Afraid of Red, Yellow, and Blue?" suggests the jarring effect that can be achieved by placing colors so far apart on the color wheel next to one another.

THEORIES OF COLOR VISION

Adults with normal color vision can discriminate up to 150 color differences across the visible spectrum (Bornstein & Marks, 1982). Different colors have different wavelengths. Although we can vary the physical wavelengths of light in a continuous manner, from shorter to longer, changes in color seem to be discontinuous, so that our perception of a color may shift suddenly from blue to green, even though the change in wavelength is smaller than that between two blues. Even though people from different cultures may classify colors in ways that seem strange to us (the primitive Hanunoo speak of "dark," "light," "dry," and "wet" colors), people from all cultural back-

Analogous Descriptive of colors that lie next to one another on the color wheel; similar or comparable.

Trichromatic theory (try-chrome-MAT-tick). The theory that color vision is made possible by three types of cones, some of which respond to red light, some to green, and some to blue.

Opponent-process theory The theory that color vision is made possible by three types of cones, some of which respond to red or green light, some to blue or yellow, and some to the intensity of light only. Red-green cones would not be able to transmit sensations of red and green at the same time.

Microspectrophotometry (my-crow-speck-tro-foe-TOM-met-tree). A method of studying the sensitivity of cones to lights of different wavelengths. (Contains the following roots: the Greek *mikro*, meaning "small"; the Latin *spectrum*, meaning "appearance"; the Greek *photos*, meaning "light"; and the Greek *metron*, meaning "measure.")

grounds divide the regions of the visible spectrum into similar groupings that correspond to the reds, yellows, greens, and blues shown in Figure 3.1.

Our ability to perceive color depends on the eye's transmission of different messages to the brain when lights of different wavelengths stimulate the cones in the retina. In this section we explore and evaluate two theories of how lights of different wavelengths are perceived as being of different colors: *trichromatic theory* and *opponent-process theory*. Then we discuss the problems of some individuals who are blind to some or all of the colors of the visible spectrum.

Trichromatic Theory   *Tri* is a word root meaning "three" (a tricycle has three wheels), and *chromatic* derives from the Greek *chroma*, meaning "color." **Trichromatic theory** is based on an experiment that was run by British scientist Thomas Young in the early 1800s. As in Figure 3.11, Young projected three lights of different colors onto a screen so that they partly overlapped. He found that he could create any color from the visible spectrum by simply varying the intensities of the lights. When all three lights fell on the same spot, they created white light, or the appearance of no color at all. The three lights manipulated by Young were red, green, and blue-violet.

German physiologist Hermann von Helmholtz saw in Young's discovery an explanation of color vision. Von Helmholtz suggested that the eye must have three different types of photoreceptors or cones. Some must be sensitive to red light, some to green, and some to blue. We see other colors when two different types of color receptors are stimulated. The perception of yellow, for example, would result from the simultaneous stimulation of receptors for red and green. Trichromatic theory is also known as the Young-Helmholtz theory, after Thomas Young and Hermann von Helmholtz.

Opponent-Process Theory   In 1870, Ewald Hering proposed the **opponent-process theory** of color vision. Opponent-process theory also holds that there are three types of color receptors, but they are not theorized to be red, green, and blue. Hering suggested that afterimages (as of the "American flag" shown in Figure 3.14) are made possible by three types of color receptors: red-green, blue-yellow, and a type that perceives differences in brightness from light to dark. A red-green cone could not transmit messages for red and green at the same time. Hering would perhaps have said that when you were staring at the green, black, and yellow flag for thirty seconds, you were disturbing the balance of neural activity. The afterimage of red, white, and blue would then have represented the eye's attempt to reestablish a balance.

Evaluation   Both theories of color vision may be partially correct (Hurvich & Jameson, 1974; Hurvich, 1978). Research with **microspectrophotometry** supports trichromatic theory. Microspectrophotometry is a modern method for analyzing the sensitivity of single cones to light of different wavelengths. This research shows that some cones are sensitive to blue, some to green, and some to yellow-red parts of the spectrum—consistent with trichromatic theory.

But studies of the bipolar and ganglion neurons suggest that messages from the cones are transmitted to the brain in an opponent-process fashion. Some neurons that transmit messages to the visual centers in the brain, for example, are excited or "turned on" by green light but inhibited or "turned off" by red light. Others can be excited by red light but are inhibited by green light. It may be that there is then a "neural rebound effect" that would help explain afterimages. With such an effect, a green-sensitive ganglion that had been excited by green light for half a minute or so might switch briefly to inhibitory activity when the light is shut off. The effect would be to perceive red, even though no red light were being shone (Haber & Hershenson, 1980).

These theoretical updates allow for the afterimage effects with the green, black, and yellow flag, and are also consistent with Young's experiments in mixing lights of different colors.

COLOR BLINDNESS

If you can discriminate the colors of the visible spectrum, you have normal color vision and are labeled a **trichromat.** This means that you are sensitive to red-green, blue-yellow, and light-dark. People who are totally color-blind are called **monochromats** and are sensitive to light-dark only. Total color blindness is quite rare. The fully color-blind see the world as trichromats would on a black-and-white television set or in a black-and-white movie.

Partial color blindness is more common than total color blindness. Partial color blindness is a sex-linked trait that strikes mostly males. The partially color-blind are called **dichromats.** Dichromats can discriminate only two colors, red and green, or blue and yellow, and the colors that are derived from mixing these colors. Figure 3.15 shows the types of tests that are used to diagnose color blindness. See also Figure 3.16.

A dichromat might put on one red sock and one green sock, but would not mix red and blue socks. Monochromats might put on socks of any color. They would not notice a difference so long as the socks did not differ in intensity, or brightness.

When we selectively breed cats and dogs, we are interested in producing coats of certain colors. But if cats and dogs bred human beings, they would not be concerned about our color, because cats and dogs are monochromats.

VISUAL PERCEPTION

Perception, as noted, is the process by which we organize or make sense of our sensory impressions. While visual sensations are caused by electromagnetic energy, visual perception also relies on our knowledge, expectations, and motivations. While sensation may be thought of as a mechanical process, perception is an active process by which we interpret the world around us.

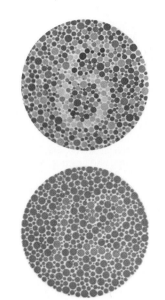

FIGURE 3.15 **PLATES FROM A TEST FOR COLOR BLINDNESS** Can you see the numbers in these illustrations? A person with red-green color blindness would not be able to see the 6, and a person with blue-yellow color blindness would probably not discern the 12. (Caution: These reproductions cannot be used for actual testing of color blindness.)

Trichromat A person with normal color vision.

Monochromat A person who is sensitive to black and white only, and hence color-blind.

Dichromat A person who is sensitive to black-white and red-green or blue-yellow, and hence partially color-blind.

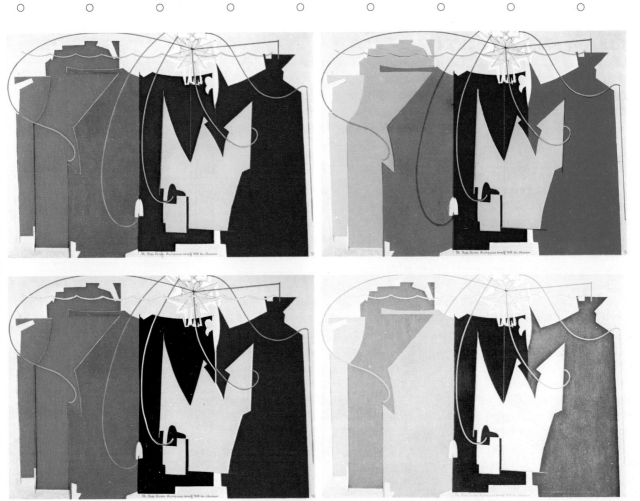

FIGURE 3.16 COLORBLINDNESS The painting in the upper left panel—Man Ray, "The Rope Dancer Accompanies Herself with Her Shadows"—appears as it would to a person with normal color vision. If you suffered from red-green blindness, the same picture would be seen as it is in the upper right panel. Similarly, the lower left and lower right panels show how the picture would look to persons with yellow-blue or total colorblindness, respectively. (Museum of Modern Art, New York. Gift of G. David Thompson)

For example, just what do you see in Figure 3.17? Random splotches of ink or a rider on horseback? If you perceive a horse and rider, it is not just because of the visual sensations provided by the drawing. Each of the blobs is meaningless in and of itself, and the pattern they form is also less than clear. Despite the lack of clarity, however, you may still perceive a horse and rider. Why? The answer has to do with your general knowledge and your desire to fit bits of information into familiar patterns.

With "horse and rider," your integration of disconnected shards of information into a meaningful whole also reflects what Gestalt psychologists refer to as the principle of **closure,** or the tendency to perceive a complete or whole figure, even when there are gaps in the sensory input. That is, in perception the whole can be much more than the sum of the parts. Collecting parts alone can be meaningless; it is their configuration that matters.

Closure The tendency to perceive a broken figure as complete or whole.

PERCEPTUAL ORGANIZATION

Earlier in the century Gestalt psychologists noted consistencies in our integration of bits and pieces of sensory stimulation into meaningful wholes and attempted to formulate rules that governed these processes. Max Wertheimer, in particular, discovered many such rules. As a group, these rules are referred to as the laws of **perceptual organization.** Let us examine a number of these rules, beginning with those concerning figure-ground perception.

Figure-Ground Perception   If you look out your window, you may see people, buildings, cars and streets, or perhaps grass, trees, birds, and clouds. In any event, the objects about you tend to be perceived as figures against backgrounds. Cars against the background of the street are easier to pick out than cars piled on each other in a junkyard. Birds against the sky are more likely to be perceived than, as the saying goes, birds in the bush. Figures are closer to us than their grounds.

When figure-ground relationships are **ambiguous,** or capable of being interpreted in different ways, our perceptions tend to be unstable, to shift back and forth. As an example, take a look at Figure 3.18—a nice leisurely look. How many people, objects, and animals can you find in this Escher

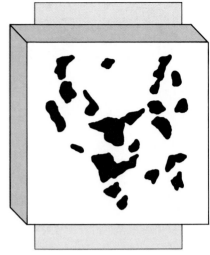

FIGURE 3.17 CLOSURE Meaningless splotches of ink or a horse and rider? This figure illustrates the Gestalt principle of closure.

Perceptual organization The tendency to integrate perceptual elements into meaningful patterns.

Ambiguous (am-BIG-you-us). Having two or more possible meanings. (From the Latin *ambigere,* meaning "to wander.")

FIGURE 3.18 How many animals and demons can you find in this Escher print? Do we have white figures on a black background, or black figures on a white background? Figure-ground perception is the tendency to perceive geometric forms against a background.

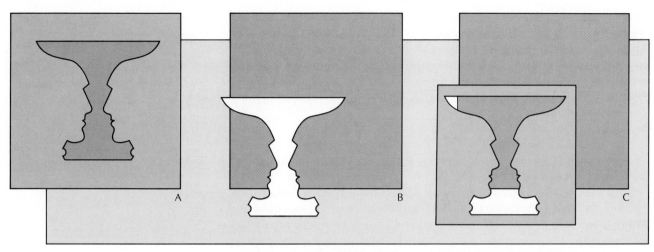

FIGURE 3.19 **THE RUBIN VASE** A favorite drawing used by psychologists to demonstrate figure-ground perception. Part *A* is ambiguous, with neither white nor black clearly figure or ground. In *B* and *C* the white areas are clearly the figures.

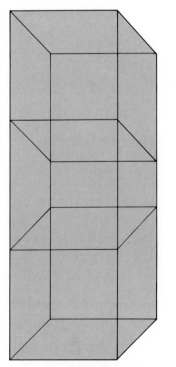

FIGURE 3.20 **A STACK OF NECKER CUBES** Ambiguity in the drawing of the cubes makes perceptual shifts possible.

print? If your eye is drawn back and forth, so that sometimes you are perceiving light figures on a dark background, and then dark figures on a light background, you are experiencing figure-ground reversals. That is, a shift is occurring in your perception of what is figure and what is ground, or backdrop. Escher was able to have some fun with us because of our tendency to try to isolate geometric patterns or figures from a background. However, in this case the "background" is as meaningful and detailed as the "figure." Therefore, our perceptions shift back and forth.

The Rubin Vase   In Figure 3.19 we see a Rubin vase, one of psychologists' favorite illustrations of figure-ground relationships. Note that the figure-ground relationship in part A of the figure is ambiguous. There are no cues that suggest which area, the white or the black, must be the figure. For this reason, our perception may shift from seeing the vase as the figure and then seeing two profiles as the figure.

There is no such problem in part B. Since it seems that a white vase has been brought forward against a black ground, we are more likely to perceive the vase than the profiles. In part C we are again more likely to perceive the profiles than the vase, because the figure seems to lie in the white square, and also because the vase is broken into patches of black and white. Of course, we can still perceive the vase in part C if we wish to, because prior experience has shown us where it is. Why not have fun with some friends by covering parts B and C and asking them what they see? (They'll catch on to you quickly if they can see all three drawings at once.)

The Necker Cube   The Necker cube (Figure 3.20) provides another example of how an ambiguous drawing can lead to perceptual shifts.

Hold this page at arm's length and stare at the center of the figure for thirty seconds or so. Try to allow your eye muscles to relax. (The feeling is of your eyes "glazing over.") After a while you will notice a dramatic shift in your perception of these "stacked boxes," so that what was once a front edge is now a back edge, and vice versa. Again, the dramatic perceptual shift is made possible by the fact that the outline of the drawing permits two interpretations.

Some Other Gestalt Rules for Organization

In addition to the law of closure, Gestalt psychologists have noted that our perceptions are guided by rules or laws of *proximity, similarity, continuity,* and *common fate,*

Verbally describe part A of Figure 3.21 without reading further. Did you say that part A consisted of six lines or of three groups of two (parallel) lines? If you said three sets of lines, you were influenced by the **proximity,** or nearness, of some of the lines. There is no other reason for perceiving them in pairs or subgroups: all lines are parallel and of equal length.

Now describe part B of the figure. Did you perceive the figure as a six by six grid, or as three columns of x's and three columns of o's? According to the law of **similarity,** we perceive similar objects as belonging together. For this reason, you may have been more likely to describe part B in terms of columns than rows or a grid.

What about part C? Is it a circle with two lines stemming from it, or is it a (broken) line that goes through a circle? If you saw it as a single (broken) line, you were probably organizing your perceptions according to the rule of **continuity.** That is, we perceive a series of points or a broken line as having unity.

According to the law of **common fate,** elements seen moving together are perceived as belonging together. A group of people running in the same direction appear unified in purpose. Birds flying together seem to be of a feather. (Did I get that right?)

Proximity Nearness. The perceptual tendency to group together objects that are near one another. (From the Latin *proximus,* meaning "nearest.")

Similarity The perceptual tendency to group together objects that are similar in appearance.

Continuity The tendency to perceive a series of points or lines as having unity.

Common fate The tendency to perceive elements that move together as belonging together (birds that flock together are assumed to be of a feather).

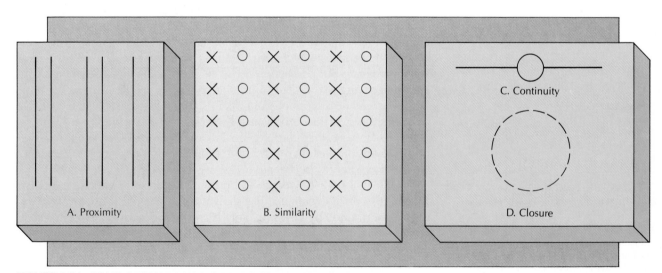

FIGURE 3.21 SOME GESTALT LAWS OF PERCEPTUAL ORGANIZATION

Part D of Figure 3.21 provides another example of the law of closure. The arcs tend to be perceived as a circle, or circle with gaps, rather than as just a series of arcs.

PERCEPTION OF MOVEMENT

It is extremely important that we be able to perceive movement. Moving objects—whether other people, animals, cars, or tons of earth plummeting down a hillside—harbor the potential for powerful rewards and punishments. As noted in Chapter 8, moving objects capture the attention of even newborn infants.

In order to understand how we perceive movement, recall what it is like to be on a train that has begun to pull out of the station while the train on the adjacent track remains stationary. If your own train does not lurch as it accelerates, you might think at first that the other train is moving. Or you might not be certain whether your train is moving forward or the other train is moving backward.

The visual perception of movement is based on change of position relative to other objects. To early scientists, whose only instrument for visual observation was the naked eye, it seemed logical that the sun circled the earth. You have to be able to imagine the movement of the earth around the sun as seen from a theoretical point in outer space—you cannot observe it directly.

So, how do you determine which train is moving when your train is pulling out of the station (or that other train is pulling in!)? One way is to look for objects you know are stable, like station platform columns, houses, signs, or trees. If you are stationary in relation to them, your train is not moving. But observing people walking on the station platform may not provide the answer, since they are also changing their position relative to stationary objects. You might also try to sense the motion of the train in your body. You would know from experience how to do these things quite well, although it might be more difficult to phrase explanations for them.

We have been considering the perception of real movement. Psychologists have also studied several types of apparent movement, or **illusions** of movement. These incluse the *autokinetic effect, stroboscopic motion,* and the *phi phenomenon.*

The Autokinetic Effect   If you were to sit quietly in a dark room and stare at a point of light projected onto the far wall, after a while it might appear that the light had begun to move, even if it remained quite still. The tendency to perceive a stationary point of light as moving in a dark room is called the **autokinetic effect.**

In one interesting experiment on the autokinetic effect (Block & Block, 1951), subjects were asked to judge how far the point of light moved. They provided estimates over a series of trials. The light, of course, did not move at all. Prejudiced subjects arrived at their final judgments more rapidly than nonprejudiced subjects. They were quicker to jump to their conclusion, given the same (erroneous) evidence.

Illusions Sensations that give rise to misperceptions. (From the Latin ''illudere,'' meaning ''to mock'' or ''to play with.'')

Autokinetic effect The tendency to perceive a stationary point of light in a dark room as moving. (From the Greek *autos,* meaning ''self,'' and *kinein,* meaning ''to move.'')

FIGURE 3.22 **STROBOSCOPIC MOTION** In a motion picture, viewing a series of stationary images at the rate of about sixteen to twenty-two per second provides the illusion of movement. This form of apparent movement is termed stroboscopic motion.

Stroboscopic Motion In **stroboscopic motion,** the illusion of movement is provided by the presentation of a rapid progression of images of stationary objects (Beck et al., 1977). In a sense, a motion picture does not move at all. Motion pictures do not consist of images that move. Rather, the audience is shown sixteen to twenty-two pictures or frames per second, like those in Figure 3.22. Each frame differs slightly from that preceding it. Showing them in rapid succession then provides the illusion of movement.

At the rate of at least sixteen frames per second, the "motion" in a film seems smooth and natural. With fewer than sixteen or so frames per second, the movement looks jumpy and unnatural. That is why slow motion is achieved through filming perhaps 100 or more frames per second. When they are played back at about twenty-two frames per second, movement seems slowed down, yet smooth and natural.

The Phi Phenomenon Have you ever seen one of those huge electronic "scoreboards" in a baseball or football stadium? When the hometeam scores, some of them seem to be shooting off fireworks. What actually happens is that a row of lights is switched on, then off. As the first row is switched off, the second row is switched on, and so on for dozens, perhaps hundreds of rows. When the switching occurs rapidly, the **phi phenomenon** occurs: the on-off process is perceived as movement.

Like stroboscopic motion, the phi phenomenon is an example of apparent motion. Both stroboscopic motion and the phi phenomenon appear to occur because of the law of continuity. We tend to perceive a series of points as having unity, and so the series of lights (points) is perceived as moving lines.

DEPTH PERCEPTION

Think of the problems you might have if you could not judge depth or distance. You might bump into other people, thinking them farther away than they are. An outfielder might not be able to judge whether to run toward the infield or the fence to catch a fly ball. You might give your front bumper a workout in stop-and-go traffic. Fortunately, both *monocular and binocular cues* help us perceive the depth of objects. Let us examine a number of them.

Monocular Cues Now that you have considered how difficult it would be to navigate through life without depth perception, ponder the problems

Stroboscopic motion A visual illusion in which the perception of motion is generated by a series of stationary images that are presented in rapid succession. (From the Greek *strobos,* meaning "twisted around," and *skopein,* meaning "to see.")

Phi phenomenon (fye or fee). The perception of movement as a result of visual stimuli arranged in consecutive order, as with lights going on and off on theater marquees or electronic scoreboards.

"Excuse me for shouting, I thought you were further away."

"I'll explain it to you, Stevie. It's called perspective."

of the artist who attempts to portray three-dimensional objects on a two-dimensional canvas. Artists use **monocular cues,** or cues that can be perceived by one eye, to create an illusion of depth. These cues—including perspective, clearness, interposition, shadows, and texture gradient—cause certain objects to appear more distant from the viewer than others.

Distant objects stimulate smaller areas on the retina than nearby objects. The sensory input from them is smaller, even though they may be the same size. The distances between far-off objects also appear smaller than equivalent distances between nearby objects. For this reason, the phenomenon known as **perspective** occurs; that is, we tend to perceive parallel lines as coming closer, or converging, as they recede from us. However, as we shall see when we discuss *size constancy,* experience teaches us that distant objects that look small will be larger when they are close by. In this way, their relative size also becomes a cue as to their distance from us.

The two engravings in Figure 3.23 represent impossible scenes in which the artists use principles of perspective to fool the viewer. In the engraving to the left, "Waterfall," note that the water appears to be flowing away from the viewer in a zigzag, because the stream becomes gradually narrower (that is, lines that we assume to be parallel are shown to be converging) and the stone sides of the aqueduct appear to be stepping down. However, given that the water arrives at the top of the fall, it must actually somehow be flowing upward. However, the spot from which it falls is no farther from the viewer than is the collection point from which it appears to (but does not) begin its flow backward.

FIGURE 3.23 **TWO IMPOSSIBLE ENGRAVINGS** In "Waterfall," to the left, how does Dutch artist M. C. Escher suggest that fallen water flows back upward, only to fall again? In "False Perspective," to the right, how did English artist William Hogarth use monocular cues for depth perception to deceive the viewer?

FIGURE 3.24 **"CHEZT-YORD"** How does Op Artist Victor Vasarely use monocular cues for depth perception to lend this picture a three-dimensional quality?

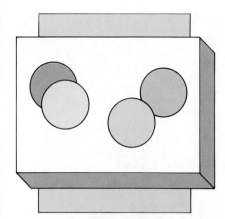

FIGURE 3.25 THE EFFECTS OF INTER-POSITION The four circles are all the same size. Which circles appear closer? The complete circles or the circles with chunks bitten out of them?

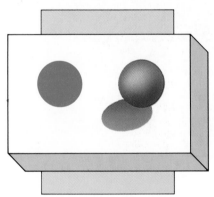

FIGURE 3.26 SHADOWING AS A CUE IN THE PERCEPTION OF DEPTH

Interposition A monocular cue for depth based on the fact that a nearby object obscures vision of a more distant object behind it.

Shadowing A monocular cue for depth based on the fact that opaque objects block light and produce shadows.

Texture gradient A monocular cue for depth based on the perception that closer objects appear to have rougher (more detailed) surfaces.

Motion parallax A monocular cue for depth based on the perception that nearby objects appear to move more rapidly in relation to our own motion. (From the Greek *para-*, meaning "alongside," and *allassein*, meaning "to change.")

Again, distant objects look smaller than nearby objects of the same size. The paradoxes in the engraving to the right, "False Perspective," are made possible by the fact that more distant objects are not necessarily depicted as being smaller than nearby objects. Thus, what at first seems to be background suddenly becomes foreground, and vice versa.

The clearness of an object also suggests its distance from us. Experience shows us that we sense more details of nearby objects. For this reason, artists can suggest that certain objects are closer to the viewer by depicting them in greater detail. Note that the "distant" hill in the Hogarth engraving (Figure 3.23) is given less detail than are the nearby plants at the bottom of the picture. Our perceptions are mocked when a man "on" that distant hill in the background is shown "conversing" with a woman leaning out a window in the middle ground. Note, too, how Vasarely uses clearness (crispness of line) to help provide a three-dimensional effect in "Chezt-Yord" (Figure 3.24).

We also learn that nearby objects can block our views of more distant objects. Overlapping, or **interposition,** is the apparent placing of one object in front of another. Experience encourages us to perceive the partly covered objects as being farther away than the objects that hide parts of them from view (Figure 3.25). In the Hogarth engraving (Figure 3.23), which looks closer: the trees in the background (background?) or the moon sign hanging from the building (or is it buildings?) to the right? How does the artist use interposition to confound the viewer?

Additional information about depth is provided by **shadowing,** and is based on the fact that opaque objects block light and produce shadows. Shadows and highlights give us information about the three-dimensional shapes of objects and about their relationships to the source of light. The left part of Figure 3.26 is perceived as a two-dimensional circle, but the right part tends to be perceived as a three-dimensional sphere because of the highlight on its surface and the shadow underneath. In the "sphere," the highlighted central area is perceived as closest to us, while the surface then recedes to the edges.

Another monocular cue is **texture gradient.** A gradient is a progressive change, and closer objects are perceived as having progressively rougher textures. In the Hogarth engraving (Figure 3.23), the building just behind the large fisherman's head has a rougher texture and thus seems closer than the building with the window from which the woman is leaning. Our surprise is thus heightened when the moon sign is shown as hanging from both buildings.

Motion Cues If you have ever driven in the country, you have probably noticed that distant objects, like mountains and stars, appear to move along with you. Objects at an intermediate distance seem stationary, but nearby objects, like roadside markers, rocks, and trees, seem to go by quite rapidly. The tendency of objects to seem to move backward or forward as a function of their distance is known as **motion parallax.** We learn to perceive objects that appear to move with us as being at greater distances.

Earlier we noted that nearby objects cause the lens to accommodate or bend more to bring them into focus. The sensations of tension in the eye

A CLOSER LOOK

TO PERCEIVE THE IMPOSSIBLE DRAWING

What's wrong with each of these drawings? Each has firm lines. Each has interesting shapes. In fact, if you look at just one corner of any of the drawings, it makes perfect sense. But take a critical view of the endless staircase in M. C. Escher's "Relativity," at the right. What would happen if you were ever to start walking up this staircase? Would you ever reach the top? Or what would happen if a ball rolled down these stairs and managed to turn all the corners? Would it ever reach bottom?

In each case the artist, working in two dimensions, has used perceptual cues carefully to encourage us to perceive a three-dimensional figure. Note that any one segment of each of these drawings makes perfect sense. It's just when you put it all together that you realize that . . . well, you can't put it all together, can you? That would be impossible.

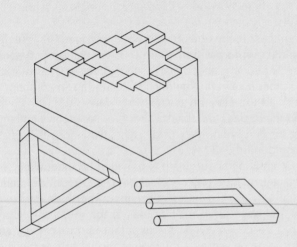

muscles also provide a monocular cue to depth, especially when we are within about four feet of the objects.

　　Binocular Cues　**Binocular cues,** or cues that involve both eyes, also help us perceive depth. Two binocular cues are *retinal disparity* and *convergence.*

　　Try a brief experiment. Hold your index finger at arm's length. Now gradually bring it closer, until it almost touches your nose. If you keep your eyes relaxed as you do so, you will see two fingers. An image of the finger will be projected onto the retina of each eye, and each image will be slightly different since the finger will be seen at different angles. The difference between the projected images is referred to as **retinal disparity,** and serves as a binocular cue for depth perception (see Figure 3.27). Note that the closer your finger comes, the farther apart the "two fingers" appear. Closer objects have greater retinal disparity.

　　If we try to maintain a single image of the approaching finger, our eyes must turn inward, or converge on it, giving us a "cross-eyed" look.

Binocular cues Stimuli suggestive of depth that involve simultaneous perception by both eyes.

Retinal disparity A binocular cue for depth based on the difference of the image cast by an object on the retinas of the eyes as the object moves closer or farther away.

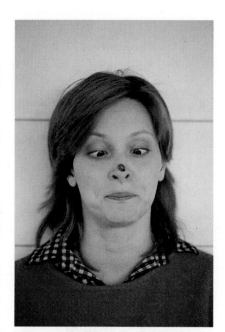

FIGURE 3.27 **RETINAL DISPARITY AND CONVERGENCE AS DEPTH CUES** As an object nears your eyes, you begin to see two images of it due to retinal disparity. If you maintain perception of a single image, your eyes must converge on the object.

Convergence is associated with feelings of tension in the eye muscles and provides another binocular cue for depth. The binocular cues of retinal disparity and convergence are strongest at near distances.

PERCEPTUAL CONSTANCIES

The world is a constantly shifting display of visual sensations. What confusion would reign if we did not perceive a doorway to be the same doorway when seen from six feet as when seen from four feet. As we neared it, we might think that it was larger than the door we were seeking and become lost. Or consider the problems of the pet owner who recognizes his dog from the side, but not from above, when the shapes differ. Fortunately, these problems tend not to occur—at least with familiar objects—because of perceptual constancies.

The image of a dog seen from twenty feet occupies about the same amount of space on your retina as an inch-long insect crawling in the palm of your hand. Yet you would not perceive the dog or cat to be as small as the insect. Through your experiences you have acquired **size constancy,** or the tendency to perceive the same object as being the same size, even though the size of its image on the retina varies as a function of its distance. Experience teaches us about perspective, that the same object seen at a great distance will appear much smaller than when it is nearby. We may joke that people or cars look like ants from airplanes, but we know that they remain people and cars. For this reason, we can say that we *perceive* them to be the same size from great distances, even though the sensory input stimulates many fewer neurons on the retina.

A case study emphasizes the role of experience in the development of size constancy. Anthropologist Colin Turnbull (1961) found that an African Pygmy, Kenge, thought that buffalo perceived across an open field were some form of insect. Turnbull had to drive Kenge down to where the animals were grazing in order to convince him that they were not insects. During the drive, as the buffalo gradually grew in size, Kenge muttered to himself and moved closer to Turnbull in fear. But even after Kenge saw that these animals were, indeed, familiar buffalo, he still wondered how they could grow large so quickly. Kenge, you see, lived in a thick forest and normally did not view large animals from great distances. For this reason he had not developed size constancy for distant objects. However, Kenge would have had no difficulty displaying size constancy with objects placed at various distances in his home.

We also have **color constancy,** or the tendency to perceive objects as retaining their color even though lighting conditions may alter their appearance. Your bright orange car may edge toward yellow-gray as the hours wend their way through twilight to nighttime. But when you finally locate it in the parking lot you will still think of it as orange. You expect an orange car and still judge it "more orange" than the (faded) blue and green cars to either side. However, it would be fiercely difficult to find it in a parking lot filled with yellow and red cars similar in size and shape.

Consider Figure 3.28. The orange squares within the blue squares are the same hue. However, the orange within the dark blue square is perceived

Convergence A binocular cue for depth based on the inward movement of the eyes as they attempt to focus on an object that is drawing nearer.

Size constancy The tendency to perceive an object as being the same size even as the size of its retinal image changes according to its distance.

Color constancy The tendency to perceive an object as being the same color even as lighting conditions change its appearance.

as purer. Why? Again, experience teaches us that the pureness of colors fades as the background grows darker. Since the orange squares are equally pure, we assume that the one in the dark background must be more saturated; we would stand ready to perceive the orange squares as equal in pureness if the square within the darker blue field actually had a bit of black mixed in with it.

Similar to color constancy is **brightness constancy.** As noted in Chapter 1, the same gray square is perceived as brighter when placed within a black background than when placed within a white background (see Figure 1.3 on p. 20). Again, consider the role of experience. If it were nighttime, we would expect gray to fade to near blackness. But the fact that the gray within the black square stimulates the eye with equal intensity suggests that it must be very much brighter than the gray within the white square.

We also perceive objects as maintaining their shapes, even if we perceive them from different angles so that the shape of the retinal image changes dramatically. This tendency is called **shape constancy.** You perceive the top of a coffee cup or a glass to be a circle, even though it is a circle when seen from above only. When seen from an angle, it is an ellipse. When seen on edge, the retinal image of the cup or glass is the same as that of a straight line. So why would you still describe the rim of the cup or glass as a circle? Perhaps for two reasons: One is that experience has taught you that the cup will look circular when seen from above. The second is that you may have labeled the cup as circular or round. Experience and labels make the world a stable place. Can you imagine the chaos that would prevail if we described objects as they stimulated our sensory organs with each changing moment, rather than according to stable conditions?

In another example, a door is a rectangle only when viewed straight on (Figure 3.29). When we move to the side or open it, the left or right edge comes closer and appears larger, changing the retinal image to a trapezoid. Yet we continue to think of doors as being rectangles.

VISUAL ILLUSIONS

The principles of perceptual organization make it possible for "our eyes to play tricks on us." Psychologists, like magicians, enjoy pulling a rabbit out of the hat now and then, and I am pleased to be able to demonstrate how the perceptual constancies trick the eye through the so-called visual illusions.

The Hering-Helmholtz and Müller-Lyer illusions (Figure 3.30) are named after the people who originated them. In the Hering-Helmholtz illusion (Figure 3.30, part A), the horizontal lines are straight and parallel. However, the radiating lines cause them to appear bent outward near the center. The two lines in the Müller-Lyer illusion are the same length, but the line on the left, with its reversed arrow heads, looks longer.

Let us try to explain the Hering-Helmholtz and Müller-Lyer illusions. Because of experience and lifelong use of perceptual cues, we tend to perceive the Hering-Helmholtz drawing as three-dimensional. Because of the tendency to perceive bits of sensory information as figures against grounds, we perceive the white area in the center as a circle in front of a series of

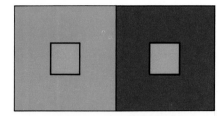

FIGURE 3.28 COLOR CONSTANCY
The orange squares within the blue squares are the same hue, yet the orange within the dark blue square is perceived as purer. Why?

Brightness constancy The tendency to perceive an object as being just as bright even though lighting conditions change its intensity.

Shape constancy The tendency to perceive an object as being the same shape although the retinal image varies in shape as it rotates.

FIGURE 3.29 SHAPE CONSTANCY
When closed, this door is a rectangle. When open, the retinal image is trapezoidal. But due to shape constancy, we still perceive the door as rectangular.

radiating lines, all of which lies in front of a white ground. Next, because of our experience with perspective, we perceive the radiating lines as parallel. We perceive the two horizontal lines as intersecting the "receding" lines, and we know that they would have to appear bent out at the center if they were to be equidistant at all points from the center of the circle.

Experience probably compels us to perceive the vertical lines in the Müller-Lyer illusion as the corners of a room as seen from inside a house, at left, and outside a house, at right (see Figure 3.30, part B). In such an example, the reverse arrowheads to the left are lines where the walls meet the ceiling and the floor. We perceive the lines as extending toward us; they push the corner away from us. The arrowheads to the right are lines where exterior walls meet the roof and foundation. We perceive them as receding from us; they push the corner toward us. The vertical line to the

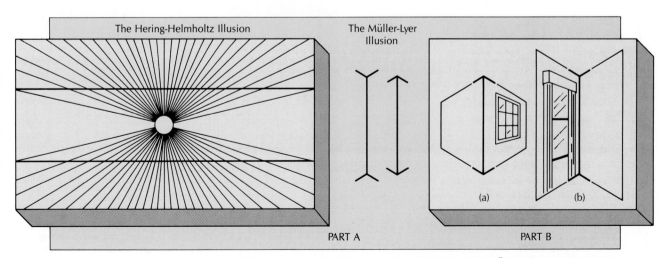

FIGURE 3.30 THE HERING-HELMHOLTZ AND MÜLLER-LYER ILLUSIONS

left is thus perceived as farther away. Since both vertical lines stimulate equal expanses across the retina, the principle of size constancy encourages us to perceive the line to the left as longer.

Figure 3.31 is known as the Ponzo illusion. In this illusion, the two horizontal lines are the same length. But do you perceive the top line as being longer? The rule of size constancy may also afford insight into this illusion. Perhaps the converging lines again strike us as parallel lines receding into the distance, like the train tracks in the cartoon on page 138. If so, we assume from experience that the horizontal line at the top is farther "down" the "track"—farther away from us. And again, the rule of size constancy tells us that if two objects appear to be the same size, and one is farther away, the farther object must be larger. So we perceive the top line as larger.

Now that you are an expert on explaining these visual illusions, look at Figure 3.32. First take some bets from friends as to whether all three cylinders are equal in height and width. Then get a ruler. Once you have made some money, however, try to explain why the cylinders to the right look progressively larger.

Now let us consider an illusion of movement. Figure 3.33, "Current," is an "optical art" painting by Bridget Riley. When you fix your gaze on any point in the painting, the surrounding areas seem to be in motion. "Current," like many other works of optical art, uses pictorial features to create the illusion of motion. In this case, the pictorial feature is a moiré

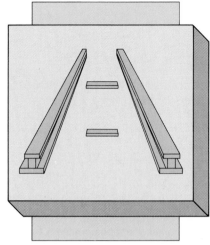

FIGURE 3.31 **THE PONZO ILLUSION** The two horizontal lines in this drawing are equal in length, but the top line is perceived as longer. Can you use the principle of size constancy to explain why?

FIGURE 3.32 **AN ILLUSION CREATED BY THE PRINCIPLE OF SIZE CONSTANCY** In this drawing, the three cylinders are the same size, yet they appear to grow larger toward the top of the picture. Can you use the principle of size constancy to explain why?

FIGURE 3.33 **"CURRENT"** In this Op Art painting by Bridget Riley, the illusion of movement is created with a moiré pattern. (Museum of Modern Art, New York. Philip Johnson Fund)

fox	_____
wolf	_____
puma	_____
deer	_____
bear	_____
beaver	_____

FIGURE 3.34 Briefly define each of the words in this list. Then turn to Figure 3.37 on page 141.

Auditory Having to do with hearing. (From the Latin *audire,* meaning "to hear." What is meant by "auditing" a course?)

pattern in which nearly identical wavy lines are placed next to each other. It is nearly impossible to perceive the continuity of any one line in the picture. Instead, our gaze tends to hop back and forth from line to line. The hopping back and forth leads to the perception of vibrations in the lines, and hence movement.

Speaking of vibrations, the time has come to discuss a way in which we can sense vibrations in the air: hearing.

HEARING

Consider the advertising slogan for the science fiction film *Alien:* "In space, no one can hear you scream." It's true. For space is an almost perfect vacuum, and hearing requires a medium, like air or water, through which sound can travel.

Sound, or **auditory** stimulation, travels through the air like waves. Sound is caused by changes in air pressure that result from vibrations. These vibrations, in turn, can be created by a tuning fork, your vocal cords, guitar strings, or the clap of a book thrown down on a desk.

Figure 3.35 suggests the way in which a tuning fork creates sound waves. During a vibration back and forth, the right prong of the tuning fork moves to the right. In so doing, it pushes together, or compresses, the molecules of air immediately to the right. Then the prong moves back to the left, and the air molecules to the right expand. By vibrating back and forth, the tuning fork actually sends air waves in many directions. A cycle

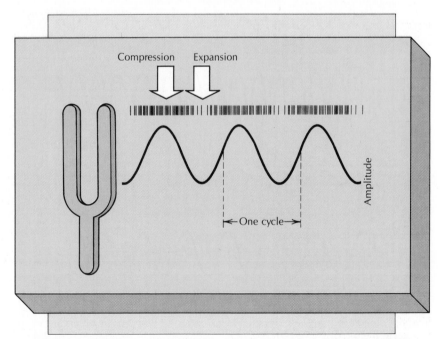

FIGURE 3.35 **CREATION OF SOUND WAVES** The vibration of the prongs of a tuning fork alternately compresses and expands air molecules, sending forth waves of sound.

of compression and expansion is considered one wave of sound. Sound waves can occur many times in one second. The human ear is sensitive to sound waves that vary from frequencies of 20 to 20,000 cycles per second.

PITCH AND LOUDNESS

Frequency   The frequency of a sound, or the number of cycles per second, is expressed in the unit **Hertz,** abbreviated *Hz*. One cycle per second is one Hz. The greater the number of cycles per second (Hz), the higher the **pitch** of the sound. The pitch of women's voices is usually higher than those of men, because women's vocal cords are usually shorter than those of men and consequently vibrate at a greater frequency. The strings of a violin are shorter than those of a viola or bass viol. They vibrate at greater frequencies, and we perceive them as higher in pitch.

Amplitude   The loudness of a sound is determined by the height, or amplitude, of sound waves. The higher the amplitude of the wave, the greater the loudness. Figure 3.36 shows records of sound waves that vary

Hertz (hurts). A unit expressing the frequency of sound waves, named after the German physicist Heinrich Hertz. One Hertz, or *1 Hz*, equals one cycle per second.

Pitch The highness or lowness of a sound, as determined by the frequency of the sound waves. (The voice of a soprano is higher in pitch, but not necessarily in loudness, than that of a bass singer.)

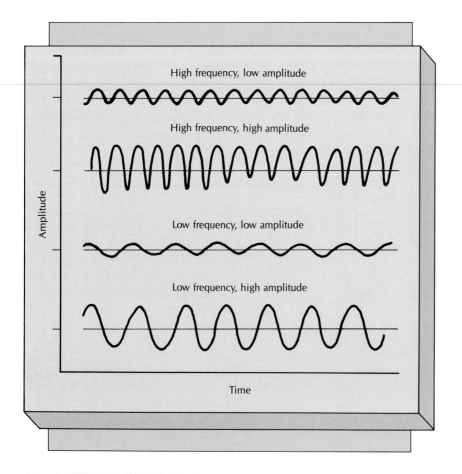

FIGURE 3.36 **SOUND WAVES OF DIFFERENT FREQUENCIES AND AMPLITUDES** Which sounds have the highest pitch? Which are loudest?

FIGURE 3.37

Use each of the words in the following list in a brief sentence:

endure _____

cope _____

carry _____

lift _____

bear _____

manage _____

How did you use the word *bear*? Would you have used it in the same way if the list had been the one shown in Figure 3.34?

If you defined *bear* as an animal in Figure 3.34 (p. 139), you may have been influenced by the context of the word. After all, the words above and below in Fig-

ure 3.34 were names of animals. But in the present list, the word *bear* was among several verbs suggestive of carrying burdens. So it would not be surprising if your short sentence involved "bearing a burden" of some kind or other.

Our perception of sensory stimulation is influenced by the context of the stimulation as well as the stimulation itself. The word *bear* is rough and wooly only in the forest. The context of a stimulus creates an expectation about the meaning of the stimulus. Gestalt psychologists refer to such expectations as *sets*.

Would you like another example? Read the following words aloud rapidly: Macarthur, Macduff, Macbeth, Macintosh, Macpherson, Machine. (Now rewrite the words and try it on a friend.)

Decibel A unit expressing the loudness of a sound. (From the Latin *deci-*, meaning "tenth," and *bel*, named for Alexander Graham Bell.) Abbreviated *dB*.

Consonant In harmony. (From the Latin *con-*, meaning "with," and *sonus*, meaning "sound.")

Dissonant Incompatible, discordant. Not in harmony. (From the Latin *dis-*, meaning "the opposite of.")

Overtones Tones of a higher frequency than those played. Overtones result from vibrations throughout a musical instrument.

Timbre (TIM-ber). The quality or richness of a sound. The quality that distinguishes the sounds of one musical instrument from those of another. (From the Greek *tympanon*, meaning "drum.")

in frequency and amplitude. Frequency and amplitude are independent dimensions. Sounds both high and low in pitch can be either high or low in loudness.

The loudness of a sound is usually expressed in the unit **decibel,** abbreviated *dB*, which is named after the inventor of the telephone, Alexander Graham Bell. Zero dB is equivalent to the threshold of hearing. How loud is that? About as loud as the ticking of a watch twenty feet away in a very quiet room (see Table 3.1).

The decibel equivalents of many familiar sounds are shown in Figure 3.38. Twenty dB is equivalent in loudness to a whisper at five feet. Thirty dB is roughly the limit of loudness at which your librarian would like to keep your college library. You may suffer hearing damage if exposed protractedly to sounds of 85–90 dB. In Chapter 14, we shall learn more about the effects of noise, and about "noise pollution."

When musical sounds (also called tones) of different frequency are played together, we also perceive a third tone that results from the difference in their frequencies. If the combination of tones is pleasant, we say that they are in harmony, or **consonant** (from Latin roots meaning "together" and "sound"). Unpleasant combinations of tones are labeled **dissonant** ("the opposite of" and "sound"). The expression that something "strikes a dissonant chord" means that we find it disagreeable.

Overtones and Timbre   In addition to producing the specified musical note, instruments like the violin also produce a number of tones that are greater in frequency. These more highly pitched sounds are called **overtones.** Overtones result from vibrations elsewhere in the instrument and contribute to the quality or richness—the **timbre**—of a sound. A $200 machine-made violin will produce the same musical notes as a $100,000 Stradivarius. But professional musicians require more expensive instruments because of the richness of their overtones—their timbre.

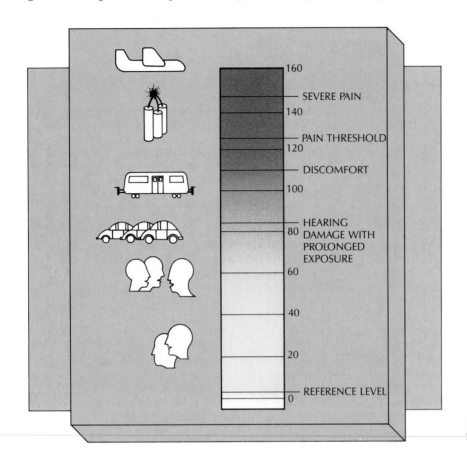

160

— SEVERE PAIN

140

— PAIN THRESHOLD

120

— DISCOMFORT

100

— HEARING
80 DAMAGE WITH
PROLONGED
EXPOSURE

60

40

20

— REFERENCE LEVEL
0

FIGURE 3.38 **DECIBEL RATINGS OF SOME FAMILIAR SOUNDS**

Noise   **Noise** is a combination of dissonant sounds. When you place a spiral shell to your ear, you do not hear the roar of the ocean. Rather, you hear the reflected noise in your vicinity. **White noise** consists of many different frequencies of sound. Yet white noise, this mixture, can lull us to sleep if the loudness is not too great.

Now let us turn our attention to the marvelous instrument that senses all these different "vibes": the human ear.

THE EAR

The human ear is good for lots of things—catching dust, combing your hair around, hanging jewelry from, and nibbling. It is also admirably suited for sensing auditory stimulation, or hearing. It is shaped and structured to capture sound waves, to vibrate in sympathy with them, and to transmit all this business to centers in the brain. In this way not only can you hear something, you can also figure out what it is.

You have an outer ear, a middle ear, and an inner ear. The outer ear is shaped to funnel, or channel, soundwaves to the **eardrum** (see Figure 3.39), a thin membrane that vibrates in response to sound waves and thereby transmits them to the middle and inner ears. The middle ear contains three

Noise A combination of dissonant sounds. (From the same Greek word from which "nausea" is derived: *nausia*, meaning "seasickness.")

White noise Discordant sounds of many frequencies, often producing a lulling effect. When you put your ear to a shell you hear white noise, not the sound of the sea.

Eardrum A thin membrane that vibrates in response to sound waves, transmitting the waves to the middle and inner ears.

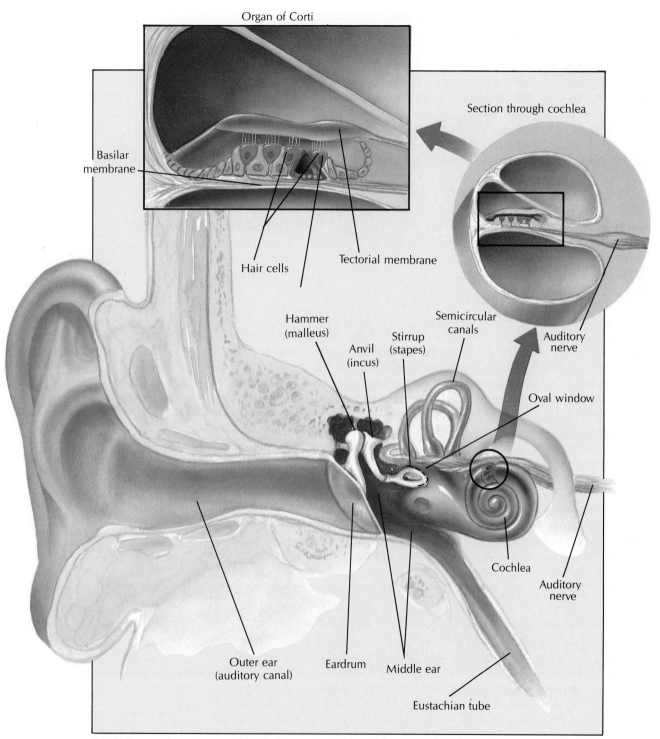

Organ of Corti

Section through cochlea

Basilar
membrane

Hair cells

Tectorial membrane

Auditory
nerve

Hammer
(malleus)

Anvil
(incus)

Stirrup
(stapes)

Semicircular
canals

Oval window

Cochlea

Auditory
nerve

Outer ear
(auditory canal)

Eardrum

Middle ear

Eustachian tube

FIGURE 3.39 THE HUMAN EAR The outer ear funnels sound to the eardrum.
Inside the eardrum, vibrations of the hammer, anvil, and stirrup transmit sound to
the inner ear. In the inner ear, vibrations in the cochlea transmit the sound to the
auditory nerve by way of the basilar membrane and the organ of Corti.

small bones, the "hammer," the "anvil," and the "stirrup," which also transmit sound by vibrating. These bones were given their names (actually the Latin *malleus, incus,* and *stapes,* which translate as hammer, anvil, and stirrup) because of their shapes.

The stirrup is attached to another membrane, the **oval window,** which transmits vibrations into the bony tube within the inner ear called the **cochlea** (from the Greek for "snail"). The cochlea, which has the shape of a snail shell, contains fluids that vibrate against the **basilar membrane** that lies coiled within the spiral of the cochlea. The **organ of Corti,** sometimes referred to as the command post of hearing, is attached to the basilar membrane. Thousands of receptor cells project like hair from the organ of Corti and bend in response to the vibrations of the basilar membrane. The bending of these receptor cells generates a neural impulse that is transmitted by the **auditory nerve** to the brain. Finally, within the brain this auditory input is projected onto the hearing areas of the temporal lobes of the cerebral cortex.

Oval window A membrane that transmits vibrations from the stirrup of the middle ear to the cochlea within the inner ear.

Cochlea (COCK-lee-uh). The bony tube within the inner ear that contains the basilar membrane and the organ of Corti.

Basilar membrane A membrane that lies coiled within the cochlea.

Organ of Corti The receptor for hearing which lies on the basilar membrane in the cochlea. It contains the receptor cells that transmit auditory information to the auditory nerve.

Auditory nerve The axon bundle that transmits neural impulses from the organ of Corti to the brain.

LOCATING SOUNDS

How do you balance the loudness of a stereo set? You sit between the speakers and adjust the volume until the sound seems equally loud in each ear. If the sound to the right is louder, the musical instruments will be perceived as being toward the right, rather than straight ahead.

There is a resemblance between balancing a stereo set and locating sounds. A sound that is louder in the right ear is perceived as coming from the right. A sound from the right side also reaches the right ear first. Loudness and sequence of stimulating the ears both provide directional cues.

But it may not be easy to locate a sound that is directly in front, in back, or overhead. Such sounds are equally loud in and distant from each ear. So what do we do? Simple—usually we turn our heads slightly to determine in which ear the sound increases. If you turn your head a few degrees to the right and the loudness increases in your left ear, the sound must be in front of you. Of course we also use vision and general knowledge in locating the source of sounds. If you hear the roar of jet engines, most of the time you will make money by betting that the airplane is overhead.

THEORIES OF HEARING

We know that sounds are heard because they cause vibration in parts of the ear and information about these vibrations is transmitted to the brain. But what determines the loudness and pitch of our perceptions of these sounds?

The loudness and pitch of sounds appear related to the number of receptor neurons on the organ of Corti that fire, and how often they fire. Psychologists are generally agreed that sounds are perceived as louder when more of these sensory neurons fire, but they are not so certain about the perception of pitch. Two theories have been advanced to explain pitch discrimination: *place theory* and *frequency theory.*

Place theory The theory that the pitch of a sound is determined by the section of the basilar membrane that vibrates in response to it.

Frequency theory The theory that the pitch of a sound is determined by the frequency with which receptor cells fire in response to the sound.

Volley principle A modification of frequency theory: The hypothesis that groups of neurons may be able to achieve the effect of firing at very high frequencies by "taking turns" firing—that is, by firing in volleys. Receptor cells would not otherwise be able to fire with adequate frequency to create the perception of very high pitches.

Odor The characteristic of a substance that makes it perceptible to the sense of smell. (A Latin word meaning "smell.")

Olfactory Having to do with the sense of smell. The olfactory membrane located high in each nostril is the receptor for smell. (From *odor* and the Latin *facere,* meaning "to make.")

Musky Having the strong, penetrating odor of musk, which is secreted by many animals.

Camphoraceous (kam-for-RAY-shuss). Having the odor of camphor, a substance that protects fabrics from moths.

Ethereal Having the odor of chemical compounds called ethers.

Pungent Having a sharp, piercing odor.

Putrid Having a rotten, foul-smelling odor.

Noxious (NOCK-shuss). Harmful, injurious. (From the Latin *noxa,* meaning "injury.")

Place Theory According to **place theory,** the pitch of a sound is determined by the place along the basilar membrane that vibrates in response to it. Different spots along the membrane would then be sensitive to tones of differing frequencies. There is one exception: The entire membrane appears responsive to tones that are low in frequency (Von Békésy, 1957).

Frequency Theory According to **frequency theory,** the frequency with which receptor neurons fire corresponds to the frequency of the sound. Individual neurons would not be capable of firing rapidly enough to transmit information about sounds of higher frequencies, however. It has been suggested that this limitation can be overcome through a **volley principle.** According to the volley principle, groups of neurons may take turns firing at high frequencies in order to transmit information about sounds of high frequency.

Place theory and frequency theory both seem to have something to offer. Future theories of pitch discrimination may incorporate elements from each.

SMELL

Smell and taste are the chemical senses. In the cases of vision and hearing, physical energy impacts upon our sensory receptors; with smell and taste, we sample molecules of the substances being sensed.

You could say that people are sort of underprivileged when it comes to the sense of smell. Dogs, for instance, devote about seven times as much area of the cerebral cortex to the sense of smell. Male dogs sniff to determine where the territories of other dogs leave off and to determine whether female dogs are sexually receptive. Dogs can even make a living sniffing out marijuana in closed packages and suitcases.

Still, smell has an important role in human behavior. If you did not have a sense of smell, an onion and an apple would taste the same to you! As lacking as our senses of smell may be when we compare them to those of the dog, we can detect the odor of 1/1,000,000th of a milligram of vanilla in a liter of air.

Odors are detected by sites on receptor neurons in the **olfactory** membrane high in each nostril. An odor is a sample of the actual substance being sensed. When a number of molecules of that substance, perhaps as few as 100 or so, come into contact with the olfactory membrane, the substance is smelled. According to various theories, there are between four and seven basic odors. These include flowery, minty, **musky, camphoraceous, ethereal, pungent,** and **putrid.**

The sense of smell tends to adapt rather rapidly to odors, even **noxious** odors. This may be fortunate if you are using a locker room or an outhouse. But it may not be so fortunate if you are being exposed to fumes from paints or other chemicals, since you may lose awareness of them even though they remain harmful.

PSYCHOLOGY IN THE WORKPLACE

WINNING A JOB BY A NOSE

So, you're off to that big job interview. You're all spruced up—freshly washed, neat as a button, and about to dab on some perfume or splash on some cologne. After all, it seems, uh, sensible to appeal to your interviewer's sense of smell as well as to his or her sense of vision, right? Not necessarily, according to research by Purdue University psychologist Robert A. Baron.

Baron (1983) found that women interviewers rate applicants who wear perfume or cologne more positively than those who abstain, but that male interviewers rate fragrant applicants—male and female alike—more negatively. For male interviewers, apparently, the smell of success is not so sweet. Male interviewers are most harsh in their ratings of women applicants who wear

perfume and also engage in "forward" body language, such as leaning toward the interviewer or persistently seeking out eye contact.

Why this sex difference? Perhaps male interviewers are more rigid than women interviewers, more susceptible to stereotypes that serious things do not come in fragrant packages. Male interviewers, that is, may believe that applicants should limit their presentations to demonstrating their ability and ambition and should not try to win by a nose.

In any event, perhaps you should reconsider if you are going to douse yourself in perfume or cologne and your interviewer is male. Using perfume with the wrong person could be rank frivolity.

SOME RECENT STUDIES IN OLFACTION: "THE NOSE KNOWS"

Let us now turn our attention to some recent research concerning the sense of smell. We shall have a brief look at *menstrual synchrony* and olfactory messengers otherwise known as *pheromones*.

Menstrual Synchrony   In Chapter 2 we saw that the menstrual cycle is regulated by hormones. In 1971, psychologist Martha McClintock reported on the phenomenon of **menstrual synchrony.** She monitored the menstrual cycles of 135 women and found that the cycles of friends and roommates converged from an average of 8.5 days apart to within five days during one school year. McClintock also found that the cycles of women who spent more time with men were shorter.

To demonstrate that menstrual synchrony is caused by odor, Russell and his colleagues (1977) recruited a colleague, Geneviève, with a regular 28-day cycle, who did not shave her underarms or use deodorants. The researchers then dabbed "essence of Geneviève" on the lips of five women subjects three times weekly over a period of four months. During this brief period the women's cycles converged from an average of 9.3 days apart to 3.4 days. Four of the women's cycles synchronized within one day of Geneviève's. A control group of six women dabbed with alcohol showed no synchronization.

In a study with laboratory rats, McClintock (1979) caused the reproductive cycles of female rats to converge by circulating air between their cages. The sense of smell was the only source of "contact" between the animals.

Pheromones: Has Science Found a Magic Potion?   For centuries people have searched for a magic potion—some formula that could cause others

Menstrual synchrony (MEN-strew-al SIN-crow-knee). The convergence of the menstrual cycles of women who spend time in close quarters. (From the Latin *syn-*, meaning "together" and *chronos*, meaning "time.")

Pheromones (FAIR-oh-moans). Chemical secretions detected by the sense of smell that stimulate stereotypical behaviors in other members of the same species.

Exaltolide (eggs-SALT-oh-lied). A musky substance that is suspected to be a sexual pheromone.

Alpha androstenol (an-DROSS-ten-all). A sexual pheromone extracted from sweat.

to fall in love with you, or at least be wildly attracted to you. Some scientists suggest that these potions may exist. They are **pheromones.**

Many organisms, from insects through mammals, are sexually aroused by these chemical secretions. They are produced by other members of the species and are detected through the sense of smell. Animals use pheromones to gather food, mark territories, sound alarms, maintain pecking orders, and send out sexual cues. Pheromones induce mating behavior mechanically in insects (Robinson & Robinson, 1979), but—perhaps to the chagrin of romantics—their sexual role becomes less vital as we rise through the ranks of the animal kingdom.

Mammals secrete pheromones in the vagina. Male mice attempt to mate with other males when urine from the female, containing pheromones, is smeared on their backs (Connor, 1972). Male mice (Cooper, 1978) and male guinea pigs (Beauchamp, 1981) show less sexual arousal when their sense of smell is blocked. Vaginal secretions also arouse male monkeys (Michael et al., 1971), but monkeys seek sexual activity even when nose drops have blocked their sense of smell (Goldfoot et al., 1978). Cognitive functioning is more complex among monkeys than mice. Monkeys are more responsive than mice to the sight of another monkey, past experience with another monkey, and observation of other monkeys involved in sexual activity.

Some people also apparently respond to pheromones, but, like monkeys, we do not need them. We can become sexually excited by a glimpse of a loved one, an erotic photo, a whiff of perfume or cologne that stirs a memory, or a lover's voice (Rathus, 1983). But still consider the case of **exaltolide,** a musky substance that is highly concentrated in the urine of adult men. Its odor is more detectable by and appealing to adult women than to children or men (Hassett, 1978). Moreover, women are most sensitive to exaltolide when they are ovulating (thus capable of conceiving).

Morris and Udry (1978) ran an experiment with married couples in which women smeared various perfumes on their breasts at bedtime. One perfume contained suspected pheromones. The couples tracked their sexual activity. One couple in five showed significantly more frequent sexual activity when they used the pheromone-laced perfume, although they did not know when the substance was being used. Pheromone-sensitive couples also engaged in sexual relations more frequently at the time of ovulation.

In other studies (Durden-Smith, 1980), photos of men and women have been rated more attractive when a suspected pheromone was in the air. People have dallied longer in pheromone-sprayed telephone booths. Although a suspected male pheromone could not be perceived consciously, women were more likely to sit on a waiting room chair that had been sprayed. Most of the sprayed seats in a theater were also occupied by women. Thus, pheromones may play some role in the sex lives of people who are sensitive to them, even if they are unnecessary.

Perfume manufacturers are betting that pheromones can play a significant role. The substance used in the studies reported by Durden-Smith, **alpha androstenol,** is extracted from human sweat. You can find it in British sex shops or in the United States, where Jovan is marketing a cologne, Andron, which contains a synthetic version of this suspected pheromone.

A CLOSER LOOK

A NEW WHODUNIT: THE CASE OF THE MALODOROUS T-SHIRTS

Now, who would pay you $10 to wear a T-shirt for 48 hours, extracting a promise that you would jog around or do pushups for at least an hour during this period? Psychologists, of course, trying to learn how sensitive we are to one form of air pollution—body odor. Body odor, as your TV set will gladly inform you through a thousand commercials, is one of America's mortal sins, although many foreign cultures do not find such odors to be offensive. (Is this one reason these cultures are foreign to us?)

Following these two-day exercises, subjects peeled the shirts off and returned them to the experimenters (McBurney et al., 1977) in tightly sealed plastic bags. In a procedure that demonstrates unparalleled commitment to the advancement of psychology, students then smelled the shirts and rated them for relative offensiveness.

There was general agreement as to which shirts smelled worse. Anonymous owners of the most putrid were rated as dirtier, less intelligent, less healthy, fatter, and less appealing to the opposite sex. Yet they were also rated stronger, more industrious, and more athletic. Apparently they were seen as tough and hard-working, but mindless and dirty drones.

Subjects also rated their own shirts as least offensive. When you live with yourself for a long time, it seems you become more tolerant—or less likely to make a stink.

Schleidt and Hold (1981) found that married couples in West Germany, Italy, and Japan could identify T-shirts worn to bed for a week by their mates—even when blindfolded. Apparently the nose knows its mate. In these studies both men and women generally considered male odors more obnoxious than female odors, although they also generally rated their mates' odor as less offensive than their own.

There was one exception. The Japanese women considered their husbands' body odors more obnoxious than their own. Why? The researchers speculate that the reason is linked to the fact that in Japan marriages are still frequently arranged by families. That is, the Japanese don't always get to sniff out a mate for themselves.

TASTE

Your cocker spaniel may jump at the chance to finish off your ice cream cones, but your Siamese cat may turn up her nose at this golden opportunity. Why? Dogs can perceive the taste quality of sweetness, as can pigs, but cats cannot (Dethier, 1978).

There are four primary taste qualities: sweet, sour, salty, and bitter. The "flavor" of a food involves its taste, but is more complex. As noted earlier, apples and onions have the same taste—or the same mix of taste qualities—but their flavor is vastly different. After all, you wouldn't chomp into a nice cold onion on a warm day, would you? The flavor of a food depends on its odor, texture, and temperature, as well as its taste. If it were not for odor, heated tenderized shoe leather might just pass for your favorite steak dish.

Taste is sensed through **taste cells,** or receptor neurons that are located on **taste buds.** You have about 10,000 taste buds, most of which are located near the edges and back of your tongue. As noted in Figure 3.40, taste buds tend to specialize a bit. Some, for example, are more responsive to sweetness, while others react to several tastes. Receptors for sweetness lie at the tip of the tongue and receptors for bitterness lie toward the back of the tongue. Sourness is sensed along the sides of the tongue, and saltiness overlaps the areas sensitive to sweetness and sourness (Figure 3.40). This is why people perceive a sour dish to "get them" at the sides of the tongue.

Taste cells Receptor cells that are sensitive to taste.

Taste buds The sensory organs for taste. They contain taste cells and are located on the tongue.

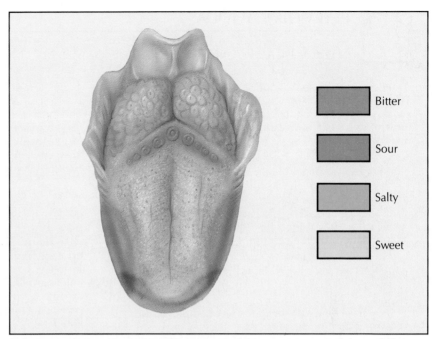

FIGURE 3.40 Taste buds on different areas of the tongue are sensitive to different primary taste qualities. The area shown in green is sensitive to sweet and salty. The area shown in purple is sensitive to sour and salty.

According to psychophysicist Linda Bartoshuk, we live in "different taste worlds" (Sheraton, 1984). Some of us, with a low sensitivity for the sweet taste could require twice the sugar to sweeten our food as others who are more sensitive to sweetness. Others of us who claim to enjoy very bitter foods may actually be taste-blind to them. Sensitivities to different tastes apparently have a strong genetic component.

By eating hot foods and scraping your tongue, you regularly kill off many taste cells. But you need not be alarmed at this unintentional display of oral aggression. Taste cells are the rabbits of the sense receptors, reproducing at the rate of complete renewal every week or so.

The number of taste cells declines with age; however, Linda Bartoshuk has also found that strong taste intensities can be elicited from very small parts of the tongue (Turkington, 1985). It is more likely, according to Bartoshuk, that the "taste" loss associated with the elderly is actually due to a decline in the sense of smell. In any event, the elderly may spice their food more heavily than the young in order to enhance its flavor. Since food is less savory, the elderly may also eat less and become malnourished.

THE SKIN SENSES

Earlier it was noted that vision is usually the most dominant of the senses, but six-month-old infants are sometimes so engrossed with the feel of objects that they may better remember changes in temperature than changes

A TASTE OF—WELL, CERTAINLY NOT HONEY Tastes can lead to powerful emotional responses.

THE CRITICAL PALATE

In the following article, food critic Mimi Sheraton describes her recent experiences in the laboratory of psychophysicist Linda Bartoshuk. In the process, we learn a bit more about how experimental psychologists go about their work.

To a food critic, the word *tasting* summons delectable images of cheese and bread, *foie gras* and caviar, chocolate and wine—the usual subjects of such comparative evaluations. But at a 90-minute tasting conducted by Dr. Linda M. Bartoshuk in her laboratory at the Yale-affiliated John B. Pierce Foundation, the only samples I was offered were tepid, clear chemical solutions. They were washed over my tongue or used as a mouth rinse as I leaned over a sink or a funnel hooked up to a waste pail.

Odorless chemical stimulants were employed to activate the four basic tastes—bitter, salty, sweet and sour. The tests were both qualitative, meaning that I was asked to identify each taste at very low concentrations, and quantitative, meaning that I was asked to rate the intensity of different concentrations. During Bartoshuk's "whole-mouth" test, when I rinsed with the diluted solutions, I wore headphones and was asked to rate the strength of sound tones administered intermittently by Dr. Lawrence E. Marks, an auditory psychophysicist. This procedure, known as magnitude matching, is used as a form of control. Psychophysicists have found that a subject's perception of strength in taste concentrations usually matches the strength rating of comparable intensities of sound.

I turned out to be a strong taster of the bitter stimuli phenylthiocarbamide (PTC) and propylthiouracil (PROP). The ability or inability to taste these stimuli is genetic. To taste very weak concentrations, as I did, indicates that the subject is probably homozygous, or has two dominant genes for bitter tasting. People who perceive PTC/PROP mildly are likely to be heterozygous, meaning that they have one dominant and one recessive gene. Non-tasters of these stimuli have two recessive genes.

It was interesting to notice how the tastes literally "felt" as they were being washed over the tongue. Salt and sweet were warm and pleasant; sweet was the most relaxing and salt was exhilarating. Bitterness curled the edges of the tongue. Sour felt icy and caused the surface of the tongue to contract.

in color (Bushnell et al., 1985). Of course, on a hot, humid July day, we may all pay more attention to an icy breeze than to a change in the color of a neighbor's beach umbrella.

Changes in temperature are just one type of event we sense by means of nerve endings in the skin. We know that the skin discriminates among five kinds of sensations—touch, pressure, warmth, cold, and pain—but how it does so is not so clear. It has been generally believed that there are sensory receptors in the skin for each type of sensation. But recent research suggests that some nerve endings may receive more than one type of sensory input.

TOUCH AND PRESSURE

Sensory receptors located around the roots of hair cells appear to fire in response to touching the surface of the skin. Other structures beneath the skin are apparently sensitive to pressure. Different parts of the body are more sensitive to touch and pressure than others. For example, our fingertips and lips are much more sensitive than our backs. This is for at least two reasons: First, nerve endings are more densely packed in the fingertips and lips. Second, a greater amount of sensory cortex is devoted to the perception of sensations in the fingertips and lips.

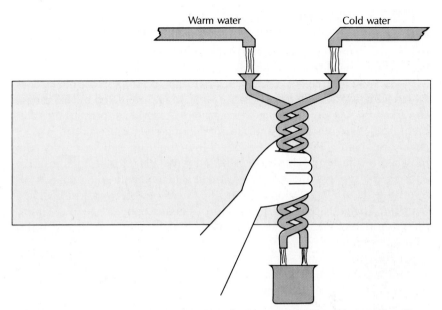

Warm water   Cold water

FIGURE 3.41 PARADOXICAL HOTNESS The perception of hotness usually relies on the simultaneous firing of receptors for cold and pain. However, we also perceive hotness when receptors for warmth and coldness are stimulated simultaneously. Would you be able to hold on to the coils if you perceived intense heat, even if you knew that one coil was filled with warm water and the other with cold water?

TEMPERATURE

It is of interest that although we have receptors that are sensitive to warmth and to coldness, we have none that are sensitive to hotness. Cold receptors fire when they are stimulated by objects below skin temperature, and also when they are stimulated by hot objects—that is, objects that are well above skin temperature. The sensation of burning apparently relies on the simultaneous firing of receptors for cold and pain.

A classic experiment in sensation and perception showed that simultaneous stimulation of receptors for warmth and coldness could also lead to perception of hotness. As shown in Figure 3.41, two coils were intertwined. Warm water was run through one of them, and cold water through the other. Yet people who grasped the coils simultaneously, as shown in the figure, perceived heat so intense that they had to let go at once. Knowing that the heat was phony made no difference. The perception of burning heat was quite convincing. I'll bet my cash that you would let go of the coils on each trial, too.

PAIN

Headaches, backaches, toothaches—these are but a few of the types of pain that most of us encounter from time to time. Some of us also suffer indescribable bouts of pain from arthritis, digestive disorders, cancer, and wounds.

Pain is a signal that something is wrong in the body. Pain is adaptive in the sense that it motivates us to do something about it. But for some of us, chronic pain—pain that even lasts once injuries or illnesses have cleared up—saps our vitality and the pleasures of everyday life.

As shown in Figure 3.42, pain originates at the point of contact, as with a stubbed toe. The pain message to the brain is initiated by the release of various chemicals, including prostaglandins, bradykinin (perhaps the most painful known substance), and the mysterious chemical called P (yes, *P* stands for "pain"). Prostaglandins not only facilitate transmission of the pain message to the brain; they also heighten circulation to the injured area, causing the redness and swelling we call inflammation. Inflammation attracts infection-fighting blood cells to the area to protect against invading bacteria. **Analgesic** drugs such as aspirin, acetaminophen (Tylenol, Datrin), diflunisal (Dolobid), and ibuprofen (Motrin) all work by inhibiting prostaglandin production.

The pain message is relayed from the spinal cord to the thalamus and then projected to the cerebral cortex, where the location and intensity of the damage become apparent.

Gate Theory   Simple remedies like rubbing and scratching the toe frequently help. Why? One possible answer lies in the so-called gate theory of pain, originated by Melzack (1980). From this perspective, only a limited amount of stimulation can be processed by the nervous system at a time. Rubbing or scratching the toe then transmits sensations to the brain that, in a sense, compete for neurons. And so, a number of nerves are prevented from transmitting pain messages to the brain. The mechanism is analogous to shutting down a "gate" in the spinal cord. It is something like too many calls flooding a switchboard at once. The flood prevents any calls from getting through.

Endorphins   In response to pain, the brain triggers the release of endorphins (see Chapter 2). A number of people who experience severe pain that cannot be relieved by available medical treatments have been found to have lower-than-normal concentrations of endorphins in their cerebrospinal fluid (Akil, 1978).

Acupuncture   Thousands of years ago the Chinese began mapping the body to learn where pins might be placed to deaden pain elsewhere. Much of the Chinese practice of acupuncture was unknown in the West, even though Western powers occupied much of China during the 1800s. But early in the 1970s, *New York Times* columnist James Reston underwent an appendectomy in China, with acupuncture the only anesthetic. He reported no discomfort. In 1972 the National Institutes of Health (NIH) undertook research to determine whether acupuncture was effective in the control of pain. And in 1975 the NIH reported that acupuncture was no more effective than hypnosis or sugar pills—that is, **placebos.**

Yet hypnosis, as you will see in Chapter 4, and sugar pills may be of help in controlling pain. Despite the NIH conclusion, there have been numerous clinical reports that acupuncture is effective with people (Pool,

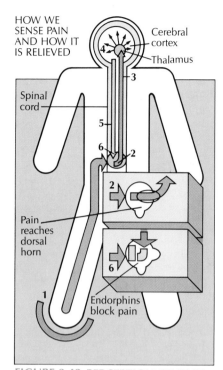

HOW WE SENSE PAIN AND HOW IT IS RELIEVED

Cerebral cortex
Thalamus
Spinal cord
Pain reaches dorsal horn
Endorphins block pain

FIGURE 3.42 **PERCEPTION OF PAIN**
Pain originates at the point of contact, and the pain message to the brain is initiated by the release of prostaglandins, bradykinin, and substance *P.*

Analgesic (an-al-GEE-zick). Giving rise to a state of not feeling pain, though fully conscious. (From the Latin *an-,* meaning "without," and *algos,* meaning "pain.")

Placebos Bogus treatments that control for the effect of expectations. See Chapter 1.

PSYCHOLOGY AND HEALTH

1973), and there is experimental evidence that it reduces perception of pain in cats and mice (Levitt, 1981). Just placing needles in certain bodily locations sometimes removes pain. At other times the needles are twirled about 120 times a minute.

SPA   In a variant of acupuncture, a small direct electric current is run through stationary needles. Levitt (1981) points out that such "stimulation-produced analgesia" (SPA) has been used successfully with many pain patients suffering from cancer or nerve or brain damage. Activating an implanted electrode (which is an electrified "needle") for 15 to 30 minutes can provide hours of relief from pain.

In a related method, transcutaneous electrical nerve stimulation (TENS), electrodes are attached to the skin at the site of pain. A mild current is passed between the electrodes across the skin. In still another method, direct electrical stimulation is applied to the brainstem.

Some of the effects of acupuncture, SPA, and TENS may be due to the releasing of endorphins. There is supportive evidence. The drug *naloxone* is known to block the pain-killing effects of morphine. The analgesic effects of SPA (Akil et al., 1976) and acupuncture are also blocked by naloxone. Therefore, it may well be that the analgesic effects of SPA and acupuncture can be linked to the morphine-like endorphins.

Interestingly, the so-called placebo effect—that is, the way in which expectation of relief sometimes leads to relief from pain and other problems—has also occasionally been attributed to release of endorphins. In future years we may well find ways of controlling pain without drugs, acupuncture, or other external means. We may learn how to control release of our bodies' own pain-killing systems more or less directly.

KINESTHESIS This dancer receives information about the position and motion of parts of her body through kinesthesis. She can intimately follow her own movements without visually observing herself.

KINESTHESIS

Try a brief experiment. Close your eyes. Then touch your nose with your index finger. If you weren't right on target, I'm sure you came close. But how? You didn't see your hand moving, and you (probably) didn't hear your arm swishing through the air.

PSYCHOLOGY AND HEALTH

BEHAVIORAL MEDICINE AND KINESTHESIS: THE MAKING OF MODERN MIRACLES

In 1895, British Nobel laureate Sir Charles S. Sherwood demonstrated the importance of kinesthetic information by cutting the sensory nerves in an animal's arm. The animal did not use the arm again, even though the nerve pathways that carried motor impulses to it were still intact.

Psychologist Neal E. Miller (1985) notes that a major use of biofeedback is to provide heightened information to the brain about what is happening in various areas of the body. In this way, the branch of psychology referred to as behavioral medicine has led to many apparent miracles. For example, psychologist Bernard Brucker of the University of Miami Medical School taught a spinal-injured man to walk by providing electronic kinesthetic feedback about the working of the leg muscles. The man's injury had deprived him of sensory information from the legs, but had not destroyed his motor ability. If the injury had prevented motor impulses from reaching the legs, this treatment would not have worked.

On the other hand, many injured patients have an unsuspected capacity for recovery. In the late 1960s, psychologist Edward Taub demonstrated that a monkey whose sensory pathways had been damaged could regain much of the use of the injured limb if use of the "good" arm was restrained. The restraints apparently motivated the monkey to attend more carefully to any kinesthetic information that was still available from the damaged arm and to learn, by trial and error, to make maximum use of it. In more recent years, Steven Wolf of the Emory University School of Medicine tried the

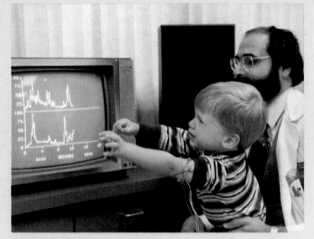

BEHAVIORAL MEDICINE Psychologist Bernard Brucker of the University of Miami Medical School uses biofeedback to help a patient.

Taub technique by restraining the movements of the "good arms" of patients who were paralyzed on one side. The restraint encouraged many patients to significantly improve their control over the damaged limbs—much more so than physical therapy alone accomplished.

In later chapters we shall explore many other uses of biofeedback and other tools in behavioral medicine.

You were able to bring your finger to your nose through your kinesthetic sense, called **kinesthesis,** after the Greek words for "motion" *(kinesis)* and "perception" *(aisthesis).* Kinesthesis is the sense that informs you about the position and motion of parts of the body. Sensory information is fed back to the brain from sensory organs in the joints, tendons, and muscles.

Imagine going for a walk without kinesthesis. You would have to watch the forward motion of each leg to be certain you had raised it high enough to clear the curb. And if you had tried our brief experiment without the kinesthetic sense, you would have had no sensory feedback until you felt the pressure of your finger against your nose (or cheek, or eye, or forehead), and you probably would have missed dozens of times.

Before we leave kinesthesis, let's try another brief experiment. Close your eyes. Then "make a muscle" in your right arm. Could you sense the muscle without looking at it or feeling it with your left hand? Of course you could. It is also kinesthesis that senses muscle contractions.

Kinesthesis (kin-ness-THEE-sis). The sense that informs us about the positions and motion of parts of our bodies.

Vestibular sense (vest-TIB-you-lar). The sense that informs us about our bodies' positions relative to gravity. Also called the sense of equilibrium. (From the Latin *vestibulum,* meaning "entrance hall," reflecting the location of the vestibular sensory organs in the "entranceway" of the ear.)

Semicircular canals Structures of the inner ear that monitor bodily movement and position.

Precognition Ability to foresee the future. (From the Latin *prae-,* meaning "before," and *cognitio,* meaning "knowledge.")

Psychokinesis Ability to manipulate objects or events by thought processes.

Extrasensory perception Perception of objects and events without sensation; abbreviated *ESP.* A controversial area of investigation. (From the Latin *extra-,* meaning "outside.")

Telepathy Direct transference of thought from one person to another.

Clairvoyance Ability to perceive things in the absence of sensory stimulation. (A French word meaning "clear-sightedness.")

THE VESTIBULAR SENSE

Your **vestibular sense** informs you whether you are upright (physically, not morally). Sensory organs located in the **semicircular canals** (Figure 3.39) and elsewhere in the ears monitor your body's motion and position in relationship to gravity. They tell you whether you are falling and provide cues as to whether your body is changing speeds, as in an accelerating airplane or automobile.

EXTRASENSORY PERCEPTION

Imagine the wealth you could amass if you had **precognition,** that is, if you were able to perceive future events. Perhaps you would check next month's stock market reports and know in advance what stocks to buy or sell. Or you could make Superbowl and World Series bets with perfect safety.

Or think of the power you would have if you were capable of **psychokinesis,** that is, of manipulating or moving objects from a distance. You may have gotten a glimpse of the types of things that could happen with psychokinesis from films like *The Power, Carrie,* and *The Fury.*

Precognition and psychokinesis are two concepts associated with **extrasensory perception** (ESP)—the perception of objects or events through means other than sensory organs. Two other concepts are **telepathy,** or the direct transmission of thoughts or ideas from person to person, and **clairvoyance,** or the perception of objects that do not stimulate the sensory organs. An example of clairvoyance is "knowing" what card is to be dealt next, although it is still in the deck and unknown to the dealer.

Now and then we hear of "psychics" who are recruited by police departments to help find missing persons or criminals (no, we don't usually hear that they have successfully located them). There was even a report in *The New York Times* that the U.S. Department of Defense was looking into the possibility of using ESP to locate enemy submarines or other hidden targets (Broad, 1984). It could be argued that this is an appropriate activity for the Department of Defense, since the Russians are also studying ESP.

ESP, in short, is extremely controversial, and most psychologists do not believe that it is an appropriate area for scientific inquiry. Scientists study natural events and ESP smacks of the supernatural, perhaps of the occult. ESP also has the flavor of a nightclub act in which a blindfolded "clairvoyant" calls out the contents of an audience member's pocketbook. However, a few psychologists believe that there is nothing wrong with investigating ESP. The issue for them is not whether ESP is sensationalistic, but whether ESP can be demonstrated in the laboratory.

Perhaps the best known of the respected ESP researchers was the late Joseph Banks Rhine of Duke University (1971), who studied ESP for several decades, beginning in the late 1920s. In a typical experiment in clairvoyance, Rhine would use a pack of 25 Zener cards, which contained five sets of the five cards shown in Figure 3.43. A subject guessing which of the five patterns was about to be turned up would be correct 20 percent of the time (one time in five) by chance alone. Rhine found that some people guessed

FIGURE 3.43 **ZENER CARDS** Zener cards have been used in research on clairvoyance to determine whether some people can guess which card is about to be turned up at above-chance levels.

correctly significantly more frequently than the 20 percent chance rate and concluded that they may have had some degree of ESP.

More recent studies have been done in clairvoyance with automated equipment, like random-number generators. Other studies have been done in psychokinesis. As of today, there are some studies that claim that individuals have performed tasks requiring ESP at above-chance levels of success. However, these studies have not been accepted by an appreciable segment of the scientific community.

There are many reasons for this skepticism, as noted by Hansel (1980). For one, negative results are rarely reported by ESP researchers. Therefore, we would expect *some* unusual findings (like an individual with a high success rate at ESP tasks over a period of several days) to surface in the literature. In other words, if you flip a coin indefinitely, eventually you will flip 10 heads in a row. The odds against this are high, but if you report your eventual "success," and do not report the weeks of failure, you give the impression that you have unique coin-flipping ability.

Second, it has not been easy to replicate ESP experiments. Subjects who have "shown" ESP with one researcher have failed to do so with another, or have refused to participate in a study with another. Third, some researchers, including a colleague of Rhine, have been found tampering with data or equipment. (Rhine himself was never accused of fraud.)

For these and other reasons, ESP research has not received much credibility. To be fair, science has shown, again and again, that "There are more things in heaven and earth" than there were once thought to be. But science has not yet found that ESP is one of those things. For the time being, the great majority of psychologists prefer to study perception that involves sensation. What is life without some sensation?

SUMMARY

1. Sensation refers to mechanical processes that involve the stimulation of sensory receptors (neurons) and the transmission of sensory information to the central nervous system. Perception is not mechanical. Perception is the active organization of sensations into a representation of the world, and perception reflects learning and expectations.

2. Vision is our dominant sense. Visible light is one part of a spectrum of electromagnetic energy.

3. The absolute threshold for a stimulus, like light, is the lowest intensity at which it can be detected. The minimum difference in intensity that can be discriminated is the difference threshold. Difference thresholds are expressed in Weber's constants.

4. The eye senses and transmits visual stimulation to the occipital lobe of the cerebral cortex. After passing through the cornea, pupil size determines the amount of light that can pass through the lens. The lens focuses light as it projects onto the retina, which is composed of photoreceptors called rods and cones.

5. The fovea is the most sensitive part of the eye. The fovea is populated by cones only, which permit perception of color. Rods are spaced most densely near the lens and transmit sensations of light and dark only. Rods are more sensitive than cones to lowered lighting, and continue to adapt to darkness once cones have reached peak adaptation.

6. Visual acuity is sharpness of vision. As people age, the lens becomes brittle, resulting in presbyopia, a condition similar to farsightedness.

7. The wavelength of light determines its color or hue. Yellows, oranges, and reds are considered warm colors, while blues and greens are considered cool. The saturation of a color is its pureness. When we mix lights of complementary colors, they dissolve into gray. The primary colors of red, blue, and yellow are not produced by mixing pigments of other hues. Secondary and tertiary colors are produced by mixing other colors.

8. There are two theories of color vision. According to trichromatic theory, there are three types of cones, some sensitive to red, others to blue or green light. Opponent-process theory proposes three types of color receptors: red-green, blue-yellow, and light-dark. Opponent-process theory better accounts for afterimages, but both theories seem to have some validity.

9. Color-blind people who can see light and dark only are called monochromats. Dichromats, who can discriminate only two colors (red and green, or blue and yellow), are more common.

10. Gestalt rules of perceptual organization influence our grouping of bits of sensory stimulation. These rules concern figure-ground relationships, proximity, similarity, continuity, common fate, and closure. Visual illusions use perceptual cues as well as twists on rules for organization to deceive the eye.

11. We perceive real movement by sensing movement across the retina and movement of objects in relation to one another. Distant objects appear to move more slowly than nearby objects, whereas middle-ground objects may give the illusion of moving backward. The autokinetic effect is the tendency to perceive a point of light in a darkened room as moving. Stroboscopic motion, used in films, is the perception of a series of still pictures as moving.

12. Depth perception involves monocular and binocular cues. Monocular cues include perspective, clearness, interposition, shadows, texture gradient, motion parallax, and accommodation. Binocular cues include retinal disparity and convergence.

13. Through experience we develop a number of perceptual constancies. For example, we learn to assume that objects retain their size, shape, brightness, and color despite their distance, their position, or changes in lighting conditions.

14. Auditory stimulation, or sound waves, require a medium. Sound waves alternately compress and expand molecules of the medium—creating vibrations.

15. The human ear can hear sounds varying in frequency from 20 to 20,000 cycles per second. The greater the frequency, the higher the pitch of a sound.

16. The loudness of a sound is measured in decibels (dB). We can suffer hearing loss if exposed to protracted sounds of 85–90 dB or more. Noise is a combination of dissonant sounds.

17. The eardrum vibrates in sympathy to sound, and transmits auditory stimulation through the bones of the middle ear to the cochlea of the inner ear. The basilar membrane of the cochlea transmits stimulation to the organ of Corti, and from there sound travels to the brain by the auditory nerve. Sounds seem louder when more neurons of the organ of Corti fire. But two theories

are competing to account for the perception of pitch: place theory and frequency theory.

18. Odors are detected by the olfactory membrane in each nostril. An odor is a sample of the substance being smelled. The sense of smell adapts rapidly to odors, even unpleasant ones.

19. Menstrual synchrony depends on the sense of smell. Pheromones, detected by the sense of smell, help control sexual behavior in lower animals, but appear to be unnecessary with people.

20. There are four primary taste qualities: sweet, sour, salty, and bitter. Flavor involves the odor, texture, and temperature of food, as well as its taste. Taste is sensed through taste cells, which are located in taste buds on the tongue.

21. There are five skin senses: touch, pressure, warmth, cold, and pain. Perception of hotness is caused by simultaneous stimulation of receptors for cold and pain, or of receptors for warmth and cold.

22. Pain originates at the point of contact and is transmitted to the brain by various chemicals, including prostaglandins, bradykinin, and substance P. According to gate theory, rubbing and scratching painful areas may reduce pain by sending competing messages to the brain. Naturally occurring endorphins also help relieve pain. Acupuncture and SPA, when effective, may also be explained by gate theory.

23. Kinesthesis is the sensing of bodily position and movement, and relies on sensory organs in the joints, tendons, and muscles. The vestibular sense is housed primarily in the semicircular canals of the ears and informs us whether we are in an upright position.

24. There has been speculation as to whether extrasensory perception (perception without sensation) is possible. Evidence for extrasensory perception has fallen into disrepute because of underreporting of experimental failures, failure to replicate research with positive results, and cases of outright fraud.

TRUTH OR FICTION REVISITED

White sunlight is actually composed of all the colors of the rainbow.

True. White light can be broken down into its components—the visible spectrum—by a prism.

On a clear, dark night you could probably see the light from a single candle burning thirty miles away.

True. This degree of brightness approximates the absolute threshold for light.

We all have blind spots in our eyes.

True. It is at the spot where axons of ganglion cells gather to form the optic nerve.

At first we may not be able to see other viewers when we enter a dark movie theater, but after several minutes we can discriminate other people and the features of the theater interior much more clearly.

True. This occurs because of the process called dark adaptation.

As we approach late adulthood, we become more likely to need reading glasses, even if our visual acuity has been perfect at younger ages.

True. This is because of increased brittleness of the lens, or presbyopia.

When we mix blue and yellow light, we attain green light.

False. By mixing blue and yellow light, we attain gray light. We attain green by mixing blue and yellow pigments.

"Motion pictures" do not move at all.

True. Stroboscopic motion—presentation of a series of still pictures—creates the illusion of movement.

We need two eyes in order to perceive depth.

False. There are several monocular (one-eyed) cues for depth perception.

The advertising slogan for the film Alien was accurate: "In space, no one can hear you scream."

True. Sound waves require a medium like air or water, and space is an almost perfect vacuum.

The menstrual cycles of women who live together tend to be synchronized.

True. This occurs because of chemical substances that are sensed by smell.

Perfume and cologne manufacturers have placed chemical substances in their products that sexually arouse us.

Not quite. Yes, manufacturers have placed suspected pheromones in some perfumes and colognes. However, most of us do not seem to be sexually responsive to these substances.

Onions and apples have the same taste.

True. But their flavor, which includes their odor and other clues, is vastly different.

We have no sensory receptors for perceiving hotness.

True. The perception of extreme heat is brought about by the simultaneous stimulation of receptors for cold and pain, or of cold and warmth.

Some people have the ability to read other people's minds.

False. Studies that suggest the existence of extrasensory perception have been found fraudulent or impossible to replicate. It may be that we can make reasonable guesses as to what others will say and do in certain situations, especially if we are well acquainted with them. Paying close attention to their facial features and postures provides us with information also. However, there is no adequate scientific evidence that any of us can directly perceive another person's thoughts.

OUTLINE

CHAPTER 4

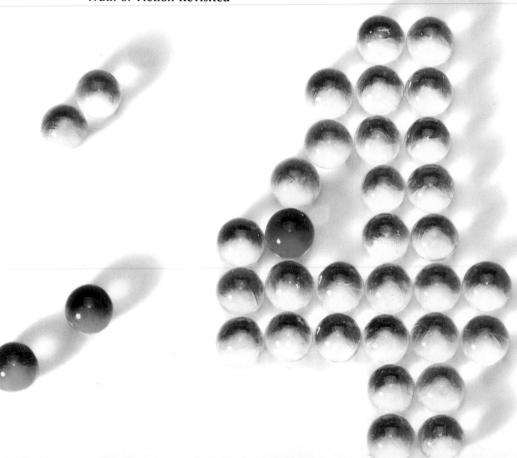

States of Consciousness

TRUTH or FICTION?

- There is no such thing as consciousness.
- Sleep becomes gradually deeper as we approach the middle of the night, and then gradually lightens until we awaken in the morning.
- People who sleep nine hours or more a night tend to be lazy and happy-go-lucky.
- We tend to act out our forbidden fantasies in our dreams.
- Many people have insomnia because they try too hard to get to sleep at night.
- Children tend to "outgrow" bed-wetting.
- It is dangerous to awaken a sleepwalker.
- Some people drink because alcohol provides them with an excuse for failure.
- Heroin was once used as a cure for addiction to morphine.
- Coca-Cola once "added life" through a powerful but now illegal stimulant.
- Cigarette smokers tend to smoke more when they are under stress.
- Smoking marijuana is harmless.
- Users of LSD can have flashbacks at any time.
- People have managed to bring high blood pressure under control through meditation.
- You can learn to increase or decrease your heart rate just by thinking about it.
- Ethical psychologists do not practice hypnosis.
- A hypnotized man experienced no pain when his arm was amputated.

It is a well-known fact of life that the few individuals who have gained insight into the mysteries of the universe wear flowing robes, have long beards streaked with white, and set up shop on some distant mountaintop. A sag in their shoulder telegraphs their weariness with knowledge and the burdens of the world.

These sages are hard to meet. You've got to wait for the end of the monsoon season, or for a thaw, to make the journey. Then you must enlist one of the last guides who recalls the route. Such guides would typically prefer to watch their donkeys graze in the backyard than make any darn fool trip. But they can be persuaded. (If they couldn't, I'd have to find another tale.)

So it is not surprising that psychologist Robert Ornstein's (1972) recounting of the experiences of a group of American travelers who were seeking just such a wise old man describes them as scrambling and stumbling through the Himalayan Mountains. As you would expect, the trip was long and arduous. Many would have turned back. But these hardy travelers were searching for the scoop on heightened consciousness, for the key to inner peace and harmony.

Finally, the travelers found themselves at the feet of the venerable **guru.** They told him of the perils and pitfalls of their journey, of the singular importance they attached to this audience. They implored the guru to share his wisdom, to help them open their inner pathways.

The guru said, "Sit, facing the wall, and count your breaths."

This was it? The secret that had been preserved through the centuries? The wisdom of several lifetimes? The prize for which our seekers had risked life and limb and bank account?

Yes, in a sense this was. Counting your breaths is one method of **meditation**—one way of narrowing your *consciousness* so that the stresses of the outside world can fade away.

In this chapter we shall explore meditation and other states of consciousness. Some of them, like sleep, are quite familiar to you. Others, like meditation, biofeedback, and hypnosis may seem more exotic. It is also in this chapter that we deal with "consciousness-altering" drugs. But first we shall tackle the $64,000 question: What *is* consciousness? This is a dangerous undertaking for at least two reasons. First, some psychologists believe that the science of psychology should not deal with the question of consciousness at all. Second, the meanings of the word are quite varied.

THE $64,000 QUESTION: WHAT *IS* CONSCIOUSNESS?

In 1904, William James wrote an intriguing article entitled "Does Consciousness Exist?" Think about that. *Does consciousness exist?* Do you feel that *you* have consciousness? That you are conscious or aware of yourself? Of the world around you? Would you bear witness to being conscious of, or experiencing, thoughts and feelings? I would bet that you would. And so, to be sure, would William James. But James did not think that con-

Guru (GOO-roo). A spiritual adviser or teacher. (A Sanskrit word meaning "venerable.")

Meditation As a method for coping with stress, a systematic narrowing of attention that slows the metabolism and helps produce feelings of relaxation.

Sensory awareness Knowledge of the environment through perception of sensory stimulation—one definition of consciousness.

Direct inner awareness Knowledge of one's own thoughts, feelings, and memories, without use of sensory organs—another definition of consciousness.

Preconscious In psychoanalytic theory, descriptive of material that is not in awareness but can be brought into awareness by focusing one's attention. (The Latin root *prae-* means "before.")

sciousness was a proper area of study for psychologists. It smacked of religion and philosophy, not of science. Consciousness was not a *thing* to James. Rather, it was "a mere echo, the faint rumor left behind by the disappearing (concept of the) 'soul'" (James, 1904, p. 477).

As noted in Chapter 1, John Watson, the "father of modern behaviorism," insisted that only observable, measurable behavior was the proper province of psychology. In "Psychology as the Behaviorist Views It," published in 1913, Watson declared, "The time seems to have come when psychology must discard all references to consciousness" (p. 163). The following year Watson was elected president of the American Psychological Association, which further cemented these ideas in the minds of many psychologists.

Despite such objections, and despite the problems involved in defining (much less measuring) consciousness, we shall attempt to explore the meanings and varieties of this most intriguing concept. Many psychologists, especially cognitive psychologists, believe that we cannot meaningfully discuss human behavior without referring to the concept of consciousness.

THE MEANINGS OF CONSCIOUSNESS

The word *consciousness* has several meanings. Let's have a look at a few of them.

Consciousness as Sensory Awareness   One meaning of consciousness is **sensory awareness** of the environment. The sense of vision permits us to be "conscious" of, or to see, the sun gleaming in the snow on the rooftops. The sense of hearing allows us to be conscious of, or to hear, a concert.

We are more conscious of, or have greater awareness of, those things to which we pay attention. Many things are going on nearby and in the world at large, yet you are conscious of, or focusing on, the words on this page (perhaps).

Consciousness as Direct Inner Awareness   Close your eyes. Imagine spilling a can of bright red paint across a black tabletop. Watch it spread across the black, shiny surface, then spill onto the floor. Although this image may be vivid, you did not "see" it literally. Your eyes and no other sensory organs were involved. You were conscious of the image through **direct inner awareness.**

We are conscious of, or have direct inner awareness of, thoughts, images, emotions, and memories. We are conscious of, or know of, the presence of all these cognitive processes without using our senses.

Sigmund Freud, the founder of psychoanalysis, differentiated thoughts and feelings of which we are conscious, or aware, from those which are preconscious and unconscious (see Figure 4.1). **Preconscious** material is not currently in awareness, but is readily available. As you answer the following questions, you will summon up "preconscious" information: What did you eat for dinner yesterday? About what time did you wake up this morning? What's happening outside the window or down the hall right now? What's your phone number? We can make these preconscious bits

SENSORY AWARENESS One of the definitions of consciousness is sensory awareness of the world around us.

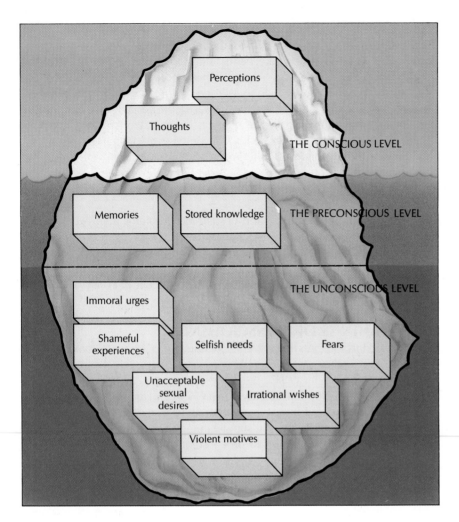

Perceptions

Thoughts

THE CONSCIOUS LEVEL

Memories

Stored knowledge

THE PRECONSCIOUS LEVEL

THE UNCONSCIOUS LEVEL

Immoral urges

Shameful experiences

Selfish needs

Fears

Unacceptable sexual desires

Irrational wishes

Violent motives

FIGURE 4.1 LEVELS OF CONSCIOUS-NESS, ACCORDING TO SIGMUND FREUD According to Freud, many memories, impulses, and feelings exist below the level of conscious awareness. We could note that any film that draws an audience seems to derive its plot from items that populate the unconscious.

of information conscious simply by directing our inner awareness, or attention, to them.

According to Freud, still other mental events are **unconscious,** or unavailable to awareness under most circumstances. Freud believed that certain memories were painful and certain impulses (primarily sexual and aggressive impulses) were unacceptable. Therefore, we would place them out of awareness, or **repress** them to escape feelings of anxiety, guilt, and shame.

Still, people do sometimes choose to stop thinking about distracting or unacceptable ideas. This conscious method of putting unwanted mental events out of awareness is termed **suppression.** We may suppress thoughts of a date when we need to study for a test. (We may also try to suppress thoughts of an unpleasant test when we are on a date so that the evening will not be ruined.)

Some bodily processes are **nonconscious**—incapable of being experienced either through sensory awareness or direct inner awareness. The growing of hair and the carrying of oxygen in the blood are nonconscious.

Self The totality of impressions, thoughts, and feelings. The sense of self is another definition of consciousness. See Chapter 9.

Altered states of consciousness States other than the normal waking state, including sleep, meditation, the hypnotic "trance," and the distorted perceptions produced by use of some drugs.

Electroencephalograph (ell-leck-tro-en-SEFF-uh-low-graph). An instrument that measures electrical activity of the brain. Abbreviated *EEG*. ("Cephalo-" derives from the Greek *kephale,* meaning "head.")

We can see that our hair has grown, but have no sense receptors that provide sensations related to the process. We can feel the need to breathe, but we cannot directly experience the exchange of carbon dioxide and oxygen.

Consciousness as Personal Unity: The Sense of Self   To the newborn, this world must seem a confusing disarray of sensory inputs. But gradually we begin to sort things out and better organize our perceptions. We also learn to differentiate us from that which is not us. We develop a sense of being persons, individuals. There is a totality to our impressions, thoughts, and feelings that comprises our conscious existence—our continuing sense of **self** in a changing world.

In this use of the word, consciousness *is* self. Cognitive psychologists view a person's consciousness as an important determinant of the person's behavior.

Consciousness as the Waking State   The least controversial meaning of the word *consciousness* describes the normal waking state as opposed, for example, to sleep. From this perspective, sleep, meditation, the hypnotic "trance," and the disordered perceptions that can accompany use of consciousness-altering drugs are considered **altered states of consciousness.**

For the remainder of this chapter we shall explore various states of consciousness and the agents that bring them about. These states and agents include sleep and dreams, a number of drugs, meditation, biofeedback, and hypnosis.

SLEEP AND DREAMS

Sleep has always been a fascinating topic. After all, we spend about one-third of our adult lives sleeping. Most of us complain when we do not sleep at least six hours or so, but some people sleep for an hour or less a day and lead otherwise healthy and normal lives.

Why do we sleep? Why do we dream? Why do some of us have trouble getting to sleep, and what can we do about it? We don't have all the answers to these questions, but we have learned a great deal.

THE STAGES OF SLEEP

When I was an undergraduate psychology student, I first heard that psychologists studied sleep by "connecting" people to the **electroencephalograph** (EEG), a device that measures the electrical activity of the brain. I had a gruesome image of people somehow being "plugged in" to the EEG. Not so. Electrodes are simply attached to the scalp or other areas with tape or paste. Later, once the brain activity under study has been duly recorded, they are simply removed. A bit of soap and water, and you're as good as new.

The EEG provides psychologists with some interesting scrawls that show the frequency and strength of the electric currents of the brain (see

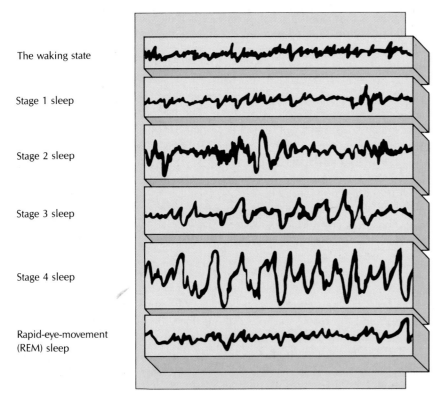

The waking state

Stage 1 sleep

Stage 2 sleep

Stage 3 sleep

Stage 4 sleep

Rapid-eye-movement
(REM) sleep

FIGURE 4.2 THE STAGES OF SLEEP This figure illustrates typical EEG patterns for the stages of sleep. During REM sleep, EEG patterns resemble those of the lightest stage of sleep, stage 1 sleep. For this reason, REM sleep is often termed *paradoxical sleep*. As sleep progresses from stage 1 to stage 4, brain waves become slower and their amplitude increases. Dreams, including normal nightmares, are most vivid during REM sleep. More disturbing night terrors tend to occur during deep stage 4 sleep.

Figure 4.2). A trip from a high point to a low point, and back, is called a cycle. During the deepest stage of sleep—or stage 4 sleep—only about one to three of these cycles occur each second. So the printouts in Figure 4.2 show what happens over a period of fifteen seconds or so. During stage 4 sleep, the brain emits slow but strong **delta waves.** Delta waves reach relatively great height or amplitude, when compared with other brain waves. Their amplitude reflects their strength. The strength or energy of brain waves is expressed in the electric unit **volts.**

Figure 4.2 shows five stages of sleep: four stages of **non-rapid-eye-movement** (NREM) sleep, and one stage of **rapid-eye-movement** (REM) sleep. When we close our eyes and begin to relax before going to sleep, our brains emit many **alpha waves.** Alpha waves are low-amplitude brain waves of about eight to twelve cycles per second. (Through biofeedback training, discussed later in the chapter, people have been taught to relax by purposefully emitting alpha waves.)

As we enter stage 1 sleep, our brain waves slow down from the alpha rhythm and enter a pattern of **theta waves.** Theta waves have a frequency

Delta waves Strong, slow brain waves usually emitted during stage 4 sleep.

Volt A unit of electrical potential.

Non-rapid-eye-movement sleep Stages of sleep 1 through 4. Abbreviated *NREM* sleep.

Rapid-eye-movement sleep A stage of sleep characterized by rapid eye movements, which have been linked to dreaming. Abbreviated *REM* sleep.

Alpha waves Rapid, low-amplitude brain waves that have been linked to feelings of relaxation.

Theta waves Slow brain waves produced during the hypnagogic state.

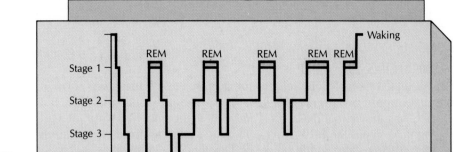

FIGURE 4.3 **SLEEP CYCLES** This figure illustrates the alternation of REM and non-REM sleep for the typical sleeper. There are about five periods of REM sleep during an eight-hour night. Sleep is deeper earlier in the night, and REM sleep tends to become prolonged toward morning.

of four to six cycles per second, and are accompanied by slow, rolling eye movements. The transition from alpha waves to theta waves may be accompanied by a **hypnagogic state,** during which we may experience brief hallucinatory, dreamlike images that resemble vivid photographs. These images may be somehow linked to creativity. Stage 1 sleep is the lightest stage of sleep. If we are awakened from stage 1 sleep, we may feel that we have not slept at all.

After thirty to forty minutes of stage 1 sleep, we undergo a rather steep descent into sleep stages 2, 3, and 4 (see Figure 4.3). Stage 4 is the deepest stage of sleep, from which it is most difficult to be awakened. During stage 2, **sleep spindles** appear. These are rather short bursts of rapid brain waves of a frequency of thirteen to sixteen cycles per second. During stages 3 and 4, we produce the slower delta waves.

After perhaps half an hour of deep stage 4 sleep, we begin a relatively rapid journey back upward through the stages until we enter REM sleep (Figure 4.3). REM sleep derives its name from the *rapid eye movements,* observable beneath our closed lids, that characterize this stage. During REM sleep we produce relatively rapid, low-amplitude brain waves that resemble those of light stage 1 sleep. REM sleep is also called paradoxical sleep. This is because the EEG patterns observed during REM sleep suggest a level of arousal similar to that of the waking state (Figure 4.2). However, we are difficult to awaken during REM sleep. If we are awakened during REM sleep, we report that we have been dreaming 80 percent of the time. (We also dream during NREM sleep, but less frequently. We report dreaming only about 20 percent of the time when awakened during NREM sleep.)

As you can see from Figure 4.3, we tend to undergo five trips through the different stages of sleep each night. These trips include about five periods of REM sleep. Our first journey through stage 4 sleep is usually longest. Sleep tends to become lighter as the night wears on. Our periods of REM sleep tend to become longer, and, toward morning, our last period of REM sleep may last upwards of half an hour.

Hypnagogic state (hip-nuh-GAHDGE-jick). The drowsy interval between waking and sleeping, characterized by brief, hallucinatory, dreamlike experiences.

Sleep spindles Short bursts of rapid brain waves that occur during stage 2 sleep.

Now that we have some idea of what sleep is like, let us examine the issue of *why* we sleep.

FUNCTIONS OF SLEEP

One outdated theory of the reasons for sleep suggested that sleep allowed the brain to rest and recuperate from the stresses of working all day. But the EEG has shown that the brain is active all night long. Moreover, at least during REM sleep, the brain waves are quite similar to those of light sleep and the waking state. So the power isn't switched off at night.

But what of sleep and the rest of the body? Most researchers would not contest the view that sleep helps rejuvenate a tired body (Levitt, 1981). Most of us have had the experience of going without sleep for a night and feeling "wrecked" the following day. Perhaps the following evening we went to bed early to "get our sleep back." Research also suggests that increased physical exertion leads to a greater proportion of time spent in NREM sleep (Walker et al., 1978). Hartmann (1973) suggests that many proteins are synthesized during NREM sleep, and that these proteins may be linked to the restorative effects of sleep. However, no one has yet discovered a relationship between sleep and the restoration of specific chemical substances.

Let us continue our study of the functions of sleep by turning to research concerning long versus short sleepers and the effects of sleep deprivation.

SLEEP Most researchers agree that sleep helps rejuvenate a tired body. There is less agreement concerning possible psychological functions of sleep and dreams.

Long vs. Short Sleepers Ernest Hartmann (1973) of Tufts University compared people who slept nine hours or more a night ("long sleepers") with people who slept six hours or less ("short sleepers"). He found that short sleepers tended to be more happy-go-lucky. They spent less time ruminating and were energetic, active, and relatively self-satisfied. The long sleepers were more concerned about personal achievement and social causes. They tended to be more creative and thoughtful, but were also more anxious and depressed. Hartmann also found that in general we tend to need more sleep during periods of change and stress, such as a change of jobs, an increase in work load, or an episode of depression. So it may be that sleep helps us recover from the stresses of life.

Hartmann also found that long sleepers spend proportionately more time in REM sleep than do short sleepers. Subtracting the amount of REM sleep experienced by both types of sleepers dramatically closed the gap between them. Perhaps REM sleep is at least partially responsible for the restorative function. Since much REM sleep is spent in dreaming, it has been speculated that dreams may somehow promote recovery.

Sleep Deprivation What will happen to you if you miss sleep for one night? For several nights? If you cut down from, say, your normal seven to ten hours to just five and a half? Anecdotal and research evidence offers some suggestions.

In 1959 disc jockey Peter Tripp remained awake for eight days. Toward the end of this episode, he became so paranoid that he could not be given psychological tests (Dement, 1972). However, seventeen-year-old Randy Gardner remained awake for 264 consecutive hours (eleven days), and did not show serious psychological disturbance (Levitt, 1981).

In another anecdote, ten of eleven military cadets who were ordered to engage in strenuous activity for 100 hours developed visual hallucinations, and most developed problems in balance and movement (Opstad et al., 1978). But, as noted by Levitt (1981), these cadets were also deprived of rest and food, not just sleep. According to sleep researcher Wilse Webb, carefully controlled experiments with people who remain sleepless for several consecutive days result in few serious disturbances. Most often, participants show temporary problems in attention, confusion, or misperception (Goleman, 1982). These cognitive lapses may reflect brief episodes of borderline sleep.

What if we were to decide that we wanted to spend a bit more of our lives in the waking state—to work, to study, to play, perchance to daydream? Would any ill effects attend curtailing our sleep to, say, five and a half hours a night? Webb followed fifteen college men who restricted their sleep to five and a half hours for sixty days. For the first few weeks, they showed an increase in deep sleep, but a decrease in REM sleep. But by the end of the first thirty days, they returned to the original level of deep sleep, but REM sleep remained at a below-normal level.

Over the sixty days the men showed little dropoff in ability to remember or to compute numbers. They did show less vigilance on one psychological test, as measured in terms of numbers of responses. But Webb suggests that this deficit may have reflected decreased motivation to perform well, rather than a falling off of perceptual sharpness. It is particularly interesting that the men reported falling asleep in class or feeling drowsy during the first week only. After that they reported *less* drowsiness than prior to the study. Did the study encourage them to permanently change their life styles? No. Despite the lack of ill effects of restricting sleep, all participants returned to their normal seven or eight hours when the study was complete.

Deprivation of REM Sleep In some studies, animals or people have been deprived of REM sleep. With people, REM-sleep deprivation is accomplished by monitoring EEG records and eye movements and waking subjects during REM sleep.

Animals deprived of REM sleep learn more slowly and forget what they have learned more rapidly (Hartmann & Stern, 1972; Pearlman & Greenberg, 1973). There is too much individual variation to conclude that people deprived of REM sleep learn more poorly than they would otherwise (McGrath & Cohen, 1978). But it does seem that such deprivation interferes with human memory—that is, the retrieval of information that has been learned earlier (Cipolli & Salzarulo, 1978; Bloch et al., 1979).

There is some recent research concerning possible links between REM sleep and various forms of abnormal behavior, such as hallucinations and depression (Levitt, 1981, p. 270). But this research is in its early stages, and it would be premature to draw any conclusions.

In any event, people deprived of REM sleep tend to show *REM-rebound*. That is, they tend to spend more time in REM sleep during subsequent sleep periods. They catch up.

As noted earlier, it is during REM sleep that we tend to dream. Let us now turn our attention to dreams, a mystery about which people have theorized for centuries.

DREAMS

Just what is the stuff of dreams? **Dreams** are a form of cognitive activity that occurs during sleep. Like vivid memories and daytime fantasies, dreams involve visual images in the absence of external visual stimulation. Some dreams are so realistic and well organized that we feel that they must be real—that we simply cannot be dreaming this time. You may have had such a dream on the night before a test. The dream would have been that you had taken the test and now it is all over. (Ah, what disappointment then prevailed when you woke up to realize that such was not the case!) Other dreams are disorganized and unformed.

Dreams are most vivid during REM sleep. Then they are most likely to have clear imagery and coherent plots, even if some of the content is fantastic. Plots are vaguer and images more fleeting during NREM sleep. You may well have a dream every time you are in REM sleep. Therefore, if you sleep for eight hours and undergo five sleep cycles, you may have five dreams. Upon waking, you may feel that time seemed to expand or contract during your dreams, so that during ten or fifteen minutes your dream content ranged over days or weeks. But dreams tend to take place in "real time": fifteen minutes of events fills about fifteen minutes of dreaming. Your dream theater is quite flexible: you can dream in black and white and in full color.

Theories of the Content of Dreams

You may recall dreams involving fantastic adventures, but according to Calvin Hall (1966), who has interviewed hundreds of dreamers and recorded the content of thousands of dreams, most dreams are simple extensions of the activities and problems of the day. Hall links dreams to life stresses. If we are preoccupied with illness or death, sexual or aggressive urges, or moral dilemmas, we are likely to dream about them. The characters in our dreams are more likely to be friends and neighbors than spies, monsters, and princes.

Sigmund Freud theorized that dreams reflected unconscious wishes and urges. He argued that through dreams we could express impulses that we would censor during the day. Moreover, the content of dreams was symbolic of unconscious fantasized objects, such as genital organs (see Table 4.1). In Chapter 12 we shall see that a major part of Freud's method of psychoanalysis involved interpretation of the dreams of his clients. Freud also believed that dreams "protected sleep" by providing imagery that would help keep disturbing, repressed thoughts out of awareness.

The view that dreams "protect sleep" has been challenged by the observation that disturbing events of the day tend to be followed by related disturbing dreams—not protective imagery (Foulkes, 1971). Our behavior

TABLE 4.1 Dream Symbols in Psychoanalytic Theory

SYMBOLS FOR THE MALE GENITAL ORGANS

airplanes	fish	neckties	tools	weapons
bullets	hands	poles	trains	
feet	hoses	snakes	trees	
fire	knives	sticks	umbrellas	

SYMBOLS FOR THE FEMALE GENITAL ORGANS

bottles	caves	doors	ovens	ships
boxes	chests	hats	pockets	tunnels
cases	closets	jars	pots	

SYMBOLS FOR SEXUAL INTERCOURSE

climbing a ladder	entering a room
climbing a staircase	flying in an airplane
crossing a bridge	riding a horse
driving an automobile	riding a roller coaster
riding an elevator	walking into a tunnel or down a hall

SYMBOLS FOR THE BREASTS

apples	peaches

Freud theorized that the content of dreams symbolized urges, wishes, and objects of fantasy that we would censor in the waking state.

in dreams is also generally consistent with our waking behavior (Carrington, 1972; Cohen, 1973). Most dreams, then, are unlikely candidates for the expression (even disguised) of repressed urges. The person who leads a moral life tends to dream moral dreams.

According to the **activation-synthesis model** proposed by J. Alan Hobson and Robert W. McCarley (1977), dreams reflect biological rather than psychological activity. According to this view, a time-triggered mechanism in the pons stimulates three kinds of responses. One is *activation* of the reticular activating system (RAS), which arouses us, but not to the point of waking. The eye muscles also respond, showing the rapid eye movement associated with dreaming. A third is general inhibition of motor (muscular) activity, so that we don't thrash about as we dream; in this way, we save ourselves (and our bed partners) a good deal of wear and tear. The RAS also stimulates neural activity in the parts of the cortex involved in vision, hearing, and memory. This activity is then automatically *synthesized* or put together by the cerebral cortex. This view explains why there is a strong tendency to dream about events of the day: the most current neural activity of the cortex would be that which represented the events or concerns of the day.

Nightmares Have you ever dreamed that something heavy was on your chest and watching as you breathed? Or that you were trying to run from a terrible threat, but couldn't gain your footing or coordinate your leg muscles?

In the Middle Ages such nightmares were thought to be the work of demons called incubi and succubi (singular: **incubus** and **succubus**). By and large, they were seen as a form of retribution. That is, they were sent to make you pay for your sins. They might sit on your chest and observe

Activation-synthesis model The view that dreams reflect stimulation of neural activity by the pons and automatic integration (synthesis) of this activity by the cerebral cortex.

Incubus (INK-cue-bus). (1) A spirit or demon thought in medieval times to lie on sleeping people, especially on women for sexual purposes. (2) A nightmare.

Succubus (SUCK-cue-bus). A female demon thought in medieval times to have sexual intercourse with sleeping men.

"NIGHTMARE" In the Middle Ages, nightmares were thought to be the work of demons who were sent to pay sleepers for their sins. In this picture, "Nightmare," by Henry Fuseli, a demon sits upon a woman who is dreaming a nightmare, and threatens to suffocate her. (The Detroit Institute of Art. Gift of Mr. and Mrs. Bert L. Smikler and Mr. and Mrs. Lawrence A. Fleischman)

you fiendishly (how else would a fiend observe, if not "fiendishly"?), as suggested in Fuseli's "Nightmare," or they might try to suffocate you. If you were given to sexual fantasies or behavior, they might have sexual intercourse with you.

Nightmares, like most pleasant dreams, are generally products of REM sleep. We shall discuss the more disturbing "night terrors" under the section on sleep disorders.

SLEEP DISORDERS

There are a number of sleep disorders. Some, like insomnia, are all too familiar. Others, like narcolepsy, seem somewhat exotic. In this section we shall discuss insomnia, narcolepsy, apnea, Sudden Infant Death Syndrome, and the deep-sleep disorders—night terrors, bedwetting, and sleepwalking.

Insomnia   **Insomnia** refers to three types of sleeping problems: difficulty falling asleep (sleep-onset insomnia), difficulty remaining asleep through the night, and awakening prematurely in the morning. Perhaps 30 million Americans suffer from insomnia (Clark et al., 1981), with women complaining of the disorder more frequently than men. Millions of sleeping pills are downed each evening.

As a group, people who suffer from insomnia show higher levels of autonomic activity as they try to get to sleep and as they sleep (Haynes et al., 1981; Johns et al., 1971; Monroe, 1967). Persons with sleep-onset insomnia obtain higher anxiety scores on questionnaires and show more

Insomnia A term for three types of sleeping problems: (1) difficulty falling asleep, (2) difficulty remaining asleep, and (3) waking early. (From the Latin *in-*, meaning "not," and *somnus*, meaning "sleep.")

Ruminative Given to prolonged turning over of thoughts. (From the Latin *ruminare*, meaning "to chew [the cud]" as a cow does.)

Tolerance Habituation to a drug, with the result that increasingly higher doses of the drug are needed to achieve similar effects.

Autogenic training A method for reducing tension involving repeated suggestions that the limbs are becoming warmer and heavier and that one's breathing is becoming more regular.

muscle tension in the forehead than nonsufferers (Haynes et al., 1974). Personality tests also find poor sleepers to be more depressed and **ruminative** than good sleepers, more concerned about physical complaints, and more shy and retiring (Freedman & Sattler, 1982; Marks & Monroe, 1976; Monroe & Marks, 1977). Insomnia comes and goes with many people, increasing during periods of anxiety and tension.

Insomniacs (that's a word that will keep you awake) tend to compound their sleep problems through their efforts to force themselves to get to sleep (Kamens, 1980; Youkilis & Bootzin, 1981). Their concern heightens autonomic activity and muscle tension. You cannot force or will yourself to get to sleep. You can only set the stage for it by lying down and relaxing when you are tired. If you focus on sleep too closely, it will elude you. Yet millions go to bed each night dreading the possibility of sleep-onset insomnia.

How (and How Not) to Get to Sleep at Night

Sleeping pills. No question about it: The most common method for fighting insomnia in the United States is popping pills. Sleeping pills may be effective—for a while. They generally work by reducing arousal. At first lowered arousal may be effective in itself. Focusing on changes in arousal may also distract you from your efforts to *get* to sleep. Expectation of success may also help.

But there are problems with sleeping pills. First, you attribute your success to the pill and not yourself, creating dependency on the pill rather than self-reliance. Second, you develop **tolerance** for sleeping pills. With continued usage you must progressively increase the dose to achieve the same effects. Third, high doses of these chemicals can be dangerous, especially if mixed with an alcoholic beverage or two. Both sleeping pills and alcohol depress the activity of the central nervous system, and their effects are additive.

Relaxing. Recently, psychological methods for coping with insomnia have been developed. These methods reduce tension directly, as with muscle-relaxation exercises. They also involve cognitive elements that distract us from striving to get to sleep.

Focusing on releasing muscle tension has been shown to reduce the amount of time needed to fall asleep and the incidence of waking during the night. It increases the number of hours slept and leaves us feeling more rested in the morning (Lick & Heffler, 1977; Weil & Gottfried, 1973). A common method for easing muscle tension is progressive relaxation, which we shall discuss in Chapter 10. Biofeedback training (Haynes et al., 1977) and **autogenic training** (Nicassio & Bootzin, 1974) have also been used successfully. Biofeedback is discussed later in this chapter. In autogenic training, one reduces muscle tension by focusing on suggestions that the limbs are growing warm and heavy and that the breathing is becoming regular. These methods also provide one with something on which to focus other than trying to fall asleep.

Coping with exaggerated fears. You need not be a sleep expert to realize that convincing yourself that the day will be ruined unless you get to sleep *right now* will increase, rather than decrease, bedtime tensions. As noted earlier, sleep does seem to restore us, especially after physical exertion. But we often exaggerate the problems that will befall us if we do not sleep. Here are some beliefs that increase bedtime tension, and some alternatives that may be of use to you:

EXAGGERATED BELIEF	*ALTERNATIVE BELIEF*
If I don't get to sleep, I'll feel wrecked tomorrow.	Not necessarily. If I'm tired, I can go to bed early tomorrow night.
It's unhealthy for me not to get more sleep.	Not necessarily. Some people do very well on only a few hours of sleep.
I'll wreck my sleeping schedule for the whole week if I don't get to sleep very soon.	Not at all. If I'm tired, I'll just go to bed a bit earlier. I'll get up about the same time with no problem.
If I don't get to sleep, I won't be able to concentrate on that big test tomorrow.	Possibly, but my fears may be exaggerated. I may just as well relax or get up and do something enjoyable for a while.

Avoiding ruminating in bed. Don't plan or worry about tomorrow in bed. When you lie down for sleep, you may organize thoughts for the day for a few minutes, but then allow yourself to relax or engage in fantasy. If an important idea comes to you, jot it down on a handy pad, so that you won't lose it. But if thoughts persist, get up and follow them elsewhere. Let your bed be a place for relaxation and sleep—not your study. A bed—even a waterbed—is not a think tank.

Establishing a regular routine. Sleeping late can encourage sleep-onset insomnia. Set your alarm for the same time each morning and get up, regardless of how many hours you have slept. By sticking to a regular time for rising, you'll be indirectly encouraging yourself to get to sleep at a regular time as well.

Using fantasy. Psychologist Jerome Singer (1975) notes that fantasies or "daydreams" are almost universal and may occur naturally as we fall asleep. You can allow yourself to "go with" fantasies that occur at bedtime, or purposefully use fantasies to get to sleep. You may be able to ease yourself to sleep by focusing on a sun-drenched beach, with waves lapping on the shore, or on a walk through a mountain meadow on a summer day. You can construct your own "mind trips" and paint their details finely. With mind trips you conserve fuel and avoid lines at airports.

Narcolepsy   In **narcolepsy,** which is in a sense the mirror image of insomnia, the person falls suddenly, irresistibly asleep. Narcolepsy afflicts as many as 100,000 people in the United States and seems to run in families. The "sleep attack" lasts about fifteen minutes, after which the person awakens, feeling refreshed. Despite being refreshing, these sleep episodes are dangerous and frightening. They can occur while a person is driving or engaged in work with sharp tools. They may also be accompanied by sudden collapse of muscle groups or even of the entire body (see Figure 4.4)— a condition called sleep paralysis—in which the person cannot move during

Narcolepsy A sleep disorder characterized by uncontrollable seizures of sleep during the waking state. (From the Greek *narke,* meaning "sleep," and *lepsia,* meaning "an attack.")

FIGURE 4.4 **NARCOLEPSY** In a narcolepsy experiment at Stanford, this poodle barks, nods, then suddenly falls asleep. The causes of narcolepsy are unknown, but it is thought to be a disorder of REM sleep functioning.

the transition from the waking state to sleep, and hallucinations occur as of a person or object sitting on the chest.

The causes of narcolepsy are unknown, but it is thought to be a disorder of REM-sleep functioning. Stimulants and antidepressant drugs have helped many narcolepsy sufferers.

Apnea **Apnea** is a potentially dangerous sleep disorder that afflicts as many as one million men, primarily the overweight. In apnea, sleepers stop breathing periodically through the night, as many as 500 times! At such times they may suddenly sit up, gasp to begin breathing again, then fall back asleep. Such sleepers are stimulated nearly, but not quite to waking, by the buildup of carbon dioxide.

Causes of apnea may include anatomical deformities that clog the air passageways, like a thick palate, or a defect in the breathing centers of the brain. Apnea can be treated with **tranquilizers** and, sometimes, by surgery.

Sudden Infant Death Syndrome (SIDS) **SIDS,** or crib death, kills 6,000 to 7,000 children during the first year of life in the United States each year. The child goes to sleep, apparently in perfect health, and is found dead in the morning. New parents often live in dread of SIDS, checking their infants regularly through the night to see that they are breathing. If they stop breathing, but are stimulated, they usually begin breathing again. Parents of children who die from SIDS also typically experience strong guilt, blaming themselves because they failed to monitor or catch their children in time. Cribs and monitors are available that will sound an alarm if the infant stops breathing.

SIDS is all the more frightening because its causes, like those of sleep apnea, are unknown. But it may reflect the immaturity of the infant's nervous system or defects in the respiratory centers of the brain. The risk also seems greatest when the infant has a cold.

Apnea (AP-knee-uh). Temporary stopping of breathing. (From the Greek a-, meaning "without," and pnoie, meaning "wind.")

Tranquilizers Drugs used to reduce anxiety and tension.

SIDS Sudden Infant Death Syndrome, also called crib death. The death, while sleeping, of apparently healthy babies who seem to stop breathing for no clear medical reason. SIDS appears to be a disorder of deep sleep.

Deep-Sleep Disorders: Night Terrors, Bed-Wetting, and Sleepwalking

Night terrors, bed-wetting, and sleepwalking all occur during deep (stage 3 or 4) sleep, are more common among children, and may reflect immaturity of the nervous system.

Night terrors are similar to but more severe than nightmares. Night terrors usually occur during deep sleep, whereas nightmares take place during REM sleep. Night terrors occur early during the night; nightmares are usually events of the morning hours (Hartmann, 1981). The dreamer may suddenly sit up with a surge in heart and respiration rates, talk incoherently, and move about wildly. The dreamer is never fully awake, returns to sleep, and may recall a brief image, as of someone pressing on the chest. But, in contrast to the nightmare, memories of the episode are not vivid. Night terrors are often decreased by a minor tranquilizer at bedtime, which reduces the amount of time spent in stage 4 sleep.

Bed-wetting is often seen as a stigma that reflects parental harshness, or the child's attempt to punish the parents, but this disorder, too, may stem from immaturity of the nervous system. In most cases, bed-wetting resolves itself before adolescence, often by age eight. Behavior-therapy methods that condition children to awaken when about to urinate have been helpful. The antidepressant drug *imipramine* often helps by increasing bladder capacity. But often all that is needed is reassurance that no one need be "to blame" for bed-wetting and that most children "outgrow" the disorder.

As many as 15 percent of children sleepwalk at least once. Sleepwalkers may roam about almost nightly, while their parents fret about the accidents that could befall them. Sleepwalkers typically do not remember their excursions, but may respond to questions while they are up and about. Contrary to myth, there is no evidence that it is dangerous or harmful to awaken a sleepwalker. Mild tranquilizers and maturity typically put an end to sleepwalking.

We have noted that drugs often play a role in the treatment of sleep disorders. But drugs are used "recreationally" or to "expand consciousness" as well as to treat problems. Let us now turn our attention to a number of such drugs.

ALTERING CONSCIOUSNESS THROUGH DRUGS

The world is a supermarket of consciousness-altering chemical substances, or drugs. The United States is flooded with hundreds of drugs that distort perceptions and change mood—drugs that take you up, let you down, and move you across town. Some people use drugs because their friends do, or because their parents tell them not to. Some are seeking pleasure. Others, like our Himalayan travelers, are seeking inner truth. We go off on our internal trips, and many times drugs provide both the vehicle and the fuel.

Following a dropoff in popularity during the 1960s, alcohol has reasserted its dominance among drugs used on college campuses. The majority of college students have tried marijuana, and perhaps one in five smokes it regularly. Many Americans take **depressants** to get to sleep at night and **stimulants** to get going in the morning. Valium, a minor tranquilizer used

Night terrors Frightening dreamlike experiences that occur during the deepest stage of NREM sleep. Nightmares, by contrast, occur during REM sleep.

Depressant A drug that lowers the rate of activity of the nervous system. (From the Latin *de-*, meaning "down," and *premere*, meaning "to press.")

Stimulant A drug that increases activity of the nervous system.

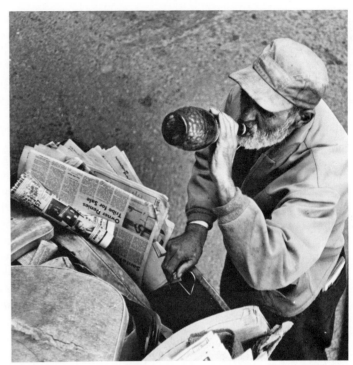

TWO FACETS OF ALCOHOL No drug has meant so much to so many as alcohol. Yet for many, alcohol is a central problem of life.

to relieve anxiety and tension, is one of the most widely prescribed drugs in the United States. Heroin may literally be the opium of the lower classes. Cocaine was until recently the toy of the well-to-do; but price breaks have allowed it to find its way into the lockers of increasing numbers of school students. Despite laws, moral pronouncements, medical warnings, and an occasional horror story, drugs are very much with us.

We shall deal with some general issues in substance abuse and dependence, and then turn our attention to specific drugs.

SUBSTANCE ABUSE AND DEPENDENCE

Where does drug *use* end and *abuse* begin? The American Psychiatric Association lists three criteria for determining substance abuse: a pattern of "pathological" use, impairment in social or occupational functioning, and a duration of the problem for at least one month (1980, p. 163). *Pathological use* typically means that the individual has difficulty limiting use or is intoxicated throughout the day. Alcohol abuse, or **alcoholism,** is drinking that repeatedly interferes with physical, personal, or social well-being. If you are missing school or work because you are drunk, or "sleeping it off," your behavior fits the definition. The amount of the drug being used is not the central factor. It is whether one's pattern of use interferes with other areas of life.

Alcoholism Drinking that persistently impairs personal, social, or physical well-being.

Substance dependence is more severe than substance abuse. It is characterized by physiological dependence, as evidenced either by *tolerance* or by an *abstinence syndrome* upon withdrawal. Tolerance is the body's habituation to a drug, so that with regular usage higher doses are required to achieve similar effects. Physiological dependence also means that there will be characteristic withdrawal symptoms, or an **abstinence syndrome,** when the level of usage is suddenly lowered. The abstinence syndrome for alcohol includes anxiety, tremors, restlessness, weakness, rapid pulse, and high blood pressure.

People who are *psychologically* dependent on a drug show concern or anxiety over going without it. Many signs of anxiety—shakiness, rapid pulse, sweating, and so on—overlap with abstinence syndromes that result from physiological dependence. Thus people may believe that they are physiologically dependent on a drug when they are psychologically dependent. Still, there are some aspects of abstinence from certain drugs that are unmistakably physiological. One example is **delirium tremens** ("the DT's"), experienced by some chronic alcoholics when they suddenly decrease or suspend drinking. The DT's are characterized by heavy sweating, restlessness, general **disorientation,** and terrifying **hallucinations**—often of creepy, crawling animals.

CAUSAL FACTORS IN SUBSTANCE ABUSE AND DEPENDENCE

There are many reasons for substance abuse and dependence. Just a handful include curiosity, peer pressure, rebelliousness, and escape from boredom or pressure (Brook et al., 1980; Conger & Petersen, 1984; Kandel, 1980). In a study of influence the social environment can play in drug use, Jerald Bachman of the University of Michigan Institute for Social Research and his colleagues (1984) surveyed young adults who were three years out of high school. For those who continued to live with their parents, use of alcohol, marijuana, and other illicit drugs remained unchanged, and for those who had gotten married, drug use decreased. But for those who moved into dormitories or apartments, or who lived with persons of the opposite sex, drug use showed an increase.

Psychological and biological theories also account for substance abuse in the following ways.

Psychoanalytic Views   Psychoanalytic explanations of substance abuse propose that drugs help people control or express unconscious needs and impulses. Alcoholism, for example, may reflect the need to remain dependent on an overprotective mother, or the effort to reduce emotional conflicts, or to cope with unconscious homosexual impulses.

Behavioral/Social-Learning Views   Learning theorists suggest that first usage of tranquilizing agents such as Valium and alcohol usually results from observing others or from a recommendation. But subsequent usage may be reinforced by the drugs' positive effects on the mood and their reduction of unpleasant sensations such as anxiety, fear, and tension. As an example, Collins, Parks, and Marlatt (1985) found that we may drink more than usual at social gatherings when others around us are drinking heavily (a modeling effect), and we may increase our drinking further as a way of reducing the unpleasantness of aversive social interactions (reinforcement). For people who are physiologically dependent, avoidance of withdrawal symptoms is also reinforcing. Carrying the substance around is reinforcing, because then one need not worry about having to go without it. Some people, for example, will simply not leave the house without taking Valium along.

Genetic Predispositions There is growing evidence that people can have a genetic predisposition toward physiological dependence on certain substances (Vaillant, 1982). For example, rats have been selectively bred to show preference for alcohol over other beverages (Sigovia-Riquelma et al., 1971). Moreover, the biological children of alcoholics who are raised by adoptive parents are more likely to develop alcohol-related problems than are the natural children of the adoptive parents (Goodwin et al., 1973; Goodwin, 1979). Cummings (1979) argues that not everyone can become physiologically dependent on heroin. Of newborn children of physiologically dependent mothers, about 92 percent show an abstinence syndrome, but the other 8 percent do not. Cummings states that this difference cannot be attributed to the quantity of heroin used by the mother.

Prenatal Factors The prenatal environment may also play a role. Julien (1986) reports that even small amounts of alcohol drunk by mothers during certain stages of pregnancy can predispose the child to alcohol-related problems.

Let us now consider the effects of some frequently used substances, including depressants, stimulants, and hallucinogenics.

DEPRESSANTS

Depressant drugs generally act by slowing the activity of the central nervous system, although there are a number of other effects specific to each drug. In this section we consider the effects of alcohol, opiates and opioids, barbiturates and methaqualone.

ALCOHOL

No drug has meant so much to so many as alcohol. Alcohol is our dinnertime relaxant, our bedtime **sedative,** our cocktail-party social facilitator. We celebrate holy days, applaud our accomplishments, and express joyous wishes with alcohol. The young assert their maturity with alcohol. The elderly use it to stimulate circulation in peripheral areas of the body. Alcohol kills germs on surface wounds. Some pediatricians even swab the painful gums of teething babies with alcohol.

Alcohol is the tranquilizer you can buy without prescription. It is the relief from anxiety you can swallow in public without criticism or stigma-

---

Sedative A drug that soothes or quiets restlessness or agitation. (From the Latin *sedare,* meaning "to settle.")

tization. A man who pops a Valium tablet may look weak. A man who chugalugs a bottle of beer may be perceived as "macho."

No drug has been so abused as alcohol. Perhaps 10 million Americans are alcoholics. Compare this figure to the 200,000 who use heroin regularly, or the 300,000 to 500,000 who abuse sedatives. Excessive drinking has been linked to lower productivity, loss of employment, and downward movement in social status (Baum-Baicker, 1984; Mider, 1984; Vaillant & Milofsky, 1982). Yet half of all Americans use alcohol, and despite widespread marijuana use, it is the drug of choice among adolescents.

Effects of Alcohol   Although the effects of drugs vary from individual to individual (Erwin et al., 1984), we can generally note that our response to a substance reflects (1) the physiological effects of that substance on us, and (2) our interpretations of those effects. Our interpretations of the effects of drugs are, in turn, influenced by our expectations. Consider the case of reverse tolerance for marijuana (with marijuana, regular usage frequently leads to the need for less of the substance in order to achieve similar effects). It may be that some of the **psychoactive** substances in marijuana smoke take a long time to be metabolized by the body. The effects of new doses would then be added to those of the chemicals remaining in the body. But regular users also expect certain effects. These expectations may interact with even mild bodily cues or sensations to produce effects previously achieved only through higher doses.

What expectations do we have of alcohol? Adolescent and adult samples tend to report the belief that alcohol will have a number of effects, including reducing tension, diverting one from worrying, enhancing pleasure, increasing social ability, and transforming experiences for the better (Brown et al., 1980, 1985; Christiansen et al., 1982; Rohsenow, 1983). What *does* alcohol do?

As a depressant, alcohol slows the activity of the central nervous system. Regular alcohol use over a year or more may contribute to feelings of depression, although short-term use may lessen feelings of depression (Aneshensel & Huba, 1983). Alcohol relaxes and deadens minor aches and pains. Alcohol also intoxicates. It impairs cognitive functioning, slurs the speech, and reduces motor coordination. Alcohol is clearly implicated in perhaps half of our automobile accidents.

Drinkers may do things they would not do if sober, because alcohol may impair the information-processing needed to inhibit impulses (Hull et al., 1983; Steele & Southwick, 1985). That is, when intoxicated, people may be less able to foresee the negative consequences of misbehavior and may be less likely to recall social and personal standards for behavior. Alcohol may also provide an excuse for unacceptable behavior (Abrams & Wilson, 1983). ("It wasn't me. It was the alcohol.") We shall pursue this important issue below. Alcohol also induces feelings of elation and **euphoria** that may help wash away self-doubts and self-criticism.

As a food, alcohol is fattening. Yet chronic drinkers may be malnourished. Though high in calories, alcohol does not contain nutrients like vitamins and proteins. A diet low in protein can lead to **cirrhosis of the**

Psychoactive Having psychological effects.
Euphoria (you-FOR-ree-uh). Feelings of well-being, elation. (From the Greek *euphoros*, meaning "healthy.")

Cirrhosis of the liver (sir-ROW-sis). A disease caused by protein deficiency in which connective fibers replace active liver cells, impeding circulation of the blood. Alcohol does not contain protein; therefore, persons who drink excessively may be prone to this disease. (From the Greek *kirrhos*, meaning "tawny," referring to the yellow-orange color of the diseased liver.)

Marry In this quotation, an alternate spelling for the name *Mary*—used to avoid disrespect for the Virgin Mary. In Shakespearean times, *Marry* was the equivalent of *My goodness.*

Nose-painting Redness of the nose caused by rupture of small blood vessels.

Lechery Unrestrained indulgence of sexual desires. (May derive from the Greek *leichein,* meaning "to lick.")

liver, which afflicts many alcoholics. In this disease, connective fibers replace active liver cells, impeding circulation of the blood. Drinking can also rupture small blood vessels, especially in the nose, leading to swelling and redness. Chronic drinking has been linked to heart disease, high blood pressure, and brain damage. Even moderate drinking by a pregnant woman can harm the fetus.

Drinking as a Strategy   We tend to think of excessive drinkers, or people who act antisocially when they drink, as "victims" of alcohol. Yet recent theory and evidence suggest that many so-called victims may purposefully use drinking as an excuse for failure and antisocial behavior.

In one experiment, volunteers were given the chance to drink alcohol (supposedly in a taste test) after having to write an essay that ran counter to their actual attitudes (Steele et al., 1981). Subjects who drank more heavily were likely to maintain their pre-experimental attitudes. Subjects who drank less showed more attitudinal change after writing the essays. The researchers theorize that some of us may drink as a way of allowing us to live with actions that run counter to our attitudes. In Chapter 1 we already saw how people tend to attribute socially unacceptable aggressive behavior to alcohol.

In another experiment (Tucker et al., 1981), volunteers were given cognitive tasks. Some had access to study materials and, consequently, had a high expectation of success. Others did not have study materials available. Subjects who could use study aids drank less than subjects who could not. The researchers suggest that subjects who were more likely to fail used alcohol as a *self-handicapping strategy*. That is, if they did fail, they could attribute their failure to the alcohol.

It should be noted that regardless of how or why one starts drinking, regular drinking can lead to physiological dependence. Once one has become physiologically dependent on alcohol, one will be motivated to drink in order to avoid withdrawal symptoms. Still, even when alcoholics have been "dried out"—withdrawn from alcohol—many return to drinking. Perhaps they are still seeking to use alcohol as an excuse for failing to live up to their expectations.

Let us now examine some experiments that suggest how we use drinking as a strategy in the area of sexual behavior.

Alcohol and Sex   Note this exchange between Macduff and a porter, two characters in Shakespeare's *Macbeth:*

PORTER: Drink, sir, is a great provoker of three things.
MACDUFF: What three things does drink especially provoke?
PORTER: **Marry,** sir, **nose-painting,** sleep, and urine. **Lechery,** sir, it provokes and unprovokes; it provokes the desire, but takes away the performance.

Does alcohol stir the sexual appetite? *Does* it inhibit sexual response ("take away the performance")? In a study of 20,000 readers of *Psychology Today,* three of five respondents wrote that alcohol increased their sexual pleasure.

QUESTIONNAIRE

WHY DO YOU DRINK?

Do you drink? If so, why? To enhance your pleasure? To cope with your problems? To help you in your social encounters? Half of all Americans use alcohol for a variety of reasons. Perhaps as many as one user in 10 is an alcoholic. College students who expect that alcohol will help them reduce tension are more likely than other students to encounter alcohol-related problems (Brown, 1985).

To gain insight into your reasons for using alcohol, respond to the following items by circling the *T* if an item is true or mostly true for you, or the *F* if an item is false or mostly false for you. Then turn to the answer key in Appendix B.

T F

____ 1. I find it very unpleasant to do without alcohol for some time.
____ 2. Alcohol makes it easier for me to talk to other people.
____ 3. I drink to appear more grown up and more sophisticated.
____ 4. When I drink, the future looks brighter to me.
____ 5. I like the taste of what I drink.
____ 6. If I go without a drink for some time, I am not bothered or uncomfortable.
____ 7. I feel more relaxed and less tense about things when I drink.
____ 8. I drink so that I will fit in better with the crowd.
____ 9. I worry less about things when I drink.
____ 10. I have a drink when I get together with the family.
____ 11. I have a drink as part of my religious ceremonies.
____ 12. I have a drink when I have a toothache or other pain.
____ 13. I feel much more powerful when I have a drink.
____ 14. You really can't blame me for the things I do when I have been drinking.
____ 15. I have a drink before a big test, date, or interview when I'm afraid of how well I'll do.
____ 16. I find I have a drink for the taste alone.
____ 17. I've found a drink in my hand when I can't remember putting it there.
____ 18. I'll have a drink when I feel "blue" or want to take my mind off my cares and worries.
____ 19. I can do better socially and sexually after having a drink or two.
____ 20. Drinking makes me do stupid things.
____ 21. Sometimes when I have a few drinks, I can't get to work.
____ 22. I feel more caring and giving after having a drink or two.
____ 23. I drink because I like the look of a drinker.
____ 24. I like to drink more on festive occasions.
____ 25. When a friend or I have done something well, we're likely to have a drink or two.
____ 26. I have a drink when some problem is nagging away at me.
____ 27. I find drinking pleasurable.
____ 28. I like the "high" of drinking.
____ 29. Sometimes I pour a drink without realizing I still have one that is unfinished.
____ 30. I feel I can better get others to do what I want when I've had a drink or two.
____ 31. Having a drink keeps my mind off my problems.
____ 32. I get a real gnawing hunger for a drink when I haven't had one for a while.

_____ 33. A drink or two relaxes me.
_____ 34. Things look better when I've had a drink or two.
_____ 35. My mood is much better after I've been drinking.
_____ 36. I see things more clearly when I've been drinking.
_____ 37. A drink or two enhances the pleasure of sex and food.
_____ 38. When I'm out of alcohol, I immediately buy more.
_____ 39. I would have done much better on some things if it weren't for alcohol.
_____ 40. When I have run out of alcohol, I find it almost unbearable until I can get some more.

Sources: Items adapted from (1) general discussion of expectancies about alcohol in Christiansen et al. (1982) and (2) smokers' self-testing items analyzed by Leventhal and Avis (1976).

Women reported these enhancing effects more often than men (Athanasiou et al., 1970). Many people believe that alcohol either increases or does not affect their sexual response, as did a group of male alcoholics studied by Wilson and his colleagues (1978).

Recent studies of response to sexually explicit films suggest that men who *believe* they have drunk alcohol (when they have not) show increases in sexual arousal, as measured by size of erection and subjective feelings of arousal. But men who have *actually* drunk alcohol, without knowing it, show decreased sexual response (Briddell & Wilson, 1976). As noted in Chapter 1, such studies are made possible by inability to taste vodka when mixed with tonic water. In this way, subjects can be led to believe they have drunk alcohol when they have not, and vice versa. Similar research shows that alcohol also decreases women's response to sexually explicit films (Wilson & Lawson, 1978). Thus our beliefs about the effects of alcohol may diverge markedly from its actual effects. The "sexy" feeling we may experience after a few drinks may stem from sensations we expect, rather than arousal stimulated by alcohol.

Many of us may drink, or encourage dates to drink, to lower inhibitions. However, there is no evidence that alcohol directly reduces feelings of guilt. In experiments similar to those described above, men who *believed* they had drunk alcohol, when they had not, spent significantly more time looking at sexually explicit pictures than men who *believed* they had not drunk alcohol. Researchers conclude that drinking may have served as an excuse for prolonged viewing of these pictures (Lang et al., 1980; Lansky & Wilson, 1981). Alcohol may give us an excuse for an assortment of behaviors we would consider unacceptable under normal circumstances.

Treatment of Alcoholism   Treatment of alcoholism has been a frustrating endeavor. *Detoxification,* or helping a physiologically dependent alcoholic safely through the abstinence syndrome, is a generally straightforward medical procedure, requiring about one week (Rada & Kellner, 1979). But assisting the alcoholic to then learn to cope with life's stresses through measures other than drinking is the heart of the problem. Several treatments have been tried, most with little documented success.

Medication. The drug *disulfuram* (brand name Antabuse) has been used most widely with alcoholics. Mixing Antabuse with alcohol can cause feelings of illness. However, current maintenance doses of Antabuse are usually too low to have this result, and there is little convincing evidence of the drug's effectiveness (Miller & Hester, 1980).

Alcoholics Anonymous. Many people consider Alcoholics Anonymous (AA), a nonprofessional organization, to offer the most effective treatment for alcoholics. At AA, alcoholics undergo a conversion in identity to that of a "recovering alcoholic." Conversion requires confession of one's drinking problems before a group of alcoholics, and the making of a public commitment not to touch another drop. The new identity becomes confirmed with the passing of each sober day, and recovering alcoholics often help other alcoholics undergo a similar conversion.

While AA commonly cites a success rate in the neighborhood of 75 percent (Wallace, 1985), critics note that figures this high usually include only persons who remain in treatment. As many as 90 percent of those who attend AA meetings drop out after a few meetings (Miller, 1982).

Behavior Therapy. Behavior therapy is proving helpful to many alcoholics. A variety of methods to be explained in depth in Chapter 12 show promising success rates. These include aversion therapy, relaxation training, covert sensitization, instruction in social skills, and self-monitoring (Elkins, 1980; Miller & Mastria, 1977; Olson et al., 1981).

Opiates (OH-pee-ates). A group of addictive drugs derived from the opium poppy that provide a euphoric "rush" and depress the nervous system.

Narcotics Drugs used to relieve pain and induce sleep. The term is usually reserved for opiates. (From the Greek *narke,* meaning "numbness" or "stupor.")

Analgesia A state of not feeling pain, although fully conscious.

Opioid (OH-pee-oid). A synthetic (artificial) drug similar in chemical composition to opiates.

Morphine An opiate introduced at about the time of the U.S. Civil War.

Heroin An opiate. Heroin, ironically, was used as a "cure" for morphine addiction when first introduced.

OPIATES AND OPIOIDS

Opiates are a group of **narcotics** derived from the opium poppy. The ancient Sumerians gave this poppy its name: it means "plant of joy." The opiates include morphine, heroin, codeine, demerol, and similar drugs whose major medical application is **analgesia.** Opiates appear to stimulate centers in the brain that lead to pleasure and to physiological dependence (Goeders & Smith, 1984; Ling et al., 1984).

In this section we discuss morphine, heroin, and the **opioid** methadone. Opioids are similar to opiates in chemical structure and effect, but are artificial (synthesized in the laboratory).

Morphine   **Morphine** was introduced at about the time of the Civil War in the United States and the Franco-Prussian War in Europe. It was used to deaden pain from wounds, and used quite liberally. Physiological dependence on morphine became known as the "soldier's disease." There was little stigma attached to dependence until morphine became a restricted substance.

Heroin   **Heroin** was given its name because, when it was derived, it was hailed as the "hero" that would cure physiological dependence on morphine. But heroin, like the other opiates, is a powerful depressant that can also provide a euphoric rush. Users of heroin claim it is so pleasurable it can eradicate any thought of food or sex. After its initial appearance,

HEROIN Users of heroin claim it is so pleasurable that it can eradicate any thought of food or sex. Many users remain dependent on heroin, because they are unwilling to undergo withdrawal symptoms or to contemplate a life devoid of drugs.

heroin was soon used to treat so many "problems" that it became known as G.O.M. ("God's own medicine").

Morphine and heroin can have distressing abstinence syndromes, beginning with flulike symptoms and progressing through tremors, cramps, chills alternating with sweating, rapid pulse, high blood pressure, insomnia, vomiting, and diarrhea. However, the syndrome can be quite variable from person to person. Many American soldiers who used heroin regularly in Vietnam are reported to have suspended usage with relatively little trouble when they returned to the United States.

Heroin is illegal. Because the penalties for possession or sale are high, it is also very expensive. For this reason many physiologically dependent people support their "habits" through dealing (selling heroin), prostitution, or selling stolen goods. But heroin does not directly stimulate criminal or aggressive behavior. On the other hand, people who use heroin regularly may be more likely than nonusers to engage in *other* criminal behavior as well. Considering the legal penalties for heroin use, most users are willing to take high risks.

Although regular users develop tolerance for heroin, high doses can cause drowsiness, stupor, altered time perception, and impaired judgment.

Methadone **Methadone** has been used to treat physiological dependence on heroin in the same way heroin was used to treat physiological dependence on morphine. Methadone is slower acting than heroin and does not provide the thrilling rush. Most people treated with it simply swap dependence on one drug for dependence on another. Because they are unwilling to undergo withdrawal symptoms, or to contemplate a life style devoid of drugs, they must be maintained indefinitely on methadone.

If methadone is injected, rather than taken orally, it can provide sensations similar to those of heroin. Another drug, *naloxone*, prevents users from becoming high if they later take heroin. Some people are placed on naloxone after being withdrawn from heroin. However, former addicts can simply choose not to take naloxone. Drugs like naloxone also do not provide former users the desire to undertake a heroin-free life style.

BARBITURATES AND METHAQUALONE

If its name ends in *-barbital,* it may well be a **barbiturate,** like amobarbital, phenobarbital, pentobarbital, and secobarbital. Barbiturates are depressants with a number of medical uses, including relief of anxiety and tension, deadening of pain, and treatment of epilepsy, high blood pressure, and insomnia. Barbiturates lead rapidly to physiological and psychological dependence.

Methaqualone, sold under the brand names Quaalude and Sopor, is a depressant similar in effect to barbiturates. Methaqualone also leads to physiological dependence and is quite dangerous.

Psychologists generally oppose using barbiturates and methaqualone for anxiety, tension, and insomnia. They lead rapidly to dependence and do nothing to teach the individual how to alter disturbing patterns of be-

---

Methadone (METH-uh-don). An artificial narcotic that is slower acting than, and does not provide the "rush" of, heroin. Methadone use allows heroin addicts to abstain from heroin without experiencing an abstinence syndrome.

Barbiturate (bar-BICH-ur-it). An addictive depressant used to relieve anxiety or induce sleep.

Methaqualone An addictive depressant. Often called "ludes."

havior. Many physicians, too, have become concerned by barbiturates. They now prefer to prescribe minor tranquilizers such as Valium and Librium for anxiety and tension, and other drugs for insomnia. However, as you will see in Chapter 12, it is now thought that minor tranquilizers may also create physiological dependence. And using them does nothing to help a person change sources of stress in his or her life.

Barbiturates and methaqualone are popular as street drugs, because they relax the muscles and produce a mild euphoric state. High doses of barbiturates result in drowsiness, motor impairment, slurred speech, irritability, and poor judgment. A physiologically dependent person who is withdrawn abruptly may experience severe convulsions and die. High doses of methaqualone may cause internal bleeding, coma, and death. Because of additive effects, it is dangerous to mix alcohol and other depressants at bedtime, or at any time.

STIMULANTS

Stimulants act by increasing the activity of the nervous system. The other effects of stimulants vary somewhat from drug to drug, and some seem to contribute to feelings of euphoria and self-confidence.

AMPHETAMINES

Amphetamines are a group of stimulants that were first used by soldiers during World War II to help them remain alert through the night. Truck drivers have used them to drive through the night. But amphetamines have become more widely known through students who have used them for all-night cram sessions, and through dieters. One of their effects is to reduce hunger.

A number of researchers report that amphetamines and a related stimulant, Ritalin, increase self-control in **hyperactive** children, increase their attention span, decrease fidgeting, and lead to academic gains (Barkley et al., 1984; Kavale, 1982; Mattes & Gittelman, 1983; O'Leary, 1980; Rapport, 1984). It may be that a combination of stimulants and behavior therapy will prove to be the most effective approach to treating hyperactivity (Hinshaw et al., 1984; Pelham et al., 1983). The paradoxical calming effect of stimulants on hyperactive children may be explained by assuming that a cause of hyperactivity is immaturity of the cerebral cortex. Amphetamines may act to stimulate the cortex to exercise control over more primitive centers in the lower brain.

Called speed, uppers, bennies (for Benzedrine), and dexies (for Dexedrine), these drugs are often used for the euphoric "rush" they can produce, especially in high doses. (The so-called antidepressant drugs, which we shall discuss in Chapter 12, do not produce any euphoric rush.) Some people swallow amphetamines in pill form or inject liquid Methedrine, the strongest form, into their veins. They may stay awake and "high" for days on end. Such highs must come to an end. People who have been on pro-

Amphetamines (am-FET-uh-means). Stimulants derived from alpha-*methyl*-beta-*phenyl*-ethyl-*amine*, a colorless liquid consisting of carbon, hydrogen, and nitrogen.

Hyperactive More active than normal.

PSYCHOLOGY TODAY

A TASTE OF ECSTASY

In the Swinging Sixties, LSD was touted as being capable of changing the world through the compelling self-insight it was supposed to afford. Two decades later, in a world still teetering on the brink, a drug called MDMA, or "Ecstasy," is the new savior on the block.

Users and proponents claim that Ecstasy allows clients in therapy to talk about things that would normally be too frightening. A Massachusetts woman took Ecstasy to enable her to discuss her terminal cancer with her family. A San Francisco rape victim used Ecstasy in order to be able to face her memories of her attack (Toufexis, 1985). Lester Grinspoon, a Harvard University psychiatrist, says that Ecstasy "helps people get in touch with feelings which are not ordinarily available to them" (Adler et al., 1985).

Ecstasy has also been credited with relaxing social inhibitions, enhancing the joys of sex, and enabling people to trust one another. But unlike stimulants, Ecstasy in normal doses is not reported to produce a rush of euphoria; unlike hallucinogenics, Ecstasy apparently does not produce hallucinations or impair the user's ability to distinguish between reality and fantasy.

A Cousin of Amphetamine   MDMA is the abbreviation for the chemical 3,4-methylenedioxymethamphetamine, and as such it is a cousin to the amphetamines.

Until recently, little was heard about any potential for MDMA abuse. But today the numbers of young people who take multiple doses to achieve amphetaminelike highs is on the rise. UCLA psychopharmacologist Ronald K. Siegel believes that MDMA has a number of unpredictable, but potentially severe, side effects, such as fluctuations in blood pressure, heavy sweating, and blurred vision (Toufexis, 1985). Although some researchers assert that the likelihood of bad reactions to MDMA is negligible or nonexistent, some government officials claim that a number of users have had psychotic episodes in response to the drug.

Prohibited   Until 1985 MDMA was as legal as aspirin and Tums, although it is much more expensive (about $10–$30 on the street for a 100-milligram dose). But then MDMA became prohibited under the Controlled Substances Act of 1984, which permits the Drug Enforcement Administration to temporarily ban drugs that are potential threats to public health. Supporters of Ecstasy are lobbying for permission to conduct legitimate research into its therapeutic uses.

As of today, the future of Ecstasy is anyone's guess.

longed highs sometimes "crash," or fall into a deep sleep or depression. Some people commit suicide when crashing.

People can become psychologically dependent on amphetamines, especially when they are using them to cope with depression. Tolerance develops rapidly, but opinion is mixed as to whether they lead to physiological dependence. High doses may cause restlessness, hallucinations, paranoid delusions (see Chapter 11), insomnia, loss of appetite, and irritability.

Cocaine

No doubt you've seen commercials claiming that Coke adds life. Given its caffeine and sugar content, "Coke"—Coca-Cola, that is—should provide quite a lift. But Coca-Cola hasn't been "the real thing" since 1906. At that time the manufacturers discontinued use of the coca leaves from which the soft drink derived its name. Coca leaves contain **cocaine,** a stimulant that produces a state of euphoria, or high, reduces hunger, deadens pain, and bolsters self-confidence.

Cocaine is brewed from coca leaves as a "tea," breathed in ("snorted") in powder form, and injected ("shot up") in liquid form.

Cocaine (co-CANE). A powerful stimulant.

"Song of Praise"   As reported in *Time* Magazine:

A cocaine high is an intensely vivid, sensation-enhancing experience—
though there is no evidence, as is often claimed, that it is aphrodisiac-
al. . . . Says a Manhattan ballerina, "It makes you shiver in tune with the
raw, volcanic energy of New York. It bleeds your sense till you see the city
as an epileptic rainbow, trembling at the speed of light." Test programs at
UCLA have shown that lab monkeys will forgo both food and sex in favor
of an injection of a cocaine solution (July 6, 1981, p. 59).

Cocaine—also called *snow* and *coke,* like the slang term for the soft
drink—has been used as a local anesthetic since the early 1800s. It came
to the attention of one Viennese neurologist in 1884, a young chap named
Sigmund Freud, who used it to fight his own depression and published an
early supportive article, "Song of Praise."

Dependence   There remains some question as to whether cocaine
leads to physiological dependence. Although many government officials
and scientists claim that it does, users may not develop tolerance for the
drug, and it is unclear as to whether there is a specific abstinence syndrome
(Van Dyke & Byck, 1982). However, there is no doubt that users can readily
become psychologically dependent. Usage can also lead to restlessness and
insomnia, tremors, severe headaches, nausea, convulsions, psychotic reactions (hallucinations and delusions), and—though rarely—respiratory and
cardiovascular collapse. Repeated "snorting" constricts blood vessels in the
nose, drying the skin, and, at times, exposing cartilege and perforating the
nasal septum. These problems require cosmetic surgery.

Although cocaine has been unavailable to the general public since
the Harrison Narcotic Act of 1914, it is still commonly the anesthetic of
choice for surgery on the nose and throat. Cocaine, by the way, *is* a stimulant, not a narcotic. Its classification as a narcotic was only a legality—
bringing the drug under the prohibitions of the narcotics act.

CIGARETTES

All cigarette packs sold in the United States carry messages such as: "Warning: The Surgeon General Has Determined That Cigarette Smoking Is Dangerous to Your Health." Cigarette advertising has been banned on the radio
and television. In 1982, Surgeon General C. Everett Koop declared that
"Cigarette smoking is clearly identified as the chief preventable cause of
death in our society and the most important public health issue of our time."

In that year, 430,000 people would die from cancer, and the Surgeon
General's report argued that 30 percent of these deaths were attributable to
smoking (Toufexis, 1982). Cigarette smoking can cause cancer of the lungs,
larynx, oral cavity, and esophagus, and may contribute to cancer of the
bladder, pancreas, and kidneys. Cigarette smoking is also linked to death
from heart disease, chronic lung and respiratory diseases, and other illnesses. Pregnant women who smoke risk miscarriage, premature birth, and
birth defects. Once it was thought that smokers' ills tended to focus on men,
but today women smokers have a 30 percent greater risk of dying from
cancer than do women nonsmokers. Because of the noxious effects of sec-

Hemoglobin The substance in the blood that carries oxygen.

Hydrocarbons Chemical compounds consisting of hydrogen and carbon.

Nicotine A stimulant found in tobacco smoke. (From the French name for the tobacco plant, *nicotiane*.)

ond-hand smoke, smoking has been banished from many public places, like elevators. Many restaurants now reserve sections for nonsmokers.

So it's no secret that cigarette smoking is dangerous. In fact, in the 1980s, peer pressure seems to be favoring *not* smoking. According to one 1980 survey, 74 percent of high school seniors thought their peers would disapprove of their smoking (ADAMHA News, February 9, 1981). It is a positive sign that the percentage of high school graduates who smoke has dropped off from about 38 percent in the mid-1970s to about 30 percent or less in the 1980s (Johnston et al., 1982).

Components of Tobacco Smoke: Where There's Smoke, There's Chemicals Tobacco smoke contains *carbon monoxide, hydrocarbons* (or *"tars"*), and *nicotine.*

Oxygen is carried through the bloodstream by **hemoglobin.** But when carbon monoxide combines with hemoglobin, it impairs the blood's ability to supply the body with oxygen. One result: shortness of breath. Some **hydrocarbons** have been shown to cause cancer in laboratory animals.

Nicotine is the stimulant in cigarettes. Nicotine can cause cold, clammy skin, faintness and dizziness, nausea and vomiting, and diarrhea—all of which account for the occasional discomforts of the novice smoker. Nicotine also stimulates discharge of the hormone adrenalin. Adrenalin creates a burst of autonomic activity, including rapid heart rate and release of sugar into the blood. It also provides a sort of mental "kick." Nicotine is responsible for the stimulating properties of cigarette smoke, but its effects are short-lived. In the long run it can contribute to fatigue.

Physiological Dependence Although there is considerable controversy as to whether smokers develop physiological dependence on cigarettes, nicotine is apparently the agent that creates dependence. The controversy over physiological dependence stems from the fact that the withdrawal symptoms from smoking cigarettes (nervousness, drowsiness, energy loss, headaches, fatigue, irregular bowels, lightheadedness, insomnia, dizziness, cramps, palpitations, tremors, and sweating) mimic an anxiety state. However, Stanley Schachter (1977) has shown that regular smokers adjust their smoking in order to maintain fairly even levels of nicotine in their bloodstream. Thus we know that smokers will avoid drops in nicotine levels. Changes in nicotine level constitute a real and measurable bodily change that results from use of cigarettes, and people who are unwilling to experience the results of this dropoff could be considered physiologically dependent.

It has also been found that nicotine is excreted more rapidly when the urine is highly acid. Stress increases the amount of acid in the urine. For this reason, smokers may need to smoke more when under stress to maintain the same blood nicotine level. They may *believe* that smoking is helping them cope with stress. However, research (Silverstein, 1982) suggests strongly that the "calming effect" attributed to cigarette smoking may amount to nothing more than suspension of the withdrawal symptoms of physiologically dependent smokers. The only source of stress with which smokers may be "coping" is the stress of withdrawal.

Quitting Smoking When it comes to stopping smoking, common sense is also good psychology. People who successfully cut their cigarette use by at least 50 percent are more highly motivated and committed to cutting down than would-be reducers (Perri et al., 1977). For successful quitters, the cons of smoking significantly outweigh the pros (Velicer et al., 1985). David Premack (1970) believes that humiliation is also a prime motivator for those who succeed. At some point we become humiliated by our inability to quit. Perhaps we torch a hole into a favorite piece of clothing or see our children fiddling with cigarettes. We then resolve to be reborn or purified as nonsmokers (Sarbin & Nucci, 1973). Our belief that we can cut down or quit is also important (Blittner et al., 1978). Once we have quit, belief in our ability to remain abstinent correlates positively with abstinence at three- and six-month follow-ups (McIntyre et al., 1983).

Evidence is mixed as to whether it is more effective to cut down gradually or quit all at once. Going cold turkey (quitting all at once) is more effective for some smokers (Flaxman, 1978), but cutting down gradually is more effective for others (Glasgow et al., 1984). Although it is most healthful to quit smoking completely, some smokers, who were not able to quit, have nevertheless learned to reduce their cigarette consumption by at least 50 percent, and to have stuck to their lower levels for up to two and a half years (Glasgow et al., 1983, 1985).

Strategies for Quitting Given the determination to quit, you or your friends may find it helpful to try some of the following suggestions:

Tell your family and friends that you're quitting—make a public commitment.

Think of specific things to tell yourself when you feel the urge to smoke: how you'll be stronger, free of fear of cancer, ready for the marathon, etc., etc.

Tell yourself that the first few days are the hardest—after that, withdrawal symptoms weaken dramatically.

Remind yourself that you're "superior" to nonquitters.

Start when you wake up, at which time you've already gone eight hours without nicotine.

Go on a smoke-ending vacation to get away from places and situations in which you're used to smoking.

Throw out ashtrays and don't allow smokers to visit you at home for a while.

Don't carry matches or light other people's cigarettes.

Sit in nonsmokers' sections of restaurants and trains.

Fill your days with novel activities—things that won't remind you of smoking.

Use sugar-free mints or gum as substitutes for cigarettes (don't light them).*

Buy yourself presents with all that cash you're socking away.

*There is a nictone gum available that may be of use to some smokers who are heavily physiologically dependent on nicotine, especially when combined with behavioral techniques (Hall et al., 1985). The gum decreases withdrawal symptoms by providing a source of nicotine, but does not contain harmful hydrocarbons or carbon monoxide.

PSYCHOLOGY AND HEALTH

A MAGIC CURE FOR SMOKING?

So, you're convinced that smoking is bad for your health and that you would like to quit if you could. But you don't believe that you have the willpower.

Well, then, what if there were a magic cure for smoking? A cure that was guaranteed to help you through the abstinence syndrome . . . with just one hitch?

The hitch? Some side effects. For two to three days after taking the cure, some people complain of nervousness and drowsiness, some of headaches, insomnia, or constipation. But these side effects are usually gone within a week. Considering the alternatives—fear of cancer and heart disease, the cost of cigarettes, the humiliation of not being able to quit—wouldn't "the cure" be worth it?

The "magic" cure exists and is readily available. It's called stopping smoking. I've simply described some common withdrawal symptoms. Sarbin and Nucci (1973) point out that we need not look upon these symptoms as awful. They are, after all, signs that the body is recovering from the effects of smoking.

Our interpretation of bodily sensations is central in coping with abstinence from any drug. It is also central in curbing overeating. We can interpret temporary, unpleasant sensations as signs that we are *winning*—not as disasters that must be avoided at all costs. After all, we wouldn't be experiencing them if we had not marshaled our willpower to take action that we felt was good for us.

Strategies for Cutting Down

Count your cigarettes to establish your smoking baseline.

Set concrete goals for controlled smoking. For example, plan to cut down baseline consumption by at least 50 percent.

Gradually restrict the settings in which you allow yourself to smoke (see Chapter 12).

Get involved in activities where smoking isn't allowed or practical.

Switch to a brand you don't like. Hold your cigarettes with your nondominant hand only.

Keep only enough cigarettes to meet the (reduced) daily goal. Never buy more than a pack at a time.

Use sugarfree candies or gum as a substitute for a few cigarettes each day.

Jog instead of having a cigarette. Or walk, swim, or make love.

Pause before lighting up. Put the cigarette in an ashtray between puffs. Ask yourself before each puff if you really want more. If not, throw the cigarette away.

Put the cigarette out before you reach the end. (No more eating the filter.)

Gradually lengthen the amount of time between cigarettes.

Imagine living a prolonged, noncoughing life. Ah, freedom!

As you smoke, picture blackened lungs, coughing fits, the possibilities of cancer and other lung diseases.

Using strategies such as the above, many individuals have gradually cut down their cigarette consumption and eventually quit. It's true that there is a high relapse rate for quitters. Be on guard: We are most likely to relapse—that is, return to smoking—when we feel highly anxious, angry, or depressed (Shiffman, 1982). But when you are tempted, you can decrease the chances of relapsing by using almost any of the strategies outlined above (Hall et al., 1984; Shiffman, 1982, 1984), like reminding yourself of reasons for quitting, having a mint, or going for a walk. And also keep in mind a note of encouragement from Stanley Schachter (1982): Despite high relapse "rates," millions of Americans have quit and been able to stay away from cigarettes permanently.

HALLUCINOGENICS

Hallucinogenic drugs are named such because they produce hallucinations—that is, sensations and perceptions in the absence of external stimulation. But hallucinogenic drugs may also have additional effects, such as relaxing the individual, creating a sense of euphoria, or, in some cases, causing panic. We shall focus on the effects of marijuana and LSD.

MARIJUANA

The *Cannabis sativa* plant grows wild in many parts of the world. This would arouse little interest but for the fact that **marijuana** is produced from it. Marijuana stirs interest because it helps some people relax and can elevate the mood. It also sometimes produces mild hallucinations, which is why marijuana is classified as a **psychedelic** or hallucinogenic drug.

The major psychedelic substance in marijuana is **delta-9-tetrahydrocannabinol** which, perhaps to save energy, is usually referred to as THC. Other substances with possible psychedelic effects that are found in marijuana include *cannabichromene* and *cannabidol*. THC is found in the branches and leaves of male and female plants, but is concentrated highly in the **resin** of the female plant. **Hashish,** or "hash," is derived from this sticky resin. It is more potent than marijuana, although the effects are similar.

In the last century, marijuana was used almost as aspirin is used today for headaches and minor aches and pains. It could be bought without prescription in any drugstore. Today marijuana use and possession are illegal in most states, but medical applications are being explored. Marijuana is known to decrease nausea and vomiting among cancer patients receiving chemotherapy. It appears to help **glaucoma** sufferers by reducing fluid pressure in the eye. It may even offer some relief from asthma. But there are also causes for concern, as noted in the "Marijuana Update."

Effects of Marijuana   Marijuana smokers report different sensations at different levels of intoxication. The early stages of intoxication are frequently characterized by restlessness, which gives way to calmness. Fair to strong intoxication is linked to reports of heightened perceptions, and increases in self-insight, creative thinking, and empathy for the feelings of others. Strong intoxication is linked to perceiving time as passing more slowly, and increased awareness of bodily sensations, such as heart beat. Smokers also report that strong intoxication heightens sexual sensations and that a song might seem to last an hour rather than a few minutes. Visual hallucinations are not uncommon. Strong intoxication may cause smokers to experience disorientation. If the mood is euphoric, loss of identity may be interpreted as harmony with the universe.

Hallucinogenic Giving rise to hallucinations.

Marijuana The dried vegetable matter of the *Cannabis sativa* plant. (A Mexican-Spanish word.)

Psychedelic (sigh-kuh-DELL-lick). Causing hallucinations, delusions, or heightening perceptions.

Delta-9-tetrahydrocannabinol (tet-truh-hide-row-can-NAB-in-all). The major active ingredient in marijuana. Abbreviated *THC*. Its name describes its chemical composition.

Resin (REH-zin). The saplike substance of plants.

Hashish (hah-SHEESH). A drug derived from the resin of Cannabis sativa. Often called "hash."

Glaucoma An eye disease characterized by increased fluid pressure within the eye. A cause of blindness. (From the Greek *glaukos*, meaning "gleaming"—referring to the appearance of the diseased eye.)

MARIJUANA Marijuana, a mild psychedelic, can relax one, provide feelings of euphoria, and enhance sensory pleasure. The jury is still out on the possible harmful effects of marijuana.

A CLOSER LOOK

MARIJUANA UPDATE: THE NATIONAL ACADEMY OF SCIENCES REPORT

In 1980 nearly 25 million Americans spent $24 billion to smoke marijuana regularly. Another 25 million have tried the drug. One reason that marijuana is the most widely used illegal substance in the United States is the tenacious belief that occasional joints do little, if any, harm. In February 1982 the Institute of Medicine of the National Academy of Sciences, chaired by Arnold Relman, editor of the prestigious *New England Journal of Medicine*, issued a long-awaited 188-page report on marijuana's effects. Based on an analysis of 1,000 research studies, the Institute concluded that widespread use of the drug "justifies serious national concern." But after its 15-month study, the academy had to admit that as yet there is insufficient research to conclude that marijuana causes irreversible long-term damage to mental functioning and physical health.

Some excerpts from the committee report:

Effects on the Nervous System and on Behavior

[Marijuana's] most clearly established acute effects are on mental functions and behavior. With a severity directly related to dose, marijuana impairs motor coordination and affects tracking ability and perceptual functions important for safe driving and the operation of other machines; it also impairs short-term memory and slows learning. Other acute effects include euphoria and other mood changes, but there are also disturbing mental phenomena, such as brief periods of anxiety, confusion, or psychosis.

[The] long-term effects of marijuana on the human brain and on human behavior remain to be defined.

Effects on the Cardiovascular and Respiratory Systems

There is . . . no evidence to indicate that a permanently [harmful] effect on the normal cardiovascular system occurs. There is good evidence to show that marijuana increases the work of the heart, usually by raising heart rate and, in some persons, by raising blood pressure. This rise in workload poses a threat to patients with hypertension, cerebrovascular disease, and coronary atherosclerosis.

Marijuana smoke . . . has many chemical components (including carbon monoxide and ["tars"]) and biological effects similar to tobacco smoke, but also some unique ingredients. This suggests the strong possibility that prolonged heavy smoking of marijuana, like tobacco, will lead to cancer of the respiratory tract and to serious impairment of lung function.

Effects on the Reproductive System

[THC] appears to have a modest reversible suppressive effect on sperm production in men, but there is no proof that it [impairs] male fertility. . . . There is convincing evidence that marijuana interferes with ovulation in female monkeys. [But] no satisfactory studies of the relation between use of marijuana and female fertility and child bearing have been carried out. Although [THC] is known to cross the placenta readily and to cause birth defects when administered in large doses to experimental animals, no adequate clinical studies have been carried out to determine if marijuana use can harm the human fetus.

But some smokers encounter negative experiences with strong intoxication. Marijuana increases the heart rate up to 140–150 beats per minute. This increase combined with heightened awareness of bodily sensations leads some smokers to fear that their hearts will "run away" with them. Some smokers find disorientation threatening, and fear failure to regain their identities. High levels of intoxication occasionally induce nausea and vomiting. Needless to say, smokers with such experiences smoke infrequently, or just once.

Some people report that marijuana helps them socialize at parties. But the friendliness characteristic of early stages of intoxication may give way to self-absorption and social withdrawal as the smoker becomes higher (Fabian & Fishkin, 1981).

Marijuana and Amotivational Syndrome It has been feared that marijuana can lead to **amotivational syndrome**—that is, destroy achievement motivation, melt away ambition, and cause difficulty in concentrating on task-oriented activities, such as work. These fears have been fueled by correlational evidence that heavy smokers in the college ranks do not strive to succeed as strenuously as do nonsmoking or infrequently smoking classmates. But we cannot confuse correlation with cause and effect. Other studies suggest that people who choose to smoke heavily may already differ from those who do not (Maugh, 1982). For instance, heavy smokers may be more concerned with emotional experience and fantasy than intellectual performance and self-control. Their approach to life could underlie both relative lack of ambition and regular use of marijuana. Still other research finds no cognitive effects from heavy use of marijuana over a seven-year period (Schaeffer et al., 1981).

LSD

LSD is the abbreviation for lysergic diethylamide acid, a synthetic hallucinogenic drug. Users sometimes just call it "acid." Supporters claim that LSD "expands consciousness" and opens new worlds. Sometimes people believe they achieved great insights while using LSD, but when it wears off they often cannot apply or clearly recall these discoveries.

As a powerful hallucinogenic, LSD produces vivid colorful hallucinations. LSD "trips" can be somewhat unpredictable. Some regular users have only "good trips." Others have one bad trip and swear off. Regular users who have had no bad trips argue that people with bad trips were psychologically unstable prior to using LSD. In fairness, Barber's review of the literature (1970) suggests that rare psychotic symptoms are usually limited to people with a history of psychological problems.

Flashbacks Some LSD users have **flashbacks**—distorted perceptions or hallucinations that occur days, weeks, or longer after usage but mimic the LSD "trip." It has been speculated that flashbacks stem from chemical changes in the brain produced by LSD, but Heaton and Victor (1976) and Matefy (1980) offer a psychological explanation for flashbacks.

Heaton and Victor (1976) found that users who have flashbacks are more oriented toward fantasy and allowing their thoughts to wander. They are also more likely to focus on internal sensations. If they should experience sensations similar to a past trip, they may readily label them flashbacks and allow themselves to focus on them indefinitely, causing an entire replay of the experience to unfold.

Matefy (1980) found that users who have flashbacks show greater capacity to become fully engrossed in role-playing, and hypothesized that flashbacks may be nothing more than enacting the role of being on a trip. This does not necessarily mean that people who claim to have flashbacks are lying. They may be more willing to surrender personal control in response to internal sensations for the sake of altering their consciousness and having peak experiences. Users who do not have flashbacks prefer to be more in charge of their thought processes and have greater concern for meeting the demands of daily life.

Other Hallucinogenics Other hallucinogenic drugs include **mescaline** (derived from the peyote cactus) and **phencyclidine** (PCP). Regular use of hallucinogenics may lead to tolerance and psychological dependence. But hallucinogenics are not known to lead to physiological dependence. High doses may induce frightening hallucinations, impaired coordination, poor judgment, mood changes, and paranoid delusions.

Let us now consider a number of ways of altering consciousness that do not rely on drugs.

ALTERING CONSCIOUSNESS THROUGH MEDITATION: WHEN EASTERN GODS MEET WESTERN TECHNOLOGY

So, back to our mountaintop and our venerable guru. Counting your breaths is one form of meditation. The Yogis stare intently at a pattern on a vase or mandala (note an example of a mandala on p. 424 in Chapter 9). The ancient Egyptians stared at an oil-burning lamp—the origin of the fable of Aladdin's magic lamp. Islamic mystics of Turkey, referred to as "whirling dervishes," may concentrate on their body movements or the rhythm of their breathing.

While meditation methods vary, they seem to have a common cognitive thread: Through passive observation, the normal relationship between the person and the environment is altered. Problem-solving, planning, worry, awareness of the events of the day are suspended. In this way consciousness—that is, the normal focuses of attention—is altered and a state of relaxation is often induced. Meditators may report that they have "merged" with the object of meditation (the vase or a repeated phrase, for example) and then transcended it, leading to "oneness with the universe," rapture, or some great insight. Psychology has no way of measuring "oneness with the universe," but psychologists can measure bodily changes, as we shall see. It is reasonable to believe that the effects of meditation, like the effects of drugs, reflect whatever bodily changes are induced by meditation *and* one's expectations about meditation.

Let us now turn our attention to **Transcendental Meditation** (TM), a simplified form of meditation brought to the United States by the Maharishi Mahesh Yogi in 1959. Hundreds of thousands of Americans practice TM by repeating **mantras,** words or sounds that are claimed to have the capacity to help one achieve an altered state of consciousness.

TM

Herbert Benson (1975) of Harvard Medical School studied TM practitioners ranging in age from seventeen to forty-one—business people, students, artists. His subjects included people who had practiced TM for nine years and novices who had practiced for a few weeks.

Benson found no scientific evidence that TM "expanded" consciousness, despite the claims of many practitioners. However, TM did produce what Benson labeled a **relaxation response.** During TM the body's metabolic rate dramatically decreased. The blood pressure of people with hypertension decreased (Benson et al., 1973). In fact, people who meditated twice daily tended to show normalized blood pressure through the entire day. Meditators produced more frequent alpha waves—brain waves associated with feelings of relaxation, but infrequent during sleep. Benson's subjects also showed lower heart and respiration rates and a decrease in blood lactate—a substance whose presence has been linked to anxiety.

A Cautionary Note   We find no major fault with Benson's research. TM does appear helpful for people with hypertension and as a general relaxing agent. But we still have no scientific evidence that TM or other forms of meditation produce a special state of consciousness (Shapiro, 1985). In fact, some researchers have shown that one's level of arousal can be lowered as much as in meditation by engaging in other relaxing activities (West, 1985), or even by resting quietly (Holmes, 1984, 1985). David Holmes and his colleagues (1983) found no differences between experienced Transcendental Meditators and novice "resters" in heart rate, respiration rate, blood pressure, and sweat in the palms of the hands (that is, galvanic skin response, or GSR). Most critics of meditation do not argue that meditation is useless, but rather that meditation may have no special effects as compared with a rest from a tension-producing routine.

Note that formerly anxious and tense individuals who practice TM have also *chosen* to alter their stress-producing life styles by taking time out for themselves once or twice a day. Just taking this time out may be quite helpful.

The final word on meditation is not yet in (Suler, 1985). Still, if you wish to try meditating, the following instructions may be of help.

HOW TO MEDITATE

In meditation, what you *don't* do is more important than what you do. Limit your awareness to a repeated or constant stimulus that holds some attraction for you. It may be a phrase, your breathing, a pleasant sight or odor, a mantra. Adopt a passive "what happens, happens" attitude. (Don't try to force it.) Make your environment quiet and predictable. Assume a comfortable sitting position or lie back with your head raised on a pillow. Try meditating once or twice a day for ten to twenty minutes.

For a concentrative device, Benson suggests "perceiving" the word *one* on every outbreath. This means "thinking" the word, but less actively than usual (good luck). Carrington (1977) suggests thinking or perceiving the word *in* while you are inhaling, and *out* or *ah-h-h* while exhaling. Carrington also suggests mantras like *ah-nam, shi-rim,* or *ra-mah.*

If you are using a mantra, you can prepare for meditation and say the mantra aloud several times. Enjoy it. Then say it more and more softly. Close your eyes and think only the mantra. Allow the thinking to become "passive," so that you only "perceive" the mantra. Again, adopt a passive

Relaxation response Benson's term for a group of responses which can be brought about by meditation. They involve lowered activity of the sympathetic branch of the autonomic nervous system.

MEDITATION People use many forms of meditation to try to expand inner awareness and experience inner harmony. The effects of meditation, like the effects of drugs, reflect the bodily changes induced by meditation *and* the meditator's expectations.

"what happens, happens" attitude. Continue to perceive the mantra. It may grow louder or softer, disappear for a while and then return. Allow yourself to drift. What happens, happens.

Some additional suggestions (from Carrington, 1977): Don't eat for an hour before meditating. Avoid drinks with caffeine for at least two. Seat yourself before a pleasant object, like a green plant or burning incense. Avoid facing direct light. Change your position as necessary. It's kosher to scratch or yawn. Play for time if you're interrupted: yawn, stretch, move slowly. You can check your watch through half-closed eyes.

Above all, "take what you get." You can't force relaxation. You can only set the stage for it and allow it to happen. If disruptive thoughts come in while you are meditating, you can try to allow them to "pass through." Don't get wrapped up in trying to squelch them. (Also note alternate methods of relaxation discussed in Chapter 10.)

ALTERING CONSCIOUSNESS THROUGH BIOFEEDBACK: GETTING IN TOUCH WITH THE UNTOUCHABLE

There is little we can take for granted in life. But two decades ago psychologists were rather secure in their distinction between *voluntary* and *involuntary* functions. Voluntary functions, like lifting an arm or leg, were conscious. They could be directly willed. But other functions, like heart rate and blood pressure, were involuntary or autonomic. Thus they were

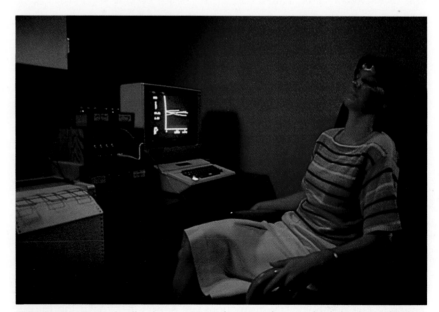

BIOFEEDBACK Biofeedback is a system that provides, or "feeds back," information about a bodily function to an organism. Through biofeedback training, people have learned to gain voluntary control over a number of functions that are normally involuntary.

beyond conscious control. We could no more consciously control blood pressure than, say, purposefully emit alpha waves.

Once in a while, to be sure, we heard tales of strange "Yoga" experts or other exotics who could make their hair stand literally on end or "will" their cheeks to stop bleeding after a nail had been put through. But such episodes were viewed as horror stories or stage tricks. Serious scientists went back to serious research.

HEADLINE: *LAB RATS "EXPAND CONSCIOUSNESS" AT ROCKEFELLER UNIVERSITY?*

"Serious scientists" went back to "serious research" except for a handful of pioneering psychologists like Neal E. Miller of Rockefeller University. In the late 1960s, Miller trained laboratory *rats* voluntarily to increase or decrease their heart rates (Miller, 1969). His procedure was simple. There is a "pleasure center" in the hypothalamus of the rat. When a small burst of electricity stimulates this center it must be quite reinforcing: rats will do whatever they can to reap this bit of shock, like learning to press a lever.

Miller implanted electrodes in the rats' pleasure centers. Some rats were then given electric shock whenever their heart rates happened to increase. Other rats received shock when their heart rates happened to decrease. One group of rats was consistently "rewarded" (that is, shocked) when their heart rates showed an increase. The other group was consistently rewarded for a decrease. After a single 90-minute training session, rats altered their heart rates by as much as 20 percent in the direction for which they had been "rewarded."

BIOFEEDBACK TRAINING (BFT): A DEFINITION

Miller's research was an early example of **biofeedback training** (BFT). Biofeedback is simply a system that provides, or "feeds back," information about a bodily function to an organism. Miller used electrical stimulation of the brain to feed back information to rats when they had engaged in a targeted bodily response (that is, raised or lowered their heart rates). Somehow the rats then used this information to raise or lower their heart rates voluntarily.

Similarly, people have learned to voluntarily change various bodily functions that were once considered beyond their control. But electrodes are not implanted in people's brains. Rather, people hear a "blip" or observe some other signal that informs them when the targeted response is being displayed.

Some Human Applications People, for instance, can learn to emit alpha waves (and feel somewhat more relaxed) through feedback from an EEG. A "blip" may increase in frequency whenever alpha waves are being emitted. The psychologist's instructions are simply to "make the blip go faster." An **electromyograph** (EMG), which monitors muscle tension, is commonly used to help people become more aware of muscle tension in

Biofeedback training The systematic feeding back to an organism of information about a bodily function so that the organism can gain control of that function. Abbreviated *BFT.*

Electromyograph An instrument that measures muscle tension. Abbreviated *EMG.* (From the Greek *mys,* meaning "mouse" and "muscle"—reflecting similarity between the movement of a mouse and the contraction of a muscle.)

the forehead and elsewhere and to learn to lower this tension. Through other instruments people have learned to lower their heart rates, their blood pressure, and the amount of sweat in the palm of the hand. All of these changes are relaxing.

People have also learned to elevate the *temperature* of a finger. Why bother, you ask? Limbs become subjectively warmer when more blood flows into them. Increasing the temperature of a finger—that is, altering patterns of blood flow in the body—helps some people control headaches which stem from too great a flow of blood into the head.

In any event, BFT is in its infancy both in the laboratory and in psychological treatment. As pointed out by psychologist Alan H. Roberts of the Scripps Clinic and Research Foundation in La Jolla, California, biofeedback has become so popular in recent years that some "patients ask for it without even knowing what it is" (1985, p. 938). But Roberts and many other psychologists (as reported in White & Tursky, 1982) express the view that much of the research into BFT has produced less clear-cut supportive evidence than is usually recognized. It is possible that some of the excitement concerning biofeedback may be premature, yet BFT is used throughout the United States today and has many thousands of supporters among patients and professionals.

ALTERING CONSCIOUSNESS THROUGH HYPNOSIS

Perhaps you have seen films in which Count Dracula hypnotized victims into a stupor. Then he could get on with a bite in the neck with no further nonsense. Perhaps a fellow student labored to place a friend in a "trance" after reading a book on hypnosis. Or perhaps you have seen an audience member hypnotized in a nightclub act. If so, chances are this person acted as if he or she had returned to childhood, imagined that a snake was about to have a nip, or lay rigid between two chairs for a while.

A BRIEF HISTORY

Hypnosis, derived from the Greek word for sleep, has only recently become a respectable subject for psychological inquiry. Hypnosis seems to have begun in its modern form with Franz Mesmer in the eighteenth century. Mesmer asserted that the universe was connected by forms of magnetism—which may not be far from the mark. But he claimed that people, too, could be drawn to one another by "animal magnetism." (No bullseye here.) Mesmer used bizarre props to bring people under his "spell." He did manage a respectable cure rate for minor ailments. But we skeptics are more likely to attribute his successes to the placebo effect than to animal magnetism.

During the second half of the last century, hypnosis contributed to the formation of psychoanalytic theory. Jean Martin Charcot, a French physician, had believed that **hysterical disorders,** such as hysterical blindness and paralysis, were caused by physical problems. But when students were

Hypnosis (hip-NO-sis). A condition in which people appear highly suggestible and behave as though they are in a trance. (From the Greek *hypnos,* meaning "sleep.")

Hysterical disorders Disorders in which a bodily function is lost because of psychological rather than biological reasons. See Chapter 11.

able to stimulate a normal woman to display hysterical symptoms through hypnosis, Charcot began to pursue psychological causes for hysterical behavior. One of his students, Pierre Janet, suggested that hysterical symptoms represented subconscious thoughts breaking through a "weakness in the nervous system."

The notion of subconscious roots for hysterical disorders was developed in Vienna, Austria. The physician Josef Breuer discovered that a female patient felt better about personal problems when he encouraged her to talk and express her feelings freely while hypnotized. Sigmund Freud later suggested that hypnosis was one avenue to the unconscious (he believed that dreams were another), and he used hypnosis to uncover what he felt were the unconscious roots of his patients' problems. Under hypnosis, for example, a number of his patients recalled traumatic childhood experiences, such as being seduced by a parent, that they could not remember during the normal state of consciousness. But after a while Freud switched from hypnosis to free association for several reasons. One is that he came to feel that some of his patients were recalling childhood fantasies instead of actual events. Other reasons are discussed in Chapter 12.

Hypnotism Today   Today hypnotism retains its popularity in nightclubs, but is also used as an anesthetic in dentistry, childbirth, even surgery. (See the nearby 60 Minutes box, "Hypnosis.") Psychologists may use hypnosis to help teach clients how to relax or help them imagine vivid imagery in techniques like systematic desensitization, which we shall discuss at length in Chapter 12. Police use hypnosis to prompt the memories of witnesses. But courtroom testimony by hypnotized people has been challenged because witnesses may pick up on suggestions communicated by the hypnotist (Press et al., 1981) and because fantasized events can seem as authentic as actual events (Stark, 1984).

HYPNOSIS Only recently has hypnosis become a respectable subject for psychological inquiry. Hypnotized subjects become passive and tend to deploy their attention according to the instructions of the hypnotist.

THE PROCESS OF HYPNOSIS

The state of consciousness called the "hypnotic trance" is usually induced by asking subjects to narrow attention to a small light, a spot on the wall, an object held by the hypnotist, or just the hypnotist's voice. There are verbal suggestions that the limbs are becoming warm, heavy, and relaxed. (Suggestions of warmth and heaviness can induce blood flow into the limbs and help calm activity of the sympathetic division of the autonomic nervous system. It has been shown that *expecting* certain bodily changes—like changes in heart rate and skin temperature—can actually produce changes in that direction [Pennebaker & Skelton, 1981].) Subjects are also told that they are becoming sleepy or falling asleep.

Hypnosis is *not* sleep, as shown by differences in EEG recordings for the hypnotic trance and the stages of sleep. But the word *sleep* is understood by subjects to suggest a hypnotic trance, and has a track record of success.

Hypnotic Suggestibility   Hypnosis is most successful with people who understand what is expected of them during the "trance state." People who are readily hypnotized are said to have hypnotic suggestibility. Generally speaking, suggestible subjects have positive attitudes and expectations about hypnosis, and are highly motivated to become hypnotized (Barber et al., 1974). Like LSD users who claim to experience flashbacks, people with high hypnotic suggestibility enjoy daydreaming, and have highly vivid and absorbing imagination styles (Crawford, 1982).

CHANGES IN CONSCIOUSNESS BROUGHT ABOUT BY HYPNOSIS

Hypnotists and hypnotized subjects report that hypnosis can bring about some or all of the following changes in consciousness.

Passivity   When being hypnotized, or in a trance, subjects await instructions and appear to suspend planning.

Narrowed Attention   Subjects may focus on the hypnotist's voice or a spot of light and avoid attending to background noise or intruding thoughts. It is claimed that subjects may not hear a loud noise behind the head if directed not to. (However, objective measures of hearing *do* suggest that subjects do not show any reduction in auditory sensitivity; rather they *report* greater deafness [Spanos et al., 1982].)

Hypermnesia   Subjects may be instructed to show heightened memory, or **hypermnesia,** by focusing on selected details and then reconstructing an entire memory. This is the method used in police investigations.

However, we may ask how accurate these memories are. A number of studies have shown that suggestible subjects "recall" more information under hypnosis than otherwise (Orne et al., 1984), but that this information is frequently incorrect (Dwyan & Bowers, 1983; Nogrady et al., 1985). Nevertheless, hypnotized subjects tend to report the incorrect information with confidence (Sheehan & Tilden, 1983), which may throw off police investigators or juries.

Suggestibility   Subjects may respond to suggestions that an arm is becoming lighter and will rise, or that the eyelids are becoming heavier and must close. They may act as though they cannot unlock hands clasped by the hypnotist, or bend an arm "made rigid" by the hypnotist. Hypnotized subjects serving as witnesses are also highly open to the suggestions of their interviewers. They may incorporate ideas and images presented by inter- viewers into their "memories" and report them as facts (Laurence & Perry, 1983).

Playing Unusual Roles   Most subjects expect to play sleepy, relaxed roles, but they may also be able to play roles calling for increased strength or alertness, such as riding a bicycle with less fatigue than usual (Banyai & Hilgard, 1976). In **age regression** subjects may play themselves as infants or children. Research shows that many supposed childhood memories and

Hypermnesia (high-purr-KNEE-she-uh). Greatly enhanced memory.

Age regression In hypnosis, taking on the role of childhood, commonly accompanied by vivid recollections of one's past.

characteristics are played inaccurately. Nonetheless, some subjects show excellent recall of such details as hair style or speech pattern. A subject may speak a language forgotten since childhood.

Perceptual Distortions   Hypnotized subjects may act as though hypnotically induced hallucinations and delusions are real. In the "thirst hallucination," for example, subjects act as if parched, even if they have just had a drink. Or subjects may behave as though they cannot hear loud noises or smell odors (Zamansky & Bartis, 1985).

Posthypnotic Amnesia   Many subjects act as though they cannot recall events that took place under hypnosis, or that they were hypnotized at all, if so directed. However, subjects can usually recall what occurred if they are hypnotized again and instructed by the hypnotist to do so (Kihlstrom et al., 1985).

The results of at least one experiment suggest that it may be advisable to take the phenomenon of posthypnotic amnesia with a grain of salt. Subjects are more likely to report recalling events while "under a trance" when they are subjected to a lie-detector test and given to believe that they will be found out if they are faking (Coe & Yashinski, 1985).

Posthypnotic Suggestion   Subjects may follow instructions according to prearranged cues of which they are supposedly unaware. For instance, a subject may be directed to fall again into a deep trance upon the single command, "Sleep!" Smokers frequently seek the help of hypnotists to break their habits, and they are frequently given the suggestion that upon "waking" cigarette smoke will become aversive. They may also be instructed to forget that this idea originated with the hypnotist.

THEORIES OF HYPNOSIS

Psychoanalytic Theory   According to Sigmund Freud's psychoanalytic theory, the hypnotic trance represents **regression.** Hypnotized adults suspend "ego functioning," or conscious control of their behavior. They permit themselves to return to childish modes of responding that emphasize fantasy and impulse, rather than fact and logic.

Role Theory   Theodore Sarbin (1972) offers a **role theory** view of hypnosis (Sarbin & Coe, 1972). He points out that the changes in behavior that are attributed to the hypnotic trance can be successfully imitated when subjects are instructed to behave *as though* they were hypnotized. Also, we cannot be hypnotized unless we are quite familiar with the hypnotic "role"—the set of behaviors that supposedly constitute the trance. Sarbin is not necessarily suggesting that hypnotic subjects *fake* the hypnotic role, but rather that they allow themselves to enact this role under the hypnotist's directions.

Research findings that "suggestible" hypnotic subjects are motivated to enact the hypnotic role (Barber et al., 1974), are good role players, and

Regression Return to a form of behavior characteristic of an earlier stage of development. See Chapter 9.

Role theory A theory that explains hypnotic events in terms of the person's ability to act *as though* he or she were hypnotized. Role theory differs from faking in that subjects cooperate and focus on hypnotic suggestions, instead of cynically pretending to be hypnotized.

60 MINUTES

HYPNOSIS

In 1842 London physician W. S. Ward amputated a man's leg after using a rather strange anesthetic: hypnosis. According to reports, the patient experienced no discomfort. Several years later operations were being performed routinely under hypnosis at the infirmary in London. Today hypnosis is used by thousands of professionals as an anesthetic in dentistry, childbirth, even some forms of surgery.

In the 60 Minutes segment "Hypnosis," correspondent Dan Rather reported that psychologist Harold Wain hypnotized physician David Ramirez, who underwent surgery on his nose under hypnosis, with no drugs. While Ramirez fantasized that he was lying under the warming sun on a beach in Puerto Rico, a doctor chiseled away at a deviated septum so that Ramirez would be able to breathe normally. After the operation Ramirez noted how his consciousness had been divided: "It's kind of funny to be lying there on the beach and have the surgeon saying, 'Well this is the piece of bone that was obstructing his breathing.'"

However, many patients who have been hypnotized report some pain (Barber et al, 1974). Others are administered analgesic (pain-relieving) drugs along with hypnotic suggestions. It also turns out that many internal organs are not particularly sensitive to pain (some register no pain at all). In such cases only a local anesthetic is required to deaden the pain of skin incisions. It is not surprising that hypnosis and a local anesthetic are a potent combination.

We must also keep in mind that anxiety and the expectation of severe pain can compound any painful experience. Witness the muscle tension and anxiety of many dental patients just sitting in the waiting room! Hypnosis can deeply relax individuals and encourage them to focus on pleasant imagery that distracts them from pain; relaxation training and guided imagery are common components of psychological programs for treating pain patients (Moore & Chaney, 1985). A state of relaxation may also enhance the ability of the nervous system to produce endorphins, which are one of the body's natural ways of combatting pain.

have vivid and absorbing imagination styles (Crawford, 1982) would all seem supportive of role theory. The fact that the behaviors shown by "hypnotized" subjects can be mimicked by role players means that we need not resort to the concept of the "hypnotic trance"—an unusual and mystifying altered state of awareness—to explain hypnotic events.

Neodissociation Theory Ernest Hilgard (1977) explains hypnotic phenomena through **neodissociation theory.** This is the view that we can selectively focus our attention on one thing (like hypnotic suggestions) and still perceive other things "subconsciously." In a sense, we do this all the time. We are not fully conscious, or aware, of everything going on about us. Rather, at any moment we selectively focus on events, like tests, dates, or television shows, that seem important or relevant. But while taking a test we may be peripherally aware of the color of the wall or of the sound of rain.

According to neodissociation theory, when people are hypnotized, they selectively attend to the hypnotist, yet they perceive other events "subconsciously" or peripherally. When told to forget they were hypnotized, they focus on other matters. But the experience of hypnosis can be focused on afterward. Let us assume a person in a "trance" is given the posthypnotic suggestion to fall into a trance again upon hearing "Sleep," but not to recall the fact that he or she was given this command. Upon "waking" the person

Neodissociation theory A theory that explains hypnotic events in terms of subconscious perception of events. People can focus selectively on hypnotic suggestions, but still perceive outside sources of stimulation.

does not focus on the posthypnotic suggestion. But hearing the command "Sleep!" leads to rapid refocusing of attention and return to the "trance." These thoughts are all, in a sense, separated or dissociated from each other. Yet the person's attention can focus rapidly on one, then another.

According to Hilgard, this subconscious level of perception functions as though we had "hidden observers" in us. Hilgard has run experiments in which hypnotized subjects immersed their left hands into buckets of ice water and verbally reported no sensation. But through **automatic writing** with the right hand, these subjects recorded painful coldness. Similarly, subjects have not responded to sudden loud noises when hypnotized, but their "hidden observers" have recorded them through automatic writing.

Note that role theory and neodissociation theory are not suggesting that the phenomena of hypnosis do not occur. Rather they suggest that we do not need to explain these events through an altered state of awareness called a trance. Hypnosis may not be special at all. Rather it is *we* who are special—through our great imaginations, our role-playing ability, and our capacity to divide our consciousness—concentrating now on one event we deem important, concentrating later on another.

Automatic writing Writing about perceived stimulation while the major portion of a person's attention is focused elsewhere.

SUMMARY

1. Consciousness has several meanings, including (1) sensory awareness; (2) direct inner awareness of cognitive processes; (3) personal unity or the sense of self; and (4) the waking state.

2. Sigmund Freud differentiated among ideas that are conscious, preconscious (available to awareness by focusing on them), and unconscious (unavailable to awareness under ordinary circumstances).

3. Electroencephalograph (EEG) records show different stages of sleep characterized by different brain waves. We have four stages of non-rapid-eye-movement (NREM) sleep and one of REM sleep. Stage 1 sleep is lightest, and stage 4 is deepest.

4. Sleep apparently serves a restorative function, but we do not know exactly how sleep restores us, or how much sleep we need.

5. Most dreams occur during REM sleep. The content of most dreams is an extension of the events of the day. Nightmares are also dreams that occur during REM sleep.

6. Anxious and tense people are more likely to suffer from insomnia. Psychological methods for dealing with insomnia include relaxing, coping with exaggerated fears, avoiding ruminating, establishing a regular routine, and using fantasy.

7. Other sleep disorders include narcolepsy, apnea, Sudden Infant Death Syndrome (SIDS), night terrors, bedwetting, and sleepwalking. Night terrors usually occur during deep sleep. Bedwetting and sleepwalking are problems of childhood that usually come to an end as the child matures.

8. Various substances or drugs alter consciousness. Substance abuse is defined as usage that impairs social or occupational functioning. Substance dependence is characterized by physiological dependence, as evidenced by tolerance or by an abstinence syndrome upon withdrawal.

9. People usually try drugs because of curiosity, but usage can be reinforced by anxiety reduction, feelings of euphoria, and other sensations. People are also motivated to avoid withdrawal symptoms once they become physiologically dependent. Some people may have genetic predispositions to become physiologically dependent on certain substances.

10. The group of substances called depressants acts by slowing the activity of the central nervous system.

11. Alcohol is an intoxicating depressant that leads to physiological dependence. Alcohol provides people with an excuse for failure or for antisocial behavior, but

has not been shown to induce antisocial behavior directly. As a depressant, alcohol also decreases sexual response, although many people expect alcohol to have the opposite effect.

12. Opiates are derived from the opium poppy, while opioids are similar in chemical structure but synthesized in the laboratory. The opiates morphine and heroin are depressants that reduce pain, but they are also bought on the street because of the euphoric rush they provide. Opiates and opioids lead to physiological dependence.

13. Barbiturates are depressants used to treat epilepsy, high blood pressure, anxiety, and insomnia. They lead rapidly to physiological dependence.

14. Stimulants act by increasing the activity of the nervous system.

15. Amphetamines are stimulants that produce feelings of euphoria when taken in high doses. But high doses may also cause restlessness, insomnia, psychotic symptoms, and a "crash" upon withdrawal. Amphetamines and a related stimulant, Ritalin, are commonly used to treat hyperactive children.

16. The stimulant cocaine was used in Coca-Cola prior to 1906. Now it is an illegal drug that provides feelings of euphoria and bolsters self-confidence. Overdoses can lead to restlessness, insomnia, and psychotic reactions.

17. Cigarette smoke contains carbon monoxide, hydrocarbons, and the stimulant nicotine. Regular smokers adjust their smoking to maintain a consistent blood level of nicotine, suggestive of physiological dependence. Cigarette smoking has been linked to death from heart disease, cancer, and many other disorders.

18. Hallucinogenic substances produce hallucinations—sensations and perceptions in the absence of external stimulation.

19. Marijuana is a hallucinogenic whose active ingredients, including THC, often produce heightened and distorted perceptions, relaxation, feelings of empathy, and reports of new insights. Hallucinations are possible. The long-term effects of marijuana usage are not fully known, although it appears that marijuana smoke is in and of itself harmful.

20. LSD is a hallucinogenic drug that produces vivid hallucinations. So-called LSD flashbacks may reflect psychological factors, like interest in attending to internal sensations and fantasy.

21. In meditation, one focuses "passively" on an object or a mantra in order to alter the normal person-environment relationship. In this way consciousness (that is, the normal focuses of attention) is altered and relaxation is often induced. TM and other forms of meditation appear to reduce high blood pressure along with producing relaxation. There is controversy as to whether meditation is more relaxing or effective in reducing blood pressure than is simple quiet sitting.

22. Biofeedback increases consciousness of bodily events by informing an organism when a targeted biological response is occurring, such as lowered heart rate or emission of alpha waves. Through biofeedback training, people and lower animals have learned to consciously control a number of autonomic functions.

23. Hypnosis in its modern form was originated by Mesmer, who explained the trance through "animal magnetism." Hypnosis typically brings about the following changes in consciousness: passivity, narrowed attention, hypermnesia (heightened memory), suggestibility, assumption of unusual roles, perceptual distortions, posthypnotic amnesia, and posthypnotic suggestion.

24. Current theories of hypnosis deny the existence of a special trance state. Rather, they focus on our abilities to enact roles with which we are familiar, and to divide our awareness, so that now we focus on one event, and now another—as our attention is redirected by the hypnotist.

TRUTH OR FICTION REVISITED

There is no such thing as consciousness.

No simple true or false answer is possible. Many people would argue that consciousness exists because of their personal experience of being conscious. However, consciousness cannot be observed or measured directly, and, therefore, some psychologists prefer not to study it. But many other psychologists, primarily cognitive psychologists, believe that human consciousness must be studied if we are to learn about human nature.

Sleep becomes gradually deeper as we approach the middle of the night, and then gradually lightens until we awaken in the morning.

False. There are several (five on the average) cycles of light and deep sleep throughout the night.

People who sleep nine hours or more a night tend to be lazy and happy-go-lucky.

False. So-called long sleepers are actually more concerned about achievement than are short sleepers.

We tend to act out our forbidden fantasies in our dreams.

False. We may "cut loose" in some of our dreams, but most dreams are a relatively unexciting rehashing of the events of the day. Moreover, we tend to adhere to our moral standards in dreams as well as during the waking state.

Many people have insomnia because they try too hard to get to sleep at night.

True. Many psychological methods for coping with insomnia in effect distract sufferers from the "task" of getting to sleep.

Children tend to "outgrow" bed-wetting.

True. Current thinking is that bed-wetting is more likely to reflect immaturity of the nervous system than deep-rooted psychological problems.

It is dangerous to awaken a sleepwalker.

False. Sleepwalkers may be confused when awakened, but there is no evidence to support the myth that they are dangerous to themselves or others.

Some people drink because alcohol provides them with an excuse for failure.

True. Drinking alcohol is referred to by some psychologists as a "self-handicapping strategy."

Heroin was once used as a cure for addiction to morphine.

True. At the time it was not recognized that heroin also led to physiological dependence.

Coca-Cola once "added life" though a powerful but now illegal stimulant.

True. Prior to 1906, Coca-Cola contained the stimulant cocaine. However, to the credit of the Coca-Cola company, cocaine was discontinued as soon as questions were raised about it—long before it became illegal.

Cigarette smokers tend to smoke more when they are under stress.

True. Smokers dependent on nicotine attempt to maintain certain nicotine levels in their bloodstream. Stress leads to more rapid excretion of nicotine. Smokers must therefore smoke more in order to achieve desired levels.

Smoking marijuana is harmless.

False. Marijuana smoke is known to contain ingredients that are harmful to the lungs in the same way cigarette smoke is. Whether there are significant long-term effects on other organ systems or on cognitive functioning remains something of an open question.

Users of LSD can have flashbacks at any time.

Probably not. Users who are prone to fantasy and allowing their thoughts to wander may encounter "flashbacks," but users who strive to maintain control over their cognitive processes are apparently less prone to them.

People have managed to bring high blood pressure under control through meditation.

True. Meditation can lower blood pressure in hypertensive people.

You can learn to increase or decrease your heart rate just by thinking about it.

True. People have learned to consciously control many autonomic functions through biofeedback.

Ethical psychologists do not practice hypnosis.

False. Although hypnosis is used sensationalistically in night club acts, psychologists have found clinical uses in helping clients cope with pain and other problems.

A hypnotized man experienced no pain when his arm was amputated.

True, according to reports of observers. However, we cannot directly observe another person's private experiences—such as that of pain. We can only say that many hypnotized people act *as though* they are not having pain under surgery.

OUTLINE

C H A P T E R   5

Learning and Memory

TRUTH OR FICTION?

- Dogs can be trained to salivate when a bell is rung.
- We can learn to change our behavior while we are sleeping.
- During World War II, a psychologist devised a plan for training pigeons to guide missiles to their targets.
- Psychologists successfully fashioned a method to teach an emaciated nine-month-old infant to stop throwing up.
- You can "hook" people on gambling by allowing them to win some money in the early stages and then tapering off the payoffs.
- Punishment doesn't work.
- Rats can be trained to climb a ramp, cross a bridge, climb a ladder, pedal a toy car, and do several other tasks—all in proper sequence.
- We must make mistakes in order to learn.
- All of our experiences are permanently imprinted on the brain, so that proper stimulation can cause us to remember them exactly.
- There is such a thing as a photographic memory.
- There is no limit to the amount of information you can store in your memory.
- You can use tricks to improve your memory.
- Rats were helped to remember their ways through mazes by being injected with the poison strychnine.

In Aldous Huxley's futuristic novel, *Brave New World,* the Director of the Central London Hatchery and Conditioning Center is leading a group of visitors on a tour. The year is 632 A.F. (that is, after Ford, or 632 years after the birth of Henry Ford, the originator of many techniques of mass production in the twentieth century).

Five classes of people populate the London of the future—Alphas, Betas, Gammas, Deltas, and Epsilons. The Alphas are the brightest. Administrators are drawn from their rank. Epsilons are least intelligent and supply menial laborers. But Epsilons are happy. Selective breeding, oxygen deprivation prior to birth, and early learning or **conditioning** combine to lead them to want only what the central planners of the brave new world decree that they should have, and not to want what it is decreed they should not have. That, notes the Director, "is the secret of happiness and virtue—liking what you've got to do. All conditioning aims at that: making people like their unescapable social destiny."

The tour arrives at the Neo-Pavlovian Conditioning Rooms, where the visitors witness a demonstration of one step in the conditioning of Delta children. Deltas belong to the **caste** just above Epsilons, and also primarily supply laborers. The social destiny of Deltas requires them to be able to focus exclusively on their assigned physical labor and not on higher forms of human activity, such as reading or even the appreciation of beauty or nature.

"Set out the books," commands the Director.

In silence the nurses obeyed his command. Between the rose bowls the books were duly set out—a row of nursery quartos opened invitingly each at some gaily colored image of beast or fish or bird.

"Now bring in the children."

They hurried out of the room and returned in a minute or two, each pushing a kind of tall dumbwaiter laden, on all its four wire-netted shelves, with eight-month-old babies, all exactly alike (a Bokanovsky Group, it was evident) and all (since their caste was Delta) dressed in khaki.

"Put them down on the floor."

The infants were unloaded.

"Now turn them so that they can see the flowers and books."

Turned, the babies at once fell silent, then [crawled] toward those clusters of sleek colors, those shapes so gay and brilliant on the white pages. . . . Small hands reached out uncertainly, touched, grasped, unpetaling the . . . roses, crumpling the . . . pages of the books. The Director waited until all were happily busy. Then, "Watch carefully," he said. And, lifting his hand, he gave the signal.

The Head Nurse, who was standing by a switchboard at the other end of the room, pressed down a little lever.

There was a violent explosion. Shriller and ever shriller, a siren shrieked. Alarm bells maddeningly sounded.

The children started, screamed; their faces were distorted with terror.

"And now," the Director shouted (for the noise was deafening), "now we proceed to rub in the lesson with a mild electric shock."

He waved his hand again, and the Head Nurse pressed a second lever. The screaming of the babies suddenly changed its tone. There was

Conditioning A simple form of learning in which associations are learned between stimuli and responses. See classical and operant conditioning.

Caste A rigid class distinction based on birth rather than achievement. (From the Latin *castus*, meaning "pure.")

something desperate, almost insane, about the sharp spasmodic yelps to which they now gave utterance. Their little bodies twitched and stiffened; their limbs moved jerkily as if to the tug of unseen wires.

"We can electrify that whole strip of floor," bawled the Director in explanation. "But that's enough," he signalled to the nurse.

The explosions ceased, the bells stopped ringing, the shriek of the siren died down from tone to tone into silence. The stiffly twitching bodies relaxed, and what had become the sob and yelp of infant maniacs broadened out once more into a normal howl of ordinary terror.

"Offer them the flowers and the books again."

The nurses obeyed, but at the image of the roses, at the mere sight of those gaily colored images of pussy and cock-a-doodle-doo and baa-baa black sheep, the infants shrank away in horror; the volume of their howling suddenly increased.

"Observe," said the Director triumphantly, "observe."

Books and loud noises, flowers and electric shocks—already in the infant mind these couples were compromisingly linked; and after 200 repetitions of the same or a similar lesson would be wedded indissolubly. What man has joined, nature is powerless to put asunder.

"They'll grow up with what psychologists used to call an 'instinctive' hatred of books and flowers. Reflexes unalterably conditioned. They'll be safe from books and botany all their lives." The Director turned to his nurses. "Take them away again."

Still yelling, the khaki babies were loaded on to their dumbwaiters and wheeled out, leaving behind them the smell of sour milk and a most welcome silence.

Brave New World, fortunately, is a work of fiction, not of fact. But the Director's program for teaching Delta infants to cringe at the sight of books and flowers has a realistic ring. It is clearly consistent with what we know of **classical conditioning,** a simple form of learning in which an originally neutral stimulus comes to bring forth, or **elicit,** the response usually brought forth by another stimulus by being paired repeatedly with that other stimulus. In *Brave New World,* the Director repeatedly paired books and flowers with stimuli that elicited fear (loud noises and electric shocks). The result was that the children learned to respond to the books and flowers as if they were loud noises and electric shocks.

This type of classical conditioning described so vividly in *Brave New World* is more specifically termed **aversive conditioning.** In aversive conditioning a neutral stimulus is paired repeatedly with an aversive stimulus. Eventually, the previously neutral stimulus acquires aversive properties itself. *Brave New World* is a work of fiction and shows how the learning discoveries of psychologists may be perverted. But many psychologists today use aversive conditioning to help clients gain control over "bad habits," as we shall see in Chapter 12. For example, clients who want to stop smoking cigarettes may use the technique of **rapid smoking,** or inhaling every six seconds, so that (previously desired) cigarette smoke takes on an aversive quality. Electric shock and nausea-producing drugs have also been used to help people gain control over problem drinking.

Classical conditioning A simple form of learning in which one stimulus comes to bring forth the response usually brought forth by a second stimulus, by being paired repeatedly with the second stimulus.

Elicit To bring forth, evoke. (From the Latin e-, meaning "out," and *lacere,* meaning "to entice.")

Aversive conditioning An instance of classical conditioning in which a previously desirable or neutral stimulus acquires aversive (repugnant) properties by being paired repeatedly with an aversive stimulus.

Rapid smoking An example of aversive conditioning designed to reduce the appeal of cigarettes. Puffs are taken in rapid succession, making the smoke aversive.

In this chapter we discuss learning and memory. We may as well admit at the outset that the very definition of **learning** stirs controversy in psychology. The concept may be defined in different ways. From a cognitive perspective, learning is *the process by which* experience leads to a relatively permanent change in behavior. Learning is *made evident* by behavioral change, but is defined as an internal, and not directly observable, process. From a behaviorist perspective, learning *is* the change in behavior that stems from experience. The behaviorist definition is **operational.** Learning is defined in terms of the measurable events or changes in behavior by which it is known. Some behaviorists prefer to use the term "acquisition of responses" rather than learning, because learning can have a cognitive meaning. Let us be aware that there is a controversy about how to define learning. However, this controversy should not affect your study of the three major forms of learning that are discussed in the chapter: *classical conditioning, operant conditioning,* and *cognitive learning.*

Learning would do us little good if we could not remember what we had learned. For this reason, this chapter also discusses memory. We may define **memory** as the processes by which learning is maintained over the passage of time. Memory is actually a complex group of processes that do not all seem to operate according to the same set of rules. (When you have completed the chapter, you may think that we should speak of *memories,* not simply of *a* memory.) We shall attempt to sort out truth from fiction, myth from reality in our study of memory. We shall see that we can use many strategies to improve memory, and that memory, like other cognitive processes, involves biological changes. In our exploration of this strange biology, we shall observe life in a goldfish bowl. We won't come to grips with why the chicken crossed the road, but we shall provide the definitive answer as to why the fish swam to the other side of the tank. We shall also learn, at long last, what makes the worm turn—or, more precisely, what made a number of worms turn in the laboratories of certain psychologists.

Learning (1) The process by which experience leads to a relatively permanent change in behavior. (2) The behaviorist definition: a relatively permanent change in behavior that results from experience.

Operational Defined in terms of the operations required to measure a concept.

Memory Processes by which learning is maintained over time.

CLASSICAL CONDITIONING

We have a distinct preference for having teachers grade our papers with A's rather than F's. We are also (usually) more likely to stop our cars for red than green traffic lights. Why? We are not born with instinctive attitudes toward the letters A and F. Nor are we born knowing that red means stop and green means go. We learn the meanings of these symbols through association. We come to understand their intended meanings through words that explain them.

STUDIES AT THE SOVIET MILITARY MEDICINE ACADEMY: PAVLOV'S RESEARCH GOES TO THE DOGS

Learning through association can also occur automatically, as Russian scientist Ivan Pavlov (1849–1936) discovered in research with laboratory dogs. A physiologist, Pavlov was attempting to identify neural receptors in the mouth that triggered a response from the salivary glands. But his research

IVAN PAVLOV Pavlov, his assistants, and a furry expert salivator at the Soviet Military Medicine Academy early in the century.

Reflex A simple unlearned response to a stimulus.

Stimulus (1) A change in the environment that leads to a change in behavior. (2) Any form of physical energy, such as light or sound, that impinges on the sensory receptors of an organism.

efforts were hampered by the fact that the dogs often salivated at undesired times, as when a laboratory assistant inadvertently clinked a food tray.

Because of its biological makeup, a dog will salivate if meat is placed on its tongue. Salivation in response to meat is unlearned, a **reflex.** Reflexes are elicited by a certain range of stimuli. A **stimulus** may be defined as a change in the environment, like dropping meat on the tongue, or a traffic light's changing from green to red. Reflexes are simple unlearned responses to stimuli. Pavlov discovered that reflexes can also be learned, or conditioned, through association. His dogs began salivating in response to clinking food trays, because this noise, in the past, had been paired repeatedly with the arrival of food. The dogs would also salivate when an assistant entered the laboratory. Why? In the past the assistant had brought food.

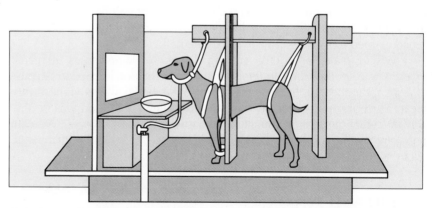

FIGURE 5.1 PAVLOV'S DEMONSTRATION OF CONDITIONED REFLEXES IN LABORATORY DOGS From behind the two-way mirror at the left, a laboratory assistant rings a bell and then places meat on the dog's tongue. After several pairings, the dog salivates in response to the bell alone. A tube collects saliva and passes it to a vial. A quantity of saliva is taken as a measure of the strength of the animal's response.

FRANK AND ERNEST by Bob Thaves

YOU'VE GOT TO STOP RINGING THAT BELL EVERY TIME YOU FEED HIM, DR. PAVLOV... YESTERDAY HE ATE THE AVON LADY

When we are faced with novel events, we sometimes have no immediate way of knowing whether or not they are important. When we are striving for concrete goals, we often ignore the unexpected, even when the unexpected is just as important, or more important, than the goal. So it was that Pavlov at first looked upon this uncalled-for canine salivation as an annoyance, an impediment to his research. But in 1901 he decided that his "problem" was worth looking into. Then he set about to show that he could train, or condition, his dogs to salivate when he wished and in response to any stimulus he chose.

Pavlov termed these trained salivary responses "conditional reflexes." They were *conditional* upon the repeated pairing of a previously neutral stimulus (like the clinking of a food tray) and a stimulus (in this case, food) that predictably evoked the target response (in this case, salivation). Today conditional reflexes are more generally referred to as **conditioned responses (CRs)**. They are responses to previously neutral stimuli that are learned, or conditioned.

Pavlov demonstrated conditioned reflexes by strapping a dog into a harness like the one in Figure 5.1. When meat was placed on the dog's tongue, it salivated. He repeated the process several times with one difference. He preceded the meat by half a second or so with the ringing of a bell on each occasion. After several pairings of meat and bell, Pavlov rang the bell but did *not* follow the bell with the powder. Still the dog salivated. It had learned to salivate in response to the bell.

Why? *Explanations for the learning of conditioned responses are made in terms of describing the conditions of learning:* The dog learned to salivate in response to the bell, *because* the ringing of the bell had been paired with meat. Psychologists do *not* say that the dog "knew" that food was on the way. We cannot speak meaningfully about what a dog "knows." We can only outline the conditions under which targeted behaviors will reliably occur.

STIMULI AND RESPONSES
IN CLASSICAL CONDITIONING: US, CS, UR, AND CR

In the demonstration described above, the meat is an unlearned or **unconditioned stimulus** (US). Salivation in response to the meat is an unlearned or **unconditioned response** (UR). The bell was at first a meaningless or neutral stimulus. It might have produced an **orienting reflex** in the dog

Conditioned response In classical conditioning, a learned response to a previously neutral stimulus. A response to a conditioned stimulus. Abbreviated *CR*.

Unconditioned stimulus A stimulus that elicits a response from an organism without learning. Abbreviated *US*.

Unconditioned response An unlearned response. A response to an unconditioned stimulus. Abbreviated *UR*.

Orienting reflex An unlearned response in which an organism attends to a stimulus.

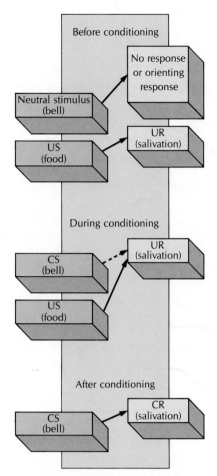

FIGURE 5.2 A SCHEMATIC REPRE-SENTATION OF CLASSICAL CONDI-TIONING Prior to conditioning, food elicits salivation. The bell, a neutral stimulus, elicits either no response or an orienting response. During conditioning, the bell is rung just before meat is placed on the dog's tongue. After several repetitions, the bell, now a CS, elicits salivation, the CR.

Conditioned stimulus A previously neutral stimulus that elicits a conditioned response because it has been paired repeatedly with a stimulus that already elicited that response. Abbreviated *CS*.

Backward conditioning A conditioning procedure in which the unconditioned stimulus is presented prior to the conditioned stimulus.

Extinction (eggs-STINK-shun). In classical conditioning, repeated presentation of the conditioned stimulus without the unconditioned stimulus, leading to suspension of the conditioned response.

because of its distinctness. But it was not yet associated with food. Then, through repeated association with the meat, the bell became a learned or **conditioned stimulus** (CS) for the salivation response. But salivation in response to the *bell (or CS)* is a learned or conditioned response (CR). A CR is a response similar to a UR, but the response elicited by the CS is by definition a CR, not a UR (Figure 5.2).

Types of Classical Conditioning Most types of classical conditioning occur most efficiently when the conditioned stimulus (CS) is presented about 0.5 seconds before the unconditioned stimulus (US). But conditioning can also take place if the CS and US are presented at the same time, or if the CS is presented a few seconds before the US. Learning is less efficient, and sometimes does not take place, when the US is presented prior to the CS. Presenting the US prior to the CS is referred to as **backward conditioning.**

EXTINCTION AND SPONTANEOUS RECOVERY

By "updating" expectations, classical conditioning helps organisms adapt to a changing environment. A dog may learn to associate a new scent (CS) with the appearance of a dangerous animal. It can then take evasive action when it perceives the scent. A child may learn to associate hearing a car pull into the driveway (CS) with the arrival of its parents (US). Thus the child may come to squeal with delight (CR) when it hears the car.

Extinction But times can change. The once dangerous animal may no longer be a threat. (What a puppy perceives as a threat may lose its power to menace once the dog matures.) After moving to a new house the child's parents may commute by public transportation. The sounds of a car in a nearby driveway may signal a neighbor's, not a parent's, homecoming. When conditioned stimuli (like the scent or the sound of a car) are no longer followed by unconditioned stimuli (a dangerous animal, a parent's homecoming), they lose their ability to elicit conditioned responses. In this way, the organism adapts to a changing environment. The process by which CSs lose the ability to elicit CRs because the CSs are no longer associated with USs is termed **extinction.**

In experiments in the extinction of CRs, Pavlov found that repeated presentations of the CS (or bell), without the US (meat), would lead to extinction of the CR (salivation in response to the bell). *Why?* It is tempting to say that the animal learns that hearing the bell no longer *means* that meat is on the way. But we cannot know what bells or other stimuli "mean" to animals. We can only make note of the observable behavior they display when presented with a stimulus. For this reason, the scientific explanation of Pavlov's experiment must be along these lines: The dog no longer salivates, because the bell (CS) was presented repeatedly in the absence of the meat (US). Therefore, the salivation response to the bell (CR) was extinguished. When we say that a response has been extinguished, rather than that a stimulus has "lost its meaning," we are referring to observable events.

Figure 5.3 shows that a dog conditioned by Pavlov began to salivate (show a CR) in response to a bell (CS) after only a couple of pairings of the

PSYCHOLOGY TODAY

THE BELL-AND-PAD METHOD FOR BEDWETTING

How do you teach a child to wake up in the middle of the night to go to the bathroom instead of wetting the bed? Think of it: the child must learn to do something *while asleep*—that is, to wake up. No amount of explanation or pleading will do the trick. However, an ingenious application of classical conditioning is successful in the majority of cases.

Normally, children at the ages of 5 or 6 waken in response to the sensations of a full bladder. They inhibit or delay urination, which is a reflexive response to bladder tension, and go to the bathroom. Bedwetters, however, frequently remain asleep when their bladders are full. As a consequence, they reflexively wet their beds.

Through the bell-and-pad method, children are taught to wake up in response to bladder tension. They sleep on a special sheet or pad that has been placed in the bed. When the child starts to urinate, an electrical circuit is closed, causing a bell or buzzer to sound and

wake the child. The bell is a *US* that wakes the child (waking is the *UR*). But through repeated pairings, stimuli that precede the bell become associated with the bell and also gain the capacity to wake the child. What are these stimuli? The sensations of a full bladder. In this way, bladder tension (the CS) gains the capacity to wake the child *even though the child is asleep during the classical conditioning procedure.*

Here is an excellent example of why the effects of classical conditioning are explained in terms of the pairing of stimuli, and not in terms of what a child "knows." How can we say that a *sleeping* child "knew" that wetting the bed would cause the bell to ring? We can only observe that by repeatedly pairing bladder tension with the bell, the child eventually learns to wake up in response to the bladder tension alone.

Similar buzzer circuits have also been built into training pants as an aid to toilet training.

bell with meat (the US). Continued pairings of the stimuli, or **trials,** led to increased salivation, measured in number of drops of saliva. After seven or eight trials, salivation leveled off at eleven to twelve drops. Then salivation to the bell (CR) was extinguished through several trials in which the CS (bell) was presented without the meat (US). After about ten extinction trials, the CR (salivation in response to the bell) was no longer shown.

Spontaneous Recovery What would happen if we were to allow a day or two to pass after we had extinguished the CR (salivation response to a bell) in a laboratory dog, and then we again presented the CS (bell)? Where would you place your money? Would the dog salivate or not?

If you bet that the dog would again show the CR (salivate in response to the bell), you were correct. Organisms tend to show **spontaneous recovery** of extinguished CRs merely as a function of the passage of time. For this reason, the term *extinction* may be a bit misleading. When a species of animal becomes extinct, all members of that species capable of reproducing have died. The species vanishes permanently. But the experimental extinction of CRs does not lead to the permanent eradication of CRs. Rather, it seems that they inhibit that response. The response does remain available for future performance.

Consider Figure 5.3 again. When spontaneous recovery of the CR does occur, the strength of the response (in this case, the number of drops of saliva) is not so great as it was at the end of the series of acquisition trials. A second set of extinction trials will also extinguish the CR more rapidly than did the first series of extinction trials. Although the CR is at first weaker

Trial In classical conditioning, a presentation of the stimuli. In conditioning trials, both the conditioned stimulus and the unconditioned stimulus are presented. In extinction trials, the conditioned stimulus is presented alone.

Spontaneous recovery In classical conditioning, the eliciting of a conditioned response by a conditioned stimulus after some time has elapsed following the extinction of the conditioned response.

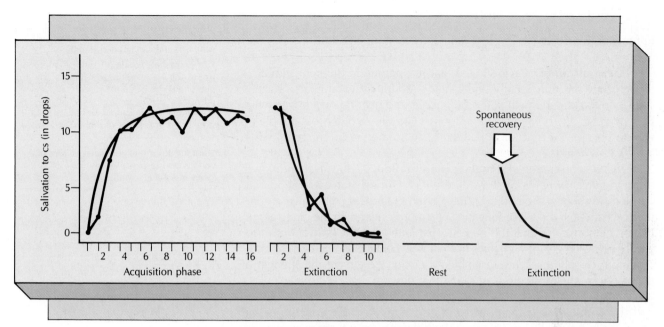

FIGURE 5.3 LEARNING AND EXTINCTION CURVES The straight lines plot actual data from Pavlov (1927). The curved lines are idealized. In the acquisition phase, a dog salivates (shows a CR) in response to a bell (CS) after only a few trials in which the bell is paired with meat (the US). Afterward, the CR is extinguished in about ten trials in which the CS is not followed by the US. After a rest period, the CR recovers spontaneously. A second series of extinction trials then leads to more rapid extinction of the CR.

the second time around, pairing the CS with the US once more will build response strength rapidly.

Spontaneous recovery, like extinction, is adaptive. What would happen if the child heard no car in the driveway for several months? It could be that the next time a car entered the driveway the child would associate the sounds with a parent's homecoming (rather than the arrival of a neighbor). This expectation could be appropriate. After all, *something* had systematically changed in the neighborhood when no car had entered the nearby driveway for so long. In the wilds a waterhole may contain water for only a couple of months during the year. But it is useful for animals to associate the waterhole with the thirst drive from time to time, so that they will return to it at the appropriate season.

As time passes and the seasons change, things sometimes follow circular paths and arrive at where they were before. Spontaneous recovery seems to provide a mechanism whereby organisms are capable of rapidly adapting to intermittently recurring situations.

GENERALIZATION AND DISCRIMINATION

No two things are exactly alike. Traffic lights are hung at slightly different heights, and shades of red and green differ slightly. The barking of two dogs differs, and the sound of the same animal differs slightly from bark to bark.

Adaptation requires that we respond similarly to stimuli that are equivalent in function, and that we respond differently to stimuli that are not.

Generalization   Pavlov noted that responding to different stimuli as though they are functionally equivalent is adaptive for animals. Rustling sounds in the undergrowth differ, but rabbits and deer do well to flee when they perceive any of many varieties of rustling. Sirens differ, but people do well to become vigilant, or to pull their cars to the side of the road, when any siren is heard.

In a demonstration of **stimulus generalization,** Pavlov first conditioned a dog to salivate when a circle was presented. During each acquisition trial, the dog was shown a circle (CS), then given meat (US). After several trials the dog exhibited the CR of salivating when presented with the circle alone. Pavlov demonstrated that the dog also exhibited the CR (salivation) in response to closed geometric figures like ellipses, pentagons, and even squares. The more closely the figure resembled a circle, the greater the strength of the response (the more drops of saliva that flowed).

Discrimination   Organisms must also learn (1) that many stimuli that are perceived as similar are functionally different; and (2) to respond adaptively to each. During the first couple of months of life babies can discriminate the voices of their mothers from those of others, and will often stop crying when they hear Mother, but not when they hear a stranger's voice.

Pavlov showed that a dog conditioned to salivate in response to circles could be trained *not* to salivate in response to ellipses. The type of conditioning that trains an organism to show a CR in response to a narrow range of stimuli (in this case, circular rather than elliptical geometric figures) is termed **discrimination training.** Pavlov trained the dog by presenting it with circles and ellipses, but associating the meat (US) with circles only. After a while, the dog no longer showed the CR (salivation) in response to the ellipse. Instead the animal showed **stimulus discrimination**. It showed the CR in response to circles only.

Pavlov then discovered that he could make the dog behave as though it were quite anxious by increasing the difficulty of the discrimination task. After the dog showed stimulus discrimination, Pavlov showed the animal increasingly rounder ellipses. Eventually the dog could no longer discriminate them from circles. Then the animal put on an infantile show. It urinated, defecated, barked profusely, and snapped at laboratory personnel.

Perhaps we would also turn nasty if we could no longer make the discriminations necessary for survival. Consider how you might behave if you could barely discriminate between a greenish-red and a reddish-green traffic light, but a person dressed in unmistakable blue was ready to hand you a traffic ticket every time you made an error.

Daily living requires appropriate generalization and discrimination. No two hotels are alike, but when traveling from one city to another it is adaptive to expect to stay in some hotel. It is encouraging that green lights in Washington have the same meaning as green lights in Honolulu. But returning home in the evening requires the ability to discriminate our homes

Stimulus generalization The eliciting of a conditioned response by stimuli that are similar to the conditioned stimulus.

Discrimination training Teaching an organism to show a conditioned response only to one of a series of similar stimuli, accomplished by pairing that stimulus with the unconditioned stimulus and presenting similar stimuli in the absence of the unconditioned stimulus.

Stimulus discrimination The eliciting of a conditioned response by only one of a series of similar stimuli.

Higher-order conditioning A form of classical conditioning in which a previously neutral stimulus comes to elicit the response brought forth by a *conditioned* stimulus by being paired repeatedly with that conditioned stimulus.

or apartments from those of others. If we could not readily discriminate our mates from those of others, we might rapidly land in divorce court.

Higher-Order Conditioning   In **higher-order conditioning,** a previously neutral stimulus comes to serve as a CS after being paired repeatedly with a stimulus that has already become a CS. Pavlov demonstrated higher-order conditioning first by conditioning a dog to salivate (show a CR) in response to a bell (a CS). He then paired the shining of a light repeatedly with the bell. After several pairings, shining the light (the higher-order CS) came to elicit the response (salivation) that had been elicited by the bell (the first-order CS).

Consider children who learn that their parents are about to arrive when they hear a car in the driveway. It might be the case that a certain cartoon show comes on television a few minutes before the car enters the driveway. The television show can come to elicit the expectations that their parents are coming by being paired repeatedly with the car's entering the driveway. In another example, a boy may burn himself touching a hot stove. After this experience, the sight of the stove may serve as a CS for eliciting a fear response. But hearing the word "stove" may elicit a cognitive image of the stove, and so hearing the word alone may evoke a fear response.

The Story of Little Albert: A Case Study in Classical Conditioning   In 1920, John B. Watson and his future wife, Rosalie Rayner, published an article describing their demonstration that emotional reactions such as fears could be acquired through principles of classical conditioning. The subject of their demonstration was an unlucky lad by the name of Little Albert. Albert was a phlegmatic fellow at the age of eleven months, not given to ready displays of emotion. But he did enjoy playing with a laboratory rat. Such are the toys to be found in psychologists' laboratories.

Using a method that some psychologists have criticized as unethical, Watson startled Little Albert by clanging steel bars behind his head when the infant played with the rat. After seven pairings, Albert showed fear of the rat, even though clanging was suspended. Albert's fear also generalized to objects similar in appearance to the rat, such as a rabbit and his mother's coat's fur collar. Albert's mother, in fact, was so outraged by her son's fear of her (because of her collar) that she removed him before Watson could attempt to reverse the process. And so Albert's conditioned fear of rats may never have become extinguished. Extinction would require perceiving rats (the conditioned stimuli) without painful consequences (in the absence of the unconditioned stimuli). But fear might have prevented Albert from facing rats. And, as we shall see in the section on operant conditioning, avoiding rats might have been *reinforced* by reduction of fear.

In any event, somewhere there may be a gentleman in his sixties who cringes when he sees furry puppies or furry muffs protecting the hands of girls in winter, and, of course, whenever rats are discussed on television.

Through classical conditioning we learn to associate stimuli, so that a simple, usually passive response made to one is then made in response to the other. In the case of Little Albert, clanging noises were associated with a rat, so that the rat came to elicit the fear response brought forth by the noise. Let us now turn our attention to operant conditioning, in which organisms learn to engage in certain behaviors because of their effects. After classical conditioning took place, Albert's avoidance of rats would be labeled *operant behavior*. Avoidance of rats would be a voluntary response that has desired effects—in this case, the reduction of fear. Similarly, the sight of a hypodermic syringe may elicit a fear response because a person once had a painful injection. But subsequent avoidance of injections is operant behavior. It has the effect of reducing fear. In other cases, we engage in operant behavior to attain rewards, not to avoid unpleasant outcomes.

OPERANT CONDITIONING

In **operant conditioning,** an organism learns to engage in certain behavior because of the effects of that behavior. Operant conditioning is also referred to as **instrumental conditioning,** or instrumental learning, because the learned behavior is *instrumental* in achieving certain effects.

We begin this section with the historic work of psychologist Edward L. Thorndike. Then we examine the more recent work of B. F. Skinner.

EDWARD L. THORNDIKE AND THE LAW OF EFFECT

In the 1890s there was a mystery in Manhattan. Stray cats were disappearing from the streets and alleyways. Many of them, it turned out, were brought to the quarters of Columbia University doctoral student Edward Thorndike. Thorndike used them as subjects in experiments in learning by trial and error.

Thorndike placed the cats in so-called puzzle boxes. If the animals managed to pull a dangling string, a latch would be released, allowing them to jump out and reach a bowl of food.

When first placed in a puzzle box, a cat would try to squeeze through any opening and would claw and bite at the confining bars and wire. It would claw at any feature it could reach. Through such **random trial-and-error** behavior, it might take three to four minutes before the cat would chance upon the response of pulling the string. Pulling the string would open the cage and allow the cat to reach the food. When placed back in the cage, it might again take several minutes for the animal to pull the string. But as these trials were repeated, it would take progressively less time for the cat to pull the string. After seven or eight trials, it might pull the string immediately when placed back in the box.

The Law of Effect Thorndike explained the cat's learning to pull the string in terms of his **law of effect.** According to this law, a response (such as string-pulling) is "stamped in" or strengthened in a particular situation (such as being inside a puzzle box) by a reward (escaping the box and eating). Rewards, that is, stamp in S-R (stimulus-response) connections. Punishments, by contrast, "stamp out" stimulus-response connections. Or-

Edward L. Thorndike.

B. F. SKINNER Skinner and some of his associates at the Harvard University laboratory.

Reinforce To follow a response with a stimulus that increases the frequency of the response.

Operant behavior Voluntary responses that are reinforced.

ganisms would learn *not* to engage in punished responses. Later we shall see that the effects of punishment on learning are not so certain.

B. F. SKINNER AND REINFORCEMENT

"What did you do in the war, Daddy?" is a question familiar to many who served during America's conflicts. Some stories involve heroism, others involve the unusual. When it comes to unusual war stories, few will top that of Harvard University psychologist B. F. Skinner's story. For as he relates the tale in his autobiography, *The Shaping of a Behaviorist* (1979), one of Skinner's wartime efforts was "Project Pigeon."

During World War II Skinner proposed that pigeons be trained to guide missiles to their targets. In their training, the pigeons would be **reinforced** with food pellets for pecking at targets projected onto a screen (see Figure 5.4). Once trained, the pigeons would be placed in missiles. Pecking at similar targets displayed on a screen within the missile would correct the flight path of the missile, resulting in a "hit" and a sacrificed pigeon. But plans for building the necessary missile—for some reason called the *Pelican* and not the *Pigeon*—were scrapped. The pigeon equipment was too bulky, and, as Skinner lamented, his suggestion was not taken seriously. Apparently the Defense Department concluded that Project Pigeon was for the birds.

Project Pigeon may have been scrapped, but the principles of learning Skinner applied to the project have found wide applications in operant conditioning. In classical conditioning, an organism learns to associate stimuli. One previously neutral stimulus (the CS) comes to elicit the response brought forth by another stimulus (the US), because they have been paired repeatedly. But in operant conditioning an organism learns to *do* something, because of its effects or consequences.

This is **operant behavior,** behavior that operates upon or manipulates the environment. In classical conditioning, involuntary responses like salivation or eyeblinks are often conditioned. In operant conditioning, *volun-*

FIGURE 5.4 During World War II, B. F. Skinner suggested training pigeons to guide missiles to their targets. In an operant-conditioning procedure, the pigeons would be reinforced for pecking targets projected on a screen. Afterward, in combat, pecking at the on-screen target would keep the missile on course.

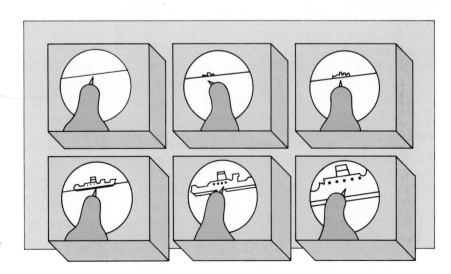

tary responses such as pecking at a target, pressing a lever, or many of the athletic skills required in playing tennis are usually acquired, or conditioned.

In operant conditioning, organisms engage in operant behaviors, also known simply as **operants,** that result in presumably desirable consequences such as food, a hug, an A on a test, attention, or social approval. Some children learn to conform their behavior to social codes and rules to earn the attention and approval of their parents and teachers. Other children, ironically, may learn to "misbehave," since misbehavior also results in attention from other people. Children may especially learn to be "bad" when their "good" behavior is routinely ignored.

Skinner Boxes and Cumulative Recorders   In order to study operant behavior efficiently, Skinner devised an animal cage termed the Skinner box (see Figure 5.5), in which conditions can be carefully controlled and laboratory animals can be carefully observed. The Skinner box saves energy; unlike Thorndike's puzzle box, a "correct" response does not result in the animal's escaping and having to be recaptured and placed back in the box.

The rat in Figure 5.5 was deprived of food and placed in a Skinner box with a lever at one end. At first it sniffed its way around the cage and engaged in **random trial-and-error behavior.** In random trial-and-error behavior, responses that meet with favorable consequences tend to occur more frequently; responses that do not meet with favorable consequences tend to be performed less frequently.

The rat's first pressing of the lever was accidental. However, because of this action a food pellet dropped into the cage. The food pellet increased the probability that the rat would press the lever again, and is thus said to have served as a reinforcement for the lever pressing.

Skinner further mechanized his laboratory procedure by making use of a **cumulative recorder,** as shown in Figure 5.6. The recorder provides a precise measure of operant behavior. The experimenter need not even be present to record correct responses. In the example used, the lever in the Skinner box is connected to the recorder, so that the recording pen moves upward with each correct response. The paper moves continuously to the left at a slow but regular pace. In the sample record shown in Figure 5.6, lever pressings (which record correct responses) were at first few and far between. But after several reinforced responses, lever pressing came fast and furious. When the rat is no longer hungry, the lever pressing will drop off and then stop.

The First "Correct" Response   In operant conditioning, it matters little how the first response that is reinforced comes to be made. The organism can happen upon it by chance, as in random trial-and-error learning. The organism can also be physically guided into the response. You may command your dog to "Sit!" then press its backside down until it is in a sitting position. Finally you reinforce sitting with food or a pat on the head and a kind word.

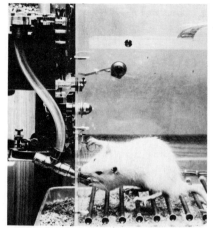

FIGURE 5.5 THE EFFECTS OF REINFORCEMENT One of the stars of modern psychology, an albino rat, earns its keep in a Skinner box. The animal presses a lever because of reinforcement—in the form of food pellets—delivered through the spout of the feeder. The habit strength of this operant can be measured as the frequency of lever pressing.

Operant An "operant" is the same as an operant behavior.

Random trial-and-error behavior Unplanned, random activity.

Cumulative recorder An instrument that records the frequency of an organism's operants (or "correct" responses) as a function of the passage of time.

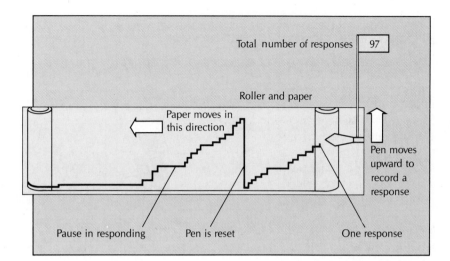

FIGURE 5.6 **A CUMULATIVE RE-CORDER** Paper moves continuously to the left while a pen automatically records each targeted response by moving upward. When the pen reaches the top of the paper, it is automatically reset to the bottom.

Animal trainers use physical guiding or coaxing to bring about the first "correct" response. Can you imagine how long it would take to train your dog if you waited for it to sit or roll over and then seized the opportunity to command it to sit or roll over? You would both age significantly in the process.

People, of course, can be verbally guided into desired responses when they are learning tasks like running a machine, spelling, or adding numbers. But they then need to be informed when they have made the correct response. Knowledge of results is often all the reinforcement that motivated people need to learn new skills.

Reinforcers Reinforcers increase the probability that an operant will be repeated. How do we know whether a stimulus is a reinforcer? Any stimulus that increases the probability that responses preceding it will be repeated serves as a reinforcer. Reinforcers include food pellets when an organism has been deprived of food, water when it has been deprived of liquid, the opportunity to mate, and the sound of a bell that has been previously associated with eating. (Yes, a CS can serve as a reinforcer.)

FIGURE 5.7 **SECONDARY REINFORCERS** Understanding other people includes being able to predict what they will find reinforcing. In this Dagwood cartoon, Dagwood apparently finds money more reinforcing than the praise of his boss, Mr. Dithers.

Skinner distinguished between positive and negative reinforcers. **Positive reinforcers** increase the probability that an operant will occur when they are applied. Food and approval usually serve as positive reinforcers. **Negative reinforcers** increase the probability that an operant will occur when they are *removed*. People often learn to plan ahead so that they need not fear that things will go wrong. Fear acts as a negative reinforcer, because *removal* of fear increases the probability that the behaviors preceding it (such as planning ahead or fleeing a predator) will be repeated.

Greater reinforcers prompt more rapid learning than do lesser reinforcers. You will probably work much harder for $1,000 than for $10. (If not, get in touch with me—I have some chores that need to be taken care of.) With sufficient reinforcement, operants become a **habit.** They show a high probability of recurrence in a certain situation.

We can also distinguish between primary and secondary or conditioned reinforcers. **Primary reinforcers** are effective because of the biological makeup of the organism. Food, water, adequate warmth (positive reinforcers), and pain (a negative reinforcer) all serve as primary reinforcers. **Secondary reinforcers** acquire their value through being associated with established reinforcers. For this reason they are also termed **conditioned reinforcers.** We may seek money because we have learned that it may be exchanged for primary reinforcers. Money, attention, social approval, all are conditioned reinforcers in our culture. We may be suspicious of, or not "understand," people who are not interested in money or the approval of others. Part of "understanding" others lies in being able to predict what they will find reinforcing (see Figure 5.7).

Extinction and Spontaneous Recovery in Operant Conditioning Extinction in classical conditioning results from repeated presentation of the CS without the US, so that the CR becomes inhibited. In operant conditioning, extinction results from repeated performance of operant behavior

Positive reinforcer A reinforcer that, when *presented*, increases the frequency of an operant. Food and approval are usually positive reinforcers.

Negative reinforcer A reinforcer that, when *removed*, increases the frequency of an operant. Pain, anxiety, and disapproval are usually negative reinforcers—that is, organisms will learn to engage in responses that permit them to *avoid* these reinforcers.

Habit A learned response that shows a high frequency of recurrence under certain conditions.

Primary reinforcer An unlearned reinforcer, such as food, water, warmth, or pain.

Secondary reinforcer A stimulus that gains reinforcement value through association with other, established reinforcers. Money and approval are secondary reinforcers.

Conditioned reinforcer Another term for a secondary reinforcer.

1 "THIS IS A STICKUP!"

2 "THIS IS A STICKUP!"

3 "THIS IS A STICKUP!"

4

5

Opie

without reinforcement. After a number of trials, the operant behavior also becomes inhibited (is no longer shown).

After some time has passed, however, an organism will usually again perform the operant when placed in a situation in which the operant had been previously reinforced. Spontaneous recovery of learned responses occurs in operant as well as classical conditioning. If the operant is reinforced at this time, it quickly regains its former strength.

Reinforcers versus Rewards and Punishments   **Rewards,** like reinforcers, are stimuli that increase the frequency of behavior. But rewards are also considered pleasant events. Skinner preferred the concept of reinforcement to that of reward, because reinforcement does not suggest trying to "get inside the head" of an organism (person or lower animal) to guess what it would find pleasant or unpleasant. A list of reinforcers is arrived at **empirically,** by observing what sorts of stimuli will increase the frequency of the behavior of organisms.

Reward A pleasant stimulus that increases the frequency of the behavior it follows. (Why did Skinner prefer to use the term "reinforcement"?)

Empirically By trial or experiment, rather than by logical deduction.

Punishments are aversive events that suppress or decrease the frequency of the behavior they follow.* Punishment can rapidly suppress undesirable behavior, and may be warranted in "emergencies," such as when a child tries to run out into the street. But many learning theorists agree that punishment is usually undesirable, especially in rearing children, for reasons such as the following:

1. Punishment does not in and of itself suggest an alternate, acceptable form of behavior.
2. Punishment tends to suppress undesirable behavior only under circumstances in which its delivery is guaranteed. It does not take children long to learn that they can "get away with murder" with one parent, or one teacher, but not with another.
3. Punished organisms may withdraw from the situation. Severely punished children may run away, cut class, or drop out of school.
4. Punishment can create anger and hostility. Adequate punishment will almost always suppress unwanted behavior—but at what cost? A child may express accumulated feelings of hostility against other children.
5. Punishment may generalize too far. The child who is punished severely for bad table manners may stop eating altogether. Overgeneralization is more likely to occur when children do not know exactly why they are being punished, and when they have not been shown alternate, acceptable behaviors.
6. Punishment may be modeled as a way of solving problems or coping with stress. We shall see that one way that children learn is by observing others. Even though children may not immediately perform the behavior they observe, they may perform it later on, even as adults, when their circumstances are similar to those of the **model.**
7. Finally, children learn responses that are punished. Whether or not children choose to perform punished responses, punishment draws their attention to them.

It is usually preferable to focus on rewarding children for desirable behavior than to punish them for unwanted behavior. By ignoring their misbehavior, or by using **time out** from positive reinforcement, we can consistently avoid reinforcing children for misbehavior.

To reward or positively reinforce children for desired behavior takes time and care. Simply never using punishment is not enough. First, we must pay attention to them when they are behaving well. If we take their desirable behavior for granted, and act as if we are aware of them only when they misbehave, we may be encouraging misbehavior. Second, we must carefully physically or verbally guide them into making the desired responses. We cannot teach children table manners by waiting for them to exhibit proper responses by random trial-and-error and then reinforcing them. If we waited by holding a half-gallon of ice cream behind our backs as a reward, we would have slippery dining room floors long before we had children with table manners.

*Recall that *negative reinforcers* are defined in terms of *increasing* the frequency of behavior, although the increase occurs when the negative reinforcer is *removed*. A punishment *decreases* the frequency of a behavior when it is *applied*.

Punishment An unpleasant stimulus that suppresses the behavior it follows. (What is the difference between a negative reinforcer and a punishment?)

Model An organism that engages in a response that is imitated by another organism.

Time out In operant conditioning, a method for decreasing the frequency of undesired behaviors: an organism is removed from a situation in which reinforcement is available when unwanted behavior is shown.

Discriminative Stimuli   B. F. Skinner might not have been able to get his pigeons into the drivers' seats of missiles during the war, but he had no problem training them to respond to traffic lights. Try the following experiment for yourself.

Find a pigeon. Or sit on a park bench, close your eyes, and one will find you. Place it in a Skinner box with a button on the wall. Drop a food pellet into the cage whenever it pecks the button. (Soon it will learn to peck the button whenever it has not eaten for a while.) Now place a small green light in the cage. Turn it on and off intermittently throughout the day. Reinforce button-pecking with food whenever the green light is on, but not when the light is off. It will not take long for this clever city pigeon to learn that it will gain as much by grooming itself or squawking and flapping around as it will by pecking the button when the light is off.

The green light will have become a **discriminative stimulus.** Discriminative stimuli act as cues. They provide information as to when an operant (in this case, pecking a button) will be reinforced (in this case, by a food pellet being dropped into the cage).

As noted above, operants that are not reinforced tend to become extinguished. For the pigeon in our experiment, pecking the button *when the light is off* becomes extinguished.

A moment's reflection will suggest many ways in which discriminative stimuli influence our behavior. Would you rather ask your boss for a raise when she is smiling or when she is frowning? Wouldn't you rather answer the telephone when it is ringing? Do you think it wise to try to get smoochy when your date is blowing smoke in your face or chugalugging a bottle of antacid tablets? One of the factors involved in gaining social skills is learning to interpret social discriminative stimuli (smiles, tones of voice, body language) accurately.

SCHEDULES OF REINFORCEMENT

In operant conditioning, some responses are maintained by **continuous reinforcement.** You probably become warmer every time you put on heavy clothing. You probably become less thirsty every time you drink water. But if you have ever watched people throwing money down the maws of slot machines, or "one-armed bandits," you know that behavior can also be maintained by **partial reinforcement.**

There is folklore about gambling that is based on solid learning theory. You can get a person "hooked" on gambling by fixing the game to allow heavy winnings at first. Then you gradually space out the gambling behaviors that are reinforced until the gambling is maintained by very infrequent winning—or even no winning at all.

New operants or behaviors are acquired most rapidly through continuous reinforcement, or, in some cases, through "one-trial learning" that meets with great reinforcement. So-called **pathological gamblers** often experienced a "big win" at the racetrack or casino or in the lottery in their late teens or early twenties (Greene, 1982). But once the operant has been acquired, it can be maintained by tapering off to a schedule of partial reinforcement.

Discriminative stimulus In operant conditioning, a stimulus that indicates that reinforcement is available.

Continuous reinforcement A schedule of reinforcement in which every correct response is reinforced.

Partial reinforcement One of several reinforcement schedules in which not every correct response is reinforced.

Pathological gambler A person who gambles habitually, despite consistent losses. A compulsive gambler.

There are four basic schedules of reinforcement. They are determined by changing either the *interval* of time that must elapse between correct responses before reinforcement is made available, or the *ratio* of correct responses to reinforcements. If the interval that must elapse between correct responses, before reinforcement becomes available, is zero seconds, the reinforcement schedule is continuous. A larger interval of time, such as thirty seconds, is a partial-reinforcement schedule. A one-to-one (1:1) ratio of correct responses to reinforcements is a continuous-reinforcement schedule. A higher ratio, such as a 2:1 or 5:1 ratio, would be a partial-reinforcement schedule.

The four basic types of schedules of reinforcement are *fixed-interval, variable-interval, fixed-ratio,* and *variable-ratio* schedules.

In a **fixed-interval schedule,** a fixed amount of time, say one minute, must elapse between the previous and subsequent times that reinforcement is made available for correct responses.

In a **variable-interval schedule,** varying amounts of time are allowed to elapse between making reinforcement available. In a three-minute variable-interval schedule, the mean amount of time that would elapse between reinforcement opportunities would be three minutes, but each interval might vary from, say, one to five minutes or from two to four minutes.

With a fixed-interval schedule, an organism's response rate falls off after each reinforcement, as if it has learned that it must wait a while before reinforcement will be made available. But the response rate remains rapid on the more unpredictable variable-interval schedule.

In a **fixed-ratio schedule,** reinforcement is provided after a fixed number of correct responses have been made.

In a **variable-ratio schedule,** reinforcement is provided after a variable number of correct responses has been made. In a 10:1 variable-ratio schedule, the mean number of correct responses that would have to be made before a subsequent correct response would be reinforced is 10, but the number of correct responses required for reinforcement might be allowed to vary from, say, one to twenty on a random basis.

Fixed-ratio and variable-ratio schedules maintain a high response rate. With a fixed-ratio schedule, it is as if the organism learns that it must make several responses before being reinforced. It then "gets them out of the way" as rapidly as possible. With a variable-ratio schedule, reinforcement can come at any time. This unpredictability also maintains a high response rate.

Shaping   If you are teaching disco-type maneuvers to people who have never danced, do not wait until they have performed a perfect Latin hustle before telling them they're on the right track. The fox-trot will be back in style before they have learned a thing.

We can teach complex behaviors by **shaping,** or at first reinforcing small steps toward the behavioral goals. At first it may be wise to smile and say "Good" when a reluctant newcomer gathers the courage to get out on the dance floor, even if your feet get flattened by his initial clumsiness. If you are teaching someone to drive a car with a standard shift, at first generously reinforce the learner simply for shifting without stalling.

Fixed-interval schedule A schedule in which a fixed amount of time must elapse between the previous and subsequent times that reinforcement is available.

Variable-interval schedule A schedule in which a variable amount of time must elapse between the previous and subsequent times that reinforcement is available.

Fixed-ratio schedule A schedule in which reinforcement is provided after a fixed number of correct responses.

Variable-ratio schedule A schedule in which reinforcement is provided after a variable number of correct responses.

Shaping In operant conditioning, a procedure for teaching complex behaviors that at first reinforces approximations to the target behavior.

BEHAVIOR MODIFICATION IN MANAGEMENT

If you think about it, the weekly, bimonthly, or monthly check at work could be considered an example of fixed-interval reinforcement. That is, there is a payoff after a certain amount of time passes. Fixed-interval schedules are linked to some inconsistency in response frequencies, of course, even though they are practical ways of paying workers. With a check coming every two weeks, there is little external reason not to slough off now and then if the manager does not keep a watchful eye.

Transfers, promotions, and raises (based on performance, not tenure) can be considered examples of variable-interval reinforcement. They tend to produce high rates of steady responses among motivated workers. Commissions on units sold and piece rates for piece work are examples of fixed-ratio schedules which, like fixed-interval schedules, are linked to some inconsistency in response rates. Bonuses, awards, and time off are examples of variable-ratio schedules and can produce high, steady response rates.

Reinforcement schedules were in operation in the work place long before managers heard of B. F. Skinner or of behavior modification. However, in recent years, companies as diverse as Chase Manhattan, Proctor & Gamble, Ford, Standard Oil of Ohio, Emery Air Freight, General Electric, B. F. Goodrich, and Connecticut General Life Insurance have all turned to principles of learning in an effort to increase productivity and enhance the quality of work life.

Steps in Using Behavior Modification The design of a behavior-modification program in the work place usually involves five steps:

1. Identifying and defining the specific behavior to be increased (or decreased, as in the case of absenteeism). "Improved attitude" is not an appropriate behavioral goal; we must specify what workers must do in order to demonstrate an improved attitude.
2. Measuring or counting the occurrences of the specified behavior.
3. Conducting an analysis of the ABCs of the behavior. This means analyzing the *Antecedents* of the behavior, the *Behavior* itself, and the *Consequences* of the

behavior. For example, concerning antecedents, we need to know whether the employee knows what is expected or has proper tools. Concerning the behavior itself, we need to know whether the employee is capable of performing it or whether something in the work place is interfering with performance. Concerning consequences, we need to know whether improvements are reinforced, i.e., whether consequences are generally weighted in favor of performance.

4. Implementing a program based on analysis of the ABCs. Implementation could include methods such as the following:

   Strategies aimed at antecedents:
   Requesting different behavior (differences specified)
   Strategies aimed at behaviors:
   Providing on-the-job training
   Strategies aimed at consequences:
   Publicly praising improved performance (positive reinforcement)
   Not responding to inadequate behavior (extinction)
   Publicly reprimanding worker for inadequate behavior (punishment)

5. Evaluating the effectiveness of the program in terms of the increase or decrease of specified behaviors. Through evaluation, effective programs can be maintained or enhanced, and ineffective programs can be eliminated or modified. Evaluation provides feedback to the manager just as the manager has provided feedback to the worker.

There are several advantages to behavior modification in the work place. One is that both managers and workers understand clearly what types of behaviors are to be increased or decreased. A second is that the consequences of improvement (or continued inadequacy) are clarified. A third is that clear specification of required behaviors and reinforcers tends to eliminate complaints about favoritism. Finally, there is concrete data to indicate whether or not improvement has taken place. Workers are not punished for intangibles such as a "poor attitude."

Successive approximations In operant conditioning, behaviors that are progressively closer to a target behavior.

But as training proceeds, we come to expect more before dispensing reinforcement. We reinforce **successive approximations** to the goal. If you want to train a rat to climb a ladder, first reinforce it (with a food pellet) when it turns toward the ladder. Then wait until it approaches the ladder before using reinforcement. Then do not drop a food pellet into the cage

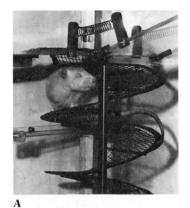

A

B

C

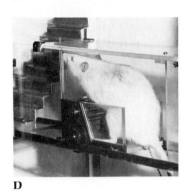

D

E

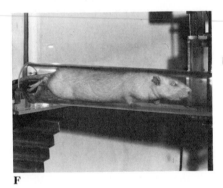

F

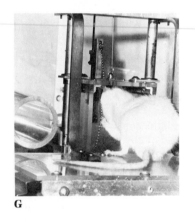

G

FIGURE 5.8 THE SHAPING UP OF BARNABUS THE RAT Psychologists at Columbia University (Pierrel & Sherman, 1963) shaped Barnabus to perform a complex behavioral chain by reinforcing each behavior in sequence. The sequence proceeded from last to first, so that each reward would trigger the next behavior in the chain. In these photos you see Barnabus (a) climb a spiral ramp, (b) cross a bridge, (c) climb a ladder, (d) pedal a toy car, (e) climb steps, (f) crawl through a tube, and (g) ride an elevator to return to the starting platform. Finally, Barnabus presses a lever to attain a food pellet (not shown). Complex behavior for a rat?

until the rat touches the ladder. In this way the rat will reach the top of the ladder more quickly than if you had waited until the target behavior had first occurred by random trial and error. This method of shaping was used to train one rat, Barnabus, to engage in the complex behavioral sequence shown in Figure 5.8.

Learning to drive a new standard-shift automobile to a new job also involves a complex sequence of operant behaviors. At first we actively seek out all the discriminative stimuli or landmarks that cue us when to turn—signs, buildings, hills, and valleys. We also focus on shifting to a lower gear as we slow down so that the car won't stall. But after many repetitions

BOX: PSYCHOLOGY AND HEALTH

USING AVOIDANCE LEARNING TO SAVE A BABY'S LIFE

The techniques of avoidance learning suggested in *Brave New World* have actually found real-life—perhaps real-life-saving—applications with children who are too young or distressed to respond to verbal forms of therapy. In one example, reported by Lang and Melamed (1969), a nine-month-old infant vomited regularly within ten to fifteen minutes after eating. Repeated diagnostic workups had found no medical basis for the problem, and medical treatments were of no avail. When the case was brought to the attention of Lang and Melamed, the infant weighed only nine pounds and was in critical condition, being fed by a pump.

The psychologists monitored the infant for the first physical indications (local muscle tension) that vomiting was to occur. When the child tensed prior to vomiting, a tone was sounded and followed by painful but (presumably) harmless electric shock. After two one-hour treatment sessions, the infant's muscle tensions ceased in response to the tone alone, and vomiting soon ceased altogether. At a one-year follow-up, the infant was still not vomiting and had caught up in weight.

How do we explain this remarkable procedure? It included classical- and operant-conditioning procedures. Through repeated pairings, the tone (CS) came to elicit expectation of electric shock (US), so that the psychologists could use the painful shock only sparingly. The electric shock and, after classical conditioning, the tone served as punishments. The infant soon learned to suppress the behaviors (muscle tensions) that were reliably followed by the punishment. In so doing, he avoided the punishment.

This learning occurred at an age long before any sort of verbal intervention could have been understood, and it apparently saved the infant's life.

these responses, these chains of behavior, become "habitual" and we need pay very little attention to them.

Have you ever driven home from school or work and been suddenly unsettled as you got out of your car that you couldn't recall exactly how you had returned home? Your entire trip may seem "lost." Were you in great danger? How could you allow such a thing to happen? Actually, it may be that your responses to the demands of the route and to driving your car had become so habitual that you did not have to focus much awareness on them. You were able to think about dinner, a problem at work, or the weekend as you drove. But if something unusual, like hesitation in your engine or a severe rainstorm, had occurred on the way, you would have deployed as much attention as was needed to arrive home. Your trip was probably quite safe, after all.

APPLICATIONS OF OPERANT CONDITIONING

Brave New World showed us how a fictitious society abused the principles of learning to condition children to want to fit into the niches deemed appropriate for them. But in the real world, operant conditioning is used every day in the **socialization** of young children. For example, as we shall see in Chapter 13, parents and peers influence children to acquire gender-appropriate behaviors through the elaborate use of rewards and punishments.

Biofeedback Training Principles of operant conditioning are used in biofeedback training, which was discussed in Chapters 3 and 4. Through BFT, people and lower animals have learned to control autonomic re-

---

Socialization Guidance of others through the systematic use of rewards and punishments and other principles of learning.

sponses to attain reinforcement. The rats in Neal Miller's laboratory, for example, were reinforced by mild shock in the pleasure centers of their brains when they accelerated or decelerated their heart rates. As part of a program to enhance their well-being, people have learned to manipulate their heart rates, blood pressure, skin temperature, even the emission of certain brain waves.

When people receive BFT, the reinforcement is *information,* not electric current in the brain. Perhaps a "bleep" sound changes in pitch or frequency of occurrence to signal that they have modified the autonomic function in the desired direction. BFT has been used with accident patients who have lost neuromuscular control of various parts of the body. A "bleep" informs them when they have contracted a muscle or sent an impulse down a neural pathway. By concentrating on changing the bleeps, they also gradually regain voluntary control over the damaged function.

Behavior therapists also apply operant conditioning to foster desired responses, such as social skills, and to extinguish unwanted behaviors, such as social withdrawal in a mental-hospital setting. Several techniques are outlined in Chapter 12.

Principles of operant conditioning have also permitted psychologists and educators to develop many beneficial innovations, such as behavior modification in the classroom and programed learning.

Behavior Modification in the Classroom   Adults frequently reinforce undesirable behavior in children by attending to them when they misbehave, but ignoring them when they behave properly. The use of behavior modification in the classroom reverses this response pattern: teachers pay attention to children when they are behaving appropriately and, when possible, ignore (avoid reinforcing) their misbehavior (Lahey & Drabman, 1981). The younger the school child, the more powerful teacher attention and approval seem to be.

One study of behavior modification in the classroom was designed to change the behavior of three elementary school children who touched others, took others' property, turned around, made noise, and mouthed objects during lessons (Madsen et al., 1968). In this program, the teacher wrote out classroom rules on the blackboard, verbally guiding the children into appropriate responses. The children repeated them out loud. During the early part of training, the teacher left the rules visible while inappropriate behavior was ignored and appropriate behavior was praised. Targeted behavior rapidly decreased.

Similar approaches have reduced aggressive behavior and increased studying in school children. Descriptive praise seems more effective than a simple "Good." Saying "It was very good the way you raised your hand and waited for me to call on you before talking out" reminds the child of the behavior that results in praise, and prompts repetition of the desired behavior.

Among older children and adolescents, peer approval is frequently a more powerful reinforcer than teacher approval. Peer approval may maintain misbehavior, and teacher ignoring of misbehavior may only allow peers

PSYCHOLOGY TODAY

COMPUTER-ASSISTED LEARNING

During the 1970s, there were few computers in the home or school. Those of us who had computers in the home used them primarily to play videogames. But today computers are being advertised as essential to the learning of children, and thousands upon thousands of parents and schools are purchasing these instruments for fear that their children will be left behind if they do not. In fact, the buzz words "computer illiteracy" strike almost as much fear into some hearts as does "illiteracy" itself. Many children are now learning the basics of programing in first grade and in summer camps, while others use existing programs as workbooks.

Programed Learning and Computers It is hard to say just how important as learning tools computers will become for children. However, so-called computer-assisted learning (CAL) is a form of instruction (used primarily in the schools) that applies the capacities of the computer to certain aspects of programed learning. That is, learning tasks are broken down into discrete steps in prewritten ("canned") programs, and students may learn at their own pace. But in contrast to pure programed learning, students can make mistakes.

In CAL, students sit at monitors and respond to questions or challenges either by typing at the keyboard or touching a certain part of the screen with an instrument called a "mouse." They receive immediate feedback as to the correctness of their answers. If they err, branching programs may be activated that teach students step by step the skills they need in order to make correct responses.

COMPUTER-ASSISTED LEARNING In CAL, students sit at monitors and respond to questions by typing at the keyboard or touching the screen with a "mouse." They can receive immediate feedback as to the correctness of their answers.

Wave of the Future? The novelty of the computer and inventiveness in programing can lend computer sessions a gamelike atmosphere. Students can proceed at their own paces and, if they make mistakes, they do so in privacy. As noted, it may be premature to suggest that CAL is one of those "waves of the future," but many school districts, at least, seem to be using CAL for fear that they will become electronic horses and carriages if they do not.

to become more disruptive. In such cases it may be necessary to separate troublesome children.

Teachers also frequently use time out from positive reinforcement to discourage misbehavior. In this method, children are placed in drab, restrictive environments for a specified time period, usually about ten minutes, when they behave disruptively. When isolated, they cannot earn the attention of peers or teachers, and no reinforcing activities are present.

It may strike you that these techniques are not startlingly new. Perhaps we all know parents who have ignored their children's misbehavior and have heard of teachers making children "sit facing the corner." Perhaps what is novel is the focus on (1) avoiding punishment, and (2) being consistent so that undesirable behavior is not reinforced intermittently. But it should be noted that punishment can also decrease undesirable behavior in the classroom. For example, after-school detention has been found to reduce disruptive classroom behavior (Brigham et al., 1985).

Programed Learning   B. F. Skinner has been instrumental in developing an educational practice called **programed learning.** Programed learning is based on the assumption that any complex task, involving conceptual learning as well as motor skills, can be broken down into a number of small steps. These steps can be shaped individually and combined in sequence to form the correct behavioral chain.

Programed learning does not punish errors. Instead, correct responses are reinforced. All children earn "100," but at their own pace. Programed learning also assumes that it is the task of the teacher (or program) to structure the learning experience in such a way that errors will not be made.

COGNITIVE LEARNING

Conditioning is a simple form of learning in which stimuli or responses become mechanically linked to certain situations. Although conditioning meets the scientific objective of explaining behavior completely in terms of public, observable events—in this case, laboratory conditions—many psychologists have come to believe that conditioning is inadequate to explain all instances of learned behavior, even in laboratory rats. They have turned to **cognitive learning** in order to describe and explain additional findings. Cognitive learning, in contrast to conditioning, is not a mechanical process. The defining feature of cognitive learning is that it involves mental representation of the environment, even when it occurs in rats and apes. In our discussion of cognitive learning, we review a number of classic studies that show why psychologists needed to develop principles of cognitive learning.

About sixty years ago, as noted in Chapter 1, German Gestalt psychologist Wolfgang Köhler became convinced that not all forms of learning could be explained by mechanical conditioning when one of his chimpan-

FIGURE 5.9 FIDDLING WITH STICKS FOR INSIGHT Gestalt psychologist Wolfgang Köhler ran experiments with chimpanzees that suggest that not all learning is mechanical. This chimp must retrieve a stick outside the cage and attach it to a stick he already has before he can retrieve the distant circular object. While fiddling with two such sticks, Sultan, another chimp, seemed to suddenly recognize that the sticks can be attached. This is an example of learning by insight.

zees, Sultan, "went bananas." Sultan had learned to use a stick to rake in bananas placed outside his cage. But now Herr Köhler (pronounced *hair curler*) placed the banana beyond the reach of the stick. He gave Sultan two bamboo poles that could be fitted together to make a single pole long enough to retrieve the delectable reward. The set-up was similar to that shown in Figure 5.9.

As if to make this historic occasion more dramatic, Sultan at first tried to reach the banana with one pole. When he could not do so, he returned to fiddling with the sticks. Köhler left the laboratory after an hour or so of frustration (his own as well as Sultan's). An assistant was assigned the thankless task of observing Sultan. But soon afterward Sultan happened to align the two sticks as he fiddled. Then, in what seemed a flash of inspiration, Sultan fitted them together and pulled in the elusive banana.

Köhler was summoned to the laboratory. When he arrived the sticks fell apart, as if on cue. But Sultan regathered them, fit them firmly together, and actually tested the strength of the fit before retrieving another banana.

LEARNING BY INSIGHT

Köhler was impressed by Sultan's rapid "perception of relationships" and used the term **insight** to describe it. He noted that such insights were not learned gradually through reinforced trials. Rather they seemed to occur "in a flash" when the elements of a problem had been arranged appropriately. Sultan also proved himself immediately capable of stringing several sticks together to retrieve various objects, not just bananas. This seemed no mechanical generalization. It appeared that Sultan understood the principle of the relationship between joining sticks and reaching distant objects.

Psychologists in the United States soon demonstrated that not even the behavior of rats was as mechanical as most behaviorists suggested. E. C. Tolman (1948), a University of California behaviorist, showed that rats behaved as if they acquired **cognitive maps** of mazes. While they would learn many paths to a food goal, they would typically choose the shortest. But if the shortest path was blocked, they would quickly switch to another. The behavior of the rats suggested that they learned *places in which reinforcement was available,* not a series of mechanical motor responses.

Bismarck, one of University of Michigan psychologist N. R. F. Maier's laboratory rats, provided further evidence for learning by insight (Maier & Schneirla, 1935). Bismarck had been trained to climb a ladder to a tabletop where food was placed. On one occasion Maier used a mesh barrier to prevent Bismarck from reaching his goal. But as shown in Figure 5.10, a second ladder to the table was provided. The second ladder was in clear view of the animal. At first Bismarck sniffed and scratched and made every effort to find a path through the mesh barrier. Then Bismarck spent some time washing his face, an activity that apparently signals frustration in rats. Suddenly Bismarck jumped into the air, turned, ran down the familiar ladder, around to the new ladder, up the new ladder, and then claimed his just desserts.

It is difficult to explain Bismarck's behavior through conditioning. It seems that Bismarck suddenly perceived the relationships between the ele-

Insight In Gestalt psychology, a sudden perception of relationships among elements of the "perceptual field," permitting the sudden solution of a problem.

Cognitive map A mental representation or "picture" of the elements in a learning situation, such as a maze.

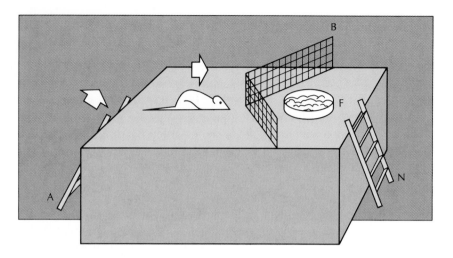

FIGURE 5.10 **BISMARCK CLAIMS HIS JUST DESSERTS** Bismarck has learned to reach dinner by climbing ladder *A*. But now the food goal *F* is blocked by a wire mesh barrier *B*. Bismarck washes his face for a while, but then, in an apparent flash of insight, runs back down ladder *A* and up new ladder *N* to claim his just desserts.

ments of his problem so that the solution occurred by insight. He seems to have had what Gestalt psychologists have termed an "Aha! experience."

LATENT LEARNING

Many behaviorists argue that organisms acquire only those responses, or operants, for which they are reinforced. However, E. C. Tolman showed that rats learn about their environments in the absence of reinforcement.

Tolman trained some rats to run through mazes for standard food goals, while other rats were permitted to explore the same mazes for several days without food goals or other rewards. The rewarded rats could be said to have found their ways through the mazes with fewer errors (fewer "wrong turns") on each trial run. But, in a sense, the unrewarded rats had no correct or incorrect turns to make, since no response led to a reward.

After the unrewarded rats had been allowed to explore the mazes for ten days, food rewards were placed in a box at the far end of the maze. The previously unrewarded explorers reached the food box as quickly as the rewarded rats after only one or two reinforced trials (Tolman & Honzik, 1950).

Tolman concluded that rats learned about mazes in which they roamed even when they were unrewarded for doing so. He distinguished between learning and performance. Rats would acquire a cognitive map of a maze and, even though they would not be motivated to follow an efficient route to the far end, they would learn rapid routes from end to end, just by roaming about within the maze. But this learning might be hidden, or **latent,** until they were motivated to follow the rapid routes for food goals.

OBSERVATIONAL LEARNING

How many things have you learned from watching other people in real life, in films, and on television? From films and television we may have gathered vague ideas about how to sky dive, ride surfboards, climb the outside of the World Trade Center, run a pattern to catch a touchdown pass in the

Latent Hidden or concealed. In latent learning, learning is not exhibited at the time of learning. But it is demonstrated when adequate reinforcement is introduced. (From the Latin *latere,* meaning "to lie hidden.")

Observational learning Acquiring operants, which may or may not be performed, by observing others engage in them. Observational learning occurs without emission and reinforcement of a response.

Superbowl, and dust for fingerprints, even if we have never tried these activities.

Social-learning theorist Albert Bandura has run numerous experiments (e.g., Bandura et al., 1963) that show that we acquire operants through observing the behavior of others. We may need some practice to refine the skills we acquire by observation, but we can acquire the required knowledge through observation alone. We may also choose to allow these skills to lie latent. For example, we may not imitate aggressive behavior unless we are provoked and believe that we are more likely to be rewarded than punished for aggressive behavior.

Observational learning may account for most human learning. It occurs when we as children observe parents cook, clean, or repair a broken appliance. There is evidence that observational learning for simple "single action" tasks, such as opening the halves of a toy barrel to look at a barrel inside, occurs as early as twelve months of age (Abravanel & Gingold, 1985). Observational learning takes place when we watch teachers solve problems on the blackboard or hear them speak in a foreign language. Observational learning is not mechanically acquired through reinforcement. We can learn by observation without engaging in overt responses at all. It appears sufficient to pay attention to the behavior of others.

As noted at the beginning of the chapter, it would be of little use to discuss how we learn, if we were not capable of remembering what we learn from second to second, from day to day, or, in many cases, for a lifetime. Let us now turn our attention to the subject of memory. How do we remember things? How much can we remember? How can we improve our ability to remember?

MEMORY

Are you in a betting mood? I bet that I can show you how to memorize the lines and shapes that correspond to the numbers 1–9 in Figure 5.11—practically instantaneously. Check them out for a minute to see if you think you can do it. Then turn to Figure 5.12.

Memory is a most important area of investigation in psychology. Without memory—that is, the ability to store and retrieve information—learning

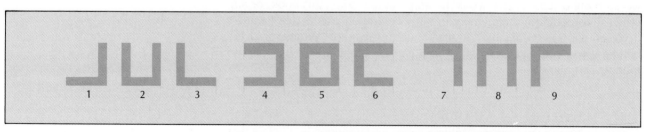

FIGURE 5.11 **AN EXERCISE IN ASSOCIATIVE LEARNING** How quickly can you memorize the shapes that correspond to each number, 1 to 9? After you have pondered this question for a while, turn to FIGURE 5.12.

MEMORY: THE UNRELIABLE WITNESS

Psychologist Jean Piaget vividly remembered an attempt to kidnap him from his baby carriage along the Champs Élysées. He recalled the gathered crowd, the scratches on the face of the heroic nurse who saved him, the policeman's white baton, the assailant running away. However vivid, Piaget's recollections were false. Years later the nurse confessed that she had made up the entire story.

A Creative Blend of Fiction and Fact Many social scientists believe that most early childhood memories are dreamlike reconstructions of stories told by parents and friends. Now [psychologist] Elizabeth Loftus has a sobering message for grownups. Their memories are almost as unreliable as children's. They are so encrusted with experiences, desires, and suggestions that they often resemble fiction as much as fact. In *Eyewitness Testimony* (1980), Loftus made a strong case against the reliability of remembrances of court witnesses. In *Memory* (1981), she indicts human recollections in general.

One problem with memory is that people do not observe well in the first place. Surprisingly often, people fail a simple test: picking out the exact copy of a real penny in a group of 15 possible designs. More important, people forget some facts and "refabricate" the gaps between the ones they do not remember accurately. They tend to adjust memory to suit their picture of the world. One example: in tests involving observations of a black man with a hat and a white man carrying a razor, people often recall the razor being in the black's hands.

Hypnosis and Truth Serums Hypnosis and "truth serums" can also produce as much fiction as fact. Far from dredging up reality, writes Loftus, "hypnosis encourages a person to relax, to cooperate, and to concentrate." Suggestibility is so heightened that people may remember events that never occurred. Studies show that after taking truth drugs, people can lie competently, garble facts, and invent stories to please their questioners. Other Loftus arguments:

Hearing memory is apparently stronger in humans than touch, sight, or smell memory. Patients who have been under total anesthesia can sometimes recall words spoken during an operation.

Most people cannot easily remember more than six or seven items in a series—a fact that bodes ill for the postal service's plan to replace five-digit zip codes with nine-digit ones. A Loftus tip: Mental shopping lists should be set up with the important purchases at the beginning or the end. As memory dims, the items in the middle tend to fade first.

Slight stress improves memory. Heavy stress erodes it. People who are about to subject themselves to danger—mountain climbing, parachute jumping, etc.—perform poorly at mental tasks.

Alcohol and marijuana seem to affect information storage more than retrieval. That is, memory may work well at the time, but some things that occur while a person is under the influence may not be recalled. Senility works in a similar way, eroding ability to store new information.

Any severe shock can produce memory loss. Rats forget tricks when given electric jolts. Amnesia, which can be the result of physical or emotional shock, is often selective. One woman, a professor of English, forgot the events and dates of her own life, but remembered those of English literature well enough to teach.

would profit us little. There would be no point to reading this book, or any other, if you could not remember it. How could you play Space Invaders if you forgot how to use the "joystick" after every shot? What would life be like if you could not remember your name, your address, your family, friends, and plans?

THE STRUCTURE OF MEMORY

Before the turn of the century, William James was intrigued by the fact that some memories were unreliable, "going in one ear and out the other," while others could be recalled for a lifetime:

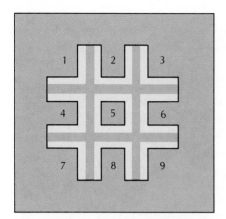

FIGURE 5.12 A FAMILIAR GRID The nine shapes in Figure 5.11 form this familiar tic-tac-toe grid when the numbers are placed inside them and they are arranged in numerical order, three shapes to a line. This method for recalling the shapes collapses nine chunks of information into one meaningful chunk. You encode them by thinking of the tic-tac-toe grid; then simply "read" the grid, shape by shape, numbering each one as you do so.

The stream of thought flows on, but most of its elements fall into the bottomless pit of oblivion. Of some, no element survives the instant of their passage. Of others, it is confined to a few moments, hours, or days. Others, again, leave vestiges which are indestructible, and by means of which they may be recalled as long as life endures (1890).

James observed correctly that there were different types or structures of memory. Each holds impressions or "elements of thought" for different lengths of time. Modern psychologists classify memory according to three such structures: *sensory memory, short-term memory (STM)*, and *long-term memory (LTM)*.

SENSORY MEMORY

The world is a constant display of sights and sounds and other sources of sensory stimulation, but only some of these are remembered. Memory first requires that you pay attention to a stimulus or image, whether a new name, a vocabulary word, or an idea. Paying attention somehow separates it from all the stimuli you find irrelevant, and are less likely to retain. In experiments on memory, for example, two-year-old boys are more likely to attend to and remember toys like cars, puzzles, and trains, while two-year-old girls are more likely to attend to and remember dolls, dishes, and teddy bears (Renninger & Wozniak, 1985). Even by this early age, children's patterns of attention have been shaped by sex-role expectations.

Note what happens when you perceive a visual stimulus, such as this list of 10 letters:

THUNSTOFAM

The visual impression lasts for only a fraction of a second in what is called **sensory memory,** or the **sensory register.** If the letters had been flashed on a screen for, say, one-tenth of a second, your ability to list them on the basis of sensory memory would be rather meager. The trace of their image would already have vanished, and you would probably recall only three or four of them.

Recollection of all ten letters would depend on whether you had successfully transformed or **encoded** the list of letters into a form in which it could be processed further by memory. Below we shall see that one way of enhancing recall would be to read (or "mentally say") the list of letters as a word. Chances of recollection would have been further enhanced by repeating the "word" to yourself, or rehearsing it.

George Sperling (1960) demonstrated the existence of sensory memory in a series of important experiments run about twenty-five years ago. In a typical procedure, three rows of numbers and letters like those below were flashed on a screen for about one-tenth of a second:

6 G R 2

V L 7 4

9 K 5 T

Viewers were asked what they had seen. On the average they remembered about three and a half numbers and letters. After that, presumably, the

Sensory memory The structure of memory first encountered by incoming information, in which sensory input, such as a visual stimulus, is maintained for only a fraction of a second.

Sensory register Another term for *sensory memory.*

Encode To transform sensory input into a form which is more readily processed by memory.

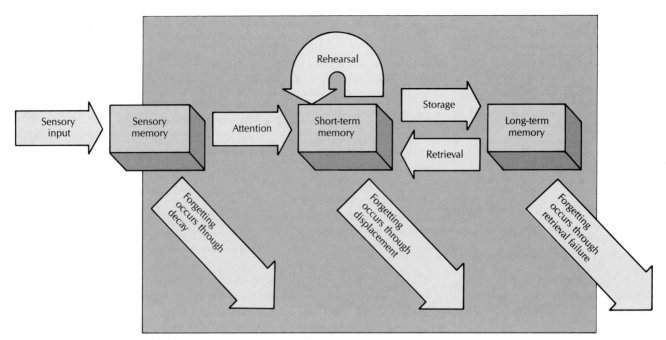

FIGURE 5.13 THE STRUCTURE OF MEMORY Sensory information impacts upon the sensory memory. If we attend to it, it is transferred to short-term memory (STM). Otherwise, the trace may decay. Once in STM, rehearsal stores the memory in long-term memory (LTM), unless it is first displaced by other chunks of information. Once in LTM, memories may be retrieved through appropriate search strategies. But if the memory is organized poorly, or misfiled, it may be lost.

sensory image faded or decayed and no more numbers were remembered. But if Sperling pointed an arrow before, during, or after presentation at the row he wanted viewers to report, they were usually successful. Arrows pointed prior to the display led to best recall. Perhaps they guided the subjects to focus their attention on the ''relevant'' material.

Sperling found that if he delayed pointing the arrow for a few fractions of a second after the display, subjects were much less successful in reporting the target row. If he allowed a quarter of a second to elapse, the arrow did not aid recall at all. Apparently stimuli decay in the sensory register within that amount of time.

SHORT-TERM MEMORY

If you focus attention on a stimulus in the sensory register, you will tend to retain it in **short-term memory** for up to thirty seconds or so after the trace of the stimulus decays. In short-term memory the image tends to fade significantly after ten to twelve seconds if it is not repeated or rehearsed (Keele, 1973). It is possible to focus on maintaining a visual image in the short-term memory (Fisher & Karsh, 1971), but it is more common to encode visual stimuli as sounds, or auditory stimulation. Then the sounds can be rehearsed.

Short-term memory The structure of memory that can hold a sensory stimulus for up to thirty seconds after the trace decays. About seven chunks of information may be maintained at once in short-term memory.

MEMORY Learning would profit us little if we could not remember what we had learned. As children mature and learn, they come to use more sophisticated strategies for storing and retrieving information.

Encoding   Let us now return to the task of remembering the list of ten letters shown at the beginning of this section. If you had coded them as the three-syllable word THUN-STO-FAM, you would probably have recalled them by mentally rehearsing (saying to yourself) the three-syllable "word" and then spelling it from the sounds. Transforming a visual stimulus into sounds in order to remember it is known as using an **acoustic code**.

A few minutes later, if someone asked whether the letters had been upper case (THUNSTOFAM) or lower case (thunstofam), you might not have been sure of the answer. You had used an acoustic code to help recall the list, and upper- and lower-case letters sound alike. When asked to list the letters, you might have said "s-t-o-*w*" rather than "s-t-o" since "stow" is an actual word that sounds like "sto."

A more elaborate way of coding the letters could have involved recognizing that they serve as an **acronym** for the familiar phrase "THe UNited STates OF AMerica." In order to recall the ten letters, you would then have had to "picture" the phrase and "read aloud" the first two letters of each word in the phrase. Since this phrase code is more complex than simply seeing the list as a single word, it might have taken you longer to recall (actually, to reconstruct) the list of ten letters. But by using the phrase you would probably remember the list of letters longer. The phrase is meaningful, and thus more likely to be recalled than the meaningless "word" THUNSTOFAM.

THUNSTOFAM is not too difficult to remember. But what if the visual stimulus had been TBXLFNTSDK? This list of letters cannot be pronounced as they are. You would have had to have found a complex acronym in order to code these letters, and within a fraction of a second—most likely an impossible task. To aid recall you would probably have chosen to try to repeat or rehearse the letters rapidly, to read each one as many times as possible before the stimulus trace faded. You would have visualized each letter as you said it, and tried to return to it before it decayed.

Auditory stimuli can be maintained longer in short-term memory than can visual stimuli (Keele, 1973). So you would probably try to use an acoustic code to remember the letters TBXLFNTSDK, rehearsing sounds. But in an effort to recall these letters, you might mistakenly report them as "TVXLFNTSTK." This would be an understandable error since the incorrect *V* and *T* sound, respectively, like the correct *B* and *D*.

Serial position effect The finding that the first and last items in a series are more readily recalled than are intervening items.

Chunk In memory theory, a discrete piece of information.

Rote A mechanical, routine way of doing something. Learning "by rote" means learning through repetition, or prolonged rehearsal.

The Serial-Position Effect   Note that you would also be likely to recall the first and last letters in the series, *T* and *K,* more accurately than the others. Why? The tendency to recall more accurately the first and last items in a series than the intervening items is known as the **serial-position effect.** This effect may occur because we pay more attention to the first and last stimuli in a series. They serve as the visual or auditory boundaries for the other stimuli. It may also be that the first item is likely to be rehearsed more frequently (repeated more times) than any other item. The last item is likely to have been rehearsed most recently, and so least likely to have faded through decay.

Chunks of Information: Is Seven a Magic Number or Did the Phone Company Get Lucky?   Rapidly rehearsing ten meaningless letters is not an easy task. With TBXLFNTSDK there are ten **chunks** of information that must be maintained simultaneously in short-term memory. With THUNSTOFAM there are only three chunks to digest at once—much easier on the digestion.

Psychologist George Miller (1956) noted that the average person was comfortable in digesting about seven integers at a time, the number of integers in a telephone number. (The three-digit area code is usually recalled as a separate chunk of information.) Most people have little trouble recalling five chunks of information, as in a zip code. Some can remember nine, which is, for all but a few, an upper limit. So seven chunks, plus or minus one or two, is the "magic" number.

How, then, do children learn the alphabet, which is 26 chunks of information? How do they learn to associate letters of the alphabet with spoken sounds? The 26 letters of the alphabet cannot be spoken like a word or phrase. There is nothing about the shape of an *A* to indicate its sound. Nor does the visual stimulus *B* sound like a *B*. Children learning the alphabet and learning to associate letters (visual stimuli) with sounds do so by **rote.** It is mechanical associative learning that requires time and repetition. If you think that learning the alphabet by rote is a simple child's task, now that it is behind you, try learning the Russian or Hebrew alphabet.

If you had recognized THUNSTOFAM as an acronym for the first two letters of each word in the phrase "THe UNited STates OF AMerica," you would have reduced the number of chunks of information that have to be recalled. We could consider the phrase a single chunk of information, and the rule that we must use the first two letters of each word of the phrase as another chunk.

Reconsider Figures 5.11 and 5.12. In Figure 5.11 you were asked to learn nine chunks of visual information. Perhaps you could have used the

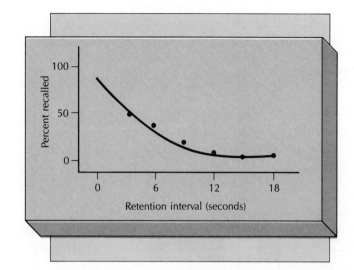

FIGURE 5.14 **INTERFERENCE** Decrease in ability to recall three-letter combinations while counting backward for eighteen seconds. Subjects in this experiment were bright college students.

acoustic codes "L" and "Square" for chunks three and five, but no obvious codes are available for the other seven chunks. But once you looked at Figure 5.12, you realized that you need only recall perhaps two chunks of information. One is the familiar tic-tac-toe grid. The other is the rule that each shape is the shape of a section of the grid, if read like words on a page (from upper left to lower right). The number sequence 1–9 presents no problem, since you learned this series by rote many years ago and have rehearsed it in countless calculations since.

Interference in Short-Term Memory   Every time I have looked up a phone number and am trying to dial, rehearsing the number repeatedly, it is guaranteed that someone will ask me the time of day. Unless I say "Just a minute!" and jot down the number on my cuff before I answer, it's back to the phonebook again. Attending to new numbers, even briefly, impairs my ability to keep the phone number in short-term memory.

In an experiment with college students, Lloyd and Margaret Peterson (1959) showed how such interference can play havoc with short-term memory. They asked students to remember three-letter combinations, like HGB, an easy three chunks of information. Then they asked students to count backward from a number like 181 by 3's (that is, 181, 178, 175, 172, and so on). The students were told to stop counting and to report the letter sequence after various brief intervals of time had passed, as shown in Figure 5.14. The percentage of combinations recalled accurately fell dramatically within just a few seconds. After eighteen seconds of interference, the letter sequences had been **displaced** by counting in almost all of these bright young students.

Eidetic Imagery   Some people have short-term memories that are capable of storing many more than seven or nine chunks of information. Only about 5 percent of children tested are capable of what has been called photographic memory, or **eidetic imagery** (Haber, 1980). Even then this ability declines with age. These children can view a complex picture for

Displace In memory theory, to cause chunks of information to be lost from short-term memory by the adding of too many new items.

Eidetic imagery (eye-DET-tick). The capacity to remember visual sensory input, such as pictures, with exceptional clarity and detail. Also called "photographic memory." (From the Greek *eidos*, meaning "shape" or "that which is seen.")

FIGURE 5.15 A TEST OF EIDETIC IMAGERY Children look at the first drawing for twenty to thirty seconds, after which it is removed. Now the children look at a neutral background for several minutes. Then they are shown the second drawing. When asked what they see, children with the capacity for eidetic imagery report seeing a face. The face is seen only by children who retain the first image and fuse it with the second, thus perceiving the third image.

twenty to thirty seconds, have the picture removed as they continue to observe a gray (neutral) background, and then respond accurately to questions about details of the picture for many minutes (Haber, 1969). The accuracy of their responses suggests that they are still "seeing" the picture.

Figure 5.15 provides an example of a test of eidetic imagery. Children are asked to look at the first drawing in the series for twenty to thirty seconds, after which it is removed. The children then continue to observe a neutral background. Several minutes later they are shown the drawing in the center. When asked what they see, many report "a face." A face would be seen only if the children fuse the retained first-seen image with the second image, yielding the last image (Haber, 1980).

Eidetic imagery appears remarkably clear and detailed. It appears to be essentially a perceptual phenomenon in which acoustic coding is not involved.

LONG-TERM MEMORY

Think of your **long-term memory** as a vast storehouse of information containing names, dates, places, what Johnny did to you in second grade, what Susan said about you when you were twelve. Psychologists are not certain how much of what you experience and think about becomes stored in long-term memory.

Long-term memory The memory structure capable of relatively permanent storage. Losses in long-term memory are thought to reflect failures at retrieval rather than decay or displacement.

How Much of What We Experience or Think Is Stored in Long-Term Memory? Some psychologists argue that every perception and idea is stored permanently. The only question is whether we shall receive appropriate stimulation to help us retrieve this information. These psychologists often point to the work of neurosurgeon Wilder Penfield (1969). By electrically stimulating parts of the brain, many of his patients reported rather vivid remembrance of things past.

Other psychologists, Elizabeth Loftus is one, note that the memories "released" by Penfield's probes were not perfectly detailed. Patients also seemed to recall more specifics when the events were ones that were important to them. We may be more likely to store permanently those perceptions and thoughts that are important or meaningful to us. We recall material better when we pay more attention to it, and encode it in a meaningful, rehearsable form. In the nearby box "Memory: The Unreliable Witness," Loftus also argues that memories are distorted by our biases and needs.

How Much Information *Can* Be Stored in Long-Term Memory? There is no evidence for any limit to the amount of information that can be stored in long-term memory. New information may replace older information in the short-term memory, but there is no evidence that memories in long-term memory are lost by displacement. Long-term memories may last days, years, or, for all practical purposes, a lifetime. From time to time it may seem that we have forgotten, or "lost," a memory in long-term memory, such as the names of elementary or high-school classmates. But it is more likely that we simply cannot find the proper cues to help us retrieve the information. (See the box, "Whatever Happened to the Class of 1965?") If it is lost, it usually becomes lost only in the same way as when we misplace an object, but know that it is still somewhere in the house or apartment. It is "lost," but not eradicated or destroyed.

Transferring Information from Short-Term to Long-Term Memory How is information transferred from short-term to long-term memory? By and large, the more often chunks of information are rehearsed, the more likely they are to be transferred to long-term memory (Rundus, 1971). But pure rehearsal, with no attempt to make information meaningful by linking it to past learning, is no guarantee of permanent storage (Craik & Watkins, 1973).

A more effective method is purposefully to relate new material to information that has already been solidly acquired. (Recall that the nine chunks of information in Figure 5.11 were made easier to reconstruct, once they were associated with the familiar tic-tac-toe grid in Figure 5.12.) Relating new material to well-known material is known as **elaborative rehearsal** (Postman, 1975). For example, have you seen this word before?

FUNTHOSTAM

Say it aloud. Do you know it? If you had used an acoustic code alone to "memorize" THUNSTOFAM, the meaningless word you first saw on page 239, it might not have been easy to recognize FUNTHOSTAM as an in-

---

Elaborative rehearsal A method for increasing the probability of recalling new information by relating it to already well-known material.

A CLOSER LOOK

WHATEVER HAPPENED TO THE CLASS OF 1965?

What's the name of your first-grade teacher? Of the first boy or girl you ever kissed? Of that hunk or fox that sat next to you in ninth-grade math? Chances are that with a bit of concentration you can recall quite a bit more than you might think.

Harry Bahrick and his colleagues (1975) found that recent high school graduates could recall an average of forty-seven names of schoolmates. People who had been out of school for at least forty years could recall the names of an average of nineteen schoolmates. The size of the school was unrelated to the number of names recalled.

On a recognition test, former students were shown photos of schoolmates interspersed with four times as many photos of strangers. Recent graduates correctly identified former schoolmates 90 percent of the time, while subjects out of school for at least forty years correctly identified former schoolmates 75 percent of the time. But a chance level of recognition would have been only 20 percent, showing rather solid long-term memory for the older subjects.

Psychologists have also found that being in the proper context dramatically increases recall (Estes, 1972; Tulving, 1974; Watkins et al., 1976). Have you ever walked the halls of an old school and been assaulted by memories of faces and names that you thought were gone forever? Have you ever walked through your old neighborhood and recalled the faces of people, or aromas of cooking that were so real that you could salivate?

Because we tend better to remember information in the context in which it was learned, it is probably better to take tests in the same room, and at the same desk, in which the subject-matter was taught. But if you can only do a long-division problem in your classroom and nowhere else, the chances are that you haven't done a good job of learning the principles involved. Textbooks ask you to solve numbers of problems with variations in details just so that you will not be "stuck" in the context of a particular problem. Varying the context and details of the problem prevents you from solving it mechanically and forces you to show that you can apply the principles and rules involved.

---

correct spelling. But let us assume that you had coded (associated) THUNSTOFAM according to the phrase "The United States of America." Such a code would have involved the "meaning" of THUNSTOFAM, and would thus have been an example of a **semantic code.** Then you would have been able to scan the spelling of the words in the phrase "The United States of America" to determine the correctness of FUNTHOSTAM. Of course, you would have found it incorrect.

You may recall that English teachers encouraged you to use new vocabulary words in sentences to help you remember them. Each new usage is an instance of elaborative rehearsal. You are building extended semantic codes that will help you retrieve their meanings in the future. Foreign-language teachers may suggest that learning classical languages "exercises the mind," so that we shall understand English better. Not exactly. The mind is not analogous to a muscle that responds to exercise. But the meanings of many English words are based on foreign tongues. A person who recognizes that *retrieve* stems from roots meaning "again" *(re-)* and "find" *(trouver* in French) is less likely to forget that *retrieval* means "finding again" or "bringing back."

Before proceeding to the next section, let me ask you to cover the above part of this page. Now, which of the following words is correctly spelled: *retrieval* or *retreival?* The spellings sound alike, so an acoustic code for reconstructing the correct spelling would fail. But a semantic code, such as the spelling rule "*i* before *e* except after *c*," would allow you to reconstruct the correct spelling: retr*ie*val.

Semantic code A code that is based on the meaning of material to be remembered.

A WHALE NURSES HER YOUNG Have you categorized whales as mammals or fish? If the answer is fish, the content of this photograph may surprise you.

Organization in Long-Term Memory   The storehouse of long-term memory is usually well-organized. Items are not just piled on the floor or thrown into closets. We tend to gather information about rats and cats into a certain section of the warehouse, perhaps the animal or mammal section. We gather oaks, maples, and eucalyptus into the tree section.

Preschoolers tend to organize their memories by grouping objects that share the same function (Lucariello & Nelson, 1985). At first, "toast" is grouped with "peanut butter sandwich" because both are eaten. Only during the early elementary school years are toast and peanut butter sandwich joined into a category with the concept "food" applied to both. Similarly, preschoolers and first graders may associate dogs and cats because they are often found together around the house (Bjorklund & de Marchena, 1984). Dogs and rabbits, however, are usually not placed in the same category until the concept "animal" is used to include them, which may not happen for a few more years.

As we develop, we tend to organize information according to a *hierarchical structure,* as shown in Figure 5.16. A **hierarchy** is an arrangement of items (or chunks of information) into groups or classes according to common or distinct features. As we work our way up the hierarchy shown in Figure 5.16, we find more encompassing or **superordinate** classes to which the items below belong. For example, all mammals are animals, but there are many types of animals other than mammals.*

When items are correctly organized in long-term memory, you are more likely to recall accurate information about them. For instance, do you

---

Hierarchy A group of objects or events arranged according to rank or categories that represent common characteristics.

Superordinate Descriptive of a higher (including) class or category in a hierarchy.

*A note to biological purists: Figure 5.16 is not intended to accurately reflect phyla, classes, orders, and so on. Rather it shows how an individual's classification scheme might be organized.

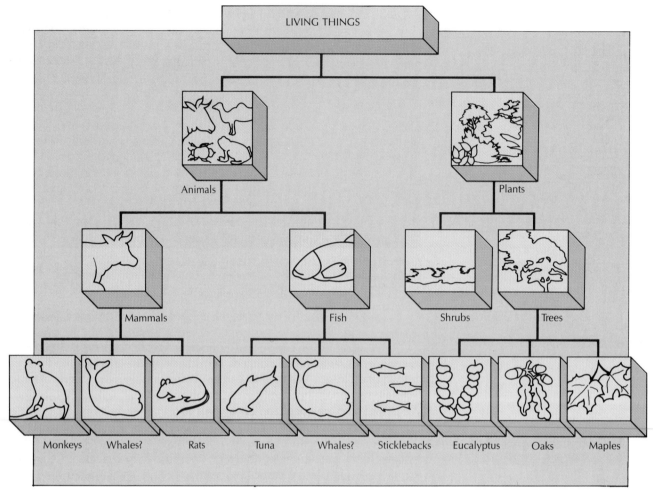

FIGURE 5.16 THE HIERARCHICAL STRUCTURE OF LONG-TERM MEMORY
Where are whales filed in the cabinets of your memory? Your classification of
whales may influence your answers to these questions: Do whales breathe underwater? Are they warm-blooded? Do they nurse their young?

remember whether whales breathe underwater? If you did not know that
whales are mammals (or, in Figure 5.16. **subordinate** to mammals), or knew
nothing about mammals, a correct answer might depend on some remote
instance of rote learning. You might recall some details from a documentary
on whales, for example. But if you *did* know that whales are mammals,
you would be able to "remember" that whales do not breathe underwater
by reconstructing information you know about mammals, the group to which
whales are subordinate. Similarly, you might "remember" that whales because they are mammals are warm-blooded, nurse their young, and are a
good deal more intelligent than, say, tunas and sticklebacks, which are fish.

Had you incorrectly classified whales as fish, you might have searched
your memory and constructed the incorrect answer that they do breathe
underwater.

Subordinate Descriptive of a lower (included) class or category in a hierarchy.

Nonsense syllables Meaningless syllables,
three letters in length, used by psychologists
to study memory.

Recognition In memory theory, the easiest
memory task, identifying objects or events
as having been encountered before.

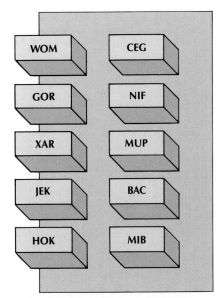

FIGURE 5.17 PAIRED ASSOCIATES
Psychologists often use paired associates, like the above, to measure recall. Retrieving CEG in response to the cue WOM is made easier by an image of a WOMan smoking a "CEG-arette."

Paired associates Nonsense syllables presented in pairs in experiments that measure recall. After viewing pairs, subjects are shown one member of each pair and asked to recall the other.

Recall Retrieval or reconstruction of learned material.

FORGETTING

What do DAR, RIK, BOF, and ZEX have in common? They are all **nonsense syllables.** Nonsense syllables are meaningless syllables three letters in length. Their usage was originated by German psychologist Hermann Ebbinghaus (1850–1909), and they have been used by many psychologists to study memory and forgetting.

Since they are intended to be meaningless, remembering nonsense syllables should depend on simple acoustic coding and rehearsal, rather than on elaborative rehearsal, semantic coding, or other ways of making learning meaningful. Nonsense syllables provide a means of measuring simple memorization ability in studies of the three basic memory tasks of *recognition, recall,* and *relearning.* Studying these memory tasks has led to several conclusions about the nature of forgetting.

Recognition To measure **recognition,** one type of memory task, psychologists may ask subjects to read a list of nonsense syllables. Then the subjects read a second list of nonsense syllables and indicate whether they recognize any of the syllables as having appeared on the first list. Forgetting is defined as failure to recognize a nonsense syllable that has been read before.

Recognition is the easiest type of memory task. This is why multiple-choice tests are easier than fill-in-the-blank or essay tests. We can recognize or identify photos of former classmates more easily than we can recall their names (Tulving, 1974).

Recall Psychologists often use lists of pairs of nonsense syllables, called **paired associates,** to measure **recall,** a second memory task. A list of paired associates is shown in Figure 5.17. Subjects read through the lists, pair by pair. Later they are shown the first member of each pair and asked to recall the second. Recall is more difficult than recognition. In a recognition task, one simply indicates whether an item has been seen before, or which of a number of items is paired with a stimulus (as in a multiple-

---

 ## A CLOSER LOOK

OH GEE, IT'S ON THE TIP OF MY TONGUE . . .

Have you ever been so close to recalling something that you felt it was "on the tip of your tongue"? But you still could not quite put your finger on it? This is a frustrating experience, like reeling in a fish but having it drop off the line just before it breaks the surface of the water. Psychologists term this experience the *tip-of-the-tongue phenomenon,* or *TOT.*

In a TOT experiment, Brown and McNeill (1966) defined some rather unusual words for students, like *sampan,* which is a small riverboat used in China and Japan. Students were then asked to recall the words they had learned. Students often had the right word

"on the tips of their tongues," but many reported words similar in meaning, like *junk, barge,* or *houseboat.* Other students reported words that sound similar, like *Saipan, Siam, sarong,* and *sanching. Sanching,* by the way, is not an actual word.

Brown and McNeill concluded that our storage systems are indexed according to both the sounds and the meanings of words, according to both acoustic and semantic codes. By scanning words that are similar in sound and meaning to the word that is on the tip of the tongue, we often eventually retrieve the word for which we are searching.

choice test). But in a recall task, the person must retrieve a syllable, with another syllable serving as a cue.

Retrieval is made easier if the two syllables can be meaningfully linked, even if the "meaning" is stretched a bit. Consider the first pair of nonsense syllables in Figure 5.17. The image of a WOMan smoking a CEG-arette may make CEG easier to retrieve when the person is presented with the cue, WOM.

As we develop through childhood, our ability to recall information increases. This memory improvement is apparently linked to our growing ability to quickly process (categorize) stimulus cues (Howard & Polich, 1985). In one study, Robert Kail and Marilyn Nippold (1984) asked eight-, twelve-, and twenty-one-year-olds to name as many animals and pieces of furniture as they could during separate seven-minute intervals. The number of items recalled increased with age both for animals and furniture. For all age groups, items were retrieved according to classes. For example, in the animal category, a series of fish might be named, then a series of birds, and so on.

It is easier to recall vocabulary words from foreign languages if you can construct a meaningful link between the foreign and English words (Atkinson, 1975). The *peso*, pronounced *pay-so*, is a unit of Mexican money. A link can be formed by finding a part of the foreign word, like the *pe* (pronounced *pay*) in *peso*, and construct a phrase like "You pay with money." When you read or hear the word *peso* in the future, you recognize the *pe-* and retrieve the link or phrase. From the phrase, you then reconstruct the translation, "a unit of money."

A similar method for prompting recall involves use of acronyms. As noted in our discussion of "THUNSTOFAM," acronyms are words that are constructed from the first letter or letters of the chunks of material to be retrieved. In Chapter 2 we saw that the acronym SAME can help us recall that *sensory* neurons are also called *afferent* neurons, and *motor* neurons are also termed *efferent*. In Chapter 3 we saw that the acronym ROY G. BIV can help us recall the colors of the visible spectrum.

In Chapter 4 we noted that some people who are hypnotized show **posthypnotic amnesia.** They are unable, for example, to recall previously learned word lists (Kihlstrom, 1980). Spanos and his colleagues (1980, 1982) hypothesize that posthypnotic amnesia occurs when hypnotized subjects interpret the suggestion not to recall information as an "invitation" to refrain from attending to retrieval cues. A hypnotized person might be told that he or she would not be able to recall the colors of the spectrum upon "awakening." This suggestion might be interpreted as an invitation *not* to focus on the acronym Roy G. Biv.

Relearning: Is Learning Easier the Second Time Around? **Relearning** is a third method of measuring retention. Do you remember having to learn all the state capitals in grade school? What were the capitals of Wyoming and Delaware? Even when we cannot recall or recognize material that had once been learned, we can relearn it more rapidly the second time, like Cheyenne for Wyoming and Dover for Delaware. Similarly, as we go through our thirties and forties we may forget a good deal of our high school French

Posthypnotic amnesia (am-KNEE-she-uh). Inability to recall material presented while hypnotized, according to a suggestion of the hypnotist.

Relearning Another measure of retention. Material is usually relearned more quickly than it is learned initially.

or geometry. But we could learn what took months or years much more rapidly the second time around.

Since time is saved when we relearn things we had once known, this method of measuring retention is also known as measuring **savings.** Quickly, now. What are the capitals of Wyoming and Delaware?

WHY PEOPLE FORGET

When we do not attend to, encode, and rehearse sensory input, we may forget it through decay of the trace of the image. Material in short-term memory can be lost through displacement, as may happen when we try to remember several new names at a party.

According to **interference theory,** we also forget material in short-term and long-term memory because newly learned material interferes with it. The two basic types of interference are *retroactive interference* (also called *retroactive inhibition*) and *proactive interference* (also called *proactive inhibition*).

Retroactive Interference   In **retroactive interference** new learning interferes with the retrieval of old learning. A medical student may memorize the bones in the leg through rote repetition. Later he or she may find that learning the names of the bones in the arm makes it more difficult to retrieve the names of the leg bones, especially if the names are similar in sound or in relative location on each limb.

Proactive Interference   In **proactive interference** older learning interferes with the capacity to retrieve more recently learned material. High school Spanish may "pop in" when you are trying to retrieve college French or Italian words. All three are Romance languages, with similar roots and spellings. German vocabulary words would probably not interfere with your ability to retrieve more recently learned French or Italian, because many German roots and sounds differ markedly from those of the Romance languages.

In terms of motor skills, you may learn how to drive a standard shift on a car with three forward speeds and a clutch that must be let up slowly after shifting. Later you learn to drive a car with five forward speeds and a clutch that must be released rapidly. For a while you make a number of errors on the five-speed car because of proactive interference. (Old learning interferes with new learning.) If you return to the three-speed car after driving the five-speed car has become "natural," you may stall it a few times. This is because of retroactive interference (new learning interfering with the old).

Repression   According to Sigmund Freud, we are motivated to forget painful memories and unacceptable ideas, because they produce anxiety, guilt, and shame. (In terms of operant conditioning, anxiety, guilt, and shame serve as negative reinforcers. We learn to do that which is followed by their removal—in this case, not to think about certain events and ideas.) In Chapter 11 we shall see that psychoanalysts believe that repression is at the heart of disorders like **psychogenic amnesia.**

Retrograde Amnesia   In retrograde amnesia, a source of trauma, like a head injury or an electric shock, prevents recent perceptions or ideas from being remembered. In this case it seems that the shock interferes with all the processes of memory. Paying attention, encoding, and rehearsal are all prevented.

It may also be that some perceptions and ideas must be allowed to rest undisturbed for a while, if they are to be remembered (Gold & King, 1974). A football player who is knocked unconscious, or a victim of an auto accident, may be unable to recall events for several minutes prior to the trauma. The football player may not recall taking to the field. The accident victim may not recall entering the car.

Now that we have looked at how and why we forget, let us consider ways of improving our ability to remember.

SOME METHODS FOR IMPROVING MEMORY

Who among us has not wished for a better memory from time to time? If we could remember more, we might earn higher grades, charm people with our stock of jokes, or even pay our bills on time. Psychologists once believed that one's memory was fixed, that one had a good or poor memory and was stuck with it (Singular, 1982). But today psychologists have found that there are a number of ways in which we can all improve our memories, such as the following.

The Method of Loci   You might be better able to remember your shopping list if you imagine meat loaf in your navel, or a strip of bacon draped over your nose. This is a meaty example of the **method of loci.** With this method you select a series of related images, like the parts of your body or the furniture in your home. Then you imagine an item from your shopping list, or another list you want to remember, attached to each image.

By placing meat loaf or a favorite complete dinner in your navel, rather than a single item like chopped beef, you can combine several items into one chunk of information. At the supermarket you recall the (familiar) ingredients for meat loaf, and simply recognize whether or not you need each one.

Mediation   In the method of **mediation,** you link two items with a third that ties them together. What if you are having difficulty remembering that John's wife's name is Tillie? Laird Cermak (1978) suggests that you can mediate between John and Tillie as follows. Reflect that the *john* is a slang term for bathroom. Bathrooms often have ceramic *tiles. Tiles,* of course, sounds like *Tillie.* So it goes: John-bathroom-tiles-Tillie.

Mnemonics   In a third method of improving memory, **mnemonics,** chunks of information are combined into a format, such as an acronym, jingle, or phrase. Recalling the phrase "Every Good Boy Does Fine" has helped many people remember the musical keys E, G, B, D, F.

How can you remember how to spell *mnemonics?* Simple—just be willing to grant "aMNesty" to those who cannot.

Method of loci (LOW-kigh). A method of improving memory in which chunks of new material are related to a series of well-established or well-known images. (*Loci* is the plural of the Latin *locus,* meaning "place.")

Mediation A method of improving memory by linking two items with a third that ties them together.

Mnemonics (neh-MON-nicks). A method of improving memory in which chunks of information are combined into a format like an acronym, jingle, or phrase.

A.C.R.O.N.Y.M.
AROUSED CITIZENS
REPRESENTING OPPRESSED
NEW YORK MINORITIES

Engram (1) An assumed electrical circuit in the brain that corresponds to a memory trace. (2) An assumed chemical change in the brain that accompanies learning. (From the Greek *en-*, meaning "in," and *gramma*, meaning "something that is written or recorded.")

Memory molecule Molecules whose chemical compositions are thought to change with experience, forming a chemical basis for memory.

THE BIOLOGY OF MEMORY:
ON ENGRAMS, EPINEPHRINE, AND MEMORY MOLECULES

Early in this century most psychologists believed that **engrams** were responsible for memory. Engrams were hypothesized electrical circuits in the brain that corresponded to the memory trace—a neurological process that was somehow thought to parallel a perceptual experience. But biological psychologists like Karl Lashley (1950) spent many fruitless years searching for these circuits or the parts of the brain in which they might be housed.

Still, contemporary psychologists have found evidence for the involvements of physiology and chemistry in learning and memory, including neurons, brain structures, and hormones such as epinephrine. Epinephrine not only generally stimulates bodily arousal and activity, as noted in Chapter 2. Epinephrine also strengthens memory when it is released into the bloodstream following instances of learning (Delanoy et al., 1982; Laroche & Bloch, 1982; McGaugh, 1983). Numerous studies of the biology of memory have also focused on the possible roles of so-called **memory molecules.** Let us examine a few experiments that are suggestive of the role of biology in memory.

The Worm Turns, *or,* **How Some Worms Got Fed Up (Literally) with Learning** A flatworm has an unusual sex life. It has both male and female sex organs. When the pickings in the outside world don't look very promising, it may just mate with itself and produce more flatworms—which are no less strange looking.

The flatworm can also *regenerate*. If you cut it in half, the head part will grow a new tail, and, more remarkably, the tail part will grow a new head, complete with a new brain.

In their efforts to locate memory functions in the flatworm, James McConnell and his colleagues (1959) devised a research program based on its ability to regenerate. Where would you think a flatworm's memory is located? Heads or tails?

To find out, the McConnell group conditioned some worms to scrunch up when a light was shone. Flatworms normally save "scrunching" for the stimulus of electric shock, but the researchers paired the light with shock. After repeated pairings, the light became a CS that elicited the response usually evoked by the shock (US).

After the classical conditioning, the worms were cut in half and given time to regenerate. As expected, the head part that grew a new tail scrunched up when a light was shone. But so did the tail part after a new head was regenerated! Memory of the light-shock association was not stored in the head alone.

In follow-up studies, the McConnell group fed chopped-up flatworms who had learned the light-shock association to other flatworms. The cannibal worms apparently got "fed up" with learning. They often scrunched up when the light was shone, even though they had not been conditioned to do so. In other experiments, flatworms were trained, by operant conditioning, to turn to the right or left at chosen points in mazes. Then they were chopped up and fed to untrained worms. The untrained worms then learned to turn right or left (assuming that they were expected to turn in the

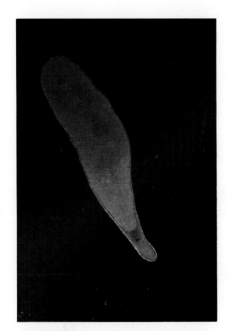

FLATWORM The flatworm can mate with itself, regenerate lost parts, and, possibly, learn "roadmaps" by eating worms that have already found the way.

same direction as their dinner) more rapidly than did untrained worms who had not been given this "brain food."

Where were memories stored in the worms that regenerated new heads? *What* did the cannibal worms eat that helped them learn mazes more rapidly than their fellows did? Additional studies by McConnell and his colleagues (1970) suggest that memories might have been stored and transmitted in molecules of **ribonucleic acid** (RNA). RNA is a protein, or **amino acid,** that is similar in structure to DNA. DNA, as noted in Chapter 2, is involved in the transmission of the genetic code from one generation of animals to another. The body's DNA is basically fixed, so that we don't suddenly become different people, but RNA is changeable.

The McConnell group transferred molecules of RNA from flatworms who had learned the light-shock association to untrained worms. The untrained worms then learned the light-shock association in fewer pairings than did worms who did not receive RNA.

Before you conclude that the best way to earn an A is to grind up your professor for dinner, we must note that McConnell's studies have not always been successfully replicated. For one thing, flatworms are not easy to condition. Similar experiments in transferring "memory molecules" between the brains of higher animals, like mice and rats, have also not consistently led to the predicted results.

But other research on the possible role of proteins in learning and memory, in which scientists have experimentally manipulated protein formation, is also suggestive of the role of memory molecules.

Life in a Goldfish Bowl: The Consolidation of Learning University of Michigan biochemist Bernard Agranoff taught goldfish that sometimes it is better to be left in the dark (Pines, 1975). He flashed a light and then the fish were given electric shock. The shock was turned off when the fish swam to the other side of the tank. After several trials the fish learned to swim to the other side of the tank whenever the light was flashed. This is an example of **avoidance learning:** by swimming across the tank the fish avoided the shock. (To be technical, the CS of light came to elicit the fear response elicited by the US of shock. Fear then acted as a negative reinforcer. The fish swam across the tank when they saw the light because they could avoid the shock in this way.)

Agranoff found that he could interfere with the fishes' learning by injecting **puromycin**—a chemical that impairs the formation of neuropeptides in the brain—after the fish were taught to associate light and electric shock. They subsequently made no effort to swim across the tank when the light was shone.

Agranoff reasoned that the puromycin prevented **consolidation** of the fishes' learning. It had prevented the memory of the association from becoming fixed in long-term memory. If, on the other hand, Agranoff waited for an hour before injecting puromycin, the learning was apparently consolidated. The fish would swim to safety as soon as the light was shone.

At the University of California at Irvine, James McGaugh's research seems to serve as the mirror image of Agranoff's. McGaugh (McGaugh et al., 1980) injected **strychnine** into laboratory rats following conditioning.

Ribonucleic acid (rye-bow-NEW-klee-ick). A substance that is involved in transmitting genetic information, and possibly in memory formation. Abbreviated *RNA*.

Amino acid An organic compound from which proteins are constructed.

Avoidance learning A conditioning procedure in which an organism learns to exhibit an operant that permits it to avoid an aversive stimulus.

Puromycin A chemical substance that inhibits protein formation in the brain, and is thought to inhibit consolidation of learning.

Consolidation In memory theory, the fixing of information in long-term memory.

Strychnine (STRICK-nine). A poison that, in small doses, aids the consolidation of learning.

Vasopressin Another term for *antidiuretic hormone*.

In large doses, strychnine is poisonous. In the smaller doses used by McGaugh, strychnine apparently promoted the formation of neuropeptides and helped the rats consolidate their learning of mazes. Here, too, the injection had to be given within an hour, while the new memories were apparently still being consolidated.

As noted earlier, current research into the chemistry of memory also involves hormones such as epinephrine. Another hormone that can play a role in memory is antidiuretic hormone (ADH).* Volunteers have received a synthetic form of ADH, or **vasopressin,** through nasal sprays and have shown significant improvement in recall (McGaugh, 1983). Excess vasopressin, unfortunately, can have serious side effects, such as constriction of the blood vessels. But research into the effects of similar chemicals, which may have fewer side effects, is under way.

The Future of Learning and Memory   Research into the biology of memory is in its infancy, but what an exciting area of research it is. What would it mean to you if you could read for a half-hour to an hour, pop a pill, and cause your new learnings to become consolidated in long-term memory? You would never have to reread the material; it would be at your fingertips for a lifetime. It would save a bit of study time, would it not?

Research into the biology of memory, like so many other psychological endeavors, remains in its infancy.

SUMMARY

1. Learning may be defined as the process by which experience leads to relatively permanent changes in behavior.

2. In classical conditioning, a previously neutral stimulus (the conditioned stimulus, or CS) comes to elicit the response evoked by a second stimulus (the unconditioned stimulus, or US) by being paired repeatedly with the second stimulus. A response to a US is called an unconditioned response (UR), and a response to a CS is termed a conditioned response (CR).

3. In the bell-and-pad method for teaching children to stop bedwetting, a bell is sounded when the child urinates, waking the child. The bell is paired with fullness in the child's bladder, so that the sensations of a full bladder (CS) gain the capacity to wake the child just as the bell (US) did.

4. Classical conditioning occurs efficiently when the CS is presented about 0.5 seconds before the US. In backward conditioning, the US is presented first.

5. After a US-CS association has been learned,

repeated presentation of the CS (for example, a bell) without the US (meat powder) will extinguish the CR (salivation). But extinguished responses may show spontaneous recovery as a function of time that has elapsed since the end of the extinction process.

6. In stimulus generalization, organisms show a CR in response to a range of stimuli similar to the CS. In stimulus discrimination, organisms learn to show a CR in response to a more limited range of stimuli by pairing only the limited stimulus with the US.

7. Edward L. Thorndike originated the law of effect, which holds that responses are "stamped in" by rewards and "stamped out" by punishments.

8. In operant conditioning, an organism learns to emit an operant that is reinforced. Initial "correct" responses may be performed by random trial and error, physical or verbal guiding. Reinforced responses occur more frequently.

9. Positive reinforcers increase the probability that operants will occur when they are applied. Negative

*See Chapters 2 and 7 for further discussion of hormones.

reinforcers increase the probability that operants will occur when they are removed. Primary reinforcers have their value because of the biological makeup of the organism. Secondary reinforcers, like money and approval, acquire their value through association with established reinforcers.

10. In operant conditioning, extinction results from repeated performance of operant behavior in the absence of reinforcement.

11. Rewards, like reinforcers, increase the frequency of behavior. But rewards differ from reinforcers in that they are pleasant stimuli. Punishments are aversive stimuli that suppress the frequency of behavior.

12. Many learning theorists prefer treating children's misbehavior by ignoring it or using time out from positive reinforcement rather than by using punishment. Punishment fails to teach desirable responses, suppresses behavior only when it is guaranteed, creates hostility, can lead to overgeneralization, and serves as a model for aggression.

13. A discriminative stimulus indicates when an operant will be reinforced.

14. Continuous reinforcement leads to most rapid acquisition of new responses, but operants are maintained most economically through partial reinforcement.

15. There are four basic schedules of reinforcement. In a fixed-interval schedule, a specific amount of time must elapse since a previous correct response before reinforcement again becomes available. In a variable-interval schedule, the amount of time is allowed to vary. In a fixed-ratio schedule, a fixed number of correct responses must be performed before one is reinforced. In a variable-ratio schedule, this number is allowed to vary.

16. In shaping, successive approximations to the target response are reinforced.

17. Research in cognitive learning suggests that not all behavior can be explained through conditioning. Köhler showed that apes can learn through sudden reorganization of perceptual relationships, or insight.

18. Tolman's work with rats suggests that they develop cognitive maps of the environment and that operant conditioning teaches organisms *where* reinforcement may be found, rather than mechanically increasing the frequency of operants. Tolman's latent learning studies suggest that organisms also learn in the absence of reinforcement and do not necessarily perform all the behaviors that they have learned.

19. Bandura and other social-learning theorists have shown that people can also learn by observing others, without emitting reinforced responses of their own. They may then choose to perform the behaviors they have observed when "the time is ripe"—that is, when they believe that they will be rewarded.

20. Memory may be divided into sensory, short-term, and long-term memory.

21. A stimulus is maintained in sensory memory only for a fraction of a second. It then decays unless it is attended to and encoded.

22. In short-term memory a perception or image may be maintained by auditory rehearsal of the encoded version. About seven (plus or minus two) chunks of information may be maintained in short-term memory at once. New chunks of information may displace older chunks that have not been transferred to long-term memory.

23. Long-term memories are organized in a hierarchical structure. Accurate organization aids the retrieval process, and the reconstruction of information that is not simply acquired by rote learning. Appropriate cues must be used if information is to be retrieved.

24. Retention is tested through three types of memory tasks—in order of ascending difficulty, recognition, recall, and relearning (savings). Recall is often measured through use of paired associates of nonsense syllables.

25. According to interference theory, people forget because learning can interfere with retrieval of other learnings. In retroactive interference, new learning interferes with old learning. In proactive interference, old learning interferes with new learning.

26. Freud suggested that we also forget threatening or unacceptable material through repression, or motivated forgetting.

27. In retrograde amnesia, shock or other trauma prevents recently learned material from being recalled, probably by interfering with consolidation.

28. Memory may be improved by the method of loci, through mediation, or through mnemonics. In each method incoming information is associated with already known material or a format constructed for the occasion.

29. Early in the century it was thought that engrams—electrical circuits in the brain corresponding to memory traces—made memory possible. Present research into the biology of memory focuses on the roles of neurotransmitters and RNA.

TRUTH OR FICTION REVISITED

Dogs can be trained to salivate when a bell is rung.

True. Pavlov accomplished this by repeatedly pairing a bell with the presentation of meat to laboratory dogs.

We can learn to change our behavior while we are sleeping.

True. In one example, the bell-and-pad method is used to condition children to wake up rather than urinate when their bladders are full.

During World War II a psychologist devised a plan for training pigeons to guide missiles to their targets.

True. B. F. Skinner proposed to accomplish this through operant conditioning. But the Defense Department apparently thought that the project was for the birds. It never got off the ground.

Psychologists fashioned a method to teach an emaciated nine-month-old infant to stop throwing up.

True, they used avoidance-learning procedures. After learning, the infant made rapid gains in weight.

You can "hook" people on gambling by allowing them to win some money in the early stages and then tapering off the payoffs.

True. Behavior can be maintained for quite a while on intermittent reinforcement schedules.

Punishment doesn't work.

False. Strong enough punishments suppress unwanted behavior, but there are a number of drawbacks to punishment, as discussed in the chapter.

Rats can be trained to climb a ramp, cross a bridge, climb a ladder, pedal a toy car, and do several other tasks—all in proper sequence.

True. The operant-conditioning methods that are used include shaping and chaining.

We must make mistakes in order to learn.

False. In programed learning, for example, it is possible to learn without making any errors.

All of our experiences are permanently imprinted on the brain so that proper stimulation can cause us to remember them exactly.

False. It seems that what we remember is a blend of truth and fiction, skewed by our biases and needs.

There is such a thing as a photographic memory.

True. This phenomenon is called eidetic imagery, and is found in about 5 percent of children. The capacity is lost by adulthood.

There is no limit to the amount of information you can store in your memory.

This is true of long-term memory, so far as we know, although there are decided limits to short-term memory (around seven or so chunks of information).

You can use tricks to improve your memory.

True. The tricks are known as mnemonic devices, and they usually work by associating new information with well-known information.

Rats were helped to remember their ways through mazes by being injected with the poison strychnine.

True. A low dose of strychnine apparently promoted the formation of neuropeptides that are involved in consolidation of learning.

OUTLINE

C H A P T E R   6

Language, Thought, and Intelligence

TRUTH OR FICTION ?

T • Psychologists have been able to teach chimpanzees and gorillas how to use sign language.

T • Apes cannot speak, because they do not have vocal tracts in their throats.

T • Deaf children do not babble.

T • Black English lacks systematic rules of grammar.

T • The fact that a two-year-old says "Daddy goed away" instead of "Daddy went away" shows that the child does not yet understand rules of English grammar.

T • Thought is not possible without language.

F • Dogs can learn the concepts of roundness and squareness.

F • The only way to solve a problem is to keep plugging away at it.

F • It may be boring, but the most efficient way to solve a problem is to use the tried and tested formula.

F • A person's "IQ" is the same thing as his or her intelligence.

F • There is no such thing as an unbiased intelligence test.

F • High intelligence runs in families.

When I was in high school, I remember being taught that human beings differed from other creatures that walked, swam, or flew, because we were the only ones to use language and tools. Then I found out that lower animals used tools too. Otters use rocks to open clam shells. Chimpanzees throw rocks as weapons and have been filmed, in the wild, using sticks to dig out grubs for food.

In recent years, our exclusive claim to the use of language has also been challenged. Advanced primates like chimps and gorillas have been taught abstract **symbols** (as in Figure 6.1), and have used these symbols to communicate by making signs with their hands or pressing keys on an electric typewriter.

Language is the communication of thoughts and feelings through symbols that are arranged according to rules of grammar. Language makes possible the efficient communication of large amounts of complex knowledge from one person to another, and from one generation to another. According to **psycholinguist** Roger Brown, "The important thing about language is that it makes life experiences cumulative; across generations and within one generation, among individuals. Everyone can know much more than he [or she] could possibly learn by direct experience" (1970, p. 212).

Language provides many of the basic units of thought, and thought is central to intelligent behavior. Chimps and gorillas may have acquired the ability to communicate a few symbols. Even so, the extraordinarily larger human capacities to acquire, manipulate, use, and create language clearly separate us from lower animals more so than any other factors. Other animals may be stronger, run faster, smell more keenly, even live longer, but only we have produced literature, music, mathematics, and science. Only we have begun to explore the reaches of space that surround the tiny rock called Earth. Our ability to manipulate the symbols of language has made this exploration possible.

Symbol Something that stands for or represents another. (From the Greek *symbolon,* meaning "sign" or "token.")

Language The communication of information through symbols that are arranged according to rules of grammar. (From the Latin *lingua,* meaning "tongue.")

Psycholinguist A psychologist who studies how we perceive and acquire language.

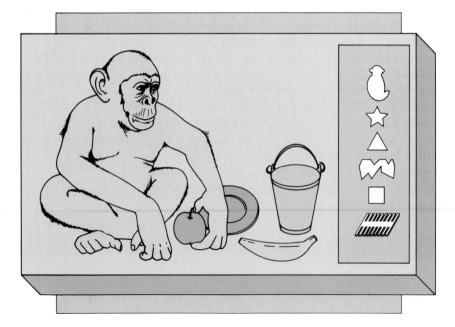

FIGURE 6.1 **THE ROLE OF OPERANT CONDITIONING IN LANGUAGE ACQUISITION** Operant conditioning was used to teach a chimp named Sarah to communicate through plastic symbols. Psychologists reinforced Sarah for selecting the proper symbols, or for following instructions made with symbols. Here Sarah will follow directions to place the apple in the pail and the banana in the dish.

In this chapter we explore the interrelated cognitive processes of language, thought, and intelligence. We shall begin by surveying efforts to teach language to apes, since these attempts afford insight into the nature of the human use of language. Next we shall discuss the building blocks and structure of language, and chronicle the orderly development of language in children. We shall explore theories of language acquisition in an effort to learn why people can use language, but tuna and turtles cannot. This will prepare us for a discussion of how language and thought are intertwined in the formation of concepts and in problem solving. Finally, we shall examine the meanings of intelligence and see how intelligence is measured. As you might be aware from the continuing publicity over "IQ tests," the definition and measurement of intelligence are quite controversial issues in psychology.

ON LANGUAGE AND APES: GOING APE OVER LANGUAGE?

Some of us may know people who insist that their dogs understand every word they say. But when we look closely, we find what the animals respond to is their human owners' excitement and a few words or commands—like "Sit," "Lunchtime," or "Out"—that have been paired repeatedly with specific acts or events. Even when dogs respond to the command "Speak," they do so with a doglike howl, bark, yap, or whine. They do not speak at all. Nor has anyone ever had a talking pet cat, horse, or elephant. So it was guaranteed that the weight of evidence of human history would make us skeptical of the first startling reports that chimpanzees had been taught to communicate by using abstract symbols.

There are a number of famous apes who have populated the literature on the psychology of language, as well as earned splashes in popular magazines. Washoe, a female chimp raised by Beatrice and Allen Gardner (1972), was the first to come to our notice. The Gardners and their assistants raised Washoe from the time she was a year of age. Instead of speaking to her, they used American Sign Language (ASL), the language used by deaf Americans. By the age of five, Washoe could use more than 160 signs, including signs for actions (verbs), like *come, gimme,* and *tickle;* signs for things (nouns), like *apples, flowers,* and *toothbrush;* and signs for more abstract concepts, like *more.* She could combine signs to form simple two-word **telegraphic** sentences, like those of young children. Note these examples: *More tickle, More banana,* and *More milk*—which doesn't sound like too bad a way to spend a lazy Sunday afternoon. As time passed Washoe showed some ability to sign longer sentences, like *Come gimme drink* and *Gimme toothbrush hurry.*

Washoe's communication efforts showed a tendency to extend the meanings of words to cover objects for which she had no words, a process called **overextension** that characterizes children's language. During the second year, for example, children may overextend the word "doggy" to refer to many animals, including dogs, horses, and cows. At two and a half,

Telegraphic Referring to speech in which only the essential words are used, as in a telegram.

Overextension Overgeneralizing the use of words into situations in which they do not apply.

60 MINUTES

TALK TO THE ANIMALS

Since the mid-1960s psychologists have been using sign language and other symbol systems to, as the fictitious Dr. Doolittle did, "Talk to the Animals."

In the 60 Minutes segment "Talk to the Animals," correspondent Morley Safer asks Penny Patterson, who has been teaching sign language to Koko and other gorillas, "Why bother?" Safer noted that people hearing of communicating with apes might say "Interesting, but why?"

One answer to this question, as noted in the nearby Psychology Today box, is that teaching sign language to apes has helped us teach retarded and brain-damaged people how to communicate. But Patterson suggested that we need not justify our infant studies in communicating with apes in terms of their usefulness alone.

Patterson noted that the apes

have intrinsic value, the same as I would attribute to myself or you. And [by] studying them, we can understand another mind. It's as though we can look into a different consciousness. We don't have to wait for the extra-terrestrials to arrive; we've got something right here we can look at.

. . . I feel that I'm privileged to know Koko, as I do, through language; that she's telling me, and maybe will tell me in the future, very important things about another form of life.

many children refer to objects and situations as "funny" or "silly," because they cannot yet use words like "interesting," "intriguing," and "delightful."

By human standards, Washoe's communications showed major failings. For example, Washoe did not attend to word order. Her words were strung together in haphazard combinations. One day she might sign *Come gimme toothbrush,* but the next day, *Hurry toothbrush gimme.* Even the language productions of human one-year-olds have reliable word order, which, as we shall see, figures into theories of language development.

Ann and David Premack (1975) taught another female chimp, Sarah, to communicate by arranging symbols on a magnet board (see Figure 6.1). Eventually Sarah learned simple telegraphic sentences like *Place orange dish.* Her word order was less haphazard than Washoe's. The Premacks consider their work with Sarah a demonstration of the role of operant conditioning in the learning of language. Sarah was reinforced for selecting the proper symbols to make a request and for following instructions that were communicated by symbols.

Some of the most impressive claims for teaching language to an ape come from Francine Patterson (1978), who taught a gorilla named Koko to use some 375 signs regularly, including signs for *friend, airplane, lollipop, belly button,* even *stethoscope.* Patterson also reports that from the ages of five to seven Koko earned scores on intelligence tests just below those of children of comparable ages. Patterson characterizes Koko's use of language as almost "human" in that Koko lies and at times does the exact opposite of what she is told to do. Patterson also reports that Koko has produced some creative insults in ASL—for example, "You dirty toilet devil" and "Rotten stink."

Patterson often took Koko on short trips for novel stimulation. Now and then Koko signed *Go there* to avoid returning home, or *Hurry go drink* when they passed a vending machine. These signings seem quite creative and spontaneous, but, given the anecdotal nature of much of Patterson's evidence, one must wonder whether Koko simply learned to associate these groupings of signs with certain types of situations.

I am not the only skeptic. Many researchers argue that Koko's language abilities are no more impressive than those of other apes, that Koko shows little if any understanding of grammar, and that Koko may simply be an excellent imitator of her teacher. Many psycholinguists believe that the ape's use of language is akin to an elaborate trick to gain a reward.

A PSYCHOLOGICAL CONTROVERSY: CAN APES REALLY UNDERSTAND AND PRODUCE LANGUAGE?

Now that we have observed the communication skills of some well-known apes, let us wrestle with the central issue: Can apes really understand and produce language? In discussing this question, we shall refer to some of the major features of human language.

Properties of Human Language: Semanticity, Productivity, and Displacement According to Roger Brown (1973), three properties distinguish human language from the communications systems of lower animals: *semanticity, productivity,* and *displacement.* **Semanticity** means that words serve as symbols for actions, objects, relational concepts (over, more, and so on), and other ideas.

Many species have systems of communication. Birds warn other birds of predators or that they claim possession of a tree by characteristic chirps and shrieks. The "waggle dances" shown by certain bees inform other bees of the approximate direction and distance of a source of food or an enemy. The purrs and howls of cats can communicate contentment or horror. Vervet monkeys emit sounds that warn their kind both of the species and distance of predators.

However, all these species-specific communications are innate and, in contrast to human language, they are largely unmodifiable by experience. Generally speaking, they also lack semanticity. Animals' sounds and waggles have not been shown to serve as symbols of objects or distances.

Productivity refers to the capacity to combine words into original sentences. In order to produce sentences they have not heard before, children must have a basic understanding of **syntax,** or the structure of grammar. Even two-year-old children string words together in original combinations, but the signs of apes are rarely combined into novel sentences.

Chimpanzees do not show as much comprehension of the importance of word order as children do (Fodor et al., 1974). Psycholinguist Herbert Terrace has concluded that apes cannot master even the basics of grammar. After reviewing videotapes and reports of researchers who taught signs to apes, Terrace (1979) reluctantly wrote, "The closer I looked, the more I regarded the many reported instances of language as elaborate tricks for obtaining rewards."

Displacement is the capacity to communicate information about events or objects in another time or place.* Language permits the efficient trans-

*The word *displacement* has a different meaning within Sigmund Freud's psychoanalytic theory, as we shall see in Chapter 9.

Semanticity A property of language: the ability to communicate meaning.

Productivity A property of language: the ability to combine words into unlimited sentences.

Syntax The rules in a language for placing words in proper order to form meaningful sentences. (From the Latin *syntaxis,* meaning "joining together.")

Displacement As a property of language: the ability to communicate information about events in other times and places.

PSYCHOLOGY TODAY

SCALING THE WALLS OF SILENCE: HOW APES HAVE TAUGHT US TO TEACH COMMUNICATIONS SKILLS TO HUMANS

Deaf, mute, and retarded since birth, twenty-three-year-old Sandra was written off as a hopeless case. But in the past two years the once hostile, violent young woman has been transformed. Today, she can request her favorite foods and communicate with her teachers—thanks to a computer-based language that was originally developed for the study of chimpanzees. "Sandra's learned to express herself," says Steve Watson, director of the Developmental Learning Center at Atlanta's Georgia Regional Hospital, where Sandra lives. "That's a way of being set free."

The language that liberated Sandra is Yerkish, named for the Yerkes Primate Center at Atlanta's Emory University, where it was developed. Invented by psychologist Duane Rumbaugh in the early 1970s, Yerkish consists of up to 225 geometric symbols that are printed on a computer keyboard. Each of the symbols represents a specific English word such as "apple," "give," "room," "yes," and "no"; sentences are formed by punching a series of keys. Scientists at the Language Research Center in Atlanta have taught Yerkish to several pygmy chimpanzees, a rare ape species that is believed to be the one closest to man in genetic makeup.

In 1981, Rumbaugh decided that it was time to use what the chimps had taught him about the beginnings of communication to help the severely retarded. With the consent of their families, fourteen retarded persons were chosen for the project. Eight of them have made significant progress—mastering anywhere from two dozen symbols (like Sandra) to more than seventy. The instructors begin by teaching the retarded pupils the symbol for their favorite food. That symbol is subsequently shifted around the keyboard, so that subjects learn to identify the symbols by shape rather than location. Additional symbols are taught, one at a time.

Temper Tantrums Using Yerkish, the retarded patients have learned to communicate their wants and needs—several so well that they have been put on a waiting list for placement with a family or group home. They have also learned to help each other, according to Mary Ann Romski, a speech pathologist who heads the program for retarded people. And she says that the researchers have learned that "retarded people know a lot of things and understand a lot of things that have not been tapped in the past, because they have had no way to tell us." As they gain confidence, their behavior often improves; Sandra, for example, has fewer temper tantrums and has been moved from the most restrictive to the least restrictive ward of the hospital.

"Ten years from now," says Rumbaugh, "I hope this looks like a very primitive beginning."

"YERKISH" Kanzi is one of the chimpanzees who have been taught "Yerkish" at Emory University's Yerkes Primate Center. Yerkish consists of geometric symbols that are printed on a computer keyboard.

mission of complex knowledge from one person to another, and from one generation to another, through records and history books. Displacement permits parents to warn children about their own experiences, and allows children to tell their parents what they did in school today, yesterday, or last week.

The "Clever Hans" Effect In *Speaking of Apes,* the husband-and-wife team of linguist Thomas Sebeok and **anthropologist** Donna Jean Umiker-Sebeok (1980) suggest that much of the language usage of these apes may be an example of the "Clever Hans" effect. Clever Hans was the name

Anthropologist A scientist who studies the physical and cultural characteristics of people. (From the Greek *anthropos,* meaning "man.")

given a German circus horse at the turn of the century. Hans could tap out, with his hoofs, the answers to problems posed by his trainer. A German psychologist finally recognized that Hans was not actually solving problems. Instead, he was responding to a host of unintended stimuli emitted by his trainer—including patterns of breathing, the size of his pupils, and changes in facial expression. Apes, who are more intelligent than horses, ought also to be able to use cues emitted by their trainers to arrive at a "correct" response.

Cognitive psychologist Ulric Niesser (1982) concludes that "language is uniquely our own" (p. 45). Now that we have more reason to appreciate the singularly human capacity to grasp the rules of grammar, let us turn our attention to the basics of language to see how it works.

THE BASICS OF LANGUAGE

ASL is a language without sound, since it is intended for use by deaf people. But the components of other languages do include sound: *phonology* (sounds), *morphology* (units of meaning), *syntax* (word order), and *semantics* (the meanings of words and groups of words).

PHONOLOGY

Phonology is the study of the basic sounds in a language. There are twenty-six letters in the English alphabet, but about forty-six basic sounds or **phonemes.** These include the *t* and *p* in *tip,* which a psycholinguist may designate with the /t/ and /p/ phonemes. The *o* in *go* and the *o* in *gone* are different phonemes—that is, although they are spelled with the same letter, they sound different. English speakers who learn French may be confused because the *o* phoneme, as in the word *go,* has various spellings in French, including *o, au, eau,* and *eaux.*

At one time or another, you may have heard someone trying to be humorous or witty by speaking English with a mock German or Japanese accent. Why can these two languages be mocked so readily in English? One answer is that different languages may use different phonemes. English speakers learning French, Spanish, or German must practice different-sounding "rolling *r*'s." German has two throaty phonemes, both spelled *ch,* which are not found in English, French, and Spanish. French and German have no *th* phonemes. So French and German speakers often compensate by pronouncing the word *the* with a sort of *zh* sound. Japanese has no *r* phoneme. For this reason, many Japanese pronounce the English words *right* and *wrong* as *light* and *long.*

MORPHOLOGY

Morphemes are the smallest units of meaning in a language. A morpheme consists of one or more phonemes pronounced in a certain order. The words *dog* and *cat* are morphemes, but not all morphemes are words. The words *dogs* and *cats* each consist of two morphemes. Adding a *z* phoneme to *dog*

Phonology The study of the basic sounds in a language. (From the Greek *phone,* meaning "sound" or "voice.")

Phoneme A basic sound in a language.

Morpheme The smallest unit of meaning in a language.

makes the word plural. Adding an *s* phoneme to *cat* serves the same function.

An *ed* morpheme at the end of a verb places it in the past tense, as with *add* and *added,* and with *subtract* and *subtracted.* A *ly* morpheme at the end of an adjective often makes the word an adverb, as with *strong* and *strongly* and *weak* and *weakly.*

Inflections   Morphemes such as *s* and *ed* tacked on to the ends of nouns and verbs are referred to as grammatical "markers," or **inflections.** Inflections change the forms of words in order to indicate grammatical relationships such as *number* (singular or plural) and *tense* (for example, present or past). Languages have grammatical rules for the formation of plurals, tenses, and other inflections.

SYNTAX

> since feeling is first
> who pays any attention
> to the syntax of things
> will never wholly kiss you . . .
> —e. e. cummings

The above lines from an e. e. cummings poem are confusing because the **syntax** permits at least two interpretations. How would the meaning be changed if we were to place a question mark at the end of the third line and remove the fourth? What would happen to the meaning if we placed *he* or *she* before the word *who?* Cummings delighted in phrasing poetry to allow various interpretations. He toyed with the syntax of English. Syntax concerns the customary arrangement of words in phrases and sentences in a language. Syntax deals with the ways words are to be strung together, or ordered, into phrases and sentences. The precise rules for word order are the *grammar* of a language.

In English, statements usually follow the pattern subject, verb, and object of the verb. Note this example:

The young boy (subject) → has brought (verb) → the book (object).

The sentence would be confusing if it were written "The young boy *has* the book *brought.*" But this is how the sentence would be written in German.

B.C.

Semantics The study of the relationships between language and objects or events. The study of the meaning of language. (From the Greek *sema,* meaning "sign" or "symbol.")

Surface structure The superficial construction of a sentence as defined by the placement of words.

Deep structure The underlying meaning of a sentence as determined by interpretation of the meanings of the words.

German syntax differs from that of English. In German, a past participle ("brought") is placed at the end of the sentence, while the helping verb ("has") follows the subject. Although the syntax of German differs from that of English, children raised in German-speaking homes* acquire German syntax readily.

SEMANTICS

Semantics concerns the meanings of a language. It is the study of the relationship between language and the objects or events language depicts. Words that sound and are spelled alike can have different meanings, depending on their usage. Compare these sentences:

A rock sank the boat.
Don't rock the boat.

In the first sentence, *rock* is a noun and the subject of the verb *sank.* The sentence probably means that the hull of a boat was ripped open by an underwater rock, causing the boat to sink. (It could also be that someone hurled a rock at the boat, but the rock would have to be rather large, and the hurler rather burly.) In the second sentence, *rock* is a verb. The sentence probably means that someone needs to be warned not to stand in a small boat or move about in it too rapidly. The second sentence could also be a figure of speech in which a person is being warned not to change things— not to "make waves" or "upset the apple cart."

Or compare these sentences:

The chicken is ready for dinner.
The lion is ready for dinner.
The shark is ready for dinner.

The first sentence probably means that a chicken has been cooked and is ready to be eaten. The second sentence probably means that a lion is hungry, or about to devour its prey. Our interpretation of the phrase "is ready for dinner" reflects our expectations concerning chickens and lions. Whether or not we expect a shark to be eaten or to do some eating would reflect on our seafood preferences or on how recently we had seen the movie *Jaws.*

We can differentiate between the *surface structure* and the *deep structure* of sentences. The **surface structure** involves the superficial construction of the sentence. The surface structure of the "ready for dinner" sentences is the same. The **deep structure** of a sentence refers to its underlying meaning. The "ready for dinner" sentences clearly differ in their deep structure. "Make me a peanut butter and jelly sandwich" has an ambiguous surface structure, allowing different interpretations of its deep meaning—the typical child's response: "Poof! You're a peanut butter and jelly sandwich!"

Now that we have looked at the structure of language, we can better appreciate the "child's task" of acquiring language, which we look at in the next section.

*No, homes do not speak German or any other language. This is an example of an English figure of speech. Such figures of speech are acquired readily by children.

A CLOSER LOOK

OUTCRY OVER "WUF TICKETS": BLACK ENGLISH VS. STANDARD USAGE IN THE COURTROOM

Many of the black kids at Ann Arbor's Green Road Housing Project in Michigan do not talk much like their well-to-do white classmates at the neighborhood King elementary school. Some of it is simple pronunciation: "We do maf work" for "We do mathematics work." Some of the differences lie in odd verb tenses: "She-ah hit us" for "She will hit us." More often the difference involves the verb "to be." Green Roaders say, "He be gone" when they mean, "He is gone a good deal of the time"; "He been gone" when they mean, "He's been gone a long while"; and "He gone" when they mean, "He is gone right now." Some is pure idiom. "To sell wolf tickets" (pronounced wuf tickets) means to challenge somebody to a fight.

Such speech, widely known as Black English, is customarily pounced upon by teachers trying to teach standard English usage. Though that would seem a normal part of pedagogy, a small group of Green Road parents felt that teachers were expressing their disapproval of Black English too harshly, causing student embarrassment and hurting the children's chances to learn. The parents filed a federal suit in Michigan's Eastern District Court, demanding that school authorities "recognize" Black English as a formal dialect with historic roots and grammatical rules of its own.

A Bridge to Standard English Like most Green Road parents, the plaintiffs want their children to use standard English, but they insisted that the school respond more sympathetically to the dialect in teaching. "Language is like clothing," said University of Michigan professor Daniel Fader, testifying on behalf of the children. "When you take it away from the child, you leave him naked." As attorney Gabe Kaimowitz insisted, "We're looking for use of Black English as a bridge to get kids to use standard English."

The suit divided Detroit's black community. "A mountain out of a molehill," said Detroit N.A.A.C.P. President Larry Washington. "The dominant language of this country is English," added Washington. "If our children are to increase their chances, that's what they have to be taught." School officials decided that the suit was unnecessary and cited as evidence an existing volunteer training course in the techniques of teaching standard English to Black English speakers.

Sensitivity Courses After three weeks of argument, U.S. District Judge Charles W. Joiner concluded that the school had not been as sympathetic as it should have been. Joiner provided the first judicial opinion that Black English is a distinct dialect, not just slovenly talk, and ordered the Ann Arbor school district to prepare a plan for teaching Black English speakers. All teachers at the King school will now be required to take "sensitivity courses" in how to steer small pupils tactfully away from "wuf tickets" and into the verb "to be."

LANGUAGE DEVELOPMENT

Now that we have become familiar with the elements of language, let us trace language development over the first several years, beginning with cries and coos.

CRYING AND COOING

Newborn infants, as parents are well aware, have one highly effective form of verbal expression: crying and more crying. Although crying can be prolonged and vigorous and vary in pitch, there are no distinct, well-formed sounds.

During the second month, children also begin **cooing.** Cooing, like crying, is unlearned. Babies use their tongues when they coo, and for this reason coos take on more distinct sounds than cries. Coos are frequently vowel-like and may resemble repeated "oohs" and "ahs." Cooing appears associated with feelings of pleasure or positive excitement.

Parents soon learn that different cries and coos can indicate different things: hunger, gas, or pleasure at being held or rocked. The nearby box

Cooing Unlearned verbalizations that are thought to express pleasure in newborn infants.

PSYCHOLOGISTS ARE LEARNING THAT BABIES' CRIES MAY SAY MORE THAN YOU THINK

Although crying babies sound helpless enough, crying may actually be an important factor in the development of feelings of self-confidence. According to psychologist Michael Lewis of the Educational Testing Service in Princeton, N.J., if crying elicits a response from the parents, the child may begin to see the world as a friendly place and develop patterns of competence.

Dr. Lewis states that "Crying should teach the child optimism about the environment, which he learns when his cries are answered. An infant as young as eight weeks is capable of understanding this, and of appreciating the fact that he can cause things to happen" (Sobel, 1981).

A Basically Disturbing Sound Infant crying is not simply a distress signal, but a powerful communicator that helps determine whether any baby will become an abused or cherished child.

As noted by psychologist Ann M. Frodi of the University of Rochester, an infant's cry is basically disturbing, possibly by evolutionary design. In her research, Frodi found that not only parents, but also childless men and women and adolescents and children have similar physiological responses to infant crying—bursts of autonomic activity highlighted by increases in heart rate, blood pressure, and sweating. The subjects generally reported that the crying made them feel irritated and anxious, and motivated them to run to the baby to try to relieve the distress.

In a series of experiments, Frodi compared the effects on adults of premature babies' cries to those of full-term infants. "A preemie's cry is a whole octave higher," she explained. "It also has different rhythm, pauses, and inhalation-exhalation patterns, and it has a much more aversive effect on the listener." Although such cries signal greater urgency, they can threaten the formation of parent-child bonds of attachment. "If there is too much crying or the sound is too grating, you may opt to relieve your own distress by trying to get away from the cry or by becoming violent," Dr. Frodi said (Sobel, 1981).

Crying as a Diagnostic Aid Cries that may be signs of infant illness or disturb parents are the research interest of Barry M. Lester of Children's Hospital Medical Center in Boston. "Mothers with a history of child abuse frequently say they couldn't stand the high-pitched, irritating cry of the baby," Dr. Lester said (Sobel, 1981). Sad to say, many conditions ranging from fetal malnutrition to high blood pressure in the pregnant mother can give her baby a high-pitched cry of 700 to 800 cycles per second, as compared to the normal 300 to 400 cycles per second.

"In these cases, you've got to support the mother," Dr. Lester said. "It's not her imagination. The crying really is a terrible noise, and the baby requires some ginger handling. With this kind of help, she can channel her energy into helping the child instead of becoming depressed or angry over the fact that he's not perfect" (Sobel, 1981).

The rhythm and pitch of infants' cries can also serve as aids in diagnosing a number of neurological disorders that cannot be easily detected in other ways.

Dr. Lester and his colleague, Sandy Zeskind, have been working to associate features of infants' cries with specific disorders. A striking example of the link between crying and a physical disorder is the syndrome called *cri du chat*, French for cry of the cat. This is a genetic disorder that produces abnormalities in the brain, atypical facial features, and, according to Dr. Lester, "a very high-pitched, squealy cry that sends chills down the spine."

Drs. Lester and Zeskind by coincidence recorded the cries of a number of babies who later died from Sudden Infant Death Syndrome. They found some unusual features of the babies' cries, but have not yet been able to identify them reliably. There is great hope in this approach, because SIDS remains very unpredictable. If infants at risk could be identified by their cries, they could be monitored carefully through the first dangerous months of life.

CRYING Infant crying is a powerful communicator that helps determine whether a baby will become an abused or cherished child.

on babies' crying reflects recent research to the effect that cries can reflect a number of medical disorders.

Remember that true language has semanticity; that is, sounds are symbols. For this reason, crying and cooing are *prelinguistic* events, not true language. Cries and coos do not represent objects or events. By about eight months of age, cooing decreases markedly. By about the fifth or sixth month, children have already begun to babble.

BABBLING

Babbling is the first vocalizing that sounds like human speech. Babbling children utter phonemes found in several languages, including the throaty German *ch*, the clicks of certain African tribes, and rolling *r*'s (Atkinson et al., 1970; McNeill, 1970). Babbling appears to be inborn. Deaf children babble even though they cannot hear the speech of others. Reinforcements for babbling—like adult smiling or pats on the stomach—can increase its frequency (e.g., Rheingold et al., 1959).

From these beginnings, children seem to single out within a few months the types of phonemes used consistently in the home. By the age of nine or ten months these phonemes are repeated regularly. "Foreign" phonemes begin to drop out. Although babbling, like crying and cooing, is a prelinguistic event, infants usually understand much of what others are saying well before they utter their own first words. Comprehension precedes production, and infants demonstrate comprehension with their actions and gestures.

THE CHILD'S FIRST WORDS(!)

Ah, that long-awaited first word! What a thrill! What a milestone! Unfortunately, many parents miss this milestone. They are not quite sure when their children utter their first word, often because first words are not pronounced clearly. "Ball," for example, may be prounounced "ba," "bee," or even "pah."

Vocabulary acquisition is slow at first. It may take children three or four months to achieve a ten-word vocabulary after the first word is spoken. By about eighteen months of age, children usually produce dozens of words, like *no, cookie, mama, hi, allgone, bye-bye,* and *eat.* During the third year, vocabulary growth accelerates markedly, as noted in Table 6.1.

TELEGRAPHIC SPEECH

Although children first use one-word utterances, these utterances may express the meanings of complete sentences. Brief one- or two-word expressions that have the meanings of sentences are examples of telegraphic speech.

The Holophrase   Single words are called **holophrases** when they are used to express complex meanings. For example, *mama* may be used by the child to signify meanings as varied as "There goes mama," "Come here, mama," and "You are mama." Similarly, *poo-cat* can signify "There

Babbling The child's first vocalizations that have the sound of speech.

Holophrase A single word used to express complex meanings. (From the Greek *holos,* meaning "whole," and *phrazein,* meaning "to speak.")

TABLE 6.1 Some Milestones in Language Development

Approximate Age	Language Performance
Birth	Cries
12 weeks	Coos, gurgles
16 weeks	Differentiates sounds and responds to human sounds
20 weeks	Makes vowel and consonant sounds
6 months	Babbles single syllable (ma, mu, da, di)
8 months	Reduplicates babbles (mama, didi), intonates
12 months	Understands some words as symbols
18 months	Still babbles, utters 2–50 words, not many joined
24 months	Shows vocabulary of 50+ words (especially nouns), uses two-word phrases
30 months	Shows fastest vocabulary increase—daily additions
36 months	Shows 1,000-word vocabulary, 80% of which is intelligible to strangers

The ages in this table are approximations. Parents need not assume that their children will have language problems if they are somewhat behind.

SOURCE: Adapted from Lenneberg (1967).

is a pussycat," "That stuffed animal looks just like my pussycat," and "I want you to give me my pussycat right now!" Most children teach their parents their intended meaning quite readily, by gesturing, using intonations, and applying rewards and punishments as if they were professional learning theorists—that is, by acting delighted when parents do as requested, and by howling fiercely when they do not.

Two-Word Utterances   Toward the end of the second year, children begin to speak in telegraphic two-word utterances. In the utterance "That ball," the words *is* and *a* are implied. There are many different types of two-word utterances, for example, agent-action ("Daddy sit"), action-object ("Hit you"), locating ("Car there"), and possessing ("Mommy cup"). The important thing to note is that the types of two-word utterances that tend to be used first in English also emerge first in languages as divergent as German, Russian, Luo (an African tongue), and Turkish (Slobin, 1973). The limited role of environmental influences can be seen as supporting the view that there is a universal, innate tendency in people to develop language according to a preprogramed schedule. This view will be amplified in the section on theories of language development.

Children's two-word utterances, while brief, nevertheless show a grasp of syntax. The child will say "Sit chair" to tell a parent to sit in a chair, not "Chair sit." (Most apes do not reliably make this distinction in ASL.) The child will say "My shoe," not "Shoe my," to show possession. "Mommy go" means Mommy is leaving, while "Go Mommy" expresses the wish for Mommy to go away. For this reason, "Go Mommy" is not heard frequently.

TOWARD MORE COMPLEX LANGUAGE

Between the ages of two and three, children's vocabularies leap impressively, and their sentence structure expands to include the words that were missing in telegraphic speech. For example, it is usually during the third

THE FAMILY CIRCUS   By Bil Keane

"He has some teeth, but his words haven't come in yet."

year that children add an impressive array of articles (a, an, the), conjunctions (and, but, or), possessive and demonstrative adjectives (your, her, that), pronouns (she, him, one), and prepositions (in, on, under, around, over, and through). Their continued use of syntax to produce words and phrases is made evident by language oddities such as "your one" instead of "yours," and "his one" instead of simply "his." It is also usually between two and three that children show knowledge of rules for combining phrases and clauses into complex sentences, such as "You goed and Mommy goed, too."

Young children try to talk about more things than they have words for. During the second year it is common for them to refer to many types of four-legged animals as doggies or horsies. At the age of two and a half, my daughter Allyn told her grandmother that "We taked Jordan [her younger sister] to the doctor to get her *fixed*." Generalizing the use of words into situations in which they do not apply is called **overextension.** Other examples of Allyn's overextensions during her third year were "That car is blue, just like us's," and "Jordan is very laughy today."

Young children are also likely to engage in **overregularization** in forming the plurals of nouns and the past tense of verbs. With regular nouns we form the plural by adding s or z sounds, and with regular verbs we add d or ed to form the past tense. *Pussycat* becomes *pussycats* and *doggy* becomes *doggies*. *Walk* becomes *walked* and *look* becomes *looked*.

If children learned these irregular plurals and verbs merely by imitating their parents, they would probably tend to form them correctly, even during the second and third years. However, children tend to form plurals and past tenses on the basis of rules rather than observation alone, and so they make many charming errors. Two- and three-year-olds, for example, may be more likely to say "I seed it" than "I saw it," and more likely to say "Mommy sitted down" than "Mommy sat down." They are likely to talk about the "gooses" and the "sheeps" they "seed" on the farm, and all about the other "childs" they ran into at the playground.

In an experiment designed to show that preschool children are not just clever mimics but have actually grasped rules of grammar, Berko (1958) showed children pictures of nonexistent animals, as in Figure 6.2. She first showed them a single animal and said, "This is a wug." Then she showed them a picture of two animals and said, "Now there are two of them." Then she said, "There are two _____," asking the children to finish the sentence. Ninety-one percent of the children said "wugs," correctly pluralizing the bogus word. This percentage was approximated in similar language tasks.

As language develops beyond the third year, children show increasing facility with pronouns and prepositions. By the fourth year, children are asking questions, taking turns talking, and engaging in lengthy conversations. By the age of six, their vocabularies have expanded, on the average, to something like 10,000 words.

Language development goes hand in hand with cognitive development, and during the early school years children come to understand words that describe relationships between people, such as *uncle* and *aunt*. Aunt Elizabeth is no longer Aunt Elizabeth because she is repeatedly designated

Overextension Overgeneralizing the use of words into situations in which they do not apply.

Overregularization The use of regular inflections (such as adding ed or s) with irregular verbs and nouns to show tense and number.

FIGURE 6.2 **"WUGS"** Many bright, sophisticated college students are unfamiliar with "wugs." Here are several wugs—actually, make-believe animals used in a study to learn whether preschool children can form the plurals of unfamiliar nouns. (They can.)

as same. She is now understood to be Aunt Elizabeth *because* she is mother's sister. Another sister of mother's could now be expected to be labeled an aunt by the child also.

By seven to nine, most children realize that words can have different meanings, and they become entertained by riddles and jokes that require semantic sophistication. If you are ready to groan, note these examples:

1. Order! Order in the court!" cries the judge.
   "A hamburger and French fries, your Honor," responds the defendant.

2. "I saw a man-eating lion at the zoo."
   "Big deal! I saw a man eating snails at a restaurant."

3. "Make me a glass of chocolate milk."
   "Poof! You're a glass of chocolate milk."

Although the sequences of development are almost invariably the same, there are great individual differences in children's rates of language development. Moreover, there are sex and social-class differences. Infant girls build their vocabularies a bit faster than boys, on the average, and pronounce words more clearly. By adolescence, girls excel in spelling, punctuation, reading comprehension, and verbal reasoning (Maccoby & Jacklin, 1974). Children from lower socioeconomic backgrounds have poorer vocabularies than more affluent children. When we consider that knowledge of the meanings of words is the single best predictor of overall scores on intelligence tests, it is not surprising that children from middle- and upper-class families attain higher test scores. In the section on intelligence, we shall explore genetic and environmental influences on these test scores.

Now that we have traced the development of language through the childhood years, let us consider theories as to why language develops as it does.

THEORIES OF LANGUAGE DEVELOPMENT

Countless billions of children have learned the languages spoken by their parents. They have continued to pass these languages down, with minor changes, from generation to generation. We can demonstrate that experience plays an indispensable role in language development. We also know of some of the biological structures involved in using language, such as the vocal cords in the throat and the speech centers in the brain. In this section we discuss the insights and limitations of learning-theory and biological approaches to understanding language development.

LEARNING-THEORY VIEWS OF LANGUAGE DEVELOPMENT

Classical Conditioning   Classical conditioning may be involved in children's learning that words are signs for objects and activities. The word *cereal*, for example, may become the conditioned stimulus (CS) for cereal (the unconditioned stimulus, or US), if the word is paired repeatedly with perception of the cereal. After conditioning has occurred, the word *cereal* (the CS) may elicit an image of cereal (a conditioned response, or CR). Learning theorist O. Hobart Mowrer (1960) drew a connection between conditioning and cognition by suggesting that many mental images are conditioned responses that are elicited by conditioned stimuli. In the case of learning the meanings of words, the conditioned responses (mental images) are objects, actions, or ideas, and the conditioned stimuli are the words that symbolize them.

There is no doubt that children can learn words for objects by pairing perception of the object with a name. Yet children as well as adults also learn words for abstract qualities (like "goodness"), complex events, and thought processes. We cannot simply point to truth, goodness, Western civilization, the creation of the universe, or memory, and name these things. Also, it matters little how frequently we point to objects and repeat their names in front of fish, birds, rats, and dogs. These animals cannot come to understand that words serve as symbols for the objects. For both reasons, classical conditioning can be at best a partial explanation for learning the meanings of words.

Operant Conditioning   When children begin to speak, parents frequently become excited and hug and kiss them. They shower them with reinforcing attention (Brown & Hanlon, 1970). Reinforcement tends to increase the frequency of behavior, including language-related behavior, and some psychologists (e.g., B. F. Skinner, 1957) have argued that language development can be largely explained by operant conditioning.

We do observe parents shaping their children's verbal behavior. They **model** certain sounds or words clearly, like *Mama* or *Dada*, and encourage children to repeat them. At first they reinforce children for approximating the sounds. Later on they may require that children utter the sound clearly, while pointing to the right person, before reinforcement is given. Some theorists suggest that sound production is "self-reinforcing" in children because of our biological makeup. They suggest that children enjoy babbling and other sounds for their own sake, even when nobody else is present or rewards them.

Critics argue that operant conditioning, like classical conditioning, can only partially explain language development. Children do not appear to learn rules of grammar by trial-and-error behavior and reinforcement.

Model As a verb, to engage in a behavior that is imitated by another.

Instead, they appear to show insight into language structure. This insight allows them to produce sentences spontaneously. According to principles of operant conditioning, children might be limited to utterances for which they have been previously reinforced.

Observational Learning   One of my friends had an eight-year-old nephew whose speech was peppered with double negatives (as in "Yes, we don't have no bananas") and frequent "Way to go!" exclamations—just as his father's speech was. Children can learn by observing their parents and other people. Observational learning may help explain why, during the first year, children begin to emphasize repetition of phonemes used by their parents, and why the accents, vocabularies, and grammatical peculiarities of some children tend to be similar to those of their parents. We also observe parents encouraging children to observe and imitate their verbal behavior by repeating words and sentences.

Observational learning can also provide only a partial explanation for language acquisition. Observational learning does not explain why children babble sounds they have not heard, or why they overregularize. As noted earlier, when a child says "Mommy goed away" rather than "Mommy went away," or "I dood it" rather than "I did it," it is not because parents were observed or heard to make these errors. It is because the child is applying grammatical rules, as they are understood, in his or her own speech. This is an ironic case in which *errors* supply powerful evidence that rules of grammar are understood.

BIOLOGICAL VIEWS OF LANGUAGE DEVELOPMENT

We have explored the ability of apes to use language and concluded that despite concerted training, apes show little capacity for grasping syntax—the grammatical structure of language. But now let's pose a related question: Why can't apes *talk*? Even if only to reproduce words ungrammatically?

Apes, it happens, have structures in their throats that look somewhat similar to human vocal tracts. But despite experiments in which apes have been reared by human families, they have never gained the ability to use these structures to produce the sounds of language reliably. Why not?

Since apes may possess a reasonably adequate vocal apparatus, and many of them have had "enriched" early environments with humans, it may be that apes lack something else that allows children to utter the sounds of language. What children probably have, and apes do not, is some kind of "neurological prewiring" that involves the speech areas* and, perhaps, other areas of the brain.

Psycholinguistic Theory   According to the **psycholinguistic theory** of language development, language acquisition involves an interaction between environmental influences, such as exposure to parental speech and parental reinforcement for language-related behaviors, and an inborn tendency to acquire language (Chomsky, 1968, 1980; Rosenthal, 1980). Evi-

---

Psycholinguistic theory The view that language learning involves an interaction between environmental influences and an inborn tendency to acquire language. The emphasis is on the innate tendency.

*Refer to Chapter 2 for a discussion of Broca's and Wernicke's areas of the brain.

dence for an inborn tendency is found in the fact that only humans can speak; in the regularity of the early production of sounds, even among deaf children; and in the largely invariable sequences of language development during the first 4–5 years, regardless of which language the child is learning. In Urdu, Russian, and English, children tend to say their first words at about one year. They use the same types of two-word utterances at the same ages, and they have largely grasped even the most complex rules of grammar by four or five.

Noam Chomsky labels this inborn tendency the **Language Acquisition Device, or** *LAD*. He believes that the LAD is a prewiring of the nervous system that makes it well suited to learn the basic rules of grammar. This is because all languages, despite their obvious differences, share what Chomsky calls a "universal grammar"—that is, an underlying deep structure that involves basic rules as to how phonemes, morphemes, and syntax are woven together to symbolize events and yield meaning.

Parents naturally influence children to learn their particular language. Parents tend to use reinforcement and other principles of learning theory to encourage their children to associate sounds with objects and ideas. Yet children's ability to grasp the syntax of a language basically reflects their neural prewiring, or LAD.

EVALUATION

Let me attempt a few summary statements about the theoretical roles of learning and biology in language development. Many words are learned by association with objects, and the associative process may be akin to classical conditioning. Concerning the possible role of operant conditioning, children certainly can be guided into verbalizing, and the frequency of verbalizations can be influenced by reinforcement. And concerning observational learning, children clearly do observe and imitate their parents and other speakers, although their "imitation" is distorted according to their levels of cognitive development and their own grasp of syntax. Learning thus plays certain roles in language development, but learning theory cannot fully account for it.

It seems clear that there is some kind of neurological prewiring (or LAD) that permits children reared to speak different tongues to grasp the deep structure of language. The prewiring appears to involve Broca's area and Wernicke's area. Prewiring accounts for the largely invariable sequence of language development found around the world, and also for the charming "errors" produced by overregularizing.

At the risk of repetition, there must be some kind of neurological prewiring that makes language development possible. Goldfish, flatworms, and rats, despite the best of environments, do not learn language. It seems foolish to think that we simply have not yet found an efficient way to teach them English or French. It is safe to assume that they lack the prewiring. Apes, on the other hand, may be partially prewired to use language. Partial prewiring could explain why they gain some facility with ASL, even though their syntax remains unreliable. And they are apparently not prewired to develop speech, even though they may possess adequate vocal tracts.

Language-Acquisition Device In psycholinguistic theory, neural "prewiring" that is presumed to facilitate the child's learning of grammar. Abbreviated *LAD*.

Now that we have some idea as to how and why language develops, let us consider how the cognitive processes of language and thought are intertwined.

LANGUAGE AND THOUGHT

Theories of language development may be of little importance to a twenty-month-old who has just polished off her plate of chocolate chip cookies and exclaims "Allgone!" In the previous section we were concerned with the question, How does the child come to say "Allgone" when she has finished her plate. Not let us ponder the question, What does her use of "Allgone" suggest about her thought processes? In other words, would the girl have *known* that there were no cookies left if she did not have a word to express this idea? Do you always think in words? Can you think *without* using language? Would you be able to solve problems without using words or sentences?

According to Jean Piaget (1976), whose theory of cognitive development will be discussed in Chapter 8, language is merely a reflection of a person's knowledge of the world. Language is not necessary for the acquisition of much of this knowledge. It is possible to have the concepts of roundness or redness even when we do not know or use the words *round* or *red*.

THE LINGUISTIC-RELATIVITY HYPOTHESIS

Language may not be necessary for all thought, but according to the **linguistic-relativity hypothesis** proposed by Benjamin Whorf (1956), language structures the ways in which we perceive the world. Consider our perceptions of microcomputers. People who understand terms like "64 K," "megabyte," and "RAM" can think about microcomputers with greater sophistication than people who do not.

According to the linguistic-relativity hypothesis, most English speakers' ability to think about snow might be rather limited when compared to that of the Eskimos. We have only a few words for snow, whereas the Eskimos have many words for snow, and they use them depending, for example, on whether the snow is hard-packed, falling, melting, ice-covered, and so on. When we think about snow, we have very few words to choose from and may have to search for descriptive adjectives. Eskimos, however, may immediately associate to a single word that fully describes a complex weather condition; perhaps it is then simpler for them to think about this variety of snow in relation to other aspects of their world. Similarly, the Hanunoo people of the Philippines used ninety-two words for rice, depending on whether the rice was husked or unhusked, and on how it was prepared.

In English we have hundreds of words to describe different colors, but those who speak Shona use only three words for colors. People who speak Bassa use only two words for colors (Gleason, 1961), corresponding to light and dark. The Hopi Indians have two words for flying objects, one for birds

Linguistic-relativity hypothesis The view that language structures the way in which one perceives the world. As a consequence, one's thoughts would be limited by the concepts available in his or her language.

and an all-inclusive word for anything else that may be found traveling through the air.

Does this mean that the Hopi are limited in their ability to think about bumblebees and airplanes that fly overhead? Are English speakers limited in their ability to think about skiing conditions? Are those who speak Shona and Bassa "color-blind" for all practical purposes?

Probably not. People who use only a few words to distinguish colors seem to perceive color variations in the same way as people with dozens of words (Rosch, 1974; Bornstein & Marks, 1982). For example, the Dani of New Guinea, like the Bassa, have just two words for colors: *mola,* which refers to warm colors, and *mili,* which refers to cool colors. Still, tasks in matching and memory show that the Dani have no difficulty in distinguishing the many colors of the spectrum when they are motivated to do so. English-speaking skiers, who are concerned about different skiing conditions, have developed a comprehensive special vocabulary about snow, including *powdèr, slush, ice, hardpack,* and *corn snow,* that may enable them to communicate and think about snow with the facility of Eskimos. The point is that when a need to expand a language's vocabulary in a given area arises, the speakers of that language apparently have little difficulty in meeting the need.

Critics of the linguistic-relativity hypothesis argue that a language's vocabulary only suggests the range of concepts that the speakers of the language have traditionally found to be important. A limited vocabulary does not mean people cannot make distinctions for which there are no words. For example, a person with limited microcomputer experience would understand readily that a computer with a capacity of 128 K is more powerful than one with a capacity of 64 K. And Hopi Indians flying from New York to San Francisco nowadays would not think that they are flying inside a bird or a bumblebee, even if they have no word for airplane.

Although language may not be necessary for all instances of thought, concepts may be. In the following section we discuss concepts and their formation.

CONCEPTS AND CONCEPT FORMATION

What's black and white and read all over? This riddle was heard quite often when I was younger. Since the riddle was spoken, you would probably assume that "read" meant "red" when you heard it. And so, in seeking an answer, you would scan your memory for an object that was red even though it was black and white. The answer to the riddle, "newspaper," would meet with a good groan.

The word *newspaper* is a **concept.** *Red, black,* and *white* are also concepts—color concepts. When we try to solve riddles or problems, we tend to try to scan our memories for all related concepts.

Concepts are symbols. They stand for groups of objects, events, or ideas that have common properties. Newspapers are indeed black and white, most of the time. They are usually read, although they can also be used for sopping up spills, paper-training your dog, and kindling and fanning fires.

Concept A symbol that stands for groups of objects, events, or ideas with common properties.

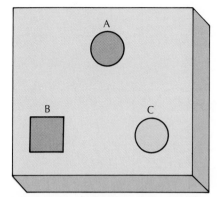

FIGURE 6.3 AN EXERCISE IN CLASSI-FICATION Where does figure *A* belong? With *B* or with *C*? Most adults prefer to classify objects according to form concepts rather than color concepts, and so they would choose *C*. Why not try this on a few adults and find out for yourself?

Material, color, shape, and purpose—these are some of the types of properties that most newspapers share. If a newspaper had full-color photos (as some do), or was made of glossy paper (as newsletters of some professional organizations are), we might think of it as an unusual newspaper.

Riddles often rely upon confusion over the way the same words or similar words may represent different concepts. Recall the sentences ''A rock sank the boat'' and ''Don't rock the boat.'' In these sentences, the same word, ''rock,'' represents different concepts. In the first sentence, ''rock'' is a noun—a hard substance. In the second sentence, ''rock'' is a verb, referring to movement from side to side.

Let us consider further the relationship between concepts and words. Words are concepts, but not all concepts are words. For instance, a dog can respond to the concept of *roundness* even though it cannot understand that the word ''round'' symbolizes the concept. This can be demonstrated through operant conditioning, as in the following example. Allow a dog to choose one of three pathways, one with a circle above it, and the other two with a square and a triangle. Alternate the size and position of these geometric figures, but reinforce the dog with food for taking the pathway marked by the circle. The round circle will become a discriminative stimulus, and the dog will reliably take the pathway marked by the circle—at least when it has been deprived of food for a while.

SUBORDINATE AND SUPERORDINATE CONCEPTS

Some concepts are more general than others. Concepts like *animal* refer to large groups of objects that have only a few properties in common. Flatworms, birds, and chimps all fit into the animal category, for example. Other concepts, like *Boston terrier, microcomputer,* and *chocolate seven-layer cake,* are more specific. There are fewer instances of more specific concepts, and specific concepts share more properties than do more general concepts. There are fewer *Boston terriers* than *animals,* and Boston terriers share more properties than do animals in general.

Concepts that are contained by others are said to be **subordinate** to them. The concepts *dog* and *bird* are said to be subordinate to the concept *animal.* Other concepts are **superordinate** to, or contain, others. The concept *animal* is superordinate to the concepts *dog, bird, chimp,* and *flatworm.*

Subordinate concepts possess all the properties ascribed to superordinate concepts. Dogs, birds, chimps, and flatworms each possess all the properties that pertain to animals, even if they differ markedly from one another in many obvious ways. Superordinate concepts do not have all the properties possessed by each subordinate concept. Birds, for instance, have all the properties of animals in general, but also have feathers and fly. Dogs, chimps, and flatworms do not have feathers or fly, but they are still animals.

Consider people for a moment. The concept *teacher* is subordinate to the concept *person.* Those things that are true of persons, like bleeding when scratched, making errors, and having emotions, are also true of teachers. But as you can see in Figure 6.4, it may be that some students place teachers in a special category. Sadly, none of my students ever seem surprised when I make errors in the classroom.

Subordinate Included, contained by another class.

Superordinate Including, containing another class.

Hi & Lois

FIGURE 6.4 ARE TEACHERS PEOPLE? You may classify teachers as people, and therefore assume that what is true of people will also hold for teachers. But children have to learn to classify concepts according to "adult" schemes.

Concepts permit us to make generalizations about the world around us without having to experience directly every object or event. If you have learned that Boston terriers are affectionate and somewhat "nervous," you will expect to find these properties in a new Boston terrier.

Knowledge of groups or classes allows us to make certain decisions efficiently. You may decide to buy a dog rather than a cat, or an Irish setter rather than a Doberman pinscher, because you know something about those classes of animals.

CONCEPT FORMATION

Simple Concepts Many simple concepts, like *dog* and *red,* may be taught by association. We simply point to a dog and say "dog" or "This is a dog" (or, more likely, "a doggy") to a child. Dogs are considered **positive instances** of the dog concept. **Negative instances,** that is, things which are *not* dogs, are then shown to the child while one says, "This is *not* a dog."

Things that are *negative instances* of one concept may be *positive instances* of another. So in teaching a child, one may be more likely to say, "This is *not* a dog, it's a *cat,*" rather than simply, "This is not a dog."

Complex Concepts More abstract concepts, like *uncle* or *square root,* may have to be learned through verbal explanations that involve more basic concepts. If one points to *uncles* (positive instances) and *not uncles* (negative instances) repeatedly, a child may eventually learn that uncles are males, or even that they are males who are not their own fathers. However, it is doubtful that this show-and-tell method would ever teach them that uncles are brothers of a parent. The concept *uncle* is best taught by explanation after a child understands the concepts *parent* (or at least *Mommy* and *Daddy*) and *brother.*

Concepts that are still more abstract, like *justice, goodness,* and *beauty,* may require complex verbal explanation and the presentation of many positive and negative instances. These concepts are so abstract and instances of them are so varied that no two people may agree on their definition. Or,

Positive instances Examples of a concept.

Negative instances Events that are *not* examples of a concept. Concept formation is aided by presentation of both positive and negative instances of the concept.

Hypothesis testing In concept formation, an active process in which we try to ferret out the meanings of concepts by testing our assumptions.

if their definitions coincide, they may argue over positive versus negative instances. An action that seems just to you may seem unjust to me. What seems a beautiful work of art to me may impress you as meaningless masses of colors. Thus, the phrase "Beauty is in the eye of the beholder."

Hypothesis Testing   We also engage in active processes called **hypothesis testing** in attempting to determine for ourselves what concepts mean. A parent may point to a fish in a tank and tell a child "That's a guppy." The child may then think that "things moving in water" are guppies. Then the parent points to another fish and says "That's an angel fish." Now the child may begin to form hypotheses about what makes up a guppy or an angel fish. The child may focus on the shapes, sizes, and colors of the fish and try to generalize to other fish, pointing and asking, "Is this a guppy, too?" The parent will say yes or no, and perhaps begin to explain that guppies are small fish with a sort of cigar shape that come in different colors. The child may then wonder if small, cigar-shaped fish with red and blue patches or with black and white stripes are also guppies, and continue to ask, "Is this a guppy, too?" The parent's continued responding "yes" and "no" gives the child further feedback as to the accuracy of his or her hypotheses.

Experiments in concept formation through hypothesis testing give us insight into the mechanics of the process (Bourne et al., 1971; Bruner et al., 1956; Horton & Turnage, 1976). Let us try a brief experiment to see how you might acquire the concept *zed*—or learn what "zeds" are so that you can describe them.

Let us imagine that we sit across a table from one another with a box of plastic shapes between us, like those in Figure 6.5. These are the rules: I ask you to pick out a piece, and each time you do so, I tell you whether or not it is a zed. When you can single out all the pieces that are zeds without making errors, I'll know that you have learned what zeds are.

You select *A1,* the small blue triangle, and I say, "No, that's not a zed." Then you pick out *B2,* and I say, "Yes, that's a zed." Do you pick out the third piece at random or on the basis of some hypotheses about what zeds might be? Have you already eliminated several hypotheses about zeds? For instance, you know already that the following hypotheses are

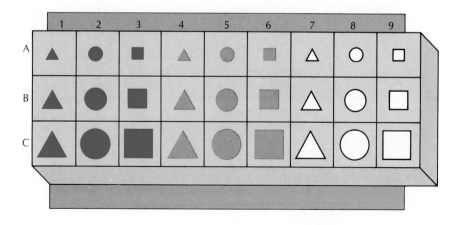

FIGURE 6.5 **GEOMETRIC FORMS OF THE TYPE USED BY PSYCHOLOGISTS IN EXPERIMENTS ON CONCEPT FORMATION**

false: All zeds are gray, all zeds are white, all zeds are square. Can you eliminate any other hypotheses at this point?

Next you pick out *B5,* and I say yes. What's your hypothesis? Do you next pick out *B8?* If you do, I say no. How do you react? You continue to select pieces. *C5* is no. *B4* is yes. *B3* is yes. *B7* is no. Would you now be able to identify those pieces that are *zed* or *not zed* without making further errors? You would if your current hypothesis is that zeds are medium-sized and blue or gray.

Studies like these suggest that even young children may use hypothesis testing to speed learning of concepts like shapes and colors. When you show a child a square and say "Square," the child may try to understand what accounts for the squareness of the figure. Is it the figure's boxiness, its size, its color, or what? After being shown several figures that are square, and several figures that are not, the child appears to develop a concept of squareness that involves other concepts like *boxy* and *sides as long as one another.* It may be many years before the child's definition involves sophisticated concepts like *closed geometric figure, four sides equal in length,* and *right angles.*

Forming and testing hypotheses is the type of cognitive activity we use to solve problems, as we see in the next section.

PROBLEM SOLVING

One of the pleasures I derived from my own introductory psychology course lay in showing friends the textbook and getting them involved in the problems in the section on problem solving. First, of course, I struggled with the problems myself. It's that time, now. And it's your turn. Get some scrap paper, take a breath, and have a go at the following problems. The answers will be discussed in the following pages, but don't peek. *Try* the problems first.

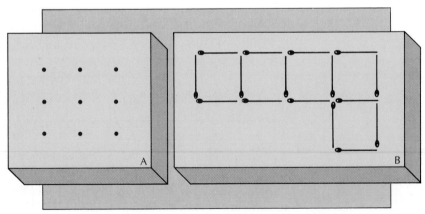

FIGURE 6.6 **TWO PROBLEMS** Draw straight lines through all the points in Part A, using only four lines. Do not lift your pencil or retrace your steps. Move three matches in Part B to make four squares equal in size. Use all the matches.

TABLE 6.2   Water–Jar Problems

Problem Number	Three Jars Are Present with the Listed Capacity (in Ounces)			Obtain This Amount of Water
	Jar A	Jar B	Jar C	
1	21	127	3	100
2	14	163	25	99
3	18	43	10	5
4	9	42	6	21
5	20	59	4	31
6	23	49	3	20
7	10	36	7	3

For each problem, how can you use some combination of the three jars given, and a tap, to obtain precisely the amount of water shown? Adapted from Abraham S. Luchins and Edith H. Luchins, *Rigidity of Behavior* (Eugene: University of Oregon Press, 1959), p. 109.

1. Provide the next two letters in the series for each of the following:
   a. ABABABAB??
   b. ABDEBCEF??
   c. OTTFFSSE??
2. Draw straight lines through all the points in part A of Figure 6.6, using only *four* lines. Do not lift your pencil from the paper or retrace your steps. (Answer shown on page 288.)
3. Move three matches in part B of Figure 6.6 to make four squares of the same size. You must use *all* the matches. (Answer shown on page 288.)
4. You have three jars, A, B, and C, which hold the amounts of water, in ounces, shown in Table 6.2. For each of the seven problems in Table 6.2, use the jars in any way you wish to arrive at the indicated amount of water. Fill or empty any jar as often as you wish. How do you obtain the desired amount of water in each problem? (The solutions are discussed on p. 286.)

STAGES IN PROBLEM SOLVING

If you are like most other problem solvers, you used three steps to solve parts a and b of problem 1. First, you sought to define the elements of the problems by discovering the structure of the *cycles* in each series. Series *1a* has repeated cycles of two letters: *AB, AB,* and so on. Series *1b* may be seen as having four cycles of two consecutive letters: *AB, DE, BC,* and so on.

Then you tried to produce *rules* that governed the advance of each series. In series *1a,* the rule is simply to repeat the cycle. Series *1b* is more complicated, and different sets of rules can be used to describe it. One correct set of rules is that odd-numbered cycles *(1 and 3,* or *AB* and *BC)* simply repeat the last letter of the previous cycle (in this case *B)* and then advance by one letter according to the alphabet. The same rule applies to even-numbered cycles *(2 and 4,* or *DE* and *EF).*

Then you used your rules to produce the next letters in the series: *AB* in series *1a,* and *CD* in series *1b.* Finally, you evaluated the effectiveness of the rules by checking your answers against the solutions in the above paragraphs.

Question: What alternate sets of rules could you have found to describe these two series? Would you have generated the same answers from these rules?

Preparation, Production, and Evaluation   People tend to use three stages in solving problems, whether the problem concerns dieting, selecting a house, or moving matchsticks to create a design. These stages include (1) preparation; (2) production; and (3) evaluation.

We prepare ourselves to solve a problem by familiarizing ourselves with its elements and clearly defining our goals. We prepare to solve high school algebra and geometry problems by outlining all the givens and trying to picture the answers as best we can. Part of preparation is proper classification of the problem. "Does this problem involve a right triangle? Does it seem similar to problems I've solved by using the quadratic equation?"

One of the difficulties in solving the problems of daily life is that they tend to be ill-defined. The elements in the problems are not clearly laid out, and the goals or desired outcomes are also cloudy. Consider the problems of people who usually get into fights when anyone casts them a negative glance or says something that could be interpreted as insulting. As we shall see in Chapter 12, there is a recently developed type of cognitive therapy called *problem-solving training* through which "explosive" people have been successfully trained to handle insults and other social provocations. First, they learn to conceptualize the provocations and their own feelings of anger as problems to be solved. Instead of acting rashly, they look at all aspects of the problem (for example, who the other person is, what he or she actually said and did, what his or her motives are likely to be) and the goal (to avert violence). Subjects consider various therapist- and self-suggested nonviolent ways of handling their anger. They try out (produce) the ones that seem most promising in practice sessions and in real-life encounters. Then they evaluate the effectiveness of their attempted solutions.

In parts a and b of Problem 1, the search for cycles and for the rules governing the cycles served as preparation for producing possible solutions.

Algorithms versus Heuristics   In solving problems, we sometimes turn to *algorithms* or *heuristic devices*. An **algorithm** is a specific procedure for solving a certain type of problem that will lead to the solution if it is used properly. Mathematical formulas, such as the quadratic equation, are examples of algorithms. They will yield correct answers to problems, *so long as the right formula is used.* Finding the right formula to solve a problem may require scanning one's memory for all formulas that contain variables that represent one or more of the elements in the problem. The quadratic equation, for example, concerns triangles with right angles. Therefore, it is appropriate to consider using this equation for problems concerning right angles, but not others.

Consider anagram problems, in which we try to reorganize groups of letters into words. In seeing how many words we can make from *DWARG,*

Algorithm A specific procedure for solving a problem that will work if used correctly; systematic calculations.

Heuristics (hue-RISS-ticks). Rules of thumb that help us simplify and solve problems. (From the Greek *heuriskein,* meaning "to invent, discover.")

Means-end analysis A heuristic device in which we try to solve a problem by evaluating the difference between the current situation and the goal.

Incubation In problem solving, a hypothesized process that sometimes occurs when one stands back from a frustrating problem for a while. Sometimes the solution "suddenly" is realized when the problem has been allowed "to incubate."

we can use the algorithm of simply listing every possible letter combination, using from one to all five letters, and then checking to see whether each result is, in fact, a word. The method is plodding, but it would certainly work.

Heuristics are rules of thumb that help us simplify and solve problems. Heuristics, in contrast to algorithms, do not guarantee a correct solution to a problem, but when they work they tend to allow for more rapid solutions. A heuristic device for solving the anagram problem would be to look for letter combinations that are found in words and then to check the remaining letters for words that include these combinations. In *DWARG,* for example, we can find the familiar combinations *dr* and *gr.* We may then quickly find *draw, drag, and grad.* The drawback to this method, however, is that we might miss some words.

One type of heuristic device is the **means-end analysis,** in which we evaluate the difference between our current situations and our goals at various steps along the way, and then do what we can to reduce this discrepancy at each step. Let's say that you are lost, but you know that your goal is west of your current location and on the "other side of the tracks." A heuristic device would be to drive toward the setting sun (west), and, at the same time, to remain alert for railroad tracks. If your road comes to an end and you must turn left or right, you can scan the distance in either direction for tracks. If you don't see any, turn right or left, but then, at the next major intersection, turn toward the setting sun again. Eventually you may get there. If not, you could use that most boring of algorithms: ask people for directions until you find someone who knows the route.

Incubation Let us return to the problems at the beginning of the section. How did you do with problem 1, part c, and problems 2 and 3? If you produced solutions that did not meet the goals, you may have become frustrated and thought, "The heck with it! I'll come back to it later." This attitude suggests a fourth stage of problem solving: **incubation.** An incubator warms chicken eggs for a while so that they will hatch. Incubation in problem solving refers to standing back from the problem for a while as some mysterious process in us seems to continue to work on it. Later, the answer may occur to us as "in a flash."

There are fascinating tales of scientists, artists, and philosophers who came away muttering from seemingly impossible problems. Later, they seemed to receive a flash of inspiration in strange settings, perhaps while walking through the woods, or while soaking in the tub. After many frustrating attempts at trying to construct a method for measuring precisely the volume of an odd-shaped object, like a crown, Archimedes, the Greek philosopher, was struck by the solution while lingering in his tub. Suddenly he realized that one could mark the line of the water in a tub, and then submerge the object, with all its nooks and crannies and points and dents. The volume of the water that rose above the line (i.e., the volume displaced) would equal precisely the volume of the odd-shaped object beneath the surface.

Some psychologists suggest that the incubation effect occurs because we have been working on the elements of the problem unconsciously. Such an answer, unfortunately, is no answer. If we cannot observe the rules by which "unconscious" problem solving occurs, they remain outside the realm of scientific discussion. One possible solution to the incubation problem is that standing-back from the problem provides us with some distance from unprofitable but persistent mental sets.

MENTAL SETS

Let us return to problem 1, part c. In order to try to solve this problem, did you seek a pattern of letters that involved cycles and the alphabet? If so, it may be because parts a and b were solved by this approach.

The tendency to respond to a new problem with the same approach that helped solve earlier, similar-looking problems is termed a **mental set.** Mental sets usually make our work easier, but they can mislead us when the similarity between problems is illusory, as in part c of problem 1. But here is a clue: Part c is no alphabet series. Each of the letters in the series *stands* for something. If you can discover what they stand for (that is, discover the rule), you will be able to generate the ninth and tenth letters. (The answer is in Figure 6.8 on page 288.)

Let us now have another look at the possible role of incubation in helping us get around hampering mental sets. Consider the seventh water-jar problem. What if we had tried all sorts of solutions involving the three water jars, and none worked? What if we were then to stand back from this water-jar problem for a day or two? Is it not possible that with a little distance we might suddenly recall a 10, a 7, and a 3—three elements of the problem—and realize that we can arrive at the correct answer by using only two water jars? Our solution might seem too easy, and we might check Table 6.2 cautiously, to make certain that the numbers are there, as remembered. Perhaps our incubation period would have done nothing more than unbind us from the mental set that problem 7 *ought* to be solved by the formula $B - A - 2C$.

While we are discussing mental sets and the water-jar problems, have another look at water-jar problem 6. The formula $B - A - 2C$ will solve this problem. Is that how you solved it? But note also that the problem could have been solved more efficiently by using the formula $A - C$. If the second formula did not occur to you, it may be because of the mental set you acquired from solving the first five problems.

FUNCTIONAL FIXEDNESS

Functional fixedness may also impair our problem-solving efforts. As an example, first ask yourself what a pair of pliers is. Is it a tool for grasping, a paperweight, or a weapon? A pair of pliers could function as any of these, but your tendency to think of them as a grasping tool is fostered by your experience with them. You have probably only used a pair of pliers for grasping things. Functional fixedness is the tendency to think of an object in terms of its name or its familiar usage. Functional fixedness can be similar to a mental set in that it can make it difficult for us to use familiar objects to solve problems in novel ways.

Mental set (1) Readiness to respond to a situation in a set manner. (2) In problem solving, a tendency to respond to a new problem with an approach that was successful with problems that are similar in appearance.

Functional fixedness The tendency to view an object in terms of its name or familiar usage. Creative problem solving often requires conceiving novel functions for familiar objects.

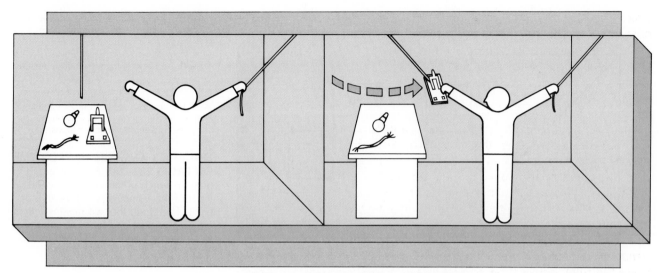

FIGURE 6.7 THE TWO-STRING PROBLEM A person is asked to tie two dangling strings together, but he cannot reach both at once. He is allowed to use any object in the room to help him—including a switch. He can solve the problem by tying the switch to one string and sending it swinging back and forth. Then he grabs the stationary string and catches the moving string when it swings his way. After removing the switch the strings are tied together. Functional fixedness could impede solution of the problem by causing the person to view the switch as electrical equipment only and not as a weight.

In a classic experiment in functional fixedness, Birch and Rabinowitz (1951) placed subjects in a room with electrical equipment, including a switch and a relay, and asked them to solve the Maier two-string problem. In this problem, a person is asked to tie together two dangling strings. But, as shown in Figure 6.7, they cannot be reached simultaneously.

In the experiment, either the switch or the relay can be used as a weight for one of the strings. If the weighted string is sent swinging, the subject can grasp the unweighted string and then wait for the weighted string to come his or her way. Subjects given prior experience with the switch as an electrical device were significantly more likely to use the relay as the weight. Subjects given prior experience with the intended function of the relay were significantly more likely to use the switch as a weight. Subjects given no prior experience with either device showed no preferences for using one or the other as the weight.

You may know that soldiers in survival training in the desert are taught to view insects and snakes as sources of food rather than as pests or threats. But it would be understandable if you chose to show civilian functional fixedness for as long as possible if you were stuck in the desert.

CREATIVITY IN PROBLEM SOLVING

A creative person may be more capable of solving problems to which there are no preexisting solutions, no tried and tested formulas.

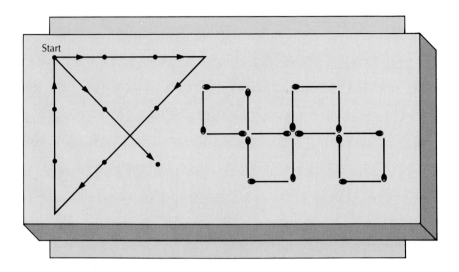

FIGURE 6.8 ANSWERS TO PROBLEMS ON PAGES 282–283 For problem 1C, note that each of the letters is the first letter of the numbers one through eight. Therefore, the two missing letters are *NT,* for *n*ine and *t*en. The solutions to problems 2 and 3 are shown in this illustration.

Creativity is an enigmatic concept. According to Robert Sternberg (1985), we tend to perceive creative people as

being willing to take chances
not accepting limitations; trying to do the impossible
appreciating art and music
being capable of using the materials around them to make unique things
questioning social norms and assumptions
being willing to take an unpopular stand
being inquisitive

A professor of mine once remarked that there is nothing new under the sun, only novel combinations of old elements. To him, the core of creativity was the ability to generate novel combinations of existing elements.

My professor's view of creativity was similar to that of many psychologists—that creativity is the ability to make unusual, sometimes remote associations to the elements of a problem, so that new combinations that meet the goals are generated. An essential aspect of a creative response is the leap from the elements of the problem to the novel solution (Amabile, 1983). A predictable solution is not particularly creative, even if it is difficult to arrive at.

In the two-string problem, the ability to associate a switch or a relay with the quality of weight rather than their intended electronic functions requires some creativity. Tying the switch or relay to the end of the string is a new combination of the familiar elements in the problem, one that meets the requirements of the situation.

Convergent Thinking and Divergent Thinking   According to Guilford (1959; Guilford & Hoepfner, 1971), creativity demands divergent thinking rather than convergent thinking. In **convergent thinking,** thought is limited to present facts as the problem solver tries to narrow thinking to find the best solution. In **divergent thinking,** the problem solver associates more

Creativity The ability to generate novel solutions to problems. A trait characterized by originality, ingenuity, and flexibility.

Convergent thinking A thought process that attempts to narrow in on the single best solution to a problem.

Divergent thinking A thought process that attempts to generate multiple solutions to problems. Free and fluent associations to the elements of a problem.

fluently and freely to the various elements of the problem. The problem solver allows "leads" to run a nearly limitless course to determine whether they will eventually combine as needed. "Brainstorming" is a popular term for divergent thinking when carried out by a group.

Successful problem solving may require both divergent and convergent thinking. At first divergent thinking generates many possible solutions. Convergent thinking is then used to select the most probable solutions and to reject the others.

Factors in Creativity   What factors contribute to creativity? Guilford (1959) has noted that creative people show flexibility, fluency (in generating words and ideas), and originality. Getzels and Jackson (1962) found that creative schoolchildren tend to express rather than inhibit their feelings, and to be playful and independent. Conger and Petersen (1984) concur that creative people tend to be independent and nonconformist. But independence and nonconformity do not necessarily make a person creative. Stereotypes of the creative personality have led to individual exaggerations of nonconformity.

Nevertheless, creative children are often at odds with their teachers because of their independence. Faced with the chore of managing upwards of 30 pupils, teachers too often label quiet and submissive children as "good" children. These studies of creativity may also explain in part why there have been many more male than female artists throughout history, even though Maccoby and Jacklin (1974) found no sex differences in creativity. As Conger and Petersen (1984) point out, traits like independence and nonconformity are more likely to be discouraged in females than in males, because such traits are inconsistent with the passive and compliant social roles traditionally ascribed to females. Because of the women's movement, the numbers of women in the creative arts and sciences are growing rapidly today. In the past the creativity of many girls may have been nipped in the bud.

INTELLIGENCE AND CREATIVITY

Intelligence and creativity sometimes, but not always, go hand in hand. Persons low in intelligence are often also low in creativity, but high intelligence is no guarantee of creativity (Crockenburg, 1972). But it sometimes happens that people of only moderate intelligence excel in creativity, especially in fields like art and music.

A recent Canadian study found that highly intelligent ("gifted") boys and girls aged nine to eleven were as a group more creative than less intelligent children, but not all of the gifted children were more creative than their less intelligent peers (Kershner & Ledger, 1985). The girls in the study were significantly more creative than their male agemates, especially on verbal tasks. Cognitive sex differences will be explored further in Chapter 13.

Tests that measure intelligence are not useful in measuring creativity. As you will see on the following pages, intelligence-test questions usually require convergent thinking to focus in on the answer. On an intelligence

QUESTIONNAIRE

THE REMOTE ASSOCIATES TEST

One aspect of creativity is the ability to freely associate to all aspects of a problem. As noted by psychologist Margaret Matlin, "Creative people can take far-flung ideas and combine them into new associations" (1983, p. 251).

Below are items from the Remote Associates Test, which measures ability to find words that are distantly related to stimulus words.

Directions: For each set of three words, try to think of a fourth word that is related to all three words. For example, the words "rough," "resistance," and "beer" suggest the word "draft," because of the phrases "rough draft," "draft resistance," and "draft beer." The answers are in Appendix B.

Give yourself some time to associate to the items. Before looking up the answers to items you could not answer, why not first let the words "incubate" for a day or two and then come back to them?

1. charming	student	valiant
2. food	catcher	hot
3. hearted	feet	bitter
4. dark	shot	sun
5. Canadian	golf	sandwich
6. tug	gravy	show
7. attorney	self	spending
8. arm	coal	peach
9. type	ghost	story

Source: M. Matlin (1983). *Cognition.* New York: Holt, Rinehart and Winston, p. 252.

test, an ingenious answer that differs from the designated answer is wrong. Tests of creativity are oriented toward determining how flexible and fluent thinking can be. Here, for example, is an item from a test used by Getzels and Jackson (1962) to measure associative ability, a factor in creativity: "Write as many meanings as you can for each of the following words: (a) duck; (b) sack; (c) pitch; (d) fair." Those who write several meanings for each word, rather than only one, are rated as more potentially creative. Those of you who wish to further explore your creativity can turn to the Remote Associates Test in the nearby box.

INTELLIGENCE

What form of life is so adaptive that it can survive in desert temperatures of 120°F, or Arctic climes of −40°F? What form of life can run, walk, climb, swim, live underwater for months on end, and fly to the moon and back? I won't keep you in suspense any longer. Human beings are that form of life. But our naked bodies do not allow us to be comfortable in these temperature extremes. It is not brute strength that allows us to live under-

Intelligence A complex and controversial concept. (1) Defined by David Wechsler as the "capacity . . . to understand the world . . . and . . . resourcefulness to cope with its challenges." (2) Defined operationally as the trait or traits required to perform well on an intelligence test. (From the Latin *inter,* meaning "among," and *legere,* meaning "to choose." Intelligence implies the capacity to make adaptive choices.)

Trait A distinguishing quality or characteristic of personality that is presumed to account for consistency in behavior. (From the Latin *trahere,* meaning "to draw a line.")

Achievement That which is attained by one's efforts and presumed to be made possible by one's abilities. (From the Middle French *achever,* meaning "to finish.")

g Spearman's symbol for general intelligence—a general factor that he believed underlay more specific abilities.

s Spearman's symbol for *specific* or *s factors* that he believed accounted for individual abilities.

Primary mental abilities According to Thurstone, the basic abilities that compose human intelligence.

water or travel to the moon. We attribute our success in adapting to these different conditions, and in challenging our physical limitations, to our **intelligence.**

You have heard about intelligence since you were a young child. At an early age we gain impressions of how intelligent we are as compared to other family members and schoolmates. Expressions like "That's a smart thing to do" and "What an idiot!" are heard each day. We think of some people as "having more" intelligence than others. We associate intelligence with academic success, advancement on the job, and appropriate social behavior. Psychologists and others use intelligence as a **trait** or characteristic in an effort to explain why people do (or fail to do) things that are adaptive and inventive.

Despite our sense of familiarity with the concept of intelligence, intelligence cannot be seen, touched, or measured physically. For this reason, intelligence is subject to various definitions, and ideas and theories about intelligence are some of the most controversial issues found in psychology today.

In this section we discuss various definitions of intelligence. We see how intelligence is measured and examine the determinants of intelligence—heredity and environment.

DEFINING INTELLIGENCE

Psychologists generally distinguish between **achievement** and intelligence. Achievement is what a person has learned, the knowledge and skills that have been gained by experience. Achievement involves specific content areas like English, history, and math. Psychologists use achievement tests to measure what students have learned in academic areas. We would not be surprised to find that a student who has taken Spanish, but not French, would score better on a Spanish than a French achievement test. The strong relationship between achievement and experience seems obvious.

Intelligence is not so easy to define (Green, 1981). Most psychologists would agree that intelligence in some way allows people to achieve in academia. Intelligence, then, has something to do with *learning ability.* But psychologists disagree about what learning ability is and how people acquire it.

Historical Views of Intelligence   In 1904 British psychologist Charles Spearman suggested that the various behaviors we consider intelligent have a common, underlying factor. He labeled this factor **g,** for "general intelligence." He supported this view by noting that people who excel in one area generally show the capacity to excel in others. He noted, however, that even the most capable people seemed more capable in some areas— perhaps music or business or poetry—than in others. For this reason, he also suggested that **s,** or specific factors, accounted for individual abilities.

American psychologist Louis Thurstone (1938) analyzed data from various tests of individual abilities and concluded that Spearman had oversimplified the concept of intelligence. Thurstone's data suggested the presence of seven basic or **primary mental abilities,** instead of a single under-

TABLE 6.3 Louis Thurstone's Primary Mental Abilities

Ability	Brief Description
Spatial ability	Visualizing forms and spatial relationships
Perceptual speed	Grasping perceptual details rapidly, perceiving similarities and differences between stimuli
Numerical ability	Computing numbers
Verbal meaning	Knowing the meaning of words
Memory	Recalling information (words, sentences, etc.)
Word fluency	Thinking of words quickly (rhyming, doing crossword puzzles, etc.)
Reasoning	Deriving rules from examples (as in problems 1a to 1c on page 283), or providing examples of rules and principles

lying trait (see Table 6.3). Thurstone suggested that a person might have high word fluency and be able to think rapidly of words that rhyme, yet not be efficient at solving mathematical problems (Thurstone & Thurstone, 1963).

This view may strike a sympathetic chord in you. Most of us know people who are "good at" math but "poor in" English, and vice versa. Nonetheless, there does seem to be some underlying link between various mental abilities. The data still show that the person with excellent reasoning ability is likely to have a larger-than-average vocabulary and better-than-average numerical ability. There are few, if any, people who exceed 99 percent of the population in one mental ability, yet are exceeded by 80 or 90 percent of the population in others.

David Wechsler, the developer of widely used intelligence tests for adults and children, defined intelligence as a general or "global capacity" (1939, p. 3). Later he described intelligence as the "capacity of an individual to understand the world around him and his resourcefulness to cope with its challenges" (1975, p. 139). Intelligence, to Wechsler, involved both a cognitive representation of the world and effective behavior.

Behavioral Views   Many behaviorally oriented psychologists prefer not to make assumptions about unobservable mental processes and mental abilities. They may prefer to speak about intelligence in terms of verbal skills or the number and quality of responses that are available to an individual in various situations.

An Operational Definition   Edwin Boring, an historian of psychology, once made the offhand remark that intelligence is "the capacity to do well in an intelligence test" (Rice, 1979). This wry definition is quite enough for those who try to avoid some of the controversies about intelligence altogether. They define intelligence *operationally*, in terms of the operations used to measure it. Intelligence, from this perspective, is defined as what is measured in intelligence tests.

Contemporary Conceptions of Intelligence   Psychologist Robert Sternberg and his colleagues (Sternberg et al., 1981; Sternberg, 1982) re-

TABLE 6.4 Factors Involved in Laypersons' and Experts' Conceptions of Intelligence

Laypersons	Experts

1. Practical Problem-Solving Ability
    Reasons logically and well
    Identifies connections among
      ideas
    Sees all aspects of a problem
    Keeps an open mind
2. Verbal Ability
    Speaks clearly and articulately
    Is verbally fluent
    Converses well
    Is knowledgeable about a
      particular field of knowledge
3. Social Competence
    Accepts others for what they are
    Admits mistakes
    Displays interest in the world at
      large
    Is on time for appointments
	1. Verbal Intelligence
	    Displays a good vocabulary
	    Reads with high comprehension
	    Displays curiosity
	    Is intellectually curious
	2. Problem-Solving Ability
	    Able to apply knowledge to
	      problems at hand
	    Makes good decisions
	    Poses problems in an optimal
	      way
	    Displays common sense
	3. Practical Intelligence
	    Sizes up situations well
	    Determines how to achieve goals
	    Displays awareness of world
	      around him or her
	    Displays interest in the world at
	      large
	    Manages self and others
	    Manages one's career

Data adapted from Sternberg et al. (1981, pp. 45–46), and from Wagner & Sternberg (1985, pp. 444, 448).

cently compared laypersons' conceptions of intelligence to those of "experts." Laypersons at the supermarket, waiting for trains, and studying in the library were asked to list behaviors characteristic of intelligence. Experts consisted of psychologists with doctoral degrees who engaged in research in intelligence.

Sternberg found that laypersons and experts have similar views of intelligent behavior. Mathematical analysis showed that each group's conception of intelligence could be broken down into three factors. Each group found that verbal ability and problem-solving ability were crucial to the definition of intelligence. Laypersons also included a factor that Sternberg labeled social competence, however, while experts included a broader category of practical intelligence (see Table 6.4). According to Richard Wagner and Robert Sternberg (1985), practical intelligence in the "real world" includes general aptitudes, formal (school) knowledge, and the abilities to manage oneself, other people, and one's career.

All in all, however, laypersons and experts structured their views of intelligence in similar ways. Although experts may be at odds in their efforts to define intelligence, laypersons apparently understand quite well what behaviors the experts are referring to.

In terms of the cognitive processes we have been discussing in this chapter, then, the people we label as intelligent have good facility with language, are good problem solvers, and are aware of and curious about their worlds.

MEASURING INTELLIGENCE

There may be theoretical disagreements about the nature of intelligence, but thousands of intelligence tests are administered by psychologists and educators every day. The results of these tests are often used to make vital choices about education and careers. First we discuss the *reliability* and *validity* of intelligence tests, and then we discuss a number of individual and group intelligence tests.

RELIABILITY AND VALIDITY

Intelligence is thought to be a relatively stable trait. It does not change much from day to day or week to week. A test that measures intelligence should yield consistent or stable results. The consistency of a means of measurement is known as its **reliability.** Psychologists use statistical techniques, especially the *correlation coefficient,* to study the reliability of tests.

Correlation coefficients and other statistics are explored in Appendix A. Here let us note that a **correlation coefficient** is a number that indicates how strongly two or more things, like height and weight, or taxes and government spending, are related. Correlation coefficients vary from − 1.00 (a perfect negative correlation) to + 1.00 (a perfect positive correlation) (Table 6.5). In order for an intelligence test to be considered reliable, correlations between a group's test results on two separate occasions should be positive and high (about + .90).

There are different ways of showing a test's reliability. **Test-retest reliability** is shown by comparing scores of tests taken on different occasions. The measurement of test-retest reliability may be confused by the fact that people often improve their scores from one occasion to the next, because of increasing familiarity with the testing procedure and the test items. In **split-half reliability,** results on half the items on a test may be correlated with scores from the other half. In **alternate-form reliability,** scores on one form of a test are correlated with scores on another form of the test. Of course, it must be shown that the forms of the test are indeed comparable.

Reliability In psychological tests and measurements, consistency of scores.

Correlation coefficient A number that is a mathematical expression of the relationship between two variables. See Appendix A.

Test-retest reliability A method for determining the reliability of a test by comparing (correlating) test-takers' scores on separate occasions.

Split-half reliability A method for determining the internal consistency of a test by correlating scores attained on half the items with scores attained on the other half of the items.

Alternate-form reliability The consistency of a test as determined by correlating scores attained on one form of the test with scores attained on another form. The Scholastic Aptitude Test (SAT), for example, has many forms.

TABLE 6.5 Interpretations of Some Correlation Coefficients

Correlation Coefficient	Interpretation
+1.00	A perfect positive correlation, as between temperatures on the Fahrenheit scale and temperatures on the centigrade scale
+0.90	High positive correlation, adequate for test reliability
+0.60 to +0.70	Moderate positive correlation, usually adequate for test validity
+0.30	Weak positive correlation, unacceptable for adequate test reliability or validity
0.00	No correlation between variables (no association indicated)
−0.30	Weak negative correlation
−0.60 to −0.70	Moderate negative correlation
−0.90	High negative correlation
−1.00	A perfect negative correlation

Validity In psychological testing, the degree to which a test measures or predicts what it is supposed to measure or predict.

Criterion Standard. Means of making a judgment.

Intelligence quotient (1) Originally, a ratio obtained by dividing a child's score (or "mental age") on an intelligence test by his or her chronological age. (2) Generally, a score on an intelligence test.

IQ Abbreviation for *intelligence quotient*. A score on a test—*not* a trait.

Mental age The accumulated months of credit that a test-taker earns on the Stanford Binet Intelligence Scale.

Standardization The process of determining how a population performs on a psychological test. This process provides data that enable psychologists to interpret individual scores as deviations from a norm.

The **validity** of a test is the degree to which it measures what it is supposed to measure. A valid intelligence test should measure intelligence, not height, musical ability, or interests. We determine whether an intelligence test is valid by correlating the intelligence test scores with an external measure or **criterion** of intelligence. First, we ask what more intelligent people can do that less intelligent people cannot do, and we then find out whether the intelligence test actually predicts that type of behavior, or criterion.

For example, psychologists generally assume that intelligence is one of the factors responsible for academic success. As a result, intelligence test scores have been correlated with school grades, which serve as the external measure of intelligence, or criterion, to see if the scores are valid. Intelligence tests correlate from about +0.60 to +0.70 with school grades (Lavin, 1965; McCall, 1975). This correlation does not approach a perfect positive relationship. This suggests that factors in addition to performance on intelligence tests contribute to academic success. Motivation and adjustment are two of them (Hrncir et al., 1985; Scarr, 1981). Yet most psychologists consider a correlation coefficient of +0.60 to be a reasonably adequate suggestion of validity.

By these standards, many individual and group intelligence tests have adequate reliability and validity. The Stanford-Binet Intelligence Scale (SBIS) and the Wechsler scales for adults and children are the most widely used and well-respected individual intelligence tests. The SBIS and Wechsler scales yield scores called **intelligence quotients,** or **IQs.** Each of them has been carefully developed and revised over the years. Each has been used by thousands of educators to help make decisions about tracking and guiding children. Each has been accused of discriminating against racial minorities like Hispanic and black children, against the foreign-born, and against socially or economically deprived children. We shall examine these and other tests and the controversy surrounding them.

INDIVIDUAL INTELLIGENCE TESTS

The Stanford-Binet Intelligence Scale The SBIS originated through the work of Frenchmen Alfred Binet and Theodore Simon early in this century. The French public-school system sought an instrument that could identify children who were unlikely to profit from the regular classroom setting, so that they could receive special attention. The Binet-Simon scale came into use in 1905. Since that time, it has undergone great revision and refinement (Table 6.6).

The Binet-Simon scale was meant for use with children and yielded a score called a **mental age,** or MA. The ability to solve intellectual problems increases with age, at least through childhood. The MA shows the intellectual level at which a child is functioning. A child with an MA of six is functioning, intellectually, like the average child aged six.

Binet also recognized that the best way to learn how the typical child of a certain age functioned intellectually was to administer his test to thousands of children of different ages. This method of determining standards for performance is termed the **standardization** of a test. Binet determined

Alfred Binet.

TABLE 6.6   Some Items from the First Binet-Simon Scale

Naming objects shown in pictures
Repeating series of numbers (digit span)
Comparing the heaviness of a series of weights; placing them in order from
    lightest to heaviest
Explaining how objects, such as a fly and a butterfly, differ from one another
Drawing designs from memory
Completing sentences with words that have been left out
Constructing sentences including three words that are given by the examiner
Defining abstract words (explaining the meanings of concepts)

SOURCE: Adapted from Willerman (1977).

empirically how many items would be answered correctly by children of different age groups. In taking the test, children earned "months" of credit for each correct answer. Their MA was determined by adding the years and months of credit they attained.

Louis M. Terman of Stanford University adapted the Binet-Simon scale for use with American children. The first version of the *Stanford* Binet Intelligence Scale (SBIS) was published in 1916. The SBIS yielded an intelligence quotient rather than simply an MA, and American educators developed interest in learning the IQs of their pupils.

The IQ reflects the relationship between a child's mental age and actual or **chronological age,** or CA. The IQ is computed by the formula IQ = 100 (Mental Age/Chronological Age), or

$$IQ = \frac{MA}{CA} \times 100$$

According to this formula, a child with an MA of 6 and a CA of 6 would have an IQ of 100. Children who can handle intellectual problems as well as older children will have IQs above 100. For instance, an eight-year-old who does as well on the SBIS as the average ten-year-old will attain an IQ of 125. Children who do not answer as many items correctly as other children of their age will attain MAs that are lower than their CAs. Consequently, their IQ scores will be below 100.

Since adults do not make gains in problem-solving ability from year to year in the same dramatic way children do, the above formula is not used in arriving at their IQ scores. For adults, IQ scores are derived from comparing their performances with those of other adults.

The Wechsler Scales   David Wechsler developed a series of scales for use with adults (Wechsler Adult Intelligence Scale), school-age children (Wechsler Intelligence Scale for Children), and younger children (Wechsler Preschool and Primary Scale of Intelligence). The first two tests have been revised in recent years and are now referred to as the WAIS-R and WISC-R. The Wechsler scales group test questions into a number of separate subtests (such as those shown in Table 6.7). Each subtest measures a different type of intellectual task. In this way the Wechsler scales help the

Empirically By trial or experiment—as opposed to by theoretical deduction.

Chronological age A person's age. (From the Greek *chronos*, meaning "time.")

TABLE 6.7 Subtests from the Wechsler Adult Intelligence Scale (WAIS-R)

Verbal Subtests	Performance Subtests
1. *Information:* "What is the capital of the United States?" "Who was Shakespeare?"	7. *Digit Symbol:* Learning and drawing meaningless figures that are associated with numbers.
2. *Comprehension:* "Why do we have zip codes?" "What does 'A stitch in time saves nine' mean?"	8. *Picture Completion:* Pointing to the missing part of a picture.
3. *Arithmetic:* "If 3 candybars cost 25 cents, how much will 18 candybars cost?"	9. *Block Design:* Copying pictures of geometric designs using multicolored blocks.
4. *Similarities:* "How are good and bad alike?"	10. *Picture Arrangement:* Arranging cartoon pictures in sequence so that they tell a meaningful story.
5. *Digit Span:* Repeating series of numbers forwards and backwards	11. *Object Assembly:* Putting pieces of a puzzle together so that they form a meaningful object
6. *Vocabulary:* "What does canal mean?"	

Items for subtests 1, 2, 3, 4, and 6 are similar but not identical to actual test items.

psychologist study a person's relative strengths and weaknesses, as well as providing a measure of over-all intellectual functioning.

Wechsler described some of his scales as measuring essentially *verbal* tasks, and others as assessing *performance* tasks (see Table 6.7). In general, verbal subtests require knowledge of verbal concepts, while performance subtests require familiarity with spatial-relations concepts. But the two groupings are not necessarily so easily distinguished. For example, the ability to name the object being pieced together in subtest 11, a sign of word fluency and general knowledge as well as of spatial-relations ability, helps the person construct it rapidly. In any event, Wechsler's scales permit the computation of verbal and performance IQs. It is not unusual for nontechnically oriented college students to attain higher verbal than performance IQs.

Wechsler also introduced the concept of the **deviation IQ.** Instead of using mental and chronological ages to compute an IQ, Wechsler examined the distribution of the number of correct answers attained by subjects of different ages. He assigned IQ scores on the basis of how much a person's number of correct answers deviated from the average number of correct answers attained by people of the same age. The average test result at any age level is defined as an IQ score of 100. Wechsler then distributed IQ scores, so that the middle 50 percent of them would fall within the broad average range from 90 to 110.

Most people's IQ scores cluster around the average (see Figure 6.10). Only 5 percent of the population have IQ scores of above 130 or below 70. Table 6.8 indicates the labels that Wechsler assigned to various IQ scores, and the approximate percentages of the population who attain IQ scores at those levels.

Deviation IQ A score on an intelligence test that is derived by calculating how far an individual's score deviates from the norm. On the Wechsler scales, the mean IQ score is defined as 100, and approximately two of three scores fall between 85 and 115.

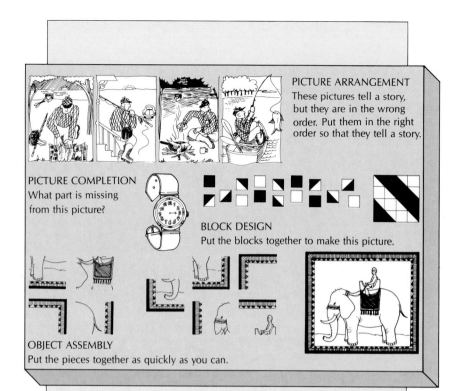

PICTURE ARRANGEMENT
These pictures tell a story, but they are in the wrong order. Put them in the right order so that they tell a story.

PICTURE COMPLETION
What part is missing from this picture?

BLOCK DESIGN
Put the blocks together to make this picture.

OBJECT ASSEMBLY
Put the pieces together as quickly as you can.

FIGURE 6.9 ITEMS RESEMBLING THOSE IN THE PERFORMANCE SUBTESTS OF THE WECHSLER ADULT INTELLIGENCE SCALE

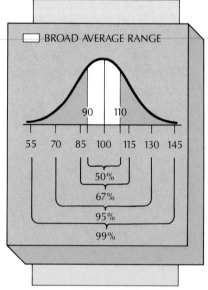

FIGURE 6.10 APPROXIMATE DISTRIBUTION OF IQ SCORES Wechsler defined the deviation IQ so that 50 percent of scores would fall within the broad average range of 90–110. This bell-shaped curve is referred to as a *normal curve* by psychologists. It describes the distribution of many traits, including height.

GROUP INTELLIGENCE TESTS

The SBIS and Wechsler scales are administered to one person at a time. This one-to-one ratio is optimal. It allows the psychologist to facilitate performance (within the limits of the standardized directions) and to observe the test taker closely. In such a setup, psychologists do more than mechanically score answers and compute IQs. They can be alert to factors that impair performance, such as language difficulties, illness, or a noisy or poorly lit room. But large institutions with few psychologists, like the armed forces and the public schools, have also wished to estimate the intellectual functioning of their charges. They have asked psychologists to provide tests that can be administered to large groups of inductees and schoolchildren.

Two such tests were rapidly developed for use with the armed forces: the *Army Alpha,* for people who can read, and the *Army Beta,* for people who cannot read or have problems with English. (See Figure 6.11 for the average IQ scores of people in various occupations, according to the Army Alpha Test.)

Group tests for schoolchildren, first developed during World War I, were administered to four million children by 1921, a couple of years after the war had ended (Cronbach, 1975). At first these tests were heralded as remarkable instruments because of their easing of the huge responsibilities

TABLE 6.8 Variations in IQ Scores

Range of Scores	Percent of Population	Brief Description*
130 and above	2	Very superior
120–129	7	Superior
110–119	16	Bright normal
100–109	25	High average
90–99	25	Low average
80–89	16	Dull normal
70–79	7	Borderline
Below 70	2	Intellectually deficient

*According to David Wechsler.

of school administrators. But as the years passed they came under increasing attack because many administrators relied on them completely to track children. They did not seek other sources of information about the children's abilities and achievements (Reschly, 1981).

THE TESTING CONTROVERSY
The use of intelligence tests has sparked a great deal of controversy because of concerns that test scores are misinterpreted and misused. The severest critics of intelligence testing charge that intelligence tests have been used as instruments of oppression.

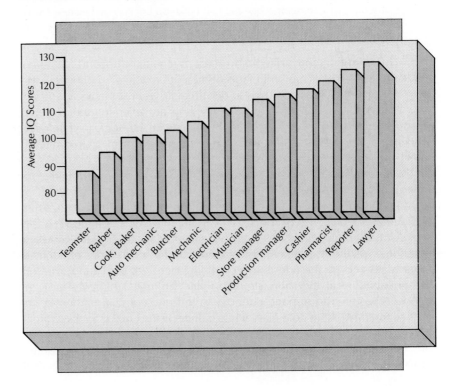

FIGURE 6.11 **AVERAGE IQ SCORES FOR PEOPLE IN VARIOUS OCCUPATIONS, ACCORDING TO THE ARMY ALPHA GROUP INTELLIGENCE TEST**

Some Notes on the Historical Misuse of Intelligence Tests During the early part of this century, intelligence tests were also misused to prevent the immigration of many Europeans and others into the United States (Kamin, 1982; Kleinmuntz, 1982). In 1917, test pioneer H. H. Goddard tested 178 newly arrived immigrants at Ellis Island and claimed that "83 percent of the Jews, 80 percent of the Hungarians, 79 percent of the Italians, and 87 percent of the Russians were feeble-minded" (Kleinmuntz, 1982, p. 333). Apparently it was of little concern to Goddard that these immigrants by and large did not understand English—the language in which the tests were administered.

Such blatant misuse of intelligence tests has led psychologists such as Leon Kamin to complain, "Since its introduction to America, the intelligence test has been used more or less consciously as an instrument of oppression against the underprivileged—the poor, the foreign born, and racial minorities" (in Crawford, 1979, p. 664). Despite these historical problems, group tests are administered to as many as 10 million children a year in the United States, although some states and municipalities no longer permit them to serve as the sole criteria by which students may be placed in special classes (Bersoff, 1981). Let us further explore the modern-day testing controversy. The important questions are whether intelligence tests are still misused and misunderstood.

A girl takes the block design subtest of an individual intelligence test.

The Modern-Day Testing Controversy

I was almost one of the testing casualties. At 15, I earned an IQ test score of 82, three points above the track of the special education class. Based on this score, my counselor suggested that I take up bricklaying because I was "good with my hands." My low IQ, however, did not allow me to see that as desirable.

This brief testimony, offered by black psychologist Robert L. Williams (1974, p. 32), echoes the sentiments of many psychologists. They feel that intelligence tests have been used to discriminate against blacks and others —or at least that the results of intelligence tests are given too much weight in educational decision making. It has been charged that some psychologists who freely admit that intelligence cannot be sensed or measured directly forget this admission as soon as they begin to compare test scores. At such times they make decisions as though an IQ were a person's intelligence instead of a score on a test.

Intelligence tests, critics point out, all measure performances, skills, and achievements. The vocabulary and arithmetic subtests on the Wechsler scales, for example, clearly reflect achievement in language skills and computational ability. It is generally assumed that the broad types of achievement measured by these tests reflect intelligence. Yet we cannot rule out the possibility that they also strongly reflect cultural familiarity with the concepts required to respond correctly to test questions. In particular, the tests seem to reflect middle-class white culture in the United States (Garcia, 1981).

If scoring well on intelligence tests requires a certain type of cultural experience, the tests are said to have a **cultural bias.** Children raised to

Cultural bias A factor hypothesized to be present in intelligence tests that provides an advantage for test-takers from certain cultural or ethnic backgrounds but does not reflect actual intelligence.

⟨?⟩ QUESTIONNAIRE

IT'S A *BITCH*
—THE BLACK INTELLIGENCE TEST
OF CULTURAL HOMOGENEITY, THAT IS

Many have complained that commonly used intelligence tests are culturally biased in favor of middle-class white children. They contain concepts that are more familiar to whites than blacks. What would happen if an intelligence test were culturally biased in favor of black children? Would whites still outperform blacks?

Vocabulary is the single best predictor of overall intelligence test scores. Black psychologist Robert L. Williams (1974) developed an "intelligence test" consisting of 100 words likely to be more familiar to blacks than to whites. Why not try a few items to see how "intelligent" you are?

Instructions: Circle the letter that indicates the correct meaning of the word or phrase.

1. *the bump*
   a. a condition caused by a forceful blow
   b. a suit
   c. a car
   d. a dance
2. *running a game*
   a. writing a bad check
   b. looking at something
   c. directing a contest
   d. getting what one wants from another person or thing
3. *to get down*
   a. to dominate
   b. to travel
   c. to lower a position
   d. to have sexual intercourse
4. *cop an attitude*
   a. leave
   b. become angry
   c. sit down
   d. protect a neighborhood
5. *leg*
   a. a sexual meaning
   b. a lower limb
   c. a white
   d. food

The "correct" answers are: 1–d, 2–d, 3–d, 4–b, 5–a. How did you do? Williams gave the BITCH to 100 white and 100 black adolescents, and the blacks outperformed the whites.

Certainly the BITCH is not a valid intelligence test. It does not predict academic success. But it dramatically highlights the importance of trying to choose test items with which all test takers have had an opportunity to become familiar.

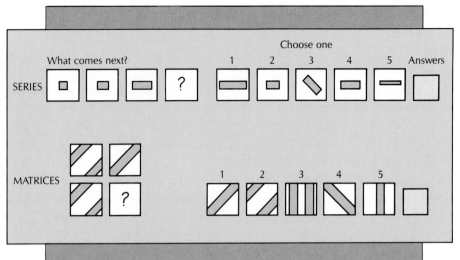

FIGURE 6.12 **SAMPLE ITEMS FROM RAYMOND CATTELL'S CULTURE-FAIR INTELLIGENCE TEST**

Culture-fair Describing a test in which cultural biases have been removed. On such a test, test-takers from different cultural backgrounds would have an equal opportunity to earn scores that reflect their true abilities.

speak Black English in black neighborhoods could be at a disadvantage, not because of differences in intelligence, but because of cultural differences. For this reason, psychologists like Raymond B. Cattell (1949) have tried to construct **culture-fair** intelligence tests. Some culture-fair tests do not rely on language at all. Instead, they evaluate reasoning ability through geometric designs, as shown in Figure 6.12.

Culture-fair tests have not lived up to their promise. First, middle-class white children still outperform blacks on them. Second, they do not appear as valid as other intelligence tests. They do not predict academic success as accurately, and academic success remains the central concern of educators.

There may really be no such thing as a culture-fair or culture-free intelligence test. Motivation to do well, for example, could be considered a cultural factor. Because of socioeconomic differences, black children in America often do not have the same motivation as whites to do well on tests. Highly motivated children attain higher scores on intelligence tests than do less well-motivated children (Zigler & Butterfield, 1968). Even basic familiarity with pencils and paper is a cultural factor. Again, white children in the United States are more likely to be familiar with these materials than are blacks.

THE DETERMINANTS OF INTELLIGENCE

In 1969 Arthur Jensen, an educational psychologist at the University of California, published an article called "How Much Can We Boost IQ and Scholastic Achievement?" in the *Harvard Educational Review*. Filled with statistics, jargon, and 123 pages long, the article gained national visibility because of Jensen's assertion that 80 percent of the variability in IQ scores is inherited—that is, that people differ in intelligence mainly because of genetic differences. This may seem like nothing to get excited about, yet Jensen became the focus of campus demonstrations and was sometimes booed loudly in class. *Why?*

As a group, blacks score about 15 points below whites on intelligence tests (Hall & Kaye, 1980), and Jensen had asserted that this difference was largely genetically determined. If so, the difference could never be decreased.

Protests from the black community were echoed by many whites, including many prominent psychologists and other scientists. Consider this emotional condemnation from behavior geneticist Jerry Hirsch: "It perhaps is impossible to exaggerate the importance of the Jensen disgrace. . . . It has permeated both science and the universities and hoodwinked large segments of government and society" (1975, p. 3).

Crawford (1979) suggested that Jensen's views met with such powerful opposition because they are incompatible with the basic American belief that children can grow up to be whatever they want to be, even President. Crawford cited a statement of this faith which he attributed to Abraham Lincoln: "If my father's son can become President, so can your father's son." (If Lincoln had made this remark today, surely he would have added "or daughter.")

What do psychologists know about the **determinants** of intelligence? What are the roles of heredity and environment?

Consider some of the problems in attempting to decide whether a person's performance on an intelligence test is mainly influenced by nature or nurture, by genetic or environmental factors. For example, if a superior child has superior parents, do we attribute the child's superiority to heredity or to the (presumably enriched) environment provided by these parents? Similarly, if a dull child comes from an impoverished home, do we attribute the dullness to the genetic potential transmitted by the parents or to the lack of intellectual stimulation in the environment?

Determinant A factor that defines or sets limits.

While no research strategy for attempting to ferret out the genetic and environmental determinants of IQ is flawless, a number of ingenious approaches have been devised. It may be that the total weight of the evidence provided through these approaches is instructive.

GENETIC INFLUENCES ON INTELLIGENCE

In considering evidence for genetic influences on intelligence, let us first describe experiments with laboratory animals in order to point up some of the difficulties and shortcomings of research into the determinants of *human* intelligence. Then we shall examine correlational research with human participants.

Selective Breeding of Rats for Maze-Learning Ability   In Chapter 2 we saw that rats have been bred selectively for maze-learning ability. "Maze-bright" parent rats tend to have maze-bright litters, and "maze-dull" parents tend to have maze-dull litters. But, as noted in that chapter, we must be cautious about generalizing such findings to people. The (spatial relations) superiority of the maze-bright rats did not generalize to all types of learning tasks, and it cannot be emphasized too strongly that maze-learning ability in rats is not comparable to the complex groupings of behavior that define human intelligence. However, the experimental technique provides a model worth noting because it cannot be replicated with human subjects.

For ethical, legal, and practical reasons, we cannot specify which people will breed together. Nor can we completely control childhood environments. These facts are fortunate from the standpoints of personal freedom and the dignity of the individual, but they also mean that experiments in selective breeding of people for the characteristic (or characteristics) of intelligence are impossible. Thus, the research on genetic influences in human intelligence must employ different strategies. Two of them involve studies of the relationships between intelligence and degree of kinship, as in the identical-fraternal twin study, and studies of the intelligence of adopted children.

Intelligence and Family Relationship   As explained, it would be unethical and impractical to run experiments in which we selectively breed people on the basis of IQ scores or other factors. Still, we can examine the IQ scores of closely and distantly related people who have been raised together or apart. If heredity is involved in human intelligence, closely related people ought to have more similar IQs than distantly related or unrelated people, even when they are raised separately.

Figure 6.13 shows the results of fifty-two studies of IQ and heredity in human beings, as summarized by the journal *Science*. The lines show the range of correlations of IQ scores for pairs of people, and the mark along each line shows the average correlation for the pairs.

Identical twins develop from one **zygote,** and their heredity is identical. Figure 6.13 shows that the IQ scores of identical twins are more alike than the scores for any other pairs, even when the twins have been reared

Zygote A fertilized egg cell.

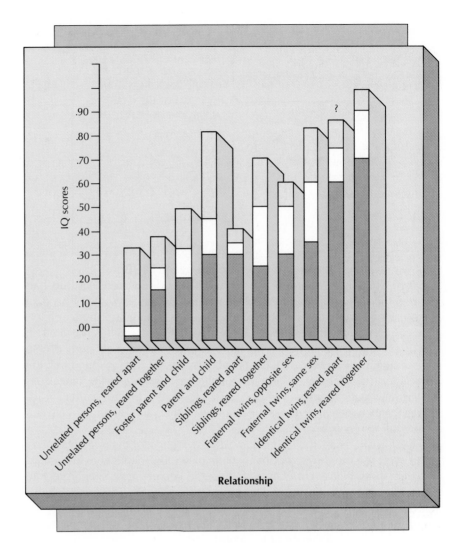

FIGURE 6.13 SUMMARY OF FINDINGS OF 52 STUDIES CONCERNING THE RELATIONSHIP BETWEEN IQ SCORES AND HEREDITY The blue and white bars show the range of correlations for pairs of individuals in each group, and the lines between the blue and white bars show the average correlation within the group. A question mark follows the data concerning "identical twins reared apart," because it was recently revealed that British psychologist Cyril Burt, whose research contributed to these figures, had falsified much of his data. Generally speaking, however, more recent research remains consistent with this summary.

apart. The average correlation is about +.90. Correlations between the IQ scores of fraternal twins (twins that develop from separate zygotes), siblings, and parents and children are generally comparable, as is their degree of genetic relationship. The correlations tend to vary from the upper +.40s to the upper +.50s. Correlations between the IQ scores of children and their biological parents are higher than those between children and foster parents.

Note that there is no relationship between the IQ scores of unrelated people who are raised separately. This is as it should be, since such pairs share neither heredity nor environment. But there is an average correlation in the +.30s for siblings separated at an early age and reared apart. And there is an average correlation in the +.70s for identical twins who were separated at an early age and raised apart.

It must be pointed out that some of the data summarized in the *Science* review are suspect. Some of it was reported by the late British psychologist Sir Cyril Burt. In a scandal of the 1970s, it was discovered that Burt had falsified the names of supposed coresearchers and fudged some of his data to support the view that heredity is the major determinant of human intelligence. However, more recent studies of kinship and intelligence are still consistent with the data shown in Figure 6.13. For instance, a study of 500 pairs of identical and fraternal twins in Louisville, Kentucky, found that the correlations in intelligence between identical twins were in the range suggested for identical twins in Figure 6.13. However, the correlations in intelligence between fraternal twin pairs were the same as those between other siblings (Wilson, 1983).

All in all, these studies provide strong evidence for the role of heredity in IQ scores. Note, however, that genetic pairs (like identical twins) reared together show higher correlations between IQ scores than similar genetic pairs (like other identical twins) who were reared apart. This finding holds for identical twins, siblings, and unrelated people. *For this reason, the same group of studies strongly suggests that the environment also plays an important role in the attaining of IQ scores.*

Studies of the Intelligence of Adoptees A second strategy for exploring genetic influences on human intelligence is to compare the correlations between adopted children and their biological and adoptive parents. Especially when children are separated from their biological parents at early ages, one can argue that strong relationships between their IQ scores and those of their biological parents reflect genetic influences. Strong relationships between their IQ's and those of their adoptive parents would reflect environmental influences.

Several recent studies with one- and two-year-old Colorado children (Baker et al., 1983), Texas children (Horn, 1983), and Minnesota children (Scarr & Weinberg, 1983) all find that there is a stronger relationship between the IQ scores of adopted children and their biological parents than there is with their adoptive parents. The Scarr and Weinberg report concerns black children reared by white adoptive parents, and we shall return to its findings in the section on environmental influences.

It must be concluded that there is a strong genetic influence on intelligence. However, we shall see that there is also a powerful environmental influence.

ENVIRONMENTAL INFLUENCES ON INTELLIGENCE

Studies on environmental influences on intelligence also employ various research strategies. One approach is simply to focus on the situational factors that determine IQ scores. Remember that an IQ is, after all, a score on a test. In some cases, therefore, we need look no further than the testing situation to explain at least part of the discrepancy between the IQ scores of middle-class children and those of children from economically disadvantaged backgrounds.

In one such study, the experimenters (Zigler et al., 1982) simply made children as comfortable as possible during the test. Rather than being cold and "impartial," the examiner was warm and friendly. Care was taken to see that the children understood the directions, and the children's test anxiety seems to have been reduced markedly as a consequence. The children's IQ scores were six points higher than those for a control group treated in a more indifferent manner, and disadvantaged children made relatively greater gains from this procedure. In other words, by doing nothing more than making testing conditions more optimal for *all* test takers, we may narrow the gap between the average IQ scores for whites and blacks.

Other research methods focus on the relationship between IQ scores and early deprivation. For example, undernourished South African children score some twenty IQ points lower than children with adequate diets (Stock & Smythe, 1963). Still others examine the effects of enriched early environments on IQ (and academic achievement). We shall see that even studies of adoptive children provide support for a strong environmental influence.

Back to the Maze-Bright/Maze-Dull Rats   Studies with rats selectively bred for maze-brightness and maze-dullness have also provided evidence for the importance of experience to learning ability.

Cooper and Zubek (1958) provided young rats descended from maze-bright and maze-dull parents with different early environments. Some rats from each group were raised in a dull, featureless environment. Others were reared in rat amusement parks with ramps, ladders, wheels, and toys. Rats raised in the impoverished environment did poorly on maze-learning tasks in adulthood, regardless of their parentage. But rats raised in the "amusement park" later learned mazes relatively rapidly. An enriched early environment caused the performances of rats with maze-dull parents to move closer to those of rats with maze-bright parents.

The Effects of the Early Environment on Children   Hundreds of studies show that the early environment of the child can lead to higher IQ scores and academic achievement. For example, Ronald McGowan and Dale Johnson (1984) found that good parent-child relationships and the maternal encouragement of independence were both positively correlated with Mexican-American children's IQ scores by the age of three. Robert

Bradley and Bettye Caldwell (1984) found that several family environment factors during the first two years of life were correlated with IQ scores at the ages of three and four and a half, and with achievement test scores during the first grade. These factors included the amount of language stimulation received by the child; parental emotional support; the number of stimulating toys and objects available to the child; the extent of home organization and safety; and the variety of experiences outside the home provided for the child.

Head Start Head Start programs are government-funded efforts to provide preschoolers with enriched early environments in order to increase their readiness for elementary school. Head Start programs were instituted in the 1960s and focus on the cognitive development and development of academically related skills of economically disadvantaged children. Children in these programs are exposed to letters and words, numbers, books, exercises in drawing, pegs and pegboards, puzzles, toy animals, dolls, and a host of other materials and activities that most middle-class children can take for granted.

Studies of Head Start programs also suggest that environmental enrichment can enhance learning ability in people (Darlington et al., 1980; Zigler & Berman, 1983). In a New York City study, for example, adolescent boys who had participated in Head Start attained average SBIS scores of 99. Boys similar in background, but who did not have preschooling, earned an average SBIS score of 93 (Palmer, 1976). In another study, twenty black children were provided with enriched day care from the age of six weeks (Heber et al., 1972). By the age of five, their IQ scores averaged about 125, as compared with an average of 95 for children from similar backgrounds who did not receive day care. Children whose IQ scores were initially lowest made the greatest gains in these programs (Zigler & Valentine, 1979).

A number of years ago there was concern that the gains of Head Start preschoolers tended to evaporate during the elementary school years. By the end of second or third grade, the performance of these children often seemed to drop back to those of peers who had not had the benefits of Head Start. However, recent studies that carefully compare the competence of Head Start graduates to that of children who were matched for IQ scores and racial and cultural variables show that Head Start children do appear to make significant and lasting intellectual gains (Lazar & Darlington, 1982). Ten years or so later, Head Start children are less likely to have been left back or placed in classes for slow learners. Head Start children outperform peers on achievement tests and are eventually significantly more likely to be graduated from high school.

And Back to the Studies of Adopted Children The Minnesota adoption studies reported by Scarr and Weinberg, as noted, suggest a powerful genetic influence on intelligence. But the same studies also suggest the importance of environmental influences. Black children who were adopted before the age of one by white parents who were above average in income and education showed IQ scores some fifteen to twenty-five points higher than those attained by black children raised by their natural parents (Scarr

HEAD START Preschoolers placed in Head Start programs have been shown to make dramatic increases in readiness for elementary school and in IQ scores.

& Weinberg, 1976). Still, the adoptees' average IQ scores, about 109, remained somewhat below those of their adoptive parents' natural children, which were about 115 (Scarr & Weinberg, 1977). Even so, the presumably enriched early environment appeared to close much of the gap between the scores of blacks and whites.

In sum, there seems to be ample evidence that *both* heredity and environment influence intelligence (Plomin & DeFries, 1980). Heredity provides the physiological potential for intelligent behavior. An impoverished environment may prevent some from living up to their potential, but an enriched environment encourages others to wring every last drop from their potential, minimizing any differences in heredity.

Perhaps we need not be concerned with "how much" of a person's IQ is due to heredity and how much is due to environment. Psychology has traditionally supported the dignity of the individual. Therefore, it might be more appropriate for us to try to identify children *of all races* whose environments seem to place them at high risk for failure to develop their potential, and then do what we can to enrich these environments.

SUMMARY

1. Language is the communication of thoughts and feelings through symbols that are arranged according to rules of grammar. Language has the properties of semanticity, productivity, and displacement.

2. Apes have been taught to use symbols to communicate, but it seems that only people have an intuitive grasp of grammar and can speak.

3. The basic components of language include phonology, morphology, syntax, and semantics. Phonology is the study of the basic sounds of a language. English has about forty-six basic sounds, or phonemes.

4. Morphemes are the smallest units of meaning in a language. Morphemes consist of one or more phonemes pronounced in a particular order. Morphemes such as *s* and *ed* tacked on to the ends of nouns and verbs are grammatical markers or inflections.

5. Syntax is the system of rules that determines how words are strung together into sentences.

6. Semantics concerns the meanings of a language. The surface structure of a sentence refers to its superficial construction, while its deep structure refers to the underlying meaning.

7. Newborn children cry and begin to coo by about two months. Babbling, the first vocalizations that have the sound of speech, appears at about six months and contains phonemes found in many languages. Babbling is innate, although it is influenced by learning.

8. Children speak their first words at about a year, and early utterances are telegraphic. Two-word telegraphic utterances appear toward the end of the second year. There are different types of two-word utterances, and their sequence of development is consistent among children who speak different languages.

9. Young children engage in overextension and overregularization. The "errors" made in overregularizing indicate a grasp of the rules of grammar.

10. Many theories, including learning theory and psycholinguistic theory, attempt to account for language development. Classical conditioning may be involved in children's learning to associate words with objects, events, and situations. A word may be a CS for an object (US). Reinforcement increases the frequency of language-related behaviors and shows children when they have made desired verbal responses. Children also imitate the speech they observe parents and others using.

11. Learning theory cannot account for the child's apparent intuitive grasp of syntax and grammar. Psycholinguistic theory asserts that some sort of neural prewiring (a "Language Acquisition Device") underlies these human abilities.

12. Thought is possible without language, but language facilitates thought. According to the linguistic-relativity hypothesis, language structures (and limits) the way in which we perceive the world. Critics argue that a vocabulary may suggest the concepts deemed important by the users of a language, but does not prevent users from making distinctions for which there are no words.

13. Concepts are symbols that stand for groups of objects, events, or ideas that have common properties. Words are concepts, but not all concepts correspond to words. Concepts permit us to generalize without experiencing each instance of the concept. Some concepts contain, or are superordinate to, others.

14. Concepts may be formed through presentation of positive and negative instances, or through explanation using other concepts. People also actively seek to acquire new concepts through hypothesis testing.

15. Problem solving involves stages of preparation, production, and evaluation. First we familiarize ourselves with the elements of the problem. Then we try to produce alternate solutions. Finally, we evaluate whether a solution has met our goals.

16. Algorithms are specific procedures for solving problems (such as formulas) that will work invariably, so long as they are applied correctly. Heuristics are rules of thumb that help us simplify and solve problems. Heuristics are less reliable than algorithms, but they allow us to solve problems more rapidly when they are effective.

17. When we cannot find a solution to a problem, distancing ourselves from the problem sometimes allows the solution to "incubate." Incubation may permit the breaking down of misleading mental sets.

18. A mental set is the tendency to solve a new problem in ways in which similar problems were solved in the past. Functional fixedness is the tendency to perceive an object in terms of its intended function or name, and can prevent novel use of familiar objects.

19. Creativity is the ability to make unusual and sometimes remote associations to the elements of a problem in order to generate new combinations that meet the goals. Creative people show flexibility, fluency, and independence. There is only a moderate relationship between creativity and intelligence.

20. Achievement is what a person has learned. Intelligence is presumed to underlie achievement, and has been defined by Wechsler as "capacity . . . to un-derstand the world . . . and . . . resourcefulness to cope with its challenges." Spearman believed that a common factor, g, underlay all intelligent behavior, but that people also have specific abilities, or s factors. Thurstone suggested that there are seven primary mental abilities, including word fluency and numerical ability. Laypersons see intelligence as involving problem-solving ability, verbal ability, and socially appropriate behavior.

21. Intelligence tests must be reliable and valid, features that are expressed in terms of correlation coefficients. Reliability is the consistency of a test. Validity is the degree to which a test measures an external criterion—that which it is supposed to measure. Validity studies typically correlate intelligence with academic success.

22. Intelligence tests yield scores called intelligence quotients, or IQs. The Stanford-Binet Intelligence Scale, originated by Alfred Binet, derives IQ scores by dividing children's mental age scores by their chronological ages, then multiplying by 100.

23. The Wechsler scales use deviation IQs, which are derived by comparing a person's performance to that of age-mates. Wechsler scales contain verbal and performance subtests.

24. Intelligence test scores reflect motivation to do well and adjustment in the school setting as well as learning ability. Some psychologists argue that intelligence tests are culturally biased in favor of middle-class white children, and efforts have been made to develop culture-fair or culture-free tests. However, culture-fair tests are weaker predictors of academic success.

25. Evidence from kinship studies, adopted-away studies, and other sources suggests that both heredity and environment are determinants of intelligence. Evidence from studies of compensatory-education programs (such as Head Start) shows that enrichment of the child's early environment can narrow the IQ gap between children of lower socioeconomic status and middle-class backgrounds.

TRUTH OR FICTION REVISITED

Psychologists have been able to teach chimpanzees and gorillas how to use sign language.

True—at least up to a point. Apes have been taught to use signs in certain situations, but questions remain as to whether their signing reliably shows features of language such as semanticity, productivity, and grasp of syntax.

Apes cannot speak because they do not have vocal tracts in their throats.

False. Apes have rather human-appearing vocal tracts. Perhaps they are not neurologically prewired to speak.

Deaf children do not babble.

False, they do. Babbling appears to be innate.

Black English lacks systematic rules of grammar.

False. The syntax of Black English is reliable and complex.

The fact that a two-year-old says "Daddy goed away" instead of "Daddy went away" shows that the child does not yet understand rules of English grammar.

False. It shows that the child does understand rules for forming the past tense. Here, however, the child is overregularizing an irregular verb.

Thought is not possible without language.

False. But language permits more efficient thinking. Language enables us to manipulate words that stand for concepts.

Dogs can learn the concepts of roundness and squareness.

True. Through operant conditioning, dogs will learn to respond to round or square shapes as discriminative stimuli. However, they show no evidence of understanding that words stand for concepts.

The only way to solve a problem is to keep plugging away at it.

False. When a persistent but unprofitable mental set impedes our problem-solving ability, it may be helpful to stand back from the problem for a while and allow the elements of the problem to "incubate." In this way the solution sometimes comes to us "in a flash."

It may be boring, but the most efficient way to solve a problem is to use the tried and tested formula.

False. It is frequently more efficient to cast about for heuristic devices.

A person's "IQ" is the same thing as his or her intelligence.

False. An IQ is an intelligence quotient, that is, a score on an intelligence test. A person's intelligence is assumed to be a trait of that person.

There is no such thing as an unbiased intelligence test.

This is most likely true. Adequate performance reflects motivation, adjustment, and basic familiarity with objects like pencils and paper, as well as intelligence.

High intelligence runs in families.

Not necessarily—it is accurate to say that high *IQs* run in families, but IQs are scores on intelligence tests, not intelligence per se. Families share heredity, but family members are also generally reared in similar environments.

OUTLINE

Motivation and Emotion

TRUTH OR FICTION?

- One out of five American adults is obese.
- Overweight people are more sensitive to stomach pangs than are normal-weight people.
- Eating salty pretzels can make you thirsty.
- "Getting away from it all" by going on a vacation from all sensory input for a few hours is relaxing.
- If quarterbacks get too "psyched up" for a big game, their performance on the field may flounder.
- A strong need to get ahead is the most powerful predictor of success in climbing the corporate ladder.
- Misery loves company.
- A frustrated need for power can lead to high blood pressure.
- You may be able to fool a lie detector by squiggling your toes.
- Romantic love is found in every culture in the world.
- Taking a date to a horror film or for a roller coaster ride may stimulate feelings of passion.

When is the last time you came face to face with a tarantula, a laser beam, or an alien from outer space? Actually, if you have been to a movie lately, it may not have been that long ago at all: *Star Wars, Raiders of the Lost Ark, Romancing the Stone, First Blood, Star Trek, Close Encounters, Indiana Jones and the Temple of Doom, Octopussy, Conan the Destroyer*. In adventure films characters like Rambo, James Bond, and Indiana Jones have been pitted against snakes, tarantulas, alligators, mythical monsters, automatic rifles, knives, swords, helicopter gunships, nuclear weapons, laser beams, crazed cultists, floods, hurricanes, blizzards, airplane crashes, shipwrecks, cosmic forces, international forces, occult forces—forces of every flavor and every size.

Most of us lead rather orderly lives, so how do we account for the huge success of these adventure films at the box office? What motivates us to flock to the audience of every film from *Gremlins* to *Goonies?*

We do not have the final answer to this question. But here are some speculations that have been advanced by psychologists, religious leaders, politicians, film critics, and your friendly neighborhood bartender:

Life is filled with vague anxieties and persistent pressures. Adventure films provide us with a temporary focus for our fears, anxieties, and frustrations.

Audiences can purge their aggressive impulses by enjoying conflicts in which other people are involved.

We are seeking coping strategies. We learn how to deal with our own frustrations and conflicts by observing the heroes and the heroines.

Adventure films make our own problems seem trivial.

Adventure films heighten awareness of the possibilities of life, giving us hope that we may someday find ourselves in exotic situations.

Most of us lead sedentary lives with uncomfortably low levels of arousal. Adventure films raise our arousal to more optimal levels, so that we feel full of vim and vigor.

Afterward, our dates may interpret their high levels of arousal from the movie as attraction to us.

We have an instinctive drive to throw away money.

We're grateful it's not happening to us.

Harrison Ford is cute.

They're fun.

The psychology of motivation is concerned with the *whys* of behavior. Why do we attend adventure films? Why do we eat and drink? Why do some of us ride motorcyles at breakneck speeds? Why do we try new things or strive to get ahead?

In this chapter we explore motivation and the closely related topic of emotion. Adventure films give rise to powerful emotional responses, and it may be that the expectation of these responses partly motivates our flocking to the theater in droves.

Let us begin with a few basic definitions. Then we shall discuss various theoretical perspectives on motivation and conclude that each has its limitations. We shall explore physiological drives, stimulus motives, and social motives. We shall pay some special attention to obesity (and what to do about it) and to the motives that lure us to—and keep us in—the work place. Finally, we shall explore various theories of emotional activation and examine a number of emotions more closely, including that most idealized human emotion—love.

MOTIVES, NEEDS, DRIVES, AND INCENTIVES

The word motive derives from the Latin *movere,* meaning "to move." **Motives** can be defined as hypothetical states within organisms that activate behavior and propel the organisms toward goals. Why do we say "hypothetical states?" This is because motives are not seen and measured directly; as are so many other psychological concepts, they are inferred from behavior. Psychologists assume that behavior does not occur at random. We assume that behavior is caused; the behavior of organisms is assumed to be largely caused by motives. *Needs, drives,* and *incentives* are closely related concepts.

The term **need** has been used in at least two different ways by psychologists. We speak both of physiological needs and psychological needs. Certain physiological needs must be met if we are to survive. Such physiological needs include the needs for oxygen, food, drink, pain avoidance, proper temperature, and the elimination of waste products. Some physiological needs, like hunger and thirst, are states of physical deprivation. For instance, when we have not eaten or drunk for a while, we develop needs for food and water. We speak of the body as having needs for oxygen, fluids, calories, vitamins, minerals, and so on.

Psychological needs include needs for achievement, power, self-esteem, social approval, and belonging, among others. Psychological needs differ from physiological needs in two important ways: First, psychological needs are not necessarily based on states of deprivation; a person with a strong need for achievement may have a history of consistent success. Second, psychological needs may be acquired through experience, or learned, whereas physiological needs reside in the physical basis of the organism. Since our biological makeups are similar, we would assume that people share similar physiological needs. And since our learning experiences differ, we would expect that people differ markedly in their psychological needs. In the section on social motives, we shall see that this indeed is the case.

Needs are said to give rise to **drives.** Depletion of food gives rise to the hunger drive, and depletion of liquids gives rise to the thirst drive. Physiological drives are the psychological counterparts of physiological needs. When we have gone without food and water our bodies may *need* these substances; however, our *experience* of drives of hunger and thirst is psychological in nature. Drives arouse us to action. Our drive levels tend to increase with the length of time we have been deprived. We are usually more highly aroused by the hunger drive when we have not eaten for several hours than when we have not eaten for, say, five minutes.

Motive A hypothetical state within an organism that propels the organism toward a goal. (From the Latin *movere,* meaning "to move.")

Need A state of deprivation.

Drive A condition of arousal in an organism that is associated with a need. The psychological correlate of a need.

Our psychological needs for approval, achievement, and belonging also give rise to drives. We can be driven to get ahead in the world of business just as surely as we can be driven to eat. For many of us the drives for achievement and power consume our daily lives.

An **incentive** is an object, person, or situation perceived as capable of satisfying a need or as desirable for its own sake. Money, food, a sexually attractive person, social approval, and attention all can act as incentives that motivate behavior. Needs and incentives can interact to influence the strength of drives. Strong needs combined with enticing incentives create the most powerful drives. Even a person who has just eaten may be tempted by a chocolate dessert. A colleague with whom I lunch once said, "That pie looks so good it creates its own drive." A rat will run down a maze more rapidly when it whiffs Limburger cheese than when it has learned to expect Purina Rat Chow. The Limburger cheese acts as an incentive that heightens the hunger drive. A dog will eat steak more rapidly than it will eat Purina Dog Chow. I'll show that I have nothing against the Purina folks by adding that you are probably more motivated to buy Purina Dog Chow when it is on a limited-time-only, half-price sale. That is, you may respond to the financial *incentive*.

Let us now turn our attention to theoretical perspectives on motivation. We shall see that psychologists and others have spawned very different views of the motives that propel us.

Incentive An object, person, or situation perceived as capable of satisfying a need. (From the Latin *in-*, meaning "in," and *canere*, meaning "to sing.")

Instinct An inherited disposition to activate specific behavior patterns that are designed to reach certain goals.

Ethologist (ee-THOLL-oh-jist). A scientist who studies the behavior patterns characteristic of different species. (From the Greek *ethos*, meaning "disposition" or "character.")

Fixed-action pattern An instinct; abbreviated *FAP*.

Releaser In ethology, a stimulus that elicits a FAP.

THEORETICAL PERSPECTIVES ON MOTIVATION

While psychologists may agree that it is important to understand why people and lower animals do things, they do not agree as to the nature of their motives. Let us have a brief look at three theoretical perspectives on motivation: instinct theory, drive reductionism, and self-actualization.

INSTINCT THEORY

Animals are born with preprogramed tendencies to behave in certain ways in certain situations. Birds reared in isolation from other birds will build nests during the mating season even when they have never observed another bird build a nest (or, for that matter, seen a nest). Siamese fighting fish reared in isolation will assume stereotypical threatening positions and attack other males when they are introduced into their tanks.

Behaviors such as these are characteristic of particular species ("species-specific") and do not rely on learning. They are labeled **instincts**—inherited dispositions that activate specific behavior patterns that appear designed to reach certain goals. Spiders spin webs and bees "dance" to communicate the location of a food source to other bees. All this activity is inborn; it is genetically transmitted from generation to generation.

Ethologists refer to instincts as instinctive **fixed-action patterns** (or FAPs). FAPs occur under certain environmental conditions, which ethologists refer to as **releasers.** As noted in Chapter 3, male members of many

A FIXED-ACTION PATTERN In the presence of another male, the Siamese Fighting Fish assumes an instinctive threatening stance in which the fins and gills are extended. If neither threatening male retreats, there will be conflict.

species become sexually aroused when they perceive pheromones secreted by females. Pheromones are releasers of the FAP of sexual response.

At the turn of the century, psychologists William James (1890) and William McDougall (1908) argued that people have various instincts that not only lead to self-survival but also to social behavior. James asserted that we have social instincts such as love, sympathy, and modesty, and McDougall catalogued 12 "basic" instincts, including hunger, sex, and self-assertion. Other psychologists put together longer lists.

The psychoanalyst Sigmund Freud also used the term *instincts* to refer to physiological needs within people. As we shall see in Chapter 9, Freud believed that instincts such as those for food, sex, and aggression give rise to *psychic energy* which is perceived as feelings of tension. Tension acts as a psychological drive that activates us to restore ourselves to a calmer, resting state. However, the behavior patterns we use to reduce the tension are largely learned. Freud also believed that people are swayed by conflicting life and death instincts that explained, at least to Freud, how it is possible for the human species to be so loving and so murderous.

It is of interest that the psychoanalytic views of Sigmund Freud coincided reasonably well with those of a group of learning theorists who presented a drive-reduction theory of learning.

DRIVE-REDUCTION THEORY

In the last chapter, rewards were defined as pleasant events that increase the frequency of behavior. In this chapter we ask the question, What's so pleasant about rewards?

According to **drive-reduction theory,** as framed by psychologist Clark Hull at Yale University some forty to fifty years ago, rewards are pleasant because they reduce drives. Hull argued that **primary drives** such as hunger, thirst, and pain trigger arousal (tension) and activate behavior, and that we learn responses that partially or completely reduce the drives. Through association, we also learn **acquired drives.** For example, we may acquire a drive for money because money is associated with food and drink, with attaining homes that enable us to escape predators and extremes of temperature, and so on. We may acquire drives for social approval and affiliation because other people, and their good will, also help us to reduce primary drives, especially when we are infants. In all cases, tension reduction is the goal.

HUMANISTIC THEORY

Humanistic psychologists, particularly Abraham Maslow, have noted that the instinct and drive-reduction theories of motivation are distorted by being basically defensive in nature. Instinct and drive-reduction theories suggest that all human behavior occurs in a rather mechanical fashion and is aimed toward survival and tension reduction. As a humanist, Maslow asserted that behavior can also be motivated by the conscious desire for personal growth. Humanists note that people will tolerate pain, hunger, and many other sources of tension in order to achieve what they perceive as personal fulfillment.

Abraham Maslow and the Hierarchy of Needs Maslow was fond of asking graduate students, "How many of you expect to achieve greatness in your careers?" He would prod them to extend themselves, because he believed that people are capable of doing more than responding to drives. Maslow believed that we are separated from lower animals by our capacity for **self-actualization,** or self-initiated striving to become whatever we believe we are capable of being. In fact, Maslow saw self-actualization to be as essential a human need as hunger.

Maslow (1970) organized human needs into a **hierarchy** from physiological needs, like hunger and thirst, through self-actualization (see Figure 7.1.) He believed that our lives would naturally travel up through this hierarchy, so long as we did not encounter insurmountable social or environmental hurdles. Maslow was optimistic about human nature. Whereas some psychologists believed in aggressive instincts, Maslow believed that people behaved antisocially only when their needs were frustrated, particularly their needs for love and acceptance.

Maslow's needs hierarchy includes:

1. *Physiological needs:* hunger, thirst, elimination, warmth, fatigue, pain avoidance, sexual release.
2. *Safety needs:* protection from the environment through housing and clothing, security from crime and financial hardship.
3. *Love and belongingness needs:* love and acceptance through intimate relationships, social groups, and friends. Maslow believed that in a gen-

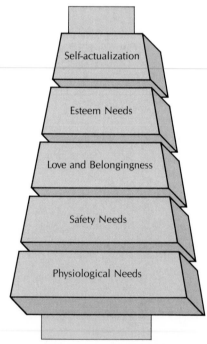

FIGURE 7.1 **MASLOW'S HIERARCHY OF NEEDS** Maslow believed that we progress toward higher psychological needs once basic survival needs have been met. Where do you fit in this picture?

A CLOSER LOOK

ARE YOU A SELF-ACTUALIZER?

Where do you stand in your journey up through Maslow's hierarchy of needs? Are you still literally hungry? Are you seeking security? Are you searching for acceptance, competence, and prestige? Or are you knocking on the door of self-actualization?

Maslow (1971) identified eight characteristics of self-actualizing people. How many of them describe you?

Experiencing life in the present, the here and now. Neither focusing excessively on past pleasures nor wishing days away while rushing toward future goals.

Making growth choices rather than fear choices. Taking reasonable risks to develop your unique potential.

Getting to know yourself. Looking inward, searching for your talents and values.

Striving toward honesty in interpersonal relationships. Stripping away the game playing and social façades that block the development of intimacy.

Becoming self-assertive, self-expressive. Maslow writes that the self-actualizer "dares to listen to himself . . . at each moment in life, and to calmly say, 'No, I don't like such and such'" (1971, p. 47).

Striving toward new goals. Becoming the best you can be.

Involving yourself in meaningful, rewarding activities. By doing so we may have "peak experiences"—brief moments of joy and fulfillment.

Being open to new experiences. Being willing to change opinions or to try new paths.

erally well-fed society, like ours, much frustration stemmed from failure to meet needs at this level.

4. *Esteem needs:* achievement, competence, approval, recognition, prestige, status.
5. *Self-actualization:* fulfillment of our unique potentials. For many individuals, self-actualization involves needs for cognitive understanding (novelty, exploration, knowledge) and aesthetic experience (music, art, poetry, beauty, order).

EVALUATION

Instinct theory has been criticized as an explanation of human behavior, because it tends to yield circular explanations of behavior. If we say that mothers love and care for their children because of a maternal instinct, and then we take maternal care as evidence for such an instinct, we have come full circle. Unfortunately, we have explained nothing; we have only repeated ourselves.

Instincts are also species-specific; that is, they give rise to stereotyped behaviors (FAPs) in all members of a species (or, perhaps, they apply to all male or to all female adults). There is so much variation in human behavior that it seems unlikely that much of it is instinctive. Consider William James's notion that sympathy is an instinct. Many people are cruel and cold-hearted; are we to assume that they somehow possess less of this instinct? If so, this assumption is incompatible with the definition of the instinct.

Drive-reduction theory appears to apply in many situations involving physiological drives, such as hunger and thirst, but it runs aground when we consider evidence that we often act to increase, rather than decrease, the tensions acting upon us. Even when hungry we sometimes go to lengthy efforts to prepare a meal rather than snack, when the snack would reduce the hunger drive just as well. We drive fast cars, ride roller coasters, and parachute-jump for sport—all activities that heighten rather than decrease arousal. We seek novel ways of doing things, because of the stimulation they afford, shunning the tried and true, although the tried and true will reliably lead to tension reduction. Later in the chapter we shall see that psychologists have also theorized the existence of so-called stimulus motives, which surmount the limitations of drive-reduction theory.

Critics of Maslow argue that there is too much individual variation for the hierarchy of motivation to apply to everyone. Some people whose physiological, safety, and love needs are met show little interest in achievement and recognition. Others seek distant, self-actualizing goals while exposing themselves to great danger. And some artists, musicians, and writers devote themselves fully to their art, even at the price of a struggle with poverty.

In sum, it may well be that none of the traditional ways of viewing motivation can fully account for the complexity of human behavior. Instinct theory applies to many species-specific behaviors, but not to the diversity of behavior that characterizes the human experience. Drive-reduction theory appears to apply to our response to physiological drives, but even here there are exceptions. While the humanists point out that motives among humans can be growth-oriented rather than defensive, there is also too much human variation for humanistic theory to be considered universal. It remains for future psychologists to integrate all aspects of human motivation into a single, satisfying theory. Nevertheless, there is a wealth of research concerning various types of motivated behavior. Let us first consider drives that arise from physiological needs; then we shall turn our attention to stimulus motives and social motives.

PHYSIOLOGICAL DRIVES

Physiological needs give rise to **physiological drives**—aroused conditions within the organism that activate behavior that will reduce these needs. Because physiological drives are unlearned, they are also referred to as primary drives. Although sexual behavior leads to survival of the species rather than survival of the individual, sex is also a primary drive.

Primary drives are inborn, but the *behavior* that people use to satisfy primary drives is strongly influenced by learning. Eating meat or fish, drinking coffee or tea, kissing lips or rubbing noses are all learned preferences.

Homeostasis   Physiological drives seem to operate largely according to principles of drive-reduction theory. Certain mechanisms in the body are triggered when we are in a state of deprivation. These mechanisms then motivate us, through sensations like hunger, thirst, and cold, to act to restore the prior balance. The bodily tendency to maintain a steady state is called **homeostasis.**

Homeostasis works much like a thermostat. When the room temperature drops below the set point, the heating system is triggered. The heat stays on until the set point is restored. Psychologists in this century have

Physiological drives Unlearned drives with a biological basis, such as hunger, thirst, and avoidance of pain.

Homeostasis (home-me-oh-STAY-sis). The tendency of the body to maintain a steady state, such as of body temperature or level of sugar in the blood. (From the Greek *homos*, meaning "same," and *stasis*, meaning "standing.")

Satiety (suh-TIE-uh-tee). The state of being satisfied. Fullness.

Sham False, pretended. (A variation of the word "shame.")

Hypothalamus A pea-sized bundle of nuclei beneath the thalamus in the brain that is involved in the regulation of body temperature and a number of drives, including hunger, thirst, and sex; see Chapter 2.

learned that the homeostatic systems of the body involve fascinating interactions between physiological and psychological processes.

In this section we explore the drives of hunger and thirst. Pain as a source of motivation was discussed in Chapter 3, and sexual motivation is discussed in Chapter 13.

HUNGER

Some of us may bounce up and down in weight because of cycles of overeating and dieting, but for most of us body weight remains remarkably constant over the years (Keesey, 1980). What are the body mechanisms that regulate the hunger drive? What psychological processes are at work? Why do many of us continue to eat when we have already supplied our bodies with the needed nutrients?

The Mouth Let us begin with the mouth—an appropriate choice since we are discussing eating. The acts of chewing and swallowing provide some sensations of **satiety.** If they did not, we might eat for a long time after we had taken in enough food, because it takes the digestive tract time to metabolize food and provide signals to the brain by way of the bloodstream.

In classic **sham** feeding experiments with dogs, a tube was implanted in the animals' throats, so that any food swallowed fell out of the body. Even though no food arrived at the stomach, the animals stopped feeding after a brief period (Janowitz & Grossman, 1949). However, they resumed feeding sooner than animals whose food did reach the stomach. Let us proceed to the stomach, too, to search for further regulatory factors in hunger.

Stomach Contractions An empty stomach will lead to stomach contractions that we call hunger pangs, but these pangs are not as influential as had once been thought. People and animals whose stomachs have been removed will still regulate food intake to maintain a normal weight level.

This finding led to the discovery of many other regulatory mechanisms, including blood sugar level, the hypothalamus, even receptors in the liver.

Blood Sugar Level When we are deprived of food, the level of sugar in the blood drops. The deficit is communicated to the **hypothalamus,** a small bundle of nuclei near the middle of the brain (see Chapter 2) involved in regulating hunger, the sex drive, body temperature, and other functions. The drop in blood sugar apparently indicates that we have been burning energy and need to replenish it by eating.

Let us examine evidence that suggests that the brain may have centers that signal us when to start and stop eating.

Experiments with the Hypothalamus: The Search for "Start Eating" and "Stop Eating" Centers in the Brain If you were just reviving from a surgical operation, fighting your way through the fog of the anesthesia, food would probably be that last thing on your mind. But when you operate on rats and make a **lesion** in the **ventromedial nucleus** (VMN) of the hypothalamus, they will grope toward their food supplies as soon as their eyes open. Then they eat vast quantities of Purina Rat Chow or whatever else they can find.

It may be that the VMN functions like a stop-eating center in the rat's brain (Novin et al., 1976). If you electrically stimulate the VMN—or "switch it on"—a rat will stop eating until the current is turned off. When the VMN is lesioned, the rat becomes **hyperphagic.** It will continue to eat until it has mushroomed to about five times its normal weight (see Figure 7.2). Then it will level off its eating and maintain the higher weight. It is as if the set point of the stop-eating center were raised to be triggered at a much higher level (Keesey & Powley, 1975; Powley, 1977).

VMN-lesioned rats are also more sensitive than normal rats to the taste of food. They will eat even greater amounts of food if sugar or fat is added, but will eat less if the food is stale or bitter (Levitt, 1981).

It may be that the **lateral hypothalamus** is a start-eating center in the rat brain. If you electrically stimulate the lateral hypothalamus, the rat will start to eat. If you make a lesion in the lateral hypothalamus, the rat may stop eating altogether—that is, become **aphagic.** But if you force-feed an aphagic rat for a while, it will begin to eat on its own, but then level off at a lower body weight. It is like turning the thermostat down from, say, 70°F to 40°F.

Receptors in the Liver   Other research suggests that receptors in the liver are also important in regulating hunger (Friedman & Stricker, 1976; Schwartz, 1978). These receptors appear sensitive to the blood sugar level. In a state of food deprivation, blood sugar is low, and these receptors send rapid messages to the brain. After a meal the blood sugar level rises, and their rate of firing decreases.

While many areas of the body work in concert to regulate the hunger drive, this is only part of the story. In human beings the hunger drive is more complex. Psychological as well as physiological factors play an important role, as we shall see in our discussion of the problem of obesity.

OBESITY

We need food to survive, but food means more than survival for many of us. Food is a symbol of family togetherness and caring. We associate food with the nurturance of the parent-child relationship, with visits home at Thanksgiving. Friends and relatives offer food when we enter their homes. Saying no may be interpreted as a personal rejection. Bacon and eggs, coffee with cream and sugar, meat and mashed potatoes, seem part of what it is to be American, part of sharing American values and agricultural abundance.

But an enormous number of us are paying the price of abundance: obesity. Consider the incidence of obesity, as reported in a couple of recent polls:

FIGURE 7.2 A HYPERPHAGIC RAT
This rodent winner of the basketball look-alike contest went on a binge after it received a lesion in the ventromedial nucleus (VMN) of the hypothalamus. It is as if the lesion pushed the "set point" for body weight up several notches, and the rat's weight is now about five times normal. But now it eats only enough to maintain its pleasantly plump stature, so you need not be concerned that it will eventually burst. If the lesion had been made in the lateral hypothalamus, the animal might have become the "Twiggy" of the rat world.

Lesion An injury that results in impaired behavior or loss of a function.

Ventromedial nucleus A central area on the underside of the hypothalamus that appears to function as a stop-eating center. (From the Latin *venter*, meaning "belly," and *medius*, meaning "middle.")

Hyperphagic (high-purr-FAY-jick). Characterized by excessive eating. (From the Greek *hyper-*, meaning "over," and *phagein*, meaning "to eat.")

Lateral hypothalamus An area at the side of the hypothalamus that appears to function as a start-eating center. (From the Latin *lateris*, meaning "side.")

Aphagic (uh-FAY-jick). Characterized by undereating.

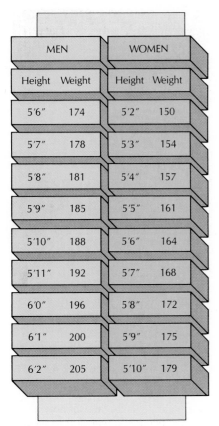

MEN		WOMEN	
Height	Weight	Height	Weight
5'6"	174	5'2"	150
5'7"	178	5'3"	154
5'8"	181	5'4"	157
5'9"	185	5'5"	161
5'10"	188	5'6"	164
5'11"	192	5'7"	168
6'0"	196	5'8"	172
6'1"	200	5'9"	175
6'2"	205	5'10"	179

FIGURE 7.3 **WEIGHTS AT WHICH OBESITY BEGINS**

Fat cells Cells that store fats.

Adipose tissue Containing animal fat. (From the Latin *adipis,* meaning "fat.")

Nearly 90 percent of Americans consider themselves at least slightly overweight, and 35 percent want to lose at least 15 pounds (Toufexis et al., 1986).

One out of five American adults (that is, 34 million of us) is obese—that is, weighs more than 20 percent above the recommended weight (Wallis, 1985) (see Figure 7.3).

Eleven million American adults are severely obese (Wallis, 1985)—that is, they exceed their desirable body weight by at least 40 percent.

About 30 percent of U.S. women and 16 percent of U.S. men were on diets in a recent year (Toufexis et al., 1986).

Within a few years, at least two-thirds of "successful" dieters regain every pound they have lost—and then some (Toufexis et al., 1986).

With few exceptions, America idealizes slender heroes and heroines. For the many Americans who measure more-than-up to television and film idols, food may have replaced sex as the central source of guilt. We feel guilt when we binge, then repent and resolve to diet. Perhaps we stick to starvation diets for a while and drop a few pounds. Then we too often return to our fattening ways and are struck by guilt again.

The obese are motivated to lose weight for more than social reasons. They encounter more than their fair share of illnesses, including heart disease, arteriosclerosis, diabetes, gout, and even certain types of cancer (Wallis, 1985).

Why do so many of us overeat? Is obesity a physiological problem, a psychological problem, or both? Research suggests that psychological and physiological factors both play a role in obesity.

On Fat Cells and Obese People Obese people may be sabotaged by microscopic units of life within their bodies in their efforts to maintain a slender profile: **fat cells.** No, fat cells are not overweight cells. They are cells that store fat, otherwise called **adipose tissue.**. Hunger may be related to the amount of fat stored in these cells. As time passes after a meal, the blood sugar level drops. Fat is then drawn from these cells to provide further nourishment. At some point, the hypothalamus is signaled of the fat deficiency in these cells, triggering the hunger drive.

People with more adipose tissue than other people will feel food-deprived earlier, even though they may be of equal weight. This is presumably because more signals are being sent to the brain. Obese people, and formerly obese people, generally have more adipose tissue than people of normal weight. It may be for this reason that many people who have dieted successfully complain that they are constantly hungry as they try to maintain normal weight levels. Psychologist Richard Keesey notes that displacing a person from his or her set point puts forces into motion that fight that displacement (1986). In fact, dieting and then regaining the weight one has lost may be particularly traumatic for one's set point. Psychologist Kelly Brownell points out that such "yo-yo dieting" may, in effect, teach the body that it will be intermittently deprived of food, causing the metabolism to greatly slow down when food intake is decreased in the future (1986).

In order to maintain their weight losses, formerly obese people may have to eat less than people of the same weight who have always been slender.

Why do some of us have more fat cells than others? We inherit different numbers of fat cells, so there may be some truth to the notion that some people are born with a greater disposition toward gaining weight than others. But the number of fat cells may also be influenced by childhood and adult dietary habits (Brownell, 1982; Sjøstrøm, 1980). Obese children develop more adipose tissue. And so childhood obesity may cause the adult dieter to feel persistent hunger, even after leveling off at a new desired weight.

But while fat cells may play a role in triggering internal sensations of hunger, they cannot compel us to eat. As we shall see in the following section, obese people seem to be *less* sensitive than normal-weight people to internal sensations of hunger.

Internal and External Eaters: Out of Sight, Out of Mouth?   During the late evening news, just as I'm settling in for sleep, a Burger King "Aren't You *Hungry?*" or frozen pizza ad assaults me from the television set. Visions of juicy meat, gooey cheese, and drippy sauce threaten to do me in. My stomach growlings are all the evidence I need that the hunger drive can be triggered by external stimuli, such as the sight of food, as well as by chemical imbalances and signals within the body.

While such commercials may stir most of our appetites, overweight people seem to be more responsive than normal-weight people to external stimulation. People who respond predominantly to their own internal stimuli are referred to as **internal eaters.** Those who must be tied to the bedpost when they see a food commercial or catch a whiff of kitchen aromas are **external eaters.** Any of us may occasionally respond to an especially appealing incentive, like a slice of chocolate cream-cheese pie (sorry, you externals). But external eaters are decidedly more swayed by external stimulation, as many experiments have shown. We shall describe just a couple of classic studies.

Balloons may not sound like your favorite breakfast treat. Still, in one classic study, Stunkard (1959) managed to recruit obese and normal-weight subjects for a study in which they swallowed stomach balloons after an all-night fast. Such balloons, filled slightly with water, will signal stomach contractions to a monitor. Subjects reported whether or not they were hungry every fifteen minutes. Normal-weight subjects were more likely than the obese to report hunger when their stomachs contracted. They were significantly more likely to respond to internal stimulation.

In another classic study, Schachter and Gross (1968) involved students in paper-and-pencil tasks in the late afternoon, when they were likely to be anticipating dinner. After fifty minutes, each student was given a box of Wheat Thins and assigned additional tasks. The students did not know that the researchers' only interest was the number of Wheat Thins they would eat during a second time period also of fifty minutes. The researchers had left a doctored clock with students during the second fifty-minute period. As a consequence, some students believed only twenty-five minutes had

Internal eaters People who eat predominantly in response to internal stimuli, such as hunger pangs.

External eaters People who eat predominantly in response to external stimuli, such as the sight or smell of food or the time of day.

passed, while others believed that an hour and forty minutes had gone by, which meant that dinnertime was very near. Obese students were slaves to the clock. Those who believed it was dinnertime ate twice as many Wheat Thins during the second time period as those who believed it was earlier in the afternoon. The belief manipulation had no such effect on normal-weight students. Hunger in the overweight was triggered by the mere expectation of food. Other studies have found that the overweight are also more responsive to the sight and smell of food and to the presence of other people who are eating.

Why are obese people more responsive than the normal-weight to external stimulation? Stanley Schachter (1971) observed similarities between the eating behavior of hyperphagic rats and obese people that led him to wonder whether many of the obese are troubled by faulty neural regulation of hunger because of problems, perhaps, in the hypothalamus.

Heavy people, like hyperphagic rats, are more sensitive than the normal-weight to the taste of food (Schachter, 1971; Schachter & Rodin, 1974). They eat relatively larger quantities of sweet foods, like vanilla milkshakes, but lower quantities of bitter foods. Obese people also take larger mouthfuls, chew less, and finish their meals more rapidly than normal-weight people (LeBow et al., 1977; Marston et al., 1977).

But the faulty-neural-mechanism theory has not yet been directly supported as a factor in obesity in human beings. For the moment we can note only that the eating behavior of obese people resembles that of hyperphagic rats. It is also possible that early dietary habits promote the greater sensitivity to external cues found among the obese (Rodin & Slochower, 1976).

Many other factors, such as emotional states, may also play a role in obesity. For example, dieting efforts may be impeded by negative emotional states like depression (Baucom & Aiken, 1981; Ruderman, 1985) and anxiety (Pine, 1985).

But now, some good news for people who would like to lose a few pounds. Psychological research has led to a number of helpful suggestions for people who would like to lose some weight and keep it off. Following a self-help manual can be successful (Wing et al., 1982).

How To Lose Weight: A Brief Manual   There is no mystery about it. Successful weight-control programs do not involve (sometimes dangerous) fad diets. Instead, they tend to focus on (1) improving nutritional knowledge, (2) decreasing calorie intake, (3) exercise, and (4) behavior modification (Epstein et al., 1985; Israel et al., 1985; Stalonas & Kirschenbaum, 1985). Losing weight means burning more calories than you consume. You can accomplish that in part by eating less and by exchanging some high-calorie foods (like ice cream and butter) for low-calorie foods (like vegetables and diet margarine). Acquiring nutritional knowledge helps the individual select low-calorie healthful foods (such as vegetables, fruits, fish and poultry, and whole grain breads and cereals).

Why exercise? For many reasons. First of all, exercise burns calories (Epstein et al., 1984b). This is one reason that dieting plus exercise is more effective than dieting alone (Epstein et al., 1984a). But there is another. When we restrict our calorie intake, our metabolic rates decrease, perhaps in an effort to conserve energy (Apfelbaum, 1978; Polivy & Herman, 1985). This decrease in metabolic rate can frustrate dieters severely. Some dieters have justly complained that they seem to reach "plateaus" where they find it extremely difficult to shed additional pounds, even though they are eating very little. Exercise, it seems, also serves the important function of maintaining the metabolic rate at normal predieting levels, even though we are restricting calories (Donahoe et al., 1984). In addition to the physical benefits of exercise, exercising can also build our sense of personal competence. We feel proud of ourselves when we see flab hardening or find that we can swim, bicycle, jog, or run longer distances than we had imagined.

And so, here are a number of suggestions for losing weight. Largely based on principles of behavior modification (see Chapter 12), they involve restricting calories and engaging in a systematic exercise program:

Establish calorie-intake goals and heighten awareness of whether you are meeting them. Acquire a book that shows how many calories are found in foods and keep a diary of your calorie intake.

Use low-calorie substitutes for high-calorie foods. Fill your stomach with celery rather than cheese cake and burritos. Eat preplanned low-calorie snacks rather than binge on a jar of peanuts or a container of ice cream.

Establish eating patterns similar to those of internal eaters. Take small bites. Chew thoroughly. Take a five-minute break between helpings. Ask yourself if you're still hungry. If not, stop eating.

Avoid sources of external stimulation (temptations) to which you have succumbed in the past. Shop at the mall with the Alfalfa Sprout, not the Gushy Gloppe Shoppe. Plan your meal before entering a restaurant and avoid ogling that tempting full-color menu. Attend to your own plate, not the sumptuous dish at the next table. (Your salad probably looks greener to them, anyhow.) Shop from a list. Walk briskly through the supermarket, preferably after dinner when you're no longer hungry. Don't be sidetracked by pretty packages (fattening things may come in them). Keep out of the kitchen. Study, watch TV, write letters elsewhere. Keep fattening foods out of the house. Prepare only enough food to remain within your calorie-intake goals.

Exercise to burn more calories and maintain your predieting metabolic rate. Reach for your mate, not your plate (to coin a phrase). Jog rather than eat an unplanned snack. Build exercise routines by a few minutes each week.

Reward yourself when you've met a weekly calorie-intake goal—but not with food. Imagine how great you'll look in that new swimsuit next summer.

Mentally rehearse solutions to problem situations. Consider how you will politely refuse when cake is handed out at the office party. Rehearse your next visit to parents or other relatives—the ones who tell you how painfully thin you look and who try to stuff you like a pig. Imagine how you'll politely refuse seconds, and thirds, despite all their protestations.

Above all, if you slip from your plan for a day, do not catastrophize. Dieters are frequently tempted to binge, especially when they insist on viewing themselves rigidly as either perfect successes or complete failures (Polivy & Herman, 1985). Do not tell yourself you're a failure and then go on a binge. Consider the *weekly* trend, not just a day, and resume your strategies the following day. And if you do binge, resume the diet the following day. Again, credit yourself for the long-term trend; do not focus excessively on the temporary lapse.

You may find other useful suggestions in the section on self-control techniques in Chapter 12.

THIRST

Our bodies need fluids as well as food in order to survive. We may survive without food for several weeks, but will only last for a few days without water. It has been speculated that thirst is a stronger drive than hunger, because animals who have been deprived of food and water will typically drink before eating, when given the opportunity to do both. Critics of this view note that hungry animals may drink first because they must take in fluids to produce saliva and other digestive fluids before eating.

Physiological mechanisms maintain a proper fluid level in the body. When there is excess fluid, we are not likely to feel thirsty, and our bodies form urine. When there is a fluid deficiency, we are likely to experience a thirst drive and our bodies are less likely to form urine.

Since we may experience thirst as dryness in the mouth and throat, it was once thought that receptors in the mouth and throat played a major role in determining thirst or satiety. But it seems that receptors in the kidney and hypothalamus play more central roles in regulating the thirst drive.

Regulation of Thirst in the Kidneys When the body is depleted of fluids, the flow of blood through the kidneys drops off. In response to this decreased flow of blood, the kidneys secrete the hormone **angiotensin.** Angiotensin, in turn, signals the hypothalamus of fluid depletion.

The Role of the Hypothalamus: On Shriveled Cells and Salty Pretzels **Osmoreceptors** in the hypothalamus can also detect fluid depletion from changes that occur within the brain. The brain, like the rest of the body, becomes fluid-depleted. Fluid depletion causes the osmoreceptor cells to shrivel, which in and of itself may trigger thirst.

Another osmoreceptor signal involves the concentration of chemicals in bodily fluids. As the volume of water in the body decreases, the concentration of chemicals in the water, such as sodium (which combines with chlorine to make salt) increases. (Think of a pool of salt water evaporating in the sun. The salt does *not* evaporate, only the water, and the remaining water becomes increasingly salty. If all the water evaporated, there would be nothing left but a crust of salt.) An increasing concentration of salt can also signal the osmoreceptors that the body's water supply is falling.

In a classic experiment, an injection of a salt solution into a goat's hypothalamus triggered heavy intake of fluids, even though the goat had

Angiotensin (an-gee-oh-TEN-sin). A hormone that signals the hypothalamus of bodily depletion of fluids. This hormone is secreted by the kidneys in response to decreased flow of blood.

Osmoreceptors Receptors in the hypothalamus that are sensitive to depletion of fluid. (From the Greek *othein,* meaning "to push"—referring to the pressure exerted by fluids.)

just drunk its fill (Andersson, 1971). (Injection of salt-free water caused the animal *not* to drink, apparently by "fooling" the osmoreceptors into behaving as though there were a higher level of fluids throughout the body.) Did you ever wonder why bartenders are usually happy to provide customers with "free" salty peanuts and salty pretzels? As the salt is dissolved into bodily fluids, the customer becomes thirsty again, even though he or she may also be making frequent trips to the bathroom in order to urinate.

The hypothalamus responds to signs of dehydration transmitted by osmoreceptors in at least two ways: (1) It signals the pituitary gland to secrete **antidiuretic hormone** (ADH). ADH increases reabsorption of urine—a water-conservation measure. (2) The hypothalamus signals the cerebral cortex. As a result, we experience the thirst drive.

Our responses to thirst are varied and largely learned. Some of us go to the tap for water. Others brew coffee or tea. Still others prefer juice or a soft drink. The time of day, social custom, and individual preferences all play a role in deciding which fluids will be drunk.

External cues may also stimulate us to drink, as they can stimulate us to eat—even in the absence of internal cues for thirst. Watching someone squeeze an orange or hearing a cork pop can make us desire orange juice or champagne. We may also drink alcohol to earn the approval of drinking buddies or for whatever incentives the sensations of intoxication may provide.

Receptors in the Mouth and Throat   Receptors in the mouth and throat do play some role in thirst, after all. Once we have begun drinking, they monitor the amount of fluid we have taken in. At some point they signal the hypothalamus, "Stop, enough." But if we have not reversed the internal processes that signal dehydration, we shall soon feel thirsty again.

Drinking, like eating, has complex origins. It can be motivated by a combination of internal and external cues.

STIMULUS MOTIVES

Physical needs give rise to the drives of hunger and thirst. In these cases, we are motivated to *reduce* tension or stimulation that impinges upon us. In the cases of the **stimulus motives,** our goals are to *increase* the amount of stimulation impinging upon us. The stimulus motives include sensory stimulation, activity, exploration, and manipulation of the environment.

Stimulus motives, like physiological motives, are generally considered innate. We shall see that people may be motivated to seek the level of stimulation that produces an *optimal level of arousal*—that is, a general level of activity or motivation at which we feel our best and behave most effectively.

Some stimulus motives provide a clear evolutionary advantage. People and lower animals who are motivated to learn about and manipulate the environment are more likely to survive. Learning about the environment increases awareness of resources and of potential dangers, and manipula-

Antidiuretic hormone A pituitary hormone that conserves bodily fluids by increasing the reabsorption of urine. Abbreviated *ADH*.

Stimulus motives Motives to increase the stimulation impinging upon an organism.

Sensory deprivation (1) In general, insufficient sensory stimulation. (2) Referring to a research method for systematically decreasing the amount of stimulation that impinges upon sensory receptors.

tion can permit us to change the environment in beneficial ways. Learning and manipulation increase our chances of surviving until sexual maturity, and of passing on whatever genetic codes may underlie these motives to future generations.

SENSORY STIMULATION AND ACTIVITY

During the 1950s some lucky students at McGill University were paid $20 a day (which, with inflation, would be nearly $100 today) for doing absolutely nothing. How would you like such "work"? Don't answer too quickly. According to the results of such experiments in **sensory deprivation,** which were run by Bexton, Heron, and Scott (1954), you might not like it much at all. In fact, you might find it intolerable.

Student volunteers were placed in isolation booths. In these quiet cubicles, they were blindfolded, their arms were bandaged, and they could hear nothing but the dull continuous hum of the air conditioning (Figure 7.4). With nothing to do, many students fell asleep for a while. After a few hours of sensory-deprived wakefulness, most students felt bored and irritable. As time went on, they became increasingly uncomfortable. A number of them reported visual hallucinations, usually restricted to simple images of dots and geometric shapes (Zubek, 1973).

Many subjects quit during the first day despite the financial incentive and the desire to contribute to scientific knowledge. Those who remained found it temporarily difficult to concentrate on even the simplest problems after several days of sensory deprivation. All in all, the experimental conditions did not provide a relaxing vacation. Instead, they proved to be a nightmare of boredom and disorientation.

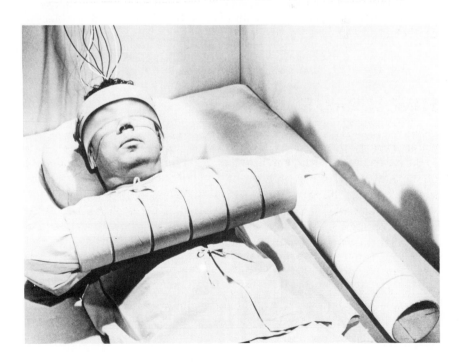

FIGURE 7.4 **A PARTICIPANT IN A SENSORY-DEPRIVATION EXPERIMENT** He sees, hears, and touches "no evil"—nor anything else, for that matter. Experimental conditions such as these do not produce a restful vacation. Instead, volunteers become quickly bored and irritable, and many quit after only a few hours, despite financial incentives. Apparently we have strong motives for sensory stimulation.

QUESTIONNAIRE

ARE YOU A SENSATION SEEKER?

Are you content reading or watching TV all day, or must you catch the big wave or bounce the bike across the dunes of the Mohave Desert? For a number of years, University of Delaware psychologist Marvin Zuckerman (1980) has been working with sensation-seeking scales that measure the level of stimulation or arousal a person will seek, and predict how well the person will fare in sensory-deprivation studies.

Zuckerman and his colleagues (1978) find four factors involved in sensation seeking: (1) seeking of thrill and adventure; (2) disinhibition (that is, the tendency to act out on impulses); (3) seeking of experience; and (4) susceptibility to boredom. Other studies show that high sensation seekers are less tolerant of sensory deprivation. They are also more likely to become involved in drugs and sexual experiences, to show public drunkenness, and to volunteer for high-risk activities and unusual experiments (Kohn et al., 1979; Malatesta et al., 1981; Zuckerman, 1974).

To gain insight into your own sensation-seeking tendencies, try this shortened version of one of Marvin Zuckerman's sensation-seeking scales. For each of the thirteen items, circle the choice, A or B, that best describes your behavior, tastes, or ideas. Then compare your responses to those in the answer key in Appendix B.

1. A. I would like a job that requires a lot of traveling.
   B. I would prefer a job in one location.
2. A. I am invigorated by a brisk, cold day.
   B. I can't wait to get indoors on a cold day.
3. A. I get bored seeing the same old faces.
   B. I like the comfortable familiarity of everyday friends.
4. A. I would prefer living in an ideal society in which everyone is safe, secure, and happy.
   B. I would have preferred living in the unsettled days of our history.
5. A. I sometimes like to do things that are a little frightening.
   B. A sensible person avoids activities that are dangerous.
6. A. I would not like to be hypnotized.
   B. I would like to have the experience of being hypnotized.
7. A. The most important goal in life is to live it to the fullest and experience as much as possible.
   B. The most important goal in life is to find peace and happiness.
8. A. I would like to try parachute-jumping.
   B. I would never want to try jumping out of a plane, with or without a parachute.
9. A. I enter cold water gradually, giving myself time to get used to it.
   B. I like to dive or jump right into the ocean or a cold pool.
10. A. When I go on a vacation, I prefer the comfort of a good room and bed.
    B. When I go on a vacation, I prefer the change of camping out.
11. A. I prefer people who are emotionally expressive even if they are a bit unstable.
    B. I prefer people who are calm and even-tempered.
12. A. A good painting should shock or jolt the senses.
    B. A good painting should give one a feeling of peace and security.
13. A. People who ride motorcycles must have some kind of unconscious need to hurt themselves.
    B. I would like to drive or ride a motorcycle.

SENSORY STIMULATION AND AC-TIVITY Why do some people leap into the sky for sport? Perhaps they are trying to raise their bodily arousal to more stimulating levels.

Some people seek higher levels of stimulation and activity than others. John may be content to sit by the TV set all evening, while Marsha doesn't feel right unless she's out on the tennis court or jogging. Cliff isn't content unless he has ridden his motorcycle over back trails at breakneck speeds, and Janet feels exuberance in the chest when she's catching the big wave or diving freefall from an airplane. One's preference for tennis, motorcycling, or skydiving will reflect one's geographical location, social class, and learning experiences. But it may just be that the levels of arousal at which we are comfortable would be too high or low for other people. It may also be that these levels are determined to some degree by innate factors.

EXPLORATION AND MANIPULATION

Have you ever brought a dog or cat into a new home? At first they may show general excitement. New kittens are even known to hide under a couch or bed for a few hours. But then they will begin to explore every corner of the new environment. When placed in novel environments, many animals appear to possess an innate motive to engage in exploratory behavior.

Once familiar with the environment, lower animals and people appear motivated to seek **novel stimulation.** For example, when they have not been deprived of food for a great deal of time, rats will often explore unfamiliar arms of mazes rather than head straight for the section of the maze in which they have learned to expect food. Animals who have just **copulated** and thereby reduced their sex drives will often show renewed interest in sexual behavior when presented with a novel sex partner. Monkeys will learn how to manipulate gadgets for the incentive of being able to observe novel stimulation through a window (see Figure 7.5). Human youngsters will spend hour after hour manipulating the controls of video games for no apparent external reward.*The question has arisen as to whether people and animals seek to explore and manipulate the environment, *because* these activities may help them reduce primary drives, like hunger and thirst, or whether they will engage in these activities for their own sake. Many psychologists do believe that such stimulating activities are reinforcing in and of themselves. Monkeys do seem to get a kick from "monkeying around" with gadgets (see Figure 7.6). They will learn how to manipulate hooks and eyes and other mechanical devices without any external incentives whatsoever (Harlow et al., 1950). Children will engage in prolonged play with "busy boxes"—boxes filled with objects that honk, squeak, rattle, and buzz. They seem to find manipulation of these gadgets pleasurable, even though manipulation does not result in food, ice cream, or even hugs from parents.

THE SEARCH FOR OPTIMAL AROUSAL

Some drives, like hunger and thirst, are associated with higher levels of **arousal** within an organism. When we eat or drink to reduce these drives,

Novel stimulation (1) New or different stimulation. (2) A hypothesized primary drive to experience new or different stimulation.

Copulate (COP-you-late). To engage in sexual intercourse. (From the Latin root for "couple.")

Arousal (1) A general level of activity or preparedness for activity in an organism. (2) A general level of motivation in an organism. (From the Middle English *rousen,* meaning "to cause to rise"—and referring to the causing of game to rise from cover during a hunt.)

---

*I say "youngsters" because college students are far too sophisticated to spend time at video games, aren't they?

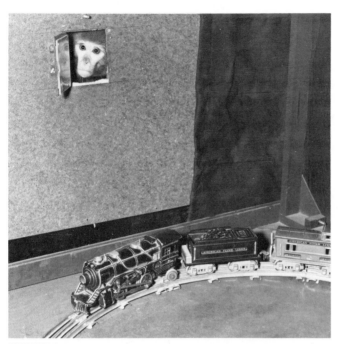

FIGURE 7.5 **THE ALLURE OF NOVEL STIMULATION** People and many lower animals are motivated to explore the environment and seek novel stimulation. This monkey has learned to unlock a door for the privilege of viewing a model train.

FIGURE 7.6 **A MANIPULATION DRIVE?** These young rhesus monkeys appear to monkey around with gadgets for the sheer pleasure of monkeying around. No external incentives or reinforcements are needed. Children similarly enjoy manipulating gadgets that honk, squeak, rattle, and buzz, even though the resultant honks and squeaks do not satisfy physiological drives such as hunger or thirst.

we are also lowering the associated level of arousal. At other times we act to increase our levels of arousal, as in going to a horror film, engaging in athletic activity, or seeking a new sex partner.

How can we explain the apparently contradictory observations that people and lower animals sometimes act to reduce arousal and at other times act to increase arousal? Some psychologists attempt to reconcile these differences by suggesting that we are motivated to seek **optimal arousal**— that is, levels of arousal that are optimal for us as individuals at certain times of the day.

Our levels of arousal can vary from quite low (see Figure 7.7), as in when we are sleeping, to quite high, as when we are frightened or intensely angered. Psychologists also hypothesize that we each have optimal levels of arousal at which we are likely to feel best and function most effectively in various situations. People whose optimal levels of arousal are relatively low may prefer sedentary lives. People whose optimal levels of arousal are high may seek activities like skydiving and motorcycling, intense problem solving (as of a difficult crossword puzzle), or vivid daydreaming. Psychologists Donald Fiske and Salvatore Maddi argue that people behave in ways that increase the impact of stimulation upon them when their levels of arousal are too low, and act to decrease the impact of stimulation when

Optimal arousal The level of arousal at which we feel and function best.

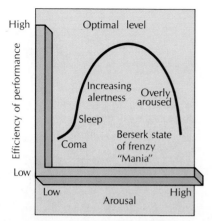

FIGURE 7.7 LEVEL OF AROUSAL AND PERFORMANCE EFFICIENCY
Our optimal levels of arousal may differ somewhat, but they tend to lie somewhere in between sleep and a state of panic. People whose optimal levels of arousal are high will seek more stimulation than people whose optimal levels are low.

Yerkes-Dodson law The principle that a high level of motivation increases efficiency in the performance of simple tasks, while a lower level of motivation permits greater efficiency in the performance of complex tasks.

their levels are too high (Maddi, 1980). The types of activity they will engage in also depend on factors like needs for meaningfulness and for variety.

The Yerkes-Dodson Law A former National Football League linebacker was reported to work himself into such a frenzy before a game that other players gave him a wide berth in the locker room. Linebacking is a relatively simple football job, requiring brute strength and something called "desire" more so than does, say, quarterbacking. This particular linebacker was no stronger than many others, but his level of arousal—or desire—helped his team reach the Superbowl on many occasions.

According to the **Yerkes-Dodson law** (see Figure 7.8), a high level of arousal increases performance on a relatively simple task, whether the task is linebacking or solving a series of simple math problems. In Chapter 14 we shall see that the presence of other people tends to increase our levels of arousal. We frequently run, swim, or ski faster during competition than when we practice alone, probably because of the higher level of arousal.

When a task is complex it seems helpful to keep one's level of arousal at lower levels. True, there are some complexities to the linebacker's job. Through experience, the linebacker must acquire the capacity to predict or "read" the play. But the quarterback's job is more complicated. He must call the plays, sometimes change them at the line of scrimmage because of an unexpected defensive realignment, and "keep a cool head" as his receivers try to break into the open and defenders try to break through the offensive line and tackle him. Similarly, it is worthwhile to try to remain somewhat relaxed on the eve of a demanding (complex) "big test."

"Cool" linebackers and "hotheaded" quarterbacks don't fare well in the professional ranks. Instead, linebackers must "psych themselves up,"

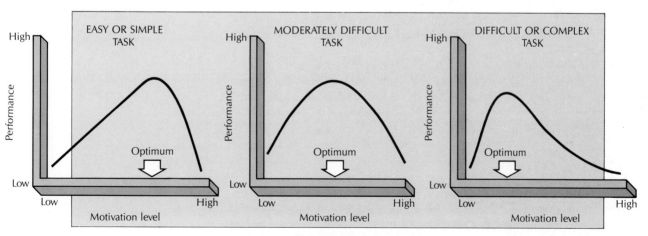

FIGURE 7.8 THE YERKES-DODSON LAW An easy or simple task may be facilitated by a high level of arousal or motivation. A highly aroused 118-pound woman is reported to have lifted the front end of a two-ton Cadillac in order to rescue a child. But a complex task, such as quarterbacking a football team or attempting to solve a math problem, requires attending to many variables at once. For this reason, a complex task is usually carried out more efficiently at a lower level of arousal.

MOTIVES FOR WORKING

Imagine your wildest fantasy. Does it have something to do with winning the lottery and quitting school or work? With lounging on beaches of tropical islands in a personal world totally devoid of pressure and responsibility?

If it does, you could be in for something of a disappointment if your dreams came true. Many million-dollar lottery winners who quit their jobs actually encounter feelings of aimlessness and dissatisfaction (Kaplan, 1978). Why?

The answer may lie in the fact that while work allows us to meet our basic needs for food, shelter, and security, work also satisfies many psychological needs, including the opportunity to engage in stimulating and satisfying activities. Other motives for working include the work ethic, self-identity, self-fulfillment, self-worth, the social values of work, and social roles:

1. *The Work Ethic.*

In works of labor, or of skill,
   I would be busy too;
For Satan finds some mischief still
   For idle hands to do.
                    —Isaac Watts

We work not only for tangible benefits. The work ethic, self-identity, self-fulfillment, and the social values of work also play roles.

and quarterbacks must "maintain their cool." Some linebackers convince themselves that the players on the opposing team represent the evil in the universe; while some quarterbacks approach their job with computer-like level-headedness.

What motivates people to get involved in contact sports like football in the first place? Stimulus motives may be a part of the answer, but learned or social motives may also have a good deal to do with it, as we see in the next section.

SOCIAL MOTIVES

Money, achievement, social approval, power, aggression—these are examples of **social motives**. Social motives differ from primary motives in that they are acquired through social learning. But like physiological drives and stimulus motives, social motives arouse us and prompt goal-directed behavior.

Harvard University Psychologist Henry Murray (1938) is one of the early researchers into social motives. He referred to social motives as psychological needs, and compiled a list of twenty-one important psychological needs, including needs for achievement, affiliation, aggression, auton-

Social motives Learned or acquired motives.

The so-called work ethic is the belief that we are morally obligated to engage in productive labor, to avoid idleness or laziness. Adherents to the work ethic view life without work as unthinkable and perhaps immoral, even for people who are financially independent.

2. *Self-Identity.* Our occupational identities become intertwined with our self-identities. We are likely to think, "I *am* a nurse," or "I *am* a lawyer," rather than "I assist in operations and bathe patients," or "I plea bargain with the district attorney and write last wills and testaments." Psychological bonds to work permit us to think of *having careers* or occupations, not as simply *holding jobs.*

3. *Self-Fulfillment.* We often express our personal needs, interests, and values through our work. We may choose a profession that allows us to express these interests. I entered psychology because I was interested in learning about other people and myself. The self-fulfilling values of the work of the astronaut, scientist, and athlete may seem obvious. But factory workers, plumbers, police officers, and fire fighters can also find self-enrichment as well as cash rewards for their work.

4. *Self-Worth.* Recognition and respect for a job well done contribute to our self-esteem. For some, self-worth may ride on accumulating money. For a writer, self-worth may hinge upon acceptance of a poem or article by a magazine. When we fail at work, our self-esteem plummets as sharply as the bank account.

5. *Social Values of Work.* The work place extends our social contacts. It introduces us to friends, lovers, even challenging adversaries. At work we are likely to meet others who share our interests and goals, and to form supportive social networks that in our highly mobile society must sometimes substitute for family.

6. *Social Roles.* Work roles help define our functions in the community. Communities have their public identities: druggist, shoemaker, teacher, doctor. Family roles are also influenced by members' roles in the social fabric. Traditionally, men have been the breadwinners and women the homemakers, but these stereotypical patterns have been changing. Today even the majority of women who view marriage with children as the most satisfying style of life still want to have a full-time job outside the home *(New York Times,* 1985). Today both spouses are likely, as one television commercial phrases it, "to bring home the bacon and fry it in a pan."

---

omy, dominance, **nurturance,** and understanding. Since we undergo different learning experiences, each of us may develop different levels of these psychological needs, or give them different priorities. Let us now consider some findings concerning the needs for achievement, affiliation, and power and the circumstances that give rise to them.

THE NEED FOR ACHIEVEMENT

We all know people who strive persistently to get ahead, to "make it," to earn vast sums of money, to invent, to accomplish the impossible. These people have a high need for achievement, abbreviated **n Ach.**

Psychologist David McClelland (1958), also of Harvard University, helped pioneer the assessment of *n* Ach through people's reported fantasies. One assessment method involves use of the **Thematic Apperception Test (TAT),** developed by Henry Murray. The TAT contains cards with pictures and drawings that are subject to various interpretations (see Chapter 9). Subjects are shown one or more TAT cards and asked to construct stories about the pictured theme; to indicate what led up to it, what the characters are thinking and feeling, and what is likely to happen.

One TAT card shows a boy with a violin (see Figure 7.9). The card itself is somewhat ambiguous: the boy may be staring into space, or his

---

Nurturance The quality of promoting development, of rearing young. (From the Latin *nutrire,* meaning "to nourish.")

n **Ach** The need for achievement—to master, to accomplish difficult things.

Thematic Apperception Test A test devised by Henry Murray to measure needs through fantasy production. Abbreviated *TAT;* see Chapter 9.

FIGURE 7.9 **TAPPING FANTASIES IN PERSONALITY RESEARCH** This is a Thematic Apperception Test card that is frequently used to measure the need for achievement. What is happening in this picture? What is the person thinking and feeling? What is going to happen? Your answers to these questions reflect your own needs as well as the content of the picture itself.

eyes may be almost closed. Consider two stories that could be told about this card:

Story 1: "He's upset that he's got to practice because his instructor is coming by and he hasn't yet learned his lesson for the week. But he'd rather be out playing with the other kids, and he'll probably sneak out to do just that."

Story 2: "He's thinking, 'Someday I'll be the world's greatest violinist. I'll be playing at Lincoln Center and the crowd'll be cheering.' He practices several hours every day."

There are formal standards that enable psychologists to derive *n* Ach scores from stories such as these, but in this case you need not be acquainted with them to see that the second story suggests more achievement motivation than the first. McClelland (1985) has found that motives as measured by the TAT permit the prediction of long-term behavior patterns.

Behavior of Individuals with High *n* Ach Classic studies find that people with high *n* Ach earn higher grades than people of comparable learning ability but low *n* Ach. They are more likely to earn high salaries and be promoted than are low-*n*-Ach people with similar opportunities. They perform better at math problems and unscrambling anagrams, such as decoding RSTA into STAR, or RATS.*

McClelland (1965) found that 83 percent of high-*n*-Ach college graduates took positions characterized by risk, decision making, and the chance for great success, such as business management, sales, or businesses of

*You can count on a psychologist not to miss an opportunity to throw a few rats into his book.

A CLOSER LOOK

THE SLUMP OF THE SECURE PLAYER

A team of psychologists has mustered statistical evidence to show that long-term contracts take some of the hustle out of professional baseball players.

Multiyear contracts became commonplace in 1977, two years after a federal arbitration panel ruled that players were no longer bound indefinitely to the teams that originally signed them, a decision that made it advantageous for owners to tie up their stars. Richard O'Brien and other psychologists at Hofstra University studied how the ruling affected players' performance. The researchers examined the records of thirty-eight pitchers during the three years before and after they signed contracts for three or more years, comparing their play with that of thirty-eight randomly chosen pitchers who signed only single-season contracts for the same period.

As long as they had to get their contracts renewed each year, the players who eventually won long-term berths improved steadily, from an average of 3.66 earned runs scored against them per game in 1974 to 2.91 in 1976. After signing their long-term agreements, how-

ever, their earned-run averages (ERAs) climbed to an average of 4.04 three years later. The pitchers with one-year contracts showed no consistent pattern during the six years.

The researchers recommend that owners combine a base salary with incentive payments for achieving goals such as a specified ERA or batting average. Negotiated performance targets, they say, "would allow equitable rewards for productive seasons for all players."

Just before the findings were published, the former Baltimore Orioles' ace pitcher, Jim Palmer, provided independent support for that conclusion in a *New York Times* interview. Having a long-term contract himself, Palmer noted that "up until 1975, my next year's salary always depended on every pitch I threw. I never relaxed. I never took anything for granted. It would seem to be hard for some players to have that kind of intensity after signing a multiyear contract. Some players are making a lot more money than they should."

their own making. Seventy percent of the graduates who chose nonentrepreneurial positions showed low *n* Ach. High-*n*-Ach individuals seem to prefer challenges and are willing to take moderate risks to achieve their goals. They see their fate as being in their own hands (McClelland et al., 1953). Workers with higher *n* Ach are also more likely to find satisfaction on the job (Reuman et al., 1984).

A report by industrial psychologist Douglas Bray (1982) finds that factors similar to *n* Ach—including need for advancement and great investment in one's work—are of moderate importance in predicting advancement through the managerial ranks at AT&T. However, two other factors are more important: administrative skills (consisting of organizational ability, decision making, and creativity) and interpersonal skills (leadership, communication ability, and adaptability). *N* Ach is an important element in success, but not the only factor.

Development of *n* Ach   Mothers with high *n* Ach tend to encourage their children to think and act independently, while low-*n*-Ach mothers tend to be more protective and restrictive. Marion Winterbottom (1958) found that mothers of sons with high *n* Ach made more demands and imposed more restrictions on their sons during the early elementary school years than did mothers of sons with low *n* Ach. Even during the preschool years, the mothers of high-*n*-Ach sons demanded that they keep their rooms and possessions neat, that they make their own decisions concerning clothes, that they select their own friends, compete as needed, and undertake difficult tasks and persist at them. But mothers of high-*n*-Ach sons also showed warmth and praised their sons profusely for their accomplishments.

David McClelland and David Pilon (1983) studied *n* Ach among children whose parents' child-rearing practices had been studied twenty-six to twenty-seven years earlier. It was found that high-*n*-Ach adults were more likely to have had parents who scheduled their feeding as infants (as opposed to allowing feeding on demand) and who were relatively demanding in their toilet-training practices.

In sum, it may be that children who develop high *n* Ach are encouraged to show independence and responsibility at early ages, and that their parents respond warmly to their efforts. Unfortunately, as we shall see in Chapter 13, parents are much more likely to encourage independence in their sons as compared to their daughters.

THE NEED FOR AFFILIATION

The need for **affiliation,** abbreviated **_n_ Aff,** prompts us to make friends, join groups, and to prefer to do things with others rather than go it alone.

N Aff contributes to the social glue that creates families and civilizations. In this sense, it is certainly a healthful trait. Yet some people have such strong *n* Aff that they find it painful to make their own decisions, or even to be by themselves over extended periods of time. Research by Stanley Schachter suggests that high *n* Aff may indicate anxiety, as when people "huddle together" in fear of some outside force.

The Schachter Studies on Anxiety and *n* Aff   In a classic experiment on the effects of anxiety on *n* Aff, Stanley Schachter (1959) manipulated subjects' anxiety by leading them to believe that they would receive either painful electric shocks (the high-anxiety condition) or mild electric shocks (the low-anxiety condition). Subjects were then asked to wait while the shock apparatus was supposedly being set up. Subjects could choose to wait alone or in a room with others. The majority (63 percent) of subjects who expected a painful shock chose to wait in a room with other people. Only one-third (33 percent) of the subjects who expected a mild shock chose to wait with others.

In a related experiment, Schachter, found that "misery loves company," but only company of a special sort. Highly anxious subjects were placed in two social conditions. In the first, they could choose either to wait alone or with other subjects who would also receive painful shocks. Sixty percent of these subjects chose to affiliate, that is, to wait with others. In the second condition, highly anxious subjects could choose to wait alone or with people they believed were not involved with the study. In this second condition, no one chose to affiliate. Schachter concluded that misery loves company so long as the company is just as miserable.

Why did Schachter's subjects wish to affiliate only with people who shared their misery? Schachter explained their choice through the **theory of social comparison.** This theory holds that in an ambiguous situation—that is, a situation in which we are not certain as to what we should do or

Affilation Association or connection with a group. (From the Latin *filius,* meaning "son.")

n Aff The need for affiliation.

Theory of social comparison The view that people look to others for cues as to how to behave when they are in confusing or unfamiliar situations.

how we should feel—we will affiliate with people with whom we can compare feelings and behaviors. Schachter's anxious recruits could compare their reactions with those of other "victims," but not with people who had no reason to feel anxious. His highly anxious subjects may also have resented uninvolved people for "getting away free."

THE NEED FOR POWER

Another social motive is the need for power (*n* Power)—the need to control organizations and other people. High-*n*-Power college students are more likely than others to be members of important committees and to hold prominent offices in student organizations (Beck, 1978). They are more likely than low-*n*-Power individuals to participate in aggressive contact sports and to seek out competitive careers, as in business and—interestingly—psychology.

The need for power has both its positive and negative features, since power can be used either for good or bad purposes. In one recent study it was found that group leaders with a high need for power may impede group decision making by failing to promote full discussion of all the facts concerning a business situation and by not encouraging full consideration of members' proposals (Fodor & Smith, 1982).

McClelland and Pilon (1983) found that high-*n*-Power adults were more likely than low-*n*-Power adults to have had parents who were permissive toward their children's sexual and aggressive behavior. That is, they were more likely to permit their children to masturbate, to engage in sex play, and to show aggression to their siblings and their parents. Perhaps allowing children to exercise power (to control themselves and others) at an early age encourages them to continue to exercise power as they develop.

PSYCHOLOGY AND HEALTH

LEADERSHIP-MOTIVE SYNDROME

For a number of years, Harvard psychologist David McClelland and his colleagues have studied a "motivational profile" referred to as the *leadership-motive syndrome*. People with this profile show a cluster of needs that includes high needs for power and self-control, and low *n* Aff. People high in the leadership-motive syndrome often rise quickly through the military or corporate ranks, assuming that they also have managerial skills. But they also often pay a price.

People with this motivational profile are also at high risk for developing stress-related illnesses, especially when they are under the stress of having their need for power inhibited or frustrated (Fodor, 1984, 1985; McClelland & Jemmott, 1980). On a physiological level, the need for power is often linked to prolonged activity of the sympathetic branch of the autonomic nervous system. Prolonged sympathetic activation can lead to high blood pressure and the breaking down of the body's immune systems (McClelland et al., 1982).

We shall learn more about behavior patterns that lead to stress and illness in Chapter 10. At this point let us note that David McClelland (1982) suggests that one of the major achievements of contemporary psychology has been the development of strategies for coping with this type of behavior. We shall also describe these strategies in some detail in Chapter 10.

USE OF THE LIE DETECTOR IN HIRING, PROMOTION, AND THE INVESTIGATION OF CRIME IN THE WORKPLACE

Imagine that you are being considered for a promotion. Your record of accomplishment is solid, and you have done well in your interviews with upper management. There is only one more hurdle: a lie-detector test.

You aren't happy about taking the test—after all, why shouldn't your word suffice in answering questions? But at least your conscience is pretty clear, because you haven't done anything at the office to worry about, with, perhaps, the exception of using the company lines to make one or two personal long-distance phone calls.

You sit by a console, and your interviewer straps you into devices that will measure your heart rate, respiration rate, blood pressure, and electrodermal response (otherwise known as Galvanic skin response, or GSR). You are then asked a number of questions about your name, address, and where you have worked in the past. But you are then asked, "Before the age of 25, did you ever steal anything from a place where you worked?" (Saxe et al., 1985). All of a sudden you become anxious. (One summer you took home a couple of hamburgers when your shift at McDonald's was finished. Another summer you might have taken something at a camp where you worked as a counselor—you're not sure.) You squirm in your seat and assume that the needles on the console must be jumping as they write out your record. "I'm not sure," you say. Then you are asked whether you have knowledge of any people who have stolen paper or pencils at your place of work. You become quite uncomfortable again, and on it goes.

These types of interviews have become quite controversial in recent years. In fact, many states no longer permit them in the case of routine hiring and promotion interviews. But they are used extensively to uncover guilt in crimes in the work place. In fact, in 1983 President Reagan declared that he was "up to my kiester in leaks" at the Department of Defense and issued a directive that federal agencies provide that "employees may be required to submit to polygraph examinations" under the threat of "adverse consequences" if they refuse (Brooks, 1985). In 1985 President Reagan ordered the testing of personnel entrusted with secret information.

The use of devices to sort out truth from lies actually has a lengthy, if not laudable, history. As told by Benjamin Kleinmuntz and Julian Szucko (1984, pp. 766–767):

The Bedouins of Arabia . . . until quite recently required conflicting witnesses to lick a hot iron; the one whose tongue was burned was thought to be lying. The Chinese, it is said, had a similar method for detecting lying: Suspects were forced to chew rice powder and spit it out; if the powder was dry, the suspect was guilty. A variation of this test was used during the Inquisition. The suspect had to swallow a "trial slice" of bread and cheese; if it stuck to the suspect's palate or throat he or she was not telling the truth.

These methods may sound primitive, even bizarre, but they are consistent with modern knowledge. Anxiety concerning being caught in a lie is linked to sympathetic arousal, and one sign of sympathetic arousal is lack of saliva, or dryness in the mouth. The emotions of fear and guilt are also linked to sympathetic arousal and, hence, dryness in the mouth.

The Polygraph Modern-day lie detectors, or *polygraphs* (see Figure 7.10), monitor four indicators of

EMOTION

Emotions color our lives. We are green with envy, red with anger, blue with sorrow. The poets paint a thoughtful mood as a brown study. Positive emotions like love and desire can fill our days with pleasure, but negative emotions like fear, depression, and anger can fill us with dread and make each day an intolerable chore.

An emotion can at once be a response to a situation (in the way that fear is a response to a threat) and have motivating properties (in the way that anger can motivate us to act aggressively). An emotion can also be a

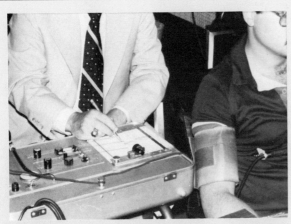

FIGURE 7.10 **A "LIE DETECTOR"** The polygraph monitors heart rate, blood pressure, respiration rate, and GSR (sweat in the palm of the hands). Is the polygraph sensitive to lying only? Is it foolproof? Because of the controversy surrounding these questions, many courts no longer admit polygraph evidence.

sympathetic arousal while a witness or suspect is being examined: heart rate, blood pressure, respiration rate, and electrodermal response. But many questions have been raised about use of the polygraph, especially since it is frequently used in the hiring process in industry and in helping to establish guilt or innocence in the courtroom.

Supporters of the polygraph claim that they are accurate in more than 90 percent of cases (Podlesny & Raskin, 1977), but conflicting research suggests that polygraphs do not approach this high accuracy rate and that they are sensitive to more than lies (Kleinmuntz & Szucko, 1984; Lykken, 1981; Saxe et al., 1985; U.S. Congress, 1983). In one experiment, subjects were able

to reduce the accuracy rate to 25 percent by thinking about exciting or disturbing events during the interview (Smith, 1971). In other studies, subjects have been yet more successful at poking holes in the accuracy rate. They dropped it to about 50 percent by biting their tongues (to produce pain) or pressing their toes against the floor (to tense muscles) while being interviewed (Honts et al., 1985).

There are other problems. One is the great variability in the reliability of the human judges of polygraph responses (Szucko & Kleinmuntz, 1981). Another is the possibility that antisocial people (discussed in Chapter 11), who show little anxiety or guilt, may escape detection because their lying is usually accompanied by low levels of arousal.

In a review of the literature, the government Office of Technology Assessment found that there was little or no valid research into the use of the polygraph in preemployment screening, in wide-scale "dragnet" investigations that attempt to ferret out the guilty from a large number of subjects, or in screening before individuals were allowed access to classified information (U.S. Congress, 1983). OTA did find a number of studies on generally criminal specific-incident investigations. But the studies' conclusions varied widely. In twenty-eight studies judged to have adequate methodology, correct detections of guilt ranged from 35 percent to 100 percent. Correct judgments of innocence ranged from 12.5 percent to 94 percent.

Because of these validity problems, results of polygraph examinations are also no longer admitted as evidence in many courtrooms. Polygraph interviews are still often conducted in criminal investigations and in job interviews, but these practices are being questioned as well.

Emotion A state of feeling that has physiological, situational, and cognitive components.

Sympathetic Of the sympathetic division of the autonomic nervous system; see Chapter 2.

Parasympathetic Of the parasympathetic division of the autonomic nervous system; see Chapter 2.

goal in and of itself. We may behave in ways that will lead us to experience joy or feelings of love.

An **emotion** is a state of feeling that has physiological, situational, and cognitive components. While no two people experience emotions in exactly the same way, it is possible to make some generalizations. Fear, for example, involves predominantly **sympathetic** arousal (rapid heartbeat and breathing, sweating, muscle tension), the perception of a threat, and beliefs to the effect that one is in danger (see Table 7.1). Anger may involve both sympathetic and **parasympathetic** arousal (Funkenstein, 1955), a frustrating or provocative situation (such as an insult), and belief that the provocateur

TABLE 7.1   Components of Three Common Emotions

Emotion	Components		
	Physiological	Situational	Cognitive
Fear	Sympathetic arousal	Environmental threat	Belief in danger, desire to avoid
Anger	Sympathetic and parasympathetic arousal	Frustration or provocation	Desire to hurt provocateur
Depression	Parasympathetic arousal	Loss, failure, or inactivity	Thoughts of helplessness, worthlessness

Emotions have physiological, situational, and cognitive components.

ought to be paid back. Depression usually involves predominantly parasympathetic arousal; a situational component of loss, failure, or inactivity; and cognitions of helplessness and worthlessness. Joy, grief, jealousy, disgust, embarrassment, liking—all have physiological, situational, and cognitive components.

The nearby box on the use of "lie detectors"—devices that are presented as being capable of distinguishing between truth and lies—highlights the link between autonomic arousal and emotion. As noted by Leonard Saxe and his colleagues at Boston University (1985), the fact of the matter is that "there is no such thing as a lie detector per se, [but] a number of approaches have been developed that are based on physiological measurement" (p. 355).

WHAT EMOTIONS ARE THERE?

How many emotions are there? What are they? These questions have prompted many speculations and observations.

Psychologist Carroll Izard (1982) suggests that newborn infants show a generalized positive feeling-state, a generalized negative feeling-state, sadness, and interest. Within the first year, additional emotions such as fear, joy, anger, and shame develop. While there is some disagreement as to how many emotions we are "born" with, with estimates ranging from one to eight or more, psychologists tend to agree that additional emotions become differentiated as we develop, reflecting physiological and cognitive changes (Mandler, 1984).

Plutchik's Classification System   Robert Plutchik (1980) theorizes that humans and many lower animals have evolved eight primary categories of inborn emotions that have survival value for the individual or for the species. As indicated in Figure 7.11, Plutchik's **primary emotions** can be arranged into a wheel, in which similar emotions lie next to one another and opposite emotions lie across from one another. Plutchik believes that each emotion motivates behavior that has a function related to survival. Fear, for example, activates escape behavior that has the function of protecting the

Primary emotions Within Plutchik's theory, basic emotions that motivate behavior with functions that promote survival.

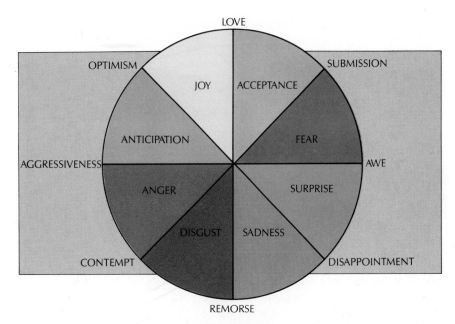

FIGURE 7.11 **PLUTCHIK'S CIRCLE OF EMOTIONS** Robert Plutchik theorizes that there are eight basic or primary emotions. On his circle of emotions, similar emotions lie next to one another, while opposite emotions lie across from one another. Secondary emotions such as love are derived from combinations of primary emotions—in this case, joy and acceptance.

organism. Anger activates destructive behavior that has the function of removing barriers that stand in the way of satisfying needs. Surprise activates orienting behavior that has the function of alerting the organism to environmental changes that may lead to other emotions and other behavioral responses. Among many lower animals, as noted in the discussion of instinct theory earlier in the chapter, behavioral responses may be stereotyped. Among higher animals and humans, however, learning, plays a major role; and among humans, value systems and personal choice also come into play.

Within Plutchik's system, other emotions are either formed from combinations of the primary emotions, or are more or less intense forms of the primary emotions. Figure 7.11 suggests that feelings of love, a **secondary emotion,** develop from the primary emotions of joy (which prompts affiliation and the incorporation of beneficial stimuli within oneself) and acceptance (which prompts reproductive behavior). Submission, awe, disappointment and so on are other secondary emotions.

Plutchik extended his wheel of emotions into a three-dimensional top-like figure to illustrate the dimension of intensity (see Figure 7.12). More intense emotions are situated across the top, and less intense emotions are placed farther down the sides of the figure. Rage, anger, and annoyance

Secondary emotion Within Plutchik's theory, an emotion that is derived from primary emotions.

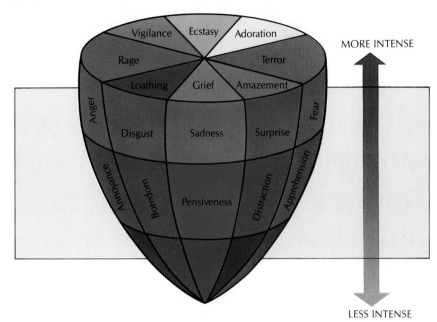

MAPPING EMOTIONAL INTENSITIES

MORE INTENSE

LESS INTENSE

FIGURE 7.12 PLUTCHIK'S EMOTION SOLID The vertical axis of this top-like figure represents varying degrees of emotional intensity. Emotional intensity increases as we journey upward; anger, for example, is more intense than annoyance, and rage is more intense than anger.

occupy a vertical strip and are all related emotions, but rage is the most intense of the three. Similarly, terror, fear, and apprehension are related, but terror is the most intense. Intense emotions prompt the most vigorous behavior. Less intense emotions such as annoyance and apprehension may stir us to heightened alertness, but we may show no overt tendencies to attack or flee unless the situation develops into more of a crisis.

The grouping of emotions, like the emotional lives of many individuals, remains somewhat in flux.

EXPRESSION OF EMOTIONS

Joy and sadness may be found in diverse cultures around the world, but how can we tell when other people are happy or despondent? It turns out that the expression of many emotions is also universal (Rinn, 1984). Smiling, for example, appears to be a universal sign of friendliness and approval (Ekman & Oster, 1979). Baring the teeth, as noted by Charles Darwin (1872) in the last century, may be a universal sign of anger. As the originator of the modern theory of evolution, Darwin believed that the universal recognition of facial expressions would have survival value; for example, they could signal that enemies are near even in the absence of language.

Research by psychologist Paul Ekman (1980) and his colleagues also supports the universality of the facial expression of emotions. Ekman took

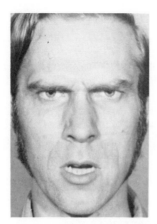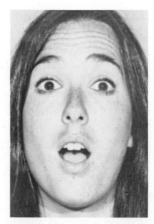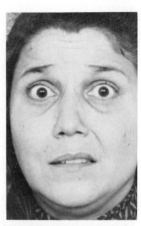

FIGURE 7.13 THE UNIVERSALITY OF THE EXPRESSION OF EMOTIONS Ekman's research suggests that there are several basic emotions whose expression is recognized around the world. These include happiness, anger, surprise, and fear.

a number of photographs of people posing the emotions of happiness, anger, surprise, and fear, as shown in Figure 7.13, and asked subjects throughout the world to indicate what emotions they depicted. Subjects ranged from European college students to the Fore, an isolated tribe who dwell in the highlands of New Guinea. All groups, including the Fore, who had almost no contact with Western culture, correctly identified the emotions being portrayed. Moreover, even the Fore displayed quite familiar facial expressions when asked how they would respond if they were the people in stories calling for basic emotional responses.

The Facial-Feedback Hypothesis We recognize that emotional states are *reflected* by facial expressions, but the **facial-feedback hypothesis** argues that the causal relationship between emotions and facial expressions can work in the opposite direction. Inducing experimental subjects to smile, for example, leads them to report more positive feelings (Kleinke & Walton, 1982) and to rate cartoons as more humorous (Laird, 1974; 1984). When subjects are induced to frown, they rate cartoons as being more aggressive (Laird, 1974; 1984). When subjects pose expressions of pain, they also rate electric shocks as more painful (Colby et al., 1977; Lanzetta et al., 1976). As Charles Darwin noted more than a hundred years ago, "The free expression by outward signs of an emotion intensifies it. On the other hand, the repression, as far as possible, of all outward signs softens our emotions" (Darwin, 1872, p. 22).

What is the link between facial feedback and emotion? One link is arousal. Posing intense facial expressions, e.g., those signifying fear, leads to increased arousal (Zuckerman et al., 1981). Our perception of heightened arousal then leads to self-report of heightened emotional activity. Other links may involve changes in brain temperature and release of neurotransmitters (Ekman, 1985; Zajonc, 1985). Perception of the contraction of facial

Facial-feedback hypothesis The view that stereotypical facial expressions can contribute to the experiencing of stereotypical emotions.

muscles involved in showing emotions may also lead us to perceive heightened emotional activation (McCaul et al., 1982).

You may have heard the British expression "to keep a stiff upper lip" as a way of handling stress. It may well be that a "stiff" lip will lower the experience of emotion so long as the lip is relaxed rather than quivering with fear or tension. But when a lip is stiffened through strong muscle tension, facial feedback could heighten autonomic activity and the perception of emotional response. In the following section we shall see that the facial feedback-hypothesis is related to the James-Lange theory of emotion.

THEORIES OF EMOTION

Emotions have physiological, situational, and cognitive components, but psychologists have disagreed as to how these components interact to produce feeling states and actions. Some psychologists argue that physiological arousal is a more basic component of emotional response than cognition, and that the type of arousal we experience strongly influences our cognitive appraisal and our labeling of the emotion (e.g., Izard, 1984; Zajonc, 1984). Other psychologists argue that cognitive appraisal and physiological arousal are so strongly intertwined that cognitive processes may determine the emotional response (e.g., Lazarus, 1984).

The so-called commonsense theory of emotions is that something happens (situation) which is cognitively appraised (interpreted) by the person, and that the feeling-state (a combination of arousal and thoughts) follows. For example, you meet someone new, appraise that person as delightful, and feelings of attraction follow. Or you flunk a test, recognize that you're in trouble, and feel down in the dumps.

However, historic and contemporary theories of how the components of emotions interact are at variance with the commonsense view. Let us consider a number of more important theories and see if we can arrive at some useful conclusions.

THE JAMES-LANGE THEORY

Just before the turn of the century, William James suggested that our emotions follow, rather than cause, our overt behavioral responses to events. This view was also proposed by a contemporary of James, the Danish physiologist Karl G. Lange. For this reason, it is referred to as the James-Lange theory of emotion.

According to James and Lange (see Figure 7.14, part A), certain external stimuli instinctively trigger specific patterns of arousal and action, such as fighting or fleeing. We then become angry *because* we act aggressively. We then become afraid *because* we run away. Emotions are simply the cognitive representations (or by-products) of automatic physiological and behavioral responses.

Walter Cannon (1927) criticized the James-Lange assertion that each emotion has distinct physiological correlates. Cannon argued that the phys-

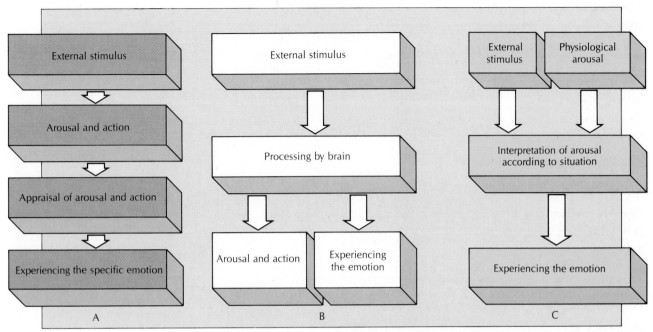

FIGURE 7.14 THEORIES OF EMOTION Several theories of emotion have been advanced, each of which has a different role for the components of emotional response. According to the James-Lange theory (part A), events trigger specific arousal patterns and actions. Emotions result from our appraisal of our bodily responses. According to the Cannon-Bard theory (part B), events are first processed by the brain. Bodily patterns of arousal, action, and our emotional responses are then triggered simultaneously. According to the theory of cognitive appraisal (part C), events and arousal are appraised by the individual. The emotional response stems from the person's appraisal of the situation and his or her level of arousal.

iological arousal that accompanies Emotion A is not so distinct from the arousal that accompanies Emotion B as the theory asserts. We can also note that the James-Lange view ascribes a very meager function to human cognition; it denies the roles of cognitive appraisal, personal values, and personal choice.

The James-Lange theory may be mainly of historical interest today, but still it is of value. It suggests that by acting in a certain way we can induce desired emotional responses. Perhaps we can overcome the emotion of fear by somehow approaching, rather than running from, dreaded objects or situations. Perhaps we can overcome the emotion of depression by engaging in, rather than withdrawing from, activities that we normally enjoy, such as bicycling or attending concerts. (This application is described in the nearby box on using pleasant events to counter feelings of depression.) Sound farfetched? These assumptions underlie many effective behavior-therapy practices that are currently used in clinics across the world. There is a kernel of truth in many outdated theories.

A CLOSER LOOK

MUST YOU REMAIN LOYAL TO DEPRESSION, OR CAN YOU USE PLEASANT EVENTS TO LIFT YOURSELF OUT OF THE DUMPS?

Some people act as though they want to remain faithful to feelings of depression. Becky's romance had recently disintegrated, and after some weeks had passed, friends became concerned that she remained weepy and withdrawn. Finally, despite her protests, they talked her into going with them to a rock concert by that new group, The Naked and the Dead.

It took some time for Becky to focus on the music and the excitement of the crowd, but after a while she began clapping and shouting with her friends. Afterwards, feelings of depression returned, but they were not so intense. Becky pushed herself more to get out and do things. She eventually dated others and dwelled less on the past.

Becky's friends had encouraged Becky to "get out and do things" because, like many people, they shared an assumption (consistent with the James-Lange theory) that by acting in a certain way we may come to experience the emotions usually linked with that activity. According to University of Oregon psychologist Peter Lewinsohn, one way to fight depression is to engage in pleasant events, events that are incompatible with depression. A number of researchers have shown that there is a significant correlation between mood and the number and type of pleasant activities with which we become involved (e.g., Lewinsohn & Graf, 1973; Lewinsohn & Libet, 1972; Rehm, 1978).

Here is a partial list of activities found by Lewinsohn and Graf to be linked with positive emotions:

Laughing
Being relaxed
Thinking about something good in the future
Thinking about people I like
Breathing clean air
Seeing beautiful scenery
Sitting in the sun
Having spare time
Listening to music
Seeing good things happen to my family or friends
Watching wild animals
Being with happy people
Being with friends
Having a frank and open conversation
Being with someone I love

Having a lively talk
Doing a project in my own way
Reading stories, novels, poems, or plays
Having peace and quiet
Wearing clean clothes
Smiling at people
Kissing
Watching people
Petting, necking
Complimenting or praising someone
Meeting someone new
Seeing old friends
Having coffee, tea, a soft drink with friends
Planning a trip or vacation
Learning to do something new

Would these activities work for you? First consider that there is a wide variety of preferences, and so we may profit from constructing our own lists. Also, experiments in using pleasant activities to lift one's mood have shown mixed results. For instance, Reich and Zautra (1981) found that engaging in pleasant activities increases feelings of well-being, but tends to relieve distress only for people under considerable stress. Biglan and Craker (1982) found that engaging in pleasant events increased the activity level of four depressed women, but did not improve self-reports of mood. So there are no guarantees.

Other research suggests that prolonged exercises such as jogging, swimming, bicycle riding, or fast walking do ameliorate feelings of depression in many cases (Doyne et al., 1983; Folkins & Sime, 1981; McCann & Holmes, 1984). As you will see in Chapter 11, there is evidence that depression may be linked to deficiencies in norepinephrine and other substances. Aerobic exercise may elevate the mood by increasing levels of these substances (Dimsdale & Moss, 1980; Carr et al., 1981) or of endorphins (see Chapter 2).

Emotions are complex, involving physiological, situational, and cognitive factors. Still, if you have been down in the dumps for a while and can't think of a good reason to stay there, it may help you to engage in some activities that seem incompatible with depression. Like chicken soup, it can't hurt. Try it—you may like it.

THE CANNON-BARD THEORY

Walter Cannon was not content to criticize the James-Lange theory. He (Cannon, 1927) and Philip Bard (1934) suggested that an event would trigger bodily responses (arousal and action) and the experience of an emotion simultaneously. As shown in Figure 7.14 (part B), when an event is perceived (processed by the brain), the brain stimulates autonomic and muscular activity (arousal and action) *and* cognitive activity (experiencing of the emotion). According to the Cannon-Bard theory, emotions *accompany* bodily responses. Emotions are not produced *by* bodily changes, as in the James-Lange theory.

The central criticism of the Cannon-Bard theory focuses on whether (1) bodily responses (arousal and action) and (2) emotions are actually stimulated simultaneously. For example, pain or the perception of danger may trigger arousal before we begin to experience distress or fear. Also, many of us have had the experience of having a "narrow escape," and then becoming aroused and shaky afterwards, when we have finally had time to consider the damage that might have occurred.

What is needed is a theory that allows for an ongoing interaction of external events, physiological changes (such as autonomic arousal and muscular activity), and cognitive activities. We need not be overly concerned with which must come first—the chicken, the egg, or the egg salad.

THE THEORY OF COGNITIVE APPRAISAL

According to Stanley Schachter (1971) and a number of other psychologists, emotions have generally similar patterns of bodily arousal. The essential way in which they vary is along a weak-strong dimension that is determined by one's level of arousal. The label we *attribute* to an emotion largely depends upon our cognitive appraisal of our situation. Cognitive appraisal is based on many factors, including our perception of external events and the ways in which other people seem to be responding to those events (see Figure 7.14, part C). Given the presence of other people, we engage in *social comparison* (see page 338) to arrive at an appropriate response.

In a classic experiment, Schachter and Jerome Singer (1962) showed that arousal can be labeled quite differently, depending on a person's situation. The investigators told subjects that their purpose was to study the effects of a vitamin on vision. Half the subjects received an injection of adrenalin, a hormone that increases autonomic arousal (see Chapter 2). A control group received an injection of an inactive **saline** solution. Subjects given adrenalin then received one of three "cognitive manipulations," as shown in Table 7.2. Group 1 was told nothing about possible emotional effects of the "vitamin." Group 2 was deliberately misinformed; group members were led to expect itching, numbness, or other irrelevant symptoms. Group 3 was informed accurately about the increased arousal they would experience.

After receiving injections and cognitive manipulations, subjects were asked to wait, in pairs, while the experimental apparatus was being set up. Subjects did not know that the person with whom they were waiting was a confederate of the experimenter. The purpose of the confederate was to model a response that the subject would believe resulted from the injection.

Some subjects waited with a confederate who acted in a happy-go-lucky manner. He flew paper airplanes about the room and tossed paper balls into a wastebasket. Other subjects waited with a confederate who

Saline Containing salt. (From the Latin *sal*, meaning "salt.")

TABLE 7.2 Injected Substances and Cognitive Manipulations in the Schachter-Singer Study

Group	Substance	Cognitive Manipulation
1	Adrenalin	No information given about effects
2	Adrenalin	Misinformation given: itching, numbness, etc.
3	Adrenalin	Accurate information: physiological arousal
4	Saline solution	None

SOURCE: Schachter & Singer (1962).

acted angrily, complaining about the experiment, tearing up a questionnaire, and departing the waiting room in a huff. As the confederates worked for their Oscars, real subjects were observed through a one-way mirror.

Subjects in Groups 1 and 2 were likely to imitate the behavior of the confederate. Those exposed to the **euphoric** confederate acted jovial and content. Those exposed to the angry confederate imitated that person's complaining, aggressive ways. But Groups 3 and 4 were less influenced by the behavior of the confederate.

Schachter and Singer concluded that Groups 1 and 2 were in an ambiguous situation. They experienced arousal from the adrenalin injection, but had no basis for attributing it to any event or emotion. Social comparison with the confederate led them to attribute their arousal either to happiness or anger, whichever was displayed by the confederate. Group 3 expected arousal from the injection with no particular emotional consequences. They did not imitate the confederate's display of happiness or anger, because they were not in an ambiguous situation. Group 4 experienced no physiological arousal for which they needed an attribution, except, perhaps, for some induced by observing the confederate. Group 4 subjects also failed to imitate the confederate.

Now happiness and anger are quite different emotions. Happiness is a positive emotion, and anger, for most of us, is a negative emotion. Yet Schachter and Singer suggest that any physiological differences between these two emotions are so slight that opposing cognitive appraisals of the same situation can lead one person to label arousal as happiness and another person to label arousal as anger. A supportive experiment suggests that it is similarly possible for people to confuse feelings of fear with feelings of sexual attraction (Dutton & Aron, 1974).

The Schachter-Singer view could not be farther removed from the James-Lange theory, which holds that each emotion has specific and readily recognized bodily sensations. The truth, it turns out, may lie somewhere in-between.

In science it must be possible to attain identical or similar results when experiments are replicated. The Schachter and Singer study has been replicated with *different* results. For instance, in studies by Rogers and Deckner (1975) and Maslach (1978), subjects were less likely to imitate the behavior of the confederate, and more likely to apply negative emotional labels to their arousal, even when exposed to a euphoric confederate.

Euphoric Characterized by feelings of well-being, elation.

Love An intense, positive emotion that involves factors such as attachment and caring.

Storge (STORE-gay). Feelings of attachment and affection.

Agape (AH-guh-pay). Feelings of generosity and charity.

Philia (FEEL-yuh). Feelings of friendship.

EVALUATION

What do we make of all this? As noted at the outset of our discussion of emotion, emotional responses are activated by physiological, situational, and cognitive factors. Recent research by Paul Ekman and his colleagues (1983) suggests that the patterns of arousal that lead us to believe we are experiencing certain emotions may be more specific than suggested by Schachter and Singer, but less specific than suggested by James and Lange. In any event, there are some reasonably distinct patterns of arousal, and these patterns are not fully interchangeable—although we may be confused as to our feelings when patterns of arousal rise up in apparently inappropriate situations. This is because our situations, and our cognitive appraisals of our situations, are also influential in activating our emotional responses. And when our situations are ambiguous, we may be at least somewhat more likely to interpret them by social comparison.

In sum, it may be that there is no reason to insist that any particular component of an experience—physiological, situational, or cognitive—is more crucial than others in activating emotional response. Perhaps the most important thing to note is that people are thinking beings who gather information from all three sources in determining their behavioral responses and in pinpointing labels for their emotional responses. The fact that none of the theories we have discussed applies to all people in all situations is comforting. Our emotions are not quite so easily understood or manipulated as theorists have suggested.

Now let us turn our attention to an enigmatic and always fascinating emotion—love.

LOVE

What makes the world go round? **Love,** of course. Love is one of the most deeply stirring emotions, the ideal for which we will make great sacrifice, the emotion that launched a thousand ships in the Greek epic *The Iliad.*

For thousands of years, poets have sought to capture love in words. A seventeenth-century poet wrote that his love was like "a red, red rose." In Sinclair Lewis's novel *Elmer Gantry,* love is "the morning and the evening star." Love is beautiful and elusive. It shines brilliantly and heavenly. Passionate or romantic love can also be earthy, involving a solid dose of sexual desire.

The Greek Heritage of Four Types of Love The concept of love can be traced back at least to the classical Greeks, who had terms for four different types of love related to its modern meaning: *storge, agape, philia,* and *eros.* **Storge** is translated as attachment and affection, the emotion that binds parents and children. **Agape** is similar to generosity and charity. It implies the wish to share one's bounty and is epitomized by anonymous donations to charity. **Philia** is close in meaning to friendship. It is based on liking and respect, and it involves the desire to do and share things with another person.

ROMANTIC LOVE In order to experience romantic love, one must be exposed to a culture that idealizes the concept.

Eros is closest in meaning to passionate or romantic love. Sigmund Freud used the concept of *eros* to describe an "instinct" that he thought motivated most human behavior (see Chapter 9). Freud believed, literally, that *eros* "makes the world go round." Our own concept of romantic love does not imply an instinct. Still, romantic love is an important determinant of behavior—in societies that believe in the concept.

Romantic Love: A Role-Playing Approach   In order to experience romantic love, one must be exposed to a culture that idealizes the concept. In Western culture, romantic love blossoms with the fairy tales of Sleeping Beauty, Cinderella, Snow White, and all their princes charming. It matures with romantic novels, television tales and films, and the personal tales of friends and relatives about dates and romances (Udry, 1971).

Consider an analogy: In Chapter 4 we noted that there may be no such thing as a hypnotic "trance." Rather, one must understand what is expected of a person in a "trance" in order to play the role of a hypnotized person. In the same way, romantic love may not reflect a natural inner state. A person must have experience with a culture that idealizes the con-

Eros Feelings of passionate or romantic love.

Ego identity Within Erikson's theory, a firm sense of who one is and what one stands for.

Idealize To magnify the positive features of another and to ignore his or her flaws.

cept of love in order to successfully play the role of a person who is "in love." This does not mean that we are being "phony" when we enact the role of someone in love (any more than "hypnotized" people need be accused of faking). It simply means that we require a clear concept of a certain pattern of behavior before we can enact it.

Unlike the Greeks, we use the label "love" to describe everything from affection to sexual intercourse ("making love"), because "love" is a more socially acceptable word for polite conversation. During adolescence, lust is often labeled love. We may refer to lust as love, because sexual desire in the absence of a committed relationship may be viewed as primitive or unworthy.

Defining Romantic Love Definitions of romantic love vary. Love is a complex concept involving intense feeling states, cognitions, and motivations (Hatfield, 1983; Sternberg & Grajek, 1984). Psychoanalysts generally speak in global concepts, such as Erich Fromm's "craving for complete fusion . . . with one other person" (1956, p. 44). Erik Erikson also sees love as the merging of two identities. To Erikson, mature love is possible only after one has established **ego identity** (see Chapters 8 and 9).

Others have avoided unmeasurable concepts like the merging or fusing of identities, and define romantic love in terms of the behavior of lovers. According to psychologist Keith E. Davis (1985), romantic love is characterized by two clusters of feelings: a "passion cluster" and a "caring cluster." As shown in Figure 7.15, the passion cluster contains feelings of fascination (preoccupation with the loved one), sexual desire, and exclusiveness (a special relationship with the loved one). The caring cluster includes championing the interests of the loved one and giving the utmost to or for the loved one, including, when necessary, sacrifice of one's own interests. College undergraduates see the desire to help or care for the loved one as more central to the concept of love than concern for how the loved one can meet one's own needs (Steck et al., 1982). Romantic lovers also **idealize** one another (Driscoll et al., 1972). They magnify each other's positive features and overlook their flaws.

Social psychologists Ellen Berscheid and Elaine Walster (Berscheid & Walster, 1978; Walster & Walster, 1978) define love in terms of physiological response and cognitive appraisal of that response. Love, to them, involves intense arousal and some reason to label that arousal love.

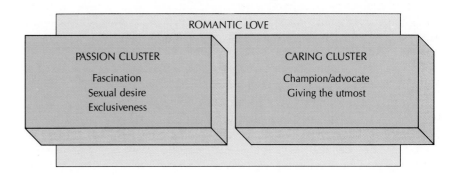

FIGURE 7.15 PASSION AND CARING Romantic love is characterized by two clusters of feelings—a passion cluster and a caring cluster.

QUESTIONNAIRE

ARE YOU IN LOVE? THE LOVE SCALE

The following love scale was developed at Northeastern University in Boston. To compare your own score (or scores, if you have been busy) with those of Northeastern University students, simply think of your dating partner or partners and fill out the scale with each of them in mind. Then compare your scores to those in Appendix B.

THE LOVE SCALE

Directions: Circle the number that best shows how true or false the items are for you according to this code:

7 = definitely true
6 = rather true
5 = somewhat true
4 = not sure, or equally true and false
3 = somewhat false
2 = rather false
1 = definitely false

1. I look forward to being with _____ a great deal.
   definitely false 1 2 3 4 5 6 7 definitely true

2. I find _____ to be sexually exciting.
   definitely false 1 2 3 4 5 6 7 definitely true

3. _____ has fewer faults than most people.
   definitely false 1 2 3 4 5 6 7 definitely true

4. I would do anything I could for _____ .
   definitely false 1 2 3 4 5 6 7 definitely true

5. _____ is very attractive to me.
   definitely false 1 2 3 4 5 6 7 definitely true

6. I like to share my feelings with _____ .
   definitely false 1 2 3 4 5 6 7 definitely true

7. Doing things is more fun when _____ and I do them together.
   definitely false 1 2 3 4 5 6 7 definitely true

8. I like to have _____ all to myself.
   definitely false 1 2 3 4 5 6 7 definitely true

9. I would feel horrible if anything bad happened to _____ .
   definitely false 1 2 3 4 5 6 7 definitely true

10. I think about _____ very often.
    definitely false 1 2 3 4 5 6 7 definitely true

11. It is very important that _____ cares for me.
    definitely false 1 2 3 4 5 6 7 definitely true

12. I am most content when I am with _____ .
    definitely false 1 2 3 4 5 6 7 definitely true

13. It is difficult for me to stay away from _____ for very long.
    definitely false 1 2 3 4 5 6 7 definitely true.

14. I care about _____ a great deal.
    definitely false 1 2 3 4 5 6 7 definitely true.

Total Score for Love Scale: _____

Romantic love An intense, positive emotion that involves arousal, a cultural setting that idealizes love, an attractive person, feelings of caring, and the belief that one is in love.

Let us define romantic love in terms of physiological, situational, and cognitive components. **Romantic love** is an intense, positive emotion that involves (1) arousal in the form of sexual attraction; (2) a cultural setting that idealizes love; (3) the actual or fantasized presence of an attractive person; (4) caring, and (5) the *belief* that one is "in love."

On Love and Arousal: If My Heart Is Pounding, It Must Mean I Love You   The Roman poet Ovid suggested that young men (his interests were admittedly sexist) might open their ladies' hearts by taking them to the gory gladiator contests. The women could attribute the pounding of their hearts and the butterflies in their stomachs to the nearness of their dates, and conclude that they were inspired by them. Research does suggest that strong arousal in the presence of a reasonably attractive person may lead us to believe that we are experiencing desire (Istvan & Griffitt, 1978). But if the person is decidedly *un*attractive, we may attribute our arousal to revulsion or disgust (White et al., 1981).

Despite the saying, love does not seem to be "blind"—just a bit nearsighted. Let us consider an experiment on arousal and feelings of passion in which male college students rated the attractiveness of *Playboy* nudes (Valins, 1966). Each rater was wired so that he could monitor his own heartbeat (he believed) through a microphone and earphone set. Heart sounds accelerated in frequency when certain slides were being shown. In general, subjects rated models as more attractive when the heartbeats were more rapid.

There was one catch. Valins had doctored the feedback arrangement so that raters were *not* listening to their own heartbeat. Instead, they were hearing heart beats that were accelerated or slowed down for randomly selected models. The men may have attributed what they believed to be their own hearts racing to the slide being shown. As a consequence, perhaps they believed that this woman *must* be particularly appealing to them.

Many sources of arousal may lead us to respond more positively to members of the opposite sex. A horror movie or a roller coaster ride may just stimulate your date's passion. It is also possible that there is, after all, a love potion. It's called adrenalin.

SUMMARY

1. A motive is a state within an organism that activates and directs behavior toward a goal. A physiological need is a state of deprivation. Needs give rise to drives, which are psychological in nature and arouse us to action. An incentive is perceived as being capable of satisfying a need.

2. According to the instinct theory of motivation, animals are born with preprogramed tendencies to behave in certain ways in certain situations. Stimuli called releasers elicit innate fixed-action patterns (FAPs).

3. According to the drive-reduction theory of motivation, rewards reduce drives and, as a consequence, we are motivated to learn to engage in behavior that leads to rewards. Drive-reduction theorists differentiate between primary (innate) drives and acquired (learned) drives.

4. Humanistic psychologists argue that behavior can be growth-oriented as people are motivated to consciously strive for self-fulfillment. Maslow hypothesized that people have a hierarchy of needs, including an innate need for self-actualization. His hierarchy includes physiological needs, safety needs, love and belonging-

ness needs, esteem needs, the need for cognitive understanding, aesthetic needs, and the need for self-actualization.

5. Physiological or primary drives are unlearned and generally function according to a homeostatic principle—the body's tendency to maintain a steady state.

6. Hunger is regulated by several internal mechanisms, including stomach contractions, blood sugar level, receptors in the mouth and liver, and the responses of the hypothalamus. The ventromedial hypothalamus functions as a stop-eating center. Lesions in this area lead to hyperphagia in rats, causing the animals to grow to several times their normal body weight, but to eventually level off. The lateral hypothalamus has a start-eating center.

7. Obese people are more responsive than normal-weight people to external cues for hunger, including the odor and taste of food, seeing other people eat, and the time of day. Effective diets tend to use combinations of the following elements: improving nutritional knowledge, decreasing calorie intake, exercise, and behavior modification.

8. Thirst is regulated by level of blood flow and the concentration of chemicals, like sodium, in the blood. Dehydration leads the kidneys to produce the hormone angiotensin, which signals the hypothalamus. Osmoreceptors in the hypothalamus detect lowered local flow of blood, which stems from dehydration or increased concentration of sodium. The hypothalamus then stimulates the pituitary to secrete antidiuretic hormone, which increases reabsorption of urine, and also signals the cortex, which prompts the thirst drive.

9. Stimulus motives are also innate. Sensory-deprivation studies show that lack of stimulation is aversive. People and many lower animals have needs for stimulation and activity, for exploration and manipulation. Sensation-seekers may seek thrills, act out on impulses, and be easily bored.

10. There is evidence that we are motivated to seek optimal levels of arousal, levels at which we feel best and function most efficiently. According to the Yerkes-Dodson law, high levels of motivation facilitate performance on simple tasks, but impede performance on complex tasks.

11. Social motives are secondary or learned. They include needs for achievement (n Ach), affiliation, and power. People with high n Ach attain higher grades and earn more money than people of comparable ability with lower n Ach.

12. The need for affiliation prompts us to join groups and make friends. Anxiety tends to increase our need for affiliation, especially with people who share our predicaments.

13. The need for power is the need to control organizations and other people. People with a frustrated need for power are prone to developing physical illness.

14. An emotion is a state of feeling with physiological, situational, and cognitive components. Emotions motivate behavior and also serve as goals.

15. So-called lie detectors (polygraphs) actually detect patterns of arousal that may be associated with lying in many individuals. However, evidence suggests that there are major problems with the validity of polygraphs.

16. According to Plutchik's classification system, there are eight primary emotions from which other emotions are derived. Plutchik argues that emotions have survival-related functions. Intense emotions prompt the most vigorous behavior, while mild emotions may only heighten alertness.

17. Research by Ekman shows that there are several basic emotions whose expression is recognized around the world.

18. The posing of intense facial expressions can heighten emotional response, perhaps because intense expressions heighten arousal and provide muscular feedback.

19. Psychologists are not agreed as to the relative importance of physiological arousal and cognitive appraisal in activating particular emotions. According to James-Lange theory, emotions have specific patterns of arousal and action that are triggered by certain external events. The emotion follows the overt response.

20. The Cannon-Bard theory proposes that processing of events by the brain gives rise simultaneously to the emotion and to bodily responses. From this view, emotions accompany bodily responses.

21. According to the theory of cognitive appraisal, emotions have largely similar patterns of arousal. The emotion a person will experience in response to an external stimulus reflects that person's appraisal of the stimulus—that is, the meaning of the stimulus to him or her.

22. Research seems to suggest that patterns of arousal are more specific than suggested by the theory of cognitive appraisal, but that cognitive appraisal does play an important role in determining our responses to events.

23. As an emotion, romantic love is found only in cultures that believe in the concept.

24. Romantic love is characterized by two clusters of feelings: passion and caring. Romantic love may be defined as a positive emotion that involves arousal, actual or fantasized presence of an attractive person, a cultural setting that idealizes love, the presence of an attractive person, caring, and the belief that one is in love.

TRUTH OR FICTION REVISITED

One out of five American adults is obese.
True. More than 30 million of us exceed our desirable body weight by at least 20 percent.

Overweight people are more sensitive to stomach pangs than are normal-weight people.
False. Normal-weight people are more sensitive to internal cues for hunger.

Eating salty pretzels can make you thirsty.
True. Increased concentrations of salt cause the hypothalamus to trigger the thirst drive.

"Getting away from it all" by going on a vacation from all sensory input for a few hours is relaxing.
False. Prolonged sensory deprivation is actually a disturbing experience.

If quarterbacks get too "psyched up" for a big game, their performance on the field may flounder.
True. The performance of complex tasks can suffer when we are very highly aroused.

A strong need to get ahead is the most powerful predictor of success in climbing the corporate ladder.
False. According to the Bray study, administrative and interpersonal skills were better predictors of getting ahead, at least at AT&T.

Misery loves company.
True, according to the Schachter study—at least when the company is also miserable.

A frustrated need for power can lead to high blood pressure.
True. Frustration is linked to overactivation of the autonomic nervous system, and chronic autonomic overactivation can lead to high blood pressure and many other ills.

You may be able to fool a lie detector by squiggling your toes.
True. Toe-squiggling can cause arousal, and the polygraph measures arousal rather than lying per se.

Romantic love is found in every culture in the world.
False. It is found only in cultures that idealize the concept.

Taking a date to a horror film or for a roller-coaster ride may stimulate feelings of passion.
True. The heightened autonomic arousal could be attributed to your charming presence.

OUTLINE

CHAPTER 8

Developmental Psychology

TRUTH OR FICTION?

- You can select the sex of your child.
- Our hearts start beating when we are only one-fifth of an inch long and weigh a fraction of an ounce.
- Newborn babies prefer their mothers' voices to those of other women.
- The way to a baby's heart is through its stomach—that is, babies become emotionally attached to those who feed them.
- Children placed in day-care facilities grow less attached to their mothers.
- Children placed in day-care facilities are more aggressive than children who are cared for in the home.
- Parents encountering financial difficulties are more likely to abuse their children.
- A four-year-old child may believe that the sky is blue because someone has painted it.
- Adolescents are biologically capable of reproduction when they first ejaculate or have their first menstrual period.
- Sexual morality is the central concern of the identity crisis of adolescence.
- Young adulthood is characterized by trying to "make it" in the career world.
- Most mothers suffer from the "empty-nest syndrome" when the youngest child leaves home.
- Forced retirement may be a death sentence.

On a summerlike day in October, Elaine and her husband Dennis rush out to their jobs as usual. While Elaine, a buyer for a New York department store, is arranging for dresses from the Chicago manufacturer to arrive in time for the spring line, a very different drama is unfolding in her body. Hormones are causing a follicle (egg container) in one of her **ovaries** to rupture and release an ovum. For a day or so following **ovulation,** Elaine will be capable of becoming pregnant. When it is released, the ovum begins a slow journey down a four-inch-long **fallopian tube** to the **uterus.** It is within this tube that one of Dennis's sperm cells will unite with it.

Like many other couples, Elaine and Dennis made love the previous night. But unlike most other couples, their timing and methodology were quite purposeful. Elaine's **gynecologist** had been tracking the consistency of her **vaginal mucus** with a **viscometer,** an instrument in his office. The viscometer had predicted that her mucus would be thinnest at about midnight. When the mucus is thinnest, sperm cells with Y sex **chromosomes** are likely to arrive in the fallopian tubes before sperm with X sex chromosomes do. If a sperm with a Y sex chromosome unites with an ovum, all of which contain X sex chromosomes, the woman will conceive a boy. In the past, two of Dennis's sperm, each containing an X sex chromosome, had resulted in Elaine's conceiving daughters.

When Elaine and Dennis made love, he ejaculated hundreds of millions of sperm, with about equal numbers of Y and X sex chromosomes. By the time of conception only a few thousand had survived the journey to the fallopian tubes. Of these, eight of ten carried Y sex chromosomes. Several bombarded the ovum, attempting to penetrate. Only one succeeded. The fertilized ovum, or **zygote,** is 1/175th of an inch long—a tiny stage for the drama yet to unfold.

The genetic material from Dennis's sperm cell combines with that in Elaine's egg cell. Later Dennis and Elaine will be pleased to learn that the sperm carried a Y sex chromosome, after all. Other genetic instructions determine that the being conceived this morning will grow arms rather than wings, a mouth rather than gills, and hair rather than scales. From the moment of conception, your stamp as an individual distinct from all others— with the possible exception of an identical twin—has been assured: whether you will have blond or black hair, someday grow bald or develop a widow's peak, or have a straight or curved nose. We do not know exactly how much influence genetic instructions have on traits like timidity, social shyness, and intelligence. Still, the effects of heredity are felt to some degree here as well (e.g., Kagan, 1984; Plomin & DeFries, 1980; Scarr et al., 1981).

Developmental psychologists would be pleased to study the behavior of Dennis and Elaine's new son from the moment of conception through his lifetime. There are a number of reasons for this. One approach to the explanation of adult behavior lies in the discovery of early influences and developmental sequences. One answer to the question of *why* we behave in certain ways lies in outlining the development of behavior patterns over the years.

There is continuing interest in sorting out what human behavior is the result of nature (heredity) and of nurture (environmental influences). What effects do genetics, early interactions with parents and **siblings,** and expe-

Ovaries Female reproductive organs located in the abdomen that produce female reproductive cells, or *ova. (Ovum* is a Latin word meaning "egg.")

Ovulation (of-you-LAY-shun). The releasing of an ovum (female reproductive cell) from an ovary.

Fallopian tube (fal-LOPE-ee-an). A tube that conducts ova from an ovary to the uterus.

Uterus (YOU-turr-us). The hollow organ within females in which the unborn child develops. (A Latin word.)

Gynecologist (guy-nah-KOLL-oh-jist). A physician who specializes in women's health problems. (From the Greek *gyne,* meaning "woman.")

Vaginal mucus Secretions that moisten and protect membranes within the vagina.

Viscometer An instrument that measures the viscosity (stickiness) of vaginal mucus.

Chromosomes Genetic structures composed of genes. See Chapter 2.

Zygote A fertilized ovum.

Siblings Brothers and sisters.

AN EXERCISE CLASS FOR PREGNANT WOMEN Years ago, the rule of thumb was that pregnant women were not to exert themselves. Today it is recognized that exercise is healthful for pregnant women, because it promotes cardiovascular fitness and increases muscle strength. Fitness and strength are assets during childbirth—and at other times.

riences in the school and the community have on traits like aggressiveness and intelligence? Clearly, the effects of nature and nurture interact in our development. Heredity matters little if one starves to death while an infant, and a rich environment cannot turn a rhesus monkey or an aardvark into a Shakespeare.

Developmental psychologists also seek insight into the causes of developmental abnormalities. This avenue of research can yield answers to pressing questions of health and psychological well-being. For instance, should pregnant women abstain from smoking and drinking? Is it safe for the unborn child if pregnant women use aspirin for a headache, or tetracycline to ward off a bacterial invasion? What are the effects of social deprivation at an early age? Need we be concerned about placing our children in day-care centers while we work? What conflicts and disillusionments can we expect as we journey through our thirties, forties, and fifties? What are the effects of forced retirement on the elderly? The information acquired by developmental psychologists can help us make decisions about how we rear our children and lead our own lives.

Of course, there is another very good reason for studying human development. Thousands of psychologists enjoy it.

THEORIES OF DEVELOPMENT

On a descriptive level, psychologists observe and record the growth and development of children and adults as faithfully as possible. But psychologists also try to understand growth and development through the creation of developmental theories. Accurate theories allow psychologists to predict aspects of growth and development and to derive suggestions for helping when things go wrong.

TABLE 8.1 An Outline of Three Major Stage Theories of Development

Approximate Age	Sigmund Freud: Psychosexual Development	Erik Erikson: Psychosocial Development	Jean Piaget: Intellectual Development
Birth–1 year	Oral	Trust vs. mistrust	Sensorimotor
1–2 years	Anal	Autonomy vs. doubt	
2–6 years	Phallic	Initiative vs. guilt	Preoperational
7–12 years	Latency	Industry vs. inferiority	Concrete Operational
Adolescence	Genital	Ego identity vs. role diffusion	Formal Operational
Young adulthood		Intimacy vs. isolation	
Middle adulthood		Generativity vs. stagnation	
Late adulthood		Ego integrity vs. despair	

These stages are not theorized to be totally age-bound. Different people may enter different stages at somewhat different ages, and many people do not reach the formal operational stage of intellectual development at all. We may also bring characteristics from earlier stages with us when we advance to new stages; for example, a person may cope with issues involving basic trust and mistrust for many years, or a lifetime. Piaget's and Erikson's stages are discussed later in this chapter, while Freud's theory is discussed in Chapter 9.

Some theories of development are **stage** theories. A stage is a distinct period of life that differs in quality from other stages. Stages also follow one another in fixed sequences.

According to Sigmund Freud's psychoanalytic theory, for example, each stage of development—oral, anal, and so on—is ushered in by biological changes. Each stage is characterized by particular behaviors and holds a distinct potential for the development of various traits and conflicts. Freud's view of development is also **psychosexual**—that is, he emphasized the sexual implications of developing biological structures.

Table 8.1 outlines three stage theories of development: Freud's stages of psychosexual development, Erik Erikson's stages of psychosocial development, and Jean Piaget's periods of intellectual development. The theories of Freud and Erikson primarily address the development of personality traits and interpersonal relationships. Piaget's theory addresses the ways in which we come to develop a cognitive representation of the world.

Not all developmental approaches involve stages. Social-learning theorists view human development as a continuous process in which the effects of learning mount gradually, with no major sudden qualitative changes. In general, stage theorists tend to place more emphasis on nature and **maturation.** They point out that the environment, even when enriched, profits us little until we are mature enough, or **ready,** to develop in a certain direction. Social-learning theorists place more emphasis on the role of the environment, or nurture.

Stage A distinct period of life that is qualitatively different from other stages. Stages follow one another in an orderly sequence.

Psychosexual Sigmund Freud's characterization of development, in which the sexual implications of maturing biological structures are emphasized. See Chapter 9.

Maturation Changes that result from heredity and minimal nutrition but do not appear to require learning or exercise. A gradual, orderly unfolding or developing of new structures or behaviors as a result of heredity. (From the Latin *maturatio,* meaning "ripening.")

Ready In developmental psychology, referring to a stage in the maturation of an organism when it becomes capable of engaging in a certain response.

PRENATAL DEVELOPMENT

The Chinese are nine months older than we are when they are the same age. Why? The Chinese date a person's age from the assumed time of conception rather than birth. The first nine months are eventful, indeed.

Following conception, the single cell formed by the union of sperm and egg will multiply—becoming two, then four, then eight, and so on, forming tissues and organs and structures that gradually take the unmistakable shape of a human being. The nine months of **prenatal** development are divided into three **trimesters** of three months each.

THE FIRST TRIMESTER

About one day after conception, the zygote suddenly divides into two cells. It then divides repeatedly, even while it is undergoing the journey to the uterus with no source of outside nourishment. Three to four days are required to reach the uterus. Then this mass of dividing cells wanders about the uterus for another three to four days before beginning to become implanted in the uterine wall. Implantation requires another week or so. The period from conception to implantation is called the **period of the ovum.**

The **embryonic period** lasts from implantation until about the eighth week of development. During the embryonic period, the major organ systems are formed. During the third week after conception, the head and the blood vessels begin to form. During the fourth week, a primitive heart begins to beat and pump blood in an organism about one-fifth of an inch long. It will continue to beat without rest every minute of every day for perhaps eighty or ninety years. "Arm buds" and "leg buds" begin to appear toward the end of the first month. Ears, nose, and mouth begin to take shape. By this time the nervous system, including the brain, has also begun to develop.

Fingers and toes become apparent at six to eight weeks. By the end of the second month the limbs are elongating, and facial features are becoming distinct—in an embryo about one inch long. During the second month the nervous system begins to transmit messages. By the end of the embryonic period, the kidneys are filtering acid from the blood, and the liver is producing red blood cells.

The **fetal stage** begins with the third month and is characterized by the growth and further development of organ systems and by dramatic gains in overall size and weight. The fetus begins to turn and respond to external stimulation at about the ninth or tenth week. By the end of the third month fingers and toes appear fully formed. The eyes can be clearly distinguished, and the sex of the fetus can be determined visually.

Hormones and Prenatal Sexual Differentiation At about five to six weeks, when the embryo is only one-fourth to one-half inch long, nondescript sex organs have been formed. By about the seventh week after conception, the genetic code (XY or XX) begins to assert itself, leading to changes in the internal and external sexual organs. If a Y chromosome is present,

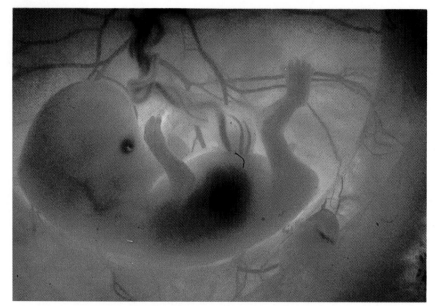

A HUMAN FETUS AT ABOUT FOUR AND A HALF MONTHS

testes will form and begin to produce male sex hormones, or **androgens.** Androgens lead to further development of internal and external male sex organs.

In the absence of male sex hormones, the internal and external sex organs will become female. Female sex hormones are not needed to induce these changes. If an embryo with an XY chromosomal structure were prevented from producing androgens, it would develop as a female—despite the genetic code.

The Amniotic Sac The unborn child—embryo and fetus—develops within an **amniotic sac,** a protective environment in the mother's uterus. The sac is surrounded by a clear membrane and contains **amniotic fluid,** which suspends the developing child. Amniotic fluid serves as a "shock absorber," preventing the child from being damaged by the mother's movements. It also helps maintain an even temperature.

The Placenta The **placenta** is a mass of tissue that permits the fetus to exchange nutrients and wastes with the mother. The placenta is unique in origin: it grows from material supplied both by mother and embryo. The fetus is connected to the placenta by the **umbilical cord.** The mother is connected to the placenta by the system of blood vessels in the uterine wall.

The circulatory systems of mother and fetus do not mix. A membrane in the placenta permits only certain substances to pass through, such as oxygen and nutrients (from the mother), carbon dioxide (from the fetus), some microscopic disease organisms—including those that cause **syphilis** and **German measles**—and some drugs, including aspirin, narcotics, alcohol, and tranquilizers. (See Table 8.2.)

Androgens Male sex hormones. See Chapters 2 and 7.

Amniotic sac (am-knee-AH-tick). A sac within the uterus that contains the embryo or fetus.

Amniotic fluid Fluid within the amniotic sac that protects the embryo or fetus from being jarred or injured. Amniotic fluid is formed largely from the unborn child's urine.

Placenta (pluh-CENT-uh). A membrane that permits the exchange of nutrients and waste products between the mother and her developing child, but does not allow the maternal and fetal bloodstreams to mix. (From the Greek *plakous,* meaning "flat object.")

Umbilical cord A tube between the mother and her developing child through which nutrients and waste products are conducted. (From the Latin *umbilicalis,* meaning "situated at the navel.")

Syphilis A sexually transmitted disease.

German measles A disease that can cause nerve damage in unborn children.

TABLE 8.2 Possible Effects on the Fetus of Certain Agents Taken During Pregnancy

Agent	Possible Effect
Accutane	Malformation, stillbirth
Alcohol	Mental retardation, addiction, hyperactivity, undersize
Aspirin (large doses)	Respiratory problems, bleeding
Bendectin	Cleft palate? Heart deformities?
Caffeine (coffee, many soft drinks, chocolate, etc.)	Stimulates fetus; other effects uncertain
Cigarettes	Undersize, premature delivery, fetal death
Diethylstilbestrol (DES—a form of estrogen formerly used to help maintain pregnancy)	Cancer of the cervix or testes
Heavy metals (lead, mercury)	Hyperactivity, mental retardation, stillbirth
Heavy sedation during labor	Brain damage, asphyxiation
Heroin, morphine, other narcotics	Addiction, undersize
Paint fumes (substantial exposure)	Mental retardation
PCB, dioxin, other insecticides	Under study (possible stillbirth)
Progestin	Masculinization of female embryos; heightened aggressiveness?
Rubella (German measles)	Mental retardation, nerve damage impairing vision and hearing
Streptomycin	Deafness
Tetracycline	Yellow teeth, deformed bones
Thalidomide	Deformed or missing limbs
Vitamin A (large doses)	Cleft palate, eye damage
Vitamin D (large doses)	Mental retardation
X-rays	Malformation of organs

A variety of chemical and other agents have been found harmful to the fetus, or are strongly implicated in fetal damage. Pregnant women should consult their physicians about their diets, vitamin supplements, and use of any drugs—including nonprescription drugs.

The placenta also secretes hormones, such as estrogen and progesterone, that preserve the pregnancy. Ultimately the placenta passes from the mother's body after delivery. For this reason it is also called the "afterbirth."

THE SECOND TRIMESTER

Between the ends of the first and second trimesters, the fetus advances from one *ounce* to two *pounds* in weight and grows three or four times in length, from about four to fourteen inches.

During the second trimester, soft, downy hair grows above the eyes and on the scalp. The skin turns ruddy because of blood vessels that show through the surface. (During the third trimester, fatty layers will give the red a pinkish hue.)

In the middle of the fourth month, the mother usually detects the first fetal movements. By the end of the second trimester, the fetus moves its limbs so vigorously that the mother may complain of being kicked. It opens and shuts its eyes, sucks its thumb, alternates between periods of wakefulness and sleep, and perceives lights and sounds. It also hiccoughs and turns somersaults, all of which are clearly perceived by the mother—often at 4:00 A.M.

THE THIRD TRIMESTER

During the last three months the organ systems of the fetus continue to mature. The fetus gains nearly six pounds and grows in length by 50 percent. Newborn boys average about seven and a half pounds and newborn girls about seven pounds.

During the seventh month, the fetus normally turns upside down in the uterus so that delivery will be head-first. As the fetus grows it becomes somewhat cramped in the uterus, and movement is constricted. Many women become concerned that their fetuses are markedly less active during the ninth month than previously, but most of the time this change is not linked to any problems.

In recent years, awareness of the risks to the fetus posed by maternal use of pain-reducing medications during labor and delivery has increased. Since many such drugs can depress the nervous-system activity of the fetus, and the breathing of the newborn, women today tend to use them as sparingly as possible. However, so-called **regional anesthetics,** such as the **epidural**—in contrast to **general anesthetics**—have less of an effect on the child.

INFANCY AND CHILDHOOD

From the dark and private prenatal world, the **neonate** is thrust into a room filled with light, noise, incomprehensible movements, and cold. Mucus and blood that may clog its respiratory tract are wiped away when its head appears. Mucus is usually aspirated from its mouth by suction, so that the passageway for breathing will not be obstructed. When the baby is completely out of the mother's body, the suctioning is usually repeated. Because of the use of suction, the baby is no longer routinely held upside down or slapped on the buttocks to help expel mucus and stimulate breathing.

Once the baby is breathing adequately on its own, the umbilical cord, through which it had received oxygen from the mother, is clamped and cut. The stump of the cord will dry up and usually drop off the baby within several days. (Whether the baby winds up with an "inny" or an "outy" has nothing to do with the preferences or expertise of the physician.)

Drops of silver nitrate or an antibiotic ointment is put into the baby's eyes to prevent eye infections that could stem from passage through the vagina. The baby also receives a vitamin K injection, since newborns do not manufacture this vitamin. Vitamin K helps ensure that the baby's blood will clot normally in case of bleeding.

In response to complaints that hospitals are cold, impersonal places to have babies, some babies today are delivered in **alternate birthing centers** or in dimly lit hospital rooms that resemble bedrooms. Rather than whisking the baby away to a nursery after the umbilical cord is cut, the

Regional anesthetics Methods that produce loss of sensation (and thus pain) in certain parts of the body. (From the Greek *an-,* meaning "without," and *aisthesis,* meaning "feeling.")

Epidural Referring to the canal surrounding the spinal column. Anesthetic injected into this canal anesthetizes the lower part of the woman's body during childbirth.

General anesthetics Methods that control pain by putting a person to sleep.

Neonate A newly born child.

Alternate birthing centers Homelike settings for childbirth in which medical care is readily available, if required.

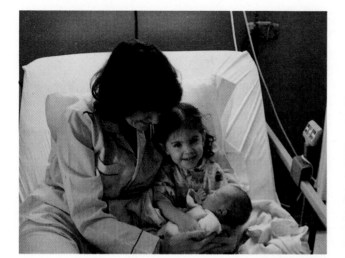

A CHANGE OF HEART This two-year-old girl has been excitedly awaiting the birth of her baby sister. By a couple of months later, however, she has learned that baby requires a good deal of attention from Mother, and she is not so certain that a baby sister was a good idea after all.

neonate is often placed on the mother's abdomen for a while and, in many instances, allowed to remain in the mother's room until discharge from the hospital. Some researchers argue that the first few hours after birth present a "maternal-sensitive" period during which the mother is particularly disposed, largely because of hormones, to form bonds of **attachment** with the neonate. In an experiment on bonding, Marshall Klaus and John Kennell (1978) arranged for an experimental group of new mothers to receive an additional sixteen hours of contact time (beyond that suggested by normal hospital procedures) with their infants over the first three days following delivery. They reported that mothers who spent more time with their newborn infants showed greater attachment (spending more time with their infants, and kissing, soothing, and talking to them more frequently) at follow-ups of one month, one, and two years. Because of such reports, many hospitals now promote as much interaction between mother and infant as is possible at this time.

The Klaus and Kennell studies seem powerful, indeed, but there are limitations. First, fathers and adoptive mothers, neither of whom have had the potentially effective chemical agents rushing through their bloodstreams, can also form powerful attachments to their children. Second, the extended-contact mothers recognized that they were in a program that went beyond normal hospital procedures. (How could they not have been aware of their special status, when other women's babies were dutifully swept away by staff according to the hands of the clock?) It could well have been knowledge of being "special" that contributed to their apparently higher levels of involvement with their infants. Other studies, moreover, have not found such differences among mothers given extended early contact with their babies (Grossmann et al., 1981). There may be no particular **critical**

Attachment (1) The tendency of infants or young organisms to remain close to other organisms, especially when fear-inducing stimuli are introduced. (2) A general description of the closeness of many parent-child relationships, involving sharing of strong, positive emotions.

period for mother-infant bonding. We shall further explore the origins of attachment later in the chapter.

In any event, early closeness is often desired by the mother, and there are no reasons, other than hospital procedures, why mothers should not be allowed to spend as much time with their **infants** as they wish. Rather than being left to pace in the waiting room, fathers are now usually present during labor and at the delivery and may help their wives through these processes by guiding them in breathing and relaxation exercises.

REFLEXES

If soon after your birth you had been held gently, face down in comfortably warm water, you would not have drowned. Instead of breathing in, you would have exhaled slowly through the mouth and engaged in swimming motions.* This response is inborn, or innate, and just one of many **reflexes** with which children are born. Reflexes are stereotypical responses that are elicited by specific stimuli. They do not involve higher brain functions; they occur automatically, without thinking.

Several months later, this swimming reflex, like many other reflexes, will have ceased to exist. But even at six to twelve months of age, children can learn readily how to swim. The transition from reflexive swimming to learned swimming can be reasonably smooth with careful, guided practice.

Many reflexes have survival value. Since newborn children do not "know" that it is necessary to eat in order to live or to reduce feelings of hunger, it is fortunate that they have **rooting** and sucking reflexes. Neonates will turn their heads (that is, root) toward stimuli that touch the cheek and will suck objects that touch their lips. Neonates reflexively withdraw from painful stimuli (the withdrawal reflex), and they draw up their legs and arch their backs in response to sudden noises, bumps, or loss of support while being held (the startle or Moro reflex). They reflexively grasp objects that press against the palms of their hands (the grasp or palmar reflex) and spread their toes when the soles of their feet are stimulated (the Babinski reflex). Babies also show sneezing, coughing, yawning, blinking, and many other reflexes. (It is guaranteed that you will learn about the **sphincter** reflex if you dress in expensive new clothes and hold an undiapered neonate on your lap for a while.) Pediatricians largely learn about the adequacy of newborn children's neural functioning by testing their reflexes.

As children develop, their muscles and neural functions mature, and they learn to coordinate sensory and motor activity. Many reflexes tend to drop out of their storehouse of responses, and many processes, like that of the elimination of wastes, come under voluntary control.

PERCEPTUAL DEVELOPMENT

Newborn children spend about sixteen hours a day sleeping and do not have much opportunity to learn about the world. Still, it seems that they are capable of perceiving the world reasonably well soon after birth (Haber & Hershenson, 1980).

*I urge readers not to test babies for this reflex. The hazards are obvious.

Critical period A period in an organism's development when it is capable of certain types of learning.

Infant A very young organism, a baby. (From Latin roots meaning "not yet speaking.")

Reflex A simple unlearned response to a stimulus.

Rooting The turning of an infant's head toward a touch, as by the mother's nipple.

Sphincter A ringlike muscle that circles a bodily opening, such as the anus. An infant will exhibit the sphincter reflex (have a bowel movement) in response to intestinal pressure. (A Greek word meaning "the act of closing.")

Pupillary reflex The automatic adjusting of the irises to permit more or less light to enter the eye.

Fixation time The amount of time spent looking at a visual stimulus. A measure of interest in infants.

FIGURE 8.1 THE CLASSIC VISUAL CLIFF EXPERIMENT This young explorer has the good sense not to crawl out onto an apparently unsupported surface, even when Mother beckons from the other side. Rats, pups, kittens, and chicks also will not try to walk across to the other side. (So don't bother asking why the chicken crossed the visual cliff.)

Visual Development   The **pupillary reflex** is present at birth; the irises of the eyes widen automatically to admit more light when it is dark, and narrow to admit less light when it is bright. Neonates are able to discriminate between light and dark and to respond to color (Bornstein et al., 1976). Newborns can fixate on a light and within days can follow, or track, a moving light with their eyes (McGurk et al., 1977). Because the lenses of the eyes do not automatically adjust according to the distances of objects, newborns are rather nearsighted, with estimates of their visual acuity ranging between about 20/600 and 20/150 (Banks & Salapatek, 1981). But by about the age of four months or so, infants appear to focus on objects about as efficiently as adults do. Their visual acuity makes dramatic gains between the ages of birth and two years, and then improves more gradually through about the ages of eleven or twelve.

Response to Complex Visual Stimulation and the Human Face   The visual preferences of infants are determined by the amount of time, termed **fixation time,** that they spend looking at one stimulus rather than another. In classical studies run by Robert Fantz (1961), two-month-old infants preferred visual stimuli that resembled the human face, as compared to newsprint, a bull's-eye, and featureless disks colored red, white, and yellow. In subsequent research (e.g., Haaf et al., 1983), babies have been shown facelike patterns that differ either according to the number of elements or the degree to which they are organized to match the human face. Five- to ten-week-old babies fixate longer on patterns that have high numbers of elements. The organization of the elements—that is, the degree to which they resemble the face—is less important. By the time infants are fifteen to twenty weeks old, the organization of the pattern also becomes significant, and they look longer at patterns tl at are most facelike.

In sum, it seems that infants have an inborn preference for complex as opposed to simple visual stimulation. However, it may well be that a preference for faces, as opposed to other stimuli of equal complexity, does not emerge until infants have had experience with other people. Nurture as well as nature appears to play a role in infant preferences.

Fear of Strangers   Although children seem intrigued by novel faces during the first few months of life, many children show fear of strangers at about six or eight months of age. At about five to seven months, their gazes take on a sober, concerned appearance. At about seven to nine months, they may whimper and cry, gaze fearfully and arch their backs in the presence of strangers. Perhaps by this age they begin to realize that other people may not be so predictable as their parents. Fear of strangers develops at about the same time in vastly different cultures, strongly suggestive that this fear is innate. Fear of strangers tends to decline at about fifteen months of age.

Depth Perception   Infants also show depth perception by the time they are able to crawl about (six to eight months or so), as well as the good sense to avoid crawling off ledges and tabletops into open space (Campos et al., 1978). Note the setup (Figure 8.1) in the classic "visual cliff" experiment run by Walk and Gibson (1961). An infant crawls about freely above the portion of the glass with a checkerboard pattern immediately beneath, but hesitates to crawl out over the portion of the glass beneath which the checkerboard has been dropped by about four feet. Since the glass alone would support the infant, this is a "visual" rather than an actual cliff.

Babies are highly likely to venture out across the visual cliff when their mothers beckon them brightly from the other side (Sorce et al., 1985), but 81 percent of the infants studied by Walk and Gibson refused to venture onto the visually unsupported glass surface, even when their mothers beckoned repeatedly. Infants also seem distressed when placed on the visually unsupported surface at the age of fifty-five days (several months before they can crawl), as measured by increases in heart rate (Campos et al., 1970).

The babies observed by Walk and Gibson avoided the visual cliff even when one of their eyes was covered, suggesting that they were able to rely on monocular cues, such as relative size, to perceive depth. The pattern on the cliff side of the apparatus consisted of apparently smaller (that is, more distant) squares, and babies can use relative size as a cue to the distance of objects by five and a half months (Yonas et al., 1985).

Hearing   When children are born, hearing may be impaired by amniotic fluid and mucus in the ears. But hearing typically improves dramatically within a few hours or days. Most newborn infants will turn their heads toward unusual sounds and suspend other activities. An old-fashioned way of testing hearing in the newborn is to see if they are startled by loud noises, or if loud noises produce increases in heart rate.

Three-day-old babies prefer their mothers' voices to those of other women, but do not show similar preferences for the voices of their fathers (DeCasper & Fifer, 1980; Prescott & DeCasper, 1981). It is possible that the human nervous system is "prewired" to show differential responsiveness to human speech, especially the speech of one's mother. But human neonates have already had several months of "experience" in the uterus, and, for a good part of this time, they have been capable of sensing sounds. Since they are predominantly exposed to prenatal sounds produced by their mothers, learning may also contribute to neonatal preferences.

Smell   Neonates can discriminate distinct odors, such as those of onions and licorice. Infants breathe more rapidly and are more active when presented with powerful odors, and they will turn away from unpleasant odors as early as from sixteen hours to five days of age (Rieser et al., 1976). The nasal preferences of newborns are similar to those of older children and adults (Steiner, 1979). Newborn infants spit, stick out their tongues, and literally wrinkle their noses at the odor of rotten eggs. But they smile and show licking motions in response to chocolate, strawberry, vanilla, butter, bananas, and honey.

Taste   Shortly after birth infants show the ability to discriminate taste. They will suck liquid solutions of sugar and milk but grimace and refuse to suck salty or bitter solutions. Infants can clearly discriminate sweetness on the day following birth. The tongue pressure of one-day-old infants sucking on a nipple correlates with the amount of sugar in their liquid diet.

Touch   Newborn babies are sensitive to touch, but they are relatively insensitive to pain, which may reflect an adaptive response to the birth process. However, their sensitivity increases dramatically within a few days.

In the next section we shall see that our sensitivity to touch apparently makes a major contribution to our becoming attached to others.

ATTACHMENT

When your newborn infant smiles at you, it may be for reasons other than your charm. Neonates smile reflexively when their cheeks are stroked, or in response to internal stimulation. But within a couple of months children show social smiling. They gratify their parents—especially their mothers—by appearing to be happy that they are there. Smiling at Mother, clinging to her, crying when she leaves—these and other behaviors are interpreted as signs of attachment.

Mother-infant attachment appears to thrive when the mother shows affection toward the child and is responsive to its needs and signals. Infants also seem to influence the process of attachment, however. Almost any infant activity that earns a response from an adult—like smiling, crying, moving, sneezing, and even soiling the diapers—may promote attachment (Bowlby, 1958).

But *why* do children become attached to their parents, especially their mothers? Is attachment learned? Is it instinctive? Let us examine three views of attachment, and then examine the influences on attachment of day care and group child-rearing (as found in the *kibbutz*).

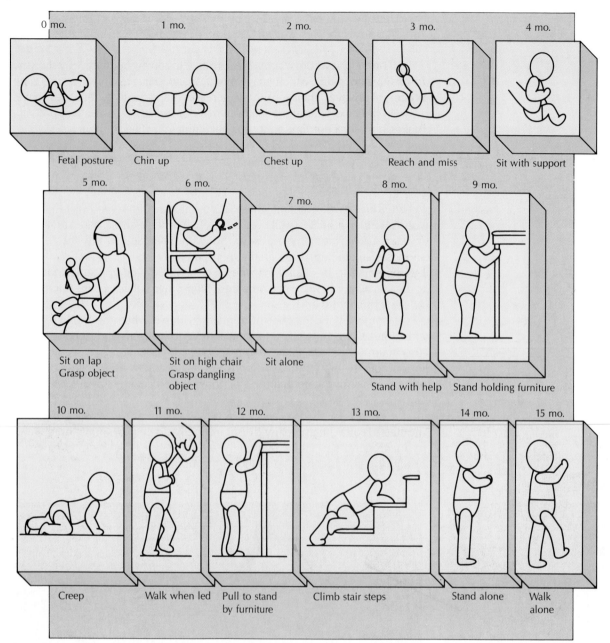

FIGURE 8.2 THE DEVELOPMENT OF LOCOMOTION IN INFANTS At birth, infants appear to be bundles of aimless "nervous energy." They have reflexive responses, but also engage in random muscular movements. Random movement is replaced by purposeful activity as they mature. Infants develop locomotion, or movement from place to place, in an orderly sequence of steps. Practice helps infants learn to coordinate muscles, but maturation is essential. During the first six months, cells in the motor and sensorimotor areas of the brain mature to allow activities like crawling and, later, walking. The times in the figure are approximate: An infant who is a bit behind may develop with no problems at all, and a slightly precocious infant will not necessarily become another Albert Einstein (or Rudolf Nureyev).

THEORETICAL VIEWS OF ATTACHMENT

A Behavioral View of Attachment: Mothers as Reinforcers Early in this century, behaviorists argued that attachment behaviors were learned through laws of conditioning. It was usually Mother who fed the infant and tended to other primary needs. So it was understandable that the infant would learn to approach its mother to meet its needs. Presence of the mother led the infant to have good feelings, since Mother would reduce the baby's primary drives.

From this perspective, a child's mother becomes a **conditioned reinforcer.** Because of repeated association with primary reinforcers, the mother herself acquires reinforcing properties. The mother's attention and approval—even her presence—can come to shape the child's future behavior.

The Harlows' View of Attachment: Mother as a Source of Contact Comfort Research begun by University of Wisconsin psychologist Harry F. Harlow in the 1950s threw doubt on the behaviorist view that attachment was learned and mechanical. Harlow had noted that infant rhesus monkeys raised without mothers or companions appeared to become attached to pieces of cloth in their cages. They clung to them as though they were security blankets. Could it be, Harlow wondered, that monkeys cling instinctively to soft and cuddly things? He conducted an ingenious series of experiments to investigate this question (Harlow, 1959).

In one study, Harlow placed rhesus monkey infants in cages with two substitute, or **surrogate,** mothers, as shown in Figure 8.3. One mother was

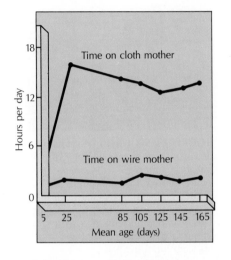

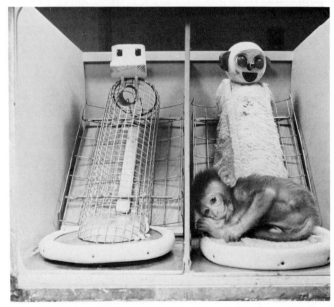

FIGURE 8.3 ATTACHMENT IN INFANT MONKEYS Although this rhesus monkey infant is fed by the "wire mother," it spends most of its time clinging to the soft, cuddly, "terrycloth mother." It knows where to get a meal, but contact comfort is apparently a more central determinant of attachment in infant monkeys (and infant humans?) than is the feeding process.

made from wire mesh from which extended a baby bottle that fed the infant. The other surrogate mother may not look much more maternal to you, but "she" was made of soft, cuddly terry cloth. Infant monkeys, as you can see from the graph in Figure 8.3, spent most of their time clinging to the cloth mother. Very disloyal, you may think, since the wire mother "fed" them. From studies like these, Harlow concluded that monkeys—and perhaps humans—have a physiological need for **contact comfort.** It may be that the way to a monkey's heart is through its skin, not its stomach.

Harlow and Zimmerman (1959) found that a surrogate mother made of terry cloth could also serve as a comforting base from which a rhesus infant could explore the environment. Toys like oversized wooden insects and stuffed bears were placed in cages with infants and their surrogate mothers (see Figure 8.4). When the monkeys were alone or had only wire surrogate mothers as companions, they cowered in fear so long as the "insect monster" or "bear monster" was present. But when the terry-cloth mothers were present, the infants clung to them for a while and then explored the intruding "monster." With human babies, too, strong bonds of mother-infant attachment appear to provide a secure base from which infants feel encouraged to express their curiosity motives.

The attachment of infant monkeys to their mothers does not seem to diminish if they are rejected. Harlow and Harlow (1966) exposed infant monkeys to different forms of "rejection" from their surrogate mothers, including being blown off by streams of compressed air and being catapulted by a spring across the cage. The infants waited until these dangers had apparently subsided and then returned to their mothers, clinging as tightly as before. It may also be that abusive human mothers will not alienate the affections of their infants.

One surrogate mother did discourage her infant from clinging—by being "coldhearted." Ice water was pumped through her, destroying the comfort of contact.

Imprinting: An Ethological View of Attachment   Ethologists have argued that for many animals attachment occurs during a critical period of life. In this period, young animals form an instinctive attachment to the first moving object they encounter. The unwritten rule seems to be, "If it moves, it must be mother." It is as if the image of the moving object becomes "imprinted" upon the young animal. In fact, the process of forming an attachment in this manner is called **imprinting.**

Ethologist Konrad Lorenz (1962, 1981) became well known when pictures of a "family" of young geese following him were made public (see Figure 8.5). How did Lorenz acquire his "following"? He was present when the goslings underwent their critical period shortly after hatching, and he allowed them to follow him. The critical period for geese and many other animals seems bounded at one end by the age at which they first engage in locomotion and, at the other end, by the age at which they develop fear of strangers. The extent of the goslings' attachment was shown in various ways. They followed "Mommy" persistently, ran to Lorenz when frightened, honked with distress at his departure, and tried to overcome barriers

FIGURE 8.4 **SECURITY** With its terry-cloth surrogate mother nearby, this infant rhesus monkey will apparently feel secure enough to explore the "bear monster" placed in its cage. But infants with only wire surrogate mothers, or with no mothers, remain cowering in a corner when the bear or other "monsters" are introduced.

Contact comfort (1) The pleasure attained from physical contact with another. (2) A hypothesized primary drive to seek physical comfort from contact with another.

Imprinting A process occurring during a critical period in the development of an organism, in which that organism responds to a stimulus in a manner that will afterwards be difficult to modify.

FIGURE 8.5 **IMPRINTING** Quite a following? Konrad Lorenz may not look like Mommy to you, but these goslings became attached to him because he was the first moving object they perceived and followed. This type of attachment process is referred to as imprinting.

placed between them and Lorenz. If you substitute crying for honking, it all sounds rather human.

If imprinting occurs with human children, it cannot follow the same mechanics that apply, say, to geese and ducks. Only 25 to 50 percent of children develop fear of strangers. When they do, it occurs at about six to eight months of age, *prior to* independent locomotion, or crawling, which usually occurs a month or two later.

But it is unlikely that children undergo imprinting. In general, the higher the species, the greater the proportion of behavior that reflects learning rather than heredity. Human attachments can also develop prior to and long after the middle of the first year of life.

Let us now turn our attention to three controversial issues in attachment: the effects of day care; the effects of group child rearing, as in the kibbutz; and the problem of child abuse.

THE EFFECTS OF DAY CARE

Between 7 and 8 million American preschool children are now placed in day-care centers. What types of experiences do they encounter in these centers? What are the effects of day care on parent-child bonds of attachment? On the children's social development? What factors contribute to a positive day-care experience?

How Do Day-Care Centers Influence Bonds of Attachment? Many parents are concerned about how day care will affect their children's bonds of attachment to them. This concern has a number of bases. One, children are spending many hours away from their parents at a young and apparently "vulnerable" age. Two, during these extended time periods, their needs will be met by outsiders. Three, parents usually have mixed feelings about

PSYCHOLOGY IN THE WORKPLACE

SELECTING A DAY-CARE CENTER

More than half of today's U.S. mothers spend the day on the job, and the ideals of the women's movement and increased financial pressure are likely to increase this number. When both parents of young children spend the day on the job, the children must be taken care of by others. Many years ago, when Americans were less mobile and there was more of an extended family life, young children were frequently farmed out to relatives. Today, however, their care is more often entrusted to the day-care center. Many children spend nine hours a day or more in day-care centers, and their parents are understandably concerned that their children will be provided with positive and stimulating experiences.

Since standards for day-care centers vary from locale to locale, licensing is no guarantee of adequate care. To become sophisticated consumers of day care, parents should weigh factors such as the following when making a choice:

1. Is the center licensed? By what agency? What standards must be met to acquire a license?
2. What is the ratio of children to caregivers? Everything else being equal, it would appear logical that caregivers can do a better job when there are fewer children in their charge. Jerome Kagan and his colleagues (1978) recommend that caregivers not have more than three infants or toddlers assigned to their care. It may also be of use to look beyond simple numbers, however, because quality is frequently more important than quantity.
3. What are the qualifications of the centers' caregivers? How well aware are they of children's patterns of development and needs? According to the findings of the National Day Care Study (Ruopp et al., 1979), children fare better when their caregivers have specific training in child development so that they are aware of the needs of their charges. Years of day-care experience and formal degrees are less important. If the administrators of a day-care center are reluctant to discuss the training and experience of their caregivers, consider another center.
4. How safe is the environment? Do toys and swings seem to be in good condition? Are dangerous objects placed out of reach? Would strangers have a difficult time breaking in? Have children been injured in this center in the past? Administrators should report previous injuries without hesitation.

DAY CARE Since more than half of today's U.S. mothers are in the work force, day care is a major influence on the lives of millions of children. Parents are understandably concerned that their children will be provided with positive and stimulating experiences.

5. What is served at mealtime? Is it nutritious, appetizing? Will *your child* eat it?
6. Which caregivers will be responsible for your child? What are their backgrounds? How do they seem to relate to children?
7. With what children will your child interact and play?
8. What toys, games, books, and other educational objects are provided?
9. What facilities are present for promoting the motor development of your child? How well-supervised are children when they try to use new objects such as swings and tricycles?
10. Are the hours offered by the center convenient for your schedule?
11. Is the location of the center convenient?
12. Do you like the overall environment and "feel" of the center?

As you can see, the variety of considerations can be overwhelming. It may be that no day-care center in your area will score perfectly on every variable. Some of them, however, are clearly more important than others. Perhaps going through the list item by item will at least help focus your concerns.

day care. If they could afford it in terms of time and money, most parents would prefer to care for their children personally. And so parents frequently have at least some guilt about "sending away" their young children for extended periods of time, and they may fear that they will be punished with loss of love for their "wrongdoing."

Whether these concerns seem rational or ill-founded, the results of studies of the effects of day care are encouraging. In their review of the literature, Jay Belsky and Laurence Steinberg (1978) concluded that day care has *not* been shown to interfere with children's bonds of attachment to their mothers.

In their large-scale, frequently cited study of day care, Jerome Kagan and his colleagues (1978, 1980) followed children placed in day care and a matched group who remained in the home from about the ages of three and a half to twenty-nine months. Both groups preferred to maintain proximity and contact with their mothers in the laboratory setting. However, the day-care children also became attached to their caregivers, as shown by their preferring them to adult strangers.

The Kagan group suggest that initial enrollment in day care is less stressful for infants when accomplished before the age of seven months or after the age of fifteen to eighteen months. In this way, the infants are usually exposed to day-care personnel before they develop strong fear of strangers and separation anxiety, or after separation anxiety is on the downswing.

How Do Day-Care Centers Influence Social Development? One of the most obvious aspects of the day-care center is that it provides an opportunity for social experiences outside the home. This fact both delights and frightens many parents. Parents generally realize that their children will need to acquire social skills for relating to outsiders, but they may also be concerned that they are not the caregivers (and protectors) who oversee their children's early social interactions.

The effects of day care on children's social development appear to have their positive and negative aspects. First, the positive. Infants with day-care experience are more peer-oriented and play at higher developmental levels. Day-care children are also more likely to share their toys with other children (Belsky & Steinberg, 1978, 1979). A follow-up study of adolescent boys who were placed in day care before the age of five found that as a group they were rated high in sociability and were liked by their peers (Moore, 1975). Thus, it appears that day care stimulates interest in peers and can have a positive influence on the formation of social skills.

Now, the negative. A number of studies have compared three- and four-year-olds who had been in full-time day care for several years with agemates just recently placed in day-care centers. The children with years of day-care experience were more impulsive, more aggressive toward peers and adults, and more egocentric than children who had generally remained in the home (Caldwell et al., 1970; Lay & Meyer, 1973; Schwartz et al., 1974). They were also less cooperative and showed less tolerance for frustration and interruptions than home-care children.

It may be that the negative characteristics found among children who had been in day care for several years all suggest a common theme: while day care can promote interest in peers and the development of social skills, children frequently do not receive the individual attention or resources (toys, books, and so on) they would like. As a result they become somewhat more aggressive in attempting to meet their needs, somewhat more selfish. Nor do day-care children fully learn to accept receiving only the partial attention of caregivers. Their lowered tolerance for frustration suggests, instead, that intermittent attention further sensitizes them to their frustrations.

Even if day care does foster impulsivity and aggressiveness, these drawbacks are not, of course, inevitable. Recall Kagan's suggestion that caregivers be assigned no more than three infants or toddlers. Unfortunately, caregivers, on the average, are assigned nearly four infants aged under eighteen months or nearly six toddlers aged eighteen to twenty-four months. In many cases, they are given twice as many or more. Two major obstructions, however, stand in the way of having one caregiver for every three children: money (that is, the increased cost of having more caregivers) and the scarcity of qualified personnel.

Now let us consider the effects of a group child-rearing method that could be considered an extended day-care type of program—the kibbutz.

THE EFFECTS OF REARING CHILDREN IN GROUPS

About 3 percent of the Israeli population live in collective farm settlements known as **kibbutzim.** In the kibbutz, children are reared in group settings from shortly after birth through adolescence. They spend their first year in a nursery, then advance to a toddler's house. The same group of children remains together from infancy, and their bonds of attachment to one another grow very strong.

Parents visit and play with their children frequently. Their major role appears to be to provide their children with emotional gratification (Beit-Hallahmi & Rabin, 1977). The children's primary care and training, however, is entrusted to a child-rearing specialist called a **metapelet.** Because parents are not involved in training chores, this arrangement reduces early parent-child conflict.

Despite the reduced parent-child contact, kibbutz life does not seem to impair parent-child bonds of attachment (Maccoby & Feldman, 1972). In fact, parent-child relations seem more cordial in the kibbutz. However, babies appear to become equally attached to their metapelet (Fox, 1977), and this outcome is unacceptable to parents who want their children to be most strongly attached to them.

It has been suggested that the kibbutz experience encourages children to be more generous and cooperative (Shapira & Madsen, 1974)—although at least one study (Levy-Shiff, 1984) found kibbutz-reared children to be less cooperative with adult strangers than were Israeli children who were reared in the city. But kibbutz-reared children seem more likely to share than Israeli city children. First- and fifth-grade kibbutz children are more likely to distribute rewards evenly between themselves and a partner than are their city counterparts (Nisan, 1984).

In contrast to American children placed in full-time day care, kibbutz children do not seem to be more impulsive and aggressive than children

A CHILD DEVELOPMENT TOY Many of today's toys are not designed simply for fun and games. Instead, they are intended also to be sources of stimulation and learning.

Kibbutz (key-BOOTS). An Israeli collective farm. Plural: *kibbutzim,* pronounced key-boots-SEEM. (A Hebrew word.)

Metapelet (meh-TAP-eh-let). An Israeli child-rearing specialist. (A Hebrew word.)

reared in the home. There are many differences between American day care and the Israeli kibbutz that may account for this finding. First, kibbutz children sleep in the kibbutz as well as spend their days there. Second, the metapelet is involved with them, as needed, on a twenty-four-hour basis; therefore, the metapelet perceives herself as the primary caregiver of the children and is probably more devoted to them than are workers in American day-care centers. Third, there are a host of cultural differences between Israel and the United States, and broad cultural expectations can also influence differences in the development of personality and social behavior.

CHILD ABUSE: WHEN ATTACHMENT FAILS

We are concerned about the company our children keep. We teach them to look both ways when they are crossing the street, and to avoid dark streets and alleyways. We know that the world at large is a violent place, but at least 625,000 children in the United States are neglected or abused each year (National Center on Child Abuse and Neglect, 1982). And so for many children, the most dangerous place is home.

Apparently a number of factors contribute to the likelihood that parents will abuse their children: situational stress; a history of child abuse in at least one of the parent's families of origin; acceptance of violence as a way of coping with stress; failure to become attached to one's children; and rigid attitudes about child-rearing (Belsky, 1984; Milner et al., 1984; Rosenberg & Reppucci, 1985; Rosenblum & Paully, 1984). Unemployment seems to be a particularly predisposing source of stress. The statistics on child abuse show increases when there has also been a jump in the rate of unemployment (National Center on Child Abuse and Neglect, 1982; Steinberg et al., 1981).

There is also the stress created by crying infants themselves. Infants who are already in pain and difficult to soothe are ironically more likely to be abused (Frodi, 1981). Parents tend to become frustrated and irritated when their babies cry for prolonged periods. Child-abusing parents, as a matter of fact, are more likely than nonabusers to draw the conclusion that their children's problem behavior is intended to disturb them (Bauer & Twentyman, 1985).

For men, child abuse is more likely to run in families, although it must be emphasized that the majority of boys who have been abused do not abuse their own children as men. According to Mindy Rosenberg of the University of Denver, for women there is no significant relationship between having been abused and abusing one's own children (Fisher, 1984). Still, as a group, abused children are more generally aggressive than nonabused children, even at preschool ages (Hoffman-Plotkin & Twentyman, 1984).

What To Do Dealing with child abuse is a frustrating issue in itself. Social agencies and courts can find it difficult to distinguish between "normal"* hitting or spanking and abuse. Because of the American ideal that parents have the right to rear their children as they wish, police and courts

*I put this word in quotes because of my own horror at child abuse, and my refusal to consider any hitting of children to be "normal."

have historically been reluctant to involve themselves in "domestic quarrels" and "family disputes."

However, the alarming incidence of child abuse has spawned new efforts at detection and prevention. Many states require helping professionals, such as psychologists and physicians, to report suspicion of abuse to public agencies. Some states require anyone who suspects abuse to report it to authorities. Efforts at prevention are directed toward enhancing the coping skills of parents; toward preventing the onset of abuse through means such as media campaigns and crisis lines; and toward targeting vulnerable populations (for example, groups of people undergoing major changes or stresses) and providing them with parent aides and visiting health workers (Rosenberg & Reppucci, 1985).

Many localities have child-abuse hotlines of one sort or another. Their telephone numbers are available from the telephone information service. If you suspect child abuse, you may call one of these numbers for advice. Parents who are having difficulty controlling aggressive impulses toward their children are also encouraged to call them. Some of these hotlines are serviced by groups such as Parents Anonymous, parents who have had difficulties of their own and who may be able to help callers diffuse feelings of frustration and anger in less harmful ways.

COGNITIVE DEVELOPMENT

When she was two and a half, one of my children confused me when she insisted that I continue to play Billy Joel on the stereo. Put aside the issue of her taste in music. My problem stemmed from the fact that when she asked for Billy Joel, the name of the singer, she could be satisfied only by my playing the first song ("Moving Out") on the album. When "Moving Out" ended and the next song, "The Stranger," began to play, she would insist that I play "Billy Joel" again. "That *is* Billy Joel," I would protest. "No! No!" she would insist, "I want Billy Joel!"

We went around in circles until it dawned on me that "Billy Joel," to her, symbolized the song "Moving Out," not the name of the singer. My daughter was conceptualizing *Billy Joel* as a *property* of a given song, not as the name of a person who could sing many songs. From the ages of two to four, children tend to show confusion between symbols and the objects that they represent. At their level of cognitive development, they do not recognize that words are arbitrary symbols for objects and events, and that people could get together and decide to use different words for things. Instead, they tend to think of words as inherent properties of objects and events.

The developing thought processes of children—their cognitive development—is explored in this section. Cognitive functioning develops over a number of years, and children have many ideas about the world that differ markedly from those of adolescents and adults. Many of these ideas are charming but illogical. Swiss psychologist Jean Piaget (1896–1980) has contributed significantly to our understanding of children's cognitive development.

TABLE 8.3   Piaget's Periods of Cognitive Development

Period	Approximate Age	Description
Sensorimotor	Birth to 2 years	Behavior suggests that child lacks language and does not use symbols or mental representations of objects in the environment. Simple responding to the environment (through reflexive schemes) draws to an end, and intentional behavior—such as making interesting sights last—begins. The child develops object permanence and acquires the basics of language.
Preoperational	2 to 7 years	The child begins to represent the world mentally, but thought is egocentric. The child does not focus on two aspects of a situation at once, and therefore lacks conservation. The child shows animism, artificialism, and objective moral judgments.
Concrete operational	7 to 12 years	The child shows conservation concepts, can adopt the viewpoint of others, can classify objects in series (for example, from shortest to longest), and shows comprehension of basic relational concepts (such as one object being larger or heavier than another).
Formal operational	12 years and above	Mature, adult thought emerges. Cognition seems characterized by deductive logic, consideration of various possibilities before acting to solve a problem (mental trial and error), abstract thought (for example, philosophical weighing of moral principles), and the formation and testing of hypotheses.

Jean Piaget.

JEAN PIAGET

During his early twenties, Jean Piaget obtained a job at the Binet Institute in Paris. His initial task was to develop a standardized version of the Binet intelligence test in French. In so doing, he questioned many children with potential items and became intrigued by their *incorrect* answers. Another investigator might have shrugged them off and forgotten them. Young Piaget realized that there were methods to his children's madness. The wrong answers seemed to reflect consistent, if illogical, cognitive processes.

Piaget hypothesized that children's cognitive processes develop in an orderly sequence (1963). While some children may be more advanced than others at particular ages, the developmental sequence does not vary. Piaget identified four major periods of cognitive development (see Table 8.3): *sensorimotor, preoperational, concrete operational,* and *formal operational.* We shall return to these periods in detail in the following pages.

Piaget's View of Human Nature Piaget regarded maturing children as natural physicists who actively intend to learn about and take intellectual charge of their worlds. In the Piagetian view, children who squish their food and laugh enthusiastically are often acting as budding scientists. In addition to enjoying earning a response from parents, they are studying the texture and consistency of their food. (Parents, of course, often prefer that their children would practice these experiments in the laboratory, not the dining room.)

Piaget's view of human nature differs markedly from formal psychoanalytic thought, which views children and adults as largely irrational and at the mercy of instinctive impulses. It also varies markedly from the early behaviorist view that people react to environmental stimuli rather than intend to interpret the world. Piaget saw people are actors, not reactors—as purposefully forming cognitive representations of and seeking to manipulate the world.

Piaget's View of Intelligence: Assimilation and Accommodation Piaget described human thought or intelligence in terms of *assimilation* and *accommodation*. **Assimilation** is responding to a new stimulus through a reflex or old habit. Infants, for example, usually try to place new objects in their mouths to suck, feel, or explore them. Piaget would say that the child is assimilating a new toy to the sucking **scheme.** A scheme is a pattern of action or a mental structure that is involved in acquiring or organizing knowledge.

Accommodation is the creation of new ways of looking at the world. In accommodation, children transform existing schemes, or ways of organizing knowledge, so that new information can be incorporated. Children (and adults) accommodate to objects and situations that cannot be integrated into existing schemes. The ability to accommodate to novel stimulation advances as a result of both maturation and learning, or experience.

Newborn children merely assimilate environmental stimulation according to reflexive schemes. Reflexive behavior, to Piaget, is not characteristic of intelligence. True intelligence involves dealing with the world through a smooth, fluid balancing of the processes of assimilation and accommodation. As the child matures and gains experience, assimilation takes on the character of play. Accommodation becomes more sophisticated in that the child comes to imitate the ways in which other people cope with novel events (Cowan, 1978). Let us now return to the periods of cognitive development.

PIAGET'S PERIODS OF COGNITIVE DEVELOPMENT

As we explore many of the milestones of cognitive development, we shall integrate them with the four periods of development hypothesized by Jean Piaget.

The Sensorimotor Period The newborn infant is capable only of assimilating novel stimulation to existing reflexes (or "ready-made schemes"), such as the rooting and sucking reflexes. But by the time an infant has

Assimilation According to Piaget, the inclusion of a new event into an existing scheme.

Scheme According to Piaget, a hypothetical mental structure that permits the classification and organization of new information. New information may be "integrated" into existing schemes.

Accommodation According to Piaget, the modification of schemes so that information that is inconsistent with existing schemes can be integrated or understood.

Object permanence Recognition that objects removed from sight still exist, as demonstrated in young children by continued pursuit.

Sensorimotor period The first of Piaget's stages of cognitive development, characterized by coordination of sensory information and motor activity, early exploration of the environment, and lack of language.

Preoperational period The second of Piaget's stages, characterized by illogical usage of words and symbols, spotty logic, and egocentrism.

Egocentric According to Piaget, assuming that others view the world as does oneself.

reached the age of one month, it will already show purposeful behavior by repeating behavior patterns that are pleasurable, such as sucking its hand. During the first month or so, infants apparently make no connection between stimulation perceived through different senses. Crude turning toward sources of auditory and olfactory stimulation has a ready-made look about it that could not be considered purposeful searching. But within the first few months the infant begins to coordinate vision with grasping, so that it simultaneously looks at what it is holding or touching.

A three- or four-month-old infant may become fascinated by its own hands and legs. It may become absorbed in watching itself open and close its fists. The infant becomes increasingly interested in acting upon the environment to make interesting results (such as the sound of a rattle) last. Behavior becomes increasingly intentional, purposeful. Between four and eight months of age the infant explores cause-and-effect relationships, such as the thump that can be made by tossing an object, or the way kicking can cause a hanging toy to bounce.

Prior to six months or so, out of sight is literally out of mind. Objects are not yet mentally represented. For this reason a child will make no effort to search for an object that has been removed or placed behind a screen. But by the age of eight to twelve months, as you can see in Figure 8.6, infants realize that objects removed from sight still exist and attempt to find them. In this way they show what is known as **object permanence.**

During the second year of life, children begin to show interest in how things are constructed. It may be for this reason that they persistently touch and finger their parents' and their own faces. Toward the end of the second year, children begin to engage in mental trial and error before they try out overt behavior. For instance, when they look for an object you have removed, they will no longer begin their search in the last place it was seen. Rather, they may follow you, assuming that you are carrying the object, even though it is not visible. It is as though they are anticipating failure in searching for the object in the place where it was most recently seen.

Since the first period of development is dominated by learning to coordinate perception of the self and of the environment with motor (muscular) activity, Piaget termed it the **sensorimotor period.** The sensorimotor period comes to a close at about the age of two, with the acquisition of the basics of language.

The Preoperational Period The **preoperational period** is characterized by children's early usage of words and symbols to represent objects and the relationships among them. But be warned—any resemblance between the logic of children between the ages of two to seven and your own very often appears purely coincidental. Children may use the same words as adults do, but this does not mean that their views of the world are similar to adults' (Piaget, 1971).

For one thing, preoperational children are decidedly **egocentric.** They cannot understand that other people do not see things as they do. They often perceive the world as a stage that has been erected to meet their own needs or for their own amusement. For instance, when asked ''Why does the sun shine?'' they may respond, ''To keep me warm.'' Or if you ask,

FIGURE 8.6 OBJECT PERMANENCE To the infant at top, who is in the early part of the sensorimotor stage, out of sight is truly out of mind. Once a sheet of paper is placed between the infant and the toy elephant, the infant loses all interest in it. From evidence of this sort, Piaget concluded that the toy is not mentally represented. The bottom series of photos shows a child in a later part of the sensorimotor stage. This child does mentally represent objects, and pushes through a towel to reach an object that has been screened from sight.

"Why is the sky blue?" they may respond "'Cause blue's my favorite color." Preoperational children also show **animism.** That is, they tend to attribute life and intentions to inanimate objects, such as the sun and the moon. They also show **artificialism,** the belief that environmental features like rain and thunder were designed and constructed by people. Again, when asked why the sky is blue, four-year-olds may answer "'Cause Mommy painted it." Examples of egocentrism, animism, and artificialism are shown in Table 8.4.

Animism The belief that inanimate objects move because of will or spirit. (From the Latin *animas,* meaning "breath" or "soul.")

Artificialism The belief that natural objects have been created by human beings.

TABLE 8.4 Examples of Preoperational Thought

Type of Thought	Sample Questions	Typical Answers
Egocentrism	Why does it get dark out?	So I can go to sleep.
	Why does the sun shine?	To keep me warm.
	Why is there snow?	For me to play in.
	Why is grass green?	Cause that's my favorite color.
	What are TV sets for?	To watch my favorite shows and cartoons.
Animism (Attributing life or intention to inanimate objects)	Why do trees have leaves?	To keep them warm.
	Why do stars twinkle?	Because they're happy and cheerful.
	Why does the sun move in the sky?	To follow children and hear what they say.
	Where do boats go at night?	They sleep like we do.
Artificialism (Assuming that natural events have been fashioned by people)	What makes it rain?	Someone emptying a watering can.
	Why is the sky blue?	Somebody painted it.
	What is the wind?	A man blowing.
	What causes thunder?	A man grumbling.
	How does a baby get in Mommy's tummy?	Just make it first. (How?) You put some eyes on it, put the head on (etc.).

SOURCES: Adapted from Cowan (1978); Turner & Helms (1983).

To gain further insight into preoperational thinking, first consider these two problems: Imagine that you pour water from a low, wide glass into a tall, thin glass. Now, does the tall, thin glass contain more than, less than, or the same amount of water as was in the low, wide glass? I won't keep you in suspense. If you said the same (with possible minor exceptions for spillage and evaporation), you were correct. Now that you're rolling, here is the other problem. If you flatten a ball of clay into a pancake, do you wind up with more, less, or the same amount of clay? If you said the same, you are correct once more. To arrive at the correct answers to these questions, you must understand the law of **conservation.** This law holds that properties of substances like their weight and mass remain the same—that is, weight and mass are *conserved*—even if you change their shape or arrangement.

Conservation requires the ability to think about, or **center,** on two aspects of a situation at once, such as height and width. Conserving the weight or mass of a substance requires recognition that a change in one dimension can compensate for a change in another. But the girl in Figure 8.7, who is in the preoperational period, focuses only on *one dimension*

Conservation According to Piaget, recognition that certain properties of substances remain constant even though their appearance may change. For example, the weight and mass of a clay ball are "conserved" even if it is flattened into a pancake.

Center According to Piaget, to focus one's attention.

at a time. When she is first presented with the two balls of clay, shown at the top, she agrees that they have the same amount of clay. Then she flattens one ball into a pancake, as shown at the bottom. Asked which piece now has more clay, she points to the pancake. Why? When she looks down on both pieces of clay, the pancake is wider. The preoperational child focuses on the most apparent dimension of the situation only—in this case, the greater width of the flattened piece of clay. She does not recognize that the decrease in height compensates for the gain in width. By the way, if you ask her whether any clay has been added or taken away in the flattening process, she will readily reply no. But if you then repeat the question as to which piece has *more* clay, she will again point to the pancake.

If all this sounds rather illogical, that is because it is illogical—or, to be precise, preoperational. But if you have any doubts concerning its accuracy, borrow a brilliant four- or five-year-old and try the clay experiment for yourself.

After you have tried the experiment with the clay, try the following. Make two rows with five pennies each. In the first row, place the pennies about half an inch apart. In the second row, place the pennies two to three inches apart. Ask a four- to five-year-old child which row has more pennies. What do you predict the child will answer? Why?

Piaget (1962) found that the moral judgment of preoperational children is usually **objective.** In judging how guilty people are for their misdeeds, preoperational children center on the amount of damage done. Older children and adults, by contrast, usually focus on the intentions or motives of the wrongdoer.

To demonstrate objective moral judgments, Piaget would tell children stories about people and ask them which character was naughtier, and why. Barry, for instance, is helping his mother set the table when he accidentally bangs the dining room door into a tray and breaks nine cups and six plates. Harmon breaks three cups as he sneaks into a kitchen cabinet to find forbidden cookies. Who is naughtier, Barry or Harmon? The typical four-year-old will say that Barry is naughtier. Why? He broke more china.

The Period of Concrete Operations   By about the age of seven, the typical child is entering the period of **concrete operations.** In this period, which lasts until about the age of twelve, children show the beginnings of the capacity for adult logic. However, their logical thought, or operations, generally involve tangible objects rather than abstract ideas. Concrete-operational children can center simultaneously on two dimensions or aspects of a problem. This attainment has implications for moral judgments, conservation, and other intellectual undertakings.

Children now become **subjective** in their moral judgments. They center on the motives of wrongdoers as well as the amount of damage done when assigning guilt. Concrete-operational children judge Harmon more harshly than Barry, since Barry was trying to help his mother when he broke the plates and cups.

Concrete-operational children show understanding of the laws of conservation. The girl in Figure 8.7, now a few years older, would say that the flattened ball still has the same amount of clay. If asked why, she might

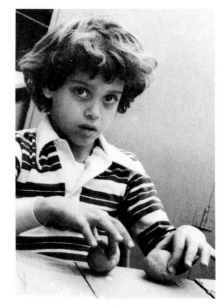

FIGURE 8.7 **CONSERVATION OF MASS**

Objective According to Piaget, objective moral judgments focus, or center, on the amount of damage done rather than on the motives of the actor.

Concrete operations Piaget's third period, characterized by logical thought concerning tangible objects, conservation, and subjective morality.

Subjective According to Piaget, subjective moral judgments center on the motives of the perpetrator.

Reversibility According to Piaget, recognition that processes can be undone, that things can be made as they were.

Formal operations Piaget's fourth period, characterized by abstract logical thought—deduction from principles.

Puberty The period of physical development during which changes occur that lead to reproductive capacity.

Syllogism (SILL-oh-jism). A form of reasoning in which a conclusion is drawn from two statements or premises. (From the Greek *syn-*, meaning "together," and *logizesthai*, meaning "to reason.")

reply, "Because you can roll it up again like the other one." An answer to this effect also suggests awareness of the concept of **reversibility**—recognition that many processes can be reversed or undone, so that things can be restored to their previous condition. Centering simultaneously on the height and the width of the clay, she recognizes that the loss in height compensates for the gain in width.

Concrete-operational children can conserve *number* as well as weight and mass. They recognize that there is the same number of pennies in each of the rows described earlier, even though one row may be spread out to look longer than the other.

Children in this period are less egocentric. They acquire the abilities to take on the roles of others and view the world, and themselves, from other peoples' perspectives. They recognize that people see things in different ways because of different situations and different sets of values.

During the concrete-operational period, children's own sets of values begin to emerge and acquire stability. Children come to understand that feelings of love between them and their parents can endure even when someone feels angry or disappointed at the moment.

The Period of Formal Operations The period of **formal operations** is the final stage in Piaget's scheme. It begins at about the time of **puberty,** and is the period of cognitive maturity. Not all children enter this period at about the time of puberty, and some people never reach it.

Formal-operational children (and adults) think abstractly. They become capable of solving geometric problems about circles and squares without reference to what the circles and squares may represent in the real world. Children derive rules for behavior from general principles and can focus, or center, on many aspects of a situation at once in arriving at judgments and solving problems.

In a sense, it is during the period of formal operations that people tend to emerge as theoretical scientists—even though they may see themselves as having little or no interest in science. As Cowan notes, it is in this period that children "discover the world of the hypothetical" (1978, p. 249). They become aware that situations can have many different outcomes, and they can think ahead, systematically "trying out" different possibilities. Children—adolescents by now—also conduct "experiments" to determine whether their hypotheses are correct. These experiments are not carried out in the laboratory. Rather, adolescents may experiment with different tones of voice, ways of carrying themselves, and ways of treating others to see which sorts of behavior are most effective for them.

Children in this period can reason deductively, or draw conclusions about specific objects or people once they have been classified accurately. Consider this **syllogism:** "All people are mortal. Socrates is a person. Therefore Socrates is mortal." Formal-operational children can follow this logic in which a statement is made about a class or group of objects ("All *people* are mortal"). Then a particular object or event (in this case, Socrates) is assigned to that class—that is, "*Socrates* is a person." Finally, it is concluded, or deduced, that what is true for the class (people) is also true for the particular object or event (Socrates)—that is, "Socrates is mortal."

Adolescents can be somewhat proud of their new logical abilities. A new sort of egocentrism can develop in which adolescents emotionally press for acceptance of their logic without recognition of the exceptions, or practical problems, that are often considered by adults. Consider this example. "It is wrong to hurt people. Industry A occasionally hurts people (perhaps through pollution or economic pressures). Therefore, Industry A must be severely punished or dismantled." This thinking is not illogical. However, by impatiently pressing for immediate major changes or severe penalties, it may not fully consider various practical problems, such as thousands of resultant layoffs.

Evaluation of Piaget's Views on Cognitive Development   Developmental psychologists are in nearly universal agreement that Piaget's studies of cognitive development are a major contribution to the understanding of children. Piaget's periods of cognitive development are widely applauded at the descriptive level, although some psychologists note that many children show some types of thinking (e.g., they can take the viewpoint of others or conserve quantities) at earlier ages than those reported by Piaget when the experimental conditions are modified.

Some psychologists argue that Piaget placed too much emphasis on the role of maturation in the development of concepts such as conservation. They suggest that attainment of these concepts can be accelerated through training (e.g., Siegler & Liebert, 1972; Miller et al., 1975).

Other psychologists take issue with the view that people actively strive to make sense of the environment. They argue that Piaget's descriptions of behavior do not show "how much" of a child's behavior is reactive to the environment and how much acts upon the environment. Behaviorists, as noted earlier, tend to see behavior as more reactive.

Still other psychologists argue that we cannot observe or directly measure a scheme, or a mental event of any sort. They believe it unscientific to use concepts that cannot be directly tied to observable behavior. However, Piaget's supporters point out that schemes like object permanence are always defined in terms of what children say and do (such as seeking and finding a hidden object), and that theories may be allowed to use some concepts which are presumed to underlie observable behavior.

It is clear that Piaget's insights into children's behavior have profoundly influenced developmental psychology. The sheer number of experiments that have been undertaken to disprove or modify his views serves as testimony to this fact.

KOHLBERG'S LEVELS AND STAGES OF MORAL DEVELOPMENT

Cognitive psychologist Lawrence Kohlberg (1981) has contributed to our understanding of moral development among children and adults—one aspect of cognitive development. Before we formally discuss Kohlberg's views, read the following tale used by Kohlberg (1969) in much of his research, and answer the questions below.

PSYCHOLOGY AND HEALTH

FIGHTING MIGRAINES WITH THE FORCE

The cast: six boys, ages ten to almost thirteen. They are all overachievers, described variously as "brightest," "head of class," and "best athlete."

The problem: All the boys suffer from migraine headaches that are not being helped by analgesics or other medication.

The scenario: Their doctor refers them to psychologists Ronald H. Rozensky and Joseph F. Pasternak for biofeedback training—a standard treatment when medication fails.

With a temperature-sensing device attached to their right index fingers, the boys are taught various relaxation techniques and are asked to raise the temperature of their hands. Feedback consists of tones and lights that change as the hand temperature rises. This hand-warming technique is based on the fact that when someone is anxious or stressed, blood flow to the periphery of the body, including the hands, is restricted, lowering their temperature.

In the film *Star Wars*, Luke Skywalker receives instruction in use of The Force from Obi-Wan Kenobi, the Jedi Master. Psychologists have successfully adapted this imagery to instruct children in relaxation techniques.

The complication: At first, feedback doesn't work at all. Instead of relaxing and letting the temperature increase just happen, the boys see handwarming as yet another goal to be conquered. They talk about "getting into the 90s" and "getting 100 percent"; they ask "What's the highest score?" Even turning off the biofeedback equipment and asking the boys simply to relax doesn't work. As soon as the machine is turned back on, they try hard again, and their temperature stops rising.

In desperation, Rozensky and Pasternak remember advice to make biofeedback imagery "concrete and interesting" to children. They invoke the image of Obi-Wan Kenobi, the Jedi Master in the *Star Wars* trilogy who taught Luke Skywalker how to use The Force. The boys are all familiar with the movies and with Kenobi's admonitions to relax and use inner strength to achieve goals. The researchers recall the instruction scenes for the boys and use some actual movie dialogue, together with other relaxation suggestions:

"Get on with your exercises."
"Remember a Jedi can feel The Force flowing through him."
"Stretch out with your feelings."
"You see, you can do it."

"Once the *Star Wars* scene was set," Rozensky and Pasternak report, "each of the six subjects immediately began handwarming and could successfully relax with little interference" (1985). Within three weeks in five cases and six weeks in the other, the boys had no migraines. Using the hand-warming/relaxation techniques at the first twinges, they headed off discomfort before it developed further. In follow-up examinations two to twenty-four months later, the boys reported no further headaches.

Why did The Force work so well? Rozensky and Pasternak mention three factors. First, treatment is most successful when it increases a person's sense of self-efficacy or mastery (in this case Jedi mastery). Second, treatment is most successful when a client believes in the therapist. In this case, they say, the therapist's "enthusiasm and trustworthiness . . . were enhanced by identification with The Force." Third, and most simply, "the familiar story simply might have been a relaxing image upon which these boys could concentrate."

In Europe a woman was near death from a special kind of cancer. There was one drug that the doctors thought might save her. It was a form of radium that a druggist in the same town had recently discovered. The drug was expensive to make, but the druggist was charging ten times what the drug cost him to make. He paid $200 for the radium and charged $2,000 for a small dose of the drug. The sick woman's husband, Heinz, went to everyone he knew to borrow the money, but he could only get together about $1,000, which was half of what it cost. He told the druggist that his wife was dying and asked him to sell it cheaper or let him pay later. But the druggist said: "No, I discovered the drug and I'm going to make money from it." So Heinz got desperate and broke into the man's store to steal the drug for his wife.

What do you think? Should Heinz have tried to steal the drug? Was he right or wrong? As you can see from Table 8.5, the issue is more complicated than a simple yes or no. Heinz's story is an example of a moral dilemma in which a legal or social rule (in this case, laws against stealing) is pitted against a strong human need (Heinz's desire to save his wife). According to Kohlberg's theory, children and adults arrive at yes or no answers for different reasons. These reasons can be classified according to the level of moral development they reflect.

As a stage theorist, Kohlberg argues that the developmental stages of moral reasoning follow an invariable sequence. Different children may progress at different rates, and not all children (or adults) reach the highest stage of development. However, children must experience stage 1 before they enter stage 2, and so on. According to Kohlberg, there are three levels of moral development and two stages within each level.

The Preconventional Level   In the **preconventional level,** which applies to most children through about the age of nine, children base their moral judgments on the consequences of their behavior. For instance, stage 1 is oriented toward obedience and punishment. Good behavior is seen as that which involves obedience and allows one to avoid punishment.

In stage 2, good behavior is that which will allow people to satisfy their own needs and, sometimes, the needs of others. (Heinz's wife needs the drug; therefore, stealing the drug—the only way of attaining it—is not wrong.)

The Conventional Level   In the **conventional level** of moral reasoning, right and wrong are judged by conformity to conventional (family, church, societal) standards of right and wrong. According to the stage 3 "good-boy orientation," it is good to meet the needs and expectations of others. During this stage moral behavior is seen as what is "normal"—that is, what the majority does. (Heinz should steal the drug, because that is what a "good husband" would do. It is "natural" or "normal" to try to help one's wife. Or, Heinz should not steal the drug because "good people do not steal.")

In stage 4 moral judgments are based on rules that maintain the social order. Showing respect for authority and doing one's duty are valued highly. (Heinz must steal the drug; it would be his responsibility if he let her die.

Preconventional level According to Kohlberg, a period during which moral judgments are based largely on expectation of rewards or punishments.

Conventional level According to Kohlberg, a period during which moral judgments largely reflect social conventions. A "law and order" approach to morality.

TABLE 8.5 Kohlberg's Levels and Stages of Moral Development

Levels	Stages	Illustrative Responses to Story of Heinz's Stealing of the Drug
Level I: Preconventional level	Stage 1: Obedience and punishment orientation	It isn't really bad to take it—he did ask to pay for it first. He wouldn't do any other damage or take anything else, and the drug he'd take is only worth $200; he's not really taking a $2,000 drug.
	Stage 2: Naively egoistic orientation	Heinz isn't really doing any harm to the druggist, and he can always pay him back. If he doesn't want to lose his wife, he should take the drug because it's the only thing that will work.
Level II: Conventional level	Stage 3: "Good-boy orientation"	Stealing is bad, but this is a bad situation. Heinz isn't doing wrong in trying to save his wife; he has no choice but to take the drug. He is only doing something that is natural for a good husband to do. You can't blame him for doing something out of love for his wife. You'd blame him if he didn't love his wife enough to save her.
	Stage 4: Respect for authority and social order. Orientation to "doing duty" and to showing respect for authority	The druggist is leading a wrong kind of life if he just lets somebody die like that, so it's Heinz's duty to save her. But Heinz can't just go around breaking laws and let it go at that—he must pay the druggist back and he must take his punishment for stealing.
Level III: Postconventional level	Stage 5: Contractual legalistic orientation	Before you say stealing is wrong, you've got to really think about this whole situation. Of course, the laws are quite clear about breaking into a store. And, even worse, Heinz would know there are no legal grounds for his actions. Yet I can see why it would be reasonable for anybody in this situation to steal the drug.
	Stage 6: Conscience or principled orientation	Where the choice must be made between disobeying a law and saving a human life, the higher principle of preserving life makes it morally right—not just understandable—to steal the drug.

SOURCE: R. J. Rest (1974).

He would pay the druggist when he could.) Many people do not mature beyond the conventional level.

Stage 3 moral judgments are found most frequently among thirteen-year-olds, and stage 4 judgments most often among sixteen-year-olds (Kohlberg, 1963). According to a review of the research, juvenile delinquents of the same ages are significantly more likely to show stage 2 moral reasoning (Blasi, 1980). Stage 2 reasoning (viewing right and wrong in terms of satisfying personal needs) is also characteristic of adult offenders who engage in robbery and other "instrumental" crimes (Thornton & Reid, 1982).

The Postconventional Level In the **postconventional level,** moral reasoning is based on the person's own moral standards. In each instance, moral judgments are derived from personal values, not from conventional standards or authority figures. In stage 5's contractual, legalistic orientation, it is recognized that laws stem from agreed-upon procedures and that many rights have great value and should not be violated. But it is also recognized that there are circumstances in which existing laws cannot bind the individual's behavior. (Although it is illegal for Heinz to steal the drug, in this case it is the right thing to do.)

In stage 6's principled orientation, people choose their own ethical principles—such as justice, **reciprocity,** and respect for individuality. Behavior that is consistent with these principles is considered right. If a law is seen as unjust, or as contradicting the rights of the individual, it is wrong to obey it.

Postconventional people look to themselves as the highest moral authority. This point has created confusion, because to some it suggests that it is right for people to break the law or ignore social conventions whenever it is convenient. But this interpretation is inaccurate. Kohlberg means that postconventional people are obligated to do what they believe is right, even if it counters social rules or laws—even if it demands great personal sacrifice.

Not all people reach the postconventional level of moral reasoning. Stage 5 and 6 moral judgments were all but absent among the seven- to ten-year-olds in Kohlberg's (1963) sample of U.S. children. Stage 5 and 6 moral judgments are found more frequently during the early and middle teens, so that by age sixteen stage 5 reasoning is shown by about 20 percent and stage 6 reasoning by about 5 percent of adolescents. However, stage 3 and 4 judgments are made more frequently at all ages, seven through sixteen, studied by Kohlberg and other investigators (Colby et al., 1983; Rest, 1983).

In sum, there is evidence that the moral judgments of children generally develop toward higher stages in a fixed sequence (Snarey et al., 1985), even though most children do not reach postconventional thought. Research suggests that formal operational thinking—which appears at about the age of thirteen—may be a prerequisite for engaging in postconventional moral reasoning (Kuhn et al., 1977), although formal operational thought does not guarantee that postconventional moral judgments will follow.

Formal operational thought and postconventional judgment are two of the cognitive features associated with adolescence. In the following section, we focus on physical, personal, and social developments of adolescence.

Postconventional level According to Kohlberg, a period during which moral judgments are derived from moral principles and people look to themselves to set moral standards.

Reciprocity Mutual action. Treating others as one is treated.

ADOLESCENCE

G. Stanley Hall, founder of the American Psychological Association, described **adolescence** as a time of *Sturm und Drang*—storm and stress. He attributed the conflicts and distress of adolescence to biological changes. However, anthropologists such as Ruth Benedict (1934) and Margaret Mead (1935) have found cross-cultural evidence that the problems of adolescence reflect cultural influences and expectations rather than hormonal changes or patterns of physical growth.

Adolescence is heralded by puberty, which begins with the appearance of **secondary sex characteristics,** such as the growth of bodily hair, deepening of the voice in males, and rounding of the breasts and hips in females. Puberty ends when the long bones make no further gains in length so that full height is attained. But adolescence ends with psychosocial markers, such as assumption of adult responsibilities. Adolescence is a psychological concept with biological correlates, but puberty is a biological concept.

CHANGES IN THE MALE

At puberty, pituitary hormones stimulate the testes to increase output of testosterone. Testosterone causes the penis and testes to grow, and pubic hair appears. Typical ages are included in the discussion of the following marker events, but there is much individual variation—which most often is no cause for concern.

By age thirteen or fourteen erections become frequent and boys may ejaculate. Ejaculatory ability usually precedes the presence of mature sperm by at least a year, so that ejaculation is not evidence of reproductive capacity. (Typically, girls also menstruate before they can reproduce.) Underarm hair appears at about age fifteen. A beard does not develop for another two or three years. At fouteen or fifteen the voice deepens because of the growth of the "voice box," or **larynx.**

Boys and girls undergo general growth spurts during puberty. Girls usually shoot up before boys, but individuals differ, and some boys spurt earlier than some girls. The muscle mass increases in weight, and there are gains in shoulder width and chest circumference. At twenty or twenty-one men stop growing taller because at about that time testosterone prevents the long bones from making further gains in length.

CHANGES IN THE FEMALE

In the female, pituitary secretions cause the ovaries to begin to secrete estrogen. Estrogen stimulates growth of breast tissue as early as ages eight or nine. Estrogen promotes growth of fatty and supportive tissue in the hips and buttocks and widens the pelvis, causing the hips to become rounded.

Small amounts of androgens produced by the female's adrenal glands, along with estrogen, stimulate growth of pubic and underarm hair. Excessive androgen production can darken or increase the quantity of facial hair. Estrogen and androgen work together to stimulate the growth of the female sex organs.

ADOLESCENTS In our society, adolescents are neither "fish nor fowl." Although they may be old enough to reproduce, and as large as their parents, adolescents are often treated quite differently.

Estrogen production becomes cyclical in puberty and regulates the menstrual cycle. First menstruation, or **menarche,** tends to occur between ages eleven and fourteen. But girls cannot become pregnant until ovulation first occurs, about two years later.

Estrogen typically brakes the female growth spurt some years earlier than testosterone brakes that of the male. Girls deficient in estrogen during their late teens may grow quite tall, but most tall girls reach their heights because of normal genetically determined variations.

ADOLESCENT BEHAVIOR AND CONFLICTS

In our society adolescents are "neither fish nor fowl," as the saying goes—neither children nor adults. Although adolescents may be old enough to reproduce, and as large as their parents, they are often treated quite differently. They may not be eligible for driver's licenses until they are sixteen or seventeen, and they cannot attend R-rated films unless accompanied by an adult. They are prevented from working long hours. They are required to remain in school usually through age sixteen. They may not marry until they reach the "age of consent."

The message is clear. Adolescents are seen as an emotional, impulsive lot. They must be restricted for their own good.

According to Roger Gould's (1975) research with 524 men and women of various age groups, a major concern of sixteen- to eighteen-year-olds is a yearning for independence from parental domination. Given the restrictions placed on adolescents, their yearning for independence, and a sex drive heightened by high levels of sex hormones, it is not surprising that many adolescents report frequent conflict with their families. Table 8.6

Menarche (men-NARK-key). The beginning of menstruation. (From the Greek *men,* meaning "month," and *arche,* meaning "beginning.")

TABLE 8.6   Sources of Stress Reported by Adolescents

Source of Stress	Percent Reporting
Receiving failing grades on a report card	28
Arguments between parents	28
Serious illness of a family member	28
Breaking up with a boyfriend or a girlfriend	24
Death in the family	22
Problems with brothers or sisters	21
Arguments with parents	21
Personal illness or injury	16

SOURCE: Meer (1985).

shows other sources of stress reported in a survey of 172 adolescents (Meer, 1985).

Despite their needs for dominance, independence, and personal responsibility, adolescents report that their current relationships with their parents involve love and closeness (Pipp et al., 1985). Sandra Pipp and her colleagues interpret this finding to suggest that adolescents view their relationships with their parents in a way that is consistent with their growing need for separation *and* their continued need for a close emotional tie.

Ego Identity vs. Role Diffusion   According to psychoanalyst Erik Erikson, the major challenge of adolescence is the creation of an adult identity. This is accomplished primarily through choosing and developing a commitment to an occupation or a role in life.

Erikson (1963) theorizes that adolescents experience a life crisis of *ego identity versus role diffusion*. If this crisis is resolved properly, adolescents develop a firm sense of who they are and what they stand for. This sense of **ego identity** can carry them through difficult times and color their achievements with meaning. If they do not resolve this life crisis properly, they may experience **role diffusion.** They then spread themselves thin, running down one blind alley after another, and placing themselves at the mercy of leaders who promise to give them the sense of identity they cannot mold for themselves.

One aspect of attaining ego identity is learning "how to connect the roles and skills cultivated earlier with the occupational prototypes of the day" (Erikson, 1963, p. 261)—that is, with jobs. But ego identity goes beyond occupational choice. It extends to sexual, political, and religious beliefs and commitments.

Caroline Waterman and Jeffrey Nevid (1977) found that the majority of first- and second-year State University of New York (SUNY) at Albany students surveyed were either in serious conflict about, or had not begun to seriously consider occupational choices. However, many students come to show commitment to career roles at some point during the college years. Many adolescents formulate their views on religion and politics only after

Ego identity According to Erikson, a sense of who one is and what one stands for.

Role diffusion According to Erikson, the probable outcome if ego identity is not established during adolescence; characterized by confusion, insecurity, and susceptibility to the suggestions of others.

they have defined their occupational roles. Bread on the table seems to be the primary concern.

But for many college students sexual-decision making and not occupational choice is a central issue. Occupational decisions can be postponed, at least for a while, but many college students face decisions about sex every week, or every weekend.

Waterman and Nevid (1977) surveyed seventy male and seventy female first- and second-year students at SUNY at Albany to learn whether the students had developed a stable set of beliefs (ego identity) about premarital sex. They also wanted to determine whether these beliefs had grown out of a serious examination of the alternatives—or, as Erik Erikson labeled it, from an **identity crisis.** Crisis or commitment in occupational choice, and in religious and political views were also investigated. It was found that sexual decision-making was extremely important to first- and second-year students. There were also interesting sex differences in the area of sexual morality. The majority of men expressed the belief that there is nothing wrong with premarital sex, but most of them had *never seriously examined* their beliefs about sexual morality. They had simply adopted the sexual double standard that is generally permissive toward male sexuality but restrictive of women.

Despite the sexual revolution, college women remain somewhat more conventional and idealistic than college men in their sexual attitudes (Hendrick et al., 1985). Most women in the Waterman and Nevid study also endorsed premarital sex, but they were more likely than men to approve of premarital sex only within the bounds of affectionate relationships. In arriving at their beliefs, the women more frequently underwent an identity crisis in which they had rejected less permissive parental values.

Although most men and women shared similar beliefs, they had arrived at them by different routes. The issue, in short, was less stressful for the men.

ADULT DEVELOPMENT

Human development continues through the years of adulthood, with people showing changing concerns and involvements. Many theorists, like Erik Erikson and Daniel Levinson, believe that these concerns are patterned in such a way that we can speak of stages of adult development. Psychologists have different schemes for dividing the adult years, but we may be able to use three broad categories without causing too much conflict: young adulthood, middle adulthood, and late adulthood.

YOUNG ADULTHOOD

Roger Gould's (1975) sample reported the twenties to be fueled with ambition. In her book *Passages,* Gail Sheehy (1976) labeled the twenties the **Trying Twenties**—a period during which people strive to advance themselves in the career world.

Identity crisis According to Erikson, a period of inner conflict during which one examines one's values and makes decisions about life roles.

Trying Twenties Sheehy's term for the third decade of life, when people are frequently occupied with advancement in the career world.

DECISION-MAKING Occupational decisions can be postponed by many college students, at least for a while, but many of them face sexual decision-making every weekend.

"MAKING IT" For many people, young adulthood is characterized by striving to advance in the career world.

Establishing Pathways in Life Sheehy interviewed 115 people drawn largely from the middle and upper classes, including many managers, executives, and other professionals. The young adults in her sample were concerned about establishing their pathways in life, finding their places in the world. They were generally responsible for their own support, made their own choices, and were largely free from parental influences.

Sheehy noted that during the twenties we often feel "buoyed by powerful illusions and belief in the power of the will [so that] we commonly insist . . . that what we have chosen to do is the one true course in life" (1976, p. 33). This "one true course" usually turns out to have many swerves and bends. As we develop, what seemed important one year can lose some of its allure in the next. That which we hardly noted can gain prominence. We can also be influenced in unpredictable ways by chance encounters with people who gain sudden influence in our lives (Bandura, 1982).

It should be noted that the Sheehy sample was overpopulated by professional men and women. Psychologists who have drawn more widely representative samples have suggested that while men's development seems guided by needs for **individuation** and **autonomy,** women are more often guided by the developing patterns of attachment and caring (Bardwick, 1980; Gilligan, 1982). In becoming adults men are likely to undergo a transition from restriction to control, according to the traditional view, whereas women, as a group, are relatively more likely to undergo a transition from

Individuation The process by which one separates from others and gathers control over his or her own behavior.

Autonomy Self-direction. (From Greek roots meaning "self" [*autos*] and "law" [*nomos*].)

being cared for to caring for others. However, career women are more likely to undergo the "male"-style transition, as we shall see further in Chapters 10 and 13.

Catch Thirties Sheehy's term for the fourth decade of life, when many people undergo major reassessments of their accomplishments and goals.

Intimacy vs. Isolation

According to Erikson (1963), a central task of young adulthood is the establishment of intimate relationships. Young adults who have evolved a firm sense of identity during adolescence are now ready to fuse their identities with those of other people through relationships like marriage and the construction of abiding friendships.

Erikson warns that we may not be capable of committing ourselves to others until we have established our own life roles. This may be one reason that teenage marriages suffer a much higher divorce rate than those formed in adulthood.

A recent study found that there is a relationship between ego identity and achievement of intimacy (Kahn et al., 1985). Men who develop a strong sense of ego identity by young adulthood get married earlier than men who do not. Women with well-developed senses of identity, on the other hand, *maintain* more stable marriages. The discrepancy may be explained by the fact that women in our society encounter greater pressure than men to get married—ready or not, so to speak (Gilligan, 1982). For women, then, the test of stability is more likely to be whether they endure in relationships, not whether they enter them (Kahn et al., 1985).

In any event, people who do not reach out to develop intimate relationships may risk retreating into isolation and loneliness.

The Challenge of the Thirties

A number of researchers have noted that women frequently encounter a crisis that begins between the ages of twenty-seven and thirty (Reinke et al., 1985). Concerns about nearing the end of the fertile years, opportunities closing down, and heightened responsibilities at home and work all make their contributions. For men and women, the lates twenties and early thirties are commonly characterized by self-questioning: "Where is my life going?" "Why am I doing this?" Sheehy (1976) labeled the thirties the **Catch Thirties**—the first period of major reassessment in life. During the thirties we often find that the life styles we adopted during the twenties do not fit so comfortably as we had anticipated.

One response to the disillusionments of the thirties, according to Sheehy, "is the tearing up of the life we have spent most of our twenties putting together. It may mean striking out on a secondary road toward a new vision or converting a dream of 'running for president' into a more realistic goal. The single person feels a push to find a partner. The woman who was previously content at home with children chafes to venture into the world. The childless couple reconsiders children [see the nearby box, 'At Long Last Motherhood']. And almost everybody who is married . . . feels a discontent" (1976, p. 34).

Many people make major life changes in their thirties, forties, and even later in life (Sheehy, 1981). Making successful life changes requires risk-taking, but risk-taking in itself is no guarantee of success. Successful life-changers also show foresight, the ability to summon up both stereotyp-

AT LONG LAST, MOTHERHOOD

Like many women of her generation, Anne Fowler went through her twenties believing it was more blessed to live than to conceive. A dedicated, and upwardly mobile, teacher at Granada High School in Livermore, California, she always wanted a family. But she could never figure out how to have babies without hurting her career. Last year, at the age of thirty-one, she stopped trying. Giving up the race for promotions—at least temporarily—Fowler and her husband decided to have their first child. "My mother told me that if people thought everything through, nobody would *ever* have children," she laughs.

They have traveled and worked late and dressed to succeed, and now they are seeking "something more." Increasingly, women over thirty are becoming mothers for the first time. "There is a profound baby hunger around these days among women who have put off having children," says psychiatrist Donald A. Bloch.

More than 3.6 million babies were born in the United States in 1980. For the most part this baby boomlet reflects the fact that, with the post-World War II baby-boom generation reaching adulthood, there are simply more potential mothers than ever before. In the last seven years the number of women of childbearing age has swelled by 6.7 million to 51.9 million. And though the overall U.S. birthrate has not risen, the rate among women in their early thirties *has* grown. What's more, the number of first births among women of that age has jumped by 37 percent in recent years. The trend is sharpest among urban professional women.

What made so many women postpone having children until now was a complex of social and economic factors. The feminist movement illuminated alternate paths women could take besides marriage and motherhood, and better methods of birth control provided the freedom of choice to pursue them. Changing sexual mores also played a part, while inflation and recession made it difficult for couples to feel secure enough financially to start a family. Women put off pregnancy while they advanced in their careers, saved for a house, [or] earned a doctorate.

UP AGAINST THE CLOCK? Many contemporary women postponed having children for reasons such as financial pressures and experimentation with alternatives to marriage and motherhood. But lately there has been a baby boom among 30–40-year-olds. Although the overall U.S. birthrate has not risen in recent years, the rate among women in their thirties has grown.

Back to the Family Throughout it all, however, counterpressures were pushing women toward motherhood. Medical breakthroughs like amniocentesis may have made later pregnancies safer and less stressful. But there was still no way of getting around the ultimate deadline of menopause. "These women don't suddenly discover God, motherhood, and apple pie," says sociologist Norma Wikler, coauthor of a study of older mothers called *Up Against the Clock.* "They have deferred and deferred and now see that deadline approaching." Other experts see traces of renewed traditionalism at work, along with peer pressure and a bit of back-to-the-family faddishness. "I think it's sort of a contagion that's going on," says New York psychologist Iris Fodor. "My patients see their friends having babies and they want their own."

ically masculine traits (like ambition) and feminine traits (like tenderness), and strong belief in their purpose.

According to Daniel Levinson and his colleagues (1978), the second half of the thirties is characterized by settling down. Sheehy similarly found that young adults who had successfully ridden out the storm of reassessments of the Catch Thirties began the process of "rooting" at this time. They felt a need to plant roots, to make a financial and emotional investment in

"*Now, see here, Harley. I was forty once, and I never went through any mid-life crisis!*"

their homes. Their concerns became more focused on promotion or tenure, career advancement, and long-term mortgages.

MIDDLE ADULTHOOD

Realizing that you're no longer as young as you used to be isn't easy. In *Passages* Gail Sheehy writes that women enter midlife about five years earlier than men do, at thirty-five rather than forty. Entering midlife triggers a sense of urgency, of a "last chance" to do certain things.

But what is so special about the age of thirty-five for women? As Sheehy notes:

Thirty-five is the average age at which women send the youngest child off to school.
Thirty-five is the beginning of the so-called "age of infidelity."
Thirty-five is the average age at which married women reenter the work force.
Thirty-*four* is the average age at which divorced women remarry.
Thirty-five is the age at which wives most frequently run away.
Thirty-five brings nearer the end of the childbearing years.

There is some point between the ages of thirty-five and forty-five when most of us realize that life may be more than halfway over. There may be more to look back upon than forward to. We'll never be president or chair-

Midlife crisis A crisis experienced by many people near age 40 when they realize that life may be halfway over. They may feel trapped in meaningless life roles.

The Dream Levinson's term for the overriding drive of youth to become someone important, to leave one's mark on history.

Empty-nest syndrome A sense of depression and loss of purpose experienced by some parents when the youngest child leaves home.

person of the board. We'll never play shortstop for the Dodgers or dance in the New York City Ballet.

The Midlife Crisis   The middle-level, middle-aged businessperson looking ahead to another ten to twenty years of grinding out accounts in a Wall Street cubbyhole may encounter a severe midlife depression. The housewife with two teenagers, an empty house from eight to four, and a fortieth birthday on the way may feel that she is coming apart at the seams. Both are experiencing a **midlife crisis,** a feeling of entrapment and loss of purpose that afflicts many middle-aged people. Some people are propelled into extramarital affairs at this time by the desire to prove to themselves that they remain attractive.

According to Levinson and his colleagues (1978), the early forties mark a turning point for men. Men in their thirties still think of themselves as part of the Pepsi Generation, older brothers to "kids" in their twenties. But at about forty, some marker event—illness, a change on the job, the death of a contemporary—leads men to realize that they are a full generation older than twenty-year-olds. They mourn their own youth and begin to adjust to the specter of old age and the finality of death.

Generativity vs. Stagnation   Erikson (1963) labels the life crisis of the middle years as that of generativity versus stagnation. If we come through this crisis positively, we may maintain or enhance our creativity, newly embrace family values, and pursue the Eriksonian ideal of helping shape the new generation. This shaping may involve raising our own children, or generally working to make the world a better place.

The Dream: Inspiration or Tyrant?   Until midlife, the men studied by the Levinson group were largely under the influence of **the Dream**—the overriding drive of youth to "become," to be the great scientist or novelist, to leave one's mark on history. At midlife we must come to terms with the discrepancies between the Dream and our achievements. Middle-aged people who free themselves from the Dream find it easier to enjoy the passing pleasures of the day.

The "Empty-Nest Syndrome": What Happens When the Last Child Leaves Home?   How do parents react when the last child goes off to college, gets married, or moves into an apartment? Do they experience a profound sense of loss, or do they heave a sigh of relief because they now have time for themselves? Research findings are mixed.

As noted by Harbeson (1971), "Too many married women arrive at middle age without having looked and planned far enough ahead, and experience difficulties in making the transition from motherhood to socially useful occupations" (p. 139). People whose lives seem meaningless when the last child leaves home are said to be suffering from the **empty-nest syndrome.**

On the other hand, many women do report increased marital satisfaction and personal changes like greater mellowness, self-confidence, and stability when the children have left home (Reinke et al., 1985). One study of life satisfaction among Americans found that men and women with children over seventeen reported more general life satisfaction and more positive feelings than parents of younger children (Campbell, 1975). Neither the "empty nest" nor menopause need be a negative or traumatic experience for women. A number of studies have found that middle-aged women show increased dominance and assertiveness, an orientation toward achievement, and greater influence in the worlds of politics and work (Serlin, 1980). It is as if they are cut free from traditional shackles by the knowledge that their child-bearing years are behind them. Slightly more than half the American women whose children have left the nest are now in the work force. Some have returned to college.

LATE ADULTHOOD

> Most people say that as you get old you have to give up things. I think you get old because you give up things.
> —Senator Theodore Francis Green, age 87, *Washington Post,* June 18, 1954

> The idea that society can provide only a limited number of jobs, and that the elderly are the logical ones to be left out, is no longer tenable. There are unlimited goods and services needed and desired in American society. Among the greatest resources that could be channeled toward these ends are the experience, skill and devotion of America's elderly millions.
> —Mae Rudolph, *Family Health,* March 1970

> How old would you be if you didn't know how old you was?
> —Satchel Paige, ageless baseball pitcher

> The true test of maturity is not how old a person is but how he reacts to awakening in the midtown area in his shorts.
> —Woody Allen, *Without Feathers*

Late adulthood begins at age sixty-five. One reason that developmental psychologists have become concerned about the later years is the so-called demographic imperative (Swensen, 1983). That is, more of us are swelling the ranks of the nation's elderly all the time. More Americans than ever before are age sixty-five or above because of improved health care and knowledge of the importance of diet and exercise. In 1900 only one American in thirty was over sixty-five, as compared to one in nine in 1970. By the year 2020, perhaps one American in five will be sixty-five or older (Eisdorfer, 1983) (Figure 8.8).

Another reason for the increased interest in aging is the recognition that, in a sense, *all* development involves aging. Developmental psychologist Bernice Neugarten (1982) suggests that development and aging are similar, perhaps synonymous, terms.

A third reason for studying the later years is to learn how we can further promote the health and psychological well-being of the elderly. The later years can be more than just the stage for preparing to die.

Some Changes That Occur during Late Adulthood A number of problematic changes do occur during the later years. Changes in calcium metabolism lead to increased brittleness in the bones and heightened risk

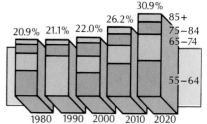

FIGURE 8.8 THE AGING OF AMERICA Because of factors such as improved health care, diet, and exercise, Americans are living longer. By the year 2020, for example, about 31 percent of us will be at least 55 years of age, as compared to about 21 percent today.

of breaks from accidents like falls. The skin becomes less elastic, subject to wrinkles and folds.

The senses become less acute. The elderly see and hear less acutely, and may use more spice to flavor their food. The elderly require more time, or **reaction time,** to respond to stimuli. Elderly drivers need more time to respond to traffic lights, other vehicles, and changing road conditions. The elderly show some decline in general intellectual ability as measured by scores on intelligence tests. The drop-off is most acute on timed items, like those on many of the "performance" scales of the Wechsler Adult Intelligence Scale (see Chapter 6).

Although changes in reaction time, intellectual functioning, and memory are common, we understand very little about *why* they occur (Storandt, 1983). Loss of sensory acuity and of motivation to do well may contribute to lower scores. Elderly psychologist B. F. Skinner (1983) argues that much of the fall-off is due to an "aging environment" rather than an aging person. That is, in many instances the behavior of elderly people goes unreinforced. Note that nursing home residents who are rewarded for remembering recent events show improved scores on tests of memory (Langer et al., 1979; Wolinsky, 1982). Skinner (1983) suggests many strategies that the elderly can adopt to enhance their sensory and motor functioning, memory, and even to cope with mental fatigue.

In some cases, supposedly "irreversible cognitive changes" may also reflect psychological problems like depression (Albert, 1981). Such changes are neither primarily cognitive nor irreversible. If the depression is treated effectively, intellectual performance may also improve.

However, the elderly often combine years of experience with high levels of motivation on the job. In these cases, forced retirement can be an arbitrary and painful penalty for no sin other than turning sixty-five or seventy. According to Kimmel,

> Up to the age of sixty-five there is little decline in learning or memory ability; factors of motivation, interest, and lack of recent educational experience are probably more important in learning complex knowledge than age per se. Learning may just take a bit longer for the elderly and occur more at the individual's own speed instead of at an external and fast pace (1974, p. 381).

Life Satisfaction among the Elderly   Despite the changes that occur with aging, one survey of people age seventy to seventy-nine found that 75 percent were generally satisfied with their lives (Neugarten, 1971). A more recent study of people retired for from 18 to 120 months found that 75 percent rated retirement as mostly good (Hendrick et al., 1982). Over 90 percent were generally satisfied with life, and more than 75 percent reported their health as good or excellent. On the other hand, poor elderly people are more likely to report ill health than are the financially secure (Birren, 1983).

Although major life changes can be stressful, retirement can be a positive step. According to psychologist Joan Crowley, who analyzed U.S. Department of Labor data on 1,200 elderly men, "most people are perfectly happy not to have to get up each morning to go to work" (1985, p. 80).

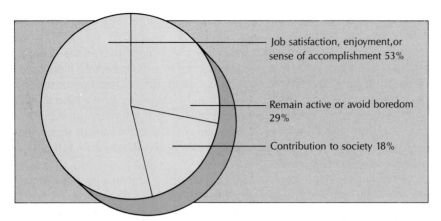

FIGURE 8.9 WHY RETIRED PEOPLE RETURN TO WORK As reported in *The Wall Street Journal,* one third of a surveyed group of retired senior executives returned to full-time work within eighteen months of retirement. Their reasons are shown in the chart.

Many retirees enjoy their leisure, and some continue to engage in part-time labor, paid or voluntary. Crowley argues that most people who deteriorate rapidly after retirement were unhealthy prior to retirement. (However, forced retirement can lead to more negative results than voluntary retirement, as noted in the nearby box, "It Takes a Long Time To Become Young.") Relocation after retirement also need not be stressful so long as careful plans are made and the retirees are financially secure (Hendrick et al., 1982).

As noted in Figure 8.9, a number of people do return to work after retiring. For them, the benefits of employment apparently outweigh the lure of leisure.

 A CLOSER LOOK

IT TAKES A LONG TIME TO BECOME YOUNG

Is youth purely a matter of chronological age, or does attitude have something to do with it? In *It Takes a Long Time To Become Young,* film director and writer Garson Kanin (1978) argues that too many people are tossed arbitrarily into the human wastebasket by forced retirement policies when they turn sixty-five or seventy.

Kanin cites data from the U.S. Bureau of Labor showing that the mean life span of forced retirees is only thirty to forty months. One of three marriages breaks up after a forced retirement, and the suicide rate among forced retirees is twelve times greater than the norms for others in this age group.

Kanin argues that choice or demonstrated incapacity to perform are the only legitimate reasons for dismissal—at age eighty-two or forty-two. The older work-er's experience often compensates for lowered stamina.

Kanin tells the story of a Connecticut town that lost its electric power. After several days of fruitless poking around, the retired engineer who installed the system was consulted. He surveyed the situation, tapped his mallet once, and there was light. He sent the town a bill for $1,000.02—two cents for tapping and $1,000.00 for knowing where to tap. Wisdom does not come cheap.

Erik Erikson (1983) also argues that the productive and creative potential of elderly people has been greatly underestimated. He believes that in the future the elderly will be expected to work till older ages than they do today.

Longevity A long span of life.

Cellular-aging theory The view that aging occurs because bodily cells lose the capacity to reproduce and maintain themselves.

Theories of Aging Although it may be hard to believe that it will happen to us, everyone who has so far walked the Earth has aged—which may not be a bad fate, considering the alternative. Why do we age? Various factors, some of which are theoretical, apparently contribute to aging.

Heredity plays a role. **Longevity** runs in families. People whose parents and grandparents lived into their eighties and nineties have a better chance of reaching these years themselves.

Environmental factors influence aging. People who exercise regularly appear to live longer. Disease, stress, obesity, and cigarette smoking can contribute to an early death. Fortunately, we can exert control over some of these factors.

According to psychologist Judith Rodin, elderly people show better health and psychological well-being when they do exert control over their own lives (Rodin & Langer, 1977; Wolinsky, 1982). Unfortunately, some elderly people are placed in nursing homes and surrender independence because of a decline in health and finances. But even in the nursing home, they fare better when they are kept well-informed and allowed to make decisions on matters that affect them.

There are several biological theories of aging. The **cellular-aging theory** suggests that the DNA within cells, which carries the genetic code of the individual, suffers damage from external factors (like ultraviolet light) and random internal changes. As the person ages, the ability to repair DNA decreases. Damage and other changes eventually accumulate to the point where affected cells can no longer reproduce or serve their bodily functions. Another view is that waste products within cells eventually accumulate so that many cells are poisoned and no longer capable of functioning. These views are currently somewhat speculative.

On Death and Dying Death is the last great taboo. Psychiatrist Elisabeth Kübler-Ross comments on our denial of death in her book *On Death and Dying:*

> We use euphemisms, we make the dead look as if they were asleep, we ship the children off to protect them from the anxiety and turmoil around the house if the [person] is fortunate enough to die at home, [and] we don't allow children to visit their dying parents in the hospitals (1969, p. 8).

From her work with terminally ill patients, Kübler-Ross found some common responses to news of impending death. She identified five stages of dying through which many patients pass: *denial, anger, bargaining, depression,* and *final acceptance.* Elderly people who suspect that death is approaching may undergo similar experiences.

In the denial stage, people feel, "It can't be me. The diagnosis must be wrong." Denial usually gives way to anger and resentment toward the young and healthy, and, sometimes, toward the medical establishment— "It's unfair. Why me?" Then people may try to bargain with God to postpone death, promising, for example, to do good deeds if they are given another six months, another year. With depression come feelings of loss and hopelessness—grief at the specter of leaving loved ones and life itself.

Ultimately an inner peace may come, a quiet acceptance of the inevitable. The "peace" does not resemble contentment; it is nearly devoid of feeling.

Reactions to nearing death are quite varied, however. Robert Kastenbaum (1977) found little evidence that people undergo stages of dying as outlined by Kübler-Ross. Some people are reasonably accepting of the inevitable; others are despondent; still others are terrorized. Some people show a rapid shifting of emotions, ranging from rage to surrender, from envy of those who are younger and healthier to moments of yearning for the inevitable (Schneidman, 1976). Richard Kalish and David Reynolds (1976) questioned several hundred young adults, middle-aged persons, and elderly people in the Los Angeles area about their feelings concerning death. Generally speaking, the elderly thought more about death, but death was somewhat less frightening for them than it was for the younger groups.

In any event, the final hours can pose a towering challenge. Kübler-Ross argues that this challenge could be better met if death and dying were dealt with as facts of life rather than denied—if the dying were helped to die in dignity in their homes rather than in an anonymous hospital.

Lying Down to Pleasant Dreams . . .   The American poet William Cullen Bryant lived for eighty-five years, from 1794 to 1878. Yet never in adulthood could he recapture the majesty of his poem "Thanatopsis," composed at eighteen.

"Thanatopsis" expresses Erik Erikson's goal of **ego integrity** during the later years. Ego integrity derives from wisdom, from the acceptance of one s life span as occurring at a certain point in the sweep of history and as being limited. We spend most of our lives accumulating things and relationships. Erikson argues that adjustment in the later years requires the wisdom to be able to let go. The alternative to ego integrity, within Erikson's view, is **despair.**

Erikson was optimistic. He believed that we can maintain a sense of trust through life. We can live so that when our time comes to "join the innumerable caravan"—the billions who have died before us—we can depart life with dignity and integrity.

Live, the poet writes, so that

. . .when thy summons comes to join
The innumerable caravan that moves
To the pale realms of shade, where each shall take
His chamber in the silent halls of death,
Thou go not, like the quarry-slave at night,
Scourged to his dungeon, but, sustained and soothed
By an unfaltering trust, approach thy grave
Like one who wraps the drapery of his couch
About him, and lies down to pleasant dreams.

Bryant, of course, wrote "Thanatopsis" at eighteen, not eighty-five. At that advanced age his feelings, his pen, might have differed. But literature and poetry, unlike science, need not reflect reality. They can serve to inspire and warm us.

Ego integrity A firm sense of identity, characterized by the wisdom to accept the fact that life is limited and by the ability to let go.

Despair Loss of hope.

SUMMARY

1. It is possible to become pregnant for a day or so following ovulation—the releasing of an ovum from an ovary. A person begins to grow and develop when a sperm cell combines with an ovum to become a zygote. Sperm cells can carry X or Y sex chromosomes, while ova always carry X sex chromosomes.

2. Developmental theories allow psychologists to predict aspects of growth and development and to derive suggestions for helping when things go wrong. According to stage theories of development, such as Freud's theory of psychosexual development, we undergo distinct periods of development that differ in quality and follow an orderly sequence. Social-learning theorists, by contrast, tend to view psychological development as a continuous process.

3. Stage theorists place relatively more emphasis on the roles of nature and maturation in development, arguing that we profit little from the environment until we are mature enough, or ready, to do so. Social-learning theorists place relatively more emphasis on the role of the environment, or nurture.

4. Prenatal development may be divided into three trimesters. The period of the ovum lasts up to two weeks following conception, during which the zygote divides as it travels through the fallopian tube and then within the uterus. Then it becomes implanted in the uterine wall.

5. During the embryo stage, which lasts until the end of the second month, the major organ systems of the unborn child undergo rapid development. Human features are formed; the nervous system becomes formed; the heart begins to beat; and sexual differentiation occurs.

6. During the fetal stage, which lasts until birth, the unborn child makes dramatic gains in length and weight.

7. The fetus is connected to the mother by the umbilical cord. Nutrients reach the fetus from the mother via a permeable membrane called the placenta, and wastes are removed from the baby's bloodstream via the placenta.

8. Infants are born with reflexes—stereotyped responses elicited by certain stimuli without involving higher brain functions. Reflexes like rooting and sucking promote survival and phase out as the infant learns survival behaviors.

9. Newborn children sleep most of the time. They can see quite well and show greater interest in complex visual stimuli than simple stimuli. Infants are capable of depth perception by the time they can crawl. Newborns can normally hear and show preferences for their mothers' voices. Newborns can discriminate different odors and tastes and show preferences for pleasant odors and sweet-tasting food.

10. Behaviorists have argued that children become attached to mothers through conditioning, because their mothers feed them and attend to other needs.

11. Harlow's studies with rhesus monkeys suggest that an innate motive, contact comfort, may be more important than conditioning in the development of attachment. His infant monkeys spent more time on soft terry-cloth surrogate "mothers" than on wire "mothers," even when their feeding bottles protruded from the wire mothers.

12. The ethological view of attachment relies on experiments with other species, such as geese and ducks. Geese and ducks show a critical period during which they will become imprinted on, or attached to, an object that they follow.

13. There is no evidence that day-care impairs mother-child attachment. Day care appears to foster peer acceptance, play, and sharing behavior, but children placed in day care are also somewhat more aggressive than children cared for in the home.

14. Rearing in the kibbutz also does not impair parent-child relations. Kibbutz-reared children seem more likely to share than do their city-reared counterparts.

15. A number of factors contribute to child abuse: situational stress; history of abuse in the family of at least one parent; acceptance of violence as a way of coping with stress; failure to become attached to one's children; and rigid attitudes about child-rearing.

16. Jean Piaget has advanced our knowledge of children's cognitive development. Piaget saw children as budding scientists who actively strive to make sense of the perceptual world. He defined intelligence as involving processes of assimilation (responding to events according to existing schemes) and accommodation (changing schemes to permit effective responses to new events).

17. Piaget's view of cognitive development includes four stages: sensorimotor (prior to use of symbols and language); preoperational (characterized by egocentric thought, animism, artificialism, and inability to center on more than one aspect of a situation); concrete

operational (characterized by conservation, less egocentrism, reversibility, and subjective moral judgments); and formal operational (characterized by abstract logic).

18. Kohlberg hypothesizes that the processes of moral reasoning develop through three "levels" and two stages within each level. In the preconventional level, judgments are based on expectation of rewards or punishments. Conventional judgments reflect the need to maintain the social order. Postconventional judgments are derived from ethical principles, and the self is seen as the highest moral authority.

19. Adolescence begins at puberty and ends with assumption of adult responsibilities. Adolescence is often stressful in our society, although cross-cultural evidence suggests that this stress stems from cultural expectations and limitations, and not from maturation. Changes that lead to reproductive capacity and secondary sex characteristics are stimulated by testosterone in the male and by estrogen and androgens in the female.

20. Adolescents frequently yearn for independence from parents. Erikson considers ego identity, or the defining of a life role, the major challenge of adolescence.

21. Adulthood is divided into young, middle, and late adulthood. Young adulthood is generally characterized by striving to advance in the business world and the development of intimate ties.

22. During the late twenties and thirties, many women encounter a crisis involving concerns about nearing the end of the fertile years, closing opportunities, and heightened responsibilities. Many adults reassess their lives in the thirties and settle down at about age thirty-five.

23. Middle adulthood is a time of crisis and further reassessment for many, a time when we must come to terms with the discrepancies between our achievements and the dreams of youth.

24. The elderly show less sensory acuity, and reaction time increases. Presumed cognitive deficits may reflect declining motivation or psychological problems like depression.

25. Most elderly people rate their life satisfaction and their health as generally good. Retirement can be a positive step, so long as it is voluntary. Having adequate financial resources is a major contributor to satisfaction among the elderly.

26. Heredity plays a role in longevity. We do not know exactly why people age, but environmental factors such as exercise, proper diet, and the maintenance of responsibility can apparently delay aging.

27. Kübler-Ross identifies five stages of dying among the terminally ill: denial, anger, bargaining, depression, and final acceptance. However, research by other investigators finds that psychological reactions to approaching death are probably more varied than Kübler-Ross suggests.

TRUTH OR FICTION REVISITED

You can select the sex of your child.

Not with certainty. But methods that help pinpoint the time of ovulation may provide better-than-chance probabilities that parents can determine whether they will have a girl or a boy.

Our hearts start beating when we are only one-fifth of an inch long and weigh a fraction of an ounce.

True. The heart starts beating during the fourth week of prenatal development. (You may need to get out a ruler to fully appreciate how small we are at this time.)

Newborn babies prefer their mothers' voices to those of other women.

True. The question is whether this preference is inherent or reflects experience with the mother's voice while in the womb.

The way to a baby's heart is through its stomach—that is, babies become emotionally attached to those who feed them.

False. Research suggests that babies may be more likely to become attached to those who comfort and hold them.

Children placed in day-care facilities grow less attached to their mothers.

False. The quality of the mother-child relationship is more important to attachment than the amount of time spent together.

Children placed in day care are more aggressive than children who are cared for in the home.

True. It may be that their aggressiveness is an adaptation to competing for limited resources and attention.

Parents encountering financial difficulties are more likely to abuse their children.

True. Stress contributes to the likelihood of child abuse.

A four-year-old child may believe that the sky is blue because someone has painted it.

True. Piaget termed this sort of preoperational thinking "artificialism."

Adolescents are biologically capable of reproduction when they first ejaculate or have their first menstrual period.

False. Mature sperm and ova are not necessarily present in early ejaculations or menstrual discharges.

Sexual morality is the central concern of the identity crisis of adolescence.

False. Occupational choice seems to be a more central concern.

Young adulthood is characterized by trying to "make it" in the career world.

True. People in their twenties typically focus on establishing themselves in their vocations.

Mothers suffer from the "empty-nest syndrome" when the youngest child leaves home.

False. Most mothers (and fathers) are well-adjusted at this time of life, and many middle-aged women are first "coming into their own" in terms of expressing and asserting themselves.

Forced retirement may be a death sentence.

True. The mortality rate is higher among forced retirees than among other members of the same age groups.

OUTLINE

Personality: Theory and Measurement

TRUTH OR FICTION?

- The human mind is like a vast submerged iceberg, only the tip of which rises above the surface into awareness.
- Biting one's fingernails or smoking cigarettes as an adult is a sign of conflict during very early childhood.
- Women who compete with men in the business world are suffering from penis envy.
- You have inherited mysterious memories that date back to ancient times.
- People who show a strong drive for superiority are actually fighting feelings of inferiority that lie deep within them.
- Airline pilots are more stable than, but not as creative as, artists and writers.
- We may believe that we have freedom of choice, but our preferences and choices are actually forced upon us by the environment.
- We are more likely to be able to accomplish difficult tasks if we believe that we can.
- Children who spend a great deal of time watching violent television shows are more likely to behave aggressively.
- We all have unique ways of looking at ourselves and at the world outside.
- Psychologists can determine whether a person has told the truth on a personality test.
- Psychological tests can help you choose an occupation.
- There is a psychological test made up of inkblots, and one of them looks something like a bat.
- A psychologist could write a believable personality report about you without interviewing you, testing you, or, in fact, having any idea who you are.

PERSONALITY AND PERSONALITY THEORIES

There is an ancient Islamic tale about several blind men who encountered an elephant for the first time. Each touched a different part of the elephant, but each was stubborn and claimed that he alone had grasped the true nature of the beast. One grabbed our gray friend by the legs and then described the elephant as firm, strong, and upright, like a pillar. To this the blind man who had touched the ear of the elephant objected. From his perspective, the animal was broad and rough, like a rug. The third man had become familiar with the animal's trunk. He was astounded at the gross inaccuracy of the others. Clearly the elephant was long and narrow, he declared, like a hollow pipe.

Each of this trio had come to know the elephant from a different perspective. Each was blind to the beliefs of his fellows, and to the real nature of the elephant—not only because of his physical limitations, but also because his initial encounter had led him to think of the elephant in a certain way.

So it is that differing ways of encountering human beings have led psychologists to view people from differing perspectives. Various theories of human **personality** have been advanced. Because personality is not something that can be touched directly, theories of personality may differ as widely as the blind men's concepts of the elephant.

Personality psychologist Walter Mischel (1986) notes that people do not even agree on what the word *personality* means. Some equate personality with liveliness, as in, "She's got a lot of personality." Others characterize a person's personality as consisting of the most striking or dominant traits, as in a "shy personality," or a "happy-go-lucky personality."

But personality theorists note a common theme that runs through most definitions of personality: Personality may be defined as the reasonably stable patterns of behavior, including thoughts and emotions, that distinguish people from one another (Mischel, 1986; Phares, 1984). Walter Mischel adds that these behavior patterns reflect a person's characteristic ways of adapting to the demands of his or her life. Personality, therefore, deals with the ways in which people differ in behavior. Personality theories may include discussion of internal variables like thoughts and emotions, as well as observable behavior.

Personality theories seek to explain how people develop distinctive patterns of behavior, and to predict how people with certain patterns will respond to the demands of life. In this chapter we shall explore four major approaches to the study of personality: psychoanalytic theory, trait theory, learning theories, and self theory. Then we shall discuss psychological methods of measuring personality.

PSYCHOANALYTIC THEORY

What if we had four, not three, men who were not blind, but who held different theories of the elephant's personality?

Personality The distinct patterns of behaviors, including thoughts and feelings, that characterize a person's adaptation to life. (From the Latin *persona*, meaning "actor's face mask.")

The person with the **psychoanalytic theory** might walk around the elephant, scratching his beard. "What we have here," he would finally say, "is the mere surface of the elephant, although I grant you it is a rather large surface. But you cannot hope to understand our mammoth friend by focusing on those floppy ears or that threatening trunk." (The elephant snorts.) "The essential elements of personality dwell deep within that gray head.

"You see, there are forces at work deep inside the elephant. They are so deep that the beast is not aware of them. Yet they determine his behavior. To understand this elephant we shall have to find a couch, a very large couch . . ."—the elephant taps the ground—"have him lie down on it, and start him talking. It may take years, but this is one way for us to learn about forces that reside deep within his unconscious mind."

"My what?" asks the elephant.

"Your unconscious mind."

"But I'm not aware of any unconscious mind," protests the elephant.

"Aha!" exclaims the psychoanalyst. "I rest my case."

SIGMUND FREUD

He was born with a shock of dark hair—in Jewish tradition, the sign of a prophet. In 1856, in a Czechoslovakian village, an old woman told his mother that she had given birth to a great man. The child was raised with great expectations. In manhood, Sigmund Freud himself would be cynical about this notion. Old women, after all, would earn greater favors through good tidings than through forecasts of doom. But, in a sense, the prophecy about Freud may have been realized. Few have shaped our thinking about human nature as deeply as the bearded, compassionate psychoanalyst from Vienna.

SIGMUND FREUD Freud taught that human personality is characterized by a dynamic struggle as basic physiological drives come into conflict with laws and social codes.

Freud's view of personality is **psychodynamic.** He taught that personality is characterized by a dynamic struggle. Basic drives such as hunger, sex, and aggression come into conflict with social pressures to behave according to laws, rules, and moral codes. The laws and social rules become internalized. We make them parts of ourselves. After doing so, the dynamic struggle becomes a clashing of opposing *inner* forces. The major struggles lie *within*. At any given moment our observable behaviors, as well as our thoughts and emotions, represent the outcome of these inner clashes.

Psychodynamic Descriptive of Freud's view that various forces move through the personality and determine behavior.

THE GEOGRAPHY OF THE MIND: WARMING UP TO THE HUMAN ICEBERG

Freud was trained as a physician. Early in his practice, he was astounded to learn that some people apparently experienced loss of feeling in a hand or paralysis of the legs without any medical disorder being present. These strange symptoms often disappeared once patients had recalled and discussed distressful events and feelings of guilt or anxiety that seemed to be associated with the symptoms. For a long time these events and feelings were hidden beneath the surface of awareness. Even so, they had the capacity to profoundly influence the behavior of patients.

Conscious, Preconscious, and Unconscious   From this sort of clinical evidence, Freud concluded that the human mind was like an iceberg (Figure 9.1). Only the tip of an iceberg rises above the surface of the water, while the great mass of it darkens the deep. Freud came to believe that people, similarly, were only aware of a small number of the ideas and the impulses that dwelled within their minds. Even though our perceptions of our own experiences may seem full and rich, Freud argued that the greater mass of the mind, our deepest images, thoughts, fears, and urges, remained beneath

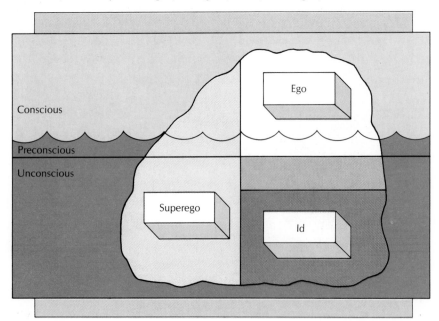

FIGURE 9.1 **THE HUMAN ICEBERG, ACCORDING TO FREUD.** According to psychoanalytic theory, only the tip of human personality rises above the surface of the mind into conscious awareness. Material in the preconscious can become conscious if we direct our attention to it, but unconscious material tends to remain shrouded in mystery.

Conscious Self-aware.

Preconscious In psychoanalytic theory, not in awareness but capable of being brought into awareness by focusing of attention.

Unconscious In psychoanalytic theory, not available to awareness by simple focusing of attention.

Repression In psychoanalytic theory, a defense mechanism that protects the person from anxiety by ejecting anxiety-evoking ideas and impulses from awareness.

Psychoanalysis In this usage, Freud's method of exploring human personality.

Self-insight In psychoanalytic theory, accurate awareness of one's motives and feelings.

Resistance In psychoanalytic theory, a blocking of thoughts whose awareness could cause anxiety; a reflection of the defense mechanism of repression.

Psychic structure (SIGH-kick). In psychoanalytic theory, a hypothesized mental structure that helps explain different aspects of behavior.

Id The psychic structure, present at birth, that represents physiological drives and is fully unconscious. (A Latin word meaning "it.")

---

the surface of conscious awareness, where little light illuminated them. He labeled the region that poked through into the light of awareness the **conscious** part of the mind. He called the regions that lay below the surface the preconscious and the unconscious.

The **preconscious** mind contains elements of experience that are presently out of awareness, but can be made conscious simply by focusing on them. The **unconscious** mind is shrouded in mystery. It contains biological instincts and urges that we only partially perceive as hunger, thirst, sexuality, and aggression. Some unconscious urges cannot be experienced consciously because mental images and words could not portray them in all their color and fury. Other unconscious urges, which are largely sexual and aggressive in nature, may be kept below the surface by *repression*.

Repression is the ejection of anxiety-evoking ideas from awareness. Repression protects us from recognizing impulses we would consider inappropriate in light of our moral values. Repression occurs automatically, without awareness. So, you ask, how do we know when we have repressed something? We do not know. By definition we cannot know. After all, if we knew that we were repressing the momentary angry impulse to destroy a loved one, we wouldn't be protecting ourselves very well from awareness of the impulse.

The unconscious is the largest part of the mind. It is here that the dynamic struggle between biological drives and social rules is fiercest. As drives seek expression, and internalized values exert counterpressures, the resultant conflict can give rise to various psychological disorders and behavioral outbursts. Since we cannot view the unconscious mind directly, Freud developed a method of mental detective work called **psychoanalysis.** In psychoanalysis people are prompted to talk about anything that "pops" into their minds while they are comfortable and relaxed. People may gain **self-insight** by pursuing some of the thoughts that pop into awareness. But they can also be motivated to avoid discussing threatening subjects. The force of repression that has made unacceptable thoughts and feelings unconscious also prompts **resistance,** the desire to avoiding thinking about or discussing them. Repression and resistance can make psychoanalysis a tedious process that lasts for years, or decades.

THE STRUCTURE OF PERSONALITY

When is a structure not a structure? When it is a mental or **psychic structure.** Sigmund Freud labeled the clashing forces of personality psychic structures. They could not be seen or measured directly, but their presence was suggested by observable behavior, expressed thoughts, and emotions. Freud hypothesized the existence of three psychic structures: the *id, ego,* and *superego.*

The Id The **id** is present at birth. It represents physiological drives and is fully unconscious. Freud described the id as "a chaos, a cauldron of seething excitations" (1964, p. 73). The conscious mind might find it inconsistent to love and hate the same person at the same time, but Freud believed that conflicting emotions could dwell side by side in the id. In the

DR. JEKYLL AND MR. HYDE Freud suggested that each of us is influenced by an id that demands instant gratification without regard for moral scruples and the needs of others. Robert Louis Stevenson had a dream in which a similar idea was expressed, and he developed it into the novel *Dr. Jekyll and Mr. Hyde*. In one film version of the tale, Dr. Jekyll, shown at right, is a loving, considerate person, suggestive of ego functioning. The monstrous Mr. Hyde, shown at left, is suggestive of the id. Stevenson's wife was horrified by the concept and destroyed an early version of the manuscript. But Stevenson was so enthralled by the idea that he rewrote the book.

id we could experience hatred for our mothers for failing to immediately gratify all of our needs, even at the same time we loved them.

The id follows what Freud termed the **pleasure principle.** It demands instant gratification of instincts without consideration of law, social custom, or the needs of others. If Freud had lived to watch the television show *Sesame Street*, he might have thought that the Cookie Monster represented the id quite well.

The Ego The **ego** begins to develop during the first year of life, largely because not all of a child's demands for gratification can be met immediately. The ego "stands for reason and good sense" (Freud, 1964, p. 76), for rational ways of coping with frustration. It curbs the appetites of the id

Pleasure principle The governing principle of the id—the seeking of immediate gratification of instinctive needs.

Ego (EE-go). The second psychic structure to develop, characterized by self-awareness, planning, and the delay of gratification. (A Latin word meaning "I.")

Reality principle Consideration of what is practical and possible in gratifying needs—characteristic of the ego.

Defense mechanism In psychoanalytic theory, an unconscious function of the ego that protects it from anxiety-evoking material by preventing accurate recognition of this material.

Superego The third psychic structure, which functions as a moral guardian and sets forth high standards for behavior.

Identification In psychoanalytic theory, the unconscious assumption of the behavior of another person, usually the parent of the same sex.

Moral principle The governing principle of the superego, which sets moral standards and enforces adherence to them.

Eros In psychoanalytic theory, the basic instinct to preserve and perpetuate life. Also see Chapter 7.

Libido (lib-BEE-doe). (1) In psychoanalytic theory, the energy of Eros; the sexual instinct. (2) Generally, sexual interest or drive.

and makes plans that are in keeping with social convention, so that a person can find gratification yet avoid the disapproval of others. The id lets you know that you are starving. The ego creates the idea of walking to the refrigerator, heating up some blueberry cheese tacos, and pouring a glass of milk.

The ego is guided by the **reality principle.** It takes into account what is practical and possible, as well as what is urged. Within Freudian theory, it is the ego that provides the conscious sense of self.

Although most of the ego is conscious, some of its business is carried out unconsciously. For instance, the ego also acts as a watchdog or censor that screens the impulses of the id. When the ego senses that socially unacceptable impulses—impulses which we would rather not admit to having—are rising into awareness, it may use psychological defenses to prevent them from surfacing. Repression is one such psychological defense, or **defense mechanism.** Other defense mechanisms will be explored in Chapter 10.

The Superego   The **superego** develops throughout middle childhood, usually incorporating the moral standards and values of parents and significant members of the community through **identification.**

The superego functions according to the **moral principle.** The superego can hold forth shining examples of ideal behavior or of an ideal self. But the superego also acts like the conscience or "voice within"—like an internal moral guardian. Throughout life, the superego monitors the intentions of the ego and hands out judgments of right and wrong. It floods the ego with feelings of guilt and shame when the verdict is in the negative.

The ego hasn't an easy time of it. It stands between id and superego, braving the arrows of each. It strives to satisfy the demands of the id and the moral sense of the superego. The id may urge, "You are sexually aroused!" But the superego may warn, "You're not married." The poor ego is caught in the middle.

From the Freudian perspective, a healthy personality has found ways to gratify most of the id's demands without seriously offending the superego. Most of the remaining demands of the id are contained or repressed. If the ego is not a good problem solver, or if the superego is overly strict, the ego will be in some hot water. Trying to negotiate an end to conflict is never easy. When the conflict is *within* a person, it can be especially difficult.

PSYCHOSEXUAL DEVELOPMENT

Freud, himself a physician, stirred controversy within the medical establishment of his day by arguing that sexual impulses, and their gratification, were central factors in the development of personality—even among children. Freud insisted that children's most basic ways of relating to the world, such as suckling their mothers' breasts and moving their bowels, involved intense sexual feelings.

Freud believed that one of the major instincts of the id was **Eros,** the instinct to preserve and perpetuate life. Eros contained a certain amount of energy, which Freud labeled **libido.** This energy was psychological in nature and involved sexual impulses, so Freud considered it *psychosexual.* This libidinal or psychosexual energy would be expressed through sexual feelings in different parts of the body, or **erogenous zones,** as the child developed. Freud saw human development as a process of **psychosexual development.** He hypothesized five stages of psychosexual development: oral, anal, phallic, latency, and genital.

The Oral Stage   During the first year of life, a child experiences much of its world through the mouth. If it fits, into the mouth it goes. This is the **oral stage.** Freud argued that oral activities like sucking and biting bring the child sexual gratification as well as nourishment.

Freud believed that children would encounter conflicts during each stage of psychosexual development. During the oral stage, conflict would center around the nature and extent of oral gratification. Early **weaning** could lead to frustration. Excessive gratification, on the other hand, could lead an infant to expect it would automatically be handed everything in life. Inadequate or excessive gratification in any stage could lead to **fixation** in that stage, and the development of traits characteristic of that stage. Oral traits include dependency, gullibility, and optimism or pessimism.

Freud theorized that adults with an **oral fixation** could experience exaggerated desires for "oral activities," such as smoking, overeating, alcohol abuse, and nail biting. Like the infant whose very survival depends on the mercy of an adult, adults with oral fixations may be disposed toward clinging, dependent interpersonal relationships.

Note that according to psychoanalytic theory our traits and "fixations" have little to do with choice or self-concept. Rather, we are portrayed as being largely at the mercy of events that occurred long before we could weigh alternatives and make decisions about how we would behave. Freud's own "oral fixation," cigar smoking, may have contributed to the cancer of the mouth and jaw that killed him in 1939.

The Anal Stage   During the **anal stage,** sexual gratification is attained through contraction and relaxation of the **sphincter** muscles that control elimination of waste products. The process of elimination, which was controlled reflexively during most of the first year of life, comes under voluntary muscular control, even if such control at first is not reliable. The anal stage is said to begin in the second year of life.

According to Freud, it is during the anal stage that children learn to delay the gratification of eliminating whenever they feel the urge. The general issue of self-control may become a source of conflict between parent and child. **Anal fixations** may stem from this conflict and lead to two sets of anal traits. So-called **anal-retentive** traits involve excessive use of self-control. They include perfectionism, a strong need for order, and exaggerated neatness and cleanliness. **Anal-expulsive** traits, on the other hand, "let it all hang out." They include carelessness, messiness, even **sadism.**

In the play *The Odd Couple,* Oscar Madison and Felix Ungar share an apartment after their wives have thrown them out. Oscar is messy. He drops everything everywhere, like a truck of junk on a bumpy road. Felix is excessively neat, the type who will follow a smoker around the room

Erogenous zone An area of the body that is sensitive to sexual sensations.

Psychosexual development In psychoanalytic theory, the process by which libidinal energy is expressed through different erogenous zones during different stages of development.

Oral stage The first stage of psychosexual development, during which gratification is hypothesized to be attained primarily through oral activities, like sucking and biting.

Weaning Accustoming the child to surrender sucking the mother's breast or a baby bottle. (From the Old English *wenian,* meaning "to accustom.")

Fixation In psychoanalytic theory, arrested development. Attachment to objects of a certain stage when one's development should have advanced so that one is attached to objects of a more advanced stage.

Oral fixation Attachment to objects and behaviors characteristic of the oral stage.

Anal stage The second stage of psychosexual development, when gratification is attained through anal activities, like eliminating wastes.

Sphincter A ringlike muscle that circles and controls the contraction of a bodily opening.

Anal fixation Attachment to objects and behaviors characteristic of the anal stage.

Anal retentive Descriptive of behaviors and traits that have to do with "holding in," or with the expression of self-control. A Freudian personality type.

Anal expulsive Descriptive of behaviors and traits that have to do with unregulated self-expression, such as messiness. A Freudian personality type.

Sadism Attaining gratification from inflicting pain on or humiliating others. (After the French Marquis de Sade.)

with an ashtray. According to psychoanalytic theory, both Felix and Oscar are fixated in the anal stage. Their behavior patterns reflect the opposing ways in which they have learned to adjust to a strict toilet-training process.

Felix became very well housebroken. His personality type is anal-retentive. He has a place for everything and everything is in its place. Neatness and spelling both count. But Oscar rebelled. His slovenliness probably symbolizes his resentment at being forced to use the potty when it was still difficult for him to exercise self-control. His personality is anal-expulsive. He is unkempt, disorganized, and careless.

The Phallic Stage Children are said to enter the **phallic stage** during the third year of life. During this stage the major erogenous zone is the phallic region (the **clitoris** in girls). Parent-child conflict is likely to develop over masturbation, which parents may treat with punishment and threats. During the phallic stage children may develop strong sexual attachments to the parent of the opposite sex and begin to view the same-sex parent as a rival for the other parent's affections. Boys may want to marry Mommy, and girls may want to marry Daddy.

Feelings of lust and jealousy are difficult for little children to handle. Home life would be tense indeed if they were aware of them. So these feelings remain largely unconscious, although their influence is felt through fantasies about marriage and through vague hostilities toward the same-sex parent. Freud labeled this conflict in boys the **Oedipus complex,** after the legendary Greek king who unwittingly killed his father and married his mother. Similar feelings in girls give rise to the **Electra complex.** According to Greek legend, Electra was the daughter of the king Agamemnon. She longed for him after his death and sought revenge against his slayers—her mother and her mother's lover.

The Oedipus and Electra complexes become resolved by about the ages five or six. Children then repress their hostilities toward and identify with the parent of the same sex. Identification leads to playing the social and sexual roles of the same-sex parent, and internalizing that parent's values. Sexual feelings toward the opposite-sex parent are repressed for a number of years. When they emerge during adolescence, they are **displaced** onto socially appropriate members of the opposite sex.

The Latency Stage By the age of five or six, Freud believed that children would have been in conflict with their parents over sexual feelings for several years. The pressures of the Oedipus and Electra complexes would motivate them to repress all sexual urges. In so doing they would enter the **latency stage,** a period of life during which sexual feelings would remain unconscious. They would use this period to focus on schoolwork and to consolidate earlier learning, most notably, of appropriate sex-role behaviors. During the latency stage it would not be uncommon for children to prefer playmates of their own sex.

The Genital Stage Freud wrote that we enter the final stage of psychosexual development, or **genital stage,** at puberty. Adolescent males again experience sexual urges toward their mothers, and adolescent females to-

Phallic stage The third stage of psychosexual development, characterized by a shift of libido to the phallic region. (From the Greek *phallos,* meaning "image of the penis.")

Clitoris (KLIT-or-riss). An external female sexual organ which is highly sensitive to sexual stimulation. (From the Greek *kleitoris,* meaning "hill.")

Oedipus complex (ED-uh-puss). A conflict of the phallic stage in which the boy wishes to possess his mother sexually and perceives his father as a rival in love.

Electra complex A conflict of the phallic stage in which the girl longs for her father and resents her mother.

Displaced Transferred. See the defense mechanism of displacement in Chapter 10.

Latency stage The fourth stage of psychosexual development, characterized by repression of sexual impulses.

Genital stage The mature stage of psychosexual development, characterized by preferred expression of libido through intercourse with an adult of the opposite sex.

A CLOSER LOOK

THE STORY OF LITTLE HANS

Sigmund Freud's experience with a psychoanalysis he conducted *by mail* contributed to his theorizing about the phallic stage. In 1908 a distraught physician wrote Freud for advice. His son, who has become known in the psychological literature as "Little Hans," would not leave the house for fear of horses, especially horses with black muzzles.

From the age of three, wrote the father, Hans had shown increasing interest in his penis and in other people's genital organs. Hans's mother had once caught Hans playing with himself and threatened that she would have a doctor cut Hans's penis off if he did not stop. Later, perhaps for reassurance, Hans asked his parents if they had "weewee makers," to which they answered yes.

Hans enjoyed coming into bed with his parents and cuddling with his mother, although his father protested that this behavior could be harmful. When Hans eventually learned that girls' "weewee makers" were not like his, he became distressed. Why? When his father left for work in the morning, Hans developed fear that he would not return. Why? At about this time Hans also developed his fear of horses. Why? We shall see below.

From these and other glimpses of the boy's history, Freud (1909) made some deductions. One, Freud suggested that Hans became upset when he discovered the facts about women's "weewee makers" because he assumed that they had been castrated, just as Hans's mother had threatened Hans. Two, Freud interpreted Hans's fear that his father would not return from work as unconsciously reflecting the possibility that Hans's *own hostility toward his father* might consume his father or drive him away. Freud, you see, also believed that Hans might be entertaining childish sexual fantasies

about his mother and wanting to possess her. Hans would then perceive his father as his rival and become hostile toward him.

Three, Freud concluded that the horse symbolized Hans's father. Hans was going through the Oedipus complex, as did all boys—or so Freud believed. Freud argued that all boys want to possess their mothers and destroy their rivals—namely, their fathers—during the phallic stage. Unconsciously, Hans would also fear that his father might retaliate, by castrating him. But conscious awareness of these feelings would have been too threatening for the little boy. So Hans transferred his fear of his father onto an animal with a large penis, like his father had, and whose blinders and black muzzle symbolized his father's spectacles and moustache. Hans could transform his castration anxiety into the fear that horses would bite him. Horses do not castrate—they bite.

Behaviorists Joseph Wolpe and Stanley Rachman (1960) accept Hans's father's descriptions of Hans's behavior, but they challenge Freud's psychoanalytic interpretation. They consider Freud's evidence for linking these events to an Oedipus complex flimsy and circumstantial. For instance, there was no evidence that Hans wanted to possess his mother sexually. Second, Hans never expressed any feelings of hatred or fear of his father. Third, it is not unusual for light-colored horses to have black muzzles; thus, there was no evidence that this feature ties the horse symbolically to Hans's father.

Freud's interpretation of the story of Little Hans remains speculative. However, it is one of the cornerstones of psychoanalytic theory and provides an example of the way in which psychoanalytic theory assumes that behavioral problems, such as irrational fears, stem from unconscious conflict with childhood origins.

---

ward their fathers. But the **incest taboo** provides ample motivation for keeping these impulses repressed and displacing them onto other adults or adolescents of the opposite sex. But boys might still seek girls "just like the girl that married dear old Dad." Girls might still be attracted to men who resemble their fathers.

People in the genital stage prefer, by definition, to find sexual gratification through intercourse with a member of the opposite sex. In Freud's view, oral or anal stimulation, masturbation, and homosexual activity would all represent **pregenital** fixations and immature forms of sexual conduct. They would not be in keeping with the life instinct Eros.

Incest taboo The cultural prohibition against marrying or having sexual relations with a close blood relative. (From the Latin *in-*, meaning "not," and *castus*, meaning "chaste.")

Pregenital Characteristic of stages less mature than the genital stage.

Penis envy In psychoanalytic theory, jealousy of the male sexual organ attributed to girls in the phallic stage.

Neo-Freudian A person who views behavior largely from the psychoanalytic perspective, but who generally attributes more behavior to conscious motives and reasoned decision-making.

A PSYCHOLOGICAL CONTROVERSY: DO WOMEN WHO COMPETE WITH MEN SUFFER FROM PENIS ENVY?

Psychoanalytic theory in many ways has been a liberating force, allowing people to admit the importance of sexuality in their lives. But it has also been claimed that Freud's views are repressive toward women. The **penis-envy** hypothesis has stigmatized women who compete with men in the business world as failing to have resolved the Electra complex.

Freud believed that little girls envy boys their penises. Why, they would feel, should boys have something that they do not? As a consequence of this jealousy, girls would resent their mothers for bringing them into the world so "ill-equipped," as Freud (1964) wrote in *New Introductory Lectures on Psychoanalysis*. They would then develop the wish to marry their fathers as a substitute for not having penises of their own.

Through a series of developmental transformations, the wish to marry the father would evolve into the desire to marry another man and bear children. A baby, especially a male child, would symbolize something growing from the genital region and bring some psychological satisfaction. Freud declared that the ideally adjusted woman would accept her husband's authority, symbolizing surrender of the wish to have a penis of her own.

Freud warned that retaining the wish to have a penis would lead to maladjustment. Persistent jealousy would cause women to develop masculine traits. They might even become competitive and self-assertive, or at worst, homosexual.

These assumptions have been attacked strongly by women and by modern-day psychoanalysts. Karen Horney (1967), a **neo-Freudian,** contended that little girls do not feel inferior to little boys, and that the penis-

A CAREER WOMAN Most psychologists today do not accept Freud's implication that career women are maladjusted and suffering from penis envy.

envy hypothesis was not supported by the evidence of actual observations of children. Horney wrote that Freud's view reflected a Western cultural prejudice that women are inferior to men—and not sound psychological theory.

Psychologist Phyllis Chesler (1972) argues that there has been a historic prejudice against self-assertive, competent women. Many people want women to remain passive and submissive, emotional, and dependent on men. In Freud's day these prejudices were more extreme. Psychoanalytic theory, in its original form, reflected the belief that motherhood and family life were the only proper avenues of fulfillment for women.

EVALUATION OF FREUD'S PSYCHOANALYTIC THEORY

Freud's psychoanalytic theory has had tremendous appeal. It is one of the richest of personality theories, explaining many varieties of human behavior and traits. But despite its richness, Freud's work has been criticized on many grounds.

Some followers of Freud, like Erik Erikson, have argued that Freud placed too much emphasis on human sexuality and neglected the relative importance of social relationships. Other followers, like Alfred Adler and Erich Fromm, have argued that Freud placed too much emphasis on unconscious motives. Adler and Fromm assert that people consciously seek self-enhancement and intellectual pleasures, rather than simply attempting to gratify the dark demands of the id.

A number of critics note that "psychic structures" like the id, ego, and superego have no substance. They are little more than useful fictions, poetic ways to express inner conflict. It is debatable whether Freud ever attributed substance to the psychic structures. He, too, may have seen them more as poetic fictions than as "things." If so, his critics have the right to use other descriptive terms and write better "poems."

Sir Karl Popper (1985) has argued that Freud's hypothetical mental processes fall short of being scientific concepts because they cannot be observed. Nor can they be used to predict observable behavior with precision, but only to "explain" it after the fact. For example, we can speculate that a client "repressed" (forgot about) an appointment because "unconsciously" he did not want to attend the session, but we cannot accurately predict when such "repression" will occur. Also, scientific propositions must be capable of being proven false. As noted by Popper, Freud's statements about mental structures are unscientific, precisely because no imaginable type of evidence can disprove them; any sort of human behavior can be explained in terms of these hypothesized (but unobservable) "structures."

Nor have the stages of psychosexual development escaped criticism. Children may begin to masturbate as early as the first year of life, rather than in the "phallic stage." As parents can testify from observing their children play "doctor," the latency stage is not so sexually "latent" as Freud believed. Much of Freud's thinking concerning the Oedipus and Electra complexes remains simple speculation. His views of female sexuality and sex-role behavior reflect the ignorance and prejudice of his times.

Analytical psychology Jung's psychoanalytic theory, which emphasizes the collective unconscious and archetypes.

Collective unconscious Jung's hypothesized store of vague racial memories.

Archetypes (ARE-keh-types). Basic, primitive images or concepts hypothesized by Jung to reside in the collective unconscious. (From the Greek *archein,* meaning "to begin," and *typos,* meaning "figure" or "model.")

Mythical Descriptive of traditional, fictitious stories often intended to explain natural phenomena or human origins. (From the Greek *mythos,* meaning "legend.")

Animus (AN-uh-mus). Jung's term for a masculine archetype of the collective unconscious. (A Latin word meaning "soul" or "disposition.")

Anima (AN-uh-muh). Jung's feminine archetype.

As noted by philosopher Adolph Grünbaum (1985), Freud's method of gathering evidence from the clinical session is also highly suspect. Psychoanalysts may subtly influence clients to produce what they had hoped to find. Analysts may also fail to separate reported facts from their own interpretations.

Once we have catalogued our criticisms of Freud's views, what of merit is left? A number of important things. Although we may find fault with the specifics of Freud's theory of psychosexual development, Freud did at least point out that childhood experiences can have far-reaching effects on adult personality. Freud also noted that people have defensive ways of looking at the world, and it does seem that our cognitive processes can be distorted by our efforts to defend ourselves against anxiety and guilt. If these ideas no longer impress us as innovative, it is largely because of the powerful influence of Sigmund Freud. Moreover, as we shall see in Chapter 12, psychoanalytic forms of therapy have been of help to many people suffering from anxiety, depression, and related problems.

OTHER PSYCHOANALYTIC THEORIES

A number of personality theorists are intellectual descendants of Sigmund Freud. Their theories, like Freud's, include roles for unconscious motivation, for motivational conflict, and for defensive responses to anxiety that involve repression and cognitive distortion of reality (Wachtel, 1982). In other respects, they differ markedly. We discuss the psychodynamic views of Carl Jung, Alfred Adler, Karen Horney, and Erik Erikson.

CARL JUNG

Carl Jung (1875–1961) was a Swiss psychiatrist who once had been a favorite of Freud's and a member of his inner circle. But he fell into disfavor with Freud when he developed his own psychoanalytic theory which he termed **analytical psychology.** Jung, like Freud, was intrigued by unconscious processes. He believed that we not only have a *personal* unconscious, which contains repressed memories and impulses, but also an inherited **collective unconscious,** which contains primitive images, or **archetypes,** that reflect the exciting history of our species.

Archetypes include vague mysterious **mythical** images. Examples of archetypes are the All-Powerful God, the young hero, the fertile and nurturing mother, the wise old man, the hostile brother, even fairy godmothers, wicked witches, and themes of rebirth or resurrection. Archetypes themselves remain unconscious, but Jung declared that they influence our thoughts and emotions and render us responsive to cultural themes in stories and films. Archetypes are somewhat accessible through the interpretation of dreams.

Jung believed that within each of us reside shadowy parts of the personality that may unfold gradually as we mature. He believed that we all have an **animus,** a masculine, aggressively competitive aspect to our personalities, and an **anima,** which is feminine, soft, supportive, and passive. Cultural influences make it likely that men will express the animus more

Carl Gustav Jung.

so than women will, and women the anima. But we are all seen as richly multifaceted.

Jung downplayed the importance of the sexual instinct. He saw it as but one of several important instincts. Despite all of his interest in the collective unconscious, Jung also granted more importance to conscious motives than Freud did. Jung believed that one of the archetypes is a **self,** a conscious, unifying force of personality that gives conscious direction and purpose to human behavior. According to Jung, heredity dictates that the self will persistently strive to achieve a wholeness or fullness. This striving takes many forms. Some people become intrigued by mystical patterns like the magic-circle archetype, or **mandala.** Others seek to express this unity through religious experience, or through inner voyages fueled by drugs or meditation.

Jung believed that an understanding of human behavior must incorporate the facts of self-awareness and self-direction as well as the impulses of the id and the mechanisms of defense. But the same Jung who insisted that importance must be attached to fully conscious functions went even further than Freud in constructing an involved, poetic inner life. Many of Jung's ideas cannot be verified through scientific study. They remain at the level of theoretical, even spiritual, speculation.

ALFRED ADLER

Alfred Adler (1870–1937), another follower of Freud, also believed that Freud had placed too much emphasis on sexual impulses. Adler believed that people are basically motivated by an **inferiority complex.** In some people feelings of inferiority may be based on physical problems and the need to compensate for them. But Adler believed that all of us encounter some feelings of inferiority because of our small size as children, and that these feelings give rise to a **drive for superiority.** For instance, the English poet Lord Byron, with a crippled leg, became a champion swimmer. Beethoven's encroaching deafness may have spurred him on to greater musical accomplishments. Adler as a child was crippled by rickets and suffered from pneumonia, and it may be that his theory developed in part from his own childhood striving to overcome repeated bouts of illness. However, there is no empirical support for the view that all of us harbor feelings of inferiority.

Adler, like Jung, believed that self-awareness plays a major role in the formation of personality. Adler spoke of a **creative self,** a self-aware aspect of personality that strives to overcome obstacles and develop the individual's potential. Because this potential is uniquely individual, Adler's views have been termed **individual psychology.**

KAREN HORNEY

Karen Horney (1885–1952), like so many other noteworthy psychologists, was born in Germany and emigrated to the United States before the outbreak of World War II. Horney agreed with Freud that childhood experiences played a major role in the development of adult personality, but, like

Self In analytical psychology, a conscious, unifying force to personality that provides people with direction and purpose.

Mandala (MON-duh-luh or man-DOLL-uh). In the Hindu and Buddhist traditions, a circular design symbolizing the wholeness or unity of life. (A Sanskrit word meaning "circle.")

Inferiority complex Feelings of inferiority hypothesized by Adler to serve as a central motivating force.

Drive for superiority Adler's term for the desire to compensate for feelings of inferiority.

Creative self According to Adler, the self-aware aspect of personality that strives to achieve its full potential.

Individual psychology Adler's psychoanalytic theory, which emphasizes feelings of inferiority and the creative self.

A MANDALA Simple artistic expression, or a reflection of a "magic circle" archetype that resides within the collective unconcious?

Alfred Adler.

Karen Horney.

Erik Erikson.

Basic anxiety Horney's term for lasting feelings of insecurity that stem from harsh or indifferent parental treatment.

Basic hostility Horney's term for lasting feelings of anger that accompany basic anxiety but are directed toward nonfamily members in adulthood.

Psychosocial development Erikson's theory of personality and development, which emphasizes social relationships and eight stages of growth.

Significant others Persons who have a major impact on one's development, including parents, peers, and lovers.

many other neoanalysts, she believed that sexual and aggressive impulses took a back seat in importance to social relationships.

Horney, like Freud, saw parent-child relationships to be of paramount importance. Small children are completely dependent, and when their parents treat them with indifference or harshness, they develop feelings of insecurity and what Horney terms **basic anxiety.** Children also resent neglectful parents, and Horney theorized that a **basic hostility** would accompany basic anxiety. Horney agreed with Freud that children would repress rather than express feelings of hostility toward their parents, because of fear of reprisal and, just as important, fear of driving them away.

Later in life, basic anxiety and repressed hostility would lead to the development of one of three neurotic ways of relating to other people: moving toward others, moving against others, or moving away from them. Of course, it is healthful to relate to other people, but the neurotic person who moves toward others has feelings of insecurity and an excessive need for approval that render him or her compliant and overly anxious to please. People who move against others also are insecure, but they attempt to cope with their insecurity by asserting power and dominating social interactions. People who move away from others cope with their insecurities by withdrawing from social interactions. By remaining aloof from others, they attempt to prevent themselves from getting hurt by them. The price, of course, is perpetual loneliness.

ERIK ERIKSON

Erik Erikson, as did other neoanalysts, believed that Freud had placed undue emphasis on sexual instincts. Erikson, like Horney, taught that social relationships are more crucial determinants of personality. The general climate of the mother-infant relationship was more important than the details of the feeding process or sexual feelings that might be stirred by the mother's nearness.

For this reason, Erikson proposes stages of psycho*social* rather than psycho*sexual* development. Rather than labeling a stage after an erogenous zone, Erikson labeled stages after the traits that might be developed during that stage (Table 8.1). Each stage was named according to the possible outcomes, which are polar opposites. For example, the first stage of **psychosocial development** is the stage of trust versus mistrust because of the two possible major outcomes: (1) A warm, loving relationship with the mother (and **significant others**) during infancy may lead to a sense of basic trust in people and the world. (2) A cold, nongratifying relationship may lead to a pervasive sense of mistrust. Erikson extended Freud's five developmental stages to eight to include the changing concerns of various stages of adulthood (discussed in Chapter 8). In recent years, Erikson (1983) has added to our knowledge concerning the problems and potentials of the elderly.

One of the richer aspects of the psychoanalytic theories is the way in which they account for the development of various traits. Let us now consider trait theory, which addresses traits from a different perspective. In trait theory the focus is on the cataloging and classifying of traits.

TRAIT THEORY

Once the psychoanalytically oriented student of personality finishes his description of the elephant, the second student walks around the elephant deliberately to study the low-hung belly and the thick legs.

"No," he says to the psychoanalyst. "You're digging too deep. Everything we need to know about our elephant is right here, right here in this massive belly. Our fat friend" (the elephant snorts) "is basically relaxed and jolly. He loves to eat—"

"Deep," interrupts the psychoanalyst. *"Deep."*

"—he loves to eat and he gets along with everybody. He's not athletic or courageous, he's not scholarly or artistic. We know all this from these rolls of flab. He loves everyone."

"You, I don't like at all," comments the elephant.

If asked to describe yourself, you would probably mention one or more of your **traits.** Traits are elements of personality that are inferred from behavior and that account for behavioral consistency. Freud linked certain traits to his stages of psychosexual development. We use traits to describe others. If you describe a friend as "shy," it may be because you observed some social anxiety or withdrawal in early meetings. Within trait theory, traits are assumed to endure and to account for behavior in various situations. Similarly, you would probably predict consistent social anxiety and withdrawal for your "shy" friend and might be surprised if he or she acted assertively.

Trait An aspect of personality that is inferred from behavior and assumed to give rise to behavioral consistency.

Cardinal trait Allport's term for pervasive traits that guide practically all of a person's behavior.

Machiavellian Characterized by craftiness and deceitfulness in the attainment of one's goals. (After Italian statesman Niccolo Machiavelli.)

Napoleonic Governed by the needs for power and aggression.

Sadistic Attaining gratification by inflicting pain on others.

Central traits Outstanding, noticeable (but not necessarily all-pervasive) characteristics of a person.

Secondary traits Traits that appear in a limited number of situations and govern a limited number of responses.

Personality structure One's total pattern of traits.

GORDON ALLPORT

According to psychologist Gordon Allport (1937, 1961), traits are rooted in the nervous system of the person. Allport considered them "neuropsychic" structures. They steered or guided people to behave consistently in various situations. For example, the trait of sociability may steer a person to invite friends along when going out, to share confidences when writing letters, and to make others feel welcome and comfortable at family gatherings. A person who lacks the trait of sociability would be disposed to behave very differently in these situations.

Allport labeled traits according to the roles they play in directing behavior. In rare cases a trait may be so outstanding and pervasive that it seems to steer practically all aspects of a person's behavior. Such a powerful trait is a **cardinal trait.** Allport (1937) offered the following adjectives as examples of cardinal traits from historic and literary figures: Christlike, **Machiavellian, Napoleonic,** and **Sadistic.**

Central traits define the outstanding characteristics of the person. They are the sort that might be mentioned in a letter of recommendation, such as "well-groomed," "honest," and "hard-working." **Secondary traits** are less influential and less noticeable. Rather than generally guiding the behavior of the individual, they appear to occur in a small range of situations and to govern a limited number of responses. Our total pattern of traits is termed our **personality structure.**

Gordon Allport.

Some fifty years ago Allport and Odbert (1936) catalogued some 18,000 human traits from a search through word lists of the sort found in dictionaries. Some were physical traits, like short, white, and brunette. Others were behavioral traits, like shy and emotional. Still others were moral traits, like honest. This exhaustive list has served as the basis for personality research by many other psychologists.

RAYMOND CATTELL

Some psychologists—Raymond Cattell (1965) is one—have used statistical techniques to reduce this universe of innumerable traits to smaller lists that show commonality in meaning. Cattell also distinguished between surface traits and source traits. **Surface traits** describe characteristic ways of behaving, i.e., cleanliness, stubbornness, thrift, and orderliness. We may observe that these traits tend to form meaningful patterns that are suggestive of underlying traits. (Cleanliness, stubbornness, and so on were all referred to as *anal retentive* traits by Freud.)

Cattell refined the Allport catalogue by removing unusual terms and grouping the remaining traits into sixteen central **source traits**—the underlying traits from which surface traits are derived. Cattell argued that psychological measurement of a person's source traits would enable us to predict his or her behavior in various situations. Cattell believed that the major work of a personality theorist lay in helping refine the list of source traits. Cattell's source traits are measured by his Sixteen Personality Factors Scale, and personality profiles based on his test are shown in the nearby box, "On Cockpits and Cocktails."

HANS EYSENCK

British psychologist Hans J. Eysenck (1960) has focused much of his research on the relationships between two source traits: **introversion-extraversion** and stability-instability, otherwise called **neuroticism.** These source traits or personality dimensions, and a number of surface traits that reflect different combinations of these source traits, are shown in Figure 9.2.

Carl Jung was first to distinguish between introverts and extraverts. Eysenck added the dimension of neuroticism to introversion-extraversion, and he has catalogued a number of personality traits according to where they are "situated" along these dimensions (refer to Figure 9.2). For instance, an anxious person would be high both in introversion and neuroticism—that is, preoccupied with his or her own thoughts and emotionally unstable. Where would you place athletes and artists in terms of the dimensions of introversion-extraversion and neuroticism?

EVALUATION OF TRAIT THEORY

Trait theory continues to generate useful psychological research, but may be criticized on several grounds. Trait theory is more descriptive than explanatory. It focuses on describing existing traits rather than tracing their origins or investigating how they may be modified. The "explanations"

Surface traits Cattell's term for characteristic, observable ways of behaving.

Source traits Cattell's term for underlying traits from which surface traits are derived.

Introversion A source trait characterized by intense imagination and the tendency to inhibit impulses.

Extraversion A source trait characterized by tendencies to be socially outgoing and to express feelings and impulses freely.

Neuroticism Eysenck's term for emotional instability. (This definition is not fully consistent with the meanings of the terms *neurotic* and *neurosis,* as discussed in Chapter 11.)

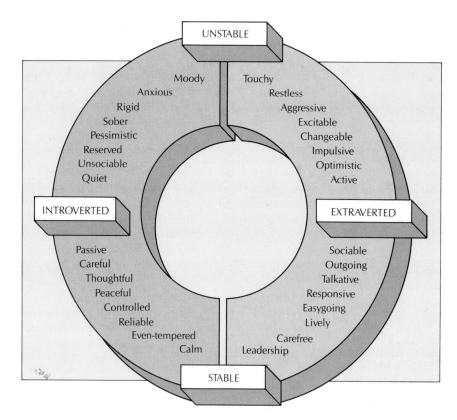

FIGURE 9.2 EYSENCK'S PERSONAL- ITY DIMENSIONS Various personality traits fall within the two major dimensions of personality suggested by Hans Eysenck.

provided by trait theory have been criticized as **circular explanations.** If we say that John failed to ask Marsha on a date *because* of shyness, we have contributed little to our understanding of the causes of John's behavior.

Allport argued that traits were *neuropsychic structures,* somehow embedded in the person's nervous system. Critics have argued that Allport failed to specify where and how these traits are embedded. In this sense, traits have no more substance than do Freud's psychic structures. Still, a number of psychologists argue that diverse traits like social shyness, aggressiveness, and neuroticism vary from person to person in ways that suggest that inborn factors play an important role (see Chapters 2 and 8).

A basic assumption of trait theory is that human behavior tends to be largely consistent from one situation to another. But research suggests that behavior varies more from situation to situation—at least for some people—than trait theory would allow (Bem & Allen, 1974; Mischel, 1977, 1986). People who are high in **private self-consciousness**—who carefully monitor their own behavior, even when others are not observing them—also try to show consistent behavior from situation to situation (Fenigstein et al., 1975; Scheier et al., 1978; Underwood & Moore, 1981). But other people show greater variability in behavior.

On the other hand, longitudinal research has shown that a number of personality traits seem to possess remarkable stability over the years. James Conley (1984, 1985), for example, studied psychological tests taken by a sample of adults during the 1930s, the 1950s, and again during the 1980s.

Circular explanation An explanation that merely restates its own concepts instead of offering additional information.

Private self-consciousness The tendency to take critical note of one's own behavior, even when unobserved by others.

PSYCHOLOGY IN THE WORKPLACE

ON COCKPITS AND COCKTAILS:
PERSONALITY PROFILES OF PILOTS, ARTISTS, AND WRITERS

What *don't* airline pilots, creative artists, and writers have in common? According to Raymond Cattell's Sixteen Personality Factors Scale, which measures the source traits he isolated, pilots are more stable, conscientious, tough-minded, practical, controlled, and relaxed than the other two groups (see Figure 9.3). But artists and writers are more intelligent, sensitive, and imaginative. You might prefer to have artists at a cocktail party, but pilots—at least those in the group tested by Cattell—seem to have the stable and controlled personality profile you would prefer to have in charge in the cockpit.

A major criticism of the trait approach is that behavior varies more widely from situation to situation than traits (examples of "personal variables") would allow. By contrast, the learning-theory approach to personality theory has focused on situational variables. But contemporary social-learning theorists believe that behavior is determined by an interaction between personal and situational variables.

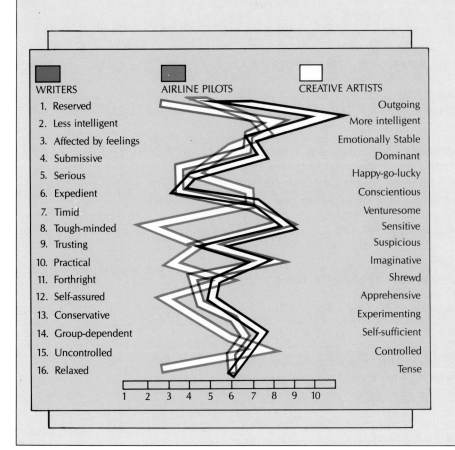

WRITERS **AIRLINE PILOTS** **CREATIVE ARTISTS**

	WRITERS	CREATIVE ARTISTS
1.	Reserved	Outgoing
2.	Less intelligent	More intelligent
3.	Affected by feelings	Emotionally Stable
4.	Submissive	Dominant
5.	Serious	Happy-go-lucky
6.	Expedient	Conscientious
7.	Timid	Venturesome
8.	Tough-minded	Sensitive
9.	Trusting	Suspicious
10.	Practical	Imaginative
11.	Forthright	Shrewd
12.	Self-assured	Apprehensive
13.	Conservative	Experimenting
14.	Group-dependent	Self-sufficient
15.	Uncontrolled	Controlled
16.	Relaxed	Tense

1 2 3 4 5 6 7 8 9 10

FIGURE 9.3 THREE PERSONALITY PROFILES ACCORDING TO CATTELL'S PERSONALITY FACTORS. How do the traits of writers, pilots, and artists compare? Where would you place yourself along these sixteen personality dimensions?

Their scores on the traits of extraversion, neuroticism, and impulsiveness showed significant consistency across five decades. While behavior may change dramatically to meet the requirements of the situation, it may well be that personality traits are more deeply embedded and more resistant to change.

LEARNING THEORIES

The psychoanalyst chides the trait theorist: "Wonderful, you've described this elephant as rotund, plump, obese, but how, my friend, did he become so huge? What motivated him to gorge himself so?" (The elephant casts a pointed glance.) "Little ghosts, perhaps? Vague cosmic forces? It is clear to anyone who cares to reflect that he is fixated in the oral stage."

"A *biting* insight," comments the trait theorist.

"The *what* stage?" asks the elephant.

"The oral stage," repeats the psychoanalyst. "Under stress, he is obviously under the command of oral impulses from the id."

"Id, shmid!" barks the learning theorist. "What's all this stuff about psychic structures?" He addresses the trait theorist: "And what's a personality *structure*? You can't observe or measure psychic structures or personality structures. You claim to be scientific, but you're both off on witch hunts for imaginary structures within an imaginary mind.

"If you want to be scientific, pull out the camera and the tape measure. Let's agree to stick to what we can all see, hear, and feel—the elephant's eating behaviors and the details of the situations in which he stuffs his trunk."

"I'm not sure I see the improvement," says the elephant.

"Rather than trying blindly to dig down deep within the elephant, let's pay some attention to the circumstances under which he eats."

There are a number of learning-theory approaches to the understanding of personality. We shall focus on two of them: behaviorism and social-learning theory. Behaviorism is important for its historical significance and still has many followers. Today, however, social-learning theory is the view with which most learning-theory oriented psychologists identify.

THE BEHAVIORIST CHALLENGE

At Johns Hopkins University in 1924, psychologist John B. Watson announced the battle cry of the **radical behaviorist** movement:

> Give me a dozen healthy infants, well-formed, and my own specified world to bring them up in and I'll guarantee to take any one at random and train him to become any type of specialist I might suggest—doctor, lawyer, merchant-chief and, yes, even beggar-man and thief, regardless of his talents, penchants, tendencies, abilities, vocations, and the race of his ancestors (p. 82).

So it was that Watson sounded the behaviorist cry that situational variables, or environmental influences—not internal, person variables—are the significant shapers of human preferences and behaviors. As a counterbalance to the psychoanalysts and structuralists of his day, Watson argued that unseen, undetectable mental structures must be rejected in favor of that which can be seen and measured. In the 1930s, Watson's hue and cry was taken up by B. F. Skinner, who agreed that we should avoid trying to see within the "black box" of the organism itself and emphasized the impact that reinforcements have upon behavior.

Do radical behaviorists see people as similar to R2D2 and C3PO for the *Star Wars* film series? Charming and entertaining, but rather mechanical when all is said and done?

The radical behaviorist outlooks of John B. Watson and B. F. Skinner largely discard the notions of personal freedom, choice, and self-direction. Let us define freedom as the right to do what you *want* to do. Most of us tend to assume that our wants somehow originate within us. But Skinner suggests that environmental influences, such as parental approval and social custom, shape us into *wanting* to do certain things and *not wanting* to do others. From the perspectives of Watson and Skinner, even our telling ourselves that we have free will is determined by the environment as surely as is our becoming startled at a sudden noise.

In his novel *Walden Two* Skinner (1948) describes a Utopian society in which people are happy and content because they are allowed to do as they please. However, they have been trained or conditioned from early childhood to engage in **prosocial** behavior and to possess prosocial attitudes. For this reason they *want* to behave in a decent, kind, and unselfish way. But they look upon themselves as being free, because society makes no effort to force them to behave as they do as adults.

Skinner elaborated his beliefs about people and society in *Beyond Freedom and Dignity* (1972). According to Skinner, adaptation to the environment requires acceptance of behavior patterns that ensure survival. If the group is to survive, it must construct rules and laws that will aid the cause of social harmony. Other people are then systematically rewarded for following these rules and laws and punished for disobeying them. Nobody is really free, although we may think of ourselves as having come freely together to establish the rules and then as choosing to follow them.

Some object to radical behaviorist notions because they degrade the importance of human consciousness and choice. Others argue that people

Prosocial Behavior that is characterized by helping others and making a contribution to society.

are not so blindly ruled by pleasure and pain. People have rebelled against the so-called necessity of survival by choosing pain and hardship over pleasure, or death over life. Many people have sacrificed their own lives to save those of others.

The radical behaviorist defense might be that the apparently individual choice of pain or death is forced upon the altruist just as inevitably as conformity to social custom is forced upon others. The altruist was also shaped by external influences. Those influences simply differed from those that affect most of us.

It may not be possible to resolve this issue logically. How can we know the difference between freedom and the illusion of freedom? How do we differentiate between a "real want" and a "perceived want"?

SOCIAL-LEARNING THEORY

Social-learning theory is a contemporary view developed by Albert Bandura (1977) and other psychologists that focuses on the importance of learning by observation and on the role of cognitive activity in human behavior. Social-learning theorists reject the radical behaviorist ideas of Watson and Skinner. Social-learning theorists see people as influencing the environment, just as the environment influences them. Theorists such as Bandura (1978), Walter Mischel (1986), and Julian B. Rotter (1972) agree that discussions of human nature should be tied to observable experiences and behaviors when possible, but assert that variables within the person must also be considered if human behavior is to be adequately explained and predicted.

Bandura, Rotter, and Mischel have in particular argued for the inclusion of cognitive points of view within the learning-theory perspective. To them, no discussion of human personality that omits the richness of our thoughts, plans, and expectations can provide a complete picture of human nature or even allow us to predict human behavior.

Social-learning theorists view behavior as stemming from an ongoing interaction between person and situational variables. **Interactionism** focuses on the ways that variables influence one another. From an interactionist perspective, we need not be concerned about whether the environment first shapes us or we first shape the environment. We need not worry about which came first—the chicken or the egg. It is enough to note that chickens and eggs develop from each other and are essential to each other's existence.

Within social-learning theory, the performance of behaviors is assumed to depend on person and situational variables (see Figure 9.4). **Person variables** include expectancies, values, behavioral competencies, and perceived self-efficacy. **Situational variables** include rewards and punishments.

Expectancies **Expectancies,** or "if-then" statements, are personal predictions about the outcome (or reinforcement contingencies) of engaging in a response. The unique human abilities to manipulate symbols and to ponder events allow us to foresee the potential consequences of our be-

Social-learning theory. A cognitively oriented learning theory in which observational learning, values, and expectations play major roles in determining behavior.

Interactionism A view of behavior that emphasizes the relationships among various determinants of behavior, instead of stressing the first cause or prime mover.

Person variables In social-learning theory, determinants of behavior that lie within the person.

Situational variables In social-learning theory, determinants of behavior that lie outside the person.

Expectancies Personal predictions about the outcomes of potential behaviors. "If-then" statements.

Walter Mischel.

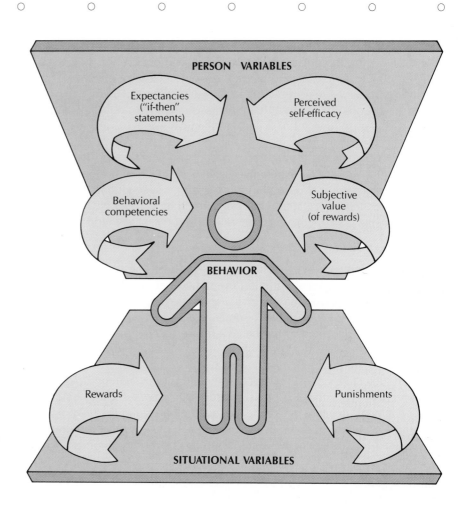

PERSON VARIABLES

Expectancies
("if-then"
statements)

Perceived
self-efficacy

Behavioral
competencies

Subjective
value
(of rewards)

BEHAVIOR

Rewards

Punishments

SITUATIONAL VARIABLES

**FIGURE 9.4 PERSON AND SITUA-
TIONAL VARIABLES** According to social-learning theory, person and situational variables interact to determine
behavior.

Julian B. Rotter.

havior. Learning and behavior, for us, is not simply a matter of trial and
error. We can learn from the experiences of others, and from the imagined
consequences of completely new behavior patterns, as well as from direct
experience.

Expectancies are frequently related to past experience in similar situations. Even though classical conditioning plays a limited role in social-
learning theory, some expectancies may be acquired through principles of
classical conditioning. Assume that we encountered pain by falling off a
bicycle or pleasure from eating a piece of cake. Now we have the opportunity to ride a bicycle or eat another piece of cake. The associated pain
or pleasure is perceived as an image, such as a mental picture of scraping
your hands and knees or of the deep chocolate flavor of the cake. The
nature of the image (negative or positive) influences us either not to repeat
(not to ride a bicycle recklessly) or to repeat (eat another piece of cake) the
response. But the nature of the image is one influence among many—we
may decide not to eat another piece of cake despite the pleasure it might
afford. (And occasionally we do decide not to eat the cake.)

A more active cognitive process, problem solving, may also be brought
to bear in arriving at expectancies. In problem solving we relate a current

situation to past similar situations. We may engage in cognitive "trial and error," predicting the outcomes of various responses. Eventually we may overtly try the response that we predict is likely to be most effective. If the response works, we may repeat it in similar situations; if not, we may discard it. But note that the central process is cognitive—our expectations and experiences influence but do not mechanically cause our behavior.

Rotter (1972) explains the fact that many of us develop reasonably stable behavior patterns through the concept of *generalized expectancies* rather than traits. That is, experience teaches us that certain types of behavior are likely to serve us well in a broad range of situations. However, these "stable" behavior patterns are not so rigid as traits; if circumstances were to change, so might our generalized expectancies, and thus our behaviors.

Values   Because of our different types of learning experiences, we may each place a different value on the same or similar stimuli. What is frightening to one person may be enticing to another. What is slightly desirable to one may be irresistible to someone else. From the social-learning perspective, as contrasted to the behaviorist perspective, we are not controlled by stimuli; instead, stimuli have various meanings for us, and these meanings may influence us in various ways.

The subjective value of a particular stimulus or reward tends to depend on past experience with it or similar rewards. This experience may be direct or observational. Because of experience, our feelings about the reward may be positive or negative. If you became nauseated the last time you drank a glass of iced tea, its subjective value as an incentive may diminish, even on a hot day.

Subjective value will also depend on social motives. A person with a high need for achievement (*n* Ach) will work harder for an A in a course than will a person with a low *n* Ach—assuming that the low *n*-Ach individual has not been promised a new car as a reward for an A. Ten dollars may also have greater subjective value as a reward to a poor person than to a rich person.

Behavioral Competencies   **Behavioral competencies** are skills. They include academic skills like reading and writing, athletic skills like swimming and tossing a football properly, social skills like knowing how to ask someone out on a date, job skills, and many others. Behavioral competencies tend to be acquired through operant conditioning and observational learning (discussed in Chapter 5). In the case of operant conditioning, we learn to engage in certain responses (operants) in certain situations, because they have been reinforced in similar situations. In the case of observational learning, which is a more sophisticated and efficient form of learning, we learn to engage in responses that we observe other people perform. We are more likely to imitate these responses if they are reinforced in the people we observe and if we believe that they are appropriate for us.

Primary and conditioned reinforcers (see Chapter 5) can lead to the acquisition of skills. Primary reinforcers include food, liquid, a comfortable temperature, and removal of pain. Conditioned reinforcers gain their re-

Behavioral competencies Skills.

inforcement value through association with established reinforcers. Conditioned reinforcers can become generalized when they are paired with several primary reinforcers. Then they are referred to as **conditioned generalized reinforcers.** Conditioned generalized reinforcers such as money, attention, and social approval can exert powerful influences on behavior. Mischel (1986) notes that many people seem to learn to seek money for its own sake. They work to pile up "paper profits," even though they never trade them in for primary reinforcers.

Radical behaviorists equated learning with behavior, but social-learning theorists usually distinguish between the learning (or acquisition) and the performance of skills. We may acquire a skill (learn how to do something) just by observing another person. We may then choose not to perform this response until we believe that we will be reinforced for it. We are more likely to engage in aggressive behavior, for example, when we believe that it is appropriate or will be socially tolerated. This is one reason that girls, for whom aggressive behavior is almost always deemed inappropriate, are less likely than boys to respond aggressively to a provocation.

Perceived Self-Efficacy According to Albert Bandura, the probability that we shall begin or persist in operant behavior is also related to our **perceived self-efficacy,** or the degree to which we believe that our efforts will bring about a positive outcome. As noted by Bandura and his colleagues Linda Reese and Nancy Adams:

> In their daily lives people must make decisions about whether to attempt risky courses of action or how long to continue, in the face of difficulties, those they have undertaken. Social-learning theory posits that . . . people tend to avoid situations they believe exceed their coping capabilities, but they undertake and perform assuredly activities they judge themselves capable of managing. . . .
> Self-judged efficacy also determines how much of an effort people will make and how long they will keep at a task despite obstacles or adverse experiences. . . . Those who have a strong sense of efficacy exert greater effort to master the challenges. . . . (1982, p. 5).

In Chapter 10 we shall review research that suggests that people can be helped to improve their performances by increasing their perceived self-efficacy. It may not be that believing in yourself is the whole story, but self-belief *in combination with* adequate skills seem to make for strong efforts.

Let us consider the important example of the observational learning of aggressive behavior from television in order to clarify some social-learning-theory concepts.

Copycats, Models, TV, and Rewards: Social-Learning Perspectives on Aggression Can we be expected to act in a civilized manner when we are exposed to a constant bombardment of violence in television shows and films? In Florida, in 1977, a teenaged boy killed an elderly woman. The defense claimed that he was not guilty by reason of insanity. Why? He had become "addicted" to TV violence and could no longer differentiate between fantasy and reality. (He was found guilty.)

"HILL STREET BLUES" "Hill Street Blues" is just one of dozens of violent television shows. With media violence so common, it may be more difficult to explain why most people who watch these shows remain nonviolent than it is to explain why a minority imitate the aggressive behavior they observe.

In 1974 a nine-year-old California girl was raped with a bottle by four other girls who admitted they had been given the idea by the television movie *Born Innocent*. The victim's family sued the network and the local station that had screened the film. The courts, however, chose not to award damages. Such a precedent, it was argued, might interfere with the right to free expression as guaranteed by the First Amendment to the Constitution.

It cannot be argued that television violence directly caused these crimes. After all, with a few unfortunate exceptions, the millions who watch television do *not* imitate antisocial behavior. But it does seem that aggressive behavior in humans is largely learned. Social-learning theory explains the acquisition of aggressive responses through operant conditioning and observational learning—with the emphasis on observation and cognitive processes.

Operant Conditioning of Aggressive Responses   A number of learning theorists (Dollard et al., 1939) once believed that frustration mechanically aroused an aggression drive, and that aggressive behavior was rewarding because it reduced that drive. Today's social-learning theorists would admit that frustration is discomforting when it is linked to highly elevated arousal and disconcerting thoughts, and that we might be motivated to engage in behavior that reduces overarousal and leads to thoughts that we have surmounted obstacles to goals. But they do not perceive aggressive responses as automatic. Sometimes these goals may be reached through aggressive responses, but a wide range of behavioral options is available, including socially appropriate self-assertion.

Still, aggressive behavior may be reinforced in some people, especially the strong and well-coordinated, because it may remove sources of frustration or external threats and earn the respect of peers. Social provocations can also lead to unpleasant increases in tension and arousal. There is some evidence that aggression can lead to pleasant declines in blood pressure (Kahn, 1966), one measure of arousal, at least when we believe that aggression is justified (Geen et al., 1975).

But do children happen upon their first aggressive responses by trial and error, as rats learn to press a lever for food in a cage? Research in social-learning theory suggests that observational learning is a more common way of acquiring aggressive responses.

Observational Learning of Aggressive Responses   Children learn not only from the effects of their own behavior, but also from observing the behavior of their parents and other adults (Bandura, 1973). In fact, children may be more likely to imitate what their parents do than to heed what they say. If adults say they disapprove of aggression, but smash furniture or slap each other when frustrated, children are likely to develop the notion that aggression is the way to handle frustration.

Now let us consider the role of television. Television is one of the major sources of observational learning in our culture. U.S. children average four hours of viewing a day by the early ages of three or four (Pearl et al., 1982; Singer & Singer, 1981). Children spend more hours at the television set than in school (Singer, 1983). This early devotion to television gives the medium the potential to be of significant benefit to children in the development of cognitive skills and general knowledge (Wright & Huston, 1983). Unfortunately, as of today television does not appear to have lived up to this potential, and it seems appropriate to suggest that we carefully examine the influence of television on the behavior of our own children (Singer & Singer, 1983).

As suggested by Figure 9.5, children may imitate the aggressive behavior they see on television, whether the aggressive **models** are cartoons or real people (Bandura et al., 1963). The probability of aggression increases when the models are similar to the observers, and when the models are rewarded for acting aggressively. Why? Again, the answer has nothing to do with mechanical learning. Instead, according to social-learning theory, children under these circumstances are more likely to come to believe that aggression is appropriate for them.

Most psychologists agree that television violence does contribute to aggression (NIMH, 1982; Rubinstein, 1983). Social-learning theorists point to at least four types of television influence:

1. *Increased arousal.* Television violence increases the level of arousal of viewers. We are more likely to engage in dominant forms of behavior, including aggressive behavior, when we have high levels of arousal.
2. *Disinhibition.* Television violence may **disinhibit** the expression of aggressive impulses that would otherwise have been controlled.
3. *Observational learning.* Television violence teaches viewers aggressive skills. Many criminals admit to imitating methods of operation observed on television.

Model In social-learning theory, an organism that exhibits behaviors that others will imitate, or acquire, through observational learning.

Disinhibit In social-learning theory, to cause the occurrence of a usually inhibited behavior (generally as a consequence of observing a model engage in that behavior).

FIGURE 9.5 A CLASSIC EXPERIMENT IN THE IMITATION OF AGGRESSIVE MODELS Children will imitate the behavior of adult models in certain situations, as shown in these pictures from a classic study by Albert Bandura and his colleagues (1963). In the top row, an adult model strikes a clown doll. The next two rows show a boy and a girl imitating the aggressive behavior.

4. *Habituation.* We become **habituated** to many stimuli that impact upon us repeatedly. Television viewers may become habituated to violence.* Continued exposure to media violence may decrease viewers' emotional response to subsequent violence (Geen, 1981; Thomas et al., 1977). If so, their own attitudes toward violence could become less condemnatory, and they might place less value on restraining their own aggressive urges.

It seems that there is a circular relationship between viewing media violence and aggressive behavior (Eron, 1982; Fenigstein, 1979). While television violence contributes to aggressive behavior, aggressive children are also more likely to watch more violent television. Eron found that aggressive children are less popular than nonaggressive children. He theorizes that aggressive children watch more television, because their peer relationships are less fulfilling and because the high incidence of television violence tends to confirm their own aggressiveness (1982, p. 210).

*In Chapter 13, we shall also see that people can become habituated to pornography.

Habituate To become accustomed to a stimulus (as determined by no longer showing a particular response in the presence of the stimulus).

It may be that television violence is one factor among many that contribute to aggressive behavior. Eron (1982) argues that parental rejection and the use of physical punishment by parents also contribute to aggression in youngsters. It may be that harsh experiences in the home further confirm the viewer's notion that the world is filled with violence, and encourage further reliance on television for companionship.

But for parents of children who will watch television violence—perhaps the great majority of children—social-learning theory offers some encouraging news. Television violence may be one factor that contributes to aggressive behavior, but televised violence does not automatically trigger aggressive behavior. Huesmann and his colleagues (1983), for example, found that children who watch violent shows are rated by peers as significantly less aggressive when they are educated about these shows according to the following principles:

1. The violent behavior they observe on television does *not* represent the behavior of most people.
2. The apparently aggressive behaviors are not real—they reflect camera tricks, special effects, and stunts.
3. Most people use other-than-violent means to resolve their conflicts.

Again, in social-learning theory, the emphasis is on the cognitive. If children believe that violence is inappropriate for them, they will probably not act aggressively even if they have acquired commanding aggressive skills.

EVALUATION OF LEARNING THEORIES

Critics note that radical behaviorism has many shortcomings in its power to explain human behavior, as noted in Chapter 5. First, behaviorism fails to explain how behaviors can be learned yet not performed. Second, behaviorism views human behavior as the summation of so many instances of conditioning; however, all instances of conditioning could never be specified, so this assertion can never be demonstrated. It must remain nothing more than an unsubstantiated belief.

Behaviorism also cannot begin to explain or even describe the richness of human behavior. We all have the experiences of thought, of complex inner maps of the world, and behaviorism in a sense deprives us of the right to search for ways to scientifically discuss what it means to us to be human. Behaviorism also seems at a loss to explain how it is that many of us will strive, against all hardships, to fulfill distant inner visions. If we only repeat behaviors that have been reinforced, how is it that we struggle—without reinforcers—to create new works and ideas? How is it that many mathematicians and composers sit almost motionless all day, and suddenly write new formulas and symphonies?

Critics of social-learning theory cannot accuse its supporters of denying the importance of cognitive activity. Still, they may contend that social-learning theory has failed to derive satisfying statements about the development of traits and to account for self-awareness. It may also be that social-learning theory—like its intellectual forebear, radical behaviorism—has not always paid sufficient attention to genetic differences among people. It appears naive to deny the role of heredity in the performance of, say, intelligent behavior, or in the development of abnormal behavior. These issues are expanded in Chapters 6 and 11.

But social-learning theorists may be beginning to repair these theoretical flaws. Mischel (1986) stresses that today's social-learning theorists view people as active, not merely as mechanical reactors to environmental pressures (as Watson saw them). Cognitive functioning is an appropriate area of study for many contemporary social-learning theorists (Wilson, 1982). In the area of abnormal behavior, social-learning theorists Gerald Davison and John Neale (1982) may speak for many of their fellows when they suggest that inherited or physiological factors often interact with situational stress to give rise to abnormal behavior.

Social-learning theory has also contributed to the formation of many strategies for helping people change maladaptive behavior. These strategies are collectively termed behavior therapy, and you will learn more about them in Chapters 10 and 12.

SELF THEORY

"Gentlemen, gentlemen," the self theorist reproves. "There may be some truth in what each of you has to say, but our elephant friend doesn't feel that you've gotten to the core of his being. None of you has asked *him* about his impressions of himself. He must feel quite left out."

"Like a specimen under a microscope," says the elephant.

"Creative," comments the trait theorist.

"Penetrating," remarks the psychoanalyst.

"A predictable response," sighs the learning theorist.

The self theorist continues. "The elephant's behavior may be influenced by unconscious dynamic forces within him. He does appear to possess traits. And reinforcement may explain some of his peanut- and popcorn-inhaling behaviors. Perhaps he also had to learn that within our culture it is expected that elephants will fear mice—" The elephant trumpets and rears on his back legs.

"All these things are true, but they are not the *essence* of the elephant," summarizes the self theorist. "They are not his *self*."

"*His* self?" mocks the trait theorist. "A rather poor grammarian."

"Don't blame him," says the learning theorist. "It's our educational system these days."

"It may reflect some deep-seated conflict," notes the psychoanalyst. "*His* is possessive. *Him* ends in *m*, the first letter in *mother*."

The self theorist is undaunted. "Gentlemen," he proceeds, "I am convinced that self-awareness is the guiding principle in the elephant's personality. I don't buy that his sense of self is but the tip of his personality, floating above the deep reaches of the unconscious," he remarks to the psychoanalyst. "Note that I did not say that he was self*ish*," he says to the trait theorist. "Nor do I believe that his freedom of choice is only an illusion," he says to the learning theorist. "His sense of self is inborn. It will urge him to develop his unique potential."

Humanistic Emphasizing the importance of self-awareness and the freedom to make choices.

Gestalt In this usage, a quality of wholeness. See Chapter 1 for a discussion of Gestalt psychology.

Innate Inborn, natural, unlearned.

Self-actualization In humanistic theory, the innate tendency to strive to realize one's potential. Self-initiated striving to become all one is capable of being.

"Fellows," the trait theorist addresses the psychoanalyst and learning theorist, "I'm thirsty. Let's get something to wet our whistles."

"Just the stimulus I needed," agrees the learning theorist.

"A little oral gratification never hurt," nods the psychoanalyst.

Moments later the elephant and self theorist are quite alone. "Your ideas sound good to me," consoles the elephant.

CARL ROGERS AND THE CONCEPT OF THE SELF

"My experience in therapy and in groups makes it impossible for me to deny the reality and significance of human choice. To me it is not an illusion that man is to some degree the architect of himself," wrote self theorist Carl Rogers (1974, p. 119). According to a survey of clinical and counseling psychologists (Smith, 1982), Rogers is the single most influential psychotherapist of recent years.

The view that people tend to shape themselves through freedom of choice and action is considered **humanistic.** Self theory is basically humanistic, but psychologists from other schools may also show a humanistic bent. Erik Erikson's view that we strive consciously to cope with identity crises and to invent ourselves is also humanistic. Many social-learning theorists who stress the importance of cognitive person variables as determinants of behavior see themselves as humanistic.

Rogers defines the self as an "organized, consistent, conceptual **gestalt** composed of perceptions of the characteristics of the 'I' or 'me' and the perceptions of the relationships of the 'I' or 'me' to others and to various aspects of life, together with the values attached to these perceptions" (1959, p. 200). Your self is your center of experience. It is your ongoing sense of who and what you are, your sense of how and why you react to the environment, and how you choose to act upon the environment. Your choices are made on the basis of your values, and your values are also parts of your self.

To Rogers the sense of self is inborn or **innate.** The self provides the experience of being human in the world. It is the guiding principle behind personality structure and behavior.

SELF-ACTUALIZATION

Humanistic personality theorists like Carl Rogers and Abraham Maslow believe that organisms are genetically programed to grow, unfold, and become themselves. This central tendency, termed **self-actualization,** is a characteristic of life itself.

It could be said that self-actualization functions as a cardinal trait. It is the steering principle that underlies behavior. Self-actualization renders behavior organized, meaningful, and whole.

THE SELF-CONCEPT AND FRAMES OF REFERENCE

Our self-concepts are our impressions of ourselves and our evaluation of our adequacy. It may help to think of us as rating ourselves along various

UNIQUE According to humanistic psychologists such as Carl Rogers, we each view the world and ourselves from a unique frame of reference. What is important to one person may have little value to another.

scales or dimensions, like good-bad, intelligent-unintelligent, strong-weak, and tall-short.

Rogers states that we all have unique ways of looking at ourselves and the world, or unique **frames of reference.** It may be that we each use a different set of dimensions in defining ourselves, and that we judge ourselves according to different sets of values. To one person achievement-failure may be the most important dimension. To another person the most important dimension may be decency-indecency. A third person may not even think in terms of decency.

SELF-ESTEEM AND POSITIVE REGARD

Rogers assumes that we all develop a need for self-regard or **self-esteem** as we grow and become aware of ourselves. Self-esteem tends first to reflect the esteem others hold for us. We are likely to seek the love and approval of parents and other important people in our lives.

Parents are likely to help their children develop self-esteem when they show them **unconditional positive regard,** when they accept them as people of intrinsic merit regardless of their behavior of the moment. But when parents show **conditional positive regard** for their children, accepting them only when they behave in a desired manner, children may learn to disown the thoughts, feelings, and behaviors that parents have rejected. Conditional positive regard may lead children to develop **conditions of worth**—that is, to think that they are worthwhile only if they behave in certain ways.

Frame of reference One's unique patterning of perceptions and attitudes, according to which one evaluates events.

Self-esteem One's evaluation and valuing of oneself.

Unconditional positive regard A persistent expression of esteem for the value of a person, but not necessarily an unqualified acceptance of all of the person's behaviors.

Conditional positive regard Judgment of another person's value on the basis of the acceptability of that person's behaviors.

Conditions of worth Standards by which the value of a person is judged.

Since each of us is thought to have a unique potential, children who develop conditions of worth must become disappointed in themselves to some degree. We cannot fully live up to the wishes of others and remain true to ourselves. This does not mean that the expression of the self inevitably leads to conflict. Rogers was optimistic about human nature. He believed that we hurt others or act in antisocial ways only when we are frustrated in our efforts to develop our potential. But when parents and others are loving and tolerant of our differentness, we, too, shall be loving—even if some of our preferences, abilities, and values differ from those of our parents.

But children in some families learn that it is bad to have ideas of their own, especially about sexual, political, or religious matters. When they perceive their parents' disapproval, they may come to see themselves as rebels and label their feelings as selfish, wrong, or evil. If they wish to retain a consistent self-concept, and self-esteem, they may have to deny many of their genuine feelings, or disown parts of themselves. In this way the self-concept becomes distorted. According to Rogers, anxiety often stems from partial perception of feelings and ideas that are inconsistent with the distorted self-concept. Since anxiety is unpleasant, we may deny that these feelings and ideas exist.

PSYCHOLOGICAL CONGRUENCE AND THE SELF-IDEAL

When we accept our feelings as our own, we experience psychological integrity or wholeness. There is a "fit" between our self-concepts and our behavior, thoughts, and emotions, which Rogers calls **congruence.**

According to Rogers, the path to self-actualization requires getting in touch with our genuine feelings, accepting them as ours, and acting upon them. This is the goal of Rogers' method of psychotherapy, person-centered therapy, which we shall discuss in Chapter 12. Here suffice it to say that person-centered therapists provide an atmosphere in which clients can cope with the anxiety that may attend focusing on disowned parts of the self.

Rogers also believes that we have mental images of what we are capable of becoming, or **self-ideals.** We are motivated to reduce the **discrepancy** between our self-concepts and our self-ideals. But as we undertake the process of actualizing ourselves, our self-ideals may gradually grow more complex. Our goals may become higher or change in quality. The self-ideal is something like a carrot dangling from a stick strapped to a burro's head. The burro strives to reach the carrot, as though it were a step or two away, without recognizing that its own progress also causes the carrot to advance. Rogers believes that the process of striving to meet meaningful goals, the good struggle, is what yields human happiness.

Maslow notes that as we actualize ourselves we may now and then encounter **peak experiences.** Peak experiences are brief moments of rapture that seem to tell us that what we are doing is right for us, that we are on the proper path. The artist may encounter such rapture upon completing a sketch that captures his or her visual experience. The machinist may find it in visualizing a more efficient way to complete an assembly-line task.

Congruence According to Rogers, a fit between one's self-concept and one's behaviors, thoughts, and feelings. (From the Latin *congruens,* meaning "coming together.")

Self-ideal A mental image of what we believe we ought to be.

Discrepancy Lack of agreement, inconsistency.

Peak experience In humanistic theory, a brief moment of rapture that stems from the realization that one is on the path to self-actualization.

We may encounter peak experiences at the birth of our children, or when our research yields major findings. We are all unique. What provides you with a peak experience may be meaningless to a friend or coworker.

EVALUATION OF SELF THEORY

Perhaps the most telling criticism of self theory is that the central concept of self-actualization cannot be proved or disproved. Like an id, or a trait, a self-actualizing force cannot be observed or measured directly. It must be inferred from its supposed effects.

Self-actualization, like trait theory, yields circular explanations for behavior. When we observe someone apparently engaged in positive striving, we gain little insight by attributing this striving to self-actualization. We have done nothing to explain the origins of the actualizing tendency. And when we observe someone who is not engaged in growth-oriented striving, it seems arbitrary to "explain" this outcome by suggesting that the self-actualizing tendency has been blocked or frustrated. It may simply be that self-actualization is an acquired need rather than an innate need, and that it is found in some, but not all, of us.

Self theory, like learning theories, also has little to say about the development of traits and personality types. Self theory assumes that we are all unique, but does not predict the sorts of traits, abilities, and interests we shall develop.

Rogers (1985) himself, in his eighties, is very aware of these criticisms, and he notes that they stem from a strict scientific approach that demands certain knowledge. But Rogers adds that one price of a strict scientific approach has been to focus on the determinants of fairly meaningless behaviors. It may be that self theory is among the more satisfying of the personality theories because it addresses the whole, active human being. Self theory, for example, agrees with many things that we like to feel are true about ourselves—that our self-awareness is important and that we have the freedom to develop ourselves in accordance with our own ideas of what we can become. How can any theory of personality seem complete if it does not deal with our own concepts and feelings of what it means to be human?

In Chapter 12 we shall see how Carl Rogers' form of psychotherapy is designed to help each of us live up to our potential.

SOME CONCLUDING THOUGHTS ABOUT THEORIES OF PERSONALITY

Our fictitious elephant, as we saw, was happiest with the self theorist's views on personality. Self theory is also usually preferred by college students for a number of reasons. One, we are aware of ourselves and the world around us, and self theory seems most clearly to recognize this self-awareness. Two, self theory seems to be suggesting that we are capable of becoming whatever we want to be, while psychoanalytic theory paints us as limited by childhood conflicts and cognitive distortions, and learning theories focus on situational influences on behavior. Put another way, psychoanalytic theory seems to portray us as victims of the past, and learning theory seems to depict us as victims of circumstances. Only self theory seems to assert that we are in full command of our selves and our futures.

The facts of human life, however, suggest that we may not always be in full command of ourselves and of our futures. We may generally attribute far too much control to the individual. Under unusual and highly stressful situations, we may even find ourselves behaving in ways that are alarming to us, as we shall see in Chapter 14.

And so, despite their diversity, it may well be that each of the personality theories discussed in this chapter has touched on some meaningful aspects of human nature. What if we were simply to put together a list of some of the basic ideas set forth by these theories? Each item on the list would not apply equally to everyone, but such a list might reflect something of what we see in ourselves and others. Let's try it out:

1. We make assumptions about personality traits based on the behavior we see in ourselves and others.
2. Our behavior is reasonably consistent under run-of-the-mill circumstances, but can differ markedly in extreme situations.
3. Early childhood experiences can have lasting influences upon us.
4. Our cognitive processes can be distorted, so that we see what we want to see and hear what we want to hear.
5. We generally seek rewards and avoid punishments.
6. We model much of our behavior after the behavior of people we observe.
7. We are to some degree the architects of ourselves.
8. We try to become like our mental images of what we are capable of being.

If it strikes you that there is some truth to each of these statements, then perhaps each of the theories of personality also has something of value to tell us. Each theory views the "elephant" from a different perspective, but perhaps each perspective sheds light on meaningful aspects of human nature.

Now that we are familiar with a number of theories of personality, let us see how psychologists measure different aspects of personality.

MEASUREMENT OF PERSONALITY

Measures of personality are used to make important decisions, such as whether a person is suited for a certain type of work, for a particular class in school, or for a drug to reduce agitation. As part of their admissions process, graduate schools will often ask professors to rate prospective students on scales that assess traits like intelligence, emotional stability, and cooperativeness. Students may take tests of **aptitudes** and interests to gather insight into whether they are suited for certain occupations. It is assumed

Aptitude A natural ability or talent. (From the Latin *apere*, meaning "to grasp" or "to reach.")

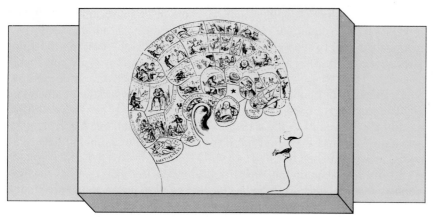

FIGURE 9.6 **A PHRENOLOGIST'S MAP OF THE "MENTAL FUNCTIONS"**

that students who share the aptitudes and interests of people who are well-adjusted in certain positions are likely to be well-adjusted themselves in those positions.

If you had wanted to learn about your personality early in the last century, an "expert" might have measured the bumps on your head with a **caliper.** This method, termed **phrenology,** was based on the erroneous belief that traits, abilities, and mental functions dwelled in specific places in the head, and could be measured from the outside. Figure 9.6 shows a "map" of these functions, as used by many phrenologists.

Today's personality measures are more scientific, if not more interesting. They involve using a sample of behavior, usually in the form of the self-report, to predict future behavior. Standardized interviews can be used, and, today, psychologists can even arrange for some routine interviews to be carried out by computer (Erdman et al., 1985). Some measures of personality are **behavior-rating scales** that assess overt behavior in settings such as the classroom or mental hospital. With behavior-rating scales, trained observers usually check off each occurrence of a specific behavior within a certain time frame, say, a fifteen-minute period. Standardized objective and projective tests are used more frequently, and they will be discussed in this section.

OBJECTIVE TESTS

Objective tests present respondents with a **standardized** group of test items in the form of questionnaires. Respondents are limited to a specific range of answers. One test may request that respondents indicate whether items are true or false for them. Another may ask respondents to select the preferred activity from groups of three.

Some tests have a **forced-choice** format in which respondents are asked to indicate which of two statements is more true of them, or which of several activities they prefer. They are not given the option of answering "none of the above." Forced-choice formats are frequently used in interest inventories that help predict whether one would be well-adjusted in a cer-

Caliper An instrument consisting of a pair of curved movable legs that is used for measuring the diameter or thickness of an object.

Phrenology The analysis of personality by measurement of the shape and protuberances of the skull. (From the Greek *phrenos,* meaning "brain.")

Behavior-rating scale A systematic means for recording the frequency with which target behaviors occur.

Objective tests Tests whose items must be answered in a specified, limited manner. Tests whose items have concrete answers that are labeled correct.

Standardized Given to a large number of respondents, so that data concerning the usual responses can be accumulated and analyzed.

Forced-choice format A method of presenting test questions that requires a respondent to select one of a number of possible answers.

Validity scales Groups of test items that indicate whether a person's responses accurately reflect that individual's traits.

Clinical scales Groups of test items that measure the presence of various abnormal behavior patterns.

Response set A tendency to answer test items according to a bias—for instance, to make oneself seem perfect or bizarre.

Hallucinations Perceptions in the absence of sensory stimulation. See Chapter 11.

tain occupation. The following item is similar to those found in interest inventories:

I would rather

a. be a forest ranger
b. work in a busy office
c. play a musical instrument

A forced-choice format is also used in the Edwards Personal Preference Schedule, which measures the relative strength of social motives (like achievement, nurturance, and others discussed in Chapter 7), by pitting them against one another consecutively in groups of two. Today it is not unusual for objective test items to be presented on a computer screen, and for clients to respond by using the keyboard (Fowler, 1985).

The Minnesota Multiphasic Personality Inventory (MMPI)   The MMPI contains 566 items presented in a true-false format. The MMPI was intended to be used by clinical and counseling psychologists to help diagnose abnormal behavior problems of the sort that will be discussed in Chapter 11, and it is the most widely used psychological test in the clinical setting* (Lubin et al., 1985). Accurate measurement of the client's problems should lead to appropriate treatment. In recent years the MMPI has also become the most widely used instrument for personality measurement in psychological research (Costa et al., 1985).

The MMPI has been given to thousands of individuals over the last few decades. This wide usage has permitted psychologists to compare the test records of clients with those of people who are known to have had certain problems. A similar test record is suggestive of the presence of similar problems. Today many psychologists send completed tests to computerized scoring services, or have them scored by on-site computers. Computers can even generate reports by interpreting the test record according to certain rules, or by comparing it to records in the computer's memory (Fowler, 1985).

The MMPI is usually scored for the four **validity scales** and ten **clinical scales** described in Table 9.1. The validity scales indicate whether there is reason to believe that the test results represent the client's thoughts, emotions, and behaviors. The validity scales in Table 9.1 assess different **response sets,** or biases, in answering the questions. People with high "L" scores, for example, may be attempting to present themselves as excessively moral and well-behaved. People with high "F" scores may be attempting to present themselves as bizarre, or answering haphazardly. In one study, F-scale scores were positively correlated with conceptual confusion, hostility, presence of **hallucinations** and other unusual thought patterns as measured on a behavior-rating scale (Smith & Graham, 1981). Many personality measures have some kind of validity scales. The clinical scales of the MMPI assess the problems shown in Table 9.1, as well as stereotypical masculine or feminine interests and introversion.

*The MMPI ranks first in use in a composite based on psychiatric hospitals, community mental-health centers, counseling centers, centers for the developmentally disabled, and Veterans Administration medical centers (Lubin et al., 1985).

TABLE 9.1 Commonly Used Validity and Clinical Scales of the MMPI

Scale	Abbreviation	Definition
Validity Scales		
Question	?	Corresponds to number of items left unanswered
Lie	L	Lies or is highly conventional
Frequency	F	Exaggerates complaints, answers haphazardly
Correction	K	Denies problems
Clinical Scales		
Hypochondriasis	Hs	Expresses bodily concerns and complaints
Depression	D	Is depressed, pessimistic, guilty
Hysteria	Hy	Reacts to stress with physical symptoms, lacks insight
Psychopathic deviate	Pd	Is immoral, in conflict with the law, involved in stormy relationships
Masculinity/ femininity	Mf	Has interests characteristic of stereotypical sex roles
Paranoia	Pa	Is suspicious, resentful
Psychasthenia	Pt	Is anxious, worried, high-strung
Schizophrenia	Sc	Is confused, disorganized, disoriented
Hypomania	Ma	Is energetic, active, easily bored, restless
Social Introversion	Si	Is introverted, timid, shy, lacking self-confidence

MMPI scales were constructed empirically, on the basis of actual clinical data, rather than on the basis of psychological theory. A test-item bank of several hundred items was derived from questions often asked in clinical interviews. Here are some of the items that were used:

My father was a good man	T	F
I am very seldom troubled by headaches	T	F
My hands and feet are usually warm enough	T	F
I have never done anything dangerous for the thrill of it	T	F
I work under a great deal of tension	T	F

The items were administered to clients and psychiatric patients with such known clinical symptoms as depression or with **schizophrenic** symptoms. Items that successfully set apart people with these problems were included on scales with appropriate names. Figure 9.7 shows the personality profile of a twenty-seven-year-old barber who consulted a psychologist because of depression and difficulty making decisions. The barber scored abnormally high on the Hs, D, Pt, Sc, and Si scales, suggestive of concern with bodily functions (Hs), persistent feelings of anxiety and tension (Pt), depression (D), insomnia and fatigue, and some difficulties relating to other people (Sc, Si). Note that the high Sc score does not in and of itself necessarily suggest that the barber is schizophrenic.

In addition to the standard validity and clinical scales, investigators of personality have derived many experimental scales, such as neuroticism, religious orthodoxy, assertiveness, substance-abuse scales, and even a

Schizophrenic (skit-so-FREN-nick). Characteristic of a major thought disorder. See Chapter 11 for a full discussion.

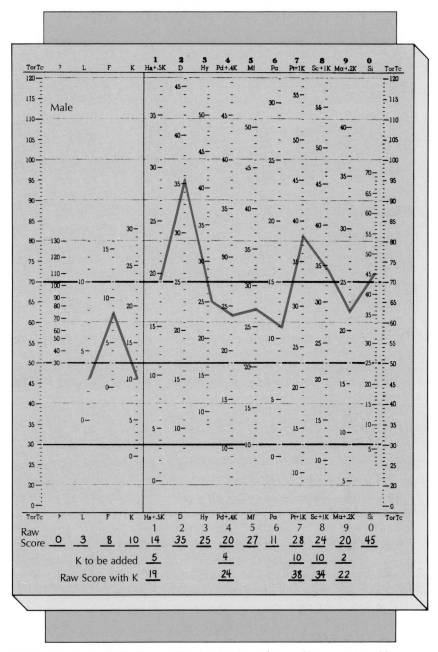

TorTc	?	L	F	K	1 Hs+.5K	2 D	3 Hy	4 Pd+.4K	5 Mf	6 Pa	7 Pt+1K	8 Sc+1K	9 Ma+.2K	0 Si	TorTc
Raw Score	0	3	8	10	14	35	25	20	27	11	28	24	20	45	
K to be added					5			4			10	10	2		
Raw Score with K					19			24			38	34	22		

FIGURE 9.7 AN MMPI PERSONALITY PROFILE This profile was attained by a depressed barber. On this form scores at the standard level of 50 are average for males, and scores above the standard score of 70 are considered abnormally high. The "raw score" is the number of items answered in a certain direction on a given MMPI scale. K is the correction scale. A certain percentage of the K-scale score is added onto several clinical scales to correct for denial of problems.

PSYCHOLOGY IN THE WORKPLACE

USING PSYCHOLOGICAL TESTS TO HELP CHOOSE AN OCCUPATION

Many high school and college students have concrete ideas about the occupations they would like to enter, but others are uncertain not only about their own likes and dislikes but also about what it means to be in a specific occupational role day after day. Psychologists have devised a number of psychological tests that can be of help. The Strong-Campbell Interest Inventory (SCII) and the Kuder Occupational Interest Survey (KOIS) are two of the tests that are widely used to predict adjustment in various occupations.

The SCII is used with high school juniors and seniors, college students, and other adults. It is the most widely used test in counseling centers (Lubin et al., 1985). Most items on the SCII require that test-takers indicate whether they like, are indifferent to, or dislike various occupations (for example, actor/actress, architect); school subjects (algebra, art); activities (adjusting a carburetor, making a speech); amusements (golf, chess, jazz or rock concerts); and types of people (babies, nonconformists). The preferences of test-takers are compared with those of people in various occupations. Areas of general interest (for example, sales, science, teaching, agriculture) and specific interest (for example, mathematician, guidance counselor, beautician) are derived from these comparisons.

The KOIS, like the SCII, is used with high school

upper classes, college students, and other adults. It consists of triads of activities, such as the following:

a. write a story about a sports event
b. play in a baseball game
c. teach children to play a game

For each triad, the test-taker indicates which activities he or she would like most and least. The KOIS reports scores for each of 126 occupational scales and for 48 college majors.

The test-retest reliability of the SCII and the KOIS are high, even when subsequent testings occur after many years have passed. Brown (1983) summarizes the data on validity for the tests by noting that about half the people who score high in an occupational area choose that area, or a closely related area, for their occupation.

Interest in an occupation does not guarantee that a person has the aptitudes required for that occupation. However, there are usually many types of jobs in a broad occupational area, and assessment of both one's interests and aptitudes can help one zero in on a potentially fulfilling choice. On the other hand, one should not interpret a score on an aptitude test as a limitation that is carved in stone.

---

measure of well-being (Costa et al., 1985; Johnson et al., 1984; Snyder et al., 1985). The MMPI remains a rich mine for unearthing elements of personality.

The California Psychological Inventory   Another personality inventory, the California Psychological Inventory (CPI), is widely used in research to assess eighteen dimensions of normal behavior, such as achievement, dominance, flexibility, self-acceptance, and self-control.

PROJECTIVE TESTS

You may have heard that there is a personality test that asks people what a drawing or inkblot looks like, and that they commonly answer "a bat." There are a number of such tests, the best known of which is the Rorschach inkblot test, named after its originator, Swiss psychiatrist Hermann Rorschach (1884–1922).

The Rorschach Inkblot Test   The Rorschach test is a **projective test.** In projective techniques there are no clear, specified answers. People are presented with **ambiguous** stimuli, like inkblots or vague drawings and may

Projective test A psychological test that presents questions to which there is no single correct response. A test that presents ambiguous stimuli into which the test-taker projects his or her own personality in making a response.

Ambiguous Having two or more possible meanings. (From the Latin *ambigere*, meaning "to wander.")

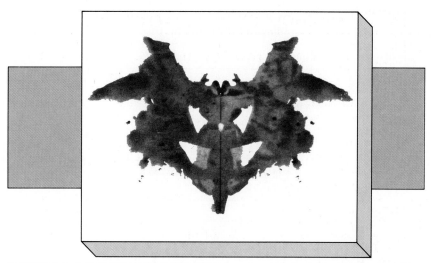

FIGURE 9.8 A RORSCHACH INKBLOT What does this look like? What could it be?

be asked to report what these stimuli look like to them, or to tell stories about them. Since there is no concrete proper response, it is assumed that people *project* their own personalities into their responses. The meanings they attribute to these stimuli are assumed to reflect their personalities as well as the drawings or blots themselves.

Actually the facts of the matter are slightly different. There may be no single "correct" response to the Rorschach inkblot shown in Figure 9.8, but some responses would clearly not be in keeping with the features of the blot. Figure 9.8 could be a bat or a flying insect, the pointed face of an animal, the face of a jack-o'-lantern or many other things. But responses like "an ice cream cone," "diseased lungs," or "a metal leaf in flames" are not suggested by the features of the blot and may suggest personality problems.

The Rorschach (1921) inkblot test contains ten cards. Five are in black and white and shades of gray. Five use a variety of colors. Subjects are given the cards, one by one, and asked what they look like, or what they could be. They can give no, one, or several responses to each card. They can hold the card upside down or sideways.

Responses are scored according to the *location, determinants, content,* and *form level.* The location is the section of the blot chosen—the whole card, or a major or minor detail. Determinants include features of the blot like shading, texture, or color that influence the response. The content is the *what* of the response, for instance a bat, a jack-o'-lantern, or a human torso. (Table 9.2 indicates the meanings attributed to certain types of content, according to many psychoanalytically oriented testers.) Form level indicates whether the response is consistent with the shape of the blot and the complexity of the response. A response that reflects the shape of the blot is a sign of adequate **reality testing.** A response that richly integrates several features of the blot is a sign of high intellectual functioning. The Rorschach is thought to provide insight into a person's intelligence, inter-

Reality testing The capacity to perceive one's environment and oneself according to accurate sensory impressions.

TABLE 9.2 Meanings Commonly Attributed to Certain Types of Content in Rorschach Responses According to Psychoanalytic Theory

Content	Interpretation
Animals	Immaturity, poor human relationships; high percentage of animal responses is normal for children
Anatomy	Concern about bodily problems, hostility
Plants	Femininity, nurturance (sexism, anyone?)
Blood	Aggression, hostility
Clouds	Intense anxiety, usually free-floating
Sex (e.g., penis, vagina)	Emotional disturbance; however, common among normal college students and other sophisticated individuals
Human (people)	Interest in other people

ests, cultural background, degree of introversion or extraversion, level of anxiety, reality testing, and a host of other variables.

The Thematic Apperception Test (TAT)   The TAT was developed in the 1930s by psychologist Henry Murray at Harvard University. It consists of drawings, like that shown in Figure 9.9, that are open to a variety of interpretations. Subjects are given the cards one at a time and asked to make up stories about them.

As noted in Chapter 7, the TAT has been widely used in research in social motives as well as in clinical practice. In an experiment described in Chapter 7, need for achievement was assessed from subjects' responses to a card of a boy and a violin. The notion is that we are likely to some degree to be preoccupied with our needs, and that our needs will be projected into our responses to ambiguous situations. The TAT is also widely used to assess attitudes toward other people, especially parents, lovers, and spouses.

A PSYCHOLOGICAL CONTROVERSY: CAN YOU WRITE A PERSONALITY REPORT THAT APPLIES TO EVERYONE?

Take this brief personality test. Indicate whether each item is mostly true or false for you. Then read the report below to learn everything you always wanted to know about your personality but were too intelligent to ask.

1. I can't unclasp my hands .... T (F)
2. I often mistake my hands for food .... T (F)
3. I never liked room temperature .... T (F)
4. My throat is closer than it seems .... T (F)
5. Likes and dislikes are among my favorites .... (T) F
6. I've lost all sensation in my throat .... T (F)
7. I try to swallow at least three times a day .... T (F)
8. My squirrels don't know where I am tonight .... T (F)
9. Walls impede my progress .... T (F)

FIGURE 9.9 A THEMATIC APPERCEPTION TEST CARD What is happening in this picture? What are the people thinking and feeling? How will it turn out?

Barnum effect The tendency to believe that a generalized personality report or prediction about oneself is accurate. (After circus magnate P. T. Barnum.)

10. My toes are numbered .... T (F)
11. My beaver won't go near the water .... T (F)
Total number of items marked true (T): __

If your total number of items marked true was between zero and eleven, the following personality report applies to you:

> The personality test you have taken has been found to predict inner potential for change. . . . In the past it has been shown that people with similar personality scores . . . have a strong capacity for change. . . . You have a great deal of unused potential you have not yet turned to your advantage. . . .
> The test also suggests that you display ability for personal integration and many latent strengths, as well as the ability to maintain a balance between your inner impulses and the demands of outer reality. Therefore, your personality is such that you have a strong potential for improvement (Halperin & Snyder, 1979, pp. 142–143).

That's you all right, isn't it? I shouldn't be surprised if you thought it sounded familiar. Psychologists Keith Halperin and C. R. Snyder (1979) administered a phony fifty-item personality questionnaire to women in an introductory psychology course at the University of Kansas. The items weren't so silly as the eleven you answered, which were thrown together by Daniel Wegner (1979) and some friends during their graduate-school days. Still, the test was meaningless. Then the students rated the same personality report, which included the paragraphs cited above, for accuracy. The average rating was "quite accurate"!

Halperin and Snyder then administered a therapy program to women who had received the phony report and to women who had not. Believe it or not, women who had received the report, which underscored their capacity for change, showed greater improvement from the treatment than women who had not. When you believe you have the capacity to improve your lot, you are probably more likely to succeed.

The tendency to believe a generalized (but phony) personality report has been labeled the **Barnum effect,** after circus magnate P. T. Barnum, who once declared that a good circus had a "little something for everybody." It is probably the Barnum effect—the tendency for general personality reports to have a "little something for everybody"—that makes fortune-tellers a living. Some psychologists argue that people who would credit such reports are simply gullible. But Layne (1979) counters that these reports are actually quite accurate, even if they are very general. We have such a variety of traits within ourselves that we may be able to find "a little something" that seems to fit us quite well (Johnson et al., 1985). Reports such as the one used by Halperin and Snyder (1979) may also increase the recipient's perceived self-efficacy, and encourage people to harness their potential.

P. T. Barnum also once declared, "There's a sucker born every minute." But in the case of the Barnum effect, it may simply be that most of us share the abilities to recognize general aspects of ourselves and to improve our lives.

EVALUATION OF MEASURES OF PERSONALITY

It seems clear that personality measures can provide useful information to help people make decisions about themselves and others. But in general, psychological tests should not be the sole criteria for making important decisions.

For example, single scales of the MMPI are reasonably accurate measures of the presence of a trait, like depression. But one could not justifiedly hospitalize a person for fear of suicide solely on the basis of a high D-scale score on the MMPI. Similarly, combinations of high MMPI scale scores seem to reflect certain clinical pictures in some populations, but not in others. A typical study found that a combination of high scores on the D, Pt, and Sc scales was likely to suggest severe disturbance in college males, but not college females (Kelley & King, 1979). There is also a controversy as to whether whites, blacks, and other racial groups score differently on the MMPI so that special norms should be established for each group (Bertelson et al., 1982; Butcher et al., 1983; Pritchard & Rosenblatt, 1980; Snyder et al., 1985). MMPI interpretation is further clouded by the fact that abnormal validity-scale scores do *not* necessarily invalidate the test for respondents who are highly disturbed.

The Rorschach inkblot test, for all its artistic appeal, has had major difficulties with validation. The TAT has been consistently shown to be a useful research tool, but its clinical validity has also met with criticism. Despite problems with projective techniques, they continue to be used regularly. The Rorschach inkblot test, in fact, remains the most widely used test in psychiatric hospitals (Lubin et al., 1985).

Psychological tests should not be used as the sole means for making important decisions. But tests that are carefully chosen and interpreted may provide useful information for supplementing other sources of information in making decisions.

SUMMARY

1. Personality can be defined as the reasonably stable patterns of behavior, including thoughts and emotions, that distinguish people from one another. These behavior patterns characterize a person's ways of adapting to the demands of his or her life.

2. Psychoanalytic theory, originated by Sigmund Freud, assumes that we are driven largely by unconscious motives. Conflict is inevitable as basic instincts of hunger, sex, and aggression come up against social pressures to follow laws, rules, and moral codes. At first this conflict is external, but as we develop it becomes intrapsychic.

3. The unconscious id is the psychic structure present at birth. The id represents psychological drives and operates according to the pleasure principle, seeking instant gratification. The ego is the sense of self or "I." The ego develops through experience and operates according to the reality principle. It takes into account what is practical and possible in gratifying the impulses of the id. Defense mechanisms protect the ego from anxiety by repressing unacceptable ideas or distorting reality. The superego is the moral sense, a partly conscious psychic structure that develops largely through identification with others.

4. People undergo psychosexual development as psychosexual energy, or libido, is transferred from one erogenous zone to another during childhood. There are five stages of development: oral, anal, phallic, latency, and genital.

5. Fixation in a stage may lead to the develop-

ment of traits associated with that stage. Fixation in the oral stage, for example, may lead to oral traits like dependency and gullibility. Anal fixation may result in cleanliness-messiness, or perfectionism-carelessness.

6. In the Oedipus and Electra complexes, which are theorized to occur during the phallic stage, children long to possess the opposite-sex parent and resent the same-sex parent. Eventually, these complexes become resolved by identifying with the same-sex parent.

7. Carl Jung's psychoanalytic theory, called analytical psychology, features a collective unconscious and a number of archetypes, both of which reflect the history of our species.

8. Alfred Adler's psychoanalytic theory, called individual psychology, features the inferiority complex and the compensating drive for superiority.

9. Karen Horney's psychoanalytic theory focuses on parent-child relationships and the possible development of feelings of basic anxiety and basic hostility. Later in life, repressed hostility can lead us to relate to others in a neurotic manner.

10. Erik Erikson's psychoanalytic theory of psychosocial development highlights the importance of early social relationships rather than the gratification of childhood sexual impulses. Erikson extended Freud's five developmental stages to eight, including stages for each period of adulthood.

11. Traits are personality elements that are inferred from behavior and account for behavioral consistency. Trait theory adopts a descriptive approach to personality.

12. Gordon Allport saw traits as neuropsychic structures. Cardinal traits dominate the personality, while central traits define the notable characteristics of the person.

13. Raymond Cattell distinguished between surface traits (characteristic ways of behaving that seem linked in an orderly manner) and source traits (underlying traits from which surface traits are derived). Cattell constructed a test that measures sixteen source traits.

14. Learning theorists of personality place more emphasis on situational determinants of behavior. John B. Watson, the father of modern behaviorism, rejected notions of mind and personality altogether. Watson and B. F. Skinner discarded notions of personal freedom, and argued that environmental contingencies can shape people into wanting to do the things that the physical environment and society requires of them.

15. Modern social-learning theory, in contrast to behaviorism, has a strong cognitive orientation and focuses on the importance of learning by observation. Social-learning theorists do not consider only situational rewards and punishments important in the prediction of behavior. They also consider the roles of person variables such as expectancies, values, behavioral competencies, and perceived self-efficacy.

16. Social-learning theory also distinguishes between the learning (acquisition) of responses and the performing of responses. People may imitate aggressive models if they believe that aggression is appropriate for them under a specific set of conditions. Televised violence may contribute to aggressive behavior by increasing the arousal of viewers, disinhibiting viewers, providing models of aggressive skills, and habituating viewers to violence.

17. Humanistic self theory begins with the assumption of the existence of the self. According to Carl Rogers, the self is an organized and consistent way in which a person perceives his or her ''I'' to relate to others and the world.

18. The self is innate and will attempt to become actualized (develop its unique potential) when the person receives unconditional positive regard. We all have needs for self-esteem. Conditions of worth lead to a distorted self-concept, disowning parts of the self, and, often, anxiety.

19. In personality measurement, psychologists take a sample of behavior to predict future behavior.

20. Objective tests present test-takers with a standardized set of test items that they must respond to in specific, limited ways (as in multiple-choice tests or true-false tests). A forced-choice format requires respondents to indicate which of two or more statements is true of them, or which of several activities they prefer.

21. The Minnesota Multiphasic Personality Inventory (MMPI) is the most widely used psychological test in the clinical setting. The MMPI is an objective personality test that uses a true-false format to assess abnormal behavior. It contains validity scales as well as clinical scales and has been validated empirically.

22. Other widely used objective personality tests include the California Psychological Inventory, which measures normal behavior patterns, and the Strong/Campbell Interest Inventory, which helps adolescents and adults make occupational choices.

23. Projective tests present ambiguous stimuli and permit the subject a broad range of responses.

24. The foremost projective technique is the Rorschach Inkblot Test, in which test-takers are asked to report what inkblots look like or could be. Rorschach responses are scored according to location, determinants (e.g., shading, texture, and color), content, and form level.

25. The Thematic Apperception Test (TAT) consists of ambiguous drawings that test-takers are asked to interpret. The TAT is widely used in research on social motives as well as in clinical practice.

26. The so-called Barnum effect refers to the research finding that people tend to believe that broadly written personality descriptions apply to them.

TRUTH OR FICTION REVISITED

The human mind is like a vast submerged iceberg, only the tip of which rises above the surface into awareness.

Probably not. This statement is consistent with Sigmund Freud's psychoanalytic theory, which proposes that there are three psychic structures: the id, which is unconscious; ego, which is partly unconscious; and the superego. However, empirical evidence is not sufficient to independently confirm the existence of these structures.

Biting one's fingernails or smoking cigarettes as an adult is a sign of conflict during very early childhood.

Probably not. This is another statement that is consistent with psychoanalytic theory—in this case, the view that adult problems can represent fixations during early stages of psychosexual development. However, empirical evidence is not sufficient to confirm this theoretical view.

Women who compete with men in the business world are suffering from penis envy.

False. This view of Freud's has been severely criticized by many other psychologists, including contemporary followers of Freud, as reflective of ignorance and prejudice.

You have inherited mysterious memories that date back to ancient times.

Probably not. This statement is consistent with Carl Jung's view that there is a collective unconscious mind that contains racial memories. However, empirical evidence does not confirm Jung's theory any more than it confirms the existence of an id, ego, and superego.

People who show a strong drive for superiority are actually fighting feelings of inferiority that lie deep within them.

Perhaps, perhaps not. This statement is consistent with Adler's psychoanalytic theory, but empirical evidence does not necessarily support this view.

Airline pilots are more stable than, but not as creative as, artists and writers.

True, according to a study run by psychologist Raymond Cattell. Stability and creativity are two of the traits measured on Cattell's Sixteen Personality Factors Scale.

We may believe that we have freedom of choice, but our preferences and choices are actually forced upon us by the environment.

Probably not. This statement is consistent with the behaviorist view that our behavior, including our preferences, is completely determined by external sources of stimulation. However, empirical evidence does not support this radical view. Contemporary social-learning theorists suggest that behavior reflects person variables as well as situational variables, and that freedom of choice is more than an illusion.

We are more likely to be able to accomplish difficult tasks if we believe that we can.

True. Perceived self-efficacy apparently motivates us to try harder.

Children who spend a great deal of time watching violent television shows are more likely to behave aggressively.

True, for two reasons: First, there is evidence that television violence contributes to aggressive behavior. Second, we also know that more aggressive children are more likely to choose to watch violent shows.

We all have unique ways of looking at ourselves and at the world outside.

Since all of us, with the exception of identical twins, are genetically unique, this assertion is probably accurate. It is also consistent with humanistic self theory.

Psychologists can determine whether a person has told the truth on a personality test.

Often they can, but not always. Some tests, like the MMPI, have built-in validity scales that frequently suggest when test-takers have not answered test items accurately.

Psychological tests can help you choose an occupation.

True. Tests such as the Strong/Campbell Interest Inventory can help pinpoint where our interests lie, and other psychological tests can help highlight our needs and abilities.

There is a psychological test made up of inkblots, and one of them looks something like a bat.

True. It is the Rorschach Inkblot Test.

A psychologist could write a believable personality report about you without interviewing you, testing you, or, in fact, having any idea who you are.

Possibly. Research into the so-called Barnum effect suggests that the majority of people will agree with broadly stated personality descriptions of themselves.

OUTLINE

Stress, Health, and Adjustment

TRUTH OR FICTION?

- Too much of a good thing can make you ill.
- Our emotional problems stem almost completely from external pressures that we have little or no ability to change or control.
- Some people are dedicated to the creation of their own stress.
- Our blood pressure rises when we are under stress.
- Stress can influence the course of cancer.
- Some people drink alcohol to purposefully handicap themselves in their ability to cope with conflict or failure.
- People who cheat on their income-tax returns often justify their behavior by claiming that government programs cost more than they're worth, or that they pay more than their fair share.
- Stressed workers have more accidents on the job.
- The belief that we can handle stress is linked to lower levels of adrenalin in the bloodstream.
- When you are about to undergo a serious operation, learning the grisly details of the surgery and the expected course of recuperation may make the experience less stressful.
- If you ask people to just relax, many will have no idea what to do.
- People who make decisions on the basis of inspiration and gut-level feelings wind up with fewer regrets than people who methodically add up all the pluses and minuses.

STRESS

Yes, too much of a good thing *can* contribute to physical illness. You may think that marrying Mr. or Ms. Right, finding a prestigious job, moving to a new home, quitting smoking, and winning the lottery—all in the same year—would propel you into a state of bliss. It's possible. But the impact of all these events occurring within a limited time frame could also lead to headaches, high blood pressure, or asthma. As pleasant as they may be, they all involve significant life changes. And according to Holmes and Rahe (1967), life changes are one source of **stress.**

The concept of stress is borrowed from physics. In physics, stress is defined as a pressure or force exerted on a body. The crushing of tons of rock against the earth, the smashing of one car into another, the stretching of a rubber band—all are types of physical stress. Psychological forces, or stresses, also "press," "push," or "pull." We may feel "crushed" by the "weight" of a major decision. We may feel "smashed," or as though we are "stretched" to the point of "snapping."

In psychology, then, stress is the demand made on an organism to adapt, to cope, to **adjust.** Some stress is necessary to keep us alert and occupied (Selye, 1980). Sensory-deprivation experiments show that the absence of stimulation is unpleasant—so much so that we may invent our own by hallucinating. Each of us functions best at moderate levels of stress that some call a "healthful tension." But stress that is too intense or too prolonged can overtax our adjustive capacity, dampen our moods from day to day (Eckenrode, 1984; Stone & Neale, 1984), and have harmful physical effects.

In this chapter we explore many sources of stress: daily hassles and life changes, pain and discomfort, anxiety, frustration, conflict, and Type A behavior. We shall see that stress can lead to physical problems that Hans Selye called "diseases of adaptation." We discuss defensive methods of coping with stress that reduce the immediate impact of **stressors** but do not confront their origins. Finally, we discuss more active coping methods that modify or eliminate stressful circumstances, or fundamentally change self-defeating ways of responding to stress.

DAILY HASSLES AND LIFE CHANGES: "GOING THROUGH CHANGES"

It is the "last" straw that will break the camel's back—so goes the saying. Similarly, stresses can pile atop each other until we can finally no longer cope. Some of these stresses are found in the form of daily "hassles"; others are life changes. University of California psychologist Richard Lazarus and his colleagues (1985) analyzed a scale that measures daily **hassles** and found that hassles could be grouped as follows:

Household hassles, such as preparing meals, shopping, and home maintenance

Health hassles, such as physical illness, concern about medical treatment, and the side effects of medication

Stress The demand made on an organism to adjust. (From the Latin *strictus,* meaning "bound tight.")

Adjust To respond to stress. To behave in ways that meet the demands of the environment. (From the Latin *ad-,* meaning "toward," and *just,* meaning "right.")

Stressor An event or stimulus that acts as a source of stress.

Hassle A source of annoyance or aggravation. (This is a colloquial term whose origin is unclear.)

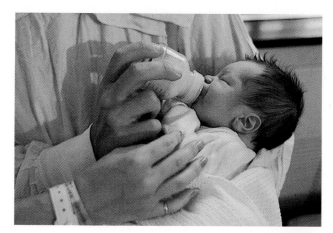

LIFE CHANGES Life changes can be stressful, even when they are positive or desired. A new baby and moving to a new home are a couple of the more demanding life changes we experience.

Time-pressure hassles, such as having too many things to do, too many responsibilities, and not enough time

Inner-concern hassles, such as being lonely and fear of confrontation

Environmental hassles, such as crime, neighborhood deterioration, and traffic noise

Financial-responsibility hassles, such as concern about owing money

Work hassles, such as job dissatisfaction, not liking one's work duties, and problems with co-workers, and

Future-security hassles, such as concerns about job security, taxes, property investments, and retirement

These hassles were linked to psychological symptoms such as nervousness, worrying, inability to get going, feelings of sadness, feelings of aloneness, and so on.

Hassles versus Life Changes   It may seem reasonable enough that hassles will have a psychological effect on us, that they may cause us to worry and may generally dampen our moods. But a number of researchers suggest that hassles can also lead to physical illness. To follow this research we must switch gears just a bit, because the research involves "life changes" rather than hassles per se. Life changes differ from "hassles" in two ways: (1) Many life changes are positive and desirable, while all hassles are negative. (2) The hassles referred to occur on a daily basis, while life changes, generally speaking, are somewhat more major events, as you can see in Table 10.1.

Let us consider a well-known study by psychiatrists Thomas Holmes and Richard Rahe (1967) into the effects of "life changes." Their approach allowed them to find some **normative data** concerning the number and types of life changes that will tax many of us to the limit.

Normative data Information concerning the behavior of a population.

TABLE 10.1 Scale of Life-Change Units

Life Event	Life-change Units
Death of one's spouse	100
Divorce	73
Marital separation	65
Jail term	63
Death of a close family member	63
Personal injury or illness	53
Marriage	50
Being fired at work	47
Marital reconciliation	45
Retirement	45
Change in the health of a family member	44
Pregnancy	40
Sex difficulties	39
Gain of a new family member	39
Business readjustment	39
Change in one's financial state	38
Death of a close friend	37
Change to a different line of work	36
Change in number of arguments with one's spouse	35
Mortgage over $10,000*	31
Foreclosure of a mortgage or loan	30
Change in responsibilities at work	29
Son or daughter leaving home	29
Trouble with in-laws	29
Outstanding personal achievement	28
Wife beginning or stopping work	26
Beginning or ending school	26
Change in living conditions	25
Revision of personal habits	24
Trouble with one's boss	23
Change in work hours or conditions	20
Change in residence	20
Change in schools	20
Change in recreation	19
Change in church activities	19
Change in social activities	18
Mortgage or loan of less than $10,000	17
Change in sleeping habits	16
Change in number of family get-togethers	15
Change in eating habits	15
Vacation	13
Christmas	12
Minor violations of the law	11

How many life-changes units did you "earn" during the past year? Holmes and Rahe linked one's number of life-change units to risk for medical problems.

SOURCE: Holmes and Rahe (1967).

*This figure was appropriate in 1967, when the Life-Change Units Scale was constructed. Today, sad to say, inflation probably puffs this figure up to at least $50,000.

Life-change units Numbers assigned by raters to various life changes that reflect the amount of stress caused by each.

Schizophrenia A major psychological disorder in which thought processes are impaired and emotions are not appropriate to the situation.

First Holmes and Rahe constructed a scale to measure the impact of life changes by assigning marriage an arbitrary weight of 50 **life-change units.** Then they asked people from all walks of life to assign units to other life changes, using marriage as the baseline. Most events shown in Table 10.1 were rated as less stressful than marriage, but a few were considered more stressful. More stressful events include death of a spouse (100 units) and divorce (73 units). Positive events such as an outstanding personal achievement and going on vacation also made the list.

Life Changes and Illness　Holmes and Rahe found that people who "earned" 300 or more life-change units within a year according to their scale were at greater risk for illness. Eight of ten developed medical problems, as compared with only one of three people whose life-change-unit totals for the year were below 150. Other researchers have found that high numbers of life-change units amassed within a year are linked to a host of physical and psychological problems, ranging from heart disease and cancer to accidents to failure in school and relapses among persons who show major psychological disorders, such as **schizophrenia** (Lloyd et al., 1980; Perkins, 1982; Rabkin, 1980; Thoits, 1983).

Criticisms of the Holmes and Rahe Approach　While the links between life changes and illness may seem quite convincing, they are correlational rather than experimental (Dohrenwend et al., 1982; Monroe, 1982). The data show that a high total of life-change units is related to medical and psychological disorders. It may seem logical that these changes caused the disorders, but the life changes were not manipulated experimentally, and rival explanations of the data are also possible. One possibility is that people who are predisposed toward medical or psychological problems amass more life-change units. For example, before medical disorders are diagnosed, they may contribute to sexual problems, arguments with one's spouse or in-laws, changes in living conditions and personal habits, changes in sleeping habits, and so on. So in many cases it may be that the physical and psychological problems precede rather than result from life changes (Dohrenwend et al., 1984; Dohrenwend & Shrout, 1985; Monroe, 1983).

Other aspects of the research into the relationship between life changes and illness have also been challenged. For instance, other researchers find that positive events may be less disturbing than negative events after all, even when the number of life-change units assigned to them is rather high (Lefcourt et al., 1981; Perkins, 1982; Thoits, 1983). That is, a change for the better in the health of a family member is usually less stressful than a change for the worse—a change for the better is a change, but it is also less of a "hassle."

Another problem with the Holmes and Rahe approach is that different kinds of people respond to life stresses in different ways. People who are "easy-going" are less likely to become ill under stress than people who are hard-driving. Factors such as self-confidence and support from family members can also alleviate many of the potential effects of life stresses (Holahan & Moos, 1985).

A Role for Cognitive Appraisal The degree of stress linked to an event will also reflect the meaning the event has for the individual. Pregnancy, for example, can be a positive or negative life change, depending on whether one wants and is prepared to have a child. As noted by Richard Lazarus and his colleagues (1985), we cognitively appraise hassles and life changes. In responding to them, we take into account our values and goals, our beliefs in our coping ability, our social support and so on. The same kind of event will be less taxing for people who have greater coping ability and support.

Still, life changes do require adjustments, and it seems wise for us to be aware of the hassles and life changes associated with our styles of life. Later in the chapter we shall explore ways of enhancing our coping ability.

Noxious Harmful, injurious.

Traumatize In psychology, to injure or wound psychologically.

Anxiety (1) A negative emotion characterized by persistent fear and dread. (2) A general emotional response to stress.

PAIN AND DISCOMFORT

Pain and discomfort impair performance and coping ability. Athletes report that pain interferes with their ability to run, swim, and so forth, even when the source of the pain does not directly weaken them.

In an experiment on the effects of pain on performance, psychiatrist Curt Richter (1957) first recorded the amount of time rats could swim to stay afloat in a tub of water. In water at room temperature, most rats could keep their noses above the surface for about eighty hours. But when Richter blew **noxious** streams of air into their faces, or kept the water uncomfortably hot or cold, the rats could remain afloat for only twenty to forty hours. When the rats were **traumatized** by having their whiskers noisily chopped off while inside a black bag before being placed in the water, some managed to remain afloat for only a few minutes. Yet the clipping itself had not physically weakened them. Rats that were allowed several minutes to recover from the clipping before being launched swam for the usual eighty hours. Later we shall see that psychologists recommend that we space aggravating tasks or chores, so that discomfort does not build to the point where it compounds stress and impairs our performance.

In Chapter 14 we shall see that people who experience discomfort from heat, crowding, and pollution often show more antisocial behavior. The discomforts of city life can also lead us to be less concerned with the plights of others.

ANXIETY

"Up-tight," "shook up," "jumpy," "on edge," "butterflies in the stomach"—these are just some of the colorful expressions used to describe the unpleasant sensations we associate with **anxiety.** The relationship between anxiety and stress is a two-way street: Anxiety may be thought of as a general emotional response to stress, but anxiety is also a source of stress. As are other emotions (see Chapter 7), anxiety is a feeling state that can have situational, physiological, and cognitive components. Anxiety is also a source of motivation that, like other sources of motivation, leads to goal-directed behavior. In the case of anxiety, the goal is usually to reduce or eliminate the anxiety.

Trait anxiety Anxiety as a personality varia-ble, or persistent trait.

Neurotic anxiety In psychoanalytic theory, feelings of anxiety that stem from uncon-scious concern that unacceptable ideas or impulses may break loose into awareness or be expressed in behavior.

Free-floating Chronic, persistent. Not tied to particular events.

State anxiety A temporary condition of anx-iety that may be attributed to a situation.

Trait vs. State Anxiety   Anxiety can be a trait or a personality variable. People who show **trait anxiety** may experience persistent feelings of dread and foreboding—cognitions that something terrible is about to happen. They are chronically worried and concerned. They experience rapid heart beat and respiration rate, muscle tension, and so forth, even when they perceive no environmental threat.

Sigmund Freud labeled this sort of persistent anxiety **neurotic anxiety.** Within psychoanalytic theory, neurotic anxiety represents the vague sensing of danger that unacceptable, unconscious impulses might break loose into awareness. For example, people may experience neurotic anxiety when they are in danger of perceiving unacceptable sexual or aggressive urges. Freud wrote that neurotic anxiety could also become generalized, or **free-floating.** We might be anxious nearly all of the time as we are chronically trying to keep a lid on our boiling impulses.

Let us note that what we observe in the case of "free-floating" anxiety is frequent or persistent anxiety. It has not been shown that such anxiety reflects efforts to repress unacceptable wishes. It could also reflect failure to pinpoint all the environmental and self-imposed stressors acting on one, or even be due to a highly active autonomic nervous system.

State anxiety, by contrast, refers to a temporary condition of arousal that is clearly triggered by a specific situation. We might experience state anxiety on the eve of a final exam, before a big date, on a job interview, or while waiting in the dentist's office. Different people experience state anxiety in different situations, because events—such as learning to use a microcomputer or speaking before a group—have different meanings for us, based on our values and our learning histories. In the following section we focus more on the cognitive components of anxiety and other negative emotions, and see how they can compound the stress we experience.

IRRATIONAL BELIEFS AND SELF-IMPOSED STRESS: THE ROLE OF COGNITIVE APPRAISAL

"There is nothing either good or bad, but thinking makes it so." In writing these lines, Shakespeare did not mean that injuries and misfortunes do not discomfort us. He did mean that our cognitive appraisals of unfortunate circumstances can heighten our discomfort.

New York psychologist Albert Ellis (1977, 1979, 1985) shares Shake-speare's view. He notes that our beliefs about events, as well as the events themselves, fashion our reaction to them, creating anxiety, depression, and other stressful emotions.

A person might be fired from a job and be miserable about it. It would be natural to assume that losing the job had caused the misery. But Ellis points out that beliefs, even if they are rapidly fleeting, actually account for much of the misery. Let us examine the situation according to Ellis's A-B-C approach: Losing the job is an *Activating event.* The eventual outcome, or *Consequence,* is misery. But between the activating event and the con-sequences lies a set of *Beliefs,* such as the following: "What an important job this was," "Losing this job means I'm worthless," "My family will starve." The process works this way:

Activating events → Beliefs → Consequences

These beliefs tend to **catastrophize** the extent of the loss and contribute to anxiety. Extensive focusing on them, or ruminating, may also distract the person from planning what to do next.

Ellis examined his early experiences as a clinical psychologist and concluded the following. (1) People in our culture are likely to harbor several of the irrational beliefs listed below; (2) these beliefs are often so automatic and fleeting that people are not aware of their role; and (3) these beliefs are responsible for a good deal of self-imposed stress in the forms of anxiety, depression, and impaired interpersonal relationships. How many of these irrational beliefs do you harbor? Are you willing to challenge them?

1. You must have sincere love and approval almost all the time from the people you find significant. (One study found that the irrational belief that one must be loved by, and earn the approval of, practically everyone was endorsed by 65 percent of anxious subjects, as compared with only 2 percent of nonanxious subjects [Newmark et al., 1973].)

2. You must prove yourself thoroughly competent, adequate, and achieving. Or you must at least have real competence or talent at something important.

3. Things must go the way you would like them to go, because you need what you want. Life proves awful, terrible, and horrible when you do not get what you prefer. (College men who believe that it is awful to be turned down for a date show more social anxiety than men who are less likely to catastrophize rejection [Gormally et al., 1981].)

4. Others must treat everyone in a fair and just manner. When people act unfairly or unethically they are rotten.

5. When dangers or fearsome things exist in your world, you must continually preoccupy yourself with and be upset about them.

6. People and things should turn out better than they do. It is awful and horrible if you do not immediately find solutions to life's hassles.

7. Your emotional misery comes almost completely from external pressures that you have little or no ability to change or control.

8. It is easier to avoid facing life's difficulties and responsibilities than to undertake more rewarding forms of self-discipline.

9. Your past life influenced you immensely and remains all-important. If something once strongly affected you, it has to keep determining your feelings and behavior today.

10. You can achieve happiness by inertia and inaction, or by passively and uncommittedly "enjoying yourself."

People whose marriages are distressed are also more likely than people with functional marriages to harbor a number of irrational beliefs (Eidelson & Epstein, 1982). They are more likely to believe that any disagreement is destructive, that their partners should be able to read their minds (and know what they want), that their partners cannot change, that they must be perfect sex partners, and that men and women differ dramatically in personality and needs. It is rational, and adjustive to a marriage, for partners to recognize that no two people can agree all the time, to express

Catastrophize (kuh-TASS-tro-fize). To exaggerate or magnify the noxious properties of events such that adjustment efforts may be hampered. To "blow out of proportion." (From the Greek *kata-*, meaning "down," and *strephein*, meaning "to turn.")

their wishes rather than depend on "mind-reading," to believe that we all can change (although change may come slowly), to tolerate intermittent sexual frustrations and blunders, and to treat each other as equals.

Ellis recognizes that it is understandable that we would like to have the approval of others, but it is irrational to believe that we cannot survive without it. It would be nice to be competent in everything we undertake, but it's not absolutely necessary—unless we convince ourselves that it is. There is a kernel of truth to most of these irrational beliefs, but many people create or compound their own stress by exaggerating their importance or necessity.

Childhood experiences may explain the origins of irrational beliefs, but it is our own cognitive appraisal of events, here and now, that causes us misery. *Here. Today.* If we wish to change the way we feel about our lives and ourselves, we must modify our cognitive appraisal of events; we must find rational alternatives for our irrational beliefs. A number of strategies for doing so will be presented as the chapter progresses.

FRUSTRATION

You may wish to play the line for the varsity football team, but you may weigh only 120 pounds or you may be a woman. You may have been denied a job or educational opportunity because of your ethnic background or favoritism. We all encounter **frustration,** the thwarting of a motive to attain a goal (see Figure 10.1, Part A). Frustration is another source of stress.

Many sources of frustration are obvious. Adolescents are used to being too young to wear makeup, drive, go out, spend money, drink, or work. Age is the barrier that requires them to delay gratification. We may frustrate ourselves if our goals are set too high, or if our self-demands are irrational. As Albert Ellis notes, if we try to earn other people's approval at all costs, or insist on performing perfectly in all of our undertakings, we doom ourselves to failure and frustration.

Anxiety and fear may also serve as barriers that prevent us from acting effectively to meet our goals. A high-school senior who wishes to attend an out-of-state college may be frustrated by fear of leaving home. A young adult may not ask an attractive person out on a date because of fear of rejection. A woman may be frustrated in her desire to move up the corporate ladder by fear that coworkers, friends, and family may view her assertiveness as compromising her femininity.

Getting ahead is often a gradual process that demands that we must be able to live with some frustration and delay gratification. Yet our **tolerance for frustration** may fluctuate. Stress heaped upon stress can lower our tolerance, just as Richter's rats, stressed from their close shaves, sank quickly to the bottom of the tub. We may laugh off a flat tire on a good day. But if it is raining, or if we have just waited for an hour in a gas line, the flat may seem like the last straw. People who have encountered frustration, but learned that it is possible to surmount barriers or find substitute goals, are more tolerant of frustration than those who have never experienced it, or those who have experienced excesses of frustration.

FRUSTRATION Most college students will have little difficulty understanding the frustration this driver is experiencing as he is stuck in traffic. Frustration results from thwarting a motive to reach a goal.

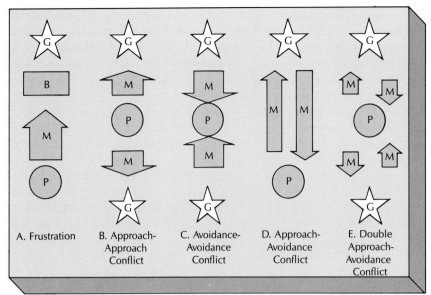

FIGURE 10.1 MODELS FOR FRUSTRATION AND CONFLICT Part A is a model for frustration in which a person (P) has a motive (M) to reach a goal (G), but is frustrated by a barrier (B). Part B shows an approach-approach conflict, in which the person cannot approach two positive goals simultaneously. Part C is an avoidance-avoidance conflict, in which avoiding one undesirable goal requires approaching another undesirable goal. Part D shows an approach-avoidance conflict, in which the same goal has both positive and negative features. Part E is a model for a double approach-avoidance conflict, in which the various goals perceived by the individual have their positive and negative features.

CONFLICT

Have you ever felt "damned if you did and damned if you didn't"? Regretted that you couldn't do two things, or be in two places, at the same time? Wanted to go to a film but had to study for a test? This is **conflict**—being torn in two or more directions by opposing motives. Conflict is frustrating and stressful. Conflict may also be looked at as a type of frustration in which the barrier to achieving a goal is an opposing impulse or motive. Let us consider four types of conflict.

Approach-Approach Conflict An **approach-approach conflict** (Figure 10.1, Part B) is the least stressful form of conflict. Here each of two goals is positive and within reach. You may not be able to decide between pizza or tacos, Tom or Dick, or a trip to Nassau or Hawaii. In such cases you may **vacillate** for a while before making a decision.

Conflicts are resolved by making decisions. Afterwards, there may be some regrets, especially if that choice falls short of expectations. You may be nauseated by the pizza. Tom may grind his teeth. It may rain in Nassau. Still, once a choice is made you are likely to become more active or work harder as you are nearing your goal. If it is satisfying, you are not likely to be too regretful about the road not taken.

Conflict A condition characterized by opposing motives, in which gratification of one motive prevents gratification of the other. (From the Latin *com-*, meaning "together," and *fligere*, meaning "to strike.")

Approach-approach conflict Conflict involving two positive but mutually exclusive goals.

Vacillate (VASS-sill-late). To move back and forth. (From the Latin *vacillare*, meaning "to sway to and fro.")

Avoidance-avoidance conflict Conflict involving two negative goals, with avoidance of one requiring approach of the other.

Approach-avoidance conflict Conflict involving a goal with positive and negative features.

Double approach-avoidance conflict Conflict involving two goals, each of which has positive and negative aspects.

Avoidance-Avoidance Conflict　An **avoidance-avoidance conflict** (Figure 10.1, Part C) is more stressful, because you are motivated to avoid each of two negative goals. However, avoiding one requires approaching the other. You may be fearful of visiting the dentist, but also fear that your teeth will decay if you do not. You may not want to contribute to the Association for the Advancement of Lost Causes, but fear that your friends will consider you cheap or uncommitted if you do not. Each goal is negative in an avoidance-avoidance conflict.

When an avoidance-avoidance conflict is highly stressful, and no resolution is in sight, some people withdraw from the conflict by focusing their attention on other matters or by suspending behavior altogether.

Approach-Avoidance Conflict　The same goal can produce both approach and avoidance motives, as in the **approach-avoidance conflict** (Figure 10.1, Part D). People and things have their pluses and minuses, their good points and their bad points. Cream cheese pie may be delicious, but oh, the calories! Why are so many attractive goals immoral, illegal, or fattening?

Goals producing mixed motives may seem more attractive from a distance, but more repulsive from nearby. Many couples repeatedly break up, then reunite. When they are apart and lonely, they may recall each other fondly and swear that they could make it work "the next time" if they got together again. But after they again spend time together, they may find themselves facing the same old aggravations and think, "How could I have ever believed this so-and-so would change?"

Double Approach-Avoidance Conflict　The most complex form of conflict is the **double approach-avoidance conflict** (Figure 10.1, Part E) in which each of two or more goals has its positive and negative aspects. Should you study on the eve of an exam or go to a film? "Studying's a drag, but I won't have to worry about flunking. I'd love to see the movie, but I'd just be worrying about how I'll do tomorrow." Should you take a job or go on for advanced training when you complete your college program? If you opt for the job, cash will soon be jingling in your pockets, but later you might wonder if you have the education to reach your potential. By furthering your education you may have to delay the independence and gratification that are afforded by earning a living, but you may find a more fulfilling position later on.

All forms of conflict entail motives that aim in opposite directions. When one motive is much stronger than the other—as when you feel "starved" and are only slightly concerned about your weight—it will probably not be too stressful to act in accord with the powerful motive and, in this case, eat. But when each conflicting motive is powerful you may encounter high levels of stress and confusion about the proper course of action. At such times you are faced with the need to make a decision, although making decisions can also be stressful, especially when there is no clear correct choice. But later in the chapter some methods for decision-making will be presented that may lead to somewhat fewer regrets.

TYPE A BEHAVIOR

Millions of us behave as though we were dedicated to the continuous creation of our own stress through the **Type A behavior** pattern. Type A people are highly driven, competitive, impatient, and aggressive (Matthews et al., 1982; Holmes & Will, 1985). They feel rushed and under pressure and keep one eye glued firmly to the clock. They are not only prompt, but frequently early for appointments (Strahan, 1981). They eat, walk, and talk rapidly, and become restless when they see others working slowly (Musante et al., 1983). They attempt to dominate group discussions (Yarnold et al., 1985). Type A people find it difficult to surrender control or to share power (Miller et al., 1985; Strube & Werner, 1985). As a consequence, they are often reluctant to delegate authority in the workplace, and in this way they increase their own workloads. Type A people also "accentuate the negative": they are merciless in their self-criticism when they fail at a task (Brunson & Matthews, 1981), and they seek out negative information about themselves in order to better themselves (Cooney & Zeichner, 1985).

Type A people find it difficult just to go out on the tennis court and bat the ball back and forth. They watch their form, perfect their strokes, and demand regular self-improvement. Albert Ellis's second irrational belief—that you must be perfectly competent and achieving in everything you undertake—seems to be the motto of Type A people.

Type B people, by contrast, relax more readily and focus more on the quality of life. They are less ambitious, less impatient, and pace themselves. Type A's perceive time as passing more rapidly than do Type B's, and they work more quickly (Yarnold & Grimm, 1982). Type A's earn higher grades and more money than Type B's of equal intelligence (Glass, 1977). Type A's also seek greater challenges than Type B's (Ortega & Pipal, 1984).

A recent study of Type A women found that they, like their male counterparts, reach higher occupational levels than their Type B peers (Kelly & Houston, 1985). Their jobs are also more stressful and demanding than those held by Type B women. However, Type A and Type B women in this study did not differ in their marital adjustment or in the amount of time spent in leisure activities.

There is an irony in the Type A person's seeking of difficult challenges; Type A's respond to challenge with higher blood pressure than Type B's do (Holmes et al., 1984). In addition, Type B's smoke less, have lower **serum cholesterol** levels, and fewer heart attacks. Numerous studies have found that Type A people are at greater risk for heart disease than are Type B's (DeBacker et al., 1983; French-Belgian Collaborative Group, 1982; Haynes et al., 1980). All in all, Type A behavior may be a stronger predictor of heart disease than smoking, lack of exercise, poor diet, or obesity (Friedman & Rosenman, 1974)—especially for Type A individuals who are hostile (Barefoot et al., 1982; Shekelle et al., 1983), and who hold in rather than express their feelings (Friedman et al., 1985).

While the evidence seems clear that Type A people are at greater risk for a number of physical ailments than Type B's, it must be pointed out that the evidence—as is the evidence that links life changes to medical and psychological disorders—is correlational and not experimental. No re-

Type A behavior Stress-producing behavior, characterized by aggressiveness, perfectionism, unwillingness to relinquish control, and a sense of time urgency.

Serum cholesterol (co-LESS-ter-all). A fatty substance (cholesterol) in the blood (serum) which has been linked to heart disease.

ARE YOU TYPE A OR TYPE B?

Are you Type A or Type B? Type A's are ambitious, hard driving, and chronically discontent with their current achievements. Type B's, by contrast, are more relaxed, more involved with the quality of life, and—according to cardiologists Meyer Friedman and Ray Rosenman—less prone to heart attacks.

The following checklist was developed from descriptions of Type A people by Friedman and Rosenman (1974), Matthews and her colleagues (1982), and Musante et al. (1983). The checklist will help give you insight into whether you are closer in your behavior patterns to the Type A or the Type B individual. Simply place a checkmark under the Yes if the behavior pattern is typical of you, and under the No if it is not. Try to work rapidly and leave no item blank. Then turn to the scoring key in Appendix B.

DO YOU: **YES NO**

1. Strongly accent key words in your everyday speech? ____ ____
2. Eat and walk quickly? ____ ____
3. Believe that children should be taught to be competitive? ____ ____
4. Feel restless when watching a slow worker? ____ ____
5. Hurry other people to get on with what they're trying to say? ____ ____
6. Find it highly aggravating to be stuck in traffic or waiting for a seat at a restaurant? ____ ____
7. Continue to think about your own problems and business even when listening to someone else? ____ ____
8. Try to eat and shave, or drive and jot down notes at the same time? ____ ____
9. Catch up on your work on vacations? ____ ____
10. Bring conversations around to topics of concern to you? ____ ____
11. Feel guilty when you spend time just relaxing? ____ ____
12. Find that you're so wrapped up in your work that you no longer notice office decorations or the scenery when you commute? ____ ____
13. Find yourself concerned with getting more *things* rather than developing your creativity and social concerns? ____ ____
14. Try to schedule more and more activities into less time? ____ ____
15. Always appear for appointments on time? ____ ____
16. Clench or pound your fists, or use other gestures, to emphasize your views? ____ ____
17. Credit your accomplishments to your ability to work rapidly? ____ ____
18. Feel that things must be done *now* and quickly? ____ ____
19. Constantly try to find more efficient ways to get things done? ____ ____
20. Insist on winning at games rather than just having fun? ____ ____
21. Interrupt others often? ____ ____
22. Feel irritated when others are late? ____ ____
23. Leave the table immediately after eating? ____ ____
24. Feel rushed? ____ ____
25. Feel dissatisfied with your current level of performance? ____ ____

searcher has randomly assigned a group of subjects to Type A behavior patterns and measured the results. People who were already Type A were compared with people who were already Type B. It may seem unlikely, but we cannot rule out the possibility that predisposition toward certain medical problems also somehow promotes Type A behavior. It may also be that personality factors, such as values, beliefs, and attitudes, lead both to Type A behavior and physical ailments. The Type A behavior pattern in itself may not be the culprit. Later we shall see that methods for coping with Type A behavior address both these attitudes and the Type A behavior pattern itself.

In any event, Type A individuals tend to show relatively greater well-being during their twenties and thirties than during their middle and later years (Strube et al., 1985). Type A behavior is more consistent with the hard-driving, achievement-oriented lifestyle of youth than with the slower pace of old age. Type B people, by contrast, seem to be relatively better adjusted during the later years than during their twenties and thirties. Even if they have a sense of well-being in their youths, Type A people may profit from reevaluating their attitudes and behavior patterns as their lives progress.

PHYSIOLOGICAL RESPONSE TO STRESS

How is it that too much of a good thing, or that anxiety, frustration, or conflict can make you ill? Why do Type A people run a greater risk of heart attacks than Type B's? We do not yet have all the answers, but those we have suggest that the body, under stress, is very much like a clock with an alarm system that does not shut off until its energy is dangerously depleted.

GENERAL-ADAPTATION SYNDROME

Hans Selye (1976) noted that the body's response to different stressors shows some similarities, whether the stressor is a bacterial invasion, a perceived danger, a major life change, an inner conflict, or a wound. He labeled this response the **general-adaptation syndrome** (GAS). The GAS consists of three stages: an alarm reaction, a resistance stage, and an exhaustion stage.

The **alarm reaction** is triggered by the impact of a stressor. It mobilizes or arouses the body in preparation for defense. Cannon (1929) had earlier termed this alarm system the **fight-or-flight reaction.** It is characterized by a high level of activity of the sympathetic branch of the autonomic nervous system (see Table 10.2). It provides more energy for muscular activity, which can be used to fight or flee from a source of danger, and decreases the body's vulnerability to wounds. The fight-or-flight reaction is inherited from a long-ago time when many stressors were life-threatening. It was triggered by a predator at the edge of a thicket, by a sudden rustling in the undergrowth. Once the threat is removed, the body returns to a lower state of arousal.

Our ancestors lived in situations in which the alarm reaction would not be activated for long. They fought or ran quickly or, to put it bluntly, they died. Sensitive alarm reactions contributed to survival. Our ancestors

General adaptation syndrome Selye's term for a hypothesized three-stage response to stress. Abbreviated *GAS*.

Alarm reaction The first stage of the GAS, which is "triggered" by the impact of a stressor and characterized by sympathetic activity.

Fight-or-flight reaction Cannon's term for a hypothesized innate adaptive response to the perception of danger.

TABLE 10.2 Components of the Alarm Reaction

Respiration rate increases
Heart rate increases
Blood pressure increases
Muscles tense
Blood shifts away from the skin
Digestion slows
Sugar is released from the liver
Adrenalin is secreted
Blood coagulability increases

The alarm reaction is triggered by various types of stressors. It is essentially defined by activity of the sympathetic branch of the autonomic nervous system, and prepares the body to fight or flee from a source of danger.

did not spend sixteen years in the academic grind or carry thirty-year adjustable-rate mortgages. Contemporary pressures may activate our alarm systems for hours, days, or months at a time, so that highly sensitive systems may now be a handicap.

If the alarm reaction mobilizes the body and the stressor is not removed, we enter the adaptation or **resistance stage** of the GAS. The level of arousal is not so high as in the alarm reaction, but it is still greater than normal. In this stage the body attempts to restore lost energy and repair whatever damage has been done.

If the stressor is still not adequately dealt with, we may enter the final or **exhaustion stage** of the GAS. Our capacity for resisting stress varies, but all of us, as even the strongest of Richter's rats, eventually become exhausted when stress persists indefinitely. Continued stress at this time may lead to deterioration, to what Selye terms "diseases of adaptation"—from allergies and hives to ulcers and heart disease—and ultimately to death.

STRESS AND ILLNESS

Stress can lead to a number of physical problems, including headaches. Most headaches result from muscle tension. We are likely to contract muscles in the shoulders, neck, forehead, and scalp during the first two stages of the GAS. Persistent stress can lead to persistent muscle tension and persistent muscle-tension headaches.

Most other headaches, including the severe migraine headache, stem from changes in the blood supply to the head. These changes may be induced by barometric pressure, pollen, specific drugs, the chemical monosodium glutamate (MSG), which is often used to enhance the flavor of food, especially in Oriental restaurants, and the tyramine found in red wines.

Regardless of the original source of the headache, we can unwittingly propel ourselves into a vicious cycle: Headache pain is a stressor that can lead us to increase, rather than relax, muscle tension in the neck and shoulders. In this way we may compound headache pain. Muscle-relaxation exercises that we shall discuss later in the chapter often relieve headache pain. Biofeedback training that alters the flow of blood to the head has been used effectively to treat migraine headache (Blanchard et al., 1980, 1982,

Resistance stage The second stage of the GAS, characterized by prolonged sympathetic activity in an effort to restore lost energy and repair damage. Also called the *adaptation stage.*

Exhaustion stage The third stage of the GAS, characterized by weakened resistance and possible deterioration.

1985). People who are sensitive to MSG or tyramine can ask that MSG be left out of their dishes and can switch to a white wine.

Hans Selye (1976) theorized that chronic stress may play a role in inflammatory diseases, such as arthritis; premenstrual distress; digestive diseases, such as colitis; even metabolic diseases such as diabetes and hypoglycemia.

Predisposing Factors   Why, under stress, do some of us develop ulcers, others develop hypertension, and still others suffer no bodily problems? It may be that there is an interaction between stress and predisposing biological and psychological differences between individuals (Davison & Neale, 1982; Walker, 1983).

Ulcers may afflict one person in ten and cause as many as 10,000 deaths each year in the United States (Whitehead & Bosmajian, 1982). People who develop ulcers under stress often have higher pepsinogen levels than those who do not (Weiner et al., 1957), and heredity may contribute to pepsinogen level (Mirsky, 1958). Research with laboratory rats suggests that intense approach-avoidance conflict may also contribute to ulcers (Sawrey et al., 1956; Sawrey & Weisz, 1956).

Hypertension may afflict 10 to 30 percent of Americans (Seer, 1979). Hypertension predisposes victims to other cardiovascular disorders such as arteriosclerosis, heart attacks, and strokes. Blood pressure rises in situations in which people must be constantly on guard against threats, whether in combat, in the work place, or in the home. Blood pressure appears to be higher among blacks than whites, and also higher among both blacks and whites who tend to hold in, rather than express, feelings of anger (Diamond, 1982; Harburg et al., 1973).

Asthma is another disorder that has been linked to stress, although this link remains controversial. In one study, for example, efforts to induce asthma attacks in sufferers by subjecting them to stress led to a slightly decreased air flow, but not to an actual attack (Weiss et al., 1976). Other

 PSYCHOLOGY AND HEALTH

STRESS AND CANCER

Relationships between stress and disease are not limited to illnesses such as headaches and ulcers. In recent years, researchers have also begun to uncover links between stress and cancer. For example, a study of children with cancer by Jacob and Charles (1980) revealed that a significant percentage had encountered severe life changes within a year of the diagnosis, often involving the death of a loved one or the loss of a close relationship.

Recent experiments with rats suggest that once cancer has affected the individual, stress can influence its course. In one such experiment, animals were implanted with small numbers of cancer cells so that their own immune systems would have a chance to successfully combat them (Visintainer et al., 1982). Some of the rats were then exposed to inescapable shocks, while others were exposed to escapable shocks or to no shock. The rats exposed to the most stressful condition—the inescapable shock—were half as likely as the other rats to reject the cancer, and two times as likely to die from it.

If stress contributes to the deadliness of cancer, then it is just possible that learning effective ways of reducing stress may be of some help to patients who are battling cancer.

Defense mechanisms In psychoanalytic theory, unconscious functions of the ego that protect it from anxiety by preventing accurate recognition of anxiety-evoking ideas and impulses.

Defensive coping A response to stress that reduces the immediate impact of the stressor, but does not change the environment or the self to permanently remove, or modify the effects of, the stressor.

Active coping A response to stress that manipulates the environment, or changes the response patterns of the individual, to permanently remove the stressor or to render it harmless.

evidence suggests that asthma sufferers can experience attacks in response to the suggestion that their air flow will become constricted (Luparello et al., 1971). In any event, in most cases the initial asthma attack follows on the heels of a respiratory infection (Alexander, 1981). Such evidence again suggests an interaction between the psychological and the physiological.

Psychologists have learned that we can do many things to reduce stress and the effects of stress on our bodies. These interventions in many cases help us eliminate some problems, such as headaches, and ameliorate many others, such as hypertension. In this chapter we have a look at a number of them.

COPING WITH STRESS

Many techniques for coping with stress are essentially defensive. They reduce the immediate impact of the stressor, but at some personal or social cost. This cost includes socially inappropriate behavior (as in alcoholism, aggression, or regression), avoidance of problems (as in withdrawal), or self-deception (as in use of **defense mechanisms** like rationalization or denial). **Defensive coping** grants us time to marshall our resources, but it does not deal with the source of stress or improve the effectiveness of our response to stress. In the long run, defensive methods can be harmful if we do not use the chance they provide to find more active ways of coping.

Direct or **active coping** begins with accepting responsibility for our own behavior, including our thoughts and our emotional responses. It includes manipulating the environment to change or eliminate sources of stress. When we cannot change the environment, it involves directly modifying cognitive and physiological responses so that the impact of stressors is reduced.

Let us explore a number of defensive and active methods for coping with stress.

DEFENSIVE COPING

In this section we discuss various methods of defensive coping. These include the use of alcohol and other drugs, aggression, withdrawal, fantasy, and the defense mechanisms of regression, denial, repression, rationalization, reaction formation, projection, intellectualization, displacement, and sublimation. Freud labeled the latter group of defensive measures "mechanisms" in keeping with the trend in his day to think of human functions in machinelike terms. He also believed that defense mechanisms operated unconsciously to protect the ego from the anxiety that might stem from recognition of unacceptable ideas and impulses. (Today many psychologists who have been influenced by computer science discuss human cognitive functioning in terms of "information processing.") But Freud's "mechanisms" may also be viewed as habitual, and not necessarily unconscious, ways of responding to stress that are reinforced by their reduction of discomfort, anxiety, or frustration.

Defense mechanisms are used by normal and abnormal people alike. They become problems when they are the only means used to cope with stress.

ALCOHOL AND OTHER DRUGS

Alcohol and a number of other drugs, including tranquilizers, act as central nervous system depressants that can directly blunt feelings of tension, anxiety, and frustration. Recent studies noted in Chapter 4 also suggest various cognitive effects of alcohol that help people cope with stress. Some behavioral scientists (e.g., Hull, 1981; Steele et al., 1981) argue that these cognitive effects allow people to decrease the negative feelings that stem from recognizing that their behavior has been inconsistent with their values or attitudes.

People also often blame alcohol for inappropriate aggressive or sexual behavior. Tucker and his colleagues (1981) found that subjects used alcohol consumption as a "self-handicapping strategy." Subjects involved in a difficult experimental task drank more when they were denied access to materials that could have aided them in the task. It may well be that they drank in order to provide themselves with an external excuse for failure: "It wasn't me—it was the alcohol." An external excuse for failure may also have allowed them to maintain their self-esteem.

Consistent use of alcohol to cope with stress constitutes psychological dependence on alcohol. People may become dependent on many drugs in order to blunt awareness of stress or distort perception of what has become—for them—an unpleasant reality. Unfortunately, many drugs have negative effects, as noted in Chapter 4. Also, the drugs do nothing to help people find direct, active ways of dealing with sources of stress.

AGGRESSION

Violence is often used to cope with threats and, sometimes, as a response to frustration. In warfare and in self-defense, aggressive behavior is usually positively valued. But most violence in our society is frowned upon, and its benefits are usually short-lived. Attacking a police officer who is writing you a traffic ticket will not earn a judge's understanding approval. Aggressive behavior, except for rare instances, heightens rather than reduces interpersonal conflict by creating motives for retaliation.

WITHDRAWAL

When you are intensely frightened, or feel helpless, or believe that any decision would be futile, you may feel pressed to withdraw from the situation. Withdrawal can be emotional, as in showing loss of interest, or physical, as in moving or changing one's life style.

Temporary withdrawal can be healthful and productive, giving us the opportunity to find more effective means of coping. But prolonged withdrawal may also exclude us from arenas of life in which we could eventually find meaningful rewards.

Regression Return, under stress, to a form
of behavior characteristic of an earlier stage
of development. A defense mechanism.
(From the Latin *re-*, meaning "back," and
gradi, meaning "to go." What are the roots
of the word *progress?*)

FANTASY

Fantasy is not for children only. Have you ever daydreamed about the future, testing career and marital choices through cognitive trial and error? Fantasy serves many functions and is useful so long as it does not become an indefinitely prolonged substitute for effective action.

DEFENSE MECHANISMS

Regression You may have been trying to explain a fine point in physics to your roommate for an hour. Then your roommate, who had "yessed" you all during the explanation, asks a question that shows that nothing you said was understood. You slam your book on the desk, shout "Jerk!," and stamp out of the room.

If you are six years old, this behavior is normal. For a college student, it is **regression**—returning to an earlier way of behaving under stress. You may know people who quit smoking or biting their nails but have returned to these habits before a big exam or after a fight with a date. These, too, are examples of regression. A psychoanalyst might consider them regression to the oral stage.

REGRESSION Stress can sometimes lead us to regress, or adopt behavior characteristic of younger people or children. Under severe stress, this woman is crawling up into a ball, putting her hand to her mouth, and clutching a stuffed animal.

Denial Many people simply deny sources of danger. Many smokers refuse to believe that they risk cancer. A person may vaguely perceive that the company is going downhill, but maintain a complacent attitude until the layoff notice arrives. Hackett and Cassem (1970) found that many cardiac patients respond with an "It can't happen to me" attitude when the patient in the next bed dies. Kübler-Ross (1969) found that many terminally ill patients greet news of impending death with **denial.**

Denial reduces the immediate impact of stressors, but denies us the chance to take effective action to ward off real threats.

Repression **Repression** is the thrusting out of awareness of unacceptable ideas or urges that are often sexual or aggressive. Repression occurs unconsciously; we are not aware of when we are repressing unacceptable ideas. Freud theorized that repression is a normal aspect of personality development, which permits us to place certain conflicts behind us and move ahead. But repressing the fact that an important paper is due in two weeks is not adjustive.

Repression must be contrasted with **suppression**—the conscious decision not to focus on a distressing topic.

Rationalization The smoker justifies his or her habit by saying, "I just can't quit." The prostitute says, "Why condemn me? I'd be out of business if wives were doing their job." These are **rationalizations**—ways of explaining unacceptable behavior that exonerate us from blame and guilt. We may also rationalize to cut our losses: "So the date didn't work out— we were too different to develop a relationship anyhow."

Rationalizations sometimes contain a kernel of truth. There may be a thin line between rationalization and rational thinking. After all, if the couple had been more compatible, perhaps the date would have worked out better.

But rationalization may also be used to justify criminal behavior. Maital (1982) found that people who cheat on their income-tax returns often rationalize that government programs cost more than they're worth, or that they pay more than their fair share of taxes. And muggers have been known to blame their victims: "Don't look at me. He was dumb for walking down that street alone with all that cash."

Reaction Formation Have you ever thought that someone who was sickeningly sweet and overpolite might be sitting on a hotbed of hostility? Has anyone denied feelings so strongly that you suspected they were actually present? Perhaps so. Freud theorized that another avenue for dealing with unacceptable impulses is **reaction formation**—taking an exaggerated position that opposes our true feelings.

Projection A motion-picture projector thrusts an image onto a screen. A person from a society without projectors might think that the image had originated in the screen.

Freud suggested that we sometimes deal with our own unacceptable impulses through **projection**—attributing them to other people, and dis-

Denial A defense mechanism in which threatening events are misperceived to be harmless.

Repression The ejection of unacceptable ideas or impulses from consciousness.

Suppression The conscious placing of stressful or threatening events or ideas out of awareness. *Not* a defense mechanism.

Rationalization A defense mechanism in which an individual engages in self-deception, finding justifications for unacceptable ideas, impulses, or behaviors.

Reaction formation A defense mechanism in which unacceptable ideas and impulses are kept unconscious through the exaggerated expression of opposing ideas and impulses.

Projection A defense mechanism in which unacceptable ideas and impulses are cast out, or attributed, to others. (From the Latin *pro-*, meaning "forward," and *jacere*, meaning "to throw." What is the origin of the word *jet?*)

Intellectualization A defense mechanism in which threatening events are viewed with emotional detachment.

Displacement A defense mechanism in which ideas or impulses are transferred from a threatening or unsuitable object to an acceptable object. (What is the role of displacement in the resolutions of the Oedipus and Electra complexes, discussed in Chapter 9?)

Sublimation A defense mechanism in which primitive impulses—usually sexual and aggressive—are channeled into positive, constructive activities.

Ego analysts A term descriptive of many Neo-Freudians, suggesting they attribute more importance to (conscious) ego functioning than Freud did.

owning them as parts of ourselves. An angry person may perceive the world as a hostile place. A sexually frustrated person who believes that sex is evil may interpret the innocent gestures of others as sexual advances.

Intellectualization   Physicians who become emotionally involved with patients may not be able to undertake painful diagnostic and surgical procedures to save their lives. Instead, they try to distance themselves from their patients' immediate discomfort, so that they can apply their knowledge and skills without excessive arousal. Similarly, psychologists who become as upset as a client over a family dispute would not be effective at suggesting coping behavior. **Intellectualization** is cognitive focusing on stress that permits emotional detachment.

While intellectualization permits us to solve problems rationally, excessive intellectualization may prevent us from experiencing life fully. Persistent intellectualizers may impress us as cold, distant, or machinelike.

Displacement   Freud considered **displacement** an essential aspect of developing mature sexual relationships. He argued that we develop lasting attachments to adults of the opposite sex by transferring, or displacing, onto them emotions that we first experienced toward our own parents. Displacement is adjustive because it permits us to substitute attainable goals for unattainable goals.

Aggressive impulses may be displaced onto targets less threatening than the person who provoked us. There is the old tale about the man who was scolded by his boss and took it out on his wife. She then scolded the child who, in turn, kicked the dog. The dog chased the cat, the cat chased the mouse, and so on. Some microscopic form of life may still be bearing the brunt of the boss's wrath.

Sublimation   Why do we build cities, sculpt statues, write poems and novels? Are our motives noble, or do they have a darker basis?

Freud suggested that these creative acts represented **sublimation**—the channeling of socially unacceptable impulses into socially productive behavior. Sublimation permits one to escape self-criticism from recognizing, or acting out, primitive impulses. An artist, for example, may gratify sexual impulses by working with nude models, while also earning a high income and critical acclaim.

This dim view of human creativity has sparked much criticism, even among Freud's contemporary followers, or **ego analysts.** Ego analysts argue that noble behavior can reflect conscious, prosocial wishes.

ACTIVE COPING

Fate, chance, luck, destiny—how many of us allow ourselves to be blown about by the wind, to endure conflict and frustration, to experience unrelenting anxiety, or engage in Type A behavior on the "fast track" to success and heart disease? How many of us, in the words of Henry David Thoreau, lead "lives of quiet desperation"?

PSYCHOLOGY IN THE WORKPLACE

STRESS AND WORK

Work for most of us involves more than forty hours a week. When we figure in commutation, preparation, lunch time, continuing education, and just thinking about the job, many of us put at least half of our waking hours into our work.

Stress at work also spills over into stress at home. Frustrations and resentments about the work place can make us tired and short-tempered, and they can contribute to arguments with one's spouse and family (Gibson et al., 1985). In a vicious cycle, marital conflict may then compound problems in the work place.

The lefthand part of Figure 10.2 shows how various features of the work place can contribute to stress (Ivancevich & Matteson, 1980). Among the aspects of the physical environment that can produce stress we find poor lighting, air pollution (including cigarette or cigar smoke produced by coworkers and clients), crowding, noise, and extremes of temperature. Individual stressors include work overload, boredom, conflict about one's work (e.g., being ordered to give an offender psychological treatment when one believes that he or she should be treated purely as a criminal), excessive responsibility, and lack of forward movement.

Group stressors include bothersome relationships with supervisors, subordinates, and peers. Organizational stressors include lack of opportunity to participate in decision making, ambiguous or conflicting company policies, too much or too little organizational structure, low pay, racism, and sexism. There are many others (Holt, 1982).

The central part of Figure 10.2 shows the worker and the sources of stress that may be acting on him or her. For example, marital or inner conflict may compound any conflicts encountered in the work place. A Type A personality may turn the easiest, most routine tasks into races to beat the clock. Irrational needs for constant approval may minimize the impact of most rewards.

The right side of the figure suggests a number of the possible outcomes of the interaction of these sources of stress. On a subjective level, stressed workers can experience anxiety, depression, frustration, fatigue, boredom, and loss of self-esteem (Gibson et al., 1985). Behaviorally, stressed workers may become accident prone, engage in excessive eating or smoking, turn to alcohol or other drugs (Bensinger, 1982; Milam & Ketcham, 1981; Peyser, 1982), and show temperamental outbursts.

The cognitive effects of excessive stress on the job include decreased attention span, poor concentration, and inability to make sound decisions. Physiological effects include high blood pressure and the "diseases of adaptation" discussed earlier in the chapter. The organizational effects of excessive stress include absenteeism, alienation from coworkers, decreased productivity, a high turnover rate, and loss of commitment and loyalty to the organization (Gibson et al., 1985; McKenna et al., 1981).

Fortunately, psychologists have found that many measures can be taken to decrease stress encountered in the work place. One can begin with an objective analysis of the work place to determine whether physical conditions are hampering rather than enhancing the quality of work life. A good deal of job stress arises from a mismatch between job demands and the abilities and needs of the employee (Chemers et al., 1985). To prevent mismatches, companies can use careful screening measures (e.g., interviewing and psychological testing) to recruit employees whose personalities are compatible with job requirements and then provide the training and education that is needed to impart the specific skills that will enable workers to perform effectively. Job requirements should be as specific and clear as possible.

STRESS MANAGEMENT IN THE WORKPLACE—1980s STYLE Companies can help workers manage stress by offering counseling and supportive therapy, education about health, and fitness centers. Such companies have made extensive investments in gyms and exercise equipment for their employees.

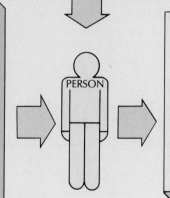

Other Sources of Stress
Hassles and life changes, marital
or inner conflict
Type A personality, physiological
predispositions for diseases of adaptation

Stressors in the Work Place
PHYSICAL ENVIRONMENT
lighting, pollution, crowding
INDIVIDUAL STRESSORS
work overload, excessive responsibilities,
role conflict, boredom
GROUP STRESSORS
poor relations with supervisors,
supervisees, peers
ORGANIZATIONAL STRESSORS
unclear or conflicting policies, too much
or too little structure, racism, sexism

PERSON

Outcomes
SUBJECTIVE
anxiety, depression, fatigue
BEHAVIORAL
accident proneness, outbursts, alcoholism
COGNITIVE
decreased attention span, poor decision-
making ability
HEALTH
High blood pressure, other diseases
of adaptation

Cognitive Appraisal
Catastrophizing of stressors and of coping
problems, irrational self-demands (e.g.,
need for constant approval)

A MODEL FOR STRESS IN THE WORKPLACE Various factors in the workplace, such as the physical environment and organizational stressors, have their impact on the worker. Workplace stressors can also interact with stresses from home and factors in the personality to produce a number of negative outcomes.

Social Support Workers need to feel that they will find social support from their supervisors if they have complaints or suggestions (Gottlieb, 1983; Rocco et al., 1980). As noted in Chapter 1, job redesign and the establishment of autonomous work groups frequently rekindle enthusiasm and the feeling that work is meaningful. Companies can also help workers manage stress by offering counseling and supportive therapy, education about health, and gyms. Kimberly-Clark, Xerox, Pepsi-Cola, Weyerhauser, and Rockwell International, for ex-ample, have all made significant investments in fitness centers that include jogging tracks, exercise cycles, and other equipment.

Workers whose companies do not help them manage stress can tackle this task on their own, using suggestions found in this chapter for coping with catastrophizing thoughts, relaxing, engaging in environmental engineering and so on. If these measures are not sufficient, they may wish to use the balance sheet to help them make decisions about whether they change jobs.

In Shakespeare's *Julius Caesar,* Cassius and Brutus listen as crowds honor Caesar as a god. But they know Caesar is only made of flesh and blood. Cassius, in fact, had once saved Caesar from drowning. So whose fault was it that Caesar now stood upon the "narrow world" like a colossal statue, while others seemed petty and fretted about beneath his legs? Cassius says to Brutus:

Men at some time are masters of their fates:
The fault, dear Brutus, is not in our stars,
But in ourselves, that we are underlings.

Similarly, if we are unhappy with our lots in life—if we are assaulted by stress heaped upon stress—it is up to us to do something about it. Rather than show socially inappropriate behavior, like aggression or regression—rather than withdraw from the social arena or use self-deception, we must bear the responsibility of coping actively if we wish to be the masters of our fates.

PERCEIVED SELF-EFFICACY AND LOCUS OF CONTROL: TAKING RESPONSIBILITY FOR YOUR OWN BEHAVIOR

Perceived Self-Efficacy   Psychologist Albert Bandura (1982) argues that our **perceived self-efficacy**—that is, our perceptions of our capacities to bring about change—influences our behavior, our thought patterns, even our emotional arousal.

When faced with fear-inducing objects, a high level of perceived self-efficacy is accompanied by *low* levels of epinephrine and norepinephrine in the bloodstream (Bandura et al., 1985). Epinephrine (also called adrenalin) generally arouses the body and can cause shakiness, "butterflies in the stomach," and feelings of nervousness, all of which can impair one's coping ability.* Thus, people with higher perceived self-efficacy may have biological as well as psychological reasons for remaining calmer. Further evidence of the importance of perceived self-efficacy to psychological well-being is found in research that shows that normal people have higher levels of perceived self-efficacy than do psychiatric subjects (Rosenbaum & Hadari, 1985).

People in whom high levels of perceived self-efficacy are experimentally induced complete experimental tasks more successfully than do people of comparable ability, and they show lower emotional arousal in the process. A combination of perceived self-efficacy *and a detailed plan* is effective at helping overweight college students lose weight (Schifter & Ajzen, 1985). People with higher levels of perceived self-efficacy are less likely to relapse when they have lost weight or quit smoking (Condiotte & Lichtenstein, 1981; Marlatt & Gordon, 1980). They are more effective in athletic competition (Weinberg et al., 1980), and they are more likely to seriously consider nontraditional and challenging career options (Betz & Hackett, 1981). They are also more likely to profit from psychotherapy for problems like

Perceived self-efficacy In social-learning theory, the degree to which an individual believes that he or she can influence the environment, or change the self, so that he or she can achieve his or her goals.

*See Chapters 2 and 7 for further discussion of adrenalin.

Locus of control The place (locus) to which an individual attributes control over the receiving of reinforcers—either inside or outside the self.

depression (Steinmetz et al., 1983). Women with higher perceived self-efficacy are more likely to persist without medication in controlling pain during childbirth (Manning & Wright, 1983).*

When intelligence and aptitudes are held constant, it appears that people with higher perceived self-efficacy regulate problem-solving behavior more effectively and bounce back more readily from failure. In these ways it seems that life's challenges may be less stressful for them.

The relationship between perceived self-efficacy and performance also appears to be a two-way street. While high perceived self-efficacy contributes to successful performances, Feltz (1982) found that improved performance (in women who were back-diving) also contributed to perceptions of self-efficacy.

Locus of Control   Julian Rotter (1966) defines a concept closely related to that of self-efficacy: **locus of control.** People who believe that they can exert a significant influence over whether or not they will attain reinforcements are said to show "internal control." That is, they perceive the site, or locus, of control to be within themselves. People who see control outside their own hands are said to show "external control."

It is easy to attribute success to internal factors. If you carry the ball seventy yards for a touchdown, it is your clear thinking and catlike agility that does the deed. If you fumble the ball, it's someone else's fault or plain bad luck. Most of us tend to credit ourselves for our successes and blame others for our shortcomings (Fitch, 1970; Lau & Russell, 1980). There are exceptions: People prone to depression are likely to blame themselves to excess for failures and shortcomings (see Chapter 11).

Persons who show internal control, or "internals," are more effective at meeting new challenges (Rotter, 1975) and attain higher grades than "externals," especially during adolescence (Findley & Cooper, 1983). Internals who quit smoking show lower relapse rates than externals. Internals show less disturbance than externals when faced with unavoidable stresses, such as spinal-cord injury (Shadish et al., 1981) or surgical operations (Shipley et al., 1978; Staub et al., 1971). Internals are more likely than externals to seek out information even about painful events, like operations. Experiments with laboratory rats suggest that knowing that a painful event is imminent results in less stress (as measured by less development of ulcers), perhaps because awareness permits the rats to brace themselves more effectively (Weiss, 1972).

Negative events, even from high school days, have more of a lingering effect on "external" than "internal" university students (Lefcourt et al., 1981). Lefcourt and his colleagues (1981) suggest that internal locus of control can help moderate the impact of negative events. In the following sections we examine several ways of moderating the impact of stressors, including controlling catastrophizing thoughts and lowering exhausting levels of bodily arousal.

*I am not promoting natural childbirth, but merely illustrating the point that people high in self-efficacy may show a greater willingness than others to persist in an endeavor, despite temporary discomfort.

QUESTIONNAIRE

LOCUS OF CONTROL SCALE

Do you believe that you are in charge of your own life? That you can exert an influence on other people and the environment to reach your goals? Or do you believe that your fate is in the "stars"? That you are ruled by luck, chance, and other people?

People who believe that they are in control of their lives are said to have an internal locus of control, or to be "internals." People who view their fates as being out of their hands are said to be "externals." Are you more of an "internal" or more of an "external"? To learn more about your perception of your locus of control, respond to the following questionnaire developed by Nowicki and Strickland (1973).

Mark your responses to the questions on the answer sheet in the next column. When you are finished, turn to Appendix B to score your test.

	YES	NO
1. Do you believe that most problems will solve themselves if you just don't fool with them?	___	___
2. Do you believe that you can stop yourself from catching a cold?	___	___
3. Are some people just born lucky?	___	___
4. Most of the time do you feel that getting good grades meant a great deal to you?	___	___
5. Are you often blamed for things that just aren't your fault?	___	___
6. Do you believe that if somebody studies hard enough he or she can pass any subject?	___	___
7. Do you feel that most of the time it doesn't pay to try hard because things never turn out right anyway?	___	___
8. Do you feel that if things start out well in the morning it's going to be a good day no matter what you do?	___	___
9. Do you feel that most of the time parents listen to what their children have to say?	___	___
10. Do you believe that wishing can make good things happen?	___	___
11. When you get punished does it usually seem it's for no good reason at all?	___	___
12. Most of the time do you find it hard to change a friend's opinion?	___	___
13. Do you think cheering more than luck helps a team win?	___	___
14. Did you feel that it was nearly impossible to change your parents' minds about anything?	___	___
15. Do you believe that parents should allow children to make most of their own decisions?	___	___
16. Do you feel that when you do something wrong there's very little you can do to make it right?	___	___
17. Do you believe that most people are just born good at sports?	___	___
18. Are most other people your age stronger than you are?	___	___
19. Do you feel that one of the best ways to handle most problems is just not to think about them?	___	___
20. Do you feel that you have a lot of choice in deciding who your friends are?	___	___
21. If you find a four-leaf clover, do you believe that it might bring you good luck?	___	___

	YES	NO
22. Did you often feel that whether or not you did your homework had much to do with what kinds of grades you got?	___	___
23. Do you feel that when a person your age is angry with you, there's little you can do to stop him or her?	___	___
24. Have you ever had a good-luck charm?	___	___
25 Do you believe that whether or not people like you depends on how you act?	___	___
26. Did your parents usually help you if you asked them to?	___	___
27. Have you felt that when people were angry with you it was usually for no reason at all?	___	___
28. Most of the time, do you feel that you can change what might happen tomorrow by what you did today?	___	___
29. Do you believe that when bad things are going to happen they are just going to happen no matter what you try to do to stop them?	___	___
30. Do you think that people can get their own way if they just keep trying?	___	___
31. Most of the time do you find it useless to try to get your own way at home?	___	___
32. Do you feel that when good things happen they happen because of hard work?	___	___
33. Do you feel that when somebody your age wants to be your enemy there's little you can do to change matters?	___	___
34. Do you feel that it's easy to get friends to do what you want them to do?	___	___
35. Do you usually feel that you have little to say about what you get to eat at home?	___	___
36. Do you feel that when someone doesn't like you there's little you can do about it?	___	___
37. Did you usually feel that it was almost useless to try in school because most other children were just plain smarter than you were?	___	___
38. Are you the kind of person who believes that planning ahead makes things turn out better?	___	___
39. Most of the time, do you feel that you have little to say about what your family decides to do?	___	___
40. Do you think it's better to be smart than to be lucky?	___	___

CONTROLLING IRRATIONAL AND CATASTROPHIZING THOUGHTS

Have you had any of these experiences?

1. You have difficulty with the first item on a test and become absolutely convinced that you will flunk?

2. You want to express your genuine feelings but think that you might make another person angry or upset?

3. You haven't been able to get to sleep for fifteen minutes and assume that you will lie awake the whole night and feel "wrecked" in the morning?

4. You're not sure what decision to make, so you try to put your conflicts out of your mind by going out, playing cards, or watching TV?

CATASTROPHIZING This football player is catastrophizing the mistakes he made on Sunday. He is telling himself that he probably lost the game for his team, and that the fans hate him. It would be more adjustive for him to tell himself that there is still time for his team to fashion a winning season, that his teammates share the responsibility for the game outcome, and that the fans have cheered him more frequently than they have booed him.

5. You decide not to play tennis or go jogging, because your form isn't perfect and you're in less than perfect condition?

If you have had these or similar experiences, it may be because you harbor a number of the irrational beliefs isolated by Albert Ellis (see page 466). Irrational beliefs and negative feelings can exacerbate each other in a vicious cycle (Ellis, 1985; Schwartz, 1982). Irrational beliefs may make you overly concerned about the approval of others (experience 2, above) or perfectionistic (experience 5). They may lead you to think that you can best relieve yourself of certain dilemmas by pretending that they do not exist (experience 4), or that a minor setback will invariably lead to greater problems (experiences 1 and 3).

How, then, do we change irrational or catastrophizing thoughts? The answer is theoretically simple: We change these thoughts by changing them. However, it may take some work, and before we can change them we must often first become more aware of them.

Cognitive psychologist Donald Meichenbaum (1976; Meichenbaum & Jaremko, 1983) suggests a three-step procedure for controlling the irrational and catastrophizing thoughts that often accompany feelings of pain, anxiety, frustration, conflict, or tension:

1. Develop awareness of these thoughts through careful self-examination. Study the examples at the beginning of this section or in Table 10.3 to see if these experiences and thought patterns characterize you. (Also

TABLE 10.3 Controlling Irrational, Catastrophizing Beliefs and Thoughts

Irrational, Catastrophizing Thoughts	Incompatible (Coping) Thoughts
"Oh my God, I'm going to lose all control"	"This is painful and upsetting, but I don't have to go to pieces."
"This will never end."	"This will come to an end, even if it's hard to see right now."
"It'll be awful if Mom gives me that look."	"It's more pleasant when Mom's happy with me, but I can live with it if she isn't."
"How can I get out there? I'll look like a fool."	"So you're not perfect; it doesn't mean you'll look stupid. And if someone thinks you look stupid, you can live with that too. Just stop worrying and have some fun."
"My heart's going to leap out of my chest! How much can I stand?"	"Easy—hearts don't leap out of chests. Stop and think! Distract yourself. Breathe slowly, in and out."
"What can I do? There's nothing I can do!"	"Easy—stop and think. Just because you can't think of a solution right now doesn't mean there's nothing you can do. Take it a minute at a time. Breathe easy."

Do irrational beliefs and catastrophizing thoughts compound the stress you experience? Cognitive psychologists suggest that we can cope with stress by becoming aware of self-defeating beliefs and thoughts and replacing them with rational, calming beliefs and thoughts.

read Ellis's irrational beliefs carefully on page 466 and ask yourself whether any of them tend to govern your behavior.) When you encounter anxiety or frustration, pay careful attention to your thoughts. Are they helping to point toward a solution, or are they compounding your problems?

2. Prepare thoughts that are **incompatible** with the irrational and catastrophizing thoughts, and practice saying them firmly to yourself. (If nobody is nearby, why not say them firmly aloud?)

3. Reward yourself with a mental pat on the back for effective changes in beliefs and thought patterns.

Coping with Test Anxiety by Controlling Irrational and Catastrophizing Thoughts   Have you or your friends experienced any of these thoughts while taking tests? "I just know I'm going to flunk." "I don't know what's wrong with me—I just can't take tests." "I know everything, but when I get in there my mind just goes blank." "The way I do on standardized tests, I'll just never get into graduate school."

Some students may use complaints of test anxiety as an excuse for performing poorly (Smith et al., 1982), but for many others, test anxiety is a frustrating handicap. Especially when we study diligently, test anxiety seems particularly cruel.

Yet we are not born with test anxiety. Test anxiety appears to reflect a combination of high bodily arousal and negative thoughts, including critical self-evaluations. People with high test anxiety show high levels of auto-

Incompatible (in-come-PAT-a-bull). Incapable of existing together. Mutually exclusive.

TABLE 10.4 Percent of Positive and Negative Thoughts for Low and High Test-Anxiety Groups of University Students

Thought	Low Test Anxiety Percent	High Test Anxiety Percent
POSITIVE THOUGHTS:		
Will do all right on test	71	43
Mind is clear, can concentrate	49	26
Feel in control of my reactions	46	23
NEGATIVE THOUGHTS:		
Wish I could get out or test was over	46	65
Test is hard	45	64
Not enough time to finish	23	49
Work I put into studying won't be shown by my grade	16	44
Stuck on a question and it's making it difficult to answer others	13	34
Mind is blank or can't think straight	11	31
Going to do poorly on test	11	28
Think how awful it will be if I fail or do poorly	11	45

High test-anxious students report fewer positive thoughts and more negative thoughts while taking tests. Moreover, their negative thoughts are linked to bodily sensations like dryness in the mouth and rapid heart rate.

SOURCE OF DATA: Galassi, Frierson, and Sharer (1981), pp. 56, 58.

nomic arousal during tests and are likely to report bodily sensations like dryness in the mouth and rapid heart rate (Galassi et al., 1981). On a cognitive level, they have more negative thoughts and are more self-critical than people with low or moderate test anxiety, even when they are performing just as well (Holroyd et al., 1978; Meichenbaum & Butler, 1980; Zatz & Chassin, 1985). Moreover, they allow their self-criticisms, and negative thoughts of the sort shown in Table 10.4, to *distract* them from working effectively on their tests (Arkin et al., 1982; Bandura, 1977; Sarason, 1978).

Marvin Goldfried and his colleagues (1978) have successfully treated test anxiety through **rational restructuring,** which is similar to the Meichenbaum technique discussed in the previous section. In rational restructuring, students first pinpoint self-defeating thoughts by imagining that they are taking tests and searching for the mental villains. Then they construct rational alternatives for each of them (see Table 10.5). They practice the rational alternatives and mentally pat themselves on the back for improved performance.

Other research suggests that the academic performance of first-year college students improves when they are informed that grade-point averages tend to increase as students reach their upperclass years (Wilson & Linville, 1982). Perhaps they then attribute academic difficulties to adjusting to college life rather than personal inadequacy, and this "restructuring" of their performance permits them to be less self-critical.

Rational restructuring The logical rethinking of threatening or anxiety-evoking events, so that coping strategies may be used instead of avoidance attempts or simple "floundering about."

TABLE 10.5 Self-Defeating Thoughts and Rational Alternatives for Decreasing Test Anxiety and Improving Grades

Self-Defeating Thought	Rational Alternative
"I'm running out of time!"	"Time is passing, but just take it item by item. Getting bent out of shape won't help."
"This is impossible! Are all the items going to be this difficult?"	"Just take it item by item. Each item is different. Don't assume the worst."
"Everybody's smarter than I am!"	"Probably not, but maybe they're not handicapping themselves by catastrophizing and distracting themselves. Just do the best you can and then relax."
"I just can't do well on tests."	"That's true only if you believe it's true. Back to the items, one by one."
"If I flunk, everything is ruined!"	"You won't make yourself happy by failing, but it won't be the end of the world either. Just take it item by item and do the best you can."

Cognitive psychologists suggest that we cope with test anxiety by substituting rational alternatives for self-defeating thoughts.

LOWERING AROUSAL

One reason that a squash does not become as aroused as a person when it is assaulted is that it does not have an autonomic nervous system. Thus it has no alarm reaction. Another reason is that it does not have a central nervous system. Therefore, it does not catastrophize.

Once you are aware that a stressor is acting upon you, and have developed a plan to cope with it, it is no longer helpful to have blood pounding so fiercely through your arteries. Psychologists and other scientists have developed many methods for teaching people to lower excessive bodily arousal. They include meditation, biofeedback (both discussed in Chapter 4), and progressive relaxation.

Meditation appears to facilitate adjustment to stress without decreasing awareness. In this way it does not reduce perception of potential threats. In one experiment, Orne-Johnson (1973) exposed meditators and nonmeditators to unpredictable loud noises. Meditators stopped showing a stress reaction—as measured by sweat in the palms of their hands (galvanic skin response, or GSR)—earlier than nonmeditators. In another experiment, Goleman and Schwartz (1976) used heart rate and GSR to measure stress reactions to a film that explicitly portrayed accidents and death. Meditators showed a greater alarm reaction than nonmeditators when the contents of the film were announced, but recovered normal levels of arousal more rapidly during the showings. Meditators in this study thus showed greater alertness to potential threat—a factor that could allow them to develop a plan for dealing with a stressor more rapidly—but also more ability to control arousal.

In one experiment with biofeedback, Sirota and his colleagues (1976) trained twenty women aged twenty-one to twenty-seven to slow their heart rates voluntarily. Afterwards, the women reported a painful electric shock to be less stressful. In another biofeedback experiment, Gatchel and Proctor (1976) showed that college students who learned to slow their heart rates reduced their speech anxiety.

Meditation seems to focus on the cognitive components of a stress reaction, while biofeedback can be directed at various functions, such as heart rate and muscle tension. Progressive relaxation focuses on muscle tension, although the instructions to slow down breathing and develop mental imagery—for instance, feelings of heaviness in the limbs—promote other responses that are incompatible with an alarm reaction. Yet all methods achieve somewhat similar effects: a combination of lowered arousal and cognitions of self-efficacy and internal locus of control.

Progressive relaxation Jacobson's method for reducing muscle tension, which involves alternate tensing and relaxing of muscle groups throughout the body.

Progressive Relaxation

Edmund Jacobson (1938) of the University of Chicago noted that people tense their muscles when they are under stress, but are often unaware of it. He reasoned that if they could learn to relax these tensions, they could lower the stress they experienced. But when he asked clients to focus on relaxing muscles, they often had no idea what to do.

Jacobson developed the method of **progressive relaxation** to teach people how to relax these tensions. In this method, people purposefully tense a muscle group before relaxing it. This sequence allows them to (1) develop awareness of their muscle tensions; and (2) differentiate between feelings of tension and relaxation. The method is "progressive" because people progress from one muscle group to another. Since its beginnings in the 1930s, progressive relaxation has undergone development by several behavior therapists, among them Joseph Wolpe of the Eastern Pennsylvania Psychiatric Institute (Wolpe & Lazarus, 1966).

Progressive relaxation decreases the sympathetic arousal of the alarm reaction (Paul, 1966b). It has been found useful with "diseases of adaptation" ranging from muscle-tension headaches (Blanchard et al., 1985; Ted-

PSYCHOLOGY IN THE WORKPLACE
"JUST RELAX": A UNION STARTS A PROGRAM TO TREAT WORKPLACE HYPERTENSION

In New York, about twenty United Store Workers union members with high blood pressure try a technique called "progressive relaxation." Psychologist Laurence Schleifer teaches them to alternately tense and relax their muscles and to associate the word "relax" with the relaxed state. He says that with practice, the workers can ease stressful situations, relieving tension.

Ernestine Harden works in Gimbel's credit department, where "I get most of the brunt of problems with bills." She practices the relaxation technique fifteen minutes daily. Her high blood pressure is down for the first time in thirty years. "I don't know if it's because of the program," she says. But she has learned "to take a deep breath and relax instead of arguing. You don't feel as frustrated after it's over."

Schleifer says 31 million workers have high blood pressure, resulting in 27 million lost work days yearly.

ers et al., 1984) to hypertension (Agras et al., 1983; Taylor et al., 1977). You can experience muscle relaxation in the arms by doing the following:

Settle down in a reclining chair, dim the lights, and loosen any tight clothing. Then use these directions to relax your arms. You can tape them or have a friend read them to you. For instructions concerning relaxation of your entire body, consult a behavior therapist or other helping professional who knows the techniques of progressive relaxation.

> Settle back as comfortably as you can. Let yourself relax to the best of your ability. . . . Now, as you relax like that, clench your right fist, just clench your fist tighter and tighter, and study the tension as you do so. Keep it clenched and feel the tension in your right fist, hand, forearm . . . and now relax. Let the fingers of your right hand become loose, and observe the contrast in your feelings. . . . Now, let yourself go and try to become more relaxed all over. . . . Once more, clench your right fist really tight . . . hold it, and notice the tension again. . . . Now let go, relax; your fingers straighten out, and you notice the difference once more. . . . Now repeat that with your left fist. Clench your left fist while the rest of your body relaxes; clench that fist tighter and feel the tension . . . and now relax. Again enjoy the contrast. . . . Repeat that once more, clench the left fist, tight and tense. . . . Now do the opposite of tension—relax and feel the difference. Continue relaxing like that for a while. . . . Clench both fists tighter and together, both fists tense, forearms tense, study the sensations . . . and relax; straighten out your fingers and feel that relaxation. Continue relaxing your hands and forearms more and more. . . . Now bend your elbows and tense your biceps, tense them harder and study the tension feelings. . . . All right, straighten out your arms, let them relax and feel that difference again. Let the relaxation develop. . . . Once more, tense your biceps; hold the tension and observe it carefully. . . . Straighten the arms and relax; relax to the best of your ability. . . . Each time, pay close attention to your feelings when you tense up and when you relax. Now straighten your arms, straighten them so that you feel most tension in the triceps muscles along the back of your arms; stretch your arms and feel that tension. . . . And now relax. Get your arms back into a comfortable position. Let the relaxation proceed on its own. The arms should feel comfortably heavy as you allow them to relax. . . . Straighten the arms once more so that you feel the tension in the triceps muscles; straighten them. Feel that tension . . . and relax. Now let's concentrate on pure relaxation in the arms without any tension. Get your arms comfortable and let them relax further and further. Continue relaxing your arms even further. Even when your arms seem fully relaxed, try to go that extra bit further; try to achieve deeper and deeper levels of relaxation (Wolpe & Lazarus, 1966, p. 177).

CHANGING THE PACE OF YOUR DAILY LIFE
Stop driving yourself—get out and walk. Too often we jump out of bed to an abrasive alarm, hop into a shower, fight commuter crowds, and arrive at class or work with no time to spare. Then we first become involved in our hectic "day." Let us examine a number of methods for changing the pace of our daily lives. Some can help us with the Type A attitudes and behaviors discussed on pages 470–472. Others can help us recognize and cope with accumulating life changes.

Confronting the Value System That Supports Type A Behavior   The first step in coping with Type A behavior is confronting the value system that supports it. Do you place too much value on competing rather than cooperating? Do you spend all your time achieving, never appreciating? Must you always "do your best"—at play as well as at work? Or can you be more selective about your efforts?

It may be useful for Type A people to challenge the irrational idea that something awful will happen if they are less than perfect at all their undertakings. Suinn (1976) suggests relaxing for several minutes once or twice a day, using environmental engineering, and slowing down.

Using Environmental Engineering   You can change your personal environment to lower stress by adopting some of the following measures:

Set your alarm clock lower or buy an alarm clock that makes a pleasant sound.

Get up earlier to sit and relax, watch the morning news with a cup of tea, or meditate. This may mean going to bed earlier.

Leave home earlier and take a more scenic route to work or school. Avoid rush-hour jams, if possible.

Don't car-pool with last-minute rushers. Drive with a group that leaves earlier or use public transportation.

Have a snack or relax at school or work before the "day" begins.

Don't do two things at once. Avoid scheduling too many classes or appointments back to back.

Use breaks to read, exercise, or meditate. Limit intake of stimulants such as caffeine.

Space chores. Why have the car and typewriter repaired, work, shop, and drive a friend to the airport all in one day?

If rushed, allow unessential work to go to the next day.

Set aside some time for yourself: for music, a hot bath, exercise, meditation, progressive relaxation. If your life will not permit this, get a new life.

Slowing Down

Move about slowly when you awake. Stretch.

Drive more slowly. This saves energy, lives, and traffic citations. It's also less stressful than racing the clock.

Don't wolf lunch. Get out, make it an occasion.

Don't tumble words out. Speak more slowly. Interrupt less frequently.

Recognizing and Controlling Hidden Life-Change Units   Become aware of the hidden life-change units in your life. Variety is the spice of life, but too much spice sours the stomach.

Do not quit smoking and diet at the same time. A dramatic increase in income does not require that you immediately take on a new mortgage and move into a better neighborhood. If you suffer a tragic personal loss, it may be foolhardy to think that moving to a new job in a new city will promote adjustment.

Keeping a log of daily activities can help you track the hidden changes in your life. After a week or so, reflect. How many activities, people, and

TYPE A AND TYPE B The Type A business executive is probably sending his blood pressure through the roof, but the Type B executive is capable of focusing on the quality of life and allowing himself to relax.

places differ from those of a few months ago? Are there major daily changes in sleeping, eating, or exercise routines? Are you a weekend runner or tennis player who tries to compensate for five sedentary weekdays by pushing your body through two days of strenuous weekend effort? Weekend athletes encounter major changes in recreational habits twice a week up to fifty-two times a year. How about your social life? Forcing yourself out of bed at 6:30 A.M. each weekday morning and staying up until 3:00 A.M. on weekends may give you chronic jet lag.

MAKING DECISIONS

When we are frustrated or in conflict, we must make decisions. We must understand the barriers that block our goals to determine whether we can overcome them and, if not, whether to search for potentially satisfying substitutes. When we are in conflict, we must carefully weigh the pluses and minuses of each possible course of action and then make a choice.

If we don't make choices, we sit on the fencepost. A personal experiment will convince you that sitting indefinitely on the fencepost causes a certain part of the anatomy to hurt. When we avoid making decisions we cannot resolve our conflicts, and conflict is painful.

Making decisions involves choosing among various goals or courses of action to reach goals. If decisions are to work out, we need to be able to predict the relative values of our goals, our ability to surmount the obstacles in our paths, and the costs of surmounting them. Janis and Mann (1977) suggest that a balance sheet can help us make more accurate predictions.

Using the Balance Sheet Experiments with the **balance sheet** show that it has helped high-school students choose a college and adults decide whether to go on diets and attend exercise classes (Janis & Wheeler, 1978). Balance sheet users show fewer regrets about "the road not taken" and are more likely to stick to their decisions. The balance sheet also increases the probability that people will respond to conflict with appropriate alertness—which Janis and Wheeler term **vigilance**—rather than deny conflict or become overly aroused.

Balance sheets help us list the pluses and minuses ("pros" and "cons") of any course of action. In using the balance sheet, we jot down the following information for each choice (see Table 10.6): (1) projected tangible gains and losses for oneself; (2) projected tangible gains and losses for others; (3) projected self-approval or self-disapproval; and (4) projected approval or disapproval of others.

Meg was a thirty-four-year-old woman whose husband beat her. She had married Bob at twenty-seven, and for two years life had run smoothly. But she had been bruised and battered, fearful of her life, for the past five. She sought psychotherapy to cope with Bob, her fears, her resentments, and her disappointments. The therapist asked if Bob would come for treat-

Balance sheet An outline of positive and negative expectations concerning a course of action. An aid to effective decision-making.

Vigilance Watchfulness. (From the Latin *vigil*, meaning "awake.")

TABLE 10.6   Meg's Balance Sheet for the Alternative of Divorcing Bob

	Positive Anticipations	Negative Anticipations
Tangible gains and losses for me	1. Elimination of fear of being beaten or killed	1. Loneliness 2. Fear of starting a new social life 3. Fear of not having children owing to age 4. Financial struggle 5. Fear of personal emotional instability
Tangible gains and losses for others	1. Mother will be relieved	1. Bob might harm himself or others (he has threatened suicide if I leave)
Self-approval or self-disapproval		1. I might consider myself a failure because I could not help Bob or save our marriage
Social approval or social disapproval		1. Some people will complain marriage is sacred and blame me for "quitting" 2. Some men may consider me "that kind of woman"—an easy mark

When making a decision, weighing up the pluses and minuses for the various alternatives can lead to more productive choices and fewer regrets. Meg's balance sheet for the alternative of divorcing an abusive husband showed her psychologist that her list of positive anticipations was incomplete.

ment too, but Bob refused. Finally, unable to stop Bob from abusing her, Meg considered divorce. But divorce was also an ugly prospect and she vacillated.

Table 10.6 shows the balance sheet, as filled out by Meg, for the alternative of divorce.

Meg's balance sheet supplied Meg and her therapist with a clear agenda of concerns to work out. It also showed that Meg's anticipations were incomplete. Would she really have no positive thoughts about herself if she divorced Bob? Would no one other than her mother applaud the decision? (And did she have an irrational need to avoid the disapproval of others?) Meg's list of negative anticipations pointed to the need to develop financial independence by acquiring job skills. Her fears about undertaking a new social life also seemed overblown. Yes, making new acquaintances might not be easy, but it was not impossible. It was, in fact, up to Meg. And what of Meg's feelings about herself? Wouldn't she be pleased that she had done what she thought was necessary, even if divorce also entailed problems?

Meg concluded that many of her negative anticipations were exaggerated. Many fears could be collapsed into one category, fear of change. Fear of change had also led her to underestimate her need for self-respect. Meg did divorce Bob, and at first she was depressed, lonely, and fearful. But after a year she was working and dating regularly. She was not blissful, but had regained a sense of forward motion, took pride in being independent, and no longer dwelled in fear. It is fortunate that this story has a relatively happy ending. Otherwise, we would have had to look for another.

Are you now putting off making any decisions in your own life? Could using the balance sheet be of any help?

SUMMARY

1. Stress is the demand made on an organism to adjust. While some stress is necessary to keep us alert and occupied, too much stress can tax our adjustive capacities and contribute to physical illness.

2. Daily sources of aggravation ("hassles") and life changes are sources of stress. Positive as well as negative life changes require adjustment, although negative life changes are more taxing than positive life changes.

3. People who "earn" more than 300 life-change units within a year, according to the Holmes and Rahe scale, are at high risk for medical or psychological disorders. These data are correlational, however, not experimental; therefore, it is possible that people about to develop illnesses lead life styles characterized by more life changes. Also, the degree of stress imposed by an event is linked to the individual's cognitive appraisal of that event.

4. Pain and discomfort impair our ability to perform, especially when severe demands shortly follow a traumatic experience.

5. Anxiety is both a general emotional response to stress and a source of stress. Trait anxiety is a personality variable, while state anxiety is situational. Freud hypothezised that neurotic anxiety (a form of trait anxiety) reflects difficulty in repressing unacceptable urges.

6. Irrational beliefs highlight the importance of the cognitive appraisal of events in determining how stressful they will be. According to Albert Ellis, irrational beliefs can lead us to have unattainable interpersonal and personal goals—such as attempting to please others or to perform perfectly all the time.

7. Frustration results from having unattainable goals or from barriers to reaching our goals.

8. Conflict results from opposing motives. We often vacillate when we are in conflict. Approach-ap-

proach conflicts are least stressful. Double approach-avoidance conflicts are most complex. Conflicts may be reduced by decision-making.

9. Type A behavior is characterized by a sense of time urgency and high competitiveness. Type A people are more aggressive and more reluctant to relinquish control or power than are Type B's. Type A people also respond to challenge with higher blood pressure than Type B's, and are at greater risk for heart attacks than Type B's, who focus more on the quality of life.

10. Under stress, Hans Selye suggested that we experience the general adaptation syndrome, which consists of three stages: alarm, resistance, and exhaustion. Alarm and resistance involve overarousal of the sympathetic branch of the autonomic nervous system. Exhaustion involves parasympathetic dominance.

11. Prolonged overarousal can lead to headaches, ulcers, hypertension, and asthma in people who are predisposed toward these disorders. There is even evidence that stress can impair the body's ability to fight off cancer.

12. Stressors in the work place originate in the physical environment, work responsibilties, relations with coworkers and supervisors, and in organizational policies and structure. They interact with personal hassles, physiological predispositions for illness, and irrational beliefs to yield various unhealthful outcomes, along with anxiety, depression, and fatigue. Methods such as improved recruitment and training and education; the providing of social support; and even the provision of gyms can all increase coping ability on the job.

13. Defensive coping methods decrease the immediate impact of a stressor and may grant us time to marshall our resources. However, there is usually a personal or social cost to defensive coping, as found in socially inappropriate behavior, withdrawal, or self-deception. Defensive methods include use of alcohol and other drugs, aggression, withdrawal, fantasy, and several defense mechanisms.

14. Defense mechanisms protect us from anxiety by helping keep unacceptable impulses out of awareness. Defense mechanisms include regression, denial, repression, rationalization, reaction formation, projection, intellectualization, displacement, and sublimation.

15. Direct or active coping methods manipulate the environment to reduce or remove sources of stress, or else they involve changing our cognitive or physiological responses to unavoidable stress, so that the harmfulness of the stress is decreased. Active coping methods, in contrast to defensive coping methods, avoid self-deception.

16. The first step in active coping is accepting responsibility for our own responses to stress. People who perceive themselves capable of coping (who have greater perceived self-efficacy) are less disturbed by stress and more effective in performance. People who also believe that they exert control over receiving reinforcements (who have an internal locus of control) are more effective at meeting challenges than people who believe that their attainment of reinforcement is out of their hands (who have an external locus of control).

17. A number of active coping methods focus on changing irrational beliefs and catastrophizing thoughts. We can modify irrational beliefs and other self-defeating thoughts by (1) becoming aware of them through careful self-examination; (2) constructing incompatible, rational alternatives, and practicing the alternatives; and (3) patting ourselves on our backs for doing so.

18. Test anxiety leads to lower performance not only by increasing our arousal, but also by distracting us from the tasks at hand. In rational restructuring for test anxiety, test-takers pinpoint self-defeating thoughts that contribute to anxiety, construct and practice alternatives to them, and return to focusing on the test items.

19. One effect of stress is to heighten our levels of arousal. Psychological methods for lowering arousal include meditation, biofeedback, and progressive relaxation.

20. In progressive relaxation, people purposefully tense then relax muscle groups in sequence. Progressive relaxation decreases the sympathetic arousal of the alarm reaction and has been found helpful with diseases of adaptation, such as headaches and hypertension.

21. We can cope with Type A behavior first by challenging Type A attitudes, then by doing some environmental engineering and slowing down.

22. Making decisions is often the way out of conflict. We can use the balance sheet more completely to list and weigh the pluses and minuses for the alternatives available to us.

TRUTH OR FICTION REVISITED

Too much of a good thing can make you ill.

True. The accumulation of a great number of life changes within a short period of time is highly stressful and increases the risk of medical or psychological disorders—even when many of the changes are positive.

Our emotional problems stem almost completely from external pressures that we have little or no ability to change or control.

False. This is one of the irrational beliefs identified by Ellis. It discourages us from trying to take charge of our lives.

Some people are dedicated to the creation of their own stress.

True. Type A people are characterized by a sense of time urgency and high competitiveness.

Our blood pressure rises when we are under stress.

True. This is just one of the responses stimulated by the sympathetic division of the autonomic nervous system under stress.

Stress can influence the course of cancer.

True. Stress exacerbates the course of cancer in laboratory rats and may have similar effects in people.

Some people drink alcohol purposefully to handicap themselves in their ability to cope with conflict or failure.

True. It appears that then they can blame the alcohol rather than themselves for their shortcomings.

People who cheat on their income-tax returns often justify their behavior by claiming that government programs cost more than they're worth, or that they pay more than their fair share.

True. These claims are often rationalizations, one kind of defense mechanism.

Stressed workers have more accidents on the job.

True. Stressed workers are also more prone to absenteeism, alcoholism, family quarrels, and so on.

The belief that we can handle stress is linked to lower levels of adrenalin in the bloodstream.

True. As a result, we are less likely to feel anxious and tense, or that we're losing control.

When you are about to undergo a serious operation, learning the grisly details of the surgery and the expected course of recuperation may make the experience less stressful.

True. Knowing the details apparently permits us to brace ourselves more effectively for the inevitable.

If you ask people to just relax, many will have no idea what to do.

True. This is why Jacobson invented progressive relaxation, a technique that clearly teaches people the difference between muscle tension and relaxation.

People who make decisions on the basis of inspiration and gut-level feelings wind up with fewer regrets than people who methodically add up all the pluses and minuses.

False. People who use the balance sheet to weigh the pluses and the minuses have fewer regrets and are more likely to stick to their decisions.

OUTLINE

C H A P T E R 11

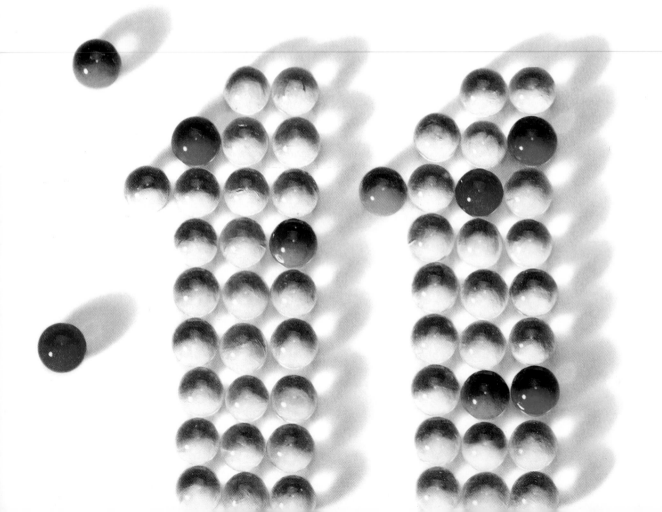

Abnormal Behavior

TRUTH OR FICTION ?

- A man shot the President of the United States in front of millions of television witnesses, yet was found not guilty by a court of law.
- Cavemen treated abnormal behavior by letting the sun shine in—or letting the evil spirits out. Therapy involved making a hole in the head.
- In the Middle Ages innocent people were drowned to prove that they were not possessed by the Devil.
- Mental disorders stem from physiological problems, such as chemical imbalances or metabolic disturbances.
- Some people are suddenly flooded with feelings of panic, even when there is no external threat.
- Some people have irresistible urges to wash their hands—over and over again.
- Some people have not one, but two or more distinct personalities dwelling within them.
- Depressed rats drive their neighbors to drink.
- Suicide is a sign of insanity.
- In some mental disorders, people may see or hear things that are not actually there.
- Supermales can leap tall buildings at a single bound.
- Many Americans have changed their sex through surgery and hormone treatments.
- Strip-teasers are exhibitionists.

The Ohio State campus lived in terror throughout the long fall of 1978. Four college women were abducted, forced to cash checks or obtain money with their instant-cash cards, then driven to unpopulated areas and raped. A mysterious phone call led to the arrest of a twenty-three-year-old drifter, William, who had been dismissed from the Navy.

William was not the boy next door.

Several psychologists and psychiatrists who interviewed William concluded that ten personalities resided within him, eight male and two female (Keyes, 1982). His personality had been "fractured" by an abusive childhood. The personalities showed distinct facial expressions, vocal patterns, and memories. They even performed differently on personality and intelligence tests.

Arthur, the most rational personality, spoke with a British accent. Danny and Christopher were normal, quiet adolescents. Christene was a three-year-old girl. It was Tommy, a sixteen-year-old, who had enlisted in the Navy. Allen was eighteen and smoked. Adelena, a nineteen-year-old **lesbian** personality, had committed the rapes. Who had made the mysterious phone call? Probably David, aged nine, an anxious child personality.

The defense claimed that William was suffering from **multiple personality.** Several distinct personalities dwelled within him. Some were aware of the others; some believed that they were the sole occupants. Billy, the core personality, had learned to sleep as a child to avoid the abuse of his father. A psychiatrist asserted that Billy had also been "asleep," in a "psychological coma," during the abductions. Therefore Billy should be found innocent by reason of **insanity.**

On December 4, 1978, Billy was found not guilty by reason of insanity. He was committed to an institution for the mentally ill and released in 1984.

In 1982, John Hinckley, was also found not guilty of the assassination attempt on President Reagan by reason of insanity. Expert witnesses testified that he was suffering from **schizophrenia.** Hinckley, too, was committed to an institution for the mentally ill.

Multiple personality and schizophrenia are two types of abnormal behavior. In this chapter we first define abnormal behavior. Then we examine various explanations for, or "models" of, abnormal behavior. In our discussion of the demonological model, we shall see that if William had lived in Salem, Massachusetts, in 1692, just 200 years after Columbus set foot in the New World, he might have been hanged or burned as a witch. At that time most people assumed that abnormal behavior was caused by possession by the Devil. Nineteen people lost their lives that year in that colonial town for allegedly practicing the arts of Satan.

Then we shall explore the ways in which abnormal behaviors are classified. Finally, we discuss various patterns of abnormal behavior, including *anxiety disorders, dissociative disorders, somatoform disorders, affective disorders, schizophrenic disorders, personality disorders,* and *psychosexual disorders.*

Lesbian Female homosexual. (After the Greek island *Lesbos,* where homosexuality among women was idealized.)

Multiple personality A dissociative disorder in which a person appears to have two or more distinct personalities. The personalities may alternate in controlling the person.

Insanity A legal term descriptive of a person judged to be incapable of recognizing right from wrong or of conforming his or her behavior to the law. (From the Latin *in-,* meaning "not," and *sanus,* meaning "healthy.")

Schizophrenia (skits-oh-FREE-knee-uh). A psychotic disorder characterized by loss of control of thought processes and inappropriate emotional responses.

60 MINUTES

BY REASON OF INSANITY

In the 60 Minutes segment "By Reason of Insanity," correspondent Morley Safer noted that

Not guilty by reason of insanity is a verdict that's been controversial since it was first used in law a hundred and forty years ago. When John Hinckley was acquitted of charges of attempted murder after successfully using the insanity defense, the debate inside the legal and psychiatric communities heated up once again.

In pleading insanity, lawyers use . . . the M'Naghton rules, named after Daniel M'Naghton, a man in England who, in 1843, had delusions that the British prime minister, Sir Robert Peel, was persecuting him. In attempting to assassinate Sir Robert, he killed his secretary. M'Naghton was found not guilty by reason of insanity. Public outrage forced the court to issue reasons for its decision. These became the M'Naghton rules which, with a few modifications, are the standards used in American law today. The central principle is that the accused does not know what he is doing when the act is committed, or—if he does know—that he does not realize it is wrong.

You can readily see how this principle leads to problems. After all, we cannot *know* whether other people understand right from wrong or "know what they are doing" at any given moment. We can only observe what they do and listen to what they say, and then we must draw our own conclusions. In the typical insanity defense, defense attorneys employ experts as witnesses—psychologists or psychiatrists who, on the basis of interviews or previous acquaintance with the client, usually testify that the accused was insane at the time of the act. The prosecution presents conflicting testimony from other expert witnesses to the effect that the accused was sane at the time of the crime.

This type of back-and-forth "expert" testimony characterized the John Hinckley trial in 1982. Hinckley tried to assassinate President Ronald Reagan, claiming that he wished to impress movie actress Jodie Foster. The defense claimed that Hinckley was suffering from schizophrenia at the time and was therefore insane. He was portrayed as a "mental cripple" living in a "fantasy world." Influenced by the movie *Taxi Driver*, he had even sought young prostitutes on the streets of New York who seemed in need of help. (Jodie Foster had

 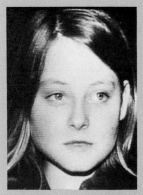

THE INSANITY PLEA Would-be Presidential assassin John Hinckley (left) is just one of the many who have evaded criminal responsibility through the insanity plea. The defense claimed that Hinckley was living in a fantasy world that involved actress Jodie Foster (right), who played a young prostitute in the film *Taxi Driver*.

played a street prostitute in *Taxi Driver*, and she was "saved" by the movie's schizophrenic "hero.")

The prosecution then brought forth witnesses who testified that Hinckley was sane. Because well-trained professionals often have conflicting views about peoples' "mental states," which are private events, the public seems to be becoming somewhat skeptical of the insanity plea.

Criminals who are found not guilty by reason of insanity are often committed to mental institutions, rather than given concrete prison terms. They are eligible for release when they are no longer behaving abnormally. The possibility of release leads the public to fear that "sick" people will be walking the streets if they show no symptoms for a while. Also, in an Associated Press-NBC News poll, 87 percent of a sample of Americans said they feared that many murderers were using the insanity plea to avoid going to jail (Caplan, 1984).

Some psychologists have suggested that we institute new verdicts such as guilty but insane, or guilty and insane. Such verdicts would allow disturbed criminals to receive treatment, in addition to being placed in prison, but they would retain responsibility for their criminal acts and would not be released from an institution simply because a judge now ruled them sane.

DEFINING ABNORMAL BEHAVIOR

What is meant by abnormal behavior? Just being different is not sufficient cause to label a person abnormal. There is only one president of the United States at a given time, yet that person is not considered abnormal (usually). Only one person holds the record for running or swimming the fastest mile. That person is different from you and me, but he or she is not abnormal.

In order for someone's behavior to be labeled abnormal, someone else must be *disturbed* by it—perhaps the person showing the behavior, a family member, a police officer, or a psychologist. If nobody is disturbed by the behavior, nobody will bother to label it abnormal. Behavior that meets one or more of the following criteria is likely to be labeled abnormal:

1. *Infrequent behavior.* Although rarity or statistical deviance is not sufficient for behavior to be labeled abnormal, it helps. Highly anxious or depressed people are not likely to be considered abnormal in a society in which nearly everyone is anxious or depressed.
2. *Socially unacceptable behavior.* Each society has standards or norms for acceptable behavior in a given context. In our society, walking naked is normal in a locker room, but abnormal on a crowded boulevard. Similarly, what is abnormal for one generation can be normal for another. Smoking marijuana and living together without benefit of marriage were almost unheard of in the early 1960s, but scarcely raise an eyebrow today.

    What is normal in one society may be abnormal in another. Citizens of our society who assume that strangers will be hostile and try to take advantage may be considered overly suspicious, even **paranoid.** But among the Mundugumor, a cannibalistic tribe studied by the anthropologist Margaret Mead (1935), perpetual suspicion was justified. Strangers, even male members of the same household, *were* hostile.
3. *Faulty perception or interpretation of reality.* I've heard it said that it's all right to say that you talk to God through prayer, but if you say that God talks back, you may be committed to a mental institution. Our society considers it normal to be inspired by religious beliefs, but abnormal to believe that God is literally speaking to you. "Hearing voices" and "seeing things" are considered **hallucinations.** Similarly, **ideas of persecution,** such as believing that the mafia or the CIA or the communists are "out to get you"—all are considered abnormal. (Unless they *are* out to get you, of course.)
4. *Personal distress.* Anxiety, depression, exaggerated fears, and other psychological states cause personal distress and can be considered abnormal. But anxiety and depression may also be appropriate responses to one's situation, a real threat or a loss, for instance. In such cases they are not abnormal unless they persevere indefinitely, long after the source of distress has been removed, or after most people would have adjusted.
5. *Self-defeating behavior.* Behavior that leads to misery rather than happiness and fulfillment may be considered abnormal. From this perspective, chronic drinking and cigarette smoking may be labeled abnormal.
6. *Dangerous behavior.* Behavior that is dangerous to the self or others is

Paranoid Characterized by oversuspiciousness and delusions of grandeur or persecution. See *paranoia* and *delusions* in this chapter.

Hallucination A sensory experience in the absence of sensory stimulation. Confusion of imagined objects and events with reality.

Ideas of persecution Erroneous beliefs that one is being victimized or persecuted. See *delusion* in this chapter.

Demonology The belief that human behavior can come under the control of evil spirits, or demons.

considered abnormal. People who threaten or attempt suicide may be considered abnormal, as may people who threaten or attack others.

NORMAL VS. ABNORMAL: HISTORICAL AND CONTEMPORARY VIEWS

There are a number of historical and contemporary views or models of abnormal behavior. They include the demonological, medical, social-learning, cognitive, and sociocultural models. The organic and psychoanalytic models are offshoots of the medical model.

THE DEMONOLOGICAL MODEL

Some archaeologists make a living by digging into human history—literally. Among their findings: a number of human skeletons dating back to the Stone Age with egg-sized holes in the skull.

The holes are taken as evidence of early **demonology**—the belief that human behavior could come under the control of evil spirits. Our ancestors apparently developed the notion that abnormal behavior represented invasion by evil spirits and used the brutal method of breaking a pathway through the skull to let those irascible spirits out. Examination of these skeletons shows that some people actually survived the ordeal.

Was the practice successful? Well, most of the time it terminated the disturbing behavior. And the "patient." We also suspect that the threat of this treatment persuaded many people to do their best to conform to the norms of their tribe or group.

TREPHINING Our ancestors may have "air-conditioned" skulls in an effort to deal with abnormal behavior. The threat of trephining could certainly encourage conformity.

Anyone who has read Homer's *Iliad* or *Odyssey* also knows that the ancient Greeks considered their gods capable of controlling human behavior. The gods drew mortals into their own conflicts, inspiring them to war to kill off the pets of rival gods. On the positive side, the gods could inspire poetry and art. The gods were also credited with punishing humans by causing confusion and madness.

Hippocrates, the Greek physician of the Golden Age of art and literature (fourth century B.C.), made the radical suggestion that abnormal behavior was not the work of the gods at all. Rather, it was caused by an abnormality of the brain. This notion that bodily processes could affect thoughts, feelings, and behaviors was to lie dormant for about 2,000 years.

The Middle Ages   During the Middle Ages in Europe, and during the early days of American civilization along the rocky coast of Massachusetts, it was generally believed that abnormal behavior was a sign of **possession** by agents or spirits of the Devil. Possession could stem from **retribution,** or God's having the Devil possess your soul as punishment for sins. Wild agitation and confusion were attributed to retribution. Possession was also believed to result from deals with the Devil in which people traded their souls for earthly power or wealth. Such traders were called witches. Witches were held responsible for unfortunate events ranging from a neighbor's infertility to a poor crop.

In either case you were in for it. An **exorcist,** whose function was to persuade these spirits to find better pickings elsewhere, might pray at your side and wave a cross at you. If the spirits didn't call it quits, you might be beaten or flogged. If your behavior was still unseemly, there were other remedies, like the rack, which have powerful influences on behavior.

In 1484 Pope Innocent VIII ordered that witches be put to death. At least 200,000 accused witches were killed over the next two centuries. Europe was no place to practice strange ways. The goings-on at Salem were trivial by comparison.

There were ingenious "diagnostic" tests for ferreting out instances of possession. One involved dunking the suspect under water. Failure to drown was interpreted as support by the Devil—in other words, possession. Then you were in real trouble.

THE MEDICAL MODEL: ORGANIC AND PSYCHOANALYTIC VERSIONS

According to the **medical model,** abnormal behavior reflects an underlying illness, and not evil spirits. The organic model and the psychoanalytic model may be considered offshoots of the medical model.

Medical Model: Organic Version   In 1883 Emil Kraepelin published a textbook of psychiatry in which he elaborated the medical model. Kraepelin argued that there were specific forms of abnormal behavior, which, within the medical model, are often called mental illnesses. (See Table 11.1 for a list of many of the commonly used terms concerning abnormal be-

Possession According to superstitious belief, a psychological state induced by demons or the Devil in which a person exhibits abnormal behavior.

Retribution Deserved punishment for evildoing. (From the Latin *re-*, meaning "back," and *tribuere*, meaning "to pay." What is "tribute"?)

Exorcist (EX-or-sist). A person who drives away evil spirits through means like ritual prayers and beatings. (From the Greek *ex-*, meaning "out," and *horkizein*, meaning "to make one swear.")

Medical model The view that abnormal behavior is symptomatic of mental illness.

TABLE 11.1   Some Commonly Used Terms Concerning Abnormal Behavior that Are Derived from the Medical Model

Mental Illness	Mental Hospital
Mental Health	Prognosis
Symptoms	Treatment
Syndrome	Therapy
Diagnosis	Cure
Mental Patient	Relapse

Organic model The view that abnormal behavior is caused by biochemical or physiological abnormalities.

Syndrome A cluster or group of symptoms suggestive of a particular disorder. (From the Greek *syn-*, meaning "with," and *dramein*, meaning "to run.")

Neurotic Of neurosis (new-ROW-sis) or neuroses. The neuroses (new-ROW-seas) are disorders characterized chiefly by anxiety. Neuroses are theorized to stem from unconscious conflict. The term *neurosis* is not recommended in the DSM-III.

Psychosis (sigh-CO-sis). A major disorder in which a person lacks insight and has difficulty meeting the demands of daily life and maintaining contact with reality.

havior that reflect the widespread influence of the medical model.) Each mental illness had specific origins, which he assumed were physiological. The assumption that biochemical or physiological problems underlie mental illness is the heart of the **organic model.**

Kraepelin argued that each mental illness, just like each physical illness, was typified by its own cluster of symptoms, or **syndrome.** Each mental illness had a specific outcome, or course, and would presumably respond to a characteristic form of treatment, or therapy.

Contemporary supporters of the organic model point to various sources of evidence. For one thing, a number of mental disorders run in families, and may therefore be transmitted from generation to generation by way of DNA (see Chapter 2). For another, imbalances in neurotransmitters and other chemical substances produce behavioral effects similar to those found in disorders such as severe depression and schizophrenia, as we shall see later in the chapter.

According to the organic model, treatment requires biological expertise and involves controlling or curing the underlying organic problem. The biological therapies discussed in Chapter 12 are largely based on the organic model.

Medical Model: Psychoanalytic Version   Sigmund Freud's psychoanalytic model argues that abnormal behavior is symptomatic of an underlying psychological rather than biological disorder. Consistent with psychoanalytic theory, the underlying disorder is usually thought to be unconscious conflict of childhood origins. The abnormal behavior (or "symptoms") often reflect difficulty in repressing primitive sexual and aggressive impulses.

Within Freudian theory, **neurotic** behavior and the experiencing of anxiety stem from the leakage of primitive impulses. Anxiety represents the impulse itself and fear of what might happen if the impulse were acted upon. In the case of **psychosis,** impulses are assumed to have broken through; behavior falls largely under the control of the id, rather than the ego or superego.

According to psychoanalytic theory, treatment (other than a sort of "band-aid" therapy) requires resolving the unconscious conflicts that underlie the abnormal behavior. As you will see in Chapter 12, this can be a protracted process.

The medical model is a major advance over demonology. It led to the view that mentally ill people should be treated by qualified professionals rather than be punished. Compassion replaced hatred, fear, and persecution.

But there are some problems with the medical model. For instance, the model suggests that the mentally ill, like the physically ill, may not be responsible for their problems and limitations. In the past, this view often led to hospitalization and suspension of responsibility (as in work and maintenance of a family life) among the mentally ill. Thus removed from the real world, the ability of the mentally ill often underwent further declines, instead of returning to normal. But today even most adherents to the medical model encourage patients to remain in the community and maintain as much responsibility as they can.

THE SOCIAL-LEARNING MODEL

From a social-learning point of view, abnormal behavior is not necessarily symptomatic of anything. Rather, the abnormal behavior is itself the problem. Abnormal behavior is believed to be acquired in the same way normal behaviors are acquired—through conditioning and observational learning. Why, then, do some people show abnormal behavior? Because their learning or reinforcement histories differ from those of most of us.

A person who lacks social skills may never have had the chance to observe people who show them. Or it may be that a minority subculture reinforced behaviors that are not approved by the majority. Punishment for early exploratory behavior, or childhood sexual activity, may lead to anxiety concerning independence or sexuality in adulthood. Inconsistent discipline (haphazard rewarding of desirable behavior and unreliable punishing of misbehavior) may lead to antisocial behavior. Children whose parents ignore or abuse them may come to pay more attention to their fantasies than the outer world, leading to schizophrenic withdrawal and inability to tell reality from fantasy.

Since social-learning theorists do not believe that all abnormal behavior reflects physiological or unconscious problems, they generally feel free to change or modify it directly. In Chapter 12 we shall see that they generally prefer *behavior therapy* to biological therapy or psychotherapy.

THE COGNITIVE MODEL

Cognitive theorists focus on the cognitive events—such as thoughts, expectations, and attitudes—that accompany and in some cases underlie abnormal behavior. Information-processing theorists, for example, compare the processes of the mind to those of the computer, and think in terms of a cycle of input of information (based on perception), storing of information, and output (based on retrieval of stored information). Information-processing theorists view abnormal behavior as disturbance in the cycle, which can be caused by the blocking or distortion of input, by faulty storage, or by faulty retrieval of information. Schizophrenic individuals, for example, frequently jump from topic to topic in a disorganized fashion, which information-processing theorists may explain as problems in storage or retrieval of information.

Other cognitive theorists, like Albert Ellis (1977), view anxiety problems as frequently reflecting irrational beliefs and attitudes, such as perfectionism and overwhelming desires for social approval (see Chapter 10). Cognitive psychiatrist Aaron Beck attributes many cases of depression to "cognitive errors" such as self-devaluation, interpretation of events in a negative light, and general pessimism (Beck et al., 1979). Some cognitive psychologists, as we shall see, attribute many cases of depression to cognitions to the effect that one is helpless to change things for the better.

Social-learning theorists like Albert Bandura straddle the borderline between the behavioral and the cognitive. They note the important role of the principles of learning in abnormal as well as normal behavior patterns, but place primary importance on our expectations (see Chapter 9). Bandura suggests, for example, that expectations that we will not be able to carry out our plans can lead to inactivity and feelings of hopelessness, two aspects of depression (1982).

THE SOCIOCULTURAL MODEL

According to British psychiatrist R. D. Laing's **sociocultural model,** abnormal behavior is a form of adjustment to an unjust society. Poverty, discrimination, and other social ills cause abnormal behavior. The schizophrenic flight into fantasy is a heroic act of defiance, not a sign of illness.

Sociocultural theorists argue that the "cure" to mental illness lies in changing society, not the person. They support their contention by pointing to evidence that mental illness is most common among the underprivileged. But we must note that low socioeconomic status is often a **consequence** rather than an **antecedent** of abnormal behavior.

Many psychologists look to more than one model to explain and treat abnormal behavior. They are considered **eclectic.** For example, many social-learning theorists believe that some, though not all, abnormal behavior patterns stem from biochemical factors or an interplay of biochemistry and learning. These eclectics are open to combining behavior therapy with drugs to treat problems such as schizophrenic and **bipolar disorders.** A psychoanalyst may also be eclectic. He or she may believe that a schizophrenic's disorganization represents control of the personality by the id rather than the ego and argue that only long-term psychoanalytic therapy can help the ego achieve permanent supremacy. But the psychoanalyst may still be willing to use drugs to calm agitation on a short-term basis.

We shall return to models for understanding abnormal behavior as we discuss the major categories of abnormal behavior. But first let us explore some issues in classifying abnormal behaviors.

CLASSIFYING ABNORMAL BEHAVIOR

Toss some people, chimpanzees, seaweed, a few fish, and sponges into a room—preferably a well-ventilated room. Stir slightly. What do you have? It depends on how you classify this conglomeration.

Classify them as plants versus animals and you lump the people, chimps, fish, and, yes, sponges together. Classify them as stuff that carries on its business on dry land rather than underwater, and we throw in our lots with only the chimps. How about those that swim and those that don't? Then the chimps, the fish, and some of us are lumped together.

The way we classify things reflects the variables that we consider important. The most widely used classification scheme for abnormal behavior patterns is the third edition of the *Diagnostic and Statistical Manual* of the American Psychiatric Association (the DSM–III), published in 1980. The DSM–III groups abnormal behavior patterns on the basis of observable common features, which seems logical enough. However, the medical model was widely adopted by the authors of previous editions of the DSM, and the medical model led the authors to lump some things together quite differently. One consequence was the category of the "neuroses." I mention

TABLE 11.2   Former and Current Labels for Some Classes of Abnormal Behaviors

DSM–II (1968)	DSM–III (1980)
Phobic neurosis	Phobic disorder
Anxiety neurosis	Generalized anxiety disorder
Obsessive-compulsive neurosis	Obsessive-compulsive disorder
Hysterical neurosis, dissociative type	Dissociative disorder
Hysterical neurosis, conversion type	Conversion disorder
Hypochondriacal neurosis	Hypochondriasis
Depressive neurosis	Dysthymic disorder

The DSM–III de-emphasizes the concept of neurosis. As compared to the DSM–II, the DSM–III makes a greater effort to tie diagnostic categories to observable behavior.

this because the terms *neurosis* and *neurotic* remain familiar in our culture at large, and, without some explanation, it might seem strange that the terms are no longer used in the major classification system of abnormal behavior. Neuroses were grouped together not on the basis of observable common features, but because of theoretical speculation that they had common origins. From Freud's psychoanalytic view, all neuroses—no matter how different the behavior patterns associated with them—stemmed from unconscious neurotic conflict. Each pattern of neurotic behavior was theorized to reflect a way of coping with unconscious fear that primitive impulses might break loose.

The DSM–III de-emphasizes neurosis, because the authors believed that the concept had outlived its usefulness (Millon, 1983). The presence of unconscious conflict is not an observable common feature; rather it is an unobservable speculation. Therefore, in the DSM–III, some former neuroses are eliminated, and alternate names for others are recommended, as shown in Table 11.2.

As compared to the DSM–II, The DSM–III also specifies more precisely when a certain diagnosis should be made. These changes have enhanced **diagnostic reliability.**

A diagnosis is reliable if it is made consistently in a given case. Studies of the reliability of diagnoses made on the basis of an earlier version of the DSM were disappointing. The percentage of agreement between a pair of psychiatrists, for example, was 53 percent for the diagnosis of schizophrenia, and ranged from 38 to 63 percent for various **affective disorders** (Beck et al., 1962). The DSM–III has clarified diagnostic features for schizophrenia and has made major changes in the area of the affective disorders. One result: a pilot study of the reliability of diagnoses made on the basis of the DSM–III found an agreement rate of 81 percent for schizophrenic disorders and 83 percent for affective disorders (Spitzer et al., 1979).

Despite these improvements over earlier versions, psychologists in general still regard the DSM–III to have a distinct medical flavor (Smith & Kraft, 1983). But the DSM–III is the major classification system in the United States, and we shall refer to it frequently in our discussion of the various patterns of abnormal behavior.

Diagnostic reliability The consistency of a diagnosis in a given case.

Affective disorders Disorders characterized primarily by prolonged disturbances of mood or emotional response. (From the Latin *ad-*, meaning "to," and *facere*, meaning "to do" in the sense of "to influence.")

ANXIETY Anxiety is characterized by nervousness, fears, feelings of dread and foreboding, and physical signs such as rapid heartbeat and sweating.

Phobic disorder (FOE-bick). Excessive, irrational fear. Fear that is out of proportion to the actual danger. Also called *phobia*. (From the Greek *phobos*, meaning "fear.")

Agoraphobia (AG-or-uh-FOE-bee-uh). Fear of open, crowded places. (From the Greek *agora*, meaning "marketplace" or "place of assembly.")

Claustrophobia (claws-tro-FOE-bee-uh). Fear of tight, small places. (From the Latin *claustrum*, meaning "box.")

Acrophobia (ack-row-FOE-bee-uh). Fear of high places. (From the Greek *akros*, meaning "top.")

Social phobias Irrational fears that involve themes of public scrutiny.

ANXIETY DISORDERS

Anxiety disorders are characterized by nervousness, fears, feelings of dread and foreboding, and signs of sympathetic overarousal that include rapid heartbeat, muscle tension, and shakiness. Let us consider four anxiety disorders: phobic, panic, generalized anxiety, and obsessive-compulsive disorders.

PHOBIC DISORDER

Phobic disorders, or *phobias,* are excessive, irrational fears of objects, situations, or activities. Some people have phobias for elevators and will not enter them. Yes, the cable *could* break. The ventilation *could* fail. One *could* be stuck in midair waiting for repairs. But these problems are infrequent, and it would be foolhardy to walk forty flights of stairs twice daily to avoid them. Similarly, some people with phobias for needles will not receive injections, even when they are the recommended treatment for serious illness. Injections can be painful, but most people with phobias for needles would gladly suffer a pinch that would cause still greater pain if it would help them fight illness.

Phobias may seriously interfere with one's life. A person may know that a phobia is irrational, yet still experience it. Although it could be argued that phobias involve faulty perception of the feared object, phobic people are not considered psychotic. The person's "irrationality" is usually limited to the phobic object.

Fears of animals and imaginary creatures are common among children, and **agoraphobia** is among the most widespread phobias of adults (Mahoney, 1980). Agoraphobia is derived from the Greek meaning "fear of the marketplace," or of being out in open, busy areas. In actual practice, however, people who receive this label are usually afraid of venturing out of their homes at all, especially when they are alone. They find it difficult or impossible to hold jobs or to carry out a normal social life.

Just a partial list of fairly familiar phobias includes **claustrophobia** (fear of tight or enclosed places), **acrophobia** (fear of heights), and fear of mice, snakes, and other creepy-crawlies. Stage fright and speech anxiety are examples of **social phobias,** in which people have an excessive fear of public scrutiny. Table 11.3 lists some phobias that may be less familiar. You could ask your professor whether memorizing them will earn you an A for achievement in this chapter—unless you have *erythrophobia*. Out of consideration for students with *triskedekaphobia*, only twelve phobias are listed.

Theoretical Views of Phobias   Since phobias tend to involve fears of specific objects and situations, theorists generally look to psychological explanations. For example, it doesn't seem to make sense that some people would inherit a tendency to fear specific objects.

Psychoanalytic theory theorizes that phobias symbolize unconscious conflicts of childhood origins. In Chapter 9 we saw that "Little Hans" was believed to have developed a phobia for horses as a result of the Oedipus complex.

TABLE 11.3 Some Exotic Species from the Museum of Phobias

Name of Phobia	Definition
Ailurophobia	Fear of cats
Arachibutyrophobia	Fear of peanut butter sticking to the roof of your mouth
Belonophobia	Fear of pins and needles
Ergasiophobia	Fear of writing
Erythrophobia	Fear of blushing
Gephydrophobia	Fear of crossing bridges
Ophidiophobia	Fear of snakes
Pnigophobia	Fear of choking
Siderodromophobia	Fear of railways
Taphophobia	Fear of being buried alive
Triskedekaphobia	Fear of the number 13
Pantaphobia	Fear of—you guessed it—everything

From the behaviorist perspective, as we saw in Chapter 5's discussion of the story of "Little Albert," phobias are conditioned fears whose origins may also stem from early childhood and be beyond memory. Avoidance of the dreaded objects or situations is reinforced by reduction of anxiety.

Social-learning theorist Albert Bandura also points out that we can acquire intense fears by observational learning. If parents squirm, grimace, shudder, and squeal at mice, dogs, blood, or dirt on the kitchen floor, young observers may acquire the tendency to do likewise. In an experiment on the observational learning of fear, Bandura and Rosenthal (1969) hooked up a confederate to a frightening array of electrical equipment. As real subjects looked on, a buzzer was sounded. The confederate's arm shot up from the chair, as if in response to shock. But this was all an Academy Award performance because no shock was given. Still, after watching a number of repetitions, the observers began to show a high level of arousal in response to the buzzer, even though they were in no personal danger of being shocked. This high level of arousal would presumably be interpreted by them as fear and could also motivate them to avoid the sound of the buzzer.

Cognitive theorists note that when fears are acquired at a young age, for whatever reason, we may later interpret them as parts of our personalities and assume that they will always be with us. We label ourselves as "people who fear (you fill it in)" and live up to the labels. Psychologists Donald Meichenbaum (1977; Meichenbaum & Jaemko, 1983) and Michael Mahoney (1974) also point out that phobic people say things to themselves that tend to perpetuate their fears when they are faced with the dreaded objects or situations. Examples include "I've got to get out of here!"; "Oh my God, it's going to be awful!"; and "I know I'll just drop dead!" Thoughts like these raise arousal further, interfere with organized thinking, contribute to the aversiveness of the object, and help motivate avoidance behavior.

Albert Bandura and his colleagues (Bandura, 1981; Bandura et al., 1982) have also shown that the belief that we shall not be able to handle a potentially painful event heightens fear. When we believe that we shall

Panic disorder The recurrent experiencing of attacks of extreme anxiety in the absence of external stimuli that usually elicit anxiety.

Generalized anxiety disorder Feelings of dread and foreboding and sympathetic arousal of at least one month's duration.

not be able to cope with a threat, we tend to become preoccupied with it and to magnify the danger. On the other hand, belief that we can cope or that we can control threatening events lessens our fear of them (Miller, 1980).

PANIC DISORDER

Panic is a sudden attack in which people typically fear that they may be losing control or going crazy. They also experience heavy sweating, trembling, and pounding of the heart (Anderson et al., 1984; Barlow et al., 1985; Norton et al., 1985). Panic seems to differ qualitatively from other kinds of anxiety disorders, in part because there is a stronger bodily component to the anxiety experienced by people with panic disorder (Barlow et al., 1985). Panic attacks may last from a minute or two to an hour or more, and afterwards victims usually feel exhausted.

Many of us—40 to 50 percent—experience panic attacks now and then (Norton & Rhodes, 1983), but the DSM–III uses the diagnosis of **panic disorder** when there have been at least three panic attacks in a three-week period. When we use this criterion, panic disorders affect only about 1 percent of the population (Meyers et al., 1984).

In contrast to the phobic disorder, there is no clear stimulus for panic disorders. They seem to descend from nowhere. Because of this unpredictability, some panic sufferers remain in the home most of the time, for fear that they could succumb to an attack in public. Given the apparent independence of attacks from external events, researchers are investigating possible organic causes for panic disorder. One possibility is that people who suffer panic attacks have overly sensitive chemical receptors in the brain that trigger attacks in response to blood levels of lactic acid and carbon dioxide that do not disturb others (Fishman & Sheehan, 1985). Another hypothesis focuses on the brain metabolism of neurotransmitters.

GENERALIZED ANXIETY DISORDER

The central feature of **generalized anxiety disorder** is persistent anxiety of at least one month's duration. As in the panic disorder, the anxiety cannot be attributed to a phobic object, situation, or activity. Rather, it seems free-floating. Symptoms may include motor tension (shakiness, inability to relax, furrowed brow, fidgeting, etc.); autonomic overarousal (sweating, dry mouth, racing heart, light-headedness, frequent urinating, diarrhea, etc.); feelings of dread and foreboding; and excessive vigilance, as shown by distractibility, insomnia, and irritability.

Psychoanalytic theory explains generalized anxiety as persistent difficulty in maintaining repression of primitive impulses. Social-learning theorists suggest that generalized anxiety is often nothing more than fear that has been associated with situations so broad that they are not readily identified—for instance, social relationships or personal achievement. Social-learning and cognitive theorists argue that generalized anxiety, like phobias, can be maintained by thinking that one is in a terrible situation and is helpless to change it.

There is some evidence that there may be a partial organic basis for persistent anxiety. For example, Sandra Scarr and her colleagues (1981) gave a battery of tests to adolescents and their parents in biologically related and adoptive families and found that **neuroticism** scores of parents and natural children correlated more highly than those of parents and adoptees. Thus it is possible that a predisposition toward generalized anxiety—perhaps in the form of a highly reactive autonomic nervous system—may be inherited.

OBSESSIVE-COMPULSIVE DISORDER

An **obsession** is a recurring thought or image that seems irrational and beyond control. Obsessions are so strong and frequent that they interfere with daily life. They may include doubts as to whether one has locked the doors and shut the windows; impulses, such as the wish to strangle one's spouse; and images, such as one mother's recurrent fantasy that her children had been run over by traffic on the way home from school. In other cases, a sixteen-year-old boy found "numbers in my head" whenever he was about to study or take a test. A housewife became obsessed with the notion that she had contaminated her hands with Sani-Flush and that the contamination was spreading to everything she touched.

A **compulsion** is a seemingly irresistible urge to engage in an act, often repeatedly, such as lengthy, elaborate washing after using the bathroom. The impulse is frequent and forceful, interfering with daily life. Some men, called *exhibitionists,* report experiencing the compulsion to expose their genitals to women strangers. The woman who felt contaminated by Sani-Flush engaged in elaborate hand-washing rituals. She spent three to four hours daily at the sink and complained, "My hands look like lobster claws."

Psychoanalysts and social-learning theorists broadly agree that compulsive behavior reduces anxiety. But psychoanalysts view obsessions as the leakage of unconscious impulses, and compulsions as acts that allow people to keep such impulses partly repressed. Social-learning theorists focus on how obsessions and compulsions themselves may allow the person to avoid a feared or unwanted event. Social-learning theorists also suggest that some obsessions or compulsions may be repeated because they have been reinforced.

The nearby box on workaholism describes one obsessive-compulsive behavior pattern that may actually make a major positive contribution to American productivity: "workaholism." Psychologists are divided on whether workaholism should be considered a disorder. In many cases, workaholism contributes to success in one's field, rather than impairing performance, although, as noted by Marilyn Machlowitz, workaholism can be hard on the people in the workaholic's personal life.

DISSOCIATIVE DISORDERS

The DSM–III lists three major **dissociative disorders:** *psychogenic amnesia, psychogenic fugue,* and *multiple personality.* In each case there is a sudden, temporary change in consciousness or self-identity.

Neuroticism A personality trait characterized largely by persistent anxiety.

Obsession A recurring thought or image that seems beyond control. (From the Latin *ob-,* meaning "toward," and *sedere,* meaning "to sit"—which refers to the ancient notion that such thoughts reflected demons "sitting on" or possessing a person.)

Compulsion An apparently irresistible urge to repeat an act or engage in ritualistic behavior, like hand-washing.

Dissociative disorders Disorders in which there are sudden, temporary changes in consciousness or self-identity.

THE WORK JUNKIES

One obsessive-compulsive behavior pattern may be abnormal in the sense that most of us do not fall prey to it, and in that it is frequently distressful to one's spouse and children. However, it is usually prized by one's supervisors at work. It is called workaholism.

When Marilyn Machlowitz was twenty-four years old, she tried to take a vacation. Packing up her sexiest sun dress and a new maillot, she headed for Martinique's Club *Meditérrané*—a holiday camp that pursues hedonism. But once on the beach, she realized something was wrong. Around her, Club Med voluptuaries laughed and flirted, frollicked and romped, while Machlowitz, an attractive brunette, checked statistics from a computer print-out. Odder still, she was having a wonderful time.

Machlowitz is a workaholic. The print-out was one step toward a Yale Ph.D. dissertation that has finally put workaholism on the academic map. "To date, alienated workers have received most of the scholarly attention," explains Machlowitz. "I thought we could learn about work from people who like it, too."

That's putting things mildly. Workaholics don't just like to work; they *live* to work. At stake, say mental-health experts, is a self-esteem based on meeting purely self-imposed standards. When a workaholic has paid the mortgage or conquered a deadline, he or she creates new excuses for nonstop toil. Mental-health workers who recognize workaholism as a syndrome are divided on its significance. Some cite the workaholic's damaging neglect of their families, while others rue the shakiness of their egos. Still others deplore hard-core workaholics as burnt-out drones who drive their subordinates crazy with incessant demands. But to Machlowitz, workaholics are neither good nor bad—simply "frustrated or fulfilled."

Mental-health workers view workaholics as obsessive-compulsives who dread inactivity. The universal worry of workaholics, according to Machlowitz, is lack of time. Even as youngsters they are afraid of wasting it and literally never learn to play. Instead of chasing butterflies or collecting baseball cards, they sell vegetables from Mommy's garden and run penny-pitch games. While some adult workaholics may be bullied into vacations, which often turn into tightly scheduled frenzies of tennis or sightseeing, the true workaholic shuns even Sundays away from the job. Machlowitz found that all workaholics cited work as a key factor in broken marriages, a conclusion that makes her wonder if workaholics might be best off wed to each other.

But for all their rushing around, and potential family conflict, Machlowitz found that workaholics, as a group, were generally happy, well-adjusted, and satisfied with their lives. Two factors that contributed to their adjustment were meaningful work and the support of family members.

Workaholics are among the world's most productive people—so what's so awful about being one? Expert opinion differs. Machlowitz is troubled by the emotional cost to their children. To Dr. Clinto Weiman, medical director of Citibank, the real victim may be the work junkie himself or herself, who sometimes pays in high blood pressure, ulcers, and migraines. Yet the corporations Machlowitz called to check on specific measures for aiding workaholics all replied incredulously, "Where can we find more of them?"

PSYCHOGENIC AMNESIA

In **psychogenic amnesia,** important personal information cannot be recalled. The memory problem cannot be attributed to organic problems, such as a blow to the head or alcoholic intoxication. Thus it is *psycho*genic. The person may not be able to recall events for a number of hours after a stressful incident, as during warfare or in the case of the uninjured survivor of an accident. In generalized amnesia, people forget their entire lives. Amnesia may last for hours or years. Termination of amnesia is also sudden.

Bower (1981) wrote that Sirhan Sirhan, the assassin of Robert Kennedy, was amnesiac for his crime and could only reconstruct the events of the fateful day during hypnosis. As noted many times in this book, we cannot enter the mind of another person, and must therefore evaluate their

---

Psychogenic amnesia A dissociative disorder marked by loss of memory of self-identity. Skills and general knowledge are usually retained.

claims—like Sirhan's claim of amnesia—on the basis of other evidence, such as behavioral observations and records of past behavior. People may claim amnesia for crimes, in the hope that they will be treated as ill or insane, rather than as criminal.

Claiming to have a disease in order to escape responsibility is known as **malingering.** Current research methods cannot guarantee that we can distinguish malingerers from people who have dissociative disorders.

Malingering Pretending to be ill in order to escape duty or work. (From a French word meaning "sickly.")

Psychogenic fugue (fyoog). A dissociative disorder in which one experiences amnesia, then flees to a new location and establishes a new life style. (From the Latin *fugere,* meaning "to flee.")

PSYCHOGENIC FUGUE

In **psychogenic fugue,** the person shows loss of memory for the past, travels suddenly from his or her home or place of work, and assumes a new identity. Either the person does not think about the past, or reports a past filled with bogus memories that are not recognized as false.

MULTIPLE PERSONALITY

Multiple personality is the name given the fascinating disorder described in the case of William (p. 500). Several "personalities," each with distinct traits and memories, "occupy" the same person, with or without awareness of the others. In the celebrated case that became the subject of the film *The Three Faces of Eve,* a timid housewife named Eve White harbored two other personalities: Eve Black, a sexually aggressive, antisocial personality, and Jane, an emerging personality who was able to accept the existence of her primitive impulses, yet show socially appropriate behavior. Finally, the three faces merged into one: Jane. Ironically, Jane (Chris Sizemore, in real life) reportedly split into twenty-two personalities later on. Chris Sizemore now tours college campuses, discussing her past. Another publicized case is that of Sybil, a woman with sixteen personalities, played by Sally Field in a recent film.

THEORIES OF THE DISSOCIATIVE DISORDERS

Psychoanalytic Theory   According to psychoanalytic theory, dissociative disorders involve massive use of repression (see Chapter 10) to prevent recognition of unacceptable impulses. In psychogenic amnesia and fugue, the person forgets a profoundly disturbing event or impulse. In multiple personality, people express unacceptable impulses through alternate personalities.

Social-Learning Theory   Social-learning theorists generally regard dissociative disorders as conditions in which people learn *not to think* about disturbing acts or impulses in order to avoid feelings of guilt and shame. Technically speaking, *not thinking about these matters* is negatively reinforced by *removal* of aversive stimuli—guilt and shame.

A related perspective suggests that many people who claim to have multiple personality can roleplay people with the disorder through observational learning. There are various things to be gained by roleplaying in-

MULTIPLE PERSONALITY. In the film *The Three Faces of Eve,* Joanne Woodward played three personalities in the same woman: the shy, inhibited Eve White (lying on couch); the flirtatious and promiscuous Eve Black (in dark dress); and a third personality ("Jane") who was healthy enough to accept her sexual and aggressive impulses and still maintain her sense of identity.

dividuals with multiple personality, such as drawing attention to themselves or escaping responsibility for criminal or other socially unacceptable behavior (Spanos et al., 1985; Thigpen & Cleckley, 1984). According to Nicholas Spanos and his colleagues (1985), movies and television shows such as *The Three Faces of Eve* and *Sybil* have made the "major components" of the multiple personality well-known, and have "provided detailed examples of the symptoms and course of multiple personality" (p. 363). I have seen "mini-epidemics" of claimed multiple personality on psychiatric wards when patients have been confronted with socially unacceptable behavior and found out that others were attributing such behavior to other personalities dwelling within them. Such evidence does not mean that there is no such thing as multiple personality; however, it does suggest that a number of individuals do attempt to escape responsibility by attributing misbehavior to forces beyond their control.

Cognitive Theory   From a cognitive perspective, the dissociative disorders may be explained in terms of where one focuses attention at a given time. Consider dissociative disorders from the perspectives of the role-playing and neodissociative theories of hypnosis, discussed in Chapter 4. Perhaps all of us are capable of acting "as if" something had not happened, or "as if" we were someone else. Perhaps all of us are capable of dividing our awareness so that we become unaware, at least temporarily, of events that we usually focus more attention on. As suggested in Chapter 4, perhaps the marvel is *not* that attention can be divided, but that human consciousness normally integrates experience into a meaningful whole.

Somatoform disorders (so-MAT-toe-form). Disorders in which people complain of physical (somatic) problems, although no physical abnormality can be found.

Conversion disorder A disorder in which anxiety or unconscious conflicts are "converted" into physical symptoms that often have the effect of helping the person cope with anxiety or conflict.

SOMATOFORM DISORDERS

In **somatoform disorders,** people show or complain of physical problems, like paralysis, pain, or the persistent belief that they have a serious disease, yet no evidence of a physical abnormality can be found. In this section we shall discuss two somatoform disorders: *conversion disorder,* and *hypochondriasis.*

CONVERSION DISORDER

Conversion disorder is characterized by a major change in or loss of physical functioning, although there are no medical findings to support the loss of functioning.

If you lost the ability to see at night, or if your legs became paralyzed, you would show understandable concern. But some victims of conversion

PSYCHOLOGY AND HEALTH

WHAT, ME HYSTERICAL?
A BIT OF ANCIENT (AND ALL-TOO-CONTEMPORARY) SEXISM

Conversion disorders were previously called *hysterical conversion reactions.* "Hysterical" or highly emotional, irrational people were thought likely to develop physical complaints as a result of stress. In an example of ancient sexism, such problems were apparently believed to be the exclusive province of women.

The Ancient Belief in the Wandering Uterus *Hysterical* derives from the Greek word *hystera,* meaning "uterus" or "womb." The ancient Greeks viewed irritability and tension as female traits because some women had difficulties prior to and during menstruation (see Chapter 2). They attributed these problems to a wandering uterus! As the uterus roamed the body, they argued, it would cause pain and sensations in odd places. Men would never complain of such nonsense.

Of course, the Greeks had not met male pilots suffering from conversion blindness during World War II.

And Today . . . Unfortunately, many women today still find that legitimate physical complaints just prior to and during menstruation are treated as "hysterical" by a predominantly male medical establishment. We now know that hormonal changes that occur at various stages of a woman's menstrual cycle can cause many painful problems, and that these problems can often be alleviated if they receive proper treatment.

The DSM–III warns that even when the professional believes that a complaint reflects a conversion disorder or hypochondriasis, every effort should be made to rule out a physical problem. A middle-aged woman with a "lump in the throat" was referred for psychological treatment because her physician thought that the problem was "hysterical." The psychologist arranged for additional medical workup, and a tumor was discovered. Physical complaints are not to be taken lightly.

La belle indifférence (lah bell an-DEEF-fay-ronce). A French term descriptive of the lack of concern sometimes shown by people with conversion disorders.

Hypochondriasis (high-poe-con-DRY-uh-sis). Persistent belief that one has a medical disorder despite lack of medical findings. (From a Greek word meaning "the soft areas of the body below the breastbone"—where anxious people often feel a sense of "heaviness.")

disorder show indifference to their symptoms, a remarkable feature referred to as **la belle indifférence.** Conversion disorder is so named because it appears to "convert" a source of stress into a physical problem. Instances are rare and of short duration, but their existence led the young Sigmund Freud to believe that subconscious processes were at work in people, as discussed in Chapters 4 and 9.

During World War II a number of bomber pilots developed night blindness. They could not carry out their nighttime missions, although no damage to the optic nerves was found. In rare cases, women with large families have been reported to become paralyzed in the legs, again with no medical findings.

Conversion disorder, like dissociative disorders, seems to serve a purpose. The "blindness" of the pilots may have afforded them temporary relief from stressful missions, or allowed them to avoid the guilt of bombing civilian populations. The paralysis of a woman who prematurely commits herself to a large family and a life at home may prevent her from doing housework or from engaging in sexual intercourse and becoming pregnant again. She "accomplishes" certain ends without having to recognize them or make decisions.

HYPOCHONDRIASIS

Persons with **hypochondriasis,** believe that they are suffering from one or a host of serious diseases, although no medical evidence can be found. Sufferers often become preoccupied with minor physical sensations, and maintain an unrealistic belief that something is wrong despite medical reassurance. "Hypochondriacs" may go from doctor to doctor, seeking the one who will find the causes of the sensations. The persistent fear may impair work or home life.

Hypochondriasis is supposed to be found more often among elderly people. However, as pointed out by Paul Costa and Robert McCrae (1985) of the National Institute on Aging, real health changes tend to occur with age, and most complaints are probably accurate reflections of people's changing health status.

There is also evidence that some hypochondriacs use their complaints as a self-handicapping strategy (Smith et al., 1983). That is, they are more likely to complain of feeling ill in situations in which illness can serve as an excuse for poor performance. In other cases, focusing on physical sensations and possible problems may serve the function of taking the person's mind off other life problems. However, every effort should be made to uncover real medical problems. Now and then a supposed hypochondriac dies from something all too real.

AFFECTIVE DISORDERS

The affective disorders are characterized by disturbance in expressed emotions. The disturbance generally involves depression or elation. We shall discuss three affective disorders: *dysthymic disorder, major depression,* and *bipolar disorder.*

DYSTHYMIC DISORDER

Depression is the "common cold" of psychological problems, according to Seligman (1973)—the most common psychological problem we face. Depressed people may feel sad, blue, or "down in the dumps." They may complain of lack of energy, loss of self-esteem, difficulty concentrating, loss of interest in other people and usually enjoyable activities, pessimism, crying, and thoughts of suicide.

The DSM–III diagnoses depression as **dysthymic disorder** when it persists for two years, even if intermittently relieved by normal moods, and when the individual, although distressed, remains capable of meeting most of the demands of daily life. We shall explore why depression may linger in some, when the rest of us seem to "snap back" from adversity, in the section on theories of depression.

MAJOR DEPRESSIVE EPISODE

To a large extent, the difference between dysthymic disorder and **major depression** is a matter of degree. In addition to the types of symptoms that define dysthymic disorder, people with major depression may show poor appetite and significant weight loss, agitation or severe **psychomotor retardation,** complaints of just "not caring" about anything anymore, and recurrent thoughts of death or suicide attempts.

Persons with major depression may also show impaired reality testing, or psychotic symptoms. These include delusions of unworthiness, guilt for imagined great wrongdoings, even ideas that one is rotting away from disease. There may also be hallucinations, as of the Devil administering just punishment or of strange sensations in the body.

THEORIES OF DEPRESSION

The causes of brief, "garden variety" depression are frequently situational. Depression is a normal reaction to a loss or to exposure to unpleasant events. Negative life events such as marital discord, physical discomfort, incompetence, failure at work, and pressure at work all contribute to feelings of depression (Eckenrode, 1984; Lewinsohn & Amenson, 1978; Stone & Neale, 1984). We are most likely to be depressed by undesirable events for which we feel responsible, such as academic problems and dropping out of school; financial problems; unwanted pregnancy; social problems, arguments, and fights; and conflict with the law (Hammen & Mayol, 1982). But many people recover from losses less readily than the rest of us. When compared to nondepressed people, depressed individuals are less likely to use problem-solving to alleviate the stresses acting upon them, and they have fewer supportive relationships to draw upon (Billings et al., 1983; Nezu & Ronan, 1985).

But let us now consider theories of lingering and major depression.

Psychoanalytic Views   Psychoanalysts suggest various explanations for depression. In one, depressed people are overly concerned about hurting

Dysthymic disorder (dis-THIGH-mick). Feelings of depression that persist for at least two years. Also referred to as *depressive neurosis.*

Major depression A depressive disorder more severe than dysthymic disorder in which the person may show loss of appetite, psychomotor symptoms, and impaired reality testing.

Psychomotor retardation Slowness in motor activity and (apparently) in thought.

Learned helplessness Seligman's model for the acquisition of depressive behavior, based on findings that organisms in aversive situations learn to show inactivity when their operants are not reinforced.

others' feelings or losing their approval. They hold in rather than express feelings of anger. This anger-turned-inward is experienced as misery and self-hatred.

Social-Learning Views   Social-learning theorists note similarities in behavior between people who are depressed and laboratory animals who are not reinforced for instrumental behavior. Inactivity and loss of interest result in each. Lewinsohn (1975) theorizes that depressed people often lack social and other skills that might lead to rewards. Some depressed people are nonassertive (Gotlib, 1984); others do have the social skills of nondepressed people, but they do not reinforce (credit) themselves as much as nondepressed people do for showing these skills (Gotlib, 1982). In any event, research by Michel Hersen and his colleagues (1984) suggests that social-skills training can ameliorate feelings of depression in many individuals.

Depression and Learned Helplessness   Research stimulated by psychologist Martin Seligman and his colleagues has explored the links between depression and **learned helplessness.** In an early study, Seligman (1975) taught dogs that they were helpless to escape an electric shock by preventing them from leaving a cage in which they were shocked repeatedly. Later a barrier to a safe compartment was removed, allowing the animals a way out. But then when they were shocked again, the dogs made no effort to escape to safety. Apparently they had learned that they were helpless.

It can also be noted that the dogs were, in a sense, reinforced for doing nothing in this experiment. That is, the shock *eventually* stopped when the dogs were showing helpless behavior—inactivity and withdrawal. Thus they would have become likely to repeat their "successful behavior"— that is, doing nothing—in a similar situation. This helpless behavior resembles that of depressed people.

Cognitive Factors in Depression   "Perfectionists" set themselves up for depression through their irrational self-demands. They are more likely than nondepressed people to fall short of their (unrealistic) expectations— that is, to fail and, as a consequence, to feel depressed (Vestre, 1984). Depressed people also tend to have negatively distorted self-images. Depressed people, for example, are less likely than nondepressed people to be satisfied with their bodies, and they see themselves as less physically attractive—even when they do not differ in their physical attractiveness from nondepressed people (Noles et al., 1985). Feelings of unattractiveness contribute to unhappiness.

Our psychological well-being is reduced by focusing on the negative outcomes of stressful events (Goodhart, 1985). Depressed people tend to respond to stressful events and interpret their shortcomings and failures in particularly negative ways (Cochran & Hammen, 1985; Hammen et al., 1985; Persons & Rao, 1985). For example, depressed people tend to attribute their failures and shortcomings to factors that they are helpless to change.

Seligman and his colleagues note that when things go wrong, we may attribute the causes of failure to *internal* or *external, stable* or *unstable, global* or *specific* factors.

Let us explain these various attributional styles through the example of having a date that does not work out. An internal attribution involves self-blame, as in "I really loused it up," whereas an external attribution places the blame elsewhere (as in "Some couples just don't take to each other," or, "She was the wrong sign for me"). A stable attribution ("It's my

A CLOSER LOOK
HEADLINE: "RATS TAKE DIVE!"
SOME NOTES ON FIGHT-FIXING AT UCLA

They didn't sell popcorn. They didn't sell beer. But on the floor of the straw-covered arena, UCLA psychologist Gaylord Ellison's (1977) rats held wrestling match after match to determine who would be the champion—Numero Uno. For this is the way rats determine the pecking order of the colony. The winners earn the privileges of eating first and choosing mates first.

One after another, rats in Ellison's experimental colonies paired off. First they would "stand and box." Then they would wrestle until one rat had been pinned to the ground. All this is normal rat behavior.

But this time Ellison was quite certain as to who the winners and losers would be. He had fixed the fights.

How? Ellison had injected some of the rats with a substance that depleted the amount of norepinephrine available to their brains. The results? The "fixed" rats lost every match. They also showed behavior characteristic of depressed people. They appeared apathetic

and withdrawn. They lay around listlessly in their burrows. Their appetites decreased and they lost weight.

Somehow the "depressed" rats were also socially disruptive. In one of Ellison's colonies, rats were given free access to water or alcohol solutions. Rats with lowered norepinephrine levels drank more water than alcohol. However, their colony-mates drank three times the amount of alcohol drunk by rats who did not have to live with norepinephrine-depleted rats.

Ellison's results may lead us to wonder whether living with someone who is depressed may eventually drive us to drink. We have no direct answer to this question; however, a study carried out at Florida State University over a three-month period found that living with a depressed roommate can lower our own moods, as measured by a standard psychological test of depression (Howes et al., 1985).

Stand and box   Top dog

personality") suggests a problem that cannot be changed, while an unstable attribution ("It was the head cold") suggests a temporary condition. A global attribution of failure ("I have no idea what to do when I'm with people") suggests that the problem is quite large. A specific attribution ("I have problems making small talk at the very outset of a relationship") chops the problem down to a manageable size. But many depressed people overgeneralize the significance of a single failure (Carver & Ganellen, 1983; Carver et al., 1985)—because of the ways in which they conceptualize their failures.

Research shows that depressed people are more likely than nondepressed people to attribute the causes of their failures to internal, stable, and global factors (Blumberg & Izard, 1985; Miller et al., 1982; Peterson et al., 1981; Pyszczynski & Greenberg, 1985; Raps et al., 1982; Seligman et al., 1979, 1984). Depressed people exaggerate the blame they deserve and view their problems as all but impossible to change. Is it any wonder that they are more likely than nondepressed people to feel helpless?

Neurotransmitters and Depression   Researchers are also searching for organic factors in depression. Martin Seligman (1975) and Jay Weiss (1982), for example, have found that dogs who had learned helplessness showed a decrease in the amount of the neurotransmitter norepinephrine available to the brain. Ellison (1977) found that rats with lowered levels of norepinephrine show behavior similar to that of depressed people (see the nearby box "Rats Take Dive!"). Helplessness and inactivity may therefore somehow lower norepinephrine levels. Once lowered, unfortunately, it could also be the case that norepinephrine deficiency tends to perpetuate inactivity.

As will be noted in Chapter 12, people whose depression has psychotic proportions often respond to antidepressant drugs. One effect of these drugs is to raise norepinephrine levels, providing further evidence suggestive of a role for norepinephrine in depression.

Other researchers argue that the neurotransmitter serotonin also plays a role in affective disorders (e.g., Berger, 1978). It has been speculated that deficiencies in serotonin may create a general disposition toward affective disorders. A deficiency of serotonin *combined with* a deficiency of norepinephrine might then be linked with depression. However, a deficiency of serotonin combined with excessive levels of norepinephrine might produce mania, which is discussed in the section on bipolar disorder. Still other researchers argue for roles for deficiencies of the neurotransmitter acetylcholine (Nadi et al., 1984) or for excesses of thyroid hormones (Whybrow & Prange, 1981) in affective disorders.

The relationships between depression and organic factors are complex and under intense study. While the causes of depression remain clouded to some degree, we know all too well that for some people suicide is one of the possible results of depression. We discuss that distressing topic next.

SUICIDE

Note a number of facts about suicide:

Suicide is more common among college students than among nonstudents. About 10,000 college students attempt suicide each year.

Suicide is the second leading cause of death among college students.

Nearly 200,000 people attempt suicide each year in the United States. About one in ten succeeds.

Three times as many women as men attempt suicide, but three times as many men succeed.

Men prefer to use guns or hang themselves, but women prefer to use sleeping pills.

Young blacks and native Americans are more than twice as likely as whites to commit suicide.

Suicide is especially common among physicians, lawyers, and psychologists, although it is found among all occupational groups and at all age levels.

No other cause of death leaves such feelings of guilt, distress, and puzzlement in friends and relatives.

Why do people take their own lives? It seems that the great majority of suicides are linked to depression (Barraclough et al., 1969; Robins et al., 1959; Leonard, 1977; Schotte & Clum, 1982). Although most people who attempt suicide show hopelessness and despair, they do not appear out of touch with reality (Leonard, 1974).

Strongly suicidal people report finding life more dull, empty, and boring than do less or nonsuicidal people. They feel more anxious, excitable, submissive, angry, guilt-ridden, helpless, and inadequate than others (Mehrabian & Weinstein, 1985; Neuringer, 1982). According to psychologist Edwin Schneidman (1985) of the UCLA Neuropsychiatric Institute, people who attempt suicide are usually experiencing unendurable psychological pain and are attempting to bring consciousness of their suffering to an end. In a Boston University study, college women who had attempted suicide were more likely than their peers to implicate their parents as a source of the pain that led to the attempt (Cantor, 1976). They were also less likely to feel able to ask parents or others for help when they felt desperate or under great stress.

Suicide attempts are more frequent following a number of stressful life events, especially "exit events" (Slater & Depue, 1981). Exit events involve loss of social support—as in death, divorce, separation, a family member's leaving home, or the loss of an unrelated but significant person. People who consider suicide following stressful experiences have also been found less capable of solving problems than are those who do not consider suicide (Schotte & Clum, 1982). That is, they are less likely to think of more productive ways to cope with stress.

Some suicides are quite logical (Shneidman & Farberow, 1970), as in the case of a terminally ill patient in unrelenting pain, whose spouse has died and who feels like a burden to the family. Suicide may also be ceremonial, as in the case of Japanese Samurai warriors who chose suicide over dishonor. A few suicides stem from thought disorders, as in paranoid schizophrenia or a "bad trip" induced by drugs.

Myths About Suicide   Some believe that people who threaten suicide are only seeking attention. The serious just "do it." Actually, 70 to 80 percent of suicides gave clear clues concerning their intentions prior to the act (Cordes, 1985; Leonard, 1977).

Some believe that those who fail at suicide attempts are only seeking attention. But 75 percent of successful suicides had made prior attempts (Cohen et al., 1966). Contrary to myth, discussion of suicide with a depressed person does not prompt suicide. In fact, extracting a promise that the person will not commit suicide before calling or visiting a mental-health worker seems to have prevented some cases of suicide.

Some believe that only insane people (meaning people who are out of touch with reality, or psychotics) would take their own lives. However, Schneidman points out that suicidal thinking is not necessarily a sign of psychosis, neurosis, or personality disorder; instead, the contemplation of suicide reflects a narrowing of the range of options that people think are available to them (Cordes, 1985). Finally, most people with suicidal thoughts, contrary to myth, will *not* act on them. Suicidal thoughts at a time of great stress are not uncommon.

Preventing Suicide   If someone tells you he or she is considering suicide, you may feel frightened and flustered, or that an enormous burden has been placed on you. In such cases, your objective should be to encourage the person to consult a professional mental health worker, or to consult a worker yourself as soon as possible. But if the person refuses to talk to anyone else and you feel that you can't break free for a consultation, there are a number of things you can do:

Draw the person out. Edwin Schneidman suggests asking questions such as "What's going on?" "Where do you hurt?" "What would you like to see happen?" (1985, p. 11). Questions such as these may encourage people to express frustrated psychological needs and provide some relief. They also give you time to assess the danger and think.

Be empathetic. Show that you understand how upset the person is. Do *not* say, "Don't be silly."

Suggest that measures other than suicide might be found to solve the problem, even if they are not evident at the time. Schneidman (1985) suggests that suicidal people can typically see only two solutions to their problems—either death or a magical resolution of their problems. Therapists thus attempt to "widen the mental blinders" of suicidal people.

Ask how the person intends to commit suicide. People with concrete plans and the weapon are at greater risk. Ask if you might hold on to the weapon for a while. Sometimes the person says yes.

Suggest that the person go *with you* to obtain professional help *now*. The emergency room of a general hospital, the campus counseling center or infirmary, the campus or local police will do. Some campuses have "hot lines" you can call. Some cities have suicide-prevention centers with hot lines that people can use anonymously.

A SUICIDE-PREVENTION HOTLINE At suicide-prevention centers across the country, trained staff stand by hotlines around the clock. If someone you know threatens suicide, consult a professional as soon as posible.

Extract a promise that the person will not commit suicide before seeing you again. Arrange a concrete time and place to meet. Get professional help as soon as you are apart.

Do *not* tell people threatening suicide that they're silly or crazy. Do *not* insist on contact with specific people, like parents or a spouse. Conflict with these people may have led to the suicidal thinking.

But above all, please remember that your primary objective must be to consult a helping professional. Don't "go it alone" for one moment more than you have to.

In the next section we discuss bipolar disorder. We shall see that a number of people with this disorder, too, take their lives.

BIPOLAR DISORDER

In bipolar disorder, formerly known as manic-depression, there are mood swings from elation to depression. These cycles seem unrelated to external events. In the elated, or **manicky** phase, people may show excessive excitement or silliness, carrying jokes too far. They may show poor judgment, sometimes destroying property, and may be argumentative (Depue et al., 1981). Roommates may avoid them, finding them abrasive. Manicky people may speak rapidly and disclose unrealistically grand, delusional schemes. They may jump from topic to topic, showing **rapid flight of ideas.** They may show extreme generosity by making unusually large contributions to

Manicky Elated, showing excessive excitement. (From the Greek *mania*, meaning "raging madness.")

Rapid flight of ideas Rapid speech and topic changes, characteristic of manicky behavior.

charity or giving away a car. They may not be able to sleep restfully or sit still.

Depression is the other side of the coin. Bipolar depressed patients often sleep more than usual and are lethargic. People with major depression are more likely to show insomnia and agitation (Davison & Neale, 1986). Bipolar depressed patients show social withdrawal and irritability. Some attempt suicide "on the way down," reporting that they fear again experiencing the full depths of depression.

Many researchers believe that bipolar disorder has at least in part an organic basis (Klein & Depue, 1985). Mood swings tend to run in families (Klein et al., 1985; Smith & Winokur, 1983); bipolar disorder is more common among identical than fraternal twins and may well reflect excesses of norepinephrine. In Chapter 12 it will also be noted that the metal lithium helps flatten out manic-depressive cycles for many sufferers, apparently by lowering levels of norepinephrine.

SCHIZOPHRENIC DISORDERS

Joyce was nineteen. Her boyfriend brought her into the emergency room because she had slit her wrists. When she was interviewed, her attention wandered. She seemed distracted by things in the air, or something she might be hearing. It was as if she had an invisible earphone.

She explained that she had cut her wrists because the "hellsmen" had told her to. Then she seemed frightened. Later she said that the hellsmen had warned her not to reveal their existence. She had been afraid that they would punish her for talking about them.

Her boyfriend told the psychiatrist that Joyce had been living with him for about a year. At first they had been together in a small apartment in town. But Joyce did not want to be near other people and had convinced him to rent a bungalow in the country. There she would make fantastic drawings of goblins and monsters during the days. Now and then she would become agitated and act as if invisible things were giving her instructions.

"I'm bad," Joyce would mutter, "I'm bad." She would begin to jumble her words. Ron, the boyfriend, would then try to convince her to go to the hospital, but she would refuse. Then the wrist-cutting would begin. Ron thought he had made the cottage safe by removing knives and blades. But Joyce would always find something.

Then Joyce would be brought to the hospital, have stitches put in, be kept under observation and medicated. She would explain that she cut herself because the hellsmen had told her she was bad and must die. After a few days she would deny hearing the hellsmen and insist on leaving the hospital.

Ron would take her home. The pattern continued.

When the admitting psychiatrist examined Joyce's wrists and heard that she believed she had been following the orders of "hellsmen," he began to suspect that she was suffering from a schizophrenic disorder. Schizophrenic disorders often touch every aspect of the victims' lives. Schizophrenic behavior is characterized by disturbances in (1) thought and language; (2)

perception and attention; (3) motor activity; and (4) mood; and by (5) withdrawal and **autism.**

Schizophrenic disorders are known primarily by disturbances in thought, which are largely inferred from verbal behavior. Schizophrenic persons may show *loosening of associations.* Unless we are daydreaming or deliberately allowing our thoughts to "wander," our thinking is normally tightly knit. We start at a certain point and the things that come to mind (the associations) tend to be logically and coherently connected. But schizophrenics often think in an illogical, disorganized manner. Their speech may be jumbled, combining parts of words or making rhymes in a meaningless fashion. Schizophrenics may also jump from topic to topic, conveying little useful information. Nor do they usually have insight that their thoughts and behavior are abnormal.

Schizophrenics may have **delusions** of grandeur, persecution, or reference. In the case of delusions of grandeur, the person may believe he is Jesus or a person on a special mission, or he may have grand, illogical plans for saving the world. Delusions tend to be unshakable, despite disconfirming evidence, as suggested by the following example. According to the New Testament there were three wise men, but only one Christ. Psychologist Milton Rokeach once placed three schizophrenic men, each of whom claimed to be Christ, on the same hospital ward. Despite eating and working together, two years later each continued to believe that he alone was Christ.

Persons with delusions of persecution may believe that they are being sought by the Mafia, CIA, FBI, or some other group or agency. A woman with delusions of reference expressed the belief that national news broadcasts contained coded information about her. A man with such delusions complained that neighbors had "bugged" his walls with "radios." Other schizophrenics may have delusions to the effect that they have committed unpardonable sins, that they are rotting away from a hideous disease, or that they or the world do not really exist.

The perceptions of schizophrenics often include hallucinations—imagery in the absence of external stimulation that the schizophrenic cannot distinguish from reality. Joyce believed she heard "hellsmen." Others may see colors or even obscene words spelled out in midair. Auditory hallucinations are most common.

Motor activity may become wild and excited or slow to a **stupor.** There may be strange gestures and peculiar facial expressions. There may be *grooming*—as in touching the hair or face or adjusting the clothing (Fairbanks et al., 1982). Emotional response may be **flat** or blunted, or inappropriate—as in giggling at bad news. Schizophrenics tend to withdraw from social contacts and become wrapped up in their own thoughts and fantasies.

It should be understood that many people diagnosed as schizophrenic show only a few of these symptoms. The DSM–III takes the view that schizophrenics at some time or another show delusions, problems with associative thinking, and hallucinations, but not necessarily all at once. There are also different kinds or types of schizophrenia, and different symptoms are predominant with each type.

Autism Self-absorption. Absorption in daydreaming and fantasy. (From the Greek *autos,* meaning "self.")

Delusions False, persistent beliefs that are unsubstantiated by sensory or objective evidence.

Stupor A condition in which the senses and thought are dulled. (From the Latin *stupidus,* meaning "stunned" or "amazed.")

Flat Monotonous, dull.

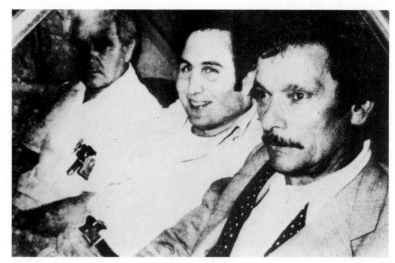

THE "SON-OF-SAM KILLER" David Berkowitz, the "Son-of-Sam killer," smiles benignly upon his arrest in 1977. Does his response to arrest seem appropriate? Because of his inappropriate emotional responses and his claim that a dog had urged him to commit his crimes, many mental-health professionals considered him schizophrenic.

TYPES OF SCHIZOPHRENIA

The DSM–III lists three major types of schizophrenia: *disorganized* (called "hebephrenic" schizophrenia in the DSM–II); *catatonic*; and *paranoid*.

Disorganized Type **Disorganized schizophrenics** tend to have disorganized delusions and vivid, abundant hallucinations that are often sexual or religious. A twenty-three-year-old female disorganized schizophrenic remarked "I see 'pennis.'" She pointed vaguely into the air before her. Asked to spell *pennis,* she replied irritatedly: "P-e-n-i-s." Apparently her social background was so inhibited that she had never heard the word for the male sex organ spoken aloud; and so she mispronounced it. Extreme social impairment is common among disorganized schizophrenics. They also often show silliness and giddiness of mood, giggling and nonsensical speech. They may neglect their appearance and hygiene, and lose control of their bladder and their bowels.

Catatonic Type **Catatonic schizophrenics** show striking impairment in motor activity. It is characterized by slowing of activity into a stupor that may change suddenly into an agitated phase. Catatonic individuals may hold unusual, even difficult postures for hours, even as their limbs grow swollen or stiff. A striking symptom is **waxy flexibility,** in which they maintain positions into which they have been manipulated by others. Immobile catatonic individuals usually will not respond to the speech of others. But after an episode of immobility they usually report that they heard what others were saying at the time.

Disorganized schizophrenics Schizophrenics who show disorganized delusions and vivid hallucinations. Formerly called *hebephrenic schizophrenics.*

Catatonic schizophrenics Schizophrenics who show striking impairment in motor activity. (From the Greek *kata-,* meaning "downward," and *tonos,* meaning "tension"—suggesting loss of muscle activity.)

Waxy flexibility A symptom of catatonic schizophrenia in which persons maintain postures into which they are placed.

Paranoid Type **Paranoid schizophrenics** are characterized by the content of their delusions. They usually show delusions of grandeur and persecution, but may also show delusions of jealousy, in which they believe that a spouse or lover has been unfaithful. They may show agitation, confusion, and fear, and experience vivid hallucinations that are consistent with their delusions. The paranoid schizophrenic often constructs a complex or systematized delusion involving themes of wrongdoing or persecution.

A rarely used, related diagnostic category is **paranoia.** People may receive this diagnosis if they show a permanent, ''unshakable'' delusional system, but do not show the confused, jumbled thinking or hallucinations suggestive of schizophrenia. Daily functioning in paranoia and in some cases of paranoid schizophrenia may be minimally impaired, or not impaired at all, so long as the person does not act on the basis of his or her delusions.

Paranoid schizophrenia A type of schizophrenia characterized primarily by delusions—commonly of persecution—and by vivid hallucinations.

Paranoia A major but rare disorder in which a person shows a persistent delusional system, but not the confusion of the schizophrenic.

POSSIBLE CAUSES OF SCHIZOPHRENIA

Psychologists have investigated various factors that may contribute to schizophrenic disorders. In this section we consider socioeconomic, psychoanalytic, social-learning, genetic, and biochemical possibilities.

Socioeconomic Status Schizophrenia is most common among lower socioeconomic groups that inhabit the inner cities (e.g., Hollingshead & Redlich, 1958). Sociocultural theorist R. D. Laing argues that poverty and social injustice cause schizophrenia. According to him, schizophrenia ''is a special sort of strategy that a person invents in order to live in an unlivable situation'' (1964, p. 186).

Critics argue that Laing's view confuses correlation with cause and effect. It may be that the causal relationship between schizophrenia and social status, if any, works in the opposite direction. Schizophrenia may lead to lowered social status. There is considerable evidence that schizophrenics tend to drift downward in socioeconomic standing (Turner & Wagonfield, 1967).

Psychoanalytic Theory Psychoanalytic theorists view schizophrenia as the overwhelming of the ego by impulses of the id. The impulses are typically hostile or sexual. They threaten the ego and lead to intense intrapsychic conflict. Under this threat the person regresses to an early phase of the oral stage in which the infant has not yet learned that it and the world are separate and distinct. Fantasies become confused with reality, giving birth to hallucinations and delusions. Primitive impulses may carry more weight than social norms.

Critics point out that schizophrenic behavior is not that similar to infantile behavior. Moreover, psychoanalysts have not predicted accurately what sorts of early experiences will later cause schizophrenic disorders.

Social-Learning Theory Social-learning theorists explain schizophrenia through conditioning and observational learning. From this per-

Concordant In agreement. (From the Latin *com-*, meaning "together," and *cor*, meaning "heart.")

spective, people show schizophrenic behavior when it is more likely than normal behavior to be reinforced. This may occur when the person is raised in a socially nonrewarding or punitive situation; inner fantasies then become more reinforcing than social realities.

In the hospital, patients may learn what is "expected" of them by observing other patients. Hospital staff may reinforce schizophrenic behavior by paying more attention to patients who behave bizarrely. This view is consistent with folklore that the child who disrupts the class earns more attention from the teacher than does the quiet, cooperative child.

Critics note that many of us grow up in socially punitive settings, but seem to show immunity to having socially appropriate responses extinguished. And some acquire schizophrenic behavior patterns without having had the opportunity to observe other schizophrenics. In Chapter 12 we shall see that behavioral methods, derived from social-learning theory, *can* decrease socially undesirable responses, but there is little evidence that they can make major changes in the expression of thought disorders.

Genetic Factors   There is a decided tendency for schizophrenic disorders to run in families. Children of schizophrenic parents are at greater than normal risks for showing certain behaviors at early ages. In a research program referred to as the *New York Project,* for example, it has been found that these children show more difficulty in social relationships, more emotional instability, and less academic motivation than control children between the ages of twelve and seventeen (Watt et al., 1982).

Persons with schizophrenic disorders constitute about 1 percent of the population, but children with two schizophrenic parents have about a 35 percent chance of becoming schizophrenic (Rosenthal, 1970). Most studies show that the identical twins of schizophrenics also show a high probability of being diagnosed as schizophrenic. A pair of individuals who receive the same diagnosis are called **concordant.** In various studies summarized by Davison and Neale (1986), the concordance rate for the diagnoses of the identical twins of schizophrenics has been found as high as 75 to 86 percent. The concordance rate for fraternal twins, whose genetic endowments are not identical, drops off dramatically, but is still at above-chance levels.

It has been pointed out quite properly that the above studies have not controlled for environmental influences. Children raised in the same family have similar environments. Parents (and outsiders) often expect (and encourage) identical behavior from identical twins. To overcome this objection, studies have been done to determine whether the natural or adoptive parents of adopted children have a greater influence on the likelihood of their being judged schizophrenic (e.g., Heston, 1966; Wender et al., 1974). In such studies, the biological parent typically places the child at greater risk than does the adoptive parent—even though the child has not been raised by the biological parent.

While evidence for a genetic role in schizophrenia seems strong, heredity cannot be the sole factor. If it were, there would be a 100 percent concordance rate for schizophrenia between pairs of identical twins. Genetics may establish a predisposition toward schizophrenia that at least sometimes must interact with other factors if the individual is to show a schizophrenic

A CLOSER LOOK

ON BEING SANE IN INSANE PLACES

What's one way to guarantee admission to a mental ward? Just show up at a hospital claiming to hear the words *empty, hollow,* and *thud.* Psychologist David Rosenhan (1973) of Stanford University coached volunteers—psychologists, physicians, a painter, and a housewife—to show up at different institutions with the single symptom. They claimed no other problems—just hearing *empty, hollow,* and *thud.*

Although the single symptom of hallucinations was not enough, according to the edition of the DSM (II) in use at the time, to make the diagnosis of schizophrenia, all but one of the phony patients was admitted with a diagnosis of schizophrenia. The other was admitted as showing a bipolar disorder. An early finding of the Rosenhan study was that many clinicians are quick to "jump at" a diagnosis on the basis of a prominent "symptom."

Following admission, the phony patients no longer claimed to hear voices and behaved normally in every way. But because they made no serious effort to gain discharge, they remained hospitalized for an average stay of nineteen days. You can interpret this average stay as administrative and staff sloppiness, caution and concern for patients with possible serious problems, or a combination of both.

During their stays, no psychiatrists or other staff members became suspicious of the phony patients. But other *patients* had noticed that they were taking notes and later reported wondering if some of them were journalists or professors "checking up on the hospital."

Upon discharge the diagnosis was schizophrenia—"in remission" (that is, no longer showing symptoms). Even though the phony patients were totally symptom-free, the diagnosis of schizophrenia, once made, stuck like glue. Once people are admitted to the mental-health system and become "patients" and receive diagnostic labels, it may be that there is a tendency to treat the label and not the person. (How do *you* treat people once you label them "impossible," "not for me," or "one of *them?*")

disorder. Perhaps heredity creates a predisposition for biochemical factors such as those discussed in the following section.

The Dopamine Theory of Schizophrenia   Over the years numerous substances have been thought to play a role in schizophrenic disorders. Current theory and research focus on the neurotransmitter **dopamine.**

The dopamine theory of schizophrenia evolved from observation of the effects of **amphetamines,** a group of stimulants discussed in Chapter 4. Researchers are confident that amphetamines act by increasing the quantity of dopamine in the brain. High doses of amphetamines lead to behavior that mimics paranoid schizophrenia in normal people, and even low doses exacerbate the symptoms of schizophrenics (Snyder, 1980). An additional source of evidence for the dopamine theory lies in the effects of a class of drugs called **phenothiazines.** Research by psychologist Ian Creese and others (1978; Turkington, 1983) suggests that the phenothiazines, which are often effective in treating schizophrenia, work by means of blocking the action of dopamine receptors.

It does not appear that schizophrenic persons produce different amounts of dopamine from other people, but that they *utilize* more of the substance. Why? It could be that they have a greater number of dopamine receptors in the brain (Snyder, 1984), but it is also possible that their dopamine receptors are more sensitive than normal.

Dopamine A neurotransmitter implicated in schizophrenia. See Chapter 2. (Acronym for dihydroxyphenyla*mine.*)

Amphetamines Stimulants whose overusage can lead to symptoms that mimic schizophrenia. See Chapter 4.

Phenothiazine (fee-no-THIGH-uh-zeen). A member of a family of drugs that are effective in treatment of many cases of schizophrenia.

Future research may suggest that schizophrenia can have multiple causes. Genetic biochemical factors may set the stage for some borderline individuals to display schizophrenic symptoms in response to impoverished environments or severe stressors. Other people may be so severely handicapped by biochemical factors that they will develop schizophrenic disorders under the most positive conditions.

In general, the more rapid the onset of the disorder, the more bizarre the behavior of the individual and the *better* the predicted outcome, or prognosis. Researchers have found that people who show higher levels of stressful life events prior to the onset of the disorder (whose disorders are thus more likely to be *reactive*), do show a better prognosis (e.g., Harder et al., 1981). If the onset has been abrupt, especially in response to a stressor that can be identified, the disorder may be less likely to reflect an unrelenting inner *process* of deterioration.

PERSONALITY DISORDERS

Personality disorders, like personality traits, are characterized by enduring patterns of behavior. Personality disorders, however, are inflexible and maladaptive. They impair personal or social functioning and are a source of distress to the individual or to others.

There are a number of personality disorders, including the *paranoid, schizotypal, schizoid,* and *antisocial personality disorders.* The defining trait of the **paranoid personality disorder** is suspiciousness. Although persons with paranoid personality disorders do not show grossly disorganized thinking, they are generally mistrustful of others, and their social relationships suffer for it. Paranoid personality disorders may be suspicious of coworkers and supervisors, but they can generally hold onto jobs.

The old DSM–II (1968) category, *simple schizophrenia,* is diagnosed as **schizotypal personality disorder** in the DSM–III (1980). The change was made because of the absence of bizarre psychotic behavior. Still, persons with schizotypal personality disorders may show some "oddities" of thought, perception, and behavior, such as excessive fantasy and suspiciousness, feelings of being unreal, or odd usage of words (DSM–III, p. 312). For these reasons, schizotypal personality disorders are often maladjusted on the job.

The **schizoid personality** is defined by one major characteristic: social withdrawal. Schizoid personalities do not develop warm, tender feelings for others. They generally prefer to be by themselves, have few friends and rarely get married. Some schizoid personalities do very well on the job, so long as continuous social interaction is not required. Hallucinations and delusions are absent (as they also are in the schizotypal personality disorder, discussed earlier).

THE ANTISOCIAL PERSONALITY

Persons with **antisocial personality disorders** persistently violate the rights of others, show indifference to commitments, and encounter conflict with

Personality disorders Enduring patterns of maladaptive behavior that are a source of distress to the individual or others.

Paranoid personality disorder A disorder characterized by persistent suspiciousness, but not the disorganization of paranoid schizophrenia.

Schizotypal personality disorder (skit-so-TYPE-al). A disorder characterized by oddities of thought and behavior, but not involving bizarre psychotic symptoms. Formerly called *simple schizophrenia.*

Schizoid personality A disorder characterized by social withdrawal.

Antisocial personality The diagnosis given a person who is in frequent conflict with society yet is undeterred by punishment, and who experiences little or no guilt and anxiety.

TABLE 11.4 Characteristics of the Antisocial Personality

Persistent violation of the rights of others
Irresponsibility as parents
Lack of formation of enduring relationships or loyalty to another person
Failure to maintain good job performance over the years
Failure to develop or adhere to a life plan
History of truancy
History of delinquency
History of running away
Persistent lying
Sexual promiscuity
Substance abuse
Impulsivity
Inability to tolerate boredom
Onset of traits before age fifteen

SOURCE: DSM–III (1980).

the law (Table 11.4). Cleckley (1964) notes that antisocial personalities often show a superficial charm and are at least average in intelligence. Perhaps their most striking feature, given their antisocial behavior, is their lack of guilt and low level of anxiety. They seem largely undeterred by punishment. Though they are likely to have earned disapproval, and often physical punishment, from others from childhood, they continue in impulsive, irresponsible styles of life.

A nineteenth-century mental-health worker described antisocial people as "morally insane." He realized that they suffered from no impairment in reality testing, but they seemed indifferent to the misery they inflicted on others.

Possible Causes of Antisocial Behavior   Various factors appear to contribute to antisocial behavior, including an antisocial father, both lack of love and parental rejection during childhood, and inconsistent discipline.

Antisocial personalities tend to run in families. Early research in family influences, however, did not control for the possibility that the contributing factor was the family environment, and not genetics. Recent studies with adopted children have found higher incidences of antisocial behavior among the biological rather than the adoptive relatives of antisocial personalities (Cadoret, 1978; Hutchings & Mednick, 1974; Mednick, 1985).

Some researchers have suggested that one genetic factor in antisocial personality was an extra Y sex chromosome. So-called **supermales,** with an XYY sex chromosomal structure, were thought to have a predisposition toward aggressiveness and crime. Supermales as a group are somewhat taller and more heavily bearded than XY males, but only about 1.5 percent of male delinquents and criminals tested show the XYY structure (Rosenthal, 1970). Moreover, there is no evidence that most supermales engage in crime or violence.

A more promising avenue of research, with genetic implications, suggests that antisocial personalities are unlikely to show anxiety or be deterred

Supermale A male with XYY sex chromosomal structure.

by punishment because they have lower-than-normal levels of arousal (Lykken, 1957, 1982). In typical experiments on this question, antisocial subjects of equal intelligence do not learn as rapidly as other subjects to avoid an impending electric shock. Once the levels of arousal of the antisocial subjects are increased by injections of adrenalin, they do engage in avoidance learning as rapidly as others (Schachter & Latané, 1964; Chesno & Kilmann, 1975). These findings tie in with the observation that many antisocial personalities are "thrill seekers"—taking high risks, racing motorcycles, fighting, and so on—who have no tolerance for boredom. It may be that dangerous, reckless activity raises their levels of arousal to more optimal and comfortable levels.

A genetically transmitted lower-than-normal level of arousal would not guarantee that a person would become antisocial. It may also be necessary that a person be raised under conditions that do not foster development of the identity of a person who abides by the law and social norms. Punishment for deviation from the norm would then be unlikely to induce feelings of guilt and shame. The individual might be "undeterred" by punishment.

Before ending this section, we must note one further finding with antisocial personalities. The one form of punishment that does seem effective with many of them is loss of money (Schmauk, 1970). Do we need any further evidence that antisocial personalities are not out of touch with reality?

PSYCHOSEXUAL DISORDERS

The DSM–III lists four classes of psychosexual disorders: *gender-identity disorders, paraphilias, psychosexual dysfunctions,* and "others," which includes *ego-dystonic homosexuality.* In **gender-identity disorders,** one feels uncomfortable with his or her anatomic sex. In the **paraphilias,** people show sexual arousal in response to unusual or bizarre objects or situations. We shall discuss homosexuality and sexual adjustment problems, or dysfunctions, in Chapter 13. Here let us note that while the DSM–II listed homosexuality as a mental disorder, the DSM–III lists only **ego-dystonic homosexuality.** That is, the current edition of the DSM–III views homosexuality as abnormal only when it is inconsistent with the self-concept of the individual and, for this reason, is a source of personal distress.

In the following sections we focus on the gender-identity disorder of *transsexualism* and on a number of paraphilias.

TRANSSEXUALISM

About thirty years ago headlines were made when an ex-GI, now known as Christine Jorgensen, had a "sex-change operation" in Denmark. Since that time some 2,500 American transsexuals, including tennis player Dr. Renée Richards, have undergone sex-reassignment surgery. Sex-reassignment surgery is cosmetic. It cannot actually change one's gender by im-

Gender-identity disorders Disorders in which a person's anatomic sex is inconsistent with his or her sense of being male or female.

Paraphilias (par-uh-FEEL-ee-uhs). Disorders in which people show sexual arousal in response to unusual or bizarre objects or situations. (From the Greek *para-,* meaning "alongside," and *philos,* meaning "loving.")

Ego-dystonic homosexuality Homosexuality that causes the individual distress, because it is inconsistent with his or her self-concept.

planting reproductive organs of the opposite sex, but it can create the appearance of the external genitals of the opposite sex—more successfully with male-to-female than female-to-male transsexuals. After these operations, transsexuals can engage in sexual activity and reach orgasm, but they cannot have children.

Transsexualism is the persistent feeling that one is of the wrong sex. Transsexuals wish to be rid of their own genitals and live as members of the opposite sex. They do not see themselves as homosexuals, even though they are sexually attracted to members of their own anatomic sex. This is because they view nature's assignment as a mistake; they see themselves as "trapped" inside a body of the wrong sex.

The causes of transsexualism are unclear, but there are broad psychological and organic views. It may be that some transsexuals are raised by disappointed parents as children of the opposite sex. But it is also possible that some transsexuals have been influenced by prenatal hormonal imbalances. It may be that the human brain can be "masculinized" or "feminized" by sex hormones at certain stages of development in the womb, and that some fetuses are exposed to hormonal "imbalances" produced by themselves or their mothers at critical periods. (See Chapters 2 and 13 for further discussion of sex hormones.)

A recent study of forty-two postoperative male-to-female transsexuals found that all but one would repeat the surgery, and the great majority found sexual activity more pleasurable as a "woman" (Bentler, 1976). Most female-to-male transsexuals rate their adjustment as positive, and are solid workers and tax payers (Person & Ovesey, 1974; Randall, 1969). Despite difficulties in surgically constructing structures that serve as external male sexual organs, a recently studied group of twenty-two postoperative female-to-male transsexuals were generally satisfied with their new bodies (Fleming et al., 1982). A follow-up study of 116 transsexuals (both female-to-male and male-to-female) at least one year after surgery found that most were pleased with the results and that the majority were acceptably adjusted (Blanchard et al., 1985).

TRANSSEXUALISM Physician Richard Raskin underwent sex reassignment surgery and became Renée Richards. For a while, Renée competed as a woman on the women's tennis circuit. More recently, Renée served as a coach to Martina Navratilova.

PARAPHILIAS

The paraphilias we shall discuss include *fetishism, transvestism, zoophilia, pedophilia, exhibitionism, voyeurism, sexual masochism,* and *sexual sadism.*

Fetishism   **Fetishism** is sexual response to a bodily part, like feet, or an inanimate object, such as an article of clothing. Sexual gratification is often achieved through masturbating in the presence of the object. Fetishes for undergarments and for objects made of leather, rubber, or silk are not uncommon.

Transvestism   **Transvestism** is recurrent, persistent dressing in clothing usually worn by the opposite sex in order to achieve sexual excitement. Transvestism may range from wearing a single female undergarment in pri-

Transsexualism A gender-identity disorder in which a person feels trapped in the body of the wrong sex. (The Latin prefix *trans-* means "across.")

Fetishism A variation of choice in sexual object in which a bodily part (like a foot) or an inanimate object (like an undergarment) elicits sexual arousal and is preferred to a person. (From the Portuguese *feitico,* meaning "a charm" as used in witchcraft.)

Transvestism Recurrent, persistent dressing in clothing worn by the opposite sex for purposes of sexual excitement. (From the Latin *trans-,* meaning "across," and *vestis,* meaning "garment.")

Zoophilia (zoe-oh-FEEL-ee-uh). Sexual contact with animals as a preferred source of sexual excitement. Also called *bestiality*.

Pedophilia (pea-doe-FEEL-ee-uh). Sexual contact with children as the preferred source of sexual excitement. (From the Greek *pais*, meaning "child," and *philia*, meaning "loving.")

Exhibitionism The compulsion to expose one's genitals in public. (From the Latin *ex-*, meaning "out of," and *habere*, meaning "to hold.")

Voyeurism Attainment of sexual gratification through observing others undress or engage in sexual activity. (From the French *voir*, meaning "to see.")

Masochism Attainment of sexual gratification through receiving pain or humiliation.

Sadism Attainment of sexual gratification through inflicting pain or humiliation on sex partners. (After the French Marquis de Sade, who wrote stories about pleasure some people obtain by inflicting pain on others.)

vate to sporting full dress at a transvestite club. Most transvestites are heterosexual and married, but they seek additional sexual gratification through dressing as women.

Zoophilia   **Zoophilia,** or *bestiality*, is sexual contact with animals as a preferred or exclusive means of achieving sexual arousal. Thus, a child or adolescent who shows some sexual response to an episode of rough-and-tumble play with the family pet is rarely showing zoophilia.

Pedophilia   **Pedophilia** is actual or fantasized sexual activity with children as a preferred means of becoming sexually aroused. Most episodes are not coerced and involve exhibitionism or fondling rather than sexual intercourse.

Exhibitionism   **Exhibitionism** is the repetitive act of exposing one's genitals to a stranger in order to surprise or shock, rather than sexually arouse, the victim. The exhibitionist is usually not interested in actual sexual contact with the victim. He may masturbate while fantasizing about or actually exposing himself.

Professional strip-teasers and scantily clad swimmers do not fit the definition of exhibitionist. Both groups may seek to sexually arouse, but usually not to shock, observers. The major motive of the strip-teaser may also be simply to earn a living.

Voyeurism   **Voyeurism** is repetitive watching of unsuspecting strangers while they are undressing or engaging in sexual activity as the preferred or exclusive means of achieving sexual arousal. We may enjoy observing spouses undress, or even the nudity in an R-rated film, without being diagnosed as voyeurs. In voyeurism, the "victim" does not know that he or she is being watched, and the voyeur prefers looking to doing.

Sexual Masochism   **Masochism** is named after the Austrian storyteller Leopold von Sacher-Masoch, who portrayed sexual satisfaction as deriving from pain or humiliation. The sexual masochist must receive pain or humiliation in order to achieve sexual gratification. It has been suggested that many masochists experience guilt about sex, but can enjoy sex so long as they see themselves as being appropriately punished for it.

Sexual Sadism   **Sadism** is named after the infamous Marquis de Sade, a Frenchman who wrote stories about the pleasures of achieving sexual gratification by inflicting pain or humiliation on others. In sadism, the person may not be able to become sexually excited unless he inflicts pain on his partner.

Psychological Explanations of the Paraphilias   According to psychoanalytic theory, paraphilias are defenses against anxiety. The exhibitionist, for example, has unconscious castration anxiety. His victim's shock at his exposure reassures him that he does, after all, have a penis. Fetishism, pedophilia, and so on protect him from fear of failure in adult heterosexual relationships.

Rathus (1983) offers a modified social-learning view of fetishism and other paraphilias. First, a fantasized or actual event—like being sexually excited when discovered by a woman while urinating behind a bush—gives the person the idea that an unusual object or situation is sexually arousing. Second, the object is used in actuality or fantasy to heighten sexual arousal. Third, recognition of the deviance of the fantasy or act may cause feelings of anxiety or guilt. These feelings, if not extreme, may further increase emotional arousal in the presence of the deviant object or activity. Heightened emotional response may then be *attributed* to the deviant object or activity. Fourth, orgasm reinforces the preceding behaviors and fantasies. Fifth, in cases in which a person is anxious about normal sexual relationships, the deviant object or activity may become the major or sole sexual outlet.

Although the causes of many patterns of abnormal behavior remain in dispute, a number of methods of therapy have been devised to deal with them. We focus on these methods in the next chapter.

SUMMARY

1. Behavior may be called abnormal when it is unusual or infrequent, socially unacceptable, involves faulty perception of reality, dangerous, self-defeating, or personally distressing.

2. Insanity is a legal, not psychological term. People may be found insane, and thus not responsible for criminal behavior, if at the time of the offense they could not distinguish right from wrong or could not prevent their behavior.

3. There are several models for explaining abnormal behavior: the demonological (the most prevalent model throughout history), medical (organic and psychoanalytic subtypes), social-learning, cognitive, and sociocultural models. Adherents to the medical model see abnormal behavior as symptomatic of underlying organic or psychoanalytic disorders. Social-learning theorists see abnormal behaviors as acquired through principles of learning, just as normal behaviors are.

4. A major system for classifying abnormal behavior is the *Diagnostic and Statistical Manual* (DSM) of the American Psychiatric Association. The DSM–III (1980) focuses more on observable behaviors than did the DSM–II (1968). The DSM–III de-emphasizes the concept of neurosis (presumed to stem from unconscious conflict), reorganizes and modifies categories, and relies relatively less heavily on the medical model than did the DSM–II.

5. Anxiety disorders are characterized by motor tension, feelings of dread, and high autonomic activity. They include irrational fears, or phobias; panic disorder, characterized by sudden attacks in which people typically fear that they may be losing control or going crazy; generalized (free-floating) anxiety; and obsessive-compulsive disorders, in which people are troubled by intrusive thoughts or impulses to repeat some activity.

6. Psychologists generally assume that phobias are a result of learning, although there is dispute as to the mechanisms of learning. Psychologists are more likely to assume that panic disorder may have an organic basis.

7. Dissociative disorders are characterized by a sudden temporary change in consciousness or self-identity. The dissociative disorders include psychogenic amnesia (motivated forgetting), psychogenic fugue (forgetting plus fleeing and adopting a new identity), and multiple personality, in which a person behaves as if distinct personalities occupied the body.

8. In somatoform disorders, people show or complain of physical problems, although no evidence of a medical abnormality can be found.

9. The somatoform disorders include conversion disorder and hypochondria. In a conversion disorder, there is loss of a bodily function with no organic basis. Hypochondriacs show consistent concern that they are suffering from illnesses, although there are no medical findings.

10. Affective disorders are characterized by disturbance in expressed emotions. Affective disorders include dysthymic disorder, major depression, and bipolar disorder.

11. In dysthymic disorder the person shows depressive behaviors for at least two years. Major depression may reach psychotic proportions, with grossly impaired reality testing. In bipolar disorder there are mood swings from elation to depression and back.

12. Recent research emphasizes the possible roles of learned helplessness, attributional styles, and the roles of neurotransmitters in depression. Depressed people are more likely than normals to make internal, stable, and global attributions for failures. It may be that deficiencies in serotonin create a predisposition toward affective disorders. Concurrent deficiencies of norepinephrine may then contribute to depression, while concurrent excesses of norepinephrine may contribute to manicky behavior.

13. Suicide is most often linked to feelings of depression and hopelessness. People who threaten suicide may well carry it out. Suicide prevention requires empathy, patience, and encouragement that solutions may be found to life's problems, and—most important—professional consultation as soon as possible.

14. Schizophrenic disorders are characterized by disturbances in thought and language (for example, loosening of associations and delusions); perception and attention (for example, hallucinations); motor activity (for example, a stupor or excited behavior); mood (for example, flat or inappropriate emotional responses); and by withdrawal and autism.

15. There are three major types of schizophrenia: disorganized (formerly, hebephrenic); catatonic; and paranoid. Disorganized schizophrenia is characterized by disorganized delusions and vivid, abundant hallucinations. Catatonic schizophrenia is characterized by impaired motor activity and waxy flexibility. Paranoid schizophrenia is characterized by paranoid delusions.

16. There is a decided tendency for schizophrenia to run in families. According to the dopamine theory of schizophrenia, schizophrenics may *utilize* more of the neurotransmitter dopamine because of a greater-than-normal number of dopamine receptors in the brain, or because of greater sensitivity to dopamine.

17. Personality disorders are inflexible, maladaptive behavior patterns that impair personal or social functioning and are a source of distress to the individual or others.

18. The defining trait of the paranoid personality is suspiciousness. Persons with schizotypal personality disorders show oddities of thought, perception, and behavior, while social withdrawal is the major characteristic of the schizoid personality.

19. Persons with antisocial personality disorders persistently violate the rights of others and encounter conflict with the law. They show little or no guilt or shame over their misdeeds and are largely undeterred by punishment.

20. Research suggests that antisocial personalities may come about from some combination of inconsistent discipline, an antisocial father, and lower-than-normal levels of arousal.

21. Psychosexual disorders include gender-identity disorders (such as transsexualism), paraphilias, psychosexual dysfunctions, and ego-dystonic homosexuality. Transsexuals feel trapped in the body of the wrong sex and seek sex-reassignment.

22. In the paraphilias, people are sexually aroused by unusual or bizarre objects or situations. The paraphilias include fetishism, transvestism, zoophilia, pedophilia, exhibitionism, voyeurism, sexual masochism, and sexual sadism.

23. According to the DSM–III, homosexuality is considered abnormal only when it is inconsistent with the person's self-concept and, consequently, a source of distress.

TRUTH OR FICTION REVISITED

A man shot the president of the United States in front of millions of television witnesses, yet was found not guilty by a court of law.

True. John Hinckley was found not guilty of the attempted assassination of President Ronald Reagan by reason of insanity.

Cavemen treated abnormal behavior by letting the sun shine in—or letting the evil spirits out. Therapy involved making a hole in the head.

Anthropological evidence strongly suggests that this is the case. This practice was an early expression of the demonological model of abnormal behavior.

In the Middle Ages innocent people were drowned to prove that they were not possessed by the Devil.

True. It was believed that the Devil or his agents, within people they "possessed," would not take kindly to drowning and would keep the person afloat.

Mental disorders stem from physiological problems, such as chemical imbalances or metabolic disturbances.

Some disorders appear to do so. Schizophrenic and affective disorders may have at least partial organic bases, but many others, like paraphilias, are not thought to.

Some people are suddenly flooded with feelings of panic, even when there is no external threat.

True. This is panic disorder, and its origins may well be biochemical.

Some people have irresistible urges to wash their hands—over and over again.

True. They are said to be suffering from a compulsion.

Some people have not one, but two or more distinct personalities dwelling within them.

Perhaps—we cannot be certain. There are several convincing case studies, but we cannot directly observe people's personalities. Personalities are inferred from behavior. Therefore, it is also possible that a number of people have convincingly behaved *as though* their behavior was governed by different personalities, even though it was not.

Suicide is a sign of insanity.

False. The great majority of suicides may be depressed, but they are not out of touch with reality.

Depressed rats drive their neighbors to drink.

It appears so. But it would be more accurate to say that the colony-mates of norepinephrine-depleted rats, whose *behavior* resembled that of depressed humans, increased their alcohol intake.

In some mental disorders, people may see or hear things that are not actually there.

True. These people are having hallucinations.

Supermales can leap tall buildings in a single bound.

False. So-called "supermales" have XYY sex chromosomal structure. They may be somewhat taller and more heavily bearded than the average male, but show little resemblance to the cartoon character Superman.

Many Americans have changed their sex through surgery and hormone treatments.

Not exactly. About 2,500 transsexuals have undergone sex-reassignment surgery, which provides the *appearance* of the external genitals of the opposite sex, but their internal sex organs cannot be changed to function like those of the opposite sex.

Strip-teasers are exhibitionists.

False. Exhibitionists attempt to surprise and shock their victims. Strip-teasers attempt to earn a living by sexually arousing their audiences.

OUTLINE

CHAPTER 12

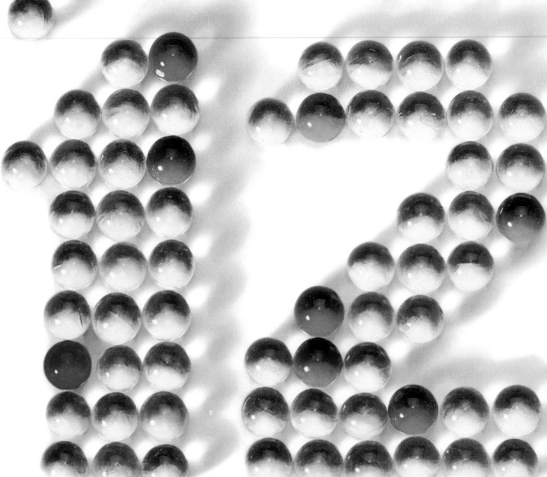

Methods of Therapy

TRUTH OR FICTION?

- People in merry old England used to visit the local insane asylum for a fun night out on the town.
- The terms *psychotherapy* and *psychoanalysis* are interchangeable.
- If you were in traditional psychoanalysis, your major tasks would be to lie back, relax, and say whatever pops into your mind.
- Some psychotherapists interpret clients' dreams.
- Some psychotherapists encourage their clients to take the lead in the therapy session.
- Other psychotherapists tell their clients precisely what to do.
- Still other psychotherapists purposefully argue with clients.
- A goal of psychotherapy is to help clients solve problems.
- You may be able to gain control over bad habits merely by keeping a record of where and when you practice them.
- Lying around in your reclining chair and fantasizing can be an effective way of confronting your fears.
- Smoking cigarettes can be an effective treatment for helping people to . . . stop smoking cigarettes.
- Staff members in a mental hospital induced reluctant patients to eat by ignoring them.
- Drugs are never a solution to abnormal behavior problems.
- Electroconvulsive shock therapy is no longer used in the United States.
- The originator of a surgical technique intended to reduce violence learned that it was not always successful—when one of his patients shot him.

Brad is having an uplifting experience—literally. Six people who minutes ago were perfect strangers have cradled him in their arms and raised him into midair. His eyes are closed. Gently they rock him back and forth and carry him about the room.

Brad is no paralyzed hospital patient. He has just joined an encounter group. He hopes to be able to learn to relate to other people as individuals, not as passing blurs on the street or as patrons asking him to cash payroll checks at the bank where he works as a teller. The group leader had directed that Brad be carried about in order to help him break down his defensive barriers and establish trust in others.

Brad had responded to a somewhat flamboyant ad in the therapy section of the classifieds in New York's *Village Voice:*

> Come to life! Stop being a gray automaton in a mechanized society! Encounter yourself and others. New group forming. First meeting free. Call 212-555-0599. Qualified therapist.

Like many who seek personal help, Brad had little idea how to go about it. His group experience may or may not work out. For one thing, he has no idea about the qualifications of the group leader and did not know to ask. If he had answered other ads in the *Voice,* including some placed by highly qualified therapists, his treatment might have looked quite different. Brad could have been:

Lying on a couch talking about anything that pops into his head and exploring the hidden meanings of a recurrent dream.

Sitting face to face with a gentle, accepting therapist who places the major burden for what happens during therapy directly on Brad's shoulders.

Listening to a frank, straightforward therapist insist that his problems stem from self-defeating attitudes and beliefs, such as an overriding need to be liked and approved of at almost all costs.

Role-playing initiating a social relationship, including smiling at a new acquaintance, making small talk, and looking the person squarely in the eye.

The form of treatment, or psychotherapy, practiced by a psychologist or another helping professional is related to that practitioner's theory of personality or model of abnormal behavior. It is not (or ought not be) a matter of chance. In this chapter we explore the history of treatment of abnormal behavior. Then we describe and evaluate several of the major current psychological treatment approaches, including *psychoanalysis, person-centered therapy, cognitive therapy, behavior therapy,* and *group therapy.* These are all forms of **psychotherapy,** which is a systematic interaction between a therapist and a client that brings psychological principles to bear on influencing the client's thoughts, feelings, or behavior in order to help that client overcome abnormal behavior or adjust to problems in living.

Quite a mouthful? True. But note the essentials:

1. Psychotherapy is a *systematic interaction.* The therapist's theoretical viewpoint and the client's problems determine how the therapist and client will relate to each other.

Psychotherapy A systematic interaction between a therapist and a client that brings psychological principles to bear on influencing the client's thoughts, feelings, or behavior in order to help that client overcome abnormal behavior or adjust to problems in living.

2. Psychotherapy brings *psychological principles* to bear on the client's problems. Psychotherapy is based on principles concerning human motivation and emotion, learning, and personality. It is not based on, say, religious or biological principles, although there is no reason why psychotherapy cannot be compatible with both.

3. Psychotherapy influences *thoughts, feelings,* or *behavior.* Psychotherapy may be aimed at any or all of these aspects of human psychology.

4. Psychotherapy helps the client *overcome abnormal behavior* or *adjust* to problems in living. Psychotherapy is concerned with people who have been diagnosed as, say, anxious or depressed, but it is also used with people who seek help in adjusting to problems such as social shyness, loss of a spouse, or confusion about the direction of one's career. Let us note also that some individuals use psychotherapy, especially insight-oriented therapies, not because there is a problem, but to learn more about the self and to achieve personal growth.

After exploring various psychotherapies, we shall turn our attention to the *biological therapies* that are used with some of the more severe forms of abnormal behavior, such as schizophrenic disorders and major depression. These include drug therapy *(chemotherapy), electroconvulsive shock therapy,* and *psychosurgery.*

HISTORICAL OVERVIEW

Ancient and medieval "treatments" of abnormal behavior often reflected the demonological model. They involved cruel practices like the Stone Age practice of breaking holes into the skull (see Chapter 11), exorcism, and death by hanging or burning, as was practiced in Europe and the United States some 300 years ago. In Europe and the United States, some people who could not meet the demands of everyday life were also thrown into prisons. Others begged in city streets, stole produce and food animals from farms, or entered marginal societal niches occupied by prostitutes and petty thieves. A few might find their ways to monasteries or other retreats that offered a kind word and some support. Generally speaking, they died young.

ASYLUMS

Asylums, which often had their origins in European monasteries, were the first institutions meant primarily for the mentally ill. Their functions were human warehousing, not treatment. Asylums mushroomed in population until the daily stresses created by noise, overcrowding, and unsanitary conditions undoubtedly heightened the problems they were meant to ameliorate. Inmates were frequently chained and beaten. Some were chained for four decades.

Humanitarian reform movements began in the eighteenth century. In Paris, Philippe Pinel unchained the patients at the asylum known as La Bicêtre. The populace was amazed that most patients, rather than running amok, profited from kindness and greater freedom. Many were later able

A CLOSER LOOK

SATURDAY NIGHT AT BEDLAM

More than 9,000 people, without care or protection . . . "bound with galling chains, bowed beneath fetters and heavy iron balls attached to drag chains, lacerated with ropes, scourged with rods and terrified beneath storms of execration and cruel blows; now subject to jibes and scorn and torturing tricks; now abandoned to the most outrageous violations."

A medieval dungeon in the damp caverns beneath a turreted castle? No. These were the conditions found in many asylums in the mid-nineteenth-century United States, as reported to Congress by New England schoolteacher Dorothea Dix.

And things were worse, much worse, at a London asylum by the name of St. Mary's of Bethlehem, which opened its gates to the unwary in 1547. Here the unfortunate were chained, whipped, and allowed to lie indefinitely in their waste products. Here the word *bedlam*, a bastardization of Bethlehem, had its origin. And to Bedlam the ladies and gents of the British upper class might wend their way on a lazy afternoon or dull evening, taking in the sights.

The admission for stopping in to have a gander at the more violently disturbed? One penny.

ST. MARY'S OF BETHLEHEM This institution is the source of the word *bedlam*.

THE UNCHAINING OF PATIENTS AT LA BICÊTRE The unchaining of patients symbolizes a landmark of the humanitarian reform movement.

to function in society again. Reform movements were later led by the Quaker William Tuke in England, and by Dorothea Dix in America.

MENTAL HOSPITALS

Mental hospitals gradually replaced asylums in the United States. In the mid-1950s, over a million people resided in state, county, Veterans Administration, or private facilities. Treatment, not warehousing, is the function of the mental hospital. Still, because of high patient populations and understaffing, many patients have received little attention. Even today, with somewhat improved conditions, it is not unusual for one psychiatrist to be responsible for the welfare of several hundred patients on a weekend.

THE COMMUNITY MENTAL-HEALTH MOVEMENT

Since the 1960s, efforts have been made to maintain as many mental patients as possible in the community. The Community Mental-Health Centers Act of 1963 provided funds for creating hundreds of community mental-health centers, in which patients would be charged according to their ability to pay, in order to accomplish this goal. These centers attempt to maintain new patients as outpatients, to serve patients from mental hospitals who have been released to the community, and to provide other services as listed in Table 12.1. Today, about 63 percent of the nation's chronically mentally ill live in the community, not the hospital (Morganthau et al., 1986).

But is it all **Valium** and roses in the community? Critics note that many mental patients who had lived in hospitals for decades were discharged to "home" communities that seemed foreign and frightening. Many discharged patients have not received adequate follow-up care in the community (Morganthau et al., 1986). Perhaps a third to a half of the nation's homeless people reflect the process of deinstitutionalization (Cordes, 1984;

Valium A popular tranquilizer that is prescribed for common anxiety and tension.

TABLE 12.1   Functions of the Community Mental-Health Center

Outpatient treatment
Short-term hospitalization
Partial hospitalization (e.g., patient sleeps in the hospital and works outside during
    the day)
Crisis intervention
Community consultation and education about abnormal behavior

The Community Mental-Health Centers Act provided funds for community agencies that attempt to intervene in mental-health problems as early as possible and to maintain mental patients in the community.

Fustero, 1984). Some former hospital inhabitants try to return to the protected world of the hospital and become trapped in a "revolving door" between the hospital and the community (Cordes, 1984).

The outlook for maintaining new patients in the community, rather than hospitalizing them, looks brighter. In a review of ten experiments in which seriously disturbed patients were randomly assigned either to hospitalization or some form of outpatient care, Kiesler (1982) did not find one case in which the outcomes of hospitalization were superior. The outpatient alternative was usually superior in terms of the patient's maintaining independent living arrangements, staying in school, and finding employment.

THE HELPING PROFESSIONALS

Throughout history people in many roles have helped others to adjust, including priests and ministers, grandparents, witch doctors, palm readers, and wise men (and women). Today qualified professionals in these roles include psychologists, psychiatrists, and social workers, among others.

Unfortunately, most states allow almost anyone to use the label *therapist.* This label indicates nothing about one's education and experience. People seeking effective therapy should never be shy about asking psychologists and others about their education and supervised experience. Here are some of the people who are genuinely qualified to help:

Psychologists   Psychologists have at least a master's degree and in many states must have a doctoral degree (Ph.D, Ed.D., Psy.D.), in order to use the label *psychologist.* The state will typically weigh the adequacy of the individual's education and supervised experience in psychology before granting a license to practice psychology. Psychologists use interviews, behavioral observations, and psychological tests to diagnose abnormal behavior problems, and psychotherapy to treat them. Most psychologists have been trained extensively in research methods. They are more likely than other helping professionals to be critically acquainted with psychological theory.

Psychiatrists   A psychiatrist is a licensed physician. Psychiatrists earn medical degrees and then undertake a psychiatric residency during which time they learn to apply medical skills, such as prescribing drugs, to treat abnormal behavior. Psychiatrists, like psychologists, may practice psychotherapy. Most psychiatrists rely on interviews for diagnostic purposes, but may refer patients to psychologists for psychological testing.

Psychiatric Social Workers   Psychiatric social workers have an M.S.W. (Master of Social Work) degree and supervised experience in helping people adjust. Many offer psychotherapy, but social workers do not use psychological tests or prescribe medical treatments. Many specialize in marital or family problems.

Psychoanalysts   Once only physicians were admitted to psychoanalytic training, but today many psychologists and social workers also practice the form of therapy originated by Sigmund Freud. The practice of psychoanalytic therapy requires years of training beyond the doctoral level, and completion of one's own psychoanalysis.

INSIGHT-ORIENTED THERAPIES

Many forms of psychotherapy are based on the assumption that abnormal behavior can be remedied if people gain **insight** into their problems. Insight involves knowledge of the experiences that led to conflicts, problems like anxiety and depression, and maladaptive behavior. Insight also involves (1) efforts to identify and *label* feelings and conflicts that lie beneath the level of conscious awareness, and (2) the ability to objectively view and to evaluate the appropriateness of one's own beliefs, attitudes, and thought processes. The insight-oriented therapies we shall discuss vary significantly in their methods, but they all share the assumption that accurate self-knowledge is required if self-defeating behavior patterns are to be changed effectively.

Let us now examine the following insight-oriented forms of psychotherapy: psychoanalysis, person-centered therapy, transactional analysis, gestalt therapy, and cognitive therapy.

PSYCHOANALYSIS: WHERE ID WAS, THERE SHALL EGO BE

> Canst thou not minister to a mind diseas'd,
> Pluck out from the memory a rooted sorrow,
> Raze out the written troubles of the brain,
> And with some sweet oblivious antidote
> Cleanse the stuff'd bosom of that perilous stuff
> Which weighs upon the heart?
> —Shakespeare, *Macbeth*

In this passage from *Macbeth*, Macbeth asks a physician to minister to Lady Macbeth after she has gone mad. In the play, her madness is at least in part caused by current events: her guilt at participating in a series of murders designed to bring her husband the throne of Scotland. But there are also hints of more deeply rooted and mysterious problems, perhaps involving infertility.

Insight In psychotherapy, knowledge of one's underlying motives or impulses.

A VIEW OF FREUD'S CONSULTING ROOM AT BERGGASSE 19 IN VIENNA Freud would sit in the chair by the head of the couch while a client free associated. The cardinal rule of free association is that no thought is to be censored, no matter how trivial or personal.

If Lady Macbeth's physician had been a psychoanalyst, he might have asked her to lie down on a couch in a slightly darkened room. He would have sat just behind her and encouraged her to talk about anything that popped into her mind, no matter how trivial, no matter how personal. In order to avoid interfering with her self-exploration, he might have said little or nothing for session after session. That would have been par for the course. After all, there would have been months of **psychoanalysis** ahead, perhaps years. . . .

Goals of Psychoanalysis   Psychoanalysis is the clinical method devised by Sigmund Freud for plucking "from the memory a rooted sorrow," for razing "out the written troubles of the brain." From Freud's perspective, as noted in Chapter 11, abnormal behavior is generally caused by inner conflict of deep-rooted origins. Psychoanalysis is the method used by Freud and his followers to "cleanse . . . that perilous stuff which weighs upon the heart"—to provide insight into the conflicts presumed to lie at the roots of a person's problems. Psychoanalysis seeks to allow the client to express emotions and impulses that are theorized to have been dammed up by the forces of repression.

Freud was fond of saying, "Where id was, there shall ego be." In part he meant that psychoanalysis could shed some light on the inner workings of the client. But Freud did not believe we should become conscious of all primitive impulses and conflicts. Instead, he sought to replace impulsive and defensive behavior with coping behavior. He believed that impulsive behavior reflected the urges of the id. Defensive behavior, such as timidly avoiding confrontations, represented the ego's compromising efforts to protect the client from these impulses and the possibility of retaliation. Coping

Psychoanalysis In this usage, Freud's method of psychotherapy.

Abreaction In psychoanalysis, expression of previously repressed feelings and impulses to allow the psychic energy associated with them to spill forth. (The Latin prefix *ab-* means "away" or "from.")

Catharsis (kuh-THAR-sis). Another term for *abreaction*.

Free association In psychoanalysis, the uncensored uttering of all thoughts that come to mind.

Compulsion to utter The urge to express ideas and impulses—in psychoanalytic theory, a reflection of the seeking of expression by impulses within the id.

Resistance The tendency to block the free expression of impulses and primitive ideas—a reflection of the defense mechanism of repression.

Interpretation An explanation of client's utterance according to psychoanalytic theory.

---

behavior would allow the client at least partially to express these impulses; but the client would do so in socially acceptable ways, thereby achieving greater gratification and also avoiding social and self-condemnation.

In this way a man with a phobia for knives might come to see that he had been repressing the urge to harm someone who had taken advantage of him. He might also find ways to confront his antagonist verbally. A woman with a conversion disorder—paralysis of the legs—could see that her disability allowed her to avoid an unwanted pregnancy without feeling guilty. Perhaps she would also taste her resentment at being pressed into a stereotypical feminine sex role and decide to expand her options.

Freud also believed that psychoanalysis should permit the client to spill forth the psychic energy theorized to have been repressed by conflicts and guilt. He called this spilling forth **abreaction,** or **catharsis**. Abreaction would provide feelings of relief.

Free Association   Early in his development as a therapist, Freud found that his clients appeared to be able to focus on repressed conflicts and talk about them under hypnosis. Hypnosis seemed an efficient way of breaking through to topics of which clients were unaware in the normal waking state.* But he found that many clients would deny the accuracy of this material once they were brought out of the trance. Other clients found these revelations premature and painful. Freud then turned to **free association** as a more gradual method of breaking down the walls of defense that he believed had prevented the ego from gaining insight into unconscious processes.

In free association, the client is made comfortable, typically by lying on a couch, and asked to talk about any topic that comes to mind. No thought is to be censored—that is the cardinal rule. While psychoanalysts ask their clients to wander "freely" from topic to topic, they do not believe that the process *within* the client is fully free. Repressed impulses constantly seek release. On a verbal level, they lead to a **compulsion to utter.** A client may begin free association by talking about various meaningless topics, but eventually the compulsion to utter will bring important repressed material to the surface.

But the ego maintains the tendency to repress unacceptable impulses and threatening conflicts. Clients will show **resistance** to recalling and talking about many frightening, threatening, or degrading ideas. Clients may claim "My mind is blank" when they are about to encounter such a thought. They may accuse the analyst of being too demanding or inconsiderate. They may "forget" their appointment when it seems that threatening material may be uncovered during that session.

During an analysis, the therapist observes this dynamic struggle between the compulsion to utter and resistance. Through discreet remarks, the analyst subtly tips the balance in favor of uttering. A gradual process of self-discovery and self-insight ensues. Now and then the analyst offers an **interpretation** of an utterance, showing how it suggests resistance, or, perhaps, the symbolic revelation of deep-seated feelings or conflicts.

*See Chapter 4 for a critical discussion of hypnosis.

Inside Woody Allen

Dream Analysis Freud considered dreams the "royal road to the unconscious." As noted in Chapter 4, the psychoanalytic theory of dreams holds that they are determined by unconscious processes as well as the remnants or "residues" of the day. Unconscious impulses tend to be expressed in dreams as a form of **wish fulfillment.**

But unacceptable impulses, usually sexual or aggressive, are likely to be displaced onto objects and situations that reflect the era and culture of the client. These objects then become **symbols** of the unconscious wishes. For instance, dream objects that are long and narrow may be **phallic symbols,** but whether the symbol takes the form of a spear, rifle, "stick shift" or spacecraft partially reflects one's cultural background.

In psychoanalytic theory, the perceived content of the dream is called its shown, or **manifest content.** The presumed hidden or symbolic content

Wish fulfillment A primitive method used by the id to attempt to gratify basic instincts.

Symbol A sign that stands for, or represents, something else.

Phallic symbol A sign that represents the penis.

Manifest content In the psychoanalytic theory of dreams, the reported content of dreams.

Latent content In the psychoanalytic theory of dreams, the symbolized or underlying content of dreams.

Transference In psychoanalysis, the generalization to the analyst of feelings toward a person in the client's life.

Countertransference In psychoanalysis, the generalization to the client of feelings toward a person in the analyst's life.

Opaque (oh-PAKE). Literally, not permitting the passage of light; thus, in psychoanalysis, the hiding of feelings by the analyst. (From the Latin *opacus*, meaning "shaded.")

of the dream is referred to as its **latent content.** A man may dream that he is flying. Flying is the manifest content of the dream. Psychoanalysts usually interpret flying as symbolic of erection, so sexual potency might be involved in the latent content of such a dream.

Freud often asked clients to jot down their dreams upon waking so that they could be interpreted during the psychoanalytic session.

Transference Freud found that his clients responded not only to his appearance and behavior, but also according to what his appearance and behavior meant to them. A young woman might see Freud as a father figure and displace, or transfer, her feelings toward her own father onto Freud. Another woman might view him as a lover and, perhaps, act seductively. Men also showed this uncalled-for generalization of feelings, or **transference.** A man might also view Freud as a father figure, or, perhaps, a competitor. Freud discovered that he could transfer his feelings onto his clients—perhaps viewing a woman as a sex object or a young man as a rebellious son. He called this placing of clients into stereotypical roles in his own life **countertransference.**

Transference and countertransference lead to uncalled-for expectations of new people in our lives and may foster maladaptive behavior. We may expect our spouses to act like our opposite-sex parents and expect too much (or too little) from them. Or we may accuse them unjustly of harboring wishes and secrets we attributed to our parents. We may not give new friends or lovers a chance when we have been mistreated by someone from the past who played a similar role in our lives or our fantasies.

In any event, psychoanalysts are trained to be **opaque** concerning their own behavior and feelings, so that they will not encourage client transference or express their own feelings of countertransference. Then, when the client acts accusingly, seductively, or otherwise inappropriately toward the analyst, the analyst can plead not guilty of encouraging the client's behavior and suggest that it reflects historical events and fantasies. In this way, transference behavior becomes grist for the therapeutic mill.

Analysis of client transference is an important element of therapy. It provides client insight and encourages more adaptive social behavior. But it may take months or years for transference to develop fully and to be resolved, which is one reason that psychoanalysis can be such a lengthy process.

Modern Psychoanalytic Approaches A number of psychoanalysts still adhere faithfully to Freud's protracted techniques. In recent years, however, briefer, less intense forms of psychoanalysis have been devised (Koss et al., 1986; Zaiden, 1982), making it possible for psychoanalysts to work with clients who cannot afford protracted therapy, or whose schedules will not permit it. These psychoanalytically oriented therapies still focus on revealing unconscious conflicts and motives and on breaking down psychological defenses and resistance, but client and therapist usually sit face to face (as opposed to using a couch), and the therapist is more directive than the traditional psychoanalyst. Therapists frequently suggest productive behavior patterns as well as promote self-insight. Briefer forms of psychoanalysis do not permit the restructuring of the client's personality.

Evaluation of Psychoanalysis   Psychoanalysis is difficult to evaluate for various reasons. As noted in Chapter 1, psychologists prefer to make evaluations on the basis of experimental evidence whenever possible. But a sound experiment to evaluate psychoanalysis could require randomly assigning people seeking therapy to psychoanalysis and to a number of other therapies for comparison. A subject might have to remain in therapy for years in order to attain a "true" psychoanalysis, but the control subjects could not be kept in briefer forms of therapy for years. Moreover, some people want psychoanalysis per se rather than psychotherapy in general. It would not be ethical, or practical, to assign them randomly to assorted treatments or to a no-treatment control group (Basham, 1986; Parloff, 1986).

Self-insight and not behavioral change is the primary goal of psychoanalysis. Since each person's self-insights must be unique, it could be impossible to measure how much insight has been gained, and whether it is accurate.

Psychoanalysts therefore claim, with some justification, that clinical judgment must be the basis for evaluating the effectiveness of analysis. Despite these evaluation problems, however, research into the effectiveness of psychoanalytically oriented therapies has been reasonably encouraging. Mary Lee Smith and Gene Glass, for example, analyzed the results of dozens of studies on psychoanalysis and concluded that people who receive psychoanalytically oriented therapy show greater well-being, on the average, than 70 to 75 percent of those who are left untreated (Smith & Glass, 1977; Smith et al., 1981). There also seems to be some consensus that psychoanalysis is most effective with well-educated, highly verbal and motivated clients (Luborsky & Spence, 1978). Psychoanalysis does not appear successful with psychotic disorders.

Despite the positive findings of Smith and Glass, critics of psychoanalysis, such as behavior therapist Joseph Wolpe (1985), argue that it has never been shown that the beneficial aspects of psychoanalysis can be attributed to the psychoanalytic method per se. Instead, it may be that the positive outcomes of such therapy should actually be attributed to the benefits of a close, emotional relationship with a therapist—benefits which may be derived from almost any sort of therapy.

In any event, during the 1940s and 1950s, psychotherapy was almost synonymous with psychoanalysis. Few other approaches to psychotherapy had any impact on psychologists or on public awareness (Garfield, 1981, 1982). But in the 1980s, according to a survey of clinical and counseling psychologists by Darrell Smith (1982), only about 14 percent of psychotherapists report that they have a psychoanalytic orientation. Sigmund Freud, once the model for almost all therapists, is currently rated third in influence, following Carl Rogers and Albert Ellis, whom we discuss in the following pages. The largest group of psychotherapists (41 percent) consider themselves eclectic (Smith, 1982, p. 804).

PERSON-CENTERED THERAPY: REMOVING ROADBLOCKS TO SELF-ACTUALIZATION

Person-centered therapy was originated by Carl Rogers (1951), who was rated as the single most influential psychotherapist in the Darrell Smith (1982) survey. Rogers has a **phenomenological** outlook; he is concerned with subjective experience. As noted in Chapter 9, Rogers sees us as free to make choices and to control our own destinies. Contrast this view to the Freudian perspective, which portrays us as driven by unconscious forces and as victims of childhood conflicts over which we have little if any control.

Rogers also believes that we have natural tendencies toward health, growth, and fulfillment. Given this view, Rogers writes that abnormal behavior stems largely from roadblocks placed in the path of our own self-actualization. Because others show us selective approval when we are young, we learn to disown the disapproved parts of ourselves. We don masks and façades to earn social approval. We may learn to be seen but not heard—not even heard, or examined fully, by ourselves. As a result we may experience stress and discomfort and the feeling that we—or the world—are not real.

Person-centered therapy may provide insight into parts of us that we have disowned, allowing us to feel whole once more. Rogers stresses the importance of creating a warm, therapeutic atmosphere that encourages client self-exploration and self-expression. Therapist acceptance of the client is thought to lead to client self-acceptance and heightened self-esteem. Self-acceptance then frees the client to make choices and decisions that foster development of his or her unique potential.

Person-centered therapy is nondirective. The client takes the lead, listing and exploring problems. The therapist reflects or paraphrases important feelings and ideas of the client, helping the client get in touch with feelings and follow the strongest leads in the quest for self-insight. (Although Rogers believes that therapy should be nondirective, he admits that "Sometimes I'll give in to a client and give a little advice. But then the client will say, 'I've already tried that'" [Bennett, 1985, p. 3].) The effective person-centered therapist also shows *unconditional positive regard, empathetic understanding, genuineness,* and *congruence.*

The therapist shows **unconditional positive regard** for clients. In this way, they are respected as important human beings with unique values and goals, and provided with a sense of security that encourages them to follow their own feelings. Person-centered therapists believe strongly that people are basically *prosocial.* If people follow their own feelings, rather than act defensively, they should not be abusive or antisocial.

Empathetic understanding is shown by accurately reflecting the client's experiences and feelings. Therapists must view the world through their clients' eyes, or **frames of reference,** by setting aside their own values and listening carefully.

Genuineness is the therapist's honesty in relationships with clients. In contrast to the opaque psychoanalyst, person-centered therapists are supposed to be open about their feelings. It would be harmful to clients if their

---

Person-centered therapy Carl Rogers' method of psychotherapy, which emphasizes the creation of a warm, therapeutic atmosphere that frees clients to engage in self-exploration and self-expression.

Phenomenological Descriptive of theoretical approaches that emphasize the importance of the human experience of the world, and which view people as free to make choices.

Unconditional positive regard Acceptance of the value of another person, although not necessarily acceptance of all of that person's behaviors. See Chapter 9.

Empathetic understanding Ability to perceive a client's feelings from the client's frame of reference. A quality of the good person-centered therapist.

Frame of reference One's unique patterning of perceptions and attitudes, according to which one evaluates events.

Genuineness Recognition and open expression of the therapist's own feelings. A quality of the good person-centered therapist.

PERSON-CENTERED THERAPY The qualities of the effective person-centered therapist include unconditional positive regard for clients, empathetic understanding, genuineness, and congruence.

therapists could not truly accept and like them, even though their values may differ from those of the therapists. Rogers admits that he has sometimes had negative feelings about clients, usually in the form of boredom; generally speaking, he has expressed these feelings rather than holding them in (Bennett, 1985). Person-centered therapists must also be able to tolerate differentness, because they believe that every client is different in important ways.

Successful person-centered therapists also show **congruence,** or a fit between their thoughts, feelings, and behavior. Congruence gives us access to inner experience (Kahn, 1985). Person-centered therapists serve as models of integrity to their clients.

Evaluation of Person-Centered Therapy   There is some difficulty in evaluating person-centered therapy because the goals of therapy—heightened self-esteem, self-acceptance, and self-actualization—pose measurement problems. Still, the analysis by Smith and Glass (1977) found that nearly 75 percent of the clients receiving person-centered therapy were better off than people who were left untreated.

Like psychoanalysis, person-centered therapy seems most effective with well-educated, highly motivated, and verbal people (Abramowitz et al., 1974; Wexler & Butler, 1976). There is no evidence of effectiveness with psychotic disorders. Despite the influence of Carl Rogers, only about 9 percent of psychotherapists place themselves within the person-centered tradition (Smith, 1982, p. 804).

Congruence A fit between one's self-concept and behaviors, thoughts, and emotions.

Transactional analysis A form of psychotherapy that deals with how people interact, and how their interactions reinforce attitudes, expectations, and "life positions." Abbreviated *TA.*

Inferiority complex Feelings of inferiority hypothesized by Alfred Adler to serve as a central motivating force. See Chapter 9.

"Parent" In TA, a moralistic "ego state."

"Child" In TA, an irresponsible, emotional "ego state."

"Adult" In TA, a rational, adaptive "ego state."

Transaction In TA, an exchange between two people.

Complementary In TA, descriptive of a transaction in which the ego states of two people interact harmoniously.

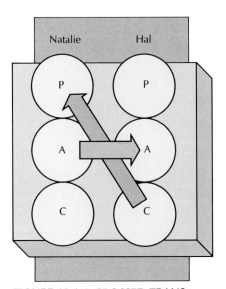

FIGURE 12.1 A CROSSED TRANSACTION Natalie asks Hal, "Did you have a good time, tonight?" Hal replies, "Why do you wanna know?" Communication is thus broken off.

TRANSACTIONAL ANALYSIS: I'M OK—YOU'RE OK—WE'RE ALL OK

Transactional analysis (TA) is rooted in the psychoanalytic and humanistic traditions. According to Thomas Harris, author of *I'm OK—You're OK* (1967), many of us suffer from the sort of **inferiority complex** described by psychoanalyst Alfred Adler. Though adults, we may continue to see ourselves as dependent children. We may think other people are OK, but not see ourselves as OK. *I'm not OK—You're OK* is one of four basic "life positions," or ways of perceiving relationships with others.

A major goal of TA is to help people adopt the life position *I'm OK—You're OK,* in which they accept others and themselves. Unfortunately, people tend to adopt "games," or styles of relating to others that are designed to confirm one of the unhealthy life positions: I'm OK—You're not OK, I'm not OK—You're OK, or I'm not OK—You're not OK.

Psychiatrist Eric Berne, the originator of TA and author of *Games People Play* (1976), described our personalities as containing three "ego states": **Parent, Child,** and **Adult.** The "parent" is a moralistic ego state. The "child" is an irresponsible and emotional ego state. The "adult" is a rational ego state. (These are three hypothesized *ego states,* or ways of coping. They are not intended to correspond exactly to the concepts of id, ego, and superego.)

People tend to relate to each other as parents, children, or adults. A social exchange between two people is called a **transaction.** A transaction is said to fit, or be **complementary,** when a social exchange follows the same lines. In one type of complementary transaction, people relate as adults. But a transaction can also be complementary, even if upsetting, when two people relate as parent and child (Parent: "You shouldn't have done that"; Child: "I'm sorry, I promise it won't happen again"). Communication breaks down when the social exchange between the parties does not follow complementary lines (as in Figure 12.1). Note these examples:

NATALIE (adult to adult): Did you have a good time tonight?
    HAL (child to parent): Why do you wanna know?

Or:

    BILL (adult to adult): Nan, did you see the checkbook?
NAN (parent to child): A place for everything and everything in its place!

TA is often carried out with couples who complain of communication problems. It encourages people to relate to each other as adults.

TA also attempts to put an end to game playing. The most commonly played marital game is "If It Weren't for You" (Berne, 1976). People who play this game marry domineering mates who prevent them from going into things they would not have the courage to do anyhow, such as taking a more challenging job or moving to a new city. By playing "If It Weren't for You," they can blame their mates for their shortcomings and excuse their own timidity.

Smith and Glass (1977) reported that people who receive TA are better off than about 72 percent of those who are left untreated.

○ ○ ○ ○ ○ ○ ○ ○ ○ ○

GESTALT THERAPY: GETTING IT TOGETHER

Like psychoanalysis and person-centered therapy, **Gestalt therapy,** originated by Fritz Perls (1893–1970), aims to provide insight into how conflicting parts of the personality create distress. Perls used the term *Gestalt* to signify his interest in shaping the conflicting parts of the personality into an integrated form. He wanted his clients to become aware of inner conflict, to live with conflict rather than deny it or keep it repressed, and to make productive choices despite fear.

Although Perls owes much to psychoanalytic theory, his form of therapy, unlike psychoanalysis, focuses on the "here and now." In Gestalt therapy, clients undergo exercises intended to make them more aware of current feelings and behavior, rather than to explore the past. Perls also believed, along with Carl Rogers, that people are free to make choices and to direct their personal growth; however, unlike person-centered therapy, Gestalt therapy is highly directive. The therapist leads the client through planned experiences.

One Gestalt technique that increases awareness of internal conflict is the **dialogue.** Clients undertake verbal confrontations between opposing wishes and ideas. An example of these clashing personality elements is "top dog" and "underdog." One's top dog may conservatively suggest, "Don't take chances. Stick with what you have or you may lose it all." Your frustrated underdog may rise up and assert, "You never try anything. How will you ever get out of this rut if you don't take on new challenges?" Heightened awareness of the elements of conflict may clear the path toward resolution, perhaps through compromise.

Body language also provides insight into conflicting feelings. Clients may be instructed to attend to responses like furrows in the eyebrow and

Gestalt therapy Fritz Perls' form of psychotherapy, which attempts to integrate conflicting parts of the personality through directive methods designed to help the person perceive his or her whole self.

Dialogue A gestalt therapy technique in which clients verbalize confrontations between conflicting parts of their personality.

Fritz Perls.

facial tension when they express ideas that they think they support whole-heartedly. In this way they often find that their body language suggests the presence of impulses that they have been denying.

In order to increase clients' understanding of opposing points of view, and to broaden their perspective, therapists may encourage them to argue ideas that are directly opposed to their own expressed ideas. They may also role play (act out) the behavior of important people in their lives to get more in touch with their points of view.

While many psychoanalysts may view dreams as the "royal road to the unconscious," Perls saw the stuff of dreams as disowned parts of the personality. He would often ask clients to role play the elements in their dreams to get in touch with these isolated parts. In *Gestalt Therapy Verbatim*, Perls —known to clients and friends alike as Fritz—describes a session in which a client, "Jim," is reporting a dream:

JIM: I just have the typical recurring dream which I think a lot of people might have if they have a background problem, and it isn't of anything I think I can act out. It's the distant wheel—I'm not sure what type it is—it's coming towards me and ever-increasing in size. And then finally, it's just above me and it's no height that I can determine, it's so high. And that's—

FRITZ: If you were this wheel, . . . what would you do with Jim?

JIM: I am just about to roll over Jim. (1971, p. 127)

Perls encourages Jim to undertake a dialogue with the wheel. Jim comes to see that the wheel represents fears about taking decisive action. Through this insight the "wheel" becomes more manageable in size, and Jim is able to use some of the "energy" that he might otherwise have spent in worrying to begin to take charge of his life.

Smith and Glass (1977) found that people who receive Gestalt therapy show greater well-being than about 60 percent of those who are left untreated.

COGNITIVE THERAPY

Cognitive therapy is the newest form of therapy presented in this book. Although there are many different cognitive therapists and more than one type of cognitive therapy, cognitive therapists in general would agree with Carl Rogers that people are free to make choices and develop in accord with their conceptions of what they are capable of becoming. Cognitive therapists would also agree with Fritz Perls that it is appropriate for clients to focus on what is happening today in therapy, instead of what happened in the distant past, and cognitive therapists are also reasonably directive in their approaches.

I include cognitive therapy as an insight-oriented therapy, because cognitive therapists, by and large, focus on the beliefs, attitudes, and automatic types of thinking that create and compound their clients' problems. Insight into clients' *current cognitions,* and not the distant past, is a primary goal of cognitive therapy. *Changing* these cognitions to reduce negative feelings like anxiety and depression, to provide more accurate perceptions of the environment, and to orient the client toward solving problems is another major goal.

Cognitive therapy A form of therapy that focuses on how clients' cognitions (expectations, attitudes, beliefs, etc.) lead to distress and may be modified to relieve distress and promote adaptive behavior.

Let us have a look at some specific cognitive-therapy approaches and methods.

Albert Ellis's Rational-Emotive Therapy   Albert Ellis, the founder of **rational-emotive therapy** and rated as the second most influential psychotherapist in the Darrell Smith (1982) survey, actively argues with clients to show them how self-defeating irrational beliefs (see Chapter 10) create or compound problems such as anxiety, depression, and feelings of helplessness. As described in Chapter 10, Ellis has found that many of us harbor a number of his ten basic irrational beliefs. These beliefs, such as the belief that we must have sincere approval from others almost all of the time, cause us to fall short of our self-demands.

Aaron Beck's Cognitive Therapy   Psychiatrist Aaron Beck (1976) also focuses on clients' cognitive distortions. He questions patients in a manner that will encourage them to see the irrationality of their own ways of thinking—how, for example, their minimizing of their accomplishments and their pessimistic assuming that the worst will happen heightens feelings of depression. Beck notes that our cognitive distortions can be fleeting and automatic, difficult to detect. His therapy methods help clients focus on their fleeting, self-defeating thoughts.

Becoming aware of and changing catastrophizing thoughts helps provide us with coping ability under stress. (Consider the example of coping with test anxiety on pp. 487–488.) In the discussion of depression in Chapter 11, it was noted that internal, stable, and global attributions of failure lead to depression and feelings of helplessness. Cognitive therapists alert clients to all these cognitive distortions as a prelude to effective behavioral change.

"Running Movies" and Cognitive Restructuring   The cognitive techniques of "running movies" and cognitive restructuring have helped people get in touch with and change cognitive errors. Consider this example: Close your eyes. Imagine that you are pushing a cart down an aisle in a supermarket. Someone pushes into you, so hard that it seems purposeful, and then says, "What the hell's the matter with you? Why don't you watch where you're going!"

What would you think? Would you think, "This so-and-so can't treat me this way! People can't be allowed to act like that!" If so you would have made the cognitive errors of taking this person's rudeness personally and expecting others to live up to your own standards. Your attitudes might prompt you to violence, to behavior you might regret afterward.

In humans, aggressive responses to aversive situations are not automatic—they involve thought processes (Berkowitz, 1983). But since many people claim that their aggressive responses seem automatic, and that they are unaware of the thoughts that lead to them, many cognitive therapists use methods such as running a movie to help them get in touch with irrational beliefs and other cognitive errors that intensify negative feelings and prompt maladaptive behavior. In running a movie about the supermarket

Albert Ellis.

Rational-emotive therapy Albert Ellis's form of cognitive psychotherapy, which focuses on how irrational expectations create anxiety and disappointment, and encourages clients to challenge and correct these expectations.

incident, a client would relive this upsetting experience in the imagination to search out fleeting thoughts that might otherwise barely be noticed.

Novaco (1974) showed how running movies, cognitive restructuring, and relaxation training helped explosive men and women deal with the supermarket-type of provocation more effectively. His strategy included three phases: education, planning, and application training. In phase 1, participants were shown how anger is intensified by the irrational beliefs that one must expect flawless behavior from others, and that an insult is a threat to one's self-esteem. In phase 2, they were taught relaxation skills and alternatives for their irrational beliefs. In phase 3, participants imagined provocations and practiced using rational beliefs and relaxation to arrive at adaptive, nonviolent responses. Subjects made dramatic gains in coping with provocations in socially acceptable ways. Many reported that they came to reconceptualize provocations as problems demanding a solution, rather than as threats requiring a violent response.

Problem-Solving Training   Another cognitive-therapy approach, problem-solving training, encourages clients to use the stages in problem solving outlined in Chapter 6 to enhance their control over their lives. Successful problem-solving involves studying all aspects of a problem (preparation), generating multiple solutions (production), and trying them out and evaluating their effectiveness (evaluation). Subjects receiving problem-solving training for controlling feelings of anger are encouraged to study sample provocations, to generate various behavioral solutions (alternative to violence), and to try out and evaluate the most promising ones (e.g., Moon & Eisler, 1983). In addition to controlling anger effectively, subjects receiving problem-solving training in the Moon and Eisler study also responded to provocations with more socially skillful behavior.

Evaluation of Cognitive Therapy   There is an increasing body of evidence that cognitive factors play an important role in adjustment problems. They are particularly pertinent to feelings of anxiety and depression that are learned or acquired through experience. This is abundantly clear in phobias, where the client believes that a particular object or situation is awful and must be avoided, and in depressive reactions that are linked to internal, stable, and global attributions of failure. Cognitive approaches have yielded many positive results with such problems. Modification of irrational beliefs has also been shown to decrease emotional distress (Lipsky et al., 1980; Smith, 1983). A number of researchers have analyzed studies that compare cognitive approaches to others in the treatment of anxiety and depression, and have found that cognitive-therapy clients show significantly greater improvement than clients receiving traditional psychoanalytic or phenomenological treatments (Andrews & Harvey, 1981; Shapiro & Shapiro, 1982).

It should be noted that many theorists consider cognitive therapy to be a collection of techniques that belong within the province of behavior therapy, which is discussed in the following section. Some members of this group prefer the name "cognitive *behavior* therapy"; others argue that the term *behavior therapy* is sufficiently broad to include cognitive therapy.

However, it seems that there is a difference in focus between many cognitive therapists and behavior therapists. To behavior therapists, the purpose of dealing with client cognitions is to change *overt* behavior. A cognitive therapist will agree that mental or cognitive change leads to overt behavioral change, but may assert that the cognitive change itself is an important and central goal.

BEHAVIOR THERAPY: ADJUSTMENT IS WHAT YOU DO

Behavior therapy—also called *behavior modification*—is the systematic application of principles of learning in order to promote desired behavioral changes. As suggested in the section on cognitive therapy, behavior therapists have increasingly come to incorporate cognitive processes in their theoretical outlook and cognitive procedures in their methodology (Wilson, 1982). For example, techniques like *systematic desensitization, covert sensitization, covert reinforcement,* and some others ask clients to engage in visual imagery or fantasy. However, behavior therapists insist that their methods be established by experimentation (Wolpe, 1985), and that therapeutic outcome be assessed in terms of observable, measurable behavior.

Behavior therapists rely heavily on principles of classical and operant conditioning and observational learning. They help clients discontinue self-defeating behavior patterns, such as overeating, smoking, and phobic avoidance of harmless stimuli. They also help clients acquire adaptive behavior patterns, such as the social skills required to initiate relationships and to say no to insistent salespeople.

Behavior therapists may help clients gain "insight," but such insight usually involves enhancing client awareness of the circumstances in which maladaptive behavior occurs, in contrast to the psychoanalytic search for its historic origins. Behavior therapists may build trusting relationships with clients that involve positive regard, but they see the special effectiveness of behavior therapy as a joint product of this sort of emotional interaction and their specific learning-based procedures (Wolpe, 1985). Behavior therapists do not, in contrast to person-centered therapists, argue that therapeutic change stems from the warm, therapeutic atmosphere and therapist traits alone.

About 17 percent of the clinical and counseling psychologists surveyed by Darrell Smith (1982) labeled themselves behavioral or cognitive-behavioral in orientation—the largest group of therapists who identified with a specific orientation. Behavior therapists Joseph Wolpe and Arnold Lazarus were ranked fourth and fifth among the ten most influential psychotherapists (Smith, 1982, p. 807).

Let us look at a number of behavior-therapy techniques.

SYSTEMATIC DESENSITIZATION

Adam has a phobia for receiving injections. His behavior therapist treats him as he reclines in a comfortable padded chair. In a state of deep mus-

Behavior therapy Systematic application of the principles of learning to the direct modification of a client's problem behaviors.

FIGURE 12.2 SYSTEMATIC DESENSITIZATION In systematic desensitization, clients engage in deep muscle relaxation, while the therapist presents a graduated series of fear-evoking stimuli.

cular relaxation, Adam observes slides projected onto a screen. A slide of a nurse holding a needle has just been shown three times, thirty seconds at a time. Each time Adam has shown no anxiety. So now a slightly more discomforting slide is shown: the nurse aiming the needle toward someone's bare arm. After fifteen seconds our armchair adventurer notices twinges of discomfort and raises a finger as a signal (speaking might disturb his relaxation). The projector operator shuts off the disturbing slide, and Adam spends two minutes imagining his "safe scene"—lying on a beach beneath the tropical sun. Then the slide is shown again. This time Adam views it for thirty seconds before feeling any anxiety.

Adam is undergoing **systematic desensitization,** a method for reducing phobic responses originated by psychiatrist Joseph Wolpe (1958, 1973). Systematic desensitization is a gradual process. Clients learn to handle increasingly disturbing stimuli as anxiety to each one is counterconditioned. About ten to twenty stimuli are arranged in a sequence or **hierarchy** according to their capacity to elicit anxiety. In imagination, or by being shown photos, the client travels gradually up through this hierarchy, approaching the **target** behavior. In Adam's case the target behavior was the ability to receive an injection without undue anxiety.

Joseph Wolpe developed systematic desensitization on the assumption that maladaptive anxiety responses, like other behaviors, are learned or conditioned. He reasoned that they can be unlearned by **counterconditioning,** or by extinction (see Chapter 5). In counterconditioning, a response that is incompatible with anxiety is made to appear under conditions that usually elicit anxiety. Muscle relaxation is incompatible with anxiety. For this reason Adam's therapist is teaching Adam to experience relaxation in the presence of (usually) anxiety-evoking slides of needles.

Systematic desensitization Wolpe's method for reducing fears by associating images of fear-evoking stimuli with deep muscle relaxation.

Hierarchy An arrangement according to rank or class structure. In this case, stimuli are arranged according to the amount of fear they evoke.

Target Goal.

Counterconditioning The repeated pairing of a stimulus that elicits a certain response (say, fear) with a stimulus that elicits an antagonistic response (say, relaxation instructions) in such a way that the first stimulus loses the capacity to elicit the problematic (fear) response.

BEHAVIOR THERAPY: ADJUSTMENT IS WHAT YOU DO   561

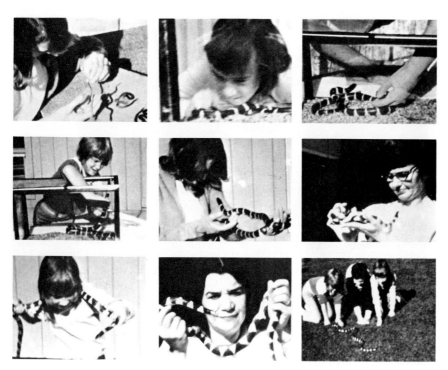

FIGURE 12.3 **PARTICIPANT MODELING** Participant modeling is a behavior-therapy technique based on principles of observational learning. In these photos, people with an aversion for snakes observe and then imitate people who are unafraid. Parents often try to convince young children that something tastes good by eating it in front of them and saying "Mmm!"

Remaining in the presence of phobic imagery, rather than running from it, is also likely to enhance our perceived self-efficacy—or our own belief in our ability to cope with the phobic object. Perceived self-efficacy is negatively correlated with levels of adrenalin in the bloodstream (Bandura et al., 1985). Thus it may be that raising clients' perceived self-efficacy helps to lower their adrenalin levels, counteract feelings of nervousness, and lessen the physical signs of anxiety.

The Symptom-Substitution Controversy Psychoanalysts have argued that phobias are symptoms of unconscious conflicts, and that systematic desensitization of a "symptom" may only lead to the appearance of another symptom—that is, to **symptom substitution.** To behavior therapists, maladaptive behavior *is* the problem, not just a symptom of the problem. Evidence suggests that systematic desensitization is effective in more than 80 percent of cases (Paul, 1969a; Smith & Glass, 1977; Marks, 1982), and symptom substitution has not been found to be a problem.

Participant Modeling A behavioral alternative to systematic desensitization is **participant modeling,** which relies on observational learning. In this method, clients observe and then imitate people who do approach and cope with the objects or situations they fear. Bandura and his colleagues (1969) found that participant modeling worked as well as systematic desensitization, and more rapidly, for a number of people who were afraid of snakes (see Figure 12.3). Participant modeling, like systematic desensiti-

Symptom substitution The exchange of one symptom for another. The term refers to the psychoanalytic belief that a phobia is a symptom of an underlying disorder, and that removal of the phobia through behavioral techniques may lead to emergence of another symptom of the disorder.

Participant modeling A behavior-therapy technique in which a client observes and imitates a person who approaches and copes with feared objects or situations.

Aversive conditioning A behavior-therapy technique in which undesired responses are inhibited by pairing repugnant or offensive stimuli with them.

zation, is likely to increase perceptions of self-efficacy in coping with feared stimuli.

In any event, systematic desensitization is a largely "painless" way to confront fears. And when given careful instructions, people seem capable of using it on their own—no therapist needed (Rosen et al., 1976).

AVERSIVE CONDITIONING

You may have read or seen the filmed version of the futuristic Anthony Burgess novel, *A Clockwork Orange*. Alex, the antisocial "hero," finds violence and rape superb pastimes. When he is caught, he is given the chance to undergo an experimental reconditioning program rather than serve a prison term. In this program, he watches films of violence and rape while he is throwing up as a result of a nausea-inducing drug. After his release, he feels ill whenever he contemplates violence. Unfortunately, Beethoven's music, which he had enjoyed, accompanies the films and feelings of nausea. So Alex acquires an aversion for Beethoven as well.

In the novel, Alex undergoes a program of **aversive conditioning**—also called *aversion therapy*—which is actually used quite frequently today, although not in prisons. It is one of the more controversial procedures in behavior therapy. In aversive conditioning, painful or aversive stimuli are paired with unwanted impulses—such as desire for a cigarette or desire to engage in antisocial behavior—in order to make the goal less appealing. For example, in order to help people control alcohol intake, tastes of different alcoholic beverages can be paired with drug-induced nausea and vomiting, or with electric shock (Wilson et al., 1975).

Aversive conditioning has been used with some success in treating problems as divergent as paraphilias (Rathus, 1983), cigarette smoking (Lichtenstein, 1982; Walker & Franzoni, 1985), and retarded children's self-injurious behavior. In one large-scale study of aversive conditioning in the treatment of alcoholism, 63 percent of the 685 people treated remained abstinent for one year afterward, and about a third remained abstinent for at least three years (Wiens & Menustik, 1983). It may seem paradoxical to use punitive aversive stimulation to stop children from punishing themselves, but people sometimes hurt themselves to obtain sympathy and attention from others. If self-injury leads to more pain than anticipated, and no sympathy, it will probably be discontinued.

OPERANT CONDITIONING

We usually prefer to relate to people who smile at rather than ignore us, and to take courses in which we do well rather than fail. We tend to repeat behavior that is reinforced. Behavior that is not reinforced tends to become extinguished. Behavior therapists have applied these principles of operant conditioning with psychotic patients as well as clients with milder problems.

The staff at one mental hospital were at a loss as to how to encourage withdrawn schizophrenic patients to eat regularly. Ayllon and Haughton (1962) observed that the staff were exacerbating the problem by coaxing patients into the dining room, even feeding them. The patients were ap-

HOT SMOKE AND COLD TURKEY

Although the medical and psychological communities are in nearly universal agreement that people should be discouraged from smoking, one method for helping clients quit smoking has an ironic and controversial twist to it. This is because clients are aided in their efforts to quit smoking by . . . smoking—more specifically, a technique called "rapid smoking."

In one rapid-smoking method, the would-be quitter inhales every six seconds. In another, the hose of a hair dryer is hooked up to a chamber with several lit cigarettes. Smoke is blown into the quitter's face as he or she also smokes a cigarette. In still another method, branching pipes are used so that the smoker draws in smoke from two or more cigarettes simultaneously.

But, you object, these procedures do not sound pleasant at all. Quite right! They are examples of *aversive conditioning*. In this behavior-therapy method, overexposure renders once-desirable cigarette smoke aversive. The quitter becomes motivated to avoid, rather than seek, cigarettes, and stops smoking at a pre-planned date. Many reports have shown a quit rate of 60 percent or higher at a six-month follow-up of former smokers.

Rapid smoking is the most widely researched aversion method for treating cigarette smoking (Lichtenstein, 1982). Rapid smoking has become popular, because it is as effective as other methods and the apparatus is readily available—the quitter's own cigarettes. But rapid smoking raises the heartbeat and blood pressure, and decreases the blood's capacity to carry oxygen. True—these changes occur with normal smoking as well, but rapid smoking also produces heart ab-

AVERSIVE CONDITIONING In this behavior-therapy method for quitting smoking, overexposure to once-desirable cigarette smoke makes smoke aversive rather than pleasurable.

normalities, as shown by the electrocardiogram, and intense discomfort (Lichtenstein & Glasgow, 1977). Nevertheless, a recent two-year follow-up study of cardiac and pulmonary patients found no negative effects from rapid smoking (Hall et al., 1984)—and, when we consider the positive benefits of quitting smoking for these patients, rapid smoking comes to elicit some hope. Still, rapid smoking should not take place without the informed consent of the smoker, medical approval, and a reasonable time limit.

parently reinforced for uncooperativeness by increased staff attention. Some rules were changed. Patients who did not arrive at the dining hall within thirty minutes after serving were locked out. Staff could not interact with patients at mealtime. With uncooperative behavior no longer reinforced, patients quickly changed their eating habits. Patients were then required to pay one penny to enter the dining hall. Pennies were earned by interacting with other patients and showing other socially appropriate behaviors. These target behaviors also increased in frequency.

Many psychiatric wards and hospitals now use **token economies** in which tokens, like poker chips, must be used by patients to purchase television-watching time, extra visits to the canteen, or private rooms. The tokens are reinforcements for productive activities like making beds, brushing teeth, and socializing. While token economies have not eliminated all

Token economy A controlled environment in which people are reinforced for desired behaviors with tokens (like poker chips) that may be exchanged for privileges.

Successive approximations In operant conditioning, a series of behaviors that gradually become more similar to a target behavior.

Assertiveness training Behavior-therapy techniques that teach clients to express feelings, seek fair treatment, and improve social skills.

symptoms of schizophrenic disorders, they have encouraged many patients to become more active and cooperative.

We can often use the operant-conditioning method of **successive approximations** in building good habits. Let us use a (not uncommon!) example: You wish to study three hours an evening, but can only maintain concentration for half an hour. Rather than attempting to increase study time all at once, you could do so gradually, say by five minutes an evening. After every hour or so of studying you could reinforce yourself with five minutes of people watching in a busy section of the library.

ASSERTIVENESS TRAINING

Are you a person who can't say no? Do people walk all over you? Brush off those footprints and get some **assertiveness training!**

Assertive behavior may be contrasted with both *nonassertive* (submissive) behavior and *aggressive* behavior. Assertive people express their genuine feelings, stick up for their legitimate rights, and refuse unreasonable requests. But they do not insult, threaten, or belittle. Assertive people also

What's wrong with this cartoon? It's true, of course, that psychologists of many theoretical persuasions encourage clients to express their feelings. However, ''qualified'' therapists also encourage clients to take responsibility for their own behavior—not to attribute their misdeeds to the suggestion of others.

"Well, I'm sorry if my remarks hurt your feelings, but I think it's a little unfair of you to blame *me*. I said those things on the advice of a highly *qualified* therapist."

QUESTIONNAIRE

THE ASSERTIVENESS SCHEDULE

How assertive are you? Do you stick up for your rights or allow others to walk all over you? Do you say what you feel or what you think other people want you to say? Do you start up relationships with attractive people, or do you shy away from them?

To find out how your assertiveness compares to that of other college students, take this self-report test of assertive behavior. Then turn to Appendix B to calculate your score and compare it to those of a sample of 1,400 students drawn from thirty-five college campuses across the United States.

Directions: Indicate how well each item describes you by using this code:

   3 = very much like me
   2 = rather like me
   1 = slightly like me
−1 = slightly unlike me
−2 = rather unlike me
−3 = very much unlike me

_____ 1. Most people seem to be more aggressive and assertive than I am.*

_____ 2. I have hesitated to make or accept dates because of "shyness."*

_____ 3. When the food served at a restaurant is not done to my satisfaction, I complain about it to the waiter or waitress.

_____ 4. I am careful to avoid hurting other people's feelings, even when I feel that I have been injured.*

_____ 5. If a salesman has gone to considerable trouble to show me merchandise that is not quite suitable, I have a difficult time saying no.*

_____ 6. When I am asked to do something, I insist upon knowing why.

_____ 7. There are times when I look for a good, vigorous argument.

_____ 8. I strive to get ahead as well as most people in my position.

_____ 9. To be honest, people often take advantage of me.*

_____ 10. I enjoy starting conversations with new acquaintances and strangers.

_____ 11. I often don't know what to say to attractive persons of the opposite sex.*

_____ 12. I will hesitate to make phone calls to business establishments and institutions.*

_____ 13. I would rather apply for a job or for admission to a college by writing letters than by going through with personal interviews.*

_____ 14. I find it embarrassing to return merchandise.*

_____ 15. If a close and respected relative were annoying me, I would smother my feelings rather than express my annoyance.*

_____ 16. I have avoided asking questions for fear of sounding stupid.*

_____ 17. During an argument I am sometimes afraid that I will get so upset that I will shake all over.*

_____ 18. If a famed and respected lecturer makes a comment which I think is incorrect, I will have the audience hear my point of view as well.

_____ 19. I avoid arguing over prices with clerks and salespeople.*

_____ 20. When I have done something important or worthwhile, I manage to let others know about it.

_____ 21. I am open and frank about my feelings.

_____ 22. If someone has been spreading false and bad stories about me, I see him or her as soon as possible and "have a talk" about it.

_____ 23. I often have a hard time saying no.*

_____ 24. I tend to bottle up my emotions rather than make a scene.*

_____ 25. I complain about poor service in a restaurant and elsewhere.

_____ 26. When I am given a compliment, I sometimes just don't know what to say.*

_____ 27. If a couple near me in a theater or at a lecture were conversing rather loudly, I would ask them to be quiet or to take their conversation elsewhere.

_____ 28. Anyone attempting to push ahead of me in a line is in for a good battle.

_____ 29. I am quick to express an opinion.

_____ 30. There are times when I just can't say anything.*

Source: Reprinted from Rathus (1973), pp. 398–406.

do not shy away from meeting and constructing relationships with new people, and they express positive feelings such as liking and love.

Assertiveness training aims to decrease social anxiety and enhance social skills through techniques like *self-monitoring, modeling,* and *behavior rehearsal.* In **self-monitoring,** the client keeps a record of upsetting social encounters in order to pinpoint instances of social avoidance, clumsiness, and feelings of frustration. The therapist may demonstrate or **model** more effective social behavior, then encourage the client to rehearse or practice this behavior while the therapist provides **feedback.** The therapist attends to the client's posture, facial expressions, and tone of voice as well as to the content of what the client is saying.

The therapist may also point out that various irrational beliefs may impede progress. Beliefs to the effect that it is awful to earn the disapproval of others, or to fumble at the first few attempts at behavioral change, are likely to increase rather than decrease social anxieties. Clients need to learn to reward themselves for gradual gains rather than condemn themselves for imperfection.

Self-monitoring Keeping a record of one's own behavior to identify problems and record successes.

Model To engage in behaviors that are imitated by others.

Feedback In assertiveness training, information as to the effectiveness of a response.

Assertiveness training can be highly effective in groups. Group members can role play important people in the lives of other members, like potential dates, spouses, or parents. The trainee then engages in **behavior rehearsal** with the role player.

Behavior rehearsal Practice.

Functional analysis A systematic study of behavior in which one identifies the stimuli that trigger it and the reinforcers that maintain it.

SELF-CONTROL TECHNIQUES

Does it sometimes seem that mysterious forces are at work? Forces that delight in wreaking havoc with your New Year's resolutions and other efforts to take charge of bad habits? Just when you go on a diet, that juicy Big Mac stares at you from the TV set. Just when you resolve to balance your budget, that sweater goes on sale. Behavior therapists have developed a number of self-control techniques to help people cope with such temptations.

Functional Analysis of Behavior   Behavior therapists first engage in a **functional analysis** of the problem behavior to determine the stimuli that seem to trigger it and the reinforcers that seem to maintain it. In a functional analysis, you jot down each instance of the behavior in a diary. You note the time of day, location, your activity (including your thoughts and feelings), and reactions (yours and others').

Functional analysis serves a number of purposes. It makes you more aware of the environmental context of your behavior. It can increase your motivation to change, and it can lead to significant behavioral change. In studies with highly motivated people, functional analysis alone has been found to increase the amount of time spent studying (Johnson & White, 1971) or talking in a therapy group (Komaki & Dore-Boyce, 1978), and to decrease the number of cigarettes smoked (Lipinski et al., 1975).

Brian used functional analysis to learn about his nail biting. Table 12.2 shows a few items from his notebook. He discovered that boredom and humdrum activities seemed to serve as triggers for nail biting. He began

TABLE 12.2   Excerpts from Brian's Diary of Nail Biting for April 14

Incident	Time	Location	Activity (Thoughts, Feelings)	Reactions
1	7:45 A.M.	Freeway	Driving to work, bored, not thinking	Finger bleeds, pain
2	10:30 A.M.	Office	Writing report	Self-disgust
3	2:25 P.M.	Conference	Listening to dull financial report	Embarrassment
4	6:40 P.M.	Living room	Watching evening news	Self-disgust

A functional analysis of problem behavior, like nail biting, increases awareness of the environmental context in which it occurs, spurs motivation to change, and, in highly motivated people, may lead to significant behavioral change.

THE SOBELL EXPERIMENT

For years the gospel had been that alcoholics must abstain completely from their habit if they were to recover—one drink and they would lose control. Linda and Mark Sobell committed heresy. They argued that through behavior modification, alcoholics could learn self-control techniques that would allow them to engage in something called *controlled social drinking*. That is, they could have a drink or two in the company of others without necessarily falling off the wagon.

The Sobell's critics generally support the AA goal of total abstinence. They argue that controlled social drinking is an impossible dream. They claim that if an alcoholic, or a recovering alcoholic, has just one drink, he or she is likely to go off on an uncontrolled drinking binge.

The critics were astounded when the Sobells published the results of their experiments with 20 alcoholic subjects who were taught behavioral self-control methods at Patton State Hospital in San Bernardino, California. Eighty-five percent of the subjects were reported by the Sobells (1973, 1976, 1984) as engaging in successful controlled social drinking at a two-year follow-up.

But psychologist Mary Pendery believed that the Sobells had made extravagant claims. As a result, she attempted to track down the men in the experiment to get their own stories. After many years of investigation, Pendery, Maltzman, and West (1982) published their own follow-up of the Sobells' subjects in *Science*. Pendery and her colleagues reported that despite the Sobells' claims, most subjects had returned to uncontrolled drinking on several occassions, and that only *one* had successfully continued to moderate his drinking. Four of the original 20 had died from alcohol-related causes.

According to psychologist Alan Marlatt, there were shortcomings in both the studies run by the Sobells and by the Pendery group (Fisher, 1982). In each case, for example, the follow-ups may have been biased because they were conducted by investigators who had an interest in showing a particular outcome.

Other investigators (e.g., Miller & Muñoz, 1983; Peele, 1984; Sanchez-Craig et al., 1984) do claim that the goal of controlled social drinking remains possible, at least for people on the road to alcoholism. The research group headed by M. Sanchez-Craig, for example, assigned 35 "early-stage problem drinkers" to controlled social drinking. After two years they reported that "Six months after treatment drinking had been reduced from an average of about 51 drinks per week to 13, and this reduction was maintained throughout the second year" (1984, p. 390).

The goal of controlled social drinking remains controversial (Foy et al., 1984; McCrady, 1985; Marlatt, 1985), and the final chapter has not yet been written.

to watch out for feelings of boredom as signals of times to practice self-control. He also planned to make some changes in his life, so that he would feel bored less often.

There are a number of self-control strategies aimed at (1) the stimuli that trigger behavior; (2) the behaviors themselves; and (3) reinforcers.

Strategies Aimed at Stimuli that Trigger Behavior

Restriction of the stimulus field. Gradually exclude the problem behavior from more environments. For example, for a while first do not smoke while driving, then extend not smoking to the office. Or practice the habit only outside the environment in which it normally occurs.

Avoidance of powerful stimuli that trigger habits. Avoid obvious sources of temptation. People who go window-shopping often wind up buying more than windows. If eating at The Pizza Glutton tempts you to forget your diet, eat at home or at The Celery Stalk instead.

SELF-CONTROL By placing yourself in a setting in which only healthful foods are available, you are less likely to be tempted by fatty or fattening foods.

Stimulus control. Place yourself in an environment in which desirable behavior is likely to occur. Maybe it's difficult to lift your mood directly at times, but you can place yourself in the audience of that uplifting concert or film. It may be difficult to force yourself to study, but how about rewarding yourself for spending time in the library?

Strategies Aimed at Behavior

Response prevention. Make unwanted behavior difficult or impossible. Impulse buying is curbed when you shred your credit cards, leave your checkbook home, and carry only a couple of dollars. You can't reach for the strawberry cream cheese pie in your refrigerator if you have left it at the supermarket (that is, have not bought it).

Competing responses. Engage in behaviors that are incompatible with the bad habits. It is difficult to drink a glass of water and a fattening milkshake simultaneously. Grasping something firmly is a useful competing response for nail biting or scratching.

Chain breaking. Interfere with unwanted habitual behavior by complicating the process of engaging in it. Break the chain of reaching for a readily available cigarette and placing it in your mouth by wrapping the pack in aluminum foil and placing it on the top shelf in the closet. Rewrap the pack after taking one. Put your cigarette in the ashtray between puffs, or put your fork down between mouthfuls of dessert. Ask yourself if you really want more.

Successive approximations. Gradually approach targets through a series of relatively painless steps. Increase studying by only five minutes a day. Decrease smoking by pausing for a minute when the cigarette is smoked halfway, or by putting it out a minute before you would wind up eating the filter. Decrease your daily intake of food by 50 to 100 calories every couple of days, or else cut out one type of fattening food every few days.

Strategies Aimed at Reinforcements

Reinforcement of desired behavior. Why give yourself something for nothing? Make pleasant activities, like going to films, walking on the beach, or reading a new novel, contingent upon meeting reasonable, daily behavioral goals. Put one dollar away toward that camera or vacation trip each day you remain within your calorie limit.

Response cost. Heighten awareness of the long-term reasons for dieting or cutting down smoking by punishing yourself for not meeting a daily goal or for practicing a bad habit. Make out a check to your most hated cause and mail it at once if you bite your nails or inhale that cheesecake.

"Grandma's method." Remember Grandma's method for inducing children to eat their vegetables? Simple: No veggies, no dessert. In this method, desired behaviors, like studying and teethbrushing, can be increased by insisting that they be done before you carry out a favored or frequently occurring activity. For example, don't watch television unless you have studied first. Don't leave the apartment until you've brushed your teeth.

Covert sensitization. Create imaginary horror stories about problem behavior. Psychologists have successfully reduced overeating and smoking by having clients imagine that they become acutely nauseated at the thought of fattening foods, or that a cigarette is made from vomit. Some horror stories are not so "imaginary." Deliberately focusing on heart strain and diseased lungs every time you overeat or smoke, rather than ignoring these long-term consequences, may also promote self-control.

Covert reinforcement. Create rewarding imagery for desired behavior. When you have achieved a behavioral goal, fantasize about how wonderful you are. Imagine friends and family patting you on the back. Fantasize about the *Playboy* or *Playgirl* centerfold for a minute.

EVALUATION OF BEHAVIOR THERAPY

Behavior therapy has provided a number of strategies for treating anxiety, mild depression, social-skills deficits, sexual disorders, and problems in self-control. They have proved effective for most clients in terms of quantifiable behavioral change. Behavior therapists have also been innovative with a number of problems, such as phobias and sexual dysfunctions,* for which

*The use of behaviorally oriented methods with sexual dysfunctions will be elaborated in Chapter 13.

there had not previously been effective treatments. Overall, Smith and Glass (1977) found behavior-therapy techniques more effective than psychoanalytic or phenomenological methods. About 80 percent of those receiving behavior-therapy treatments, such as systematic desensitization and strategies for self-control, showed greater well-being than people who were left untreated (as compared to percentages in the low to middle 70s for psychoanalytic and phenomenological approaches). In an analysis of studies that directly compared treatment techniques, behavior-therapy approaches also showed an edge over psychoanalytic and phenomenological approaches.

Behavior therapy has also been effective in helping manage institutionalized populations, including schizophrenics and the mentally retarded. However, there is little evidence that behavior therapy alone is effective in treating the thought disorders involved in severe psychotic disturbance (Wolpe, 1985).

There is also some question as to *why* behavior therapy works. Is it because clients replace self-defeating habits with adaptive habits, or because they cognitively reappraise disturbing stimuli and relationships? No broad, simple answer to this question is possible. Nevertheless, behavior therapists can point with pride to a wide and growing body of experimental evidence that their techniques are effective with the vast majority of the clients they treat.

GROUP THERAPY

When a psychotherapist has several clients with similar problems—whether stress management, adjustment to divorce, lack of social skills, or anxiety—it often makes sense to treat clients in groups of six to twelve rather than conduct individual therapy. The methods and characteristics of the group will reflect the needs of the members and the theoretical orientation of the leader. Clients may interpret one anothers' dreams in a psychoanalytic group. They may provide an accepting atmosphere for self-exploration in a client-centered group. Clients in a TA group may comment on the games played by others. Behavior-therapy groups may undergo joint desensitization to anxiety-evoking stimuli or model and rehearse social skills.

There are several advantages to group therapy: (1) It is more economical, allowing several clients to be seen at once. (2) There is a greater fund of information and experience from which clients may draw. (3) Appropriate behavior receives the emotional support of several group members rather than just the therapist. (4) Group members who show improvement provide hope for others. (5) Group members can rehearse social skills in relating to one another in a relatively nonthreatening atmosphere. Still, many clients prefer individual therapy, because they do not wish to disclose their problems to a group, are inhibited about relating to others, or desire individual attention. It is the responsibility of the therapist to explain that group disclosures must be kept confidential, to establish a supportive atmosphere, and to see that group members receive the attention they need.

A TOUCHING EXERCISE Many groups use touching exercises to help members grow comfortable with one another. This encourages them to be open about feelings and to try out new, adaptive behavior patterns.

As noted, many forms of therapy can be conducted individually or in groups. Encounter groups and family therapy can be conducted in group-format only.

ENCOUNTER GROUPS

Encounter groups are not appropriate for treating serious psychological problems. Rather, they are intended to promote personal growth through heightening awareness of one's own needs and feelings and those of others. This goal is sought through intense confrontations, or encounters, between strangers. Like ships in the night, group members come together out of the darkness, touch one another briefly, then sink back into the shadows of one anothers' lives. But something is thought to be gained from the contact.

Encounter groups stress interactions between group members in the here and now. Discussion of the past may be outlawed. Interpretation is out. Expression of genuine feelings toward others is encouraged. When group members think that a person's social mask is phony, they may descend en masse to rip it off.

Professionals recognize that encounter groups can be damaging when they urge overly rapid disclosure of intimate matters, or when several members attack one member in unison. Responsible leaders do not tolerate these abuses and try to keep groups moving in growth-enhancing directions.

FAMILY THERAPY

In **family therapy,** one or more families constitute the group. Family therapy may be undertaken from various theoretical viewpoints. One common viewpoint is the "systems approach," for which much credit can be given to family therapist Virginia Satir (1967). In Satir's method, the family system of interaction is analyzed (not in the psychoanalytic sense of the word) and modified.

It is often found that family members with low self-esteem cannot tolerate different attitudes and behaviors from other family members. Faulty family communications also create problems. It is also not uncommon for the family to present an "identified patient"—that is, the family member who has *the* problem and is *causing* all the trouble. However, family therapists usually assume that the identified patient is a scapegoat for other problems within and among family members. It is a sort of myth: Change the bad apple (identified patient) and the barrel (the family) will be functional once more.

The family therapist—who is often a specialist in this field—attempts to teach the family to communicate more effectively, and to encourage growth and the eventual **autonomy** of each family member. In doing so, the family therapist will also show the family how the identified patient has been used as a focus for the problems of other members of the group.

There are many other types of groups: marathon groups, sensitivity training, and psychodrama, to name just a few. Space limitations prevent us from examining each of them.

Encounter group A type of group that aims to foster self-awareness by focusing on how group members relate to each other in a setting that encourages open expression of feelings.

Family therapy A form of therapy in which the family unit is treated as the client.

Autonomy Self-direction.

EVALUATION OF GROUP THERAPY

An evaluation of group therapy must consider the intentions and goals of the various group formats. Generally speaking, it is easiest to demonstrate the effectiveness of behavior-therapy groups, because of the emphasis on measurable outcomes. Group desensitization, for example, works about as well as individual desensitization. A study of encounter groups suggests that they may hurt as many people as they help (Lieberman et al., 1973).

Generally speaking, people who desire a group experience should make certain that the leader is a qualified member of a helping profession, and that their personal goals are consistent with group goals and methods.

BIOLOGICAL THERAPIES

In the 1950s Fats Domino popularized the song "My Blue Heaven." Fats was singing about the sky and happiness. But today "blue heavens" is the street name for the ten-milligram dose of one of the most widely used prescription drugs in the world: Valium. The **minor tranquilizer** Valium became popular, because it reduces feelings of anxiety and tension and the manufacturer once claimed that people could not become addicted to Valium nor readily kill themselves with overdoses. Today Valium looks more dangerous. Some people who have been using high doses of Valium are reported to go into convulsions when use is suspended. And now and then someone dies from mixing Valium with alcohol, or someone shows unusual sensitivity to the drug.

Psychiatrists and other physicians prescribe Valium and other drugs as chemical therapy, or **chemotherapy,** for various forms of abnormal behavior. In this section we discuss chemotherapy, *electroconvulsive therapy,* and *psychosurgery,* three biological or medical approaches to treating abnormal behavior.

CHEMOTHERAPY

If you visit a mental hospital, you will notice that many patients stroll up to the nurses' stations several times a day, toss pills from small paper cups into their mouths, and swallow them with water. Some patients have been taking the same pills for nearly twenty years. Some patients take pills to cope with feelings of anxiety, some to lift themselves from fearsome depressions, some to reduce violent agitation. Occasionally patients take pills because they, and perhaps the hospital staff, are afraid to learn what would happen if they stopped taking them.

In this section we discuss minor tranquilizers, major tranquilizers, antidepressants, and lithium.

Minor Tranquilizers Valium is but one of many (many) minor tranquilizers. Some of the others are Librium, Miltown, Atarax, Serax, and Equanil. These drugs are usually prescribed for outpatients who complain of anxiety or tension, although many people also use them as sleeping pills.

"It's no use, Marvin. We tried tenderness and we tried Valium and you're still impossible."

Valium and other tranquilizers are theorized to depress the activity of the central nervous system, which, in turn, decreases sympathetic activity, reducing the heart rate, respiration rate, and feelings of nervousness and tension (Caplan et al., 1983).

Unfortunately, with regular usage people come to tolerate small dosages of these drugs very quickly. Dosages must be increased in order for the drug to remain effective. It is not unusual for the patient to become embroiled in a tug-of-war with the prescribing physician, if the physician becomes concerned about the dose the patient is using. In a typical confrontation, the physician wants the patient to cut down for his or her own benefit. The patient resents the physician for getting him or her "involved" with the drug and then playing the moralist.

Another problem associated with many minor tranquilizers is **rebound anxiety.** Many patients who have been using these drugs regularly report that their anxiety returns in exacerbated form once they discontinue them.

Rebound anxiety Strong anxiety that can attend the suspension of usage of a tranquilizer.

Some users may simply be experiencing fear of doing without the drugs, but for others rebound anxiety may reflect biochemical processes that are as of yet only poorly understood (Chouinard et al., 1983).

Valium, interestingly, is usually ineffective with panic disorder, suggesting that panic has quite different bodily correlates than other anxiety disorders. Antidepressant medications, discussed later, do often help panic sufferers, giving rise to speculation that panic may involve faulty metabolism of norepinephrine (Fishman & Sheehan, 1985).

Major Tranquilizers   Patients with schizophrenic and schizophreniform disorders are likely to be treated with **major tranquilizers** or "antipsychotic drugs." Many of these drugs, including Thorazine, Mellaril, and Stelazine, belong to the chemical class of **phenothiazines,** and are thought to act by blocking the action of dopamine in the brain. Research along these lines tends to support the dopamine theory of schizophrenia (see Chapter 11).

In most cases, major tranquilizers reduce agitation, delusions, and hallucinations (May, 1975; Watson et al., 1978). Major tranquilizers account in large part for the lessened need for various forms of restraint and supervision (padded cells, straitjackets, hospitalization, and so on) used with schizophrenic patients. More than any other single form of treatment, major tranquilizers have allowed hundreds of thousands of patients to lead largely normal lives in the community, holding jobs and maintaining family lives.

Unfortunately, in many cases the blocking of dopamine action leads to symptoms like those of Parkinson's disease, including tremors and muscular rigidity, as described in Chapter 2 (Calne, 1977; Levitt, 1981). These "side effects" can usually be controlled by drugs that are used for Parkinsonism. However, in a minority of patients long-term use of phenothiazines leads to motor problems that are not so readily controlled (Jus et al., 1976.)

Antidepressants   **Antidepressant** drugs are often given patients with major depression. They are believed to work by increasing the amount of norepinephrine and serotonin available in the brain. As noted in Chapter 11, deficiencies of these neurotransmitters have been linked to depression. Antidepressant drugs tend to alleviate the physical aspects of depression. For example, they tend to increase the activity level of the patient and to reduce eating and sleeping disturbances (Lyons et al., 1985; Weissman et al., 1981). In this way patients may become more receptive to psychotherapy, which addresses the cognitive and social aspects of depression.

Severely depressed people often have insomnia, and it is not unusual for antidepressant drugs, which have a strong **sedative** effect, to be given at bedtime. Typically, antidepressant drugs like Tofranil and Elavil must "build up" to a therapeutic level, which may take ten days to three weeks. For this reason, some patients are hospitalized during this period to prevent suicidal behavior. Overdoses of antidepressant drugs can be lethal. It can be a risky business to prescribe these drugs for depressed people who remain outpatients.

Major tranquilizer A drug that decreases severe anxiety or agitation in psychotic patients or in violent individuals.

Phenothiazines A family of drugs that act as major tranquilizers and are effective in treating many cases of schizophrenic disorders.

Antidepressant Acting to relieve depression.

Sedative A drug that relieves nervousness or agitation.

Lithium You could say that the ancient Greeks and Romans were among the first to use the metal lithium as a psychoactive drug. They would prescribe mineral water for patients with bipolar affective disorder. Although they had no inkling as to why this treatment was sometimes effective, it may have been because mineral water contains lithium. A salt of the metal lithium, in tablet form, flattens out cycles of manicky behavior and depression for most persons with this disorder, apparently by moderating the level of norepinephrine available to the brain.

Since lithium is more **toxic** than most drugs, the dose must be carefully monitored through repeated analysis of blood samples during early phases of therapy. It may be necessary for persons with bipolar disorder to use lithium indefinitely, just as a medical patient with diabetes must continue use of insulin to control the illness.

Evaluation of Chemotherapy There is little question that major tranquilizers, antidepressants, and lithium have been found effective in helping patients with severe psychiatric disturbances. They have enabled thousands of formerly hospitalized patients to return to the community and resume— or for the first time engage in—productive lives. Problems in using these drugs are often related to their dosage and side effects.

Minor tranquilizers are frequently abused by overuse. Many people request them to dull the arousal that stems from anxiety-producing life styles or interpersonal problems. Rather than make the often painful decisions required to confront their problems and change their lives, they find it easier to pop a pill. At least for a while. Then the dosage must be increased if the drug is to remain effective, and they frequently begin to worry about drug dependence. Many family physicians, and a few psychiatrists, find it easier to prescribe minor tranquilizers than to help patients examine their lives and change anxiety-evoking conditions. The physician's lot is not eased by the fact that many clients want pills, not conversation.

ELECTROCONVULSIVE THERAPY

Electroconvulsive therapy (ECT) was introduced by Italian psychiatrist Ugo Cerletti in 1939 for use with psychiatric patients. Cerletti had noted that some slaughterhouses used electric shock to render animals unconscious. The shocks also produced convulsions, and Cerletti erroneously believed, as did other European researchers of the period, that convulsions were incompatible with schizophrenia and other major disorders.

After the advent of major tranquilizers, use of ECT was generally limited to treatment of people with major depression. The discovery of antidepressant medications limited use of ECT even further—to patients who do not respond to these drugs. But even as a therapy of last resort, ECT is still used with about 60,000 to 100,000 people a year in the United States (Sackeim, 1985).

ECT patients typically receive one treatment three times a week for several weeks. ECT induces unconsciousness, and so patients do not recall the shock. Still, they are usually put to sleep with a sedative prior to treatment. In the past, ECT patients flailed about wildly during the convulsions, sometimes breaking bones. Today they are given muscle-relaxing drugs, and convulsions are barely perceptible to onlookers. ECT is not given to patients with high blood pressure or heart ailments.

ECT is controversial for many reasons. First, ECT seems barbaric to many professionals. The thought of passing electric shock through the head and producing convulsions (even if they are suppressed by drugs) is distressing. Second are the side effects. ECT disrupts recall of recent events, and although memory functioning usually seems near normal for most patients a few months after treatment, some patients appear to suffer permanent memory impairment (Roueche, 1980). Third, nobody knows *why* ECT works. For reasons like these, ECT was outlawed in Berkeley, California, by voter referendum in 1982. This decision was later overturned in the courts, but it marked the first time that a specific treatment found its way to the ballot box. Still, some helping professionals maintain that ECT is the treatment of choice when antidepressant drugs fail.

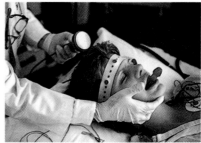

ELECTROCONVULSIVE THERAPY In ECT, electrodes are placed on each side of the patient's head, and a current is passed between them. Sufficient voltage induces a seizure. ECT is used mostly in cases of major depression where antidepressant drugs fail. ECT is quite controversial: Many find it barbaric, and there are negative side effects.

PSYCHOSURGERY

Psychosurgery is more controversial than ECT. It is a method for treating people who show abnormal behavior that could be said to have originated with the cavemen who broke holes into others' skulls. The best-known modern technique, the **prefrontal lobotomy,** has been used with severely disturbed patients and crudely severs with a picklike instrument the nerve pathways that link the prefrontal lobes of the brain to the thalamus. The prefrontal lobotomy was pioneered by the Portuguese neurologist Antonio Egas Moniz and was brought to the United States in the 1930s. It was performed on more than a thousand mental patients by 1950. Although the prefrontal lobotomy often reduces violence and agitation, it is not universally successful. One of Dr. Moniz's failures shot him, leaving a bullet lodged in his spine and causing paralysis in the legs.

The prefrontal lobotomy also has a host of side effects, including hyperactivity and distractibility, impaired learning ability, overeating, apathy and withdrawal, epileptic-type seizures, reduced creativity, and, now and then, death. Because of these side effects and because of the advent of major tranquilizers, the prefrontal lobotomy has been largely discontinued.

In recent years a number of more refined psychosurgery techniques have been devised for a variety of purposes. Generally speaking, they focus on smaller areas of the brain and leave less damage in their wake than does the prefrontal lobotomy. As pointed out by Elliot Valenstein (1980), these operations have been performed to treat problems ranging from aggression to depression, psychotic behavior, chronic pain, and epilepsy. Follow-up studies of the effectiveness of these contemporary procedures find slightly more than half of them to result in marked improvement (Corkin, 1980; Mirsky & Orzack, 1980). Moreover, no major neurological damage was attributable to these operations.

In sum, biological forms of therapy, particularly chemotherapy, seem desirable for some major psychiatric disorders that do not respond to psy-

Psychosurgery Surgery intended to promote psychological changes or to relieve disordered behavior.

Prefrontal lobotomy (lo-BOT-to-me). The severing or destruction of a section of the frontal lobe of the brain. A form of psychosurgery.

chotherapy or behavior therapy alone. But common sense as well as research evidence suggests that psychological methods of therapy are preferable with problems like anxiety, mild depression, and interpersonal conflict. No chemical can show a client how to change a thought or to solve an interpersonal problem. Chemicals can only dull the pain of failure and put off the day when the client must eventually deal with reality. ECT and psychosurgery are probably still to be considered experimental, and their use seems appropriately limited to severe cases in which all else fails.

SUMMARY

1. Psychotherapy is a systematic interaction between a therapist and a client that brings psychological principles to bear on influencing the client's thoughts, feelings, or behavior to help that client overcome abnormal behavior or to adjust to problems in living.

2. The history of treatment of abnormal behavior varies from the ancient opening of skulls and the exorcism of the Middle Ages to asylums and prisons, mental hospitals, and the contemporary community mental-health movement.

3. The helping professionals include psychologists, psychiatrists (who are also trained as physicians), psychiatric social workers, psychoanalysts, and others.

4. Many forms of psychotherapy, including psychoanalysis, person-centered therapy, transactional analysis, and Gestalt therapy are designed to foster self-insight. We have discussed cognitive therapy as an insight-oriented therapy, because of the common view that cognitive change is the central feature of client gains. Behavior therapy helps clients substitute productive behavior for maladaptive behavior with or without benefit of self-insight.

5. Sigmund Freud's method of psychoanalysis attempts to shed light on unconscious conflicts that are presumed to lie at the roots of clients' problems, and to substitute coping behavior for impulsive behavior and avoidance of life's challenges. Freud also believed that psychoanalysis would allow clients to engage in catharsis; that is, to spill forth psychic energy theorized to have been repressed by conflicts and guilt.

6. The major method in psychoanalysis is free association, in which clients utter what comes to mind without censorship, thus eventually bringing repressed material to the surface. Psychoanalysis also focuses on the hidden meanings of dreams and on resolving the transference relationship between analyst and client.

7. Contemporary psychoanalytic approaches are briefer and less intense than Freud's.

8. Carl Rogers' person-centered therapy is a nondirective method that provides clients with a warm, accepting atmosphere that enables them to explore and overcome roadblocks to self-actualization. The characteristics shown by the person-centered therapist include unconditional positive regard, empathetic understanding, genuineness, and congruence.

9. Eric Berne's transactional analysis (TA) focuses on people's life positions (such as "I'm OK—You're not OK"), and how people play games to confirm unhealthy life positions. TA also encourages clients to function according to their rational "adult" ego states, rather than their impulsive "child" ego states or their moralistic "parent" ego states.

10. Fritz Perls' Gestalt therapy provides directed exercises that are designed to help clients integrate disowned parts of the personality. In the Gestalt technique of dialogue, people undertake a verbal confrontation between conflicting parts of the personality.

11. Cognitive therapy addresses the ways in which clients' beliefs, attitudes, and automatic types of thinking create and compound their clients' problems.

12. In his type of cognitive therapy called rational-emotive therapy, Albert Ellis confronts clients with the ways in which self-defeating irrational beliefs contribute to problems such as anxiety, depression, and feelings of hopelessness.

13. Aaron Beck's cognitive therapy encourages clients to see how their minimizing of their accomplishments and their pessimism heighten feelings of depression.

14. "Running movies" is one of the ways in which cognitive therapists help clients get in touch with rapidly fleeting thoughts that contribute to negative emotional

responses and maladaptive behavior. Other cognitive methods include cognitive restructuring and problem-solving training.

15. Behavior therapy is the systematic application of principles of learning to bring about desired behavioral changes. The behavior therapist focuses on changing observable behavior rather than thoughts or feelings, although behavior therapists may also develop warm relationships with clients.

16. The behavior-therapy technique of systematic desensitization helps clients deal with irrational fears. In this method, they gradually confront more anxiety-evoking stimuli while they remain in a state of deep relaxation.

17. In the behavior-therapy method of aversive conditioning, undesired responses are decreased in frequency by being associated with aversive stimuli. An example is the rapid-smoking method of helping clients quit smoking.

18. Through behavior-therapy operant-conditioning methods, desired responses are reinforced and undesired responses are extinguished. Examples include the use of the token economy and of successive approximations.

19. In the behavior-therapy method of assertiveness training, clients learn to express themselves and seek their legitimate rights. Assertiveness-training methods include self-monitoring, modeling, and behavior rehearsal.

20. In behavior-therapy self-control methods, clients first engage in a functional analysis of their problem behavior to learn what stimuli trigger and maintain the behavior. Then they are taught how to manipulate the antecedents and consequences of their behavior, and the behavior itself, to increase the frequency of desired responses and decrease the frequency of undesired responses.

21. Group therapy can be more economical than individual therapy. It permits the therapist to help several clients at once, and clients have one anothers' knowledge and emotional support as resources.

22. Encounter groups seek to promote personal growth through intense confrontations that deal with relating to other group members in the here and now.

23. Family therapy usually uses a systems approach to boost family members' coping skills and self-esteem, and to promote the growth of each member. In family therapy, clients are encouraged to tolerate each other's differentness, and are given insight into how one family member often becomes the "identified patient" or scapegoat for family problems.

24. Biological therapies have a distinct place in the treatment of abnormal behavior. Major tranquilizers have permitted thousands of schizophrenics to lead productive lives in the community. Antidepressants have relieved many instances of major depression, and lithium helps flatten out the cycles of bipolar disorder.

25. Unfortunately, minor tranquilizers, used for common anxiety and tension, are frequently abused. Patients develop tolerance for these drugs rapidly, and the drugs do nothing to show them how to manage their problems in more productive ways.

26. Electroconvulsive therapy (ECT) is a controversial treatment that is still used in many cases to treat major depression when antidepressant drugs fail. Memory impairment is a frequent side effect of ECT.

27. Psychosurgery is also controversial. The operation called the prefrontal lobotomy was once used to treat violently agitated patients, but its side effects and the advent of chemotherapy have largely brought its usefulness to an end.

TRUTH OR FICTION REVISITED

People in Merry Old England used to visit the local insane asylum for a fun night out on the town.

True. People with severe disturbances were often chained and mistreated, and the public was frequently much amused.

The terms psychotherapy and psychoanalysis are interchangeable.

False. Psychoanalysis is just one type of psychotherapy, the type originated by Sigmund Freud.

If you were in traditional psychoanalysis, your major task would be to lie back, relax, and say whatever pops into your mind.

True. The central method in a traditional psychoanalysis is free association.

Some psychotherapists interpret clients' dreams.

True. Psychoanalysts and Gestalt therapists are a couple of examples.

Some psychotherapists encourage their clients to take the lead in the therapy session.

True. Psychoanalysts and person-centered therapists frequently use this approach.

Other psychotherapists tell their clients precisely what to do.

True. Gestalt therapists, cognitive therapists, and behavior therapists may be highly directive, depending upon the client's needs and situation.

Still other psychotherapists purposefully argue with clients.

True. Certain methods in cognitive therapy, for example, involve convincing clients, through persuasive arguments, that their ways of interpreting events are irrational and self-defeating.

A goal of psychotherapy is to help clients solve problems.

True. In fact, the name of one type of cognitive therapy is "problem-solving training."

You may be able to gain control over bad habits merely by keeping a record of where and when you practice them.

True. Self-monitoring of behavior has been shown to help highly motivated people increase the frequency of desired behaviors and decrease the frequency of unwanted behaviors.

Lying around in your reclining chair and fantasizing can be an effective way of confronting your fears.

True. In the behavior-therapy technique of systematic desensitization, a client gradually travels up a hierarchy of fear-evoking stimuli, while remaining as relaxed as possible.

Smoking cigarettes can be an effective treatment for helping people to . . . stop smoking cigarettes.

True. The specific technique is rapid smoking, in which the person inhales every six seconds.

Staff members in a mental hospital induced reluctant patients to eat by ignoring them.

True. They used operant conditioning to extinguish uncooperative patient behavior.

Drugs are never a solution to abnormal behavior problems.

False. Drugs (or chemotherapy) are frequently helpful in disorders such as schizophrenia, major depression, and bipolar affective disorder.

Electroconvulsive shock therapy is no longer used in the United States.

False. ECT is still used with some 60,000 severely depressed patients each year.

The originator of a surgical technique intended to reduce violence learned that it was not always successful—when one of his patients shot him.

True. Antonio Moniz, the originator of the prefrontal lobotomy, was shot by a former patient.

OUTLINE

CHAPTER 13

Sex Roles and Sexual Behavior

TRUTH OR FICTION?

- Women are expected to be more vain than men.
- Teachers are more likely to accept calling out in class from boys than from girls.
- Working women remain more likely than their husbands to do the cooking and take care of the laundry, even when the women are presidents or vice-presidents of their companies.
- Men behave more aggressively than women do.
- Men show greater math and spatial-relations abilities than women do.
- Women with higher testosterone levels view themselves as more enterprising but not so warm as women with lower testosterone levels.
- Parents treat sons and daughters differently, even when they are under one year of age.
- Stimulating male rats in a certain part of the brain causes them to engage in sexual foreplay.
- Women make natural mothers.
- Only men are sexually stimulated by hard-core pornography.
- Homosexuals suffer from hormonal imbalances.
- Any healthy woman can successfully resist a rapist if she really wants to.
- Orgasm is a reflex.
- People with psychosexual dysfunctions can often effectively treat themselves by using self-help manuals.

Two children were treated at Johns Hopkins University Hospital for the same disorder. But the treatments and the outcomes were vastly different. Each child was genetically female, and each had the internal sex organs of a girl. But because of excessive exposure to male sex hormones while they were being carried by their mothers, each had developed external sex organs that resembled a boy's (Money & Ehrhardt, 1972).

The problem was identified in one child (let's call her Deborah) at a very early age. The masculinized sex organs were surgically removed when she was two years old. Like many other girls, Deborah was tomboyish during childhood, but she was always feminine in appearance and had a female **gender identity.** As she developed, she dated boys, and her fantasies centered around marriage to a man.

The other child (let's call him Mitch) was at first mistaken for a genetic male whose external sex organs were stunted. This error was discovered at the age of three and a half. But by then Mitch had a firm male gender identity. So instead of undergoing surgery to remove his external sex organs, Mitch had surgery to further masculinize them. At puberty, hormone therapy promoted the development of bodily hair, male musculature, and other male secondary sex characteristics.

As an adolescent, Mitch did poorly in school. Possibly in an effort to compensate for his poor grades, he joined a gang of semidelinquents. He was accepted as one of the boys. In contrast to Deborah, Mitch was sexually attracted to women.

Deborah and Mitch both had **androgenital syndrome,** a hormonal disorder in which prenatal exposure to androgens masculinizes the sex organs of genetic females. In the case of Deborah, the child was assigned to the female gender and raised as a girl. The other child, Mitch, was labeled male and raised as a boy. Through information received from others, each child then gradually acquired the gender identity of the assigned sex.

When children are born with androgenital syndrome, it is important to make gender assignments reasonably early. Most children acquire a firm gender identity by the age of 36 months (Marcus & Corsini, 1978; McConaghy, 1979; Money, 1977).

The problems encountered by Deborah and Mitch are quite rare. Still, they raise questions about what it means to be male or female in our society. Let us explore this issue further by discussing masculine and feminine sex-role stereotypes. Then we examine research on sex differences in cognitive functioning and personality and explore how we develop "masculine" and "feminine" traits. Next we turn our attention to a number of controversial issues in sexual motivation: pornography, homosexuality, and forcible rape. We consider the sexual-response cycle—the bodily changes that take place as we become sexually aroused and reach orgasm. Finally, we discuss problems in becoming sexually aroused and reaching orgasm (the "psychosexual dysfunctions"), and the treatment of these problems. We shall see that although most people of the same sex possess reasonably similar sexual equipment, our sex-role behaviors and our sexual experiences can differ widely.

Gender identity One's sense of being male or female.

Androgenital syndrome A hormonal disorder in which prenatal exposure to male sex hormones (androgens) masculinizes the external genitals of genetic females.

"YUPPIES" ON THEIR WAY TO WORK Sex-role stereotypes appear to reflect the traditional distribution of men into breadwinning roles and women into homemaker roles. Working women are less likely to be perceived as sharing stereotypical feminine traits—when they work because of choice, that is, and not because of financial necessity.

SEX ROLES AND SEX DIFFERENCES

Do you recall the song from the musical *My Fair Lady,* "Why Can't a Woman Be More Like a Man?" The singer laments that women are emotional and fickle, while men are logical and dependable. The emotional woman is a **stereotype**—a fixed conventional idea about a group. The logical man is also a stereotype.

In this section we first explore stereotypes and sex roles of men and women in our culture. Then we discuss the ugly side of sex-role stereotyping—sexism. We examine research on individuals who show both "masculine" and "feminine" personality traits and behaviors, and, finally, we examine evidence concerning actual cognitive and personality sex differences.

SEX ROLES AND STEREOTYPES

Cultural expectations of men and women involve clusters of stereotypes that we call **sex roles.** Laypeople tend to see the traditional feminine stereotype as dependent, gentle, helpful, kind, mild, patient, and submissive (Cartwright et al., 1983). The typical masculine stereotype is perceived as tough, protective, gentlemanly, heading the house and providing for the family (Myers & Gonda, 1982).

In one study of the cultural conception of masculine and feminine sex roles, Inge Broverman and her colleagues (1972) first had undergraduate psychology students list traits and behaviors that they thought differentiated men from women. A list of 122 traits, each of which was mentioned at least twice, was generated. Each trait was made into a bipolar scale, such as:

Stereotype A fixed, conventional belief about a group.

Sex roles Complex groups or clusters of ways in which men and women are expected to behave in given social settings.

TABLE 13.1 Stereotypical Sex-Role Traits

INSTRUMENTALITY CLUSTER (Masculine Pole Perceived as More Desirable)

Feminine	Masculine
Nonaggressive	Aggressive
Dependent	Independent
Emotional	Not emotional
Submissive	Dominant
Dislikes math and science	Likes math and science
Noncompetitive	Competitive
Home-oriented	Worldly
Sneaky	Direct
Feelings easily hurt	Feelings not easily hurt
Has difficulty making decisions	Makes decisions easily
Not self-confident	Self-confident
Unable to separate feelings from ideas	Easily able to separate feelings from ideas

WARMTH-EXPRESSIVENESS CLUSTER (Feminine Pole Perceived as More Desirable)

Feminine	Masculine
Doesn't use harsh language	Uses harsh language
Talkative	Not talkative
Tactful	Blunt
Gentle	Rough
Empathetic	Not empathetic
Vain	Not vain
Neat	Sloppy
Strong need for security	Little need for security
Enjoys art and literature	Doesn't enjoy art and literature
Easily expresses tender feelings	Doesn't easily express tender feelings

Adapted from I. K. Broverman et al., "Sex-role Stereotypes: A Current Appraisal," *Journal of Social Issues*, 28(2), 63.

Not at all aggressive .... Very aggressive

Another group of students indicated which pole of the scale was more descriptive of the "average" man or woman. Only 41 of the 122 traits achieved a 75 percent agreement rate, and many of them are shown in Table 13.1.

Further analysis broke the list down into two broad factors. One centered around competency in the realm of objects, including the business world (which we label "instrumentality"). The second involved emotional warmth and expression of feelings (the Brovermans' "warmth-expressiveness cluster"). Other samples then rated the items as more desirable for men or women. In general, masculine traits in the instrumentality cluster were rated as more desirable for men, while feminine traits in this cluster were rated as more desirable for women. The people in this study felt it was desirable for women to be less rational than men, less aggressive, less competitive, and less dominant, but more emotional and dependent. The ideal woman was also seen as neater, gentler, more empathetic, and more emotionally expressive than a man.

As pointed out by Alice Eagly and Valerie Steffen (1984), these stereotypes largely reflect the traditional distribution of men into breadwinning roles and women into homemaking roles. When the wife works, she is less likely to be perceived as sharing stereotypical feminine traits—that is, so long as she works because of choice, and not because of financial necessity (Atkinson & Huston, 1984).

SEXISM

Sexism is the prejudgment that a person, because of gender, will possess negative traits. These traits may be assumed to prevent adequate performance in certain types of jobs or social situations. Until recently, sexism excluded women from many occupations, with medicine and law being the most visible examples.

Sexism may lead us to interpret the same behavior in different ways when shown by women or by men. We may see the male as "self-assertive," but the female as "pushy." We may view him as "flexible," but her as "fickle" and "indecisive." He may be "rational," when she is "cold." He is "tough" when necessary, but she is "bitchy." When the business-woman dons stereotypical masculine behaviors, the sexist reacts negatively by branding her abnormal or unhealthy.

Sexism can also make it difficult for men to show stereotypical feminine behaviors. A "sensitive" woman is simply sensitive, but a sensitive man may be seen as a "sissy." A woman may seem "polite," when a man showing the same behavior is labeled "passive" or "weak." Only recently have men begun to enter occupational domains restricted largely to women in this century, such as nursing, secretarial work, and teaching elementary school.

Let us examine some studies of the power of sexism. For example, what happens once women have gained footholds in traditional male preserves like medicine and engineering? Do sexists say, "I guess I was wrong about women's abilities, after all"? Not according to a study at the University of Tulsa (Touhey, 1974). The Touhey study suggests, rather, that sexists downgrade the value of the profession, as if the profession must be lowering its standards when women are admitted. College students downgraded the prestige of architecture, college teaching, medicine, and science when they received exaggerated reports that these professions were being flooded by women. Women students, products of the same culture, shared men's sexist expectations; they also downgraded these fields.

In another study, Sandra and Daryl Bem (1973) had college students rate the quality of professional articles in several fields. When the same article was attributed to a woman, it received lower ratings than when it was attributed to a man. As in the Touhey study, women raters were as guilty as men at assuming male superiority. This rating pattern was maintained with works of art as well as essays.

The above studies were carried out with college students. Would sophisticated mental-health professionals like psychologists, psychiatrists, and social workers show fewer stereotypical attitudes? In the 1980s, with the increased attention sexism has received, they might. But in the 1970s, it

B.C.

seemed that one answer to the question "Why Can't a Woman Be More Like a Man?" was that she might be labeled mentally unhealthy.

The Brovermans and their colleagues (Broverman et al., 1970) gave mental-health workers a list of bipolar traits similar to those in Table 13.1 and asked them to identify the pole that typified the "healthy adult woman" and the "healthy adult man." The healthy woman was described as submissive, dependent, vain, emotional, and uninterested in math and science. But the healthy man was described as competitive, independent, firm, objective, decisive, and skilled in the worlds of business and science. It does not require lengthy consideration to conclude that the healthy man has a more positive stereotype than the healthy woman. Women professionals were as guilty of stereotyping as their male counterparts.

Rachel Hare-Mustin (1983) argues that women are still misunderstood by mental-health professionals. Women, for example, are more frequently depressed than men, which has been traditionally interpreted as meaning that women more often show a psychological problem than men do. But, suggests Hare-Mustin, women more often than men are forced to live with low social status, discrimination, and helplessness. Their depression is often an appropriate response to their more stressful situations. The appropriate "treatment" of women whose depression stems from these problems is social and economic change—not psychotherapy.

School Days, School Days—Dear Old Sexist School Days? Now that the public has been aware of the existence of sexism for more than a decade, you might expect that sexism would have greatly diminished, especially among schoolteachers. Schoolteachers, after all, are generally well-educated and fair-minded. They are also trained to be sensitive to the needs of their young charges in today's changing society.

However, recent studies by investigators such as Myra and David Sadker (1985) suggest that we have not heard the last of sexism. Field researchers enlisted by the Sadkers observed students in fourth-, sixth-, and eighth-grade classes in four states and in the District of Columbia. Teachers and students were drawn from various racial backgrounds and from urban, suburban, and rural settings. However, in almost all cases, findings were quite similar.

Boys generally dominated classroom communication, whether the subject was math (a traditionally "masculine" area) or language arts (a traditionally "feminine" area). Boys, in fact, were eight times more likely than girls to call out answers without raising their hands. So far, it could be said, we have evidence of a sex difference—but not of sexism. However, teachers were less than impartial in responding to boys and girls when they called out. Teachers, male and female, were significantly more likely to accept boys' responses when they called out. Girls were significantly more likely to—as the song goes—receive "teachers' dirty looks," or to be reminded that they should raise their hands and wait to be called on. Boys, it appears, are expected to be "boys"—that is, impetuous—but girls are reprimanded for "unladylike behavior."

Despite boys' dominance of classroom communication, the Sadkers (1985) found evidence that teachers unwittingly adhere to the stereotype

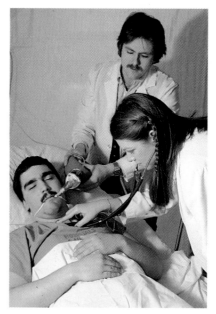

BUCKING THE STEREOTYPES Women in increasing numbers are pursuing careers that have been traditionally labeled masculine.

SEXISM IN THE CLASSROOM Despite boys' dominance of classroom communication, research has found that teachers unwittingly continue to adhere to the stereotype that girls talk more often than boys.

that girls talk more often than boys. In a clever experiment, the researchers showed teachers and administrators films of classroom discussions. Afterward they asked who was doing more talking, the boys or the girls. Most teachers reported that the girls were more talkative, even though, in the film, the boys actually spent three times as much time talking as the girls.

The Sadkers also report other instances of sexism in the classroom:

At the preschool level, teachers praise boys more often than girls and are more likely to give them detailed instructions.

Girls are less likely to take courses in math and science, even when their aptitude in these areas equals or exceeds that of boys.

Girls, as a group, begin school with greater skills in basic computation and reading, but have lower SAT scores in quantitative and verbal subtests by the time they are graduated from high school. It seems unlikely that girls carry genetic instructions that cause academic potential to self-destruct as the years go on. Instead, it would appear that the educational system does relatively more to encourage boys to develop academic skills.

The irony is that our educational system has been responsible for the lifting of generation upon generation of the downtrodden into the mainstream of American life. Sad to say, the system appears to be doing more for males than for females—even in the 1980s.

We have been considering the effects of sex-role stereotypes on our perceptions and expectations of men and women. Let us now turn our attention to people who combine stereotypical masculine and feminine traits and behavior patterns.

QUE/TIONNAIRE

DO YOU ENDORSE A TRADITIONAL OR A LIBERAL MARITAL ROLE?

What do you believe? Should the woman cook and clean, or should housework be shared? Should the man be the breadwinner, or should each couple define their own roles? Are you traditional or nontraditional in your views on marital roles for men and women?

The following items permit you to indicate the degree to which you endorse traditional roles for men and women in marriage. Answer each one by circling the letters (AS, AM, DM, or DS), according to the code given below. Then turn to the key at the end of the chapter to find out whether you tend to be traditional or nontraditional in your views. (Ignore the numbers beneath the codes for the time being.) You may also be interested in seeing whether the answers of your date or your spouse show some agreement with your own.

AS = Agree Strongly
AM = Agree Mildly
DM = Disagree Mildly
DS = Disagree Strongly

1. A wife should respond to her husband's sexual overtures even when she is not interested.

AS	AM	DM	DS
1	2	3	4

2. In general, the father should have greater authority than the mother in the bringing up of children.

AS	AM	DM	DS
1	2	3	4

3. Only when the wife works should the husband help with housework.

AS	AM	DM	DS
1	2	3	4

4. Husbands and wives should be equal partners in planning the family budget.

AS	AM	DM	DS
4	3	2	1

5. In marriage, the husband should make the major decisions.

AS	AM	DM	DS
1	2	3	4

6. If both husband and wife agree that sexual fidelity isn't important, there's no reason why both shouldn't have extramarital affairs if they want to.

AS	AM	DM	DS
4	3	2	1

7. If a child gets sick and his wife works, the husband should be just as willing as she to stay home from work and take care of that child.

AS	AM	DM	DS
4	3	2	1

8. In general, men should leave the housework to women.

AS	AM	DM	DS
1	2	3	4

TOWARD PSYCHOLOGICAL ANDROGYNY

We usually think of masculinity and femininity as opposite poles of one continuum (Storms, 1980). We assume that the more masculine a person is, the less feminine he or she must be, and vice versa. For this reason, a man who shows the "feminine" traits of nurturance, tenderness, and emotionality is also often considered to be less masculine than other men. This is also why girls who compete with boys in sports or, at later ages, in the business world are not only seen as more masculine than other girls, but also as less feminine.

But in recent years many psychologists have argued that masculinity and femininity comprise independent personality dimensions. That is, a person who scores high on a measure of masculine traits, whether male or female, need not necessarily score low on feminine traits. A person who shows stereotypical masculine *instrumentality* can also show stereotypical feminine *warmth-expressiveness* (see Table 13.1). Such people show **psychological androgyny.** People high in instrumentality *only* are stereotypically masculine. People high in expressiveness *only* are stereotypically feminine. People who are low in both instrumentality and expressiveness are "undifferentiated" according to the stereotypical sex-role dimensions. Undifferentiated people seem to encounter distress. Undifferentiated women, for example, are viewed less positively than more feminine or more masculine women, even by their friends (Baucom & Danker-Brown, 1983), and they are less satisfied with their marriages (Baucom & Aiken, 1984). However, psychologically androgynous people, as we shall see, may be more resistant to stress.

Research is mixed as to whether psychologically androgynous people are physically healthier than highly masculine or feminine people (Hall & Taylor, 1985). However, there is some evidence that androgynous people may be relatively well-adjusted, because they can summon both "masculine" and "feminine" traits to meet the demands of various situations. For example, in terms of Erik Erikson's concepts of ego identity and intimacy, androgynous college students are more likely than feminine, masculine, and undifferentiated students to show a combination of "high identity" and "high intimacy" (Schiedel & Marcia, 1985). That is, they are more likely

Psychological androgyny Possessing personality traits attributed to both men and women. Possession of "instrumental" and "expressive" traits. (From the Latin *andros,* meaning "man," and *gyne,* meaning "woman.")

to show a firm sense of who they are and what they stand for (identity), and to have a greater capacity to form intimate, sharing relationships.

Psychologically androgynous people of both sexes show "masculine" independence under group pressures to conform and "feminine" nurturance in interactions with a kitten or a baby (Bem, 1975; Bem et al., 1976). They feel more comfortable performing a wider range of activities, including (the "masculine") nailing of boards and (the "feminine") winding of yarn (Bem & Lenney, 1976; Helmreich et al., 1979). In adolescence, they report greater interest in pursuing nontraditional occupational roles (Motowidlo, 1982). They show greater maturity in moral judgments, greater self-esteem (Flaherty & Dusek, 1980; Spence et al., 1975), and greater ability to bounce back from failure (Baucom & Danker-Brown, 1979). They are more likely to try to help others in need. Androgynous people are more willing to share the leadership in mixed sex groups, whereas masculine people attempt to dominate and feminine people tend to be satisfied with taking a back seat (Porter et al., 1985). Androgynous women rate stressful life events as less undesirable than do feminine women (Shaw, 1982).

These findings on adjustment have not gone unchallenged. Self-esteem is an important factor in our psychological well-being. On the basis of an analysis of thirty-five studies on the relationship between sex roles and self-esteem, Bernard Whitley (1983) argues that the self-esteem benefits of psychological androgyny do *not* derive from the combination of masculine and feminine traits. Rather, they reflect the presence of "masculine" traits, whether they are found in males or females. That is, traits such as independence and assertiveness contribute to high self-esteem in both sexes.

The Whitley study does not address all the correlates of psychological androgyny, of course. Nor does it suggest that it is disadvantageous for either sex to show stereotypical feminine traits, such as nurturance. Other research, in fact, suggests that "feminine" traits contribute to marital happiness. Antill (1983) found not only that husbands' happiness was positively related to their wives' femininity, but also that wives' happiness was positively related to their husbands' femininity. Wives of psychologically androgynous husbands were far happier than women whose husbands adhered to a strict, stereotypical masculine sex role. Androgynous men are more tolerant of their wives' or lovers' faults and more likely to express loving feelings than are "macho" males (Coleman & Ganong, 1985), and women, like men, appreciate spouses who are sympathetic, warm, tender, and who love children.

Criticism of the view that psychological androgyny is a worthwhile goal has also been voiced by some feminists—for a quite different reason. The problem, from the feminist perspective, is that psychological androgyny is defined as the possession of both masculine and feminine personality traits. However, this very definition relies upon the presumed rigidity of masculine and feminine sex-role stereotypes, and feminists like Bernice Lott (1981, 1985) would prefer to see the dissolution of these stereotypes.

In any event, Sandra Bem (1974) has found that about 50 percent of her samples of college students have adhered to their own sex-role stereotypes on her test for measuring psychological androgyny—the Bem Sex Role Inventory. About 15 percent have been cross-typed (described by traits stereotypical of the opposite sex), and 35 percent have been androgynous. The incidence of psychological androgyny is probably higher among college students than among the general population, yet many young people today seem to be challenging stereotypical sex roles and deciding that they are free both to show competence in the realm of objects and to express feelings of warmth and tenderness.

Now that we have considered the masculine and feminine stereotypes, let us examine research concerning the actual behavioral differences between the sexes.

SEX DIFFERENCES: VIVE LA DIFFÉRENCE OR VIVE LA SIMILARITÉ?

We have surveyed sex-role stereotypes, but now let us address the question, What are the actual psychological differences between men and women? Let us consider differences in cognitive functioning and in personality.

Differences in Cognitive Functioning   It was once believed that men were more intelligent than women because of their greater knowledge of world affairs and skill in science and industry. We now recognize that greater male knowledge and skill reflected the systematic exclusion of women from world affairs, science, and industry. Two generations of experience

PSYCHOLOGY IN THE WORKPLACE

SEX ROLES, SEXISM, AND WORKING WIVES

The numbers of women in the work force have changed dramatically in recent years. According to the U.S. Bureau of Labor Statistics, during the twelve-year span between 1973 and 1985, the percentage of working wives with children under age eighteen jumped by 20 points—from 42 to 62 (Lublin, 1984; *New York Times*, 1985). In 1985, even 50 percent of women with children younger than three years old worked.

Working wives, especially mothers, are in situations that can create role conflict. Sometimes the conflict is caused by the stereotype that "a woman's place is in the home." Sometimes conflict is caused by the fact that the woman would like to be in two places at once—with her children and at work. Conflict can also occur when women earn more than their husbands, especially when their husbands feel that their traditional role as breadwinner is being compromised. But despite all these sources of potential conflict, it is instructive to note that women are more likely to feel that they are overloaded and are being pulled in different directions in the role of mother than in the role of paid worker (Barnett & Baruch, 1985).

Since so many of today's women are bucking tra-

dition, let us examine what is known about how working affects a woman's marital happiness and general life satisfaction.

In terms of personal satisfaction, it seems that the reasons why a wife is working are more important than the simple fact of her being in the labor force (Hofferth & Moore, 1979). Wives who choose to work, who have the support of their husbands, who work part-time, or who enter the work force when their children have begun school seem more satisfied than women who are under pressure to work or who would rather have remained in the home with very young children.

***The Wall Street Journal*/Gallup Survey**   Women may still account for the majority of secretaries and school teachers, as you can see in Figure 13.1, but they have also made dramatic recent gains in the professions, now accounting, for example, for about 40 percent of bank officials and financial managers.

The Wall Street Journal and the Gallup Organization recently ran a joint survey of 772 women executives, all of whom had reached a position of vice-president, or (continued on p. 594)

WORKING MOTHER Working mothers are generally more satisfied with themselves and with their lives than are nonworking mothers—so long as they choose to work.

higher, in their firms. Of this group, the married women executives were more satisfied with their lives than were unmarried women executives (Rogan, 1984a). However, 57 percent of the executives who were earning *less* than their husbands were totally satisfied with their lives, as compared with only 38 percent of the women executives who brought home *more* than their husbands. It may be that husbands of women who outearn them feel insecure or threatened by their wives' success, or that very high earners spend more energy bringing home the bacon than enjoying it with their spouses.

The Ferree Study A frequently cited study by sociologist Myra Marx Ferree (1976) surveyed 135 predominantly working-class wives who had children in the first or second grade. Forty-five percent of them were housewives. Twenty-six percent held full-time jobs, and 29 percent held part-time jobs. There were no group differences in marital happiness, but the working women were more satisfied with themselves and with their lives in general. Part-time workers were happiest. Their jobs apparently offered the social and psychological benefits of employment, while also allowing them more time for family life.

The working wives in the Ferree study did not hold glamorous occupations. Most filled stereotypical female positions such as typist, waitress, cashier, or office-machine operator. But even these jobs apparently provided the benefits of a paycheck, a sense of accomplishment, and expanded social contacts.

Ferree attributes the dissatisfaction of many full-time homemakers to a breaking down of the supportive family and social network as people have emigrated to the suburbs or followed the breadwinners' jobs to new towns and cities. Nowadays there may be little companionship for a woman at home during the day other than television game shows or soap operas. Some homemakers complained, "I feel like I'm going crazy staying home," "I feel like I'm in jail," or "I don't see anything but four walls a day."

Working Mothers and Their Children The major reason that women have been expected to remain in the home is so that they can "be there" for their children. What are the effects of maternal employment on children? Must mother be available for round-the-clock love and attention if her children are to thrive? Not necessarily.

Developmental psychologists (e.g., Easterbrooks & Goldberg, 1985; Hoffman, 1985) have found no consistent evidence that maternal employment is harmful to children. Generally speaking, the children of working women do not differ from those of full-time housewives in terms of anxiety, incidence of antisocial behavior, dependence, or complaints of stress-related disorders such as headaches and upset stomachs. In fact, the children of working women see their mothers as more competent and hold fewer stereotypical sex-role attitudes (Gold & Andres, 1978a, 1978b, 1978c). Children of working women are more helpful with the housework. The daughters of working women are more achievement oriented and set themselves higher career goals than do the daughters of nonworking women.

In some cases, the stereotypical sex roles are reversed and the father stays at home (serves as "house-husband"), while the mother takes the morning trek to the factory or the office. Children in these families also show fewer stereotypical sex-role attitudes, higher intelligence-test scores, and a greater internal locus of control (Radin, 1982; Russell, 1982). But we cannot necessarily attribute these findings to the father's remain-

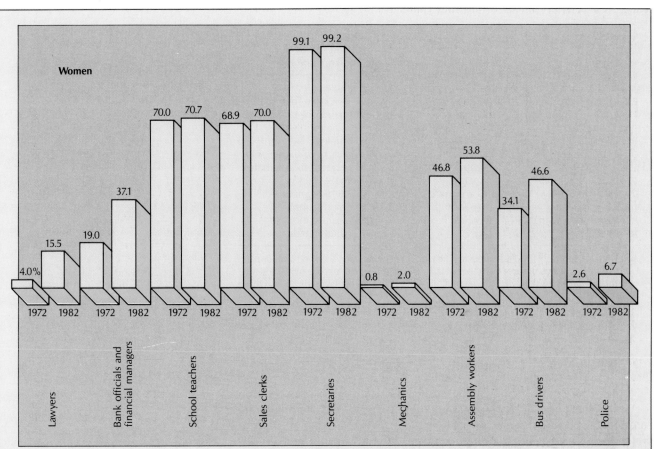

Women

	1972	1982
Lawyers	4.0%	15.5
Bank officials and financial managers	19.0	37.1
School teachers	70.0	70.7
Sales clerks	68.9	70.0
Secretaries	99.1	99.2
Mechanics	0.8	2.0
Assembly workers	46.8	53.8
Bus drivers	34.1	46.6
Police	2.6	6.7

FIGURE 13.1 RECENT CHANGES IN THE PERCENTAGES OF WOMEN IN VARIOUS FIELDS Women may still account for the majority of secretaries and school teachers, but they have also made dramatic recent gains in the professions, including the world of finance.

ing in the home. It may be that the same egalitarian or nonconformist attitudes that led to the parental decision to reverse roles also led to the differences in the children.

All in all, working women spend half as much time caring for their infant children as do housewives, but these children develop normal attachments to them (Moore & Hofferth, 1979). It appears that the quality of the time parents and children spend together, along with the making of adequate child-care arrangements, outweighs the number of hours (Bralove, 1981; Easterbrooks & Goldberg, 1985). When mothers choose to work and find their work fulfilling, they are happier with their lives. They and their husbands are more egalitarian in the distribution of chores in the home as well as in the breadwinning role (Gold & Andres, 1978a, 1978b, 1978c). Perhaps the working mothers' feelings of competence and high self-esteem transfer into

more productive relationships with their children in the home.

However, despite the greater egalitarianism found in homes where mothers work, the *Wall Street Journal/Gallup* survey found that married women executives were still much more likely than their husbands to have the major responsibility for certain traditional household chores (Rogan, 1984b): For example, 52 percent of the women executives saw that the laundry got done, as compared to 7 percent of their husbands. Women executives were also more likely than their husbands to plan meals and shop for food (47% vs. 8%), shop for the children's clothes (70% vs. 3%), and stay home with their children when they got ill (30% vs. 5%).*

*These percentages do not add up to 100 because in many cases the responsibilities were shared. These women, remember, were all vice-presidents, or higher.

TABLE 13.2 Vive la Différence? Just How Different Are the Two Sexes?

Differences Borne Out by Some Research Studies	Differences About Which There Is Greater Doubt	Assumed Differences that Research Has Shown To Be False
Males tend to be more aggressive than females.	Females are more timid and anxious than males?	Females are more sociable than males.
Females have greater verbal ability than males.	Males are more active than females?	Females are more suggestible than males.
Males have greater visual-spatial ability than females.	Males are more competitive than females?	Males have higher self-esteem than females.
Males have greater ability in math than females.	Males are more dominant than females?	Females lack achievement motivation.
		Males are more logical than females.

It has been commonly assumed that there are great differences between men and women, and that these differences reflect heredity or the natural order of things. Yet psychological research has shown the supposed differences to be much smaller than had been assumed. And those differences that remain, such as greater math ability in males and greater verbal ability in females, may reflect cultural expectations and not heredity.

SOURCE: Based on data from Maccoby & Jacklin (1974).

with assessment of intelligence have dispelled myths about overall differences in cognitive functioning between the sexes.

Still, in their review of cognitive and personality differences between the sexes, Maccoby and Jacklin (1974) found suggestions that women are somewhat superior to men in verbal ability. More recent research confirms that girls begin to speak earlier, pronounce their words more distinctly, and read better than boys. As a matter of fact, remedial reading programs are two to three times more heavily populated by boys than girls (Funnichi & Childs, 1981). But men appeared somewhat superior in math and visual-spatial abilities (Table 13.2). According to the recent second Science International Study, this difference persists (Walton, 1985). In fact, on the Scholastic Aptitude Math test, seven or eight boys score above 600 for every girl who does (Benbow & Stanley, 1983).

However, a number of factors should caution us not to attach too much importance to these cognitive gender differences. It is true we can point to notable differences in the extreme ends of the distribution of skills, as with the comparative numbers of boys and girls in reading remediation and scoring above 600 on the SAT math test (Wittig, 1985). But overall sex differences in reading and math abilities and other cognitive skills are small and somewhat inconsistent (Caplan et al., 1985; Hyde, 1981). Second, they represent group differences, and variation in these skills is larger within, than between, the sexes. Despite group differences, millions of men exceed the "average" woman in writing and spelling skills, and millions of women outdistance the "average" man in mathematics and spatial relations. Third, the small differences that appear to exist may reflect cultural expectations and environmental influences, not innate potential (Tobias, 1982). Women receiving even brief training in various visual-spatial skills, such as rotating geometric figures, show no performance deficit in these skills when compared to men (Stericker & LeVesconte, 1982). In fact, when we consider the high school curriculums of boys and girls, it is not surprising that boys do better on the SAT math test; boys take more math classes in high school than girls do (Caplan et al., 1985).

Differences in Personality   In almost all cultures, with a couple of fascinating exceptions (Ford & Beach, 1951; Mead, 1935), it is the men who march off to war and who battle for glory and shaving-cream commercial contracts in the arenas. In psychological studies, boys and men consistently behave more aggressively than girls and women.

The research does seem to bear out some stereotypes, at least among married couples. Michael Barnes and David Buss (1985) of Harvard University recruited ninety-three Boston-area couples through newspaper advertisements and flyers for one study, and asked them to indicate how often they had engaged in certain behaviors during the last three months. Wives reported performing the following types of acts with significantly greater frequency: "coercive-manipulative" ("I cried in order to get my way," "I persuaded him/her to do something he/she didn't want to do," etc.); "communal" ("I cooked dinner for the group," "I visited someone who needed company"); and wearing "flashy attire" ("I dressed in flashy clothes"). Husbands more often than their wives reported performing "initiative" acts ("I helped a stranger with directions," "I took the initiative in the sexual encounter," "I walked alone at night"). Answers to some of the Barnes and Buss items may reflect cultural expectations and limitations rather than personality differences. For example, in the flashy-attire category was the item, "I wore sexy clothes to impress someone." Since our culture does not encourage men to think of themselves as wearing "sexy" clothes, even when they are wearing clothes calculated to attract women, it is understandable that women would report this act more often. Similarly, it is understandable that men would be more likely to report "I helped a friend with a difficult assignment." But does this finding truly reflect "initiative" as suggested by the authors, or the fact that men are more likely than women to be in the work force and, therefore, more likely to help friends with assignments? It is also understandable that men are more likely to report "I walked alone at night," but, again, does this item really reflect "initiative"? Perhaps it simply reflects the reality that it is less dangerous for men to walk alone at night.

Despite the stereotype of women as gossips and "chatterboxes," research in communication styles suggests that men in many situations spend more time talking than women do. Men are also more likely to introduce new topics and to interrupt others (Deaux, 1976; Kramer, 1974). Yet women do seem more willing to reveal their feelings and personal experiences (Cozby, 1973) and to develop more intimate relationships with members of their own sex (Reis et al., 1985). Women are less likely than men to curse—with the exception of women who are bucking sex-role stereotypes.

Women appear to require less **personal space** than men do. They tend to stand and sit closer to one another than men do, as noted in naturalistic-observation studies of window shoppers and visitors to art exhibits (Fisher

Personal space A psychological boundary that surrounds a person and permits that person to maintain a protective distance from others.

et al., 1984), and in experiments (Sussman & Rosenfeld, 1982). Women also prefer to have friends sit next to them, while men prefer friends to sit across from them (Sommer, 1969; Fisher & Byrne, 1975). Social psychologists suggest that differences in seating preferences and personal space requirements reflect greater male competitiveness. Men, that is, perceive close encounters as confrontations in which they face potential adversaries. Thus, they need to keep an eye on them from a safe distance.

In a statistical analysis of forty-six studies on **gender** and conformity, Cooper (1979) concluded that women do tend to conform to group pressures more than males do. Conformity among women appears linked to acceptance of the stereotypical feminine role. Bem (1975) found that psychologically androgynous women are less likely to conform than are women who score as highly "feminine" on her sex-role inventory.

In the following section, we shall see that boys and men are consistently more likely than girls and women to behave aggressively. However, we shall also see that females have the capacity to act aggressively, and that cultural stereotypes and expectations inhibit aggressive behavior in women.

Clearly, there are important anatomical differences between the sexes. However, in many cases it seems that differences in cognitive functioning are small, even in those cases where they may exist. Many differences in "personality" clearly reflect cultural expectations. The French have a saying, "Vive la différence." For those who have felt restricted by their sex roles, perhaps we can also exclaim, "Vive la similarité."

Gender One's classification according to sex.

Differentiation The modification of tissues and organs in structure or function during the course of development.

ON BECOMING A MAN OR A WOMAN: THE DEVELOPMENT OF SEX DIFFERENCES IN BEHAVIOR

Like mother like daughter, like father like son—at least often, if not always. Why is it that little boys (often) grow up to behave according to the cultural stereotypes of what it means to be male? That little girls (often) grow up to behave like female stereotypes? Let us have a further look at the ways in which hormonal and psychological factors may contribute to the development of sex differences in cognitive functioning, personality, and behavior.

THE INFLUENCE OF SEX HORMONES

Sex hormones are responsible for the **differentiation** of sex organs within the mother's womb. At the beginning of the chapter, it was noted that the sex organs of genetic females who are exposed to excess androgens in utero may become masculinized. It has been argued that sex hormones in utero not only influence the development of male or female sex organs, but also physically "masculinize" or "feminize" the brain, and thus create behavioral predispositions that are consistent with some sex-role stereotypes (Diamond, 1977; Money, 1977; Turkington, 1984).

Diamond takes an extreme view, suggesting that brain masculinization in utero can cause tomboyishness, self-assertiveness, even preference for trousers over skirts and for playing with toys designed for boys. Money is more moderate. He agrees that certain predispositions may be created in utero, but argues that psychological processes, such as social learning, play a stronger role in the development of gender identity, personality traits, and preferences. In fact, Money claims that social learning is so powerful that it can counteract any prenatal masculine or feminine predispositions.

Some evidence for the possible role of hormonal influences derives from animal studies. For example, male rats are generally superior to females in maze-learning ability, a task that requires spatial skills. However, female rats who are exposed to androgens in the uterus or soon after birth learn maze routes as well as male rats do (Beatty, 1979; Goy & McEwen, 1982).

There is little experimental research on prenatal hormonal influences in children. Ethical considerations prevent us from experimentally manipulating prenatal levels of sex hormones in humans. However, now and then sex hormones are manipulated for other reasons and we can observe the results. For example, many women have been given androgens (male sex hormones) in order to help them maintain their pregnancies. Sex hormones pass through the placenta into the bloodstreams of unborn children. Anke Ehrhardt and Susan Baker (1975) were consequently able to study the effects of prenatal androgens on seventeen children.

As compared to sisters who had not been exposed to androgens in utero, androgenized girls were more active during play and more likely to perceive themselves as tomboys. They were less vain about their appearance. Androgenized girls did not enjoy caring for babies or show much interest in eventually marrying. The boys whose mothers had received hormone treatments engaged yet more frequently than their brothers in outdoor sports and rough-and-tumble play.

While some have interpreted the Ehrhardt and Baker report as strong evidence for the effects of prenatal hormones on personality and behavior, a number of problems should be noted. First, the sample was not chosen at random. It consisted of the children of women who feared that they might miscarry. The biological basis for this fear as well as the androgens might have influenced their children. A double-blind study including a control group of women who also feared they might miscarry, but who were given a placebo in the place of androgens, could have met this shortcoming. However, it would have been unethical to deceivingly withhold a desired treatment for the sake of science. Second, the prenatal androgen levels of the children required that they receive regular doses of the steroid cortisone after birth. Cortisone has a number of side effects, among them an increased level of activity. Thus, play styles among the children studied could have reflected the cortisone therapy as well as prenatal androgen levels.

In more recent research, Donald Baucom and his colleagues (1985) found relationships between levels of testosterone and personality traits among women college students. Eighty-four female undergraduates took a number of paper-and-pencil tests, including masculinity and femininity scales and Sandra Bem's Sex Role Inventory. Their testosterone levels were determined from samples of saliva. Masculine-sex-typed, androgynous, and undifferentiated women all had higher testosterone levels than feminine-sex-typed women. Women with higher testosterone levels perceived themselves as more enterprising, unconventional, spontaneous, and resourceful than women with lower testosterone levels, but as less "civilized," rational, helpful, and warm. All in all, high concentrations of testosterone were linked to stereotypical masculine behaviors.

Schindler found a link between testosterone levels and women's needs and vocational choices (1979). Women with high testosterone levels also showed higher needs for achievement and autonomy than women with lower concentrations, as measured by the Edwards Personal Preference Schedule. Women lawyers also showed higher levels than women teachers, nurses, and athletes. Why women athletes had lower testosterone concentrations than women lawyers is a mystery.

Despite their intrigue, keep in mind that the Baucom and Schindler studies were correlational, not experimental. Although testosterone levels and masculine traits, needs, and vocations were linked, we cannot conclude that the hormone levels gave rise to the traits and needs. It is also possible that the traits and needs influenced the hormone levels, or that other, undetected factors influenced both. Moreover, we still have to wonder why the women athletes had lower testosterone levels than the lawyers.

PSYCHOLOGICAL INFLUENCES

Psychoanalytic, social-learning, and cognitive approaches to personality development offer the following views of the development of sex differences.

A Psychoanalytic View   Psychoanalytic theory explains the acquisition of sex roles in terms of identification. Within psychoanalytic theory, identification is the incorporation of the behaviors and what we perceive as the thoughts and feelings of other people. Sigmund Freud believed that gender identity is rather flexible until the resolution of the Oedipus and Electra complexes at about the age of five or six. Freud argued that the assumption of sex-appropriate sex roles required that boys identify with their fathers and surrender the wish to possess their mothers. Girls would have to identify with their mothers and surrender the wish to have a penis.

There is little evidence for Freud's views on the psychodynamics of identification. Also, children engage in stereotypical sex-role behaviors long before the ages of five or six. Within the first year of life, boys' play shows more exploration and independence, while girls are more quiet, dependent, and restrained (Goldberg & Lewis, 1969). By eighteen to thirty-six months, girls are more likely than boys to play with soft toys and dolls, and to dance. Eighteen- to thirty-six-month-old boys are more likely to play with hard objects, blocks, and toy cars, trucks, and airplanes (Fagot, 1974; O'Brien & Huston, 1985).

Social-Learning Views   Social-learning theorists explain the acquisition of sex roles and sex differences in terms of identification and socialization. The psychoanalytic concept of identification centers on Oedipal conflict; social-learning theorists, however, view identification as a broad,

ACQUIRING SEX ROLES According to social-learning theory, the imitation of same-sex adults plays a major part in the acquisition of sex roles.

continuous learning process in which children are influenced by rewards and punishments to imitate adult role models. These models include their parents—particularly the parent of the same sex—and same-sex adults in general (Bronfenbrenner, 1960; Kagan, 1964; Storms, 1980). In identification children not only imitate certain behavior patterns; they also try to become broadly like the model.

Socialization also plays an important part in teaching children to assume sex roles. Parents and other adults—even other children—provide children with messages about how they are expected to behave. Through approval and affection, parents reward children for behavior they consider sex-appropriate, and punish (or fail to reinforce) children for behavior they consider inappropriate. Girls are given dolls while they still sleep in cribs. They are encouraged to rehearse care-taking behaviors as preparation for traditional feminine adult roles.

Many parents believe that they treat their children reasonably equally, regardless of whether they are boys or girls. But a number of observational studies and experiments suggest that boys are often more equal than girls, especially when they try to engage in vigorous physical activity or to explore the environment.

Through observational studies, Beverly Fagot (1974, 1978) found that boys and girls are responded to quite differently, even when they show the same behavior. Mothers are more likely, for example, to encourage their young daughters to follow them around the house, while boys of the same age are pushed to act independently. Both parents are more likely to reinforce sons for exploring the environment and manipulating objects, while girls are more likely to be criticized or warned about the prospects of getting hurt. Other researchers have found that boys are told to run errands outside the home at earlier ages than girls (Saegert & Hart, 1976).

Experiments have shown that parents treat six- and fourteen-month-old infants significantly differently on the basis of sex (Frisch, 1977; Smith & Lloyd, 1978). In these studies, the sex of infants introduced in the laboratory was visually concealed, and the parents were told at random that they were either boys or girls. Parents who believed that the infants were boys were more likely to encourage them to engage in motor activities, such as crawling, and to play with blocks, hammers, and tricycles. Parents who believed that the children were girls spent more time talking to them and cuddling them, and were more likely to encourage them to play with dolls and baby bottles.

The Role of the Father   Generally speaking, mothers more so than fathers have the major responsibility for the day-to-day caregiving and nurturance of children (Belsky, 1984; Belsky et al., 1984). Fathers tend more to interact playfully with their children and to communicate cultural norms for sex-typed behaviors (Lamb, 1981).

Fathers, moreover, are more likely than mothers to treat sons and daughters differently. In one study, sex differences in fathers' play with sons and daughters were noted when the children were only twelve months old (Snow et al., 1983). Fathers prohibited their sons from touching or playing with breakable or potentially harmful objects more frequently. Fathers held their daughters and gave them dolls more frequently.

Research has also shown that boys in father-absent families show a weaker preference for the traditional masculine sex role, tend to be more dependent, and perform less well in school than boys raised by both parents. But boys in father-absent homes who have had one or more older brothers are relatively more masculine in their behavior, less dependent, and earn higher grades in school (Santrock, 1970; Wohlford et al., 1971). Boys with older sisters are more likely than boys with older brothers or no siblings to show a number of feminine sex-stereotyped behaviors (Sutton-Smith & Rosenberg, 1970), and girls with older brothers are also more likely to show stereotypical masculine behaviors.

The Role of Peers   Children are also motivated to engage in "sex-appropriate" behaviors in order to earn the approval, and avoid the disapproval, of their peers. In one study, the researchers (Serbin et al., 1979) observed children in a playroom under three conditions: alone, with a peer of the same sex, or with a cross-sex peer. Many toys were available in the room. When peers of either sex were present, the children were significantly more likely to restrict their play to toys that were consistent with the stereotypes for their sex. Boys, that is, were more likely to choose toy soldiers or transportation toys when in the presence of a peer than when they were alone. Girls, similarly, were more likely to play with dolls, tea sets, and housekeeping toys when they were in the company of their agemates. Several children sort of looked back over their shoulders at the peer when they

Sex norms Social rules or conventions that govern the ways in which males and females interact.

picked up a toy that did not fit their stereotypes; they then tended to select another toy, even when the peer did not seem to be paying attention.

Children have good reason to select stereotypically sex-appropriate toys in the presence of their peers (Lamb & Roopnarine, 1979; Lamb et al., 1980). Three-year-olds frequently avoid boys who play with dolls or tea sets, or girls who play with toy guns, firetrucks, and hammers. Five-year-olds are often openly critical. They usually criticize the choices of the other children and encourage them to choose "appropriate" toys. Sometimes they physically prevent others from playing with the "wrong" toys. But they need not usually go to such extremes; children usually drop cross-gender behaviors quickly when others show disapproval.

The Social Learning of Sex Differences in Aggressive Behavior   Concerning the greater aggressiveness of boys, Maccoby and Jacklin note that:

> Aggression in general is less acceptable for girls, and is more actively discouraged in them, by either direct punishment, withdrawal of affection, or simply cognitive training that "that isn't the way girls act." Girls then build up greater anxieties about aggression, and greater inhibitions against displaying it (1974, p. 234).

Girls frequently learn to respond to social provocations by feeling anxious about the possibility of acting aggressively, while boys are generally encouraged to retaliate (Frodi et al., 1977).

Several experiments highlight the importance of social-learning factors in female aggressiveness. Studies by Albert Bandura and his colleagues (1963) found that boys are more likely than girls to imitate film-mediated aggressive models, because the social milieu more often frowns upon aggressiveness in girls. Other investigators (Taylor & Epstein, 1967; Richardson et al., 1979) have also found that the development of aggressive behavior in females is strongly influenced by situational variables, such as the nature of the provocation and the possibility that someone will disapprove of them.

In the Taylor and Epstein study, aggressive behavior was measured by the strength of the electric shock selected for delivery to another person. Subjects took turns shocking other participants in the study when they failed to respond quickly enough to a stimulus. Subjects could select the strength of the shock themselves. When men set low or moderate shock levels for women subjects, the women generally chose somewhat lower shock levels for the men when their turn came. In this way, they adhered to the feminine stereotype of nonaggressiveness. But when the men violated the **sex norm** of treating women favorably by setting high levels of shock for them, the women retaliated by setting shock levels that were equally high. Apparently the women decided that what was sauce for the goose was sauce for the gander—if men could violate sex norms and treat women aggressively, women could violate sex norms and respond aggressively.

The experiment by the Richardson group suggests that the development of aggressive behavior in girls is strongly influenced by the responses of those who monitor her behavior and reward or punish her. In this study, college women competed with men in responding quickly to a stimulus. They could not see their opponents. The loser of each trial received an electric shock whose intensity was set by the opponent. Women competed under one of three experimental conditions: "public," "private," or with a "supportive other." In the public condition, another woman observed her silently. In the private condition, there was no observer. In the supportive-other condition, another woman urged her to retaliate strongly when her opponent selected high shock levels. As shown in Figure 13.2, women in the private and supportive-other conditions selected increasingly higher levels of shock in retaliation. Presumably, the women in the study assumed that an observer—though silent—would frown on aggressive behavior. It is logical that such an assumption would reflect their own early socialization experiences. Women who were unobserved or urged on by a supportive-other apparently felt free to violate the sex norm of nonaggressiveness when their situations called for aggressive responses.

A Cognitive-Developmental View of the Development of Sex Differences   According to Lawrence Kohlberg's (1966) cognitive-developmental view of the development of sex differences, gender identity itself motivates children to imitate the behavior of adult role models of the sex to which they perceive themselves as belonging. Once children see themselves as being male and female, Kohlberg argues that they actively seek to learn what behaviors are considered masculine or feminine and to imitate them.

Much knowledge of what is "masculine" or "feminine" is acquired by observational learning, as suggested by an experiment by David Perry and Kay Bussey (1979). In this study, children learned which behaviors are stereotypically masculine or feminine by observing the *relative frequencies* with which adult men and women role models performed them. The models expressed arbitrary preferences for objects such as oranges over apples, and toy cows over toy horses. All in all, the models made choices for one of each of sixteen pairs of items while eight- and nine-year-old boys and girls looked on. Then the children were asked to show their own preferences. Boys selected an average of fourteen of sixteen items that agreed with the "preferences" of the men models. Girls selected an average of only three of sixteen items that agreed with the choices of the men. In a related experiment, Perry and Bussey (1979) found that children tended to imitate the behavior of a same-sex adult role model *only when they believed that that particular adult* usually behaved in accord with traditional sex-role stereotypes. Even before the age of ten, the children were unwilling to be "misled" by role models whose behavior was nontraditional.

According to the cognitive-developmental view, then, children actively seek to identify with adults of their own gender. While they gain information through observation, changes in behavior cannot be attributed to reinforcement in a mechanical sense. If reinforcement by parents, other adults, and peers plays a role in the development of sex differences, it is because reinforcement *provides information* as to what behavior is considered appropriate. But from Kohlberg's perspective, children want and actively seek this information.

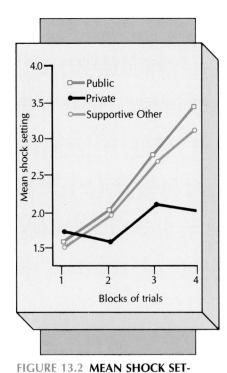

FIGURE 13.2 **MEAN SHOCK SETTINGS CHOSEN BY WOMEN IN RETALIATION AGAINST MALE OPPONENTS IN THE RICHARDSON STUDY** In this study, the intensity of the aggressiveness shown by women was influenced by who was watching them. Women who were alone or in the company of a supportive person behaved more aggressively than women in the company of a person who they believed would disapprove of aggressiveness in women.

SEXUAL MOTIVATION

We may describe people as "hungering" or "thirsting" for sex, but the sex drive differs from the hunger and thirst drives in that sex may be necessary for the survival of the species, but not for the survival of the individual (despite occasional claims to the effect, "I'll simply *die* unless you . . .").

But there are also important similarities between the hunger, thirst, and sex drives. All three can be triggered by external cues as well as internal processes. The sex drive, for example, can be triggered by the sight (or memory) of a loved one, a whiff of perfume, attractive strangers, provocative photographs or films, or a wink.

In Chapter 3 we noted that chemicals detected through the sense of smell—pheromones—play a major role in sexual behavior among lower animals, and appear to play a motivational role in the sexual behavior of some human beings. In this section, we focus on a number of issues concerning sexual motivation, including the organizing and activating influences of sex hormones, the "maternal drive," and the controversial issues of pornography, homosexuality, and forcible rape.

ORGANIZING AND ACTIVATING EFFECTS OF SEX HORMONES

Sex hormones not only promote sexual differentiation and regulate the menstrual cycle. They also have **organizing effects** and **activating effects** on sexual behavior. They predispose lower animals toward masculine or feminine mating patterns (an organizing effect); they influence the sex drive and facilitate sexual response (activating effects).

Male rats who have been castrated at birth—and thus deprived of testosterone—make no effort to mate as adults. But when they receive *female* sex hormones in adulthood, they become receptive to the sexual advances of other *males* and assume typical female mating stances (Harris & Levine, 1965). Male rats who are castrated in adulthood also show no sexual behavior. But if they receive injections of testosterone, they resume stereotypical male sexual behaviors.

Female mice, rats, cats, and dogs are receptive to males only during **estrus,** when female sex hormones are plentiful. The sex organs of female rodents exposed to large doses of testosterone **in utero** (because they share the uterus with many brothers, or because of injections) become masculinized in appearance, and these females are predisposed toward masculine mating behaviors. If they are given testosterone as adults, they attempt to **mount** other females about as often as males do (Goy & Goldfoot, 1975). The earlier doses of testosterone may have permanently organized the brain in the masculine direction, predisposing them toward masculine sexual behaviors in adulthood, when "activated" by additional testosterone.

Testosterone is also important in the behavior of human males. Men who are castrated or given **antiandrogen** drugs usually show gradual loss of sexual desire and of the capacities for erection and orgasm. Still, many castrated men remain sexually active for years, suggesting that for many people fantasies, memories, and other cognitive stimuli are as important as hormones in sexual motivation. Beyond minimal levels, there is no clear link between testosterone level and sexual arousal. For example, sleeping men are *not* more likely to have erections during surges in the testosterone level (Schiavi et al., 1977).

Unlike females of most other species, women are sexually responsive during all phases of the menstrual cycle, even during menstruation itself, when hormone levels are low, and even after **menopause.** But androgens may influence female as well as male sexual response. Women whose adrenal glands and ovaries have been removed (so that they no longer produce androgens) may gradually lose sexual interest and the capacity for sexual response. An active and enjoyable sexual history seems to ward off loss of sexual capacity, suggestive of the importance of cognitive and experiential factors in human sexual motivation.

Discussion of the so-called maternal drive will provide further insight into the roles of sex hormones among various species.

THE "MATERNAL DRIVE"—DO WOMEN MAKE NATURAL MOTHERS?

We often hear that men are naturally clumsy at child-rearing tasks such as making faces, feeding infants, and changing diapers. Women, however, supposedly make "natural" mothers. Consider the expression "A mother *knows.*" Somehow a mother is expected to know how to raise children properly. *Do* mothers "know"? If so, *how* do they know? Does maternal behavior reflect a primary drive in human beings, or is it learned?

The Maternal Drive in Lower Animals In many lower animals, parental behavior is **innate** and governed by hormones. For example, the *male* members of some species of fish will guard their young in their mouths at time of danger when they are influenced by certain hormones. But when the levels of these hormones drop off, their own young will become just another meal if they have not yet swum off on their own.

Maternal behavior in rats also appears largely under the control of hormones: estrogen, progesterone, and **prolactin.** Hormones are carried in the bloodstream. When the blood from a new mother rat is transfused into another female rat, the second female will also show maternal behaviors (Terkel & Rosenblatt, 1972). But at least one situational factor also triggers mechanical maternal behaviors in rats. Female rats will show maternal behaviors in response to being presented a litter of rat pups. *And so will males.* Male rats presented with a litter will maintain a nest and hover above the pups in a typical nursing stance.

Maternal Behavior Among Primates With monkeys, learning plays a more prominent role. At the University of Wisconsin Primate Center, Harry F. Harlow and his colleagues (Harlow & Harlow, 1966; Ruppenthal et al., 1976) reared female monkeys in isolation. At maturity they did not show normal sexual or social interests or behaviors. If they bore children, they frequently showed impatience and lack of interest. This pattern of

Menopause The cessation of menstruation.

Innate Inborn. Responding to a situation in an unlearned, stereotypical manner.

Prolactin A hormone involved in the secretion of milk in mammals, and, among lower mammals, in the regulation of maternal behavior.

neglect and abuse was termed the "motherless-mother syndrome." This syndrome suggests that mothering is learned among primates, and that important related learnings occur at early ages.

Gorillas are yet more advanced primates. Female gorillas raised in captivity often do not have the opportunity to observe adult gorillas functioning in natural social groups. They must often learn how to raise offspring by observing human models going through the motions if they are to be successful mothers.

Maternal Behavior Among Humans   Human beings are also primates, the most advanced primates. (We write the textbooks.) With people, as other primates, sexual and mothering behaviors must also be learned.

If maternal behaviors are learned, why does parenthood often seem to come naturally to women but not to men? As noted earlier, girls are usually given dolls and guided into play that prepares them for the caretaking roles their parents expect them to assume in adulthood. Given this background, it is not surprising that so many women seem to take "naturally" to motherhood. If the L. A. Raiders had all been urged to change siblings' diapers and baby-sit during adolescence, they, too, might fit the mothering role "naturally."

DO WOMEN MAKE NATURAL MOTHERS? Becoming pregnant and bearing children are natural functions. However, caring for children adequately is learned behavior among humans.

PORNOGRAPHY

Since the late 1960s, when the Supreme Court ruled that prohibiting **explicit** sexual materials violated freedom of expression, **pornography** has been a boom industry in the United States. Sections of major American cities—like Times Square in New York and the "Combat Zone" in Boston—garishly display their sex films and other wares. In just a few years we have developed "porno classics" like *Deep Throat* and *The Devil in Miss Jones*. Marilyn Chambers, the willowy star of the porno film *Behind the Green Door*, was fired as "the Ivory Soap girl" for appearing in the movie. Ivory Soap wished to retain its image as 99 and 44/100ths percent pure.

Some people complain that the availability of **erotica** has led to a breakdown in moral standards. Women's groups have argued that pornography inspires crimes of violence against women. In this section we review research bearing on two important questions concerning pornography: What are the effects of pornography? Does pornography inspire antisocial behavior?

What Are the Effects of Pornography?   In the 1960s, congress created a presidential Commission on Obscenity and Pornography to review research on pornography and conduct its own studies. The Commission concluded that married couples exposed to pornography reported feeling sexually aroused, but were not motivated to try observed sexual activities that were "deviant" for them (Abelson et al., 1970). More recent studies with participants ranging from middle-aged couples to college students have attained similar results (Brown et al., 1976; Hatfield et al., 1978; Heiby & Becker, 1980; Herrell, 1975; Schmidt et al., 1973). Observers were sexually aroused and may have been motivated to masturbate or engage in

Explicit Clearly shown. Leaving nothing implied.

Pornography (pour-NOG-graph-fee). Explicit, uncensored portrayals of sexual activity that are intended to excite the observer sexually. (From the Greek *porne*, meaning "prostitute," and *graphein*, meaning "to write.")

Erotica Sexual material that stimulates a sexual response.

PORNOGRAPHY What are the effects of pornography? Does pornography inspire antisocial behavior?

sexual activity with their usual sex partners. But they did not lose self-control or become notably distressed or disturbed.

But these have generally been "one-shot" experiments. What of people who have prolonged exposure to pornography? Howard and his colleagues (1973) exposed male college students to pornography for ninety minutes a day over a fifteen-day period. Personality variables as measured by psychological tests showed no change at the end of the study. Sexual arousal was measured by self-report and a **penile strain gauge,** which measures size of erection. Sexual arousal according to both measures was highest at the outset of the study, then waned gradually. Toward the end of the study many men reported increasing boredom and stated they would not have completed the study except for the financial incentive ($100) or their commitment to the research.

In a similar study, undergraduates of both sexes were exposed to six pornographic films a week over a six-week period (Zillmann & Bryant, 1983). As in the Howard study, the students showed less sexual response to new pornographic films at the end of the study. However, the films in the Zillmann and Bryant study included examples of sadomasochism and sex with animals, and, at the end of the study, the students also showed less revulsion to these activities. As with TV violence (see Chapter 9), overexposure to deviant sex can apparently desensitize the viewer.

It is folklore that men are most sexually responsive to explicit, "hardcore" sexual materials and fantasies. Women, however, are considered more romantic, and thus more likely to be sexually aroused by affectionate, "soft-core" themes. But psychologist Julia Heiman (1975) found that hardcore erotica is not for men only. She played audiotapes with romantic or sexually explicit content while college students' responses were measured by the penile strain gauge and the **vaginal photoplethysmograph.** She found

Penile strain gauge An instrument that measures the size of erection.

Vaginal photoplethysmograph (FOE-toe-pleth-THIZZ-mow-graph). An instrument that measures sexual arousal in women as a function of reflected light in the vaginal wall. The amount of light is related to blood pressure. (From the Greek *phos*, meaning "light," *plethyein*, meaning "to increase," and *graphein*, meaning "to write.")

that explicit sex, with or without romantic trappings, was sexually arousing to both women and men.

Research also shows that women who have strong feelings of guilt about sex report less sexual arousal in response to pornography than women with low sex-guilt report. However, the women with high sex guilt show *greater* physiological responsiveness to pornography than do women with low sex guilt, as measured by the vaginal photoplethysmograph (Morokoff, 1985). Perhaps guilt about sex causes us to misread our bodies' responses to erotic stimulation. But we must also keep in mind that there is a difference between physiological arousal and cognitive processes: physiological response in humans does not necessarily mean that one is cognitively ready for sexual activity. The emotion of guilt is associated with arousal and may facilitate physiological responsiveness to explicit materials, but that need not mean that the person is mentally "turned on."

Does Pornography Inspire Antisocial Behavior?   In addition to reviewing the results of studies of pornography, the president's Commission surveyed over 3,000 mental-health professionals, including psychologists and psychiatrists. Eighty percent of the helping professionals reported having never seen a case in which pornography seemed to be a causal factor in antisocial behavior. Only 7 percent felt they had definitely encountered such a case. Only 12 percent thought that "obscene" books played a causal role in juvenile delinquency.

How do we summarize these results? By noting that the overwhelming majority of mental-health workers found little connection between pornography and antisocial behavior? Or by arguing that a significant minority reported such cases? The data can be used to support either conclusion. But the data are also subject to all of the errors in self-report discussed in Chapter 1.

However, in recent years feminists and others have been arguing that pornography is degrading to women and generally supportive of stereotypes of women as submissive to the needs of men (Blakely, 1985). They have also charged that pornography that depicts sexual and other types of violence against women encourages male viewers to abuse women. Recent well-controlled experiments with aggressive-erotic films do appear to support their concerns, even though normal men and women are usually more sexually aroused by films that portray affectionate coitus than by films showing sex with aggression (Malamuth, 1981).

In one study (Donnerstein, 1980), 120 college men were either provoked or treated neutrally by a male or female confederate of the experimenter. Subjects were then shown neutral, erotic, or aggressive-erotic films. In the latter film, a man forced himself into a woman's home and raped her. Subjects were then given the opportunity to aggress against the male or female confederate of the experimenter through a fake electric-shock apparatus. The measure of aggression was the intensity of the shock chosen. As expected, provoked subjects selected higher shock levels. But even nonprovoked men shown aggressive-erotic films showed greater aggression toward women confederates. And provoked men who were shown aggressive-erotic films chose the highest shock levels against women.

A second study (Malamuth et al., 1980) found that college men and women usually reported greater sexual response to a story about mutually desired sex than to a story about rape. But in variations of the study, Malamuth and his colleagues portrayed the rape victim as experiencing an involuntary orgasm, with or without pain. The addition of the involuntary orgasm raised student self-reports of sexual arousal to levels that equaled the response to mutually desired sex. Women subjects were most responsive when the woman in the story did not have pain, but men were most aroused when she did. The researchers speculate that the woman's orgasm legitimized the violence. Thus, the sexual responsiveness of the observers was **disinhibited.** The story may have reinforced the cultural myth that some women need to be dominated and will be "turned on" by an overpowering man. Exposure to aggressive-erotic films may increase violence, even among normal college men (Donnerstein & Linz, 1984).

However, even these well-controlled experiments have some limitations. For example, they both involved selection of a (phony) electric shock in a laboratory. Neither measured violence against women outside the lab. Still, if legislation were to be considered to answer the legitimate concerns of women who argue against the availability of aggressive-erotic materials, it might be that the Swedish approach of outlawing portrayals of *violence* rather than of sexual behavior could be considered. There remains no evidence that pornography without violence stimulates antisocial behavior. But it may be that any legislation that would curtail the production or sale of pornographic materials could be interpreted as impeding freedom of expression. Such legislation could be found in conflict with the First Amendment and therefore unconstitutional (Blakely, 1985). Even the feminist community is split on the issue, with some feminist writers, like Kate Millett, arguing that "We're better off hanging tight to the First Amendment so that we have freedom of speech" (Press et al., 1985). The question as to what, if anything, should and can be done about pornography is a controversial issue that is likely to be with us for some time to come.

HOMOSEXUALITY

Homosexuality, or a homosexual sexual *orientation,* is defined as sexual preference for members of one's own sex. Sexual activity with member's of one's own sex in and of itself may reflect limited sexual opportunities rather than homosexuality. For instance, adolescent boys may masturbate one another while fantasizing about girls. Men in prisons may similarly turn to each other for sexual outlets.

Kinsey and his colleagues (1948, 1953) estimated that as many as 37 percent of the men and 13 percent of the women in his sample had had at least one homosexual encounter, while only about 4 percent of his male and 1 to 3 percent of his female subjects had a homosexual orientation. About 2 percent of the men and 1 percent of the women in a more recent survey reported a homosexual orientation (Hunt, 1974).

Adjustment of Homosexuals   Despite the slings and arrows of an often outraged society, it seems that homosexuals are about as well-adjusted

Disinhibit In social-learning theory, to stimulate a response that is normally inhibited by showing a model engaging in that response.

Homosexuality Preference for sexual activity and the forming of romantic relationships with members of one's own sex. (From the Greek *homos,* meaning "same.")

GAY RIGHTS In recent years, homosexuals have become more open about expressing their sexual orientations and demanding equal rights.

as heterosexuals. Saghir and Robins (1973) could not distinguish gay males from heterosexuals in terms of anxiety, depression, and psychosomatic complaints like headaches and ulcers. Adelman (1977) found that professionally employed lesbians were somewhat more socially isolated than professional heterosexual women, but could not otherwise be differentiated.

Bell and Weinberg (1978) found that the adjustment of San Francisco homosexuals was linked to their life styles. Homosexual "close couples" who lived as though married appeared as well-adjusted as married people. Homosexuals who led other life styles showed various levels of adjustment. Older homosexuals who lived by themselves and had few if any sexual contacts were poorly adjusted—as are many heterosexuals who lead a similar life style.

Homosexuality and AIDS   Since the disease Acquired Immune Deficiency Syndrome (AIDS) came into public awareness during the early 1980s, 70 to 75 percent of the afflicted persons in the United States have been homosexual males (Clark et al., 1985; Wallis et al., 1985; Masters et al., 1985). AIDS impairs the body's ability to fight off run-of-the-mill infections, and the vast majority of those who contract full-blown cases die (Clark et al., 1985; Wallis et al., 1985).*

AIDS develops from a viral infection and can be sexually transmitted by men or women. Anal intercourse seems to be a common method of transmitting the AIDS virus, perhaps because it can rupture the rectal lining and allow infected semen to easily enter the bloodstream of the recipient

---

*It should be noted, however, that the majority of those who carry the AIDS virus—homosexual and heterosexual alike—have not *yet* developed full-blown cases (Wallis et al., 1985).

(Clark et al., 1985; Wallis et al., 1985). Since anal intercourse is practiced more frequently by male homosexuals than by the general population (Masters et al., 1985), this practice may explain why gay males are at greater risk for acquiring AIDS than are most other groups. It has also been learned that gay males who have large numbers of sex partners are at greater risk for AIDS than those with relatively few (Darrow, 1983; Jaffe et al., 1983). For these reasons, many gay males have limited their sexual behavior to safer practices and have restricted their sexual contacts to one or a few well-known partners (Gelman et al., 1985; Meredith, 1984).

Fear of AIDS has had wider effects. It has even been suggested that concern about AIDS and a number of other sexually transmitted diseases has helped bring the "sexual revolution" of the 1960s and 1970s to a crashing halt (Gelman et al., 1985).

Causes of Homosexuality The origins of homosexuality are complex and controversial. It was once thought that homosexuality might be genetically transmitted. Kallmann (1952) found a 100 percent **concordance** rate for homosexuality among the **probands** of forty identical twins. However, more recent studies (e.g., Parker, 1964; Zuger, 1976; McConaghy & Blaszczynski, 1980) have failed to replicate Kallmann's findings.

Sex hormones influence the mating behavior of lower animals, and it was thought that gay males might be deficient in testosterone while lesbians might have lower-than-normal levels of estrogen and higher-than-normal levels of androgens in their bloodstreams. However, recent studies have shown no reliable differences in current hormone levels between heterosexuals and homosexuals (Feder, 1984).

Still, there are other ways in which sex hormones may be related to sexual preference. Men have small amounts of estrogen in their bloodstreams, and there are some indications that the brains of male homosexuals may be more responsive to estrogen than are the brains of male heterosexuals (Blake, 1985). Perhaps as part of "masculinizing" or "feminizing" the brain, prenatal hormonal influences create a basic predisposition toward heterosexuality or homosexuality by establishing certain levels of sensitivities to the sex hormones that will be found in the bloodstream later on.

Psychoanalytic theory (Bieber, 1976) suggests that homosexuals resolve the Oedipus and Electra complexes differently from the heterosexual majority. In men this faulty resolution stems from a "classic pattern" of a close-binding mother and a detached-hostile father. But we should note that many gay males have had excellent relationships with both parents and that the childhoods of many heterosexuals have fit the "classic pattern."

Social-learning theory suggests that pleasurable early sexual interactions with people of our own sex may induce a homosexual orientation. However, many gay males and lesbians felt their preferences before they had had any overt sexual contacts (Bell et al., 1981). Other people have had numerous homosexual experiences in childhood, but never doubted their heterosexual orientations.

The causes of human homosexuality are indeed mysterious—as mysterious as the causes of human heterosexuality.

Concordance Agreement.

Proband The family member first studied or tested. (From the Latin *probare*, meaning "to test" or "to prove.")

FORCIBLE RAPE

Forcible rape is the seeking of sexual gratification against the will of another person. There are more than 90,000 reported cases of rape in the United States each year (Allgeier & Allgeier, 1984). Since it has been estimated that only one rape in five is reported, it may be that as many as 450,000 rapes take place in the United States each year. An additional 400,000 to 2 million instances of forced sex may take place within marriage each year, although women are not likely to define forced sex by their husbands as rape (Groth & Gary, 1981).

If we add to these figures instances in which women are subjected to forced kissing and petting, the numbers grow even more alarming. For example, nearly 70 percent of 282 women in one college sample had been assaulted (usually by dates and friends) at some time since entering college (Kanin & Parcell, 1977). At a major university, 40 percent of 201 male students surveyed admitted to using force to unfasten a woman's clothing, and 13 percent reported that they had forced a woman to engage in sexual intercourse (Rapaport & Burkhart, 1984).

Causes of Rape   Why do men rape women? Many social scientists argue that sexual motivation frequently has little to do with rape. Rape, they argue, is more often a man's way of expressing anger toward, or power over, women (e.g., Groth & Burgess, 1980). In fact, many rapists have long records as violent offenders (Amir, 1971). With some rapists, violence also appears to enhance sexual arousal, so that they are motivated to combine sex with aggression (Quinsey et al., 1984).

Many social critics also assert that our culture socializes men into becoming rapists (Burt, 1980). Males, who are often reinforced for aggressive and competitive behavior, could be said to be asserting culturally expected dominance over women. Sexually coercive college males, as a group, are more likely to believe that aggression is a legitimate form of behavior than are noncoercive college males (Rapaport & Burkhart, 1984).

Women, on the other hand, may be socialized into the victim role. The stereotypical feminine role encourages passivity, nurturance, warmth, and cooperation. Women are often taught to sacrifice for their families, and not to raise their voices. Thus a woman may be totally unprepared to cope with an assailant. She may lack aggressive skills and believe that violence is inappropriate for women. Mary Beth Myers and her colleagues (1984) found that rape victims are less dominant and self-assertive than nonvictims—that is, their behavior is more consistent with what society expects of women.

Gary Wieder (1985) argues that the conclusion that nonassertive, less socially effective women are more likely to become victims of rape is, in a sense, blaming the victim for her assault. The implication is that women should project a more assertive image which, in fact, sometimes prompts rapists to become yet more violent and aggressive. Mary Beth Myers and her associates (1985) reply that they did not mean to suggest that women are responsible for their victimization. They only noted that victimization is not a random process, and that women who appear vulnerable are more

QUESTIONNAIRE

CULTURAL MYTHS THAT CREATE A CLIMATE THAT SUPPORTS RAPE

Martha Burt (1980) has compiled a number of statements concerning rape. Read each of them and indicate whether you believe it to be true or false by writing T or F in the blank. Then turn to Appendix B to learn of the implications of your answers.

T F

_____ 1. A woman who goes to the home or apartment of a man on their first date implies that she is willing to have sex.

_____ 2. Any female can get raped.

_____ 3. One reason that women falsely report a rape is that they frequently have a need to call attention to themselves.

_____ 4. Any healthy woman can successfully resist a rapist if she really wants to.

_____ 5. When women go around braless or wearing short skirts and tight tops, they are just asking for trouble.

_____ 6. In the majority of rapes, the victim is promiscuous or has a bad reputation.

_____ 7. If a girl engages in necking or petting and she lets things get out of hand, it is her own fault if her partner forces sex on her.

_____ 8. Women who get raped while hitchhiking get what they deserve.

_____ 9. A woman who is stuck-up and thinks she is too good to talk to guys on the street deserves to be taught a lesson.

_____ 10. Many women have an unconscious wish to be raped, and may then unconsciously set up a situation in which they are likely to be attacked.

_____ 11. If a woman gets drunk at a party and has intercourse with a man she's just met there, she should be considered "fair game" to other males at the party who want to have sex with her too, whether she wants to or not.

_____ 12. Many women who report a rape are lying because they are angry and want to get back at the man they accuse.

_____ 13. Many, if not most, rapes are merely invented by women who discovered they were pregnant and wanted to protect their reputation.

likely than others to be attacked. Generally speaking, criminologists know that people who look vulnerable are more likely to be victims of many kinds of crime.

Social Attitudes and Myths that Encourage Rape   Many people, including professionals who work with rapists and victims, believe a number of myths about rape. These include "Only bad girls get raped," "Any healthy woman can resist a rapist if she wants to," and "Women only cry rape when they've been jilted or have something to cover up" (Burt, 1980, p. 217). These myths tend to deny the impact of the assault, and also to place blame on the victim rather than her assailant. They contribute to a social

60 MINUTES

DEPO-PROVERA

Are rapists in control of their own behavior? Should convicted rapists be thrown into prison?

One new treatment for rapists suggests that at least some rapists are not always in charge of their own behavior. And, to the dismay of many rape victims, judges, and others, they are participating in experimental treatment programs rather than spending terms in prison.

As reported on a 60 Minutes segment by correspondent Ed Bradley, the experimental treatment is a drug called Depo-Provera, which has the effect of lowering testosterone levels in rapists. According to Dr. Fred Berlin of Johns Hopkins University Hospital, who was interviewed on the segment, many rapists are career criminals without a conscience, and drugs are not the answer for them. However—again according to Berlin—some rapists have unusually high levels of testosterone in their blood, and high levels of this hormone create intense sex drives that they have difficulty controlling.

Although conclusive findings are not yet in, a San Antonio rapist interviewed on the segment stated,

> I'm not the monster [people] think I am. I'm a person with a problem. And if it's controllable, why put me in prison for five years and let me back out

on the street with the same problem? And [Depo-Provera] reduces the sex drive to where I can change. With—with the drug, I have no sex drive.

Berlin did not explain why these men with high levels of testosterone raped strangers instead of engaging in more frequent sexual activity with wives or girlfriends—or why they chose rape over masturbation. Judge Tom Rickhoff, also interviewed, argued that rapists in this program should be sent to prison like other rapists. Why? Rickhoff argued:

> [Prison] tells him that there is a punishment for crime. It forces him to recognize that he doesn't just have a psychological problem or a chemical problem in his body. His problem is he's raping people. . . . If he's going to get through life thinking he's got a chemical imbalance, what's to prevent him from going out and committing another violent rape? What's to prevent him is the punishment of confinement. That's why we have prisons, punishment.

Ed Bradley also asked a woman rape victim whether she thought that prison would do the rapist any good. She replied, "I'm sorry, Ed, but I'm not very much concerned with what's going to do *him* any good."

"climate" that is too often lenient toward rapists and unsympathetic toward victims.

Do you believe cultural myths that have the effect of supporting rape? Why not take the questionnaire on p. 614 and find out?

Preventing Rape In *The New Our Bodies, Ourselves,* The Boston Women's Health Book Collective (1984) lists a number of suggestions that women can use to lower the likelihood of rape: Establish signals and arrangements with other women in an apartment building or neighborhood. List only first initials in the telephone directory or on the mailbox. Use dead-bolt locks. Keep windows locked and obtain iron grids for first-floor windows. Keep entrances and doorways brightly lit. Have keys ready for the front door or the car. Do not walk alone in the dark. Avoid deserted areas.

Also: Never allow a strange man into your apartment or home without checking his credentials. Drive with the car windows up and the door locked. Check the rear seat of the car before entering. Avoid living in an unsafe building. Do not pick up hitchhikers. Do not talk to strange men in the street. Shout "Fire!" not "Rape!" People crowd around fires but avoid scenes of violence.

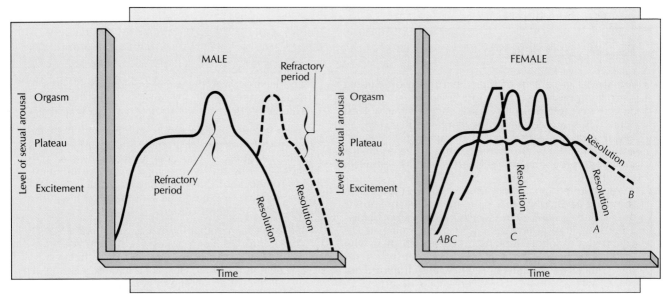

FIGURE 13.3 **THE MALE AND FEMALE SEXUAL RESPONSE CYCLES** The pattern of male sexual response shows that men undergo a refractory period following orgasm during which they are not responsive to further sexual stimulation. But they may be restimulated to orgasm after sufficient time passes. Pattern A, for women, shows that women may be restimulated to orgasms in quick succession (multiple orgasms). In Pattern B, a woman has been highly excited for a protracted period, but has not reached orgasm. Eventually her excitement subsides. In Pattern C, a woman quickly reaches orgasm and her excitement also rapidly subsides. Men may also experience patterns B and C. Source: Masters and Johnson (1966).

THE SEXUAL-RESPONSE CYCLE

During the 1960s William Masters and Virginia Johnson became renowned for their research in human sexual response and **psychosexual dysfunctions.** They disdained the standard questionnaire and interview approaches to sex research. Instead, they arranged for volunteers to engage in sexual activity in the laboratory while their physiological responses were monitored.

Masters and Johnson (1966) found that sexual stimulation leads to many types of responses. Two of them are largely reflexive: **myotonia,** or muscle tension, and **vasocongestion,** or the flow of arterial blood into the genitals and other parts of the body, such as the breasts. These responses, and others, can be described in terms of a sexual-response cycle that applies to both men and women. The four phases of this cycle are the excitement, plateau, orgasm, and resolution phases (Figure 13.3).

THE EXCITEMENT PHASE

The **excitement phase** is the first phase of physiological response to sexual stimulation. The heart rate, blood pressure, and respiration rate increase.

Psychosexual dysfunction A problem that has psychological roots and is characterized by difficulty in becoming sexually aroused or in reaching orgasm.

Myotonia (my-oh-TONE-knee-uh). Muscle tension. (From the Greek *myos*, meaning "muscle.")

Vasocongestion (vaz-oh-con-JEST-shun). Accumulation of blood, particularly in the genital region. (From the Latin *vas*, meaning "vessel," as in "blood vessel.")

Excitement phase The first phase of the sexual-response cycle, in which erection occurs in the male, and vaginal lubrication and clitoral swelling occur in the female.

Clitoris A female sex organ that is highly sensitive to sexual stimulation.

Sex flush A reddish hue on body surfaces that is caused by vasocongestion.

Plateau phase (plat-toe). An advanced state of sexual arousal that precedes orgasm.

Semen (SEE-men). The fluid that is ejaculated during coitus, containing sperm.

Refractory period A period following orgasm when a male is insensitive to further sexual stimulation.

Multiple orgasms The experiencing of one or more additional orgasms as a result of sexual stimulation during the resolution phase. Two or more orgasms in rapid succession.

In the male, blood vessels in chambers of loose tissue within the penis dilate reflexively to allow blood to flow in. Filling or engorgement with blood results in erection. Despite the slang terms for an erection, "boner" and "muscle," the process of erection relies neither on bone nor muscle.

In the female, the breasts swell and the nipples become erect. Blood engorges the genital region, and the **clitoris**—a protrusion on the genitals that is highly sensitive to sexual stimulation—expands. The inner part of the vagina—the tubelike organ that contains the penis during coitus—lengthens and dilates. Within ten seconds to half a minute, vaginal lubrication reflexively appears. A **sex flush,** or mottling of the skin, may appear late in this phase.

THE PLATEAU PHASE

The **plateau phase** describes a heightening of sexual arousal that prepares the body for orgasm. The heart rate, blood pressure, and respiration rate continue to rise. In the man, further engorgement causes the ridge around the head of the penis to turn a deep purple. The testes increase in size and elevate in order to allow a full ejaculation.

In the woman, the outer vagina becomes so engorged that its diameter is reduced about one-third. Engorgement of the area around the clitoris causes the clitoris to "withdraw" beneath a fold of skin called the clitoral hood. Further swelling of the breasts causes the nipples to appear to have become smaller, although they have not. The sex flush becomes pronounced.

THE ORGASM PHASE

During orgasm, breathing, blood pressure, and heart rate reach a peak, and there are involuntary muscle contractions throughout the body. In the man, muscles at the base of the penis contract and expel **semen** through the penis. In the woman, muscles surrounding the outer third of the vagina contract rhythmically. Most authorities agree that there is no female ejaculation, just vaginal lubrication.* For both sexes the initial contractions are most intense and spaced at about 0.8-second intervals (five contractions every four seconds). Subsequent contractions are weaker and spaced farther apart.

Following orgasm, men enter a **refractory period** during which they are unresponsive to further sexual stimulation, although some men are capable of reaching orgasm twice before sexual arousal subsides. Women can experience numerous or **multiple orgasms,** as many as fifty in rapid succession. This capacity has given some women the feeling that they ought not be satisfied with only one—the flip side of the old myth that sexual pleasure is meant for men only. In sex, as in other areas of life, our oughts and shoulds often place arbitrary demands on us that evoke anxiety and feelings of inadequacy (Rathus & Nevid, 1986).

*See Ladas and her colleagues (1982) for a divergent view.

PSYCHOLOGY AND HEALTH

SEXUAL RESPONSE AND THE AGING

"Just because there's snow on the roof doesn't mean there's no fire in the furnace"—so goes the saying. Yet, for various reasons, we may think of sex as for young people only. It may be difficult for us to imagine our parents engaged in sexual activity; we may not understand why the elderly would be attracted to one another; and we may link sex with reproduction (Rathus, 1983). Still, Kinsey and his colleagues (1948) found that half of the men aged seventy-five in his sample achieved erections regularly. Masters and Johnson (1966) found women at this age capable of multiple orgasms.

Some changes do occur with advancing age. By age fifty or so, men may require increased sexual stimulation to achieve erection and may not be able to reattain erection for from eight to twenty-four hours after ejaculation (Kaplan & Sager, 1971). But from the woman's perspective, her mate may become a more effective lover. It may take older men longer to ejaculate, and so the couple may be able to prolong intercourse. Many men continue to have intercourse into their eighties, but some lose the ability to attain erection. This falloff may stem from decreased production of testosterone and health problems, but can also reflect psychological factors, such as loss of interest in one's sex partner.

Along with menopause, women may experience vaginal dryness and loss of vaginal elasticity, reflecting decreased estrogen production. This condition may be corrected through use of artificial lubrication or estro-

SEXUAL RESPONSE AND THE AGING Men and women with positive sexual attitudes can enjoy sexual activity for a lifetime.

gen-replacement therapy (ERT). However, ERT is controversial, because prolonged use has been linked to cancer. Menopause signals the end of a woman's reproductive capacity, but certainly not of her sexual capacity. Women in their eighties can reach orgasm. Men and women with positive sexual attitudes can enjoy sexual activity for a lifetime.

Orgasm is a reflex. We can set the stage for it by receiving adequate sexual stimulation of a physical and, perhaps, cognitive nature (by focusing on the attractiveness of our partner, erotic fantasies, and so forth), but we cannot force or will an orgasm to happen. Efforts to force orgasm can be counterproductive, as we shall see in our discussion of the psychosexual dysfunctions.

THE RESOLUTION PHASE

After an orgasm that is not followed by additional sexual stimulation, a **resolution phase** occurs in which the body gradually returns to its resting state. The heart rate, blood pressure, and respiration rate all return to normal levels. Blood that has engorged the genitals is dispelled from this region throughout the body.

If a lengthy plateau phase is not followed by orgasm (as in pattern B in Figure 13.3), genital engorgement may take longer to dissipate, leading to pelvic tension or discomfort in both men and women.

Resolution phase The final phase of the sexual-response cycle, during which the body returns gradually to its prearoused state.

Inhibited sexual desire Lack of interest in sexual activity usually accompanied by absence of sexual fantasies.

Inhibited sexual excitement Persistent lack of sexual response during sexual activity.

Inhibited orgasm Inability to reach orgasm in a person who is sexually excited.

Premature ejaculation Ejaculation that occurs before the couple is satisfied with the duration of coitus.

PSYCHOSEXUAL DYSFUNCTIONS AND SEX THERAPY

Many of us will be troubled by some form of psychosexual dysfunction, or difficulty in becoming sexually aroused or reaching orgasm, at one time or another. Masters and Johnson (1970) estimated that at least half the marriages in this nation are sexually dysfunctional. Fourteen to 15 percent of the middle-class married men and women surveyed by Frank and his colleagues (1978) reported their sexual relations as "not very satisfying" or "not satisfying at all." The incidence of psychosexual dysfunction may be higher among single people, since they are less likely to feel secure in their sexual relationships and to be familiar with their partner's sexual preferences.

In this section we define the various psychosexual dysfunctions, then discuss their origins and their treatment.

TYPES OF PSYCHOSEXUAL DYSFUNCTIONS

The psychosexual dysfunctions listed in the DSM–III include inhibited sexual desire, inhibited sexual excitement, inhibited orgasm, premature ejaculation, dyspareunia, and vaginismus.

In the case of **inhibited sexual desire,** the person shows lack of interest in sexual activity and frequently reports an absence of sexual fantasies. Note that the label of *inhibited* desire presumes that sexual fantasies and interests are normal response patterns that may be blocked by anxiety or other factors.

Sexual excitement in the male is characterized by erection of the penis. Men who have difficulty attaining or sustaining an erection were once called "impotent," a term that has been changed in part because of its implication that a man with this problem is weak or sterile. In the female, sexual excitement is characterized by a lubricating of the vaginal walls that makes entry by the penis possible. Almost all men now and then have difficulty attaining erection or maintaining an erection through intercourse, and almost all women now and then have difficulty becoming or remaining lubricated. But in the case of **inhibited sexual excitement,** the lack of sexual response during sexual activity is persistent and understandably troubling.

In **inhibited orgasm,** the man or woman, although sexually excited, is persistently delayed in reaching orgasm, or does not reach orgasm at all. Inhibited orgasm is more common among women than men. In some cases, an individual can reach orgasm without difficulty while engaging in sexual relations with one partner, but not with another. Inhibited orgasm in women was once called "frigidity," implying that women with this psychosexual dysfunction were uninterested in sex or generally "cold" as people. However, women with inhibited orgasm may be generally warm and loving.

In **premature ejaculation** the male persistently ejaculates too soon to permit his partner or himself to fully enjoy sexual relations.

In **functional dyspareunia,** sexual intercourse is associated with recurrent pain in the genital region. When the problem is caused by a medical disorder, it is considered organic, not functional.

Functional vaginismus is involuntary spasm of the muscles surrounding the vagina. Vaginismus makes sexual intercourse painful or impossible.

ORIGINS OF SEXUAL DYSFUNCTIONS

It was once assumed that sexual dysfunctions almost invariably stemmed from organic or physical causes. But there has been recent recognition that most dysfunctions reflect psychosocial factors like troubled relationships, lack of sexual skills, irrational beliefs, and anxiety, and can therefore be considered *psychosexual.* Physical factors may also interact with psychological factors. For instance, anxiety has physiological correlates like rapid heart and respiration rates. In small doses, as typical of a first date, anxiety may enhance sexual excitement, but severe anxiety can block sexual response. Let us now examine various physical and psychological causes of sexual dysfunction.

Physical Factors   Since perhaps 10 to 20 percent of sexual dysfunctions stem from disease, people seeking sex therapy usually receive a thorough physical examination first. Inhibited sexual excitement, for example, can reflect diabetes and diseases of the heart and lungs.

The single most common cause of dyspareunia in women is lack of sufficient vaginal lubrication, which, in turn, usually reflects inadequate foreplay, marital dissatisfaction, anxiety, or other factors. But dyspareunia may also result from a vaginal infection, an **episiotomy** scar, collection of secretions underneath the clitoral hood, and other physical causes. Dyspareunia in men can reflect infection of the **prostate gland, gonorrhea,** or even high sensitivity to the natural acidity of the vagina.

Fatigue may lead to inhibited sexual excitement and inhibited orgasm. But these incidents will be isolated unless we attach too much meaning to them and become overly concerned about future sexual performance.

Depressants like alcohol, narcotics, and tranquilizers may impede sexual response. Antiadrenergic drugs (used to treat high blood pressure), adrenal steroids like cortisone and ACTH (used to treat allergic reactions and inflammation), and anticholinergic drugs (used to treat ulcers and glaucoma) may also contribute to sexual dysfunctions.

Sex-Negative Attitudes   Certain stereotypical attitudes suggest that, although men may find sex pleasurable, sex is a duty for women. Women who share these sex-negative attitudes may be so anxious about sex that they become a self-fulfilling prophecy. Men, too, may be handicapped by misinformation and sexual taboos.

Psychosexual Trauma   **Psychosexual trauma** refers to physically or psychologically painful sexual experiences that cause future sexual response to be blocked by anxiety. Rape victims may encounter sexual adjustment

Functional dyspareunia (dis-par-OOH-knee-uh). Painful coitus that has psychological origins.

Functional vaginismus (vadge-in-IS-muss). Involuntary contraction of the muscles surrounding the outer part of the vaginal barrel.

Episiotomy (ep-peas-ee-OTT-to-me). A surgical incision that eases childbirth.

Prostate gland A gland that secretes the bulk of seminal fluid (semen).

Gonorrhea (gone-or-EE-yuh). A sexually transmitted disease that can inflame the pelvic region.

Psychosexual trauma A distressing sexual experience that may have lingering psychological effects.

problems such as vaginismus or inhibited orgasm. Masters and Johnson (1970) report several cases of men with inhibited sexual excitement who had had anxiety-evoking encounters with prostitutes.

Troubled Relationships A sexual relationship is usually no better than other aspects of the relationship or marriage (Perlman & Abramson, 1982). Communication problems are an excellent predictor of marital dissatisfaction (Markman, 1981; Snyder, 1979; Schultz, 1980). Couples who have problems expressing their sexual desires are at a disadvantage in teaching their partners how to provide pleasure. We shall see that sex-therapy techniques enhance a couple's communication skills. Couples who communicate are also less likely to build resentments over nonsexual issues that spill over into the bedroom.

Lack of Sexual Skills Sexual skills, as are other behavioral competencies, are learned largely from operant conditioning and observational learning. We learn what makes us and others feel good through trial and error, talking and reading about sex, and, perhaps, by watching sex films. But many people do not acquire sexual skills, because they lack the opportunity to experiment. Or perhaps anxiety that stems from sex-negative beliefs inhibits their exploration.

Sex therapy addresses the teaching of sexual skills, and also deals with anxiety that may interfere with their acquisition.

Irrational Beliefs Albert Ellis (1977) and other cognitive psychologists point out that irrational beliefs and attitudes may contribute to psychosexual dysfunctions. For instance, if we believe that we need others' approval at all times, we may catastrophize the importance of one disappointing sexual episode. Similarly, if we believe that events are essentially beyond our control, we may assume that we are powerless to change our sexual "fates." Each of the ten basic irrational beliefs discussed in Chapter 10 may be applied to sexual behavior. Sex therapists attempt to be sensitive to client's anxiety-evoking, self-defeating irrational beliefs.

Performance Anxiety Two thousand years ago it was said, "All roads lead to Rome"—the heart of the empire. In most cases of psychosexual dysfunction, the physical and psychological factors we have outlined lead to yet another psychological factor—**performance anxiety,** or fear as to whether we shall be able to perform sexually. People with performance anxiety may focus on recollections of past failures and expectations of another disaster, rather than lose themselves in their erotic sensations and fantasies (Barlow, 1986).

Performance anxiety can make it difficult for a man to attain erection, yet spur him to ejaculate prematurely (see Chapter 2). Inhibited sexual excitement and premature ejaculation are often found in the same man. Performance anxiety can also prevent a woman from becoming adequately lubricated or can contribute to vaginismus.

At the heart of performance anxiety is the cognition that something is

---

Performance anxiety Excessive concern about whether one will be able to become sexually aroused or reach orgasm.

being sexually *demanded* of someone. Therefore, sex-therapy programs suggest that an individual or a couple begin retraining themselves under nondemanding circumstances.

SEX THERAPY

When Kinsey was making his surveys of sexual behavior in the 1940s, there was no effective treatment for the sexual dysfunctions. But a number of useful methods based on the behavioral model, collectively called **sex therapy,** have been developed in recent years.

Sex therapists assume that psychosexual dysfunctions can be treated by directly modifying the problem behavior. Treatment of most dysfunctions is enhanced by the cooperation of a patient sex partner, so it may be necessary to work on the couple's relationship before sex therapy is undertaken.

Sex therapy focuses on (1) reducing performance anxiety; (2) changing self-defeating expectations; and (3) learning sexual skills or behavioral competencies. When possible, both sex partners are involved in therapy. The sex therapists educate the couple and guide them through a series of homework assignments. Masters and Johnson argue that sex therapists should work in male-female teams, but research suggests that sex therapy is equally effective whether carried out by a single therapist or a team, and regardless of whether the single therapist is the same sex as the person with the dysfunction (LoPiccolo et al., 1985). Masters and Johnson also use a standard two-week treatment format with couples who live in residence at their clinic during this period. However, in many instances "bibliotherapy"—or treatment of problems through reading self-help manuals—has also been successful in treating psychosexual dysfunctions (e.g., Dodge et al., 1982).

Let us have a look at a sample of the techniques that have been effective in treating inhibited sexual excitement in the male, premature ejaculation, and inhibited orgasm in the female.

Inhibited Sexual Excitement   A man with erectile problems learns that he need not "do" anything to attain erection. He need only receive sexual stimulation under relaxed circumstances, so that anxiety does not inhibit the erectile reflex.

In order to reduce performance anxiety, the partners engage in contacts that do not demand that the man attain erection. At first they use **sensate-focus exercises** in which they massage one another without touching the genitals. Each partner learns to "pleasure" the other and to "be pleasured" by receiving and giving verbal instructions and guiding the other's hands. Thus communication skills as well as sexual skills are acquired. After a couple of sessions, sensate focus extends to the genitals. When the man attains erection the couple does not immediately attempt coitus, since this might recreate performance anxiety. Once erection is attained reliably, the couple engages in a graduated series of sexual activities, culminating in intercourse.

Masters and Johnson (1970) report that this technique resulted in a "reversal" of inhibited sexual excitement in about 72 percent of the couples they treated for the problem. But it should be noted that Masters and John-

Sex therapy A collection of predominantly behavioral methods that treat sexual dysfunctions by (1) reducing performance anxiety; (2) changing self-defeating expectations; and (3) teaching sexual skills.

Sensate-focus exercises Planned sessions in which couples take turns giving and receiving physical pleasure.

THE IMPORTANCE OF COMMUNICATION In order to overcome psychosexual dysfunctions (as well as other problems), couples must learn to communicate.

son have been criticized for their evaluation of the effectiveness of their treatments. Their shortcomings include (1) failure to operationally define degrees of improvement in clients; and (2) inadequate follow-up of treated clients to determine whether treatment "reversals" remain reversed (Adams, 1980; Zilbergeld & Evans, 1980).

Premature Ejaculation Sensate-focus exercises are also often used in treatment of premature ejaculation, so that couples will learn to give and receive pleasure under relaxed, rather than sexually demanding, circumstances. Then, when the couple is ready to begin sexual interaction, Masters and Johnson (1970) teach them the "squeeze technique," in which the tip of the penis is squeezed when the man feels he is about to ejaculate. This method, which is best learned through personal instruction by sex therapists, prevents ejaculation. Gradually the man learns to prolong coitus without ejaculating. Masters and Johnson report this technique successful with 182 of 196 men treated.

In 1956, urologist James Semans suggested a simpler method called the "stop-and-go" technique, in which a man simply suspends sexual stimulation whenever he feels he is about to ejaculate. With this method, too, the man learns gradually to prolong sexual stimulation without ejaculating.

Inhibited Orgasm Women who have difficulty reaching orgasm with a particular partner may be best advised to become involved in sex therapy with that partner. But women who have never experienced orgasm may benefit, at least at first, from individual treatment. These women often harbor beliefs that sex is dirty, and they may have been taught never to touch themselves. They are typically anxious about their sexuality, and may not have had the chance to learn, through trial and error, what types of sexual stimulation will excite them and bring them to orgasm.

Masters and Johnson have treated such women by working with the couples involved, but other sex therapists suggest that it is preferable to use masturbation (Andersen, 1981; Barbach, 1975; Heiman et al., 1976; LoPiccolo & Stock, 1986; McMullen & Rosen, 1979). Masturbation provides women with a chance to learn about their own bodies and to give themselves pleasure without depending on a sex partner. Once women can reach orgasm by masturbating, they may need additional treatment to transfer their training to sex with a partner (Leiblum & Ersner-Hershfield, 1977; Schneidman & McGuire, 1976; Zeiss et al., 1977).

On the other hand, women who are morally opposed to masturbation may elect to involve themselves in sex therapy with their partners for that reason. Opposition to masturbation need not necessarily suggest that the woman possesses broad sex-negative attitudes that will impair her ability to reach orgasm with her husband or other partner.

The actual masturbation programs have several elements in common. Women first learn about their own anatomy through reading, discussion groups, and use of a mirror. They experiment with self-caresses at their own pace, learning gradually to bring themselves to orgasm while pleasure helps countercondition sexual anxiety.

When inhibited orgasm reflects a woman's relationship with or feelings about her sex partner, treatment requires dealing with the couple—if the woman chooses to maintain the relationship. Masters and Johnson again begin with sensate-focus exercises to decrease performance anxiety, open communication channels, and enhance the couple's sexual skills. During genital massage and then coitus, the woman guides her partner in the caresses and movements that she finds sexually exciting. Masters and Johnson (1970) report that the dysfunctions of 81 percent of 183 women treated for this problem were reversed.

Sex therapists tend to agree that success rates for treating these problems would be much greater if every person and couple they worked with were fully committed to productive change. In a sense, this observation applies to every area of life. Aren't we generally more successful at those undertakings to which we are fully committed?

SUMMARY

1. A sex role is a cluster of stereotypical traits ascribed to men or women.

2. The masculine sex-role stereotype includes aggressiveness, skill in business, interest in math and science, logic, and decisiveness.

3. The feminine sex role includes dependence, warmth, vanity, nurturance, and expression of feelings.

4. Sexism is the prejudgment that a person, because of gender, will possess negative traits. Generally speaking, sexists tend to have negative expectations of women.

5. The same works are generally rated as lower in quality when they are attributed to women. Boys generally dominate classroom communication, but girls are erroneously perceived as more talkative. Calling out in class is more often tolerated from boys than from girls.

6. People who possess both stereotypically "masculine" instrumentality and stereotypically "feminine" warmth-expressiveness are said to be psychologically androgynous. Other people may be stereotypically masculine, stereotypically feminine, or undifferentiated (low in masculine and feminine traits).

7. Psychologically androgynous people may be relatively well-adjusted because they can summon both instrumental traits and warmth-expressiveness to meet the demands of their situations. Psychologically androgynous people are more likely to pursue nontraditional careers, to show higher self-esteem, and greater ability to bounce back from failure.

8. Women who choose to work are more satisfied with their lives than women who are obliged to work by financial pressure but would rather remain in the home. A woman's earning more than her husband can be a source of marital confict. A mother's working has not been shown to be harmful to her children, and the children of working women are less likely to harbor traditional sex-role stereotypes.

9. Males are more aggressive than females, and, concerning cognitive skills, males as a group do better in math and science while females show greater verbal skills.

10. Research into sex differences in cognitive functioning shows that they are small, and that differences within the sexes are greater than differences between the sexes.

11. Sex hormones are responsible for physical sexual differentiation, but it is unclear how or if they lead to different behavior patterns in men and women. Some scientists argue that brain masculinization in utero can lead to masculine traits like tomboyishness and self-assertiveness; others believe that social learning is a more powerful influence.

12. According to psychoanalytic theory, the development of stereotypical masculine and feminine traits depends upon the resolution of the Oedipus and Electra complexes and consequent identification with (usually) the same-sex parent at about the age of five or six.

13. Social-learning theorists explain the acquisition of sex roles and sex differences in terms of identification and socialization. Through approval and affection, parents reward children for establishing gender identities and behavior patterns that they perceive as consistent with their anatomic sex.

14. Research shows that girls can be as aggressive as boys when they believe that their situations call for aggression and they have the aggressive skills that are required.

15. According to the cognitive-developmental view of the development of sex differences, gender identity itself motivates children to imitate the behavior of adult role models of the same sex. Children acquire information as to what is "masculine" and what is "feminine" through observational learning.

16. Sex hormones have organizing and activating effects on sexual behavior. They predispose lower animals toward masculine or feminine mating patterns (an organizing effect) and influence the sex drive (an activating effect).

17. In lower animals, such as rats, maternal behavior is largely under the control of the hormones estrogen, progesterone, and prolactin. Among higher animals (monkeys and apes) and humans, maternal behavior is essentially learned.

18. Pornography appears to arouse women sexually as well as men. There is no reliable evidence that films with explicit sexual content contribute to antisocial behavior; however, recent experiments suggest that aggressive-erotic (rape) films may lead to increased aggression by men toward women.

19. Homosexuality is sexual preference for members of one's own sex. Homosexual episodes do not necessarily reflect a homosexual orientation. Homosexuals are generally about as well-adjusted as heterosexuals, although homosexuals who lead different life styles show different levels of adjustment. The causes of homosexuality are complex and mysterious, but it may be that prenatal hormonal influences, in combination with subsequent learning experiences or with the utilization of sex hormones in adulthood, are implicated in homosexuality.

20. Forcible rape is the seeking of sexual gratification against the will of another person. Rape is more likely to be motivated by anger or the desire to dominate the victim than by sexual needs. Various cultural myths help maintain a climate that has the effect of supporting rape.

21. The human sexual-response cycle consists of four phases: excitement, plateau, orgasm, and resolution. The responses that characterize these phases occur reflexively when adequate sexual stimulation is received in the absence of inhibitory anxiety. Women are capable of multiple orgasms.

22. The elderly usually retain the physical capacity to respond sexually, although many elderly people discontinue sex for psychological reasons.

23. Psychosexual dysfunctions are problems in becoming sexually aroused or reaching orgasm. These dysfunctions include inhibited sexual desire, inhibited

sexual excitement, inhibited orgasm, premature ejaculation, dyspareunia, and vaginismus.

24. Sexual dysfunctions now and then reflect physical factors, such as disease or fatigue. However, most instances reflect psychosocial factors such as sex-negative attitudes, psychosexual trauma, troubled relationships, lack of sexual skills, and irrational beliefs. Any of these factors may lead to performance anxiety, which compounds sexual problems.

25. Sex-therapy methods are based largely on the behavioral model. Sex therapy deals with the psychosexual dysfunctions through brief treatment programs that reduce performance anxiety, challenge irrational expectations and beliefs, and impart sexual skills. While these programs can be quite varied in their particulars, they generally involve dysfunctional individuals or couples in guided, nondemand sexual activities in which they proceed at their own pace.

TRUTH OR FICTION REVISITED

Women are expected to be more vain than men.
True. Vanity is one feature of the feminine sex-role stereotype.

Teachers are more likely to accept calling out in class from boys than from girls.
True. Teachers generally insist that girls act in a "ladylike" manner but are more tolerant of boys.

Working women remain more likely than their husbands to do the cooking and take care of the laundry, even when the women are presidents or vice-presidents of their companies.
True.

Men behave more aggressively than women do.
True. The question is whether their greater aggressiveness is innate or reflects cultural expectations.

Men show greater math and spatial-relations abilities than women do.
True, but the differences are small. Differences within the sexes also exceed differences between the sexes.

Women with higher testosterone levels view themselves as more enterprising but not as warm as women with lower testosterone levels.
True, according to research by Donald Baucom and his colleagues.

Parents treat sons and daughters differently, even when they are under one year of age.
True. Parents encourage more motor activity in boys and cuddle and talk more to girls.

Stimulating male rats in a certain part of the brain causes them to engage in sexual foreplay.
True. Sexual behavior patterns seem largely instinctive among lower animals.

Women make natural mothers.
False. Women must learn effective maternal behavior.

Only men are sexually stimulated by hard-core pornography.
False. Women can also be sexually stimulated by explicit sexual materials.

Homosexuals suffer from hormonal imbalances.

False. Their current levels of sex hormones do not differ from those of heterosexuals. However, prenatal imbalances in sex hormones and differential responsiveness to sex hormones may be implicated in homosexuality.

Any healthy woman can successfully resist a rapist if she really wants to.

False. This myth is just one expression of the tendency to blame the victim in rape.

Orgasm is a reflex.

True. The rhythmic muscle contractions that define orgasm occur reflexively in the presence of adequate sexual stimulation.

People with psychosexual dysfunctions can often effectively treat themselves through using self-help manuals.

True. "Bibliotherapy" has been found effective in many cases with inhibited sexual excitement, inhibited orgasm, and other problems.

OUTLINE

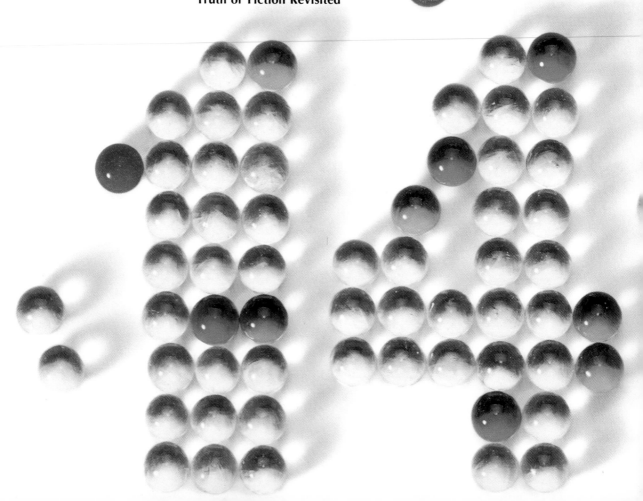

Social Psychology

TRUTH OR FICTION?

- Admitting your product's weak points in an ad is the death knell for sales.
- Most of us are swayed by ads that offer useful information, not by emotional appeals or celebrity endorsements.
- People who are highly worried about what other people think of them are likely to be low in sales resistance.
- We appreciate things more when we have to work hard for them.
- We tend to divide the social world into "us" and "them."
- First impressions have powerful effects on our social relationships.
- We hold others responsible for their misdeeds, but tend to see ourselves as victims of circumstances when our behavior falls short of our standards.
- Beauty is in the eye of the beholder.
- Physical attractiveness is the most important trait we seek in our partners for long-term, meaningful relationships.
- Opposites attract: We are more likely to be drawn to people who disagree with our attitudes than to people who share them.
- Most people would refuse to deliver painful electric shock to an innocent party, even under powerful social pressure.
- Bicycle riders and runners tend to move more rapidly in competition than when they are practicing alone.
- Nearly forty people stood by and did nothing while a woman was being stabbed to death.
- High noise levels can raise our blood pressure.
- Auto fumes may lower your children's IQ.

Candy and Stretch. A new technique for controlling weight gains? No, these are the names Bach and Deutsch (1970) give two people who have just met at a camera club that doubles as a meeting place for singles.

Candy and Stretch stand above the crowd—literally. Candy, an attractive woman in her early thirties, is almost six feet tall. Stretch is more plain-looking, but wholesome, in his late thirties, and six feet five inches.

Stretch has been in the group for some time. Candy is a new member. Let's listen in on them as they make conversation during a coffee break. As you will see, there are some differences between what they say and what they are thinking:

THEY SAY	THEY THINK
STRETCH: Well, you're certainly a welcome addition to our group.	(Can't I ever say something clever?)
CANDY: Thank you. It certainly is friendly and interesting.	(He's cute.)
STRETCH: My friends call me Stretch. It's left over from my basketball days. Silly, but I'm used to it.	(It's safer than saying my name is David Stein.)
CANDY: My name is Candy.	(At least my nickname is. He doesn't have to hear Hortense O'Brien.)
STRETCH: What kind of camera is that?	(Why couldn't a girl named Candy be Jewish? It's only a nickname, isn't it?)
CANDY: Just this old German one of my uncle's. I borrowed it from the office.	(He could be Irish. And that camera looks expensive.)
STRETCH: May I? (He takes her camera, brushing her hand and then tingling with the touch.) Fine lens. You work for your uncle?	(Now I've done it. Brought up work.)
CANDY: Ever since college. It's more than being just a secretary. I get into sales, too.	(So, okay, what if I only went for a year. If he asks what I sell, I'll tell him anything except underwear.)
STRETCH: Sales? That's funny. I'm in sales, too, but mainly as an executive. I run our department. I started using cameras on trips. Last time it was in the Bahamas. I took—	(Is there a nice way to say used cars? I'd better change the subject.) (Great legs! And the way her hips move—)
CANDY: Oh! Do you go to the Bahamas, too? I love those islands.	(So I went just once, and it was for the brassière manufacturers' convention. At least we're off the subject of jobs.)
STRETCH: (She's probably been around. Well, at least we're off the subject of jobs.) I did a little underwater work there last summer. Fantastic colors. So rich in life.	(And lonelier than hell.)
CANDY:	(Look at that build. He must swim like a fish. I should learn.)

THEY SAY	THEY THINK
I wish I'd had time when I was there. I love the water.	(Well, I do. At the beach, anyway, where I can wade in and not go too deep.)

And so begins a relationship. Candy and Stretch have a drink and talk, sharing their likes and dislikes. Amazingly, they seem to agree on everything—from cars to clothing to politics. The attraction is very strong, and neither is willing to risk turning the other off by disagreeing.

They spend the weekend together and feel that they have fallen in love. They still agree on everything they discuss, but they scrupulously avoid one topic: religion. Their religious differences became apparent when they exchanged last names. But that doesn't mean they have to talk about it.

They also put off introducing each other to their parents. The O'Briens and the Steins are narrow-minded about religion. If the truth be known, so are Candy and Stretch. They narrow their relationships to avoid tension with one another, and as the romance develops, they feel progressively isolated from family and friends.

What happens in this tangled web of deception? Candy becomes pregnant. After some deliberation, and not without misgivings, the couple decides to get married. Do they live happily ever after? We cannot say—"ever after" hasn't arrived yet.

We may not have all the answers, but we do have some questions. Candy and Stretch's relationship began with a powerful attraction. What is *attraction?* How do we determine who is attractive? Did Candy and Stretch pretend to share each other's attitudes? What are *attitudes?* Why were Candy and Stretch so reluctant to disagree?

Candy and Stretch were prejudiced about religion. What is *prejudice?* Why didn't Candy and Stretch introduce each other to their parents? Did they fear that their parents would want them to *conform* to their own standards? Would their parents try to *persuade* them to date within their religions? Would they *obey?*

And—as long as we're asking questions—what do you think might have happened if their parents had tried to break up the relationship? Would they have succeeded, or would Candy and Stretch, like the star-crossed lovers in *Romeo and Juliet,* have been pressed closer by family opposition?

Attraction, attitudes, prejudice, conformity, persuasion, obedience— these topics are the province of the branch of psychology called **social psychology.** Social psychologists study the factors that influence our thoughts, feelings, and behaviors in social situations.

In this chapter we first discuss attitudes, social perception, obedience to authority, and the nature of group behavior. We shall examine theory and research that concerns many of the questions posed about Candy and Stretch. Then we explore some of the issues that have been raised in a new area of inquiry, **environmental psychology.** Environmental psychologists study relationships between people and their physical environment, such as the effects of noise, air pollution, and city life.

Social psychology The field of psychology that studies the factors that influence our thoughts, feelings, and behaviors in social situations.

Environmental psychology The field of psychology that studies the ways in which behavior influences, and is influenced by, the physical environment.

There is some controversy about environmental psychology. Some psychologists regard it as a subfield of social psychology, while others consider it a field of its own. I am firmly determined to avoid taking a stand on this matter.

ATTITUDES

Psychologists are a rather independent bunch, so it is not surprising to find different definitions of **attitudes.** Some view attitudes primarily as cognitive evaluations. Others consider attitudes feelings with an evaluative, cognitive component. We define attitudes in terms of (1) cognitive, (2) emotional, and (3) behavioral components—as enduring systems of beliefs, feelings, and behavioral tendencies concerning people, groups, religion, politics, and so on.

Attitudes can change, but they tend to remain stable unless shoved a little. Most people do not change their religion or political affiliation without serious deliberation.

This definition implies that our behavior is consistent with our beliefs and feelings. When we are free to do as we wish, it often is, even though social psychologists have found that the relationships between attitudes and behavior are quite complex (Bagozzi, 1981; Bentler & Speckart, 1981; Borgida & Campbell, 1982). But just as Candy and Stretch were reluctant to express attitudes that might turn each other off, we may be influenced to behave in ways that are inconsistent with our beliefs. Finally, in this section we explore the nature of a particularly troublesome type of attitude—prejudice.

ORIGINS OF ATTITUDES

You were not born a Republican or Democrat. You were not born a Catholic or a Jew—although your parents may practice one of these religions. Political, religious, and other attitudes are learned.

Classical and Operant Conditioning   Conditioning may play a role in the acquisition of attitudes. For instance, children who enjoy slim hamburgers and slimmer French fries could acquire a positive attitude toward one emblem of twentieth-century American architecture—the McDonald's golden arches. Through **classical conditioning,** the golden arches may lead children to respond positively, because the arches have been repeatedly associated with eating. Laboratory experiments have shown that attitudes toward national groups can be influenced simply by associating them with positive words (like "gift" or "happy") or negative words (like "ugly" and "failure") (Lohr & Staats, 1973).

In examples of **operant conditioning,** parents often reward children for saying and doing things consistent with their own attitudes. Children may be shown approval for wearing Daddy's "No nukes" button or carrying Mommy's "My body is my own" placard. Experiments have shown that

Attitude An enduring system of beliefs, feelings, and behavioral tendencies concerning people, objects, or ideas.

Classical conditioning A simple form of learning in which one stimulus acquires the capacity to elicit the response usually brought forth by a second stimulus by being paired repeatedly with the second stimulus. See Chapter 5.

Operant conditioning A simple form of learning in which reinforcement increases the frequency of a response. See Chapter 5.

people who are rewarded consistently for favorable descriptions of even nonexistent groups will later express more positive attitudes toward these groups (Kerpelman & Himmelfarb, 1971). How much more positive would they be if the groups did exist?

Observational Learning Although attitudes formed through direct experience may be stronger and easier to recall (Fazio & Cooper, 1983), we also acquire attitudes from friends and the mass media. The approval or disapproval of peers molds adolescents to prefer short or long hair, or blue jeans or preppy sweaters. Television shows us that body odor, bad breath, and the frizzies are dreaded diseases—and, perhaps, that people who use harsh toilet paper are vaguely un-American.

Cognitive Appraisal Yet all is not so mechanical. Now and then we also evaluate information and attitudes on the basis of evidence. Research suggests that we may revise stereotypes on the basis of new evidence (Weber & Crocker, 1983). We are especially likely to examine our attitudes when we know that we shall have to justify them to people who may disagree with them (Tetlock, 1983).

Still, early attitudes tend to serve as cognitive "anchors." In this way, attitudes we learn about later are often judged in terms of how much they "deviate" from the first set. Accepting larger deviations appears to require greater adjustments in information-processing (Quattrone, 1982). For this reason, perhaps, they are more likely to be resisted. Yet attitudes can be changed by persuasion, as we see in the following section.

CHANGING ATTITUDES THROUGH PERSUASION

There are at least two routes to persuading others to change attitudes (Petty & Cacioppo, 1981). The first, or central route, views attitude change as resulting from careful consideration of arguments and evidence. The second, or peripheral route, involves association of the objects of attitudes with positive or negative "cues." These cues include rewards (like McDonald's French fries) and punishments (like parental disapproval), and factors such as the trustworthiness and attractiveness of the communicator. Advertisements, which are a form of persuasive communication, also rely on central and peripheral routes. Some advertisements focus on the quality of the product (central route), while others attempt to associate the product with appealing images (peripheral route) (Fox, 1984). Ads for Total cereal, which emphasize its nutritional benefits, provide information about the quality of the product (Snyder & DeBono, 1985). So too do the "Pepsi challenge" taste-test ads, which claim that Pepsi tastes better than Coca-Cola. The Marlboro cigarette ads, by contrast, focus on the masculine, rugged image of the "Marlboro man" and offer no information about the product itself (Snyder & DeBono, 1985).

The success of most persuasive communications often relies on a combination of central and peripheral cues, such as speech content and voice quality (O'Sullivan et al., 1985). In this section we examine one central factor in persuasion—that is, the nature of the message itself—and three peripheral factors: (1) the person delivering the message; (2) the context in which the message is delivered; and (3) the audience.

The Persuasive Message: Say What? Say How? Say How Often? How do we respond when television commercials are repeated until we have memorized every dimple on the actors' faces? Research suggests that familiarity breeds content, not contempt.

You might not be crazy about *zabulons* and *afworbus* at first, but Zajonc (1968) found that people began to react favorably toward these bogus Turkish words on the basis of repeated exposure. Political candidates who become highly familiar to the public through frequent television commercials attain more votes (Grush, 1980). People respond more favorably to abstract art (Heingartner & Hall, 1974), classical music (Smith & Dorfman, 1975), even photographs of black people (Hamm et al., 1975) and of college students (Moreland & Zajonc, 1982) simply on the basis of repetition. Love for classical art and music may begin through exposure in the nursery—not the college appreciation course. The more complex the stimuli, the more likely it is that frequent exposure will have favorable effects (Saegert & Jellison, 1970; Smith & Dorfman, 1975). The 100th repetition of a Bach concerto may be less tiresome than the 100th repetition of a pop tune.

Two-sided arguments, in which the communicator recounts the arguments of the opposition in order to refute them, can be especially effective when the audience is at first uncertain about its position (Hass & Linder, 1972). Theologians and politicians sometimes expose their followers to the arguments of the opposition. By refuting them one by one, they give their followers a sort of psychological immunity to them. Swinyard found that

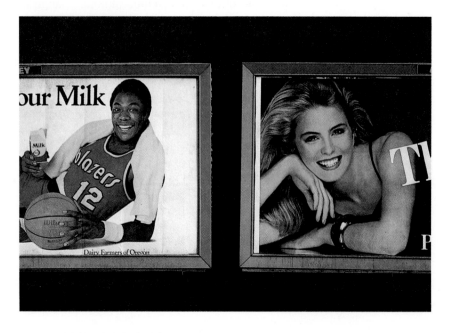

Advertisers use both central and peripheral cues to sell their wares. What elements contribute to the persuasiveness of messages? To the persuasiveness of communicators?

two-sided product claims, in which advertisers admitted their product's weak points as well as highlighting its strengths, were most believable (in Bridgwater, 1982).

It would be nice to think that people are too sophisticated to be persuaded by an **emotional appeal.** However, grisly films of operations on cancerous lungs are more effective than matter-of-fact presentations aimed at changing smoking attitudes (Leventhal et al., 1972). Films of bloodied gums and decayed teeth are also more effective than logical discussions intended to increase toothbrushing (Dembroski et al., 1978). Fear appeals are most effective when they are strong, when the audience believes the dire consequences, and when the recommendations offered seem practical (Mewborn & Rogers, 1979). Induced feelings of guilt as well as of fear facilitate persuasion (Regan et al., 1972; Wallington, 1973).

Audiences also tend to believe arguments that appear to run counter to the personal interests of the communicator (Wood & Eagly, 1981). People may pay more attention to a whaling-fleet owner's claim, than to a conservationist's, that whales are becoming extinct. If the president of General Motors complained that auto fumes were becoming increasingly poisonous, you can bet we would prick up our ears.

The Persuasive Communicator: Whom Do You Trust?   Would you buy a used car from a person convicted of larceny? Would you attend weight-control classes run by a 350-pound leader? Would you leaf through fashion magazines featuring clumsy models? Probably not. Research shows that persuasive communicators show expertise (Hennigan et al., 1982), trustworthiness, attractiveness, or similarity to their audiences (Baron & Byrne, 1984).

Health professionals enjoy high status in our society and are considered experts. It is not surprising that toothpaste ads boast that their products have the approval of the American Dental Association.

Even though we are raised not to judge books by their covers, we are more likely to find attractive people persuasive. Corporations do not gamble millions on the physically unappealing to sell their products. Some advertisers seek out the perfect combination of attractiveness and plain, simple folksiness with which the audience can identify. Ivory Soap commercials sport "real" people with attractive features who are so freshly scrubbed that you may think you can smell Ivory Soap emitting from the TV set.

The Context of the Message: "Get 'Em in a Good Mood"   You are too clever and insightful to allow someone to persuade you by buttering you up, but perhaps someone you know would be influenced by a sip of wine, a bite of cheese, and a sincere compliment. Seduction attempts usually come at the tail end of a date—after the Szechuan tidbits, the nouveau Fresno film, the disco party, and the wine that was sold at its time. An assault at the outset of a date would be viewed as . . . well, an assault. Experiments suggest that food and pleasant music increase acceptance of persuasive messages (Janis et al., 1965; Galizio & Hendrick, 1972).

It is also counterproductive to call your dates fools when they disagree with you—even though their views are bound to be foolish if they do not agree with yours. Agreement and praise are more effective at encouraging others to accept your views (Baron, 1971; Byrne, 1971). Appear sincere, or else your compliments will look manipulative. It seems a bit immoral to give out this information.

The Persuaded Audience: Are You a Person Who Can't Say No? Why do some people have "sales resistance," while others enrich the lives of every door-to-door salesperson? People with high self-esteem and low social anxiety are more likely to resist social pressure (Santee & Maslach, 1982). Broad knowledge of the areas that a communicator is discussing also tends to decrease persuadability (Wood, 1982).

A study by Schwartz and Gottman (1976) shows how the social anxiety that makes it difficult for some of us to say no is linked to what we are thinking when requests are made. Schwartz and Gottman found that people who comply with unreasonable requests are more likely to report thinking: "I was worried about what the other person would think of me if I refused"; "It is better to help others than to be self-centered"; or "The other person might be hurt or insulted if I refused." People who did not comply reported thoughts like "It doesn't matter what the other person thinks of me"; "I am perfectly free to say no"; or "This request is an unreasonable one" (p. 916).

In Chapter 10 we noted cognitive strategies that may be used by people who are concerned that irrational attitudes—such as fearing the disapproval of the person who makes the request—lower their sales resistance. Assertiveness training, discussed in Chapter 12, focuses both on client attitudes as well as fostering social skills.

Let us now turn our attention to the issue of what happens when we perceive our own attitudes to be inconsistent or imbalanced.

BALANCE THEORY

According to **balance theory,** we are motivated to maintain harmony among our perceptions, beliefs, and attitudes (Heider, 1958). When people we like share our attitudes, there is balance and all is well. If we dislike others, we do not care about their attitudes. They may disagree with us, but this state of **nonbalance** leaves us indifferent (Newcomb, 1981).

But when someone you care about expresses a discrepant attitude, you are likely to be concerned. The relationship will survive if you like chocolate and your friend prefers vanilla, but what if the discrepancies concern important attitudes about religion, politics, or raising children? Now a state of **imbalance** exists. Candy was Catholic and Stretch Jewish. Each was painfully aware of the imbalance in religious preferences. How did they handle the imbalance? At first they misperceived the other's preference. Later they tried not to think about it.

What else can people do to end a state of imbalance? We can try to convince others to change their attitudes. (Candy and Stretch could have asked each other to change religions.) Or we can change our feelings about the other person. (Candy or Stretch might have "realized" that the other was a jerk, after all.) Cognitive-dissonance theory, however, might suggest

Balance theory The view that people have a need to organize their perceptions, opinions, and beliefs in a harmonious manner.

Nonbalance In balance theory, a condition in which persons whom we dislike do not agree with us.

Imbalance In balance theory, a condition in which persons whom we like disagree with us. We are motivated to bring such a discrepancy into "balance."

that Candy and Stretch's feelings for each other could grow even stronger as a result of discovering their religious differences, as we shall see.

COGNITIVE-DISSONANCE THEORY

According to cognitive-dissonance theory, which was originated by Leon Festinger (Festinger, 1957; Festinger & Carlsmith, 1959), people dislike inconsistency. As with balance theory, we do not like to think that our attitudes (cognitions) are inconsistent; nor do we like to think that our attitudes are inconsistent with our behavior. Awareness that two cognitions are dissonant, or that our cognitions and our behavior are inconsistent, is sufficient to motivate us to reduce the discrepancy. Cognitive dissonance is an unpleasant state (Fazio & Cooper, 1983) that is accompanied by increased physiological arousal (Croyle & Cooper, 1983). Thus a physiological motive for eliminating cognitive dissonance might be to reduce our arousal to a more optimal level.

In the first and best-known study on cognitive dissonance, one group of subjects received $1.00 for telling someone else that a just-completed boring task was very interesting (Festinger & Carlsmith, 1959). A second group of subjects received $20.00 to describe the task positively. Both groups were paid to engage in **attitude-discrepant behavior**—that is, behavior that ran counter to their actual thoughts and feelings. After "selling" the task to others, the subjects were asked to rate their own liking for the task. Ironically, the group paid *less* rated the task as significantly more interesting. *Why?*

From a learning-theory point of view, this result would be confusing; after all, shouldn't we learn to like that which is highly rewarding? But cognitive-dissonance theory would predict this "less-leads-to-more effect" for the following reason: the cognitions "I was paid very little" and "I told someone that this task was interesting" are dissonant. You see, another

---

Attitude-discrepant behavior Behavior that runs counter to one's thoughts and feelings.

concept in cognitive-dissonance theory is **effort justification,** and subjects in studies like these can only justify their behavior to themselves by drawing the conclusion that their attitudes might not have been as discrepant with their behavior as they originally believed.*

Effort justification The tendency to seek justification (reasons) for strenuous efforts.

Consider another situation. Cognitive dissonance would be created if we were to believe that our preferred candidate were unlikely to win the U.S. presidential election. One cognition would be that our candidate is better for the country, or, at an extreme, would "save" the country from harmful forces. A second and dissonant cognition would be that our candidate does not have a chance to win. Research shows that in the presidential elections from 1952–1980, people by a four-to-one margin helped reduce such dissonance by expressing the belief that their candidate would win (Granberg & Brent, 1983). They frequently held these beliefs despite lopsided polls to the contrary. Among highly involved but poorly informed people, the margin of self-deception was even higher.

Concerning Candy and Stretch, cognitive-dissonance theory might predict that their discovery that they held different religious views might have *strengthened* rather than destroyed their relationship. Why? After finding out about the other's religion, each might have thought, "Stretch (Candy) must be *very* important to me if I can feel this way about him (her), knowing that he (she) is Jewish (Catholic)."

Let us consider a real-life case study in order to further see how attitude-discrepant behavior may influence our thoughts and feelings—even our senses of who we are and what we stand for.

Can One's Self-Identity Be Converted Through Attitude-Discrepant Behavior? The Strange Case of Patty Hearst In February, 1974, newspaper heiress Patty Hearst, an undergraduate student at Berkeley, was abducted by a revolutionary group known as the Symbionese Liberation Army (SLA). Early messages from the SLA directed the Hearst family to distribute millions of dollars' worth of food to the poor if they wished their daughter to live. There was no suggestion that Patty was a willing prisoner.

But a couple of months later, SLA communiqués contained statements by Patty that she had willingly joined them. Patty declared her revolutionary name to be Tania and sent a photograph in which she wore a guerrilla outfit and held a machine gun. She expressed contempt for her parents' capitalist values and called them pigs. But her family did not believe that Patty's attitudes had really changed. They had raised her for twenty years. She had been with the SLA for only two months. Surely her statements were designed to earn good treatment from her captors.

In April, Patty and other SLA members robbed a San Francisco bank. Patty was videotaped brandishing a rifle. She was reported to have threatened a guard. But, the Hearsts maintained, the rifle could have been unloaded. Patty might still have been acting out of fear of losing her life. Then Patty became involved in another incident. She acted as a cover for SLA members William and Emily Harris, firing an automatic rifle as they fled from a store they had robbed. Patty seemed unsupervised at the time.

*The notion that we have greater appreciation for the things for which we must work hard is another example of effort justification.

EFFECTS OF ATTITUDE-DISCREPANT BEHAVIOR Patty Hearst as the "urban guerrilla" Tania (left), and in manacles (right) on her way to testify in court. After her abduction by the Symbionese Liberation Army, Patty was forced into attitude-discrepant revolutionary behavior. Engaging in antisocial acts like armed robbery appears to have converted her self-identity from that of a typical (though wealthy) college student to that of a revolutionary. After her capture, her identity appeared to revert to that of Patty. Patty's experience raises a challenging question: How can any of us know where the influences of others end and our "real selves," or true identities, begin?

Patty and the Harrises were captured in San Francisco late in 1975. At first Patty was defiant. She gave a revolutionary salute and identified herself as Tania. But once she was in prison, her identity appeared to undergo another transformation. She asked to be called Patty. At her trial she seemed quite remorseful. The defense argued that had it not been for the social influence of the SLA, Patty would never have engaged in criminal behavior or adopted revolutionary values. When President Jimmy Carter signed an order for Patty's early release from prison in 1979, he was operating under an admission from Patty's original prosecutors that they, too, believed that Patty would not have behaved criminally without being abducted by the SLA and experiencing dread in the days that followed.

How is it that a college undergraduate with typical American values came to express attitudes that were opposed to her lifelong ideals?

It may be that such conversions in identity can be explained through cognitive-dissonance theory. After Patty's kidnapping, she was exposed to fear and fatigue and forced into attitude-discrepant behavior. She had to express agreement with SLA values, engage in sexual activity with SLA members, and train for revolutionary activity. So long as she clung firmly to her self-identity as Patty, these repugnant acts created great cognitive dissonance. But by adopting the suggested revolutionary identity of Tania, Patty could look upon herself as "liberated" rather than as a frightened captive or criminal. In this way her cognitive dissonance would be reduced, and her behavior would no longer be so stressful. Supportive research shows that we do draw conclusions about our attitudes from our decisions to engage in particular behavior (Fazio et al., 1982; Nisbett & Ross, 1980).

Cognitive-dissonance theory is not without its critics (e.g., Bem, 1967; Chapanis & Chapanis, 1964). But it leads to the hypothesis that we can change people's attitudes by getting them somehow to behave in a manner consistent with the attitudes we wish to promote. Research does show that people may indeed change attitudes when attitude-discrepant behavior is rewarded (Calder et al., 1973; Cooper, 1980). It is at once a frightening and promising concept. For instance, it sounds like a prescription for totalitarianism. Yet it also suggests that prejudiced individuals who are prevented from discriminating—who are compelled, for example, by open-housing laws to allow people from different ethnic backgrounds to buy homes in their neighborhoods—may actually become less prejudiced. In the following section, we turn our attention to the problems of prejudice and discrimination.

PREJUDICE

A few years ago Iowa schoolteacher Jane Elliot taught her all-white class of third-graders some of the effects of prejudice. She divided the class into blue-eyed and brown-eyed children. The brown-eyed children were labeled inferior, made to wear collars that identified their group, and denied classroom privileges. After a few days of discrimination, the brown-eyed children lost self-esteem and earned poorer grades. They cried often and expressed the wish to stay at home.

Then the pattern was reversed. Blue-eyed children were assigned the inferior status. After a few days they, too, learned how painful it is to be victims of discrimination. Weiner and Wright (1973) later found that making children victims of discrimination in this fashion led them to show less discrimination toward blacks. Why? Perhaps being discriminated against made the children more mindful of the sensitivities and feelings of members of outgroups. Unless we are encouraged to actively consider our attitudes toward others, we may automatically rely upon previously conceived ideas, and these ideas are very often prejudiced (Langer et al., 1985).

Prejudice is an attitude toward a group that leads people to evaluate members of that group negatively. On a cognitive level, prejudice is linked to expectations that the target group will behave badly, in the workplace, say, or by engaging in criminal activity. On an affective level, prejudice is associated with negative feelings like dislike or hatred. Behaviorally, prejudice is associated with avoidance behavior, aggression, and, as we shall see, discrimination. There is an interaction between our cognitions, affects,

Prejudice The belief that a person or group, on the basis of assumed racial, ethnic, sexual, or other features, will possess negative characteristics or perform inadequately. An attitude toward members of a group that is not supported by facts.

STEREOTYPING How well is this child performing on her test? An experiment by Darley and Gross showed that our expectations concerning a child's performance on a test are linked to our awareness of that child's socioeconomic background.

and behaviors. In one recent study, nonangered white people apparently adopted new **egalitarian** norms by acting less aggressively toward blacks than toward other whites. But angered whites acted more aggressively toward blacks than whites, suggesting persistence of underlying prejudices (Rogers & Prentice-Dunn, 1981).

Discrimination One form of negative behavior that results from prejudice is called **discrimination.** Many groups have been discriminated against from time to time in the United States. They include, but are not limited to, Jews, Catholics, blacks, Native Americans, Hispanic Americans, homosexuals, and women. Discrimination takes many forms, including denial of access to certain jobs, housing, even the voting booth. Many people have forgotten that American blacks gained the right to vote several decades before it was obtained by American women.

Stereotypes Are Jews shrewd and ambitious? Are blacks superstitious and musical? If you believe such ideas, you are falling for a **stereotype**—a prejudice about a group that can lead us to interpret observations in a biased fashion. In one experiment, subjects who watched videotapes of a child taking an academic test rated her performance as superior when told that she came from a high socioeconomic background. Other subjects were told that she came from a low socioeconomic background. They watched the same videotape, but rated her performance as below grade level (Darley & Gross, 1983).

Egalitarian Descriptive of the belief that all people should have equal rights.

Discrimination The denial of privileges to a person or group on the basis of prejudice. A behavioral aspect of prejudice.

Stereotype A fixed, conventional idea about a group.

In recent studies of stereotypes (Sagar & Schofield, 1980; Smedley & Bayton, 1978), whites viewed middle-class blacks as ambitious, intelligent, conscientious, and responsible, but saw *lower-class* blacks as ignorant, rude, dangerous, and self-pitying. Blacks shared whites' negative impressions of lower-class individuals of the other race. But blacks also negatively evaluated *middle-class* whites as biased, sly, and deceitful, even though they also considered middle-class whites conscientious and ambitious.

Despite the persistence of some stereotypes, white children in recent years seem more willing to work with and befriend blacks than they were during the 1960s (Moe et al., 1981).

Sources of Prejudice   The sources of prejudice are many and varied. Let us briefly consider several possible contributors.

As we shall see later in the chapter, we are prone to feeling attracted to and liking people who share our attitudes. In forming impressions of others, we are influenced by attitudinal similarity and dissimilarity as well as by race (Goldstein & Davis, 1972; Rokeach et al., 1960). People of different religions and races often have different backgrounds and values, giving rise to dissimilar attitudes. But even when people of different races share important values, they are likely to assume that they will not.

There is also a lengthy history of social and economic conflict between people of different races and religions. Conflict and competition lead to negative attitudes (Sherif, 1966).

Based on psychoanalytic theory and their interpretation of the **Holocaust,** some social scientists (e.g., Adorno et al., 1950) have argued that racial and religious minorities serve as **scapegoats** for majority groups. The Germans, for instance, submitted to Nazi **authoritarianism,** because they had been raised to submit to authority figures. They then displaced unconscious hostility toward their fathers onto Jews. These Freudian concepts have been criticized by many psychologists, but authoritarian people do appear to harbor more prejudices than nonauthoritarians (e.g., Stephan & Rosenfield, 1978).

As noted in Chapter 8, children tend to acquire certain attitudes from others, especially parents, through identification and socialization. Children often broadly imitate their parents, and parents often reinforce their children for doing so. In this way, prejudices are likely to be transferred from generation to generation.

Another explanation of prejudice stems from the fact that people often divide the social world into two categories: "us" and "them." People also usually view those who belong to their own groups—the "ingroup"—more favorably than those who do not—the "outgroup" (Hemstone & Jaspars, 1982; Wilder & Thompson, 1980). Moreover, there is a tendency for us to assume that outgroup members are more alike in their attitudes and behaviors than members of our own groups (Park & Rothbart, 1982). Our relative isolation from outgroups does not encourage us to break down our stereotypes.

Let us now turn our attention to some of the factors involved in our formation of impressions of other people.

Holocaust The name given the Nazi murder of millions of Jews during World War II. A great or total destruction of life, especially by fire. (From the Greek *holos,* meaning "whole," and *kaustos,* meaning "burnt.")

Scapegoat A person or group upon whom the blame for the mistakes or crimes of others is cast. (From the ancient Jewish practice of confessing sins over a goat that was subsequently allowed to escape.)

Authoritarianism Belief in the importance of unquestioning obedience to authority. A characteristic of a society that demands unquestioning obedience.

Social perception A subfield of social psychology that studies the ways in which we form and modify impressions of others.

Primacy effect The tendency to evaluate others in terms of first impressions.

Recency effect The tendency to evaluate others in terms of the most recent impression.

SOCIAL PERCEPTION

Getting to know you,
Getting to know all about you . . .

So goes the song from *The King and I*. How do we get to know other people, get to know all about them? In this section we explore some factors that contribute to **social perception:** primacy and recency effects, attribution theory, and body language. In the following section we explore the determinants of attraction to others.

PRIMACY AND RECENCY EFFECTS: THE IMPORTANCE OF FIRST IMPRESSIONS

Why do you wear your best outfit to an interview for an attractive job? Why do defense attorneys dress their clients immaculately before they are seen by the jury? Because first impressions are important.

When I was a teenager, a young man was accepted or rejected by his date's parents the first time they were introduced. If he was considerate and made small talk, her parents would allow them to stay out past curfew, even to attend submarine races at the beach. If he was boorish or uncommunicative, he was a cad forever. Her parents would object to him, no matter how hard he worked to gain their favor later on.

First impressions often make or break us. This is the **primacy effect.** As noted in Chapter 9, we infer traits from behavior. If we act considerately at first, we are labeled considerate. The trait of considerateness is used to explain and predict our future behavior. If, after being labeled considerate, one keeps a date out past curfew, this behavior is likely to be seen as an exception to a rule—as justified by circumstances or external causes. But if at first one is seen as inconsiderate, several months of considerate behavior may be perceived as a cynical effort to "make up for it."

In a classic experiment on the primacy effect, Luchins (1957) had subjects read different stories about "Jim." The stories consisted of one or two paragraphs. One-paragraph stories portrayed Jim as friendly or unfriendly. These paragraphs were also used in the two-paragraph stories, but presented to different subjects in opposite order. Of subjects reading only the "friendly" paragraph, 95 percent rated Jim as friendly. Of those who read just the "unfriendly" paragraph, 3 percent rated him as friendly. Seventy-eight percent of those who read two-paragraph stories in the "friendly-unfriendly" order labeled Jim as friendly. But when they read the paragraphs in the reverse order, only 18 percent rated Jim as friendly.

How can we encourage people to pay more attention to more recent impressions? Luchins accomplished this by allowing time to elapse between presenting the paragraphs. In this way, fading memories allowed more recent information to take precedence. This is the **recency effect.** Luchins found a second way to counter first impressions: He simply counseled subjects to avoid snap judgments and to weigh all the evidence.

ATTRIBUTION THEORY

One of the central issues in psychology could be summed up in the question, "Why do people do the things they do?" We have tried to explain why people do some of the things they do throughout the book, but in this section we focus on the question, "Why do *we assume that* people do the things they do?" An assumption as to why people do things is called an **attribution** for behavior. Our inference of the motives and traits of others through the observation of their behavior is called the **attribution process.** We now focus on attribution theory, or the processes by which people draw conclusions about the factors that influence one anothers' behavior.

Attribution theory is very important because our attributions lead us to perceive others either as purposeful actors or as victims of circumstances.

Dispositional and Situational Attributions When Patty Hearst was sent to prison, her sentence was harsh, because the court believed that she had willfully chosen to break the law. The court, that is, had *attributed* Patty's behavior to internal factors—to her personality dispositions and to choice. The court may be said to have made a **dispositional attribution** about Patty's behavior. When President Jimmy Carter ordered Patty Hearst's release, he was acting on the belief that Patty had been a victim of circumstances. The President attributed Patty's behavior largely to external, situational factors. He may be said to have made a **situational attribution** about the same behavior.

In another example, when parents and children argue about the children's choice of friends or dates, the parents tend to see their children as being stubborn, difficult, and independent. The children may perceive their parents as bossy and controlling. Parents and children alike attribute the others' behavior to internal causes. That is, they make dispositional attributions about the behavior of others.

But how do the parents and children perceive themselves? The parents probably see themselves as forced into conflict by their children's foolishness. If they become insistent, it is in response to their children's stubbornness. The children probably see themselves as responding to peer pressures, and, perhaps, to sexual urges that may come from within but do not seem "of their own making." The parents and children tend to see their own behavior as motivated by external factors. That is, they make situational attributions about their own behavior.

Biases in the Attribution Process When we see ourselves and others engaging in behavior that we do not like, we tend to see the others as willful, but to perceive ourselves as victims of circumstances. The tendency to attribute the behavior of others to internal, dispositional factors, and our own behavior to external, situational influences is called the **actor-observer effect.** The actor-observer effect is just one of the biases frequently at work in the attribution process (Jellison & Green, 1981; Jones, 1979; Reeder, 1982; Safer, 1980).

The actor-observer effect also extends to our perceptions of the ingroup (an extension of ourselves) and the outgroup. Consider conflicts between nations. Each side may engage in brutal acts of violence. However,

Attribution An assumption as to why people behave as they do.

Attribution process The process by which people draw conclusions about the motives and traits of others.

Dispositional attribution An assumption that a person's behavior is determined by internal causes, such as personal attitudes or goals.

Situational attribution An assumption that a person's behavior is determined by external circumstances, such as the social pressure found in a situation.

Actor-observer effect The tendency to attribute our own behavior to situational factors, but to attribute the behavior of others to dispositional factors.

Fundamental attribution error The tendency to assume that others act predominantly on the basis of their dispositions, even when there is evidence suggestive of the importance of their situations.

Consensus (con-SEN-suss). General agreement. (From the Latin *com-*, meaning "with," and *sentire*, meaning "to feel.")

each side usually also considers the other to be willful, stubborn and, perhaps, evil. Yet each side also typically views its own people as victims of circumstances, and its own violent actions as justified, or as required by the circumstances. After all, we may look at the other side as being in the wrong, but can we expect the outgroup to agree with us?*

According to Glenn Reeder (1982), there is also a strong tendency to attribute too much of other people's behavior to dispositional factors. This general bias is called the **fundamental attribution error.** Apparently, when we observe the behavior of others, we focus excessively on their actions and too little on the context within which their actions take place. But we tend to be more aware of the networks of forces acting on ourselves.

Another bias is that we tend to see ourselves as less self-centered than others (Rempel et al., 1985). Also, as noted in Chapter 10, we are more likely to attribute our successes to internal, dispositional factors, but our failures to external, situational influences. When we have done well on a test or impressed a date, we are more likely to attribute these outcomes to our intelligence and charm. But when we fail, we are more likely to attribute these outcomes to bad luck, an unfairly difficult test, or our date's "bad mood."

It seems that we can extend these biases in the attribution process to our perceptions of why we win or lose when we gamble. A study by Gilovich (1983) found that when we win bets on football games, we tend to attribute our success to the greater ability of the winners (a dispositional factor). But when we lose our bets, we tend to attribute the game outcome to a fluke, such as an erroneous call by a referee—some unpredictable external factor.

There are some exceptions. We are more likely to own up to our responsibility for our failures when we think that other people will not accept situational attributions (Reiss et al., 1981). And, as noted in Chapter 11, depressed people are more likely than nondepressed people to attribute their failures to internal factors, even when dispositional attributions are not justified.

Another interesting bias in attribution is a sex difference in attributions for friendly behavior. Men are more likely than women to interpret a woman's friendliness toward men as a sign of promiscuity or seductiveness (Abbey, 1982). Traditional sex-role expectations apparently still lead men to believe that "decent" women are socially passive.

Consensus, Consistency, and Distinctiveness   According to Harold Kelley (1979; Kelley & Michela, 1980), our attribution of behavior to internal or external causes can also be influenced by three factors: ***consensus,*** *consistency,* and *distinctiveness.* When few people act in a certain way—that is, when consensus is low—we are likely to attribute behavior to dispositional (internal) factors. Consistency refers to the degree to which the same person acts in the same way on other occasions. Highly consistent

---

*I am not suggesting that all nations are equally blameless (or blameworthy) for their violence toward other nations. I am merely pointing out that the people of any nation generally stand ready to perceive their own nation as forced into unwanted behavior, while they perceive other nations as willful and guided by national dispositions.

TABLE 14.1 Factors Leading to Internal or External Attributions of Behavior

	Internal Attribution	External Attribution
Consensus	Low: Few people behave this way.	High: Most people behave this way.
Consistency	High: The person behaves this way frequently.	Low: The person rarely behaves this way.
Distinctiveness	Low: The person behaves this way in many situations.	High: The person behaves this way in few situations.

We are more likely to attribute behavior to internal, dispositional factors when it is low in consensus, high in consistency, and low in distinctiveness. In the example given in the text, we will be most likely to attribute Morris's dating of a beautiful woman to internal factors if few men date beautiful women, but Morris does so frequently and generally acts as if such behavior is typical of him.

behavior is usually attributed to dispositional factors. Distinctiveness is the extent to which the person responds differently in different situations. If the person acts similarly in different situations, distinctiveness is low and we are likely to attribute his or her behavior to dispositional factors.

Let us apply the criteria of consensus, consistency, and distinctiveness to a hypothetical situation involving our dull classmate, Morris. Morris, it turns out, is on a date with a woman for whom many sovereign nations would go to war. Our question is: Does Morris have a secret way with women? (Is his success due to internal, dispositional causes?) Or did Morris luck out on a blind date (an external cause)?

Morris's dating experience ranks low in consensus, low in consistency, and high in distinctiveness (see Table 14.1). Few men have such attractive dates (low consensus); Morris has not dated this woman before (low consistency); and, in fact, Morris rarely dates at all (high distinctiveness). That's two out of three (consistency and distinctiveness) in favor of an external attribution. The chances are that we shall infer that Morris's date was a fluke, and that his date may have had to go out with him because she lost a bet. If they go out repeatedly, however—and consistency thereby increases—we may have to reconsider.

BODY LANGUAGE

Body language is an important factor in our perception of others. At an early age we learn that the ways that people carry themselves provide cues as to how they feel and are likely to behave. You may have noticed that when people are "uptight," their bodies may also be rigid and straight-backed. People who are relaxed are more likely to literally "hang loose." It seems that various combinations of eye contact, posture, and distance between people provide broadly recognized cues as to their moods and as to their feelings toward their companions (Schwartz et al., 1983).

When people face us and lean toward us, we may assume that they like us or are interested in what we are saying. If we are privy to a conversation between a couple and observe that the woman is leaning toward the man but that he is sitting back and toying with his hair, we are likely to infer that he is not having any of what she is selling (Clore et al., 1975; DePaulo et al., 1978).

Touching also communicates. Women are more likely than men to touch other people when they are interacting with them (Stier & Hall, 1984). In one touching experiment, Kleinke (1977) showed that appeals for help can be more effective when the distressed person engages in physical contact with people being asked for aid. A woman received more dimes for phone calls when she touched the person she was asking for money on the arm. In another experiment, women about to undergo operations reported lower anxiety and showed lower blood pressure when nurses explaining the procedures touched them on the arm (Whitcher & Fisher, 1979). But men who were touched while the procedures were explained reported higher anxiety and showed elevated blood pressure. How do we account for this sex difference? Female patients may have interpreted touching as a sign of warmth, while male patients may have seen it as a threatening sign of the nurse's superior status in the hospital.

Body language can also be used to establish and maintain territorial control (Brown & Altman, 1981), as anyone who has had to step aside because a football player was walking down the hall can testify. Werner and her colleagues (1981) found that players in a game arcade used touching as a way of signaling others to keep their distance. Solo players engaged in more touching than did groups, perhaps because they were surrounded by strangers.

Gazing and Staring: The Eyes Have It   We usually feel we can learn much from eye contact. When others "look us squarely in the eye," we may assume that they are assertive or open with us. Avoidance of eye contact may suggest deception or depression (Knapp, 1978; Siegman & Feldstein, 1977). In a study designed to validate a scale to measure romantic love, Rubin (1970) found that couples who attained higher "love scores" also spent more time gazing into each other's eyes.

Gazes are different, of course, from persistent "hard" stares. Hard stares are interpreted as provocations or signs of anger (Ellsworth & Langer, 1976). Adolescent males sometimes engage in "staring contests" as an assertion of dominance. The male who looks away first "loses."

Hard staring is found among many primates and may elicit instinctive responses. Rhesus monkeys use hard stares to establish and maintain dominance hierarchies (Exline, 1972). High status in these hierarchies affords privileges in feeding and mating. Exline has found that when people venture hard stares at a rhesus monkey, the monkey first returns the stare. Then it opens its mouth and begins to bob its head. If these "threats" fail to induce withdrawal, the rhesus literally springs to the attack. A submissive rhesus monkey shows more "discretion" than an occasional experimental psychology student; it suspends hard staring before eliciting an attack.

In a series of field experiments, Phoebe Ellsworth and her colleagues (1972) subjected drivers stopped at red lights to hard stares from riders of motor scooters (see Figure 14.1). Recipients of the stares crossed the intersection more rapidly than nonrecipients when the light changed. Greenbaum and Rosenfeld (1978) found that recipients of hard stares from a man

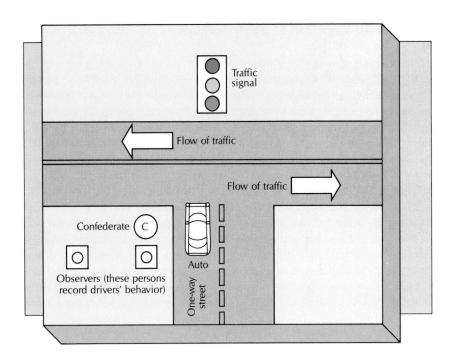

FIGURE 14.1 **DIAGRAM OF AN EX-PERIMENT IN HARD STARING AND AVOIDANCE** In the Greenbaum and Rosenfeld study, the confederate of the experimenter stared at some drivers and not at others. Those stared at drove across the intersection more rapidly once the light turned green. Why?

seated near an intersection also drove off more rapidly after the light turned green. Other research shows that recipients of hard stares show higher levels of physiological arousal than people who do not receive the stares (Strom & Buck, 1979). It may be that many of us rapidly leave situations in which we are stared at in order to achieve pleasant declines in arousal and avoid the threat of danger.

INTERPERSONAL ATTRACTION

Whether we are talking about a pair of magnetic toy animals or a couple in a singles bar, **attraction** is a force that draws bodies, or people, together. In social psychology, attraction has been defined as an attitude of liking or disliking (Berscheid, 1976). Factors such as physical appearance, attitudinal similarity, family opposition, reciprocity, propinquity, and whether the other person seems "hard to get" all contribute to interpersonal attraction.

PHYSICAL ATTRACTIVENESS: HOW IMPORTANT IS LOOKING GOOD?

You might like to think that we are all so intelligent and sophisticated that we rank physical appearance low on the roster of qualities we seek in a date—below sensitivity and warmth, for example. But in experimental "Coke dates" and computer dates, physical appearance has been found the central factor in attraction and consideration of partners for future dates, sexual activity, and marriage (Byrne et al., 1970; Walster et al., 1966b).

Attraction A force that draws bodies or people together. In social psychology, an attitude of liking or disliking (negative attraction). (From the Latin *ad-*, meaning "to," and *trahere*, meaning "to draw" or "to pull.")

Today Christie Brinkley contributes to setting the standard for female beauty in our culture. Are attractive people more successful? Do they make better spouses and parents?

What determines physical attractiveness? Are our standards fully subjective, or is there broad agreement on what is attractive?

Is Beauty in the Eye of the Beholder?   It may be that there are no universal standards for beauty (Ford & Beach, 1951), but there are some common standards for physical attractiveness in our culture. Tallness is an asset for men (Berkowitz et al., 1971), but tall women are not viewed so positively. Undergraduate women prefer their dates to be about six inches taller than they are, while undergraduate men, on the average, prefer women who are about four and a half inches shorter (Gillis & Avis, 1980).

Women generally prefer men with a V-taper, whose backs and shoulders are medium-wide, but whose waists, buttocks, and legs taper from medium-thin to thin (Lavrakas, 1975; Horvath, 1981). Men, weaned on *Playboy* magazine perhaps, desire women with larger-than-average breasts, medium-length legs, and small to medium buttocks (Wiggins et al., 1968). Yet women with medium bust sizes are better liked than women with large or small busts. Women with large breasts are also often viewed as less intelligent, competent, moral, and modest than women with smaller breasts (Kleinke & Staneski, 1980). Neither sex pays too much attention to the knees, ankles, or ears of the opposite sex (Nevid, 1984).

Both sexes perceive obese people as unattractive (Harris et al., 1982), but there remain some sex differences in perceptions of the most desirable body shape. Male college undergraduates as a group believe that their current figure is quite similar to the ideal male figure and to the figure women will find most attractive (Fallon & Rozin, 1985). Women undergraduates, by contrast, generally see themselves as significantly heavier than the figure that is most attractive to males, and heavier, still, than the ideal female figure (Figure 14.2). But both sexes err in their estimates of the preferences of the opposite sex. Men actually prefer women to be heavier than women expect—about halfway between the girth of the average woman and what the woman thinks is most attractive. And women prefer their men somewhat thinner than men expect. There is a saying that you can't be too rich or too thin, but women's concepts of how they should look may be too thin for most men.

An experiment at the University of Illinois found that the same people are perceived as being more attractive when they smile as compared to when they are posing sad faces (Mueser et al., 1984). So it may be that, as the song goes, there is ample reason to "put on a happy face" when you're looking for a date.

Jeffrey Nevid (1984) of St. John's University found that college men and women are relatively more concerned about their partners' attractiveness and "builds" or figures when they are involved in a relationship that they perceive as largely sexual. When they are involved in "meaningful," long-term relationships, psychological traits such as honesty, fidelity, warmth, and sensitivity play more prominent roles. Overall, however, Nevid also found that men were more swayed by the physical characteristics of their partners than women were, both for sexual and meaningful relationships. Women placed relatively greater emphasis on personal qualities such as warmth, assertiveness, need for achievement, and wit. What was the single

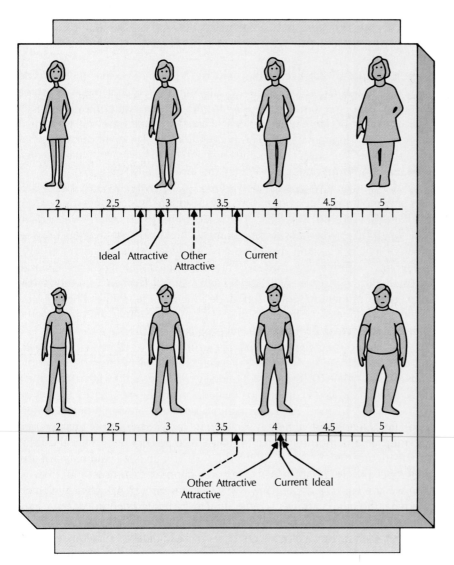

FIGURE 14.2 **CAN YOU EVER BE TOO THIN?** Research suggests that most college women believe that they are heavier than they ought to be. However, men actually prefer women to be a bit heavier than women assume they would like them to be.

most important personal quality that men and women both sought in their long-term partners? Honesty.

Do Good Things Come in Pretty Packages? By and large, we rate what is beautiful as good. We expect attractive people to be poised, sociable, popular, and mentally healthy; to be persuasive, hold prestigious jobs, be good parents, feel fulfilled, and even have stable marriages (Berscheid & Walster, 1974; Brigham, 1980; Dion et al., 1972; O'Grady, 1982; Unger et al., 1982).

But attractive people are also seen as more self-centered and likely to have extramarital affairs (Dermer & Thiel, 1975). Yet even these "negative" assumptions have a positive side. After all, don't they mean that we think attractive people have more to be self-centered about, and that their affairs reflect their greater sexual opportunities?

WHAT DO YOU LOOK AT FIRST?

When you meet someone of the opposite sex, what do you look at first? Are you impressed by small, even features? Do you search for sensitive eyes? Do bright teeth snap up your attention? Or, for you, do clothes tend to make the man, or woman?

According to a poll by the Roper Organization (*Psychology Today*, 1984), the largest number of women (35 percent) first notice how a man is dressed, while 29 percent of men are initially influenced by a woman's clothing. The largest group of men (45 percent) immediately responds to the woman's figure or build, while 29 percent of women share this interest in what is happening below the neck. Other things that men and women tend to notice first include the eyes (30 percent of women; 22 percent of men), the face (27 percent of women; 34 percent of men), and hair (16 percent for both sexes). The teeth, height, hands, and legs earn our less immediate interest, if we focus on them at all.

What do we look at first when meeting a person of our own sex? Women (41 percent) and men (39 percent) are both most likely to note how the person is dressed. Women and men are about equally impressed by the person's face (26 percent of women; 28 percent of men) and figure (20 percent of women; 16 percent of men). Women pay more attention to the new person's hair (27 percent of women; 13 percent of men), while men are more likely to rapidly focus in on the new person's height (15 percent of men; only 2 percent of women).

Is there a message in all this? Perhaps. Although we are brought up not to judge books by their covers, clothing apparently makes a significant contribution to our first impressions of others. There may be limits to how much we can enhance our faces, but our figures are also important, and most of us may be able to maximize their presentability through diet, exercise, and—yes—strategic dressing. That's two (clothing and figure) out of three, and that isn't too bad.

Attractive people are more likely to be found innocent of burglary and cheating in mock jury experiments. When found guilty, they are handed down less severe sentences (Efran, 1974). Perhaps we assume that more attractive people are less likely to need to resort to deviant behavior to achieve their goals. Even when they have erred, perhaps they will have more opportunity for personal growth and be more likely to change their evil ways.

The beautiful are also perceived as more talented. In one experiment, students rated essays as higher in quality when their authorship was attributed to a more attractive woman (Landy & Sigall, 1974).

Attractive children learn early of the high expectations of others. Even during the first year of life, adults tend to rate physically attractive babies as good, smart, likable, and unlikely to cause their parents problems (Stephan & Langlois, 1984). Parents, teachers, and other children expect them to do well in school and be popular, well behaved, and talented. Since our self-esteem reflects the admiration of others, it is not surprising that the physically attractive have higher self-esteem (Maruyama & Miller, 1975).

Physical Attractiveness in Social Interaction: Do Good Looks Somehow Translate into Social Skills? If we expect that "good things come in pretty packages," we shall probably treat pretty packages—that is, good-looking people—relatively favorably. Our great expectations may induce higher self-expectations and self-confidence, both of which may lead to the development of social skills.

In one experiment, male telephone callers were told at random that their telephone partner was attractive or unattractive. Actually all women in the study had been rated as equal in appearance (Snyder et al., 1977). Judges who heard only the woman's side of the conversation rated women who had been labeled attractive as more likable, sociable, and friendly. Apparently, male callers who believed that their telephone partners were attractive somehow elicited more competent social behavior from them.

In another study, Goldman and Lewis (1977) found that attractive people were more likely to be rated by telephone partners as socially skillful and likable, even though their conversants were blind to their appearance. Physically attractive people seem to acquire and maintain the socially competent behavior that is fostered in them.

Attractive college men engage in more social interaction with women and less interaction with men than do their less attractive peers (Reis et al., 1980, 1982). Their increased contacts with women appear to be at the expense of relationships with men. There is no such link between attractiveness and social interactions among college women. More attractive college women spend more time on dates and at parties than do their less attractive peers, but increased heterosexual interactions do not spill over into other areas of social contact. The satisfaction derived from opposite-sex interactions is positively related to attractiveness for both sexes.

The Matching Hypothesis: Who Is "Right" for You? Have you ever refrained from asking out an extremely attractive person for fear of rejection? Do you feel more comfortable with someone who's a bit less attractive?

If so, you're not alone. Although we may rate highly attractive people as most desirable, we are more likely to try to construct relationships with and marry people who are similar to ourselves in attractiveness (Murstein & Christy, 1976). This tendency is predicted by the **matching hypothesis** (Berscheid et al., 1971). A major motivating factor is fear of rejection by more attractive people. In a recent study, Shanteau and Nagy (1979) found that college women chose prospective dates who were moderately attractive but highly likely to accept the date, as opposed to more attractive men who were considered likely to reject them.

But the process of "settling" for someone other than the local Robert Redford or Cheryl Tiegs look-alike need not be an unhappy one. We tend to rate our mates as slightly more attractive than ourselves—as if we had somehow "gotten the better of the deal" (Murstein, 1972). We tend to idealize loved ones (see Chapter 7), but other explanations are also possible. By focusing on their positive features we may feel happier with our marriages. Too, we may be aware of our own struggles to present ourselves to the world each day, but take our mates' appearance more or less for granted.

There are exceptions. Now and then we find a beautiful woman married to a plain man, or vice versa. How do we explain it? According to Bar-Tal and Saxe (1976), we may assume that such men are wealthy—as in the Jackie Kennedy-Aristotle Onassis match—highly intelligent, or otherwise successful. We seek an unseen factor that will maintain the balance in the match. Similarly, a study of lonely-hearts advertisements, published under the provocative title *Let's Make a Deal* (Harrison & Saeed, 1977), found

Matching hypothesis The view that people tend to choose persons similar to themselves in attractiveness and attitudes in the formation of interpersonal relationships.

that there were exceptions to the matching rule of only attractive people seeking attractive partners. For instance, physically unappealing but wealthy men and women often advertised for physically attractive partners. Wealth and physical appeal are both positively valued in our society. In this way it could be argued that such couples were "matches," after all. But it should also be noted that couples mismatched for attractiveness were found more likely to break up than matched couples over a nine-month period (White, 1980).

The matching hypothesis applies not only to physical attractiveness. We are also more likely to get married to people who are similar to us in their needs (Meyer & Pepper, 1977), personality (Buss, 1984; Lesnik-Oberstein & Cohen, 1984), and attitudes, as we shall see below.

ATTITUDINAL SIMILARITY: BIRDS OF A FEATHER FLOCK TOGETHER

It has been observed since ancient times that we tend to like people who agree with us (Jellison & Oliver, 1983). Birds of a feather, so to speak, flock together.

Byrne and his colleagues (1970) found that college students were most attracted to computer match-ups who were physically appealing and expressed similar attitudes. Ratings of physically attractive dates with dissimilar attitudes approximated those of unattractive dates with similar attitudes. The more dogmatic we are, the more likely we are to reject people who disagree with us (Palmer & Kalin, 1985). Physical appeal and attitudes are both important determinants of whom we shall like and whom we shall dislike.

But there is also evidence that we may tend to *assume* that physically attractive people share our attitudes (Marks et al., 1981). Can this be a sort of wish-fulfillment? When physical attraction is very strong, as it was with Candy and Stretch, perhaps we like to think that all the kinks in a relationship will be small, or capable of being ironed out. Similarly, we tend to assume that preferred presidential candidates share our political and social attitudes (Brent & Granberg, 1982). We may even fail to remember statements they make that conflict with our attitudes (Johnson & Judd, 1983). Then, once they are in office, we may become disillusioned when they swerve from our expectations.

All attitudes are not necessarily equal. Men on computer dates at the University of Nevada were more influenced by sexual than religious attitudes (Touhey, 1972). But women were more attracted to men whose religious views coincided with their own. These findings suggest that women may have been less interested than men in a physical relationship, but more concerned about creating a family with cohesive values. Considering changing values and the ongoing "sexual revolution," it would be interesting to learn whether these findings would hold in the 1980s, and whether they would be consistent across the United States.

Grush and Yehl (1979) found that nontraditional college women (who, for example, endorsed the views of the National Organization for Women) and traditional college men were more attracted to opposite-sex strangers

SIMILARITY According to the matching hypothesis, we tend to form relationships with people who are similar to ourselves in attractiveness. We also tend to be more attracted to people who possess similar attitudes, whether the relationship is a love relationship or a friendship.

who they believed shared their sex-role attitudes. They showed stronger preferences for dating, marriage, and work partners who shared their beliefs. Traditional women and nontraditional men were not so strongly influenced by attitudinal similarity. These findings may seem confusing at first, but recall from Chapter 13 that the traditional (stereotypical) masculine role includes traits of competitiveness and outspokenness. These traits are more likely shared by *non*traditional than traditional women. Thus, traditional men and nontraditional women may be less tolerant of people who disagree with them, or at least more willing to confront those who disagree.

Similarity in tastes and distastes is also important in the development of relationships. For example, May and Hamilton (1980) found that college women rate photos of male strangers as more attractive when they are listening to music they prefer (in most cases, rock) as compared to music that they don't like (in this experiment, "avant-garde classical"). If a dating couple's taste in music does not overlap, one member may look more appealing at the same time the second is losing appeal in the other's eyes, all because of what is on the stereo.

THE "ROMEO AND JULIET EFFECT": WHEN PARENTS SAY NO

Would parental opposition drive a wedge between you and your date, or would you fight to maintain the relationship? In the Shakespearean play, the young lovers Romeo and Juliet drew closer to each other against the bloody backdrop of a family feud. But that was literature. What about real life?

Psychologists sought an answer through a survey of dating and married couples at the University of Colorado (Driscoll et al., 1972). Student questionnaires suggested that parental opposition intensified feelings of love between couples during the first six to ten months of the relationship. But parental opposition did not affect feelings between married couples.

During the early stages of a relationship, parental opposition may intensify needs for security within a couple, so that they cling together more strongly. But for couples who have already made a strong commitment, as in a lengthy courtship or a marriage, parental opposition may become irrelevant.

RECIPROCITY: IF YOU LIKE ME, YOU MUST HAVE EXCELLENT JUDGMENT

Has anyone told you how good-looking, brilliant, and mature you are? That your taste is refined? If so, have you been impressed by his or her fine judgment?

When people praise us, we are more susceptible to the messages they are delivering. When we are admired and complimented, we tend to return these feelings and behaviors. This is **reciprocity.** When people tell you that you are terrific, you may wonder why you didn't pay more attention to them before.

Reciprocity In interpersonal attraction, the tendency to return feelings and attitudes that are expressed about us.

PROPINQUITY: IF YOU'RE NEAR ME, I MUST BE ATTRACTED TO YOU

Why did Sarah Abrams walk down the aisle with Allen Ackroyd and not Danny Schmidt? Sarah and Danny actually had more in common. But Sarah and Al exchanged smoldering glances throughout eleventh-grade English, because their teacher had used an alphabetical seating chart. Danny sat diagonally across the room. Sarah, to him, was only a name called when attendance was taken.

Attraction is more likely to develop between people who are placed in frequent contact with one another. This is the effect of nearness, or **propinquity.** Students are more likely to develop friendships when they sit next to one another (Segal, 1974). Homeowners are most likely to become friendly with next-door neighbors, especially those with adjacent driveways (Whyte, 1956). Apartment dwellers tend to find friends among those who live nearby on the same floor (Nahemow & Lawton, 1975).

PLAYING HARD TO GET: *"I ONLY HAVE EYES FOR YOU"*

Are you likely to be more or less attracted to people who play "hard to get"?

Elaine Walster and her colleagues (1973) recruited male subjects for an experiment in which they were given the opportunity to rate and select dates. They were given phony initial reactions of their potential dates to them and to the other men in the study. One woman was generally hard to get. She reacted indifferently to all the men. Another woman was uniformly easy to get. She responded positively to all male participants. A third showed the fine judgment of being attracted to the rater only. Men were overwhelmingly more attracted to this woman—the one who had eyes for them only. She was selected for dates 80 percent of the time.

Now that we have seen how our feelings of attraction are influenced by physical features, attitudinal similarity, and so on, let us consider the psychology of social influence.

SOCIAL INFLUENCE

Most of us would be reluctant to wear blue jeans to a funeral, to walk naked on city streets, or, for that matter, to wear clothes at a nudist colony. Other people and groups can exert enormous pressure on us to behave according to their wishes or according to group norms. **Social influence** is the area of social psychology that studies the ways in which people alter the thoughts, feelings, and behaviors of others. Earlier in the chapter we saw how attitudes can be changed through persuasion or by inducing attitude-discrepant behavior. In this section we describe a couple of classic experiments to show how people can influence others to engage in destructive obedience and to conform to group norms.

OBEDIENCE TO AUTHORITY

Richard Nixon resigned the Presidency of the United States in August, 1974. For two years the business of the nation had almost ground to a halt while Congress investigated the 1972 burglary of a Democratic party campaign office in the Watergate office and apartment complex. It turned out that Nixon supporters had authorized the break-in. Nixon himself might have been involved in the cover-up of this connection later on. For two years Nixon and his aides had been investigated by the press and by Congress. Now it was over. Some of the bad guys were thrown into jail. Nixon was exiled to the beaches of southern California. The nation returned to work. The new President, Gerald Ford, declared "Our national nightmare is over."

But was it over? Have we come to grips with the implications of the Watergate affair?

According to Stanley Milgram (*APA Monitor*, January 1978), a prominent Yale University psychologist, the Watergate cover-up, like the Nazi slaughter of the Jews, was made possible through the compliance of people who were more concerned about the approval of their supervisors than about their own morality. Otherwise they would have refused to abet these crimes. The broad question is: How pressing is the need to obey authority figures at all costs?

THE MILGRAM STUDIES: SHOCKING STUFF AT YALE

Stanley Milgram also wondered how many of us would resist authority figures who made immoral requests. To find out, he ran a series of experiments at Yale University. In an early phase of his work, Milgram (1963) placed ads in New Haven, Connecticut, newspapers for subjects for studies on learning and memory. He enlisted forty men ranging in age from twenty to fifty—teachers, engineers, laborers, salespeople, men who had not completed elementary school, men with graduate degrees. The sample composed a cross-section of the population of this Connecticut city.

Let us suppose you had answered an ad. You would have shown up at the university for a fee of $4.50, for the sake of science and your own curiosity. You might have been impressed. After all, Yale was a venerable institution that dominated the city. You would not have been less impressed by the elegant labs where you would have met a distinguished behavioral scientist dressed in a white laboratory coat and another newspaper recruit—like you. The scientist would have explained that the purpose of the experiment was to study the *effects of punishment on learning*. The experiment would require a "teacher" and a "learner." By chance you would be appointed the teacher, and the other recruit the learner.

You, the scientist, and the learner would enter a laboratory room containing a rather threatening chair with dangling straps. The scientist would secure the learner's cooperation and strap him in. The learner would express some concern, but this was, after all, for the sake of science. And this was Yale University, was it not? What could happen to a person at Yale?

You would follow the scientist to an adjacent room from which you would do your "teaching." This teaching promised to be effective. You

FIGURE 14.3 **THE "AGGRESSION MACHINE"** In the Milgram studies on obedience to authority, pressing levers on the "aggression machine" was the operational definition of aggression.

would punish the "learner's" errors by pressing levers marked from 15 to 450 volts on a fearsome looking console (Figure 14.3). Labels described twenty-eight of the thirty levers as running the gamut from "Slight Shock" to "Danger: Severe Shock." The last two levers resembled a film unfit for anyone under age seventeen: They were rated simply "XXX." Just in case you had no idea what electric shock felt like, the scientist gave you a sample 45-volt shock. It stung. You pitied the fellow who might receive more.

Your learner was expected to learn word pairs. Pairs of words would be read from a list. After hearing the list once, the learner would have to produce the word that was paired with the stimulus word. He would do so by pressing a switch that would signify his choice from a list of four alternatives. The switch would light one of four panels in your room. If it was the correct panel, you would proceed to the next stimulus word. If not, you would deliver an electric shock. With each error, you would increase the voltage of the shock.

You would probably have some misgivings. Electrodes had been strapped to the learner's wrists, and the scientist had applied electrode paste to "avoid blisters and burns." You were also told that the shocks would cause "no permanent tissue damage," although they might be extremely painful. Still, the learner was going along, and, after all, this was Yale.

The learner answered some items correctly and then made some errors. With mild concern you pressed the levers up through forty-five volts. You had tolerated that much yourself. Then a few more mistakes were made. You pressed the sixty-volt lever, then seventy-five. The learner made another mistake. You paused and looked at the scientist. He was reassuring: "Although the shocks may be painful, there is no permanent tissue damage, so please go on." Further errors were made, and quickly you were up to a shock of 300 volts. But now the learner was pounding on the other side of

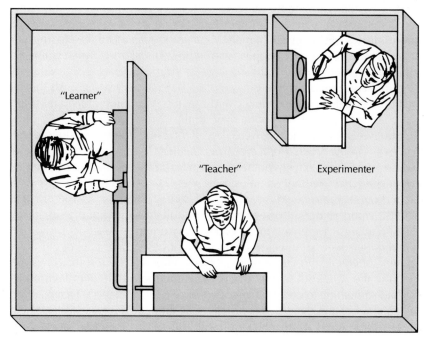

FIGURE 14.4 **THE EXPERIMENTAL SET-UP IN THE MILGRAM STUDIES** When the "learner" makes an error, the experimenter prods the "teacher" to deliver a painful electric shock.

"Learner"

"Teacher" Experimenter

the wall! Your chest tightened and you began to perspire. Damn science and the $4.50, you thought. You hesitated and the scientist said, "The experiment requires that you continue." After the delivery of the next stimulus word, there was no answer at all. What were you to do? "Wait for five to ten seconds," the scientist instructed, "and then treat no answer as a wrong answer." But after the next shock, there was again that pounding on the wall! Now your heart was racing and you were convinced that you were causing extreme pain and discomfort. Was it possible that no lasting damage was being done? Was the experiment that important, after all? What to do? You hesitated again. The scientist said, "It is absolutely essential that you continue." His voice was very convincing. "You have no other choice," he said. "You *must* go on." You could barely think straight, and for some unaccountable reason you felt laughter rising in your throat. Your finger shook above the lever. What were you to do?

On Truth at Yale   Milgram (1963, 1974) found out what most people would do. Of the forty men in this phase of his research, only five refused to go beyond the 300-volt level, at which the learner first pounded the wall. Nine more teachers defied the scientist within the 300-volt range. But 65 percent of the participants complied with the scientist throughout the series, believing that they were delivering 450-volt, XXX-rated shocks.

Were these newspaper recruits simply unfeeling? Not at all. Milgram was impressed by their signs of stress. They trembled, they stuttered, they bit their lips. They groaned, they sweated, they dug their fingernails into their flesh. There were fits of laughter, though laughter was inappropriate. One salesperson's laughter was so convulsive that he could not continue with the experiment.

Milgram wondered if college students, heralded for independent thinking, would show more defiance. But a replication of the study with Yale undergraduates yielded similar results. What about women, who were supposedly less aggressive than men? Women, too, shocked the "learners." But surely this could only happen within the walls of Yale, where subjects would be overpowered by the prestige of the setting! Not so. Milgram attained the same results in a dingy storefront in a nearby town. All this in a nation that values independence and the free will of the individual. Our "national nightmare" may not be over at all.

But we still have not answered a very pressing question: *Why did the "teachers" obey orders from the experimenter?* We do not have all the answers, but we can offer hypotheses. Despite the expressed American ideal of independence, we are socialized to obey others (such as parents and teachers) from the time we are little children. In Milgram's experimental settings, experimenters also seemed to have full command of the situation, while "teachers" were very much on their own; and so teachers could not compare their ideas and feelings with those of others. We cannot attribute teachers' obedience to the prestige of Yale—after all, the results were replicated in the storefront setting. But perhaps the foot-in-the-door technique also had something to do with their obedience (Gilbert, 1981). That is, after teachers had begun the process of delivering graduated shocks to learners, perhaps they found it progressively more difficult to extricate themselves

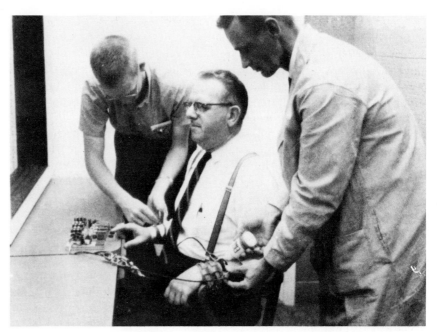

A "LEARNER" IN THE MILGRAM STUDIES ON OBEDIENCE TO AUTHORITY
This man could be in for quite a shock.

from the project. Finally, as noted in Chapter 7, we become subject to conflicting thoughts and motives as our levels of arousal shoot up. As teachers in the Milgram experiments became more and more aroused, it might have become progressively more difficult for them to make decisions.

On Deception at Yale   You are probably skeptical enough to wonder whether the "teachers" in the Milgram study actually shocked the "learners" when they pressed the levers on the console. They didn't. The only real shock in this experiment was the forty-five-volt sample given the teachers. Its purpose was to lend credibility to the procedure.

The learners in the experiment were actually confederates of the experimenter. They had not answered the newspaper ads, but were in on the truth from the start. "Teachers" were the only real subjects. Teachers were led to believe that they were chosen at random for the teacher role, but the choosing was rigged so that newspaper recruits would always become teachers.

Milgram's research has alerted us to a real and present danger—the tendency of most people to obey authority figures, even when their demands contradict their moral attitudes and values. It has happened before. Unhappily, unless we remain alert, it may happen again. Who are the authority figures in your life? How do you think you would have behaved if you had been a "teacher" in the Milgram studies? Are you sure?

In the section on conformity we describe another classic study, and you may try again to imagine how you would behave if you were involved in it.

CONFORMITY

Earlier we noted that most of us would be reluctant to wear blue jeans to a funeral, to walk naked on city streets, or to wear clothes at a nudist colony. The tendency to **conform** to group norms is often a good thing; many group norms have evolved because they favor comfort and survival. But group pressure can also promote maladaptive behavior, such as wearing coats and ties in summer in buildings cooled only to 78° F. At that high temperature the main motive for conforming to a dress code may be to show that we have been adequately socialized and are not threats to social rules.

Let us have a look at a classic experiment on conformity run by Solomon Asch in the early 1950s. Then we shall examine factors that promote conformity.

SEVEN LINE JUDGES CAN'T BE WRONG: THE ASCH STUDY

Do you believe what you see with your own eyes? Seeing is believing, is it not? Not if you were a participant in the Asch (1952) study.

You would enter a laboratory room with seven other subjects for an experiment on visual discrimination. If you were familiar with psychology experiments, you might be surprised: There were no rats and no electric-shock apparatus in sight, only a man at the front of a room with some cards with lines drawn on them.

The eight of you would be seated in a series. You would be given the seventh seat, a minor fact at the time. The man would explain the task. There was a single line on the card on the left. Three lines were drawn on the card at the right (Figure 14.5). One line was the same length as the line on the other card. You and the other subjects need only call out, one at a time, which of the three lines—1, 2, or 3—was the same length. Simple.

You would try it out. Those to your right spoke out in order: "3," "3," "3," "3," "3," "3." Now it was your turn. Line 3 was clearly the same length as the line on the first card, so you said "3." Then the fellow after you chimed in "3." That's all there was to it. Then two other cards were set up in the front of the room. This time line 2 was clearly the same

Conform To behave in accordance with group norms and expectations.

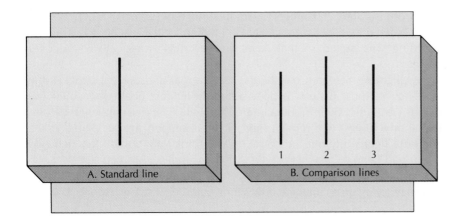

A. Standard line

1   2   3
B. Comparison lines

FIGURE 14.5 CARDS USED IN THE ASCH STUDY ON CONFORMITY Which line on card B—1, 2, or 3—is the same length as the line on card A? Line 2, right? But would you say "2" if you were a member of a group and six people answering ahead of you all said "3"? Are you sure?

THE SET-UP OF THE ASCH EXPERIMENT IN CONFORMITY The experimenter is at the right, and the unsuspecting subject is seated sixth from the left. All other "subjects" are actually in league with the experimenter.

length as the line on the first card. "2," "2," "2," "2," "2," "2." Your turn again. "2," you said, and perhaps your mind began to wander. Your stomach was gurgling a bit. That night you would not even mind dorm food particularly. "2," said the fellow after you.

Another pair of cards was held up. Line 3 was clearly the correct answer. The 6 people on your right spoke in turn: "1," "1. . . ." Wait a second! ". . . 1," "1—" You forgot about dinner and studied the lines briefly. No, 1 was too short, by a good half an inch. ". . . 1," "1," and suddenly it was your turn. Your hands had quickly become sweaty and there was a lump in your throat. You wanted to say 3, but was it right? There was really no time and you had already paused noticeably. "1," you said. "1," the last fellow confirmed matter-of-factly.

Now your attention was riveted on the task. Much of the time you agreed with the other seven line judges, but sometimes you did not. And for some reason beyond your understanding, they were in perfect agreement, even when they were wrong—assuming that you could trust your eyes. The experiment was becoming an uncomfortable experience, and you began to doubt your judgment.

The discomfort in the Asch study was caused by the pressure to conform. Actually, the other seven recruits were confederates of the experimenter. They prearranged a number of incorrect responses. The sole purpose of the study was to see whether you would conform to the erroneous group judgments.

How many of Asch's subjects caved in? How many went along with the crowd rather than assert what they thought to be the right answer? Seventy-five percent. *Three of four agreed with the majority wrong answer at least once.*

What about you? Would you wear blue jeans if everyone else wore slacks and skirts? A number of more recent experiments (Wheeler et al., 1978) show that the tendency to conform did not go out with the Fabulous Fifties.

FACTORS INFLUENCING CONFORMITY: NUMBERS, SUPPORT, AND SEX

Several personal and situational factors promote conformity. Personal factors include low self-esteem, high self-consciousness, social shyness (Krech et al., 1962; Santee & Maslach, 1982), gender (Cooper, 1979), and familiarity with the task. As noted in Chapter 13, women who accept the feminine sex-role stereotype are more likely than men to conform (Bem, 1975). One interesting recent experiment (Eagly et al., 1981) found that men conform to group opinions as frequently as women do when their conformity or independence will be private. But when their conformity would be made known to the group, they conform less often than women do, apparently because nonconformity is more consistent with the masculine sex-role stereotype of independence. That is, men may often show independence just to conform with the male sex-role stereotype of rugged individualism. It's a little bit like "doublethink" in the Orwell novel *1984*: "Nonconformity is conformity." (As with experiments showing that we are more "altruistic" when we are rewarded for being altruistic, sometimes you just can't win.)

Familiarity with the task at hand promotes self-reliance (Eagly, 1978). In one experiment, for example, Sistrunk and McDavid (1971) found that women were more likely to conform to group pressure on tasks involving identification of tools (such as wrenches) that were more familiar to men. But men were more likely to conform on tasks involving identification of cooking utensils, with which women, in our society, are usually more familiar.

Situational factors include the number of people who hold the majority opinion and the presence of at least one other who shares the discrepant opinion. Probability of conformity, even to incorrect group judgments, increases rapidly as a group grows to five members. Then it increases at a slower rate up to eight members (Gerard et al., 1968; Wilder, 1977), at which point maximum probability of conformity is reached. But finding just one other person who supports your minority opinion is apparently enough to encourage you to stick to your guns (Morris et al., 1977). In a variation of the Asch experiment, recruits were provided with just one confederate who agreed with their minority judgments (Allen & Levine, 1971). Even though this confederate seemed to have a visual impairment, as evidenced by thick glasses, his support was sufficient to lead actual subjects not to conform to incorrect majority opinions.

Studies in conformity highlight some of the ways in which we are influenced by groups. In the following section, we discuss other aspects of group behavior.

GROUP BEHAVIOR

To be human is to belong to groups. Families, classes, religious groups, political parties, circles of friends, bowling teams, sailing clubs, conversation groups, therapy groups—to how many groups do you belong? How do groups influence the behavior of individuals?

In this section we have a look at a number of aspects of group be-

Social facilitation The process by which a person's performance is increased when other members of a group engage in similar behavior.

Evaluation apprehension Concern that others are evaluating our behavior.

havior: social facilitation, group decision-making, mob behavior, and the bystander effect.

SOCIAL FACILITATION

One effect of groups on individual behavior is **social facilitation,** or the effects on performance that result from the presence of others. Bicycle riders and runners tend to move more rapidly when they are members of a group. This effect is not limited to humans: dogs and cats eat more rapidly when others are present; even roaches run more rapidly when other roaches are present (Zajonc, 1980).

According to psychologist Robert Zajonc (1980), the presence of others influences us by increasing our levels of arousal, or motivation. When our levels of arousal are highly increased, our performance of simple, dominant responses is facilitated, but our performance of complex, recently acquired responses may be impaired. For this reason, a well-rehearsed speech may be delivered more masterfully before a larger audience, but our performance in an offhand speech or at a question-and-answer session may be hampered by a large audience.

Social facilitation may be influenced by **evaluation apprehension** as well as level of arousal (Bray & Sugarman, 1980; Markus, 1981). Our performance before a group may be affected not only by the physical presence of others, but also by our concern that they are evaluating our performance. When giving a speech, we may "lose our thread" if we become distracted by the audience and begin to focus too much on what they may be thinking of us (Seta, 1982). If we believe that we have begun to flounder, our evaluation apprehension may skyrocket and, as a consequence, our performance may deteriorate further.

The presence of others can also decrease performance when we are not acting *before* a group, but when we are anonymous members *of* a group (Latané et al., 1979; Williams et al., 1981). Workers, for example, may "goof off" or engage in "social loafing" on humdrum tasks when they feel that they will not be found out and held accountable (see the nearby box on "social loafing"). There is then no evaluation apprehension. Group members may also reduce their efforts if an apparently capable member makes no contribution, but tries to "ride free" on the efforts of other group members (Kerr, 1983). The belief that other group members are not likely to work as hard as we do also contributes to social loafing (Jackson & Harkins, 1985).

POLARIZATION AND THE RISKY SHIFT

You might think that a group decision would be more conservative than an individual decision. After all, a few "mature" individuals should be able to balance the opinions of daredevils. But in general you would be wrong.

As an individual, you might recommend that your company risk $10,000 on a new product. Other company executives, polled individually, might risk similar amounts. But if you were gathered for a group decision, it is likely that you would either recommend well above this figure or nothing

PERIL OF WORK WITHIN GROUP: SOCIAL LOAFING

Science works its wonders in homely ways. Alexander Fleming saw a mold growing in a dish—and came upon penicillin. Benjamin Franklin flew a kite in a thunderstorm and demonstrated that lightning is electricity.

Professor Bibb Latané listened to a bunch of college students hollering and clapping—and decided that he had uncovered a root cause of America's productivity problems: social loafing.

The Presence of Others Dr. Latané concludes that there is a "diffusion of responsibility" in groups. Each person feels less responsibility to help because others are present.

Latané and his colleagues (1981) organized student volunteers into groups of varying sizes and asked them to clap or shout as loud as they could. In some tests, students wore blindfolds and headphones, and the headphones sometimes transmitted taped sounds of yelling and clapping so students couldn't judge the sound output of other subjects.

The researchers measured the volume generated by students alone and in groups. In one experiment, students were told over the headphones that they would shout in pairs, but in fact they shouted alone. In other trials they were told they would shout alone, and did. In this and other experiments, the researchers found that when subjects either were in a group or believed they were, they consistently made less noise per person than when they shouted or clapped alone.

The Workplace Dr. Latané says his group plans to extend its basic research into the workplace by examining a secretarial pool, an executive committee meeting, and an air-traffic control center.

Despite what his research suggests, Dr. Latané doesn't think the solution to social loafing is breaking up groups and turning the U.S. work force into a collection of loners. Rather, the researchers suggest that managers channel group motivation to intensify rather than diffuse individual effort.

A Japanese Idea Many corporate managers already endorse that conclusion. Organizational psychologist Harry Levinson notes the "almost fad-like move to quality circles," the teamwork concept many companies have imported from Japan. General Motors is one of them.

SOCIAL FACILITATION OR SOCIAL LOAFING? Under what circumstances does working in a group facilitate performance? Under what circumstances does it promote social loafing?

Its Fitzgerald, Georgia, battery-making plant has run on a team system since it opened in 1975. There, semiautonomous teams set their own production goals and work schedules, administer their own discipline, and evaluate their own performance—with great success.

"And now at this point in the meeting I'd like to shift the blame away from me and onto someone else."

at all (Myers & Lamm, 1976). This group effect is called **polarization,** or the taking of an extreme position. Yet if you had to gamble on which way the decision would go, you would do better to place your money on movement toward the higher sum—that is, to bet on a **risky shift.** Why?

One possibility is that a group member may reveal information which the others had not been aware of, and that this information clearly points in one direction or the other. With doubts removed, the group becomes polarized—moving decidedly in the appropriate direction. It may also be that social facilitation occurs in the group setting, and that increased motivation prompts more extreme decisions.

But why do groups tend to take greater rather than smaller risks than those that would be ventured by their members? One answer is **diffusion of responsibility** (Burnstein, 1983; Myers, 1983). If the venture flops, it will not be you alone to blame. You can always say (and tell yourself) that it was, after all, a group decision. And if the venture pays off handsomely, I have no doubt that you will trumpet abroad your influential role in the group decision-making process.

THE SHARING OF INFORMATION IN GROUP DECISION-MAKING: ARE CAMELS REALLY HORSES MADE BY COMMITTEES?

Are camels horses made by committees? Are two or three heads (or humps) really better than one?

Polarization In social psychology, the taking of an extreme position or attitude on an issue.

Risky shift The tendency to make riskier decisions as a member of a group than as an individual acting independently.

Diffusion of responsibility The spreading or sharing of responsibility for a decision or behavior among a group.

Since we need information to make proper decisions, and since several people presumably have more information available than one person, you might think that groups would arrive at fairer, more knowledgeable decisions than individuals. However, according to a recent study by Garold Stasser and William Titus (1985), groups do not necessarily avail themselves of the knowledge of all group members. In a simulation of a political caucus, in which groups of Miami University students pretended to be selecting political candidates, group members did not effectively pool their information. Instead, group discussion was dominated by (1) information that was known to all group members prior to the caucus, and (2) information that supported the group members' premeeting preferences.

Groups, sad to say, can sometimes serve as forums for the validation of pre-existing prejudices rather than opportunities for the rational weighing of the available information and unbiased decision-making.

On the other hand, groups do have the potential for making high-quality decisions. The elements required for group processes to lead to good decisions include knowledgeable group participants, a strong and fair chairperson, an explicit procedure for arriving at decisions, and a process of give and take, all of which encourage the exchange of relevant information (Vinokur et al., 1985).

MOB BEHAVIOR AND DEINDIVIDUATION: DO CROWDS BRING OUT THE BEAST IN US?

Gustave Le Bon (1960), the French social thinker, did not endear himself to feminists and liberals when he wrote that men in mobs show the gullibility and ferocity of "primitive beings" like women, children, members of the lower classes, and savages. He branded mobs and crowds irrational, like a "beast with many heads." Mob actions like race riots and lynchings sometimes seem to operate on a psychology of their own. Do mobs elicit the beast in us? How is it that mild-mannered people will commit mayhem as members of a mob? In seeking an answer, let us examine a lynching and the baiting type of crowd that often seems to attend threatened suicides.

The Lynching of Arthur Stevens   In *Social Learning and Imitation,* Neal Miller and John Dollard (1941) vividly described a southern lynching. Arthur Stevens, a black man, was accused of murdering his lover, a white woman, when she wanted to break up with him. Stevens was arrested and confessed to the crime. The sheriff feared violence and moved Stevens to a town 200 miles distant during the night. But his location was uncovered. The next day a mob of a hundred persons stormed the jail and returned Stevens to the scene of the crime.

Outrage spread from person to person like a plague bacillus. Laborers, professionals, women, adolescents, and law-enforcement officers alike were infected. Stevens was tortured, emasculated, and murdered. His corpse was dragged through the streets. Then the mob went on a rampage in town, chasing and assaulting other blacks. The riot ended only when troops were sent in to restore law and order.

Deindividuation (dee-in-div-vid-you-AY-shun). The process by which group members may discontinue self-evaluation and adopt group norms and attitudes.

Deindividuation   When we act as individuals, fear of consequences and self-evaluation tend to prevent antisocial behavior. But as members of a mob, we may experience **deindividuation,** a state of reduced self-awareness and lowered concern for social evaluation (Mann et al., 1982). Many factors lead to deindividuation, including anonymity, diffusion of responsibility, arousal due to noise and crowding (Zimbardo, 1969), and focusing of individual attention on the group process (Diener, 1980). Individuals also tend to adopt the emerging norms and attitudes of the group (Turner & Killian, 1972). Under these circumstances, crowd members behave more aggressively than they would as individuals.

Police know that mob actions are best averted early, by dispersing the small groups that may gather into a crowd. On an individual level, perhaps we can resist deindividuation by instructing ourselves to stop and think whenever we begin to feel highly aroused as group members. If we dissociate ourselves from such groups when they are in the formative process, we shall be more likely to retain critical self-evaluation and avoid behavior that we shall later regret.

The Baiting Crowd in Cases of Threatened Suicide   As individuals, we often feel compassion when we observe people who are so distressed that they are considering suicide. Why is it, then, that when people who are considering suicide threaten to jump from a ledge the crowd often baits them, urging them on?

Such baiting occurred in ten of twenty-one cases of threatened suicide studied by Leon Mann (1981). Analysis of newspaper reports suggested a number of factors that might have prompted deindividuation among crowd members, all contributing to anonymity: The crowds were large. It was dark out (past 6 P.M.) The victim and the crowd were distant from one another (with the victim, for example, on a high floor). Baiting by the crowd was also linked to high temperatures (the summer season) and a long duration of the episode, suggestive of stress and fatigue among crowd members.

HELPING BEHAVIOR AND THE BYSTANDER EFFECT: SOME WATCH WHILE OTHERS DIE

In 1964 America was shocked by the murder of twenty-eight-year-old Kitty Genovese in New York City. Murder was not unheard of in the "big apple," but Kitty had screamed for help as her killer had repeatedly stabbed her. Nearly forty neighbors had heard the commotion. Many watched. Nobody helped. Why? As a nation are we a callous bunch who would rather watch than help when others are in trouble? Penn State Psychologist R. Lance Shotland notes that in the two decades since the murder (Dowd, 1984), more than a thousand books and articles have been written attempting to explain the behavior of bystanders in crises. According to Stanley Milgram, the Genovese case "touched on a fundamental issue of the human condition. If we need help, will those around us stand around and let us be destroyed or will they come to our aid?" (in Dowd, 1984).

What factors determine whether we will come to the aid of others who are in trouble?

The Helper: Who Helps?   Some psychologists (e.g., Hoffman, 1981) suggest that **altruism** is a part of human nature. In keeping with sociobiological theory (see Chapter 1), they argue that self-sacrifice will sometimes help guarantee that a close relative will succeed. In this way, self-sacrifice is actually "selfish" from a genetic point of view: It helps us perpetuate a genetic code similar to our own in future generations.

Most psychologists focus on the roles of helper mood and personality traits. By and large, we are more likely to help others when we are in a good mood (Manucia et al., 1984; Rosenhan et al., 1981). Yet we may help others when we are miserable ourselves, if our own problems work to increase our empathy or sensitivity to the plights of others (Batson et al., 1981; Thompson et al., 1980). People with a high need for approval may act "altruistically" in order to earn approval from others (Satow, 1975). People who are empathic, who can take the perspective of others, are also likely to help (Archer et al., 1981).

Highly masculine people might be expected to try to "take charge" of most situations, and thus be expected to be more likely to come to the aid of others in emergencies. However, Dianne Tice and Roy Baumeister (1985) found that highly masculine subjects, as measured by Sandra Bem's Sex Role Inventory, were *less* likely than others to help others in distress. The researchers suggest that highly masculine people may have a greater fear of potential embarrassment and loss of poise than most people—that is, they have a "tougher" image to protect. These fears then inhibit them from intervening in emergencies.

There are many other reasons why bystanders frequently do not come to the aid of others in distress. For example, if bystanders do not fully understand what they are seeing, they may not recognize that an emergency exists. That is, the more ambiguous the situation, the less likely it is that bystanders will try to help (Shotland & Heinold, 1985). Second, the presence of others may lead to diffusion of responsibility, so that no one assumes responsibility for helping others (as we shall see in a following section). Third, if bystanders are not certain that they possess the behavioral competencies to take charge of the situation, they may also stay on the sidelines for fear of making a social blunder and being subject to ridicule (Pantin & Carver, 1982)—or for fear of getting hurt themselves.

Bystanders who believe that others "get" what they deserve may rationalize not helping by thinking that a person would not be in trouble unless this outcome was just (Lerner et al., 1975). A sense of personal responsibility increases the likelihood of helping. Such responsibility may stem from having made a verbal commitment to help (e.g., Moriarty, 1975) or from having been designated by others as responsible for carrying out a helping chore (Maruyama et al., 1982).

The Victim: Who Is Helped?   Although sex roles have been changing, it is traditional for men to help women in our society. Latané and Dabbs (1975) found that women were more likely than men to receive help, especially from men, when they dropped coins in Atlanta (a southern city) than in Seattle or Columbus (northern cities). The researchers explain this differ-

Altruism (AL-true-izm). Unselfish concern for the welfare of others. (From the Latin *alter*, meaning "another.")

ence by noting that traditional sex roles are persevering more strongly in the South.

Women are also more likely than men to be helped when their cars have broken down on the highway or they are hitchhiking (Pomazal & Clore, 1973). There may be sexual overtones to some of this "altruism." Women are most likely to be helped by males when they are attractive and when they are alone (Snyder et al., 1974; Benson et al., 1976).

As in the research on interpersonal attraction, similarity also seems to promote helping behavior. Poorly dressed people are more likely to succeed in requests for a dime with poorly dressed strangers, while well-dressed people are more likely to get money from well-dressed strangers (Hensley, 1981).

Situational Determinants of Helping: "Am I the Only One Here?" It may seem logical that a group of people would be more likely to have come to the aid of Kitty Genovese than would a lone person. After all, a group could more effectively have overpowered her attacker. Yet research by Darley and Latané (1968) suggests that a lone person may have been more likely to try to help her.

In their experiment, male subjects were performing meaningless tasks in cubicles when they heard a (convincing) recording of a person apparently having an epileptic seizure. When the subjects thought that four other persons were immediately available to help, only 31 percent made an effort to do so. But when they thought that no one else was available, 85 percent of them tried to offer aid. As in other areas of group behavior, it seems that diffusion of responsibility inhibits helping behavior in groups or crowds. When we are in a group, we are often willing to let George (or Georgette) do it. When George isn't around, we are more willing to help others ourselves.

Note that the bystanders in most studies on the bystander effect are strangers (Latané & Nida, 1981). Research shows that bystanders who are acquainted with victims are more likely to respond to the social norm of helping others in need (Rutkowski et al., 1983). After all, aren't we more likely to give to charity when asked directly by a co-worker or supervisor in the socially exposed situation of the office, as compared to in response to a letter received in the privacy of our own homes?

We are more likely to help others when we can clearly see what is happening (for instance, if we can see clearly that the woman whose car has broken down is alone), and when the environment is familiar to us (for instance, when we are in our home town rather than a strange city).

Speaking of strange and familiar environments, let us now turn our attention to environmental psychology.

ENVIRONMENTAL PSYCHOLOGY

Only recently have psychologists begun to systematically study how people and the physical environment influence each other. This is an important field of inquiry, for it is within the environment that we survive from day to day and hope to enhance the quality of life.

Let us explore some findings of environmental psychology concerning the effects of noise, heat, air pollution, and crowding.

Decibel A unit expressing the loudness of a sound. Abbreviated *dB*. See Chapter 3.

NOISE: OF ROCK 'N' ROLL, TRAFFIC, AND LOW-FLYING AIRCRAFT

Noise, especially loud noise, can be aversive. How do you react when chalk is scraped on the blackboard or when an airplane screeches low overhead?

The unit for expressing the loudness of noise is the **decibel** (dB). The hearing threshold is defined as zero dB. Your school library is probably about 30–40 dB. A freeway is about 70 dB. One hundred forty dB is painfully loud, and 150 dB can rupture your eardrums. After eight hours of exposure to 110–120 dB your hearing may be damaged (rock groups play at 110–120 dB). High noise levels lead to increases in blood pressure, neurological and intestinal disorders (National Academy of Sciences, 1981), ulcers (Colligan & Murphy, 1982), and other stress-related illnesses.

Children who are exposed to greater traffic noise on the lower floors of apartment complexes (Cohen et al., 1973), or to loud noise from low-flying airplanes in their schools (Cohen et al., 1980), show signs of stress, hearing loss, and impairments in learning and memory. Time to adjust and subsequent noise abatement do not seem to reverse their cognitive and perceptual deficits (Cohen et al., 1981).

Couples may enjoy high noise levels at the disco, but less desirable noises of 80 dB seem to decrease feelings of attraction, causing couples to space themselves farther apart. Loud noise also puts a damper on helping behavior. People are less likely to help pick up a dropped package when the background noise of a construction crew is at 92 dB than when it's at 72 dB (Page, 1977). They're even less willing to make change for a quarter.

If you and your date have had a fight and are then exposed to a sudden blowout, look out. Angered people are more likely to behave aggressively when exposed to a sudden noise of 95 dB than one of 55 dB (Donnerstein & Wilson, 1976).

EXTREMES OF TEMPERATURE

When a car's engine is too hot, there may be great demands on the circulatory system, causing the water to overheat and the radiator to pop its cap. Extremes of heat can also make excessive demands on our bodies' circulatory systems, leading to conditions such as dehydration, heat exhaustion, heat stroke, and, in severe enough cases, a heart attack.

When it is too cold, the body responds by attempting to generate and retain heat. The metabolism increases; we shiver; and blood vessels in the skin constrict, decreasing flow of blood to the periphery of the body, where its warmth can be transmitted more easily to the outside.

Despite their obvious differences, both hot and cold temperatures are aversive events with some similar consequences, the first of which is increased arousal. Beyond this, it is difficult to generalize (Bell, 1982). How-

AT THE DISCO Couples may enjoy high noise levels (up to 140 dB) at the disco, but less desirable noises of only 80 dB can decrease feelings of attraction, put a damper on helping behavior, and even help prompt aggressive behavior.

ever, a number of studies suggest that moderate shifts in temperature may facilitate learning and behavior, increase feelings of attraction, and have generally positive effects. But when temperatures become extreme, performance and activity levels tend to deteriorate.

The "Long, Hot Summer Effect"   Campus and city riots broke out with regularity during the broiling summers of the 1960s (Figure 14.6). Each spring, news commentators wondered whether we would be in for another "long, hot summer." Yet it can also be too hot for a riot. The United States Riot Commission (1968) found that riots occurred only rarely in temperatures exceeding 100° F.

AIR POLLUTION: FUSSING AND FUMING

Auto fumes, industrial smog, cigarette smoke, fireplaces, burning leaves— these are a handful of the sources of air pollution that affect us. The lead in auto fumes may impair children's intellectual functioning in the same way chewing lead paint does (Fogel, 1980). Carbon monoxide, a colorless, odorless gas found in cigarette smoke and auto fumes, decreases the capacity of the blood to carry oxygen (see Chapter 4). Carbon monoxide impairs learning ability and perception of the passage of time (Beard & Wertheim, 1967). It may also contribute to highway accidents.

BASKING Research suggests that people are more cooperative and generous when the sun is shining. When the skies are grim, people are more likely to be grim also.

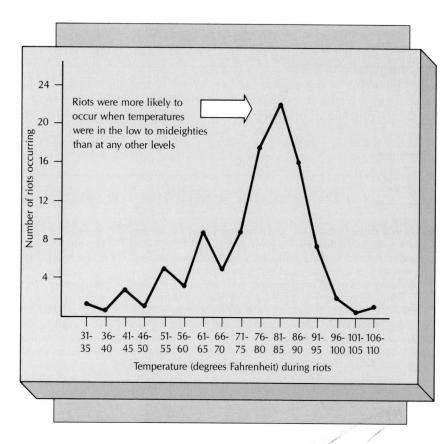

FIGURE 14.6 **THE "LONG, HOT SUMMER EFFECT"** Most riots of the 1960s occurred when temperatures were in the uncomfortable mid-80s. There was a rapid decrease in the incidence of rioting as temperatures increased further. When the heat is really on, perhaps people "cool it" by themselves.

Air pollution can kill more directly. In December, 1952, stagnation of industrial smog over London was linked to 3,500 deaths, with sulfur dioxide considered the specific culprit (Goldsmith, 1968). Los Angeles residents are accustomed to warnings to remain indoors or to be inactive in order to reduce air consumption when atmospheric inversions allow smog to accumulate for several days near ground level.

There is mounting evidence that odorous air pollutants, like other forms of aversive stimulation, decrease feelings of attraction and heighten aggression (Fisher et al., 1984). In people sensitive to it, even the atmospheric electricity that accompanies changing weather patterns can lead to tension, irritability, and crimes of violence (Baron et al., 1985; Charry & Hawkinshire, 1981; Rotton & Frey, 1985).

Mortality Death, especially on a large scale, as from disease or war. (From the Latin *mortis*, meaning "death.")

CROWDING AND PERSONAL SPACE

Sometimes you do everything you can for rats. You give them all they can eat, sex partners, a comfortable temperature, and protection from predators like owls and pussycats. And how do they reward you? By acting like, well, rats.

Calhoun's "Rat Universe"   John Calhoun (1962) allowed rats to reproduce with no constraints but for the limited space of their laboratory environment (Figure 14.7). At first all was bliss in rat city. The males scurried about, gathered females into harems, and defended territories. They did not covet their neighbors' wives. They rarely fought. The females, unliberated, built nests and nursed their young. They resisted the occasional advance of the passing male.

But unrestricted population growth proved to be the snake in rat paradise. Beyond a critical population, the **mortality** rate rose. Family structure broke down, packs of delinquent males assaulted inadequately defended

A CLOSER LOOK

"HERE COMES THE SUN": A TIME FOR FAVORS AND BIG TIPS?

Do our dispositions vary with the sunshine? Do we become bright and open, or grim and cloudy, as do the skies? Recent research suggests that we may indeed become more cooperative and generous when the sun shines down upon us (Cunningham, 1979).

Student passers-by at the University of Minnesota were more likely to agree to fill out a lengthy public-opinion poll when the sun was shining than on cloudy days of equal temperature. Temperature, wind velocity, and humidity also played roles. Helping behavior peaked when the temperature was an ideal 65° F and dropped off when the thermometer moved up or down. Wind velocity was positively linked to helping in the summer, when cooling breezes are favored, but nega-

tively linked in winter, when the wind-chill factor chilled the hearts of passers-by. Students were more helpful when the humidity was low.

Sunshine streaming in through restaurant windows apparently warms customers' hearts as measured by the size of tips. Waitresses at a Chicago restaurant with large windows tracked their tips for several weeks. The temperature and humidity in the restaurant were kept constant throughout the period. But when the sun shone, it shone into the restaurant as well, and tips were significantly larger.

If misfortune should befall us, so that we are in need of help, let us hope that the sun is shining, the temperature is 65° F, and the humidity is low.

FIGURE 14.7 **THE "RAT UNIVERSE"** In Calhoun's "rat universe," an unlimited food supply and easy access between compartments (with the exception of compartments 1 and 4, between which there was no direct access) caused compartments 2 and 3 to become a "behavioral sink." The "sink" was characterized by overpopulation, breakdown of the social order, and a higher mortality rate. Do some human cities function as behavioral sinks?

females. Some males shunned all social contact. Some females avoided sexual advances and huddled with fearsome males. Upon dissection, many rats showed bodily signs of stress—unhealthy changes in organs and gland malfunctions.

High Density Among People People are also influenced by crowding. You may have been shoehorned with several roommates into a dorm room intended for two. Under such crowded conditions, students are more likely to withdraw from social interaction, when possible (Paulus, 1979); they are also less satisfied with their roommates and rate them as less cooperative (Baron et al., 1976). Crowded prison inmates show higher blood pressure, more mental disorders, and a higher mortality rate than uncrowded prisoners (Fisher et al., 1984).

There is also a "tripling effect." When three students live together, a coalition frequently forms between two of them, so that the third feels isolated. The isolate finds the crowding more aversive than his or her room-mates do (Aiello et al., 1981; Reddy et al., 1982). Findings such as these suggest that with humans it is not crowding per se that is so aversive. Instead, it may be the sense that one does not have *control* over the situation.

Many examples from everyday life suggest that a sense of control over the situation—of choice—is an aid to adjustment. When we are at a concert, a disco, or a sports event, we may encounter greater crowding than we do in those frustrating registration lines. But we may be having a wonderful time. Why? We have *chosen* to be at the concert and are focusing on our good time (unless a tall or noisy person sits in front of us). We feel in control.

Another example: Women seem to find such crowding less aversive than men do. This may be because women feel freer to express their dis-comfort (Karlin et al., 1976). Men who conform to the rugged, independent masculine stereotype tend to keep a "stiff upper lip." Women may thus form a supportive social network under the same circumstances in which men remain isolated.

Architecture, too, can do much to eliminate the feelings of stress that often attend crowding. Students in suite arrangements, who share a com-mon gathering place and bathroom, find their roommates more cooperative and encounter less stress than do students who live along a lengthy central hall (Baum & Davis, 1980). The suite arrangement allows them to exercise more control over their social contacts.

Some Effects of City Life   As compared with suburbanites and rural folk, people who live in the big city encounter greater stimulus overload and fear of crime. Overwhelming crowd stimulation, bright lights, shop windows, and so on cause them to narrow their perceptions to a particular face, destination, or job.

City dwellers are less willing to shake hands with (Milgram, 1977), make eye contact with (Newman & McCauley, 1977), or help strangers (Glass & Singer, 1972; Milgram, 1970). People who move to the city from more rural areas adjust by becoming more deliberate in their daily activities (Franck et al., 1974). They plan ahead to take safety precautions, and they increase their alertness to potential dangers.

Farming, anyone?

Personal Space: "Don't Burst My Bubble, Please"   One aversive effect of crowding is the invasion of **personal space**. Personal space is an invisible boundary, something like a bubble, that surrounds you. You are likely to become anxious and, perhaps, angry when others invade your space, as in sitting down across from or next to you in an otherwise empty cafeteria, or standing too close in an elevator.

Personal space appears to serve protective and communicative func-tions. Violent people are likely to expect violent reactions from others, and violent prisoners require three times the personal space sought by nonvi-olent prisoners (Kinzel, 1970). Anxious people position themselves farther from others than do nonanxious people (Karabenick & Meisels, 1972). We need more personal space when we are in small rooms with others (White,

Personal space A psychological boundary that surrounds a person and permits that person to maintain a protective distance from others.

1975) or indoors rather than outdoors (Pempus et al., 1975). We apparently seek a safe distance from others when escape or exit could be a problem. Persons with an internal locus of control (see Chapter 10) require less personal space than externals (Duke & Nowicki, 1972). Perhaps they feel more competent to handle potential threats.

As a form of communication, the distance between people limits the possible interactions (Hall, 1968). Up to one and a half feet permits an intimate relationship in which touch is important, as in lovemaking, comforting, and contact sports like wrestling. Close friends and everyday acquaintances tend to remain from one and a half to four feet apart. Impersonal business contacts remain four to twelve feet apart, and formal contacts, as between performer and audience or lawyer and judge, remain at least twelve feet apart.

People sit and stand closer to people of the same race, similar age, or similar socioeconomic status. Dating couples come closer together as the attraction between them increases. As noted in Chapter 13, men are made more uncomfortable by strangers who sit across from them, while women feel more "invaded" by strangers who sit next to them. In libraries men tend to pile books protectively in front of them, while women strategically place books and coats to discourage others from taking adjacent seats (Fisher et al., 1984). Consider the possibilities for miscommunicating your intentions to the opposite sex. A man might seat himself next to a woman rather than across from her in order to avoid threatening her. Yet she might find his behavior forward and offensive.

Perhaps such communications problems have a bright side. They help keep a number of psychologists in business.

"Space Invaders" and Arousal, OR Psychology Goes to the John   *Up periscope!* was the thrilling cry of submarine warfare during World War II. These cigar-shaped vessels poked their periscopes above the water to search for prey without alerting their victims.

Recently a periscope was used in a less dramatic but more unusual theater of action: a men's room (Figure 14.8). Psychologists (Middlemist et al., 1976) were pioneering an ingenious method for seeing whether personal space invasions lead to stress, as reflected by higher levels of arousal. High arousal, you see, interferes with urinating. When people are aroused, it takes them longer to begin to urinate (there is "delay of onset"), and the duration of urinating is shorter.

The men's room had three urinals and a toilet stall. When a male subject was about to urinate in the urinal next to the stall, his personal space was invaded by another male who was a confederate of the experimenter. The "space invader" would use either the urinal adjacent to his or the one at the far end of the row. While this drama was taking place, an unseen experimenter in the innocent-looking stall used a periscope to observe time of onset and duration of urination. Sure enough, close encounters led to increased delay of onset and shorter duration of urination—the target signs of heightened arousal (Figure 14.9).

This experiment received some acid commentary from other psychologists. Gerald Koocher (1977), for one, complained that it invaded the

FIGURE 14.8 **RESEARCH ON "SPACE INVADERS" IN A CAMPUS RESTROOM** A periscope is quite obvious in the photo at the left. But in the experiment by Middlemist and his colleagues, the periscope was hidden from view by the wall of a stall, enabling the researchers to observe subjects' bathroom behavior surreptitiously.

privacy as well as the space of the subjects. The subjects might also have suffered psychological damage if they had known they were being observed. Middlemist and his colleagues (1977) replied that men in a pilot study reported no concern when they were told that they had been secretly observed while urinating.

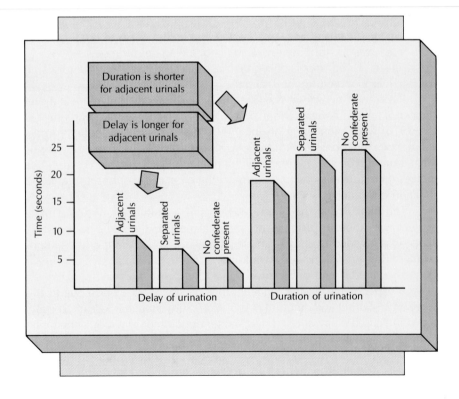

FIGURE 14.9 **EFFECTS OF THE REST-ROOM "SPACE INVADERS"** The graph shows that men whose personal space was invaded by a person using the adjacent urinal showed (1) delay of onset and (2) shorter duration of urination. Both effects are interpreted as signs of stress.

It is hard to determine whether some experiments are ethically justified. Some experiments can be run only by secretly observing or deceiving subjects. In each case we must weigh the value of the potential knowledge to be gained against the possible negative consequences to the people involved.

In any case, I'm sure that the restroom down the hall from you is free from experimenters.

SUMMARY

1. Social psychologists study the factors that influence our thoughts, feelings, and behaviors in social situations.

2. Attitudes are enduring systems of beliefs with cognitive, emotional, and behavioral components. People frequently, but not always, behave in ways that are consistent with their attitudes.

3. Attitudes may be acquired through conditioning, observational learning, and cognitive appraisal.

4. Persuading people to change attitudes can take place through central and peripheral routes. The central route views change as occurring through consideration of arguments and evidence. Peripheral routes involve association of the objects of attitudes with positive or negative cues, such as attractive communicators.

5. Repeated messages generally "sell" better than messages delivered once. People tend to show greater response to emotional appeals than to purely factual presentations, especially when emotional appeals offer concrete advice for avoiding negative consequences. Persuasive communicators tend to show expertise, trustworthiness, attractiveness, or similarity to the audience. People who are easily persuaded frequently show low self-esteem and high social anxiety.

6. According to the foot-in-the-door effect, people are more likely to accede to large requests after they have acceded to smaller requests.

7. According to balance theory, we are motivated to maintain harmony among our perceptions, beliefs, and attitudes. When people we care about express attitudes that differ from ours, we are in a state of imbalance, and we are motivated to try to restore the balance.

8. According to cognitive-dissonance theory, which is similar to balance theory, people dislike inconsistency between their attitudes and their behavior. Attitude-discrepant behavior apparently induces cognitive dissonance, which people can then reduce by

changing their attitudes. People also engage in effort justification; that is, they tend to justify attitude-discrepant behavior to themselves by concluding that their attitudes might differ from what they thought they were.

9. The case of Patty Hearst may illustrate cognitive-dissonance theory. Patty was a conservative college student who was forced into attitude-discrepant behavior by a radical group who kidnapped her and threatened her life. Patty's attitudes appear to have become radicalized while she was under the influence of the group.

10. Prejudice is an attitude toward a group that includes negative evaluations, negative affect, and avoidance behavior or discrimination. Sources of prejudice include attitudinal dissimilarity (or the assumption that members of outgroups hold different attitudes), social conflict, social learning, authoritarianism, and the tendency to divide the social world into two categories: "us" and "them."

11. The psychology of social perception concerns our perception of others. We often perceive others in terms of first impressions (primacy effect), although recent impressions (recency effect) can become important when time passes between observations.

12. Our inference of the motives and traits of others through the observation of their behavior is called the attribution process. In dispositional attributions, we attribute people's behavior to internal factors, such as their personality traits and decisions. In situational attributions, we attribute people's behavior to their circumstances or external forces.

13. According to the actor-observer effect in attribution theory, we tend to attribute the behavior of others to internal, dispositional factors, while we tend to attribute our own behavior to external, situational factors. The so-called fundamental attribution error is the tendency to attribute too much of other people's behavior to dispositional factors.

14. Our attribution of behavior to internal or external causes is also influenced by the behavior's consensus, consistency, and distinctiveness. We are likely to attribute behavior to internal factors when it is low in consensus (few people act that way), high in consistency (the person behaves that way consistently), and low in distinctiveness (the person acts similarly in different situations).

15. At an early age we learn to "read" body language. People who feel positively toward one another position themselves close together and touch. Gazing into another's eyes can be a sign of love, but a "hard stare" is an aversive challenge.

16. In social psychology, attraction is an attitude of liking (positive attraction) or disliking (negative attraction). In our culture, slenderness is found attractive in both men and women, and tallness is valued in men.

17. We are more attracted to good-looking people, and we tend to assume that attractive people are more likely to be talented and less likely to engage in criminal behavior. According to the matching hypothesis, we tend to seek dates and mates at our own level of attractiveness, largely because of fear of rejection. Attitudinal similarity, propinquity, reciprocity, parental opposition, and playing hard to get can all enhance feelings of attraction.

18. Social influence is the area of social psychology that studies the ways in which people alter the thoughts, feelings, and behavior of others. Areas within the study of social influence include obedience and conformity. Most people comply with the demands of authority figures, even when these demands seem immoral, as shown in the Milgram studies on obedience.

19. People experience increasing pressure to conform to group norms and opinions as groups grow to eight persons. The presence of a person who shares one's minority view and familiarity with the task at hand decrease conforming behavior.

20. Social facilitation refers to the effects on performance that result from the presence of others. The presence of others may facilitate performance for reasons such as increased arousal and evaluation apprehension. However, when we are anonymous group members, task performance may fall off; this phenomenon is referred to as social loafing.

21. Group decisions tend to be more polarized and risky than individual decisions, largely because groups diffuse responsibility. Group decisions may be highly productive when group members are knowledgeable, there is an explicit procedure for arriving at decisions, and there is a process of give and take.

22. Highly emotional crowds may induce attitude-discrepant behavior through the process of deindividuation, which is a state of reduced self-awareness and lowered concern for social evaluation.

23. According to the bystander effect, people are unlikely to aid others in distress when they are members of crowds. Crowds tend to diffuse responsibility. We are more likely to help people in need when we think we are the only one available, when we have a clear view of the situation, and when we are not afraid that we shall be committing a social blunder.

24. Environmental psychologists study the ways in which people and the physical environment influence one another. For example, high noise levels can lead to stress and to cognitive and perceptual deficits.

25. Hot and cold temperatures are aversive events that both increase arousal. While moderate shifts in temperature may facilitate learning and behavior, performance deteriorates under extremes of temperature.

26. Air pollution can be physically harmful, foster aggression, and decrease feelings of attraction.

27. Crowding is stressful and leads people to rate others as less cooperative. We seek a certain amount of personal space, which seems to serve both protective and communicative functions. Invasions of our personal space can lead to anxiety and irritation.

TRUTH OR FICTION REVISITED

Admitting your product's weak points in an ad is the death knell for sales.

False. Admitting weaknesses while also stressing strengths can build credibility.

Most of us are swayed by ads that offer useful information, not by emotional appeals or celebrity endorsements.

False. Emotional appeals are more effective than information presented matter-of-factly, and the appeal of the endorser often seems to rub off on the product.

People who are worried about what other people think of them are likely to be low in sales resistance.

True. Focusing on the feelings of salespersons rather than on whether or not one needs a product makes it more difficult to refuse.

We appreciate things more when we have to work hard for them.

True. According to the principle of effort justification, we would be seeking reasons to justify our labors, and these reasons would probably have something to do with the value of the goal.

We tend to divide the social world into "us" and "them."

True. This tendency is one of the roots of prejudice.

First impressions have powerful effects on our social relationships.

True. We tend to interpret subsequent behavior in terms of our first impressions.

We hold others responsible for their misdeeds, but tend to see ourselves as victims of circumstances when our behavior falls short of our standards.

True. This bias is the kernel of the fundamental attribution error—the tendency to underestimate the importance of the situation in making attributions of the behaviors of others.

Beauty is in the eye of the beholder.

False. There are some rather consistent cultural standards for beauty.

Physical attractiveness is the most important trait we seek in our partners for long-term, meaningful relationships.

False. Personal qualities take on relatively more importance when we are contemplating long-term relationships, and the single most important personal quality we look for is honesty.

Opposites attract: We are more likely to be drawn to people who disagree with our attitudes than to people who share them.

False. Physical attraction and attitudinal similarity are the two most powerful contributors to the development of relationships.

Most people would refuse to deliver painful electric shock to an innocent party, even under powerful social pressure.

False. The great majority complied with an authority figure in the Milgram studies.

Bicycle riders and runners tend to move more rapidly in competition than when they are practicing alone.

True. This is an example of social facilitation.

Nearly forty people stood by and did nothing while a woman was being stabbed to death.

True. We are more likely to help others when we believe we are the only ones available to do so.

High noise levels can raise our blood pressure.

True. Loud noises are stressful aversive stimuli.

Auto fumes may lower your children's IQ.

True. Auto fumes contain lead, carbon monoxide, and other pollutants, a number of which have been shown to impair learning and memory.

APPENDIX A:
Statistics

Imagine that some visitors from outer space arrive outside Madison Square Garden in New York City. Their goal this dark and numbing winter evening is to learn all they can about the inhabitants of planet Earth. They are drawn inside the Garden by lights, shouts, and warmth. The spotlighting inside rivets their attention to a wood-floored arena where the New York Apples are hosting the California Quakes in a briskly contested basketball game.

Our visitors use their sophisticated instruments to take some measurements of the players. Some surprising **statistics** are sent back to the planet of their origin: It appears that (1) 100 percent of Earthlings are male, and (2) the height of Earthlings ranges from six feet one inch to seven feet two inches.

Statistics is the name given the science concerned with obtaining and organizing numerical measurements or information. Our imagined visitors have sent home some statistics about the sex and size of human beings that are at once accurate and misleading. They accurately measured the basketball players, but their small **sample** of Earth's **population** was quite distorted. Fortunately for us Earthlings, about half of us are female. And the **range** of heights observed by the aliens, of six feet one to seven feet two, is both restricted and too high. People vary in height by more than one foot and one inch. And our **average** height is not between six one and seven two but several inches below.

Psychologists, like our imagined visitors, are vitally concerned with measuring human as well as animal characteristics and traits—not just physical characteristics like sex and height, but also psychological traits like intelligence, aggressiveness, anxiety, or self-assertiveness. By observing the central tendencies (averages) and variations in measurements from person to person, psychologists can state that some person is average or above average in intelligence, or that another person is less assertive than, say, 60 percent of the population.

Statistics Numerical facts assembled in such a manner that they provide significant information about measures or scores. (From the Latin word *status*, meaning "standing" or "position.")

Sample Part of a population.

Population A complete group from which a sample is selected.

Range A measure of variability; the distance between extreme measures or scores.

Average Central tendency of a group of measures, expressed as means, median, and mode.

Descriptive statistics The branch of statistics that is concerned with providing information about a distribution of scores.

Frequency distribution An ordered set of data that indicates how frequently scores appear.

But psychologists, unlike our aliens, are careful in their attempts to select a sample that accurately represents the entire population. Professional basketball players do not represent the human species. They are taller, stronger, and more agile than the rest of us, and they make more shaving-cream commercials.

In this appendix we shall survey some of the statistical methods used by psychologists to draw conclusions about the measurements they take in research activities. First we shall discuss *descriptive statistics* and learn what types of statements we can make about the height of basketball players and some other human traits. Then we shall discuss the *normal curve* and learn why basketball players are abnormal—at least in terms of height. We shall explore *correlation coefficients* and provide you with some less-than-shocking news: More intelligent people attain higher grades than less intelligent people. Finally, we shall have a brief look at *inferential statistics* and see why we can be bold enough to say that the difference in height between basketball players and other people is not just a chance accident, or fluke. Basketball players are in fact *statistically significantly* taller than the general population.

DESCRIPTIVE STATISTICS

Being told that someone is a "ten" is not very descriptive unless you know something about how possible scores are distributed and how frequently one finds a ten. Fortunately—for tens, if not for the rest of us—one is usually informed that someone is a ten on a scale of one to ten, and that ten is the positive end of the scale. If this is not sufficient, one will also be told that tens are few and far between—rather unusual statistical events.

This business of a scale from one to ten is not very scientific, to be sure, but it does suggest something about **descriptive statistics.** We can use descriptive statistics to clarify our understanding of a distribution of scores, such as heights, test grades, IQs, or increases or decreases in measures of sexual arousal following drinking of alcohol. For example, descriptive statistics can help us to determine measures of central tendency, or averages, and to determine how much variability there is in the scores. Being a ten loses some of its charm if the average score is an eleven. Being a ten is more remarkable in a distribution whose scores range from one to ten than in one that ranges from nine to ten.

Let us now examine some of the concerns of descriptive statistics: the *frequency distribution, measures of central tendency* (types of averages), and *measures of variability.*

THE FREQUENCY DISTRIBUTION

A **frequency distribution** takes scores, or items of raw data, puts them into order, as from lowest to highest, and groups them according to class intervals. Table A.1 shows the rosters for a recent California Quakes–New York Apples basketball game. The members of each team are listed according to

TABLE A.1 Rosters of Quakes vs. Apples at New York

California		New York	
2 Callahan	6'-7"	3 Roosevelt	6'-1"
5 Daly	6'-11"	12 Chaffee	6'-5"
6 Chico	6'-2"	13 Baldwin	6'-9"
12 Capistrano	6'-3"	25 Delmar	6'-6"
21 Brentwood	6'-5"	27 Merrick	6'-8"
25 Van Nuys	6'-3"	28 Hewlett	6'-6"
31 Clemente	6'-9"	33 Hollis	6'-9"
32 Whittier	6'-8"	42 Bedford	6'-5"
41 Fernando	7'-2"	43 Coram	6'-2"
43 Watts	6'-9"	45 Hampton	6'-10"
53 Huntington	6'-6"	53 Ardsley	6'-10"

A glance at the rosters for a recent California Quakes–New York Apples basketball game shows you that the heights of the teams, combined, ranged from 6 feet one inch to seven feet two inches. Are the heights of the team members representative of those of the general male population?

the numbers of their uniforms. Table A.2 shows a frequency distribution of the heights of the players of both teams combined, with a class interval of one inch.

It would also be possible to use three-inch class intervals, as in Table A.3. In determining how large a class interval should be, a researcher attempts to collapse that data into a small enough number of classes to ensure that they will appear meaningful at a glance, but attempts also to maintain a large enough number of categories to ensure that important differences are not obscured.

Table A.3 obscures the fact that no players are six feet four inches tall. If the researcher feels that this information is extremely important, a class interval of one inch may be maintained.

TABLE A.2 Frequency Distribution of Heights of Basketball Players, with a One-inch Class Interval

Class Interval	Number of Players in Class
6-1 to 6-1.9	1
6-2 to 6-2.9	2
6-3 to 6-3.9	2
6-4 to 6-4.9	0
6-5 to 6-5.9	3
6-6 to 6-6.9	3
6-7 to 6-7.9	1
6-8 to 6-8.9	2
6-9 to 6-9.9	4
6-10 to 6-10.9	2
6-11 to 6-11.9	1
7-0 to 7-0.9	0
7-1 to 7-1.9	0
7-2 to 7-2.9	1

TABLE A.3 Frequency Distribution of Heights of Basketball Players, with a Three-inch Class Interval

Class Interval	Number of Players in Class
6-1 to 6-3.9	5
6-4 to 6-6.9	6
6-7 to 6-9.9	7
6-10 to 7-0.9	3
7-1 to 7-3.9	1

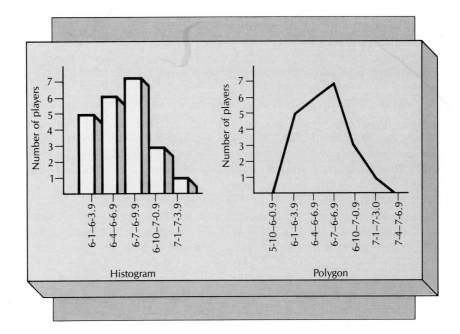

Histogram

Polygon

Figure A.1 shows two methods for representing the information in Table A.3 with graphs. Both in frequency **histograms** and frequency **polygons** the class intervals are typically drawn along the horizontal line, or X-axis, and the number of scores (persons, cases, or events) in each class is drawn along the vertical or Y-axis. In a histogram the number of scores in each class interval is represented by a rectangular solid, so that the graph resembles a series of steps. In a polygon the number of scores in each class interval is plotted as a point, and the points are then connected to form a many-sided geometric figure. Note that class intervals were added at both ends of the horizontal axis of the frequency polygon, so that the lines could be brought down to the axis to close the geometric figure.

MEASURES OF CENTRAL TENDENCY

There are three types of measures of central tendency, or averages: *mean, median,* and *mode.* Each tells us something about the way in which the scores in a distribution may be summarized by a typical or representative number.

The **mean** is what most people think of as "the average." The mean is obtained by adding up all the scores in a distribution and then dividing this sum by the number of scores. In the case of our basketball players it would be advisable first to convert all heights into one unit, such as inches (6'1" becomes 73", and so on). If we add all the heights in inches, then divide by the number of players, or 22, we obtain a mean height of 78.73", or 6'6.73".

The **median** is the score of the middle case in a frequency distribution. It is the score beneath which 50 percent of the cases fall. In a distribution

Histogram A graphic representation of a frequency distribution that uses rectangular solids. (From the Greek *historia,* meaning "narrative," and *gramma,* meaning "writing" or "drawing.")

Polygon A closed figure. (From the Greek *polys,* meaning "many," and *gōnia,* meaning "angle.")

Mean A type of average calculated by dividing the sum of scores by the number of scores. (From the Latin *medius,* meaning "middle.")

Median The score beneath which 50 percent of the cases fall. (From the Latin *medius,* meaning "middle.")

with an even number of cases, such as the distribution of the heights of the twenty-two basketball players in Table A.2, the median is determined by finding the mean of the two middle cases. Listing these twenty-two cases in ascending order, we find that the eleventh case is 6'6" and the twelfth case is 6'7". Thus the median is (6'6" + 6'7")/2, or 6'6½".

In the case of the heights of the basketball players, the mean and the median are similar, and either serves as a useful indicator of the central tendency of the data. But suppose we are attempting to determine the average savings of thirty families living on a suburban block. Let us assume that twenty-nine of the thirty families have savings between $8,000 and $12,000 adding up to $294,000. But the thirtieth family has savings of $1,400,000! The mean savings for a family on this block would thus be $56,467. A mean can be greatly distorted by one or two extreme scores, and for such distributions the median is a better indicator of the central tendency. The median savings on our hypothetical block would lie between $8,000 and $12,000, and so would be more representative of the central tendency of savings. Studies of the incomes of American families usually report median rather than mean incomes just to avoid the distortions that would result from treating incomes of the small numbers of multimillionaires in the same way as other incomes.

The **mode** is simply the most frequently occurring score in a distribution. The mode of the data in Table A.1 is 6'9" because this height occurs most often. The median class interval for the data in Table A.3 is 6'6½" to 6'9½". In these cases the mode is somewhat higher than the mean or median height.

In some cases the mode is a more appropriate description of a distribution than the mean or median. Figure A.2 shows a **bimodal** distribution, or a distribution with two modes. In this hypothetical distribution of the test scores the mode at the left indicates the most common class interval for students who did not study, and the mode at the right indicates the most frequent class interval for students who did. The mean and median test scores would probably lie within the 55-59 class interval, yet use of that interval as a measure of central tendency would not provide very meaning-

Mode The most frequently occurring number or score in a distribution. (From the Latin *modus,* meaning "measure.")

Bimodal Having two modes.

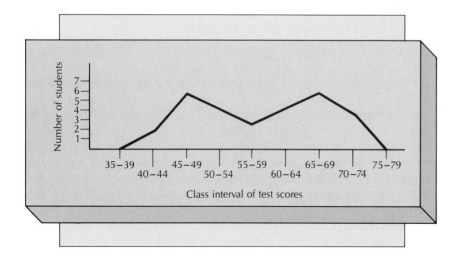

Class interval of test scores

FIGURE A.2 A BIMODAL DISTRIBUTION This hypothetical distribution represents the scores of students on a test. The mode at the left represents the central tendency of students who did not study, and the mode at the right represents the mode of students who studied.

Range The difference between the highest and the lowest scores in a distribution.

ful information about the distribution of scores. It might suggest that the test was too hard—not that a number of students chose not to study. One would be better able to visualize the distribution of scores if it is reported as bimodal. Even in similar cases in which the modes are not exactly equal, it might be more appropriate to describe a distribution as being bimodal or even multimodal.

MEASURES OF VARIABILITY

Measures of variability of a distribution inform us about the spread of scores, or about the typical distances of scores from the average score. Measures of variability include the *range* of scores and the *standard deviation*.

The **range** of scores in a distribution is defined as the difference between the highest score and the lowest score, and it is obtained by subtracting the lowest score from the highest score. The range of heights in Table A.2 is 7'2" minus 6'1", or 1'1". It is important to know the range of temperatures if we move to a new climate so that we may anticipate the weather and dress appropriately. A teacher must have some understanding of the range of abilities or skills in a class in order to teach effectively. Classes of gifted students or slow learners are formed so that teachers may attempt to devise a level of instruction that will better meet the needs of all members of a particular class.

The range is an imperfect measure of variability because of the manner in which it is influenced by extreme scores. In our earlier discussion of the savings of thirty families on a suburban block, the range of savings is $1,400,000 to $8,000, or $1,392,000. This tells us little about the typical variability of savings accounts, which lie within a restricted range of $8,000 to $12,000. The standard deviation is a statistic that indicates how scores are distributed about a mean of a distribution.

The standard deviation considers every score in a distribution, not just the extreme scores. Thus the standard deviation for the distribution on the right in Figure A.3 would be smaller than that of the distribution on the left.

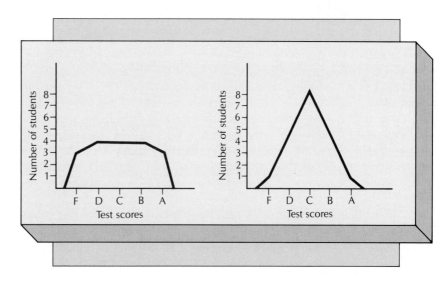

FIGURE A.3 HYPOTHETICAL DISTRIBUTIONS OF STUDENT TEST SCORES Each distribution has the same number of scores, the same mean, and even the same range, but the standard deviation is greater for the distribution on the left because the scores tend to be farther from the mean.

TABLE A.4   Hypothetical Scores Attained from an IQ Testing

IQ Score	d (Deviation Score)	d^2 (Deviation Score Squared)
85	15	225
87	13	169
89	11	121
90	10	100
93	7	49
97	3	9
97	3	9
100	0	0
101	− 1	1
104	− 4	16
105	− 5	25
110	− 10	100
112	− 12	144
113	− 13	169
117	− 17	289

Sum of IQ scores = 1500   Sum of d^2 scores = 1426

$$\text{Mean} = \frac{\text{Sum of scores}}{\text{Number of scores}} = \frac{1500}{15} = 100$$

$$\text{Standard Deviation (S.D.)} = \sqrt{\frac{\text{Sum of } d^2}{\text{Number of scores}}} = \sqrt{\frac{1426}{15}} = \sqrt{95.07} = 9.75$$

Note that each distribution has the same number of scores, the same mean, and the same range of scores. But the standard deviation for the distribution on the right will be smaller than that of the distribution on the left because the scores tend to cluster more closely about the mean.

The **standard deviation** (S.D.) is calculated by the following formula:

$$\text{S.D.} = \sqrt{\frac{\text{Sum of } d^2}{N}}$$

where d equals the deviation of each score from the mean of the distribution, and N equals the number of scores in the distribution.

Let us find the mean and standard deviation of the IQ scores listed in column 1 of Table A.4. To obtain the mean, we add all the scores, attain 1500, and then divide by the number of scores (15) to obtain a mean of 100. We obtain the deviation score (d) for each IQ score by subtracting the score from 100. The d for an IQ of 85 equals 100 minus 85, or 15, and so on. Then we square each d and add these squares. The S.D. equals the square root of the sum of squares (1426) divided by the number of scores (15), or 9.75.

As an additional exercise, we can show that the S.D. of the test scores on the left (in Figure A.3) is greater than that for the scores on the right by assigning the grades points according to a 4.0 system. Let A = 4, B = 3, C = 2, D = 1, and F = 0. The S.D. for each distribution of test scores is

Standard deviation A measure of the variability of a distribution, attained by the formula

$$\sqrt{\frac{\text{Sum of } d^2}{N}}$$

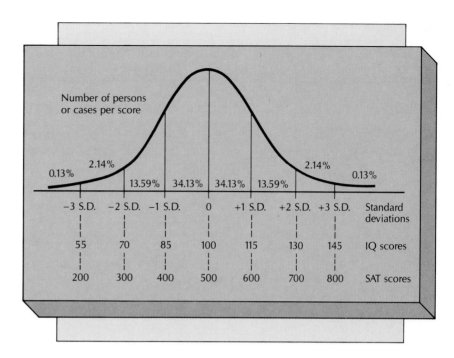

Number of persons
or cases per score

0.13% 2.14% 13.59% 34.13% 34.13% 13.59% 2.14% 0.13%

−3 S.D.	−2 S.D.	−1 S.D.	0	+1 S.D.	+2 S.D.	+3 S.D.	Standard deviations
55	70	85	100	115	130	145	IQ scores
200	300	400	500	600	700	800	SAT scores

FIGURE A.4 **A BELL-SHAPED OR NORMAL CURVE** In a normal curve approximately 68 percent of the cases lie within a standard deviation (S.D.) from the mean, and the mean, median, and mode all lie at the same score. IQ tests and scholastic aptitude tests have been constructed so that distributions of scores approximate the normal curve.

computed in Table A.5. The greater S.D. for the distribution on the left indicates that the scores in that distribution are more variable, or tend to be farther from the mean.

THE NORMAL CURVE

Many human traits and characteristics, such as height and intelligence, seem to be distributed in a pattern known as a normal distribution. In a **normal distribution** the mean, median, and mode all fall at the same data point or score, and scores cluster most heavily about the mean, fall off rapidly in either direction at first—as shown in Figure A.4—and then taper off more gradually.

The curve in Figure A.4 is bell-shaped. This type of distribution is also called a **normal curve.** It is hypothesized to reflect the distribution of variables in which different scores are determined by chance variation. Height is thought to be largely determined by chance combinations of genetic material. A distribution of the heights of a random sample of the population approximates normal distributions for men and women, with the mean of the distribution for men a few inches higher than the mean for women.

Test developers traditionally assumed that intelligence was also randomly or normally distributed among the population. For that reason they constructed intelligence tests so that scores would be distributed as close to "normal" as possible. In actuality, IQ scores are also influenced by environmental factors and chromosomal abnormalities, so the resultant curves are not perfectly normal. Most IQ tests have means defined as scores of

Normal distribution A symmetrical distribution in which approximately 68 percent of cases lie within a standard deviation of the mean.

Normal curve Graphic presentation of a normal distribution, showing a bell shape.

TABLE A.5 Computation of Standard Deviations for Test Score Distributions in Figure A.3

Distribution at Left:			Distribution at Right:		
Grade	d	d^2	Grade	d	d^2
A (4)	2	4	A (4)	2	4
A (4)	2	4	B (3)	1	1
A (4)	2	4	B (3)	1	1
B (3)	1	1	B (3)	1	1
B (3)	1	1	B (3)	1	1
B (3)	1	1	C (2)	0	0
B (3)	1	1	C (2)	0	0
C (2)	0	0	C (2)	0	0
C (2)	0	0	C (2)	0	0
C (2)	0	0	C (2)	0	0
C (2)	0	0	C (2)	0	0
D (1)	-1	1	C (2)	0	0
D (1)	-1	1	C (2)	0	0
D (1)	-1	1	D (1)	-1	1
D (1)	-1	1	D (1)	-1	1
F (0)	-2	4	D (1)	-1	1
F (0)	-2	4	D (1)	-1	1
F (0)	-2	4	F (0)	-2	4

Sum of grades = 36
Mean grade = 36/18 = 2
Sum of d^2 = 32

$$S.D. = \sqrt{\frac{32}{18}} = 1.33$$

Sum of grades = 36
Mean grade = 36/18 = 2
Sum of d^2 = 16

$$S.D. = \sqrt{\frac{16}{18}} = 0.94$$

100 points, and the Wechsler scales are constructed to have standard deviations of 15 points, as shown in Figure A.4. This means that 50 percent of the Wechsler scores fall between 90 and 110 (the "broad average" range), about 68 percent (or two of three) fall between 85 and 115, and more than 95 percent fall between 70 and 130—that is, within two S.D.'s of the mean. The Stanford-Binet Intelligence Scale has an S.D. of 16 points.

The Scholastic Aptitude Tests (SATs) were constructed so that the mean scores would be 500 points, and an S.D. would be 100 points. Thus a score of 600 would equal or excel that of some 84 to 85 percent of the test takers. Because of the complex interaction of variables determining SAT scores, the distribution of SAT scores is not exactly normal either. The normal curve is an idealized curve.

THE CORRELATION COEFFICIENT

What is the relationship between intelligence and educational achievement? Between cigarette smoking and lung cancer in human beings? Between introversion and frequency of dating among college students? We cannot run experiments to determine whether the relationships between these variables are causal, because we cannot manipulate the independent variable.

Correlation coefficient A number between −1.00 and +1.00 that indicates the degree of relationship between two variables.

Scatter diagram A graphic presentation showing the plotting of points defined by the intersections of two variables.

For example, we cannot randomly assign a group of people to cigarette smoking and another group to nonsmoking. People must be permitted to make their own choices, and so it is possible that the same factors that lead people to choose to smoke may also lead to lung cancer. However, the **correlation coefficient** may be used to show that there is a relationship between smoking and cancer. If a strong correlation is shown between the two variables, and we add supportive experimental evidence with laboratory animals who are assigned to conditions in which they inhale tobacco smoke, we wind up with a rather convincing indictment of smoking as a determinant of lung cancer.

The correlation coefficient is a statistic that describes the relationship between two variables. It varies from +1.00 to −1.00; therefore a correlation coefficient of +1.00 is called a perfect positive correlation, a coefficient of −1.00 is a perfect negative correlation, and a coefficient of 0.00 shows no correlation between variables. In order to examine the meanings of different correlation coefficients, let us first discuss the *scatter diagram*.

THE SCATTER DIAGRAM

A **scatter diagram,** or scatter plot, is a graphic representation of the relationship between two variables. As shown in Figure A.5, a scatter diagram is typically drawn with an *X* axis (horizontal) and *Y* axis (vertical).

Let us assume that we have two thermometers. One measures temperature according to the Fahrenheit scale and one measures temperature according to the centigrade scale. Over a period of several months we record the temperatures Fahrenheit and centigrade at various times of the day. Then we randomly select a sample of eight Fahrenheit readings and jot down the corresponding centigrade readings, as shown in Figure A.5.

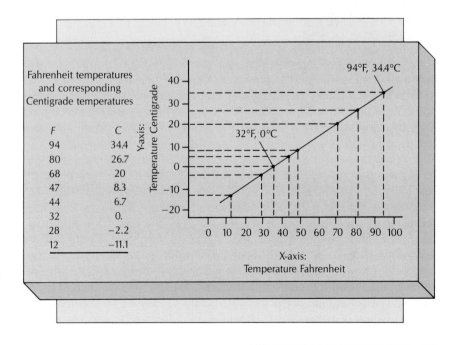

FIGURE A.5 A SCATTER DIAGRAM SHOWING THE PERFECT POSITIVE CORRELATION BETWEEN FAHRENHEIT TEMPERATURES AND THE CORRESPONDING CENTIGRADE TEMPERATURES Scatter diagrams have *X* and *Y* axes, and each point is plotted by finding the spot where an *X* value and the corresponding *Y* value meet.

Fahrenheit temperatures and corresponding Centigrade temperatures

F	C
94	34.4
80	26.7
68	20
47	8.3
44	6.7
32	0.
28	−2.2
12	−11.1

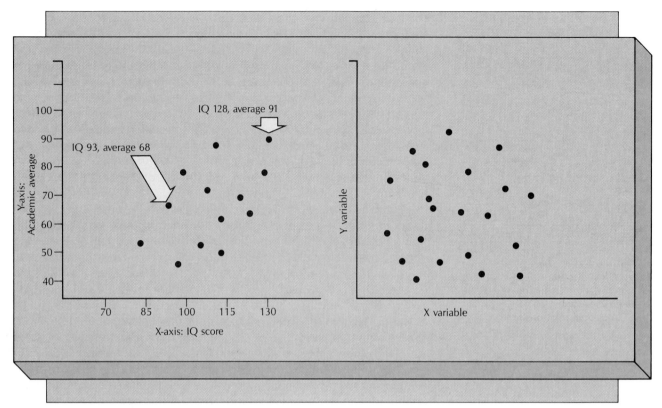

FIGURE A.6 A HYPOTHETICAL SCATTER DIAGRAM SHOWING THE RELATIONSHIP BETWEEN IQ SCORES AND ACADEMIC AVERAGES Such correlations usually fall between +0.60 and +0.70, which is considered an adequate indication of validity for intelligence tests, since such tests are intended to predict academic performance.

FIGURE A.7 A scatter diagram showing a correlation coefficient of 0.00 between the X and Y variables.

Figure A.5 shows a perfect positive correlation. One variable increases as the other increases, and the points on the scatter diagram may be joined to form a straight line. We usually do not find variables forming a perfect positive (or perfect negative) correlation, unless they are related according to a specific mathematical formula. The temperatures Fahrenheit and centigrade are so related (degrees Fahrenheit = 9/5 degrees centigrade + 32).

A positive correlation of about +0.80 to +0.90, or higher, between scores attained on separate testings is usually required to determine the **reliability** of psychological tests. Intelligence tests such as the Stanford-Binet Intelligence Scale and the Wechsler scales have been found to yield **test-retest reliabilities** that meet these requirements. Somewhat lower correlation coefficients are usually accepted as indicators that a psychological test is **valid,** when test scores are correlated with scores on an external criterion. Figure A.6 shows a hypothetical scatter diagram that demonstrates the relationship between IQ scores and academic averages for children in grade school. The correlation coefficient that would be derived by mathematical formula would be between +0.60 and +0.70. Remember that correlation

Reliability Consistency; see Chapter 6.

Test-retest reliability Consistency of a test as determined by a comparison of scores on repeated testings.

Validity The degree to which a test measures what it is supposed to measure; see Chapter 6.

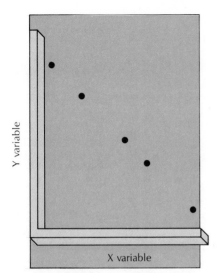

FIGURE A.8 A scatter diagram showing a correlation coefficient of −1.00 between the X and Y variables, or a perfect negative relationship.

does not show cause and effect. Figure A.6 suggests a relationship between the variables but cannot be taken as evidence that intelligence causes achievement.

Figure A.7 shows a scatter diagram in which there is a correlation coefficient of about 0.00 between the X and Y variables, suggesting that they are fully independent of each other. A person's scores on spelling quizzes taken in California ought to be independent of the daily temperatures in Bolivia. Thus we would expect a correlation coefficient of close to 0.00 between the variables.

Figure A.8 shows a scatter diagram in which there is a perfect negative correlation between two variables: As one variable increases, the other decreases systematically.

Correlations between 0.80 and 1.00 are considered very high (whether they are positive or negative). Correlations between 0.60 and 0.80 are high, between 0.40 and 0.60 moderate, from 0.20 to 0.40 weak, and between 0.00 and 0.20 very weak.

It cannot be overemphasized that correlation coefficients do not show cause and effect. For instance, a relationship between intelligence and academic performance could be explained by suggesting that the same cultural factors that lead some children to do well on intelligence tests also lead them to do well on academic tasks. According to this view, intelligence does not cause high academic performance. Instead, a third variable determines both intelligence and academic performance.

However, many psychologists undertake correlational research as a first step in attempting to determine causal relationships between variables. Correlation does not show cause and effect; but a lack of correlation between two variables suggests that it may be fruitless to undertake experimental research in order to determine whether they are causally related.

INFERENTIAL STATISTICS

In a study reported in Chapter 6 children enrolled in a Head Start program earned a mean IQ score of 99, whereas children similar in background who were not enrolled in Head Start earned a mean IQ score of 93. Is this difference of six points in IQ significant, or does it represent chance fluctuation of scores? In a study reported in Chapter 1, subjects who believed they had drunk alcohol chose higher levels of electric shock to be applied to persons who had provoked them than did subjects who believed they had not drunk alcohol. Did the difference in level of shock chosen reflect an actual difference between the two groups of subjects, or could it have been a chance fluctuation? Inferential statistics help us make decisions as to whether differences found between such groups reflect real differences or just fluctuations.

Figure A.9 shows the distribution of heights of a thousand men and a thousand women selected at random. The mean height for men is greater than the mean height for women. Can we draw the conclusion, or **infer,** that this difference in heights represents the general population of men and

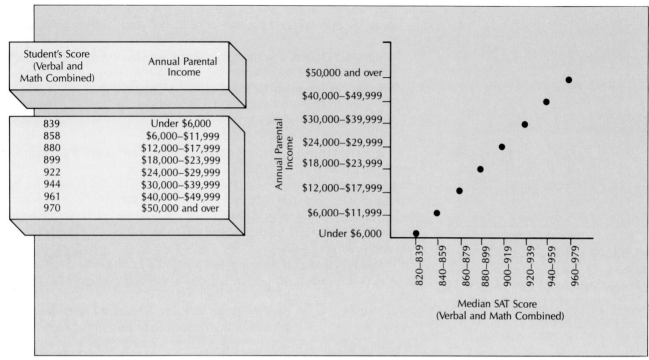

Student's Score (Verbal and Math Combined)	Annual Parental Income
839	Under $6,000
858	$6,000–$11,999
880	$12,000–$17,999
899	$18,000–$23,999
922	$24,000–$29,999
944	$30,000–$39,999
961	$40,000–$49,999
970	$50,000 and over

A scatter diagram showing the relationship between income of a student's family and the student's score on the Scholastic Aptitude Test (SAT) taken during 1980-1981. Scores are a combination of scores on the Verbal and Mathematics sub-tests, and may vary from 400-1600. Scores shown are for white students only. SAT scores predict performance in college. Note the strong positive correlation between SAT scores and parental income. Does the relationship show that a high-income family is better able to expose children to concepts and skills measured on the SAT? Or that families who transmit genetic influences that may contribute to high test performance also tend to earn high incomes? Correlation is *not* cause and effect. For this reason, the data cannot answer these questions.

women? Or must we avoid such an inference and summarize our results by stating only that the sample of a thousand men in the study had a higher mean height than that of the sample of a thousand women in the study?

If we could not draw inferences about populations from studies of samples, our research findings would be very limited indeed—limited only to the specific subjects studied. However, the branch of statistics known as **inferential statistics** uses mathematical techniques in such a way that we can make statements about populations from which samples have been drawn, with a certain level of confidence.

STATISTICALLY SIGNIFICANT DIFFERENCES

In determining whether differences in measures taken of research samples may be applied to the populations from which they were drawn, psychologists use mathematical techniques that indicate whether differences are

Inferential statistics The branch of statistics concerned with the confidence with which conclusions drawn about samples may be extended to the populations from which they were drawn.

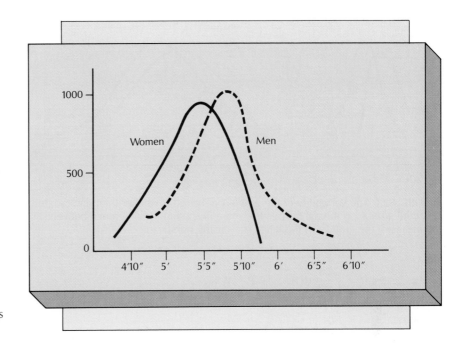

FIGURE A.9 **DISTRIBUTION OF HEIGHTS FOR RANDOM SAMPLES OF MEN AND WOMEN** Inferential statistics permit us to apply our findings to the populations sampled.

statistically significant. Was the difference in IQ scores for children attending and those not attending Head Start significant? Did it represent only the children participating in the study, or can it be applied to all children represented by the sample? Is the difference between the height of men and the height of women in Figure A.9 statistically significant? Can we apply our findings to all men and women?

Psychologists use formulas involving the means and standard deviations of sample groups in order to determine whether group differences are statistically significant. As you can see in Figure A.10, the farther apart the group means are, the more likely it is that the difference between them is statistically significant. This makes a good deal of common sense. After all, if you were told that your neighbor's car had gotten one-tenth of a mile more per gallon of gasoline than your car had last year, you might assume that this was a chance difference. But if the differences were farther apart, say fourteen miles per gallon, you might readily believe that this difference

FIGURE A.10 Psychologists use group means and standard deviations in order to determine whether the difference between group means is statistically significant. The difference between the means of the groups on the right is greater and thus more likely to be statistically significant.

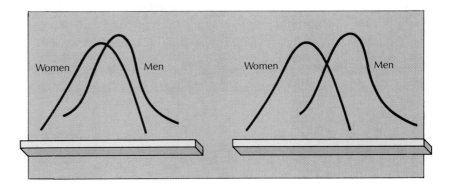

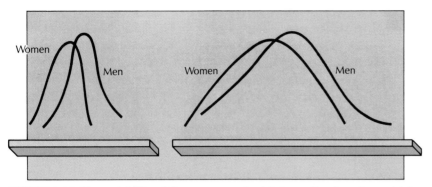

FIGURE A.11 The variability of the groups on the left is smaller than the variability of the groups on the right. Thus it is more likely that the difference between the means of the groups on the left is statistically significant.

reflected an actual difference in driving habits or efficiency of the automobiles.

As you can see in Figure A.11, the smaller the standard deviations (a measure of variability) of the two groups, the more likely it is that the difference of the means is statistically significant. As an extreme example, if all women sampled were exactly 5'5" tall, and all men sampled were exactly 5'10", we would be highly likely to assume that the difference of five inches in group means is statistically significant. But if the heights of women varied from 2' to 14', and the heights of men varied from 2'1" to 14'3", we might be more likely to assume that the five-inch difference in group means could be attributed to chance fluctuation.

SAMPLES AND POPULATIONS

Inferential statistics are mathematical tools that psychologists apply to samples of scores in order to determine whether they can generalize their findings to populations of scores. Thus they must be quite certain that the samples involved actually represent the populations from which they were drawn.

As you saw in Chapter 1, psychologists often use the techniques of random sampling and stratified sampling of populations in order to draw representative samples. If the samples studied do not accurately represent their intended populations, it matters very little how sophisticated the statistical techniques of the psychologist may be. We could use a variety of statistical techniques on the heights of the New York Apples and California Quakes, but none would tell us much about the height of the general population.

APPENDIX B:
Answer Keys for Questionnaires

This appendix contains scoring keys, answer keys, and normative data for the various Questionnaires presented in the text.

SCORING KEY FOR THE "SOCIAL DESIRABILITY SCALE" (CHAPTER 1, PP. 40–41)

Place a check mark on the appropriate line of the scoring key each time your answer *agrees* with the one listed on the scoring key. Add the check marks and place the total number of check marks in the box marked "Total Score."

SCORING KEY

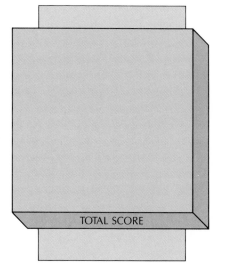

TOTAL SCORE

1.	T _____	12.	F _____	23.	F _____
2.	T _____	13.	T _____	24.	T _____
3.	F _____	14.	F _____	25.	T _____
4.	T _____	15.	F _____	26.	T _____
5.	F _____	16.	T _____	27.	T _____
6.	F _____	17.	T _____	28.	F _____
7.	T _____	18.	T _____	29.	T _____
8.	T _____	19.	F _____	30.	F _____
9.	F _____	20.	T _____	31.	T _____
10.	F _____	21.	T _____	32.	F _____
11.	F _____	22.	F _____	33.	T _____

Interpreting your score. LOW SCORERS (0–8). About one respondent in six earns a score between 0 and 8. Such respondents answered in a socially *undesirable* direction much of the time. It may be that they are more willing than most people to respond to tests truthfully, even when their answers might meet with social disapproval.

AVERAGE SCORERS (9–19). About two respondents in three earns scores between 9 and 19. They tend to show an average degree of concern for the social desirability of their responses, and it may well be that their actual behavior represents an average degree of conformity to social rules and conventions.

HIGH SCORERS (20–33). About one respondent in six earns a score between 20 and 33. These respondents may be highly concerned about social approval and respond to test items in such a way as to avoid the disapproval of people who may read their responses. Their actual behavior may show high conformity to social rules and conventions.

SCORING KEY FOR THE "WHY DO YOU DRINK?" QUESTIONNAIRE (CHAPTER 4, PP. 182–183)

Why do you drink? Score your questionnaire by seeing how many items you answered for each of the following reasons for drinking. Consider the key as *suggestive* only. For example, if you answered several items in such a way that you scored on the *addiction* factor, it may be wise to seriously examine what your drinking means to you. However, a few test-item scores cannot be interpreted as binding evidence of addiction.

Addiction	Anxiety/Tension Reduction	Pleasure/Taste	Transforming Agent
1. T	7. T	2. T	2. T
6. F	9. T	5. T	4. T
32. T	12. T	16. T	19. T
38. T	15. T	27. T	22. T
40. T	18. T	28. T	28. T
	26. T	35. T	30. T
	31. T	37. T	34. T
	33. T		36. T

Social Reward	Celebration	Religion	Social Power
3. T	10. T	11. T	2. T
8. T	24. T		13. T
23. T	25. T		19. T
			30. T

Scapegoating (Using alcohol as an excuse for failure or social misconduct)	Habit
14. T	17. T
15. T	29. T
20. T	
21. T	
39. T	

SCORING KEY FOR THE "REMOTE ASSOCIATES TEST" (CHAPTER 6, P. 290)

1. Prince
2. Dog
3. Cold
4. Glasses
5. Club
6. Boat
7. Defense
8. Pit
9. Writer

SCORING KEY FOR "ARE YOU A SENSATION SEEKER?" (CHAPTER 7, P. 330)

Since this is a shortened version of a questionnaire, no norms are available. However, the following answers are suggestive of sensation seeking:

1. A
2. A
3. A
4. B
5. A
6. B
7. A
8. A
9. B
10. B
11. A
12. A
13. B

NORMS FOR THE LOVE SCALE (CHAPTER 7, P. 354)

Table B.1 gives the scores of 220 undergraduate students at Northeastern University, aged between 19 and 24, with the largest single age group 21. Students were asked to indicate whether they were absolutely in love, probably in love, not sure, probably not in love, or definitely not in love. Scores of men and women in the five conditions did not differ, so they are lumped together. A number of students broke into arguments after taking the Love Scale: their love for one another "differed" by a couple of points! Please do not take scales like this too seriously. They are fun, but will not hold up in court as grounds for divorce. Rely on your feeling, not your scores.

TABLE B.1   Love-Scale Scores of Northeastern University Students

Condition	N*	Mean Scores
Absolutely in love	56	89
Probably in love	45	80
Not sure	36	77
Probably not in love	40	68
Definitely not in love	43	59

*N = Number of students.

ANSWER KEY FOR "ARE YOU TYPE A OR B?" QUESTIONNAIRE (CHAPTER 10, P. 471)

Yesses suggest the Type A behavior pattern, which is marked by a sense of time urgency and constant struggle. In appraising your "type," you need not be overly concerned with the precise number of "yes" answers; we have no normative data for you. But as Friedman and Rosenman note, you will have little difficulty spotting yourself as "hard core" or "moderately afflicted" (1974, p. 85)—that is, if you are honest with yourself.

SCORING KEY FOR THE "LOCUS OF CONTROL SCALE"
(CHAPTER 10, PP. 484–485)

Credit yourself with one point each time your answer agrees with the answer on the scoring key below. Write the total number of answers in agreement in the box marked "Total Score."

SCORING KEY

1. Yes ____	11. Yes ____	21. Yes ____	31. Yes ____
2. No ____	12. Yes ____	22. No ____	32. No ____
3. Yes ____	13. No ____	23. Yes ____	33. Yes ____
4. No ____	14. Yes ____	24. Yes ____	34. No ____
5. Yes ____	15. No ____	25. No ____	35. Yes ____
6. No ____	16. Yes ____	26. No ____	36. Yes ____
7. Yes ____	17. Yes ____	27. Yes ____	37. Yes ____
8. Yes ____	18. Yes ____	28. No ____	38. No ____
9. No ____	19. Yes ____	29. Yes ____	39. Yes ____
10. Yes ____	20. No ____	30. No ____	40. No ____

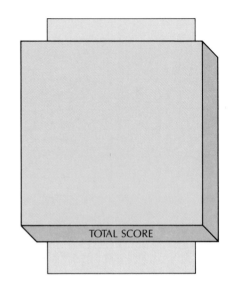

TOTAL SCORE

Interpreting your score. LOW SCORERS (0–8). About one respondent in three earns a score of from 0 to 8. Such respondents tend to have an internal locus of control. They see themselves as responsible for the reinforcements they attain (and fail to attain) in life.

AVERAGE SCORERS (9–16). Most respondents earn from 9 to 16 points. Average scorers may see themselves as partially in control of their lives. Perhaps they see themselves as in control at work, but not in their social lives—or vice versa.

HIGH SCORERS (17–40). About 15 percent of respondents attain scores of 17 or above. High scorers largely tend to see life as a game of chance, and success as a matter of luck.

SCORING KEY FOR THE "ASSERTIVENESS SCHEDULE"
(CHAPTER 12, PP. 566–567)

Tabulate your score as follows: Change the signs of all items followed by an asterisk (*). Then add the 30 item scores. For example, if the response to an asterisked item was 2, place a minus (−) sign before the 2. If the response to an asterisked item was −3, change the minus sign to a plus sign (+) by adding a vertical stroke.

Scores on this test can vary from +90 to −90. Table B.2 will show you how your score compared with those of 764 college women and 637 college men from 35 campuses all across the United States. For example, if you are a woman and your score was 26, it exceeded that of 80 percent of the women in the sample. A score of 15 for a male exceeds that of 55–60 percent of the men in the sample.

TABLE B.2   Percentiles of Scores on the Rathus Assertiveness Schedule for College Women and Men

Women's Scores	Percentile	Men's Scores	Women's Scores	Percentile	Men's Scores
55	99	65	6	45	8
48	97	54	2	40	6
45	95	48	−1	35	3
37	90	40	−4	30	1
31	85	33	−8	25	−3
26	80	30	−13	20	−7
23	75	26	−17	15	−11
19	70	24	−24	10	−15
17	65	19	−34	5	−24
14	60	17	−39	3	−30
11	55	14	−48	1	−41
8	50	11			

Source: Nevid & Rathus (1978).

SCORING KEY FOR THE "DO YOU ENDORSE A TRADITIONAL OR A LIBERAL MARITAL ROLE?" SCALE (CHAPTER 13, PP. 590–591)

Below each of the scoring codes (AS, AM, DM, and DS) in the questionnaire, there is a number. Underline the numbers beneath each of your answers. Then add the underlined numbers to attain your total score.

The total score can vary from 10 to 40. A score of 10–20 shows moderate to high traditionalism concerning marital roles. A score of 30–40 shows moderate to high liberalism. A score between 20–30 suggests that you are a middle-of-the-roader.

Your endorsement of a traditional or a liberal marital role is not a matter of right or wrong. However, if you and your partner endorse highly different marital roles, there may be role conflict ahead. It may be worthwhile for the two of you to have a frank talk about your goals and values to determine whether you do have major disagreements and, if so, whether you are willing to work to resolve them.

ANSWER KEY FOR "CULTURAL MYTHS THAT SUPPORT RAPE" QUESTIONNAIRE (CHAPTER 13, P. 614)

Actually, each item on the questionnaire, with the exception of number 2, represents a cultural myth that tends to support rape. Agreement with any of these items shows endorsement of such a myth.

REFERENCES

Abbey, A. (1982). Sex differences in attributions for friendly behavior. *Journal of Personality and Social Psychology, 42,* 830–838.

Abelson, H., Cohen, R., Heaton, E., & Slider, C. (1970). Public attitudes toward and experience with erotic materials. In *Technical Reports of the Commission on Obscenity and Pornography,* Vol. 6. Washington, D.C.: U.S. Government Printing Office.

Abramowitz, C. V., Abramowitz, S. I., Roback, H. B., & Jackson, C. (1974). Differential effectiveness of directive and nondirective group therapies as a function of client internal-external control. *Journal of Consulting and Clinical Psychology, 42,* 849–853.

Abrams, D. B., & Wilson, G. T. (1983). Alcohol, sexual arousal, and self-control. *Journal of Personality and Social Psychology, 45,* 188–198.

Abravanel, E., & Gingold, H. (1985). Learning via observation during the second year of life. *Developmental Psychology, 21,* 614–623.

Adair, J. G., Dushenko, T. W., & Lindsay, R. C. L. (1985). Ethical regulations and their impact on research practice. *American Psychologist, 40,* 59–72.

Adams, V. (1980). Sex therapies in perspective. *Psychology Today, 14* (8), 35–36.

Adelman, M. R. (1977). A comparison of professionally employed lesbians and heterosexual women on the MMPI. *Archives of Sexual Behavior, 6,* 193–202.

Adelson, J. (1982). Still vital after all these years. *Psychology Today, 16* (4), 52–59.

Adler, J., Abramson, P., Katz, S., & Hager, M. (1985, April 15). Getting high on "ecstasy." *Newsweek,* p. 96.

Adorno, T. W., Frenkel-Brunswick, E., & Levinson, D. J. (1950). *The authoritarian personality.* New York: Harper.

Agras, W. S., Southam, M. A., & Taylor, C. B. (1983). Long-term persistence of relaxation-induced blood pressure lowering during the working day. *Journal of Consulting and Clinical Psychology, 51,* 792–794.

Akil, H. (1978). Endorphins, beta-LPH, and ACTH: Biochemical pharmacological and anatomical studies. *Advances in Biochemical Psychopharmacology, 18,* 125–139.

Akil, H., Mayer, D. J., & Liebeskind, J. L. (1976). Antagonism of stimulation-produced analgesia. *Science, 191,* 961–962.

Albert, M. S. (1981). Geriatric neuropsychology. *Journal of Consulting and Clinical Psychology, 49,* 835–850.

Alexander, A. B. (1981). Asthma. In S. N. Haynes, & L. Gannon (eds.), *Psychosomatic disorders: A psychophysiological approach to etiology and treatment.* New York: Praeger.

Allen, V. L., & Levine, J. M. (1971). Social support and conformity: The role of independent assessment of reality. *Journal of Experimental Social Psychology, 7,* 48–58.

Allgeier, E. R., & Allgeier, A. A. (1984). *Sexual interactions.* Lexington, MA: Heath.

Allport, G. W. (1937). *Personality: A psychological interpretation.* New York: Holt, Rinehart and Winston.

Allport, G. W. (1961). *Pattern and growth in personality.* New York: Holt, Rinehart and Winston.

Allport, G. W., & Odbert, H. S. (1936). Trait names: A psycholexical study. *Psychological Monographs, 47,* 2–11.

Amabile, T. M. (1983). The social psychology of creativity: A componential conceptualization. *Journal of Personality and Social Psychology, 45,* 357–376.

American Psychiatric Association (1980). *Diagnostic and statistical manual–III.* Washington, D.C.: American Psychiatric Association.

American Psychological Association (1981). Ethical principles of psychologists. *American Psychologist, 36,* 633–638.

Amir, M. (1971). *Patterns in forcible rape.* Chicago: University of Chicago Press.

Anastasi, A. (1983). Evolving trait concepts. *American Psychologist, 38,* 175–184.

Andersen, B. L. (1981). A comparison of systematic desensitization and directed masturbation in the treatment of primary orgasmic dysfunction in females. *Journal of Consulting and Clinical Psychology, 49,* 568–570.

Anderson, D. J., Noyes, R., Jr., & Crowe, R. (1984). A comparison of panic disorder and generalized anxiety disorder. *American Journal of Psychiatry, 141,* 572–575.

Andersson, B. (1971). Thirst—and brain control of water balance. *American Scientist, 59,* 408.

Andrews, G., & Harvey, R. (1981). Does psychotherapy benefit neurotic patients? *Archives of General Psychiatry, 38,* 1203–1208.

Aneshensel, C. S., & Huba, G. J. (1983). Depression, alcohol use, and smoking over one year: A four-wave longitudinal causal model. *Journal of Abnormal Psychology, 92,* 134–150.

Antill, J. K. (1983). Sex role complementarity versus similarity in married couples. *Journal of Personality and Social Psychology, 52,* 260–267.

APA Monitor, February 1978, 4.

APA Monitor, January 1978, 5, 23.

Apfelbaum, M. (1978). Adaptation to changes in caloric intake. *Progress in Food and Nutritional Science, 2,* 543–559.

Archer, R. L., Diaz-Loving, R., Gollwitzer, P. M., Davis, M. H., & Foushee, H. C. (1981). The role of dispositional empathy and social evaluation in the empathic mediation of helping. *Journal of Personality and Social Psychology, 40,* 786–796.

Arkin, R. M., Detchon, C. S., & Maruyama, G. M. (1982). Roles of attribution, affect, and cognitive interference in test anxiety. *Journal of Personality and Social Psychology, 43,* 1111–1124.

Asch, S. E. (1952). *Social psychology.* Englewood Cliffs, NJ: Prentice-Hall.

Atkinson, J., & Huston, T. L. (1984). Sex role orientation and division of labor early in marriage. *Journal of Personality and Social Psychology, 46,* 330–345.

Atkinson, K., MacWhinney, B., & Stoel, C. (1970). An experiment on recognition of babbling. In *Papers and Reports on Child Language Development.* Stanford, CA: Stanford University Press.

Atkinson, R. C. (1975). Mnemotechnics in second-language learning. *American Psychologist, 30,* 821–828.

Ayllon, T., & Haughton, E. (1962). Control of the behavior of schizophrenic patients by food. *Journal of the Experimental Analysis of Behavior, 5,* 343–352.

Bach, G. R., & Deutsch, R. M. (1970). *Pairing.* New York: Peter H. Wyden.

Bachman, J. G., O'Malley, P. M., & Johnston, L. D. (1984). Drug use among young adults: The impacts of role status and social environment. *Journal of Personality and Social Psychology, 47,* 629–645.

Bagozzi, R. P. (1981). Attitudes, intentions, and behaviors: A test of some key hypotheses. *Journal of Personality and Social Psychology, 41,* 607–627.

Bahrick, H. P., Bahrick, P. O., & Wittlinger, R. P. (1975). Fifty years of memory for names and faces: A cross-sectional approach. *Journal of Experimental Psychology: General, 104,* 54–75.

Baker, L. A., DeFries, J. C., & Fulker, D. W. (1983). Longitudinal stability of cognitive ability in the Colorado adoption project. *Child Development, 54,* 290–297.

Bandura, A. (1973). *Aggression: A social learning analysis.* Englewood Cliffs, NJ: Prentice-Hall.

Bandura, A. (1977). *Social learning theory.* Englewood Cliffs, NJ: Prentice-Hall.

Bandura, A. (1978). The self system in reciprocal determinism. *American Psychologist, 33,* 344–358.

Bandura, A. (1981). Self-referrant thought: A developmental analysis of self-efficacy. In J. H. Flavell & L. Ross (eds.), *Social cognitive development: Frontiers and possible futures.* Cambridge, England: Cambridge University Press.

Bandura, A. (1982). The psychology of chance encounters and life paths. *American Psychologist, 37,* 747–755.

Bandura, A. (1982). Self-efficacy mechanism in human agency. *American Psychologist, 37,* 122–147.

Bandura, A., Blanchard, E. B., & Ritter, B. (1969). The relative efficacy of desensitization and modeling approaches for inducing behavioral, affective, and cognitive changes. *Journal of Personality and Social Psychology, 13,* 173–199.

Bandura, A., Reese, L., & Adams, N. E. (1982). Microanalysis of action and fear arousal as a function of differential levels of perceived self-efficacy. *Journal of Personality and Social Psychology, 43,* 5–21.

Bandura, A., & Rosenthal, T. L. (1966). Vicarious classical conditioning as a function of arousal level. *Journal of Personality and Social Psychology, 3,* 54–62.

Bandura, A., Ross, D., & Ross, S. A. (1963a). A comparative test of the status envy, and the secondary reinforcement theories of identificatory learning. *Journal of Abnormal and Social Psychology, 67,* 527–534.

Bandura, A., Ross, S. A., & Ross, D. (1963b). Imitation of film-mediated aggressive models. *Journal of Abnormal and Social Psychology, 66,* 3–11.

Bandura, A., Taylor, C. B., Williams, S. L., Mefford, I. N., & Barchas, J. D. (1985). Catecholamine secretion as a function of perceived coping self-efficacy. *Journal of Consulting and Clinical Psychology, 53,* 406–414.

Banks, M., & Salapatek, P. (1981). Infant pattern vision: A new approach based on the contrast selectivity function. *Journal of Experimental Child Psychology, 31,* 1–45.

Banyai, E. I., & Hilgard, E. R. (1976). A comparison of active-alert hypnotic induction with traditional relaxation induction. *Journal of Abnormal Psychology, 85,* 218–224.

Barbach, L. G. (1975). *For yourself: The fulfillment of female sexuality.* Garden City, NY: Doubleday.

Barber, T. X. (1970). *LSD, marihuana, yoga, and hypnosis.* Chicago: Aldine.

Barber, T. X., Spanos, N. P., & Chaves, J. F. (1974). *Hypnosis, imagination, and human potentialities.* New York: Pergamon Press.

Bard, P. (1934). The neurohumoral basis of emotional reactions. In C. A. Murchison (ed.), *Handbook of General Experimental Psychology.* Worcester, MA: Clark University Press.

Bardwick, J. M. (1971). *Psychology of women: A study of biocultural conflicts.* New York: Harper & Row.

Bardwick, J. M. (1980). The seasons of a woman's life. In D. G. McGuigan (ed.), *Women's lives: New theory, research, and policy.* Ann Arbor: University of Michigan, Center for Continuing Education of Women.

Barefoot, J. C., Dahlstrom, W. G., & Williams, R. B., Jr. (1983). Rapid communication, hostility, CHD incidence, and total mortality: a 25-year follow-up study of 225 physicians. *Psychosomatic Medicine, 45,* 59–63.

Barkley, R. A., Karlsson, J., Strzelecki,

E., & Murphy, J. V. (1984). Effects of age and Ritalin dosage on the mother-child interactions of hyperactive children. *Journal of Consulting and Clinical Psychology, 52,* 750–758.

Barlow, D. H. (1986). Causes of sexual dysfunction: The role of anxiety and cognitive interference. *Journal of Consulting and Clinical Psychology, 54,* 140–148.

Barlow, D. H., Vermilyea, J., Blanchard, E. B., Vermilyea, B. B., Di Nardo, P. A., & Cerny, J. A. (1985). The phenomenon of panic. *Journal of Abnormal Psychology, 94,* 291–297.

Barnes, M. L., & Buss, D. M. (1985). Sex differences in the interpersonal behavior of married couples. *Journal of Personality and Social Psychology, 48,* 654–661.

Barnett, R. C., & Baruch, G. K. (1985). Women's involvement in multiple roles and psychological distress. *Journal of Personality and Social Psychology, 49,* 135–145.

Baron, R. A. (1971). Behavioral effects of interpersonal attraction: Compliance with requests from liked and disliked others. *Psychonomic Science, 25,* 325–326.

Baron, R. A. (1973). The "foot-in-the-door" phenomenon: Mediating effects of size of first request and sex of requester. *Bulletin of the Psychonomic Society, 2,* 113–114.

Baron, R. A. (1983). *Behavior in organizations.* Boston: Allyn and Bacon.

Baron, R. A., & Byrne, D. (1984). *Social psychology: Understanding human interaction,* 3d ed. Boston: Allyn and Bacon.

Baron, R. A., Mandel, D. R., Adams, C. A., & Griffen, L. M. (1976). Effects of social density in university residential requirements. *Journal of Personality and Social Psychology, 34,* 434–446.

Baron, R. A., Russell, G. W., & Arms, R. L. (1985). Negative ions and behavior: Impact on mood, memory, and aggression among Type A and Type

B persons. *Journal of Personality and Social Psychology, 48,* 746–754.

Barraclough, B. M., Nelson, B., Bunch, J., & Sainsbury, P. (1969). The diagnostic classification and psychiatric treatment of 100 suicides. Proceedings of the Fifth International Conference for Suicide Prevention. London.

Bart, P. B. (1970). Mother Portnoy's complaints. *Trans-action, 8,* 69–74.

Bar-Tal, D., & Saxe, L. (1976). Perceptions of similarly and dissimilarly physically attractive couples and individuals. *Journal of Personality and Social Psychology, 33,* 772–781.

Basham, R. B. (1986). Scientific and practical advantages of comparative design in psychotherapy outcome research. *Journal of Consulting and Clinical Psychology, 54,* 88–94.

Batson, C. D., Duncan, B. D., Ackerman, P., Buckley, T., & Birch, K. (1981). Is empathic emotion a source of altruistic motivation? *Journal of Personality and Social Psychology, 40,* 290–302.

Baucom, D. H., & Aiken, P. A. (1981). Effect of depressed mood on eating among obese and nonobese dieting and nondieting persons. *Journal of Personality and Social Psychology, 41,* 577–585.

Baucom, D. H., & Aiken, P. A. (1984). Sex role identity, marital satisfaction, and response to behavioral marital therapy. *Journal of Consulting and Clinical Psychology, 52,* 438–444.

Baucom, D. H., Besch, P. K., & Callahan, S. (1985). Relationship between testosterone concentration, sex role identity, and personality among females. *Journal of Personality and Social Psychology, 48,* 1218–1226.

Baucom, D. H., & Danker-Brown, P. (1979). Influence of sex roles on the development of learned helplessness. *Journal of Consulting and Clinical Psychology, 47,* 928–936.

Baucom, D. H., & Danker-Brown, P. (1983). Peer ratings of males and females possessing different sex role identities. *Journal of Personality Assessment, 44,* 334–343.

Bauer, R. H., & Fuster, J. M. (1976). Delayed-matching and delayed-response deficit from cooling dorsolateral prefrontal cortex in monkeys. *Journal of Comparative and Physiological Psychology, 90,* 293–302.

Bauer, W. D., & Twentyman, C. T. (1985). Abusing, neglectful, and comparison mothers' responses to child-related and non-child-related stressors. *Journal of Consulting and Clinical Psychology, 53,* 335–343.

Baum, A., & Davis, G. E. (1980). Reducing the stress of high density living: An architectural intervention. *Journal of Personality and Social Psychology, 38,* 471–481.

Baum-Baicker, C. (1984). Treating and preventing alcohol abuse in the workplace. *American Psychologist, 39,* 454.

Baumrind, D. (1985). Research using intentional deception: Ethical issues revisited. *American Psychologist, 40,* 165–174.

Bazar, J. (1980). Catching up with the ape language debate. *APA Monitor, 11* (1), 4–5, 47.

Beard, R. R., & Wertheim, G. A. (1967). Behavioral impairment associated with small doses of carbon monoxide. *American Journal of Public Health, 57,* 2012–2022.

Beatty, W. W. (1979). Gonadal hormones and sex differences in nonreproductive behaviors in rodents: Organizational and activational influences. *Hormones and Behavior, 12,* 112–163.

Beauchamp, G. (1981). Paper presented to the Conference on the Determination of Behavior by Chemical Stimuli. Hebrew University, Jerusalem.

Beck, A. T. (1976). *Cognitive therapy and the emotional disorders.* New York: International Universities Press.

Beck, A. T., Rush, A. J., Show, B. F., & Emery, G. (1979). *Cognitive therapy of depression.* New York: Guilford Press.

Beck, A. T., Ward, C. H., Mendelson, M., Mock, J. E., & Erbaugh, J. K. (1962). Reliability of psychiatric diagnoses II: A study of consistency of clinical judgments and ratings. *American Journal of Psychiatry, 119,* 351–357.

Beck, J., Elsner, A., & Silverstein, C. (1977). Position uncertainty and the perception of apparent movement. *Perception and Psychophysics, 21,* 33–38.

Beck, R. C. (1978). *Motivation: Theories and principles.* Englewood Cliffs, NJ: Prentice-Hall.

Becker, R. D. (1979). Brain pollution. *Psychology Today, 13* (2), 124.

Beit-Hallahmi, B., & Rabin, A. I. (1977). The kibbutz as a social experiment and a child-rearing laboratory. *American Psychologist, 32,* 532–544.

Bell, A. P., & Weinberg, M. S. (1978). *Homosexualities: A study of diversity among men and women.* New York: Simon & Schuster.

Bell, A. P., Weinberg, M. S., & Hammersmith, S. K. (1981). *Sexual preference: Its development in men and women.* Bloomington, IN: University of Indiana Press.

Bell, P. A. (1982, August). Theoretical interpretations of heat stress. Paper presented to the American Psychological Association, Washington, D.C.

Belsky, J. (1984). The determinants of parenting: A process model. *Child Development, 55,* 83–96.

Belsky, J., Gilstrap, B., & Rovine, M. (1984). The Pennsylvania infant and family development project, I: Stability and change in mother-infant and father-infant interaction in a family setting at one, three, and nine months. *Child Development, 55,* 692–705.

Belsky, J., & Steinberg, L. D. (1978). The effects of day care: A critical review. *Child Development, 49,* 929–949

Belsky, J., & Steinberg, L. D. (1979, July–August). What does research teach us about day care? A follow-up report. *Children Today,* pp. 21–26

Bem, D. J. (1967). Self-perception: An alternative interpretation of cognitive dissonance phenomena. *Psychological Review, 74,* 183–200.

Bem, D. J. (1972). Self-perception theory. In L. Berkowitz (ed.), *Advances in experimental social psychology,* Vol. 6. New York: Academic Press.

Bem, D. J., & Allen, A. (1974). On predicting some of the people some of the time: The search for cross-situational consistencies in behavior. *Psychological Review, 81,* 506–520.

Bem, S. L. (1974). The measurement of psychological androgyny. *Journal of Consulting and Clinical Psychology, 42,* 151–162.

Bem, S. L. (1975). Sex role adaptability: One consequence of psychological androgyny. *Journal of Personality and Social Psychology, 31,* 634–643.

Bem, S. L. (1981). Gender schema theory: A cognitive account of sex typing. *Psychological Review, 88,* 354–364.

Bem, S. L., & Bem, D. J. (1973). Training the woman to know her place: The power of a nonconscious ideology. In L. S. Wrightsman & J. C. Brigham (eds.), *Contemporary issues in social psychology,* 2d ed. Monterey, CA: Brooks/Cole.

Bem, S. L., & Lenney, E. (1976). Sex typing and the avoidance of cross-sexed behaviors. *Journal of Personality and Social Psychology, 33,* 48–54.

Bem, S. L., Martyna, W., & Watson, C. (1976). Sex typing and androgyny: Further explorations of the expressive domain. *Journal of Personality and Social Psychology, 34,* 1016–1023.

Benbow, C. P., & Stanley, J. C. (1983). Sex differences in mathematical reasoning ability: More facts. *Science, 210,* 1029–1020.

Benedict, R. (1934). *Patterns of culture.* Boston: Houghton Mifflin.

Bennett, D. (1985). Rogers: More intuition in therapy. *APA Monitor, 16* (10), 3.

Bensinger, P. B. (1982, November–December). Drugs in the workplace. *Harvard Business Review,* 48–60.

Benson, H. (1975). *The relaxation response.* New York: Morrow.

Benson, H., Manzetta, B. R., & Rosner, B. (1973). Decreased systolic blood pressure in hypertensive subjects who practiced meditation. *Journal of Clinical Investigation, 52,* 8.

Benson, P. L., Karabenick, S. A., & Lerner, R. M. (1976). Pretty pleases: The effects of physical attractiveness, race, and sex on receiving help. *Journal of Experimental Social Psychology, 12,* 409–415.

Bentler, P. M. (1976). A typology of transsexualism: Gender identity theory and data. *Archives of Sexual Behavior, 5,* 567–584.

Bentler, P. M., & Speckart, G. (1981). Attitudes "cause" behaviors: A structural equation analysis. *Journal of Personality and Social Psychology, 40,* 226–238.

Berger, P. A. (1978). Medical treatment of mental illness. *Science, 200,* 974–981.

Berko, J. (1958). The child's learning of English morphology. *Word, 14,* 150–177.

Berkowitz, L. (1983). Aversively stimulated aggression: Some parallels and differences in research with animals and humans. *American Psychologist, 38,* 1135–1144.

Berkowitz, L., & Donnerstein, E. (1982). External validity is more than skin deep: Some answers to criticisms of laboratory experiments. *American Psychologist, 37,* 245–257.

Berkowitz, W. R., Nebel, J. C., & Reitman, J. W. (1971). Height and interpersonal attraction: The 1960 mayoral election in New York City. Paper presented at the annual convention of the American Psychological Association. Washington, D.C.

Berne, E. (1976a). *Beyond games and scripts.* New York: Grove.

Berne, E. (1976b). *Games people play.* New York: Ballantine.

Berscheid, E. (1976). Theories of interpersonal attraction. In B. B. Wolman & L. R. Pomeroy (eds.), *International encyclopaedia of neurology, psychiatry, psychoanalysis, and psychology.* New York: Springer.

Berscheid, E., Dion, K., Walster, E., &

Walster, G. W. (1971). Physical attractiveness and dating choice: A test of the matching hypothesis. *Journal of Experimental Social Psychology, 7,* 173–189.

Berscheid, E., & Walster, E. (1974a). A little bit about love. In T. L. Huston (ed.), *Foundations of interpersonal attraction.* New York: Academic Press.

Berscheid, E., & Walster, E. (1974b). Physical attractiveness. In L. Berkowitz (ed.), *Advances in experimental social psychology,* Vol. 7. New York: Academic Press.

Berscheid, E., & Walster, E. (1978). *Interpersonal attraction.* Reading, MA: Addison-Wesley.

Bersoff, D. N. (1981). Testing and the law. *American Psychologist, 36,* 1159–1166.

Bertelson, A. D., Marks, P. A., & May, G. D. (1982). MMPI and race: A controlled study. *Journal of Consulting and Clinical Psychology, 50,* 316–318.

Betz, N. E., & Hackett, G. (1981). The relationships of career-related self-efficacy expectations to perceived career options in college women and men. *Journal of Counseling Psychology, 28,* 399–410.

Bexton, W. H., Heron, W., & Scott, T. H. (1954). Effects of decreased variation in the sensory environment. *Canadian Journal of Psychology, 8,* 70–76.

Bieber, I. A. (1976). Discussion of "Homosexuality: The ethical challenge." *Journal of Consulting and Clinical Psychology, 44,* 163–166.

Biglan, A., & Craker, D. (1982). Effects of pleasant-activities manipulation on depression. *Journal of Consulting and Clinical Psychology, 50,* 436–438.

Billings, A. G., Cronkite, R. C., & Moos, R. H. (1983). Social-environmental factors in unipolar depression: Comparisons of depressed patients and nondepressed controls. *Journal of Abnormal Psychology, 92,* 119–133.

Birch, H. G., & Rabinowitz, H. S. (1951). The negative effect of previous experience on productive thinking. *Journal of Experimental Psychology, 42,* 121–125.

Birren, J. E. (1983). Aging in America: Roles for psychology. *American Psychologist, 38,* 298–299.

Bjorklund, D. F., & de Marchena, M. R. (1984). Developmental shifts in the basis of organization in memory: The role of associative versus categorical relatedness in children's free recall. *Child Development, 55,* 952–962.

Blackler, F. H. M., & Brown, C. A. (1978). *Job redesign and management control: Studies in British Leyland and Volvo.* New York: Praeger.

Blake, R. (1985). Neurohormones and sexual preference. *Psychology Today, 19* (1), 12–13.

Blakely, M. K. (1985). Is one woman's sexuality another woman's pornography? The question behind a major legal battle. *Ms., 13* (10), 37–47, 120–123.

Blanchard, E. B., Andrasik, F., Ahles, T. A., Teders, S. J., & O'Keefe, D. M. (1980). Migraine and tension headache: A meta-analytic review. *Behavior Therapy, 11,* 613–631.

Blanchard, E. B., Andrasik, F., Neff, D. F., Arena, J. G., Ahles, T. A., Jurish, S. E., Pallmeyer, T. P., Saunders, N. L., Teders, S. J., Barron, K. D., & Rodichok, L. D. (1982). Biofeedback and relaxation training with three kinds of headache: Treatment effects and their prediction. *Journal of Consulting and Clinical Psychology, 50,* 562–575.

Blanchard, E. B., Andrasik, F., Evans, D. D., Neff, D. F., Appelbaum, K. A., & Rodichok, L. D. (1985). Behavioral treatment of 250 chronic headache patients: A clinical replication series. *Behavior Therapy, 16,* 308–327.

Blanchard, R., Steiner, B. W., & Clemmensen, L. H. (1985). Gender dysphoria, gender reorientation, and the clinical management of transsexualism. *Journal of Consulting and Clinical Psychology, 53,* 295–304.

Blasi, A. (1980). Bridging moral cognition and moral action: A critical review of the literature. *Psychological Bulletin, 88,* 1–45.

Blittner, M., Goldberg, J., & Merbaum, M. (1978). Cognitive self-control factors in the reduction of smoking behavior. *Behavior Therapy, 9,* 553–561.

Bloch, V., Hennevin, E., & Leconte, P. (1979). Relationship between paradoxical sleep and memory processes. In M. A. B. Braszier (ed.), *Brain mechanisms in memory and learning: From the single neuron to man.* New York: Raven Press.

Block, J., & Block, J. (1951). An investigation of the relationship between intolerance of ambiguity and ethnocentrism. *Journal of Personality, 19,* 303–311.

Blumberg, S. H., & Izard, C. E. (1985). Affective and cognitive characteristics of depression in 10- and 11-year-old children. *Journal of Personality and Social Psychology, 49,* 194–202.

Bolles, R. C., & Faneslow, M. S. (1982). Endorphins and behavior. *Annual Review of Psychology, 33,* 87–101.

Borgida, E., & Campbell, B. (1982). Belief relevance and attitude-behavior consistency: The moderating role of personal experience. *Journal of Personality and Social Psychology, 42,* 239–247.

Bornstein, M. H., Kessen, W., & Weiskopf, S. (1976). The categories of hue in infancy. *Science, 191,* 201–202.

Bornstein, M. H., & Marks, L. E. (1982). Color revisionism. *Psychology Today, 16* (1), 64–73.

Boston Women's Health Book Collective. (1984). *The new our bodies, ourselves.* New York: Simon & Schuster.

Bourne, L. E., Ekstrand, B. R., & Dominowski, R. L. (1971). *The psychology of thinking.* Englewood Cliffs, NJ: Prentice-Hall.

Bower, G. H. (1981). Mood and memory. *American Psychologist, 36,* 129–148.

Bowlby, J. (1973). Separation. *Attachment and loss,* Vol. 2. New York: Basic Books.

Boyatzis, R. E. (1974). The effect of alcohol consumption on the aggressive behavior of men. *Quarterly Journal for the Study of Alcohol, 35,* 959–972.

Bradley, R. H., & Caldwell, B. M. (1984). The relation of infants' home environments to achievement test performance in first grade: A follow-up study. *Child Development, 55,* 803–809.

Bralove, M. (1981, December 7). Keeping work world out of family life is growing problem for two-job couples. *The Wall Street Journal.*

Bray, D. W. (1982). The assessment center and the study of lives. *American Psychologist, 37,* 180–189.

Bray, R. M., & Sugarman, R. (1980). Social facilitation among interaction groups: Evidence for the evaluation-apprehension hypothesis. *Personality and Social Psychology Bulletin, 6,* 137–142.

Brazleton, T. B. (1970). Effects of prenatal drugs on the behavior of the neonate. *American Journal of Psychiatry, 126,* 95–100.

Brecher, E. M., & Editors of *Consumer Reports.* (1975). Marijuana: The legal question. *Consumer Reports, 40,* 265–266.

Brehm, J. W. (1972). *Responses to loss of freedom: A theory of psychological reactance.* Morristown, NJ: General Learning Press.

Brent, E., & Granberg, D. (1982). Subjective agreement with the presidential candidates of 1976 and 1980. *Journal of Personality and Social Psychology, 42,* 393–403.

Briddell, D. W., & Wilson, G. T. (1976). Effects of alcohol and expectancy set on male sexual arousal. *Journal of Abnormal Psychology, 85,* 225–234.

Bridgwater, C. A. (1982). What candor can do. *Psychology Today, 16* (5), 16.

Brigham, J. C. (1980). Limiting conditions of the "physical attractiveness stereotype": Attributions about divorce. *Journal of Research in Personality, 14,* 365–375.

Brigham, T. A., Hopper, C., Hill, B., De Armas, A., & Newsom, P. (1985). A self-management program for disruptive adolescents in the school: A clin-

ical replication analysis. *Behavior Therapy, 16,* 99–115.

Broad, W. J. (1984, January 10). Pentagon is said to focus on ESP for wartime use. *The New York Times.*

Bronfenbrenner, U. (1960). Freudian theories of identification and their derivatives. *Child Development, 31,* 15–40.

Bronfenbrenner, U. (1973). The dream of the kibbutz. In *Readings in Human Development.* Guilford, CT: Dushkin Publishers.

Brook, J. S., Lukoff, J. F., & Whiteman, M. (1980). Initiation into marihuana use. *Journal of Genetic Psychology, 137,* 133–142.

Brooks, J. (1985). Polygraph testing: Thoughts of a skeptical legislator. *American Psychologist, 40,* 348–354.

Brooks-Gunn, J., & Ruble, D. N. (1980). The menstrual attitude questionnaire. *Psychosomatic Medicine, 42,* 503–511.

Brown, B. B., & Altman, I. (1981). Territoriality and residential crime. In P. A. Brantingham & P. L. Brantingham (eds.), *Urban crime and environmental criminology.* Beverly Hills, CA: Sage.

Brown, F. G. (1983). *Principles of educational and psychological testing,* 3d ed. New York: Holt, Rinehart and Winston.

Brown, M., Amoroso, D., & Ware, E. (1976). Behavioral aspects of viewing pornography. *Journal of Social Psychology, 98,* 235–245.

Brown, R. (1970). The first sentences of child and chimpanzee. In R. Brown (ed.), *Psycholinguistics.* New York: Free Press.

Brown, R. (1973). *A first language: The early stages.* Cambridge, MA: Harvard University Press.

Brown, R., & Hanlon, C. (1970). Derivational complexity and order of acquisition in child speech. In J. R. Hayes (ed.), *Cognition and the development of language.* New York: Wiley.

Brown, R., & McNeill, D. (1966). The tip-of-the-tongue phenomenon. *Jour-

nal of Verbal Learning and Verbal Behavior, 5,* 325–337.

Brown, S. A. (1985). Expectancies versus background in the prediction of college drinking patterns. *Journal of Consulting and Clinical Psychology, 53,* 123–130.

Brown, S. A., Goldman, M. S., & Christiansen, B. A. (1985). Do alcohol expectancies mediate drinking patterns of adults? *Journal of Consulting and Clinical Psychology, 53,* 512–519.

Brown, S. A., Goldman, M. S., Inn, A., & Anderson, L. R. (1980). Expectations of reinforcement from alcohol. *Journal of Consulting and Clinical Psychology, 48,* 419–426.

Brown, W. A., Monti, P. M., & Corriveau, D. P. (1978). Serum testosterone and sexual activity and interest in men. *Archives of Sexual Behavior, 7,* 97–103.

Brownell, K. D. (1982). Obesity: Understanding and treating a serious, prevalent, and refractory disorder. *Journal of Consulting and Clinical Psychology, 50,* 820–840.

Brownell, K. D. (1986). In Toufexis, A., Garcia, C., & Kalb, B. (1986, January 20). Dieting: The losing game. *Time Magazine,* 54–60.

Bruner, J. S., Goodnow, J. J., & Austin, G. A. (1956). *A study of thinking.* New York: Wiley.

Brunson, B. I., & Matthews, K. A. (1981). The Type-A coronary-prone behavior pattern and reactions to uncontrollable stress. *Journal of Personality and Social Psychology, 40,* 906–918.

Burnstein, E. (1983). Persuasion as argument processing. In M. Brandstatter, J. H. Davis, & G. Stocker-Kreichgauer (eds.), *Group decision processes.* London: Academic Press.

Burt, M. R. (1980). Cultural myths and supports for rape. *Journal of Personality and Social Psychology, 38,* 217–230.

Bushnell, E. W., Shaw, L., & Strauss, D. (1985). Relationship between visual and tactual exploration by 6-month-olds. *Developmental Psychology, 21,* 591–600.

Buss, D. M. (1984). Toward a psychology of person-environment (PE) correlation: The role of spouse selection. *Journal of Personality and Social Psychology, 47*, 361–377.

Butcher, J. N., Braswell, L., & Raney, D. (1983). A cross-cultural comparison of American Indian, black, and white inpatients on the MMPI and presenting symptoms. *Journal of Consulting and Clinical Psychology, 51*, 587–594.

Byrne, D. (1971). *The attraction paradigm*. New York: Academic Press.

Cadoret, R. J. (1978). Psychopathology in adopted-away offspring of biologic parents with antisocial behavior. *Archives of General Psychiatry, 35*, 176–184.

Calder, B. J., Ross, M., & Inkso, C. A. (1973). Attitude change and attitude attribution: Effects of incentive, choice, and consequences. *Journal of Personality and Social Psychology, 25*, 84–99.

Caldwell, B. M., Wright, C. M., Honig, A. S., & Tannenbaum, J. (1970). Infant day care and attachment. *American Journal of Orthopsychiatry, 40*, 397–412.

Calhoun, J. B. (1962). Population density and social pathology. *Scientific American, 206*, 139–148.

Calne, D. B., (1977). Developments in the pharmacology and therapeutics of Parkinsonism. *Annals of Neurology, 1*, 111–119.

Campbell, A. (1975). The American way of mating: Marriage si, children only maybe. *Psychology Today, 8*, 37–43.

Campos, J. J., Hiatt, S., Ramsey, D., Henderson, C., & Svejda, M. (1978). The emergence of fear on the visual cliff. In M. Lewis & L. Rosenblum (eds.), *The origins of affect*. New York: Plenum Press.

Campos, J. J., Langer, A., & Krowitz, A. (1970). Cardiac responses on the visual cliff in prelocomotor infants. *Science, 170*, 196–197.

Cannon, W. B. (1927). The James-Lange theory of emotions: A critical examination and an alternative theory. *American Journal of Psychology, 39*, 106–124.

Cannon, W. B. (1929). *Bodily changes in pain, hunger, fear, and rage*. New York: Appleton.

Cantor, P. C. (1976). Personality characteristics found among youthful female suicide attempters. *Journal of Abnormal Psychology, 85*, 324–329.

Caplan, L. (1984, July 2). The insanity defense. *The New Yorker*, 45–78.

Caplan, P. J., MacPherson, G. M., & Tobin, P. (1985). Do sex-related differences in spatial abilities exist? A multilevel critique with new data. *American Psychologist, 40*, 786–799.

Carlson, N. R. (1981). *Physiology of behavior*. Boston: Allyn & Bacon.

Carr, D. B. et al. (1981). Physical conditioning facilitates the exercise-induced secretion of beta-endorphins and beta-lipotropin in women. *New England Journal of Medicine, 305*, 560–563.

Carrington, P. (1972). Dreams and schizophrenia. *Archives of General Psychiatry, 26*, 343–350.

Carrington, P. *Freedom in meditation*. New York: Anchor Press/Doubleday, 1977.

Cartwright, R. D. (1978). *A primer on sleep and dreaming*. Reading, MA: Addison-Wesley.

Cartwright, R. D., Lloyd, S., Nelson, J. B., & Bass, S. (1983). The traditional-liberated woman dimension: Social stereotype and self-concept. *Journal of Personality and Social Psychology, 44*, 581–588.

Carver, C. S., & Ganellen, R. J. (1983). Depression and components of self-punitiveness: High standards, self-criticism, and overgeneralization. *Journal of Abnormal Psychology, 92*, 330–337.

Carver, C. S., Ganellen, R. J., & Behar-Mitrani, V. (1985). Depression and cognitive style: Comparisons between measures. *Journal of Personality and Social Psychology, 49*, 722–728.

Cattell, R. B. (1949). *The culture-free intelligence test*. Champaign, IL: Institute for Personality and Ability Testing.

Cattell, R. B. (1965). *The scientific analysis of personality*. Baltimore: Penguin.

Cattell, R. B. (1973). Personality pinned down. *Psychology Today, 7*, 40–46.

Cattell, R. B., Kawash, G. F., & DeYoung, G. E. (1972). Validation of objective measures of ergic tension: Response of the sex erg to visual stimulation. *Journal of Experimental Research in Personality, 6*, 76–83.

Cautela, J. R. (1967). Covert sensitization. *Psychological Reports, 74*, 459–468.

Cautela, J. R. (1970). Covert reinforcement. *Behavior Therapy, 1*, 33–50.

Cermak, L. (1978). *Improving your memory*. New York: McGraw-Hill.

Chapanis, N. P., & Chapanis, A. C. (1964). Cognitive dissonance: Five years later. *Psychological Bulletin, 61*, 1–22.

Charry, J. M., & Hawkinshire, F. B. W., Jr. (1981). Effects of atmospheric electricity on some substrates of disordered social behavior. *Journal of Personality and Social Psychology, 41*, 185–197.

Chemers, M. M., Hays, R. B., Rhodewalt, F., & Wysocki, J. (1985). A person-environment analysis of job stress: A contingency model explanation. *Journal of Personality and Social Psychology, 49*, 628–635.

Chesler, P. (1972). *Women and madness*. Garden City, NY: Doubleday.

Chesno, F. A., & Kilmann, P. R. (1975). Effects of stimulation intensity on sociopathic avoidance learning. *Journal of Abnormal Psychology, 84*, 144–151.

Chomsky, N. (1965). *Aspects of the theory of syntax*. Cambridge: MIT Press.

Chomsky, N. (1968). *Language and mind*. New York: Harcourt Brace Jovanovich.

Chomsky, N. (1980). Rules and representations. *Behavior and Brain Science, 3*, 1–15.

Chouinard, G., Labonte, A., Fontaine,

R., & Annable, L. (1983). New concepts in benzodiazepine therapy: Rebound anxiety and new indications for the more potent benzodiazepines. *Progress in Neuro-psychopharmacology and Biological Psychiatry, 7,* 669–673.

Christiansen, B. A., Goldman, M. S., & Inn, A. (1982). Development of alcohol-related expectancies in adolescents. *Journal of Consulting and Clinical Psychology, 50,* 336–344.

Cipolli, C., & Salzarulo, P. (1978). Sleep and memory: Reproduction of syntactic structures previously evoked within REM-related reports. *Perceptual and Motor Skills, 46,* 111–114.

Clark, H. H., & Clark, E. V. (1977). *Psychology and language: An introduction to psycholinguistics.* New York: Harcourt Brace Jovanovich.

Clark, M., Gosnell, M., Shapiro, D., & Hager, M. (1981, July 13). The mystery of sleep. *Newsweek,* 48–55.

Clark, M., Gosnell, M., Witherspoon, D., Hager, M., & Coppola, V. (1985, August 12). AIDS. *Newsweek,* 19–27.

Cleckley, H. (1964). *The mask of sanity, 4th ed.* St. Louis: Mosby.

Clore, G. L., Wiggins, N. H., & Itkin, S. (1975). Gain and loss in attraction: Attributions from nonverbal behavior. *Journal of Personality and Social Psychology, 31,* 706–712.

Cochran, S. D., & Hammen, C. L. (1985). Perceptions of stressful life events and depression: A test of attributional models. *Journal of Personality and Social Psychology, 48,* 1562–1571.

Cochran, W. G., Mosteller, F., & Tukey, J. (1954). *Statistical problems of the Kinsey report on sexual behavior in the human male.* Washington, D.C.: American Statistical Association.

Coe, W. C., & Yashinski, E. (1985). Volitional experiences associated with breaching posthypnotic amnesia. *Journal of Personality and Social Psychology, 48,* 716–722.

Cohen, D. B. (1973). Sex-role orientation and dream recall. *Journal of Abnormal Psychology, 82,* 246–252.

Cohen, E. J., Motto, A., & Seiden, R. H. (1966). An instrument for evaluating suicide potential: A preliminary study. *American Journal of Psychiatry, 122,* 886–891.

Cohen, S., Evans, G. W., Krantz, D. S., & Stokols, D. (1980). Physiological, motivational, and cognitive effects of aircraft noise on children. *American Psychologist, 35,* 231–243.

Cohen, S., Evans, G. W., Krantz, D. S., Stokols, D., & Kelly, S. (1981). Aircraft noise and children: Longitudinal and cross-sectional evidence on adaptation to noise and the effectiveness of noise abatement. *Journal of Personality and Social Psychology, 40,* 331–345.

Cohen, S., Glass, D. C., & Singer, J. E. (1973). Apartment noise, auditory discrimination, and reading ability in children. *Journal of Experimental Social Psychology, 9,* 407–422.

Colby, A., Kohlberg, L., Gibbs, J., & Lieberman, M. (1983). A longitudinal study of moral judgment. *Monographs of the Society for Research in Child Development, 48* (Serial No. 200).

Colby, C. Z., Lanzetta, J. T., & Kleck, R. E. (1977). Effects of the expression of pain on autonomic and pain tolerance response to subject-controlled pain. *Psychophysiology, 14,* 537–540.

Coleman, M., & Ganong, L. H. (1985). Love and sex role stereotypes: Do macho men and feminine women make better lovers? *Journal of Personality and Social Psychology, 49,* 170–176.

Colligan, M. J., & Murphy, L. R. (1982). A review of mass psychogenic illness in work settings. In M. J. Colligan, J. W. Pennebaker, & L. R. Murphy (eds.), *Mass psychogenic illness.* Hillsdale, NJ: Erlbaum.

Collins, R. L., Parks, G. A., & Marlatt, G. A. (1985). Social determinants of alcohol consumption: The effects of social interaction and model status on the self-administration of alcohol. *Journal of Consulting and Clinical Psychology, 53,* 189–200.

Comarr, A. E. (1970). Sexual function among patients with spinal cord injury. *Urologia Internationalis, 25,* 134–168.

Condiotte, M. M., & Lichtenstein, E. (1981). Self-efficacy and relapse in smoking cessation programs. *Journal of Consulting and Clinical Psychology, 49,* 648–658.

Conger, J. J., & Petersen, A. (1984). *Adolescence and youth: Psychological development in a changing world.* New York: Harper & Row.

Conley, J. J. (1984). Longitudinal consistency of adult personality: Self-reported psychological characteristics across 45 years. *Journal of Personality and Social Psychology, 47,* 1325–1333.

Conley, J. J. (1985). Longitudinal stability of personality traits: A multitrait-multimethod-multioccasion analysis. *Journal of Personality and Social Psychology, 49,* 1266–1282.

Connor, J. (1972). Olfactory control of aggressive and sexual behavior in the mouse. *Psychonomic Science, 27,* 1–3.

Conover, M. R. (1982). Modernizing the scarecrow to protect crops from birds. *Frontiers of Plant Science, 35,* 7–8.

Conway, E., & Brackbill, Y. (1970). Delivery medication and infant outcome: An empirical study. *Monographs of the Society for Research in Child Development, 35* (4), 24–34.

Cooney, J. L., & Zeichner, A. (1985). Selective attention to negative feedback in Type A and Type B individuals. *Journal of Abnormal Psychology, 94,* 110–112.

Cooper, A. J. (1978). Neonatal olfactory bulb lesions: Influences on subsequent behavior of male mice. *Bulletin of the Psychonomic Society, 11,* 53–56.

Cooper, H. M. (1979). Statistically combining independent studies: A meta-analysis of sex differences in conformity research. *Journal of Personality and Social Psychology, 37,* 131–146.

Cooper, J. (1980). Reducing fears and increasing assertiveness: The role of dissonance reduction. *Journal of Experimental Social Psychology, 16,* 199–213.

Cooper, R., & Zubek, J. (1958). Effects of enriched and restricted early environments on the learning ability of bright and dull rats. *Canadian Journal of Psychology, 12,* 159–164.

Cordes, C. (1984). The plight of the homeless mentally ill. *APA Monitor, 15* (2), 1, 13.

Cordes, C. (1985). Common threads found in suicide. *APA Monitor, 16* (10), 11.

Corkin, S. (1980). A prospective study of cingulotomy. In E. S. Valenstein (ed.), *The psychosurgery debate.* San Francisco: W. H. Freeman.

Costa, P. T., Jr., & McCrae, R. R. (1985). Hypochondriasis, neuroticism, and aging: When are somatic complaints unfounded? *American Psychologist, 40,* 19–28.

Costa, P. T., Jr., Zonderman, A. B., McCrae, R. R., & Williams, R. B., Jr. (1985). Content and comprehensiveness in the MMPI: An item factor analysis in a normal adult sample. *Journal of Personality and Social Psychology, 48,* 925–933.

Cowan, P. A. (1978). *Piaget with feeling.* New York: Holt, Rinehart and Winston.

Cozby, P. C. (1973). Self-disclosure: A literature review. *Psychological Bulletin, 79,* 73–91.

Craik, F. I. M., & Watkins, M. J. (1973). The role of rehearsal in short-term memory. *Journal of Verbal Learning and Verbal Behavior. 12,* 599–607.

Crawford, C. (1979). George Washington, Abraham Lincoln, and Arthur Jensen: Are they compatible? *American Psychologist, 34,* 664–672.

Crawford, H. J. (1982). Hypnotizability, daydreaming styles, imagery vividness, and absorption: A multidimensional study. *Journal of Personality and Social Psychology, 42,* 915–926.

Creese, I., Burt, D. R., & Snyder, S. H. (1978). Biochemical actions of neuroleptic drugs. In L. L. Iversen, S. D. Iversen, & S. H. Snyder (eds.), *Hand-*

book of psychopharmacology, Vol. 10. New York: Plenum Press.

Crockenburg, S. B. (1972). Creativity tests: A boon or boondoggle for children? *Review of Educational Research, 42,* 27–45.

Cronbach, L. J. (1975). Five decades of public controversy over mental testing. *American Psychologist, 30,* 1–14.

Crowley, J. (1985). Cited in Zuckerman, D. (1985). Retirement: R & R or risky? *Psychology Today, 19* (2), 80.

Croyle, R. T., & Cooper, J. (1983). Dissonance arousal: Physiological evidence. *Journal of Personality and Social Psychology, 45,* 782–791.

Cummings, N. A. (1979). Turning bread into stones: Our modern antimiracle. *American Psychologist, 34,* 1119–1129.

Cunningham, M. R. (1979). Weather, mood, and helping behavior. *Journal of Personality and Social Psychology, 37,* 1947–1956.

Curtiss, S. R. (1977). *Genie: A psycholinguistic study of a modern-day "wild child."* New York: Academic Press.

Dale, P. S. (1976). Language development: Structure and function. Hinsdale, IL: Dryden Press.

Dalton, K. (1968). Menstruation and examinations. *Lancet, 2,* 1386–1388.

Dalton, K. (1972). *The menstrual cycle.* New York: Warner Books.

Dalton, K. (1980). Cyclical criminal acts in premenstrual syndrome. *Lancet, 2,* 1070–1071.

Darley, J. M., & Gross, P. H. (1983). A hypothesis-confirming bias in labeling effects. *Journal of Personality and Social Psychology, 44,* 20–33.

Darley, J. M., & Latané, B. (1968). Bystander intervention in emergencies: Diffusion of responsibility. *Journal of Personality and Social Psychology, 8,* 377–383.

Darlington, R. B., Royce, J. M., Snipper, A. S., Murray, H. W., & Lazar, I. (1980). Preschool programs and later school competence of children from low-income families. *Science, 208,* 202–204.

Darrow, W. W. (1983, November). Social and psychological aspects of Acquired Immune Deficiency Syndrome. Paper presented at the annual meeting of the Society for the Scientific Study of Sex, Chicago, IL.

Darwin, C. A. (1872). *The expression of the emotions in man and animals.* London: J. Murray.

Dauber, R. B. (1984). Subliminal psychodynamic activation in depression: On the role of autonomy issues in depressed college women. *Journal of Abnormal Psychology, 93,* 9–18.

Davis, K. E. (1985). Near and dear: Friendship and love compared. *Psychology Today, 19* (2), 22–30.

Davison, G. C., & Neale, J. M. (1986). *Abnormal psychology,* 4th ed. New York: Wiley.

Deaux, K. (1976). *The behavior of men and women.* Monterey, CA: Brooks/Cole.

Deaux, K. (1984). From individual differences to social categories: Analysis of a decade's research on gender. *American Psychologist, 39,* 105–116.

DeBacker, G., et al. (1983). Behavior, stress, and psychosocial traits as risk factors. *Preventative Medicine, 12,* 32–36.

DeCasper, A. J., & Fifer, W. P. (1980). Of human bonding: Newborns prefer their mothers' voices. *Science, 208,* 1174–1176.

DeGree, C. E., & Snyder, C. R. (1985). Adler's psychology (of use) today: Personal history of traumatic life events as a self-handicapping strategy. *Journal of Personality and Social Psychology, 48,* 1512–1519.

Delanoy, R. L., Merrin, J. S., & Gold, P. E. (1982). Moderation of long-term potentiation (LTP) by adrenergic agonists. *Neuroscience Abstracts, 8,* 316.

Dembroski, T. M., Lasater, T. M., & Ramirez, A. (1978). Communicator similarity, fear-arousing communications, and compliance with health care recommendations. *Journal of Applied Social Psychology, 8,* 254–269.

Dement, W. (1972). Sleep and dreams.

In A. M. Freedman & H. I. Kaplan (eds.), *Human behavior: Biological, psychological, and sociological.* New York: Atheneum.

DePaulo, B. M., Rosenthal, R., Eisenstat, R. A., Rogers, P. L., & Finkelstein, S. (1978). Decoding discrepant nonverbal cues. *Journal of Personality and Social Psychology, 38,* 313–323.

Depue, R. A., Slater, J. F., Wolfstetter-Kausch, H., Klein, D., Goplerud, E., & Farr, D. (1981). A behavioral paradigm for identifying persons at risk for bipolar depressive disorder. *Journal of Abnormal Psychology, 90,* 381–438.

Dermer, M., & Thiel, D. L. (1975). When beauty may fail. *Journal of Personality and Social Psychology, 31,* 1168–1176.

Derner, G. (1977, May 7). Biofeedback Workshop. Adelphi University, Garden City, NY.

Dethier, V. G. (1978). Other tastes, other worlds. *Science, 201,* 224–228.

Diamond, E. L. (1982). The role of anger and hostility in essential hypertension and coronary heart disease. *Psychological Bulletin, 92,* 410–433.

Diamond, M. (1977). Human sexual development: Biological foundations for social development. In F. A. Beach (ed.), *Human sexuality in four perspectives.* Baltimore: Johns Hopkins University Press.

Diamond, M. (1978). Aging and cell loss: Calling for an honest count. *Psychology Today, 12* (9), 126.

Diamond, M. (1984). A love affair with the brain. *Psychology Today, 18,* (11), 62–73.

Dickson, P. (1975). *The future of the workplace: The coming revolution in jobs.* New York: Weybright and Talley.

Diener, E. (1980). Deindividuation: The absence of self-awareness and self-regulation in group members. In P. Paulus (ed.), *The psychology of group influence.* Hillsdale, NJ: Erlbaum.

Dill, C. A., Gilden, E. R., Hill, P. C., & Hanselka, L. L. (1982). Federal human subjects regulations: A methodological artifact. *Personality and Social Psychology Bulletin, 8,* 417–425.

Dimsdale, J. E., & Moss, J. (1980). Plasma catecholamines in stress and exercise. *Journal of the American Medical Association, 243,* 340–342.

Dion, K. K., Berscheid, E., & Walster, E. (1972). What is beautiful is good. *Journal of Personality and Social Psychology, 24,* 285–290.

Dodge, L. J. T., Glasgow, R. E., & O'Neill, H. K. (1982). Bibliotherapy in the treatment of female orgasmic dysfunction. *Journal of Consulting and Clinical Psychology, 50,* 442–443.

Dohrenwend, B. P., & Shrout, P. E. (1985). ''Hassles'' in the conceptualization and measurement of life stress variables. *American Psychologist, 40,* 780–785.

Dohrenwend, B. S., Dohrenwend, B. P., Dodson, M., & Shrout, P. E. (1984). Symptoms, hassles, social supports and life events: The problem of confounded measures. *Journal of Abnormal Psychology, 93,* 222–230.

Dohrenwend, B. S., Krasnoff, L., Askenasy, A. R., & Dohrenwend, B. P. (1982). The psychiatric epidemiology research interview life events scale. In L. Goldberger & S. Breznitz (eds.), *Handbook of stress: Theoretical and clinical aspects.* New York: Free Press.

Dollard, J., Doob, L. W., Miller, N. E., Mowrer, O. H., & Sears, R. R. (1939). *Frustration and aggression.* New Haven, CT: Yale University Press.

Donahoe, C. P., Jr., Lin, D. H., Kirschenbaum, D. S., & Keesey, R. E. (1984). Metabolic consequences of dieting and exercise in the treatment of obesity. *Journal of Consulting and Clinical Psychology, 52,* 827–836.

Donnerstein, E. (1980). Aggressive erotica and violence against women. *Journal of Personality and Social Psychology, 39,* 269–277.

Donnerstein, E., & Linz, D. (1984). Sexual violence in the media: A warning. *Psychology Today, 18,* (1), 14–15.

Donnerstein, E., & Wilson, D. W. (1976). Effects of noise and perceived control on ongoing and subsequent aggressive behavior. *Journal of Personality and Social Psychology, 34,* 774–781.

Dowd, M. (1984, March 12). 20 years after the murder of Kitty Genovese, the question remains: Why? *The New York Times,* B1, B4.

Dowlin, N. (1981, May). Deer fences protecting crops. *Impacts of Crop Research in Pennsylvania,* 8–10.

Doyne, E. J., Chambless, D. L., & Bentler, L. E. (1983). Aerobic exercise as treatment for depression in women. *Behavior Therapy, 14,* 434–440.

Driscoll, R., Davis, K. E., & Lipetz, M. E. (1972). Parental interference and romantic love. *Journal of Personality and Social Psychology, 24,* 1–10.

Duke, M. P., & Nowicki, S. (1972). A new measure and social learning model for interpersonal distance. *Journal of Experimental Research in Personality, 6,* 119–132.

Durden-Smith, J. (1980, November/December.) How to win the mating game by a nose. *Next,* 85–89.

Dutton, D. G., & Aron, A. P. (1974). Some evidence for heightened sexual attraction under conditions of high anxiety. *Journal of Personality and Social Psychology, 30,* 510–517.

Dywan, J., & Bowers, K. S. (1983). The use of hypnosis to enhance recall. *Science, 222,* 184–185.

Eagly, A. H. (1974). Comprehensibility of persuasive arguments as a determinant of opinion change. *Journal of Personality and Social Psychology, 29,* 758–773.

Eagly, A. H. (1978). Sex differences in influenceability. *Psychological Bulletin, 85,* 86–116.

Eagly, A. H., & Steffen, V. J. (1984). Gender stereotypes stem from the distribution of women and men into social roles. *Journal of Personality and Social Psychology, 46,* 735–754.

Eagly, A. H., Wood, W., & Fishbaugh, L. (1981). Sex differences in conformity: Surveillance by the group as a determinant of male conformity. *Journal of Personality and Social Psychology, 40,* 384–394.

Easterbrooks, M. A., & Goldberg, W. A. (1985). Effects of early maternal employment on toddlers, mothers, and fathers. *Developmental Psychology, 21,* 774–783.

Eckenrode, J. (1984). Impact of chronic and acute stressors on daily reports of mood. *Journal of Personality and Social Psychology, 46,* 907–918.

Efran, M. G. (1974). The effect of physical appearance on the judgment of guilt, interpersonal attraction, and severity of recommended punishment in a simulated jury task. *Journal of Research in Personality, 8,* 45–54.

Ehrhardt, A. A., & Baker, S. W. (1975). Hormonal aberrations and their implications for the understanding of normal sex differentiation. In P. H. Mussen, J. J. Conger, & J. Kagan (eds.), *Basic and contemporary issues in developmental psychology.* New York: Harper & Row.

Eibl-Eibesfeldt, I. (1974). *Love and hate: The natural history of behavior patterns.* New York: Schocken Books.

Eidelson, R. J., & Epstein, N. (1982). Cognition and relationship maladjustment: Development of a measure of dysfunctional relationship beliefs. *Journal of Consulting and Clinical Psychology, 50,* 715–720.

Eisdorfer, C. (1983). Conceptual models of aging: The challenge of a new frontier. *American Psychologist, 38,* 197–202.

Ekman, P. (1980). *The face of man.* Garland STPM Press.

Ekman, P. (1985). Cited in Bower, B. (1985, July 6). The face of emotion. *Science News, 128,* 12–13.

Ekman, P., Levenson, R. W., & Friesen, W. V. (1983). Autonomic nervous system activity distinguishes among emotions. *Science, 221,* 1208–1210.

Ekman, P., & Oster, H. (1979). Facial expressions of emotion. *Annual Review of Psychology,* Vol. 30. Palo Alto, CA: Annual Reviews.

Elkins, R. L. (1980). Covert sensitization treatment of alcoholism. *Addictive Behaviors, 5,* 67–89.

Ellis, A. (1977). The basic clinical theory of rational-emotive therapy. In A. Ellis & R. Grieger (eds.), *Handbook of rational-emotive therapy.* New York: Springer.

Ellis, A. (1979). Rational-emotive therapy: Research data that support the clinical and personality hypotheses of RET and other modes of cognitive-behavior therapy. In A. Ellis & J. M. Whiteley (eds.), *Theoretical and empirical foundations of rational-emotive therapy.* Monterey, CA: Brooks/Cole.

Ellis, A. (1985). Cognition and affect in emotional disturbance. *American Psychologist, 40,* 471–472.

Ellison, G. D. (1977). Animal models of psychopathology: The low-norepinephrine and low-serotonin rat. *American Psychologist, 32,* 1036–1045.

Ellsworth, P. C., Carlsmith, J. M., & Henson, A. (1972). The stare as a stimulus to flight in human subjects. *Journal of Personality and Social Psychology, 21,* 302–311.

Ellsworth, P. C., & Langer, E. J. (1976). Staring and approach: An interpretation of the stare as a nonspecific activator. *Journal of Personality and Social Psychology, 33,* 117–122.

Epstein, L. H., Wing, R. R., Koeske, R., & Valoski, A, (1984a). Effect of diet plus exercise on weight change in parents and children. *Journal of Consulting and Clinical Psychology, 52,* 429–437.

Epstein, L. H., Wing, R. R., Woodall, K., Penner, B. C., Kress, M. J., & Koeske, R. (1985). Effects of family-based behavioral treatment on obese 5-to-8-year-old children. *Behavior Therapy, 16,* 205–212.

Epstein, L. H., Woodall, K., Goreczny, A. J., Wing, R. R., & Robertson, R. J. (1984b). The modification of activity patterns and energy expenditure in obese young girls. *Behavior Therapy, 15,* 101–108.

Erdman, H. P., Klein, M. H., & Greist, J. H. (1985). Direct patient computer interviewing. *Journal of Consulting and Clinical Psychology, 53,* 760–773.

Erikson, E. H. (1963). *Childhood and society.* New York: Norton.

Erikson, E. H. (1975). *Life history and the historical moment.* New York: Norton.

Eriksson, K. (1972). Behavior and physiological differences among rat strains specially selected for their alcohol consumption. *Annals of the New York Academy of Science, 197,* 32–41.

Eron, L. D. (1982). Parent-child interaction, television violence, and aggression of children. *American Psychologist, 37,* 197–211.

Erwin, G., Plomin, R., & Wilson, J. (1984, March 17). Alcohol test may be inaccurate. *Science News,* 171.

Estes, W. K. (1972). An associative basis for coding and organization in memory. In A. W. Melton & E. Martin (eds.), *Coding processes in human memory.* Washington, DC: Winston.

Exline, R. V. (1972). Visual interaction: The glances of power and preference. In J. K. Cole (ed.), *The Nebraska symposium on motivation,* Vol. 19. Lincoln, NE: University of Nebraska Press.

Eysenck, H. J. (1960). Classification and the problem of diagnosis. In H. J. Eysenck (ed.), *Handbook of abnormal psychology.* London: Pitman.

Eysenck, H. J. (1972, November). Obscenity—officially speaking. *Penthouse,* 95–102.

Fabian, W. D., Jr., & Fishkin, S. M. (1981). A replicated study of self-reported changes in psychological absorption with marijuana intoxication. *Journal of Abnormal Psychology, 90,* 546–553.

Fagot, B. I. (1974). Sex differences in toddlers' behavior and parental reaction. *Developmental Psychology, 10,* 554–558.

Fagot, B. I. (1978). The influence of sex of child on parental reactions to toddler children. *Child Development, 49,* 459–465.

Fairbanks, L. A., McGuire, M. T., & Harris, C. J. (1982). Nonverbal interaction of patients and therapists during psychiatric interviews. *Journal of Abnormal Psychology, 91,* 109–119.

Fallon, A. E., & Rozin, P. (1985). Sex differences in perceptions of desirable body shape. *Journal of Abnormal Psychology, 94,* 102–105.

Fantz, R. L. (1961). The origin of form perception. *Scientific American, 204* (5), 66–72.

Farthing, G. W., Venturino, M., & Brown, S. W. (1984). Suggestion and distraction in the control of pain: Test of two hypotheses. *Journal of Abnormal Psychology, 93,* 266–276.

Fazio, R. H., & Cooper, J. (1983). Arousal in the dissonance process. In J. T. Cacioppo & R. E. Petty (eds.), *Social psychophysiology.* New York: Guilford Press.

Fazio, R. H., Sherman, S. J., & Herr, P. M. (1982). The feature-positive effect in the self-perception process: Does not doing matter as much as doing? *Journal of Personality and Social Psychology, 42,* 404–411.

Feder, H. H. (1984). Hormones and sexual behavior. *Annual Review of Psychology, 35,* 165–200.

Felsenthal, N. (1976). *Orientations to mass communications.* Chicago: Science Research.

Feltz, D. L. (1982). Path analysis of the causal elements in Bandura's theory of self-efficacy and an anxiety-based model of avoidance behavior. *Journal of Personality and Social Psychology, 42,* 764–781.

Fenigstein, A., Scheier, M. F., & Buss, A. H. (1975). Public and private self-consciousness: Assessment and theory. *Journal of Consulting and Clinical Psychology, 43,* 522–527.

Ferree, M. M. (1976). Working class jobs: Housework and paid work as sources of satisfaction. *Social Problems, 23,* 431–441.

Festinger, L. (1957). *A theory of cognitive dissonance.* Evanston, IL: Row, Peterson.

Festinger, L., & Carlsmith, J. M. (1959). Cognitive consequences of forced compliance. *Journal of Abnormal and Social Psychology, 58,* 203–210.

Findley, M. J., & Cooper, H. M. (1983). Locus of control and academic achievement: A literature review. *Journal of Personality and Social Psychology, 44,* 419–427.

Finnuchi, J., & Childs, B. (1981). Are there really sex differences in dyslexia? In A. Ansara, N. Geschwind, A. Galaburda, M. Albert, & N. Gartrell (Eds.), *Sex differences in dyslexia.* Towson, MD: The Orton Dyslexia Society.

Fisher, D. F., & Karsh, R. (1971). Modality effects and storage in sequential short-term memory. *Journal of Experimental Psychology, 87,* 410–414.

Fisher, J. D., Bell, P. A., & Baum, A. (1984). *Environmental psychology,* 2d ed. New York: Holt, Rinehart and Winston.

Fisher, J. D., & Byrne, D. (1975). Too close for comfort: Sex differences in response to invasions of personal space. *Journal of Personality and Social Psychology, 32,* 15–21.

Fisher, K. (1982). Debate rages on 1973 Sobell study. *APA Monitor, 13* (11), 8–9.

Fisher, K. (1984). Family violence cycle questioned. *APA Monitor, 15* (12), 30.

Fisher, L. E. (1980). Relationships and sexuality in contexts and culture: The anthropology of eros. In B. B. Wolman & J. Money (eds.), *Handbook of human sexuality.* Englewood Cliffs, NJ: Prentice-Hall.

Fisher, S. (1973). *Female orgasm: Psychology, physiology, fantasy.* New York: Basic Books.

Fisher, W. A., & Byrne, D. (1978b). Sex differences in response to erotica? Love versus lust. *Journal of Personality and Social Psychology, 36,* 117–125.

Fishman, S. M., & Sheehan, D. V. (1985). Anxiety and panic: Their cause and treatment. *Psychology Today, 19* (4), 26–32.

Fitch, G. (1970). Effects of self-esteem, perceived performance, and choice on causal attribution. *Journal of Personality and Social Psychology, 16,* 311–315.

Flaherty, J. F., & Dusek, J. B. (1980). An investigation of the relationship between psychological androgyny and components of self-concept. *Journal of Personality and Social Psychology, 38,* 984–992.

Flaxman, J. (1978). Quitting smoking now or later: Gradual, abrupt, immediate, and delayed quitting. *Behavior Therapy, 9,* 260–270.

Fleming, J. D. (1974). Field report: The state of the apes. *Psychology Today, 8,* 31–46.

Fleming, M. Z., MacGowan, B. R., Robinson, L., Spitz, J., & Salt, P. (1982). The body image of the postoperative female-to-male transsexual. *Journal of Consulting and Clinical Psychology, 50,* 461–462.

Fodor, E. M. (1984). The power motive and reactivity to power stresses. *Journal of Personality and Social Psychology, 47,* 853–859.

Fodor, E. M. (1985). The power motive, group conflict, and physiological arousal. *Journal of Personality and Social Psychology, 49,* 1408–1415.

Fodor, E. M., & Smith, T. (1982). The power motive as an influence on group decision making. *Journal of Personality and Social Psychology, 42,* 178–185.

Fodor, J. A., Bever, T. G., & Garrett, M. F. (1974). *The psychology of language.* New York: McGraw-Hill.

Fogel, M. L. (1980). Warning: Auto fumes may lower your kid's IQ. *Psychology Today, 14* (1), 108.

Folkins, C. H., & Sime, W. E. (1981). Physical fitness training and mental health. *American Psychologist, 36,* 373–389.

Ford, C. S., & Beach, F. A. (1951). *Patterns of sexual behavior.* New York: Harper & Row.

Foulkes, D. (1971). Longitudinal studies of dreams in children. In J. Masserman (ed.), *Science and psychoanalysis.* New York: Grune & Stratton.

Fowler, R. D. (1985). Landmarks in computer-assisted psychological assessment. *Journal of Consulting and Clinical Psychology, 53,* 748–759.

Fox, N. (1977). Attachment of kibbutz infants to mother and metapelet. *Child Development, 48,* 1228–1239

Fox, S. (1984). *The mirror makers.* New York: Morrow.

Foy, D. W., Nunn, L. B., & Rychtarik, R. G. (1984). Broad-spectrum behavioral treatment for chronic alcoholics: Effects of training controlled drinking skills. *Journal of Consulting and Clinical Psychology, 52,* 218–230

Franck, K. D., Unseld, C. T., & Wentworth, W. E. (1974). Adaptation of the newcomer: A process of construction. Unpublished manuscript, City University of New York.

Frank, E., Anderson, C., & Rubinstein, D. (1978). Frequency of sexual dysfunction in "normal" couples. *New England Journal of Medicine, 299,* 111–115.

Freedman, J. L., & Fraser, S. C. (1966). Compliance without pressure: The foot-in-the-door technique. *Journal of Personality and Social Psychology, 4,* 195–202.

Freedman, J. L., Wallington, S. A., & Bless, E. (1967). Compliance without pressure: The effect of guilt. *Journal of Personality and Social Psychology, 7,* 117–124.

Freedman, R. R., & Sattler, H. L. (1982). Physiological and psychological factors in sleep-onset insomnia. *Journal of Abnormal Psychology, 91,* 380–389.

French, G. M., & Harlow, H. F. (1962). Variability of delayed-reaction performance in normal and brain-damaged rhesus monkeys. *Journal of Neurophysiology, 25,* 585–599.

French-Belgian Collaborative Group. (1982). Ischemic heart disease and psychological patterns: Prevalence and incidence in Belgium and France. *Advances in Cardiology, 29,* 25–31.

Freud, S. (1909). Analysis of a phobia in a five-year-old boy. In *Collected papers,* Vol. 3, trans. A. and J. Strachey. New York: Basic Books, 1959.

Freud, S. (1927). A religious experience. In *Standard edition of the complete psychological works of Sigmund Freud,* Vol. 21. London: Hogarth Press, 1964.

Freud, S. (1930). *Civilization and its discontents,* trans. J. Strachey. New York: Norton, 1961.

Freud, S. (1933). New introductory lectures. In *Standard edition of the complete psychological works of Sigmund Freud,* Vol. 22. London: Hogarth Press, 1964.

Friedman, M., & Rosenman, R. H. (1974). *Type A behavior and your heart.* New York: Knopf.

Friedman, M. I., & Stricker, E. M. (1976). The physiological psychology of hunger: A physiological perspective. *Psychological Review, 83,* 409–431.

Frisch, H. L. (1977). Sex stereotypes in adult-infant play. *Child Development, 48,* 1671–1675.

Frodi, A. M. (1981). Contribution of infant characteristics to child abuse. *American Journal of Mental Deficiency, 85,* 341–349.

Frodi, A. M., Macauley, J., & Thome, P. R. (1977). Are women always less aggressive than men? A review of the experimental literature. *Psychological Bulletin, 84,* 634–660.

Fromm, E. (1956). *The art of loving.* New York: Harper & Row.

Funkenstein, D. (1955, May). The physiology of fear and anger. *Scientific American.*

Fustero, S. (1984). Home on the street. *Psychology Today, 18* (2), 56–63.

Galanter, E. (1962). Contemporary psychophysics. In R. Brown et al. (eds.), *New directions in psychology.* New York: Holt, Rinehart and Winston.

Galassi, J. P., Frierson, H. T., & Sharer, R. (1981). Behavior of high, moderate, and low test anxious students during an actual test situation. *Journal of Consulting and Clinical Psychology, 49,* 51–62.

Galizio, M., & Hendrick, C. (1972). Effect of musical accompaniment on attitude: The guitar as a prop for persuasion. *Journal of Applied Social Psychology, 2,* 350–359.

Gallup, G. G., Jr., & Suarez, S. D. (1985). Alternatives to the use of animals in psychological research. *American Psychologist, 40,* 1104–1111.

Garcia, J. (1981). The logic and limits of mental aptitude testing. *American Psychologist, 36,* 1172–1180.

Gardner, B. T., & Gardner, R. A. (1972). Two-way communication with an infant chimpanzee. In A. M. Schrier & F. Stollnitz (eds.), *Behavior of nonhuman primates,* Vol. 4. New York: Academic Press.

Gardner, H. (1978, March). The loss of language. *Human Nature, 1,* 76–84.

Gardner, R. A., & Gardner, B. T. (1977). Comparative physiology and language acquisition. In K. Salzinger & F. Denmark (eds.), *Psychology: The state of the art.* New York: Annals of the New York Academy of the Sciences.

Garfield, S. L. (1981). Psychotherapy: A 40-year appraisal. *American Psychologist, 36,* 174–183.

Garfield, S. L. (1982). Eclecticism and integration in psychotherapy. *Behavior Therapy, 13,* 610–623.

Gash, D. M. (1981). Brain transplants are next. *Psychology Today, 15* (12) 116.

Gatchel, R. J., & Proctor, J. D. (1976). Effectiveness of voluntary heart rate control in reducing speech anxiety. *Journal of Consulting and Clinical Psychology, 44,* 381–389.

Gazzaniga, M. S. (1972). One brain—two minds? *American Science, 60,* 311–317.

Gazzaniga, M. S. (1983). Right hemisphere language following brain bisection: A 20-year perspective. *American Psychologist, 38,* 525–537.

Gazzaniga, M. S. (1985). The social brain. *Psychology Today, 19* (11), 29–38.

Geen, R. G. (1981). Behavioral and physiological reactions to observed violence: Effects of prior exposure to aggressive stimuli. *Journal of Person-*

ality and Social Psychology, 40, 868–875.

Geen, R. G., Stonner, D., & Shope, G. L. (1975). The facilitation of aggression by aggression: Evidence against the catharsis hypothesis. Journal of Personality and Social Psychology, 31, 721–726.

Geffen, G. (1976). Development of hemispheric specialization for speech perception. Cortex, 12, 337–346.

Gelman, D., Abramson, P., Raine, G., McAlevey, & McKillop, P. (1985, August 12). The social fallout from an epidemic. Newsweek, 28–29.

Gerard, H. B., Wilhelmy, R. A., & Conolley, E. S. (1968). Conformity and group size. Journal of Personality and Social Psychology, 8, 79–82.

Gerbner, G., & Gross, L. (1976). The scary world of TV's heavy viewer. Psychology Today, 9, 41–45.

Getzels, J. W., & Jackson, P. W. (1962). Creativity and intelligence: Explorations with gifted students. New York: Wiley.

Gibson, J. L., Ivancevich, J. M., & Donnelly, J. H., Jr. (1985). Organizations: Behavior, structure, processes, 5th ed. Plano, TX: Business Publications, Inc.

Gilbert, S. J. (1981). Another look at the Milgram obedience studies: The role of the gradated series of shocks. Personality and Social Psychology Bulletin, 7, 690–695.

Gilligan, C. (1982). In a different voice. Cambridge, MA: Harvard University Press.

Gillis, J. S., & Avis, W. E. (1980). The male-taller norm in mate selection. Personality and Social Psychology Bulletin, 6, 396–401.

Gilovich, T. (1983). Biased evaluation and persistence in gambling. Journal of Personality and Social Psychology, 44, 1110–1126.

Glasgow, R. E., Klesges, R. C., Godding, P. R., & Gegelman, R. (1983). Controlled smoking, with or without carbon monoxide feedback, as an alternative for chronic smokers. Behavior Therapy, 14, 396–397.

Glasgow, R. E., Klesges, R. C., Godding, P. R., Vasey, M. W., & O'Neill, H. K. (1984). Evaluation of a work-site-controlled smoking program. Journal of Consulting and Clinical Psychology, 52, 137–138.

Glasgow, R. E., Klesges, R. C., Klesges, L. M., Vasey, M. W., & Gunnarson, D. F. (1985). Long-term effects of a controlled smoking program: A 2 1/2 year follow-up. Behavior Therapy, 16, 303–307.

Glass, D. C. (1977). Stress and coronary-prone behavior. Hillsdale, NJ: Erlbaum.

Glass, D. C., & Singer, J. E. (1972). Urban stress. New York: Academic Press.

Gleason, H. A., Jr. (1961). An introduction to descriptive linguistics, rev. ed. New York: Holt, Rinehart and Winston.

Goeders, N. E., & Smith, J. E. (1983). Cortical dopaminergic involvement in cocaine reinforcement. Science, 221, 773–775.

Gold, D., & Andres, D. (1978a). Comparisons of adolescent children with employed and nonemployed mothers. Merrill-Palmer Quarterly, 24, 243–254.

Gold, D., & Andres, D. (1978b). Developmental comparisons between ten-year-old children with employed and nonemployed mothers. Child Development, 49, 75–84.

Gold, D., & Andres, D. (1978c). Relations between maternal employment and development of nursery school children. Canadian Journal of Behavioral Science, 10, 116–129.

Gold, P. E., & King, R. A. (1974). Retrograde amnesia: Storage failure versus retrieval failure. Psychological Review, 81, 465–469.

Goldberg, L. W. (1978). Differential attribution of trait-descriptive terms to oneself as compared to well-liked, neutral, and disliked others. Journal of Personality and Social Psychology, 36, 1012–1028.

Goldberg, S., & Lewis, M. (1969). Play behavior in the year-old infant: Early

sex differences. Child Development, 40, 21–31.

Goldfoot, D. A., Essock-Vitale, S. M., Asa, C. S., Thornton, J. E., & Leshner, A. I. (1978). Anosmia in male rhesus monkeys does not alter copulatory activity with cycling females. Science, 199, 1095–1096.

Goldfried, M. R., Linehan, M. M., & Smith, J. L. (1978). Reduction of test anxiety through cognitive restructuring. Journal of Consulting and Clinical Psychology, 46, 32–39.

Goldman, W., & Lewis, P. (1977). Beautiful is good: Evidence that the physically attractive are more socially skillful. Journal of Experimental Social Psychology, 13, 125–130.

Goldsmith, H. H. (1983). Genetic influences on personality from infancy to adulthood. Child Development, 54, 331–355.

Goldsmith, J. R. (1968). Effects of air pollution on human health. In A. C. Stearn (ed.), Air pollution, 2d ed. New York: Academic Press.

Goldstein, M., & Davis, E. E. (1972). Race and belief: A further analysis of the social determinants of behavioral intentions. Journal of Personality and Social Psychology, 22, 345–355.

Goleman, D. J. Staying up. (1982). Psychology Today, 16 (3), 24–35.

Goleman, D. J., & Schwartz, G. E. (1976). Meditation as an intervention in stress reactivity. Journal of Consulting and Clinical Psychology, 44, 456–466.

Golub, S. (1976). The effect of premenstrual anxiety and depression on cognitive function. Journal of Personality and Social Psychology, 34, 99–104.

Goodhart, D. E. (1985). Some psychological effects associated with positive and negative thinking about stressful event outcomes. Journal of Personality and Social Psychology, 1985, 198–215.

Goodwin, D. W. (1979). Alcoholism and heredity. Archives of General Psychiatry, 36, 57–61.

Goodwin, D. W., Schulsinger, F., Hermansen, L., Guze, S. B., & Winokur, G. A. (1973). Alcohol problems in adoptees raised apart from alcoholic biological parents. *Archives of General Psychiatry, 128,* 239–243.

Gormally, J., Sipps, G., Raphael, R., Edwin, D., & Varvil-Weld, D. (1981). The relationship between maladaptive cognitions and social anxiety. *Journal of Consulting and Clinical Psychology, 49,* 300–301.

Gotlib, I. H. (1982). Self-reinforcement and depression in interpersonal interaction: The role of performance level. *Journal of Abnormal Psychology, 91,* 3–13.

Gotlib, I. H. (1984). Depression and general psychopathology in university students. *Journal of Abnormal Psychology, 93,* 19–30.

Gould, R. (1975). Adult life stages: Growth toward self-tolerance. *Psychology Today, 8,* 74–81.

Goy, R. W., & Goldfoot, D. A. (1976). Neuroendocrinology: Animal models and problems of human sexuality. In E. A. Rubenstein et al. (eds.), *New directions in sex research.* New York: Plenum.

Goy, R. W., & McEwen, B. S. (1982). *Sexual differentiation of the brain.* Cambridge, MA: MIT Press.

Graham, J. (1977). *The MMPI: A practical guide.* New York: Oxford University Press.

Granberg, D., & Brent, E. (1983). When prophecy bends: The preference-expectation link in U.S. presidential elections. *Journal of Personality and Social Psychology, 45,* 477–491.

Green, B. F. (1981). A primer of testing. *American Psychologist, 36,* 1001–1011.

Greenbaum, P., & Rosenfeld, H. M. (1978). Patterns of avoidance in response to interpersonal staring and proximity: Effects of bystanders on drivers at a traffic intersection. *Journal of Personality and Social Psychology, 36,* 575–587.

Greene, J. (1982). The gambling trap. *Psychology Today, 16* (9), 50–55.

Gregory, R. L. (1973). *Eye and brain,* 2d ed. New York: World Universities Library.

Grossmann, K., Thane, K., & Grossmann, K. E. (1981). Maternal tactual contact of the newborn after various post-partum conditions of mother-infant contact. *Developmental Psychology, 17,* 158–169.

Groth, A. N., & Burgess, A. W. (1980). Male rape: Offenders and victims. *American Journal of Psychiatry, 137,* 806–810.

Groth, A. N., & Gary. (1981). Cited in Allgeier, E. R., & Allgeier, A. R. (1984). *Sexual interactions.* Lexington, MA: Heath.

Grünbaum, A. (1985). Cited in D. J. Goleman. Pressure mounts for analysts to prove theory is scientific. *The New York Times,* January 15, 1985, C1, C9.

Grush, J. E. (1980). The impact of candidate expenditures, regionality, and prior outcomes on the 1976 Democratic presidential primaries. *Journal of Personality and Social Psychology, 38,* 337–347.

Grush, J. E., & Yehl, J. G. (1979). Marital roles, sex differences, and interpersonal attraction. *Journal of Personality and Social Psychology, 37,* 116–123.

Guilford, J. P. (1959). Traits of creativity. In H. H. Anderson (ed.), *Creativity and its cultivation.* New York: Harper & Row.

Guilford, J. P. (1967). *The nature of human intelligence.* New York: McGraw-Hill.

Guilford, J. P., & Hoepfner, R. (1971). *The analysis of intelligence.* New York: McGraw-Hill.

Haaf, R. A., Smith, P. H., & Smitley, S. (1983). Infant response to facelike patterns under fixed trial and infant-control procedures. *Child Development, 54,* 172–177.

Haber, R. N. (1969). Eidetic images. *Scientific American, 220,* 36–55.

Haber, R. N. (1980). Eidetic images are not just imaginary. *Psychology Today, 14* (11), 72–82.

Haber, R. N., & Hershenson, M. (1980). *The psychology of visual perception.* New York: Holt, Rinehart and Winston.

Hackett, T. P., & Cassem, N. H. (1970). Psychological reactions to life-threatening illness: Acute myocardial infarction. In H. S. Abram (ed.), *Psychological aspects of stress.* Springfield, IL: Charles C. Thomas.

Hall, C. (1966). *The meaning of dreams.* New York: McGraw-Hill.

Hall, E. T. (1968). Proxemics. *Current Anthropology, 9,* 83–107.

Hall, J. A., & Taylor, M. C. (1985). Psychological androgyny and the masculinity femininity interaction. *Journal of Personality and Social Psychology, 49,* 429–435.

Hall, R. G., Sachs, D. P. L., Hall, S. M., & Benowitz, N. L. (1984). Two-year efficacy and safety of rapid smoking therapy in patients with cardiac and pulmonary disease. *Journal of Consulting and Clinical Psychology, 52,* 574–581.

Hall, S. M., Rugg, D., Tunstall, C., & Jones, R. T. (1984). Preventing relapse to cigarette smoking by behavioral skill training. *Journal of Consulting and Clinical Psychology, 52,* 372–382.

Hall, S. M., Tunstall, C., Rugg, D., Jones, R. T., & Benowitz, N. (1985). Nicotine gum and behavioral treatment in smoking cessation. *Journal of Consulting and Clinical Psychology, 53,* 256–258.

Hall, V. C., & Kaye, D. B. (1980). Early patterns of cognitive development. *Monographs of the Society for Research in Child Development, 45,* (2), Serial No. 184.

Halperin, K. M., & Snyder, C. R. (1979). Effects of enhanced psychological test feedback on treatment outcome: Therapeutic implications of the Barnum effect. *Journal of Consulting and Clinical Psychology, 47,* 140–146.

Hamm, N. H., Baum, M. R., & Nikels, K. W. (1975). Effects of race and exposure on judgments of interpersonal favorability. *Journal of Experimental Social Psychology, 11,* 14–24.

Hammen, C., Marks, T., Mayol, A., & deMayo, R. (1985). Depressive self-schemas, life stress, and vulnerability to depression. *Journal of Abnormal Psychology, 94,* 308–319.

Hammen, C., & Mayol, A. (1982). Depression and cognitive characteristics of stressful life-event types. *Journal of Abnormal Psychology, 91,* 165–174.

Hansel, C. E. M. (1980). *ESP and parapsychology: A critical evaluation.* Buffalo, NY: Prometheus Books.

Hansen, G. O. (1975). Meeting house challenges: Involvement—the elderly. In *Housing issues.* Lincoln, NE: University of Nebraska Press.

Harbeson, G. E. (1971). *Choice and challenge for the American woman,* rev. ed. Cambridge: Schenckman.

Harburg, E., Erfurt, J. C., Hauenstein, L. S., Chape, C., Schull, W. J., & Schork, M. A. (1973). Socioecological stress, suppressed hostility, skin color, and black-white male blood pressure: Detroit. *Psychosomatic Medicine, 35,* 276–296.

Harder, D. W., Gift, T. E., Strauss, J. S., Ritzler, B. A., & Kokes, R. F. (1981). Life events and two-year outcome in schizophrenia. *Journal of Consulting and Clinical Psychology, 49,* 619–626.

Hardy-Brown, K., & Plomin, R. (1985). Infant communicative development: Evidence from adoptive and biological families for genetic and environmental influences on rate differences. *Developmental Psychology, 21,* 378–385.

Hare-Mustin, R. (1983). An appraisal of the relationship between women and psychotherapy: 80 years after the case of Dora. *American Psychologist, 38,* 593–601.

Harlow, H. F. (1959). Love in infant monkeys. *Scientific American, 200,* 68–86.

Harlow, H. F., & Harlow, M. K. (1966). Learning to love. *American Scientist, 54,* 244–272.

Harlow, H. F., Harlow, M. K., & Meyer, D. R. (1950). Learning motivated by a manipulation drive. *Journal of Experimental Psychology, 40,* 228–234.

Harlow, H. F., & Zimmermann, R. R. (1959). Affectional responses in the infant monkey. *Science, 130,* 421–432.

Harlow, M. K., & Harlow, H. F. (1966). Affection in primates. *Discovery, 27,* 11–17.

Harrell, T. W., & Harrell, M. S. (1945). Army General Classification Test scores for civilian occupations. *Educational and Psychological Measurement, 5,* 229–239.

Harris, G. W., & Levine, S. (1965). Sexual differentiation of the brain and its experimental control. *Journal of Physiology, 181,* 379–400.

Harris, M. B., Harris, R. J., & Bochner, S. (1982). Fat, four-eyed, and female: Stereotypes of obesity, glasses, and gender. *Journal of Applied Social Psychology, 12,* 503–516.

Harris, T. A. (1967). *I'm OK—You're OK.* New York: Harper & Row.

Harrison, A. A., & Saeed, L. (1977). Let's make a deal: An analysis of revelations and stipulations in lonely hearts advertisements. *Journal of Personality and Social Psychology, 35,* 257–264.

Hart, B. (1967). Sexual reflexes and mating behavior in the male dog. *Journal of Comparative and Physiological Psychology, 66,* 388–399.

Hartmann, E. L. (1973). *The functions of sleep.* New Haven, CT: Yale University Press.

Hartmann, E. L. (1981). The strangest sleep disorder. *Psychology Today, 15* (4), 14–18.

Hartmann, E. L., & Stern, W. C. (1972). Desynchronized sleep deprivation: Learning deficit and its reversal by increased catecholamines. *Physiology and Behavior, 8,* 585–587.

Harvey, J. H., Ickes, W. J., & Kidd, R. F. (eds.). (1976). *New directions in attributional research,* Vol. 1. Hillsdale, NJ: Erlbaum.

Harvey, J. H., Ickes, W. J., & Kidd, R. F. (eds.). (1978). *New directions in attributional research,* Vol. 2. Hillsdale, NJ: Erlbaum.

Hass, R. G., & Linder, D. E. (1972). Counterargument availability and the effects of message structure on persuasion. *Journal of Personality and Social Psychology, 23,* 219–233.

Hassett, J. (1978). Sex and smell. *Psychology Today, 12* (10), 40–42, 45.

Hatfield, E. (1983). What do women and men want from love and sex? In E. R. Allgeier & N. B. McCormick (eds.), *Changing boundaries: Gender roles and sexual behavior.* Palo Alto, CA: Mayfield.

Hatfield, E., Sprecher, S., & Traupman, J. (1978). Men's and women's reaction to sexually explicit films: A serendipitous finding. *Archives of Sexual Behavior, 6,* 583–592.

Havighurst, R. J. (1972). *Developmental tasks and education,* 3d ed. New York: McKay.

Hayes, S. L. (1981). Single case design and empirical clinical practice. *Journal of Consulting and Clinical Psychology, 49,* 193–211.

Haynes, S. G., Feinlieb, M., & Kannel, W. B. (1980). The relationship of psychosocial factors to coronary heart disease in the Framingham study: III. Eight-year incidence of coronary heart disease. *American Journal of Epidemiology, 111,* 37–58.

Haynes, S. N., Adams, A., & Franzen, M. (1981). The effects of presleep stress on sleep-onset insomnia. *Journal of Abnormal Psychology, 90,* 601–606.

Haynes, S. N., Follingstad, D. R., & McGowan, W. T. (1974). Insomnia: Sleep patterns and anxiety level. *Journal of Psychosomatic Research, 18,* 69–74.

Haynes, S. N., Sides, H., & Lockwood, G. (1977). Relaxation instructions and frontalis electromyographic feedback intervention with sleep-onset insomnia. *Behavior Therapy, 8,* 644–652.

Haynes, S. N., Woodward, S., Moran, R., & Alexander, D. (1974). Relaxation treatment of insomnia. *Behavior Therapy, 5,* 555–558.

Heaton, R. K., & Victor, R. G. (1976). Personality characteristics associated with psychedelic flashbacks in natural and experimental settings. *Journal of Abnormal Psychology, 85,* 83–90.

Heber, R., Garber, H., Harrington, S., & Hoffman, C. (1972, December). Rehabilitation of families at risk for mental retardation. Progress report, University of Wisconsin at Madison.

Heiby, E., & Becker, J. D. (1980). Effect of filmed modeling on the self-reported frequency of masturbation. *Archives of Sexual Behavior, 9,* 115–122.

Heider, F. (1958). *The psychology of interpersonal relations.* New York: Wiley.

Heiman, J. R. (1975). The physiology of erotica: Women's sexual arousal. *Psychology Today,* 90–94.

Heiman, J. R., LoPiccolo, L., & LoPiccolo, J. (1976). *Becoming orgasmic: A sexual growth program for women.* Englewood Cliffs, NJ: Prentice-Hall.

Heingartner, A., & Hall, J. V. (1974). Affective consequences in adults and children of repeated exposure to auditory stimuli. *Journal of Personality and Social Psychology, 29,* 719–723.

Helmreich, R. L., Spence, J. T., & Holahan, C. K. (1979). Psychological androgyny and sex-role flexibility: A test of two hypotheses. *Journal of Personality and Social Psychology, 37,* 1631–1644.

Hemstone, M., & Jaspars, J. (1982). Explanations for racial discrimination: The effects of group decision on intergroup attributions. *European Journal of Social Psychology, 12,* 1–16.

Hendrick, C., Wells, K. S., & Faletti, M. V. (1982). Social and emotional effects of geographical relocation on elderly retirees. *Journal of Personality and Social Psychology, 42,* 951–962.

Hendrick, J., & Hendrick, C. D. (1977). *Aging in mass society: Myths and realities.* Cambridge, MA: Winthrop.

Hendrick, S., Hendrick, C., Slapion-Foote, M. J., & Foote, F. H. (1985). Gender differences in sexual attitudes. *Journal of Personality and Social Psychology, 48,* 1630–1642.

Hennigan, K. M., Cook, T. D., & Gruder, C. L. (1982). Cognitive tuning set, source credibility, and the temporal persistence of attitude change. *Journal of Personality and Social Psychology, 42,* 412–425.

Hensley, W. E. (1981). The effects of attire, location, and sex on aiding behavior: A similarity explanation. *Journal of Nonverbal Behavior, 6,* 3–11.

Herrell, J. M. (1975). Sex differences in emotional responsiveness to "erotic literature." *Journal of Consulting and Clinical Psychology, 43,* 921.

Hersen, M., Bellack, A. S., Himmelhoch, J. M., & Thase, M. E. (1984). Effect of social skill training, amiltriptyline, and psychotherapy in unipolar depressed women. *Behavior Therapy, 15,* 21–40.

Heston, L. L. (1966). Psychiatric disorders in foster-home-reared children of schizophrenic mothers. *British Journal of Psychiatry, 112,* 819–825.

Hilgard, E. R. (1977). *Divided consciousness: Multiple controls in human thought and action.* New York: Wiley-Interscience.

Hinshaw, S. P., Henker, B., & Whalen, C. K. (1984). Cognitive-behavioral and pharmacologic interventions for hyperactive boys: Comparative and combined effects. *Journal of Consulting and Clinical Psychology, 52,* 739–749.

Hirsch, J. (1975). Jensenism: The bankruptcy of "science" without scholarship. *Educational Theory, 25,* 3–28.

Hite, S. (1976). *The Hite report: A nationwide study on female sexuality.* New York: Macmillan.

Hite, S. (1981). *The Hite report on male sexuality.* New York: Knopf.

Hobson, J. A., & McCarley, R. W. (1977). The brain as a dream state generator: An activation-synthesis hypothesis of the dream process. *American Journal of Psychiatry, 134,* 1335–1348.

Hofferth, S. L., & Moore, K. A. (1979). Women's employment and marriage. In R. E. Smith (ed.), *The subtle revolution: Women at work.* Washington, D.C.: The Urban Institute.

Hoffman, L. W. (1985, August). Work, family, and the child. Master lecture delivered at the meeting of the American Psychological Association, Los Angeles.

Hoffman, M. L. (1981). Is altruism part of human nature? *Journal of Personality and Social Psychology, 40,* 121–137.

Hoffmann-Plotkin, D., & Twentyman, C. T. (1984). A multimodal assessment of behavioral and cognitive deficits in abused and neglected preschoolers. *Child Development, 55,* 794–802.

Holahan, C. J., & Moos, R. H. (1985). Life stress and health: Personality, coping, and family support in stress resistance. *Journal of Personality and Social Psychology, 49,* 739–747.

Hollingshead, A. B., & Redlich, F. C. (1958). *Social class and mental illness: A community study.* New York: Wiley.

Holmes, D. S. (1984). Meditation and somatic arousal reduction: A review of the experimental evidence. *American Psychologist, 39,* 1–10.

Holmes, D. S. (1985). To meditate or to simply rest, that is the question: A response to the comments of Shapiro. *American Psychologist, 40,* 722–725.

Holmes, D. S., McGilley, B. M., & Houston, B. K. (1984). Task-related arousal of Type A and Type B persons: Level of challenge and response specificity. *Journal of Personality and Social Psychology, 46,* 1322–1327.

Holmes, D. S., Solomon, S., Cappo, B. M., & Greenberg, J. L. (1983). Effects of transcendental meditation versus resting on physiological and subjective arousal. *Journal of Personality and Social Psychology, 44,* 1244–1252.

Holmes, D. S., & Will, M. J. (1985). Expression of interpersonal aggression by angered and nonangered persons with the Type A and Type B behavior patterns. *Journal of Personality and Social Psychology, 48,* 723–727.

Holmes, T. H., & Rahe, R. H. (1967). The social readjustment rating scale. *Journal of Psychosomatic Research, 11,* 213–218.

Holroyd, K. A., Westbrook, T., Wolf, M., & Badhorn, E. (1978). Performance, cognition, and physiological responding in test anxiety. *Journal of Abnormal Psychology, 87,* 442–451.

Holt, R. R. (1982). Occupational stress. In L. Goldberger & S. Breznitz (eds.), *Handbook of stress.* New York: Free Press.

Honts, C., Hodes, R., & Raskin, D. (1985). *Journal of Applied Psychology, 70* (1).

Horn, J. M. (1983). The Texas adoption project: Adopted children and their intellectual resemblance to biological and adoptive parents. *Child Development, 54,* 268–275.

Horney, K. (1967). *Feminine psychology.* New York: Norton.

Horton, D. L., & Turnage, T. W. (1976). *Human learning.* Englewood Cliffs, NJ: Prentice-Hall.

Horvath, T. (1981). Physical attractiveness: The influence of selected torso parameters. *Archives of Sexual Behavior, 10,* 21–24.

Howard, J. L., Liptzin, M. B., & Reifler, C. B. (1973). Is pornography a problem? *Journal of Social Issues, 29,* 133–145.

Howard, L., & Polich, J. (1985). P300 latency and memory span development. *Developmental Psychology, 1985,* 283–289.

Howes, M. J., Hokanson, J. E., & Loewenstein, D. A. (1985). Induction to depressive affect after prolonged exposure to a mildly depressed individual. *Journal of Personality and Social Psychology, 49,* 1110–1113.

Hrncir, E. J., Speller, G. M., & West, M. (1985). What are we testing? *Developmental Psychology, 21,* 226–232.

Huesmann, L. R., Eron, L. D., Klein, R., Brice, P., & Fischer, P. (1983). Mitigating the imitation of aggressive behaviors by changing children's attitudes about media violence. *Journal of Personality and Social Psychology, 44,* 899–910.

Hull, J. G., Levenson, R. W., Young, R. D., & Sher, K. J. (1983). Self-awareness-reducing effects of alcohol consumption. *Journal of Personality and Social Psychology, 44,* 461–473.

Hunt, M. (1974). *Sexual behavior in the 1970s.* Chicago: Playboy Press.

Hunter, J. E., & Schmidt, F. L. (1983). Quantifying the effects of psychological interventions on employee job performance and work-force productivity. *American Psychologist, 38,* 473–478.

Huntley, C. W., & Davis, F. (1983). Undergraduate study of value scores as predictors of occupation 25 years later. *Journal of Personality and Social Psychology, 45,* 1148–1155.

Hurvich, L. M. (1978). Two decades of opponent processes. In F. W. Billmeyer & G. Wyszecki (eds.), *Color 77.* Bristol, England: Adam Hilger.

Hurvich, L. M., & Jameson, D. (1974). Opponent processes as a model of neural organization. *American Psychologist, 29,* 88–102.

Hutchings, B., & Mednick, S. A. (1974). Registered criminality in the adoptive and biological parents of registered male adoptees. In S. A. Mednick, F. Schulsinger, J. Higgins, & B. Bell (eds.), *Genetics, environment, and psychopathology.* New York: Elsevier.

Huxley, A. (1939). *Brave new world.* New York: Harper & Row.

Hyde, J. S. (1981). How large are cognitive gender differences? *American Psychologist, 36,* 892–901.

Ibrahim, A. (1976). The home situation and the homosexual. *Journal of Sex Research, 12,* 263–282.

Israel, A. C., Stolmaker, L., & Andrian, C. A. G. (1985). The effects of training parents in general child management skills on a behavioral weight loss program for children. *Behavior Therapy, 16,* 169–180

Istvan, J., & Griffitt, W. (1978). Emotional arousal and sexual attraction.

Unpublished manuscript, Kansas State University.

Ivancevich, J. M., & Matteson, M. T. (1980). *Stress and work: A managerial perspective.* Glenview, IL: Scott, Foresman.

Ivey, M. E., & Bardwick, J. M. (1968). Patterns of affective fluctuation in the menstrual cycle. *Psychosomatic Medicine, 30,* 336–345.

Izard, C. E. (ed.). (1982). *Measuring emotions in infants and children.* New York: Cambridge University Press.

Izard, C. E. (1984). Emotion-cognition relationships and human development. In C. E. Izard, J. Kagan, & R. B. Zajonc (eds.), *Emotions, cognition, and behavior.* New York: Cambridge University Press.

Jackson, J. M., & Harkins, S. G. (1985). Equity in effort: An explanation of the social loafing effect. *Journal of Personality and Social Psychology, 49,* 1199–1206.

Jacobs, T. J., & Charles, E. (1980). Life events and the occurrence of cancer in children. *Psychosomatic Medicine, 42,* 11–24.

Jacobson, E. (1938). *Progressive relaxation.* Chicago: University of Chicago Press.

Jaffe, H. W., Bregman, D. J., & Selik, R. M. (1983). Acquired immune deficiency syndrome in the United States. *Journal of Infectious Diseases, 148,* 339–345.

James, W. (1890). *The principles of psychology.* New York: Henry Holt.

James, W. (1904). Does "consciousness" exist? *Journal of Philosophy, Psychology, and Scientific Methods, 1,* 477–491.

Janda, L. H., & O'Grady, E. E. (1980). Development of a sex anxiety inventory. *Journal of Consulting and Clinical Psychology, 48,* 169–175.

Janis, I., & Mann, L. (1977). *Decision-making.* New York: Free Press.

Janis, I., & Wheeler, D. (1978). Thinking clearly about career choices. *Psychology Today, 12* (12), 66–76, 121–122.

Janis, I., Kaye, D., & Kirschner, P. (1965). Facilitating effects of "eating while reading" on responsiveness to persuasive communications. *Journal of Personality and Social Psychology, 1,* 181–186.

Janowitz, H. D., & Grossman, M. I. (1949). Effect of variations in nutritive density on intake of food in dogs and cats. *American Journal of Physiology, 158,* 184–193.

Jellison, J. M., & Green, J. (1981). A self-presentation approach to the fundamental attribution error: The norm of internality. *Journal of Personality and Social Psychology, 40,* 643–649.

Jellison, J. M., & Oliver, D. F. (1983). Attitude similarity and attraction: An impression management approach. *Personality and Social Psychology Bulletin, 9,* 111–115.

Johns, M. W., Masterson, J. P., & Bruce, D. W. (1971). Relationship between sleep habits, adrenocortical activity and personality. *Psychosomatic Medicine, 33,* 499–507.

Johnson, J. H., Butcher, J. N., Null, C., & Johnson, K. N. (1984). Replicated item level factor analysis of the full MMPI. *Journal of Personality and Social Psychology, 48,* 105–114.

Johnson, J. T., Cain, L. M., Falke, T. L., Hayman, J., & Perillo, E. (1985). The "Barnum effect" revisited: Cognitive and motivational factors in the acceptance of personality descriptions. *Journal of Personality and Social Psychology, 49,* 1378–1391.

Johnson, J. T., & Judd, C. M. (1983). Overlooking the incongruent: Categorization biases in the identification of political statements. *Journal of Personality and Social Psychology, 45,* 978–996.

Johnson, P. B. (1981). Achievement motivation and success: Does the end justify the means? *Journal of Personality and Social Psychology, 40,* 374–375.

Johnson, S. M., & White, G. (1971). Self-observation as an agent of behavioral change. *Behavior Therapy, 2,* 488–497.

Johnston, L. D., Bachman, J. G., & O'Malley, P. M. (1982). Student drug use, attitudes, and beliefs, 1975–1982. DHHS Publication No. ADM 82–1260. Washington, DC: National Institute on Drug Abuse.

Jones, E. (1961). *The life and work of Sigmund Freud.* New York: Basic Books.

Jones, E. (1979). The rocky road from acts to dispositions. *American Psychologist, 34,* 107–117.

Jones, M. (1975). Community care for chronic mental patients: The need for a reassessment. *Hospital and Community Psychiatry, 26,* 94–98.

Julien, R. M. (1986). *A primer of drug action,* 2d Ed. San Francisco: Freeman.

Jung, C. G. (1964). *Man and his symbols.* Garden City, NY: Doubleday.

Jus, A., Pineau, R., Lachance, R., Pelchat, G., Jus, K., Pires, P., & Villeneuve, R. (1976). Epidemiology of tardive dyskinesia. *Diseases of the Nervous System, 37,* 210–214.

Kagan, J. (1964). Acquisition and significance of sex-typing and sex-role identity. In M. L. Hoffman & L. W. Hoffman (eds.), *Review of child development research,* Vol. 1. New York: Russell Sage.

Kagan, J. (1984). *The nature of the child.* New York: Basic Books.

Kagan, J., Kearsley, R. B., & Zelazo, P. R. (1976). The effects of infant daycare on psychological development. Paper presented at the meeting of the Association for the Advancement of Science, Boston.

Kagan, J., Kearsley, R. B., & Zelazo, P. R. (1980). *Infancy: Its place in human development.* Cambridge, MA: Harvard University Press.

Kahn, E. (1985). Heinz Kohut and Carl Rogers: A timely comparison. *American Psychologist, 40,* 893–904.

Kahn, M. (1966). The physiology of catharsis. *Journal of Personality and Social Psychology, 3,* 278–286.

Kahn, S., Zimmerman, G., Csikszent-mihalyi, M., Getzels, J. W. (1985). Relations between identity in young adulthood and intimacy at midlife. *Journal of Personality and Social Psychology, 49,* 1316–1322.

Kail, R., & Nippold, M. A. (1984). Unconstrained retrieval from semantic memory. *Child Development, 55,* 944–951.

Kalish, R. A., & Reynolds, D. K. (1976). *Death and ethnicity: A psycho-cultural study.* Los Angeles: University of Southern California Press.

Kallmann, F. J. (1952). Comparative twin study on the genetic aspects of male homosexuality. *Journal of Nervous and Mental Disease, 115,* 283–298.

Kamens, L. (1980). Cognitive and attribution factors in sleep-onset insomnia. Unpublished doctoral dissertation, Southern Illinois University at Carbondale.

Kamin, L. J. (1973, May). Heredity, intelligence, politics, and psychology. Paper presented at the meeting of the Eastern Psychological Association, Washington, D.C.

Kamin, L. J. (1982). Mental testing and immigration. *American Psychologist, 37,* 97–98.

Kandel, D. B. (1980). Drug and drinking behavior among youth. *Annual Review of Sociology, 6,* 235–285.

Kanfer, F., & Goldfoot, D. (1966). Self-control and tolerance of noxious stimulation. *Psychological Reports, 18,* 79–85.

Kanin, E. J., & Parcell, S. R. (1977). Sexual aggression: A second look at the offended female. *Archives of Sexual Behavior, 6,* 67–76.

Kanin, G. (1978). *It takes a long time to become young.* Garden City, NY: Doubleday.

Kaplan, H. S., & Sager, C. J. (1971). Sexual patterns at different ages. *Medical Aspects of Human Sexuality, 5* (6), 10–23.

Karacan, I. (1978). Advances in the psychophysiological evaluation of male erectile impotence. In J. LoPiccolo & L. LoPiccolo (eds.), *Handbook of sex therapy.* New York: Plenum.

Karlin, R. A., McFarland, D., Aiello, J. R., & Epstein, Y. M. (1976). Normative mediation of reactions to crowding. *Environmental Psychology and Non-Verbal Behavior, 1,* 30–40.

Kastenbaum, R. (1977). *Death, society, and human behavior.* St. Louis: Mosby.

Katzell, R. A., & Guzzo, R. A. (1983). Psychological approaches to productivity improvement. *American Psychologist, 38,* 468–472.

Kavale, K. (1982). The efficacy of stimulant drug treatment for hyperactivity: A meta-analysis. *Journal of Learning Disabilities, 15,* 280–289.

Kazdin, A. E. (1981). Drawing valid inferences from case studies. *Journal of Consulting and Clinical Psychology, 49,* 183–192.

Kazdin, A. E., & Wilcoxin, L. A. (1976). Systematic desensitization and nonspecific treatment effects: A methodological evaluation. *Psychological Bulletin, 83,* 729–758.

Keele, S. W. (1973). *Attention and human performance.* Santa Monica, CA: Goodyear.

Keesey, R. E. (1980). A set-point analysis of the regulation of body weight. In A. J. Stunkard (ed.), *Obesity.* Philadelphia: W. B. Saunders.

Keesey, R. E. (1986). In Toufexis, A., Garcia, C., & Kalb, B. (1986, January 20). Dieting: The losing game. *Time Magazine,* 54–60.

Keesey, R. E., & Powley, T. L. (1975). Hypothalamic regulation of body weight. *American Scientist, 63,* 558–565.

Kelley, C. K., & King, G. D. (1979). Behavioral correlates of the 2–7–8 MMPI profile type in students at a university mental health center. *Journal of Consulting and Clinical Psychology, 47,* 679–685.

Kelley, H. H. (1979). *Personal relationships: Their structures and processes.* Hillsdale, NJ: Erlbaum.

Kelley, H. H., & Michela, J. L. (1980). Attribution theory and research. *Annual Review of Psychology, 31,* 457–501.

Kelly, K. E., & Houston, B. K. (1985). Type A behavior in employed women: Relation to work, marital, and leisure variables, social support, stress, tension, and health. *Journal of Personality and Social Psychology, 48,* 1067–1079.

Kerpelman, J. P., & Himmelfarb, S. (1971). Partial reinforcement effects in attitude acquisition and counterconditioning. *Journal of Personality and Social Psychology, 19,* 301–305.

Kerr, N. L. (1983). Motivation losses in small groups: A social dilemma analysis. *Journal of Personality and Social Psychology, 45,* 819–828.

Kershner, J. R., & Ledger, G. (1985). Effect of sex, intelligence, and style of thinking on creativity: A comparison of gifted and average IQ children. *Journal of Personality and Social Psychology, 48,* 1033–1040.

Kesey, K. (1962). *One flew over the cuckoo's nest.* New York: Viking.

Keverne, E. B. (1977). Pheromones and sexual behavior. In J. Money & H. Musaph (eds.), *Handbook of sexology.* Amsterdam: Excerpta Medica.

Keye, W. R. (1983). Update: Premenstrual syndrome. *Endocrine and Fertility Forum, 6* (4), 1–3.

Keyes, D. (1982). *The minds of Billy Milligan.* New York: Bantam Books.

Kiesler, C. A. (1982). Mental hospitalization and alternative care. *American Psychologist, 37,* 349–360.

Kihlstrom, J. F. (1980). Posthypnotic amnesia for recently learned material: Interactions with "episodic" and "semantic" memory. *Cognitive Psychology, 12,* 227–251.

Kihlstrom, J. F., Brenneman, H. A., Pistole, D. D., & Shor, R. E. (1985). Hypnosis as a retrieval cue in posthypnotic amnesia. *Journal of Abnormal Psychology, 94,* 264–271.

Kimmel, D. C. (1974). *Adulthood and aging: An interdisciplinary developmental view.* New York: Wiley.

Kinsey, A. C., Pomeroy, W. B., & Martin, C. E. (1948). *Sexual behavior in the human male.* Philadelphia: Saunders.

Kinsey, A. C., Pomeroy, W. B., Martin, C. E., & Gebhard, P. H. (1953). *Sexual behavior in the human female.* Philadelphia: Saunders.

Klaus, M. H., & Kennell, J. H. (1978). In J. H. Stevens, Jr., & M. Mathews (eds.), *Mother/child, father/child relationships.* Washington, D.C.: National Association for the Education of Young Children.

Klein, D. N., & Depue, R. A. (1985). Obsessional personality traits and risk for bipolar affective disorder: An offspring study. *Journal of Abnormal Psychology, 94,* 291–297.

Klein, D. N., Depue, R. A., & Slater, J. F. (1985). Cyclothymia in the adolescent offspring of parents with bipolar affective disorder. *Journal of Abnormal Psychology, 94,* 115–127.

Kleinke, C. L. (1977). Compliance to requests made by gazing and touching experimenters in field settings. *Journal of Experimental Social Psychology, 13,* 218–223.

Kleinke, C. L., & Staneski, R. A. (1980). First impressions of female bust size. *Journal of Social Psychology, 110,* 123–134.

Kleinke, C. L., & Walton, J. H. (1982). Influence of reinforced smiling on affective responses in an interview. *Journal of Personality and Social Psychology, 42,* 557–565.

Kleinmuntz, B. (1982). *Personality and psychological assessment.* New York: St. Martin's.

Kleinmuntz, B., & Szucko, J. J. (1984). Lie detection in ancient and modern times: A call for contemporary scientific study. *American Psychologist, 39,* 766–776.

Knapp, M. L. (1978). *Nonverbal communication in human interaction.* New York: Holt, Rinehart and Winston.

Koffka, K. (1925). *The growth of the mind.* New York: Harcourt Brace Jovanovich.

Kohlberg, L. (1963). Moral development and identification. In H. W. Stevenson (ed.), *Child psychology: 62nd yearbook of the National Society for the Study of Education.* Chicago:

University of Chicago Press.

Kohlberg, L. (1966). A cognitive-developmental analysis of children's sex-role concepts and attitudes. In E. E. Maccoby (ed.), *The development of sex differences*. Stanford, CA: Stanford University Press.

Kohlberg, L. (1969). *Stages in the development of moral thought and action*. New York: Holt, Rinehart and Winston.

Kohlberg, L. (1981). *The philosophy of moral development: Moral stages and the idea of justice*. San Francisco: Harper & Row.

Köhler, W. (1925). *The mentality of apes*. New York: Harcourt Brace Jovanovich.

Kohn, P. M., Barnes, G. E., & Hoffman, F. M. (1979). Drug-use history and experience seeking among adult male correctional inmates. *Journal of Consulting and Clinical Psychology, 47,* 708–715.

Kolko, D. J., & Rickard-Figueroa, J. L. (1985). Effects of video games on the adverse corollaries of chemotherapy in pediatric oncology patients: A single-case analysis. *Journal of Consulting and Clinical Psychology, 53,* 223–228.

Komacki, J., & Dore-Boyce, K. (1978). Self-recording: Its effects on individuals high and low in motivation. *Behavior Therapy, 9,* 65–72.

Koocher, G. P. (1977). Bathroom behavior and human dignity. *Journal of Personality and Social Psychology, 35,* 120–121.

Koss, M. P., Butcher, J. L., & Strupp, H. H. (1986). Brief psychotherapy methods in clinical research. *Journal of Consulting and Clinical Psychology, 54,* 60–67.

Kramer, C. (1974, February). Women's speech: Separate but unequal? *Quarterly Journal of Speech,* 14–24.

Krech, D., Crutchfield, R. S., & Ballachey, E. L. (1962). *Individual in society*. New York: McGraw-Hill.

Krieger, D. T. (1983). Brain peptides: What, where, and why? *Science, 222,* 975–985.

Kübler-Ross, E. (1969). *On death and dying*. New York: Macmillan.

Kuhn, D., Kohlberg, L., Langer, J., & Haan, N. (1977). The development of formal operations in logical and moral judgment. *Genetic Psychology Monographs.*

LaChance, C. C., Chestnut, R. W., & Lubitz, A. (1978). The "decorative" female model: Sexual stimuli and the recognition of advertisements. *Journal of Advertising.*

Ladas, A. K., Whipple, B., & Perry, J. D. (1982). *The G spot and other recent discoveries about human sexuality*. New York: Holt, Rinehart and Winston.

Lahey, B. B., & Drabman, R. S. (1981). Behavior modification in the classroom. In W. E. Craighead, A. E. Kazdin, & M. J. Mahoney (eds.), *Behavior modification: Principles, issues, and applications,* 2d ed. Boston: Houghton Mifflin.

Laing, R. D. (1964). Is schizophrenia a disease? *International Journal of Social Psychiatry, 10,* 184–193.

Laird, J. D. (1974). Self-attribution of emotion: The effects of expressive behavior on the quality of emotional experience. *Journal of Personality and Social Psychology, 29,* 475–486.

Laird, J. D. (1984). The real role of facial response in the experience of emotion: A reply to Tourangeau and Ellsworth, and others. *Journal of Personality and Social Psychology, 47,* 909–917.

Lamb, M. E. (1981). The development of father-infant relationships. In M. E. Lamb (ed.), *The role of the father in child development*. New York: Wiley.

Lamb, M. E., Easterbrooks, M. A., & Holden, G. W. (1980). Reinforcement and punishment among preschoolers: Characteristics, effects, and correlates. *Child Development, 51,* 1230–1236.

Lamb, M. E., & Roopnarine, J. L. (1979). Peer influences on sex-role development in preschoolers. *Child Development, 50,* 1219–1222.

Landy, D., & Sigall, H. (1974). Beauty is talent: Task evaluation as a function of the performer's physical attractiveness. *Journal of Personality and Social Psychology, 30,* 299–304.

Lang, A. R., Goeckner, D. J., Adesso, V. J., & Marlatt, G. A. (1975). Effects of alcohol on aggression in male social drinkers. *Journal of Abnormal Psychology, 84,* 508–518.

Lang, A. R., Searles, J., Lauerman, R., & Adesso, V. J. (1980). Expectancy, alcohol, and sex guilt as determinants of interest in and reaction to sexual stimuli. *Journal of Abnormal Psychology, 89,* 644–653.

Lang, P. J., & Melamed, B. B. (1969). Case report: Avoidance conditioning therapy of an infant with chronic ruminative vomiting. *Journal of Abnormal Psychology, 74,* 1–8.

Langer, E. J., Bashner, R. S., & Chanowitz, B. (1985). Decreasing prejudice by increasing discrimination. *Journal of Personality and Social Psychology, 49,* 113–120.

Langer, E. J., Rodin, J., Beck, P., Weinman, C., & Spitzer, L. (1979). Environmental determinants of memory improvement in late adulthood. *Journal of Personality and Social Psychology, 37,* 2003–2013.

Lansky, D., & Wilson, G. T. (1981). Alcohol, expectations, and sexual arousal. *Journal of Abnormal Psychology, 90,* 35–45.

Lanzetta, J. T., Cartwright-Smith, J., & Kleck, R. E. (1976). Effects of nonverbal dissimulation on emotional experience and autonomic arousal. *Journal of Personality and Social Psychology, 33,* 354–370.

Laroche, S., & Bloch, V. (1982). Conditioning of hippocampal cells and long-term potentiation: An approach to mechanisms of posttrial memory facilitation. In C. Ajmone Marsan, & H. Matthies (eds.), *Neuronal plasticity and memory formation*. New York: Raven.

Larson, C. C. (1982). Taub conviction revives centuries-old debate. *APA Monitor, 13* (1), 1, 12–13.

Lashley, K. S. (1950). In search of the engram. In *Symposium of the Society for Experimental Biology*, Vol. 4. New York: Cambridge University Press.

Latané, B., & Dabbs, J. M. (1975). Sex, group size, and helping in three cities. *Sociometry, 38,* 180–194.

Latané, B., & Nida, S. (1981). Ten years of research on group size and helping. *Psychological Bulletin, 89,* 308–324.

Latané, B., Williams, K., & Harkins, S. (1979). Many hands make light the work: The causes and consequences of social loafing. *Journal of Personality and Social Psychology, 37,* 822–832.

Lau, R. R., & Russell, D. (1980). Attributions in the sports pages. *Journal of Personality and Social Psychology, 39,* 29–38.

Laurence, J. R., & Perry, C. (1983). Hypnotically created memory among highly hypnotizable subjects. *Science, 222,* 523–524.

Lavin, D. E. (1965). *The prediction of academic performance: A theoretical analysis and review of research.* New York: Russell Sage.

Lavrakas, P. J. (1975, May). Female preferences for male physiques. Paper presented at the Midwestern Psychological Association, Chicago.

Lay, M., & Meyer, W. (1973). Teacher/child behaviors in an open environment day care program. Syracuse, NY: Syracuse University Children's Center.

Layne, C. (1979). The Barnum effect: Rationality versus gullibility? *Journal of Consulting and Clinical Psychology, 47* 219–221.

Lazar, I., & Darlington, R. (1982). Lasting effects of early education: A report from the Consortium of Longitudinal Studies. *Monographs of the Society for Research in Child Development, 47* (2–3), Serial No. 195.

Lazarus, R. S., DeLongis, A., Folkman, S., & Gruen, R. (1985). Stress and adaptational outcomes: The problem of confounded measures. *American Psychologist, 40,* 770–779.

Leak, G. K., & Christopher, S. B. (1982). Freudian psychoanalysis and sociobiology: A synthesis. *American Psychologist, 37,* 313–322.

LeBon, G. (1895). *The crowd.* New York: Viking, 1960.

LeBow, M. D., Goldberg, P. S., & Collins, A. (1977). Eating behavior of overweight and nonoverweight persons in the natural environment. *Journal of Consulting and Clinical Psychology, 45,* 1204–1205.

Leerhsen, C., & Abramson, P. (1985, May 6). *Newsweek,* 82–83.

Lefcourt, H. M., Miller, R. S., Ware, E. E., & Sherk, D. (1981). Locus of control as a modifier of the relationship between stressors and moods. *Journal of Personality and Social Psychology, 41,* 357–369.

Leiblum, S., & Ersner-Hershfield, R. (1977). Sexual enhancement groups for dysfunctional women: An evaluation. *Journal of Sex and Marital Therapy, 3,* 139–152.

Lenneberg, E. H. (1967). *Biological foundations of language.* New York: Wiley.

Lenneberg, E. H. (1969). On explaining language. *Science, 164,* 635–643.

Leonard, C. V. (1974). Depression and suicidality. *Journal of Consulting and Clinical Psychology, 42,* 98–104.

Leonard, C. V. (1977). The MMPI as a suicide predictor. *Journal of Consulting and Clinical Psychology, 45,* 367–377.

Lerner, M. J., Miller, D. T., & Holmes, J. G. (1975). Deserving versus justice: A contemporary dilemma. In L. Berkowitz & E. Walster (eds.), *Advances in experimental social psychology,* Vol. 12. New York: Academic Press.

Leslie, G. R., & Leslie, E. M. (1977). *Marriage in a changing world.* New York: Wiley.

Lesnik-Oberstein, M., & Cohen, L. (1984). Cognitive style, sensation seeking, and assortive mating. *Journal of Personality and Social Psychology, 46,* 112–117.

Leventhal, H. (1970). Findings and theory in the study of fear communication. In L. Berkowitz (ed.), *Advances in experimental social psychology,* Vol. 5. New York: Academic Press.

Leventhal, H., & Avis, N. (1976). Pleasure, addiction, and habit: Factors in verbal report or factors in smoking behavior? *Journal of Abnormal Psychology, 85,* 478–488.

Leventhal, H., Watts, J. C., & Paogano, F. (1967). Effects of fear and instructions on how to cope with danger. *Journal of Personality and Social Psychology, 6,* 313–321.

Levinson, D. J., Darrow, C. N., Klein, E. B., Levinson, M. H., & McKee, B. (1978). *The seasons of a man's life.* New York: Knopf.

Levitt, R. A. (1981). *Physiological psychology.* New York: Holt, Rinehart and Winston.

Levy, J. (1985). Right brain, left brain: Fact and fiction. *Psychology Today, 19,* (5), 38–44.

Levy-Shiff, R. (1983). Adaptation and competence in early childhood: Communally raised kibbutz children versus family raised children in the city. *Child Development, 54,* 1606–1614.

Lewinsohn, P. M. (1975). The behavioral study and treatment of depression. In M. Hersen, R. M. Eisler, & P. M. Miller (eds.), *Progress in behavior modification,* Vol. 1. New York: Academic Press.

Lewinsohn, P. M., & Amenson, C. S. (1978). Some relations between pleasant and unpleasant mood-related events and depression. *Journal of Abnormal Psychology, 87,* 644–654.

Lewinsohn, P. M., & Graf, M. (1973). Pleasant activities and depression. *Journal of Consulting and Clinical Psychology, 41,* 261–268.

Lewinsohn, P. M., & Libet, J. (1972). Pleasant events, activity schedules, and depression. *Journal of Abnormal Psychology, 79,* 291–295.

Lichtenstein, E. (1982). The smoking problem: A behavioral perspective.

Journal of Consulting and Clinical Psychology, 50, 804–819.

Lichtenstein, E., & Glasgow, R. E. (1977). Rapid smoking: Side effects and safeguards. *Journal of Consulting and Clinical Psychology, 45,* 815–821.

Lick, J. R., & Heffler, D. (1977). Relaxation training and attention placebo in the treatment of severe insomnia. *Journal of Consulting and Clinical Psychology, 45,* 153–161.

Lieberman, M. A., Yalom, I. D., & Miles, M. (1973). *Encounter groups: First facts.* New York: Basic Books.

Ling, G. S. F., MacLeod, J. M., Lee, S., Lockhart, S. H., & Pasternak, G. W. (1984). Separation of morphine analgesia from physical dependence. *Science, 226,* 462–464.

Lipinski, D. P., Black, J. L., Nelson, R. O., & Ciminero, A. R. (1975). Influence of motivational variables on the reactivity and reliability of self-recording. *Journal of Consulting and Clinical Psychology, 43,* 637–646.

Lipsky, M., Kassinove, H., & Miller, N. (1980). Effects of rational-emotive therapy, rational role reversal and rational-emotive imagery on the emotional adjustment of community mental health center patients. *Journal of Consulting and Clinical Psychology, 48,* 366–374.

Lloyd, C., Alexander, A. A., Rice, D. G., & Greenfield, N. S. (1980). Life events as predictors of academic performance. *Journal of Human Stress, 6,* 15–25.

Loehlin, J. C., Willerman, L., & Horn, J. M. (1982). Personality resemblances between unwed mothers and their adopted-away offspring. *Journal of Personality and Social Psychology, 42,* 1089–1099.

Logan, D. D. (1978, August). Variations on "the curse": Menstrual euphemisms in other countries. Paper presented at the meeting of the American Psychological Association, Toronto.

Lohr, J. M., & Staats, A. (1973). Attitude conditioning in Sino-Tibetan languages. *Journal of Personality and Social Psychology, 26,* 196–200.

Lombardo, M. M., & McCall, M. W. (1984). The intolerable boss. *Psychology Today, 18* (1), 44–48.

LoPiccolo, J., Heiman, J. R., Hogan, D. R., & Roberts, C. W. (1985). Effectiveness of single therapists versus cotherapy teams in sex therapy. *Journal of Consulting and Clinical Psychology, 53,* 287–294.

LoPiccolo, J., & Stock, W, E. (1986). Treatment of sexual dysfunction. *Journal of Consulting and Clinical Psychology. 54,* 158–167.

Lorenz, K. (1962). *King Solomon's ring.* London: Methuen.

Lorenz, K. (1966). *On aggression.* New York: Harcourt Brace Jovanovich.

Lorenz, K. (1981). *The foundations of ethology.* New York: Springer-Verlag.

Lott, B. (1981). A feminist critique of androgyny: Toward the elimination of gender attributions for learned behavior. In C. Mayo & N. M. Henley (eds.), *Gender and nonverbal behavior.* New York: Springer.

Lott, B. (1985). The potential enhancement of social/personality psychology through feminist research and vice versa. *American Psychologist, 40,* 155–164.

Lubin, B., Larsen, R. M., Matarazzo, J. D., & Seever, M. (1985). Psychological test usage patterns in five professional settings. *American Psychologist, 40,* 857–861.

Lublin, J. S. (1984, March 8). Couples working different shifts take on new duties and pressures. *The Wall Street Journal, 33.*

Luborsky, L., & Spence, D. P. (1978). Quantitative research on psychoanalytic therapy. In S. L. Garfield & A. E. Bergin (eds.), *Handbook of psychotherapy and behavior change: An empirical analysis.* New York: Wiley.

Lucariello, J., & Nelson, K. (1985). Slot-filler categories as memory organizers for young children. *Developmental Psychology, 21,* 272–281.

Luchins, A. S. (1957). Primacy-recency in impression formation. In C. I. Hovland (ed.), *The order of presentation in persuasion.* New Haven, CT: Yale University Press.

Luparello, T. J., McFadden, E. R., Lyons, H. A., & Bleecker, E. R. (1971). Psychologic factors and bronchial asthma. *New York State Journal of Medicine, 71,* 2161–2165.

Lykken, D. T. (1957). A study of anxiety in the sociopathic personality. *Journal of Abnormal and Social Psychology, 55,* 6–10.

Lykken, D. T. (1981). *A tremor in the blood: Uses and abuses of the lie detector.* New York: McGraw-Hill.

Lykken, D. T. (1982). Fearlessness: Its carefree charm and deadly risks. *Psychology Today, 16* (9), 20–28.

Lyons, J. S., Rosen, A. J., & Dysken, M. W. (1985). Behavioral effects of tricyclic drugs in depressed inpatients. *Journal of Consulting and Clinical Psychology, 53,* 17–24.

Maccoby, E. E., & Feldman, S. S. (1972). Mother-attachment and stranger reactions in the third year of life. *Monographs of the Society for Research in Child Development, 37* (1).

Maccoby, E. E., & Jacklin, C. N. (1974). *The psychology of sex differences.* Stanford, CA: Stanford University Press.

Maddi, S. R. (1980). *Personality theories: A comparative analysis.* Homewood, IL: Dorsey.

Madsen, C. H., Becker, W. C., & Thomas, D. R. (1968). Rules, praise, and ignoring: Elements of elementary classroom control. *Journal of Applied Behavior Analysis, 1,* 139–150.

Mahoney, M. J. (1974). *Cognition and behavior modification.* Cambridge, MA: Ballinger.

Mahoney, M. J. (1980). *Abnormal psychology.* New York: Harper & Row.

Maier, N. R. F., & Schneirla, T. C. (1935). *Principles of animal psychology.* New York: McGraw-Hill.

Maital, S. (1982). The tax-evasion virus. *Psychology Today, 16* (3), 74–78.

Malamuth, N. M. (1981). Rape fantasies as a function of exposure to violent sexual stimuli. *Archives of Sexual Behavior, 10,* 33–48.

Malamuth, N. M., Heim, N., & Feshbach, S. (1980). Sexual responsiveness of college students to rape depictions: Inhibitory or disinhibitory effects. *Journal of Personality and Social Psychology, 38,* 399–408.

Malatesta, V. J., Sutker, P. B., & Treiber, F. A. (1981). Sensation seeking and chronic public drunkenness. *Journal of Consulting and Clinical Psychology, 49,* 292–284.

Mandler, G. (1984). *Mind and body: The psychology of emotion and stress.* New York: Norton.

Mann, L. (1981). The baiting crowd in episodes of threatened suicide. *Journal of Personality and Social Psychology, 41,* 703–709.

Mann, L., Newton, J. W., & Innes, J. M. (1982). A test between deindividuation and emergent norm theories of crowd aggression. *Journal of Personality and Social Psychology, 42,* 260–272.

Manning, M. M., & Wright, T. L. (1983). Self-efficacy expectancies, outcome expectancies, and the persistence of pain control in childbirth. *Journal of Personality and Social Psychology, 45,* 421–431.

Manucia, G. K., Baumann, D. J., & Cialdini, R. B. (1984). Mood influences on helping: Direct effects or side effects? *Journal of Personality and Social Psychology, 46,* 357–364.

Marcus, T. L., & Corsini, D. A. (1978). Parental expectations of preschool children as related to child gender and socioeconomic status. *Child Development, 49,* 243–246.

Markman, H. J. (1981). Prediction of marital distress: A five-year follow-up. *Journal of Consulting and Clinical Psychology, 49,* 760–762.

Marks, G., Miller, N., & Maruyama, G. (1981). Effect of targets' physical attractiveness on assumption of similarity. *Journal of Personality and Social Psychology, 41,* 198–206.

Marks, I. M. (1982). Toward an empirical clinical science: Behavioral psychotherapy in the 1980s. *Behavior Therapy, 13,* 63–81.

Marks, P. A., & Monroe, L. J. (1976). Correlates of adolescent poor sleepers. *Journal of Abnormal Psychology, 85,* 243–246.

Markus, H. (1981). The drive for integration: Some comments. *Journal of Experimental Social Psychology, 17,* 257–261.

Marlatt, G. A. (1985). Controlled drinking: The controversy rages on. *American Psychologist, 40,* 374–375

Marlatt, G. A., & Gordon, J. R. (1980). Determinants of relapse: Implications for the maintenance of behavior change. In P. O. Davidson & S. M. Davidson (eds.), *Behavioral medicine: Changing health lifestyles.* New York: Brunner/Mazel.

Marlatt, G. A., & Rohsenow, D. J. (1981). The think-drink effect. *Psychology Today, 15* (12), 60–69.

Marston, A. R., London, P., Cohen, N., & Cooper, L. M. (1977). In vivo observation of the eating behavior of obese and nonobese subjects. *Journal of Consulting and Clinical Psychology, 45,* 335–336.

Maruyama, G., Fraser, S. C., & Miller, N. (1982). Personal responsibility and altruism in children. *Journal of Personality and Social Psychology, 42,* 658–664.

Maruyama, G., & Miller, N. (1975). *Physical attractiveness and classroom acceptance.* Social Science Research Institute Report no. 75–2, University of Southern California.

Maslach, C. (1978). Emotional consequences of arousal without reason. In C. E. Izard (ed.), *Emotions and psychopathology.* New York: Plenum.

Maslow, A. H. (1970). *Motivation and personality,* 2d ed. New York: Harper & Row.

Maslow, A. H. (1971). *The farther reaches of human nature.* New York: Viking.

Masters, W. H., & Johnson, V. E. (1966). *Human sexual response.* Boston: Little, Brown.

Masters, W. H., & Johnson, V. E. (1970). *Human sexual inadequacy.* Boston: Little, Brown.

Masters, W. H., & Johnson, V. E. (1979). *Homosexuality in perspective.* Boston: Little, Brown.

Masters, W. H., Johnson, V. E., & Kolodny, R. C. (1985). *Human sexuality,* 2d Ed. Boston: Little, Brown.

Matefy, R. (1980). Role-playing theory of psychedelic flashbacks. *Journal of Consulting and Clinical Psychology, 48,* 551–553.

Matlin, M. (1983). *Cognition.* New York: Holt, Rinehart and Winston.

Mattes, J. A., & Gittelman, R. (1983). Growth of hyperactive children on maintenance regimen of methylphenidate. *Archives of General Psychiatry, 40,* 317–321.

Matthews, K. A., Krantz, D. S., Dembroski, T. M., & MacDougall, J. M. (1982). Unique and common variance in structured interview and Jenkins Activity Survey measures of the Type A behavior pattern. *Journal of Personality and Social Psychology, 42,* 303–313.

Maugh, T. H. (1982). Marijuana "justifies serious concern." *Science, 215,* 1488–1489.

May, J. L., & Hamilton, P. A. (1980). Effects of musically evoked affect on women's interpersonal attraction toward and perceptual judgments of physical attractiveness of men. *Motivation and Emotion, 4,* 217–228.

May, P. R. (1975). A follow-up study of treatment of schizophrenia. In R. L. Spitzer & D. F. Klein (eds.), *Evaluation of psychological therapies.* Baltimore: The Johns Hopkins University Press.

McAuliffe, K., & McAuliffe, S. (1983, November 6). Keeping up with the genetic revolution. *The New York Times Magazine,* 40–44, 92–97.

McBurney, D. H., & Collings, V. (1977). *Introduction to sensation/perception.* Englewood Cliffs, NJ: Prentice-Hall.

McBurney, D. H., Levine, J. M., & Cavanaugh, P. H. (1977). Psychophysical and social ratings of human body odor. *Personality and Social Psychology Bulletin, 3,* 135–138.

McCall, R. B. (1975). *Intelligence and heredity.* Homewood, IL: Learning Systems Company.

McCann, I. L., & Holmes, D. S. (1984). Influence of aerobic exercise on depression. *Journal of Personality and Social Psychology, 46,* 1142–1147.

McCaul, K. D., & Haugvedt, C. (1982). Attention, distraction, and cold-pressor pain. *Journal of Personality and Social Psychology, 43,* 154–162.

McCaul, K. D., Holmes, D. S., & Solomon, S. (1982). Voluntary expressive changes and emotion. *Journal of Personality and Social Psychology, 42,* 145–152.

McClearn, G. E., & DeFries, J. C. (1973). *Introduction to behavioral genetics.* San Francisco: Freeman.

McClelland, D. C. (1958). Methods of measuring human motivation. In J. W. Atkinson (ed.), *Motives in fantasy, action, and society.* Princeton, NJ: Van Nostrand.

McClelland, D. C. (1965). Achievement and entrepreneurship: A longitudinal study. *Journal of Personality and Social Psychology, 1,* 389–392.

McClelland, D. C. (1982). Understanding psychological man. *Psychology Today, 16* (5), 55–56.

McClelland, D. C. (1985). How motives, skills, and values determine what people do. *American Psychologist, 40,* 812–825.

McClelland, D. C., Alexander, C., & Marks, E. (1982). The need for power, stress, immune functions, and illness among male prisoners. *Journal of Abnormal Psychology, 91,* 61–70.

McClelland, D. C., Atkinson, J. W., Clark, R. A., & Lowell, E. L. (1953). *The achievement motive.* New York: Appleton.

McClelland, D. C., & Jemmott, J. B., III. (1980). Power, motivation, stress and physical illness. *Journal of Human Stress, 6* (4), 6–15.

McClelland, D. C., & Pilon, D. A. (1983). Sources of adult motives in patterns of parent behavior in early childhood. *Journal of Personality and Social Psychology, 44,* 564–574.

McClintock, M. K. (1971). Menstrual synchrony and suppression. *Nature, 229,* 244–245.

McClintock, M. K. (1979). Estrous synchrony and its mediation by airborne chemical communication. *Hormones and Behavior, 10,* 264.

McConaghy, M. J. (1979). Gender permanence and the genital basis of gender: Stages in the development of constancy of gender identity. *Child Development, 50,* 1223–1226.

McConaghy, N., & Blaszczynski, A. (1980). A pair of monozygotic twins discordant for homosexuality: Sex-dimorphic behavior and penile volume responses. *Archives of Sexual Behavior, 9,* 123–132.

McConnell, J. V., Jacobson, A. L., & Kimble, D. P. (1959). The effects of regeneration upon retention of a conditioned response in the planarian. *Journal of Comparative and Physiological Psychology, 52,* 1–5.

McConnell, J. V., Shigehisa, T., & Salive, H. (1970). Attempts to transfer approach and avoidance responses by RNA injections in rats. In K. H. Pribram & D. E. Broadbent (eds.), *Biology of memory.* New York: Academic Press.

McCrady, B. S. (1985). Comments on the controlled drinking controversy. *American Psychologist, 40,* 370–371

McDougall, W. (1908). *Social psychology.* New York: G. P. Putnam.

McGaugh, J. L. (1983). Preserving the presence of the past: Hormonal influences on memory storage. *American Psychologist, 38,* 161–174.

McGaugh, J. L., Martinez, J. L., Jr., Jensen, R. A., Messing, R. B., & Vasquez, B. J. (1980). Central and peripheral catecholamine function in learning and memory processes. In *Neural mechanisms of goal-directed behavior and learning.* New York: Academic Press.

McGowan, R. J., & Johnson, D. L. (1984). The mother-child relationship and other antecedents of childhood intelligence: A causal analysis. *Child Development, 55,* 810–820.

McGrath, J. J., & Cohen, D. B. (1978). REM sleep facilitation of adaptive waking behavior: A review of the literature. *Psychological Bulletin, 85,* 24–57.

McGurk, H., Turnura, C., & Creighton, S. J. (1977). Auditory-visual coordination in neonates. *Child Development, 48,* 138–143.

McIntyre, K. O., Lichtenstein, E., & Mermelstein, R. J. (1983). Self-efficacy and relapse in smoking cessation: A replication and extension. *Journal of Consulting and Clinical Psychology, 51,* 632–633.

McKenna, J. F., Oritt, P. L., & Wolff, H. K. (1981). Occupational stress as a predictor in the turnover decision. *Journal of Human Stress, 7* (12), 12–17.

McMullen, S., & Rosen, R. C. (1979). Self-administered masturbation training in the treatment of primary orgasmic dysfunction. *Journal of Consulting and Clinical Psychology, 47,* 912–918.

McNeill, D. (1970). The development of language. In P. H. Mussen (ed.), *Carmichael's manual of child psychology,* Vol. 1, 3d ed. New York: Wiley.

Mead, M. (1935). *Sex and temperament in three primitive societies.* New York: Morrow.

Mednick, S. A. (1985). Crime in the family tree. *Psychology Today, 19* (3), 58–61.

Meer, J. (1985). Turbulent teens: The stress factors. *Psychology Today, 19,* (5), 15–16.

Mehr, J. J. (1983). *Abnormal psychology.* New York: Holt, Rinehart & Winston.

Mehrabian, A., & Weinstein, L. (1985). Temperament characteristics of suicide attempters. *Journal of Consulting and Clinical Psychology, 53,* 544–546.

Meichenbaum, D. (1976). Toward a cognitive theory of self-control. In G. Schwartz & D. Shapiro (eds.), *Consciousness and self-regulation: Ad-*

vances in research. New York: Plenum.

Meichenbaum, D. (1977). *Cognitive behavior modification: An integrative approach*. New York: Plenum.

Meichenbaum, D., & Butler, L. (1980). Toward a conceptual model for the treatment of test anxiety: Implications for research and treatment. In I. G. Sarason (ed.), *Test anxiety: Theory, research, and application*. Hillsdale, NJ: Erlbaum.

Meichenbaum, D., & Jaremko, M. E. (eds.) (1983). *Stress reduction and prevention*. New York: Plenum.

Melzack, R. (1973). *The puzzle of pain*. New York: Basic Books.

Melzack, R. (1980). Psychological aspects of pain. In J. J. Bonica (ed.), *Pain*. New York: Raven.

Meredith, N. (1984). The gay dilemma. *Psychology Today, 18* (1), 56–62

Mewborn, C. R., & Rogers, R. W. (1979). Effects of threatening and reassuring components of fear appeals on physiological and verbal measures of emotion and attitudes. *Journal of Experimental Social Psychology, 15,* 242–253.

Meyer, J. P., & Pepper, S. (1977). Need compatibility and marital adjustment in young married couples. *Journal of Personality and Social Psychology, 35,* 331–342.

Meyers, J. K., Weissman, M. M., Tischler, G. L., Holzer, C. E., Leaf, P. J., Orvaschel, H., Anthony, J. C., Boyd, J. H., Burke, J. D., Kramer, M., & Stoltsman, R. (1984). Six-month prevalence of psychiatric disorders in three communities. *Archives of General Psychiatry, 41,* 959–967.

Michael, R. P., Keverne, E. B., & Bonsall, R. W. (1971). Pheromones: Isolation of male sex attractants from a female primate. *Science, 172,* 964–966.

Mider, P. A. (1984). Failures in alcoholism and drug dependence prevention and learning from the past. *American Psychologist, 39,* 183.

Middlemist, R. D., Knowles, E. S., & Matter, C. F. (1976). Personal space invasions in the lavatory: Suggestive evidence for arousal. *Journal of Personality and Social Psychology, 33,* 541–546.

Middlemist, R. D., Knowles, E. S., & Matter, C. F. (1977). What to do and what to report: A reply to Koocher. *Journal of Personality and Social Psychology, 35,* 122–124.

Milam, J. R., & Ketcham, K. (1981). *Under the influence: A guide to the myths and realities of alcoholism*. Seattle: Madrove Publishers.

Milgram, S. (1963). Behavioral study of obedience. *Journal of Abnormal and Social Psychology, 67,* 371–378.

Milgram, S. (1970). The experience of living in cities. *Science, 167,* 1461–1468.

Milgram, S. (1974). *Obedience to authority*. New York: Harper & Row.

Milgram, S. (1977). *The individual in a social world*. Reading, MA: Addison-Wesley.

Miller, G. A. (1956). The magical number seven, plus or minus two: Some limits on our capacity for processing information. *Psychological Review, 63,* 81–97.

Miller, I. W., Klee, S. H., & Norman, W. H. (1982). Depressed and non-depressed inpatients' cognitions of hypothetical events, experimental tasks, and stressful life events. *Journal of Abnormal Psychology, 91,* 78–81.

Miller, N. E. (1969). Learning of visceral and glandular responses. *Science, 163,* 434–445.

Miller, N. E. (1982). Understanding psychological man. *Psychology Today, 16* (5), 51–52.

Miller, N. E. (1985). Rx: Biofeedback. *Psychology Today, 19* (2), 54–59.

Miller, N. E. (1985). The value of behavioral research on animals. *American Psychologist, 40,* 423–440.

Miller, N. E., & Dollard, J. (1941). *Social learning and imitation*. New Haven, CT: Yale University Press.

Miller, P. H., Heldmeyer, K. H., & Miller, S. A. (1975). Facilitation of conservation of number in young children. *Developmental Psychology, 11,* 253.

Miller, P. M., & Mastria, M. A. (1977). *Alternatives to alcohol abuse: A social learning model*. Champaign, IL: Research Press.

Miller, S. M. (1980). Why having control reduces stress: If I can stop the roller coaster I don't want to get off. In J. Garber & M. E. P. Seligman (eds.), *Human helplessness: Theory and research*. New York: Academic Press.

Miller, S. M., Lack, E. R., & Asroff, S. (1985). Preference for control and the coronary-prone behavior pattern. *Journal of Personality and Social Psychology, 49,* 492–499.

Miller, W. R. (1982). Treating problem drinkers: What works? *The Behavior Therapist, 5* (1), 15–18.

Miller, W. R., & Hester, R. K. (1980). Treating the problem drinker. In W. R. Miller (ed.), *The addictive behaviors*. New York: Pergamon Press.

Miller, W. R., & Muñoz,, R. F. (1983). *How to control your drinking*, 2d ed. Albuquerque: University of New Mexico Press.

Millon, T. (1983). The DSM–III: An insider's perspective. *American Psychologist, 38,* 804–814.

Milner, J. S., Gold, R. G., Ayoub, C., & Jacewitz, M. M. (1984). Predictive validity of the child abuse potential inventory. *Journal of Consulting and Clinical Psychology, 52,* 879–884.

Mirsky, A. F., & Orzack, M. H. (1980). Two retrospective studies of psychosurgery. In E. S. Valenstein (ed.), *The psychosurgery debate*. San Francisco: W. H. Freeman.

Mirsky, I. A. (1958). Physiologic, psychologic, and social determinants in the etiology of duodenal ulcer. *American Journal of Digestive Diseases, 3,* 285–315.

Mischel, W. (1977). On the future of personality measurement. *American Psychologist, 32,* 246–254.

Mischel, W. (1986). *Introduction to personality*, 4th ed. New York: Holt, Rinehart and Winston.

Moe, J. L., Nacoste, R. W., & Insko, C. A. (1981). Belief versus race as determinants of discrimination: A study of Southern adolescents in 1966 and 1979. *Journal of Personality and Social Psychology, 41,* 1031–1050.

Molfese, D. L., Freeman, R. B., Jr., & Palermo, D. S. (1975). The ontogeny of brain lateralization for speech and nonspeech stimuli. *Brain and Language, 2,* 356–368.

Molfese, D. L., & Molfese, V. J. (1979). Hemisphere and stimulus differences as reflected in the cortical responses of newborn infants to speech stimuli. *Developmental Psychology, 15,* 505–511.

Money, J. (1960). Phantom orgasm in the dreams of paraplegic men and women. *Archives of General Psychiatry, 3,* 373–382.

Money, J. (1974). Prenatal hormones and posthormonal socialization in gender identity differentiation. In J. K. Cole & R. Dienstbier (eds.), *Nebraska symposium on motivation.* Lincoln, NE: University of Nebraska Press.

Money, J. (1977). Human hermaphroditism. In F. A. Beach (ed.), *Human sexuality in four perspectives.* Baltimore: Johns Hopkins.

Money, J. (1980). *Love and love sickness.* Baltimore: Johns Hopkins.

Money, J., & Ehrhardt, A. (1972). *Man and woman, boy and girl.* Baltimore: Johns Hopkins.

Monroe, L. J. (1967). Psychological and physiological differences between good and poor sleepers. *Journal of Abnormal Psychology, 72,* 255–264.

Monroe, L. J., & Marks, P. A. (1977). MMPI differences between adolescent poor and good sleepers. *Journal of Consulting and Clinical Psychology, 45,* 151–152.

Monroe, S. M. (1982). Life events and disorder: Event-symptom associations and the course of disorder. *Journal of Abnormal Psychology, 91,* 14–24.

Monroe, S. M. (1983). Major and minor life events as predictors of psychological distress: Further issues and findings. *Journal of Behavioral Medicine, 6,* 189–205.

Monte, C. F. (1980). *Beneath the mask: An introduction to theories of personality.* New York: Holt, Rinehart and Winston.

Moon, J. R., & Eisler, R. M. (1983). Anger control: An experimental comparison of three behavioral treatments. *Behavior Therapy, 14,* 493–505.

Moore, J. E., & Chaney, E. F. (1985). Outpatient group treatment of chronic pain: Effects of spouse involvement. *Journal of Consulting and Clinical Psychology, 53,* 326–334.

Moore, K. A., & Hofferth, S. L. (1979). Women and their children. In R. E. Smith (ed.), *The subtle revolution: Women at work.* Washington, D.C.: The Urban Institute.

Moore, T. (1975). Exclusive early mothering and its alternatives: The outcome to adolescence. *Scandinavian Journal of Psychology, 16,* 255–272.

Moreland, R. L., & Zajonc, R. B. (1982). Exposure effects in person perception: Familiarity, similarity, and attraction. *Journal of Experimental Social Psychology, 18.*

Morganthau, T., Agrest, S., Greenberg, N. F., Doherty, S., & Raine, G. (1986, January 6). Abandoned: The chronic mentally ill. *Newsweek,* 14–19.

Moriarty, T. (1975). Crimes, commitment, and the responsive bystander: Two field experiments. *Journal of Personality and Social Psychology, 31,* 370–376.

Morokoff, P. J. (1985). Effects of sex guilt, repression, sexual "arousability," and sexual experience on female sexual arousal during erotica and fantasy. *Journal of Personality and Social Psychology, 49,* 177–187.

Morris, N. M., & Udry, J. R. (1978). Pheromonal influences on human sexual behavior: An experimental search. *Journal of Biosocial Science, 10,* 147–157.

Morris, W. N., Miller, R. S., & Spangenberg, S. (1977). The effects of dissenter position and task difficulty on conformity and response conflict. *Journal of Personality, 45,* 251–256.

Motowidlo, S. T. (1982). Sex role orientation and behavior in a work setting. *Journal of Personality and Social Psychology, 42,* 935–945.

Mowrer, O. H. (1960). *Learning theory and the symbolic processes.* New York: Wiley.

Mueser, K. T., Grau, B. W., Sussman, S., & Rosen, A. J. (1984). You're only as pretty as you feel: Facial expression as a determinant of physical attractiveness. *Journal of Personality and Social Psychology, 46,* 469–478.

Murray, H. A. (1938). *Explorations in personality.* New York: Oxford.

Murstein, B. I. (1972). Physical attractiveness and marital choice. *Journal of Personality and Social Psychology, 22,* 8–12.

Murstein, B. I., & Christy, P. (1976). Physical attractiveness and marital adjustment in middle-aged couples. *Journal of Personality and Social Psychology, 34,* 537–542.

Musante, L., MacDougall, J. M., Dembroski, T. M., & Van Horn, A. E. (1983). Component analysis of the Type A coronary-prone behavior pattern in male and female college students. *Journal of Personality and Social Psychology, 45,* 1104–1117.

Myers, A. M., & Gonda, G. (1982). Utility of the masculinity-femininity construct: Comparison of traditional and androgyny approaches. *Journal of Personality and Social Psychology, 43,* 514–523.

Myers, D. G. (1983). Polarizing effects of social interaction. In H. Brandstatter, J. H. Davis, & G. Stocker-Kreichgauer (eds.), *Group decision processes.* London: Academic Press.

Myers, D. G., & Lamm, H. (1976). The group polarization phenomenon. *Psychological Bulletin, 85,* 602–627.

Myers, M. B., Templer, D. I., & Brown, R. (1984). Coping ability of women who become victims of rape. *Journal of Consulting and Clinical Psychology, 52,* 73–78.

Myers, M. B., Templer, D. I., & Brown, R. (1985). Reply to Wieder on rape victims: Vulnerability does not imply responsibility. *Journal of Consulting and Clinical Psychology, 53,* 431.

Nadi, N. S., Nurnberger, J. I., Jr., & Gershon, E. S. (1984). Muscarinic cholinergic receptors on skin fibroblasts in familial affective disorder. *New England Journal of Medicine, 311,* 225–230.

Nahemow, L., & Lawton, M. P. (1975). Similarity and propinquity in a friendship formation. *Journal of Personality and Social Psychology, 32,* 205–213.

National Academy of Sciences (1981). *The effect on human health from long-term exposure to noise* (Report of Working Group 81). Washington, D.C.: National Academy Press.

National Center on Child Abuse and Neglect Report (1982, January–February). *Children Today,* 27–28.

National Institute of Mental Health (1982). Television and behavior: Ten years of scientific progress and implications for the eighties. Washington, D.C.: National Institute of Mental Health.

Neugarten, B. (1971). Grow old with me, the best is yet to be. *Psychology Today, 5* (5), 45–49.

Neugarten, B. (1982). Understanding psychological man. *Psychology Today, 16* (5), 54–55.

Neuringer, C. (1982). Affect configurations and changes in women who threaten suicide following a crisis. *Journal of Consulting and Clinical Psychology, 50,* 182–186.

Nevid, J. S. (1984). Sex differences in factors of romantic attraction. *Sex Roles, 11* (5/6), 401–411.

Nevid, J. S., & Rathus, S. A. (1978). Multivariate and normative data pertaining to the RAS with the college population. *Behavior Therapy, 9,* 675.

Newcomb, T. M. (1981). Heiderian balance as a group phenomenon. *Journal of Personality and Social Psychology, 40,* 862–867.

Newman, J., & McCauley, C. (1977). Eye contact with strangers in city, suburb, and small town. *Environment and Behavior, 9,* 547–558.

Newmark, C. S., Frerking, R. A., Cook, L., & Newmark, L. (1973). Endorsement of Ellis's irrational beliefs as a function of psychopathology. *Journal of Clinical Psychology, 29,* 300–302.

New York Times (1985, May 12). Poll finds many women seek marriage plus jobs. P. 19.

New York Times (1985, December 29). Should leaves for new parents be mandatory? P. 16E.

Nezu, A. M., & Ronan, G. F. (1985). Life stress, current problems, problem solving, and depressive symptoms: An integrative model. *Journal of Consulting and Clinical Psychology, 53,* 693–697.

Nicassio, P., & Bootzin, R. (1974). A comparison of progressive relaxation and autogenic training as treatments for insomnia. *Journal of Abnormal Psychology, 83,* 253–260.

Niesser, U. (1982). Understanding psychological man. *Psychology Today, 16* (5), 44–48.

NIMH. (1982). See Pearl, Bouthilet, & Lazar (1982).

Nisan, M. (1984). Distributive justice and social norms. *Child Development, 55,* 1020–1029.

Nisbett, R. E., & Ross, L. (1980). *Human inference: Strategies and shortcomings of social judgment.* Englewood Cliffs, NJ: Prentice-Hall.

Nogrady, H., McConkey, K. M., & Perry, C. (1985). Enhancing visual memory: Trying hypnosis, trying imagination, and trying again. *Journal of Abnormal Psychology, 94,* 195–204.

Noles, S. W., Cash, T. F., & Winstead, B. A. (1985). Body image, physical attractiveness, and depression. *Journal of Consulting and Clinical Psychology, 53,* 88–94.

Norton, G. R., Harrison, B., Hauch, J., & Rhodes, L. (1985). Characteristics of people with infrequent panic attacks. *Journal of Abnormal Psychology, 94,* 216–221.

Norton, G. R., & Rhodes, L. (1983). *Characteristics of people with infre-*quent panic attacks: A preliminary analysis. Unpublished manuscript: University of Winnipeg.

Novaco, R. (1974). A treatment program for the management of anger through cognitive and relaxation controls. Doctoral dissertation, Indiana University.

Novaco, R. (1977). A stress inoculation approach to anger management in the training of law enforcement officers. *American Journal of Community Psychology, 5,* 327–346.

Novin, D., Wyrwick, W., & Bray, G. A. (eds.) (1976). *Hunger: Basic mechanisms and clinical implications.* New York: Raven Press.

Nowlis, G. H., & Kessen, W. (1976). Human newborns differentiate differing concentrations of sucrose and glucose. *Science, 191,* 865–866.

O'Grady, K. E. (1982). Sex, physical attractiveness, and perceived risk for mental illness. *Journal of Personality and Social Psychology, 43,* 1064–1071.

O'Leary, K. D. (1980). Pills or skills for hyperactive children. *Journal of Applied Behavior Analysis, 13,* 191–204.

Olson, R. P., Ganley, R., Devine, D. T., & Dorsey, G. (1981). Long-term effects of behavior versus insight-oriented therapy with inpatient alcoholics. *Journal of Consulting and Clinical Psychology, 49,* 866–877.

Opstad, P. K., Ekanger, R., Nummestad, M., & Raabe, N. (1978). Performance, mood and clinical symptoms in men exposed to prolonged, severe physical work and sleep deprivation. *Aviation Space and Environmental Medicine, 49,* 1065–1073.

Orne, M. T., Soskis, D. A., & Dinges, D. F. (1984). Hypnotically-induced testimony and the criminal justice system. In G. L. Wells & E. F. Loftus (eds.), *Eyewitness testimony: Psychological perspectives.* New York: Cambridge.

Orne-Johnson, D. (1973). Autonomic stability and transcendental meditation. *Psychosomatic Medicine, 35,* 341–349.

Ortega, D. F., & Pipal, J. E. (1984). Challenge seeking and the Type A coronary-prone behavior pattern. *Journal of Personality and Social Psychology, 46,* 1328–1334.

O'Sullivan, M., Ekman, P., Friesen, W., & Scherer, K. (1985). What you say and how you say it: The contribution of speech content and voice quality to judgments of others. *Journal of Personality and Social Psychology, 48,* 54–62.

Page, R. A. (1977). Noise and helping behavior. *Environment and Behavior, 9,* 311–334.

Paige, K. E. (1971). Effects of oral contraceptives on affective fluctuations associated with the menstrual cycle. *Psychosomatic Medicine, 33,* 515–537.

Paige, K. E. (1973). Women learn to sing the menstrual blues. *Psychology Today, 7* (4), 41.

Paige, K. E. (1977). Sexual pollution: Reproductive sex taboos in American society. *Journal of Social Issues, 33,* 144.

Paige, K. E. (1978). The declining taboo against menstrual sex. *Psychology Today, 12* (7), 50–51.

Palmer, D. L., & Kalin, R. (1985). Dogmatic responses to belief dissimilarity in the "bogus stranger" paradigm. *Journal of Personality and Social Psychology, 48,* 171–179.

Palmer, F. H. (1976). *The effects of minimal early intervention on subsequent IQ scores and reading achievement.* Report to the Education Commission of the States, contract 13–76–06846, State University of New York at Stony Brook.

Pantin, H. M., & Carver, C. S. (1982). Induced competence and the bystander effect. *Journal of Applied Social Psychology, 12,* 100–111.

Park, B., & Rothbart, M. (1982). Perception of outgroup homogeneity and levels of social categorization: Memory for the subordinate attributes of in-group and out-group members. *Journal of Personality and Social Psychology, 42,* 1051–1068.

Parker, N. (1964). Homosexuality in twins: A report on three discordant pairs. *British Journal of Psychiatry, 110,* 489–495.

Parloff, M. B. (1986). Placebo controls in psychotherapy research: A sine qua non or a placebo for research problems? *Journal of Consulting and Clinical Psychology, 54,* 79–87.

Patterson, F. (1978). Conversations with a gorilla. *National Geographic, 154,* 438–465.

Paul, G. L. (1969a). Outcome of systematic desensitization II: Controlled investigations of individual treatment, technique variations, and current status. In C. M. Franks (ed.), *Behavior therapy: Appraisal and status.* New York: McGraw-Hill.

Paul, G. L. (1969b). Physiological effects of relaxation training and hypnotic suggestion. *Journal of Abnormal Psychology, 74,* 425–437.

Pavlov, I. (1927). *Conditioned reflexes.* London: Oxford.

Pearl, D., Bouthilet, L., & Lazar, J. (eds.). (1982). *Television and behavior: Ten years of scientific progress and implications for the eighties,* Vols. 1 & 2. Washington, D.C.: U.S. Government Printing Office.

Pearlman, C. A., & Greenberg, R. (1973). Posttrial REM sleep: A critical period for consolidation of shuttlebox avoidance. *Animal Learning and Behavior, 1,* 49–51.

Peele, S. (1984). The cultural context of psychological approaches to alcoholism: Can we control the effects of alcohol? *American Psychologist, 39,* 1337–1351

Pelham, W. E. (1983). The effects of psychostimulants on academic achievement in hyperactive and learning-disabled children. *Thalamus, 3,* 1–49.

Pempus, E., Sawaya, C., & Cooper, R. E. (1975). "Don't fence me in": Personal space depends on architectural enclosure. Paper presented to the American Psychological Association, Chicago.

Pendery, M. L., Maltzman, I. M., & West, L. J. (1982). Controlled drinking by alcoholics? New findings and a reevaluation of a major affirmative study. *Science, 217,* 169–174.

Penfield, W. (1969). Consciousness, memory, and man's conditioned reflexes. In K. H. Pribram (ed.), *On the biology of learning.* New York: Harcourt Brace Jovanovich.

Pennebaker, J. W., & Skelton, J. A. (1981). Selective monitoring of physical sensations. *Journal of Personality and Social Psychology, 41,* 213–223.

Perkins, D. (1982). The assessment of stress using life events scales. In L. Goldberger & S. Breznitz (eds.), *Handbook of stress: Theoretical and clinical aspects.* New York: Free Press.

Perlman, S. D., & Abramson, P. R. (1982). Sexual satisfaction among married and cohabiting individuals. *Journal of Consulting and Clinical Psychology, 50,* 458–460.

Perls, F. S. (1971). *Gestalt therapy verbatim.* New York: Bantam.

Perri, M. G., Richards, C. S., & Schultheis, K. R. (1977). Behavioral self-control and smoking reduction: A study of self-initiated attempts to reduce smoking. *Behavior Therapy, 8,* 360–365.

Perry, D. G., & Bussey, K. (1979). The social learning theory of sex differences: Imitation is alive and well. *Journal of Personality and Social Psychology, 37,* 1699–1712.

Person, E., & Ovesey, L. (1974). The psychodynamics of male transsexualism. In R. Friedman et al. (eds.), *Sex differences in behavior.* New York: Wiley.

Persons, J. B., & Rao, P. A. (1985). Longitudinal study of cognitions, life events, and depression in psychiatric inpatients. *Journal of Abnormal Psychology, 94,* 51–63.

Peterson, C., Schwartz, S. M., & Seligman, M. E. P. (1981). Self-blame and depressive symptoms. *Journal of Per-*

sonality and Social Psychology, 41, 253–259.

Peterson, L. R., & Peterson, M. J. (1959). Short-term retention of individual verbal items. Journal of Experimental Psychology, 58, 193–198.

Petty, R. E., & Cacioppo, J. T. (1981). Attitudes and persuasion: Classic and contemporary approaches. Dubuque, Iowa: Wm. C Brown.

Peyser, H. (1982). Stress and alcohol. In L. Goldberger & S. Breznitz (eds.), Handbook of stress. New York: Free Press.

Phares, E. J. (1984). Introduction to personality. Columbus, OH: Charles E. Merrill.

Piaget, J. (1962). The moral judgment of the child. New York: Collier.

Piaget, J. (1963). The origins of intelligence in children. New York: Norton.

Piaget, J. (1971). The construction of reality in the child. New York: Ballantine.

Piaget, J. (1976). The grasp of consciousness. Cambridge, MA: Harvard.

Pierrel, R., & Sherman, J. G. (1963, February). Train your pet the Barnabus way. Brown Alumni Monthly, 8–14.

Pine, C. J. (1985). Anxiety and eating behavior in obese and nonobese American Indians and White Americans. Journal of Personality and Social Psychology, 49, 774–780.

Pines, M. (1975, October 26). Head head start. New York Times Magazine.

Pipp, S., Shaver, P., Jennings, S., Lamborn, S., & Fischer, K. W. (1985). Adolescents' theories about the development of their relationships with parents. Journal of Personality and Social Psychology, 48, 991–1001.

Pliner, P., Hart, H., Kohl, J., & Saari, D. (1974). Compliance without pressure: Some further data on the foot-in-the-door technique. Journal of Experimental Social Psychology, 10, 17–22.

Plomin, R. (1982). Quoted in Pines, M., Behavior and heredity: Links for specific traits are growing stronger. The New York Times, June 29, 1982, C1–C2.

Plomin, R., & DeFries, J. C. (1980). Genetics and intelligence: Recent data. Intelligence, 4, 15–24.

Plutchik, R. (1980). Emotion: A psychoevolutionary synthesis. New York: Harper & Row.

Podlesny, J. A., & Raskin, D. C. (1977). Physiological measures and the detection of deception. Psychological Bulletin, 84, 782–799.

Polivy, J., & Herman, C. P. (1985). Dieting and binging: A causal analysis. American Psychologist, 40, 193–201.

Pomazal, R. J., & Clore, G. L. (1973). Helping on the highway: The effects of dependency and sex. Journal of Applied Social Psychology, 3, 150–164.

Pomeroy, W. B. (1966). Parents and homosexuality: I. Sexology, 32, 508–511.

Pool, J. L. (1973). Your brain and nerves. New York: Scribner.

Popper, K. (1985). Cited in D. J. Goleman, Pressure mounts for analysts to prove theory is scientific. The New York Times, January 15, 1985, C1, C9.

Porter, N., Geis, F. L., Cooper, E., & Newman, E. (1985). Androgyny and leadership in mixed-sex groups. Journal of Personality and Social Psychology, 49, 808–823.

Postman, L. (1975). Verbal learning and memory. Annual Review of Psychology, 26, 291–335.

Powley, T. L. (1977). The ventromedial hypothalamic syndrome, satiety, and a cephalic phase hypothesis. Psychological Review, 84, 89–126.

Premack, A. J., & Premack, D. (1975). Teaching language to an ape. In R. C. Atkinson (ed.), Psychology in progress. San Francisco: Freeman.

Premack, D. (1970). Mechanisms of self-control. In W. A. Hunt (ed.), Learning mechanisms in smoking. Chicago: Aldine.

Prescott, P., & DeCasper, A. J. (1981). Do newborns prefer their fathers' voices? Apparently not. Paper presented to the meeting of the Society for Research in Child Development, Boston.

Press, A., Clausen, P., & Contreras, J. (1981, October 19). The trials of hypnosis. Newsweek, 96.

Press, A., Namuth, T., Agrest, S., Gander, M., Lubenow, G. C., Reese, M., Friendly, D. T., & McDaniel, A. (1985, March 18). The war against pornography. Newsweek, 58–66.

Pritchard, D., & Rosenblatt, A. (1980). Racial bias in the MMPI: A methodological review. Journal of Consulting and Clinical Psychology, 48, 129–142.

Pyszczynski, T., & Greenberg, J. (1985). Depression and preference for self-focusing stimuli after success and failure. Journal of Personality and Social Psychology, 49, 1066–1075.

Quattrone, G. A. (1982). Overattribution and unit formation: When behavior engulfs the person. Journal of Personality and Social Psychology, 42, 593–607.

Quinsey, V. L., Chaplin, T. C., & Upfold, D. (1984). Sexual arousal to nonsexual violence and sadomasochistic themes among rapists and non-sex-offenders. Journal of Consulting and Clinical Psychology, 52, 651–657.

Rabkin, J. G. (1980). Stressful life events and schizophrenia: A review of the literature. Psychological Bulletin, 87, 408–425.

Rabkin, L. Y., & Rabkin, K. (1974). Children of the kibbutz. In Readings in psychology today, 3d ed. Del Mar, CA: CRM Books.

Rada, R. T., & Kellner, R. (1979). Drug treatment in alcoholism. In J. Davis & D. J. Greenblatt (eds.), Recent developments in psychopharmacology. New York: Grune & Stratton.

Radin, N. (1982). Primary caregiving and role-sharing behaviors. In M. E. Lamb (ed.), Nontraditional families: Parenting and child development. Hillsdale, NJ: Erlbaum.

Randell, J. (1969). Preoperative and

postoperative status of male and female transsexuals. In R. Green & J. Money (eds.), *Transsexualism and sex reassignment*. Baltimore: Johns Hopkins.

Rapaport, K., & Burkhart, B. R. (1984). Personality and attitudinal characteristics of sexually coercive college males. *Journal of Abnormal Psychology, 93*, 216–221.

Rapport, M. D. (1984). Hyperactivity and stimulant treatment: *Abusus non tollit usum*. *The Behavior Therapist, 7*, 133–134.

Raps, C. S., Peterson, C., Reinhard, K. E., Abramson, L. Y., & Seligman, M. E. P. (1982). Attributional style among depressed patients. *Journal of Abnormal Psychology, 91*, 102–108.

Rathus, S. A. (1973). A 30-item schedule for assessing assertive behavior. *Behavior Therapy, 4*, 398–406.

Rathus, S. A. (1983). *Human sexuality*. New York: Holt, Rinehart and Winston.

Rathus, S. A., & Nevid, J. S. (1977). *Behavior therapy*. Garden City, NY: Doubleday.

Rathus, S. A., & Nevid, J. S. (1986). *Adjustment and growth: The challenges of life*, 3d ed. New York: Holt, Rinehart and Winston.

Reckless, J., & Geiger, N. (1978). Impotence as a practical problem. In J. LoPiccolo & L. LoPiccolo (eds.), *Handbook of sex therapy*. New York: Plenum.

Reeder, G. D. (1982). Let's give the fundamental attribution error another chance. *Journal of Personality and Social Psychology, 43*, 341–344.

Regan, D. T., Williams, M., & Sparling, S. (1972). Voluntary expiation of guilt: A field experiment. *Journal of Personality and Social Psychology, 24*, 42–45.

Rehm, L. P. (1978). Mood, pleasant events, and unpleasant events. *Journal of Consulting and Clinical Psychology, 46*, 854–859.

Reich, J. W., & Zautra, A. (1981). Life events and personal causation: Some relationships with satisfaction and distress. *Journal of Personality and Social Psychology, 41*, 1002–1012.

Reich, W. (1983, January 30). The world of Soviet psychiatry. *The New York Times Magazine*, 20–26, 50.

Reinke, B. J., Holmes, D. S., & Harris, R. L. (1985). The timing of psychosocial changes in women's lives: The years 25 to 45. *Journal of Personality and Social Psychology, 48*, 1353–1364.

Reis, H. T., Nezlek, J., & Wheeler, L. (1980). Physical attractiveness in social interaction. *Journal of Personality and Social Psychology, 38*, 604–617.

Reis, H. T., Senchak, M., & Solomon, B. (1985). Sex differences in the intimacy of social interaction. *Journal of Personality and Social Psychology, 48*, 1204–1217.

Reis, H. T., Wheeler, L., Spiegel, N., Kernis, M. H., Nezlek, J., & Perri, M. (1982). Physical attractiveness in social interaction: II. Why does appearance affect social experience? *Journal of Personality and Social Psychology, 43*, 979–996.

Reiss, I. L. (1967). *The social context of premarital sexual permissiveness*. New York: Holt, Rinehart and Winston.

Reiss, M., Rosenfeld, P., Melburg, V., & Tedeschi, J. T. (1981). Self-serving attributions: Biased private perceptions and distorted public descriptions. *Journal of Personality and Social Psychology, 41*, 224–231.

Rempel, J. K., Holmes, J. G., & Zanna, M. P. (1985). Trust in close relationships. *Journal of Personality and Social Psychology, 49*, 95–112.

Renninger, K. A., & Wozniak, R. H. (1985). Effect of interest on attentional shift, recognition, and recall in young children. *Developmental Psychology, 21*, 624–632.

Reschly, D. J. (1981). Psychological testing in educational classification and placement. *American Psychologist, 36*, 1094–1102.

Rest, J. R. (1983). Morality. In P. H. Mussen, J. Flavell, & E. Markman (eds.), *Handbook of child psychology*, Vol. 3: *Cognitive development*, 4th ed. New York: Wiley.

Restak, R. (1975, August 9). José Delgado: Exploring inner space. *Saturday Review*.

Reuman, D. A., Alwin, D. F., & Veroff, J. (1984). Assessing the validity of the achievement motive in the presence of random measurement error. *Journal of Personality and Social Psychology, 47*, 1347–1362.

Rheingold, H. F., Gewirtz, J. L., & Ross, H. W. (1959). Social conditioning of vocalizations in the infant. *Journal of Comparative and Physiological Psychology, 51*, 68–73.

Rhine, J. B. (ed.). (1971). *Progress in parapsychology*. Durham, NC: Parapsychology Press.

Rice, B. (1979). Brave new world of intelligence testing. *Psychology Today, 13* (9), 27.

Richardson, D. C., Bernstein, S., & Taylor, S. P. (1979). The effect of situational contingencies on female retaliative behavior. *Journal of Personality and Social Psychology, 37*, 2044–2048.

Richter, C. P. (1957). On the phenomenon of sudden death in animals and man. *Psychosomatic Medicine, 19*, 191–198.

Ridon, J., & Langer, E. J. (1977). Long-term effects of control-relevant intervention with the institutionalized aged. *Journal of Personality and Social Psychology, 35*, 897–902.

Rieser, J., Yonas, A., & Wilkner, K. (1976). Radial localization of odors by human newborns. *Child Development, 47*, 856–859.

Rinn, W. E. (1984). The neuropsychology of facial expression: A review of the neurological and psychological mechanisms for producing facial expressions. *Psychological Bulletin, 95*, 52–77.

Roberts, A. H. (1985). Biofeedback: Research, training, and critical roles. *American Psychologist, 40*, 938–941.

Robins, E. J., Gassner, J., Kayes, J., Wilkinson, R., & Murphy, G. E. (1959). The communication of suicidal intent: A study of 134 successful (completed) suicides. *American Journal of Psychiatry, 115*, 724–733.

Robinson, M. H., & Robinson, B. (1979). By dawn's early light: Matutinal mating and sex attractants in a neotropical mantid. *Science, 205*, 825–826.

Rock, I., & Victor, J. (1964). Vision and touch: An experimentally created conflict between the two senses. *Science, 143*, 594–596.

Rodin, J., & Slochower, J. (1976). Externality in the obese: The effects of environmental responsiveness on weight. *Journal of Personality and Social Psychology, 33*, 338–344.

Rogan, H. (1984a, October 29). Women executives feel that men both aid and hinder their careers. *The Wall Street Journal, 35*, 59.

Rogan, H. (1984b, October 30). Executive women find it difficult to balance demands of job, home. *The Wall Street Journal, 33*, 55.

Rogers, C. R. (1951). *Client-centered therapy*. Boston: Houghton Mifflin.

Rogers, C. R. (1959). A theory of therapy, personality and interpersonal relationships, as developed in the client-centered framework. In S. Koch (ed.), *Psychology: A study of science*, Vol. 3. New York: McGraw-Hill.

Rogers, C. R. (1974). In retrospect: 46 years. *American Psychologist, 29*, 115–123.

Rogers, C. R. (1985). Cited in Cunningham, S. (1985). Humanists celebrate gains, goals. *APA Monitor, 16* (5), 16, 18.

Rogers, R. W., & Deckner, C. W. (1975). Effects of fear appeals and physiological arousal upon emotions, attitudes, and cigarette smoking. *Journal of Personality and Social Psychology, 32*, 222–230.

Rogers, R. W., & Prentice-Dunn, S. (1981). Deindividuation and anger-mediated interracial aggression: Unmasking regressive racism. *Journal of Personality and Social Psychology, 41*, 63–73.

Rohsenow, D. J. (1983). Drinking habits and expectancies about alcohol's effects for self versus others. *Journal of Consulting and Clinical Psychology, 51*, 752–756.

Rokeach, M., Smith, D. W., & Evans, R. I. (1960). Two kinds of prejudice or one? In M. Rokeach (ed.), *The open and closed mind*. New York: Basic Books.

Rollin, B. E. (1985). The moral status of research animals in psychology. *American Psychologist, 40*, 920–926.

Ronen, S. (1981). *Flexible working hours*. New York: McGraw-Hill.

Rorschach, H. (1921). *Psychodiagnostics*. Berne: Hans Huber.

Rosch, E. (1974). Linguistic relativity: In A. Silverstein (ed.), *Human communication: Theoretical perspectives*. New York: Halsted Press, 1974.

Rose, R. M. (1975). Testosterone, aggression, and homosexuality: A review of the literature and implications for future research. In E. J. Sachar (ed.), *Topics in psychoendocrinology*. New York: Grune & Stratton.

Rosen, G. M., Glasgow, R. E., & Barrera, M., Jr. (1976). A controlled study to assess the efficacy of totally self-administered systematic desensitization. *Journal of Consulting and Clinical Psychology, 44*, 208–217.

Rosenbaum, M., & Hadari, D. (1985). Personal efficacy, external locus of control, and perceived contingency of parental reinforcement among depressed, paranoid, and normal subjects. *Journal of Personality and Social Psychology, 49*, 539–547.

Rosenberg, M. S., & Reppucci, N. D. (1985). Primary prevention of child abuse. *Journal of Consulting and Clinical Psychology, 53*, 576–585.

Rosenblum, L. A., & Paully, G. S. (1984). The effects of varying environmental demands on maternal and infant behavior. *Child Development, 55*, 305–314.

Rosenhan, D. (1973). On being sane in insane places. *Science, 179*, 250–258.

Rosenhan, D., Salovey, P., & Hargis, K. (1981). The joys of helping. *Journal of Personality and Social Psychology, 40*, 899–905.

Rosenthal, D. (1970). *Genetic theory and abnormal behavior*. New York: McGraw-Hill.

Rosenthal, D. M. (1980). The modularity and maturation of cognitive capacities. *Behavior and Brain Science, 3*, 32–34.

Rosenzweig, M. R. (1969). Effects of heredity and environment on brain chemistry, brain anatomy, and learning ability in the rat. In M. Manosovitz et al. (eds.), *Behavioral genetics*. New York: Appleton.

Rotter, J. B. (1966). Generalized expectancies for internal versus external control of reinforcement. *Psychological Monographs, 80* (609).

Rotter, J. B. (1971). External control and internal control. *Psychology Today, 5*, 37–42, 58–59.

Rotter, J. B. (1972). Beliefs, social attitudes, and behavior: A social learning analysis. In J. B. Rotter, J. E. Chance, & E. J. Phares (eds.), *Applications of a social learning theory of personality*. New York: Holt, Rinehart and Winston.

Rotter, J. B. (1975). Some problems and misconceptions related to the construct of internal versus external control of reinforcement. *Journal of Consulting and Clinical Psychology, 43*, 56–67.

Rotton, J., & Frey, J. (1985). Air pollution, weather, and violent crimes: Concomitant time-series analysis of archival data. *Journal of Personality and Social Psychology, 49*, 1207–1220.

Roueche, B. (1980). *The medical detectives*. New York: Truman Talley.

Rovet, J., & Netley, C. (1983). The triple X chromosome syndrome in childhood: Recent empirical findings. *Child Development, 54*, 831–845.

Rozensky, R. H., & Pasternak, J. F. (1985). Cited in Horn, J. C. (1985). Fighting migraines with The Force. *Psychology Today, 19* (11), 74.

Rubinstein, E. A. (1983). Television and behavior: Research conclusions of the

1982 NIMH report and their policy implications. *American Psychologist, 38,* 820–825.

Ruderman, A. J. (1985). Dysphoric mood and overeating: A test of restraint theory's disinhibition hypothesis. *Journal of Abnormal Psychology, 94,* 78–85.

Rundus, D. (1971). Analysis of rehearsal processes in free recall. *Journal of Experimental Psychology, 89,* 63–77.

Ruopp, R. (1979). *Children at the center: Final report of the national day care study.* Cambridge, MA: Abt Associates.

Ruppenthal, G. C., Arling, G. L., Harlow, H. F., Sackett, G. P., & Suomi, S. J. (1976). A ten-year perspective of motherless-mother monkey behavior. *Journal of Abnormal Psychology, 85,* 341–349.

Russell, G. (1982). Shared-caregiving families: An Australian study. In M. E. Lamb (ed.), *Nontraditional families: Parenting and child development.* Hillsdale, NJ: Erlbaum.

Russell, M. J., Switz, G. M., & Thompson, K. (1977, June). Olfactory influences on the human menstrual cycle. Paper presented at the meeting of the American Association for the Advancement of Science.

Rutkowski, G. K., Gruder, C. L., & Romer, D. (1983). Group cohesiveness, social norms, and bystander intervention. *Journal of Personality and Social Psychology, 44,* 545–552.

Sackeim, H. A. (1985). The case for ECT. *Psychology Today, 19* (6), 36–40.

Sadker, M., & Sadker, D. (1985). Sexism in the schoolroom of the 1980s. *Psychology Today, 19* (3), 54–57.

Saegert, S. C., & Hart, R. (1976). The development of sex differences in the environmental competence of children. In P. Burnett (ed.), *Women in society.* Chicago: Maaroufa Press.

Saegert, S. C., & Jellison, J. M. (1970). Effects of initial level of response competition and frequency of exposure to liking and exploratory behavior. *Journal of Personality and Social Psychology, 16,* 553–558.

Safer, M. A. (1980). Attributing evil to the subject, not the situation: Student reactions to Milgram's film on obedience. *Personality and Social Psychology Bulletin, 6,* 205–209.

Sagar, H. A., & Schofield, J. W. (1980). Racial and behavioral cues in black and white children's perceptions of ambiguously aggressive acts. *Journal of Personality and Social Psychology, 39,* 590–598.

Saghir, M. T., & Robins, E. (1973). *Male and female homosexuality: A comprehensive investigation.* Baltimore: Williams & Wilkins.

Sanchez-Craig, M., Annis, H. M., Bornet, A. R., & MacDonald, K. R. (1984). Random assignment to abstinence or controlled drinking: Evaluation of a cognitive-behavioral program for problem drinkers. *Journal of Consulting and Clinical Psychology, 52,* 390–403

Santee, R. T., & Maslach, C. (1982). To agree or not to agree: Personal dissent amid social pressure to conform. *Journal of Personality and Social Psychology, 42,* 690–700.

Santrock, J. W. (1970). Paternal absence, sex typing, and identification. *Developmental Psychology, 2,* 264–272.

Sarason, I. G. (1978). The test anxiety scale. In C. D. Spielberger & I. G. Sarason (eds.), *Stress and anxiety,* Vol. 5. New York: Halsted-Wiley.

Sarbin, T. R., & Coe, W. C. (1972). *Hypnosis: A social psychological analysis of influence communication.* New York: Holt, Rinehart and Winston.

Sarbin, T. R., & Nucci, L. P. (1973). Self-reconstitution processes: A proposal for reorganizing the conduct of confirmed smokers. *Journal of Abnormal Psychology, 81,* 182–195.

Satir, V. (1967). *Conjoint family therapy.* Palo Alto, CA: Science and Behavior Books.

Satow, K. L. (1975). Social approval and helping. *Journal of Experimental Social Psychology, 11,* 501–509.

Sawrey, W. L., Conger, J. J., & Turrell, E. S. (1956). An experimental investigation of the role of psychological factors in the production of gastric ulcers in rats. *Journal of Comparative and Physiological Psychology, 49,* 457–461.

Sawrey, W. L., & Weisz, J. D. (1956). An experimental method of producing gastric ulcers. *Journal of Comparative and Physiological Psychology, 49,* 269–270.

Saxe, L., Dougherty, D., & Cross, T. (1985). The validity of polygraph testing: Scientific analysis and public controversy. *American Psychologist, 40,* 355–366.

Scarr, S. (1981). Testing *for* children: Assessment and the many determinants of intellectual competence. *American Psychologist, 36,* 1159–1166.

Scarr, S., Webber, P. L., Weinberg, R. A., & Wittig, M. A. (1981). Personality resemblance among adolescents and their parents in biologically related and adoptive families. *Journal of Personality and Social Psychology, 41,* 885–898.

Scarr, S., & Weinberg, R. A. (1976). IQ test performance of black children adopted by white families. *American Psychologist, 31,* 726–739.

Scarr, S., & Weinberg, R. A. (1977). Intellectual similarities within families of both adopted and biological children. *Intelligence, 1,* 170–191.

Scarr, S., & Weinberg, R. A. (1983). The Minnesota adoption studies: Genetic differences and malleability. *Child Development, 54,* 260–267.

Schachter, S. (1959). *The psychology of affiliation.* Stanford, CA: Stanford.

Schachter, S. (1971a). *Emotion, obesity, and crime.* New York: Academic Press.

Schachter, S. (1971b). Some extraordinary facts about obese humans and rats. *American Psychologist, 26,* 129–144.

Schachter, S. (1982). Recidivism and self-cure of smoking and obesity. *American Psychologist, 37,* 436–444.

Schachter, S., & Gross, L. P. (1968). Manipulated time and eating behavior. *Journal of Personality and Social Psychology, 10,* 98–106.

Schachter, S., Kozlowski, L. T., & Silverstein, B. (1977). Effects of urinary pH on cigarette smoking. *Journal of Experimental Psychology: General, 106,* 13–19.

Schachter, S., & Latané, B. (1964). Crime, cognition, and the autonomic nervous system. In D. Levine (ed.), *Nebraska symposium on motivation.* Lincoln, NE: University of Nebraska Press.

Schachter, S., & Rodin, J. (1974). *Obese humans and rats.* Washington, D.C.: Erlbaum/Halsted.

Schachter, S., & Singer, J. E. (1962). Cognitive, social, and physiological determinants of emotional state. *Psychological Review, 69,* 379–399.

Schaeffer, J., Andrysiak, T., & Ungerleider, J. T. (1981). Cognition and long-term use of ganja (cannabis). *Science, 213,* 465–466.

Scheier, M. F., Buss, A. H., & Buss, D. M. (1978). Self-consciousness, self-report of aggressiveness, and aggression. *Journal of Research in Personality, 12,* 133–140.

Schiavi, R. C., Davis, D. M., Fogel, M., White, D., Edwards, A., Igel, G., Szechter, R., & Fisher, C. (1977). Luteinizing hormone and testosterone during nocturnal sleep: Relation to penile tumescent cycles. *Archives of Sexual Behavior, 6,* 97–104.

Schiedel, D. G., & Marcia, J. E. (1985). Ego identity, intimacy, sex-role orientation, and gender. *Developmental Psychology, 21,* 149–160.

Schifter, D. E., & Ajzen, I. (1985). Intention, perceived control, and weight loss: An application of the theory of planned behavior. *Journal of Personality and Social Psychology, 49,* 843–851.

Schindler, G. L. (1979). *Testosterone concentration, personality patterns, and occupational choice in women.*

Unpublished doctoral dissertation, University of Houston.

Schleidt, M., & Hold, B. (1981). Paper presented to the conference on the determination of behavior by chemical stimuli. Hebrew University, Jerusalem.

Schmauk, F. J. (1970). Punishment, arousal, and avoidance learning in sociopaths. *Journal of Abnormal Psychology, 76,* 443–453.

Schmidt, G., Sigüsch, V., & Schafer, S. (1973). Responses to reading erotic stories: Male-female differences. *Archives of Sexual Behavior, 2,* 181–199.

Schneidman, B., & McGuire, L. (1976). Group therapy for nonorgasmic women: Two age levels. *Archives of Sexual Behavior, 5,* 239–247.

Schneidman, E. S. (ed.) (1976). *Deaths of man.* New York: Quadrangle.

Schneidman, E. S. (1985). Cited in Cordes, C. (1985). Common threads found in suicide. *APA Monitor, 16* (10), 11.

Schneidman, E. S., Farberow, N. L., & Litman, R. E. (eds.). (1970). *The psychology of suicide.* New York: Science House.

Schotte, D. E., & Clum, G. A. (1982). Suicide ideation in a college population: A test of a model. *Journal of Consulting and Clinical Psychology, 50,* 690–696.

Schultz, D. P. (1978). *Psychology and industry today.* New York: Macmillan.

Schwartz, J. C., Strickland, R. G., & Krolick, G. (1973). Infant day care: Behavioral effects at preschool age. *Developmental Psychology, 10,* 502–506

Schwartz, L. M., Foa, U. G., & Foa, E. B. (1983). Multichannel nonverbal communication: Evidence for combinatory rules. *Journal of Personality and Social Psychology, 45,* 274–281.

Schwartz, M. (1978). *Physiological psychology.* Englewood Cliffs, NJ: Prentice-Hall.

Schwartz, M. F., Saffran, E. M., & Marin, O. S. M. (1980). The word order problem in agrammatism: I: Compre-

hension. *Brain and Language, 10,* 249–262.

Schwartz, R. M. (1982). Cognitive behavior modification: A conceptual review. *Clinical Psychology Review, 2,* 267–293.

Schwartz, R. M., & Gottman, J. M. (1976). Toward a task analysis of assertive behavior. *Journal of Consulting and Clinical Psychology, 44,* 910–920.

Scott, J. P., & Fuller, J. L. (1965). *Genetics and the social behavior of the dog.* Chicago: University of Chicago Press.

Sears, R. R., Maccoby, E. E., & Levin, H. (1957). *Patterns of child rearing.* New York: Harper & Row.

Sebeok, T., & Umiker-Sebeok, J. (1980). *Speaking of apes.* New York: Plenum.

Seer, P. (1979). Psychological control of essential hypertension: Review of the literature and methodological critique. *Psychological Bulletin, 86,* 1015–1043.

Segal, M. W. (1974). Alphabet and attraction: An unobtrusive measure of the effect of propinquity in the field setting. *Journal of Personality and Social Psychology, 30,* 654–657.

Segovia-Riquelma, N., Varela, A., & Mardones, J. (1971). Appetite for alcohol. In Y. Israel & J. Mardones (eds.), *Biological basis of alcoholism.* New York: Wiley.

Seligman, M. E. P. (1973). Fall into helplessness. *Psychology Today, 7,* 43–48.

Seligman, M. E. P., Abramson, L. Y., Semmel, A., & von Baeyer, C. (1979). Depressive attributional style. *Journal of Abnormal Psychology, 88,* 242–247.

Seligman, M. E. P., Peterson, C., Kaslow, N. J., Tanenbaum, R. L., Alloy, L. B., & Abramson, L. Y. (1984). Attributional style and depressive symptoms among children. *Journal of Abnormal Psychology, 93,* 235–238.

Selye, H. (1976). *The stress of life,* rev. ed. New York: McGraw-Hill.

Selye, H. (1980). The stress concept today. In I. L. Kutash, L. B. Schlesinger, et al. (eds.), *Handbook on stress and anxiety*. San Francisco: Jossey-Bass.

Semans, J. (1956). Premature ejaculation: A new approach. *Southern Medical Journal, 49*, 353–358.

Serbin, L. A., Conner, J. M., Burchardt, C. J., & Citron, C. C. (1979). Effects of peer presence on sex typing of children's play behavior. *Journal of Experimental Child Psychology, 27*, 303–309.

Serlin, E. (1980). Emptying the nest: Women in the launching stage. In D. G. McGuigan (ed.), *Women's lives: New theory, research, and policy*. Ann Arbor: University of Michigan, Center for Continuing Education of Women.

Seta, J. J. (1982). The impact of comparison processes on coactors' task performance. *Journal of Personality and Social Psychology, 42*, 281–291.

Shadish, W. R., Hickman, D., & Arrick, M. C. (1981). Psychological problems of spinal injury patients: Emotional distress as a function of time and locus of control. *Journal of Consulting and Clinical Psychology, 49*, 297.

Shanteau, J., & Nagy, G. (1979). Probability of acceptance in dating choice. *Journal of Personality and Social Psychology, 37*, 522–533.

Shapira, A., & Madsen, M. C. (1974). Between and within group cooperation and competitive behavior among kibbutz and nonkibbutz children. *Developmental Psychology, 10*, 140–145.

Shapiro, D. (1985). Clinical use of meditation as a self-regulation strategy: Comments on Holmes' conclusions and implications. *American Psychologist, 40*, 719–722.

Shapiro, D. A., & Shapiro, D. (1982). Meta-analysis of comparative therapy outcome studies: A replication and refinement. *Psychological Bulletin, 92*, 581–594.

Shaw, J. S. (1982). Psychological androgyny and stressful life events. *Journal of Personality and Social Psychology, 43*, 145–153.

Sheehy, G. (1976). *Passages: Predictable crises of adult life*. New York: Dutton.

Sheehy, G. (1981). *Pathfinders*. New York: Morrow.

Sheraton, M. (1984, June 4). You can argue with taste. *Time Magazine*, 74–75.

Shekelle, R. B., Gale, M., Ostfeld, A. M., & Paul, O. (1983). Hostility, risk of coronary heart disease, and mortality. *Psychosomatic Medicine, 45*, 109–114.

Sherif, C. W. (1980). A social psychological perspective on the menstrual cycle. In J. E. Parsons (ed.), *The psychobiology of sex differences and sex roles*. New York: McGraw-Hill, Hemisphere.

Sherif, M. (1966). *In common predicament: Social psychology of intergroup conflict and cooperation*. Boston: Houghton Mifflin.

Shiffman, S. (1982). Relapse following smoking cessation: A situational analysis. *Journal of Consulting and Clinical Psychology, 50*, 71–86.

Shiffman, S. (1984). Coping with temptations to smoke. *Journal of Consulting and Clinical Psychology, 52*, 261–267.

Shipley, R. H. (1981). Maintenance of smoking cessation: Effect of follow-up letters, smoking motivation, muscle tension, and health locus of control. *Journal of Consulting and Clinical Psychology, 49*, 982–984.

Shipley, R. H., Butt, J. H., Horwitz, B., & Farbry, J. E. (1978). Preparation for a stressful medical procedure: Effect of amount of stimulus preexposure and coping style. *Journal of Consulting and Clinical Psychology, 46*, 499–507.

Shotland, R. L., & Heinold, W. D. (1985). Bystander response to arterial bleeding: Helping skills, the decision-making process, and differentiating the helping response. *Journal of Personality and Social Psychology, 49*, 347–356.

Sieber, J. E. (1983). Deception in social research III: The nature and limits of debriefing. *IRB: A Review of Human Subjects Research, 5* (3), 1–4.

Siegler, R. S., & Liebert, R. M. (1972). Effects of presenting relevant rules and complete feedback on the conservation of liquid quantity task. *Developmental Psychology, 7*, 133–138.

Siegman, A. W., & Feldstein, S. (eds.). (1977). *Nonverbal behavior and communication*. Hillsdale, NJ: Erlbaum.

Silverstein, B. (1982). Cigarette communication. Hillsdale, NJ: Erlbaum.

Silverstein, B. (1982). Cigarette smoking, nicotine addiction, and relaxation. *Journal of Personality and Social Psychology, 42*, 946–950.

Silverstein, B., Kozlowski, L. T., & Schachter, S. (1977). Social life, cigarette smoking, and urinary pH. *Journal of Experimental Psychology: General, 106*, 20–23.

Singer, D. G. (1983). A time to reexamine the role of television in our lives. *American Psychologist, 38*, 815–825.

Singer, J. L. (1975). *The inner world of daydreaming*. New York: Harper & Row.

Singer, J. L., & Singer, D. G. (1981). *Television, imagination, and aggression: A study of preschoolers*. Hillsdale, NJ: Erlbaum.

Singer, J. L., & Singer, D. G. (1983). Psychologists look at television: Cognitive, developmental, personality, and social policy implications. *American Psychologist, 38*, 826–834.

Singular, S. (1982). A memory for all seasonings. *Psychology Today, 16* (10), 54–63.

Sirota, A. D., Schwartz, G. E., & Shapiro, D. (1976). Voluntary control of human heart rate: Effect on reaction to aversive stimulation: A replication and extension. *Journal of Abnormal Psychology, 85*, 473–477.

Sistrunk, F., & McDavid, J. W. (1971). Sex variable in conforming behavior. *Journal of Personality and Social Psychology, 17*, 200–207.

Sjøstrøm, L. (1980). Fat cells and body

weight. In A. J. Stunkard (ed.), *Obesity*. Philadelphia: W. B. Saunders.

Skinner, B. F. (1938). *The behavior of organisms: An experimental analysis*. New York: Appleton.

Skinner, B. F. (1948). *Walden two*. New York: Macmillan.

Skinner, B. F. (1957). *Verbal behavior*. New York: Appleton.

Skinner, B. F. (1960). Pigeons in a pelican. *American Psychologist, 15*, 28–37.

Skinner, B. F. (1972). *Beyond freedom and dignity*. New York: Knopf.

Skinner, B. F. (1979). *The shaping of a behaviorist*. New York: Knopf.

Skinner, B. F. (1983). Intellectual self-management in old age. *American Psychologist, 38*, 239–244.

Slobin, D. I. (1971). *Psycholinguistics*. Glenville, IL: Scott, Foresman.

Slobin, D. I. (1973). Cognitive prerequisites for the development of grammar. In C. A. Ferguson & D. I. Slobin (eds.), *Studies of child development*. New York: Holt, Rinehart and Winston.

Slobin, J. F., & Depue, R. A. (1981). The contribution of environmental events and social support to serious suicide attempts in primary depressive disorder. *Journal of Abnormal Psychology, 90*, 275–285.

Smedley, J. W., & Bayton, J. A. (1978). Evaluative race-class stereotypes by race and perceived class of subjects. *Journal of Personality and Social Psychology, 36*, 530–535.

Smith, B. M. (1967, January). The polygraph. *Scientific American*.

Smith, B. M. (1971). *The polygraph in contemporary psychology*. San Francisco: Freeman.

Smith, C. P., & Graham, J. R. (1981). Behavioral correlates for the MMPI *F* scale and for a modified *F* scale for black and white psychiatric patients. *Journal of Consulting and Clinical Psychology, 49*, 455–459.

Smith, D. (1982). Trends in counseling and psychotherapy. *American Psychologist, 37*, 802–809.

Smith, D., King, M., & Hoebel, B. G.

(1970). Lateral hypothalamic control of killing: Evidence for a cholinoceptive mechanism. *Science, 167*, 900–901.

Smith, D., & Kraft, W. A. (1983). DSM–III: Do psychologists really want an alternative? *American Psychologist, 38*, 777–785.

Smith, G. F., & Dorfman, D. (1975). The effect of stimulus uncertainty on the relationship between frequency of exposure and liking. *Journal of Personality and Social Psychology, 31*, 150–155.

Smith, M. L., & Glass, G. V. (1977). Meta-analysis of psychotherapy outcome studies. *American Psychologist, 32*, 752–760.

Smith, M. L., Glass, G. V., & Miller, R. L. (1981). *The benefits of psychotherapy*. Baltimore: Johns Hopkins.

Smith, R. E., & Winokur, G. (1983). Affective disorders. In R. E. Tarter (ed.), *The child at psychiatric risk*. New York: Oxford.

Smith, S. S., & Richardson, D. (1983). Amelioration of deception and harm in psychological research: The important role of debriefing. *Journal of Personality and Social Psychology, 44*, 1075–1082.

Smith, T. W. (1983). Change in irrational beliefs and the outcome of rational-emotive psychotherapy. *Journal of Consulting and Clinical Psychology, 51*, 156–157.

Smith, T. W., Snyder, C. R., & Handelsman, M. M. (1982). On the self-serving function of an academic wooden leg: Test anxiety as a self-handicapping strategy. *Journal of Personality and Social Psychology, 42*, 314–321.

Smith, T. W., Snyder, C. R., & Perkins, S. C. (1983). The self-serving function of hypochondriacal complaints: Physical symptoms as self-handicapping strategies. *Journal of Personality and Social Psychology, 44*, 787–797.

Snarey, J. R., Reimer, J., & Kohlberg, L. (1985). Development of social-moral reasoning among kibbutz adolescents: A longitudinal cross-cultural

study. *Developmental Psychology, 21*, 3–17.

Snow, M. E., Jacklin, C. N., & Maccoby, E. E. (1983). Sex-of-child differences in father-child interaction at one year of age. *Child Development, 54*, 227–232.

Snyder, D. (1979). Multidimensional assessment of marital satisfaction. *Journal of Marriage and the Family, 41*, 813–823.

Snyder, D. K., Kline, R. B., & Podany, E. C. (1985). Comparison of external correlates of MMPI substance abuse scales across sex and race. *Journal of Consulting and Clinical Psychology, 53*, 520–525.

Snyder, M., & Cunningham, M. R. (1975). To comply or not to comply: Testing the self-perception explanation of the ''foot-in-the-door'' phenomenon. *Journal of Personality and Social Psychology, 31*, 64–67.

Snyder, M., & DeBono, G. (1985). Appeals to image and claims about quality: Understanding the psychology of advertising. *Journal of Personality and Social Psychology, 49*, 586–597.

Snyder, M., Grether, J., & Keller, K. (1974). Staring and compliance: A field experiment on hitchhiking. *Journal of Applied Social Psychology, 4*, 165–170.

Snyder, M., Tanke, E. D., & Berscheid, E. (1977). Social perception and interpersonal behavior: On the self-fulfilling nature of social stereotypes. *Journal of Personality and Social Psychology, 35*, 656–666.

Snyder, S. H. (1977). Opiate receptors and internal opiates. *Scientific American, 236*, 44–56.

Snyder, S. H. (1980). *Biological aspects of mental disorder*. New York: Oxford.

Snyder, S. H. (1984). Drug and neurotransmitter receptors in the brain. *Science, 224*, 22–31.

Sobel, D. (1981, November 3). Baby's cry, it turns out, can speak volumes. *The New York Times*, C1, C3.

Sobell, M. B., & Sobell, L. C. (1973).

Alcoholics treated by individualized behavior therapy: One year treatment outcomes. *Behaviour Research and Therapy, 11,* 599–618.

Sobell, M. B., & Sobell, L. C. (1976). Second year treatment outcome of alcoholics treated by individualized behavior therapy: Results. *Behaviour Research and Therapy, 14,* 195–215

Sobell, M. B., & Sobell, L. C. (1984). The aftermath of heresy: A response to Pendery et al.'s critique of "Individualized behavior therapy for alcoholics." *Behaviour Research and Therapy, 22,* 413–440

Sommer, R. (1969). *Personal space.* Englewood Cliffs, NJ: Prentice-Hall.

Sorce, J. F., Emde, R. N., Campos, J. J., & Klinnert, M. D. (1985). Maternal emotional signaling: Its effect on the visual-cliff behavior of 1-year-olds. *Developmental Psychology, 21,* 195–200.

Spanos, N. P., Jones, B., & Malfara, A. (1982). Hypnotic deafness: Now you hear it—now you still hear it. *Journal of Abnormal Psychology, 91,* 75–77.

Spanos, N. P., McNeil, C., Gwynn, M. I., & Stam, H. J. (1984). Effects of suggestion and distraction on reported pain in subjects high and low on hypnotic suggestibility. *Journal of Abnormal Psychology, 93,* 277–284.

Spanos, N. P., Radtke, H. L., & Dubreuil, D. L. (1982). Episodic and semantic memory in posthypnotic amnesia: A reevaluation. *Journal of Personality and Social Psychology, 43,* 565–573.

Spanos, N. P., & Radtke-Bodorik, H. L. (1980, April). Integrating hypnotic phenomena with cognitive psychology: An illustration using suggested amnesia. *Bulletin of the British Society for Experimental and Clinical Hypnosis,* 4–7.

Spanos, N. P., Weekes, J. R., & Bertrand, L. D. (1985). Multiple personality: A social psychological perspective. *Journal of Abnormal Psychology, 94,* 362–376.

Spence, J. T., Helmreich, R., & Stapp, J. (1975). Ratings of self and peers on sex-role attributes and their relation to self-esteem and concepts of masculinity and femininity. *Journal of Personality and Social Psychology, 32,* 29–39.

Sperling, G. (1960). The information available in brief visual presentations. *Psychological Monographs, 74,* 498.

Sperry, R. W. (1974). Lateral specialization in the surgically separated hemispheres. In F. O. Schmitt & F. G. Worden (eds.), *The neurosciences: Third study program.* Cambridge: MIT Press.

Spitzer, R. L., Forman, J. B. W., & Nee, J. (1979). DSM–III field trials: Initial interrater diagnostic reliability. *American Journal of Psychiatry, 136,* 815–817.

Stalonas, P. M., & Kirschenbaum, D. S. (1985). Behavioral treatments for obesity: Eating habits revisited. *Behavior Therapy, 16,* 1–14.

Stapp, J., Tucker, A. M., & VandenBos, G. R. (1985). Census of psychological personnel: 1983. *American Psychologist, 40,* 1317–1351.

Stark, E. (1984). Hypnosis on trial. *Psychology Today, 18* (2), 34–36.

Stasser, G., & Titus, W. (1985). Pooling of unshared information in group decision making: Biased information sampling during discussion. *Journal of Personality and Social Psychology, 48,* 1467–1478.

Staub, E., Tursky, B., & Schwartz, G. (1971). Self-control and predictability: Their effects on reactions to aversive stimulation. *Journal of Personality and Social Psychology, 18,* 157–162.

Steck, L., Levitan, D., McLane, D., & Kelley, H. H. (1982). Care, need, and conceptions of love. *Journal of Personality and Social Psychology, 43,* 481–491.

Steele, C. M., & Southwick, L. L. (1985). Alcohol and social behavior I: The psychology of drunken excess. *Journal of Personality and Social Psychology, 48,* 18–34.

Steele, C. M., Southwick, L. L., &

Critchlow, B. (1981). Dissonance and alcohol: Drinking your troubles away. *Journal of Personality and Social Psychology, 41,* 831–846.

Steinberg, L. D., Catalano, R., & Dooley, D. (1981). Economic antecedents of child abuse and neglect. Paper presented to the meeting of the Society for Research in Child Development, Boston.

Steiner, J. E. (1979). Facial expressions in response to taste and smell discrimination. In H. W. Reese, & L. P. Lipsitt (eds.), *Advances in child development and behavior,* Vol. 13. New York: Academic Press.

Steinmetz, J. L., Lewinsohn, P. M., & Antonuccio, D. O. (1983). Prediction of individual outcome in a group intervention for depression. *Journal of Consulting and Clinical Psychology, 51,* 331–337.

Stephan, C. W., & Langlois, J. H. (1984). Baby beautiful: Adult attributions of infant competence as a function of attractiveness. *Child Development, 55,* 576–585.

Stephan, W. G., & Rosenfield, D. (1978). Effects of desegregation on racial attitudes. *Journal of Personality and Social Psychology, 36,* 795–804.

Stericker, A., & LeVesconte, S. (1982). Effect of brief training on sex-related differences in visual-spatial skill. *Journal of Personality and Social Psychology, 43,* 1018–1029.

Sternberg, R. J. (1982). Who's intelligent? *Psychology Today, 16* (4), 30–39

Sternberg, R. J. (1985). Implicit theories of intelligence, creativity, and wisdom. *Journal of Personality and Social Psychology, 49,* 607–627.

Sternberg, R. J., Conway, B. E., Ketron, J. L., & Bernstein, M. (1981). People's conceptions of intelligence. *Journal of Personality and Social Psychology, 41,* 37–55.

Sternberg, R. J., & Grajek, S. (1984). The nature of love. *Journal of Personality and Social Psychology, 47,* 312–329.

Stier, D. S., & Hall, J. A. (1984). Gender differences in touch: An empirical and theoretical review. *Journal of Person-*

ality and Social Psychology, 47, 440–459.

Stock, M. B., & Smythe, P. M. (1963). Does undernutrition during infancy inhibit brain growth and subsequent intellectual development? Archives of Disorders in Childhood, 38, 546–552.

Stone, A. A., & Neale, J. M. (1984). Effects of severe daily events on mood. Journal of Personality and Social Psychology, 46, 137–144.

Storandt, M. (1983). Psychology's response to the graying of America. American Psychologist, 38, 323–326.

Storms, M. D. (1978). Sexual orientation and self-perception. In P. Plier et al. (eds.), Advances in the study of communication and affect, Vol. 5. New York: Plenum.

Storms, M. D. (1980). Theories of sexual orientation. Journal of Personality and Social Psychology, 38, 783–792.

Strahan, R. F. (1981). Time urgency, Type A behavior, and effect strength. Journal of Consulting and Clinical Psychology, 49, 134.

Strauss, M. A., Gelles, R., & Steinmetz, S. (1979). Behind closed doors: A survey of family violence in America. Garden City, NY: Doubleday.

Strom, J. C., & Buck, R. W. (1979). Staring and participants' sex: Physiological and subjective reactions. Personality and Social Psychology Bulletin, 5, 114–117.

Strube, M. J., Berry, J. M., Goza, B. K., & Fennimore, D. (1985). Type A behavior, age, and psychological well being. Journal of Personality and Social Psychology, 49, 203–218.

Strube, M. J., & Werner, C. (1985). Relinquishment of control and the Type A behavior pattern. Journal of Personality and Social Psychology, 48, 688–701.

Stunkard, A. J. (1959). Obesity and the denial of hunger. Psychosomatic Medicine, 1, 281–289.

Suinn, R. M. (1976). How to break the vicious cycle of stress. Psychology Today, 10, 59–60.

Suler, J. R. (1985). Meditation and somatic arousal: A comment on Holmes's review. American Psychologist, 40, 717.

Sussman, N. M., & Rosenfeld, H. M. (1982). Influence of culture, language, and sex on conversational distance. Journal of Personality and Social Psychology, 42, 66–74.

Sutton-Smith, B., & Rosenberg, B. G. (1970). The sibling. New York: Holt, Rinehart and Winston.

Sutton-Smith, B., Rosenberg, B. G., & Landy, F. (1968). The interaction of father absence and sibling presence on cognitive abilities. Child Development, 39, 1213–1221.

Swensen, C. H. (1983). A respectable old age. American Psychologist, 38, 327–334.

Szucko, J. J., & Kleinmuntz, B. (1981). Statistical versus clinical lie detection. American Psychologist, 36, 488–496.

Tavris, C., & Sadd, S. (1977). The Redbook report on female sexuality. New York: Delacorte.

Taylor, C. B., Farquhar, J. W., Nelson, E., & Agras, D. (1977). Relaxation therapy and high blood pressure. Archives of General Psychiatry, 34, 339–343.

Taylor, S. P., & Epstein, S. (1967). Aggression as a function of the interaction of the sex of the aggressor and the sex of the victim. Journal of Personality, 35, 474–486.

Taylor, W. N. (1985). Super athletes made to order. Psychology Today, 19 (5), 62–66.

Teders, S. J., Blanchard, E. B., Andrasik, F., Jurish, S. E., Neff, D. F., & Arena, J. G. (1984). Relaxation training for tension headache: Comparative efficacy and cost-effectiveness of a minimal-therapist-contact versus a therapist-delivered procedure. Behavior Therapy, 15, 59–70.

Télégdy, G. (1977). Prenatal androgenization of primates and humans. In J. Money & H. Musaph (eds.), Handbook of sexology. Amsterdam: Excerpta Medica.

Terkel, J., & Rosenblatt, J. S. (1972). Hu-moral factors underlying maternal behavior at parturition: Cross transfusion between freely moving rats. Journal of Comparative and Physiological Psychology, 80, 365–371.

Terrace, H. (1979). Nim. New York: Knopf.

Tetlock, P. E. (1983). Accountability and complexity of thought. Journal of Personality and Social Psychology, 45, 74–83.

Thigpen, C. H., & Cleckley, H. M. (1984). On the incidence of multiple personality disorder. International Journal of Clinical and Experimental Hypnosis, 32, 63–66.

Thoits, P. A. (1983). Dimensions of life events as influences upon the genesis of psychological distress and associated conditions: An evaluation and synthesis of the literature. In H. B. Kaplan (ed.), Psychosocial stress: Trends in theory and research. New York: Academic Press.

Thomas, M. H., Horton, R. W., Lippincott, E. C., & Drabman, R. S. (1977). Desensitization to portrayals of real-life aggression as a function of exposure to television violence. Journal of Personality and Social Psychology, 35, 450–458.

Thompson, W. C., Cowan, C. L., & Rosenhan, D. L. (1980). Focus of attention mediates the impact of negative affect on altruism. Journal of Personality and Social Psychology, 38, 291–300.

Thornton, D., & Reid, R. L. (1982). Moral reasoning and type of criminal offense. British Journal of Social Psychology, 21, 231–238.

Thurstone, L. L. (1938). Primary mental abilities. Psychometric Monographs, 1.

Thurstone, L. L., & Thurstone, T. G. (1963). SRA primary abilities. Chicago: Science Research.

Tice, D. M., & Baumeister, R. F. (1985). Masculinity inhibits helping in emergencies: Personality does predict the bystander effect. Journal of Personality and Social Psychology, 49, 420–428.

Tobias, S. (1982). Sexist equations. *Psychology Today, 16* (1), 14–17.

Tolman, E. C., & Honzik, C. H. (1930). Introduction and removal of reward, and maze performance in rats. *University of California Publications in Psychology, 4,* 257–275.

Toufexis, A. (1981, July 27). Coping with Eve's curse. *Time Magazine,* 59.

Toufexis, A. (1982, March 8). Report from the surgeon general. *Time Magazine,* 72–73.

Toufexis, A. (1985, June 10). A crackdown on Ecstasy. *Time Magazine,* 64.

Toufexis, A., Garcia, C., & Kalb, B. (1986, January 20). Dieting: The losing game. *Time Magazine,* 54–60.

Touhey, J. C. (1972). Comparison of two dimensions of attitude similarity on heterosexual attraction. *Journal of Personality and Social Psychology, 23,* 8–10.

Touhey, J. C. (1974). Effects of additional women professionals on ratings of occupational prestige and desirability. *Journal of Personality and Social Psychology, 29,* 86–89.

Tryon, R. C. (1940). Genetic differences in maze learning in rats. *Yearbook of the National Society for Studies in Education, 39,* 111–119.

Tucker, J. A., Vuchinich, R. E., & Sobell, M. B. (1981). Alcohol consumption as a self-handicapping strategy. *Journal of Abnormal Psychology, 90,* 220–230.

Turkington, C. (1983). Drugs found to block dopamine receptors. *APA Monitor, 14,* 11.

Turkington, C. (1984). Hormones in rats found to control sex behavior. *APA Monitor, 15,* (11), 40–41.

Turkington, C. (1985). Taste inhibitors. *APA Monitor, 16* (10), 3.

Turnbull, C. M. (1961). Notes and discussions: Some observations regarding the experiences and behavior of the Bambute pygmies. *American Journal of Psychology, 7,* 304–308.

Turner, R. H., & Killian, L. M. (1972). *Collective behavior.* Englewood Cliffs, NJ: Prentice-Hall.

Turner, R. J., & Wagonfield, M. O. (1967). Occupational mobility and schizophrenia. *American Sociological Review, 32,* 104–113.

Udry, J. R. (1971). *The social context of marriage.* Philadelphia: Lippincott.

Underwood, B., & Moore, B. S. (1981). Sources of behavioral consistency. *Journal of Personality and Social Psychology, 40,* 780–785.

Unger, R. K., Hilderbrand, M., & Madar, T. (1982). Physical attractiveness and assumptions about social deviance: Some sex-by-sex comparisons. *Personality and Social Psychology Bulletin, 8,* 293–301.

U.S. Congress, Office of Technology Assessment (1983, November). *Scientific validity of polygraph testing: A research review and evaluation* (OTA-TM-H-15). Washington, D.C.: Office of Technology Assessment.

U.S. Riot Commission (1968). *Report of the National Advisory Commission on civil disorders.* New York: Bantam.

Vaillant, G. E. (1982). *The natural history of alcoholism.* Cambridge: Harvard.

Vaillant, G. E., & Milofsky, E. S. (1982). The etiology of alcoholism. *American Psychologist, 37,* 494–503.

Valenstein, E. S. (ed.). (1980). *The psychosurgery debate.* San Francisco: W. H. Freeman.

Valins, S. (1966). Cognitive effects of false heart-rate feedback. *Journal of Personality and Social Psychology, 4,* 400–408.

Van Dyke, C., & Byck, R. (1982). Cocaine. *Scientific American, 44* (3), 128–141.

Velicer, W. F., DiClemente, C. C., Prochaska, J. O., & Brandenburg, N. (1985). Decisional balance measure for assessing and predicting smoking status. *Journal of Personality and Social Psychology, 48,* 1279–1289.

Vestre, N. D. (1984). Irrational beliefs and self-reported depressed mood. *Journal of Abnormal Psychology, 93,* 239–241.

Vinokur, A., Burnstein, E., Sechrest, L., & Wortman, P. M. (1985). Group decision making by experts: Field study of panels evaluating medical technologies. *Journal of Personality and Social Psychology, 49,* 70–84.

Visintainer, M. A., Volpicelli, J. R., & Seligman, M. E. P. (1982). Tumor rejection in rats after inescapable or escapable shock. *Science, 216* (23), 437–439.

Von Békésy, G. (1957, August). The ear. *Scientific American,* 66–78.

Wachtel, P. L. (1982). What can dynamic therapies contribute to behavior therapy? *Behavior Therapy, 13,* 594–609.

Wagner, R. K., & Sternberg, R. J. (1985). Practical intelligence in real-world pursuits: The role of tacit knowledge. *Journal of Personality and Social Psychology, 49,* 436–458.

Waldholz, M. (1985, July 22). Breakthroughs in prenatal testing give hope to high-risk couples. *The Wall Street Journal,* 21.

Wales, E., & Brewer, B. Graffiti in the 1970s. (1976). *Journal of Social Psychology, 99,* 115–123.

Walker, B. B. (1983). Treating stomach disorders: Can we reinstate regulatory processes? In W. E. Whitehead & R. Holzl (eds.), *Psychophysiology of the gastrointestinal tract.* New York: Plenum Press.

Walker, J. M., Floyd, J. C., Fein, G., Cavness, C., Lualhati, R., & Feinberg, I. (1978). Effect of exercise on sleep. *Journal of Applied Physiology, 44,* 945–951.

Walker, W. B., & Franzini, L. R. (1985). Low-risk aversive group treatments, physiological feedback, and booster sessions for smoking cessation. *Behavior Therapy, 16,* 263–274.

Wallace, J. (1985). The alcoholism controversy. *American Psychologist, 40,* 372–373

Wallington, S. A. (1973). Consequences of transgression: Self-punishment and depression. *Journal of Personality and Social Psychology, 29,* 1–7.

Wallis, C. (1985, February 25). Gauging the fat of the land. *Time, 72.*

Walsh, R. N., et al. (1981). The menstrual cycle, sex and academic performance. *Archives of General Psychiatry, 38,* 219–221.

Walster, E., Aronson, E., Abrahams, D., & Rottman, L. (1966). Importance of physical attractiveness in dating behavior. *Journal of Personality and Social Psychology, 4,* 508–516.

Walster, E., & Walster, G. W. (1978). *A new look at love.* Reading, MA: Addison-Wesley.

Walster, E., Walster, G. W., Piliavin, J., & Schmidt, L. (1973). "Playing hard to get": Understanding an illusive phenomenon. *Journal of Personality and Social Psychology, 26,* 113–121.

Walton, S. (1985). Girls and science: The gap remains. *Psychology Today, 19* (6), 14.

Waterman, C. K., & Nevid, J. S. (1977). Sex differences in the resolution of the identity crisis. *Journal of Youth and Adolescence, 6,* 337–342.

Watkins, M. J., Ho, E., & Tulving, E. (1976). Context effects on recognition memory for faces. *Journal of Verbal Learning and Verbal Behavior, 15,* 505–518.

Watson, J. B. (1913). Psychology as the behaviorist views it. *Psychological Review, 20,* 158–177.

Watson, J. B. (1924). *Behaviorism.* New York: Norton.

Watson, J. B., & Rayner, R. (1920). Conditioned emotional reactions. *Journal of Experimental Psychology, 3,* 1–14.

Watson, S. J., Berger, P. A., Akil, H., Mills, M. J., & Barchas, J. D. (1978). Effects of naloxone on schizophrenia: Reduction in hallucinations in a subpopulation of subjects. *Science, 201,* 73–76.

Watt, N. F., Grubb, T. W., & Erlenmeyer-Kimling, L. (1982). Social, emotional, and intellectual behavior among children at high risk for schizophrenia. *Journal of Consulting and Clinical Psychology, 50,* 171–181.

Weber, R., & Crocker, J. (1983). Cognitive processes in the revision of stereotypic beliefs. *Journal of Personality and Social Psychology, 45,* 961–977.

Wechsler, D. (1939). *The measurement of adult intelligence.* Baltimore: Williams & Wilkins.

Wechsler, D. (1975). Intelligence defined and undefined: A relativistic appraisal. *American Psychologist, 30,* 135–139.

Wegner, D. M. (1979). Hidden Brain Damage Scale. *American Psychologist, 34,* 192–193.

Weil, G., & Goldfried, M. R. (1973). Treatment of insomnia in an eleven-year-old child through self-relaxation. *Behavior Therapy, 4,* 282–294.

Weinberg, R. S., Yukelson, S., & Jackson, A. (1980). Effect of public and private efficacy expectations on competitive performance. *Journal of Sport Psychology, 2,* 340–349.

Weiner, H., Thaler, M., Rieser, M. F., & Mirsky, I. A. (1957). Relation of specific psychological characteristics to rate of gastric secretion. *Psychosomatic Medicine, 17,* 1–10.

Weiner, M. J., & Wright, F. E. (1973). Effects of undergoing arbitrary discrimination upon subsequent attitudes toward a minority group. *Journal of Applied Social Psychology, 3,* 94–102.

Weiss, J. M. (1982, August). A model for the neurochemical study of depression. Paper presented to the American Psychological Association, Washington, D.C.

Weiss, J. M., Glazer, H. I., & Pohorecky, L. A. (1976). Coping behavior and neurochemical changes: An alternative explanation for the original "learned helplessness" experiments. In G. Serban & A. Kling (eds.), *Animal models of human psychobiology.* New York: Plenum Press.

Weissman, M., Klerman, C., Prusoff, B., Sholomkas, D., & Padian, N. (1981). Depressed outpatients. Results one year after treatment with drugs and/or interpersonal psychotherapy. *Archives of General Psychiatry, 18,* 51–55.

Wender, P. H., Rosenthal, R., Kety, S., Schulsinger, S., & Weiner, J. (1974). Cross-fostering: A research strategy for clarifying the role of genetic and experiential factors in the etiology of schizophrenia. *Archives of General Psychiatry, 30,* 121–128.

Werner, C. M., Brown, B. B., & Damron, G. (1981). Territorial marking in a game arcade. *Journal of Personality and Social Psychology, 41,* 1094–1104.

West, M. A. (1985). Meditation and somatic arousal reduction. *American Psychologist, 40,* 717–719.

Wexler, D. A., & Butler, J. M. (1976). Therapist modification of client expressiveness in client-centered therapy. *Journal of Consulting and Clinical Psychology, 44,* 261–265.

Wheeler, L., Deci, L., Reis, H., & Zuckerman, M. (1978). *Interpersonal influence.* Boston: Allyn & Bacon.

Whitcher, S. J., & Fisher, J. D. (1979). Multidimensional reaction to therapeutic touch in a hospital setting. *Journal of Personality and Social Psychology, 37,* 87–96.

White, G. L. (1980). Inducing jealousy: A power perspective. *Personality and Social Psychology Bulletin, 6,* 222–227.

White, G. L., Fishbein, S., & Rutstein, J. (1981). Passionate love and the misattribution of arousal. *Journal of Personality and Social Psychology, 41,* 56–62.

White, L., & Tursky, B. (eds.). (1982). *Clinical biofeedback: Efficacy and mechanisms.* New York: Guilford.

White, M. (1975). Interpersonal distance as affected by room size, status, and sex. *Journal of Social Psychology, 95,* 241–249.

Whitehall, M. H., Gainer, H., Cox, B. M., & Molineaux, C. J. (1983). Dynorphin-A-(1-8) is contained within vasopressin neurosecretory vesicles in rat pituitary. *Science, 222,* 1137–1139.

Whitehead, W. E., & Bosmajian, L. S. (1982). Behavioral medicine approaches to gastrointestinal disorders. *Journal of Consulting and Clinical Psychology, 50,* 972–983.

Whitley, B. E., Jr. (1983). Sex role orientation and self-esteem: A critical meta-analysis. *Journal of Personality and Social Psychology, 44,* 765–778.

Whorf, B. (1956). *Language, thought, and reality.* New York: Wiley.

Whybrow, P. C., & Prange, A. J. (1981). A hypothesis of thyroid-catecholamine-receptor interaction. *Archives of General Psychiatry, 38,* 106–113.

Whyte, W. W. (1956). *The organization man.* New York: Simon & Schuster.

Wieder, G. B. (1985). Coping ability of rape victims: Comment on Myers, Templer, & Brown. *Journal of Consulting and Clinical Psychology, 53,* 429–431.

Wiens, A. N., & Menustik, C. E. (1983). Treatment outcome and patient characteristics in an aversion therapy program for alcoholism. *American Psychologist, 38,* 1089–1096.

Wiggins, J. S., Wiggins, N., & Conger, J. C. (1968). Correlates of heterosexual somatic preference. *Journal of Personality and Social Psychology, 10,* 82–90.

Wilder, D. A. (1977). Perception of groups, size of opposition, and social influence. *Journal of Experimental Social Psychology, 13,* 253–268.

Wilder, D. A., & Thompson, J. E. (1980). Intergroup contact with independent manipulations of in-group and out-group interaction. *Journal of Personality and Social Psychology, 38,* 589–603.

Willerman, L. (1977). *The psychology of individual and group differences.* San Francisco: Freeman.

Williams, K., Harkins, S., & Latané, B. (1981). Identifiability as a deterrent to social loafing. *Journal of Personality and Social Psychology, 40,* 303–311.

Williams, R. L. (1974). Scientific racism and IQ: The silent mugging of the black community. *Psychology Today, 8* (5).

Wilson, G. T. (1982). Psychotherapy process and procedure: The behav-ioral mandate. *Behavior Therapy, 13,* 291–312.

Wilson, G. T., & Lawson, D. M. (1978). Expectancies, alcohol, and sexual arousal in women. *Journal of Abnormal Psychology, 87,* 358–367.

Wilson, G. T., Lawson, D. M., & Abrams, D. B. (1978). Effects of alcohol on sexual arousal in male alcoholics. *Journal of Abnormal Psychology, 87,* 609–616.

Wilson, G. T., Leaf, R. C., & Nathan, P. E. (1975). The aversive control of excessive alcohol consumption by chronic alcoholics in the laboratory setting. *Journal of Applied Behavior Analysis, 8,* 13–26.

Wilson, T. D., & Linville, P. W. (1982). Improving the performance of college freshmen: Attribution therapy revisited. *Journal of Personality and Social Psychology, 42,* 367–376.

Wilson, R. S. (1983). The Louisville twin study: Developmental synchronies in behavior. *Child Development, 54,* 298–316.

Wing, R. R., Epstein, L. H., & Shapira, B. (1982). The effect of increasing initial weight loss with the Scarsdale diet on subsequent weight loss in a behavioral treatment program. *Journal of Consulting and Clinical Psychology, 50,* 446–447.

Winterbottom, M. (1958). The relation of need for achievement to learning experiences in independence and mastery. In J. Atkinson (ed.), *Motives in fantasy, action, and society.* Princeton, NJ: Van Nostrand.

Witkin, H. A., Mednick, S. A., Schulsinger, F., Bakkestrøm, E., Christiansen, K. O., Goodenough, D. R., Hirschhorn, K., Lundsteen, C., Owen, D. R., Philip, J., Rubin, D. B., & Stocking, M. (1976). Criminality in XYY and XXY men. *Science, 193,* 547–555.

Wittig, M. A. (1985). Metatheoretical dilemmas in the psychology of gender. *American Psychologist, 40,* 800–811.

Wohlford, P., Santrock, J. W., Berger, S., & Liberman, D. (1971). Older brothers' influence on sex-typed, ag-gressive, and dependent behavior in father-absent children. *Developmental Psychology, 4,* 124–134.

Wolfe, L. (1981). *The Cosmo report.* New York: Arbor House.

Wolinsky, J. (1982). Responsibility can delay aging. *APA Monitor, 13* (3), 14, 41.

Wolpe, J. (1958). *Psychotherapy by reciprocal inhibition.* Stanford, CA: Stanford.

Wolpe, J. (1973). *The practice of behavior therapy.* New York: Pergamon Press.

Wolpe, J. (1985). Existential problems and behavior therapy. *The Behavior Therapist, 8* (7), 126–127.

Wolpe, J., & Lazarus, A. A. (1966). *Behavior therapy techniques.* New York: Pergamon Press.

Wolpe, J., & Rachman, S. (1960). Psychoanalytic "evidence": A critique based on Freud's case of Little Hans. *Journal of Nervous and Mental Disease, 131,* 135–147.

Wood, W. (1982). Retrieval of attitude-relevant information from memory: Effects on susceptibility to persuasion and on intrinsic motivation. *Journal of Personality and Social Psychology, 42,* 798–810.

Wood, W., & Eagly, A. H. (1981). Steps in the positive analysis of causal attributions and message comprehension. *Journal of Personality and Social Psychology, 4,* 246–259.

Wright, J. C., & Huston, A. C. (1983). A matter of form: Potentials of television for young viewers. *American Psychologist, 38,* 835–843.

Yarnold, P. R., & Grimm, L. G. (1982). Time urgency among coronary-prone individuals. *Journal of Abnormal Psychology, 91,* 175–177.

Yarnold, P. R., Mueser, K. T., & Grimm, L. G. (1985). Interpersonal dominance of Type A's in group discussion. *Journal of Abnormal Psychology, 94,* 233–236.

Yonas, A., Granrud, C. E., & Pettersen, L. (1985). Infants' sensitivity to relative size information for distance.

Developmental Psychology, 21, 161–167.

Youkilis, H. D., & Bootzin, R. R. (1981). A psychophysiological perspective on the etiology and treatment of insomnia. In S. N. Haynes & L. R. Gannon (eds.), *Psychosomatic disorders.* New York: Praeger.

Zaiden, J. (1982). Psychodynamic therapy: Clinical applications. In A. J. Rush (ed.), *Short-term psychotherapies for depression.* New York: Guilford Press.

Zajonc, R. B. (1968). Attitudinal effects of mere exposure. *Journal of Personality and Social Psychology, 9* (Monograph Supplement 2), 1–27.

Zajonc, R. B. (1980). Compresence. In P. Paulus (ed.), *The psychology of group influence.* Hillsdale, NJ: Erlbaum.

Zajonc, R. B. (1984). On the primacy of affect. *American Psychologist, 39,* 117–123.

Zajonc, R. B. (1985). Cited in Bower, B. (1985, July 6). The face of emotion. *Science News, 128,* 12–13.

Zamansky, H. S., & Bartis, S. P. (1985). The dissociation of an experience. *Journal of Abnormal Psychology, 94,* 243–248.

Zatz, S., & Chassin, L. (1985). Cognitions of test-anxious children under naturalistic test-taking conditions. *Journal of Consulting and Clinical Psychology, 53,* 393–401.

Zeiss, A., Rosen, G., & Zeiss, R. (1977). Orgasm during intercourse: A treatment strategy for women. *Journal of Consulting and Clinical Psychology, 45,* 891–895.

Zigler, E., Abelson, W. D., Trickett, P. K., & Seitz, V. (1982). Is an intervention program necessary to improve economically disadvantaged children's IQ scores? *Child Development, 53,* 340–348.

Zigler, E., & Berman, W. (1983). Discerning the future of early childhood intervention. *American Psychologist, 38,* 894–906.

Zigler, E., & Butterfield, E. C. (1968). Motivational aspects of change in IQ test performance of culturally deprived nursery school children. *Child Development, 39,* 1–14.

Zilbergeld, B., & Evans, M. (1980). The inadequacy of Masters and Johnson. *Psychology Today, 14* (8), 29–34, 47–53.

Zillmann, D., & Bryant, J. (1983). Effects of massive exposure to pornography. In N. M. Malamuth & E. Donnerstein (eds.), *Pornography and sexual aggression.* New York: Academic Press.

Zimbardo, P. G. (1969). The human choice: Individuation, reason, and order versus deindividuation, impulse, and chaos. In W. J. Arnold & D Levine (eds.), *Nebraska symposium on motivation,* Vol. 17. Lincoln, NE: University of Nebraska Press.

Zubek, J. P. (1973). Review of effects of prolonged deprivation. In J. E. Rasmussen (ed.), *Man in isolation and confinement.* Chicago: Aldine.

Zuckerman, M. (1974). The sensation-seeking motive. In B. Maher (ed.), *Progress in experimental personality research,* Vol. 7. New York: Academic Press.

Zuckerman, M. (1980). Sensation seeking. In H. London & J. Exner (eds.), *Dimensions of personality.* New York: Wiley.

Zuckerman, M., Eysenck, S., & Eysenck, H. J. (1978). Sensation seeking in England and America: Cross-cultural, age, and sex comparisons. *Journal of Consulting and Clinical Psychology, 46,* 139–149.

Zuckerman, M., Klorman, R., Larrance, D. T., & Spiegel, N. H. (1981). Facial, autonomic, and subjective components of emotion. *Journal of Personality and Social Psychology, 41,* 929–944.

Zuger, B. (1976). Monozygotic twins discordant for homosexuality: Report of a pair and significance of the phenomenon. *Comprehensive Psychiatry, 17,* 661–669.

page 19 (left), Yale Joel/Life Picture Service; (right), Animal Behavioral Enterprises; (bottom), The National Library of Medicine; *page* 21, The Three Lions; *page* 24, Jim Amos/Photo Researchers, Inc.; *page* 28, courtesy of Dr. Albert Bandura; *page* 30, Gary Sigman; *page* 38, © Charles Addams/The New Yorker Magazine, Inc.; *page* 46, Jeff Albertson/Stock, Boston.

CHAPTER 2: *page* 53 (left, top, and bottom), from Leeson and Leeson, *Descriptions and Explanations: Practical Histology, A Self-Instructional Laboratory Manual in Filmstrip*, Philadelphia: W. B. Saunders Company, 1973; (right), from Curtis, Jacobson, and Marcus, *An Introduction to the Neurosciences* (filmstrip), Philadelphia: W. B. Saunders Company, 1972; *page* 56, Bettmann Newsphotos; *page* 81, courtesy of Dr. José M. R. Delgado; *page* 81 (bottom), drawing by Opie, © 1951 by The New Yorker Magazine, Inc.; *page* 86, Charlie Newman/Sygma; *page* 100, courtesy of the March of Dimes.

CHAPTER 3: *page* 114, Scanning electron microphotograph of Necturus rods and cones by Frank Werblin and Edwin Lewis, University of California, Berkeley; *page* 118, Erika Stone; *page* 119 (bottom), Inmont Corporation; *page* 124, American Optical Corporation from their AO Pseudo Isochromatic Color Tests; *page* 130 (bottom), Gahan Wilson/The New Yorker Magazine, Inc.; *page* 132 (bottom), drawing by © Tobey/The New Yorker Magazine, Inc. *page* 134, M. C. Escher, *Relativity*. © Beelbdrecht, Amsterdam/VAGA, New York, 1982. Collection Haags Gemeentemuseum The Hague. *page* 135, Teri Leigh Stratford; *page* 149, Susan McElhinnery/Archive Pictures; *page* 153, Larry Gordon/The Image Bank; *page* 154, courtesy of Dr. Bernard Brucker.

CHAPTER 4: *page* 168, courtesy of Spencer A. Rathus; *page* 175, Chris Springman; *page* 177 (left), Randy Miller/The Image Bank; (right), Timothy Eagan/Woodfin Camp & Associates; *page* 184, Jane Schreibman/Photo Researchers, Inc.; *page* 196, Mike Button/EKM-Nepenthe; *page* 200, David Parker/Photo Researchers, Inc.

CHAPTER 5: *page* 214, Thaves © 1974, NEA, Inc.; *page* 220, courtesy of Teachers College, Columbia University; *page* 222, Pfizer, Inc.; *page* 223, "B.C." by permission of Johnny Hart and Field Enterprises, Inc.; *page* 224, © King Feature Syndicate, Inc. 1974; *page* 225 © Opie/The New Yorker Magazine, Inc.; *page* 233, courtesy of IBM; *page* 241, Allen Green/Photo Researchers, Inc.; *page* 247, Russ Kinne/Photo Researchers, Inc.; *page* 252, © Dana Fradon/The New Yorker Magazine, Inc.; *page* 253, J. A. L. Cook/Animals, Animals.

CHAPTER 6: *page* 266, "B.C." by permission of Johnny Hart and Field Enterprises; *page* 269, © B. Ullmann/Taurus Photos; *page* 271, "The Family Circus" by Bill Keane, courtesy of the Register and Tribune Syndicate, Inc.; *page* 280, © King Feature Syndicate, Inc.; *page* 300, Nancy Hays/Monkmeyer Press Photo; *page* 302, © Archie Comic Publications, Inc.; *page* 306, "B.C." by permission of Johnny Hart and Field Enterprises, Inc.; *page* 308, Ellis Herwig/Stock, Boston.

CHAPTER 7: *page* 317, G. H. Thompson/Animals, Animals; *page* 322, Dr. Neal E. Miller, Yale University; *page* 332 (left), Harry F. Harlow, University of Wisconsin Primate Laboratory; *page* 332 (right), Yerkes Regional Primate Research Center; *page* 334, Peter Paz/The Image Bank; *page* 341, Truth Verification; *pages* 343 and 344, courtesy of Dr. Robert Plutchik; *page* 345, courtesy of Dr. Paul Ekman; *page* 351, Diego Goldberg/Sygma; *page* 352, © 1971, United Features Syndicate, Inc.

CHAPTER 8: *page* 361 © Hazel Hankin; *page* 364, Science Source/Photo Researchers, Inc.; *page* 369, Enrico Ferorelli; *page* 373 (left and right) and *page* 374, Harry F. Harlow, University of Wisconsin, Primate Laboratory; *page* 375 (left and right), Nina Leen/Life Picture Service; *page* 376, Jerry Howard/Positive Images; *page* 378, courtesy of Creative Playthings; *page* 384, George Zimbel/Monkmeyer Press Photo; *page* 386, Mimi Forsyth/Monkmeyer Press Photo; *page* 389, Museum of Modern Art/Film Stills Archive: *page* 394, George Zimbel/Monkmeyer Press Photo; *page* 397 (left), Stock/Boston; (right), Roger Tully; *page* 399, Samantha M. Eisenstein; *page* 400, © Ed Arno/The New Yorker Magazine, Inc.

CHAPTER 9: *page* 416, Museum of Modern Art/Film Stills Archive; *page* 421, Roger Tully; *page* 423, The National Library of Medicine; *page* 424, The Bettmann Archive; *page* 425 (top), Association for the Advancement of Psychoanalysis of the Karen Horney Psychoanalytic Institute and Center; (bottom), Harvard University News Office; *page* 426, Archives of the History of American Psychology, University of Akron; *page* 431, Museum of Modern Art/Film Stills Archive; *page* 432, courtesy of Dr. Walter Mischel; *page* 433, courtesy of Dr. Julian Rotter; *page* 436, courtesy of NBC; *page* 438, courtesy of Dr. Albert Bandura.

CHAPTER 10: *page* 461 (left), © Junebug Clark, 1982/Photo Researchers, Inc.; (right), © M. E. Warren/Photo Researchers, Inc.; *page* 467, © Freda Leinwand/Monkmeyer Press Photo; *page* 477, Karen Coolidge/Photo Researchers, Inc; *page* 480, Jim Wilson; *page* 486, Jeff Jacobson/Archive Pictures; *page* 493 (left), Dick Durrance II/Woodfin Camp & Associates; (right), Will McIntyre/Photo Researchers, Inc.

CHAPTER 11: *page* 501 Wide World Photos; *page* 503, The University of Pennsylvania Museum; *page* 509, Ed Lettau/Photo Researchers, Inc.; *page* 515, Museum of Modern Art/Film Stills Archive; *page* 524, B. Kliewe/Jeroboam; *pages* 527 and 534, Bettmann Newsphotos.

CHAPTER 12: *pages* 544 and 545, The Bettmann Archive; *page* 548, courtesy of Edmund Engelman; *page* 550, from *Non-Being and Somethingness* by Woody Allen, drawn by Stuart Hample, © 1978 by IWA Enterprises, Inc., and Hackenbush Productions, Inc., and reprinted by permission of Random House, Inc.; *page* 554, Frank Keillor/Jeroboam; *page* 558, courtesy of Dr. Albert Ellis; *page* 561, © Van Bucher, 1978, Photo Researchers, Inc.; *page* 562, courtesy of Dr. Albert Bandura; *page* 564, Lester Sloan/Woodfin Camp & Associates; *page* 565, drawing by Handelsman, © 1978 by The New

Yorker Magazine, Inc.; *page* 570, Bill Strode/Woodfin Camp & Associates; *page* 573, Paul Fusco/Magnum; *page* 575, drawing by Handelsman, © The New Yorker Magazine; *page* 578, Will McIntyre/Photo Researchers.

CHAPTER 13: *page* 584, Cecile Brunswick; *page* 587, "B.C." by permission of Johnny Hart and Field Enterprises, Inc.; *page* 588, Richard Wood/The Picture Cube; *page* 589, Cary Wolinsky/Stock, Boston; *page* 594, Michael Kagan/ Monkmeyer Photo Press; *page* 601 (left), Betsy Lee Taurus; (right), David Strickler/Monkmeyer Photo Press; *page* 607, Ed Lettau/Photo Researchers, Inc.; *page* 608, Newsweek; *page* 611, Ron Cooper/EKM-Nepenthe; *page* 618, Carol Simowitz/ The Image Bank; *page* 623, W. S. Silver/The Picture Cube.

CHAPTER 14: *page* 634, Robert V. Eckert, Jr./EKM-Nepenthe; *page* 639, Wide World Photos; *page* 641, © John Coletti/Stock, Boston; *page* 649, Wide World Photos; *page* 653, Larry Dale Gordon/The Image Bank; *pages* 656 (top) and 659, the Estate of Stanley Milgram; *page* 661, courtesy of William Vandivert; *page* 664, Steve Niedorf/The Image Bank; *page* 665, © Maslin, 1985/The New Yorker Magazine, Inc.; *page* 670, José Fernandez/Woodfin Camp & Associates; *page* 671, Sam Falk/Monkmeyer Press Photo; *page* 676, Eric Knowles.

Copyright Acknowledgments

TABLE 1.2 (p. 11) Copyright 1985 by Newsweek, Inc. All rights reserved. Reprinted by permission.

QUESTIONNAIRE (p. 40) From Crowne, D. P., and Marlowe, D. A new scale of social desirability independent of pathology. *Journal of Consulting Psychology, 24*:351, Table 1. Copyright 1960 by The American Psychological Association. Reprinted by permission of the publisher and authors.

NEWS ITEM (p. 86) Copyright © 1981 by The New York Times Company. Reprinted by permission.

NEWS ITEM (p. 86) Adapted from *Newsweek*. Copyright 1981 by Newsweek, Inc. All rights reserved. Reprinted by permission.

TABLE 3.1 (p.110) Adapted from E. Galanter, Contemporary psychophysics. In R. Brown et al. (eds.), *New Directions in Psychology*. Copyright 1962 by Holt, Rinehart and Winston. Reprinted by permission.

BOX (p. 146) Copyright 1984 Time Inc. All rights reserved. Reprinted by permission from *Time*.

(Pp. 210–211) Abridged from pages 21–24 in *Brave New World* by Aldous Huxley. Copyright 1932, 1960 by Aldous Huxley. Reprinted by permission of Harper & Row, Publishers, Inc.

NEWS ITEM. (p. 238) Copyright 1980 Time Inc. All rights reserved. Reprinted by permission from *Time*.

NEWS ITEM (p. 264) Copyright 1985 by Newsweek, Inc. All rights reserved. Reprinted by permission.

(P. 266) Lines from "since feeling is first" from IS 5 poems by e. e. cummings reprinted by permission of Liveright Publishing Corporation. Copyright ©1985 by e. e. cummings Trust. Copyright 1926 by Horace Liveright. Copyright ©1954 by e. e. cummings. Copyright ©1985 by George James Firmage.

NEWS ITEM (p. 268) Copyright 1979 Time Inc. All rights reserved. Reprinted by permission from *Time*.

TABLE 6.1 (p. 271) Adapted from E. H. Lenneberg, *Biological Foundations of Language*, p. 128. Copyright 1967 by John Wiley & Sons. Reprinted by permission.

TABLE 6.2 (p. 283) Adaptation reprinted by permission. From Luchins, Abraham S., and Luchins, Edith H., *Rigidity of Behavior,* University of Oregon Books, 1959, p. 109. Also in *Wertheimer's Seminars Revisited: Problem Solving and Thinking* (Albany, N. Y.: SUNY/Albany Faculty-Student Association, 1970), vol. iii, p. 4.

BOX (p. 290) The Remote Associates Test, p. 252, from *Cognition* by Margaret Matlin. Copyright © 1983 by CBS College Publishing. Adapted by permission of CBS College Publishing.

TABLE 6.4 (p. 293) Data adapted from Robert J. Sternberg et al., People's conception of intelligence, *Journal of Personality and Social Psychology, 41* (1980):45–46, and from R. J. Wagner, Practical intelligence in real-world pursuits: The role of tacit knowledge, *Journal of Personality and Social Psychology, 49* (1985):436–458. Copyright 1980, 1985 by the American Psychological Association. Adapted by permission of the publisher and authors.

TABLE 6.6 (p. 296) Some items from the first Binet-Simon scale, adapted from L. Willerman, *The Psychology of Individual and Group Differences.* Copyright 1977, W. H. Freeman and Company, San Francisco. Adaptation reprinted by permission.

BOX (p. 301) Reprinted with permission from *Psychology Today* magazine. Copyright © 1982 American Psychological Association.

TABLE 7.2 (p. 350) From Schachter, S., and Singer, J. E. Cognitive, social and psychological determinants of emotional state, *Psychological Review, 69* (1962): 379–399. Copyright 1962 by the American Psychological Association. Reprinted by permission of the publisher.

FIGURE 8.4 (p. 374) Adapted from *Lifespan Development,* 2nd ed., by Jeffrey S. Turner and Donald B. Helms. Copyright © 1983 by CBS College Publishing. Copyright © 1979 by W. B. Saunders Company. Also adapted from *Piaget with Feeling: Cognitive, Social, and Emotional Dimensions* by Philip A. Cowan. Copyright ©1978 by Holt, Rinehart and Winston. Adaptations by permission of CBS College Publishing.

BOX (p. 389) Reprinted with permission from *Psychology Today* magazine. Copyright ©1985 American Psychological Association.

TABLE 8.5 (p. 391) From James R. Rest, The hierarchical nature of moral judgment: A study of patterns of comprehension and preference of moral stages, *Journal of Personality, 41* (March 1973): 92–93. Copyright ©1973 Duke University Press.

TABLE 8.6 (p. 395) Reprinted with permission from *Psychology Today* magazine. Copyright ©1985 American Psychological Association.

QUESTIONNAIRE (p. 614) From Martha R. Burt, Cultural myths and supports for rape, *Journal of Personality and Social Psychology, 38:* 217–230. Copyright 1980 by the American Psychological Association. Reprinted by permission of the publisher and author.

Page 652 from "Getting to Know You," from *The King and I.* Copyright ©1951 by Richard Rodgers and Oscar Hammerstein II. Copyright renewed; Williamson Music Co., owner of publication and allied rights throughout the Western Hemisphere and Japan. International copyright secured. All rights reserved. Used by permission.

NEWS ITEM (p. 664) Reprinted by permission of *The Wall Street Journal,* © Dow Jones & Company, Inc. 1981. All rights reserved.

INDEXES

NAME INDEX

Abbey, A., 645
Abramowitz, S. I., 554
Abrams, D. B., 180, 183
Abramson, P., 83
Abramson, P. R., 621
Abravenel, E., 237
Adams, N. E., 435
Adams, V., 623
Adelman, M. R., 611
Adelson, J., 16
Adler, A., 422, 424, 555
Adler, J. 187
Adolph, E. F., 328
Adorno, T. W., 642
Agranoff, B., 254
Agras, W. S., 491
Aiken, P. A., 325, 591
Ajzen, I., 482
Akil, H., 153
Albert, M. S., 403
Alexander, A. B., 475
Allen, A., 428
Allen, V. L., 662
Allen, W., 402
Allgeier, A. A., 613
Allgeier, E. R., 613
Allport, G. W., 426–427, 428
Altman, I., 647
Amabile, T. M., 288
Amenson, C. W., 518
Amir, M., 613
Andersen, B. L., 624
Anderson, D. J., 511
Andersson, B., 328
Andres, D., 594, 595
Andrews, G., 559

Aneshensel, C. S., 180
Antill, J. K., 592
Anuszkiewicz, R., 119
Apfelbaum, M., 326
Archer, R. L., 668
Archimedes, 285
Aristotle, 15, 16, 73
Arkin, R. M., 488
Aron, A. P., 350
Asch, S. E., 660–661
Athanasiou, R., 181
Atkinson, J., 587
Atkinson, K., 270
Atkinson, R. C., 250
Avis, N., 183
Avis, W. E., 649
Ayllon, T., 563

Bach, G. R., 630
Bachman, J., 178
Bagozzi, R. P., 632
Bahrick, H. P., 246
Baker, L. A., 306
Baker, S. W., 599
Bandura, A., 28, 237, 397, 432, 435,
    437, 482, 488, 506–507, 510,
    562, 603
Banks, M., 369
Banyai, E. I., 201
Barbach, L. G., 624
Barber, T. X., 194, 201, 202, 203
Bard, P., 348–349
Bardwick, J. M., 88, 397
Barefoot, J. C., 470
Barkley, R. A., 180
Barlow, D. H., 511

Barnes, M. L., 597
Barnett, R. C., 593
Barnum, P. T., 453
Baron, R. A., 146, 635, 636, 637,
    672, 673
Barraclough, B. M., 522
Bar-Tal, D., 652
Bartis, S. P., 202
Bartoskuk, L. M., 149, 150
Baruch, G. K., 593
Batson, C. D., 668
Baucom, D. H., 325, 591, 592, 599, 600
Bauer, R. H., 76
Bauer, W. D., 379
Baum, A., 674
Baum-Baicker, C., 180
Baumeister, R. F., 668
Baumrind, D., 44, 45
Bayton, J. A., 642
Bazar, J., 90
Beach, F. A., 597, 649
Beard, R. R., 671
Beatty, W. W., 599
Beauchamp, G., 147
Beck, A. T., 506, 558
Beck, J., 508
Beck, R. C., 339
Becker, J. D., 607
Beit-Hallahmi, B., 378
Bell, A. G., 141
Bell, A. P., 611, 612
Bell, P. A., 670
Belsky, J., 377, 379, 602
Bem, D. J., 428, 587, 592, 640
Bem, S. L., 587, 592, 598, 599, 662,
    668

SUBJECT INDEX

Terms in the running glossary are indicated by page numbers in boldface type.

Despair, **406**
Determinants, **23, 303**
Detoxification, 183
Development,
  cognitive, 25, 272–273, 380–392
  intellectual, 362
  language, 268–271
  moral, 386, 388, 390–392
  perceptual, 368–371
  prenatal, 363–366
  psychosexual, **362**, 417, **418**–422, 423
  psychosocial, 362, **424**, 425
  social and day care, 377–378
  stages of, 362
  theories of 361–362
  visual, 369–370
Developmental psychologists, 9
Developmental psychology, 358–409
Deviation, standard, 685, **686**, 687
Deviation IQ, **297**
Diabetes mellitis, 84
Diagnostic reliability, **508**
Diagnostic and Statistical Manual of Mental Disorders, 507–508
Diagram, scatter, **689**–691
Dialogue, **556**, 557
Dichromat, **124**
Difference threshold, **109**
Differentiation (sex organs), **598**
Diffusion, of responsibility, **665**
Dignity, human, 6
Direct inner awareness, **163**–165
Discomfort, stress and, 464
Discrepancy, **443**
Discrimination, 218–219, 300, 302,**641**
  stimulus, **218**
Discrimination training, **218**
Discriminative stimulus, **227**
Diseases of adaptation, 473, 490–491
Disinhibition, **437, 610**
Disorders,
  affective, **508**, 517–525
  anxiety, 509–512, 513
  bipolar, 524–525
  conversion, **516**–517
  dissociative, **512**–516
  dysthymic, **518**
  gender-identity, **533**–534
  generalized anxiety, **511**–512
  hysterical, **199**–200
  obsessive-compulsive, 512, 513
  panic, **511**, 576
  personality, **531**–533
  phobic, **509**–511
  psychosexual, 533–536
  schizophrenic, 525–531
  sleep, 172–176

somatoform, **516**–517
Disorganized schizophrenics, **527**
Disorientation, **178**
Displacement (defense mechanism), **419, 479**
  coping and, 479
Displacement (language property), **263**–264
Displacement (memory theory), **243**
Dispositional attribution, **644**
Dissociative disorders, **512**–516
  theories of, 514–516
Dissonant (tones), **141**
Distinctiveness, 646
Distribution, normal, **687**
Disulfuram, 184
Divergent thinking, **288**–289
Dizygotic twins, **94**, 305, 306, 529
DNA (see Deoxyribonucleic acid)
Dominant trait, **94**
Dopamine, **61, 530**
  schizophrenia and, 530, 576
Double approach-avoidance conflict, **469**
Double-blind study, **33**
Down syndrome, **94**, 96
Dream, the (Levinson), **401**
Dream analysis, 550–551
Dream symbols, in psychoanalytic theory, 170, 171, 550–551
Dreams, 167, **170**–172, 550–551, 557
  content of, 170–171, 550–551
Drinking, reasons given for, 182–183, 696
See also Alcohol; Alcoholism
Drive(s), **315**–316
  acquired, **318**
  hunger, 321–322
  maternal, 606–607
  physiological, 315, 319, **320**–328
  primary, **318**, 320
  psychological, 316
  sex, 605
  for superiority, **424**
  thirst, 327–328
Drive-reduction theory, 317–**318**, 319–320
Drugs, altering consciousness through, 176–195
  coping and, 476
  hallucinogenic, **192**–195
  physiological effects and expectations and, 178
  psychedelic, **192**
  sexual dysfunctions and, 620
Ductless glands, 83–89
Ducts (glands with), **83**
Dying, 405–406
Dynorphin, **63**

Dyslexia, **8**
Dyspareunia, functional, **620**
Dysthymic disorder, **518**

Ear, 142–144, 145
Eardrum, **142**
Eclecticism, **507**
Ecstasy (MDMA), 187
Educational psychologists, 8–9
Edwards Personal Preference Schedule, 447
EEG, *see* Electroencephalograph
Effect, law of (Thorndike), **220**–221
Efferent neurons, **56**
Effort justification, **638**
Egalitarian (norms), **641**
Ego, **416**–417, 422, 505, 528, 548, 549
Ego analysts, **479**
Ego-dystonic homosexuality, **533**
Ego identity, **353, 395**
  role diffusion vs., 395–396
Ego integrity, **406**
Ego states, 555
Egocentrism, **383**–384, 388
Eidetic imagery, **243**–244
Ejaculation, premature, 73, **619**, 623
Elaborative rehearsal, **245**–246
Elavil, 576
Elderly, sexual responses of, 618
Electra complex, **419**, 421, 422
Electrical stimulation of the brain, 24, 79–82, 245
Electroconvulsive therapy, **577**–578, 579
Electroencephalograph, **165**
Electromyograph, 198–**199**
Elicit (response), **211**
Embryonic period, **363**
Emotion(s), 340, **341**–351
  Cannon-Bard theory of, 248–249
  classification of, 342–344
  cognitive appraisal theory of, 349–350
  expression of, 344–346
  facial feedback hypothesis of, 344–345
  James-Lange theory of, 346–347, 350, 351
  primary, **342**–343
  secondary, **343**
Emotional appeal, **635**
Empathetic understanding, **553**
Empirical, **29, 225, 296**
Empty nest syndrome, **401**–402
Encoding **239**, 241–242
Encounter groups, 27, 542, **573**, 574
Endocrine system, 52, 82, **83**–89
Endorphins, **62**–63, 152, 153, 348

Engram, **253**
Enkaphalins, **63**
Environment, intelligence and, 306, 307–309
Environmental engineering, using, to lower stress, 492
Environmental psychologists, 9–10
Environmental psychology, **631**–637, 669–677
Epidural (anesthetic), **366**
Epilepsy, **70**, 79
Epinephrine (see Adrenalin)
Episiotomy, **620**
Erogenous zones, **418**
Eros, **352, 417**, 420
Erotica, **607**
ESP, see Extrasensory perception
Esteem needs, 319
Estrogen, 85, **89**, 393, 394
Estrus, **605**
Ethereal (odor), **145**
Ethics, 6, **43**–46
    psychology and, 6, 43–46, 677
Ethologist, **316**
Euphoria, **180, 351**
Evaluation apprehension, **663**
Evolutionary theory, 17
Exaltolide, **147**
Excitatory synapse, **61**
Excitement phase (sexual response cycle), **616**–617
Exercise, for depression, 348
    weight loss and, 325–326
Exhaustion stage, **473**
Exhibitionism, 512, **535**
Exorcism, 543
Exorcist, **504**
Expectancies, **432**–434
Experiment, **31**
Experimental method, 31–35
Experimental psychologists, 11
Experimental subjects, **32**
Explicit (sexual materials), **607**
Exploration, 331
External eaters, **324**–325
Extinction, **215**–216, 224–225
Extrasensory perception, **155**–156
Extraversion, **91, 427**
Eye, 111–116
Eye contact, 647–648

Face, infant's response to, 369
Facial expressions, emotions and, 343–345
Facial-feedback hypothesis, 344–345
Fallopian tube, **360**
Family, adolescents and, 394–395
    Intelligence and, 304, 305
Family therapy, **573**

Fantasy,
    coping and, 476
    for pain, 153
    sleep and, 174
Farsightedness, **116**
Fat cells, **323**–324
Father, sex differences and, 602
Fear, 341, 342
    coping with, 511
    sleep and, 173–175
    of strangers, 369, 375
    See also Phobias
Feedback (in assertiveness training), **567**
Fetal stage, **363**
Fetishism, **534**, 535–536
Fetus, 363, 364–366
    sex of the, 96
Fight-or-flight reaction, **472**, 473
Figure-ground perception, 126–127
First impressions, importance of, 643
Fissures, **70**
Fixation time, **369**
Fixations, **418**
Fixed-action pattern (FAP), **316**–317, 319
Fixed-interval schedule, **228**
Fixed-ratio schedule, **228**
Flashbacks, **194**–195
Flat (emotional response), **526**
Flextime, **12**
Food, taste and, 148–149, 150
Forced-choice format, **446**–447
Forcible rape, 613–615
Forensic psychologist, 14
Forgetting, 249–252
    reasons for, 251–252
Formal operations period (cognitive development), 381, **387**–388
Fovea, **113**, 114
Frame of reference, 441–**442, 553**
Fraternal twins, 94, 305, 306, 529
Free association, **549**
Free-floating anxiety, **465**
Free will, 431
Freedom, 431, 432
Frequency (sound), 140, 145
Frequency distribution, **681**–683
Frequency theory (sound), **145**
Frontal lobe, **74**
Frustration, 436, 437, **467**
    stress and, 467
    tolerance for, **467**
Fugue, psychogenic, **514**
Functional analysis, **568**–569
Functional dyspareunia, **620**
Functional fixedness, **286**–287
Functional vaginismus, **620**
Functionalism, 16–**17**
Fundamental attribution error, **645**

g, **291**
Galvanic skin response, 489
Gambler, pathological, **227**
Gambling, 227
Ganglia, **63**
    basal, **70**
Ganglion cells, **111**
Gate theory of pain, 152
Gazing, **647**
Gender, **598**
Gender identity, **584**–585, 604
Gender-identity disorders, **533**–534
General-adaptation syndrome (GAS), **472**–473, 489
General anesthetics, **365**
Generalization(s), **34**–35, 218, 280
    stimulus, **218**
Generalized anxiety disorder, **511**–512
Genes, **23**, 24, **90**
Genetic abnormalities, 94–96
Genetic code, 363, 364
Genetic counseling, **100**
Genetic engineering, 99
Genetics, 90, **91**–100
    antisocial personality and, 532–533
    mental disorders and, 505, 512
    schizophrenia and, 529–530
    See also Heredity
Genital stage (psychosexual development), **419**–420
Genotype, **91**
Genuineness, **553**–554
German measles, **364**
Gestalt, **441**
Gestalt psychology, **18**, 19–21, 126, 128–129
Gestalt therapy, 27, **556**–557
Gland(s), 82–89
    adrenal, 83, 85, 86–88, 393
    ductless, 83–89
    with ducts, 83
    ovaries, 85, 89, 393
    pancreas, **84**–85
    pituitary, **83**–84, 85, 393
    prostate, **620**
    testes, 85, 89
    thyroid, 85, 86
    uterus, 85
Glaucoma, **192**
Glial cells, **53**
Glucagon, **84**, 85
Gonorrhea, **620**
Grammar, 266, 272, 276
Gray matter (spinal cord), **64**, 66
Grooming, 526
Group behavior, 662–669
Group decision making, 663, 665–666
Group therapy, 572–574
    evaluation of, 574

long-term, **244**–248
permanence of, 238
photographic, 243–244
retrieval of information, and, 245, 246, 250
sensory, **239**–240
short-term, **240**–244
structure of, 238–239
Memory modecules, **253**
Menarche, **394**
Menopause, **606**, 618
Menstrual cycle, hormonal regulation of, 89
Menstrual synchrony, **146**
Menstruation, 88, **89**, 516
Mental age, **295**, 296
Mental hospitals, 530, 545
Mental illnesses (*see* Abnormal behavior)
Mental process, studying, 5
Mental set, **286**
Mescaline, **195**
Metabolism, **86**, 196
Metapelet, **378**, 379
Methadone, **185**
Methaqualone, **185**–186
Methedrine, 186
Method of loci, **252**
Microspectrophotometry, **123**–124
Middle adulthood, 400–402
Midlife crisis, **401**
Migraine headache, 389, 473
Mind, 25, 73, 414–415, 422
Minnesota Multiphasic Personality Inventory (MMPI), 447–450, 454
Minor tranquilizers, 178, 186, **574**–576, 577
Mitosis, **91**–92
Mnemonics, **56, 252**
Mob behavior, 666–667
Mode, **684**–685
Modeling, participant, **562**–563
Models, **226, 274, 437, 567**, 604
Mongolism (*See* Down syndrome)
Monochromat, **124**
Monocular cues, 130, **131**, 133
Monosodium glutamate (MSG), 473, 475
Monozygotic twins, **93**, 304–305, 306, 525, 592
Moral development, 386, 388, 390–392
Moral principle, **417**
Morphemes, **265**–266
Morphine, 23, 62, **184**, 185
Morphology, 265–266
Mortality, **672**
Motherhood, in later years, 398, 399

Motion
cues, 133–134
perception of, 129–130
stroboscopic, **130**
Motherless-mother syndrome, 606–607
Motion parallax, **133**
Motivation, 303, 314–339
anxiety as source of, 464
sexual, 605–615
theoretical perspectives on, 316–320
Motive(s), **315**
social, **334**–339
stimulus, **328**–334
for working, 334–335
Motor cortex, **74**
Mount (mating), **605**
Mouth, hunger and, 321
receptors in, thirst and, 328
Müller-Lyer illusion, 137–138
Multiple orgasms, **617**, 618
Multiple personality, **500**, 514–515
Mundugumor, 502
Musky (odor), **145**
Mutations, **92**
Myelin sheath, **54**
Myotonia, **616**
Mythical (images), **423**

N ach **335**–338
N aff, **338**–339
Naloxone, 153, 185
Napoleonic (trait), **426**
Narcolepsy, **174**–175
Narcotics, **184**–185
Naturalistic observation method, 29, **30**–31
Nature (behavior genetics), **91**
Nature-nurture controversy, 91, 360–361, 362
Nearsightedness, **116**
Necker cube, 127–128
Need(s) **315**, 316
achievement, 335–338
affiliation, 338–339
esteem, 319
hierarchy of (Maslow), 318–319, 320
love and belongingness, 318–319
physiological, 315, 318
power, 339
psychological, 315
safety, 318
self-actualization, 319
Negative correlation, **43**
Negative instances, **280**
Negative reinforcer, **224**, 226
Neoanalysts, 27
Neodissociation theory (hypnosis), **203**–204

Neo-Freudian, **421**, 479
Neonates, **366**
Nerve, **63**
Nervous system, 52, 63–73
autonomic, **64**–73
central, **64**–70
peripheral, **64**, 70–73
somatic, **71**
Neural impulse, **57**–59
Neurons, 52, **53**–63
afferent, **56**
efferent, **56**
Neuropeptides, **62**–63
Neuropsychic structures, 426, 428
Neuroses, **507**–508
Neurotic (behavior), 425, **505**
Neurotic anxiety, **465**
Neuroticism, **91, 427, 512**
Neurotransmitters, **53**, 60–62, 505, 511, 520, 521
Nicotine, 189
Night blindness, conversion, 516, 517
Night terrors, **176**
Nightmares, 171–172, 176
Nodes of Ranvier, **54**
Noise, 142, 670
white, **142**
Nonbalance, **636**
Nonconscious, **164**–165
Non-rapid-eye-movement (NREM) sleep, **166**–167, 170
Nonsense syllables, **248**, 249, 250
Noradrenalin, **88**
See also Norepinephrine
Norepinephrine, **61**–62, 348, 482, 520, 521, 525, 576
Normal curve, **687**–688
Normal distribution, **587**
Normative data, **461**
Nose-painting, 181
Novel stimulation, **331**
Noxious (odors), **145**
Nuclei, **63**
Nurturance, **335**
Nurture (behavior genetics), **91**

Obedience, authority and, 656–659
Obesity, 322–327
Object permanence, **383**
Objective (morality) **386**
Objective (sensations), **16**
Objective tests, **446**–450
Observation, naturalistic, 23, **30**–31
Observational learning, **236**–237, 434
aggression and, 437–439
attitudes and, 633
language development and, 274, 276
phobias and, 510

Radical behaviorist, **28, 430**–431, 435
Rage response, **23**
Random sample, **38**–39
Random trial-and-error behavior, **220, 222**
Range, **680**, 685
Rape, forcible, 613–615
  questionnaire on, 614, 699
Rapid-eye-movement (REM) sleep, **166**, 167, 168, 169–170
  deprivation of, 169–170
  rebound, 170
Rapid flight of ideas, **524**
Rapid smoking, **211**, 564
Rathus Assertiveness Schedule, 566–567, 698–699
Rational-emotive therapy, **558**
Rational restructuring, **488**
Rationalization, **478**
  coping and, 478
Reaction formation, **478**
  coping and, 478
Reaction time, **403**
Readiness, **362**
Reality principle, **417**
Reality testing, **451**, 518
Rebound anxiety, **575**–576
Recall, **249**–250
Recency effect, **643**
Receptor site, **60**
Recessive trait, **94**
Reciprocity, **392, 654**
Recognition, **248**, 249
Reflex(es), 66–67, 213, **368**
  orienting, **214**–215
  pupillary, **369**
  sphincter, **368**
  spinal, **64**
  swimming, 368
Refractory period,
  absolute, **58**–59
  relative, **59**
  in sexual response cycle, 617
Regard, conditional positive, **442**
  unconditional positive, **442**
Regional anesthetics, **360**
Regression, **202, 447**, 528
  age, **201**–202
  hypnosis and, 202
Rehearsal, elaborative, **245**–246
Reinforce, **221**
Reinforcement, **18**, 221–234, 262, 274
  continuous, **227**
  covert, 571
  partial, **227**
  schedules of, 227–228
Reinforcers, 223–224
  conditioned, **223, 373**, 434–435
  conditioned generalized, **435**

negative, **224**, 226
positive, **224**
primary, **224**, 434
rewards and punishments vs, 225–226
secondary, **224**
Relative refractory period, **59**
Relaxation, deep muscle, 560–561
  sleep and, 133
  training, 559
Relaxation, progressive, **490**
  lowering arousal through, 490–491
Relaxation response, **196**
Relearning, **250**–251
Releaser, **316**–317
Reliability, **690**
  alternate-form, **294**
  diagnostic, 508
  split-half, **294**
  test, **294**, 295, **690**
  test-retest, **294, 690**
REM (see Rapid-eye-movement sleep)
Replication, **35**
Repression, 9, **164**, 251, **415**, 417, 422, 425, **478**
  coping and, 478
Research, animal, 45, 46
  applied, **6**, 7
  deception in, 44–45
  human subject, 44
  pure (basic), **6**–7
Resin, **192**
Resistance, **415, 549**
Resistance stage, **473**
Resolution phase (sexual response cycle), **618**
Response, **17**
  conditioned, **214**
  unconditioned, **214**
Response set, **447**
Responsibility, diffusion of, **665**
Resting potential, **58**
Retardation, psychomotor, **518**
Reticular activating system, **68**, 171
Retina, **111**, 113
Retinal disparity, **134**, 135
Retirement, 403–404
Retribution, **504**
Retrieval of information, 245, 246, 250
Retroactive interference, **251**
Retrograde amnesia, 252
Reversibility, **387**
Rewards, **225**, 226
  subjective value of, 434
Ribonucleic acid, (RNA), **254**
Risky shift, **665**
Ritalin, 186
RNA (see Ribonucleic acid)
Rods, 111, **114**, 115

Role diffusion, **395**–396
Role-playing, 202–203, 352–353, 514–515, 542, 557
Role theory, **202**–203, 704
Romantic love, 352–**355**
"Romeo and Juliet effect," 654
Rooting, 368
Rorschach inkblot test, 66, 450–452, 454
Rote, **242**, 243
Rubin vase, 127
Ruminative (sleepers), **173**, 174
"Running movies," 558–559

s, **291**
Sadism, sexual, **418, 535**
Sadistic (trait), **421**
Safety needs, 318
Saline (solution), **348**
Sample, **34, 680**, 694
  random, **38**–39
  stratified, **39**
Satiety, **321**
Saturation (color), **118**
Savings, 251
Scapegoats, **642**
Scatter diagram, **689**–691
Schedules, reinforcement, 227–228
Scheme, **382**
Schizoid personality, **531**
Schizophrenia, **463, 500**, 501, 505, 506, 508, 525–531, 576
  causes of, 61, 528–531, 576
  hallucinations and, 526, 527, 528, 530
  simple, 531
  types of, 527–528
Schizophrenic disorders, 525–531
Schizophrenic (symptoms), **448**
Schizophrenics,
  catatonic, **527**
  disorganized, 527
  paranoid, **528**
Schizotypal personality disorder, **531**
School psychologists, 8
Secondary colors, **118**, 119–120
Secondary emotions, **343**
Secondary reinforcer, **224**
Secondary sexual characteristics, **89, 393**
Secondary traits, **426**
Sedative, **179, 576**
Selective breeding, 96, 98–99
Self, **165, 424**
  creative, **424**
Self-acceptance, 553, 554
Self-actualization, **318**, 319, 320, **441**, 443, 444, 553–554
Self-awareness, 26, 424

Self-belief, 435
Self-blame, depression and, 520
Self-concept, 441–442, 443
Self-consciousness, private, **428**
Self-control techniques, 568–571, 572
Self-direction, 424
Self-efficacy, perceived, **435,**
482–483, 562
Self-esteem, **442**–443, 553, 554, 592
Self-exploration, 553
Self-expression, 553
Self-handicapping strategy, 181, 517
Self-ideal, **443**
Self-identity, conversion of, 638–640
Self-image, depression and, 519
Self-insight, **415,** 552
Self-monitoring, **587**
Self report, **5,** 35
Self-sacrifice, 668
Self-theory, 440–445
evaluation of, 444
Semantic code, **246**
Semanticity, **263**
Semantics, **267**
Semen, **617**
Semicircular canals, **154**
Sensate-focus exercises, **622**–623, 624
Sensation, 104–106, **107**–159
Sensation-seeking, 330
questionnaire on, 330, 697
Sensitization, covert, 571
Sensorimotor period (cognitive development), 381, 382–**383**
Sensory awareness, **163**
Sensory cortex, **74**
Sensory deprivation, **271**
Sensory memory, **239**–240
Sensory register, **239**
Sensory stimulation, 329–331
Serial position effect, **242**
Serotonin, **62,** 521, 576
Serum cholesterol, **470**
Sex,
Alcohol and, 181, 183
premarital, 396
Sex chromosomes, **93**
Sex differences, 87, 273, 396,
397–398, 593, 596–604
Sex drive, 605
Sex flush, **617**
Sex guilt, 609
Sex hormones, 534, 584, 598–600,
605–606, 612
Sex-negative attitudes, 620
Sex norms, 603
Sex-reassignment surgery, 533–534
Sex roles, 10, **585**–604, 645, 654,
662, 669
Sex therapy, **622**–624

Sex-typing, **9**
See also Stereotypes, sex role
Sex surveys, 36–37, 39, 610, 622
Sexism, 516, **587**–591, 593–595
Sexual activity, anxiety and, 71, 73,
620
Sexual arousal, pheromones and,
146–147
Sexual desire, inhibited, **619**
Sexual differentiation, prenatal,
363–364, 598–599, 605
Sexual dysfunctions (*see* Psychosexual
dysfunctions)
Sexual excitement, inhibited, **619,**
622–623
Sexual motivation, 605–615
Sexual response, reflexes and, 66–67
Sexual-response cycle, 616–618
Shadowing, **133**
Sham (experiments), **321**
Shape constancy, **136**
Shaping, **228**–231
Short-term memory, **240**–244
interference in, 243
transferring information to long-term
memory from, 245–246
Siblings, **360**
SIDS (*see* Sudden infant death syndrome)
Sight, *see* Eye; Vision
Signal detection theory, **111**
Significant others, **424,** 425
Similarity, **128**
attitudinal, 653–654
Situational attribution, **644**
Situational variables, **432**
Sixteen Personality Factors Scale, 427,
429
Size constancy, **135**
Skills, 434–435
social, 519, 651–652
Skin senses, 149–153
Skinner box, 222
Sleep, 165–176
deprivation of, 168–169
disorders, 172–176
functions of, 168–170
inducement of, 173–174
non-rapid-eye-movement (NREM),
166–167, 170
rapid-eye-movement (REM), **166,**
167, 168, 169–170
stages of, 165–167
Sleep paralysis, 174–175
Sleep spindles, **167**
Sleeping pills, 173
Sleepwalking, 176
Smell, 145–147, 148
neonates and, 370

Smiling, 344, 345, 371
Smoking, 188–192
cutting down on, 191
quitting, 190, 191–192, 563, 564
rapid, **211,** 564
Snellen Chart, 116
Social comparison, theory of, **338**–339
Social Desirability Scale, 40–41,
695–696
Social development, day care and,
377–378
Social facilitation, **663**
Social influence, **655**–662
Social-learning model (abnormal behavior), 506
Social learning theory, **28,** 29, 362,
429, **432**–440, 441
evaluation of, 440–441
Social loafing, 663, 664
Social motives, **334**–339
Social perception, **643**–648
Social phobias, **509**
Social psychologists, 9
Social psychology, 630–**631,**
632–669
Social skills, 651–652
Social-skills training, 519
Social workers, psychiatric, 547
Socialization, **231,** 601–602, 642
Sociobiology, **24**–25, 668
Sociocultural model (abnormal behavior), **507**
Socioeconomic status, mental illness
and, 507
schizophrenia and, 528
Soma, **54**
Somatic nervous system, **71**
Somatoform disorders, **516**–517
Sopor, 185
Sound, 139–145, 670
Sound waves, 139–140
Sounds, locating, 144
Source traits, **427,** 429
SPA (*see* Stimulation-produced analgesia)
Space, personal, **674**–677
Sphincter (muscles), **418**
Sphincter (reflex), **368**
Spinal cord, **64**–67
Spinal reflex, **64**
Split-brain operation, **79**
Split-half reliability, **294**
Spontaneous recovery, **216**–217,
225
Sports, men vs. women in, 87
Stage, **362**
Stages, developmental, 362
Standard deviation, 685, **686,** 687
Standardization, **295, 446**

Stanford-Binet Intelligence Scale, 295–296, 298
"Stamping in" and "stamping out" responses, 220–221
Staring, 647–648
State anxiety, **465**
Statistically significant differences, 692–694
Statistics, **680**–694
descriptive, **681**–687
inferential, 691–**692**, 693–694
Steroids, 83, **87**–88
Stereotypes, **9**, **585**, **641**–642
sex-role, 585–595, 654, 662
Stimulants, **176**, 186–188
Stimulation, novel, **331**
Stimulation-produced analgesia (SPA), 153
Stimulus, **17**, **213**, 434
ambiguous, **450**–451
conditioned, **215**
discriminative, **227**
unconditioned, **214**
Stimulus discrimination, **218**
Stimulus generalization, **218**
Stimulus motives, **328**–334
Stomach contractions, 321
Storge, **351**
Strangers, fear of, 369, 375
Stratified sample, **39**
Stress, 458–**460**, 461–497
in adolescence, 394–395
aggression and, 476
anxiety and, 464–465
chronic, 474
conflict and, 468–469
coping with, 189, 475–495
denial and, **478**
depression and, 519
discomfort and, 464
frustration and, 467
headaches and, 473–474
illness and, 339, 461–463, 470, 472, 473–475
lowering, environmental engineering and, 492
pain and, 464
physiological response to, 472–475
regression and, **477**
schizophrenia and, 531
self-imposed, 465–467
smoking and, 189
suicide and, 522
Type A behavior and, **470**–472
work and, 480–481
See also Coping; Hassles
Stressor, **460**
Strip-teasers, 535

Stroboscopic motion, **130**
Strong-Campbell Interest Inventory (SCII), 450
Structuralism, **16**
Strychnine, **254**–255
Stupor, **526**, 527
Subjective, **16**, **386**
Subjects, **31**
animal, 45, 46
control, **32**
experimental, **32**
human, 44
Sublimation, **479**
coping and, 479
Subordinate (categories), **248**
Subordinate (concepts), **279**
Substance abuse, 177, 178–179
See also Drugs
Substance dependence, **178**–179
See also Drugs
Successive approximations, **229**–230, **565**, 571
Succubus, **171**–172
Sudden infant death syndrome (SIDS), **175**, 269
Suicide, 521–524, 667
myths about, 523
preventing, 523–524
Sunshine, 672
Superego, **417**, 422, 505
Superfemales, 95
Superiority, drive for, **424**
Supermales, 94, **532**
Superordinate (categories), **247**
Superordinate (concepts), **279**
Suppression, **164**, **478**
Surface structure, **267**
Surface traits, **427**
Surrogate (mothers), **373**–374
Survey, **36**
Survey method, 35–39
Swimming reflex, 368
Syllogism, **387**
Symbionese Liberation Army (SLA), 638–640
Symbols, **260**, **550**
dream, 550–551
phallic, **550**
Sympathetic (arousal), **341**
Sympathetic division, autonomic nervous system, **71**, 73, 341
Symptom substitution, **562**
Synapse, **59**
excitatory, **61**
inhibitory, **61**
Syndrome, **85**, **505**
Syntax, **263**, **266**–267
Syphilis, **364**

Systematic desensitization, **560**–563, 572

Tactile (impressions), **79**
Target (behavior), **561**
Tasaday, 30
Taste, 148–149, 150
infants and, 370–371
Taste buds, **148**
Taste cells, **148**, 149
TAT (*see* Thematic Apperception Test)
Tay-Sachs disease, 96
Telegraphic (speech), **261**, 262, 270–271
Telepathy, **155**
Television violence and, 435–436, 437–439
Temperature, 149–150, 151, 670–671
Temporal lobe, **74**
TENS (*see* Transcutaneous nerve stimulation)
Tension, 317
Terminals, **54**
Tertiary colors, **120**
Test anxiety, coping with, 487–488, 489
Test-retest reliability, **294, 690**
Testes, 85, 89, 393, 617
Testing,
hypothesis, **281**–282
method, 39
Testosterone, 85, **89**, 393, 599–600, 605, 606
Tests
creativity, 290
culture-fair, 301, **302**–303
intelligence, 289–290, 294–303, 403
objective, **446**–450
personality, 445–454
projective, **450**–452, 454
psychological, 39, 428–429
reliability of, **294**, 295, 690
validity of, **295**, 454, 690
Texture gradient, **133**
Thalamus, **69**
Thanatos, **27**
Thematic Apperception Test (TAT), **335**–336, 452, 454
Theory, **5**–6
attribution, 644
balance, **636**–637
cognitive appraisal, 349–350
cognitive-dissonance, 636–640
drive-reduction, 317–**318**, 319
frequency, **145**
humanistic, 318–319, 320
interference, **251**